# CONTENTS



**Fodor's Features**

## MAPS

Fodor's

# THE CAROLINAS & GEORGIA

**FODOR'S THE CAROLINAS & GEORGIA**

**Writers:** Christine Anderson, Rickey Bevington, Melissa Bigner, Liz Biro, Mary Coy, Anna Evans, Kinsey Gidick, Sally Mahan, Debbie Michaud, Ashley Morris, Rachel Roberts Quartarone, Patrick Rodgers, Stina Sieg, Summer Teal Simpson, Lan Sluder, Rob Young
**Editors:** Salwa Jabado, *lead project editor;* Maria Teresa Hart
**Editorial Contributors:** Bethany Beckerlegge, Luke Epplin, John Rambow, Amanda Theunissen

**Production Editor:** Jennifer DePrima
**Maps & Illustrations:** Mark Stroud, Moon Street Cartography; and David Lindroth, *cartographers;* Rebecca Baer, *map editor;* William Wu, *information graphics*
**Design:** Fabrizio La Rocca, *creative director*; Tina Malaney, Chie Ushio, Jessica Ramirez, *designers*; Melanie Marin, *associate director of photography;* Jennifer Romains, *photo research*
**Cover Photo:** Front cover: Ian Dagnall/Alamy (Drayton Hall Plantation House and Gardens near Charleston, SC). Back cover (left to right): NC Tourism - Bill Russ; Library of Congress Prints and Photographs Division; Dave Allen Photography/ Shutterstock. Spine: Jill Lang/iStockphoto.
**Production Manager:** Angela McLean

**COPYRIGHT**



20th Edition

ISBN 978–0–89141–949–5

ISSN 1525–5832

**SPECIAL SALES**

This book is available at special discounts for bulk purchases for sales promotions or premiums. Special editions, including personalized covers, excerpts of existing books, and corporate imprints, can be created in large quantities for special needs. For more information, write to Special Markets/Premium Sales, 1745 Broadway, MD 3-1, New York, NY 10019, or e-mail specialmarkets@randomhouse.com.

**AN IMPORTANT TIP & AN INVITATION**

Although all prices, opening times, and other details in this book are based on information supplied to us at press time, changes occur all the time in the travel world, and Fodor's cannot accept responsibility for facts that become outdated or for inadvertent errors or omissions. So **always confirm information when it matters,** especially if you're making a detour to visit a specific place. Your experiences—positive and negative—matter to us. If we have missed or misstated something, **please write to us.** Share your opinion instantly through our online feedback center at fodors.com/contact-us.

PRINTED IN COLOMBIA

10 9 8 7 6 5 4 3 2 1

# ABOUT THIS GUIDE

### Fodor's Ratings

Everything in this guide is worth doing—we don't cover what isn't—but exceptional sights, hotels, and restaurants are recognized with additional accolades. **Fodor's Choice** ★ indicates our top recommendations; ★ highlights places we deem highly recommended. Care to nominate a new place? Visit Fodors.com/contact-us.

### Trip Costs

We list prices wherever possible to help you budget well. Hotel and restaurant price categories from **$** to **$$$$** are noted alongside each recommendation. For hotels, we include the lowest cost of a standard double room in high season. For restaurants, we cite the average price of a main course at dinner or, if dinner isn't served, at lunch. For attractions, we always list adult admission fees; discounts are usually available for children, students, and senior citizens.

### Hotels

Our local writers vet every hotel to recommend the best overnights in each price category, from budget to expensive. Unless otherwise specified, you can expect private bath, phone, and TV in your room. For expanded hotel reviews, facilities, and deals visit Fodors.com.

### Restaurants

Unless we state otherwise, restaurants are open for lunch and dinner daily. We mention dress code only when there's a specific requirement and reservations only when they're essential or not accepted. To make restaurant reservations, visit Fodors.com.

### Credit Cards

The hotels and restaurants in this guide typically accept credit cards. If not, we'll say so.

**Ratings**

- ★ Fodor's Choice
- ★ Highly recommended
- Family-friendly

**Listings**

- Address
- Branch address
- Telephone
- Fax
- Website
- E-mail
- Admission fee
- Open/closed times
- Subway
- Directions or Map coordinates

**Hotels & Restaurants**

- Hotel
- Number of rooms
- Meal plans
- Restaurant
- Reservations
- Dress code
- No credit cards
- Price

**Other**

- See also
- Take note
- Golf facilities

# Experience the Carolinas and Georgia

1

# THE CAROLINAS AND GEORGIA TODAY

## The People

No matter who you meet in the Carolinas and Georgia, rest assured they'll be friendly. Folks in this part of the Southeast like to say hello—or rather hey, howdy, and how y'all doing. Such openness dates back to genteel 18th- and 19th-century plantation days when scattered neighbors in remote, rural areas had only each other to depend on.

Late-20th-century migrations from the Northeast and Midwest changed the region's previous agrarian lifestyle. Coastal and metropolitan areas boomed. The mild climate and reasonable cost of living attracted businesses. Thousands of retirees and vacationers came seeking leisure, especially golf and seaside homes. New job opportunities brought people from all over the world. Asians and Latinos round out the 64% white, 26% black population at 8% and 2.4% respectively. Nearly a fourth of the population hold college degrees, and cities host some of America's best-known schools, including Duke University in Durham, North Carolina; Emory University in Atlanta, Georgia; and Clemson University in Clemson, South Carolina. Needless to say, college sports rivalries run deep.

## Economy

It used to be that nearly everyone in the Carolinas and Georgia had agricultural ties. Colonists planted the first crops for sustenance, but by the mid-1800s the region's economy depended on cotton and tobacco, and slave labor was used to work large plantations. Civil War ravages and subsequent Reconstruction forced economic diversity.

Farm fields still characterize the region—Georgia alone produces half of America's peanuts—but the larger employers are government, retail, manufacturing, education, health, and tourism.

Marine Corps bases like Camp Lejeune, the nation's largest amphibious training base, employ thousands of troops and civilians in North Carolina's coastal plain. Georgia hosts massive Fort Benning Army base. South Carolina houses various military complexes, too, most famously the major Marine recruit base Parris Island.

Military and other government employers like the Centers for Disease Control and Prevention in Atlanta help cushion the region from economic recession. Still, unemployment rates hovered around 10% starting in 2009, South Carolina leading with 12%. The region has since started to recover, with unemployment rates in Georgia, North Carolina, and South Carolina dropping to around 9%. Various contributors fuel each state's economy. Georgia ranks high in aerospace exports and hosts 14 Fortune 500 companies. The state's numerous corporate headquarters include Coca-Cola and Delta Airlines in Atlanta. North Carolina's Piedmont is a research and science hub, and Charlotte is a major U.S. banking center. South Carolina claims BMW vehicle and Honda ATV and personal watercraft plants, as well as a Boeing aircraft-assembly plant. Tourism and service industries are important sectors throughout the area, especially along the beaches.

## Sports

During one week each spring, work stops in many Georgia and the Carolinas locations—and bosses don't mind. No doubt they're all drawn to the same thing: college basketball.

This is Atlantic Coast Conference (ACC) country, and when the mighty league hosts its annual March college basketball

tournament, fans here have many teams to cheer. Schools in these three states make up half of the ACC's 12, soon to be 14, members. North Carolina alone owns the powerhouse Carolina Tar Heels, Duke Blue Devils, and Wake Forest Demon Deacons.

The region is represented in the Southern, Southeastern, and Big South conferences, too, and basketball isn't the only hot game. College football is just as significant.

Professional sports are dearly loved, too. Tailgaters root for the National Football League's Atlanta Falcons and Carolina Panthers. Mild winters can't deter hockey madness in Raleigh, North Carolina, home to the Carolina Hurricanes, 2006 Stanley Cup champions. Baseball fans have the Atlanta Braves, and hoops lovers the National Basketball Association's Atlanta Hawks and Charlotte Bobcats.

NASCAR races were born on North Carolina's mountain roads, where drivers ran bootleg whiskey during prohibition. The first NASCAR "strictly stock" car race happened in 1949 in Charlotte. Today, the region boasts the major NASCAR tracks Charlotte Motor Speedway in Concord, North Carolina; Atlanta Motor Speedway in Atlanta, Georgia; and Darlington Raceway in Darlington, South Carolina. Charlotte's 150,000-square-foot NASCAR Hall of Fame features 18 historic cars.

Golf lovers relish the region's hundreds of courses, some of the world's most challenging. Pinehurst in North Carolina has staged more golf championships than any other American golf resort and hosts the 2014 U.S. Open and U.S. Women's Open. The Masters Gold Tournament is played annually in Augusta, Georgia. In 2012, South Carolina's Kiawah Island Golf Resort hosted the 94th PGA Championship.

### Cuisine

Early explorers arriving in what would become the Carolinas and Georgia found Native Americans eating corn, beans, pecans, and seafood. These humble foods combined with imported ingredients shaped the regional cuisine and inspired cooks to create distinctive local fare.

Soul food and Southern cooking can be found throughout the area, but Georgia's rich African-American culture may lay claim to fried chicken. Slaves brought deep-fat frying to the area, along with many favorites like candied yams and stewed collards with cornbread.

African and Caribbean influences season Lowcountry cuisine, associated mainly with South Carolina's shore but stretching south to Savannah, Georgia, and north to Wilmington, North Carolina. Bountiful seafood and coastal rice plantations provided ingredients for famous dishes like shrimp and grits, she-crab soup, and the rice-and-black-eyed-pea dish named hoppin' John.

Barbecue debates rage in North Carolina. Westerners prefer tomato-based sauce while Easterners want vinegar-based sauce. One thing is agreed upon: barbecue means pork butts, pork shoulders, or whole hogs roasted slowly over a wood or charcoal fire and then shredded or "pulled" after cooking.

Each state also claims popular foodstuffs. Coca-Cola was invented in Georgia, Pespi in North Carolina, and Firefly Iced Tea Vodka in South Carolina. North Carolina is home to Cheerwine and Krispy Kreme.

# WHAT'S WHERE

*The following numbers refer to chapters in the book.*

**2 The North Carolina Coast.** Nothing in the region compares with the Outer Banks. This thin band of barrier islands with wind-twisted oaks and gnarled pines has some of the East Coast's best beaches.

**3 Central North Carolina.** The New South comes alive in three major metropolitan centers—Charlotte; the Triangle, which consists of Raleigh, Durham, and Chapel Hill; and the Triad, which consists of Greensboro, Winston-Salem, and High Point. Shopping, dining, and nightlife abound, and sports get top billing here, from college football games to NASCAR races. The Sandhills region, with Pinehurst, is known for its world-class golf.

**4 Asheville and the North Carolina Mountains.** Western North Carolina is home to more than 1 million acres of stupendous vertical scenery. In addition to opportunities for outdoor adventures, visitors will find edgy art galleries and sophisticated eateries in Asheville. The nation's largest private residence, the Biltmore House, sits nearby.

**5 Great Smoky Mountains National Park.** Nine million visitors annually can't be wrong; while the Smokies is the most visited of the national parks, there is more than enough beauty and deserted woodland on the 276,000 acres of the North Carolina side for peaceful communion with nature.

**6 Myrtle Beach and the Grand Strand, SC.** South Carolina's Grand Strand, a 60-mile-long expanse of white sandy beach, offers varied pleasures: the quiet refuge of Pawleys Island and its sometimes shabby, sometimes elegant summer homes; Brookgreen Gardens, with its magnificent sculptures and landscaped grounds; dozens of golf courses; and the bustle of Myrtle Beach.

**7 Charleston, SC.** Charleston anchors the Lowcountry in high style. The harbor town's past, dating to 1670, is evident in cobblestone streets, antebellum mansions and plantations, and Gullah accents. It also hosts the renowned Spoleto performing arts festival. Lately, Charleston has garnered a reputation as a foodie hub. The city hosts award-winning chefs, top-rated restaurants, and a celebrated food and wine festival.

**8 Hilton Head, SC, and the Lowcountry.** The coastal lowlands feature picturesque landscapes of coastal forests

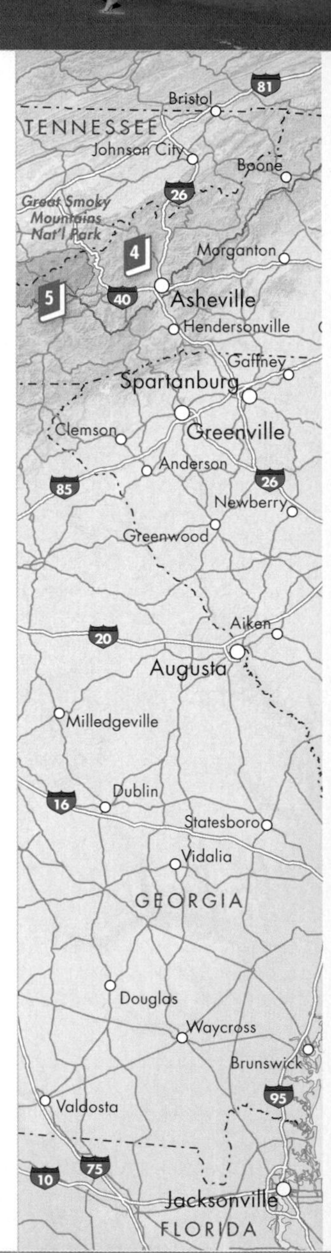

VIRGINIA
77
85
Winston-Salem
Reidsville
Greensboro
Henderson
Roanoke Rapids
Elizabeth City
Blue Ridge Parkway
3
Wake Forest
Durham
Rocky Mount
40
Chapel Hill
Statesville
Lexington
RALEIGH
Greenville
Salisbury
Asheboro
95
NORTH CAROLINA
Pamlico Sound
Sanford
Goldsboro
2
85
Gastonia
Albemarle
Kinston
Southern Pines
New Bern
Charlotte
Havelock
Fayetteville
Cape Hatteras National Seashore
Laurinburg
Jacksonville
Lumberton
40
77
SOUTH CAROLINA
Cape Lookout National Seashore
95
Wilmington
20
Florence
COLUMBIA
Sumter
Conway
Myrtle Beach
Orangeburg
6
7
26
95
ATLANTIC OCEAN
Charleston
Beaufort
8
Hilton Head
Savannah
Cumberland Island National Seashore
0
50 mi
0
50 km

# WHAT'S WHERE

and wide-open marshes, undisturbed beaches, and fishing villages with quaint waterfront areas. Farther south, Hilton Head Island is home to 29 world-class golf courses and even more resorts, hotels, and top restaurants.

9 **The Midlands and Upstate, SC.** Radiating out from Columbia, South Carolina's engaging capital, the small towns of the area have their claims to fame: Aiken is a national equestrian center; Camden is the place to go for well-priced antiques; Abbeville is steeped in Civil War history.

10 **Savannah, GA.** Georgia's oldest and grandest city, Savannah is known for its elegant mansions, Spanish moss, and summer heat. It has more than 1,200 restored or reconstructed buildings dating from its founding in 1733.

11 **Georgia's Coastal Isles and the Okefenokee.** Stretching southward from Savannah, Georgia's coastal isles are "almost Florida" but more appealing. For wildlife watchers, the Cumberland Island National Seashore and the wild and mysterious Okefenokee Swamp are must-sees. Upscale visitors favor Little St. Simons Island and Sea Island, while St. Simons Island and Jekyll Island have something for everyone.

12 **Southwest Georgia.** The serenity of this quiet corner of Georgia has been thoroughly enjoyed by two U.S. presidents. Franklin Delano Roosevelt had a summer home, The Little White House, in Warm Springs. Jimmy Carter, a Plains native, returned to begin work as one of America's most active former presidents.

13 **Atlanta, GA.** Georgia Aquarium, World of Coca-Cola, High Museum of Art, great shopping, and restaurants keep visitors busy in the capital of the New South. The Martin Luther King Jr. National Historic Site brings to life Atlanta's racially divided past and its ties to the civil rights movement.

14 **Central and North Georgia.** Stretching from Augusta to Macon, Central Georgia lies at the heart of the Old South. White-columned mansions and shady verandas evoke a romanticized past. The pace picks up in Athens, home to the University of Georgia. Near the town of Dahlonega, site of America's first gold rush, vineyards produce new "gold" for the region. In the northwest, walk the hallowed ground of Chickamauga, the site of one of the Civil War's bloodiest battles.

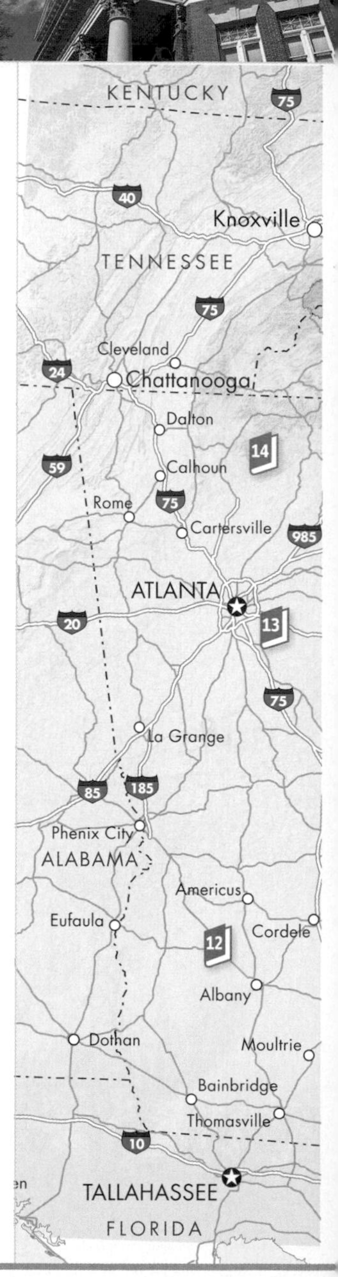

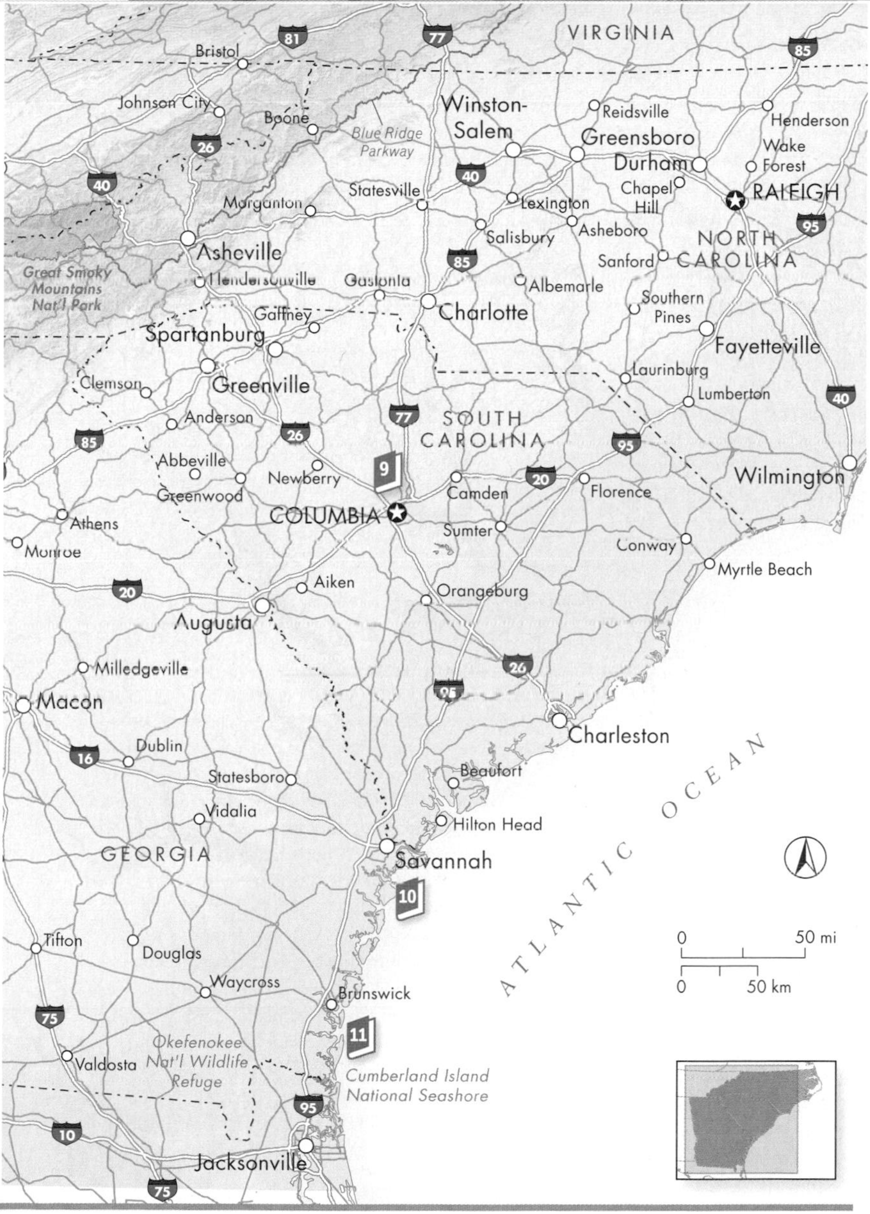

VIRGINIA
NORTH CAROLINA
SOUTH CAROLINA
GEORGIA
ATLANTIC OCEAN
Bristol
Johnson City
Boone
Blue Ridge Parkway
Winston-Salem
Reidsville
Greensboro
Henderson
Wake Forest
Durham
Chapel Hill
RALEIGH
Statesville
Lexington
Morganton
Asheboro
Salisbury
Asheville
Great Smoky Mountains Nat'l Park
Hendersonville
Gastonia
Albemarle
Sanford
Southern Pines
Charlotte
Gaffney
Spartanburg
Fayetteville
Laurinburg
Clemson
Greenville
Lumberton
Anderson
Abbeville
Newberry
Greenwood
Camden
Florence
Wilmington
Athens
COLUMBIA
Sumter
Monroe
Conway
Myrtle Beach
Aiken
Orangeburg
Augusta
Milledgeville
Macon
Charleston
Dublin
Beaufort
Statesboro
Vidalia
Hilton Head
Savannah
Tifton
Douglas
Waycross
Brunswick
Valdosta
Okefenokee Nat'l Wildlife Refuge
Cumberland Island National Seashore
Jacksonville
9
10
11
0
50 mi
0
50 km
81
77
85
26
40
95
20
16
75
10

# CAROLINAS AND GEORGIA PLANNER

## When to Go

Spring is the best time to see the Carolinas and Georgia in bloom. Fall can bring spectacular foliage in the mountains and stunning coastal sunsets.

### CLIMATE

Spring and fall daytime temperatures are delightful; bring a jacket for cool nights. Summer is hot and humid, especially along the coast. In winter, mild weather is punctuated by brief bouts of cold. Short afternoon thunderstorms are common in spring and summer.

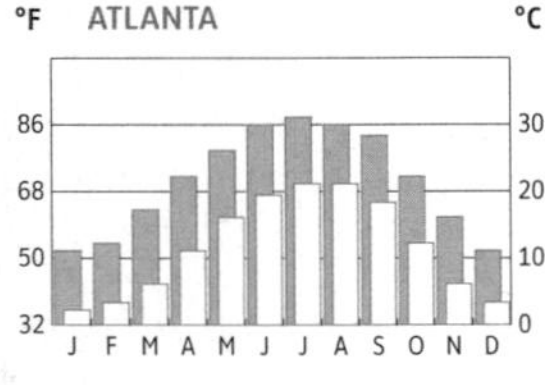


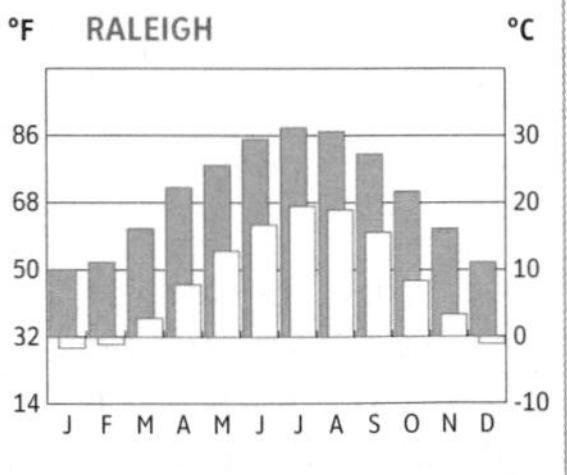


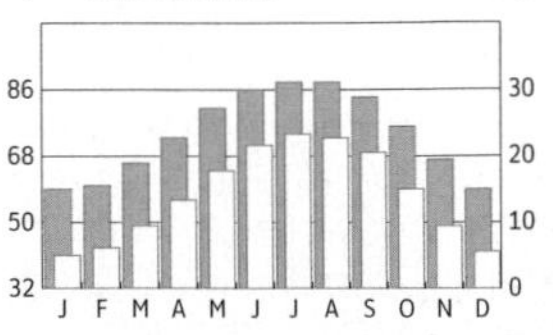


## Getting Here

Due to the sheer number of flights into Hartsfield-Jackson Atlanta International Airport (ATL), it's often the most logical, if hectic, choice for the region's south end. Flying here means navigating a crowded airport and Atlanta's notorious traffic snarls. If you are staying in Atlanta, especially in Downtown, Midtown, or Buckhead, consider taking the MARTA train from the airport to your hotel. Charlotte Douglas International Airport (CLT) in North Carolina is a good option for travelers heading to both Carolinas. Raleigh-Durham International Airport (RDU) is in the heart of the state, making it convenient for North Carolina's eastern and central areas. Asheville Regional Airport (AVL) provides access to the mountains and adjoining areas. Piedmont Triad International Airport (GSO) serves Greensboro, Winston-Salem, and High Point. For links to these airports, the airlines that serve them, and more, go to 🌐 *www.airlineandairportlinks.com*.

## Getting Around

Once in the region, major highways—such as Interstates 75, 85, 20, 40, and 95—lead to major cities and many other destinations. For beachgoers, the route to hit is U.S. Highway 17, which hugs the coast of the Carolinas and Georgia. In the mid-Carolinas, Interstates 40 and 77 are important connectors. Especially around big cities such as Charlotte and Atlanta, plan your trips to avoid rush hours. If staying in town, check with hosts for expected road conditions, even on the weekends, when concerts, ball games, and special events can delay traffic. In Georgia, the Department of Transportation's 🌐 *www.georgia-navigator.com* provides real-time traffic data, including trip times and construction and accident information on major highways statewide. Myrtle Beach, South Carolina, is likely to feel effects of travelers jamming in on Highway 17 during holiday weekends. Sports fans rush into college towns such as Clemson, South Carolina; Athens, Georgia; Chapel Hill and Raleigh, North Carolina; and Atlanta, Georgia, during big game days. Come equipped with directions, atlases, or a GPS system.

## Beat the Heat

Southerners like to say, "It's not the heat, it's the humidity." From late June to September's end, high temperatures and humidity can take your breath away in the Piedmont and along the coast. Don't let the weather dampen your fun. Plan plenty of indoor, air-conditioned breaks. Be prepared, too, by packing hats, sunblock, water bottles, UVB-blocker sunglasses, and lots of light-color and lightweight clothing. You'll want to change your T-shirt often. And remember, summer heat and moisture means mosquitoes, too—carry insect repellent or wear clothing that will protect you from bites, especially at dusk.

## Festivals

Celebrate Southern culture at festivals that happen every month in some part of the Carolinas and Georgia. Join North Carolina's great barbecue debate in October by sampling western-style pork barbecue with tomato-based sauce at **Lexington's Barbecue Festival.** In April, sometimes late March, head to the coast for eastern-style 'cue with vinegar-based sauce at the **Newport Pig Cookin' Contest** in Newport, North Carolina. During Macon, Georgia's March **International Cherry Blossom Festival**, the city's more than 300,000 cherry trees glow pink and white. Beaufort, South Carolina's **Gullah Festival** on the May weekend before Memorial Day highlights fine arts, customs, language, and dress of Lowcountry African Americans. Find out about the region's festivals at 🌐 *www.southfest.com.*

## Friendly Advice

Whether you want to attend a festival, take a winery tour, hike a mountain trail, explore the many Civil War sites that dot the Carolinas and Georgia, or just laze on the beach and contemplate your sandy toes, state tourism agencies are available to help devise your vacation.

**North Carolina Division of Tourism:** ☎ *800/847–4862* 🌐 *www.visitnc.com.*

**South Carolina Department of Parks, Recreation, and Tourism:** ☎ *866/224–9339* 🌐 *www.discoversouthcarolina.com.*

**Georgia Department of Economic Development:** ☎ *800/847–4842* 🌐 *www.exploregeorgia.org.*

## Southernisms

Use this knowledge of Southernisms and Southern culture while navigating around.

### FOOD AND DRINK

**Sweet tea,** made by dissolving cupfuls of sugar in hot orange pekoe tea and then adding ice, is the aptly named universal beverage of the South.

Many Southern restaurants offer **meat-and-three** menus. Think of them as you would a cafeteria: your choice of a meat or seafood main accompanied by three sides.

Whenever possible, order **biscuits,** so light they seem as if they could float on air. Smother them with butter and molasses or sausage gravy.

**Boiled peanuts,** found at roadside stands and country stores, are nothing like their roasted Virginia cousins. The texture is akin to boiled beans. The peanuts are served hot or cold, salty and wet, many times packed in their juice. They're a real taste of the South—if an acquired one.

### SPEAK YOUR PIECE

"Fixin' to" find a store that carries postcards? Ask the clerk, but don't be startled if the reply is: "sure don't." That's not said to be "ugly," or ill mannered, but to be polite, Southern style.

Even in their disdain, Southerners show a certain grace, couching insults or pity in phrases like "poor thing" and "bless your heart."

# NORTH CAROLINA TOP ATTRACTIONS

A

B

C

D

### Cape Hatteras National Seashore

**(A)** The mighty Atlantic Ocean meeting a 70-mile ribbon of sand composes one of America's most beautiful beaches. Find some of the country's best fishing, surfing, and seaside strolling, not to mention maritime history. Three lighthouses mark the coast, including the Cape Hatteras Lighthouse, the nation's tallest brick beacon, and Ocracoke Lighthouse, the second-oldest operating U.S. lighthouse.

### Airlie Gardens, Wilmington

**(B)** Southern hospitality and flowery scents fill this 67-acre garden dating to 1901. A wealthy industrialist's wife planted it to accommodate her many guests and lavish parties. The estate features more than 100,000 azalea cultivars, along with dozens of camellias and magnolias framing two freshwater lakes. The massive circa-1545 Airlie oak tree anchors it all.

### North Carolina Museum of Art, Raleigh

**(C)** Thirty works by French sculptor Auguste Rodin are among the 300-plus European and American artworks, making this museum the leading repository of Rodin's work in this country. One of the nation's largest collections of Jewish ceremonial art is here, too, and other items date to ancient Egypt. Touring exhibitions have ranged from Michelangelo Merisi da Caravaggio's dramatic realism to Norman Rockwell's feel-good Americana.

### Duke Chapel, Durham

**(D)** Stone piers, pointed arches, and flying buttresses delight architectural history buffs, but this medieval-looking Duke University centerpiece is more modern than it looks. The neo-Gothic chapel was built in the 1930s using 17 shades of stone from a nearby quarry. The bell tower rises 210 feet. Three different pipe organs sup-

E

F

H

G

ply music, which visitors can hear from 12:30 to 1:30 pm most weekdays.

### Old Salem Museum and Gardens, Winston-Salem

**(E)** One of the nation's most well-documented colonial sites comes to life at a 100-acre complex of heirloom gardens and 80 original and reconstructed buildings. Costumed interpreters and craftsmen demonstrate daily life at this former backcountry trading center founded in 1766. Learn about Moravian settlers and then head to the gift shop for samples of their super-thin spice cookies.

### Biltmore Estate, Asheville

**(F)** Much of America's largest private home and its gardens are open to the public. The French Renaissance chateau was built in the 1890s. Exquisite art and antiques that the Vanderbilts collected fill the home's 250 rooms. Frederick Law Olmsted, designer of New York's Central Park, landscaped the original 125,000-acre estate, now 8,000 acres, 75 acres of which are formal gardens.

### Blue Ridge Parkway

**(G)** Connecting the Great Smoky Mountains in North Carolina and Shenandoah National Park in Virginia, the parkway is among America's most scenic roadways. Relax and enjoy the view on the meandering 469-mile road, 252 miles of which are in North Carolina. You can stop at 162 scenic overlooks along the way.

### Levine Museum of the New South, Charlotte

**(H)** Study central North Carolina's difficult Reconstruction era to flourishing modern times. The 8,000-square-foot Cotton Fields to Skyscrapers exhibit brings visitors into a one-room tenant house and one of the South's first African-American hospitals. The museum also hosts historic Charlotte walking tours in May.

# SOUTH CAROLINA TOP ATTRACTIONS

A

B

D

C

### Brookgreen Gardens, Murrells Inlet

This idyllic sculpture garden—America's oldest—showcases 1,400 pieces of American sculpture in outstanding outdoor garden galleries. Daniel Chester French, Frederic Remington, and Anna Hyatt Huntington pieces are on display. Plus, the Lowcountry Zoo is kid-friendly.

### Spoleto Festival USA, Charleston

**(A)** Elegant Charleston becomes an entertainment paradise for more than two weeks each May and June. Dance, opera, theater, and music events—from symphony to rap—have been filling churches, auditoriums, and open-air sites since the festival's 1977 debut.

### NASCAR SpeedPark, Myrtle Beach

**(B)** Experience high-speed thrills in NASCAR replica cars you get to drive. Choose from seven tracks, some slick, some winding, some with high banking. Even kids get to take the wheel. When everyone's tired of driving, mini-golf, bumper boats, and carnival rides supply the fun.

### Old Slave Mart Museum, Charleston

**(C)** Likely South Carolina's only existing slave market building on one of the city's last cobblestone streets, the circa-1859 structure offers a poignant look at a troubling U.S. period. The complex includes a kitchen, a morgue, and the jail where slaves were held before public auctions. A museum recounts the lives of people who passed through the market.

### Battery Park, Charleston

**(D)** This promenade affords lovely Charleston Harbor views, the city's most beautiful historic mansions, White Point Gardens' massive oaks, and views of Fort Sumter, where the Civil War's first shot was fired. Along the way you'll also see the Civil War prison Castle Pinckney, the Revolutionary War's Fort Moultrie, and the World War II aircraft carrier USS *Yorktown*.

### Middleton Place, Charleston

**(E)** America's oldest landscaped garden, begun in 1741, is a fairy-tale setting where peacocks roam acres of camellias, magnolias, azaleas, and roses. Swans glide on pools, and terraced lawns overlook butterfly-wing-shape lakes. The Civil War claimed the main mansion, but gentleman guest quarters contain some of the Middletons' original furnishings. Garden wine tastings and a fine Lowcountry restaurant add contemporary panache.

### St. Helena Island

**(F)** The heart of Gullah culture is a starting point for anyone interested in Lowcountry history. Penn Center, the South's first school for freed slaves, today is a museum that explains the area's past. Residents here still speak their native tongue and use hand-tied nets to harvest shrimp.

### Congaree Swamp National Park, Hopkins

**(G)** High bluffs border this 22,200-acre South Carolina park. Some of the oldest and largest trees in the southeastern United States fill America's biggest old-growth, bottomland hardwood forest. Miles of hiking and canoe trails ensure views of varied wildlife, even wild boar. Primitive camping is available, and naturalists lead evening tours into the dark, creepy forest.

### Riverbanks Zoo and Garden, Columbia

**(H)** Siberian tigers, siamang apes, lemurs, giraffes, koalas, and zebras are among more than 2,000 animals that roam natural habitats. More than 4,200 native and exotic species fill five separate gardens, including one dedicated to old roses. See Civil War ruins here, too.

# GEORGIA TOP ATTRACTIONS

A

C

D

B

### The Georgia Aquarium, Atlanta

**(A)** Breathtaking beluga whales and whale sharks, the largest fish on the globe, reside at the world's largest aquarium. Pass through the 100-foot long underwater tunnel to see thousands of saltwater species, from sharks to manta rays. The 10-million-gallon aquarium, home to more aquatic life than any other aquarium, also has sea lions, otters, penguins, and a coral reef with tropical fish.

### MLK National Historic District, Atlanta

**(B)** Make a pilgrimage to Atlanta's Sweet Auburn neighborhood to learn about Reverend Martin Luther King Jr.'s role in the civil rights movement. King's tomb and that of his wife, Coretta Scott King, are here, as well as a number of Dr. King's personal effects. Take a guided tour of the modest home where King was born, and then visit Ebenezer Baptist Church, where members of the King family preached for three generations.

### Chickamauga and Chattanooga National Military Park

**(C)** Nine thousand acres of preserved and enhanced battlefields honor upward of 34,000 Union and Confederate soldiers killed or injured here in one of the Civil War's bloodiest conflicts. More than 1,400 monuments and historical markers chronicle the September 1863 battles.

### Cumberland Island

The largest of Georgia's coastal islands remains a mostly unspoiled wonderland of beaches, lakes, ponds, and maritime forest. Wild horses roam the shore. Sand roads and foot trails tunnel below live oaks. John F. Kennedy Jr. and Carolyn Bessette were married in the First African Church, established here in 1893.

### City Squares and Forsythe Park, Savannah

**(D)** Five beautifully landscaped public squares, each with historical significance and some with fancy fountains,

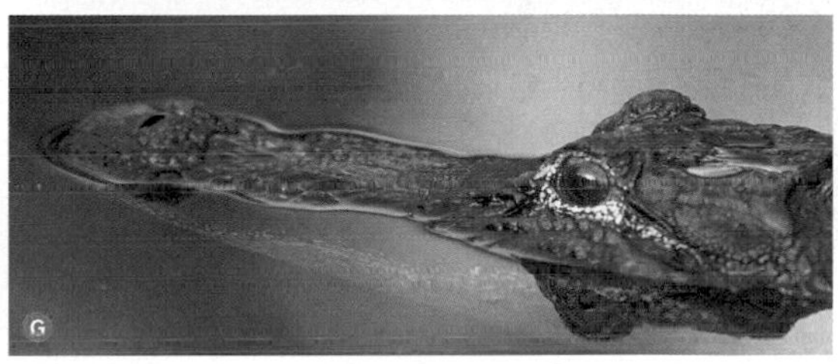


monuments, and shady resting areas, lead down Savannah's central Bull Street to magnificent Forsythe Park. Thirty acres host a showy 1858 fountain, Civil and Spanish-American war memorials, a fragrant garden for the blind, and a grand, tree-shaded pedestrian boulevard.

### Owens Thomas House and Museum, Savannah

**(E)** Considered *the* historic home to see in Savannah, Owens is among the country's finest examples of English Regency architecture. Curving walls, Greek-inspired ornamental molding, half-moon arches, stained glass, and a second-floor, hardwood bridge that spans the stairwell delight history buffs. Rare, urban slave quarters on the property contain original furnishings and slave-made haint-blue paint, a color folklore claims wards off evil spirits.

### Amicalola Falls State Park and Lodge, Dawsonville

**(F)** The Southeastern United States' tallest waterfall cascades down 729 feet of massive rock steps, which in fall are surrounded by a rainbow display of changing leaf colors. View the beauty from a heart-pumping foot trail or over a relaxing buffet brunch at the park's Maple Restaurant. Camp, reserve a cottage, or stay in the park lodge.

### Okefenokee National Wildlife Refuge

**(G)** The famous Okefenokee Swamp is just a small part of this 730-square-mile rugged landscape containing the United States' largest intact freshwater wetlands. Alligators, otters, bald eagles, and black bears populate the complex's varied landscapes, including rivers, lakes, forests, aquatic prairies, sandy pine islands, subtropical hammocks, and many bogs where the earth quivers like gelatin.

# TOP EXPERIENCES

### Eat Your Way Through Charleston

Taste your way through Charleston, South Carolina, America's new foodie hotspot. Plan delicious experiences around March's **Charleston Wine + Food Festival,** where you might meet top chefs like Rachael Ray, John Besh, Daniel Boulud, and Charleston's own James Beard Award–winning Sean Brock, whose **Husk** restaurant in 2011 was voted best new restaurant by both *Southern Living* and *Bon Appetit*. Top-ranked restaurants offer special deals during fall's **Restaurant Week.** Autumn also brings the **Taste of Charleston** food-sampling fair while winter means the **Lowcountry Oyster Festival.**

### Learn Secrets from the Vintners

On Georgia's Wine Trail, oenophiles can savor award-winning wines, walk among the vineyards, admire outstanding views, and learn secrets about the grapes from the vintners themselves. From vintners David Harris at **BlackStock Winery,** near Dahlonega, and John Ezzard at **Tiger Mountain Vineyards,** near Clayton, the information flows as easily as the fine wines.

### Hit a Hole-in-One Like the Pros

The Southeast is known for outstanding golf courses. While no one but members can play the **Augusta National Golf Course,** longtime home of the Masters Tournament, the hundreds of courses in the region provide ample opportunities to get in some practice. While the Masters Tournament sells out quickly, Augusta National offers a limited number of practice-round tickets sold in advance by application only. Applications must be filed by mid-July for the next year's tournament. Lucky winners are notified in early September for the next year's round.

### Swim or Dive with the Fishes

Make a splash at the **Georgia Aquarium** by becoming part of an educational program allowing a limited number of landlubbers to pay for a swim or dive in the Ocean Voyager's 6.3-million-gallon tank. They cavort with whale sharks, manta rays, schools of tarpon, cownose rays, and many more ocean creatures.

### Touch the Clouds

By car or by trail, check out the clouds and gorgeous scenery at the tip-top of North and South Carolina and Georgia. And don't forget to bring a camera to record the visit! Taking top honors is **Mount Mitchell,** near Burnsville, North Carolina, the highest point east of the Mississippi at 6,686 feet. **Sassafras Mountain,** with an elevation of 3,560 feet, is located in northwestern South Carolina. In Georgia, **Brasstown Bald** near Hiawassee claims the honor at 4,784 feet.

### Live Like Royalty for a Day

Tour the luxurious **Biltmore Estate** chateau and grounds, taste the estate-made wine, and enjoy a meal at one of the estate's restaurants. You can even stay the night on the 8,000-acre property at the **Inn on Biltmore Estate.** A visit during the holiday season means sparkling Biltmore decorations, special events, and live music. Another memorable Asheville, North Carolina, splurge is spending the night at the legendary **Grove Park Inn,** enjoying a fine dinner, drinks, and music in front of the massive fireplace in the lobby. Wake up to pampering at the more than 43,000-square-foot spa, featuring swimming and mineral pools, waterfalls, and hot tubs. It's been named one of the country's finest spas.

### Take a Hike—All the Way to Maine

The **Appalachian National Scenic Trail** begins at Springer Mountain in Georgia and meanders 2,175 miles north to Maine. Walkers, day hikers, or backpackers can catch portions of the trail in parks and at highways that cross it. Hiking is especially spectacular in the spring, when wildflowers bloom, and fall, when the leaves paint the mountains red, orange, and yellow. If you're just looking for a great photo op featuring a massive AT-engraved rock, head to Dicks Creek Gap, on U.S. 76 near Clayton, Georgia.

### Drive Like a Speed Demon

**Richard Petty Driving Experience** participants can drive a 600-horsepower, NASCAR Sprint Cup–style stock car at high speeds around the Charlotte Motor Speedway track in Concord, North Carolina, or they can choose to go along for a ride with an instructor at speeds as high as 165 mph. Laps allowed 'round the track vary from 3 to 50, depending on the package selected. The adventure is a hands-on, inside look at the sport from the driver's perspective. For many fans, it's a lifelong dream fulfilled. Reservations are required for driving; ride-alongs are available on a first come, first served basis. Ride-along participants must be at least 14 years old and accompanied by a parent or legal guardian if younger than 18. Drivers must be at least 16 and have a valid driver's license.

### Chill Out at the Beach

Whether your preferred beach experience means shag music, tacky T-shirts, and water parks, which you'll find in ample supply at South Carolina's **Myrtle Beach,** or quiet days spent contemplating one of the most beautiful shorelines, looking for dolphins, and shell collecting on Georgia's **Jekyll Island,** the Carolinas–Georgia coast has universal appeal. Treat yourself to a truly Southern experience and rent a cottage—or grand home—right on the shore for a vacation retreat.

### Shopping Spree

Southerners know how to look gorgeous in the most humid weather and to dress their homes to dispense the grandest Southern hospitality. That takes great shopping experience and demand for quality. Check out upscale **King Street** in Charleston for Bob Ellis Shoe Store, Ann Taylor, and antiques and specialty shops aplenty. Atlanta's **Phipps Plaza** and **Lenox Square** are quintessential shopping destinations. Conveniently, the two sit catty-corner on Peachtree Road. **Concord Mills** in Concord, North Carolina, near Charlotte, keeps shoppers more than satisfied with Bass Pro Shops Outdoor World, Polo Ralph Lauren Factory Store, Bose Factory Outlet, NASCAR SpeedPark, Sak's Fifth Avenue OFF 5TH, and Brooks Brothers. **North Georgia Premium Outlets** offers Restoration Hardware, Ann Taylor, Burberry, Coach, and many more.

### Time Travel to the Antebellum South

While the Yankees occupied the small mill town of Roswell, Georgia, in 1864 and burned its cotton and woolen mills, they spared its antebellum mansions, mill workers' homes, and churches on their trek toward the Battle of Atlanta. Today visitors tour a 640-acre historic district. Highlights are three historic homes open daily: **Bulloch Hall,** where Teddy Roosevelt's mother was married; **Barrington Hall,** a stunning Greek Revival home; and the **Archibald Smith Plantation,** once part of a 300-acre cotton farm. Catch weekend ghost tours featuring tales of haunted houses.

# QUINTESSENTIAL CAROLINAS & GEORGIA

### Serious BBQ

Barbecue is one of the region's most revered traditions. Eating barbecue is a social event—from church lunches to July 4th parties to family get-togethers. Even at restaurants, customers often share long tables filled usually with pork barbecue (served chopped, sliced, or pulled from the bone), extra sauce, white bread or buns and never-ending glasses of sweet tea. Locals are fiercely loyal to their favorite 'cue haunts and sauces. Visitors quickly learn that while most sauces are based on ketchup, mustard or vinegar, along with spicy peppers, there are exceptions. On the coast in all three states, but especially in eastern North Carolina, barbecue is served with a flavorful mixture of vinegar, spices, and hot peppers. Central South Carolina is known for its mustard barbecue. Richer sauces containing ketchup, molasses, and onion show up in the mountains.

### The Big Game

It's hard not to feel like a local when you're surrounded by thousands of sports fans yelling, screaming, or, in the case of Georgia Bulldog boosters, barking for their favorite college teams. During football season a party atmosphere overtakes the entire region, when cars festooned with colorful flags, decals, and bumper stickers stream toward the stadiums. Basketball is legendary, too, with powerhouse teams playing in packed arenas in all three states. Even for games featuring famous rivals—the University of South Carolina and Clemson, the University of North Carolina and North Carolina State University, and the University of Georgia and Georgia Tech—tickets are generally available.

**If you want to get a sense of contemporary culture in the Carolinas and Georgia, start by getting familiar with the rituals of daily life. These are a few things visitors can take part in with relative ease.**

### On the Waterfront

Blue ribbons of rivers, creeks, and streams do more than decorate the Carolinas and Georgia's green landscapes. They're among the region's most popular destinations for outdoor enthusiasts. Jet Skis and pontoon boats skim glassy lakes. Canoes and kayaks are great for exploring mysterious swamps hung with Spanish moss. In the mountains, roaring rapids promise a wild ride for white-water rafters, and quieter stretches are perfect for a lazy afternoon in an inner tube. Anglers won't be disappointed, either. Children here don't just learn how to fish; they set crab traps with chicken necks and maneuver nets to bring home a mess of shrimp. The ocean is never far away, and more-remote shores such as North Carolina's Corolla and Ocracoke Island offer peace and privacy.

### Back Roads and Country Stores

Short car rides lead from the Carolinas and Georgia cities into the countryside, where folks still sit around little stores to discuss matters of the day, whether it's politics or the recent church supper's best layer cake. Along the way, you'll find makeshift produce stands, signs offering farm-fresh eggs, even fishermen hawking their catch. Pick a two-lane road and simply explore or follow trusted paths like Georgia's 100-mile Antebellum Trail between Macon and Athens that mainly follows Route 441 through charming towns. South Carolina's Cherokee Foothills Scenic Highway, Route 11 near Greenville, winds under a covered bridge and by places to buy peach cider. North Carolina's Route 52 passes stunning scenery on the way from Winston-Salem to the quintessential small town of Mt. Airy, the basis for *The Andy Griffith Show*'s Mayberry.

# IF YOU LIKE

## Southern Dining

Although Southerners still thrive on meat-and-three menus, cooking with fresh regional foods and herbs has also caught on in the South.

Charleston, South Carolina, in particular, has become a foodie hub, boasting nationally recognized chefs, restaurants, and food festivals. Favorite-son chef Sean Brock, winner of the 2010 James Beard Best Chef Southeast award, leads the pack with New South cuisine focused on local foods. Sample inventive dishes at his restaurant, **McCrady's.** At **Husk,** named America's best new restaurant in 2011 by *Bon Appetit* magazine, Brock features heirloom products and crafts menus throughout each day, depending on what local purveyors bring to his kitchen.

Central North Carolina nips at Charleston's tasty heels. With its bountiful farmers market, ethnic food mix and contemporary and traditional Southern fare, Durham was recognized by the *New York Times* as an "exciting, unexpected food hub." Chapel Hill is home to lauded **Lantern,** where 2011 James Beard Best Chef Southeast Andrea Reusing uses North Carolina ingredients in Asian dishes.

Raleigh boasts **Poole's Diner,** where yet another James Beard Award winner Ashley Christensen serves seasonally changing menus in a retro-chic setting.

True to tradition, Mildred Edna Cotton Council opened her **Mama Dip's** restaurant in Chapel Hill in 1976, and serves up old-fashioned Southern home cooking. To-go picnics include fried chicken, potato salad, pickles, and pecan tarts, all tucked inside a wicker basket. Savannah, Georgia, cook Paula Deen reintroduced America to traditional Southern fare through her wildly successful **Lady and Sons** restaurant in Savannah and her Food Network cooking programs.

On your way into the Greek Revival mansion that houses Savannah's **Elizabeth on 37th,** you might see the staff snipping herbs that flavor remarkable dishes.

Elsewhere in Georgia, Summerland Farm grows organic herbs and produce for use in Anne Quatrano and Clifford Harrison's award-winning Atlanta restaurant **Bacchanalia. Quinones at Bacchanalia,** another Quatrano and Harrison restaurant, emphasizes Southern ingredients in a nightly changing tasting menu.

## Golfing

The Carolinas' and Georgia's mild climate allows play all year, and the scenery is as good as the game. Courses abound, but the chance to play top links during high seasons—spring and fall—can be a bigger challenge than getting a hole-in-one. Resorts and country clubs offer first-choice tee times to guests. If any times are left open, it is possible to get reservations.

Golf legend Bobby Jones called **Pinehurst** in North Carolina "the St. Andrews of United States golf." As the site of more championships than any other golf resort in the country, the resort is consistently ranked among the best in the world. Among its eight courses, the Donald Ross–designed Number Two is considered the masterpiece.

All 18 holes of Kiawah Island Golf Resort's **Ocean Course** offer sea views. The greens wind through salt marshes and seaside forests filled with wildlife, including the occasional alligator. This South Carolina course has one of most dramatic last holes in golf.

In the shadow of the Harbor Town Lighthouse, Hilton Head Island's **Harbour Town**

**Golf Links** is devilishly difficult. Although deceptively short by today's standards, this top South Carolina course leaves no room for error.

Often called the "granddaddy of golf," **Pine Lakes Country Club** has long been a landmark in Myrtle Beach. The columned clubhouse, resembling an antebellum mansion, was built in 1927.

## Grand Gardens

The temperate climate in the Carolinas and Georgia, combined with the region's huge diversity of flora, makes this area a draw for garden lovers.

Henry Middleton, First Continental Congress president, began the lush, semi-tropical gardens of Charleston's **Middleton Place** in 1741. Restoration of the gardens began during World War I. Today they are among the most beautiful in the world, ablaze with camellias, azaleas, roses, and magnolias. Also in the area is one of America's oldest gardens, **Magnolia Plantation and Gardens**, first planted in the mid-1680s. Among the sights is the **Audubon Swamp Garden** traversed with boardwalks and bridges over waters that host, yes, alligators.

Two outstanding gardens are in Asheville, North Carolina. The 434-acre **North Carolina Arboretum** was established in 1986 as a part of the University of North Carolina. Find a quilt garden, with plantings patterned after local quilt designs. The castlelike grandeur of **Biltmore Estate**, the country's largest private residence, has gorgeous grounds designed by Frederick Law Olmsted of New York City's Central Park fame.

Superb **Callaway Gardens** are part of a resort, but that shouldn't dissuade a visit to this outstanding spot in Pine Mountain, Georgia. **Overlook Azalea Garden** has some 700 varieties of azaleas, and the **Callaway Brothers Azalea Bowl** has 3,400 hybrid azalea plants that should not to be missed in the spring.

## Civil War History

The Civil War forever changed the South's character, particularly the bastions of plantation life in the Carolinas and Georgia. In the region's many museums, period furnishings offer glimpses into antebellum life, and heart-wrenching letters tell of the toll the war took on families—rich and poor. Photographs show the hardships suffered by slaves.

A huge painting that encircles the viewer inside the **Atlanta Cyclorama & Civil War Museum** depicts the 1864 Battle of Atlanta in detail. Inside the museum there's an impressive collection of period weapons, uniforms, maps, and photographs.

The site of one of the Civil War's worst conflicts, Chickamauga battlefield saw around 34,000 soldiers killed or injured during a three-day struggle in September 1863. North Georgia's **Chickamauga and Chattanooga National Military Park and Visitor Center** offers a glimpse into the strategies used by both sides during the campaign. Visitors can take a 7-mile driving tour to see many of the 1,400 monuments and historical markers.

Although it was built to protect Charleston after the War of 1812, **Fort Sumter** became a symbol of Southern resistance after it became the site of the first battle of the Civil War. The first shots were fired here on April 12, 1861.

Near Charleston, **Drayton Hall** is the only plantation along Ashley River Road not destroyed during General William Tecumseh Sherman's march through South Carolina.

# GREAT PLANTATIONS OF THE CAROLINAS AND GEORGIA

by Rachel Roberts Quartarone

Southern belles in hoop skirts and gentlemen smoking cigars are part of the cultural image of the Old South. Grand white-columned mansions, like Tara, the storied plantation home in *Gone with the Wind,* were the stage where life's dramas played out. Having survived the Civil War and the collapse of a way of life, today the "big houses," restored and open to the public, provide a way to see the Old South in a new light.

At the plantations of the Carolinas and Georgia, you can experience history, tour impressive and elaborate homes, and wander beautiful grounds and gardens. Fulfilling the mission to present a more balanced view of history, these heritage sites also tell the stories of enslaved people on the plantation. Visiting these historic places provides insight into the real lives of people—free and enslaved—in a time often shrouded in romance and myth.

Above, Drayton Hall

## LIFE IN THE BIG HOUSE

### IMITATING THE EUROPEANS

The planter elite fashioned their homes after the European aristocracy they came from or strove to emulate. Greek Revival was the architectural style of the day, hence the white Doric columns, gabled roofs, and broad porches now associated with the South.

Wealthy planters enjoyed throwing lavish parties. Most grand houses, like Drayton Hall in South Carolina, contained a large sitting room that could easily be transformed into a ballroom. Plantation owners traveled abroad and prized European-style furnishings and ornamental gardens like those found at Middleton Place and Magnolia Plantation near Charleston, South Carolina.

To escape the oppressive heat, bugs, and disease, planters and their families summered up north or in nearby cities like Charleston or Savannah, Georgia, where they owned townhomes. Their plantation homes, meanwhile, were left to be operated by an overseer—sometimes a trusted slave.

### HOUSES LARGE . . . AND SMALL

The oldest and grandest mansions are along South Carolina's coast in the heart of rice country. While grand for their time, some plantation homes may appear small and plain by today's standards. At their core, plantations were large working farms. Most plantations were diversified, growing a cash crop, such as cotton, but also corn, wheat, and vegetables families needed for subsistence. The wealthiest planters like the Draytons and Middletons of South Carolina usually owned a network of large plantations.

While the planter elite enjoyed a lavish lifestyle, these families comprised only a small percentage of the population. By 1860, a year before the Civil War, only 25% of Southerners owned slaves and only 12% of them owned more than 20 enslaved people. Especially on smaller plantations, the entire family worked in the fields alongside their slaves and plantation mistresses cooked, preserved food, and sewed.

The plantation house of the Magnolia Plantation, Charleston, South Carolina

## LIFE IN THE SLAVE QUARTERS

Slaves of Thomas F Drayton of Magnolia Plantation, South Carolina, 1862.

### CHARLESTON AND THE SLAVE TRADE

The story of slavery in the Carolinas and Georgia begins in Charleston, a key port in the British colonies. Throughout the 18th century, ships with human cargo arrived from Africa. Those who survived the perilous Middle Passage across the Atlantic were auctioned on the public square outside of Charleston's Exchange Building. It is estimated that 40 to 60 percent of the approximately 500,000 Africans who were brought to America during the slave trade came through Charleston's port. Although the U.S. government banned the importation of African slaves in 1808, Charleston continued to be a major center of interstate slave trading up until 1865.

### THE PLANTATION COMMUNITY

Once on the plantation, most slaves lived in rudimentary shacks where an entire family might share a space about the size of a modern-day bedroom. Slave quarters were usually clustered together a good distance away from the owner's compound. As a result, the enslaved formed close family and community ties. They shared and passed down African music, folklore and other cultural traditions, and did their best to survive the grueling living conditions.

Old Slave Mart Museum in Charleston

Georgia politician Alexander H. Stephens with a servant, formerly a slave

### OLD SLAVE MART

For a quick history lesson about the transatlantic slave trade and to get a sense of how enslaved people were treated, bought, and sold, head to the Old Slave Mart Museum in Charleston. African-Americans were sold here as part of the domestic slave trade from 1856 to 1863. Documents, shackles, and other eye-opening artifacts bring home the inhumanity of this sordid chapter in history. ⇨ *See Chapter 7.*

# BEST NORTH CAROLINA PLANTATIONS

Poplar Grove Plantation

Fodor's Choice ★ HISTORIC STAGVILLE
Notable For: Original two-story slave cabins

HISTORIC LATTA PLANTATION
Notable For: Living history farm

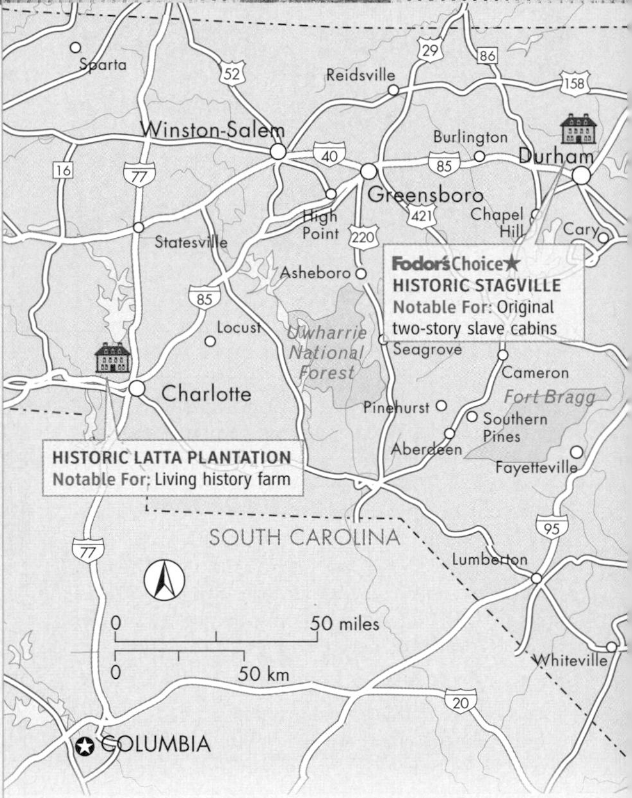

While North Carolina plantation homes have the reputation of being more plain and utilitarian than their Deep South counterparts, these amazingly preserved plantations and yeomen farmsteads shed light on the realities of life in the Old South.

**HISTORIC LATTA PLANTATION,** Huntersville. The last remaining Catawba River plantation open to the public, this living history site interprets 19th-century farm life in North Carolina's backcountry. James Latta, a traveling merchant, built the plantation's Federal-style home in 1800 and soon became a cotton planter. According to family documents, the entire Latta family and their 34 slaves assisted with production on the 742-acre farm. Today, visitors can tour the home as well as reconstructed slave quarters and a yeoman farmer's home. Historically appropriate farm animals and special weekend programs, such as folk craft demonstrations, round out the experience. ⇨ *See Chapter 3.*

**POPLAR GROVE PLANTATION,** Wilmington. Peanuts, not rice, were the claim to fame at this coastal plantation. James Foy, Jr., purchased the 628-acre plantation in 1795. The Foy family became pioneers in the peanut industry, which helped the plantation to survive the post–Civil War economy. An 1850 Greek Revival–style home, smokehouse, kitchen, and tenant farmer's home recreate a 19th-century working plantation. Blacksmiths and weavers regularly demonstrate their crafts—skills likely held by the Foy slaves. ⇨ *See Chapter 2.*

Somerset Place

**SOMERSET PLACE,** Creswell. Located in the rural upstate, Somerset Place was one of the largest plantations in North Carolina. The 100,000-acre plantation actively produced rice, corn, wheat and timber from 1785 to 1865. Home to 800 enslaved African Americans, the plantation was practically a small town with

a thriving slave community, hospital, chapel, sawmills, smokehouse, salting house, and dairy in addition to the owners' complex. Some of the original buildings remain, while others are reconstructed. The 1½-hour tour includes the Collins' 1830 Greek Revival home as well as the slave quarters and outbuildings. Self-guided tours are another option. ⇨ *See Chapter 2.*

Historic Stagville

**Fodor's Choice★**

**HISTORIC STAGVILLE,** Durham. Owned by the Bennehan and Cameron families, Stagville once stretched to 30,000 acres and was one of the largest plantations in the Southeast. The plantation's two-story wood frame home, completed in 1799, may seem plain and even austere by today's standards. In its time, however, the house was quite a status symbol as it stood tall on a hill overlooking the fields. About 900 slaves lived at Stagville. Remarkably preserved are the unusual two-story slave cabins, built between 1851 and 1860, to help prevent disease among the slave population. Also impressive is the Great Barn, built and engineered by enslaved craftspeople throughout the 1850s. Guided tours of the property include the main house and other interesting buildings like the Horton Home, a yeoman farmer's homestead that owner Richard Bennehan purchased in 1823. The pre-Revolutionary War home was typical of other farm homes in the region—simple, sturdy and practical. The home was likely adapted to house an overseer or slave family. It's interesting to note that corn, not tobacco, was the cash crop here. While tobacco was grown here, it did not become the primary crop of the region until after the Civil War. ⇨ *See Chapter 3.*

# BEST SOUTH CAROLINA PLANTATIONS

Drayton Hall

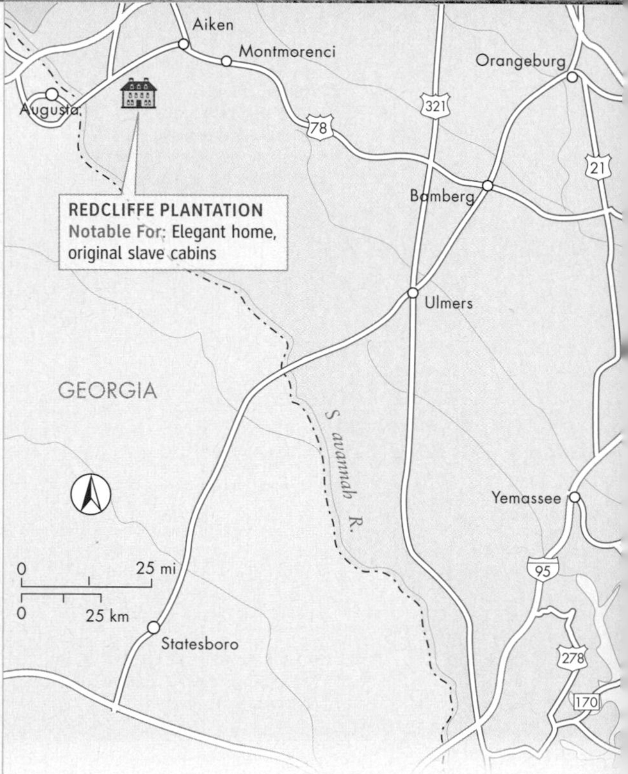

**REDCLIFFE PLANTATION**
**Notable For:** Elegant home, original slave cabins

Some of the oldest and most ornate plantation homes are found in South Carolina. Planters here sought slaves from the Windward Coast of Africa (modern-day Senegal, Sierra Leone, and Liberia) because they were experienced in rice cultivation. Rice farming was especially arduous work, but because enslaved Africans were knowledgeable and their owners were not, they were able to bargain for a task system of labor that sometimes allowed for a shorter workday. Rice cultivation brought with it tremendous wealth you'll see reflected in the grand showplaces of the Lowcountry.

**DRAYTON HALL,** Charleston. Built between 1738 and 1742, Drayton Hall is the oldest plantation house in the nation that remains in preserved form. The Drayton family ran an empire of rice plantations, but this home was built to be the primary residence and showplace, not a working plantation. House tours focus on the immaculate Georgian Palladian architecture and slave craftsmanship that made its construction possible. Offered daily, a separate "Connections" program focuses on African American history at the plantation. ⇨ *See Chapter 7.*

Drayton Hall

**MAGNOLIA PLANTATION,** Charleston. Another home of the Drayton family, the plantation boasts a massive informal garden with some parts remaining true to its original 1685 design. After the Civil War, rice production ceased and the gardens became the focus of the property. The "From Slavery to Freedom" tour provides a look at restored cabins that were occupied by African-Americans at the plantation from 1850 through to the 1960s. A guided boat tour takes you through former rice fields. ⇨ *See Chapter 7.*

**REDCLIFFE PLANTATION,** Beech Island. Completed in 1859, this Greek Revival showplace was home to James Henry Hammond, the statesmen

Middleton Place

Magnolia Plantation

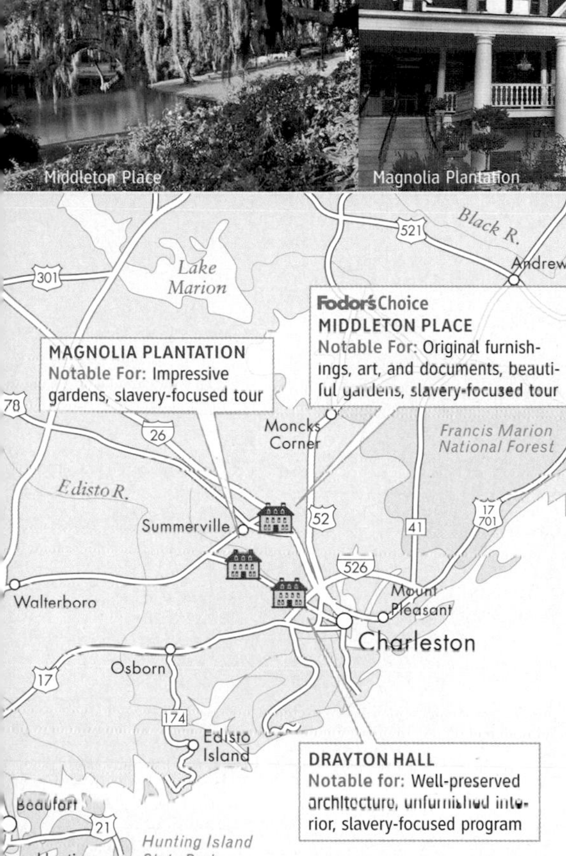


who coined the phrase "Cotton is King." Aided by some 300 slaves, Hammond grew cotton on his three other Beech Island plantations. Redcliffe served as the primary residence and grounds for experimentation with sugar cane, viniculture, and indigo. Now a state park, tours of the home and grounds—including original slave cabins—are offered Thursday through Monday. ⇨ *See Chapter 9.*

Middleton Place

**Fodor's Choice★**

**MIDDLETON PLACE,** Charleston. Established around 1742, Middleton Place was at the center of the Middleton family's empire of rice plantations which consisted of 63,000 acres and 3,500 slaves on properties throughout the South Carolina Lowcountry. With its massive three-story brick manor home and prized gardens, Middleton Place was a grand statement of wealth. The original manor home was destroyed in the Civil War, but one of its flanking buildings, which served as the gentlemen's guest quarters, was salvaged and transformed into the family's post-bellum residence. Still quite a showplace, the home displays original furnishings, documents, and works of art belonging to the Middletons. Restored in the 1920s, the breathtakingly beautiful gardens are considered the oldest landscaped gardens in the country.

To get the complete picture of life on a rice plantation, be sure to allow time for the African American Focus tour. The tour begins at Eliza's House, a restored 1870s sharecropper's home. Inside the house, a small exhibit provides details on the lives of the Middleton slaves. Next door, the reconstructed stableyards features farm animals and demonstrations by skilled craftspeople in period attire. ⇨ *See Chapter 7.*

# BEST GEORGIA PLANTATIONS

Archibald Smith Plantation

A coastal rice plantation and former cotton plantations, including the showplace of the Cherokee nation, are among the historic plantation homes that remain in Georgia.

**Fodor's Choice★**
**CHIEF VANN HOUSE HISTORIC SITE**
**Notable For:** Owned by a Cherokee leader

**ARCHIBALD SMITH PLANTATION**
**Notable For:** Owner's history and conflicted views on slavery

**ARCHIBALD SMITH PLANTATION,** Roswell. Among the group of prominent families who moved from the Georgia coast to former Cherokee lands to found the city of Roswell, Archibald Smith was the only planter. Built in 1845, the home's Plantation Plain style architecture is typical of most plantations in the region. Smith owned about 40 slaves, but held conflicted views on the practice. He experimented with paying his slaves wages and contemplated ways to teach them self-governance. An outbuilding, believed to have been slave quarters, is furnished appropriate to the time period and provides more information about slaves on the property. ⇨ *See Chapter 13.*

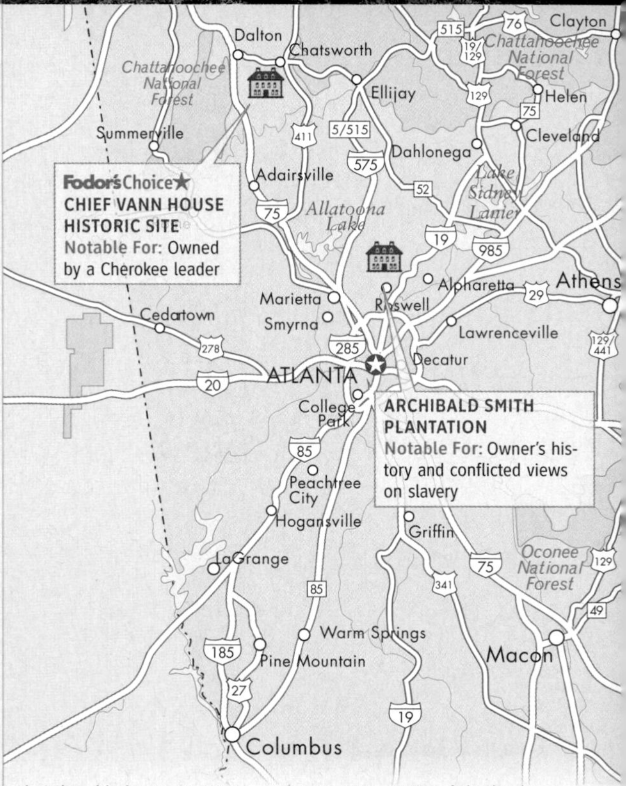

**CALLAWAY PLANTATION,** Washington. You can trace the Callaways' rise to prominence as cotton planters on the Georgia frontier from their humble beginnings in a settler's log cabin (1785) to their grand redbrick mansion (1869). Guided tours allow a glimpse into the mansion while the other buildings, such as a kitchen, blacksmith's shop and schoolhouse, are self-guided. ⇨ *See Chapter 14.*

Callaway Plantation

**HOFWYL-BROADFIELD PLANTATION,** Brunswick. Now a state park, this former rice plantation owned by the Troup and Dent families is representative of the kind of rice plantations that once flourished on the Georgia coast. The two-story Hofwyl House was built in the 1850s, although the plantation (known as Broadfield) dates to 1806. The museum and visitor center offer a short film and exhibits about the planter families, rice cultivation, and the lives of the enslaved people who worked and lived here. The home is furnished with original family pieces. ⇨ *See Chapter 11.*

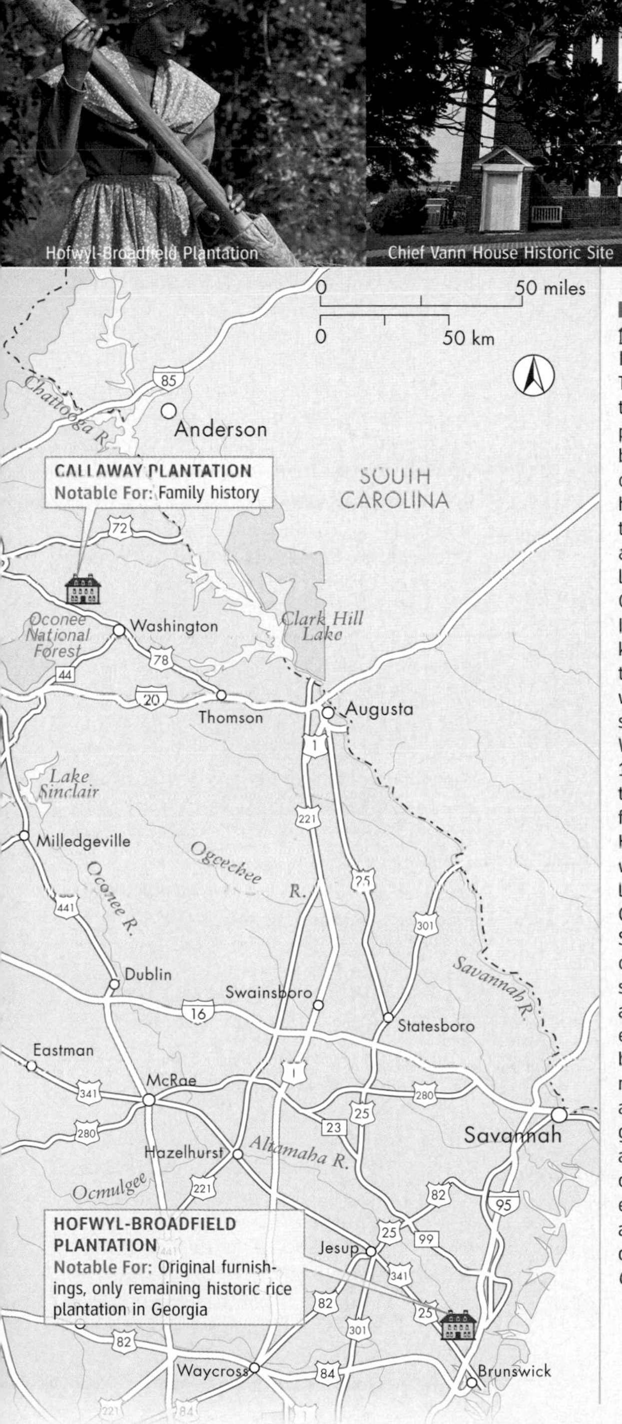


Hofwyl-Broadfield Plantation

Chief Vann House Historic Site

**Fodor's Choice★**

**CHIEF VANN HOUSE HISTORIC SITE,** Chatsworth. This beautiful home with all the trappings of the wealthy planter lifestyle is fascinating because of the intermingling of cultures that took place here. Known as Diamond Hill, this historic site was home to a 1000-acre plantation—the largest and most prosperous in Cherokee history.

In 1804 James Vann, a Cherokee leader, built the plantation's stately redbrick mansion with the help of Moravian missionaries and enslaved workers. When Vann was murdered in 1809, his son Joseph took over the property until he was forcefully evicted in 1835. Diamond Hill and surrounding lands were then given away in a land lottery to white settlers, its Cherokee origins wiped away. Start your visit in the visitor center where you can view a short film and browse exhibits about the site's history. Rangers lead tours of the home, but outdoor exhibits, such as a recreated Cherokee farmstead and plantation kitchen, are self-guided. The kitchen outbuilding also houses an exhibit focused on the daily lives of the 110 enslaved people who resided at Diamond Hill before Vann's departure in 1835. ⇨ *See Chapter 14.*

# WITH KIDS

Try these sights and events for guaranteed family fun.

## Wet and Wild

NASCAR's slick **Charlotte Motor Speedway** in Concord holds up to 140,000 fans on race days. On non–race days, racetrack tours—including a drive around the track—are available for kids and adults.

Get a look at 18 historic stock cars or get the driver's experience by sitting inside a racing simulator that provides virtual laps around a speedway at the **NASCAR Hall of Fame** in Charlotte.

Atlanta's **Georgia Aquarium** is the largest in the world, with sea creatures in 10 million gallons of water. Special programs are aimed at toddlers, and families with kids ages 5–10 can take a behind-the-scenes tour to learn about the aquarium's sharks and how they are managed.

**Riverbanks Zoo and Garden** in Columbia, South Carolina, supplies grounds for exotic animals like Siberian tigers, siamang apes, lemurs, and giraffes. More than 2,000 animals occupy natural habitats, while around 4,200 native and exotic plant species fill gardens. Civil War ruins dot the landscape, too.

## Back to the Future

Take a self-guided tour or follow guides in native costume at the **Oconaluftee Indian Village,** which tracks back 225 years with demonstrations of weaving, hunting techniques, and canoe construction. The nearby **Museum of the Cherokee Indian** contains artifacts and displays that cover 11,000 years. Nature walks, dance programs, and traditional Cherokee dinners are available, in addition to museum tours. Both the village and the museum are near Cherokee, North Carolina, and the entrance to the Great Smoky Mountains National Park.

Kids can climb Big Devil Hill where Wilbur and Orville Wright tested their gliders at the **Wright Brothers National Memorial,** south of Kitty Hawk, North Carolina. Stand right on the spot where the Ohio bicyclists first took flight on December 17, 1903, and examine a replica of their *Flyer.* There's also a kite-building demonstration for kids followed by a chance for them to fly their own homemade kites.

## Hands-on Adventures

Along the way to major attractions, take side trips to spots guaranteed to please. **EdVenture Children's Museum** in Columbia, South Carolina, is nothing but hands-on fun, from science experiments to anchoring a newscast.

Myrtle Beach is awash with activities guaranteed to bring smiles—and squeals—from the 30-plus rides at **Family Kingdom Amusement Park** to **Myrtle Waves,** South Carolina's largest water park, and many colorful mini- and putt-putt golf courses.

Kids of all ages never tire of classic **Six Flags Over Georgia,** the state's major theme park. Start with easy family rides, move on to scream-drawing roller coasters, and then cool down with water attractions.

## Easy on Mom and Dad

Kids can collect shells while parents stroll the beach on **Pawleys Island,** South Carolina. Challenge energetic youngsters to climb the East Coast's tallest sand dune (80 to 100 feet) at **Jockey's Ridge State Park** in Nags Head, North Carolina, or test adventurous teens with a visit to the "mile-high" swinging bridge at **Grandfather Mountain,** North Carolina, in the Smoky Mountains. Join the kids as they splash through the Fountain of Rings at **Atlanta's Centennial Olympic Park.**

# SOUTHERN SOUNDS

Trace bluegrass, blues, and gospel to the Carolinas and Georgia. Each distinctive genre was nurtured and passed to future generations in the region's homes, churches, and social clubs.

### Old-time and Bluegrass

Ballads, fiddles, and pluck-string instruments are well known throughout the region thanks to Africans and Scotch-Irish immigrants in Appalachia. North Carolina's continuing old-time music tradition influenced bluegrass and country. Top performers Doc Watson, Del McCoury, and the famous Earl Scruggs, known for his revolutionary three-finger banjo-plucking style, all were born in North Carolina. The state is a hotbed of music festivals, including late April's famous **MerleFest**, in Wilkesboro, where players gather to honor bluegrass and Appalachian music. **Folkmoot USA** brings folk music and dance to Waynesville during the last two weeks of July.

### Gospel to Rhythm and Blues

Spirituals that slaves in the South sang enriched gospel's signature repetitive lyrics and simple tunes, creating soulful songs that define gospel music. Georgia natives James Brown and Little Richard fused gospel with blues and boogie-woogie to create soul music and rhythm and blues. In the 1960s, Georgia's Gladys Knight and Otis Redding added strong emotion. The state's gospel, soul, and rhythm and blues pioneers are celebrated at the **Georgia Music Hall of Fame** in downtown Macon.

African Americans' unique finger-picking guitar style shaped ragtime-based rhythms of Piedmont blues. A favorite was the Rev. Gary Davis, born in Laurens, South Carolina, in 1896. While living in Durham in the 1920s, he collaborated with other Piedmont blues players, and this part of North Carolina remains a go-to area for shows. North Carolina's **Piedmont Blues Preservation Society** compiles information about live performances at 🌐 *www.piedmontblues.org.*

### Beach Music

Blues, jazz, big-band swing, R&B, doo-wop, boogie, rockabilly, and old-time rock and roll make up the Carolinas' easy-going Beach Music. Legendary bands like the Tams, the Embers, and Band of Oz supply the sound's shuffle-foot "shag" dance done to titles like "Summertime's Calling Me" and "Under the Boardwalk." Myrtle Beach FM radio station 94.9 FM plays all Beach Music, and it lists live music shows and other events at its website 🌐 *www.949thesurf.com,* but many stations from North Carolina south to Georgia broadcast Beach Music. Each November, North Myrtle Beach hosts the Carolina **Beach Music Awards**, when bands perform at famous clubs like **Fat Harold's**.

### New South Sounds

To find today's Southern sounds, all you have to do is look to the college towns in the Carolinas and Georgia. Athens, Georgia; Chapel Hill, North Carolina; and Columbia, South Carolina, host clubs where Hootie and the Blowfish, Ben Folds Five, R.E.M., and the B-52s got their start. Check equally cool urban centers, too. The Avett Brothers formed their punk/bluegrass band in Charlotte, North Carolina. Atlanta's famous nightclub Opera is the place for hip-hop and house music, but don your best duds: a strict dress code is enforced. Hear the latest country sounds at Swallow at the Hollow in Roswell, just outside Atlanta.

# GREAT ITINERARIES

## ASHEVILLE AND THE GREAT SMOKY MOUNTAINS

### The South's hippest city meets America's most visited National Park, 4 days

The soft mountain peaks, blue fog, and fall leaves of the Great Smoky Mountains have long inspired painters, writers, and musicians. Art-centric Asheville edges this great American landscape and makes the perfect launch pad for mountain touring. Pack your hiking boots to see the natural beauty up close.

#### DAY 1: DOWNTOWN ASHEVILLE

Drive into **Asheville** *(p. 191)* or land at pleasant **Asheville Regional Airport** *(p. 189)*, one of the South's best small airports, and rent a car. Stay downtown at **Haywood Park Hotel** *(p. 206)*—the expansive suites are close to the action. Hip Asheville is a center of North Carolina's craft beer and local food movements, so lunch at lively **Lexington Avenue Brewery,** better known as LAB. Pair a beer flight with small plates like chorizo nachos and mussels vindaloo in the historic building that was once the city's oldest store. Hit the sidewalks for a look at Asheville's art and architecture. Elaborate bricked and polychrome-tiled **Basilica of St. Lawrence** *(p. 192)* is a few blocks from LAB, as is **Black Mountain College Museum + Arts Center** *(p. 193)*. The legendary college nurtured maverick 20th-century artists. Alternately, kick around the architectural wonder that is **Grove Arcade Public Market** *(p. 193)*, built in 1929. Armies of stone gargoyles guard numerous locally owned stores and restaurants. Make advanced reservations for a dinner of extraordinary tapas at **Cúrate** *(p. 199)*, the hottest restaurant in town, which is partially owned by Chef Felix Meana, formerly of the famed elBulli restaurant on the Costa Brava of Spain. Or, if you're craving a "meat and three" Southern meal made with quality local ingredients, head to **Early Girl Eatery** *(p. 199)*. An early dinner allows time for a show at **Asheville Community Theater,** which stages productions year-round.

#### DAY 2: GREAT SMOKY MOUNTAINS

*(1½ hours by car)*

Rise early to visit one of Asheville's more than 50 tailgate markets, including **Asheville City Market** *(p. 200)*. Stock up on locally made foods for the ride to **Great Smoky Mountains National Park** *(p. 237)*. Interstate 40 heading west is the quickest route out of Asheville. Take the highway to U.S. 19, which links to the spectacular **Blue Ridge Parkway** *(p. 218)* just west of Maggie Valley. The parkway leads into Great Smoky Mountains National Park. At the park entrance, stop by **Oconaluftee Visitor Center** *(p. 243)* for maps and information. Spend the day exploring by vehicle and by foot. **Newfound Gap Road**/U.S. 441 *(p. 245)* is one of the park's most scenic drives and leads to **Clingmans Dome Trail** *(p. 254)*. This moderately difficult 1-mile trail ends at a 54-foot tall observation tower affording amazing mountain views. The round-trip hike takes about an hour, a nice warm-up before a picnic lunch and then another hike along **Trillium Gap Trail to Grotto Falls** *(p. 275)*. The 1.3-mile, moderately difficult hike ends at the 30-foot-high falls, the only falls in the park that you can walk behind. Stick around the park for sunset views at **Chimney Tops Overlook** *(p. 272)*. Camp at the park or depart for two luxurious nights at nearby **Grove Park Inn Resort & Spa** *(p. 207)*. The grand hotel, built in 1913 with locally mined

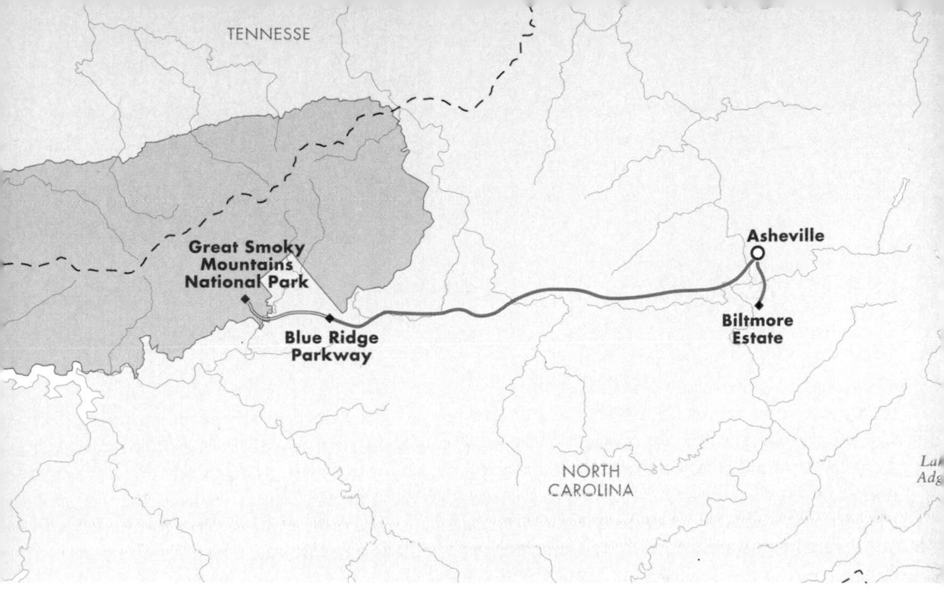


stone, is home to the world's largest collection of Arts and Crafts furniture. The tony spa offers massages, outdoor whirlpools, and a subterranean sanctuary to ease tired hiking muscles.

**DAY 3: BILTMORE ESTATE**

*(15 minutes by car from Asheville)*

Stick around Grove Park Inn for a sunrise breakfast. If the weather is warm, book a day of kayaking, canoeing, or whitewater rafting via the Grove Park Inn's Nantahala Outdoor Center. The center also offers mountain biking, hiking, climbing, fishing and horseback riding adventures in the Blue Ridge and Great Smoky mountains.

If the weather is chilly, set off instead for a morning tour of **Biltmore Estate** *(p. 196)*, America's largest private home. Built in the 1890s as George Vanderbilt's private residence, this castle of sorts has 250 rooms, including its own bowling alley, and 75 acres of gardens and grounds. Be sure to visit the complex's state-of-the-art winery and tasting rooms, as well as the winery's Bistro restaurant, one of four Biltmore spots that serve lunch.

Spend late afternoon at the **North Carolina Arboretum** *(p. 197)*, created by Fredrick Law Olmsted, designer of New York City's Central Park, and part of the original Biltmore Estate. See 65 acres of cultivated gardens and a bonsai exhibit of native trees. You may also explore a 10-mile network of trails.

Biltmore Village boasts many fine eateries, including **Corner Kitchen** *(p. 205)*. The renovated Victorian cottage has a fireplace in one dining room. The restaurant serves American classics with a twist like pecan-crusted mountain trout with bourbon sauce or sweet-mustard-glazed three-meat meatloaf.

**DAY 4: HEAD HOME**

If you're flying out of Asheville, enjoy breakfast at Grove Park Inn, where window-lined dining rooms provide fantastic views. If you're driving home, check out early and head to downtown Asheville's funky **Tupelo Honey Café** *(p. 202)* for down-home Southern cooking with an uptown twist. Think maple-peppered bacon strips, goat cheese grits, and sweet-potato pancakes with whipped peach butter and spiced pecans. Don't forget a souvenir: a Tupelo Honey Café brown-butter pecan pie to go.

## THE LOWCOUNTRY

### Savannah to Charleston, 7 days

Stretching from genteel Savannah, Georgia, to lively Charleston, South Carolina, the Lowcountry serves up history, culture, stunning coastlines, urban flair, and culinary adventures. Unspoiled natural areas and captivating seaside communities dot the easy 150-mile drive between these two Southern hospitality centers. Secure reservations at popular restaurants before you leave home.

#### DAYS 1 AND 2: SAVANNAH

Drive into **Savannah** *(p. 477)* or arrive by plane at **Savannah/Hilton Head International Airport** *(p. 483)* and rent a car. Immerse yourself in the feel of old Savannah with a stay at elegant but inviting **Foley House Inn** *(p. 506)*, where you'll be treated to complimentary breakfast, afternoon tea, and evening wine and hors d'oeuvres.

Once refreshed, spend a few leisurely hours strolling Bull Street. Enjoy beautifully landscaped squares and the **Green-Meldrim House,** a Gothic Revival mansion where General Sherman once lived, on the way to **Forsyth Park** *(p. 489)*. Massive, moss-draped oaks line wide park lanes leading to war memorials, an old fort, and a magnificent fountain.

For dinner, leave the beaten path for **Leoci's Trattoria** *(p. 500)*. Housemade pasta, inspired by the owner's Sicilian grandmother, is especially nice on the patio.

Savannah's various tours offer fun and easy overviews of the city's rich history. On day two, step back in time on a morning horse-drawn history tour with **Carriage Tours of Savannah** *(p. 484)*. The 50-minute journey winds through the historic district as drivers narrate. Afterwards, set out on foot for the **Owens-Thomas House and Museum** *(p. 490)*, one of America's finest examples of English Regency architecture. Grab lunch at **Angel's BBQ** *(p. 481)*, a favorite for brisket, pork barbecue, and stewed collard greens with a side of peanut sauce. Spend the afternoon shopping at **Riverfront/Factors Walk** *(p. 489)*, where a network of iron crosswalks and stairways leads to renovated warehouses hosting shops, cafes, and pubs. Splurge for dinner with the seven-course tasting menu at award-winning **Elizabeth on 37th** *(p. 499)*.

#### DAY 3: HILTON HEAD ISLAND

*(1 hour by car from Savannah)*

**Hilton Head Island** *(p. 421)* beaches span 12 miles, offering respite after busy Savannah. **Burkes Beach** *(p. 432)*, mid-island, is a quiet place to stroll or sunbathe before being pampered at **Spa at Palmetto Bluff** *(p. 439)*, where you may also book accommodations. Wraps, massages, and soothing baths on the veranda are first-class. Soak up more island beauty at **Old Fort Pub** *(p. 426)*. Tucked under an umbrella of old oaks hung with Spanish moss, the restaurant has near panoramic views of stunning sunsets and sweeping marshlands, not to mention an impressive wine list and a tasting menu. Lowcountry crawfish cakes might share space with hazelnut-crusted beef tenderloin alongside a sweet potato tart. **The Jazz Corner** *(p. 431)* serves a musical nightcap.

#### DAY 4: ST. HELENA ISLAND

*(1 hour by car from Hilton Head Island)*

The Lowcountry is rooted in Gullah culture. The Gullah people, descendants of 18th-century slaves, maintain their dialect and heritage, much of it centered on **St. Helena Island** *(p. 440)*, where Gullahs still catch shrimp with hand-tied nets. **Penn Center** *(p. 440)*, the first school for freed slaves, is official Gullah headquarters

and part of the Penn School Historic District, which includes old burial grounds and Gantt Cottage, where Martin Luther King Jr. stayed. At **York W. Bailey Museum** *(p. 441)*, see Gullah indigo stamping, wood-burning art, and sweetgrass basket-making demonstrations. **Gullah Grub** restaurant features authentic Lowcountry cooking.

**DAYS 5 AND 6: CHARLESTON**

*(2½ hours by car from Hilton Head Island)*

Charleston's status as the South's foodie capital gives the city a delicious layer of appeal atop all the art, architecture, history, and natural beauty there. Arrive in time for freshly made breakfast crepes and cold-pressed coffee at **Queen Street Grocery** *(p. 378)*. Walking **Charleston's Historic District** *(p. 354)* is a great way to see key landmarks such as the 1752 **St. Michael's Episcopal Church** *(p. 362)*, the city's oldest surviving church, and nosh along the way. For lunch, **Alluette's Café** *(p. 369)* serves "holistic soul food," including fried shrimp, inspired by Geechee-Gullah culture. Or weekdays take a seat at the chef's table at **Slightly North of Broad** *(p. 379)*, which looks into the kitchen, giving you a view of all that goes into your meal preparation at this energetic Lowcountry bistro.

No culinary tour of Charleston is complete without visiting James Beard Award–winning chef Sean Brock's **McCrady's** *(p. 377)* and **Husk** *(p. 376)* restaurants. Book dinner at McCrady's and lunch the next day at Husk. Both spots highlight new Southern cooking and local ingredients. Husk is also earning a reputation for cool cocktails. Their Carriage Tour Punch blends St. Germain, blood orange liqueur, gin, chamomile, and honey syrup.

With a Husk lunch reservation secured, spend Day 6 working up an appetite by touring Charleston's magnificent plantations. **Magnolia Plantation Gardens** *(p. 367)* has a huge array of blooming plants, a 19th-century plantation house, and 500 acres of trails. Stunning **Middleton Place** *(p. 367)* has terraced lawns, butterfly-shaped lakes and, for dinner, Lowcountry specialties at Middleton Place Restaurant.

After dinner, toast this grand dame of Southern cities at swanky outdoor Pavilion Bar atop **Market Pavilion Hotel** *(p. 387)*. Terrific views and creative cocktails make this Charleston's best rooftop bar.

**DAY 7: FUEL UP FOR TAKE-OFF**

Have breakfast of housemade sausage with fresh ginger pumpkin bread at homespun **Hominy Grill** *(p. 375)* before catching a flight or driving home.

## ATLANTA

### Discover the New South, 3 days

Traditional but always forward-looking Atlanta earns its place as the New South's capital. A city that began as a railroad terminus in 1837 grew to become Georgia's cosmopolitan center. Old-school Southern hospitality meets business and industry here. America's busiest airport and a clean, safe, above-ground rail line make Atlanta an easy weekend getaway.

**DAY 1: ARRIVE IN ATLANTA**

Landing early at **Hartsfield-Jackson Atlanta International Airport** *(p. 582)* means plenty of time to dive into Atlanta's thrilling urban scene. Sleek, glass, steel and stone towers and grand city views at **Omni Hotel at CNN Center** *(p. 616)* set the mood and are close to public transportation. Right at the hotel, start with a 55-minute, behind-the-scenes tour of **CNN Center** *(p. 587)*. Next stop: **Georgia Aquarium** *(p. 587)*. That this landlocked city is home to the world's largest aquarium (10 million gallons of water) is testimony to Atlanta's progressive attitude. Take the MARTA subway to Midtown for a contemporary Southern lunch at **JCT Kitchen & Bar** *(p. 607)*. Billed as a "farmstead bistro" with Southern flair, JCT is the place for deviled eggs with country ham, pimento cheese fry bread, grilled okra, and chicken and dumplings made with chicken confit and potato dumplings. Don't leave Midtown without checking the evening lineup at **Fox Theatre** *(p. 593)*. The vintage movie palace built in 1929 is worth seeing for its Moorish-Egyptian style alone. The ceiling has moving clouds and twinkling stars. These days, it's a venue for dance, concerts, musicals, and film festivals. Head back to the hotel to ready for a night on the town, whether it's a Fox Theatre show or one of Midtown's hot clubs. In the Crescent Street Entertainment District you'll find **Opera** *(p. 626)*, a hopping theaterlike dance club with balcony VIP boxes and personal cocktail service. Don your fancy garb; there's a strict dress code.

**DAY 2: ART AND HISTORY**

*(15 minutes by subway)*

Sleep in, stick around the hotel for breakfast, and then find your way to Atlanta's **Sweet Auburn** *(p. 589)* district to tour the area where civil rights leader Reverend Martin Luther King Jr. was born, raised, and later returned, making Atlanta a center for social change. Sign up early for a guided tour of the **Martin Luther King Jr. National Historic Site and Birth Home** *(p. 590)*. A limited number of visitors are allowed to visit the house each day; arriving early is the surest way to get inside. Also visit **Ebenezer Baptist Church** (p. 589), where King was baptized and later preached alongside his father. Stroll the **International Civil Rights Walk of Fame** *(p. 577)*. Granite markers recognize civil rights leaders like Rosa Parks. Pay tribute to King and his compatriots at **The King Center** *(p. 577)*, which houses the Eternal Flame and the Kings' final resting place. Note the inscription on King's white marble tomb: "Free at last, free at last, thank God almighty I'm free at last." End a tour of this inspiring district at **Sweet Auburn Curb Market** *(p. 591)*, named for the days when whites were allowed to shop inside while African Americans had to shop along the curb. Cafés, meats, and fresh produce fill the market.

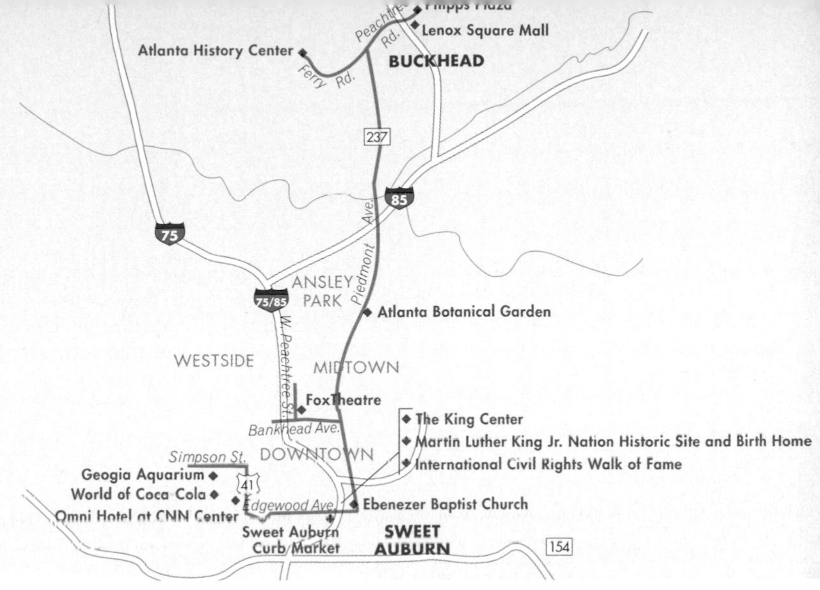


Have lunch at the market or move on to fashionable **Buckhead.** With its history museums, cool shopping, and hot restaurants, the neighborhood is a perfect example of Atlanta's Old South/New South blend. Hip **Eclipse di Luna** *(p. 609)* is a fun place for a glass of wine and shared tapas like honey and goat cheese–stuffed piquillo peppers with tomato sauce, although you may want to hoard your own sweet-and-spicy brisket on a biscuit.

While in Buckhead, visit **Atlanta History Center** *(p. 597)*, which focuses on Atlanta, the South, and the Civil War. A plantation house and a 1928 mansion are on the 33-acre complex, too. Stick around Buckhead for shopping and dinner, followed by smooth jazz at **Dante's Down the Hatch** *(p. 627)*. If you have your own vehicle or a rental car, head to **The Swallow at the Hollow** *(p. 615)*, a legendary barbecue restaurant and country-music venue all in one in nearby Roswell.

### DAY 3: BRUNCH AND STROLL

*(15 minutes by subway)*

Breakfast at **Flying Biscuit** *(p. 612)*. With six Atlanta locations, the spot is an easy mark for tall, pillowy biscuits with cranberry apple butter or a full breakfast, perhaps orange-scented French toast or grilled flat-iron steak and eggs. Don't forget to get some biscuits to go. Choosing the Midtown location will put you near the 30-acre **Atlanta Botanical Garden** *(p. 592)* inside Piedmont Park. There's an orchid center, hardwood forest with walking trails, and a 2-acre interactive kids garden. Atlanta's economic success is evident at **Phipps Plaza** *(p. 632)*, a shopping center with big names like Gucci, Saks Fifth Avenue, and Tiffany & Co. **Lenox Square Mall** *(p. 632)* has more than 200 stores including BVLGARI and Louis Vuitton. Before departing the hotel for home, stop by the nearby **World of Coca-Cola** *(p. 587)*, a shrine to the famous soda whose corporate headquarters are based in Atlanta. Sample the many different Cokes sold around the world, see the company's more-than-a-century's worth of marketing and, of course, buy a refrigerator magnet before you head home in the afternoon or early evening.

2

# The North Carolina Coast

## WORD OF MOUTH

"Buy a kite, hike up the sand dunes and literally go fly a kite! There's a great kite store in Kitty Hawk. . . . If you have a four-wheel-drive vehicle, go to the northern part of the outer banks to Corolla where you can drive on the beach and see wild horses. Make sure to let some air out of your tires first or you WILL get stuck."

—gillybrit

# WELCOME TO THE NORTH CAROLINA COAST

## TOP REASONS TO GO

★ **Water, water everywhere:** Surfers delight in Cape Hatteras's formidable waves. Kayakers and boaters prefer the Crystal Coast's sleepy estuaries. Beach strollers love Ocracoke's remote, unspoiled shore.

★ **Pirate lore and hidden booty:** The Graveyard of the Atlantic is littered with shipwrecks to dive. See artifacts from Blackbeard's flagship *Queen Anne's Revenge* at Beaufort's North Carolina Maritime Museum.

★ **Lighting the darkness:** North Carolina's seven lighthouses each has its individual personality.

★ **The Lost Colony:** In a mystery for the ages, 117 settlers disappeared without a trace. Their story is presented both in historical context and dramatic entertainment in Manteo.

★ **Fresh seafood:** You can get fresh seafood of every variety fixed in practically every method—fried, grilled, stuffed, blackened, or raw.

**1 The Outer Banks.** Long stretches of wild beach are intermingled with small, lively towns on this ribbon of sand. The north end is a tourist mecca of shops, resorts, restaurants, beach cottages, and historic sites. Quieter villages and open, undeveloped beach mark the south end where travelers often hear nothing but surf and shorebirds. With just one two-lane road stretching the length of the Outer Banks, locals speak of mile markers instead of street numbers.

**2 Cape Hatteras National Seashore.** With challenging waves, myriad fish, and the impressive Cape Hatteras lighthouse anchoring the south end, this wide-open beach is a surfer's playground, an angler's dream, and a history buff's treasure.

**3 The Crystal Coast and New Bern.** History here ranges from colonial sites to the birthplace of Pepsi, while extensive ocean, sound, and river fronts please boaters, anglers, water-sports lovers, and those who just want to relax on a big Southern porch with a glass of sweet tea.

**4 Wilmington and the Cape Fear Coast.** Part cosmopolitan, part old-fashioned Southern charm, the Cape Fear region has attracted people from all over the world since explorers first landed here in the early 1500s. You can still cast a line off an old wooden pier or spend the day roaming art galleries and wine bars.

## GETTING ORIENTED

You could pick a destination and stick to it, but touring the entire Carolina coast is doable in four to five days, especially in spring and fall when traffic is lighter. Drive here from nearby locales or fly into airports at Wilmington or New Bern, North Carolina; Myrtle Beach, South Carolina; or Norfolk, Virginia; then rent a car. A vehicle is essential for navigating the coast here, as little public transportation is available. State-operated vehicle ferries and smaller private ferries run between islands and provide an enjoyable, relaxing tour. Boat touring is another option. Dozens of marinas line the shore, and the intracoastal waterway runs the length of the North Carolina coast.

# NORTH CAROLINA BEACHES

"Endless beaches" is hardly an overstatement when it comes to North Carolina's coast. From the north end's Outer Banks to the Central Coast's unspoiled Cape Lookout and the cottage-lined southern shores, white sands, and the pristine sea seem endless.

(above) All kids need is a pail and a shovel to enjoy a day at Wrightsville Beach. (lower right) The Cape Fear Kite Festival features large show kites. (upper right) Surfers gather near piers where sandbars create better waves.

Continuous barrier islands comprise 300-plus miles of coastline. Explore lighthouses, aquariums, museums, woodlands, and historic sites galore. Playtime means golf, carnival rides, fishing, and water sports. The Outer Banks range from the north end's quiet Corolla, where wild horses roam, to shopping and nightlife in Nags Head, to untouched beaches on the far south end. The Crystal Coast proceeds with the quaint maritime town of Beaufort and onto family-friendly Bogue Banks beach towns. Wilmington's eclectic downtown scene gives the Cape Fear region an urban beat, while Wrightsville Beach, Pleasure Island, and the Brunswick County shore provide everything from old-fashioned boardwalks to exciting surfing safaris.

—Liz Biro

### HANG TEN

You can hardly walk a North Carolina beach without encountering a surfer. Watching them ride waves large and small might convince you to grab a "stick" and give the sport a try. The Outer Banks and Wrightsville Beach are surfing hot spots, especially near piers and jetties. It's best to take a class rather than try to teach yourself to surf. Check out the local surf shop for information on classes.

## NORTH CAROLINA'S BEST BEACHES

### NAGS HEAD

Couples, families and friends all find options along **Nags Head**'s 11 miles of beach. Plenty of accommodations—homes, hotels, and cozy inns—line the shore, but with 41 public access points, many with lifeguards and handicap access, getting on the beach is no problem, even if you have to drive there.

### CAPE HATTERAS NATIONAL SEASHORE

The place for recreation and reflection, the many unspoiled beaches hidden behind tall dunes along this 60-mile stretch provide opportunities for shelling, surfing, birding, fishing, camping, lighthouse exploring, or simply getting lost in thought. The park's undeveloped **Coquina Beach** and **Ocracoke Island beaches** are considered by locals to be the Outer Banks' loveliest shorelines.

### CAPE LOOKOUT NATIONAL SEASHORE

Exchange real-world stress for the magical wonderlands of this 56-mile stretch extending from the historic Portsmouth Island village to **Shackleford Banks'** wild horses. The 28,400 acres of uninhabited land and marsh include remote, sandy islands linked to the mainland by nothing more than private ferries. You can climb an old lighthouse, see historic buildings in abandoned fishing villages, set up camp, stay in an old-timey cabin, or keep a lookout for loggerhead sea turtles nesting at night.

### BOGUE BANKS

This 21-mile-long island is anchored by the family-friendly towns of **Atlantic Beach** at the east end and Emerald Isle at the west end. Both offer shopping, fishing, parking, and kids' activities.

### WRIGHTSVILLE BEACH

Quiet and upscale, with longtime family homes and striking contemporary cottages jamming the lifeguard-protected shore, **Wrightsville Beach** is a perfect family or couples retreat. The white-sand beaches are sports-lovers' favorites. Surfers, kayakers, paddle boarders, and body boarders dig Wrightsville's tasty waves while anglers love its concrete fishing pier. College kids fill downtown clubs at night. Arrive early, as paid parking spaces fill up quickly.

### KURE AND CAROLINA BEACHES

Aptly named, **Pleasure Island** offers all sorts of fun for families and singles. On the south end kids will love **Kure Beach**'s aquarium, while history buffs can discover a Civil War fort. Beaches are wide, with plenty of room for fishing and surfing. There's even an old wooden pier. Head north to **Carolina Beach** for charter-boat fishing excursions and the nostalgic charm of an old-fashioned boardwalk with arcades, carnival rides, candy, and ice cream.

# NORTH CAROLINA LIGHTHOUSES

A flashing beacon in the distance marks one of North Carolina's "mighty seven" lighthouses that still guide mariners along the state's treacherous shore. Each tower has its own tale to tell and, oftentimes, a staircase to climb.

(above) Cape Lookout Lighthouse. (lower right) Currituck Beach Lighthouse. (upper right) Bodie Island Lighthouse.

Set along what mariners long ago named the Graveyard of the Atlantic, the lights guided ships along rough currents and shifting shoals, thereby saving many mariners' lives.

The first lighthouse was a wooden, pyramid-shape structure built in 1794 on Ocracoke Island; its early lights were fired with whale oil. Today, the lighthouses sport modern lenses and refurbished staircases that delight tourists more than mariners, who have the luxury of electronic navigation tools. Still, the beacons remain comforting signals, which assure travelers that a safe return to shore is not far away.

—Liz Biro

### SHODDY CONSTRUCTION

Building a lighthouse was not easy in the mid-1800s and mistakes did happen. Former customs official Thomas Blount oversaw construction of the first Bodie Island Lighthouse in 1847 and unwittingly ordered it constructed with an unsupported brick foundation. His lack of engineering experience became apparent when the 54-foot tower began to lean two years later. It was abandoned in 1859.

### CURRITUCK BEACH LIGHTHOUSE

The last major lighthouse constructed is the first you reach traveling from north to south. Currituck Lighthouse's redbrick exterior was left unpainted to distinguish it from other lighthouses. Now visitors may marvel over how builders in 1875 could perfectly place bricks in circles winding to the top of the 162-foot-tall structure.

### BODIE ISLAND LIGHTHOUSE

In 1837, the U.S. government determined that more vessels wrecked off Bodie Island than anywhere else off North Carolina. Ten years later, the first light was erected but fell victim to shoddy construction. During the Civil War in 1861, Confederate troops blew up the second light so that Union soldiers could not use it. The current Bodie Island Lighthouse was built in 1872, stands 156 feet tall, and is covered in broad horizontal black-and-white stripes.

### CAPE HATTERAS LIGHTHOUSE

Built in 1870, America's tallest brick lighthouse—you can climb its 248 cast-iron steps—reaches 210 feet into the sky. After saving hundreds of ships from deadly fates, the light itself became threatened by the Atlantic Ocean's eroding forces and had to be relocated 2,900 feet inland in 1999. The tower's black and white candy stripes are known worldwide.

### OCRACOKE LIGHTHOUSE

The second-oldest lighthouse in the United States still in continuous service, the 77-foot-tall, pure white tower was rebuilt after a fire in 1823. The bright exterior, matched by a charming picket fence, is a photographer's dream.

### CAPE LOOKOUT LIGHTHOUSE

The distinctive black-and-white diamonds on Cape Lookout Lighthouse aren't just pretty decoration, they serve a navigational purpose. The black diamonds are oriented in a north–south direction, the white in an east–west direction, pointing ships away from shallow waters and toward deeper water respectively.

### BALD HEAD ISLAND LIGHTHOUSE

Built in 1817 and nicknamed "Old Baldy," North Carolina's oldest lighthouse is 90 feet tall and stands on an island accessible only by boat. The octagonal shape and weathered gray exterior set the simple tower apart.

### OAK ISLAND LIGHTHOUSE

Close to the border between North Carolina and South Carolina, the 169-foot-tall Oak Island Lighthouse is the United States' youngest lighthouse. Built in 1958, it lacks the elegance of its older siblings but contains the last manually operated light in the world. The completely cylindrical tower has three broad horizontal stripes—black, white, and gray.

# DAY TRIP: NORTH CAROLINA COASTAL DRIVE

(above) Spot a brown pelican and other shore birds at Pea Island National Wildlife Refuge. (upper right) If you're feeling peckish, stop for lunch at Rusty's Surf & Turf.

North Carolina's coast is a string of stunning barrier islands with long, two-lane roads and hidden gems that beg exploration. The most relaxing drives happen in late fall and early spring, when crowded beach roads become easy byways allowing you to contemplate shoreline views.

The tour begins at the entrance to Cape Hatteras National Seashore at the junction of U.S. 64/264/158 and Route 12. The entire tour follows along Route 12 south, passing tall, sea-oat-covered dunes on the ocean side and Pamlico Sound in the opposite direction. About 23 miles down Route 12, you can visit **Bodie Island Lighthouse.** Three miles later, your very small place in the world is apparent when crossing the tall Bonner Bridge over Oregon Inlet, where enormous Pamlico Sound meets the Atlantic Ocean's mighty waves. After crossing the bridge, look for shorebirds as you pass through **Pea Island National Wildlife Refuge** along the 12 miles to **Rodanthe.**

—Liz Biro

### PLANNING YOUR TIME

You'll take Route 12 south from the Cape Hatteras National Seashore entrance for this entire 80-mile drive. It takes from four to eight hours, depending on stops, so get an early start and allow a full day for the drive, ferry waiting time, and stopping at sights along the way.

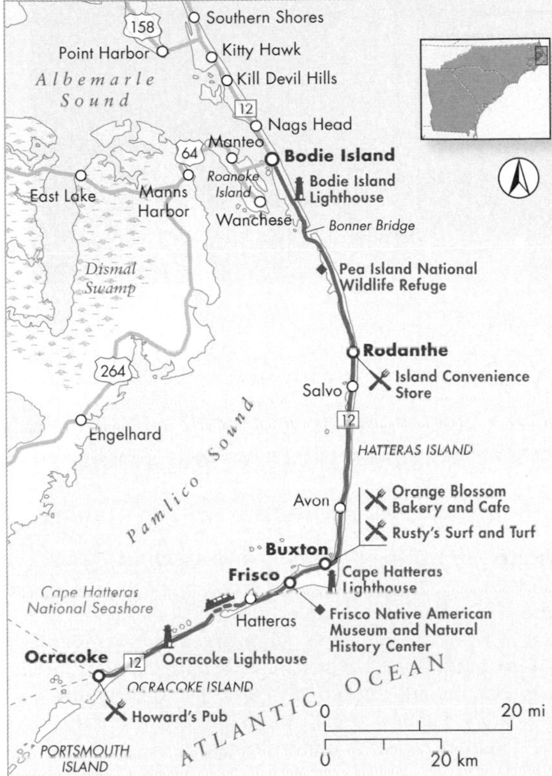


From Rodanthe, drive 23 miles of winding roads to Buxton, where you'll find **Cape Hatteras Lighthouse,** the tallest lighthouse in the United States. If you are here before mid-October, you can climb the tower's 248-step, iron spiral staircase. A little farther down Route 12 in Frisco, a nationally recognized collection of Native American artifacts fills **Frisco Native American Museum & Natural History Center.** Galleries display native art from across the United States, as well as relics from the first inhabitants of Hatteras Island.

Afterward, proceed 12 miles to the 30-minute state ferry that leaves every half hour from Hatteras to **Ocracoke Island.** On Ocracoke, you can walk wild beaches or photograph the stark white **Ocracoke Lighthouse,** the second-oldest lighthouse in the United States still in continuous service. If you packed a picnic, enjoy it on the beach. Otherwise, stop at **Howard's Pub,** a friendly restaurant where you can check out a list of 200 bottled beers from around the world and enjoy thick burgers, hand-cut fries, or varied seafood dishes.

## QUICK BITES

**Island Convenience.** Part grocery store, part souvenir shop, this convenience store stocks just about everything you need, whether it's gas, fishing tackle, or Wi-Fi. Best of all are the biscuits and homemade chicken salad sandwiches at the store's deli counter. ✉ *23523 Hwy. 12, Rodanthe* ☎ *252/987-2239.*

**Rusty's Surf & Turf.** This colorful restaurant offers local seafood, steaks, burgers, and sandwiches, as well as some Mexican dishes like fish tacos. Try the seared sea scallops with lemon rosemary aioli or the wahoo with Margarita Mojo Salsa. ✉ *47355 Hwy. 12, Buxton* ☎ *252/995-4184* 🌐 *www.rustyssurfnturf.com* ⏲ *Memorial Day–Labor Day, daily 5–9; call for off-season hrs.*

**Orange Blossom Bakery and Café.** This bakery-café is famous for fried doughnuts called "uglies," which come with apples or are smothered in chocolate. ✉ *47206 Hwy. 12, Buxton* ☎ *252/995-4109* 🌐 *www.orangeblossombakery.com* ⏲ *Daily 6:30–11 am.*

Updated by Liz Biro

Three hundred miles of breathtaking barrier islands make North Carolina's coastline a beach lover's dream. White sands and pristine waters, lighthouses, and all sorts of wonderful vacation homes mark the shore. Athletes, history buffs, anglers, shoppers, and children find plenty do here, but snoozing along the quiet shore is just as appealing.

Distinctive port cities dot broad rivers that lead inland from the sounds. There are American Revolution and Civil War battle sites, elegant golf links, and kitschy putt-putt courses. Aquariums, fishing charters, and museum outreach programs put you up close and personal with the seashore critters. North Carolina's small towns (mostly of 1,000 to 3,000 people) offer genuine warmth and hospitality.

The coast is divided into three broad sections that include islands, shoreline, and coastal plains: the Outer Banks (Corolla south through Ocracoke, including Roanoke Island), the Crystal Coast (Core and Bogue Banks, Beaufort, Morehead City, and the inland river city of New Bern), and the greater Cape Fear region (Wrightsville Beach through the Brunswick County islands, including Wilmington). The Outer Banks are visible from space: the thin, delicate white tracings are barrier islands that form a buffer between the Atlantic Ocean and the mainland.

Although other states' coasts have wall-to-wall hotels and condominiums, much of North Carolina's coast belongs to the North Carolina Division of Parks and Recreation and the U.S. National Park Service. This arrangement keeps large chunks of the coast accessible to the public for exploration, athletic activities, picnicking, and camping. Still, property values have skyrocketed as summer residents' dream houses continually replace generations-old beach cottages.

Some of the coast closes during midwinter, but even the colder season is a special time to visit. You can escape both crowds and peak prices but still enjoy seafood, beaches, and museums. Whether you're seeking peace or adventure, you can find it on the coast.

# PLANNING



## WHEN TO GO

North Carolina's coast shines in spring (April and May) and fall (September and October), when the weather is most temperate and the water reasonably warm. Traveling during these times means you can avoid long lines and higher prices associated with the peak summer tourist season.

## PLANNING YOUR TIME

The North Carolina coast is a string of beach and inland towns, each with its own character. Pick one and plan day trips from there. Boisterous Nags Head and Wilmington provide dining, shopping, and nightlife, but they are also short drives from lovely gardens, quiet beaches, dense woodlands, and historic landmarks. Beaufort is a brief, private ferry ride away from barrier islands where wild horses roam. Just an hour inland are New Bern's charming downtown and historic Tryon Palace and gardens. In summer, on secondary roads and some major highways you're bound to pass fresh seafood and produce stands.

## GETTING HERE AND AROUND

### AIR TRAVEL

The closest large, commercial airports to the Outer Banks are Raleigh-Durham, a 5-hour drive, and Norfolk International in Virginia, a 1½-hour drive. Coastal Carolina Regional Airport in New Bern has connector flights, charter service, and car rentals available. Wilmington International Airport serves the Cape Fear Coast.

Barrier Island Aviation provides charter service between the Dare County Regional Airport and major cities along the East Coast. US Airways Express and Delta ASA fly into Coastal Carolina Regional Airport in New Bern. US Airways, Delta, and Allegiant serve Wilmington International Airport.

**Air Contacts Barrier Island Aviation** ✉ *407 Airport Rd., Manteo* ☎ *252/473-4247* 🌐 *www.barrierislandaviation.com.* **Coastal Carolina Regional Airport** ✉ *200 Terminal Dr., New Bern* ☎ *252/638-8591* 🌐 *www.newbernairport.com.* **Dare County Regional Airport** ✉ *410 Airport Rd., Manteo* ☎ *252/475-5570* 🌐 *www.co.dare.nc.us/airport.* **Norfolk International** ✉ *2200 Norview Ave.* ☎ *757/857-3351* 🌐 *www.norfolkairport.com.* **Wilmington International Airport** ✉ *1740 Airport Blvd.* ☎ *910/341-4125* 🌐 *www.flyilm.com.*

### CAR TRAVEL

On the one hand, navigation in the Outer Banks is a snap because there's only one road—Route 12. On the other hand, traffic can make that single road two lanes of pure frustration on a rainy midsummer day when everyone is looking for something besides sunbathing. Low-lying areas of the highway are also prone to flooding.

Highways into the other areas along the coast—U.S. 158 into Kitty Hawk and Nags Head; U.S. 64 around Nags Head and Manteo; Interstate 40, which can take you from Wilmington all the way to Las Vegas or California if you desire, or Raleigh if you're catching a plane; and U.S. 17, which services Wilmington and New Bern—run smoothly during all but weekday rush hours and the busiest days of the high summer season.

Driving on the beaches is allowed in designated areas, and permits are usually required. The strictly enforced speed limit on the beaches is 25 mph, and pedestrians always have the right of way. Driving on sand can be tricky, so be careful.

### TAXI TRAVEL

Beach Cab, based in Nags Head, runs 24-hour service from Norfolk to Ocracoke and towns in between. The Connection is a shuttle service with passenger vans large enough to handle families, camping gear, surfboards, and bikes. It's a bargain at $155 from Norfolk to Nags Head. Beach Limousine, headquartered in Kill Devil Hill, serves the entire area and Norfolk International Airport and runs around the clock; getting to the airport in a van costs about $160 from Nags Head.

**Taxi Contacts Beach Cab** ✉ *6933 South Croatan Hwy.* ☎ *252/261-3133* 🌐 *www.islandtaxicab.com.* **Beach Limousine** ☎ *252/255-5466* 🌐 *www.obxbeachlimo.com.* **The Connection** ☎ *252/449-2777* 🌐 *www.calltheconnection.com.*

## RESTAURANTS

Raw bars serve oysters and clams on the half shell; some seafood houses sell each day's local catch, be it tuna, wahoo, mahi, mackerel, shrimp, or blue crabs. This is, after all, the coast, though highly trained chefs are settling in the region and increasingly diversifying menus. Seafood dishes—broiled, fried, grilled, or steamed—are listed alongside entrées fusing Asian, European, and Latin flavors with traditional Southern ingredients such as black-eyed peas.

Expect up to hour-long waits, sometimes longer, at many restaurants during summer and festival periods. Many places don't accept reservations. Restaurant hours are frequently reduced in winter, and some restaurants in remote beach communities close for a month or more. Only the most upscale, pricey restaurants call for a tie; usually a collared shirt will do. Casual dress (shorts and polo shirts) is acceptable in most restaurants. *Prices in the reviews are the average cost of a main course at dinner or, if dinner is not served, at lunch.*

## HOTELS

Hundreds of rental properties are available. Small beach cottages can be had, but increasingly so-called sand castles—large multistory homes—suit large groups. Motels and hotels clustered all along the Outer Banks are still the more affordable way to go.

Throughout the coast, the main choices are cottages, condos, and waterfront resorts. Chain hotels have outlets here, too, but you can also stay at a surprising number of small, family-run lodgings. You might also consider one of many quaint bed-and-breakfasts often filled with antiques and managed by accommodating hosts. Always ask about special packages (price breaks on multiple-night stays) and off-season rates. Most hotels, inns, and B&Bs on the coast offer free parking on their property, a few have street parking only, but you can expect not to pay parking fees even at the priciest hotels. *Prices in the reviews are the lowest cost of a standard double room in high season.*

### VISITOR INFORMATION

**Contacts National Park Service's Group Headquarters** ✉ *1401 National Park Dr., Manteo* ☎ *252/473–2111* 🌐 *www.nps.gov/caha.*



## THE OUTER BANKS

North Carolina's Outer Banks stretch from the Virginia state line south to Cape Lookout. Think of the OBX (shorthand used on popular bumper stickers) as a series of stepping stones in the Atlantic Ocean. Throughout history, the treacherous waters surrounding these islands have been the nemesis of shipping, gaining them the nickname "Graveyard of the Atlantic." A network of lighthouses and lifesaving stations, which grew around the need to protect seagoing craft, attracts curious travelers, just as the many submerged wrecks attract scuba divers. The islands' coves and inlets, which sheltered pirates—the notorious Blackbeard lived and died here—now give refuge to anglers, sunbathers, and bird-watchers.

The region is divided into four coastal sections: the Northern Beaches, followed by Roanoke Island, Hatteras Island, and then Ocracoke Island. For many years the Outer Banks remained isolated, with only a few hardy commercial fishing families. Today the islands are linked by bridges and ferries, and much of the area is included in the Cape Hatteras and Cape Lookout national seashores. The largest towns are also the most colorfully named: Kitty Hawk, Kill Devil Hills, Nags Head, and Manteo. Vacation rentals here are omnipresent—thousands of weekly rental cottages line the Outer Banks.

You can travel the region from the south end by taking a car ferry from Cedar Island to Ocracoke Island, then another from Ocracoke Island to Hatteras Island. Starting from the north, driving the 120-mile stretch of Route 12 from Corolla to Ocracoke can be managed in a day, but be sure to start very early in the morning and allow plenty of time in summer for delays due to heavy traffic, for ferry waiting times, and for exploring the undeveloped beaches, historic lighthouses, and interesting beach communities along the way. Mile markers (MM) indicate addresses all along the Outer Banks.

Sudden squalls frequently blow up on the Outer Banks in summer, and the Atlantic hurricane season runs from June 1 to November 30. Be aware that during major storms and hurricanes, evacuations are mandatory and roads and bridges become clogged with traffic following the blue-and-white evacuation-route signs.

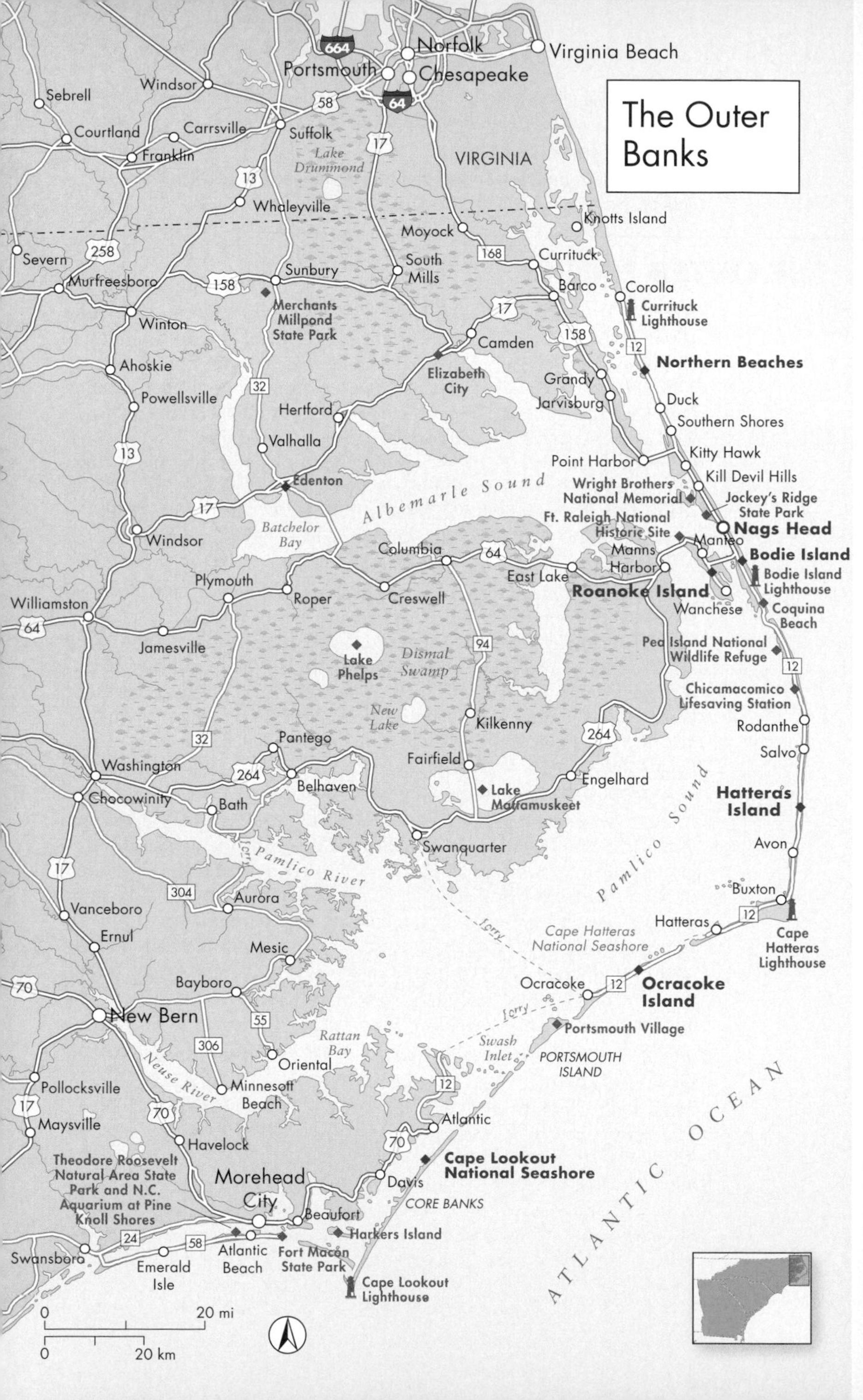
The Outer Banks
Norfolk
Virginia Beach
Portsmouth
Chesapeake
Windsor
Sebrell
Courtland
Carrsville
Suffolk
Franklin
Lake Drummond
VIRGINIA
Whaleyville
Knotts Island
Moyock
Severn
Currituck
South Mills
Sunbury
Murfreesboro
Barco
Corolla
Currituck Lighthouse
Merchants Millpond State Park
Winton
Camden
Northern Beaches
Ahoskie
Elizabeth City
Grandy
Jarvisburg
Duck
Powellsville
Southern Shores
Hertford
Valhalla
Point Harbor
Kitty Hawk
Kill Devil Hills
Wright Brothers National Memorial
Edenton
Albemarle Sound
Jockey's Ridge State Park
Ft. Raleigh National Historic Site
Nags Head
Batchelor Bay
Windsor
Manteo
Columbia
Manns Harbor
Bodie Island
East Lake
Bodie Island Lighthouse
Plymouth
Roanoke Island
Williamston
Roper
Creswell
Wanchese
Coquina Beach
Jamesville
Pea Island National Wildlife Refuge
Lake Phelps
Dismal Swamp
Chicamacomico Lifesaving Station
New Lake
Kilkenny
Rodanthe
Pantego
Salvo
Washington
Fairfield
Belhaven
Engelhard
Hatteras Island
Chocowinity
Bath
Lake Mattamuskeet
Pamlico Sound
Swanquarter
Avon
Pamlico River
Buxton
Aurora
Vanceboro
Hatteras
Ernul
Cape Hatteras National Seashore
Cape Hatteras Lighthouse
Mesic
Bayboro
Ocracoke
Ocracoke Island
New Bern
Portsmouth Village
Rattan Bay
Swash Inlet
PORTSMOUTH ISLAND
Oriental
Pollocksville
Minnesott Beach
Neuse River
Maysville
Atlantic
Havelock
Cape Lookout National Seashore
ATLANTIC OCEAN
Theodore Roosevelt Natural Area State Park and N.C. Aquarium at Pine Knoll Shores
Morehead City
Davis
CORE BANKS
Beaufort
Harkers Island
Swansboro
Emerald Isle
Atlantic Beach
Fort Macon State Park
Cape Lookout Lighthouse
0
20 mi
0
20 km
664
64
58
17
13
258
168
158
17
158
12
32
13
17
64
94
64
264
32
264
17
304
12
70
12
55
306
12
17
70
70
24
58
Ferry
Ferry
Ferry

## NORTHERN BEACHES

*Corolla: 91 miles south of Norfolk, VA, via U.S. 17, U.S. 158, and Rte. 12; 230 miles east of Raleigh via U.S. 64, U.S. 17, and Rte. 12. Duck: 16 miles south of Corolla. Kitty Hawk: 19 miles south of Corolla; 7 miles south of Duck.*

2

The small northern beach settlements of Corolla and Duck are largely seasonal, residential enclaves full of summer rental homes and condominiums. Drive slowly in Corolla: here freely wandering wild horses always have the right of way. Upscale Duck has lots of restaurants and shops. Kitty Hawk, with a few thousand permanent residents, has fewer rental accommodations. Given these communities' contiguous nature and similar looks, the uninitiated may not realize when they've crossed from Kitty Hawk into Kill Devil Hills. The towns' respective roles in the drama of the first powered flight occasionally create some confusion as well. When arriving at the Outer Banks, the Wright brothers first stayed in the then-remote fishing village of Kitty Hawk, but their flight took place some 4 miles south on Kill Devil Hills, a gargantuan sand dune where today the Wright Brothers National Memorial stands.

### GETTING HERE AND AROUND

Most people drive to the northern beaches via U.S. 17, 64, and 264, which all link to the local U.S. 158 and Route 12. Some commercial and charter flights are available from nearby airports. Plan your time wisely, as heavy traffic can lead to long travel delays in summer. Marked paths and wide shoulders accommodate bikers and walkers along some main roads. Guided tours are available, too. Still, a car is essential for getting around on your own time.

### ESSENTIALS

**Visitor Information Aycock Brown Welcome Center** ✉ *5230 N. Croatan Hwy., MM 1, Kitty Hawk* ☎ *877/629–4386* 🌐 *www.outerbanks.org/outerbanks-forms-and-other-information.*

### EXPLORING

**Currituck Beach Lighthouse.** The northernmost lighthouse on the Outer Banks, the Currituck Lighthouse was completed in 1875 and was built from about 1 million bricks, which remained unpainted. Except in high winds or thunderstorms, you can climb 214 steps to the top. ✉ *1101 Corolla Village Rd., Rte. 12, north of Whalehead Club sign, Corolla* ☎ *252/453–4939* 🌐 *www.currituckbeachlight.com* 🎫 *$7 cash or check only* 🕑 *Easter–Thanksgiving, daily 9–5; Thurs. 9–8 in summer.*

**The Whalehead Club.** This 21,000-square-foot monument to gracious living was built between 1922 and 1925 as the private residence of a Northern couple taken with the area's reputation for waterfowl hunting (the home was given its current name by the second owner). After having been abandoned, sold, and vandalized, it was restored by a team of specialists and is listed on the National Register of Historic Places. A floral motif is carried throughout the art-nouveau home in Tiffany lamps with flower detailing and mahogany woodwork carved with water lilies. ✉ *1100 Club Way, Currituck Heritage Park, off Rte. 12, Corolla* ☎ *252/453–9040* 🌐 *www.whaleheadclub.com* 🎫 *$10* 🕑 *Mon–Sat. 9–5.*

CLOSE UP

## First in Flight

First successful flight of the *Wright Flyer.*

December 17, 1903, was a cold and windy day on the Outer Banks, but Wilbur and Orville Wright took little notice. The slightly built brothers from Ohio were undertaking an excellent adventure. With Orville at the controls, Wilbur running alongside, and the men of the nearby Lifesaving Service stations acting as ground crew, the fragile *Wright Flyer* lifted off from the Kill Devil Hills dune near Kitty Hawk and flew 120 feet in 12 seconds.

Outer Banker John Daniels photographed the instant the world forever changed: a heavier-than-air machine was used to achieve controlled, sustained flight with a pilot aboard. To prove they were not accidental aviators, the Wrights took two flights each that day, and in Wilbur's second attempt, he flew 852 feet in 59 seconds.

Others were attempting—and dying in the attempt of—powered flight as the Wright brothers opened their Dayton bicycle-repair shop in 1892. Using information on aerodynamics from the Smithsonian Institution and observation of birds in flight, they began experimenting with a box kite roughly shaped like a biplane and a makeshift wind tunnel. Strong, steady winds drew them to the then-remote Outer Banks, where they could test their next phase, manned glider flights, in privacy. In time, they added power to the three-axis control they developed and eventually solved the problems of mechanical flight, lift, and propulsion that had vexed scientists for hundreds of years.

Their success is honored at the Wright Brothers National Memorial in Kill Devil Hills and by the North Carolina boast emblazoned on millions of license plates: "First in flight."

★ **Wright Brothers National Memorial.** A 60-foot granite monument that resembles an airplane's tail stands as a tribute to Wilbur and Orville Wright. The two bicycle mechanics from Ohio took to the air here on December 17, 1903. You can see a replica of their *Flyer* and stand on the spot where it made four takeoffs and landings, their longest flight a distance of 852 feet. Exhibits and an informative talk by a National Park Service ranger bring the event to life. The Wrights had to transport in the unassembled airplane by boat, along with all their food and supplies for building a camp. They made four trips to the site beginning in

1900. The First Flight is commemorated annually. ✉ *1000 N. Croatan Hwy, off U.S. 158 at MM 7.5, 5 miles south of Kitty Hawk, Kill Devil Hills* ☎ *252/441–7430* 🌐 *www.nps.gov/wrbr* *$4* ⏲ *Daily 9–5.*

## WHERE TO EAT

$$$$ SEAFOOD ★ **Blue Point Bar & Grill.** Sleek, modern decor meets casual Southern style and local seafood at this upscale spot with an enclosed porch overlooking Currituck Sound. Try the ever-popular crab cakes or thick, rich she-crab soup made with cream, sherry, herbs, Old Bay seasoning, and, of course, crab roe. Lunch is served Tuesday–Sunday. [$] *Average main: $30* ✉ *1240 Duck Rd., Duck* ☎ *252/261–8090* 🌐 *www.thebluepoint.com* ⏲ *No lunch Mon.*

$$$$ FRENCH FUSION **Elizabeth's Café & Winery.** This small bistro evokes big-time romance and sophistication even though it's in a shopping center. Eat in the French-country dining room or in the stone grotto. À la carte and fixed menus including wine change to reflect the day's market purchases, whether it's lamb chops with pinot noir barrel-made-molasses reduction, Angus beef tenderloin au poivre, or the freshest produce for interesting vegetarian options such as pecan-crusted sweet-onion torte drizzled with aged-balsamic reduction. The restaurant's wine list features hundreds of wines. [$] *Average main: $35* ✉ *Scarborough Faire Shopping Village, 1177 Duck Rd., #11, Duck* ☎ *252/261–6145* 🌐 *www.elizabethscafe.com* ⏲ *No lunch.*

$$ AMERICAN **Outer Banks Brewing Station.** Craft beer rules here—six suds are on tap, including lemongrass wheat, which won a 2009 World Beer Cup silver medal—but kids are welcome, and there is even a playground and pirate ship to explore outside. Casual fare compliments the beer. Rare, seared, local tuna tops a garden salad. Béarnaise sauce and lump crabmeat crown beef filets. Pizza, sandwiches, bar munchies, and steamed and fried seafood are served, too. Cooper accents, lots of wood, and fun, retro touches (a Superman doll denotes the men's room; Wonder Woman, the ladies' room) characterize this huge white building, modeled after a turn-of-the-19th-century lifesaving station. Even more interesting is a wind turbine that partially powers both the restaurant and brewery. [$] *Average main: $20* ✉ *600 S. Croatan Hwy., U.S. 158, MM 8.5, Kill Devil Hills* ☎ *252/449–2739* 🌐 *www.obbrewing.com* *Reservations not accepted.*

## WHERE TO STAY

*Hotel reviews have been abbreviated in this book. For expanded reviews, please go to Fodors.com.*

$$$ B&B/INN ★ **Advice 5¢.** A roof with varied pitches and eaves tops this contemporary, steely blue-gray beach house with white trim and multipane windows rising from the dunes. **Pros:** quiet and secluded but walking distance to commercial area. **Cons:** no ocean view; no pets allowed; no kids under age 16. [$] *Rooms from: $225* ✉ *111 Scarborough La., Duck* ☎ *252/255–1050, 800/238–4235* 🌐 *www.advice5.com* *4 rooms* ⏲ *Closed mid-Nov.–mid-Mar.* *Breakfast.*

$$$$ B&B/INN **The Inn at Corolla Light.** The inn is a part of the Corolla Light Resort and sits along Currituck Sound, about 10 miles from Duck. **Pros:** lots of resort amenities available; shuttle service to beach, some rooms have

fireplaces for cozy or romantic fall and winter vacations. **Cons:** you'll have to walk several blocks to the ocean; no refund for reservations canceled seven days or less prior to arrival. *Rooms from: $299* *1066 Ocean Trail, Corolla* *252/453–3340, 800/215–0772* *www.corolla-inn.com* *30 rooms, 13 suites* *Closed Dec.–Feb.* *Breakfast.*

$$$$ RESORT ★ **The Sanderling Resort & Spa.** Located on a remote beach 5 miles north of Duck, the Sanderling is a fine place to be pampered, go swimming, or go for a stroll. **Pros:** on-site spa; natural surroundings; plush robes in every room. **Cons:** main pool across a busy street; DVD players and microwaves must be requested at the front desk. *Rooms from: $299* *1461 Duck Rd., Duck* *252/261–4111, 800/701–4111* *www.thesanderlinginn.com* *88 rooms, 5 homes* *Breakfast.*

### SPORTS AND THE OUTDOORS

**Sea Scape Golf Links.** Winds from the nearby ocean and sound make this short course an unexpected challenge while sand dunes and a maritime forest provide a serene setting. *300 Eckner St., MM 2.5, Kitty Hawk* *252/261–2158* *www.seascapegolf.com* *18 holes. 6131 yds. Par 70. Green Fee: $50/$99.* *Facilities: Putting green, practice bunker, golf carts, rental clubs, pro shop, restaurant.*

## NAGS HEAD

*9 miles south of Kitty Hawk.*

It's widely accepted that Nags Head got its name because pirates once tied lanterns around the necks of their horses to lure merchant ships onto the shoals hoping to wreck the vessels and profit from their cargo. Dubious citizenry aside, Nags Head was established in the 1830s and has become a North Carolina tourist haven.

The town—one of the largest on the Outer Banks, yet still with a population of only about 3,000 people—lies between the Atlantic Ocean and Pamlico Sound, along and between U.S. 158 ("the bypass") and Route 12 ("the beach road" or Virginia Dare Trail). Both roads are congested in the high season, and the entire area is commercialized. Many lodgings, whether they're dated cottages, shingled older houses, or sprawling new homes with plenty of bells and whistles, are available through the area's plentiful vacation rentals. Numerous restaurants, motels, hotels, shops, and entertainment opportunities keep the town hopping day and night.

Nags Head has 11 miles of beach with 41 public access points from Route 12, some with paved parking and some with restrooms and showers. ■ **TIP→** It's easy to overlook the flagpoles stationed along many area beaches; but if there's a red flag flying from one of them, it means the water is too rough even for wading. These are not suggestions—ignoring them can mean hefty fines.

### GETTING HERE AND AROUND

From the east, arrive by car on U.S. 64 or from the north on U.S. 17 and U.S. 158. Although many people cycle and walk on designated paths, most exploring requires a car.

At Jockey's Ridge State Park you can hike to the top of the tallest natural sand dune in the Eastern United States.

### ESSENTIALS

**Visitor Information Whalebone Welcome Center** ✉ *2 N.C. 12 Hwy., MM 17* ☎ *877/629–4386* 🌐 *www.outerbanks.org/outerbanks-forms-and-other-information.*

## EXPLORING

**Jockey's Ridge State Park.** Jockey's Ridge State Park has 420 acres that encompass the tallest sand dune on the East Coast (about 80 to 100 feet). Walk along the 360 foot boardwalk from the visitor center to the edge of the dune. The climb to the top is a challenge; nevertheless, it's a popular spot for hang gliding, kite flying, and sand boarding. You can also explore an estuary, a museum, and a self-guide trail through the park. In summer, join the free Sunset on the Ridge program: watch the sun disappear while you sit on the dunes and learn about their local legends and history. Covered footwear is a wise choice here, as the loose sand gets quite hot in the summer months. ✉ *300 W. Carolista Dr., MM 12* ☎ *252/441–7132* 🌐 *www.jockeysridgestatepark.com* 🎫 *Free* 🕐 *June–Aug., daily 8 am–9 pm; Mar.– May, Sept., and Oct., daily 8–8; Nov.–Feb., daily 8–6.*

OFF THE BEATEN PATH

**Somerset Place.** Drive about an hour inland to see one of North Carolina's best preserved historic plantations. Located 52 miles west of Nags Head on Highway 64, Somerset Place once sat on 100,000 acres of land that bordered Lake Phelps and was one of the largest plantations in the state. The plantation produced rice, corn, oats, peas, beans, and flax, and its sophisticated sawmills handled thosands of feet of lumber from 1785 to 1865. The 800 slaves who resided here throughout the plantation's 80 years planted and harvested crops, cooked, and washed. Some slaves were also skilled laborers like carpenters, brick masons, cobblers, and weavers. The site has seven original 19th-century buildings and three others have been reconstructed including slave quarters. Tours of the builidngs and grounds last 90 minutes. ✉ *2572 Lake Shore Rd., Creswell* ☎ *252/797–4560* 🌐 *www.nchistoricsites.org/somerset* 🎫 *Free* 🕑 *Apr.–Oct., Tues.–Sat. 9–5; Nov.–Mar., Tues.–Sat. 10–4.*

**SIFTING ECOLOGY**

The vegetation on the sand dunes is practically all that's keeping them from blowing away in the wind. Dune conservation is very serious for the survival of the beaches, and the vegetation also provides shelter to turtles, rabbits, snakes, and other wildlife. Please don't disturb it!

**USS *Huron*.** The first North Carolina Historic Shipwreck Site, the 175-foot *Huron* lies underwater 250 yards off the beach at Nags Head Pier and is a favorite with scuba divers. The iron-hulled ship sank in a November storm in 1877, taking all but a handful of her 124-man crew with her. ✉ *Offshore between MM 11 and MM 12* 🌐 *www.archaeology.ncdcr.gov/ncarch/underwater/huron.htm.*

### WHERE TO EAT

$$$ SEAFOOD ★ ✕ **Basnight's Lone Cedar Café.** Hearts were broken when this restaurant, owned by powerful North Carolina Senator Marc Basnight and family, burned in 2007, but the rebuilt contemporary setting with simple pine tables, large windows with waterfront views, and a huge glass-walled wine rack in the main dining room is sleeker and more spacious than the original. North Carolina produce and seafood star here. Soft-shell crabs in season come from an on-site shedding facility, and a stunning, extensive herb garden provides fresh seasoning. Try local favorites such as clear clam chowder, pan-blackened bluefish, or whole fried flounder. Beef, chicken, pork, and pastas are also on the menu. Brunch is served on Sunday. $ *Average main: $25* ✉ *Nags Head–Manteo Causeway, 7623 S. Virginia Dare Trail* ☎ *252/441–5405* 🌐 *www.lonecedarcafe.com* ✍ *Reservations not accepted* 🕑 *Closed Jan.–early Feb. No lunch.*

$$$$ SEAFOOD Fodor's Choice ★ ✕ **Owens' Restaurant.** This family-owned restaurant, in business since 1946, is housed in a replica of a lifesaving station like those found on the Outer Banks in the early 19th century. The classic clapboard building has pine paneling and is filled with maritime artifacts. Stick with fresh-off-the-boat local seafood or prime beef; the kitchen staff excels at both. Miss O's crab cakes are ever popular, as is filet mignon topped with lump crabmeat and asparagus with béarnaise sauce. Pecan-encrusted sea scallops are plump and tender. The 14-layer chocolate cake is delicious. In summer, arrive early and expect to wait. The brass-and-glass Station Keeper's Lounge has entertainment Friday and Saturday nights in summer and early fall. $ *Average main: $30* ✉ *U.S. 158, MM 16.5, 7114 S. Virginia Dare Trail* ☎ *252/441–7309* 🌐 *www.owensrestaurant.com* ✍ *Reservations not accepted* 🕑 *Closed Jan.-early March. No lunch.*

$$ SEAFOOD ✕ **Pier House Restaurant.** The restaurant is literally *on* the old, crooked, wooden Nags Head Fishing Pier, and if you catch and clean your own fish, the chef will cook it to your liking. If fishing was bad, no worries;

2

the restaurant has a homestyle American menu including seafood and breakfast. *Average main: $15 ✉ 3335 S. Virginia Dare Trail, U.S. 158, MM 11.5 ☎ 252/441–4200 🌐 www.nagsheadpier.com/food ✍ Reservations not accepted ⏲ Closed Thanksgiving–Easter.*

$$$ SEAFOOD **✕ RV's Sugar Creek.** If fiery red sunsets and marinated tuna entice you, this is the place to eat. Locals come to eat, drink, and take in Roanoke Sound's serene views. Portions of everything—from clam chowder to barbecued shrimp to crab cakes and calamari—are huge. You can also get steak, ribs, and chicken. The turtle cake, with chocolate, pecans, and caramel, is a dieter's nightmare. There's a little pier outside and an attached outdoor gazebo where you can get a drink. Visit the Sugar Shack next door for the raw bar or quick to-go orders of sandwiches, steamed seafood, or fresh catch to cook yourself. Both businesses are on the causeway between Nags Head and Roanoke Island. *Average main: $22 ✉ Nags Head–Manteo Causeway, MM 16.5, 7340 S. Virginia Dare Trail ☎ 252/441–4963 🌐 www.sugarcreekseafood.com ✍ Reservations not accepted ⏲ Call for off-season hrs.*

$$ ECLECTIC **✕ Seaside Gourmet to Go.** When lazing around the beach house trumps waiting in line at a restaurant, this all-take-out shop is the place to stop. Chef Jason Ward takes advantage of local seafood and produce to create regional and international dishes packed and ready to eat or heat-and-eat. Selections change daily, depending on what's fresh. Choices may range from Asian five-spice marinated tuna over cilantro-scallion sticky rice to shrimp-and-crab enchiladas. Vegetarians get big nods with tempeh wrap sandwiches and artichoke- and Havarti-stuffed risotto cakes. *Average main: $15 ✉ 3701 North Croatan Highway, Kitty Hawk ☎ 252/255–5330 🌐 www.seasidegourmet.com ✍ Reservations not accepted.*

$ SEAFOOD **✕ Sam & Omie's.** This no-nonsense niche, named after two fishermen who were father and son, opened in 1937 and is one of the Outer Banks' oldest restaurants. Fishing illustrations hang on the walls, and country music plays in the background. Locals love breakfast here; dinner brings all manner of seafood. Try the crab and eggs Benedict or fine marinated tuna steak. The kitchen has been using the same she-crab soup recipe for 24 years. Die-hard fans claim that Sam & Omie's serves the best oysters on the beach. *Average main: $15 ✉ U.S. 158, MM 16.5, 7228 Virginia Dare Trail ☎ 252/441–7366 🌐 www.samandomies.net ✍ Reservations not accepted ⏲ Closed Dec.–Feb.*

## WHERE TO STAY

*Hotel reviews have been abbreviated in this book. For expanded reviews, please go to Fodors.com.*

$$ B&B/INN Fodor's Choice ★ **First Colony Inn.** Stand on the verandas that encircle this old, three-story, cedar-shingle inn and admire the ocean views. **Pros:** homey accommodations feel like grandma's house; some in-room hot tubs; microwaves in rooms. **Cons:** on a busy highway; you'll have to cross a road to get to the beach. *Rooms from: $189 ✉ 6715 S. Croatan Hwy., U.S. 158 MM 16 ☎ 252/441–2343, 800/368–9390 🌐 www.firstcolonyinn.com 27 rooms Breakfast.*

$ HOTEL **The Nags Head Inn.** Being an independent property, not a chain, is not the only thing that makes this motel stand out—the blocky, white stucco exterior with blue accents is in sharp contrast to the cottages that surround it. **Pros:** shaded parking; on the beach; microwaves in rooms. **Cons:** continental breakfast only; a small, no-frills lobby. *Rooms from: $125 ✉ Rte. 12, MM 14, 4701 S. Virginia Dare Trail ☎ 252/441–0454, 800/327–8881 🌐 www.nagsheadinn.com 100 rooms ⏲ Closed late Nov.–Dec.*

## SPORTS AND THE OUTDOORS

### BEACHES

**Coquina Beach.** In the Cape Hatteras National Seashore but just a few miles south of Nags Head, Coquina is considered by locals to be the loveliest beach in the Outer Banks. The wide-beam ribs of the shipwreck *Laura Barnes* rest in the dunes here. Driven onto the Outer Banks by a nor'easter in 1921, she ran aground north of this location; the entire crew survived. The wreck was moved to Coquina Beach in 1973 and displayed behind ropes, but subsequent hurricanes have scattered the remains and covered them with sand, making it difficult, if not impossible, to discern. **Amenities:** parking, showers, toilets. **Best for:** swimming. *✉ Off Rte. 12, MM 26, 8 miles south of U.S. 158 🌐 www.nps.gov/caha.*

★ **Jennette's Pier.** Built in 1939, Jennette's Pier was North Carolina's oldest wooden ocean-fishing pier until 2003 when Hurricane Isabel knocked it down. In 2009, the state of North Carolina came to the rescue, breaking ground for not only a new concrete pier but also a public beach access point with 262 free parking spaces. Fish, surf, build a sand castle, or just laze on the wide, clean beach in the heart of Nags Head just north of the U.S. 64/Route 12 intersection. When you get tired of sunbathing and swimming, check out some of the 16,000-square-foot pier house's various exhibits. **Amenities:** food and drink, parking, toilets. **Best for:** swimming. *✉ 72223 S. Virginia Dare Trail, just north of the U.S. 64/Rte. 12 intersection 🌐 www.jennettespier.net.*

**Nags Head Beaches.** Forty-one public beach access points make Nags Head the perfect place to hit the shore no matter your needs. Access points are marked with white signs clearly stating "Public beach access." Fifteen points are handicapped accessible, and beach wheelchairs are available at the Bonnett and Hargrove accesses. The Eighth Street access has a stability mat that makes getting a stroller or wheelchair on the beach easy. Many other areas have lifeguards and bathhouses. The town lists all the accesses and provides a map of them on its website. No matter where you land, expect clean sand and water. **Amenities:** food and drink, lifeguards, parking, showers, toilets. **Best for:** sunrise, sunset, swimming. *✉ Nags Head Town Hall, 5401 S. Croatan Hwy. ☎ 252/441–5508 🌐 www.townofnagshead.net.*

### GOLF

**Nags Head Golf Links.** This beautiful, Scottish-links-style course borders Roanoke Sound, which is visible from five holes. Wild sea grass and rolling dunes separate most tees and greens. Coastal winds and a rugged shoreline create one of the area's most challenging courses. *✉ 5615 S. Seachase Dr., off Rte. 12, MM 15 ☎ 252/441–8073 🌐 www.*

Golf courses along the Outer Banks often have beautiful water views.

*nagsheadgolflinks.com* *18 holes. 6126 yds. Par 71. Green Fee: $55/$120.* ☞ *Facilities: Driving range, putting green, golf carts, pro shop, restaurant, bar.*

### HANG GLIDING

**Kitty Hawk Kites.** The premier hang-gliding outfitter in the country, Kitty Hawk Kites—in business since 1974—gives beginner dune lessons. The only requirement is that you must be able to run approximately 10 yards; kids as young as 4 and persons with most types of physical challenges can be accommodated. Jockey's Ridge is a favorite spot to learn, and instruction packages start at $99. Those with the gumption can try a high-altitude tandem flight that soars up to a mile high. History buffs can try flying a reproduction of the Wright Brothers' 1902 glider. Kitty Hawk Kites also sells wind toys and gives kayaking, kiteboarding, parasailing, and paddleboarding classes and leads guided walking tours. You can pick up sports gear and sportswear, plus souvenirs. ✉ *U.S. 158, MM 12.5, 3925 S. Croatan Hwy.* ☎ *252/449–2210, 800/483–2808* 🌐 *www.kittyhawk.com.*

### WATER SPORTS

**Outer Banks Boarding Company.** Rent surfboards, sign-up for private lessons, or browse the retail shop at Outer Banks Boarding Company. ✉ *103 E. Morning View Pl., U.S. 158, MM 11* ☎ *252/441–1939* 🌐 *www.obbconline.com.*

**Outer Banks Dive Center.** This outfitter has equipment rental, diving instruction, guided offshore charters, and leads off-the-beach dives to shipwrecks. ✉ *3917 S. Croatan Hwy.* ☎ *252/449–8349* 🌐 *www.obxdive.com.*

### SHOPPING

**Morales Art Gallery.** For 35 years, Gallery Row has been a small cluster of art-related businesses that sell everything from beach crafts to original seascapes to diamond earrings. Morales Art Gallery is the fine-arts store that started it all. Most of the gallery owners live on-site. ✉ *207 E. Gallery Row* ☎ *252/441–6484, 800/635–6035.*

**Tanger Outlet Center.** Find two dozen stores—including Bass, Coach, Gap Outlet, and Polo Ralph Lauren—selling designer clothes, shoes, casual attire, books, sunglasses, and more. ✉ *U.S. 158 bypass, MM 16* ☎ *252/441–5634, 800/720–6747* 🌐 *www.tangeroutlets.com.*

## ROANOKE ISLAND

*10 miles southwest of Nags Head.*

On a hot July day in 1587, 117 men, women, and children left their boat and set foot on Roanoke Island to form the first permanent English settlement in the New World. Three years later, when a fleet with supplies from England landed, the settlers had disappeared without a trace, leaving a mystery that continues to baffle historians. Much of the 12-mile-long island, which lies between the Outer Banks and the mainland, remains wild. Of the island's two towns, Wanchese is the fishing village and Manteo is tourist-oriented, with sights related to the island's history, as well as an aquarium.

#### GETTING HERE AND AROUND

From the east, drive to the island on U.S. 64; from the Outer Banks, follow U.S. 158 to U.S. 64. Although Manteo's main drag and downtown waterfront have sidewalks, a car is useful for visiting the town's various sites. Charter flights are available at Dare County Regional Airport.

#### ESSENTIALS

**Visitor Information Outer Banks Welcome Center on Roanoke Island** ✉ *1 Visitors Center Circle, Manteo* ☎ *877/629–4386* 🌐 *www.outerbanks.org/outerbanks-forms-and-other-information.*

### EXPLORING

★ **Elizabethan Gardens.** The lush gardens are a 10-acre re-creation of 16th-century English gardens, established as an elaborate memorial to the first English colonists. Walk through the brick-and-wrought-iron entrance to see antique statuary, wildflowers, rose gardens, and a sunken garden, all sponsored by the Garden Club of North Carolina. The gatehouse, designed in the style of a 16th-century orangery, serves as a reception center and gift and plant shop. Many weddings are held in one tranquil garden or another. ✉ *1411 National Park Dr., 3 miles north of downtown Manteo* ☎ *252/473–3234* 🌐 *www.elizabethangardens.org* 🎟 *$8* ⏲ *Dec.–Feb., daily 10–4; Mar., Oct., and Nov., daily 9–5; Apr., May, and Sept., daily 9–6; June–Aug., daily 9–7.*

★ **Fort Raleigh National Historic Site.** Fort Raleigh is a restoration of the original 1585 earthworks that mark the beginning of English-colonial history in America. Be sure to see the orientation film before taking a guided tour of the fort. A nature trail through the 513-acre grounds leads to an outlook over Albemarle Sound. Native American and Civil

War history is also preserved here. ✉ *1401 National Park Dr., Manteo* ☎ *252/473–5772* 🌐 *www.nps.gov/fora* 🎟 *Free.*

The Lost Colony. Pulitzer Prize–winner Paul Green's drama was written in 1937 to mark the 350th birthday of Virginia Dare, the first English child born in the New World. Except from 1942 to 1947, during World War II when enemy German U-boats prowled the nearby Atlantic Ocean, it has played every summer since in Fort Raleigh National Historic Site's Waterside Theatre. It reenacts the story of the first colonists, who settled here in 1587 and mysteriously vanished. Cast alumni include Andy Griffith and Lynn Redgrave. Reservations are essential. ✉ *1409 National Park Dr., off U.S. 64, 3 miles north of downtown Manteo* ☎ *252/473–2127 office, 252/473–6000 box office* 🌐 *www.thelostcolony.org* 🎟 *$26.50–$35* ⏲ *May–Aug., Mon.–Sat. at 8:30 pm.*

**North Carolina Aquarium at Roanoke Island.** The aquarium occupies 68,000 square feet of space overlooking Croatan Sound. There are touch tanks, but *The Graveyard of the Atlantic* is the centerpiece exhibit. It's a 285,000 gallon ocean tank containing the re-created remains of the USS *Monitor,* sunk off Hatteras Island. The aquarium hosts a slew of activities and field trips, from feeding fish to learning about medicinal aquatic plants to a workshop allowing kids to diagnose and treat a replica of an injured sea turtle before releasing it back into the sea. The aquarium also manages the 1,000 foot long wood-and-concrete Jennette's Pier at MM 16.5 in Nags Head. Visitors may fish or walk on the pier or check out educational programs and exhibits offered in the two-story, 16,000-square-foot pier house. Additionally, the pier is a beach access point with 262 parking spaces. ✉ *374 Airport Rd., off U.S. 64, 3 miles northeast of Manteo* ☎ *252/473–3493, 800/832–3474 for aquarium, 252/473–3494 for educational programs* 🌐 *www.ncaquariums.com* 🎟 *$8* ⏲ *Daily 9–5.*

**Roanoke Island Festival Park.** This multifunctional attraction sits on the waterfront in Manteo. Costumed interpreters conduct tours of the 69-foot ship, *Elizabeth II,* a representation of a 16th-century vessel, but you can also help them set the sails, plot a course, and swab the decks. The 25-acre state park also has an interactive museum representing 400 years of Outer Banks history as well as a gift shop, a re-created 16th-century settlement site, a Native American exhibit, a fossil pit, plays and concerts at indoor and outdoor venues, arts-and-crafts exhibitions, and special programs. ✉ *Waterfront off Budleigh St., 1 Festival Park, Manteo* ☎ *252/475–1500, 252/475–1506 for event hotline* 🌐 *www.roanokeisland.com* 🎟 *$10 good for two consecutive days* ⏲ *Mar.–Dec., daily 9–5.*

## WHERE TO EAT

$ DINER **Big Al's Soda Fountain and Grill.** This fun and popular spot has '50s decor, Coca-Cola memorabilia, a game room, and a dance floor, not to mention a line out the door. Burgers, patty melts, seafood, and blue-plate specials like pork chops in brown gravy or meatloaf glazed with Coca-Cola barbecue sauce dominate the menu. Hot-fudge sundaes, banana splits, milkshakes, malts, and all sorts of other ice-cream con-

At Roanoke Island Festival Park, you can help costumed 16th-century "sailors" set the sails and swab the decks of the *Elizabeth II*.

fections hit the spot for dessert or an afternoon treat. $ *Average main: $15* ✉ *716 S Hwy 64, Manteo* ☎ *252/473–5570* 🌐 *www.bigalsobx.com.*

$$ AMERICAN ★ ✕ **Full Moon Café and Grille.** Located in a renovated gas station, this wonderfully cheerful bistro has large front windows and lots of patio seating. The herbed hummus with toasted pita is fantastic, as are the fat crab cakes and baked crab-dip appetizer. Other choices include salads, veggie wraps, seafood enchiladas, burgers of all kinds, and hearty sandwiches. Light eaters beware: even the Waldorf salad comes with a million pecans and apples; expect lots of cheese on any dish that includes it. The café also serves specialty cocktails, maintains a thoughtfully selected wine list, and offers North Carolina beers. $ *Average main: $20* ✉ *208 Queen Elizabeth Ave., Manteo* ☎ *252/473–6666* 🌐 *www.thefullmooncafe.com.*

$ AMERICAN ✕ **Poor Richard's Sandwich Shop.** In business since 1984, there is always a long line at the rear of this downtown Manteo breakfast-and-lunch institution. Homemade sweet-potato biscuits are breakfast favorites, while cold and grilled classic sandwiches like BLTs, Reubens, chicken salad, and tuna melts fuel hungry noon crowds. Enjoy your stacks in the friendly, honey-blond wood bar and dining room up front or on the waterfront deck around back. $ *Average main: $7* ✉ *303 Queen Elizabeth Ave., Manteo* ☎ *252/473–3333* 🌐 *www.poorrichardsmanteo.com* ✍ *Reservations not accepted.*

### WHERE TO STAY

*Hotel reviews have been abbreviated in this book. For expanded reviews, please go to Fodors.com.*

$ B&B/INN **Island House of Wanchese.** Antiques, hope chests, and handmade quilts decorate rooms at this circa-1900 house that retains original wood floors and wavy glass windows. **Pros:** lots of interesting antiques on display; serene setting; cozy gardens; some pets allowed. **Cons:** far from business and beach districts; no kids allowed unless approved by owners. *Rooms from: $140 ✉ 104 Old Wharf Rd., Wanchese ☎ 252/473–5619 🌐 www.islandhouse-bb.com 3 rooms, 1 suite Breakfast.*

#### GONE FISHING

When you're considering chartering a boat, in addition to asking the price, find out the answer to these questions: How long will you actually be fishing once the travel time is factored out? Where will you go, and for what will you be fishing? Will they supply the rods and tackle? How many people are required for a trip? Will there be other fishing parties on board? Are food and drinks provided? Will they clean the catch and ice it down?

2

$ B&B/INN **Scarborough Inn.** Two stories of wraparound porches surround the Scarborough, which is modeled after a turn-of-the-20th-century inn. **Pros:** nicely groomed garden areas; B&B feel at a good price. **Cons:** located on a busy road; small lobby; innkeeper may step out and lock front office. *Rooms from: $85 ✉ 524 U.S. 64/264, Manteo ☎ 252/473–3979 🌐 www.scarborough-inn.com 14 rooms Breakfast.*

$$$ B&B/INN ★ **Tranquil House Inn.** This charming, waterfront, 19th-century-style inn is just steps from shops, restaurants, and Roanoke Island Festival Park. **Pros:** easy walking distance from shops and restaurants; complimentary evening wine reception; children up to age 18 stay free in their parents' rooms. **Cons:** located on a busy commercial waterfront; small, cramped lobby. *Rooms from: $199 ✉ 405 Queen Elizabeth Ave., Box 2045, Manteo ☎ 252/473–1404, 800/458–7069 🌐 www.tranquilhouseinn.com 25 rooms Breakfast.*

### SPORTS AND THE OUTDOORS

**Oregon Inlet Fishing Center.** This full-service marina leads fishing excursions and has supplies such as bait, tackle, ice, and fuel for the fisherman. The National Park Service maintains an adjacent boat launch. *✉ 98 Rte. 12, north end of Oregon Inlet Bridge ☎ 252/441–6301, 800/272–5199 🌐 www.oregon-inlet.com.*

**Pirates Cove Yacht Club and Marina.** This yacht club and marina has a deep-water, charter dock as well as a restaurant, a kiddy pool and playground, a fitness center, and a pavilion for private events. *✉ 2000 Sailfish Dr., Manteo ☎ 252/473–3906, 800/367–4728 🌐 www.fishpiratescove.com.*

# CAPE HATTERAS NATIONAL SEASHORE

Longtime visitors to the Outer Banks have seen how development changes these once unspoiled barrier islands, so it's nice to know that the 70-mile stretch of the Cape Hatteras National Seashore will remain protected. Its pristine beaches, set aside as the first national seashore in 1953, stretch from the southern outskirts of Nags Head to Ocracoke Inlet, encompassing three narrow islands: Bodie, Hatteras, and Ocracoke.

These waters provide some of the East Coast's best fishing and surfing, and they're ideal for other sports such as windsurfing, diving, and boating. Parking is allowed only in designated areas. Fishing piers are in Rodanthe and Avon.

With 300 miles of coastline, there are plenty of beaches that don't have lifeguards on duty. ■**TIP→** **To identify beaches with trained staff, contact the Ocean Rescue in the town, or if you're in a national park, the Park Service.**

## BODIE ISLAND

*7 miles south of Nags Head.*

Natives pronounce it "Bah-dy" not "Bow-dy." Folklore claims the local pronunciation harks back to the days when this corner of the Graveyard of the Atlantic was known as "Bodies Island" because of all the dead seafarers who washed onto the shores. The island remains mostly barren, but the boardwalks and observation decks on its marshes offer excellent opportunities to watch wading birds and to kayak or canoe through the inlets.

#### GETTING HERE AND AROUND

From the north, reach Bodie Island via U.S. 158 to Route 12. From the east, take U.S. 64/264 to U.S. 158 and then Route 12. South of the Outer Banks, U.S. 70 leads to Route 12 but requires a couple of ferry rides. Some commercial and charter flights are available from nearby airports. Tour buses visit major sites, but a car is necessary to travel around freely.

#### ESSENTIALS

**Visitor Information Whalebone Welcome Center** ✉ *2 N.C. 12 Hwy., MM 17, Nags Head* ☎ *877/629–4386* 🌐 *www.outerbanks.org/outerbanks-forms-and-other-information.*

### EXPLORING

**Bodie Island Lighthouse.** Designer Dexter Stetson was also the brains behind the Cape Hatteras Lighthouse, which explains why the two look so much alike. Bodie, with its wide (22 feet tall) black-and-white horizontal stripes, stands 156 feet tall and is capped by a black cast-iron lantern. It's actually the third lighthouse to guard this area of the coast. The first, built in 1847, was simply abandoned because of its shoddy construction. A second, build in 1859, was blown up in 1861 by retreating Confederate soldiers because they feared it would be used as a Yankee observation tower. The current lighthouse was completed in

1872, and is in the midst of a two-part renovation scheduled for completion in 2013. Only the keeper's house and museum can be toured. ✉ *8210 Bodie Island Lighthouse Rd., Nags Head* ☎ *252/441–5711, 252/473–2111* 🌐 *www.nps.gov/caha/historyculture/bodie-island-light-station.htm* 🎫 *Free* 🕓 *Daily 9–5.*



## HATTERAS ISLAND

*15 miles south of Nags Head.*

The Herbert C. Bonner Bridge arches for 3 miles over Oregon Inlet and carries traffic to Hatteras Island, a 42-mile-long curved ribbon of sand jutting out into the Atlantic Ocean. At its most distant point (Cape Hatteras), the island is 25 miles from the mainland. About 85% of the island belongs to Cape Hatteras National Seashore, and the remainder is privately owned in seven small, quaint villages strung along Route 12, the island's fragile lifeline to points north. Among its nicknames, Hatteras is known as the blue marlin (or billfish) capital of the world. The fishing's so great here because the Continental Shelf is 40 miles offshore, and its current, combined with the nearby Gulf Stream and Deep West Boundary Current, create an unparalleled fish habitat. The total population of the towns—Rodanthe, Waves, Salvo, Avon, Buxton, Frisco, and Hatteras Village—is around 3,000, according to the 2010 Census.

#### GETTING HERE AND AROUND

From the north, reach Hatteras Island via U.S. 158. From the east, take U.S. 64 to U.S. 158. South of the Outer Banks, U.S. 70 leads to Route 12 and requires a couple of ferry rides. Some commercial and charter flights are available from nearby airports.

#### ESSENTIALS

**Visitor Information Hatteras Welcome Center** ✉ *57190 Kohler Rd., Hatteras Village* ☎ *252/986–2203* 🌐 *www.outerbanks.org.*

### EXPLORING

★ **Cape Hatteras Lighthouse.** The Cape Hatteras Lighthouse, authorized by Congress in 1794 to help prevent shipwrecks, was the first lighthouse built in the region. The original structure was lost to erosion and Civil War damage; this 1870 replacement is, at 210 feet, the tallest brick lighthouse in the United States. Endangered by the sea, in 1999 the lighthouse was actually raised and rolled some 2,900 feet inland to its present location. A visitor center is located near the base of the lighthouse. In summer the principal keeper's quarters are open for viewing, and you can climb the lighthouse's 248 steps (12 stories) to the viewing balcony. Children under 42 inches tall aren't allowed to climb the lighthouse. Offshore lay the remains of the USS *Monitor,* a Confederate ironclad ship that sank in 1862. ✉ *Lighthouse Rd., off Rte. 12, 30 miles south of Rodanthe, Buxton* ☎ *252/995–4474* 🌐 *www.nps.gov/caha/planyourvisit/climbing-the-cape-hatteras-lighthouse.htm* 🎫 *Visitor center and keeper's quarters free, lighthouse tower $7* 🕓 *Visitor center and keeper's quarters: Memorial Day–Labor Day, daily 9–6; 9–5 rest of yr. Lighthouse tower: mid-Apr.–Memorial Day and Labor Day–mid-Oct., daily 9–4:30; Memorial Day–Labor Day, daily 9–5:30.*

Learn about the lifesaving stations that once dotted the North Carolina coast at the Chicamacomico Lifesaving Station.

**Chicamacomico Lifesaving Station.** Pronounced "chik-a-ma-*com*-i-co," the restored 1911 lifesaving station is now a museum that tells the story of the brave people who manned 29 stations that once lined the Outer Banks. These were the precursors to today's Coast Guard, with staff who rescued people and animals from seacraft in distress. There's more here than meets the eye. Eight buildings on 7 acres include a cookhouse, bathhouse, stables, workshop, and the original 1874 lifesaving station. You'll see original equipment and tools, artifacts, and exhibits. Living-history reenactments are performed late May through August, and a 1907 cottage moved to the site portrays turn-of-the-19th-century life along the Outer Banks. ✉ *23645 N.C. Hwy. 12, at MM 39.5, Rodanthe* ☎ *252/987–1552* 🌐 *www.chicamacomico.net* 🎟 *$6* 🕒 *Mid-Apr.–Nov., weekdays 10–5.*

**Frisco Native American Museum & Natural History Center.** A nationally recognized collection of Native American artifacts fills the museum. Galleries display native art from across the United States as well as relics from the first inhabitants of Hatteras Island. The museum has been designated as a North Carolina Environmental Education Center. Several acres of nature trails wind through a maritime forest, a pavilion overlooks a salt marsh, and a bird observation room overlooks a garden with plants selected to attract birds. Beginning birding and archaeology summer programs are included in the ticket price, and admission tickets are valid for a full week. ✉ *Rte. 12, 53536 N.C. Hwy. 12, Frisco* ☎ *252/995–4440* 🌐 *www.nativeamericanmuseum.org* 🎟 *$5* 🕒 *Tues.–Sun. 10:30–5. Winter hrs may vary, call ahead.*

**Pea Island National Wildlife Refuge.** This refuge is made up of more than 5,800 acres of marsh on the Atlantic Flyway. To bird watchers' delight, more than 365 species have been sighted from its observation platforms and spotting scopes and by visitors who venture into the refuge. Pea Island is home to threatened peregrine falcons, piping plovers, and tundra swans, which winter here. A visitor center on Route 12 has an information display and maps of the two trails. Remember to douse yourself in bug spray, especially in spring. Guided canoe tours are available for a fee. ✉ *Pea Island Refuge Headquarters, 15440 N.C. Hwy. 12, Rodanthe* ☎ *252/987–2394* 🌐 *www.fws.gov/peaisland* 🎫 *Free* 🕑 *Daily 9–4.*

### WHERE TO EAT AND STAY

*Hotel reviews have been abbreviated in this book. For expanded reviews, please go to Fodors.com.*

$$$ SEAFOOD ✕ **Breakwater.** Fat Daddy crab cakes, rolled in potato chips then fried and served with pineapple jalapeño salsa, is one of the more creative signature dishes at Breakwater. You also get more standard seafood options, such as shrimp lightly breaded and fried or broiled with white wine and butter, as well as Filet Oscar with crab and sauce bearnaise. The restaurant sits atop Oden's Dock. Given the casual nature of life here, Breakwater stands out with tables dressed in white linen. The dining room is a bit small, but waiting for a table in comfortable chairs on the deck overlooking Pamlico Sound is not a chore. $ *Average main: $25* ✉ *Waterfront, Rte. 12, 57896 N.C. Hwy. 12, Hatteras Village* ☎ *252/986–2733* 🌐 *www.odensdock.com* *Reservations not accepted* 🕑 *Closed Sun.–Wed. Labor Day Memorial Day. No lunch.*

$$ AMERICAN ✕ **The Captain's Table.** South of the entrance for the Cape Hatteras Lighthouse, this place is popular for its well-prepared food and homey manner. Stuffed flounder, fried soft-shell crabs, homemade crab salad, burgers, and assorted sandwiches are favorites though the menu also lists pasta, chicken, beef, and pulled pork. Weathered wood-shingle siding outside and maritime art and objects inside give the feel of an old fashioned beach house. $ *Average main: $17* ✉ *Rte. 12, 47048 Hwy. 12, MM 61, Buxton* ☎ *252/995–5988* 🕑 *Closed late Nov.–late March.*

$$ HOTEL **Sea Gull Motel.** The 1950s-era, family-operated Sea Gull offers beachside rooms in a two-story building as well as two adjacent cottage properties, each of which sleeps up to six (available for rent [$$$$] by the week only during high season). **Pros:** quiet setting; oceanfront pool; family-friendly; microwaves in room. **Cons:** remote location; no breakfast. $ *Rooms from: $150* ✉ *56883 N.C. Hwy. 12, between MM 70 and 71, Hatteras Village* ☎ *252/986–2550* 🌐 *www.seagullhatteras.com* *15 rooms, 1 suite, 2 cottages.*

## OCRACOKE ISLAND

*Ocracoke Village: 15 miles southwest of Hatteras Village.*

Around 950 people live here, the last inhabited island in the Outer Banks. The island can be reached only by water or air. The village itself is in the widest part of the island, around a harbor called Silver Lake. Man-dredged canals form the landscape of a smaller residential area called Oyster Creek.

## DID YOU KNOW?

Due to erosion, the Cape Hatteras Lighthouse had to be moved from its original location farther inland. It was raised and rolled some 2,900 feet over 23 days to its present location in 1999.

Centuries ago, Ocracoke was the stomping ground of Edward Teach, the pirate known as Blackbeard. A major treasure cache from 1718 is still rumored to be hidden somewhere on the island. Fort Ocracoke was a short-lived Confederate stronghold that was abandoned in August 1861 and blown up by Union forces a month later.

Although the island remains a destination for people seeking peace and quiet, silence can be hard to find in summer, when tourists and boaters swamp the place. About 90% of Ocracoke is part of Cape Hatteras National Seashore; the island is on the Atlantic Flyway for many migrating land and water birds. A free ferry leaves hourly from Hatteras Island and arrives 40 minutes later; toll ferries connect with the mainland at Swan Quarter (2½ hours) and at Cedar Island (2¼ hours). Reserve well in advance.

### GETTING HERE AND AROUND

The only way to reach Ocracoke Island is by ferry or private boat. State car ferries land at either end of the island and depart as late as 8 pm to Cedar Island and midnight to Hatteras Island. Only one road, Route 12, traverses the island. Quiet streets shoot off to the left and right at the south end. Lots of cyclists come to Ocracoke, and many inns have bikes guests may use, but be careful when biking Route 12 from one end of the island to the other in summer; traffic can be heavy, and the designated bike path doesn't travel the highway's entire 13-mile length.

### ESSENTIALS

**Visitor Information National Park Service Visitor Center** ✉ *Rte. 12* ☏ *252/928–4531* 🌐 *www.nps.gov/caha/planyourvisit/visitor-centers.htm.*

## EXPLORING

**British Cemetery.** On May 11, 1942, the HMS *Bedfordshire,* an armed British trawler on loan to the United States, was torpedoed by a German U-boat and sank with all 37 hands lost off the coast of Ocracoke Island. The men were buried on Ocracoke in a corner of the community graveyard. The wreck was discovered in 1980 and some artifacts were recovered. It's still frequented by divers. ✉ *British Cemetery Rd. off Rte. 12, Ocracoke Village* ☏ *252/926–9171* 🌐 *www.nps.gov/caha/historyculture/british-cemetery.htm.*

**Ocracoke Lighthouse.** Built in 1823, this is the second-oldest operating lighthouse in the United States (Sandy Hook, New Jersey, has the oldest). It was first fueled by whale oil, then kerosene, and finally electricity. The white finish was once achieved with a whitewash blend of unslaked lime, glue, rice, salt, and powdered fish. The squat whitewashed structure, 77 feet, 5 inches tall, is unfortunately not open to the public for climbing. The lighthouse is a photographer's dream. ✉ *Live Oak Rd. off Rte. 12, Ocracoke Village* ☏ *No phone.* 🌐 *www.nps.gov/caha/historyculture/ocracoke-island-lighthouse.htm.*

**Ocracoke Pony Pen.** From the observation platform, you can look out at the descendants of the Banker Ponies that roamed wild before the island came under the jurisdiction of Cape Hatteras National Seashore. The Park Service took over management of the ponies in the early 1960s and has helped maintain the population of 25–30 animals; the wild herd once numbered nearly 500. All the animals you see today

See the descendants of the wild Banker Ponies that used to roam Ocracoke Island at the Ocracoke Pony Pen.

were born in captivity and are fed and kept on a 180-acre range. Legends abound about the arrival of the island's Banker Ponies. Some believe they made their way to the island after the abandonment of Roanoke's Lost Colony. Others believe they were left by early Spanish explorers or swam to shore following the sinking of the *Black Squall*, a ship carrying circus performers. ✉ *Rte. 12, 6 miles southwest of Hatteras-Ocracoke ferry landing* ☎ *No phone.* 🌐 *www.nps.gov/caha/historyculture/ocracokeponies.htm.*

**Ocracoke Preservation Society Museum.** Run by the local preservation society, the museum contains photographs and artifacts illustrating the island's lifestyle and history. The summer outdoor "Porch Talks" series of presentations cover various topics including storytelling, sea songs, history, photography, and island life history. ✉ *49 Water Plant Rd., off Rte. 12 across from the Cedar Island ferry dock, Ocracoke Village* ☎ *252/928–7375* 🌐 *www.ocracokepreservation.org* 🎟 *Free* ⏲ *April–late Nov., weekdays 10–4, Sat. 11–4.*

## WHERE TO EAT AND STAY

*Hotel reviews have been abbreviated in this book. For expanded reviews, please go to Fodors.com.*

**$$$** SEAFOOD ✕ **Back Porch Restaurant.** At what looks like a cozy little cottage in the woods, seafood stars, whether it's crab beignets or cream and butter baked scallops. Find notable beef, chicken, and vegetarian dishes, including pecan-crusted chicken breast in bourbon sauce and spinach and chick pea curry over rice. You have the choice of enjoying your meal indoors or on a screened porch. The wine bar has a respectable wine list. The Back Porch Lunchbox, just a block away on Highway

12, offers sandwiches, snacks, and sweets to go. *Average main: $20* *110 Back Rd., Ocracoke* *252/928–6401* *No lunch.*

$$ AMERICAN **Howard's Pub.** The atmosphere is boisterous and friendly at this restaurant, which is open every day of the year for lunch and dinner (really, every day). The polite, quick-footed staff aims to please locals and travelers alike no matter what time of year they arrive. Don't miss the fresh-cut fries, fine burgers, or the grilled fresh catch. Best of all are appetizers like conch fritters or creamy shrimp and crab dip paired with any of the 24 beers on tap or nearly 200 bottled beers from around the world. Check out the many license plates, college banners, and beer towels adorning the walls, or strike up a conversation with whoever is sitting next to you in the large, friendly dining room or on the screened porch. *Average main: $18* *1175 Irvin Garrish Hwy., Ocracoke Village* *252/928–4441* *www.howardspub.com* *Reservations not accepted.*

$ B&B/INN **The Island Inn Villas.** The historic, white-clapboard Island Inn, built in 1901 and listed on the National Register of Historic Places, really shows its age. **Pros:** quiet; walking distance to shops and restaurants; friendly innkeeper; whirlpool tubs. **Cons:** no breakfast; no restaurant; main inn lobby may be cluttered and messy. *Rooms from: $69* *25 Lighthouse Rd., off Rte. 12, Box 9* *252/928–4351, 877/456–3466* *www.ocracokeislandinn.com* *16 rooms; 12 villas.*

$ HOTEL **Sand Dollar Motel.** The Sand Dollar is small and unassuming, but well run and features both a garden and a secluded swimming pool. **Pros:** picnic area with grill; microwave in rooms; walking distance to shops, restaurants, and historic sites. **Cons:** small rooms; no breakfast; no restaurant. *Rooms from: $79* *70 Sand Dollar Rd.* *252/928–5571, 866/928–5571* *www.sanddollarmotelocracoke.com* *12 rooms, 1 apartment, 2 cottages* *Closed Nov.–Mar.*

## SPORTS AND THE OUTDOORS

### BEACHES

★ **Ocracoke Island Beaches.** The 16 miles of undeveloped shoreline here was named America's number one beach in 2007 by Dr. Beach (Stephen P. Leatherman, director of the Laboratory for Coastal Research at Florida International University). These beaches are among the least populated and most beautiful on the Cape Hatteras National Seashore. The shelling is amazing, the solitude unparalleled. Four public-access areas are close to the main beach road, Route 12, and easy to spot; just look for large brown and white wooden signs. **Amenities:** parking, toilets. **Best for:** solitude, sunrise, sunset, surfing, swimming, windsurfing. *Rte. 12* *www.hydecounty.org/attractions/OcracokeBeach.htm.*

## SHOPPING

**Styron's General Store.** In 1920 Albert Styron set up Styron's General Store in Ocracoke; three generations later, the store is a place to pick up not dry goods and fishing equipment but souvenirs and gifts. Still, the building is interesting to see in that it is one of the island's oldest structures. An old red Coca-Cola cooler today holds Nehi, Cheerwine, and Sun-Drop sodas and serves as a candy stand. *Lighthouse Rd.* *252/928–2609.*

## BEACH CAMPING

Camping is permitted in four designated areas along the Cape Hatteras National Seashore. These campgrounds have spaces for tents, trailers, and motor homes. All camping at Cape Lookout National Seashore is primitive. Be sure to take extra-long tent stakes for sand, and don't forget insect repellent and bags for taking all your trash with you when you leave. All sites are available on a first-come, first-served basis, except Ocracoke, where reservations are accepted. For information about private campgrounds, contact the Outer Banks Visitors Bureau.

**Contacts Cape Hatteras National Seashore** *Rooms from: $20 ✉ 1401 National Park Dr., Manteo ☎ 252/473–2111 🌐 www.nps.gov/caha.* **Cape Lookout National Seashore** *Rooms from: $54 ✉ 131 Charles St., Harkers Island ☎ 877/444–6777 🌐 www.nps.gov/calo.* **Outer Banks Visitors Bureau** *Rooms from: $54 ✉ 1 Visitors Center Cir., Manteo ☎ 877/629–4386 🌐 www.outerbanks.org/outerbanks-campgrounds-and-rv-parks.*

## CAPE LOOKOUT NATIONAL SEASHORE

*Southwest of Ocracoke Island via Cedar Island.*

Extending for 55 miles from Portsmouth Island to Shackleford Banks, Cape Lookout National Seashore includes 28,400 acres of uninhabited land and marsh. The remote, sandy islands are linked to the mainland by private ferries. Loggerhead sea turtles, which have been placed on the federal list of threatened and endangered species, nest here. To the south, wild ponies roam Shackleford Banks. Four-wheel-drive vehicles are allowed on the beach, and primitive camping is allowed. There are primitive cabins (with and without electricity, no linens or utensils) with bunk beds. Private ferry service is available from Beaufort and Morehead City to Shackleford Banks, Beaufort, and Harkers Island to the Cape Lookout Lighthouse area, from Davis to Shingle Point, from Atlantic to North Core Banks and Long Point, and from Ocracoke Village to Portsmouth Village.

### GETTING HERE AND AROUND

The park's various islands are accessible by boat only. Various private ferries run back and forth to the island, and a list of authorized ferry services can be found at the park's website: 🌐 *www.nps.gov/calo/planyourvisit/ferry.htm.*

### ESSENTIALS

**Cape Lookout Visitor Center.** The visitor center is on Harkers Island, at the end of U.S. 70 East, near a private ferry terminal. *✉ 131 Charles St., Harkers Island ☎ 252/728–2250 for visitor center, 252/728–0942, 877/444–6777 for cabins 🌐 www.nps.gov/calo/planyourvisit/visitorcenters.htm Park free, ferry ride $10–$35 or $75–$400 for vehicles ⏲ Visitor center daily 9–5.*

## EXPLORING

**Cape Lookout Lighthouse.** When the original red-and-white-striped 1812 lighthouse proved too short and unstable, the 1859 structure was built to replace it. The double walls allow the tower to rise as tall as required—169 feet—without making the building unstable. This lighthouse on Core Banks island withstood retreating Confederate troops' attempts to blow it up to keep it out of Union hands (they stole the lens instead). With its white-and-black diamond markings, the beacon continues to function as a navigational aid. A small museum inside the Cape Lookout Visitor Center on Harkers Island tells the story of the lighthouse from its first incarnation in 1812. From there, you must take a private ferry to get to the lighthouse. Anyone 44 inches or taller may climb the tower's 207 steps (12 stories) from mid-May to mid-September, but reservations are highly recommended. The climb is worth it for an incomparable view of Cape Lookout's wild shores. ✉ *Cape Lookout Visitor Center, 131 Charles St., Harkers Island* ☎ *252/728–0708 for lighthouse ticket reservations; purchase tickets at the visitor center, 252/728–2250* 🌐 *www.nps.gov/calo* 🎫 *$8 to climb tower* ⏲ *Mid-May–mid-Sept., Wed.–Sat. 10–3:45.*

**Portsmouth Village.** Inhabited from 1753 until the early 1970s, the village listed 685 permanent residents at its peak in 1860, according to the census that year. It was a "lightering" town, where ships heavy with cargo had to unload to smaller boats that could navigate the shallow Ocracoke Inlet. But the Civil War and the dredging of a deeper inlet at Hatteras were the beginning of the end for Portsmouth. By 1956 there were 17 inhabitants; the last 2 left in 1971. Today the public can tour the visitor center, the one-room schoolhouse, the post office and general store, the Methodist church, and the turn-of-the-20th-century Life Saving Station (a multiroom Coast Guard station). Guided tours are available June 1 to Sept. 1. The walking trails can be difficult because of standing water, sandy soil, and mosquitoes. Public restrooms are not abundant; bring your own food and water. ✉ *Portsmouth Island* ✣ *Take ferry from Ocracoke* ☎ *252/728–2250* 🌐 *www.friendsofportsmouthisland.org* 🎫 *Free* ⏲ *Visitor center and buildings Apr.–Nov.*

## SPORTS AND THE OUTDOORS

### BEACHES

★ **Cape Lookout Beach.** White sand beaches, blue-green waters, and a tall lighthouse mark this quiet beach at the southern tip of Cape Lookout National Seashore. A boat is the only way to get here. Land on the sound side, then walk across a path to the beach, where you'll be greeted by a long beach strand full of seashells. You can also climb the lighthouse tower or tour a museum in the keeper's quarters. **Amenities:** none. **Best for:** solitude, sunrise, sunset, swimming. ✉ *Private passenger ferries leave from Harkers Island, Beaufort, Morehead City, and Ocracoke* 🌐 *www.nps.gov/calo.*

**Shackleford Banks.** Wild, wooded, and undeveloped, this 7½-mile-long barrier island, part of Cape Lookout National Seashore, is made even more magical by myriad seashells along the shore and free-roaming horses. Folklore offers two reasons for the Banker Ponies' presence.

One tale claims they swam ashore from a long-ago Spanish shipwreck, but some locals say early settlers first put these horses to pasture on the island. The horses may look friendly, but it's best to view them from a distance. The island hosted various settlements in the 1800s, but storms drove residents inland. Today, gravestones here and there are the only remaining evidence of the people who lived here. Island access is by private ferry only, and although primitive camping is allowed (at no fee), there are no amenities aside from composting toilets. **Amenities:** toilets. **Best for:** solitude, sunrise, sunset, swimming. ✉ *2 miles southeast of Beaufort. Private passenger ferries leave from Beaufort.*

## THE CRYSTAL COAST AND NEW BERN

Carteret County, with nearly 80 miles of ocean coastline, is known as the Crystal Coast. It's composed of the south-facing beaches along the barrier island Bogue Banks (Atlantic Beach, Pine Knoll Shores, Indian Beach, Salter Path, and Emerald Isle), three major mainland townships (Morehead City, Beaufort, and Newport), and a series of small, unincorporated "down-east" communities traversed by a portion of U.S. 70, designated a Scenic Byway.

Cape Lookout National Seashore is a great place for surf fishing year-round, but the best seasons are spring and fall.

Neighboring Craven County—which contains New Bern, a good chunk of the 157,000-acre Croatan National Forest, and massive Cherry Point Marine Corps air station—is by turns genteel and historic, modern and commercialized, rural and wild. Golfers, boaters, and a growing number of retirees find the area a haven.

## BEAUFORT

*20 miles west of Harkers Island–Cape Lookout ferry; 150 miles southeast of Raleigh.*

There's a feeling of having stepped back in time in the small seaport with a charming boardwalk; residents take great pride in the city's restored public buildings and homes—and in their homes' histories, which sometimes include tales of pirates and sea captains. **■ TIP→** Don't make the mistake of pronouncing the town's name as "BEW-furt." South Carolinians call that state's city of Beaufort "BEW-furt." North Carolina's Beaufort is pronounced "BOW-furt." Established in 1713, the third-oldest town in North Carolina was named for Henry Somerset, duke of Beaufort, and it's hard to miss the English influence here. Streets, at least those in the historic district, are named after British royalty and colonial leaders.

#### GETTING HERE AND AROUND

Beaufort is near the far eastern end of U.S. 70, which links to U.S. 17 to the north at New Bern. The town has a small airstrip but no commercial flights. For boaters, it's located along the intracoastal waterway, and downtown docks are available. The closest major airport is in New

Bern. The town is a perfect park-and-stroll location, with historic sites, museums, and a retail center all within walking distance of each other.

### ESSENTIALS

**Visitor Information Beaufort Historic Site Visitor Center** ✉ *150 Turner St.* ☎ *252/728–5225* 🌐 *www.beaufortthistoricsite.org.*

## EXPLORING

Today the town still has a strong connection with the sea—everything from motorized dinghies to graceful sailboats to fabulous yachts from around the world anchors here. Boat rides of all types—dolphin watches, dinner cruises, lighthouse excursions, party jaunts, and scenic harbor tours—are available for a fee. Restaurants and shops line the waterfront. Also on the harbor is the private Duke University Marine Laboratory, with the National Science Foundation's huge research vessel, the *Cape Hatteras,* moored out back.

**Beaufort Historic Site.** In the center of town, the historic site consists of 10 buildings dating from 1732 to 1859, 8 of which have been restored, including the 1796 **Carteret County Courthouse** and the 1859 **Apothecary Shop and Doctor's Office.** Don't miss the **Old Burying Grounds** (1709), where Otway Burns, a privateer in the War of 1812, is buried under his ship's cannon; a nine-year-old girl who died at sea is buried in a rum keg; and an English soldier saluting the king is buried upright in his grave. Tours, either on an English-style double-decker bus or by guided walk, depart from the visitor center. ✉ *150 Turner St.* ☎ *252/728–5225, 800/575–7483* 🌐 *www.beaufortthistoricsite.org* 🎫 *Tour $8* 🕒 *Mon.–Sat., walking tours at 10, 11:30, 1, and 3. Bus tour: Apr.–Oct., Mon., Wed., Fri., and Sat. at 11 and 1:30. Burying Ground tour: June–Sept., Tues.–Thurs. at 2:30.*

★ **North Carolina Maritime Museum.** An exhibit about the infamous pirate Blackbeard includes artifacts recovered from the discovery of his flagship, *Queen Anne's Revenge,* near Beaufort Inlet. Other exhibits feature coastal culture and the state's rich marine-science history. You'll see seashells, fossils, duck decoys, and commercial fishing gear. Educational programs might include birding treks, sailing lessons, and history tours. You can also roam the library's extensive maritime collection. The associated **Watercraft Center,** across the street, has lectures and classes on boatbuilding and you can see various projects under construction by professional and amateur boatbuilders. ✉ *315 Front St.* ☎ *252/728–7317* 🌐 *www.ncmaritime.org* 🎫 *Free* 🕒 *Weekdays 9–5, Sat. 10–5, Sun. 1–5.*

## WHERE TO EAT

$$$ MODERN AMERICAN

✕ **Blue Moon Bistro.** Beaufort native Chef Kyle Swain returned home to put into use the lessons he learned apprenticing with some of North Carolina's top chefs. He pairs classical French technique with creative presentations, many emphasizing local seafood and produce. Try shrimp sautéed scampi-style with prosciutto, plum tomatoes, and basil or pan-seared salmon over meat-filled ravioli in mushroom sauce. Though the emphasis is on local seafood, meat, poultry, and interesting vegetarian dishes like asparagus-shiitake-goat-cheese risotto, are among the entrées. The restaurant occupies the 1827 Dill House, which has

CLOSE UP

## North Carolina's Pirates

North Carolina's coast was a magnet for marauding sea dogs during the Golden Age of Piracy, a period in the first quarter of the 18th century. Among those who visited was Stede Bonnet, the so-called gentleman pirate. For this successful owner of a sugar plantation, piracy seemed the result of a midlife crisis. He should have stayed on the farm: he was cheated by Blackbeard, captured by authorities, and hanged in 1718.

Anne Bonny was the Irish illegitimate daughter of a lawyer. Married at 16 to a small-time pirate, she fell in love with "Calico Jack" Rackham, and the two ran away together and put together a pirate crew. In 1720 they were attacked and most of the scalawags were too drunk to defend themselves. Rackham was sentenced to be hanged; Bonny claimed she was pregnant and was eventually pardoned. She disappeared from history before the age of 25.

Of course, the most notorious buccaneer of them all was Blackbeard, whose two-year reign of terror began in 1716. He cultivated fear by strapping on six pistols and six knives, tying his luxuriant beard into pigtails and, legend has it, tucking lighted matches into it during battle.

Illustration from the cover of *Blackbeard, Buccaneer* by Ralph D. Paine.

A polygamist with at least 12 wives, Blackbeard attacked ships in the Caribbean and settlements along the coasts of Virginia and the Carolinas. At least three of his ships sank in North Carolina's waters; archaeologists are studying artifacts from what is likely the flagship, *Queen Anne's Revenge,* which ran aground on a sandbar near Beaufort Inlet in May 1718.

The following November a seafaring posse caught Blackbeard in one of his favorite playgrounds, Ocracoke Inlet. The pirate was decapitated and his head was hung from one of the conquering ships. Blackbeard's other lost ships and his reputedly fabulous treasure are still being sought today.

---

been dressed up with oak woodwork, wainscoting, and suns and moons made of pressed tin. *Average main: $20 ✉ 119 Queen St. ☎ 252/728–5800 🌐 www.bluemoonbistro.biz ⏲ Closed Sun. and Mon. No lunch.*

$$ CONTEMPORARY **Clawson's 1905 Restaurant & Pub.** Housed in what was a grocery store in the early 1900s, Clawson's is stuffed with memorabilia. It gets crowded in summer, so arrive early for both lunch and dinner. Hearty food such as ribs, steaks, pasta, and seafood are part of the attraction. The pub has a selection of North Carolina microbrews. *Average main: $18 ✉ 425 Front St. ☎ 252/728–2133 🌐 www.clawsonsrestaurant.com ⏲ Closed Sun. Labor Day–Memorial Day.*

$$$ SEAFOOD **The Spouter Inn.** Dining at a shaded table on the Spouter's deck overlooking Beaufort Harbor and Taylor's Creek is one of life's treats. Boats

## VACATION RENTALS

Vacation rentals, booked primarily through agencies, are increasingly popular, as properties are available to meet almost every taste and budget. If you're looking for a rental home, some of our favorite local agencies are:

**Emerald Isle Realty** *7501 Emerald Dr., Emerald Isle 866/586-6980 www.emeraldislerealty.com.*

**Intracoastal Realty** *1900 Eastwood Rd., No. 38, Wilmington 910/256-4503, 800/346-2463 www.intracoastalrentals.com.*

**Midgett Realty** *57783 Hwy. 12, Hatteras 252/986-2841, 800/527-2903 www.midgettrealty.com.*

glide by, you see a wild horse or two on Carrot Island just across the way, and a waiter appears with a cold drink and plate of steamed shrimp. The prime rib and maple bourbon barbecue ribs are popular alternatives to seafood. The attached bakery produces all kinds of cakes and pies: the carrot cake is outstanding. Sunday brunch choices include quiche, omelets, and eggs Benedict with crab cakes. There's indoor seating as well. *Average main: $25 218 Front St. 252/728-5190 www.thespouterinn.com Closed Jan.–mid-Feb.*

### WHERE TO STAY

*Hotel reviews have been abbreviated in this book. For expanded reviews, please go to Fodors.com.*

$ B&B/INN **The County Home B&B.** Billed as something between a country inn and a bed-and-breakfast, the inn was renovated in 1996 and is listed on the National Register of Historic Places. **Pros:** private baths in each room; large porch with rockers; pets allowed. **Cons:** located just over a mile from the historic downtown area, but on a route too busy for pedestrians; no communal dining room. *Rooms from: $110 299 N.C. Hwy. 101 252/728-4611 www.countyhomeb-b.com 10 rooms.*

$ B&B/INN **Pecan Tree Inn.** Local lore has it that when this 1866 Queen Anne building with gingerbread trim was converted from a Masonic Lodge and schoolhouse to a private home, it was the first in Beaufort to have gas lighting, indoor plumbing, and a telephone. **Pros:** quiet location; no smoking; friendly hosts; close to two of the area's best restaurants. **Cons:** no elevator; children under age 10 not allowed. *Rooms from: $115 116 Queen St. 252/728-6733, 800/728-7871 www.pecantree.com 7 rooms Breakfast.*

## MOREHEAD CITY

*3 miles west of Beaufort via U.S. 70.*

The quiet commercial waterfront at Morehead City is dotted with restaurants and shops that have put new life in its old buildings. The largest town on the Crystal Coast, it hosts a state port and charter fishing arena. It's also home to sizable marine research facilities for the

National Oceanic and Atmospheric Administration, the University of North Carolina at Chapel Hill, and North Carolina State University.

Arendell Street (U.S. 70) is Morehead City's main drag. Running parallel to the waterfront, it and some side streets contain the Fish Walk, a series of colorful sculptures in clay relief depicting indigenous fish and other types of sea life, as well as gift shops, restaurants, and the Crystal Coast Tourism Authority.

Outside the city, you can fish, swim, picnic, and hike at Fort Macon State Park. Route 58 passes through all the beach communities on Bogue Banks, a barrier island across Bogue Sound from Morehead City. There are a number of popular family beaches, including Atlantic Beach and Emerald Isle. Points of public access along the shoreline are marked by orange-and-blue signs. Lifeguards monitor only a few beaches.

#### GETTING HERE AND AROUND

Morehead City is near the far east end of U.S. 70. A small regional airport is in nearby Beaufort, and a commercial airport is about an hour away in New Bern. There is no public bus service in this busy town; a car is essential.

#### ESSENTIALS

**Visitor Information** **Crystal Coast Visitor Center** ✉ *3409 Arendell St.* ☎ *800/786–6962* 🌐 *www.crystalcoastnc.org.*

### EXPLORING

★ **Fort Macon State Park.** The centerpiece of the park is the 1834 pentagon-shaped fortress used first to protect the coast against foreign invaders and pirates, then against Yankees during the Civil War. You can explore on your own or take a guided tour. The 365-acre park set in a maritime forest also offers picnic areas, hiking trails, a mile-long beachfront with a large bathhouse and refreshments, and summer concerts. Rangers offer a wide selection of nature talks and walks, including Civil War weapons demonstrations, bird or butterfly hikes, and beach explorations. Follow the boardwalk over the dunes to the beach, which, due to strong currents, has lifeguards on duty June through Labor Day from 10 to 5:45. ✉ *East end of Rte. 58, Bogue Banks, 3 miles south of Morehead City* ☎ *252/726–3775* 🌐 *www.ncparks.gov/Visit/parks/foma/main.php* 🎟 *Free* 🕒 *Daily 9–5:30.*

**The History Place.** A large artifact collection reflects the history of Carteret County and the Cape Lookout region from Native American through modern times. There's also a gift shop, tearoom, and a public research library with a notable genealogy collection. ✉ *1008 Arendell St.* ☎ *252/247–7533* 🌐 *www.thehistoryplace.org* 🎟 *Free* 🕒 *Tues.–Fri. and the first Sat. of each month 10–4.*

Fodor's Choice ★ **North Carolina Aquarium at Pine Knoll Shores.** Touch a stingray, look a shark in the eye, or see a rare white sea turtle at various exhibits featuring marine and coastal animals. Exhibits include river otters; a touch pool with live horseshoe crabs; and a 306,000-gallon, 64-foot-long tank containing tiger sharks and hundreds of fish that swim around the replica of a German submarine sunk off the North Carolina coast in 1942. There's a large selection of programs, walks, and excursions.

Watch fish school around the replica of a German U-boat sunk off the North Carolina coast in 1942 at the North Carolina Aquarium at Pine Knoll Shores.

Learn to cook seafood or kayak the Theodore Roosevelt Natural Area. Kids will love seeing the aquarium menagerie getting fed or spending a night at a slumber party in front of the Living Shipwreck exhibit. The Birds in Flight program features live owls, hawks, falcons, and other shorebirds, some of which fly overhead during the indoor show. ✉ *1 Roosevelt Blvd., Pine Knoll Shores* ☎ *252/247–4003, 800/832–3474 for activities* 🌐 *www.ncaquariums.com* 🎟 *$8* ⏲ *Daily 9–5.*

### WHERE TO EAT AND STAY

*Hotel reviews have been abbreviated in this book. For expanded reviews, please go to Fodors.com.*

$$ ECLECTIC ★ ✕ **Bistro by the Sea.** The bar's atrium is decorated as a grape arbor, which speaks to the importance of wines at this Mediterranean-style spot, although the cuisine defies any particular theme. Beef, chicken, and local seafood all share space on the menu—but the flavor is as likely to be Asian as Italian. Don't miss the tuna sushi. There's a vodka and piano bar, too. $ *Average main: $18* ✉ *4031 Arendell St.* ☎ *252/247–2777* 🌐 *www.bistro-by-the-sea.com* ⏲ *Closed Sun. and Mon. No lunch.*

$$$$ SEAFOOD ✕ **Chefs 105 and 105 Oyster Bar.** Named for its street address in a 1929 Gulf Oil Corp. warehouse, this casual restaurant has a hip feel. Chef Andy Hopper, of Chicago's Spiaggia Cafe fame, offers rustic, seasonally changing takes on meats and fresh, local seafood. Smoked gouda seasons the creamy crab dip, pimento cheese enriches shrimp and grits, and lamb ragù is braised for eight hours before landing on pappardelle. Lunch is served in summer only and includes options such as a tasty bison burger or fried oyster salad with warm champagne hollandaise. An adjoining oyster bar features steamed seafood, oyster shooters, and

she-crab soup. The second-story deck has particularly nice views. *Average main: $25 ✉ 105 S. 7th St. ☎ 252/240–1105 ⊕ www.chefs105.com ⊙ No lunch, except during summer.*

$$$ SEAFOOD ★ **Sanitary Fish Market.** It can get busy (hourlong waits) and noisy (600 seats), but locals and people from around the world (their photos, many celebrities among them, line the walls) gush about the seafood and don't mind the no-frills atmosphere. In 1938 when the Sanitary was founded, many fish houses were ill kept. The owners wanted to signal that theirs was different; *clean, simple,* and *generous* are still the bywords at this waterfront place where diners sit at long wooden tables. Have seafood prepared almost any way you want it—steamed, fried, grilled, or broiled. The two-course deluxe shore dinner has, among other things, shrimp, oysters, crabs, and fish. Hush puppies and coleslaw come with every meal. *Average main: $20 ✉ 501 Evans St. ☎ 252/247–3111 ⊕ www.sanitaryfishmarket.com ⊙ Closed late Nov. to early Feb.*

$$ HOTEL **Windjammer Inn.** What you get here is straightforward—a large, simple, comfortable room with a private balcony, an ocean view, and easy access to the beach. **Pros:** outdoor Jacuzzi; all rooms are oceanfront; beach is right outside the door and feels private. **Cons:** small lobby; no breakfast. *Rooms from: $167 ✉ 103 Salter Path Rd., Atlantic Beach ☎ 252/247–7123, 800/233–6466 ⊕ www.windjammerinn.com 46 rooms No meals.*

## SPORTS AND THE OUTDOORS

### BEACHES

★ **Atlantic Beach.** Just over the high-rise bridge from Morehead City to the beach, Atlantic Beach was once known for boisterous nightclubs on the infamous Circle. In recent years, Atlantic Beach has become a more family-friendly spot enjoyed by couples and retirees, too. These days, free outdoor movies, playgrounds, volleyball, soccer, and carnival rides are featured on the town's Circle. A boardwalk fronts part of the clean, wide beach, where buoys mark lifeguard-protected swimming areas. **Amenities:** food and drink, lifeguards, toilets. **Best for:** surfing, swimming, windsurfing. *✉ The Circle comprises East Dr., Central Dr., and West Atlantic Blvd., Atlantic Beach ⊕ www.atlanticbeach-nc.com.*

★ **Bogue Banks Beaches.** Fort Macon State Park anchors the east end, and family-friendly Emerald Island is positioned at the west end of this 21-mile stretch of beach. In between are the quiet oceanfront towns of Indian Beach and Pine Knoll Shores. The shoreline is the same from town to town, but off-beach experiences vary. Fort Macon offers a Civil War fort to explore, as well as lifeguards, bathhouses, and free parking. Pine Knoll Shores and Indian Beach are full of posh and cozy vacation rentals, as well as putt-putt and real golf. Emerald Isle is full-on family fun, with a fishing pier, waterslide, an active town recreation center, and plenty of shopping. **Amenities:** food and drink, lifeguards, parking (some with fee, some no fee), toilets. **Best for:** sunrise, sunset, surfing, swimming, windsurfing. *✉ Rte. 58 ✣ From the west follow Rte. 24 to Rte. 58 in Emerald Isle; from the east take U.S. 70 to Rte. 58 at Atlantic Beach ⊕ www.crystalcoastnc.org.*

### SCUBA DIVING

Two wreck sites popular for scuba diving are the former 255-foot German gunship *Schurz,* seized by the United States and sunk following a collision in 1918, and the *Papoose,* a 412-foot tanker sunk by a German torpedo in 1942, which is now inhabited by docile sand tiger sharks.

**Olympus Dive Center.** With three dive boats Olympus Dive Center offers full- and half-day charters, special charters for divers seeking decompression certification, equipment rental, and lessons. In addition to wreck excursions, it sponsors spearfishing charters and shark expeditions. ✉ *713 Shepard St.* ☎ *252/726–9432* 🌐 *www.olympusdiving.com.*



### SHOPPING

**Carteret County Curb Market.** The oldest continuously operating curb market in North Carolina, Carteret County Curb Market has hosted vendors since 1931. It is open each Saturday from 7:30 am to 11 am beginning on the first Saturday in May through Labor Day. It's the place to find everything from flowers to flounder, locally grown vegetables, fresh seafood, baked goods of all descriptions, and a variety of North Carolina crafts. ✉ *13th and Evans Sts.* ☎ *252/222–6352* ⏲ *May–Labor Day, Sat. 7:30 am–11 am.*

**Dee Gee's Gifts & Books.** Offering a wide variety of books with regional interest, Dee Gee's Gifts & Books frequently holds book signings by local authors. The store also stocks a large selection of North Carolina crafts, cards, bride and baby gifts, jewelry, nautical charts, and art. ✉ *508 Evans St.* ☎ *252/726–3314, 800/333–4337* 🌐 *www.deegees.com.*

## NEW BERN

*36 miles northeast of Morehead City via U.S. 70.*

This city of 29,899 was founded in 1710 by a Swiss nobleman who named it after his home: Bern, Switzerland. Since "bern" means "bear" in German, black bears are New Bern's mascot, peering from carvings, the city's seal, and town souvenirs. New Bern boasted the state's first printing press in 1749, the first newspaper in 1751, and the first publicly funded school in 1764. For nearly 30 years it was the state capital until it moved to Raleigh in 1792. George Washington even slept in New Bern . . . *twice.* In 1898, New Bern cemented its place in pop-culture history when pharmacist Caleb Bradham mixed up a digestive aid that would become known as Pepsi-Cola.

Today New Bern has a 20-block historic district that includes more than 150 significant buildings, some 50 of which are on the National Register. The diverse architecture covers colonial, Georgian, Federal, Greek Revival, and Victorian styles. Since 1979, more than $200 million has been spent preserving and revitalizing the downtown area, now a pleasant mix of shops, restaurants, and museums. Sailors and sun seekers enjoy the area, too, as the Neuse and Trent rivers are perfect for such activities as waterskiing and crabbing. The town has several marinas, and, if water sports aren't your thing, five public or semipublic golf courses.

### GETTING HERE AND AROUND

The east–west U.S. 70 and north–south U.S. 17 intersect at New Bern, allowing highway access from all directions. The city also has a medium-size airport offering commercial flights. You can walk around downtown, but you'll need a car to maneuver around the city.

### ESSENTIALS

**Visitor Information Craven County Convention and Visitors Bureau** ✉ *203 S. Front St.* ☎ *252/637–9400* 🌐 *www.visitnewbern.com.*

**Air Contact Coastal Carolina Regional Airport** ✉ *200 Terminal Dr.* ☎ *252/638–8591* 🌐 *www.newbernairport.com.*

## EXPLORING

**Birthplace of Pepsi-Cola.** In honor of the soda's 100th anniversary, the local bottling company opened the Birthplace in the same corner store where teacher-turned-pharmacist Caleb Bradham brewed his first batch of "Brad's Drink." He later renamed it Pepsi-Cola, began marketing the syrup to other soda fountains, and a conglomerate was born. This old-fashioned pharmacy shop feels like a museum, with its reproduction of Bradham's fountain and exhibits of memorabilia and gift items. Enjoy a Pepsi float while roaming the new addition next door, full of Pepsi history and souvenirs ranging from T-shirts to thimbles. ✉ *256 Middle St.* ☎ *252/636–5898* 🌐 *www.pepsistore.com* ⏲ *Mon.–Sat. 10–6.*

Fodor's Choice ★ **Tryon Palace.** This elegant reconstructed 1770 Georgian building was the colonial capitol and originally the home of Royal Governor William Tryon. The palace burned to the ground in 1798, and it wasn't until 1952 that a seven-year, $3.5-million effort to rebuild it took place. Today only the stable and one basement wall are original, but the structure and furnishings are so authentic—reconstructed from architect plans, maps, and letters—that 82% of the books in the library are the same titles as those that were there 200 years ago. It's furnished with English and American antiques corresponding to Governor Tryon's inventory. The stately **John Wright Stanly House** (circa 1783), the **George W. Dixon House** (circa 1830), the **Robert Hay House** (circa 1805), and the **New Bern Academy** (circa 1809) are all part of the 13-acre Tryon Palace complex. You can also stroll through the 18th-century formal gardens, which bloom year-round but are especially popular during spring tulip and fall mum seasons. The complex's 60,000-square-foot **North Carolina History Center** contains two museums providing interactive displays that trace the history of New Bern and the central North Carolina coast. Concerts, lectures, and theater performances also are staged there. ✉ *529 S. Front St.* ☎ *252/639–3500* 🌐 *www.tryonpalace.org* 🎟 *Gardens $6; galleries $12; guided tours buildings and grounds $20* ⏲ *Mon.–Sat. 9–5, Sun. 1–5.*

## WHERE TO EAT

$$$ AMERICAN ★ **Captain Ratty's Seafood & Steakhouse.** Everyone from businessmen to vacationing families finds something to like at Captain Ratty's. Sandwiches and generous salads are popular lunch items; steaks and seafood, especially lump crab cakes, are the prime choices for evening meals, though you can also get oysters on the half shell. Five separate dining areas include the new, tony, second-floor Grapes of Rat wine bar

boasting 300 labels (20 offered by the glass) and weekly tastings. An outdoor rooftop dining area provides a bird's-eye view of downtown. Takeout and kid's menus are available. *Average main: $20 ✉ 202 Middle St. ☎ 252/633–2088 🌐 www.captainrattys.com ⏲ No breakfast Mon.–Fri.*

$$$ MODERN AMERICAN **The Chelsea.** Situated in the former drugstore of the pharmacist who invented Pepsi-Cola—a two-story restored 1912 building—this casual dining spot is a magnet for weekday business lunches as well as weekenders wanting a quick sandwich or large salad. Evening entrées in the romantic, upstairs dining room include shrimp and grits and Southern osso buco (a roasted pork shank in red wine sauce with capers and fire-roasted tomatoes). The bar is well stocked, and Pepsi products are, as might be expected, the nonalcoholic drinks of choice. Look for historical architectural details, such as the tin ceiling. *Average main: $20 ✉ 335 Middle St. ☎ 252/637–5469 🌐 www.thechelsea.com.*

$ CAFÉ **Cow Cafe.** Nearly everything is "moolicious" at this black-and-white spotted café—New Bern's only "4-hoof" restaurant—created by the Maola Milk and Ice Cream Company. Today the café is privately owned, but cows still rule here, making children squeal with delight. Gifts and toys have something to do with the animals, but the ice cream is most popular. Choose Udder Pecan, Mooberry Mousse, and Blue Moo M&Ms. Sandwiches, hot dogs, "cowsadillas," housemade caramel corn, and apple pie "à la moo" are served, too. *Average main: $7 ✉ 319 Middle St. ☎ 252/672–9269 🌐 www.cowcafenewbern.com Reservations not accepted.*

$$ AMERICAN **Harvey Mansion Historic Inn and Restaurant.** This circa 1804, three-story home's intimate dining areas, not to mention three spacious bedrooms for rent in a top-floor B&B ($), feel like a fancy colonial residence and are suitable for both special occasions and casual dinners. The menu features an array of Continental and new-American dishes such as crab cakes, bacon-wrapped meat loaf, and lamb osso bucco. Seafood lovers relish the Crab Stack: three fried soft-shell crabs, a crab cake, and sautéed lump crabmeat over mashed potatoes, all finished with lobster cream sauce. Early-bird dinner specials, including salad and bread, are fun to share at the copper-top bar, where exposed beams lend a publike atmosphere. *Average main: $18 ✉ 221 S. Front St. ☎ 252/635–3232 🌐 www.theharveymansion.com ⏲ No lunch; breakfast for B&B guests only.*

$$ AMERICAN **Morgan's Tavern & Grill.** Skylights illuminate exposed redbrick walls, Windsor-style chairs, and weathered wooden ceiling beams at this downtown, circa 1912 building that started out as a garage and filling station. Today patrons drive here for hand-cut steaks, fried seafood, half-pound burgers, and all sorts of salads and sandwiches. More refined dishes include lasagna, lobster bisque, mussels in champagne sauce, and grilled chicken cordon bleu. *Average main: $15 ✉ 235 Craven St. 🌐 www.morganstavernnewbern.com.*

$ AMERICAN **Pollock Street Deli.** Good-size crowds gather in the tiny rooms of this cozy, historic-district colonial house—and at its sidewalk tables—for breakfast, classic lunchtime deli treats (the Reuben is renowned; the chicken salad a winner), and sometimes dinner (schedule changes, call ahead). Service is friendly and walls covered with funky comics and

Stroll through 16 acres of 18th-century formal gardens at Tryon Place.

license plates from all over the world stir great conversations. *Average main: $8 ✉ 208 Pollock St. ☎ 252/637–2480 ⊙ No dinner Sat.–Thurs.*

## WHERE TO STAY

*Hotel reviews have been abbreviated in this book. For expanded reviews, please go to Fodors.com.*

$ B&B/INN **Hanna House.** Innkeepers Camille and Joe Klotz's renovation of the Rudolph Ulrich House (circa 1896) resulted in accommodations that attract guests again and again—think sleek, modern plumbing and bath fixtures in antiques-filled rooms. **Pros:** a short walk from downtown shops and a riverfront park; special breakfast requests taken. **Cons:** no pets allowed; no small children; no phones or televisions in rooms. *Rooms from: $89 ✉ 218 Pollock St. ☎ 252/635–3209, 866/830–4371 ⊕ www.hannahousenc.net ⇨ 5 rooms 🍴 Breakfast.*

$ B&B/INN ★ **Harmony House Inn.** Crafty wreaths, quilts, and embroidery complement the mix of antiques and reproductions in guest rooms at this quaint inn that lodged Yankee soldiers during the Civil War. **Pros:** on a quiet downtown side street; easy walking distance to shops, restaurants, and the waterfront park; whirlpool baths in some suites. **Cons:** no pets allowed; smoking permitted on front porch. *Rooms from: $119 ✉ 215 Pollock St. ☎ 252/636–3810, 800/636–3113 ⊕ www.harmonyhouseinn.com ⇨ 7 rooms, 3 suites 🍴 Breakfast.*

## SHOPPING

The success of the downtown revitalization process is obvious in the variety of businesses in these old buildings.

**Bear Essentials.** This shop specializes in earth-friendly products ranging from cosmetics to lotions. A selection of 100% organic cotton baby clothes and women's wear made from bamboo fiber is also sold. ✉ *309 Middle St.* ☎ *252/637–6663.*

**Bern Bear Gifts Inc.** Bear-themed souvenirs and gifts imported from Europe fill Bern Bear Gifts Inc., a tribute to the city's mascot, the bear, and the Swiss nobleman who founded New Bern. ✉ *301 Pollock St.* ☎ *252/637–2300.*

**Carolina Creations.** Regional and national artists of every genre are represented at Carolina Creations art gallery and gift shop. You can find blown glass, pottery, jewelry, wood carvings, and all manner of paintings and prints. ✉ *317A Pollock St.* ☎ *252/633–4369* 🌐 *www.carolinacreationsnewbern.com.*

**The Four C's.** The Coastal Casual Clothing Co. is the best place to pick out sportswear and camping gear. ✉ *252 Middle St.* ☎ *252/636–3285.*

**Fraser's Wine & Cheese Gourmet Shoppe.** This specialty food shop has an enviable international wine selection as well as imported chocolates. ✉ *210 Middle St.* ☎ *252/634–2580.*

# WILMINGTON AND THE CAPE FEAR COAST

The greater Cape Fear region stretches from Topsail Island north of Wilmington south to Oak Island. The Cape Fear River basin begins in the Piedmont region and meanders several hundred miles before spilling into the Atlantic Ocean about 20 miles south of downtown Wilmington.

Miles and miles of sand stretch northward to Topsail Island and southward to the South Carolina state line. The beaches offer activities from sunbathing to kayaking, fishing, parasailing, and scuba diving, and towns here have varied accommodations. Approximately 100 points of public access along the shoreline are marked by orange-and-blue signs.

First settled in 1729, Wilmington is one of North Carolina's two deep-water ports. It also has a 300-block downtown historic district and a picturesque riverfront listed on the National Register of Historic Places. South of Wilmington, three distinct island communities are an easy day trip from the city: Wrightsville Beach, Kure (pronounced "*cure*-ee") Beach, and Carolina Beach. Southport, which sits along the west side of Cape Fear River's mouth, has a revitalized waterfront, shaded streets, grand homes, and year-round golf. Such is the personality of the region that it has something for artists, sportspeople, history buffs, naturalists, shoppers, sunbathers, and filmmakers alike. EUE/Screen Gems Studios, the largest full-service motion-picture facility in the United States east of California, is headquartered in Wilmington, making the city ripe for celebrity sightings.

# WILMINGTON

*89 miles southwest of New Bern via U.S. 17 and 117; 130 miles south of Raleigh via I–40.*

The city's long history, including its part in the American Revolution, is revealed in sights downtown and in the surrounding area. The Cotton Exchange is a complex of old mills, warehouses and cotton export buildings now used as shopping and entertainment centers. *Henrietta III,* a boat resembling paddle wheelers that once plied the Cape Fear River, has been put into service as a tourist vessel. Wilmington, also a college town, hosts special annual events such as the Azalea Festival, North Carolina Jazz Festival, Christmas candlelight tours, fishing tournaments, and the Cucalorus Film Festival. The city also hosts EUE/Screen Gems Studios, which claims more than 300 film, television, and commercial productions, including the popular CW network shows *Dawson's Creek* and *One Tree Hill.*

### GETTING HERE AND AROUND

Wilmington is at the crossroads of U.S. 17 and the Interstate 40 terminus. Commercial flights land at Wilmington International Airport. The downtown historic district along the riverfront is easily walkable and also offers free trolley service. As you move away from this immediate area, however, a car becomes necessary for visits to places such as the Cameron Art Museum, Airlie Gardens, and the USS *North Carolina* Battleship Memorial. In summer and during rush hours year round, the major thoroughfares are busy, so allow more time than the distance would indicate. Route 132 (College Road), the main north–south road through the city, continues south where Interstate 40 leaves off. U.S. 76/U.S. 17 (Market Street) runs from downtown east to the vicinity of Wrightsville Beach; U.S. 421 goes south to Carolina and Kure beaches.

### ESSENTIALS

**Visitor Information Cape Fear Coast Convention and Visitors Bureau** ✉ *24 N. 3rd St.* ☎ *910/341–4030, 877/406–2356* 🌐 *www.capefearcoast.com.*

### TOURS

**Wilmington Walking Tours.** Give yourself chills even on a sultry night. Choose between the Ghost Walk of Old Wilmington, with its stories of privateers, murderers, and unmarked graves; the Haunted Pub Crawl, where you wash down tales of madmen and saucy wenches with Dutch courage (must be 21); or Hollywood Location Walk that will take you to real locations and actual sets of movies and television shows that have been or are being filmed in Wilmington. ✉ *Tours depart from riverfront at Market and Water Sts., Downtown* ☎ *910/794–1866* 🌐 *www.hauntedwilmington.com* 🎫 *Ghost walk $12; pub crawl $15, drinks not included; Hollywood Location Walk $12.*

## EXPLORING

### TOP ATTRACTIONS

**Burgwin-Wright Museum House.** The house General Cornwallis used as his headquarters in April 1781 was built in 1770 on the foundations of a jail. After a fine, furnished restoration, this colonial gentleman's town house was turned into a museum that includes seven distinct period

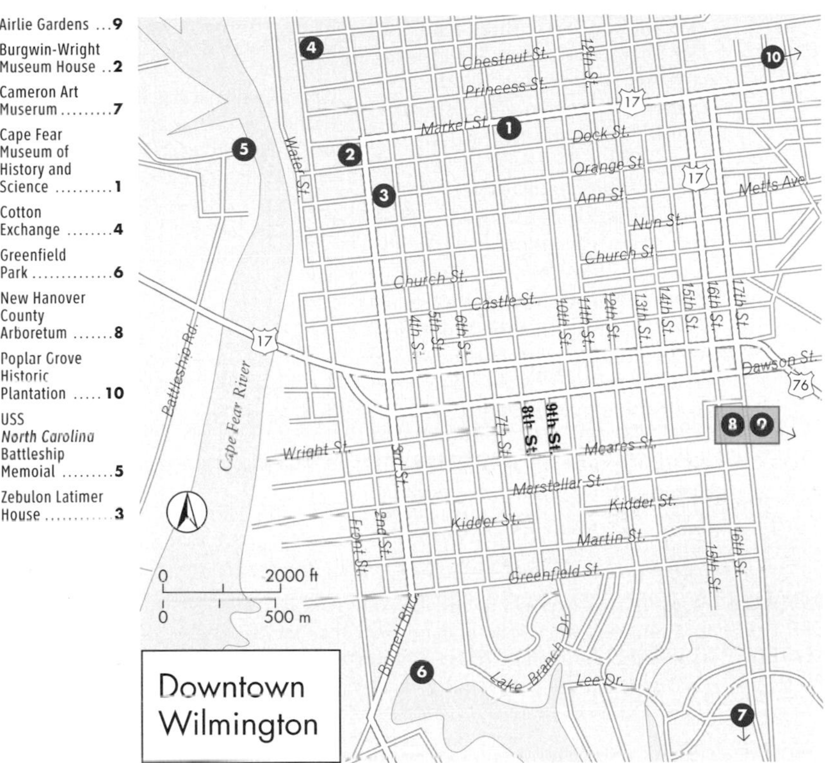


gardens. ✉ *224 Market St., Downtown* ☎ *910/762–0570* 🌐 *www.burgwinwrighthouse.com* 🎟 *$10* 🕑 *Tues.–Sat. 10–4. Closed Jan.*

**Cameron Art Museum.** The museum, formerly known as the St. John's Museum of Art, is dedicated to the fine art and crafts of North Carolina. It presents exhibitions and public programs of both historical and contemporary significance, with six to eight changing exhibitions annually. The displayed permanent collection, contained in a sleek 40,000-square-foot facility, varies and includes originals by Mary Cassatt and folk artist Clyde Jones. On the 10-acre grounds are restored Confederate defense mounds built during a battle in the waning days of the Civil War. The museum's Cafe Johnnie focuses on local foods and Southern recipes with a modern twist. ✉ *3201 S. 17th St., 4 miles south of Downtown, South Metro* ☎ *910/395–5999* 🌐 *www.cameronartmuseum.com* 🎟 *$8* 🕑 *Tues., Wed., Fri. and weekends 10–5; Thurs. 10–9.*

**Cape Fear Museum of History and Science.** Trace the natural, cultural, and social history of the lower Cape Fear region from its beginnings to the present. The interactive Cape Fear Stories exhibit provides a chronological history of the region from early Native Americans to the 20th century. The Michael Jordan Discovery Gallery encourages kids to get in touch with the area's enviroment. They can make sand dunes and feed Venus Flytraps. Also check out the fossilized skeleton of an ancient

(1.5 million years old), giant (20 feet long, 6,000 pounds) sloth discovered in 1991 during the construction of a Wilmington retention pond. ✉ *814 Market St., Downtown* ☎ *910/798–4350* 🌐 *www.capefearmuseum.com* 🎫 *$7* 🕑 *Memorial Day–Labor Day, Mon.–Sat. 9–5, Sun. 1–5; Labor Day–Memorial Day, Tues.–Sat. 9–5, Sun. 1–5.*

**WORD OF MOUTH**

"Downtown Wilmington is quite beautiful. Almost every block has a sign explaining its historic significance, and there are statues, fountains and lovely homes. Many huge, live oak trees border the streets. The Riverwalk is inviting, as it sits between the river and shops and restaurants. It's about a mile long and a good place to spend a relaxing few hours. The Riverboat was a perfect way to wind up our visit."

—sluggo

**Cotton Exchange.** In an area along the Cape Fear River that has flourished as a trading center since pre–Civil War days stands a shopping mall in a rambling renovated warehouse, once headquarters of the largest cotton exporter in the world. There are also restaurants, including a German eatery, on-site. ✉ *321 N. Front St., Downtown* ☎ *910/343–9896* 🌐 *www.shopcottonexchange.com* 🕑 *Mon.–Sat. 10–5:30, Sun. 12–4.*

OFF THE BEATEN PATH

**Moore's Creek National Battlefield.** American patriots not only ambushed charging Loyalists on this site on February 27, 1776, but they also seized the equivalent of $1 million in British sterling. The battle is reenacted on the anniversary each year, and a 10-minute film shot on the site and shown in the visitor center tells the story, with professional actors playing the parts. See it before walking an interpretive trail lining the battlefield. Exhibits also fill the visitor center, and the 85-acre park is a wildlife habitat. ✉ *40 Patriots Hall Dr., 20 miles northwest of Wilmington on Rte. 210, Currie* ☎ *910/283–5591* 🌐 *www.nps.gov/mocr* 🎫 *Free* 🕑 *Daily 9–5.*

**USS *North Carolina* Battleship Memorial.** Take a self-guided tour of a ship that participated in every major naval offensive in the Pacific during World War II. Exploring the floating city, with living quarters, a post office, chapel, laundry, and even an ice-cream shop, takes about two hours. A climb down into the ship's interior is not for the claustrophobic. A 10-minute orientation film is shown throughout the day. ■ **TIP→** Don't miss the Independence Day fireworks display that lights up the ship. The ship can be reached by car or by taking the river taxi from Riverfront Park that runs daily Memorial Day through Labor Day and weekends May 1 to Memorial Day and Labor Day to mid-November, at a cost of $4 per person. ✉ *1 Battleship Rd., junction of U.S. 74/76 and U.S. 17 and 421, west bank of Cape Fear River, Downtown* ☎ *910/251–5797* 🌐 *www.battleshipnc.com* 🎫 *$12* 🕑 *Memorial Day–Labor Day, daily 8–8; Labor Day–late May, daily 8–5.*

### WORTH NOTING

**Airlie Gardens.** Designed first as a European-style garden showcasing plants in all four seasons, Airlie has suffered its share of hurricane damage since it was built in the early 1900s, but has come back each time

Kids love touring the USS *North Carolina* battleship, a floating city that saw combat in World War II.

and is now owned by New Hanover County. There are 67 acres in this lush Southern garden—azaleas, magnolias, and camellias abound—as well as two freshwater lakes that attract waterfowl. The greatest specimen of them all is the gargantuan 468-year-old Airlie oak. May through October you can flutter among 300–400 butterflies in the huge butterfly house. The last tickets for the day are sold one hour before closing. ✉ *300 Airlie Rd., 8 miles east of Downtown via U.S. 76, Midtown* ☎ *910/798–7700* 🌐 *www.airliegardens.org* 🎫 *$5* ⏲ *Mid-Mar.–Dec., daily 9–5; Jan.–mid-Mar., Tues.–Sun. 9–5.*

**Greenfield Park.** Come to this city park for picnic spots, bike paths, nature trails, playgrounds, tennis courts, and a skateboard park. There are also canoe, kayak, and paddleboat rentals on a 150-acre lake bordered by cypress trees laden with Spanish moss. In April, the 250-acre park is ablaze with azaleas. ✉ *1739 Burnett Blvd., 1 mile south of Downtown, South Metro* ☎ *910/341–7852* 🌐 *www.wilmingtonnc.gov/community_services/parks_landscaping.aspx* 🎫 *Free* ⏲ *Daily sunrise–sunset.*

**New Hanover County Arboretum.** Lose yourself in numerous natural exhibits, among dozens of varieties of shade-loving camellias on seven acres. There are magnolia and patio gardens, a water garden, and a children's garden. ✉ *6206 Oleander Dr., 6 miles east of Downtown via U.S. 76, Midtown* ☎ *910/798–7660* 🌐 *www.nhcgov.com/arboretum/pages/thegardens.aspx* 🎫 *Free* ⏲ *Daily dawn–dusk.*

**Poplar Grove Historic Plantation.** Take a tour of what was once the first major peanut farm in North Carolina, the 1850 Greek Revival manor house, and its outbuildings. You can also see blacksmith, weaving, and basket-making demonstrations as well as farm animals (goats, sheep, horses, geese, and chickens). On Wednesday, from 8 to 1, April through December, there is a farmers' market selling local foods, plants, and crafts. The site adjoins the 67-acre Abbey Nature Preserve, where birding and hiking are offered. ✉ *10200 U.S. 17, 9 miles northeast of Downtown, North Metro* ☎ *910/686–9518* 🌐 *www.poplargrove.com* 🎫 *Guided tours $10* ⏲ *Early Feb.–late Dec., Mon.–Sat. 9–5, Sun. noon–5.*

**Zebulon Latimer House.** Built in 1852 in the Italianate style, this home museum, with thousands of Victorian items in its collection, is a reminder of opulent antebellum living. The Historical Society of the Lower Cape Fear is based here; it leads 1½-hour, guided walking tours of the downtown historic district at 10 am each Saturday. ✉ *126 S. 3rd St., Downtown* ☎ *910/762–0492* 🌐 *www.latimerhouse.org* 🎫 *$10* ⏲ *Mon.–Sat. 10:30–3:30.*

## WHERE TO EAT

$$ BISTRO Fodor's Choice ★ ✕ **Caprice Bistro.** White-lace curtains at the windows and tables dressed in white signal master French Chef Thierry Moity's "solid bistro cooking." Onion soup, *pommes frites* (fries) served with aioli, classic steak au poivre, and crisp duck confit come at unexpectedly low prices. The wine list has American labels as well as French. The art-filled upstairs lounge offers a late-night menu and stays open until 2 am. A nightly, three-course, $25 prix-fixe special is one of the city's best dining deals. $ *Average main: $20* ✉ *10 Market St., Downtown* ☎ *910/815–0810* 🌐 *www.capricebistro.com* ⏲ *No lunch.*

$$ SEAFOOD ★ ✕ **Catch.** Native Wilmingtonian chef Keith Rhodes is a James Beard Award nominee who sources local seafood for inspired Asian- and Southern-influenced dishes that lately have attracted celebrities like Robert Downey Jr. and Gwyneth Paltrow. Copper fish sculptures decorate the dining room's sky blue walls. Cognac cream tops fried Firecracker Shrimp sprinkled with sesame seeds. Sherry, chorizo, and shiitake mushrooms enliven shrimp and grits. Locals love the classic fried seafood platters. Landlubbers get smoked paprika-seasoned ribs and duck confit with black truffled fried rice. $ *Average main: $25* ✉ *6623 Market St.* ☎ *910/799–3847* 🌐 *www.catchwilmington.com* ⏲ *No lunch weekends.*

$ MEXICAN FUSION ✕ **K38 Baja Grill.** Named for a popular surfers' point break in Baja, Mexico, where some friends once shared memorable roadside fish tacos, the K38 menu heavily references Baja culinary traditions. Mexican-American fusion dishes feature seafood, such as tacos with crisp beer-battered fish. Chicken and beef are also available. Close quarters are fun and colorful. The restaurant has two nearby outposts—Tower 7 at Wrightsville Beach and Las Olas and K38 Baja Grill in north Wilmington. $ *Average main: $10* ✉ *5410 Oleander Dr., Midtown* ☎ *910/395–6040* 🌐 *www.liveeatsurf.com* $ *Average main: $10* ✉ *Porter's Neck Shopping Center, 8211 Market St., North Wilmington* ☎ *910/686–8211* 🌐 *www.liveeatsurf.com* ✍ *Reservations not accepted* $ *Average main: $10* ✉ *Tower 7, 4 N. Lumina Ave., Wrightsville Beach* ☎ *910/256–8585* 🌐 *www.liveeatsurf.com* ✍ *Reservations not accepted.*

$ DINER **Nick's Diner.** Every corner of this colorful, downtown place is jammed with cool art and collectibles, everything from Coca-Cola trays to wind-up toys. A huge Batman painting hangs by the front door. A frame holds one of late rocker Kurt Cobain's sweaters. The counter is shaped like a Beatles guitar. Don't be fooled by the decor though, this third-generation family diner serves breakfast all day, serious comfort food, and a few unexpected surprises. **TIP→** Try the creamy macaroni and cheese baked in mini cast-iron skillets—you can get them topped with prime rib or even a whole, steamed lobster. Soft-shell crab is as common on the menu as the signature Ohio City Burger topped with ham, bacon, sausage, and a fried egg. *Average main: $8* *127 N. Front St.* *910/341–7655* *Reservations not accepted.*

2

## WHERE TO STAY

*Hotel reviews have been abbreviated in this book. For expanded reviews, please go to Fodors.com.*

$$ B&B/INN **Graystone Inn.** Less B&B than elegant mansion, Graystone is downtown but feels as quiet and remote as the countryside. **Pros:** luxurious lobby, considerate touches like umbrellas at the door; spacious rooms. **Cons:** on a busy street; "proper attire" required in common areas—that means clean shoes, neat shirts, and no swimsuits; no red wine allowed; no children younger than 12. *Rooms from: $199* *100 S. 3rd St., Downtown* *910/763–2000, 888/763–4773* *www.graystoneinn.com* *6 rooms, 3 suites* *Breakfast.*

$ HOTEL **Jameson Inn.** Midway between downtown Wilmington and Wrightsville Beach, this small hotel with large rooms offers all the comforts of home, including recliners in some rooms. **Pros:** pet-friendly; near two key thoroughfares; walking distance to shopping and chain restaurants. **Cons:** small bathrooms; far from the downtown historic district; surrounded by congested roads. *Rooms from: $124* *5102 Dunlea Ct., Market* *910/452–5660* *www.jamesoninns.com* *67 rooms* *Breakfast.*

$ HOTEL ★ **The Wilmingtonian.** Members of the entertainment industry often frequent the Wilmingtonian. **Pros:** walking distance to several restaurants and downtown business/historic district; private courtyard; free parking; celebrity spotting. **Cons:** no restaurant; no breakfast; dated decor; building starting to show age. *Rooms from: $129* *101 S. 2nd St., Downtown* *910/343–1800, 800/525–0909* *www.thewilmingtonian.com* *32 suites.*

## NIGHTLIFE AND THE ARTS

The city has its own symphony orchestra, oratorio society, civic ballet, community theater, and concert association. The North Carolina Symphony makes four appearances here each year. The old riverfront area—with its restaurants and nightclubs, strolling couples, and horse-drawn carriages—really jumps on weekend nights.

**Level 5 at City Stage.** At the top of an old Masonic temple, Level 5 is a rooftop bar with live music and a fantastic open-air view of downtown Wilmington. Attached City Stage is a 250-seat venue for offbeat productions and comedy troupes. *21 S. Front St., Downtown* *910/342–0272 Level 5, 910/264–2602 City Stage* *www.citystagenc.com.*

**Thalian Hall Center for the Performing Arts.** A restored opera house in continuous use since 1858, Thalian Hall Center for the Performing Arts hosts dozens of theater, dance, stand-up comedy, cinema society, and musical performances each year. ✉ *310 Chestnut St., Downtown* ☎ *910/632–2241, 800/523–2820* 🌐 *www.thalianhall.com.*

### SPORTS AND THE OUTDOORS

**Aquatic Safaris.** Wrecks such as the World War II oil tanker *John D. Gill,* sunk by Germans in 1942 on her second-ever voyage, make for exciting scuba diving off the Cape Fear Coast. Aquatic Safaris leads trips to see the wrecks and rents scuba equipment. ✉ *6800-1A Wrightsville Ave.* ☎ *910/392–4386* 🌐 *www.aquaticsafaris.com.*

**Cape Fear Riverboats, Inc.** From April through December, Cape Fear Riverboats, Inc. runs several types of cruises, including dinner and murder mystery journeys, aboard a three-deck, 156-foot riverboat, the *Henrietta III,* which departs from docks at Water and Dock streets. ✉ *101 S. Water St., Downtown* ☎ *910/343–1611, 800/676–0162* 🌐 *www.cfrboats.com.*

### SHOPPING

**Old Books on Front Street.** You can smell well-worn pages as soon as you step inside Old Books on Front Street. Among its thousands of treasures are rare paperbacks and recent novels. Tons of gently used cookbooks are shelved next to Sugar, a friendly, in-store coffee shop serving homey sweets. ✉ *249 N. Front St.* ☎ *910/762–6657* 🌐 *www.oldbooksonfrontst.com.*

## WRIGHTSVILLE BEACH

*12 miles east of Wilmington.*

Wrightsville Beach is a small (5-mile-long), upscale, and quiet island community. Many beach houses have been in the same families for generations, but lots of striking contemporary homes are here, too.

The beaches are havens for serious sunning, swimming, surfing, and surf fishing, and the beach patrol is vigilant about keeping ATVs, glass containers, alcohol, pets, and bonfires off the sands. In summer, when the population skyrockets, parking can be a problem if you don't arrive early; towing is enforced.

#### GETTING HERE AND AROUND

A short drive from Wilmington, Wrightsville Beach is a good day-trip destination. U.S. 74/76 (Eastwood Drive) is the only road access to this small, friendly town. In town you can walk and bike or boat on the intracoastal waterway.

#### ESSENTIALS

**Visitor Information Wrightsville Beach Visitor Center** ✉ *305 Salisbury St.* ☎ *910/256–8116* 🌐 *www.visitwrightsville.com.*

### WHERE TO EAT AND STAY

*Hotel reviews have been abbreviated in this book. For expanded reviews, please go to Fodors.com.*

$ AMERICAN ★ **Causeway Café.** Sipping coffee supplied by the efficient staff, patrons waiting to be seated in the no-frills dining room or on the wrap-around porch contemplate what to order this time—malted pancakes? Eggs Benedict? A country-ham sandwich? Cinnamon-raisin-sourdough French toast? Shrimp and grits? Though the lunch menu is perfectly respectable, breakfast (served all day) is what packs 'em into the place, which is less than ¼ mile from the bridge separating Wilmington from Wrightsville Beach Island. Arrive before 8 am summer weekends if you don't want to wait for a table. *Average main: $10 114 Causeway Dr. 910/256–3730 Reservations not accepted No credit cards No dinner.*

### WATCH THOSE RAYS!

It's tempting to overdo it your first day at the beach, but be careful to avoid a sunburn that could ruin the remainder of your vacation. Apply sunscreen at least 15 minutes before you go out since it takes a little while for sunscreens to start working. Carry a hat, sunglasses, and a long-sleeve cover up. Gradually increase your exposure over a period of days. And remember, the water vapor in clouds magnifies the sun's rays—you can get a nasty burn in weather so overcast you don't need sunglasses.

$$ SEAFOOD **South Beach Grill.** Tight parking on a cramped lot doesn't deter diners from this friendly restaurant where standard and creative fare suits families as well as singles. The fried seafood is good, but the chef shows off with dishes like Lowcountry mac and cheese with backfin crabmeat and crawfish, or the eggplant and shrimp stack with tasso ham, roasted red peppers, and boursin-Asiago cheese sauce. Beef, pork, chicken, steak, and vegetarian options please landlubbers. Sit inside or on the patio. *Average main: $20 100 S. Lumina Ave. 910/256–4646 www.southbeachgrillwb.com.*

$$$$ RESORT **Holiday Inn Resort Wrightsville Beach.** If you like to be pampered, this is the only place on Wrightsville Beach to fit the bill—but you'll pay a premium for the amenities. **Pros:** activities for kids; indoor and outdoor pools; steps from the beach. **Cons:** expensive rates; mediocre restaurant. *Rooms from: $279 1706 N. Lumina Ave. 910/256–2231, 877/330–5050 www.wrightsville.holidayinnresorts.com 184 rooms, 8 suites.*

$$ HOTEL **Silver Gull Motel.** This beach mainstay, in business since 1971, might be showing its age a little, but the rooms are clean and reasonably priced, and the kitchens and the west wing have been renovated. **Pros:** good oceanfront value; next door to a concrete fishing pier; shaded parking. **Cons:** no breakfast; no-frills decor. *Rooms from: $180 20 E. Salisbury St. 910/256–3728, 800/842–8894 32 rooms.*

## SPORTS AND THE OUTDOORS

### BEACHES

★ **Wrightsville Beach.** Clean, wide beaches here provide the setting for all sorts of water sports. Surfers dominate fine morning waves while newbies take lessons on the beach before hitting the respectable swells. Kayakers, parasailors, paddleboarders, bodyboarders, and windsurfers all share the waters here while shoreline runners and walkers hit the sand,

Dining on the pier in Wrightsville Beach offers a spectacular view of the Atlantic Ocean.

which is also perfect for sunbathing, sand-castle-building, and people-watching. Anglers can cast lines from the surf or the Johnny Mercer concrete fishing pier. Get to the beach early; parking lots jam up by 9 am in summer. Meters cost $2 per hour, though parking in Wrightsville Beach is free after 6 pm. Meters take nickels, dimes, and quarters, and you can get change at the town's Parking Office on 5 Live Oak Street. Keep time on the meters; parking enforcement is strict. **Amenities:** food and drink, lifeguards, parking (fee). **Best for:** sunrise, sunset, surfing, swimming, windsurfing. ✉ *N. Lumina Ave.* ✣ *Take U.S. 76 (Causeway Dr.) to N. Lumina Ave. and turn left or right to find parking* 🌐 *www.visitwrightsville.com.*

## KURE BEACH AND CAROLINA BEACH

*17 miles southwest of Wrightsville Beach; 21 miles southwest of Wilmington via U.S. 421.*

A resort community on a strip of sand locals know as Pleasure Island, Kure Beach contains Fort Fisher State Historic Site and one of North Carolina's three aquariums. In some places twisted live oaks still grow behind the dunes. The community has miles of beaches; public access points are marked by orange-and-blue signs. **■ TIP→ A stroll down the old-fashioned Carolina Beach boardwalk, lighted at night, is fun for the family or a romantic cap to an evening.**

### GETTING HERE AND AROUND

Drive to Kure Beach on U.S. 421 or take the ferry from Route 211 in Southport. Once at the beach, you'll want a car to get up and down the island, although some people walk and bike along the narrow, main highway.

### ESSENTIALS

**Visitor Information Pleasure Island Visitor Center** ✉ *1121 N. Lake Park Blvd., Ste. B, Carolina Beach* ☎ *910/458–8434* 🌐 *www.pleasureislandnc.org.*

## EXPLORING

**Carolina Beach.** A few miles northeast of Kure Beach, this town, established in 1857, has an old-fashioned boardwalk that has been dressed up and revitalized. A semi-open arcade features vintage games, a doughnut shop still fries its rounds daily and, in summer, there are fireworks and carnival rides. Bars and marinas line a central business district. The town's popularity with young people once earned it the nickname "Pleasure Island," but affluent families snapping up waterfront property are changing the demographics. Fishing is a major activity, and anglers can test their skills on the pier, in the surf, and on deep-sea charter excursions. You can also take a nightly party cruise. ✉ *3 miles northeast of Kure Beach via U.S. 421* 🌐 *www.wilmingtonandbeaches.com/Carolina-Beach.*

**Fort Fisher State Historic Site.** This is one of the South's largest and most important earthworks fortifications from the Civil War, so tough it was known as the Southern Gibraltar. A reconstructed battery, Civil War relics, a fiber-optic battle map, and artifacts from sunken blockade runners are on-site. The fort is part of the Fort Fisher Recreation Area, with 4 miles of undeveloped beach. It's also known for its underwater archaeology sites. At least two guided tours are available daily. ✉ *U.S. 421, 1610 Fort Fisher Blvd.* ☎ *910/458–5538* 🌐 *www.nchistoricsites.org/fisher* 🎫 *Free* 🕑 *Memorial Day–Labor Day, Tues.–Sat. 9–5, Sun. 1–5; Labor Day–Memorial Day, Tues.–Sat. 9–5.*

**North Carolina Aquarium at Fort Fisher.** The oceanfront aquarium features a 235,000-gallon saltwater tank that's home to sharks, stingrays, and the most recent additions, a Goliath grouper and green moray eel. Twice a day, scuba divers enter the multistory tank and answer questions from the onlookers. Other exhibits feature creatures of the deep from every undersea corner of the earth. There's a touch tank, a tank with glowing jellyfish, an albino alligator, and turtle ponds. Kids love the life-size replica of a megladon shark, complete with fossilized teeth found in North Carolina. ✉ *900 Loggerhead Rd., off U.S. 421* ☎ *800/832–3474* 🌐 *www.ncaquariums.com* 🎫 *$8* 🕑 *Daily 9–5.*

## WHERE TO EAT AND STAY

*Hotel reviews have been abbreviated in this book. For expanded reviews, please go to Fodors.com.*

$$$$ AMERICAN ✕ **Jack Mackerel's Island Grill.** Step through the wood-and-glass hatch into a dining room where tropical blues, greens, and thatch huts mingle with portholes, a bar top that seems fashioned from a wooden boat deck, and a roof curved like a luxury teak cabin. The Caribbean cruise theme carries to the menu. Grilled mahi is brushed with sweet chili lime glaze.

Grilled pineapple accompanies seared, bacon-wrapped jumbo shrimp. Dark-rum glaze colors the grilled chicken breast, and ribs are basted with jalapeño-ginger barbecue sauce. A kids' menu features pasta, burgers, and, of course, chicken tenders. *Average main: $25 113 K Ave. 910/458–7668 www.jackmackerelsrestaurantkurebeach.com Reservations not accepted.*

$$$ SEAFOOD **Shuckin' Shack.** The front doors of this main-drag raw bar are wide open even in wintertime, giving the casual restaurant a backyard-oyster-roast feel. Servers are efficient, the crowd fun and friendly, with locals reminiscing over the newspaper clippings that plaster the bar. Shorts and jeans rule the scene, and bottled beer is de rigueur. Fat, salty local oysters are served fall and winter; shrimp and clams year-round. For munchies try deep-fried jalapeño coins, jumbo Buffalo wings, and hush puppies with a sweet edge. *Average main: $20 6A N. Lake Park Blvd., Carolina Beach 910/458–7380 www.pleasureislandoysterbar.com Reservations not accepted.*

$$ B&B/INN **Beacon House Inn.** Back in the 1950s, these pine-panel rooms were a boardinghouse, and Beacon House is filled with reminders of those days. **Pros:** quiet; off the main drag; close to the beach; private bathrooms. **Cons:** can be difficult to find; pets are only allowed in the cottages, and you have to pay a fee; breakfast not included with cottages; children under 12 are welcome only in the cottages, as the main house is not childproofed. *Rooms from: $150 715 Carolina Beach Ave. N, Carolina Beach 910/458–6244, 877/232–2666 www.beaconhouseinnb-b.com 5 rooms, 2 suites, 3 cottages Breakfast.*

## SPORTS AND THE OUTDOORS

### BEACHES

**Carolina Beach.** With ice-cream cones and paddleboats, flashing arcade lights and seashell souvenirs, Carolina Beach's old-fashioned boardwalk is steeped in nostalgic charm. Hand-holding, outdoor movies, and bicycles built for two are still favorite pastimes here. That's not to say you won't find adventure. Stalk giant game fish offshore aboard a choice charter boat. Join surfers riding the waves or skateboarders and in-line lovers winding the local skate park. **Amenities:** food and drink, lifeguards, parking. **Best for:** sunrise, sunset, surfing, swimming, windsurfing. *U.S. 421 Take U.S. 17 from the north or south to U.S. 421 www.wilmingtonandbeaches.com/Carolina-Beach.*

★ **Kure Beach.** Family memories are made on tall ocean piers where kids reel in their first big catches. You can kiteboard over the big blue sea or scuba dive down to find some of the Cape Fear Coast's dozens of shipwrecks. Wildlife excursions set off from various nature trails, birding sites, and miles of undeveloped beach. Shorebirds and loggerhead sea turtles inhabit the remote reserve named Zeke's Island. At Fort Fisher, the Confederacy's largest earthen fort, you can track Kure Beach's history. **Amenities:** food and drink, lifeguards, parking. **Best for:** sunrise, sunset, surfing, swimming, windsurfing. *U.S. 421 Take U.S. 17 from the north or south to U.S. 421 www.wilmingtonandbeaches.com/Kure-Beach.*

CLOSE UP

## Mini-Golf

There seems to be an unspoken competition among miniature golf courses to come up with the most outrageous themes and outlandish decor. Trams that resemble old mining trains roll through manmade caves and under waterfalls. Stocks await unruly pirates, and giant giraffes hide in bushy corners. It's all in good fun, and putt-putt provides great family entertainment. Many facilities also have snack grills, arcades, and batting cages. Here are some of our favorites:

**Lost Treasure Golf.** More than the usual mix of palm trees and waterfalls, Lost Treasure Golf also features bumper boats and a go-kart track that both kids and adults find irresistible before, after, or instead of playing golf. ✉ *976 Salter Path Rd., Salter Path* ☎ *252/247-3024* 🌐 *www.losttreasuregolf.com/miniature-golf-locations/salter-path-nc.*

**Carolina Beach Jungle Mini Golf.** Swing a club or a bat at Carolina Beach Jungle Mini Golf. This jungle-themed course includes batting cages and some interesting holes. At No. 10, you'll hit the ball into the water then watch it float to the hole. ✉ *906 Lake Park Blvd., Carolina Beach* ☎ *910/458-8888.*

**Lost Treasure Golf.** Check out the pirate ship or take a mini mining cart train to the top of a mountain in the middle of what resembles a Wild West mission town. The cart takes you to the first holes, making the course extra fun for kids. ✉ *1600 N. Croatan Hwy., Kill Devil Hills* ☎ *252/480-0142* 🌐 *www.losttreasuregolf.com/miniature-golf-locations/kill-devil-hills-nc.*

## SOUTHPORT

*10 miles southwest of Kure Beach via U.S. 421 and ferry; 30 miles south of Wilmington via Rte. 133.*

This small town, which sits quietly at the mouth of Cape Fear River, is listed on the National Register of Historic Places. An increasingly desirable retirement spot, Southport retains its village charm and character. Stately and distinctive homes, antiques stores, gift shops, and restaurants line streets that veer to accommodate ancient oak trees. The town, portrayed in Robert Ruark's novel *The Old Man and the Boy,* is ideal for walking; it's also popular with moviemakers—*Crimes of the Heart* was filmed here.

### GETTING HERE AND AROUND

From U.S. 17, Routes 211 and 133 both land in Southport. A state car ferry arrives every 45 minutes from Kure Beach to the north. Once downtown, you can park your car and walk or bike all over the waterfront area. Commercial airports are located at nearby Wilmington and Myrtle Beach, South Carolina.

### ESSENTIALS

**Visitor Information Southport Visitor Center** ✉ *203 E. Bay Street* ☎ *800/388-9635* 🌐 *www.cityofsouthport.com.*

## EXPLORING

**Southport–Fort Fisher Ferry.** If you're approaching the town from Kure Beach and Fort Fisher via U.S. 421, the state-operated car ferry provides a river ride between Old Federal Point at the tip of the spit and the mainland. **Bald Head Island Lighthouse** on Bald Head Island is seen en route, as well as the **Oak Island Lighthouse** and the ruins of Price's Creek Lighthouse—in fact, this is the only point in the United States where you can see three lighthouses at the same time. It's best to arrive early (30 minutes before ferry departure), as it's first-come, first-served. ✉ *2422 S. Fort Fisher Blvd., Kure Beach* ☎ *800/368–8969* 🌐 *www.ncdot.org/ferry* 🎟 *$5 per car, one-way* 🕒 *Call for schedule.*

OFF THE BEATEN PATH

**Brunswick Town State Historic Site.** You can explore the excavations of a colonial town, see the Civil War earthworks Fort Anderson, take in a colonial-era cooking demonstration, hear costumed interpreters, or just have a picnic. Special events include reenactments of Civil War encampments. ✉ *8884 St. Phillip's Rd. SE, off Rte. 133, about 10 miles north of Southport, Winnabow* ☎ *910/371–6613* 🌐 *www.nchistoricsites.org/brunswic/brunswic.htm* 🎟 *Free* 🕒 *Tues.–Sat. 9–5.*

## WHERE TO EAT AND STAY

*Hotel reviews have been abbreviated in this book. For expanded reviews, please go to Fodors.com.*

$ FAST FOOD

✕ **Trolly Stop.** An institution in the Cape Fear region (there are also locations in Wrightsville Beach, Carolina Beach, and Wilmington), this long, narrow hot-dog joint is known for various wieners, all with individual names. The North Carolina comes with chili, slaw, and mustard. The Surfer Dog is topped with cheese and vegetarian bacon bits. For the health conscious, there are also vegetarian or fat-free dogs and other sandwiches. $ *Average main: $3* ✉ *111 S. Howe St.* ☎ *910/457–7017* 🌐 *www.trollystophotdogs.com* *Reservations not accepted* 💳 *No credit cards.*

$$$$ RESORT ★

**Bald Head Island Resort.** Reached by ferry from Southport, this entire island bills itself as a resort though it's actually a self-contained, carless community, complete with a grocery store, restaurants, an inn, and ample rental properties from shingled cottages to luxury homes. **Pros:** friendly small-town feel; secluded and quiet; lots of natural areas; children's programs. **Cons:** island is accessible only by ferry; no cars allowed on the island; activities at the island's recreation clubs are not available to all accommodations. $ *Rooms from: $300* ✉ *Bald Head Island* ☎ *910/457–5000, 800/432–7368, 910/457–5003 for ferry reservations* 🌐 *www.baldheadisland.com* *195 condos, villas, and cottages; 16 rooms in 1 inn.*

# Central North Carolina

## THE TRIANGLE, TRIAD, CHARLOTTE, AND SANDHILLS

### WORD OF MOUTH

"Allen and Son BBQ is still on Highway 54, next to the railroad tracks just north of [Chapel Hill] before you get to the interstate. It still has the same cheap wood paneling and shaky chairs and tables they had when I was in grad school, and I am now retired. . . . [T]hey still make the Best Barbecue in the World."

—Ackislander

# WELCOME TO CENTRAL NORTH CAROLINA

## TOP REASONS TO GO

★ **Raleigh museums:** More than a dozen museums and historical sites—several within an easy walk of one another—cover every aspect of North Carolina life, from its prehistoric roots to its arts achievements and sports heroes.

★ **Old Salem:** Costumed guides fill this restored village in the heart of Winston-Salem, founded by the Moravian sect in the mid-18th century.

★ **Golf:** Many of the best golf courses in the Southeast (and some would argue, in the world) surround tiny Pinehurst, a village in the Sandhills.

★ **Wineries:** North Carolina has more than 90 wineries, and many of the finest are in the Piedmont. Sample a few fine vintages in their tasting rooms.

★ **Seagrove:** This Sandhills community has been renowned for its pottery for two centuries. More than 100 potters now sell their wares, including charmingly ugly face jugs as well as mugs, plates, and other treasures.

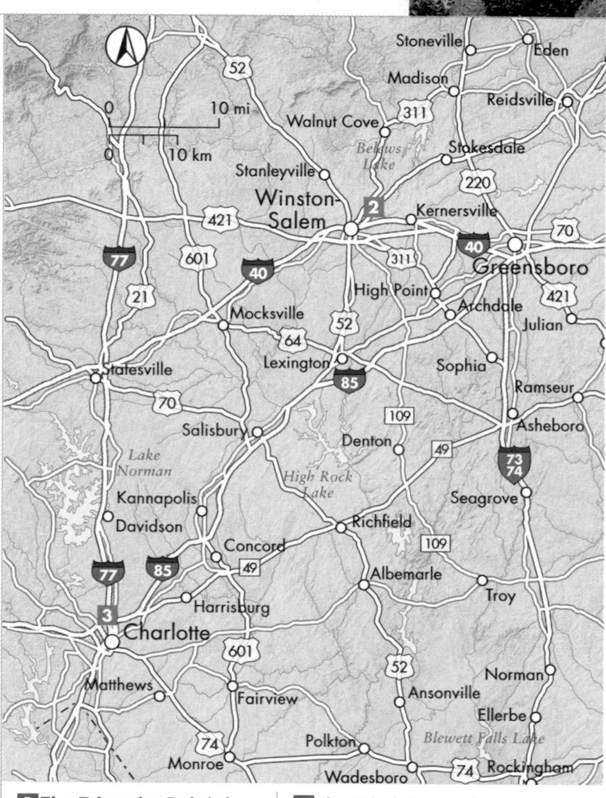


**1 The Triangle: Raleigh, Durham, and Chapel Hill.** Since the region is home to Duke University, North Carolina State University, and the University of North Carolina at Chapel Hill, life in the Triangle revolves around basketball and higher education. Leafy campuses offer architectural delights, and the surrounding communities reflect the universities' progressive spirits with a vibrant farm-to-table food scene.

**2 The Triad: Greensboro, Winston-Salem, and High Point.** The past and present fuse in these vastly different cities. History comes alive in the restored Moravian village of Old Salem, and twice a year the furniture-making traditions of the Piedmont thrive at the High Point Market, a home furnishings show. Greensboro, famous for its role in the Civil Rights movement, is one of the most diverse cities in the state.

## GETTING ORIENTED

North Carolina's dramatic mountains and beaches tend to overshadow the state's central Piedmont and Sandhills regions. However, visitors who take the time to experience the woodlands and hills that grace the heart of the state will find themselves enchanted by the same sturdy beauty that has nurtured generations of intellectuals and artists, from early 20th-century wit O. Henry to the modern master of humor David Sedaris.

**3 Charlotte.** The Queen City's contemporary facade dazzles, and its skyline gleams with the most impressive modern architecture in the region. Alongside fans cheering the NFL's Carolina Panthers and partyers hitting the city's sleek nightspots, you'll find traditional Southern hospitality and a lot of good eating inspired by regions around the world.

**4 The Sandhills.** This quiet regions draws golfers on a pilgrimage to the famed Pinehurst courses, particularly Donald Ross's No. 2. Fort Bragg, home to the Army's storied 82nd Airborne Division; the North Carolina Zoo; and the vast Seagrove pottery district also draw visitors to the region.

# NORTH CAROLINA BARBECUE

The birthplace of barbecue is as hotly contested as a grand champion title at one of the nation's ubiquitous BBQ festivals.

(above) Wilber's Barbecue pit-cooks their hogs over oak. (lower right) Pepper and vinegar flavor Eastern-style North Carolina barbecue. (upper right) A pulled-pork sandwich with coleslaw and pickles.

North Carolina, however, states its claim as the "Cradle of Cue," arguing it is home to the longest continuous barbecue tradition—a tradition variously linked to Native Americans, African slaves, and Scottish-Irish settlers. Enhancing its bid (or perhaps diluting it if you come from a state competing for top barbecue billing) is the fact that North Carolina is home to two distinct styles of barbecue. Expect a vinegar-and-pepper-based sauce in the east, while the western barbecue mixes sweet with smoky flavors.

Over the past decade many barbecue restaurants have switched to cheaper, faster gas or electric cooking. Yet plenty of family-run barbecue joints remain, where pitmasters savor smoky flavors as they bring love and patience to secret recipes for slow-cooking the pig over wood or charcoal flames.

Ultimately, the debate ends in agreement over three things that barbecue always represents: good food, good friends, and a good time.

—Jenn Goddu

## EAST VS. WEST

North Carolinians have distinct ideas about the proper preparation of this Southern meal. Easterners (typically east of Interstate 95), prefer a vinegar-and-pepper-based seasoning after the entire hog is cooked long hours and the meat is pulled (shredded) off the bone. Expect a sweeter, thicker "Lexington-style" secret sauce (is it ketchup? brown sugar?) in western barbecue joints, where just the pork shoulder is sliced or chopped.

*Here are some of our favorite North Carolina BBQ joints:*

**Lexington Barbecue #1.** The town of Lexington is the base for Carolina's sweet, red-sauce style of barbecue. At Lexington Barbecue #1, meat is pulled from smoked pork shoulders and served up as a sandwich in a soft bun topped with red slaw. Finish with peach cobbler—unless it's the first of the month, when Berry Berry Cobbler is served. ✉ *100 Smokehouse La., Lexington* ☎ *336/249–9814* ⏲ *Closed Sun.*

**Red Bridges Barbecue Lodge.** For old-fashioned western-style barbecue, take a bright-blue seat here, where the meat cooks in a pit over hickory all night long. The meat comes minced (almost a mash), chopped, or sliced with crunchy hush puppies and tangy sweet-and-sour dipping sauce served warm. Try the particularly smoky shoulder meat known as "outside brown" for a real woodsy taste. ✉ *2000 E. Dixon Blvd., Shelby* ☎ *704/482–8567* 🌐 *www.bridgesbbq.com* ⏲ *Closed Mon. and Tues.*

**Skylight Inn.** The big flavor tradition of Down East barbecue thrives in the little town of Ayden, where this family-owned, no-frills spot does it right. There's no menu and no waitstaff. Order a BBQ sandwich and you'll get smoky, oh-so-tender pork mixed with tiny morsels of pork skin for crunch, served with slightly sweet slaw and corn bread.

✉ *4618 Lee St., Ayden* ☎ *252/746–4113* ⏲ *Closed Sun.*

**Stamey's.** Here the chopped, eastern-style BBQ is mostly shoulder meat already sauced in the kitchen, though there's also plenty of vinegary Stamey's Secret Sauce at your table. If you're looking for something other than pork, try the Brunswick Stew, a traditional Southeastern thick tomato-based stew. ✉ *2206 High Point Rd., Greensboro* ☎ *336/299–9888* 🌐 *www.stameys.com* ⏲ *Closed Sun.*

**Wilber's Barbecue.** Here you'll find pit-cooked (oak wood) barbecue. (There's even a 100-foot woodpile on the premises.) This flavorful chopped BBQ mixes ham, shoulder, loin, and side meat. You sauce it yourself, using bottles of "spicy good" eastern peppery vinegar sauce. Try the white slaw for more vinegary tang. Wilber's been celebrated since it opened in 1962—come see why. ✉ *4172 U.S. Hwy. 70 E, Goldsboro* ☎ *919/778–5218* 🌐 *www.wilbersbarbecue.com.*

3

# NORTH CAROLINA WINERIES

For a gentle introduction to the world of wine, look no further than North Carolina.

(above) Taste the wine and tour Raffaldini Vineyards' gorgeous estate. (lower right) RayLen Vineyards makes a perfect day trip from Winston-Salem. (upper right) Relax at Raffaldini Vineyards.

With nearly 100 wineries sprinkled throughout its valleys, mountains, and coastal plain, the state's wine industry is huge yet intimate in its approach.

When touring and tasting around these parts, don't be surprised if you end up sipping your vintage alongside the owner or head grower. Even the wildly successful folks at RayLen and Westbend Vineyards remain approachable and focus on producing quality wine. This is especially true in the Yadkin Valley, the biggest wine-producing region in the state, located on and near the western edge of the Piedmont. Here, dozens of wineries have made a name for themselves by bucking North Carolina's centuries-old tradition of producing sweet Muscadine and Scuppernong wines and opting instead for the drier European varieties of the vinifera family. Though they were originally labeled rebels by the state's old-school wine producers, the Yadkin growers are now considered some of the finest in the state. A few of the hot varietals to watch include the white Viognier and the red Cabernet Franc.

—Stina Sieg

### WINE FLIGHT

Sipping a glass of Yadkin Valley wine is as simple as stepping off a plane. Located in the Charlotte Douglass International Airport, the Yadkin Valley Wine Bar serves vintages from across North Carolina's biggest wine region. The friendly and knowledgeable staff make customers feel like they're in the small tasting rooms found throughout the famous valley. Located between Terminals D and E.

*Here is a guide to some of the best wineries in the state:*

**Childress Vineyards.** Modeled after an Italian villa, this winery is as over-the-top as you might expect from a vineyard created by famous NASCAR driver and team owner Richard Childress. Open since 2004, the winery offers many varieties, including its popular Reserve Chardonnay and Signature Meritage. Within its opulent 35,000-square-foot building, visitors can witness winemaking firsthand, or have lunch at the Bistro, which overlooks the vineyards. ✉ *1000 Childress Vineyards Rd., Lexington* ☎ *336/236–9463* 🌐 *www.childressvineyards.com.*

**Raffaldini Vineyards.** Taste the famous Raffaldini Vermentino (President Barack Obama presented Italian president Giorgio Napolitano with a bottle in 2009) and other vineyard favorites like Sangiovese, Pinot Grigio, and Montepulciano at Raffaldini's countryside estate. Walking tours of the vineyard are available Wednesday through Sunday. ✉ *450 Groce Rd., Ronda* ☎ *336/835–9463* 🌐 *www.raffaldini.com* ⏲ *Closed Tues.*

**RayLen Vineyards.** An approximate 20-minute drive from Winston-Salem makes RayLen an easy escape from city life. In its low-key country setting you can discover some of the state's most famous wines, including RayLen's

Bordeaux-blend showstopper, Category 5 (yes, named after the strength of a hurricane). Tours are offered six days a week. ✉ *3577 Hwy. 158, Mocksville* ☎ *336/998–3100* 🌐 *www.raylenvineyards.com* ⏲ *Closed Sun.*

**Shelton Vineyards.** Shelton has long been considered one of the most prominent wineries of the Yadkin Valley. Here, you can choose between a variety of wine experiences, from inexpensive group tours to pricier vineyard-side and reserve tastings. The Harvest Grill offers an array of dishes that pair nicely with Shelton's most popular wines, including Cabernet Franc, Cabernet Sauvignon, and Chardonnay. ✉ *286 Cabernet La., Dobson* ☎ *336/366–4724* 🌐 *www.sheltonvineyards.com.*

**Westbend Vineyards.** Westbend was a pioneer of the Yadkin Valley wine scene when it opened in 1988—and has remained at the top ever since. The vineyard remains a low-key affair, with tours offered on weekends and by special request. The Chardonnay Sauvignon and Cabernet Sauvignon are of particular note. ✉ *5394 Williams Rd., Lewisville* ☎ *336/945–5032* 🌐 *www.westbendvineyards.com* ⏲ *Closed Mon.*

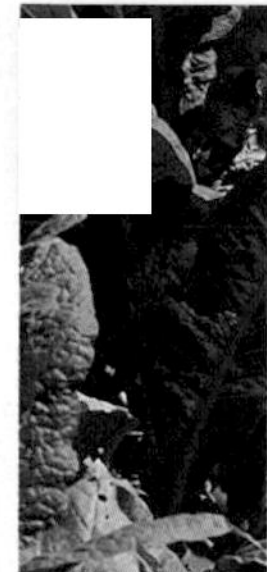

Updated by Stina Sieg

While visiting the Piedmont, it's easy to forget what state you're in. Though located in the geographic heart of North Carolina, this collection of growing urban areas and college towns is like nothing else in the Tar Heel State. This is a region looking ahead and on the move, and while it does lack a certain amount of tradition and charm, it has something that's perhaps just as special. Here, things are changing all the time, and often for the better. This constant evolution keeps the local culture vital.

The Piedmont's gently rolling hills are home to North Carolina's three major metropolitan areas—the Triangle (Raleigh, Durham, and Chapel Hill), the Triad (Winston-Salem, Greensboro, and High Point), and Charlotte. Though their histories differ, these sprawling population clusters now have much in common. They're full of big-city highlights, like huge sports complexes, sparkling new museums, and upscale restaurants. Hip, progressive elements abound, too, including farmers' markets, indie cinemas, and monthly art walks, which show off the area's growing creative scene. The transition is not only fascinating to watch but also fun to take part in. You should never be at a loss for things to eat, see, or do.

The Sandhills, which lies south of the Piedmont, is another world entirely. There, tradition is all-important, especially when it comes to the area's two main draws: golf and pottery. People come from around the world to play the Sandhills' famous fairways and buy ceramics from its renowned potters. Beyond that, there isn't much in the way of sightseeing, but if you're like most visitors, you won't mind. Instead, you'll spend most of your time on scenic drives or at one of the area's many resorts, considered some of the best in the state.

# PLANNING

## WHEN TO GO

North Carolina's Piedmont and Sandhills regions shine particularly in spring (April and May) and fall (September and October), when the weather is most temperate and the trees and flowers burst with color.

## PLANNING YOUR TIME

Because the areas within the Piedmont are fairly compact, it makes sense to tackle them one at a time. Downtown Raleigh, with its expanding array of restaurants and hotels, makes a good base for exploring Durham and Chapel Hill on day trips. Take on Charlotte and the Triad separately. In Charlotte, Uptown is centrally located and provides plenty of entertainment, dining, and lodging within walking distance. The Sandhills, which covers the area from Asheboro southeast to Fayetteville, is more diverse and a bit more cumbersome. Staying in one of the luxurious resorts in Southern Pines or Pinehurst would put you close to the pottery region of Seagrove. Give yourself more driving time when exploring this part of the state.

## GETTING HERE AND AROUND

### AIR TRAVEL

The Raleigh-Durham International Airport (RDU), off Interstate 40 between the two cities, is served by most major airlines. RDU Airport Taxi Service provides taxi service from the airport.

Charlotte-Douglas International Airport (CLT), served by most major airlines, is west of Charlotte off Interstate 85. From the airport, taxis charge a set fee to designated zones; the cost is $13 to $25 (plus $2 for each additional passenger after the first two) to most destinations in Charlotte. Just west of Greensboro, the Piedmont Triad International Airport (PTI) is off Route 68 north from Interstate 40; it's served by Allegiant Air, American Eagle, Continental Express, Delta, United, and US Airways. Taxi service to and from PTI is provided by Piedmont Triad Airport Transportation.

**Air Contacts Charlotte-Douglas International Airport** *(CLT). ✉ 5501 Josh Birmingham Pkwy., Airport/Coliseum, Charlotte ☎ 704/359–4013 🌐 www.charlotteairport.com.* **Piedmont Triad International Airport** *(PTI). ✉ 6451 Bryan Blvd., Greensboro ☎ 336/665–5666 🌐 www.flyfrompti.com.* **PTI Airport Transportation** *✉ 6415 Bryan Blvd., Greensboro ☎ 336/668–9808.* **Raleigh-Durham International Airport** *(RDU). ✉ 1600 Terminal Blvd., Morrisville ☎ 919/840–2123 🌐 www.rdu.com.* **RDU Airport Taxi Service** *✉ 1600 Terminal Blvd., Raleigh-Durham ☎ 919/840–7277 🌐 www.rdutaxiinc.com.*

### BUS TRAVEL

Capital Area Transit is Raleigh's public transport system, Chapel Hill Transit serves Chapel Hill and Carrboro, and Durham Area Transit Authority is Durham's intracity bus system. The fare for the Raleigh and Durham systems is $1. Chapel Hill Transit is free.

Triangle Transit, which links downtown Raleigh with Cary, Research Triangle Park, Durham, and Chapel Hill, runs weekdays except major holidays. Rates start at $2.

**Bus Contacts Capital Area Transit** ☎ *919/485–7433* 🌐 *www.raleighnc.gov/transit.* **Chapel Hill Transit** ☎ *919/969–4900* 🌐 *www.townofchapelhill.org.* **Durham Area Transit Authority** ☎ *919/485–7433* 🌐 *www.durhamnc.gov.* **Triangle Transit** ☎ *919/485–7433* 🌐 *www.triangletransit.org.*

### CAR TRAVEL

Although it's possible to use buses and trains for travel within the Piedmont and Sandhills, they're usually not convenient or quick. Interstates 40, 85, and 77, as well as several state highways, offer easy access to most of the region's destinations. Traffic is an issue in the metropolitan areas during morning and evening rush hours, but this is no D.C. or L.A.

U.S. 1 runs north–south through the Sandhills and the Triangle, and is the recommended route from the Raleigh-Durham area to Southern Pines.

Charlotte is a transportation hub; Interstate 77 comes in from Columbia, South Carolina, to the south, and then continues north to Virginia, intersecting Interstate 40 on the way. Interstate 85 arrives from Greenville, South Carolina, to the southwest, and then goes northeast to meet Interstate 40 in Greensboro. From the Triangle, Interstate 85 continues northeast and merges with Interstate 95 in Petersburg, Virginia.

Greensboro and Winston-Salem are on Interstate 40, which runs east–west through North Carolina. From the east Interstate 40 and Interstate 85 combine coming into the Triad, but in Greensboro, Interstate 85 splits off to go southwest to Charlotte. High Point is off a business bypass of Interstate 85 southwest of Greensboro.

U.S. 1 runs north–south through the Triangle and links to Interstate 85 going northeast. U.S. 64, which makes an east–west traverse across the Triangle, continues eastward all the way to the Outer Banks. Interstate 95 runs northeast–southwest to the east of the Triangle and the Sandhills, crossing U.S. 64 and Interstate 40, from Virginia to South Carolina.

### TAXI TRAVEL

Taxis and airport vans service all the area towns and airports and are an alternative to renting a car if you don't plan on doing a lot of sightseeing. Reputable companies include Blue Bird Taxi in Greensboro, Central Piedmont Transportation in Winston-Salem, and Crown Cab and Yellow Cab in Charlotte.

**Taxi Contacts Blue Bird Taxi** ✉ *1205 W. Bessemer Ave., Suite 208, Greensboro* ☎ *336/272–5112* 🌐 *www.bluebirdtaxigreensboro.com.* **Central Piedmont Transportation** ✉ *6415 Bryan Blvd., Greensboro* ☎ *336/668–9808.* **Crown Cab** ✉ *1541 St. George Pl., Charlotte* ☎ *704/334–6666* 🌐 *www.crowncabinc.com.* **Yellow Cab** ✉ *4257 Golf Acres Dr., Charlotte* ☎ *704/332–6161* 🌐 *www.yellowcabofcharlotte.net.*

## RESTAURANTS

In the Piedmont it's almost as easy to grab a bagel, empanada, or spanakopita as a biscuit. The region is still a center of barbecue: wood-fired, pit-cooked, chopped or sliced pork traditionally served with coleslaw and hush puppies. Southern specialties such as catfish, fried green tomatoes, grits, collard greens, fried chicken, sweet potatoes, and pecan pie are also favorites. *Prices in the reviews are the average cost of a main course at dinner or, if dinner is not served, at lunch.*

### HOTELS

It's not usually a problem to find a place to stay in one of the Piedmont's resorts, bed-and-breakfasts, or motels or hotels. But during the High Point Market, a home-furnishings show held in spring and fall, tens of thousands of people descend on the area, making rooms almost impossible to find. May is graduation time for the region's colleges and universities. If you're planning on visiting the Triangle during these peak times, book accommodations well in advance. **■TIP→** Because many of the cities in the Piedmont are destinations for business travelers, hotel rates are often much higher during the week than the weekend. You can also expect lots of up-charges in fancier business-oriented hotels for such things as breakfast, parking, and Internet fees.

Most lodging options in the Sandhills fall into the resort category; pricing plans and options are extensive and often confusing. However, there are some chain motels in Southern Pines as well as numerous B&Bs. The high seasons for golf, which bring the most expensive lodging rates, are from mid-March to mid-May and from mid-September to mid-November. *Prices in the reviews are the lowest cost of a standard double room in high season.*

3

## THE TRIANGLE: RALEIGH, DURHAM, AND CHAPEL HILL

Known collectively as the Triangle, the cities of Raleigh (to the east), Durham (to the north), and Chapel Hill (to the west) attract scientists, academics, and businesspeople from all over the world. But it's also a nucleus of young, hip energy. Here, things are always in motion, with new "it" bars, galleries, and eateries opening all the time. What never changes, however, is the deep pride in—and rivalry between—the area's three major universities. College basketball is an extremely hot topic, and the NCAA championship tends to trade hands among the three schools.

## RALEIGH

*85 miles east of Greensboro; 143 miles northeast of Charlotte.*

For a state capital, Raleigh is surprisingly approachable. The very walkable downtown, smaller than you might think, is not only home to a multitude of government buildings, but also many friendly pubs and cafés. The shaded parks and the quiet Oakwood Historic District nearby add to the city's comfortable feel. Raleigh has both a sense of history and cutting-edge coolness about it. Home to seven universities and colleges, this bustling, modern city is a great place to get your fill of urban living (and some great food). Take in a play, visit a museum, and stroll along the wide city streets filled with tall and impressive buildings. When you finally feel the need to connect with nature once more, do as the locals do and grab your running shoes or bike and hit the Capital Area Greenway, Raleigh's well-loved series of trails, 68 miles in length and still growing.

### GETTING HERE AND AROUND

Like Washington, D.C., Raleigh has a highway that loops around the city. The terms "Inner Beltline" and "Outer Beltline" refer to your direction: the Inner Beltline runs clockwise; the Outer Beltline runs counterclockwise. Don't confuse the Outer Beltline with the Outer Loop, which refers to Interstate 540.

If you come by train or bus, you'll step off in Raleigh's Warehouse District, a developing area of cool clubs and restaurants a few blocks west of Downtown. RDU International is a 15-minute cab ride, depending on rush-hour traffic, from Downtown. Buses and taxis serve all parts of the city, including the suburbs. **■TIP→** **This is the easiest city in the Triangle to get around without a car. Not having your own transportation will make exploration outside the city a pain, however.**

**Historic Raleigh Trolley Tours.** You can board a trolley run by Historic Raleigh Trolley Tours for a narrated hour-long tour of historic Raleigh. Between March and December, the trolley runs Saturday at 11 am, noon, and 1 and 2 pm. Although the tour starts and ends at Mordecai Historic Park, you can hop aboard at any stop along the route, including the State Capital Bicentennial Plaza, the Joel Lane House, and City Market. The cost is $10 per person. ☎ *919/857–4364* ⊕ *www.raleighnc.gov/arts/content/PRecRecreation.*

### ESSENTIALS

**Visitor Information Greater Raleigh Convention and Visitors Bureau** ✉ *500 Fayetteville St.* ☎ *919/834–5900* ⊕ *www.visitraleigh.com.* **Capital Area Visitor Services** ✉ *5 E. Edenton St.* ☎ *919/807–7950* ⊕ *www.ncmuseumofhistory.org/vs.*

## EXPLORING

### TOP ATTRACTIONS

**City Market.** Specialty shops, art galleries, restaurants, and a small farmers' market are found in this cluster of cobblestone streets. A free trolley shuttles between City Market and other downtown restaurant and nightlife locations from 5:30 pm to 11:30 pm Thursday through Saturday. ✉ *Martin and Blount Sts., Downtown* ☎ *919/821–8023* ⊙ *Most stores Mon.–Sat. 10–5:30; most restaurants Mon.–Sat. 7 am–1 am, Sun. 11:30–10.*

**Executive Mansion.** Since 1891, this 37,500-square-foot brick Queen Anne–style structure with elaborate gingerbread trim and manicured lawns has been the home of the state's governors. Reservations for tours must be made at least two weeks in advance. ✉ *200 N. Blount St., Downtown* ☎ *919/807–7900 tours* ⊕ *www.nchistoricsites.org* 🎫 *Free* ⊙ *Call for tour times and dates, which change seasonally.*

**Joel Lane Museum House.** Dating to the 1760s, the oldest dwelling in Raleigh was the home of Joel Lane, known as the "father of Raleigh" because he once owned the property on which the capital city grew. Costumed docents lead tours of the restored house and beautiful period

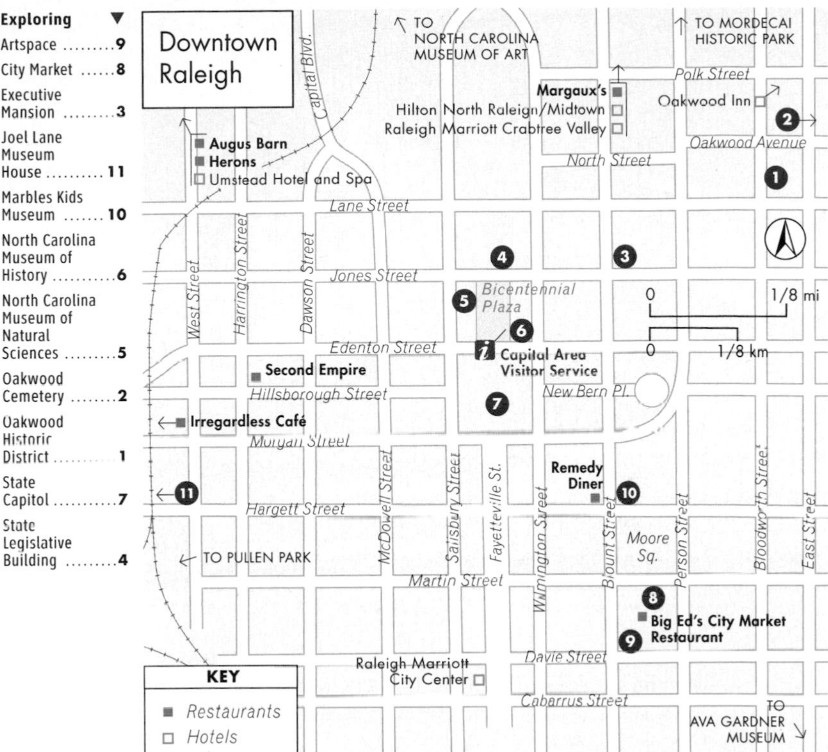


gardens. The last tour starts an hour before closing. ✉ *728 W. Hargett St., at St. Mary's St., Downtown* ☎ *919/833–3431* 🌐 *www.joellane.org* 🎫 *$5* ⏲ *Mar.–mid-Dec., Wed.–Fri. 10–2, Sat. 1–4; mid-Dec.–Feb., Sat. 1–4.*

**North Carolina Museum of History.** Founded in 1902, the museum is now in a state-of-the-art facility on Bicentennial Plaza. It houses the N.C. Sports Hall of Fame, which displays memorabilia from hundreds of inductees, from college heroes to pro superstars to Olympic contenders. You can see Richard Petty's race car, Arnold Palmer's Ryder cup golf bag, and Harlem Globetrotter Meadowlark Lemon's uniforms. ■ **TIP→** The Capital Area Visitor Services, in the same building, is a great place to plan your downtown itinerary, pick up brochures, or arrange area tours. ✉ *5 E. Edenton St., Downtown* ☎ *919/807–7900* 🌐 *www.ncmuseumofhistory.org* 🎫 *Free* ⏲ *Mon.–Sat. 9–5, Sun. noon–5.*

★ **North Carolina Museum of Natural Sciences.** At over 200,000 square feet, this museum is the largest of its kind in the Southeast. Exhibits and dioramas celebrate the incredible diversity of species in the state's various regions. There are enough live animals and insects—including butterflies, snakes, and a two-toed sloth—to qualify as a midsize zoo. Rare whale skeletons are also on display. The pièce de résistance, however, is the "Terror of the South" exhibit, featuring the dinosaur skeleton of

Meet "Acro," the world's only acrocanthosaurus dinosaur, at the North Carolina Museum of Natural Sciences.

"Acro," a giant carnivore that lived in the region 110 million years ago. The impressive bones belong to the world's only discovered acrocanthosaurus dinosaur. In the Nature Research Center, where visitors can have live conversations with scientists. ✉ *11 W. Jones St., Downtown* ☎ *919/733–7450, 877/462–8724* 🌐 *www.naturalsciences.org* 🎫 *Free* ⏲ *Mon.–Wed., Fri., and Sat. 9–5, Thu. 9–9, Sun. noon–5.*

**Oakwood Historic District.** Several architectural styles—including Victorian buildings, which are especially notable—can be found in this tree-shaded 19th-century neighborhood. Brochures for self-guided walking tours of the area, which encompasses 20 blocks bordered by Person, Edenton, Franklin, and Watauga–Linden streets, are available at the Capital Area Visitor Services on Edenton Street.

**Oakwood Cemetery**. Established in 1869, Oakwood Cemetery is the resting place of 2,800 Confederate soldiers, Civil War generals, governors, and numerous U.S. senators. The carefully cultivated grounds feature willows, towering oaks, and crepe myrtles. The House of Memory next to the Confederate burial ground recalls North Carolinians' involvement in the U.S. military. ✉ *701 Oakwood Ave., Oakwood Historic District* ☎ *919/832–6077* 🌐 *www.historicoakwoodcemetery.org.*

**State Capitol.** This beautifully preserved example of Greek Revival architecture from 1840 once housed all the functions of state government. Today it's part museum, part executive offices. Under its domed rotunda, the capitol contains a copy of Antonio Canova's statue of George Washington, who's depicted as a Roman general, with a tunic, tight-fitting body armor, and a short cape. Guided tours are given Saturday starting at 11 and 2. ✉ *Capitol Sq., 1 E. Edenton St., Downtown*

☎ *919/733–4994* 🌐 *www.nchistoricsites.org/capitol* 🎟 *Free* 🕓 *Weekdays 9–5, Sat. 9–4.*

**State Legislative Building.** One block north of the State Capitol, this complex hums with lawmakers and lobbyists when the legislature is in session. It's fun to watch from the gallery. A free guided tour is also available through Capital Area Visitor Services. ✉ *16 W. Jones St., Downtown* ☎ *919/733–7928* 🌐 *www.ncleg.net* 🎟 *Free* 🕓 *Weekdays 8–5, Sat. 9–5, Sun. 1–5.*

3

### WORTH NOTING

**Artspace.** A nonprofit visual-arts center, Artspace offers open studios, where artists are happy to talk to you about their work. The gift shop showcases the work of the resident artists. ■ **TIP→** The place bustles with visitors during the monthly First Friday art walk, when galleries and museums throughout the city host public receptions to show off new work. ✉ *201 E. Davie St., Downtown* ☎ *919/821–2787* 🌐 *www.artspacenc.org* 🎟 *Free* 🕓 *Tues.–Sat. 10–6.*

**Marbles Kids Museum.** This 84,000-square-foot cathedral of play and learning is aimed at children 10 and younger. Everything is hands-on, so your child is free to fill a shopping cart in the marketplace, don a fireman's hat, clamber through the cab of a city bus, scale the crow's nest of a three-story pirate ship, or splash in numerous water stations. Older children can play chess with 2-foot pawns, perform simple science experiments, or learn about the value of cash at the Moneypalooza exhibit. Toddler Hollow, designed with an enchanted forest in mind, is meant for kids under 2. The space's wide-open design and its architectural details, including a suspension bridge and a courtyard with a 6-foot marble fountain, give adults something to look at as well. There's also an IMAX theater. ✉ *201 E. Hargett St., Downtown* ☎ *919/834–4040* 🌐 *www.marbleskidsmuseum.org* 🎟 *Museum $5; museum and IMAX $10–17* 🕓 *Tues.–Sun. 9–5.*

### OUTER RALEIGH

The city is spread out, so you'll need a car to visit museums and parks beyond downtown.

**Ava Gardner Museum.** Located in the hometown of the legendary movie star, this museum has an extensive collection of memorabilia tracing Gardner's life, from childhood on the farm to her Hollywood glory days. It's about 30 miles southeast of Raleigh in downtown Smithfield. ✉ *325 E. Market St., Smithfield* ☎ *919/934–5830* 🌐 *www.avagardner.org* 🎟 *$7* 🕓 *Mar.–Nov., Mon.–Sat. 9–5, Sun. 2–5; Dec.–Feb., Mon.–Sat. 9–5.*

**Mordecai Historic Park.** You can see the Mordecai family's Greek Revival plantation home and other historically significant structures that have been moved onto the 2-acre property, including the house where President Andrew Johnson was born in 1808. Moses Mordecai, a well-respected lawyer, married two granddaughters of Joel Lane, the "Father of Raleigh." Mordecai's descendants lived in the house until 1964. There are guided tours hourly from 10 to 3 Tuesday to Saturday, and from 1 to 3 on Sunday. ■ **TIP→** The historical figure's name is pronounced MOR-de-key. Using a long "i" will mark you as a newcomer immediately. ✉ *1*

*Mimosa St., at Wake Forest Rd., Downtown* ☎ *919/857–4364* 🌐 *www.raleighnc.gov/mordecai* 🎫 *Free; guided tour $5* ⏲ *Daily sunrise–sunset.*

★ **North Carolina Museum of Art.** On the west side of Raleigh, the NCMA houses 5,000 years of artistic heritage, including one of the nation's largest collections of Jewish ceremonial art. The museum hosts touring exhibitions of works by such artists as Caravaggio and Rodin. There are tours at 1:30 Tuesday to Sunday. A 164-acre park featuring nine monumental works of art, which visitors can view on foot or by bike, adjoins the museum. The in-house restaurant, Blue Ridge, looks out on mammoth modernistic sculptures that, when viewed from above, spell the words "Picture this." ✉ *2110 Blue Ridge Rd., Northwest/Airport* ☎ *919/839–6262* 🌐 *www.ncartmuseum.org* 🎫 *Free* ⏲ *Tues.–Thurs. and weekends 10–5, Fri. 10–9.*

**Pullen Park.** Attracting more than 1 million visitors annually, this park near North Carolina State University draws folks who come to ride the train, the paddleboats, or the 1911 Dentzel carousel. You can also swim in a large indoor aquatic center, play a game of tennis, or, if the timing is right, see a summer play at the Theater in the Park. ✉ *520 Ashe Ave., University* ☎ *919/996–6468* 🎫 *Free* ⏲ *Nov.–Feb., daily 10–5; Mar., Apr., and Oct., daily 10–6; May–Aug., daily 10–9; Sept., daily 10–8.*

## WHERE TO EAT

$$$$ STEAKHOUSE Fodor's Choice ★

✕ **Angus Barn.** Dinner at this huge, rustic barn is a real event, and certainly worth the sizable prices. With its big portions, kitschy interior, and 85-page wine and beer list, this steak house is both traditional and fun. Under the supervision of Iron Chef Walter Royal, the steaks, prime rib, fresh seafood, baby back ribs, and homemade desserts are all delicious. This is the place to come for a special occasion, as the attentive staff seemed trained to make every patron feel special. Popular with large groups, the restaurant can seat more than 700 when filled to capacity and has several private dining areas. In the Meat Locker, a popular smoking lounge that's disconnected from the main dining hall, tobacco enthusiasts can puff away while enjoying their dinner. $ *Average main: $39* ✉ *9401 Glenwood Ave., Northwest/Airport* ☎ *919/781–2444* 🌐 *www.angusbarn.com* ✍ *Reservations essential* ⏲ *No lunch.*

$ SOUTHERN

✕ **Big Ed's City Market Restaurant.** This homey breakfast and lunch spot was founded by Big Ed Watkins, who claims some of the recipes were handed down from his great-grandfather, a Confederate mess sergeant. Southern cooking doesn't get much more traditional than this place; make sure you get the biscuits. The restaurant is filled with antique farm implements and political memorabilia, including snapshots of presidential candidates who have stopped by. Every Saturday morning a Dixieland band plays. $ *Average main: $9* ✉ *220 Wolfe St., City Market, Downtown* ☎ *919/836–9909* ⏲ *No dinner.*

$$$$ SOUTHERN

✕ **Herons.** At this elegant hotel restaurant, the menu shifts with the seasons and is always filled with new twists on traditional Southern dishes and international fare. Truly farm to fork, the restaurant uses produce from its own sustainable farm, which is less than a mile away. Previous offerings have included Scottish salmon, served with a blue-crab custard, a pancetta-fennel relish, buttered mussels, and pickled walnuts. Don't forget dessert, which is artfully constructed by the place's own pastry chef. *Average main: $35 ✉ Umstead Hotel & Spa, 100 Woodland Pond Dr., Northwest/Airport ☎ 919/447–4200 ⊕ www.theumstead.com/dining/herons-en.html Reservations essential ⏲ No dinner Sun.*

$$ ECLECTIC **Irregardless Café.** This café's menu—a combination of dishes inspired by the seasons for meat eaters as well as vegetarians and vegans—changes daily. Salads are amply portioned, and the breads, soups, and yogurts are made on the premises. Whenever possible, the eatery uses locally grown produce, just as it has since it opened its doors in 1975. There's live music every night and during Saturday and Sunday brunch, and dancing on Saturday nights starting at 9:30. The blond wood, brightly hued contemporary art, sunny dining areas, and well-spaced tables all add to the relaxing vibe. The restaurant is midway between North Carolina State University and downtown. **■ TIP→ Check Irregardless's detailed Web site for up-to-date menus and a full music schedule.** *Average main: $18 ✉ 901 W. Morgan St., University ☎ 919/833–8898 ⊕ www.irregardless.com ⏲ Closed Mon. No dinner Sun.*

$$$ ECLECTIC ★ **Margaux's.** At this North Raleigh fixture, the eclectic menu changes daily and might include peppercorn-crusted beef fillet with crispy fried oysters or phyllo-wrapped salmon with Brie, cranberry jam, and asparagus. A stone fireplace warms the room in winter; on the walls a wide range of frequently changing art hangs here, there, and everywhere. *Average main: $24 ✉ Brennan Station Shopping Center, 8111 Creedmoor Rd., North Hills ☎ 919/846–9846 ⊕ www.margauxsrestaurant.com ⏲ Closed Sun. No lunch Sat.–Wed.*

$ AMERICAN **Remedy Diner.** This small café is good for what ails you. Expect customers and staff alike to be young and tattooed, almost as colorful as the restaurant's mural-covered bathrooms. The vegetarian- and vegan-friendly menu includes plenty of salads, sandwiches, and homemade desserts. For a fiery kick, try the Flame Job, a tempeh sandwich with pepper-Jack cheese, fresh jalapeños, and chipotle mayo grilled on sourdough. The full bar adds to the edgy attitude of the place, which stays open until midnight on weekends. *Average main: $10 ✉ 137 E. Hargett St., Downtown ☎ 919/835–3553 ⊕ www.theremedydiner.com Reservations not accepted.*

$$$$ AMERICAN ★ **Second Empire.** Wood paneling, muted lighting, and well-spaced tables make for an elegant dining experience in this restored 1879 house. The menu, which changes seasonally, has a regional flavor. The food is intricately styled so that colors, textures, and tastes fuse. Previous standouts have included pan-roasted sea scallops served with grits and applewood-smoked bacon and five-spiced duck confit with green lentils and orzo. A brick tavern on the lower level has a less expensive menu that has included bison short ribs and grilled North Carolina trout. *Average main: $28 ✉ 330 Hillsborough St., Downtown ☎ 919/829–3663 ⊕ www.second-empire.com ⏲ Closed Sun. and Mon. No lunch.*

3

The Umstead's spectacular spa and vanishing pool make it ideal for a girls' getaway.

## WHERE TO STAY

*Hotel reviews have been abbreviated in this book. For expanded reviews, please go to Fodors.com.*

$ HOTEL **Hilton North Raleigh/Midtown.** This easily accessed hotel is a favorite spot for corporate meetings. **Pros:** close to Interstate 440; free airport shuttle available between 6 am and 10 pm. **Cons:** busy location makes getting in and out of the hotel at rush hour tough; unexciting views from many rooms. *Rooms from: $109 3415 Wake Forest Rd., North Hills 919/872–2323, 800/445–8667 www.hilton.com 338 rooms, 7 suites No meals.*

$ B&B/INN **Oakwood Inn.** This 1871 Victorian B&B, one of the first to be built in what is now the Oakwood Historic District, is on the National Register of Historic Places; each of its individually decorated rooms has a working fireplace, high ceilings, and walls with rich, solid colors. **Pros:** good value; the only B&B in the Oakwood Historic District; the surrounding Victorian homes and tree-lined streets make for good strolling. **Cons:** long walk from many Raleigh attractions; the abundance of Victorian furnishings isn't for everyone. *Rooms from: $139 411 N. Bloodworth St., Oakwood Historic District 919/832–9712, 800/267–9712 www.oakwoodinnbb.com 6 rooms Breakfast.*

$$ HOTEL **The Raleigh Marriott City Center.** The 17-story hotel, very close to the city's convention center, is right in the heart of things and has rooms with lots of amenities. **Pros:** great central location with good views; upscale rooms. **Cons:** pricier than the chain hotels farther from the city center; parking and Internet usage cost extra; busy during conventions. *Rooms from: $169 500 Fayetteville St., Downtown*

☎ *919/833–1120* 🌐 *www.marriott.com* 🛏 *390 rooms, 10 suites* 🍴 *No meals.*

$ HOTEL **Raleigh Marriott Crabtree Valley.** Fresh flowers adorn the elegant public rooms of one of the city's most comfortable, yet affordable, hotels. **Pros:** some of the best shopping in the Triangle is right across the street at Crabtree Valley Mall; there is a free airport shuttle between 7 am and 10 pm; free Wi-Fi in the lobby. **Cons:** traffic from the mall can be terrible; not in walking distance to anywhere charming; high daily rate for Internet. $ *Rooms from: $109* ✉ *4500 Marriott Dr., U.S. 70 near Crabtree Valley Mall, University* ☎ *919/781–7000, 800/909–8289* 🌐 *www.marriott.com* 🛏 *370 rooms, 5 suites* 🍴 *No meals.*

**RALEIGH'S GREENER SIDE**

Raleigh has nearly 70 miles of scenic trails for biking or walking throughout the downtown area and beyond. A map of the **Capital Area Greenway** can be found at 🌐 *www.mappery.com/Raleigh-greenway-map.*

$$$$ HOTEL Fodor's Choice ★ **The Umstead Hotel and Spa.** Though close to the airport, this modern and luxurious hotel feels light years away from the traffic of Interstate 40. **Pros:** luxurious hotel with a restaurant, bar, and spa; lovely natural setting. **Cons:** outside of Raleigh and not in walking distance to any sights; allows pets but only at a very high onetime fee. $ *Rooms from: $259* ✉ *5 SAS Campus Dr.(100 Woodland Pond Rd.), Cary* ☎ *919/447–4000, 866/877–4141* 🌐 *www.theumstead.com* 🛏 *123 rooms, 27 suites* 🍴 *No meals.*

## NIGHTLIFE AND THE ARTS

### THE ARTS

**Progress Energy Center for the Performing Arts.** The Progress Energy Center for the Performing Arts has several different performance spaces. The 2,277-seat **Memorial Auditorium**, the crown jewel of the complex, is home to the North Carolina Theatre and the nationally acclaimed Carolina Ballet. The 1,700-seat **Meymandi Concert Hall** hosts the North Carolina Symphony. The 600-seat **Fletcher Opera Theater** provides a showcase for the A.J. Fletcher Opera Institute. The 170-seat **Kennedy Theater** stages shows by smaller, more alternative theater groups. ✉ *2 E. South St., Downtown* ☎ *919/831–6011* 🌐 *www.progressenergycenter.com.*

**Time Warner Cable Music Pavilion at Walnut Creek.** Accommodating up to 20,000 fans, this amphitheater hosts whatever big touring musicians happen to be in town. ✉ *3801 Rock Quarry Rd., Southeast Metro* ☎ *919/831–6666* 🌐 *www.livenation.com.*

### NIGHTLIFE

**Berkeley Café.** Rock and roll, metal, country, bluegrass, and electronic all play on this bar and restaurant's stage. ✉ *217 W. Martin St., Downtown* ☎ *919/821–0777* 🌐 *www.berkeleycafe.net.*

**Goodnight's Comedy Club.** This club near the university combines dinner with a night of laughs. Past performers include Jerry Seinfeld, Chris Rock, and Ellen DeGeneres. ✉ *861 W. Morgan St., University* ☎ *919/828–5233* 🌐 *www.goodnightscomedy.com.*

## DID YOU KNOW?

In addition to trying to inspire awe and reverence, the architects of Duke Chapel also added a touch of whimsy. Look for two wooden mice hidden within the intricate woodwork—one is in the choir stalls near the altar; the other is on top of a wooden pillar on the organ. If you still can't find them, take the tour.

**Raleigh Times Bar.** Faces of early-20th-century newsboys stare out from a 20-foot photo mural covering one wall at this 1906 newspaper office, artfully restored into a gastropub. The bar features a great selection of Belgian beers and thoughtful wine and cocktail lists. ✉ *14 E. Hargett St., Downtown* ☎ *919/833–0999* 🌐 *www.raleightimesbar.com.*

## SPORTS AND THE OUTDOORS

### BASKETBALL

**Wolfpack.** Raleigh's Atlantic Coast Conference entry plays basketball in the PNC Center, which is also home to the Carolina Hurricanes. ☎ *919/865–1510* 🌐 *www.gopack.com.*



### GOLF

**Hedingham Golf Club.** Designed by architect David Postlethwait, this semiprivate course has water hazards on eight holes. Watch out for Hole 1, where a large pond affects your play three times. ✉ *4801 Harbour Towne Dr.* ☎ *919/250–3030* 🌐 *www.hedingham.org* *18 holes. 6609 yds. Par 71. Green Fee: $25–$45.* ☞ *Facilities: Golf carts, golf academy/lessons.*

**Lochmere Golf Club.** Designed by Carolina PGA Hall of Famer Gene Hamm, this course meanders through the tree-lined links, challenging players with several different types of water hazards. A tiered green makes Hole 3 a difficult par 3. ✉ *2511 Kildaire Farm Rd., Cary* ☎ *919/851–0611* 🌐 *www.lochmere.com* *18 holes. 6627 yds. Par 71. Green Fee: $20–$59.* ☞ *Facilities: Driving range, putting green, golf carts, rental clubs, pro shop, golf academy/lessons, restaurant.*

**Neuse Golf Club.** About 20 minutes from downtown Raleigh, this semiprivate course feels far from the city's hustle and bustle. The 1993 John LaFoy–designed course, which follows the Neuse River, is characterized by rolling fairways and rock outcroppings. ✉ *918 Birkdale Dr., Clayton* ☎ *919/550–0550* 🌐 *www.neusegolf.com* *18 holes. 7010 yds. Par 72. Green Fee: $40–$60.* ☞ *Facilities: Driving range, putting green, rental clubs, pro shop, golf academy/lessons.*

### JOGGING

**Shelley Lake Park.** Runners are drawn to this scenic 53-acre lake and its winding 2-mile paved trail. ☎ *919/420–2331* 🌐 *www.raleighnc.gov/arts.*

**Capital Area Greenway.** Nearly 40 years in the making, this series of trails links the city's parks for runners and bikers. It currently consists of 77 miles that connect 3,700 acres, but new trails open regularly. ☎ *919/996–4776 for map* 🌐 *www.raleighnc.gov/arts.*

## SHOPPING

### SHOPPING MALLS

**Cameron Village Shopping Center.** Raleigh's first shopping center is an upscale assemblage of boutiques and restaurants. ✉ *1900 Cameron St., Cameron Village* ☎ *919/821–1350* 🌐 *www.shopcameronvillage.com.*

**Triangle Town Center.** The Triangle Town Center contains some 165 stores, including Abercrombie & Fitch, Coldwater Creek, Louis Vuitton, Saks Fifth Avenue, and Williams-Sonoma. ✉ *5959 Triangle Town Blvd., North Raleigh* ☎ *919/792–2222* 🌐 *www.triangletowncenter.com.*

### FOOD

**State Farmers' Market.** Open year-round, this 60-acre market is the place to go for locally grown fruits and vegetables, flowers and plants, and North Carolina crafts. There's also a cavernous restaurant serving down-home cooking. ✉ *1201 Agriculture St., Southwest Metro* ☎ *919/733–7417* 🌐 *www.ncagr.gov/markets/facilities/markets/raleigh.*

## DURHAM

*23 miles northwest of Raleigh.*

For many, Durham and Duke University are synonymous, and for good reason. Duke's well-manicured lawns, tree-lined streets, and stately buildings run right into town. With more than 20,000 employees, the university is also the city's biggest employer and famous for its renowned medical and research facilities. Having a university of such magnitude in their backyard means that Durhamites, and visitors alike, can attend all kinds of world-class lectures, exhibits, and sports events. This is not purely a college town, however, but a former tobacco-company town continually growing into a more arts-minded, urbane city. For years, old brick factory buildings have been slowly turned into shopping malls, theater spaces, and trendy restaurants. While neighboring Chapel Hill often steals its thunder when it comes to attracting visitors, many locals prefer Durham's calmer and more mature vibe. Add Durham's long list of historic sites and museums to its ever-evolving sense of self, and you've got a city that is definitely worth exploring.

### GETTING HERE AND AROUND

Durham's city center has grown rather haphazardly around its universities and commercial districts in the past 100 years. One-way streets and roads that change names can make navigation tricky. Using Durham Freeway, aka Highway 147, as a guide helps. This thoroughfare bisects the city diagonally, connecting Interstates 85 and 40, and most places of interest can be reached via its exits.

### ESSENTIALS

**Visitor Information Durham Convention and Visitors Bureau** ✉ *101 E. Morgan St.* ☎ *919/687–0288, 800/446–8604* 🌐 *www.durham-nc.com.*

## EXPLORING

### TOP ATTRACTIONS

**Duke Chapel.** A Gothic-style gem built in the early 1930s, this chapel is the centerpiece of Duke University. Modeled after England's Canterbury Cathedral, it has a 210-foot-tall bell tower. Weekly services are held here Sunday at 11 am. ■ **TIP→ The chapel is a popular wedding spot, so check the Web site before trying to visit on Saturday.** ✉ *West Campus, Chapel Dr., Duke University* ☎ *919/681–1704* 🌐 *www.chapel.duke.edu* ⊙ *Sept.–May, daily 8 am–10 pm; June–Aug., daily 8–8.*

**Duke Homestead.** Washington Duke, patriarch of the now famous Duke family, moved into this house in 1852. It wasn't until he heard how the Union soldiers were enjoying smoking his tobacco that he decided to market his "golden weed." Explore the family's humble beginnings at this State Historic Site, which includes the first ramshackle "factory" as

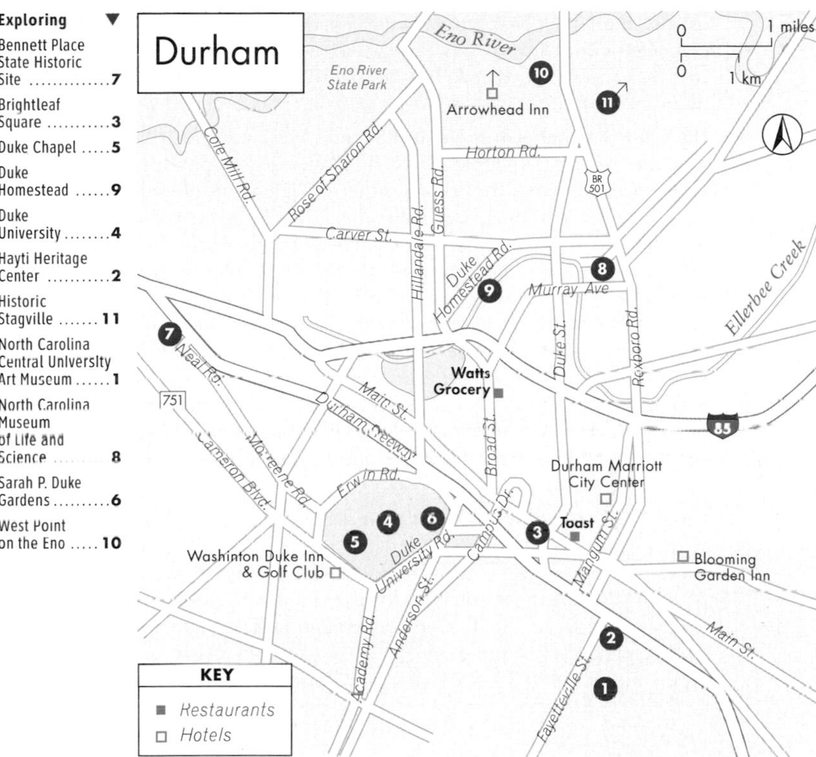


well as the world's largest spittoon collection. Guided tours demonstrate early manufacturing processes; the visitor center exhibits early tobacco advertising. ✉ *2828 Duke Homestead Rd., Downtown* ☎ *919/477–5498* 🌐 *www.history.ncdcr.gov* 🎟 *Free* 🕘 *Tues.–Sat. 9–5.*

**Duke University.** A stroll along the tree-lined streets of this campus, founded in 1924, is a lovely way to spend a few hours. The university, known for its Georgian and Gothic Revival architecture, encompasses 525 acres in the heart of Durham. Tours of the campus, available during the academic year, can be arranged in advance. ✉ *Office of Special Events, Smith Warehouse, 114 S. Buchanan Blvd., Duke University* ☎ *919/684–8111* 🌐 *www.duke.edu.*

**Nasher Museum of Art.** A highlight of any Duke visit, this museum displays African, American, European, and Latin American artwork. The collection includes works by Rodin, Picasso, and Matisse. ✉ *2001 Campus Dr., Duke University* ☎ *919/684–5135* 🌐 *www.nasher.duke.edu*

**Fodor's Choice ★**

**Historic Stagville.** Owned by the Bennehan and Cameron families, Stagville was one of the largest plantations in antebellum North Carolina, at 30,000 acres and with about 900 slaves. The plantation today sits on 161 acres and has many original buildings, including the Bennehan's two-story wood frame home, built in 1799; four two-story slave cabins; the Great Barn, built by enslaved craftspeople; and the family cemetery. Guided tours of the property are given on the hour from 10 to 3. ✉ *5828 Old Oxford Hwy.* ☎ *919/620–0120* 🌐 *www.stagville.org* 🎟 *Free* 🕑 *Tues.–Sat. 10–4.*

★ **North Carolina Museum of Life and Science.** Here you can ride in a flying machine, sail a radio-controlled boat on an outdoor pond, view artifacts from space missions, and ride a train through a wildlife sanctuary. The nature center contains such animals as black bears, red wolves, and lemurs. The three-story Magic Wings Butterfly House lets you walk among tropical species in a rain-forest conservatory. In the Insectarium you can see and hear live insects under high magnification and amplification. One of the museum's newest exhibits, the Dinosaur Trail, gives you a glimpse of what life was like millions of years ago, and comes complete with massive dinosaur replicas. ■ **TIP→** The museum will be closed Mondays through May 2013. After that date, check for Monday times. ✉ *433 Murray Ave., off I–85, Downtown* ☎ *919/220–5429* 🌐 *www.ncmls.org* 🎟 *Museum $14, train ride $3, bungee ride $5* 🕑 *Tue.–Sat. 10–5, Sun. noon–5.*

**Sarah P. Duke Gardens.** A wisteria-draped gazebo and a Japanese garden with a lily pond teeming with fat goldfish are a few of the highlights of these 55 acres in Duke University's West Campus. More than 5 miles of pathways meander through formal plantings and woodlands. The Terrace Café serves lunch Monday through Friday and brunch Saturday and Sunday. ✉ *426 Anderson St., at Campus Dr., West Campus, Duke University* ☎ *919/684–3698* 🌐 *www.hr.duke.edu/dukegardens* 🎟 *Free* 🕑 *Daily 8–dusk.*

### WORTH NOTING

**Bennett Place State Historic Site.** In April 1865 Confederate General Joseph E. Johnston surrendered to U.S. General William T. Sherman in this house, 17 days after Lee's surrender to Grant at Appomattox. The two generals then set forth the terms for a "permanent peace" between the South and the North. Live historical events, held throughout the year, demonstrate how Civil War soldiers drilled, lived in camps, got their mail, and received medical care. ✉ *4409 Bennett Memorial Rd., Downtown* ☎ *919/383–4345* 🌐 *www.nchistoricsites.org/bennett* 🎟 *Free* 🕑 *Tues.–Sat. 9–5.*

**Brightleaf Square.** In the former Watts and Yuille warehouses, Brightleaf Square is named for the tobacco that once filled these buildings. The two long structures—now filled with stores like James Kennedy Antiques, Offbeat Music, and Wentworth and Leggett Rare Books and Prints—sandwich an attractive brick courtyard. ✉ *Main and Gregson Sts., Duke University* ☎ *919/682–9229* 🌐 *www.historicbrightleaf.com.*

**Hayti Heritage Center.** One of Durham's oldest houses of worship, St. Joseph's AME Church, houses this center for African-American art and culture. In addition to exhibitions of traditional and contemporary art by local, regional, and national artists, the center hosts events like the Bull Durham Blues Festival and the Black Diaspora Film Festival. ✉ *804 Old Fayetteville St., Downtown* ☎ *919/683–1709* 🌐 *www.hayti.org* 🎟 *Free* 🕑 *Mon. 5–8, Tues.–Fri. 10–5, Sat. 10–3* 🕑 *Closed Sun.*

**North Carolina Central University Art Museum.** Located in the first publicly supported liberal-arts college for African-Americans, this gallery showcases work by black artists. The permanent collection includes 19th-century masterpieces and 20th-century works created during the Harlem Renaissance. Pieces by outsider artists, as well as students and staff, are also on display. ✉ *580 E. Lawson St., South/NCCU* ☎ *919/530–6211* 🌐 *www.nccu.edu/artmuseum* 🎫 *Free* ⏲ *Tues.–Fri. 9–4:30, Sun. 2–4.*

**West Point on the Eno.** This city park on the banks of the Eno River boasts a restored mill dating from 1778—one of 32 that once dotted the area. Also on site are a 19th-century Greek Revival farmhouse that was occupied by John Cabe McCown, the onetime owner of the mill, and a museum that showcases early-20th-century photographer Hugh Mangum's pictures of the surrounding area. The three-day Festival for the Eno, held around July 4, includes musicians, artists, and craftspeople from around the region. ✉ *5101 N. Roxboro Rd., U.S. 501N, North Metro* ☎ *919/471–1623* 🎫 *Free* ⏲ *Park daily 8–dark; buildings weekends 1–5.*

3

## WHERE TO EAT

$ ITALIAN

✕ **Toast.** Tucked into a plain storefront, this low-key Italian sandwich shop has quite a fan base—you'll likely become a believer, too. Crowd favorites include panini filled with grilled chicken, roasted peppers, and mozzarella; and crostini topped with goat cheese, honey, and cracked black pepper. If none of that suits your fancy, try some homemade soup, bruschetta, or a bite of biscotti. Chow down outside or in the cute and simple dining room, awash in robin's-egg blue. There's usually a crowd at lunch, but it's worth it. [$] *Average main: $7* ✉ *345 W. Main St., Five Points* ☎ *919/683–2183* 🌐 *www.toast-fivepoints.com* ⏲ *Closed Sun. No lunch Sat.*

$$$ SOUTHERN ★

✕ **Watts Grocery.** When slow food enthusiasts say "eat local," this is what they mean. The menu of dressed-up regional dishes reflects both the chef's Southern roots and her French training. Expect the freshest seasonal ingredients and locally raised meats. The smooth and savory meat terrines, served with homemade pickles, and the grilled pork tenderloin over corn pudding are standouts on the summer menu. Sunday brunch draws a crowd that comes for the full bar as well as must-try indulgences like biscuits and gravy and homemade churros, served with a dark chocolate dipping sauce. [$] *Average main: $21* ✉ *1116 Broad St., Trinity Park* ☎ *919/416–5040* 🌐 *www.wattsgrocery.com* ⏲ *Closed Mon.*

## WHERE TO STAY

*Hotel reviews have been abbreviated in this book. For expanded reviews, please go to Fodors.com.*

$$ B&B/INN ★

🏨 **Arrowhead Inn.** This plantation home circa 1775 is a nice treat for those looking for something a little special. **Pros:** comfortable inn offers suites and roomy cottages; beautiful country setting; upscale dinners can be arranged. **Cons:** it's a 15-minute drive to the city center; nothing nearby in the way of entertainment. [$] *Rooms from: $165* ✉ *106 Mason Rd., North Metro* ☎ *919/477–8430, 800/528–2207* 🌐 *www.arrowheadinn.com* 🛏 *7 rooms, 1 cabin, 1 cottage* 🍴 *Breakfast.*

**DID YOU KNOW?**

Brightleaf Square used to house the Watts and Yuille tobacco warehouses, which were used for storing, aging, and fermenting tobacco for cigarettes. These warehouses were named after George W. Watts and Thomas B. Yuille, both members of the Duke family. Today, the buildings house shops and restaurants.

Brightleaf Square
Brightleaf Square
Restaurants

$ B&B/INN **Blooming Garden Inn.** With its yellow exterior and lush gardens, this B&B is literally and figuratively a bright spot in the Holloway Historic District. **Pros:** great location near downtown; highly regarded service; very comfortable rooms. **Cons:** quiet setting may be too quiet for those seeking nightlife action; older bathroom fixtures; most rooms don't have TVs. *Rooms from: $115 ✉ 513 Holloway St., Downtown ☎ 919/687–0801 www.bloominggardeninn.com 3 rooms, 2 suites Breakfast.*

$ HOTEL **Durham Marriott City Center.** Given this nine-story hotel's excellent downtown location, the rates here are reasonable. **Pros:** located near plenty of sights; free airport shuttle; warm-toned hallways and room interiors. **Cons:** not a whole lot of frills; small bathrooms; can get busy when conventions are in town. *Rooms from: $129 ✉ 201 Foster St., Downtown ☎ 919/768–6000 www.marriott.com 187 rooms, 2 suites No meals.*

$$ HOTEL ★ **Washington Duke Inn & Golf Club.** On the campus of Duke University, this luxurious hotel evokes the feeling of an English country inn. **Pros:** well appointed and service-oriented; luxury travelers will feel right at home; allows all pets (for a fee). **Cons:** must be booked well in advance for any stays during graduation or other Duke events; many of the rooms have views of the parking lot. *Rooms from: $199 ✉ 3001 Cameron Blvd., Duke University ☎ 919/490–0999, 800/443–3853 www.washingtondukeinn.com 271 rooms, 42 suites No meals.*

### THE STATE OF THINGS

If you're curious about the people, places, and issues that matter to the Triangle and beyond, you might want to tune in *The State of Things*, a live, one-hour public radio show with Frank Stasio. Beamed right out of the American Tobacco Campus in Durham, the interview program feels unscripted and fresh, and it always features a variety of guests, both famous and obscure. You can hear it every weekday at noon on WUNC, 91.5 FM.

## NIGHTLIFE AND THE ARTS

### THE ARTS

**American Dance Festival.** This internationally known festival, held annually in June and July, brings performances to various locations throughout town. *✉ 715 Broad St. ☎ 919/684–6402 www.americandancefestival.org.*

**Carolina Theatre.** Dating from 1926, this Beaux Arts space hosts classical, jazz, and rock concerts, as well as April's Full Frame Documentary Film Festival and August's North Carolina Gay and Lesbian Film Festival. Check online for a full calendar of indie, retro, and all-around interesting films. *✉ 309 W. Morgan St., Downtown ☎ 919/560–3030 www.carolinatheatre.org.*

**Manbites Dog Theater.** Manbites Dog Theater performs edgy, socially conscious plays. *✉ 703 Foster St., Downtown ☎ 919/682–3343 www.manbitesdogtheater.org.*

Check out modern dance performances at the American Dance Festival in June and July.

### NIGHTLIFE

**American Tobacco Campus.** This complex, adjacent to the Durham Bulls Athletic Park, houses offices, bars, and restaurants in a series of beautifully refurbished warehouses left over from the city's cigarette-rolling past. Free summer concerts are staged on a central lawn, in the shadow of a Lucky Strike water tower. ✉ *318 Blackwell St., Downtown* ☎ *919/433–1566* 🌐 *www.americantobaccohistoricdistrict.com.*

**James Joyce Irish Pub.** With 19 beers on tap, this Irish bar is a popular meeting place. Expect frequent live music, trivia nights, and open mics. ✉ *912 W. Main St., Downtown* ☎ *919/683–3022* 🌐 *www.jamesjoyceirishpub.com.*

## SPORTS AND THE OUTDOORS

### BASEBALL

**Durham Bulls.** Immortalized in the hit 1988 movie *Bull Durham* and a tradition since 1902, this AAA affiliate of the Tampa Bay Rays plays in the 10,000-seat Durham Bulls Athletic Park. ✉ *Durham Bulls Athletic Park, 409 Blackwell St., North Metro* ☎ *919/687–6500* 🌐 *www.dbulls.com.*

### BASKETBALL

**Blue Devils.** Durham's Atlantic Coast Conference team plays home games at the 8,800-seat Cameron Indoor Stadium. ☎ *919/681–2583* 🌐 *www.goduke.com.*

### GOLF

**Duke University Golf Club.** Twice host of the NCAA men's championship, this course was designed in 1957 by the legendary Robert Trent Jones; his son, Rees Jones, completed a renovation of the links in 1993.

The whopping 455-yard par 4 on Hole 18 separates serious players from duffers. ✉ *3001 Cameron Blvd., at Science Dr.* ☎ *919/681–2288, 800/443–3853* 🌐 *www.golf.duke.edu* *18 holes. 7136 yds. Par 72. Green Fee: $55–$100.* ☞ *Facilities: Driving range, golf carts, rental clubs, pro shop, golf academy/lessons, restaurant, bar.*

**Hillandale Golf Course.** The oldest course in the area, Hillandale was designed by the incomparable architect Donald Ross, but then redesigned by George Cobb following the course's move in 1960. The course, with a couple of doglegs and a creek running through it, gives even experienced golfers a strategic workout. ✉ *1600 Hillandale Rd.* ☎ *919/286–4211* 🌐 *www.hillandalegolf.com* *Reservations essential* *18 holes. 6339 yds. Par 71. Green Fee: $20–$24.* ☞ *Facilities: Driving range, golf carts, rental clubs, pro shop, golf academy/lessons, restaurant, bar.*

### HIKING

**Eno River State Park.** This 4,231-acre park includes miles of hiking trails, a picnic area, and backcountry camping sites. Though only 15 minutes from downtown Durham, Eno is a slice of secluded wilderness. ✉ *6101 Cole Mill Rd., North Metro* ☎ *919/383–1686* 🌐 *www.ncparks.gov.*

### TENNIS

**Parks and Recreation Department.** Durham's Parks and Recreation Department can provide information on the city's 72 public tennis courts. ☎ *919/560–4355* 🌐 *www.ci.durham.nc.us/departments/parks.*

## SHOPPING

### SHOPPING AREAS AND MALLS

**9th Street.** Durham's funky 9th Street is lined with shops and restaurants. ✉ *9th St. at Markham Ave., West Durham* ☎ *919/572–8808.*

**Streets of Southpoint Mall.** At the heart of Durham's shopping scene, this village-like mall has restaurants, a movie theater, and upward of 150 stores, including Nordstrom and Restoration Hardware. ✉ *6910 Fayetteville Rd., off I–40, Southeast Metro* ☎ *919/572–8800* 🌐 *www.streetsatsouthpoint.com.*

### CRAFTS

**One World Market.** Browse 2,000 square feet of unique, affordable home accessories, children's toys, and other arts and crafts collected from around the world. As a nonprofit enterprise, the market sells crafts from fair-trade vendors, which aim to provide artisans in developing countries (and poor areas of the U.S.) a living wage. ✉ *811 9th St., Duke University* ☎ *919/286–2457* 🌐 *www.oneworldmarket.info.*

**Outsiders Art & Collectibles.** This small, quirky gallery is the only place in town to show a mixture of outsider and folk art. Here, you can see work by 99 local and regional artists, mostly untrained and self-taught. The gallery's tiny annex, **Outsiders**, is located downtown at 721 Broad St. ■ **TIP→** The main gallery's monthly art receptions, open to the public, are some of the best parties in town. ✉ *718-C Iredell St* ☎ *919/451–3231* 🌐 *www.outsiders-art.com* 🕒 *Mon.–Sat. 10–6.*

#### FOOD

**Parker and Otis.** Much more than just a grocery store, this shop offers local produce and specialty foods as well as international spices, wines, chocolates, teas, coffees, and scads of candy. Breakfast is served until 11, and lunch lasts until 7. Gift baskets can be shipped all over the country. ✉ *112 S. Duke St., Downtown* ☎ *919/683–3200* 🌐 *www.parkerandotis.com.*

## CHAPEL HILL



*28 miles northwest of Raleigh; 12 miles southwest of Durham.*

Chapel Hill is the smallest city in the Triangle, but it probably has the biggest personality. Home to the nation's first state university, the University of North Carolina, this is a college town through and through. Though not as quaint as it once was, this little city has never lost its quirky edge, thanks in no small part to its constant influx of young people. With its prestigious yet offbeat reputation, UNC draws all kinds of students, from West Coast hippies to fraternity-loving members of the Southern aristocracy. Part of the fun of the area is the push–pull between this motley crew of students and the wealthy retirees who call Chapel Hill home. While there are fancy restaurants and hotels, there are also cheap pizza joints and dive bars. Franklin Street, located in the heart of downtown, caters to both these communities with a mixture of boutiques, restaurants, and galleries. It's just as good a place to buy incense as it is to purchase a designer shirt—and it makes for great people-watching.

#### GETTING HERE AND AROUND

Chapel Hill is a wonderful place to walk around, and a terrible place to park a car. Find a parking space in one of the lots along Rosemary Street, one block off Franklin, and give yourself a chance to enjoy the Carolina blue skies. Start at the Old Well on Cameron Avenue and wander through campus, or eat, sip, and shop your way down Franklin Street, beginning at the Old Post Office and heading west to Carrboro.

#### ESSENTIALS

**Visitor Information Chapel Hill/Orange County Visitors Bureau** ✉ *501 W. Franklin St.* ☎ *919/968–2060* 🌐 *www.visitchapelhill.org.*

### EXPLORING

**Morehead Planetarium and Science Center.** The original Apollo astronauts trained here, at one of the largest planetariums in the country. You can see planetarium shows, science demonstrations, and exhibits for children and adults. ✉ *250 E. Franklin St., University* ☎ *919/962–1236* 🌐 *www.moreheadplanetarium.org* 🎟 *$7.25* 🕓 *Sat. 10–3:30, Sun. 1–4:30, closed Mon., hrs vary during the week. Call or check Web site before visiting.*

**North Carolina Botanical Garden.** Part of the University of North Carolina, this ode to native plants includes wildflowers, shrubs, trees, ferns, and grasses of the Southeast. Other highlights include nature trails that wind through a 300-acre Piedmont forest, a green education center, and an impressive collection of herbs and carnivorous plants. ✉ *100 Old*

*Mason Farm Rd., South Metro* ☎ *919/962–0522* 🌐 *www.ncbg.unc.edu* 🎫 *Free* ⏲ *June–Aug., weekdays 8–5, Sat. 9–6, Sun. 1–6; Sept.–May., weekdays 8–5, Sat. 9–5, Sun. 1–5.*

**University of North Carolina.** Franklin Street runs along the northern edge of the campus, which is filled with oak-shaded courtyards and stately old buildings. Regarded as one of the top public institutions in the United States, UNC Chapel Hill is also one of the country's oldest public universities and was the first to admit students (it opened its doors in 1795). To this day, it remains the very heart of Chapel Hill, which has grown up around it for more than two centuries. ✉ *Visitor Center, 250 E. Franklin St.* ☎ *919/962–1630 visitor center* 🌐 *www.unc.edu/visitors.*

**Ackland Art Museum.** Come and see one of the Southeast's strongest collections of Asian art, plus an outstanding selection of drawings, prints, and photographs as well as Old Master paintings and sculptures. ✉ *101 S. Columbia St., University* ☎ *919/966–5736* 🌐 *www.ackland.org.*

**Louis Round Wilson Library.** Visit this library for the largest single collection of North Carolina literature in the nation. ✉ *153A Country Club Rd., University* ☎ *919/962–1172* 🌐 *www.lib.unc.edu/wilson.*

## WHERE TO EAT

$ BARBECUE

✕ **Allen and Son Barbecue.** If you're hankering for the tang of vinegar-based BBQ sauce, this is the 'cue for you. Located a bit out of town, this family-owned spot has been serving slow-cooked pork plates, sandwiches, and all the traditional fixins' for decades. Though the interior is a bit worn and the hours can be unpredictable, all kinds of people make the pilgrimage to this out-of-the-way landmark daily. Make a point to try the famous hush puppies. [$] *Average main: $10* ✉ *6203 Millhouse Rd.* ☎ *919/942–7576* ⏲ *Closed Sun. and Mon. No dinner Tues. and Wed.*

$$$ SOUTHERN ★

✕ **Crook's Corner.** In business since 1982, this small restaurant has always been an exemplar of Southern chic. The menu, which changes nightly, highlights local produce and regional specialties such as green-pepper chicken with hoppin' John (black-eyed peas), crab gumbo, buttermilk pie, and honeysuckle sorbet. A wall of bamboo and a waterfall fountain make the patio a delightful alfresco experience (it's heated for wintertime dining). Crook's also does a nice Sunday brunch, though it's closed for lunch on other days. Look for the faded pink pig atop the building. [$] *Average main: $20* ✉ *610 W. Franklin St., Downtown* ☎ *919/929–7643* 🌐 *www.crookscorner.com* ⏲ *Closed Mon. No lunch.*

$$$$ ITALIAN

✕ **Il Palio.** This small and inviting place is a real find for food lovers willing to stray from Chapel Hill's lively downtown. Il Palio serves high-class Italian fare with an emphasis on local and seasonal ingredients. The menu even includes a long list of nearby farms and purveyors used. Although the dishes change frequently, previous offerings have included pappardelle Bolognese and pan-seared scallops served with corn succotash. Much more than just a hotel restaurant, this independently owned eatery is a destination in its own right. [$] *Average main: $31* ✉ *Siena Hotel, 1505 E. Franklin St.* ☎ *919/929–4000* 🌐 *www.ilpalio.com* ⏲ *No dinner Sun.*

$ SOUTHERN **Mama Dip's Country Kitchen.** In Chapel Hill, Mildred Edna Cotton Council—better known as Mama Dip—is just about as famous as Michael Jordan. That's because she and her restaurant, which serves authentic home-style Southern meals in a roomy but simple setting, have been on the scene since the early '60s. Chicken and dumplings, ribs, and country ham as well as fish, beef, salads, a mess of fresh vegetables, and melt-in-your-mouth buttermilk biscuits appear on the lengthy menu. **TIP→** Mama Dip's two cookbooks explain her famed "dump cooking" method and have up more than 450 recipes. *Average main: $12 408 W. Rosemary St., Downtown 919/942–5837 www.mamadips.com.*

3

## WHERE TO STAY

*Hotel reviews have been abbreviated in this book. For expanded reviews, please go to Fodors.com.*

$ HOTEL **Aloft Chapel Hill.** Self-conscious about its cool but still a lot of fun, this hip hotel has intentionally sparse rooms that are all furnished with a desk, mini couch and plain white bed. **Pros:** good value for an expensive area; unique hotel experience; enthusiastic staff. **Cons:** the no-frills approach and youthful vibe might not go over well with those seeking luxury; not in walking distance to the university. *Rooms from: $129 1001 S. Hamilton Rd., Downtown 919/932–7772 www.alofthotels.com/chapelhill 130 rooms No meals.*

$$$$ B&B/INN ★ **Fearrington House Country Inn.** The crown jewel of Fearrington Village, this inn sits on a 200-year-old farm that has been remade to resemble a country hamlet. **Pros:** a country inn with up-to-date luxuries; surrounded by plenty of shops and restaurants; fantastic breakfast. **Cons:** visitors may mind the 15-minute drive to the center of Chapel Hill, and it might be too quiet for some; very expensive. *Rooms from: $299 2000 Fearrington Village Center, Pittsboro 919/542–2121 www.fearringtonhouse.com 19 rooms, 13 suites Breakfast.*

$$ HOTEL Fodor's Choice ★ **The Franklin Hotel.** Guests come to this boutique hotel, which is just minutes from the UNC campus, to be pampered. **Pros:** great location, luxurious amenities and friendly staff make stays memorable; cook-to-order breakfast. **Cons:** Franklin Street can get noisy when the campus is buzzing with students; no pool; reservations are scarce during busy times. *Rooms from: $189 311 W. Franklin St., University 919/442–9000 www.franklinhotelnc.com 60 rooms, 7 suites Breakfast.*

$$ HOTEL **Siena Hotel.** Experience a taste of Italy at this fanciful and friendly hotel, where the lobby and rooms are filled with imported carved-wood furniture, fabrics, and artwork that conjure up the Renaissance. **Pros:** the setting is elegant and close to shopping at Eastgate Mall; friendly staff are extremely helpful; great restaurant. **Cons:** not within walking distance to downtown; furnishings in some rooms feel a little dated. *Rooms from: $169 1505 E. Franklin St., North Metro 919/929–4000, 800/223–7379 www.sienahotel.com 67 rooms, 12 suites No meals.*

CLOSE UP

## Piedmont Gardens

Exploring the gorgeous gardens in North Carolina's Piedmont is a year-round pleasure. For starters, there are lots of them, and they are diverse in size, style, and plant life. Many offer the charm of surprise, as they can be found in little-known or unlikely places. From April until the first frost in November, for example, wildflowers offer dazzling bursts of color along the roadsides. Here's a sample of the state's standouts:

**Asheboro:**

**North Carolina Zoo.** In the Uwharrie Mountains are the city of Asheboro and its North Carolina Zoo, home not just to creatures great and small, but also botanicals from the Arctic to the tropics. ✉ *4401 Zoo Pkwy., Asheboro* ☎ *336/879–7000, 800/488–0444* 🌐 *www.nczoo.org.*

**Belmont:**

**Daniel Stowe Botanical Garden.** This bright garden is known for its painterly display of colors in a vast perennial garden, wildflower meadow, Canal Garden, an orchid conservatory, and other themed areas. ✉ *6500 S. New Hope Rd., 20 miles west of downtown Charlotte* ☎ *704/825–4490* 🌐 *www.dsbg.org.*

**Charlotte:**

**Wing Haven Garden & Bird Sanctuary.** Set in one of the city's most exclusive neighborhoods, this four-acre garden is a serene environment for feathered visitors and others. ✉ *248 Ridgewood Ave.* ☎ *704/331–0664* 🌐 *www.winghavengardens.com.*

**Fayetteville:**

**Cape Fear Botanical Garden.** Spanning 79 acres at the confluence of the Cape Fear River and Cross Creek, these gardens boast 2,000 varieties of ornamental plants, an old-growth forest, a heritage garden, and separate gardens dedicated to daylilies, camellias, and hostas. ✉ *536 N. Eastern Blvd., 45 miles east of Aberdeen* ☎ *910/486–0221* 🌐 *www.capefearbg.org.*

Wildflower bloom in the Piedmont.

**Greensboro:**

**Bicentennial Gardens & Bog Garden.** Sandwiched between two busy roads, the Bicentennial Gardens & Bog Garden flourish almost despite themselves. The garden beds are carefully tended, especially compared to the nearby bog, whose natural setting includes wooden walkways over water and wetlands. ✉ *Hobbs Rd. and Starmount Farms Dr.* ☎ *336/373–2199* 🌐 *www.greensborobeautiful.org.*

**Raleigh:**

**JC Raulston Arboretum at North Carolina State University.** The university's working, research, and teaching garden holds the most diverse collection of hardy temperate-zone plants in the southeastern United States, a white garden, and a 450-foot-long perennial border. ✉ *4415 Beryl Rd.* ☎ *919/515–3132* 🌐 *www.ncsu.edu/jcraulstonarboretu.*

## NIGHTLIFE AND THE ARTS

### THE ARTS

**Dean E. Smith Center.** Basketball games as well as concerts and other special events are hosted here. ✉ *300 Skipper Bowles Dr., University* ☎ *919/962–2296, 800/722–4335* 🌐 *www.goheels.com.*

**Playmakers Repertory Company.** This professional theater company performs a variety of work, from old-time radio dramas to large-scale musicals, in the Paul Green Theatre. ✉ *250 Country Club Rd., University* ☎ *919/962–7529* 🌐 *www.playmakersrep.org.*



### NIGHTLIFE

The Chapel Hill area is a great place to hear live rock and alternative bands. Many of the best music venues are in adjacent Carrboro, while Chapel Hill's Franklin Street is the spot to create your own pub crawl. As a rule of thumb, the younger crowd heads east of Columbia Street, while the older, post-college set steers west of it.

**Cat's Cradle.** A stalwart of the club scene, this dark and funky venue hosts local and regional bands as well as nationally known indie acts. ✉ *300 E. Main St., Carrboro* ☎ *919/967–9053* 🌐 *www.catscradle.com.*

**The Crunkleton.** You'll have to "join" this classy bar—technically a private club—before you get the pleasure of drinking in it. But don't worry, it's more than worth the $5. A mix of students and locals come for the wine, beer, and more than 300 distilled spirits, served by knowledgeable mixologists. ✉ *320 W. Franklin St., Downtown* ☎ *919/969–1125* 🌐 *www.thecrunkleton.com.*

**Southern Rail.** This crowd pleaser is a unique place for drinking and schmoozing. Set near active train tracks, the bar/restaurant/music venue is scattered throughout old train station buildings and railcars. ✉ *201-C E. Main St., Carrboro* ☎ *919/967–1967* 🌐 *www.thestationcarrboro.com.*

**West End Wine Bar.** An affluent crowd seeks out this tony bar for its comprehensive wine list (more than 50 by the glass), tapas menu, and rooftop patio. Downstairs, the speakeasy-style Cellar has two pool tables and beers on tap. ✉ *450 W. Franklin St., Downtown* ☎ *919/967–7599* 🌐 *www.westendwinebar.com.*

## SPORTS AND THE OUTDOORS

### BASKETBALL

**Tar Heels.** The University of North Carolina's Tar Heels are Chapel Hill's Atlantic Coast Conference team. They play in the Dean E. Smith Student Activities Center, commonly known as the "Dean Dome." ☎ *919/962–2296, 800/722–4335* 🌐 *www.goheels.com.*

### GOLF

**UNC Finley Golf Course.** This public golf course was designed by golf legend Tom Fazio, who gave the links wide fairways and fast greens. ✉ *Finley Golf Course Rd.* ☎ *919/962–2349* 🌐 *www.goheels.com* ⛳ *18 holes. 6231 yds. Par 72. Green Fee: $46–$68.* ☞ *Facilities: Driving range, putting green, golf carts, pro shop, golf academy/lessons, restaurant.*

### SHOPPING

#### SHOPPING CENTERS

**Eastgate Shopping Center.** Minutes from downtown, this lively collection of shops offers everything from antiques to wine. ✉ *1800 E. Franklin St., at U.S. 15/501 bypass, North Metro* 🌐 *www.shoppingeastgate.com.*

**Fearrington Village.** Nestled in the countryside 8 miles south of Chapel Hill on U.S. 15/501, this Pittsboro-based complex has upscale shops selling art, garden items, handmade jewelry, and more. Shoppers can also relax in a spa or one of the center's several restaurants. ✉ *2000 Fearrington Village Center, Pittsboro* ☎ *919/542–4000* 🌐 *www.fearrington.com.*

#### BOOKS

**McIntyre's Books.** You can read by the fire in one of this little shop's cozy rooms. The independent bookstore has a big selection of mysteries, as well as gardening and cookbooks. It also hosts weekly readings. ✉ *Fearrington Village, 2000 Fearrington Village Center, Pittsboro* ☎ *919/542–3030* 🌐 *www.fearrington.com/village/mcintyres.asp.*

#### FOOD

**A Southern Season.** A Southern Season stocks a dazzling variety of items for the kitchen, from classic recipe books to the latest gadgets. Many of the foods, such as barbecue sauces, peanuts, and hams, are regional specialties. Custom gift baskets can be sent anywhere in the world. ✉ *Eastgate Shopping Center, 201 S. Estes Dr., North Metro* ☎ *919/929–7133, 800/253–3663* 🌐 *www.southernseason.com.*

## THE TRIAD: GREENSBORO, WINSTON-SALEM, AND HIGH POINT

They may be neighbors, but the cities of the Triad are each very distinct. Greensboro, to the east, is a business and cultural hub with a varied, youthful, and surprisingly alternative art scene. Winston-Salem, to the west, is calmer, smaller, and steeped in the past, with two historic villages still preserved for visitors. To the south is Highpoint, which is off most visitors' radar, unless they're headed to one of its museums or involved in the furniture industry. It's home to the largest furniture trade show in the world.

## GREENSBORO

*96 miles northeast of Charlotte; 26 miles east of Winston-Salem; 58 miles west of Durham.*

With its aging brick buildings and outer ring of small-city sprawl, Greensboro might not seem all that romantic at first. But let it grow on you. There's an energy here, an excitement, a feeling of possibility created by a constant influx of new residents, which include college students, businesspeople, and immigrants from around the world. This mixture of new folks and natives makes this unassuming city diverse in pretty much every aspect of daily life. For a night out, choose between an edgy play, live music, or a second-run movie at the super-cheap

cinema outside of town. You can also have your pick of fried chicken, foie gras, or pho. Though Greensboro is best known for its textile industry, now mostly gone, and its role in the fight for civil rights (the famous lunch counter sit-ins of the mid-sixties started here, after all), this place is creating a brand-new face. To watch this funky work in progress, take an early-evening stroll along South Elm Street, which has housed the city's creative mojo for years. You'll find everything from vintage stores to bubble tea. Things are always evolving in this section of town. With any luck, that represents the future of the city as a whole.

#### GETTING HERE AND AROUND

Interstates 40 and 85 diverge just to the northeast of Greensboro, which means getting here is easy. Navigating the city is easy, too, especially in the booming and walkable downtown.

#### ESSENTIALS

**Visitor Information Greensboro Area Convention and Visitors Bureau** ✉ *2200 Pinecroft Rd., Suite 200* ☎ *336/274–2282* 🌐 *www.greensboronc.org.*

## EXPLORING

### TOP ATTRACTIONS

★ **Elsewhere Artist Collaborative.** Set inside a former thrift store, this Greensboro original—a combination art museum, studio, and school—brings complete sensory overload via an astounding explosion of art and artifacts collected over several decades by its former owner, Sylvia Gray. When the store was in business, Gray sold hardly anything, but that didn't keep her from constantly expanding her vast collection (or hoard, you could say) of whatnots and thingamajigs. These days, a colorful cast of resident artists creates new work from this musty treasure trove. Expect colorful plumes of fabric hanging from the walls and toys, books, jewelry, and so much more stuffed into every corner of this large space. You can't buy anything here, but you can touch it all. **TIP→ A great time to see Elsewhere is during First Friday, when galleries and shops throughout downtown host an open house and art walk. Check out the scene every first Friday of the month, 6–9 pm.** ✉ *606 S. Elm St., Downtown* 🌐 *www.goelsewhere.org* 🎟 *$1* 🕒 *Mar.–Nov., Wed.–Sat. 1–10.*

**The Greensboro Children's Museum.** The exhibits at this fun museum are designed for children under 12, who can tour an airplane cockpit, explore a fire truck or police car, scale a climbing wall, create crafts out of recycled materials, or learn about buildings in the construction zone. **TIP→** Admission is reduced to $4 Friday 5–8 pm. ✉ *220 N. Church St., Downtown* ☎ *336/574–2898* 🌐 *www.gcmuseum.com* *$8* *Tues.–Thurs. and Sat. 9–5, Fri. 9–8, Sun. 1–5.*

## O. HENRY

It's easy to overlook a three-piece sculpture celebrating writer O. Henry. Before adopting his pen name, William Sydney Porter spent his youth in Greensboro. The life-size sculpture, on the corner of North Elm and Bellemeade streets, depicts the writer, his faithful dog, and a huge bronze book revealing some of his most famous characters.

★ **The International Civil Rights Center and Museum.** With an unflinching eye, this new museum documents the beauty and horror of America's civil rights movement of the 1960s. The star attraction is the actual Woolworth lunch counter where countless African Americans staged sit-ins to protest segregation for more than six months in 1960. A guided tour shows viewers how this act of defiance spread to more than 50 cities throughout the South and helped finally bring segregation to an end. Other exhibits uncover the brutality of America's racism throughout the South. ⚠ Many of the museum's graphic images of historical violence may be too intense for young eyes. Even adults should prepare themselves. ✉ *134 S. Elm St., Downtown* ☎ *336/274–9199* 🌐 *www.sitinmovement.org* *$10* *Oct.–Mar., Tues.–Sat. 10–6, Sun. 1–5; Apr.–Sept., Tues.–Thurs. 9–6, Fri. and Sat. 9–7, Sun. 1–6.*

**Natural Science Center of Greensboro.** You can roam through a room filled with dinosaurs, learn about gems and minerals, and see the lemurs and other creatures at this kid-friendly museum. A planetarium, a petting zoo, and a reptile and amphibian house are on the premises. Animal Discovery, a 22-acre science museum and zoological garden, is also here. ✉ *4301 Lawndale Dr., Northwest Metro* ☎ *336/288–3769* 🌐 *www.natsci.org* *Center $8, planetarium $3–$5* *Daily 9–5. Animal Discovery daily 10–4.*

**Old Greensborough.** Elm Street, with its turn-of-the-20th-century architecture, is the heart of this appealing district. Listed on the National Register of Historic Places, it has become one of Greensboro's most vibrant areas, with lively galleries, trendy nightspots, and interesting boutiques and antiques shops. "Friday After Five" brings weekly live music to the district in summer. **TIP→** There's Wi-Fi access throughout the area. ✉ *Elm St. between Market and Lee Sts., Downtown* 🌐 *www.downtowngreensboro.net.*

### WORTH NOTING

**The Blandwood Mansion.** The elegent home of former governor John Motley Morehead is considered the prototype of the Italian-villa architecture that swept the country during the mid-19th century. Noted architect Alexander Jackson Davis designed the house, which has a stucco exterior and towers and still contains many of its original furnishings. ✉ 447

*W. Washington St., Downtown* ☎ *336/272–5003* 🌐 *www.blandwood.org* 🎟 *$8* 🕒 *Tours Tues.–Sat. 11–4, Sun. 2–5.*

**Greensboro Cultural Center.** Home to the offices of more than a dozen art, dance, music, and theater organizations, the cultural center also has several art galleries, a studio theater, an outdoor amphitheater, a sculpture garden, and a restaurant with outdoor seating. ✉ *200 N. Davie St., Downtown* ☎ *336/373–7523* 🌐 *www.greensboro-nc.gov.*

ArtQuest. This hands-on art gallery for children was the first of its kind in the state. ✉ *200 N. Davies St.* ☎ *336/333–7460* 🌐 *www.greenhillcenter.org.*

**Greensboro Historical Museum.** Set in a Romanesque-style church dating from 1892, the museum has displays about the city's own O. Henry and Dolley Madison. There's also an exploration of the Woolworth sit-in, which launched the civil rights movement's struggle to desegregate eating establishments. Permanent exhibits include collections of Confederate weapons and Jugtown pottery. Behind the museum are the graves of several Revolutionary War soldiers. ✉ *130 Summit Ave., Downtown* ☎ *336/373–2043* 🌐 *www.greensborohistory.org* 🎟 *Free* 🕒 *Tues.–Sat. 10–5, Sun. 2–5.*

**Guilford Courthouse National Military Park.** Established in 1917, the park has more than 200 acres with wooded hiking trails. It memorializes one of the earliest events in the area's recorded history and a pivotal moment in the life of the colonies. On March 15, 1781, the Battle of Guilford Courthouse so weakened British troops that they surrendered seven months later at Yorktown. ✉ *2332 New Garden Rd., Northwest Metro* ☎ *336/288–1776* 🌐 *www.nps.gov/guco* 🎟 *Free* 🕒 *Daily 8:30–5.*

**Colonial Heritage Center.** Situated near Guilford Courthouse National Military Park, this historic park draws you into the life of early settlers with a hands-on approach to history. Among the buildings you'll find here is the restored 19th-century Hoskins House. The center has one of the country's most outstanding collections of original colonial settlement maps. ✉ *2200 New Garden Rd., Northwest Metro* ☎ *336/545–5315* 🎟 *Free* 🕒 *Fri.–Sun. 8:30–5.*

**Weatherspoon Art Museum.** Set on the campus of North Carolina at Greensboro, the museum consists of six galleries and a sculpture garden. It's known for its permanent collection, which includes lithographs and bronzes by Henri Matisse, and for its changing exhibitions of 20th-century American art. ✉ *Tate and Spring Garden Sts., University* ☎ *336/334–4110* 🌐 *weatherspoon.uncg.edu* 🎟 *Free* 🕒 *Tues., Wed., and Fri. 10–5; Thurs. 10–9; weekends 1–5.*

## WHERE TO EAT

$$$ AMERICAN

**Liberty Oak Restaurant & Bar.** Situated in the middle of one of Greensboro's most pleasant areas, this inviting eatery serves upscale food in non-stuffy surroundings. The constantly shifting menu always includes an array of seafood, steaks, pasta and vegetarian dishes. Be sure to check out the restaurant's full bar, which has a wide selection of international beers, and its Sunday brunch. $ *Average main: $23*

*✉ 100-D W. Washington St., Downtown ☎ 336/273–7057 🌐 www.libertyoakrestaurant.com.*

$$$$ ITALIAN **✕ Nico's.** Head to this upscale, centrally located spot for stellar Southern Italian. With its walls of windows, a chic bar, and servers who exude urban elegance, Nico's has all the trappings of an upscale restaurant. But it's really the food that matters. While the menu changes with the seasons, you can always expect Southern Italian favorites bursting with fresh ingredients and complex flavors. Handmade tortellini with prosciutto and cream sauce is a year-round favorite. Most of the pasta, some of the cheese, and all of the desserts are made in-house—and the owner, Nico Scavone, might tell you so himself. The Italian-born chef sometimes comes by to chat with customers during dinner hours. *$ Average main: $28 ✉ 201 N. Elm St., Suite 105, Downtown ☎ 336/285–9866 🌐 www.nicosrestaurantandbar.com ⏲ Closed Sun. No lunch Sat.*

$ ASIAN **✕ Pho Hien Vuong.** Don't be fooled by the unassuming appearance of this storefront restaurant, decorated with a few items that speak to the owners' Vietnamese and Thai ancestry. There's nothing unassuming about the food. The flavors and textures of the dishes are excellent, permeating everything from the fabulous *pho* to the vegetable curry to the sliced grilled pork. If you want the food to have extra kick, request it "hot." *$ Average main: $9 ✉ 4109-A Spring Garden St., Coliseum ☎ 336/294–5551.*

$$$$ AMERICAN Fodor's Choice ★ **✕ Table 16.** This magnificent little restaurant is one of the best parts of Greensboro's ever-expanding downtown. The menu changes every month to adapt to seasonal produce, and locally grown ingredients are used whenever possible. The modern menu features plenty of meats and seafood, but there's always a vegetarian selection as well. Some past offerings have included roasted duck served with black mission fig, basmati rice with parsley, and a molasses vinaigrette; and molten chocolate ganache cake, accompanied by raspberry mousse and chantilly cream. Though pricey, the dishes are worth every bite, and the extra-attentive staff help make every meal feel special. It's a good idea to call for a reservation on weekends and holidays as this place is in demand. *$ Average main: $28 ✉ 600 S. Elm St., Downtown ☎ 336/279–8525 🌐 www.table16restaurant.com ⏲ Closed Sun. and Mon. No lunch.*

## WHERE TO STAY

*Hotel reviews have been abbreviated in this book. For expanded reviews, please go to Fodors.com.*

$ HOTEL **Biltmore Greensboro Hotel.** In the heart of the central business district, this historic spot has an old-world, slightly faded feel, with 16-foot ceilings, a cage elevator, and a lobby with walnut-panel walls and a fireplace. **Pros:** fans of old hotels will find the setting appealing; great downtown location; one of the best values in town. **Cons:** not very modern; small bathrooms; breakfast is Continental only. ■ **TIP→** Dogs of any size are welcome. For a set fee, pooches get a bed to use and a treat and toy to take home. *$ Rooms from: $99 ✉ 111 W. Washington St., Downtown ☎ 336/272–3474, 800/332–0303 🌐 www.thebiltmoregreensboro.com 24 rooms, 2 suites 🍴 Breakfast.*

$$$$ HOTEL Fodor's Choice ★ **O. Henry Hotel.** This boutique hotel, named for the renowned author who grew up in Greensboro, was constructed in the late 1990s but evokes turn-of-the-20th-century charm; expect lots of wood paneling, leather sofas, mohair club chairs, and an extremely friendly staff. **Pros:** nostalgic setting with modern comforts; in walking distance to the popular Friendly Shopping Center; free airport shuttle (often in a checkered cab or London taxi, no less). **Cons:** some rooms have views of unattractive commercial properties, so ask for a scenic view if you want one; not in walking distance from Greensboro's city center; expensive. *Rooms from: $269 624 Green Valley Rd., Friendly 336/854–2000, 800/965–8259 www.ohenryhotel.com 121 rooms, 10 suites Breakfast.*

$$$$ HOTEL ★ **Proximity Hotel.** With its high ceilings, big windows, and exposed beams, this environmentally friendly place makes you feel like you're in the future—or perhaps just a bigger city than Greensboro. **Pros:** a "green" hotel that blends luxury and urban cool; free airport shuttle. **Cons:** the super-sleek interior isn't for everyone; outside the city center; expensive. *Rooms from: $259 704 Green Valley Rd., Friendly 336/379–8200 www.proximityhotel.com 147 rooms No meals.*

$ HOTEL **Sheraton Greensboro Hotel at Four Seasons.** It's no surprise that business travelers dominate this place, as it's adjacent to the convention center. **Pros:** lots to do without ever leaving the hotel mall complex; the big rooms have a lot of amenities due to business clientele. **Cons:** hotel is geared to conventioneers, so individuals seeking a quiet getaway may feel overwhelmed by large crowds; it's easy to get lost in the massive parking lot; not in walking distance to downtown. *Rooms from: $145 3121 High Point Rd., Coliseum 336/292–9161, 800/242–6556 www.sheratongreensboro.com 910 rooms, 80 suites No meals.*

## NIGHTLIFE AND THE ARTS

### THE ARTS

**Broach Theatre.** Now more than a quarter century old, this playhouse stages six professional shows each year in the Old Greensborough historic district. Little-known comedy gems are its specialty. *520-C S. Elm St., Downtown 336/333–7469 www.broachtheatre.org.*

**Carolina Theatre.** What opened in 1927 as a vaudeville theater has matured and diversified over the years. It now serves as one of the city's principal performing-arts centers, showcasing dance, music, films, and plays. *310 S. Greene St., Downtown 336/333–2605 www.carolinatheatre.com.*

**Eastern Music Festival.** The Eastern Music Festival, whose guests have included Billy Joel, André Watts, and Wynton Marsalis, brings a month of more than four dozen classical-music concerts to Greensboro's Guilford College and music venues throughout the city. It starts in late June. *200 N. Davie St., Downtown 336/333–7450, 877/833–6753 www.easternmusicfestival.org.*

**Greensboro Coliseum Complex.** The vast Greensboro Coliseum Complex hosts arts and entertainment events throughout the year, including the Central Carolina Fair as well as roller derby. And the Greensboro Symphony and the Greensboro Opera Company perform here. ✉ *1921 W. Lee St.* ☎ *336/373–7474* 🌐 *www.greensborocoliseum.com.*

**Triad Stage.** In the heart of town, this professional theater company mixes classic and original plays. ✉ *232 S. Elm St., Downtown* ☎ *336/274–0067* 🌐 *www.triadstage.org.*

### NIGHTLIFE

**Blind Tiger.** A Greensboro institution, this is one of the best places in the Triad to hear live music. Previous headliners have included Ben Folds Five (their first show, no less) and members of the Neville Brothers. ✉ *1819 Spring Garden St., Coliseum* ☎ *336/272–9888* 🌐 *www.theblindtiger.com.*

**Natty Greene's Pub & Brewing Company.** Located on lively South Elm Street, this tavern has 10 of its own beers on tap, from a pale ale to a stout. The food is typical bar food, but the potato chips are made in-house. Upstairs is a sports bar with pool tables. In nice weather, you can sit on the patio. ✉ *345 S. Elm St., Downtown* ☎ *336/274–1373* 🌐 *www.nattygreenes.com.*

## SPORTS AND THE OUTDOORS

### GOLF

**Bryan Park & Golf Club.** These two public courses, 6 miles north of Greensboro, have 36 holes of great golf. The Players Course, designed by Rees Jones in 1988, features 79 bunkers and eight water hazards. Jones outdid himself on the lovely 1990 Champions Course, in which seven holes hug Lake Townsend. ✉ *6275 Bryan Park Rd., Browns Summit* ☎ *336/375–2200* 🌐 *www.bryanpark.com* 🏌 *2 18-hole courses. Players: 7057 yds. Champions: 7255 yds. Players: Par 72. Champions: Par 72. Green Fee: $36–$59.* ☞ *Facilities: Driving range, golf carts, pro shop, golf academy/lessons, restaurant.*

**Grandover Resort & Conference Center.** Greensboro's only resort hotel tempts you with 36 holes on the East and West courses, designed by golf architects David Graham and Gary Panks. Golf packages are available; the deluxe package includes dinner for two at the resort's Di Valletta Restaurant. The resort is parallel to Interstate 85, but it's set so deep into 1,500 acres that you'll never think about the traffic. ✉ *1000 Club Rd.* ☎ *336/294–1800* 🌐 *www.grandoverresort.com* 🏌 *2 18-hole courses. East: 7100 yds. West: 6800 yds. East: Par 72. West: Par 72. Green Fee: $61–$69.* ☞ *Facilities: Driving range, putting green, golf carts, rental clubs, pro shop, golf academy/lessons, restaurant, bar.*

**Greensboro National Golf Club.** The clubhouse is known for its hot dogs, so you know this course lacks the pretense of others in the area. Called "a golf course for guys who like golf courses," the Don-and-Mark-Charles-designed public links feature wide fairways, expansive greens, and layouts that are challenging without resorting to blind spots and other trickery. ✉ *330 Niblick Dr., Summerfield* ☎ *336/342–1113* 🌐 *www.greensboronatl.com* 🏌 *18 holes. 6261 yds. Par 72. Green Fee: $35–$47.* ☞ *Facilities: Driving range, golf carts, pro shop, golf academy/lessons, restaurant, bar.*

Costumed guides lead tours at Old Salem Museum & Gardens, a living history museum.

### SHOPPING

**Replacements, Ltd.** Located between Greensboro and Burlington, this is the world's largest seller of discontinued and active china, crystal, flatware, and collectibles. It stocks more than 12 million pieces in 286,000 patterns. The cavernous showroom is open 9 to 7 daily, and free tours begin every half hour between 9:30 and 6:30. ✉ *I–85/I–40 at Mt. Hope Church Rd., Exit 132* ☎ *800/737–5223* 🌐 *www.replacements.com*.

## WINSTON-SALEM

*26 miles west of Greensboro; 81 miles north of Charlotte.*

Even in the heart of downtown, there's something not entirely modern about Winston-Salem. And that's a good thing. The second-largest city in the Triad blends the past and the present nicely, creating a pleasant and low-key place for both history-minded tourists and nose-to-the-grindstone businesspeople.

Two historical areas—Old Salem and Bethabara—celebrate the hardworking members of the Moravian Church, a Protestant sect that arose in what's now the Czech Republic in the 15th century. For nearly a hundred years, starting in the mid–18th century, the Winston-Salem region was almost entirely populated by Moravian settlers. With its Colonial Williamsburg–like period reconstruction (and tasty, tasty cookies), Old Salem in particular shouldn't be missed, even if you have only an afternoon to spend here.

For a taste of present-day Winston-Salem, check out the Downtown Arts District, centered around the intersection of 6th and Trade streets. Once known for its bustling tobacco market, this area is now a sea of happening galleries.

With two impressive art museums, a symphony orchestra, a film festival, and the internationally respected North Carolina School of the Arts, there's plenty to do within the city limits.

### GETTING HERE AND AROUND

Easily accessed by Interstate 40, Winston-Salem is laid out in an orderly grid. Parts of the city are great for walking, especially Old Salem and the neighborhoods surrounding it. Parking near most sights is not a problem.

### TOBACCO BARNS

As you're driving through the Piedmont, you'll notice two-story wood structures in various states of disrepair. The differences in architecture are subtle, but fascinating: a wide tin awning, a small overhang, a roof patched together as abstract art. These are tobacco barns, where tobacco was hung to be cured. Although most have been left to fall apart, some have been transformed into workshops, studios, garages, and small apartments.

### ESSENTIALS

**Visitor Information Winston-Salem Convention and Visitors Bureau** ☎ *336/728–4200* ⊕ *www.visitwinstonsalem.com.*

## EXPLORING

### TOP ATTRACTIONS

**Historic Bethabara Park.** Set in a wooded 180-acre wildlife preserve, this was the site of the first Moravian settlement in North Carolina. The 1753 community—whose name means "house of passage"—was never intended to be permanent. It fell into decline after Salem's completion. You can tour restored buildings, such as the 1788 Gemeinhaus congregation house, or wander the colonial and medicinal gardens. God's Acre, the first colony cemetery, is a short walk away. Children love the reconstructed fort from the French and Indian War. Brochures for self-guided walking tours are available year-round at the visitor center. ✉ *2147 Bethabara Rd., University* ☎ *336/924–8191* ⊕ *www.bethabarapark.org* *$4* ⊙ *Apr.–Dec., Tues.–Fri. 10:30–4:30, weekends 1:30–4:30.*

★ **Museum of Early Southern Decorative Arts.** Dedicated to the decorative arts of the early South, this unique museum has twelve galleries that showcase the furniture, painting, ceramics, and metalware used through 1820. The bookstore carries hard-to-find books on Southern culture and history. It's on the southern edge of Old Salem. ✉ *924 S. Main St., Old Salem* ☎ *336/721–7369, 888/653–7253* ⊕ *www.mesda.org* *$21, includes admission to Old Salem Museum & Gardens* ⊙ *Tue.–Sat. 10–5, Sun. 1–5.*

Fodor's Choice ★ **Old Salem Museum & Gardens.** Founded in 1766 as a backcountry trading center, Old Salem is one of the nation's best-documented colonial sites. This living-history museum, a few blocks from downtown Winston-Salem, is filled with dozens of original and reconstructed buildings. Costumed guides explain household activities common in the late-18th and early-19th century Moravian communities. Tours include a stop by the 1861 St. Philip's Church, the state's oldest-standing African-American church. Old Salem also has a children's museum, a great bakery, and a restaurant. ■ **TIP→** Don't miss the "world's largest coffeepot," a 12-foot-tall vessel built by Julius Mickey in 1858 to advertise his tinsmith shop. After surviving two separate car collisions, it was moved to its present location at the edge of Old Salem in 1959. ✉ *600 S. Main St., Old Salem* ☎ *336/721–7300, 888/653–7253* 🌐 *www.oldsalem.org* 🎫 *$21, includes admission to Museum of Early Southern Decorative Arts* 🕐 *Tues.–Sat. 9:30–4:30, Sun. 1–4:30.*



QUICK BITES

**Winkler Bakery. No trip to the Old Salem Museum & Gardens is complete without a stop at the Winkler Bakery, where you can buy bread and their pillowy, best-selling sugar cakes baked in the traditional brick ovens. Moravian ginger cookies, paper-thin and dense with spice, are a classic treat. You can also try them dipped in chocolate.** ✉ ***525 S. Main St.*** ☎ ***336/721–7302*** 🌐 ***www.oldsalem.org/winkler-bakery.html.***

## WORTH NOTING

**Reynolda House Museum of American Art.** Katharine Smith Reynolds and her husband Richard Joshua Reynolds, founder of the R. J. Reynolds Tobacco Company, once called this house their home. The 1917 dwelling is filled with paintings, prints, and sculptures by such artists as Thomas Eakins, Frederic Church, and Georgia O'Keeffe. There's also a costume collection, as well as clothing and toys used by the Reynolds children. The museum is next to **Reynolda Village,** a collection of shops, restaurants, and gardens that fill the estate's original outer buildings. ✉ *2250 Reynolda Rd., University* ☎ *336/758–5150, 888/663–1149* 🌐 *www.reynoldahouse.org* 🎫 *$10* 🕐 *Tues.–Sat. 9:30–4:30, Sun. 1:30–4:30.*

**SciWorks.** This complex has 45,000 square feet of interactive and hands-on exhibits. There's also a 120-seat planetarium and a 15-acre environmental park with barnyard animals and paved walking trails. ✉ *100 W. Hanes Mill Rd., North Metro* ☎ *336/767–6730* 🌐 *www.sciworks.org* 🎫 *$11* 🕐 *Labor Day–May, weekdays 10–4, Sat. 11–5; June–Labor Day, Mon.–Sat. 10–5.*

**Southeastern Center for Contemporary Art.** Near the Reynolda House Museum of American Art, this museum showcases artwork by nationally and internationally known artists. ✉ *750 Marguerite Dr., University* ☎ *336/725–1904* 🌐 *www.secca.org* 🎫 *Free* 🕐 *Tue.–Sat. 10–5, Thurs. 10–8, Sun. 1–5.*

## WHERE TO EAT

$ GREEK ✕ **Grecian Corner.** In a white building with blue trim, this eatery has been dishing up gyros and chicken and pork souvlakia since 1970. Patrons, including workers at the nearby hospital and local families, appreciate the friendly service and ample portions of moussaka, spanakopita, and salads, plus more-familiar fare like hamburgers and pizza. The wine list includes Greek reds and whites. [$] *Average main: $8* ✉ *101 Eden Terr., Downtown* ☎ *336/722–6937* 🌐 *www.greciancorner.com* 💳 *No credit cards* 🕐 *Closed Sun.*

$$$$ SOUTHERN ★ **Noble's Grille.** New Southern flavors with European accents are the key to the menu here. Typical entrées, grilled or roasted over an oak-and-hickory fire, include pan-seared filet mignon, and Pamlico Sound shrimp and grits with bacon. The dining room, with tall windows and track lighting, has a view of the grill. *Average main: $25 ✉ 380 Knollwood St., Thruway ☎ 336/777–8477 www.noblesgrille.com Closed Sun. No lunch Sat.*

$$ AMERICAN **The Tavern in Old Salem.** Now under new owners, this landmark has two very distinct personalities. By day, costumed staff serve dishes that hark back to Moravian times. By night, it morphs into something fancier, with staff wearing black aprons and serving contemporary fare to candle-lit tables. While this is a big change for the historic spot, much of its past remains: the trademark chicken pies and gingerbread with lemon ice cream are still on the menu. Extra touches at this family-run establishment include desserts and breads made from scratch. *Average main: $19 ✉ 736 S. Main St., Old Salem ☎ 336/748–8585 www.thetaverninoldsalem.ws Closed Mon. No dinner Sun.*

## WHERE TO STAY

*Hotel reviews have been abbreviated in this book. For expanded reviews, please go to Fodors.com.*

$ B&B/INN ★ **Augustus T. Zevely Inn.** The only lodging in this historic part of town and the sole B&B in all of Winston-Salem, the Zevely has made a name for itself as a romantic getaway. **Pros:** only lodging in Old Salem; guests get a strong sense of history here; despite the old-time setting, the inn has modern conveniences like TVs and free Wi-Fi. **Cons:** awfully quiet at night. *Rooms from: $100 ✉ 803 S. Main St., Old Salem ☎ 336/748–9299, 800/928–9299 www.winston-salem-inn.com 11 rooms, 1 suite Breakfast.*

$ HOTEL ★ **Brookstown Inn.** No two rooms are the same in this historic, affordable, and very pleasant lodging, a former textile mill built in 1837. **Pros:** historic setting is unique; walking distance to Old Salem; nice extras. **Cons:** not as posh as newer hotels; some rooms have dim lighting; families might miss having a pool, especially in the sweltering summer. *Rooms from: $95 ✉ 200 Brookstown Ave., Old Salem ☎ 336/725–1120, 800/845–4262 www.brookstowninn.com 40 rooms, 30 suites Breakfast.*

$$ HOTEL **Marriott Winston-Salem.** This central and reliable chain is part of Twin City Quarter, a shopping and dining area in downtown Winston-Salem. **Pros:** it's an easy walk to the arts district and jazz clubs; pool comes in handy on hot days; weekend rates are a good deal. **Cons:** not overly luxurious; standard chain-hotel experience. *Rooms from: $199 ✉ 425 N. Cherry St., Downtown ☎ 336/725–3500, 877/888–9762 www.marriott.com 309 rooms, 6 suites No meals.*

## NIGHTLIFE AND THE ARTS

### THE ARTS

**Festival Stage of Winston-Salem.** The sister company of the group behind North Carolina Shakespeare Festival stages three contempory plays a year at the Hanesbrands Theatre. *✉ 209 N. Spruce St., University ☎ 336/747–1414 box office festivalstage.org.*

**National Black Theatre Festival.** Every other August, the North Carolina Black Repertory Company hosts this weeklong showcase of African-American arts, which attracts tens of thousands of people to venues all over the city. The next festival is scheduled for July 29 to August 3, 2013. ✉ *610 Coliseum Dr., University* ☎ *336/723–2266* 🌐 *www.nbtf.org.*

**Stevens Center.** Many North Carolina School of the Arts musical and dramatic performances are held at this restored 1929 movie palace. ✉ *405 W. 4th St., Downtown* ☎ *336/721–1945* 🌐 *www.uncsa.edu/stevenscenter.*



### NIGHTLIFE

**6th and Vine.** For a classy and yet quirky evening out, try this wine bar/café. Outdoor seating, North Carolina wines and frequent dance parties make this a good all-around option. ✉ *209 W. 6th St., Downtown* ☎ *336/725–5577* 🌐 *www.6thandvine.com.*

**The Garage.** Check out one of the best places to drink a beer and hear a sampling of mostly regional musicians. Expect live music about half the week. ✉ *110 W. 7th St., Downtown* ☎ *336/777–1127* 🌐 *www.the-garage.ws.*

## SPORTS AND THE OUTDOORS

### BASKETBALL

**Demon Deacons.** Winston-Salem's Atlantic Coast Conference entry plays in Lawrence Joel Veterans Memorial Coliseum. ☎ *336/758–3322, 888/758–3322* 🌐 *wakeforestsports.cstv.com.*

### GOLF

**Reynolds Park Golf Course.** This is the elder statesman of local links: a public course designed by Ellis Maples, which opened in 1940. The final hole tests any player's stamina: there's a 425-yard fairway that ends on an elevated green. ✉ *2391 Reynolds Park Rd.* ☎ *336/650–7660* 📠 *336/650–7664* ⛳ *18 holes. 6379 yds. Par 71. Green Fee: $29–$33.* ☞ *Facilities: Driving range, putting green, golf carts, rental clubs, pro shop, golf academy/lessons.*

**Tanglewood Park Golf Club.** In addition to Tanglewood Park's Reynolds Course, there's the Championship Course, which was long home to the Vantage Championship. Both courses were designed by Robert Trent Jones in the mid-'50s, and both feature pine lined fairways (narrower on the Reynolds course) and lakes that come into play several times. ✉ *U.S. 158 off I–40, Clemmons* ☎ *336/778–6320* 🌐 *www.tanglewoodpark.org* ⛳ *3 18-hole courses. Reynolds: 6086 yds. Championship: 6637 yds. Reynolds: Par 72. Championship: Par 72. Green Fee: $26–$48.* ☞ *Facilities: 2 driving ranges, golf carts, rental clubs, pro shop, golf academy/lessons, restaurant, bar.*

## SHOPPING

### CRAFTS

**Piedmont Craftsmen's Shop & Gallery.** Contemporary and traditional works from more than 350 craftspeople fill this gallery/shop, located in Winston-Salem's arty hub. The organization has held an annual fair in November since the 1960s. ✉ *601 N. Trade St., Downtown* ☎ *336/725–1516* 🌐 *www.piedmontcraftsmen.org* ⏲ *Closed Sun. and Mon.*

Don't miss the World's Largest Chest of Drawers in High Point, a city known for its superlative furniture.

OFF THE BEATEN PATH

**Bob Timberlake Gallery.** North Carolina's most successful artist is best known for his landscapes of the rural South, especially his native Lexington. Many of his original paintings, done in a highly detailed "American Realist" style, are exhibited in this gallery about 20 miles from Winston-Salem. You'll also find his personal collections of canoes, decoys, and quilts. ✉ *1714 E. Center St. Extension, Exit 94 off I–85, Lexington* ☎ *800/244–0095* 🌐 *www.bobtimberlake.com* 🎫 *Free* ⏲ *Tues.–Sat. 10–5.*

## HIGH POINT

*18 miles southeast of Winston-Salem; 76 miles northeast of Charlotte; 20 miles southwest of Greensboro.*

High Point earned its name through simple geography: it was the highest point on the railroad line between Goldsboro and Charlotte. Nowadays the city's "high point" is hosting the semi-annual High Point Market, the largest wholesale furniture trade show in the world. Each spring and fall for about a week, so many people flood the town that its population of 104,000 nearly doubles. The rest of the year, the city can be pretty sleepy. Note that High Point does not have that many memorable restaurants. For more varied eats, check out nearby Greensboro or Winston-Salem.

### GETTING HERE AND AROUND

High Point is one of the Piedmont's smaller cities, with very little traffic. Navigating it by car is fairly simple, and if you happen to get turned around, friendly folks are ready to offer help with directions

## ESSENTIALS

**Visitor Information High Point Convention and Visitors Bureau** ✉ *300 S. Main St.* ☎ *336/884–5255* 🌐 *www.highpoint.org.*

## EXPLORING

**High Point Museum & Historical Park.** You can wander through the 1786 Haley House and the 1801 Hoggatt House, where rotating exhibits highlight Piedmont history and Quaker heritage with local artifacts. Tours of the buildings, conducted by costumed staff, are available on Saturday. Ever wonder about candle-dipping and writing with a quill? You can try these and other activities during the museum's monthly living-history events. ✉ *1859 E. Lexington Ave.* ☎ *336/885–1859* 🌐 *www.highpointmuseum.org* 🎟 *Free* ⏲ *Museum Wed.–Sat. 10–4:30, park Sat. 10–4.*

**Mendenhall Plantation.** A well-preserved example of 19th-century domestic architecture, this park lies a few miles northwest of High Point. As Quakers, the Mendenhalls opposed slavery, and here you can find one of the few surviving false-bottom wagons, used to help slaves escape to freedom on the Underground Railroad. ■ **TIP→ Come in July, when kids can learn how to make a corn-husk doll or design a quilt square during the Village Fair.** ✉ *603 W. Main St., Jamestown* ☎ *336/454–3819* 🌐 *www.mendenhallplantation.org* 🎟 *$2* ⏲ *Tues.–Fri. 11–3, Sat. 1–4, Sun. 2–4.*

**World's Largest Chest of Drawers.** In the 1920s this building shaped like an 18th-century chest of drawers was constructed to call attention to the city's standing as the "furniture capital of the world." The 40-foot-high building, complete with a 6-foot-long pair of socks dangling from one of its drawers, remains one of the strangest sights in North Carolina to this day. It now houses the offices for the High Point Jaycees. ✉ *508 N. Hamilton St.*

## WHERE TO EAT AND STAY

$$$$ AMERICAN ✕ **Blue Water Grille.** This intimate spot is one of the best surprises in High Point's sparse culinary scene. The menu, which changes several times a year, is always full of fresh seafood dishes and other low-county favorites, often presented with an Asian flair and a bit of French influence. The ahi tuna appears in different dishes depending on the season, and it always stands out. Sauces are always made to order, as well. With its black leather chairs, soft lighing, and full bar, this is a classy pick for a date or just a nice night out on the town. $ *Average main: $25* ✉ *126 State St.* ☎ *336/886–1010* 🌐 *www.bluewatergrillenc.net* ⏲ *Closed Sun. No lunch.*

$ HOTEL 🏨 **Best Western High Point.** The central location makes this hotel a favorite with people arriving for weekend shopping trips. **Pros:** close to popular furniture shops and downtown; reasonable rates; reliable chain. **Cons:** downtown High Point is usually dead at night; the hotel's bar hours are very inconsistent; some rooms feel dated. $ *Rooms from: $107* ✉ *135 S. Main St.* ☎ *336/889–8888* 🌐 *www.bestwestern.com* *242 rooms, 10 suites* 🍴 *No meals.*

## THE ARTS

**North Carolina Shakespeare Festival.** With many shows at the High Point Theatre, this festival's professional troupe performs at least one of the Bard's plays in September and *A Christmas Carol* every December. ✉ *Spirit Center, 807 W. Ward Ave.* ☎ *336/887–3001* 🌐 *www.ncshakes.org.*

**Theatre Art Galleries.** Solo and group shows rotate through the two exhibition spaces at this gallery, in the same building as the High Point Theatre. The frequent art openings are always open to the public. ✉ *220 E. Commerce Ave.* ☎ *336/887–2137* 🌐 *www.tagart.org.*

## SPORTS AND THE OUTDOORS

### GOLF

**Oak Hollow.** The Pete Dye–designed public course makes use of its lakeside position by including peninsula greens and an island tee on its par-4 6th hole. ✉ *3400 N. Centennial St.* ☎ *336/883–3260* 🌐 *www.oakhollowgc.com* 🏌 *18 holes. 6564 yds. Par 72. Green Fee: $17–$38.* ☞ *Facilities: Driving range, golf carts, pro shop, golf academy/lessons, restaurant.*

### HIKING

**Piedmont Environmental Center.** The 376-acre Piedmont Environmental Center has 11 miles of hiking trails and a 10-mile paved greenway adjacent to City Lake Park. ✉ *1220 Penny Rd.* ☎ *336/883–8531* 🌐 *www.piedmontenvironmental.com.*

### TENNIS

**J. Brooks Reitzel Tennis Center.** Reservations are a must to play at this center, which has both clay and hard courts, indoor and outdoor. High Point has 30 additional public courts. ✉ *Oak Hollow Lake Park, 3401 N. Centennial St.* ☎ *336/883–3493.*

## SHOPPING

**Furniture Land South.** A visit to this sprawling campus, home to the biggest furniture retailer in the world, could easily take all day. With more than 1 million square feet of showroom space, the store goes far beyond an average shopping experience. Customers register with the front desk and are given tips by a Furniture Land consultant on how to maximize their visit to the massive store, which includes innumerable galleries from leading manufacturers and a discount center. Meals and refreshments are available at Starbucks Café and Furniture Land South Café, both on-site. ✉ *5635 Riverdale Dr., Jamestown* ☎ *866/436–8056* 🌐 *www.furniturelandsouth.com.*

**High Point Furniture Sales.** Deep discounts are part of the draw to this furniture store. Expect more than 150 well-known brands and some pieces offered at below manufacturer direct prices. The **Discount Furniture Warehouse & Furniture Value & Clearance Center**, at 2035 Brentwood St., is only one exit from the main store. ✉ *2000 Baker Rd.* ☎ *336/841–5664, 800/334–1875* 🌐 *www.highpointfurnituresales.com.*

# CHARLOTTE

Don't expect to hear many Southern accents in this melting pot, the biggest city in the state. Visiting Charlotte is much more of an urban experience than a down-home one, but that's all part of the fun of being in this bustling, forward-focused place. Here, local custom is not to preserve the old, but build new. While controversial, this tradition is responsible for the ultramodern feel of the city's Uptown. With little doubt, it's also why Charlotte is home to so many brand-new sports complexes, museums, and chic lofts. This lack of dwelling in the past brings people from across the country to start new lives—and also to start restaurants, galleries, and high-concept bars.



Things are always in motion here, but history lovers shouldn't despair. Bits and pieces of Charlotte's past still linger. With their antique architecture and shaded streets, neighborhoods like Dilworth and the Fourth Ward offer lovely glimpses of what once was. Other areas, like hip Plaza Midwood, are becoming a fusion of the new and old. There, historic houses have been converted into wine bars and late-night eateries.

Be aware that heavy development has created some typical urban problems throughout town. Yes, the traffic and parking can be terrible, and restaurants are packed on weekends. But don't let that scare you away from the Queen City. When visiting the Piedmont, Charlotte is not to be missed.

### GETTING HERE AND AROUND

Charlotte is a driver's town, but its light-rail system makes going sans car possible for visitors sticking to central areas. Though its route is short and limited, the LYNX blue line is clean and fast. It runs from Uptown, through the convention center, to Interstate 485. Check for routes and schedules at 🌐 *www.charmeck.org/departments/cats/lynx*.

You'll be able to walk around Uptown and the historic Fourth Ward.

### ESSENTIALS

**Visitor Information Visit Charlotte/Main Street Charlotte** ✉ *330 S. Tryon St., Uptown* ☎ *704/331–2700, 800/231–4636* 🌐 *www.charlottesgotalot.com.*

# UPTOWN CHARLOTTE

Uptown Charlotte, the city's "downtown," is ideal for walking. The city was laid out in four wards around Independence Square, at Trade and Tryon streets. The Square, as it is known, is the center of the Uptown area. In recent years, Uptown has become increasingly user-friendly, with restaurants, bars, and museums tightly packed into a small area. If you're in town for only a short while, this is the place to be.

## EXPLORING

### TOP ATTRACTIONS

**Bechtler Museum of Modern Art.** With the famed "Firebird" sculpture out front, there's no way you can miss this 2010 addition to Uptown's art scene. Covered in mirrors and colored class, Niki de Saint Phalle's 17-foot, birdlike creature is just a taste of what Bechtler has to offer, however. The rotating collection might include Warhol's pop art,

Giacometti's dark sculptures, and ceramics by Picasso. Founded by Swiss-born Andreas Bechtler, the museum highlights his family's love affair with art, as well as their deep connections with many of the artists on display. ✉ *420 S. Tryon St., Uptown* ☎ *704/353–9200* 🌐 *www.bechtler.org* 🎫 *$8* ⏲ *Wed.–Mon. 10–5, Sun. noon–5.*

★ ☺ **Discovery Place.** Allow at least two hours for the **aquariums,** the three-story **rain forest,** and the **IMAX Dome Theater.** Lie on a bed of nails, conduct experiments in the interactive labs or get in touch with your inner innovator as you create shoes from garbage. Check the schedule for special exhibits. ✉ *301 N. Tryon St., Uptown* ☎ *704/372–6261, 800/935–0553* 🌐 *www.discoveryplace.org* 🎫 *$12, $17 with IMAX* ⏲ *Weekdays 9–4, Sat. 10–6, Sun. noon–5.*

★ **Mint Museum Uptown.** With five stories and 145,000 square feet of space, this is a must-see for art lovers of all stripes visiting the city. Expect rotating special exhibits as well as permanent collections of American and contemporary work, plus craft and design. Be sure not to miss the museum's dramatic atrium, which houses a 60-foot-tall glass curtain that offers amazing views of the surrounding cityscape. ■ **TIP→ Use your ticket stub for free entrance to Mint Museum Randolph (good for two days). Admission is free at both Mint museums Tuesday 5–9 pm.** ✉ *Levine Center for the Arts, 500 S. Tryon St., Uptown* ☎ *704/337–2000* 🌐 *www.mintmuseum.org* 🎫 *$10* ⏲ *Tues.–Sat. 10–5, Sun. noon–5.*

**Fodor's Choice** ★ ☺ **NASCAR Hall of Fame.** This 150,000-square-foot mega-museum is a NASCAR lover's paradise and has enough going on to intrigue non-fans as well. A complete visual overload, the racing palace features exhibits of famous NASCAR autos, an enormous theater, and countless rotating exhibits. Best of all, the interactive exhibits allow visitors to travel through the museum as one of their favorite NASCAR heroes. ✉ *400 E. Martin Luther King Blvd., Uptown* ☎ *704/654–4400* 🌐 *www.nascarhall.com* 🎫 *$19.95* ⏲ *Daily 10–6, check website for time fluctuations.*

### WORTH NOTING

**Bank of America Corporate Center.** Architecture fans should make time for a trip to see one of the city's most striking buildings. The Cesar Pelli–designed structure rises 60 stories to a crownlike top. The main attractions are three monumental lobby frescoes by the world-renowned local painter Ben Long, whose themes are making/building, chaos/creativity, and planning/knowledge. Also in the tower are the **North Carolina Blumenthal Performing Arts Center** and the restaurants, shops, and exhibition space of **Founders Hall.** ✉ *100 N. Tryon St., Uptown.*

**Fourth Ward.** Charlotte's popular old neighborhood began as a political subsection created for electoral purposes in the mid-1800s. The architecture and sensibility of this quiet, homespun neighborhood provide a glimpse of life in a less hectic time. A brochure with 18 places of historic interest can be picked up at the Visit Charlotte visitor center, at Tryon Street and Martin Luther King Jr. Boulevard.

**Levine Museum of the New South.** With an 8,000-square-foot exhibit, "Cotton Fields to Skyscrapers: Charlotte and the Carolina Piedmont in the New South," as a jumping-off point, this museum offers

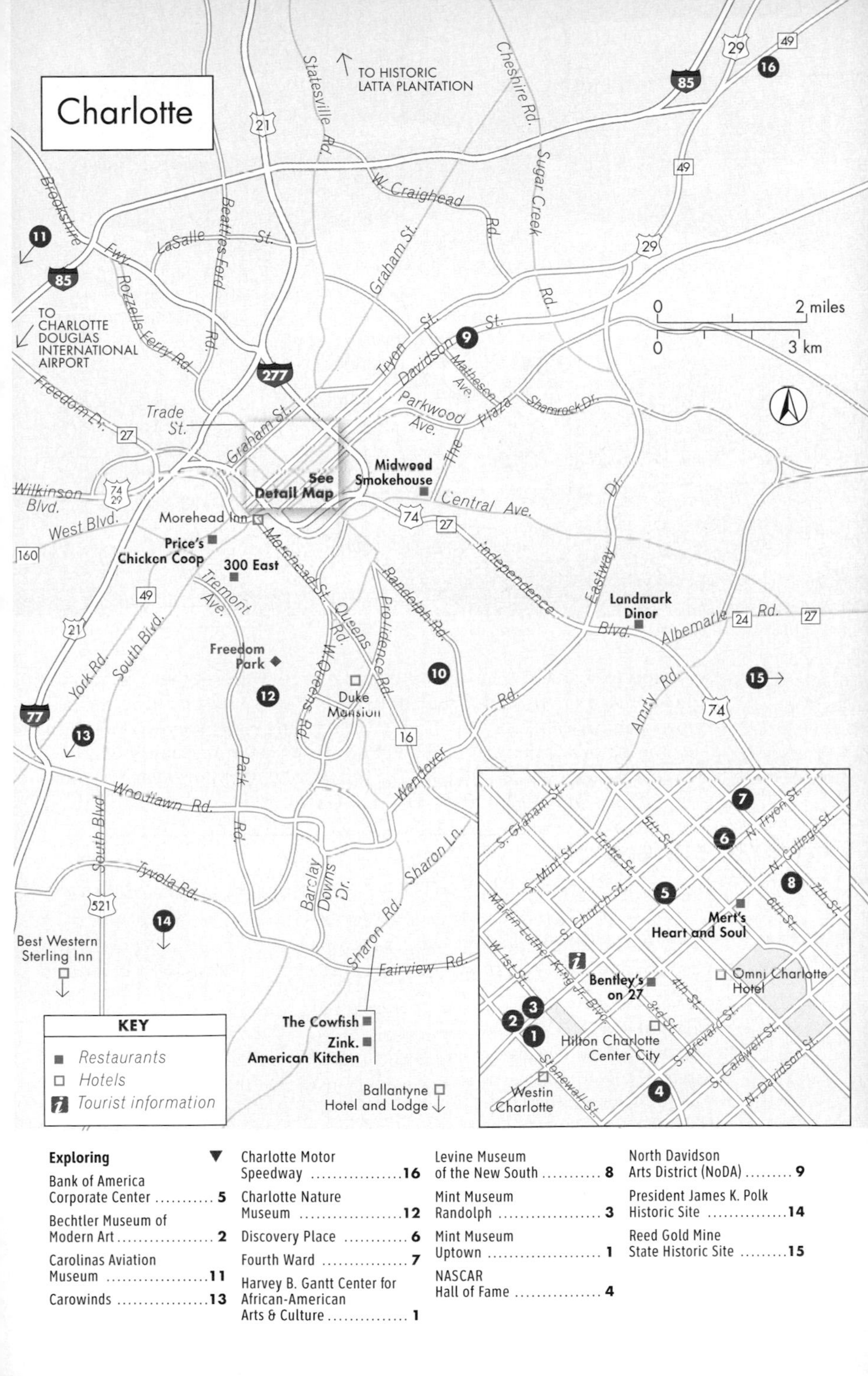

Charlotte
TO HISTORIC LATTA PLANTATION
TO CHARLOTTE DOUGLAS INTERNATIONAL AIRPORT
Statesville Rd.
Cheshire Rd.
Sugar Creek Rd.
W. Craighead Rd.
Brookshire Fwy.
LaSalle St.
Beatties Ford Rd.
Rozzells Ferry Rd.
Graham St.
Tryon St.
Davidson St.
Matheson Ave.
Parkwood Ave.
The Plaza
Shamrock Dr.
Freedom Dr.
Trade St.
Wilkinson Blvd.
West Blvd.
See Detail Map
Midwood Smokehouse
Central Ave.
Morehead Inn
Price's Chicken Coop
300 East
Tremont Ave.
Morehead St.
Queens Rd.
W. Queens Rd.
Providence Rd.
Randolph Rd.
Independence Blvd.
Eastway Dr.
Landmark Diner
Albemarle Rd.
Amity Rd.
Wendover Rd.
Freedom Park
Duke Mansion
South Blvd.
York Rd.
Park Rd.
Woodlawn Rd.
Tyvola Rd.
Barclay Downs Dr.
Sharon Ln.
Sharon Rd.
Fairview Rd.
Best Western Sterling Inn
The Cowfish
Zink. American Kitchen
Ballantyne Hotel and Lodge
0 2 miles
0 3 km
KEY
Restaurants
Hotels
Tourist information
S. Graham St.
S. Mint St.
Trade St.
5th St.
N. Tryon St.
N. College St.
S. Church St.
Martin Luther King Jr. Blvd.
W. 1st St.
Mert's Heart and Soul
6th St.
7th St.
Bentley's on 27
4th St.
3rd St.
Omni Charlotte Hotel
Hilton Charlotte Center City
S. Brevard St.
S. Caldwell St.
N. Davidson St.
Stonewall St.
Westin Charlotte
Exploring
Bank of America Corporate Center ........... 5
Bechtler Museum of Modern Art .................. 2
Carolinas Aviation Museum ...................11
Carowinds .................13
Charlotte Motor Speedway .................16
Charlotte Nature Museum ...................12
Discovery Place ........... 6
Fourth Ward ............... 7
Harvey B. Gantt Center for African-American Arts & Culture ............... 1
Levine Museum of the New South ........... 8
Mint Museum Randolph .................. 3
Mint Museum Uptown ..................... 1
NASCAR Hall of Fame ................ 4
North Davidson Arts District (NoDA) ......... 9
President James K. Polk Historic Site ...............14
Reed Gold Mine State Historic Site .........15

The NASCAR Hall of Fame displays historic cars and racing memorabilia.

a comprehensive interpretation of post–Civil War Southern history. Interactive exhibits and different "environments"—a tenant farmer's house, an African-American hospital, a bustling street scene—bring to life the history of the region. **■ TIP➜** Admission is free on Sunday. ✉ *200 E. 7th St., Uptown* ☎ *704/333–1887* 🌐 *www.museumofthenewsouth.org* 🎫 *$8* 🕙 *Mon.–Sat. 10–5, Sun. noon–5.*

## GREATER CHARLOTTE

Many of Charlotte's most interesting sights lie outside the city center. From gardens to museums to a racing speedway, there are plenty of reasons to leave Uptown if you have time—and wheels. While you can reach some of these spots by city bus, a car is essential for others.

### EXPLORING

#### TOP ATTRACTIONS

★ **Charlotte Motor Speedway.** This state-of-the-art facility, holding 167,000 fans, is considered the heart of NASCAR. An estimated 90% of driving teams live within 50 miles. Hosting more than 350 events each year, this is one of the busiest sports venues in the United States. Racing season runs April to November, and tours are offered on non–race days. The Speedway Club, an upscale restaurant, is on the premises. **■ TIP➜** When there's a race, the population of Concord can jump from 60,000 to more than 250,000. Make sure you book your hotel well in advance. ✉ *5555 Concord Pkwy. S, northeast of Charlotte, Concord* ☎ *704/455–3200, 800/455–3267* 🌐 *www.charlottemotorspeedway.com.*

**Richard Petty Driving Experience.** If you want to indulge your inner racecar driver, take lessons through the Richard Petty Driving Experience. You can drive a NASCAR-style stock car at speeds up to 140 mph around Charlotte Motor Speedway. If you want the thrill of the ride without being in the driver's seat, you can ride with an instructor and go up to 165 mph. Classes are available throughout the year, though only when there's no event at the speedway. Prices vary, but start at $449 for eight laps around the track. **■TIP➔** You must have a valid driver's license and be able to drive a manual (stick shift) transmission car to drive, and you'll need to reserve ahead of time. ☎ *704/455–9443* 🌐 *www.1800bepetty.com.*

**Charlotte Nature Museum.** You'll find a butterfly pavilion, bugs galore, live animals, nature trails, a puppet theater, and hands-on exhibits just for children at this museum, which is affiliated with Discovery Place. ✉ *1658 Sterling Rd., Freedom Park* ☎ *704/372–0471* 🌐 *www.discoveryplace.org* 🎫 *$6* 🕒 *Weekdays 9–5, Sat. 10–5, Sun. noon–5.*

**The Harvey B. Gantt Center for African-American Arts + Culture.** This museum is in a section of Uptown that was once a thriving African-American neighborhood. Historic Brooklyn, as it was known, is long gone, but this celebration of black art, history, and culture serves its memory well. Past exhibits have included Tavis Smiley's "American I AM," detailing the imprint of nearly 500 years of black contributions to American culture. While the exhibits change frequently, you can always see John and Vivian Hewitt's collection of African-American visual art. ✉ *401 N. Myers St., Uptown* ☎ *704/547–3700* 🌐 *www.ganttcenter.org* 🎫 *$12* 🕒 *Tues.–Sat. 10–5, Sun. 1–5.*

OFF THE BEATEN PATH

**Historic Latta Plantation.** This plantation and grounds lie about 12 miles northwest of Charlotte, within the Latta Plantation Nature Preserve. The two-story Federal style home was built by James Latta, a traveling merchant, in 1800. Thirty-three slaves toiled on the 742-acre farm. The farm animals here are all of historically appropriate breeds. Guided tours of the home, including a video, are offered on the hour, with the last beginning at 4. ✉ *5225 Sample Rd., Huntersville* ☎ *704/875–2312* 🌐 *www.lattaplantation.org* 🎫 *$7* 🕒 *Tues.–Sat. 10–5, Sun. 1–5.*

★ **Mint Museum Randolph.** Built in 1836 as the first U.S. Mint, this building has been a home for art since 1936. The holdings in its impressive permanent collections include fashion, ceramics, coins and currency, and art of the ancient Americas. **■TIP➔** Your ticket stub gets you free admission to the Mint Museum Uptown (good for two days). ✉ *2730 Randolph Rd., East Charlotte/Merchandise Mart* ☎ *704/337–2000* 🌐 *www.mintmuseum.org* 🎫 *$10* 🕒 *Tues. 10–9, Wed.–Sat. 10–6, Sun. noon–5.*

**North Davidson Arts District.** Located 2 miles north of Uptown, Charlotte bills NoDa as "SoHo's little sister." While this small, historic neighborhood is quite a bit sleepier than its New York City sibling, it's still undeniably cool. Creative energy flows through the reclaimed textile mill and little houses, cottages, and commercial spaces. Here you'll find both the kooky and traditional—artists, musicians, dancers, restaurateurs, and even knitters—sharing space. 🌐 *www.noda.org.*

## PLAZA MIDWOOD

Plaza Midwood, one of Charlotte's most diverse areas, is a fascinating place to spend an afternoon or evening. Located northeast of Uptown, on and near Central Avenue and the Plaza, it houses a funky-cool collection of restaurants, shops, and galleries. After dark, it morphs into a colorful nightlife scene. This is a great spot to simply stroll and people-watch.

**House of Africa.** Visit with the chatty owners as you browse through a massive selection of African-made goods from every country on the continent. Their motto, "If you can't get to Africa, we'll bring Africa to you," rings true. ✉ *1215 Thomas Ave., Plaza Midwood* ☎ *704/376–6160.*

**The Penguin.** Here, rumbling stomachs can be soothed with greasy goodness. Always busy, this neighborhood icon is worth the wait. Its burgers were once voted best in the nation by *Gourmet* magazine. ✉ *1921 Commonwealth Ave., Plaza Midwood* ☎ *704/375–1925* 🌐 *www.penguindrive-in.com.*

**Thomas Street Tavern.** This little bar is one of the best places in Plaza Midwood to grab a beer and catch live tunes. ✉ *1218 Thomas Ave., Plaza Midwood* ☎ *704/376–1622.*

**Twenty Two.** If you like to look at art with a drink in hand, visit this gallery/bar. The space serves beer, wine, and sake nightly, and new art monthly. ✉ *1500 Central Ave., Plaza Midwood* ☎ *704/334–0122.*

**Evening Muse.** Hear live music nightly at this popular listening room, or wait for "Find Your Muse," as its frequent open mics are called. ✉ *3227 N. Davidson St.* ☎ *704/376–3737* 🌐 *www.eveningmuse.com.*

### WORTH NOTING

**Carolinas Aviation Museum.** The star here is the "Miracle on the Hudson" plane—the famed Airbus A320-214 that was safely landed in the Hudson River in January 2009 by the pilot Capt. Chesley B. Sullenberger after both engines failed. A working DC-3, F-14D Super TomCat, and about a dozen other aircraft are also on display. ✉ *Charlotte-Douglas International Airport, 4672 First Flight Dr.* ☎ *704/359–8442* 🌐 *www.carolinasaviation.org* 🎫 *$12* ⏲ *Weekdays 10–4, Sat. 10–5, Sun. 1–5.*

**Carowinds.** This 100-acre amusement park, 15 miles from Charlotte, has dozens of rides and attractions. Star entertainers and touring shows perform at the Paladium Amphitheatre and Carowinds Theatre. ■ **TIP→** **Check Carowinds's Web site for deals. It's usually cheaper to buy tickets online than at the gate.** ✉ *14523 Carowinds Blvd., off I–77 at Carowinds Blvd., South Charlotte/Pineville* ☎ *704/588–2600, 800/888–4386* 🌐 *www.carowinds.com* 🎫 *$45* ⏲ *Late Mar.–May and mid-Aug.–late Oct., weekends; June–mid-Aug., daily. Park opens at 9; closing hrs vary.*

**President James K. Polk State Historic Site.** This state historic site 10 miles south of central Charlotte marks the humble birthplace and childhood home of the 11th U.S. president, nicknamed "Napoleon of the Stump." Guided tours of the log cabins (replicas of the originals) show what life was like for settlers back in 1795. ✉ *12031 Lancaster Hwy., Pineville*

*704/889–7145 www.polk.nchistoricsites.org Free Tues.–Sat. 9–5.*

**Reed Gold Mine State Historic Site.** This historic site, about 22 miles east of Charlotte, is where America's first documented gold rush began, after Conrad Reed discovered a 17-pound nugget in 1799. Forty-minute guided underground tours of the gold mine are available, as well as seasonal gold panning, walking trails, and a stamp mill. *9621 Reed Mine Rd., north of Rte. 24/27, Midland 704/721–4653 www.nchistoricsites.org/reed Free; gold panning $3 Tues.–Sat. 9–5.*

3

## WHERE TO EAT

$$ AMERICAN ★ **300 East.** Operated out of an old home in pleasant Dilworth, this comfortable little spot is the perfect place to hang out and people-watch. The always-changing menu, which has its roots in Southern and Californian styles, includes modern, sophisticated takes on various meat and fish dishes, pizza, salads, and pastas. A few items always available (thankfully) include sweet potato ravioli, drowned in a rich and gooey Gorgonzola cream sauce, and The Usual, a chicken-salad sandwich that has been a local favorite for years. Friendly and attentive service adds to the homey atmosphere. This is the kind of place where longtime regulars have their names engraved on the back of bar stools. *Average main: $17 300 East Blvd., Dilworth 704/332–6507 www.300east.net Reservations essential.*

$$$$ FRENCH **Bentley's on 27.** Where to look? To one side is the city skyline, viewed from the 27th floor. To the other is the impressive display at the *guéridon,* a French cooking cart. The food itself is elegant in its simplicity: a salad of baby greens, shallots, tomatoes, and a champagne vinaigrette dressing, for instance, or a filet mignon with roasted potatoes, pearl onions, wild mushrooms, spinach leaf, and red wine reduction. You could close your eyes to savor the taste, but then you'd miss the view. *Average main: $48 Charlotte Plaza, 201 S. College St., Uptown 704/343–9201 www.bentleyson27.com Closed Sun.*

$ ECLECTIC **The Cowfish.** Feel like burgers? Feel like sushi? How about "burgushi?" There's an entire section of the menu devoted to this concept that blends, you guessed it, burgers and sushi. It's all about unexpected combinations: sushi packed with burger and beef components, and burgers stuffed with rice, tempura, rare ahi tuna, and other traditional sushi elements. But even if you're not so adventurous, this fun and always-packed spot will surely have something for you. The menu is made to be personalized, with a sprawling selection of available proteins, buns, and toppings for its burgers, and all manner of fillings to go in and on its sushi. If you're not in a build-your-own mood, try a taste of Doug's Filet Roll, a black truffle cheeseburger, or a selection of the popular mini-burgers. With late hours, a full bar, and often a line out the door, this place stays very buzzy—and it's also much more than a hip gimmick. *Average main: $12 4310 Sharon Rd., South Park 704/365–1922 www.thecowfish.com.*

$ AMERICAN **Landmark Diner.** This informal diner is a cut above the competition. Best of all, it's open until 1 am on weeknights, 4 am Friday and

You can learn about yeoman farmers' lives at the Historic Latta Plantation, a living-history farm and museum.

Saturday, and midnight Sunday. The chef's salad with grilled chicken is a standout, as is chicken Sorrento made with sautéed artichokes, spinach, and sun-dried tomatoes. For dessert there's chocolate-cream pie. *Average main: $8 ✉ 4429 Central Ave., East Charlotte/Merchandise Mart ☎ 704/532–1153.*

$ SOUTHERN Fodor's Choice ★ **Mert's Heart and Soul.** Business executives and arts patrons make their way to Mert's—named for Myrtle, a favorite customer with a sunny disposition. Owners James and Renee Bezzelle serve large portions of Lowcountry and Gullah staples, such as fried chicken with greens, macaroni and cheese, corn bread, shrimp-and-salmon omelets, and red beans and rice. Buckwheat and sweet-potato pancakes draw a weekend brunch crowd. *Average main: $10 ✉ 214 N. College St., Uptown ☎ 704/342–4222 www.mertscharlotte.com.*

$ BARBECUE **Midwood Smokehouse.** It's notoriously hard to find good barbecue in Charlotte, but this spot bucks the trend. Located in the funky Plaza Midwood neighborhood, it offers a full range of sauces and meats, and keeps its wood-fired smoker burning 24/7. With late hours and a full bar, this is no hole-in-the-wall joint, but instead a fun and modern-looking place with something for just about every kind of BBQ lover. The beef brisket is excellent, especially with a half-lean, half-fatty plate. For a special treat, order the banana pudding. It's some of the best in the city—or anywhere. *Average main: $10 ✉ 1401 Central Ave., Plaza Midwood ☎ 704/295–4227 www.midwoodsmokehouse.com.*

$ SOUTHERN **Price's Chicken Coop.** If you want to know where the locals eat, just follow the scent of oil to this storefront institution in the historic South End neighborhood, just across Interstate 277 from Uptown. The place isn't much to look at, but that's OK because the food is to-go only. And the chicken is the reason to go—and go again and again. A light, crispy coating covers meat so juicy you'll begin to understand that there is indeed an art to running a deep fryer. Take some back to your hotel in Uptown and make everyone on the elevator jealous with the scent of Southern-fried goodness. *Average main: $7 1614 Camden Rd., SouthEnd 704/333–9866 www.priceschickencoop.com Reservations not accepted No credit cards Closed Sun. and Mon.*

$$$ MODERN AMERICAN **Zink. American Kitchen.** Right at home in the posh South Park Mall, Zink offers a good selection of American favorites, many with an upscale twist. A convergence of high-end and down-home, this elegant eatery offers its signature dishes, such as lobster mac and cheese, alongside a revolving menu of seasonal meat and fish entrées. Fans also come for the local produce, wood-fired cooking, and house-made flatbreads. The 30-foot-long zinc bar and outdoor seating make this a nice spot to mix and mingle or just kick back and take a break in the middle of a shopping marathon. *Average main: $24 1310 Sharon Rd., Suite W01, South Park 704/909–5500 www.harpersgroup.com/zink.asp.*

3

## WHERE TO STAY

*Hotel reviews have been abbreviated in this book. For expanded reviews, please go to Fodors.com.*

$$$ RESORT **Ballantyne Hotel and Lodge.** On 2,000 acres, this beautiful and stately resort hotel is the best of the best when it comes to luxury in Charlotte. **Pros:** luxury defined; beautiful setting with equally lovely rooms. **Cons:** not convenient for exploring city center; not in walking distance to any interesting sights. *Rooms from: $199 10000 Ballantyne Commons Pkwy., South Charlotte 704/248–4000, 866/248–4824 www.ballantyneresort.com 202 rooms, 12 suites Multiple meal plans.*

$ HOTEL **Best Western Sterling Inn.** If you're looking for an inexpensive, friendly, and reliable place to spend a night while in transit, this is the spot. **Pros:** great location for those traveling by car or plane; friendly staff. **Cons:** a little noisy; no pool; dark hallways and rooms. *Rooms from: $70 242 E. Woodlawn Rd., Airport/Coliseum 704/525–5454 97 rooms Breakfast.*

$$$ B&B/INN **Duke Mansion.** Spending a night at this historic, luxurious inn seems more like borrowing a wealthy friend's estate than spending a night in a hotel. **Pros:** guests get a real sense of history and a neighborhood feel; the surrounding area is a great place to stroll. **Cons:** some bathrooms have older fixtures; not in walking distance to nightlife spots. *Rooms from: $209 400 Hermitage Rd., Myers Park 704/714–4400 www.dukemansion.com 20 rooms Breakfast.*

$ HOTEL **Hilton Charlotte Center City.** This comfortable hotel is right in the heart of things, just down the block from the Charlotte Convention Center. **Pros:** central location; YMCA on the premises. **Cons:** some rooms have showers only; like most Charlotte hotels, rates vary dramatically depending on the day and time of year. *Rooms from: $129 222 E. 3rd St., Uptown 704/377–1500, 800/445–8667 www.charlottecentercity.hilton.com 386 rooms, 14 suites No meals.*

$$ B&B/INN **Morehead Inn.** Built in 1917, this grand Colonial Revival house has rooms filled with period antiques, including several with impressive four-poster beds. **Pros:** cozy and historic; known for its cooked-to-order breakfast. **Cons:** a popular spot for weddings and parties, so it can be noisy; though in a beautiful area, it's not in walking distance to nightlife. *Rooms from: $179 1122 E. Morehead St., Dilworth 704/376–3357, 888/667–3432 www.moreheadinn.com 12 rooms Breakfast.*

$ HOTEL **Omni Charlotte Hotel.** This 16-story hotel is downtown, within walking distance of the convention center as well as many arts and sports venues. **Pros:** location and amenities are great for downtown; adjacent to a mall with tons of restaurant options. **Cons:** busy setting might be too much for some travelers; charges for parking and Internet use add up. *Rooms from: $149 132 E. Trade St., Uptown 704/377–0400, 800/843–6664 www.omnicharlotte.com 374 rooms, 33 suites No meals.*

$$ HOTEL **Westin Charlotte.** For an upscale taste of Uptown, it's hard to get much better than this business hotel that's next to the convention center. *Rooms from: $165 601 S. College St., Uptown 704/375–2600 www.westin.com/charlotte 700 rooms No meals.*

## NIGHTLIFE AND THE ARTS

### THE ARTS

**Blumenthal Performing Arts.** Along with the 2,100-seat Belk Theatre, this performing arts center houses several resident companies, including the Charlotte Symphony Orchestra, North Carolina Dance Theatre, and Opera Carolina. *130 N. Tryon St., Uptown 704/372–1000 www.blumenthalcenter.org.*

**Neighborhood Theatre.** Once called the Astor Theater this circa-1945 former movie palace is now a 700-seat venue that has hosted concerts by the likes of the Indigo Girls, Little Feat, and the Nitty Gritty Dirt Band. *511 E. 36th St. 704/358–9298 www.neighborhoodtheatre.com.*

**NoDa Gallery Crawl.** On the first and third Friday of every month, Charlotte's North Davidson (NoDa) neighborhood really gets going during its evening gallery crawl, basically an all-out block party held at various galleries and shops from around 6 to 9:30. *www.noda.org.*

**Paladium Amphitheater.** Family-friendly acts are presented at this amusement park's amphitheater from spring to fall. *Carowinds, 14523 Carowinds Blvd., South Charlotte/Pineville 704/588–2600, 800/888–4386 www.carowinds.com.*

**Verizon Wireless Amphitheater.** The Verizon Wireless Amphitheater spotlights big-name concerts—Norah Jones, Tim McGraw, Melissa Etheridge—spring through fall. *707 Pavilion Blvd., Speedway 704/549–5555 www.livenation.com.*

### NIGHTLIFE

**Crave Dessert Bar.** Charlotte's only dessert bar serves a wide range of upscale sweets and signature cocktails into the early-morning hours. Crave brings in a young, well-dressed crowd, drawn not only by the place's hip feel, but its wide selection of cupcakes, pies, ice cream, and more. Hookahs are also available, with several different flavors for patrons to toke. ✉ *500 W. 5th St., Uptown* ☎ *704/335–0588* 🌐 *www.cravedessertbar.com.*

**Double Door Inn.** In business since 1973, this laid-back venue is a staple of the national blues circuit. Eric Clapton, Junior Walker, and Stevie Ray Vaughn are among the legends who've played here. ✉ *1218 Charlottetown Ave., Uptown* ☎ *704/376–1446* 🌐 *www.doubledoorinn.com.*

**Rí Rá.** Irish for "uproar," this lively, busy joint serves up traditional Irish food and ale. It's one of the better options in the Uptown bar scene, with live music Fridays and Saturdays and often weeknights, too. ✉ *208 N. Tryon St., Uptown* ☎ *704/333–5554.*

3

## SPORTS AND THE OUTDOORS

### AUTO RACING

**Charlotte Motor Speedway.** NASCAR races, such as May's Coca-Cola 600, draw huge crowds to this well-known speedway. ⇨ *See Greater Charlotte's Top Attractions for more details.* ✉ *5555 Concord Pkwy. S, northeast of Charlotte, Concord* ☎ *704/455–3200, 800/455–3267* 🌐 *ww.charlottemotorspeedway.com.*

### BOATING

**North Carolina Division of Parks and Recreation.** Inlets on Lake Norman are ideal for canoeing. You can rent canoes and paddleboats for $5 for the first hour and $3 for each additional hour from the North Carolina Division of Parks and Recreation. ☎ *704/528–6350* 🌐 *www.ncparks.gov.*

**Catawba Queen.** On Lake Norman, the *Catawba Queen* paddle wheeler gives lunch and dinner cruises and tours. The *Lady of the Lake*, a 90-foot yacht, offers dinner cruises. ✉ *1459 River Hwy., Mooresville* ☎ *704/663–2628* 🌐 *www.queenslanding.com.*

### FISHING

**North Carolina Wildlife Resources Commission.** You can find good fishing in Charlotte's neighboring lakes and streams. A license can be bought at local bait-and-tackle shops or over the phone from the North Carolina Wildlife Resources Commission. A 10-day, out-of-state license is $10, or $20 if you want to fish for mountain trout. Game fish in Lake Norman waters include crappie, bluegill, and yellow perch, as well as striped, largemouth, and white bass. ☎ *888/248–6834* 🌐 *www.ncwildlife.org.*

### FOOTBALL

**Carolina Panthers.** Charlotte's National Football League team plays from August through December—and hopefully into the postseason playoffs, too—in the 74,000-seat Bank of America Stadium. ✉ *800 S. Mint St., Uptown* ☎ *704/358–7800* 🌐 *www.panthers.com.*

### GOLF

**Larkhaven Golf Club.** The oldest public course in Charlotte, Larkhaven opened in 1958. Mature trees have narrowed the fairways, and there's a 60-foot elevation drop on Hole 9, a par 3. ✉ *4801 Camp Stewart*

*Rd.* ☎ *704/545–4653* 🌐 *www.larkhavengolf.com* 🏌 *18 holes. 6328 yds. Par 72. Green Fee: $32–$46.* ☞ *Facilities:Putting green, pitching area, rental clubs, golf carts, pro shop, restaurant, bar.*

**Paradise Valley Golf Center.** This short course is perfect for players without much time: a round takes under two hours. But don't let that fool you: the course can challenge the best of them. Unique elements include two island tees. There's also a miniature golf course called the Lost Duffer set in a 19th-century mining town. ✉ *110 Barton Creek Dr.* ☎ *704/548–1808* 🌐 *www.charlottepublicgolf.com/paradise-valley.php* 🏌 *18 holes. 1264 yds. Par 54. Green Fee: $9–$13.* ☞ *Facilities:Putting green, golf carts, pull carts, rental clubs, pro shop.*

**Woodbridge Golf Links.** This semiprivate course is lovely to look at and challenging to play. You have to be careful with the water hazards; there are water features on 13 holes. ✉ *7101 Highland Creek Pkwy.* ☎ *704/875–9000* 🏌 *18 holes. 7043 yds. Par 72. Green Fee: $49–$69.* ☞ *Facilities: Driving range, putting green, pitching area, golf carts, pro shop, golf academy/lessons, restaurant, bar.*

## SHOPPING

Charlotte is the largest retail center in the Carolinas. Most stores are in suburban malls; villages and towns in outlying areas have shops selling regional specialties.

### SHOPPING MALLS

**Carolina Place Mall** ✉ *11025 Carolina Place Pkwy., off I–485, South Charlotte/Pineville* ☎ *704/543–9300* 🌐 *www.carolinaplace.com.*

**Concord Mills.** Destination shopping has been raised to an art form at this large outlet mall, which sells hundreds of brand names and discounted designer labels. Look for stores carrying Ralph Lauren, Coach, Guess, and Banana Republic. ✉ *8111 Concord Mills Blvd., off I–85, Concord* ☎ *704/979–5000* 🌐 *www.simon.com/mall/?id=1239.*

**SouthPark Mall.** Shoppers flock to this spendy spot for such high-end stores as Tiffany & Co., Montblanc, Coach, and Hermès. ✉ *4400 Sharon Rd., South Park* ☎ *704/364–4411.*

### SPECIALTY STORES

#### ANTIQUES

The nearby towns of Waxhaw, Pineville, and Matthews are the best places to find antiques.

**International Collectibles & Antique Show.** You can find a good selection of antiques and collectibles at this sprawling show, held the first weekend of every month. ✉ *Metrolina Trade Show Expo, 7100 N. Statesville Rd., off I–77, North Charlotte/Lake Norman* ☎ *704/714–7909* 🌐 *www.icashow.com.*

#### FOOD

**Charlotte Regional Farmers Market.** This is the spot for local produce, eggs, plants, and crafts. ✉ *1801 Yorkmount Rd., Airport/Coliseum* ☎ *704/357–1269* 🌐 *www.ncagr.gov/markets/facilities/markets/charlotte.*

# THE SANDHILLS

Though only a few hours from North Carolina's biggest cities, this land of pine trees, lakes, and country estates feels like a completely different world. Used as an escape from daily life for generations of city folk, the Sandhills are a little like a posh summer camp for adults, with all the high-end shopping and fancy hotels and restaurants anyone could want.

While plenty of visitors play tennis or ride horses here, golf is the real star. A panel of experts assembled by *Golf Digest* magazine recently named the region one of the top three golfing destinations in the world. Players come from all over the globe to hit these well-loved links, several of which were designed by legend Donald Ross himself.

Although most of the area's quaint villages live and breathe the game, little Seagrove is the exception. Instead, it's home to a large community of potters who sell their wares from roadside shops and galleries.

## SOUTHERN PINES

*104 miles east of Charlotte; 71 miles southwest of Raleigh.*

The center of the Sandhills, Southern Pines is a good place to begin exploring the region. Perhaps because its golf resorts are out of town, this little spot feels homier than its bordering villages and attracts a more low-key crowd. This is a great place to stroll, window shop, eat a leisurely lunch, and generally lose yourself between tee times.

### GETTING HERE AND AROUND

Southern Pines is easy to reach from the Triangle in the east via U.S. 1. From Charlotte the route is a bit more roundabout and involves driving southeast on U.S. 74, then heading north on U.S. 1. Once you've arrived, you will find Southern Pines to be laid out in a neat grid, with Broad Street at the center.

### ESSENTIALS

**Visitor Information Pinehurst/Southern Pines/Aberdeen Area Convention and Visitors Bureau** ✉ *1480 U.S. 15/501, Box 2270* ☎ *910/692–3330* 🌐 *www.homeofgolf.com.*

## EXPLORING

**Sandhills Horticultural Gardens.** The garden has a wetland area that can be observed from elevated boardwalks. It's part of a 32-acre series of gardens showcasing roses, fruits and vegetables, herbs, conifers, hollies, a formal English garden, pools, and a waterfall. ✉ *Sandhills Community College, 3395 Airport Rd., Pinehurst* ☎ *910/695–3882* 🌐 *www.sandhillshorticulturalgardens.com* 🎫 *Free* ⏲ *Daily sunrise–sunset.*

> **WORD OF MOUTH**
>
> "You might enjoy visiting Seagrove—near Asheboro—about an hour and a half from Charlotte. It is an incredible pottery area. You could spend days, but there are clusters of potteries. Or go to Jugtown—also near—and there is a nice sales center." —Gretchen

**Shaw House.** This 1820 structure is typical of the sturdy homes built by the Scottish families who settled the region. It serves as headquarters for the Moore County Historical Association. Two other restored cabins, both of which date to the 1700s, help illustrate the lives of early settlers. ✉ *110 W. Morganton Rd.* ☎ *910/692–2051* 🌐 *www.moorehistory.com* 🎫 *Free* ⏲ *Tues.–Fri. 1–4.*

**Weymouth Woods Sandhills Nature Preserve.** On the eastern outskirts of town, this 900-acre wildlife preserve has 6 miles of hiking trails. A staff naturalist will answer your questions about the beaver pond and other interesting sights. ✉ *1024 N. Fort Bragg Rd., off U.S. 1* ☎ *910/692–2167* 🌐 *www.ncparks.gov* 🎫 *Free* ⏲ *Apr.–Oct., daily 8–7; Nov.–Mar., daily 8–6.*

OFF THE BEATEN PATH

**Cameron.** This quaint little town, with a district on the National Register of Historic Places, has pockets that don't look that different than they looked in the 19th century. This is the place to shop for antiques, with dozens of dealers operating out of 12 stores. Though hours may vary, most shops are open Tuesday through Saturday 10 to 5, Sunday 1 to 5. The town holds antiques fairs with more than 300 dealers twice a year on the first Saturday in October and May. ✉ *Off U.S. 1, 12 miles north of Southern Pines* ☎ *910/245–7001 for information on antiques shops* 🌐 *www.antiquesofcameron.com.*

## WHERE TO EAT AND STAY

*Hotel reviews have been abbreviated in this book. For expanded reviews, please go to Fodors.com.*

$$$ ECLECTIC ✕ **Ashten's.** Emphasizing local and organic food, and with a menu that's equally divided between pub favorites and fusiony takes on Southern classics, Ashten's does its best to avoid being boring or overly traditional. Diners can choose between Ashten's standard dining room, private dining, and a comfy pub area, where you eat at coffee tables and couches. For a taste of something truly different, try the famous Reuben egg rolls, which are stuffed with corned beef, sauerkraut, and Swiss cheese. 💲 *Average main: $20* ✉ *140 E. New Hampshire Ave.* ☎ *910/246–3510* 🌐 *www.ashtens.com* ⏲ *Closed Mon. No lunch.*

$ CAFÉ ✕ **Sweet Basil.** This cozy corner café is run by a family whose considerable expertise is plain to see: lots of homemade breads, hefty sandwiches, and lush salads. The soups and rich desserts are especially good here. Make sure to arrive early to avoid the lunch rush. *Average main: $8 ✉ 134 N.W. Broad St. ☎ 910/693–1487 ⊙ Closed Sun. and Mon. No dinner.*

$ RESORT **Mid Pines Inn & Golf Club.** In a building dating from 1921, this elegant resort is the sibling of Pine Needles Lodge. **Pros:** elegant historic setting has loads of charm; good value for a pricey area. **Cons:** not a good fit for those who need modern decor and up-to-the-minute amenities; in order to use a pool or gym, guests must walk across the street to the Pine Needles. *Rooms from: $140 ✉ 1010 Midland Rd. ☎ 910/692–2114 ⊕ www.pineneedles-midpines.com 103 rooms, 7 villas No meals.*

$ RESORT **Pine Needles Lodge & Golf Club.** One of the bonuses of staying at this resort is the chance to meet Peggy Kirk Bell, a champion golfer who built the place with her late husband. **Pros:** comfortable inn that's a bit more relaxed than some of its neighbors; for tennis lovers, the lodge's grass courts are a bonus. **Cons:** if you're looking for the ultimate luxury experience, this one probably isn't for you; not within walking distance to the cute downtown. *Rooms from: $150 ✉ 1005 Midland Rd. ☎ 910/692–7111, 800/747–7272 ⊕ www.pineneedles-midpines.com 78 rooms No meals.*

## SPORTS AND THE OUTDOORS

### GOLF

**Longleaf Golf and Country Club.** Photos from the 1970s reveal how this golf course was built on the site of a training track for thoroughbreds. Some elements of the horse track still can be spotted on Holes 3, 4, 7, and 8. *✉ 10 N. Knoll Rd. ☎ 910/692–6100 ⊕ www.longleafgolf.com 18 holes. 6627 yds. Par 71. Green Fee: $55–$79. ☞ Facilities: Driving range, putting green, pitching area, golf carts, pro shop, restaurant.*

**Mid Pines Golf Club.** This course remains the same today as it was in 1921, when Donald Ross designed it. It is shorter than what's at the Pine Needles Golf Club, but its hillier terrain means it provides an ample challenge. *✉ 1010 Midland Rd. ☎ 910/692–2114, 800/323–2114 ⊕ www.pineneedles-midpines.com 18 holes. 6600 yds. Par 72. Green Fee: $95–$180. ☞ Facilities: Driving range, putting green, pitching area, golf carts, rental clubs, pro shop, golf academy/lessons, restaurant, bar.*

**Pine Needles Golf Club.** A 2005 renovation restored the course to its original Donald Ross design, with long line greens. The par-5 Hole 10 presents a particular challenge, with a sand trap along the inside curve of a dogleg. *✉ 1005 Midland Rd. ☎ 910/692–8611, 800/747–7272 ⊕ www.pineneedles-midpines.com 18 holes. 7015 yds. Par 71. Green Fee: $125–$235. ☞ Facilities: Driving range, putting green, pitching area, practice course, golf carts, pull carts, pro shop, golf academy/lessons, restaurant, bar.*

**Talamore Golf Club.** When Talamore opened in 1991, it had a great gimmick—llama caddies. The furry helpers quickly put the course on the map and gave golfers great anecdotes for more than a decade. In recent years, the caddy program has fallen by the wayside, but the llamas remain. Even though they won't be accompanying your round, you can still meet the llamas, which live a charmed life overlooking the course. *✉ 48 Talamore Dr. ☎ 910/692–5884, 800/552–6292 ⊕ www.*

*talamoregolfresort.com* 🏌 *18 holes. 6840 yds. Par 71. Green Fee: $69–$120.* ☞ *Facilities: Driving range, golf carts, rental clubs, restaurant.*

### SHOPPING

**The Country Bookshop.** Located in the center of the historic downtown, this independently run shop stocks a lot of everything, including books by Southern authors and children's books and puzzles. It also hosts frequent author readings. ✉ *140 N.W. Broad St.* ☎ *910/692–3211* 🌐 *www.thecountrybookshop.biz* ⏲ *Closed Sun.*

**Swank Coffee Shoppe & Handmade Market.** For gifts with personality, try Swank Coffee Shoppe & Handmade Market, which sells a surprisingly wide assortment of locally made clothing, art, and hip knickknacks. It's also great place to grab a cup of coffee or a freshly baked sweet. ✉ *124 W. Pennsylvania Ave.* ☎ *910/692–8068.*

## PINEHURST

*6 miles west of Southern Pines.*

Pinehurst is a New England–style village with quiet, shaded streets and immaculately kept homes ranging from massive Victorians to tiny cottages. It was laid out in the late 1800s in a wagon-wheel pattern by Frederick Law Olmsted, who also designed Ashville's Biltmore and New York City's Central Park. Annie Oakley lived here for a number of years and headed the local gun club. Today Pinehurst is renowned for its golf courses.

While golfers will be in heaven, their non-golfing friends and family might be at a loss for entertainment around these sleepy parts. Don't expect to find much nightlife here or practically anything open late. Instead, this is a good place to stroll and sleep in. The town operates at a different pace than most the world, and that's a big part of its charm. ■ **TIP→** There are hardly any restaurants in Pinehurst that are not attached to hotels and lodges. When booking your trip, make sure to check out packages that include meals where you're staying.

#### GETTING HERE AND AROUND

A manicured traffic circle directs travelers coming from five directions to the village center and resorts. Golf courses line the 5-mile stretch of N.C. 22 (aka Midland Road) between Southern Pines and Pinehurst. The community's namesake resort is just east of the village center.

### EXPLORING

**Tufts Archives.** These archives recount the founding of Pinehurst through James Walker Tufts's letters, pictures, and news clippings, dating from 1895. Pinehurst owes its origins to Tufts, who once served as president of the United States Golf Association. The history of Pinehurst can be traced back to his decision to build a health retreat here. ✉ *Given Memorial Library, 150 Cherokee Rd.* ☎ *910/295–6022, 910/295–3642* 🌐 *www.tuftsarchives.org* 🎟 *Free* ⏲ *Weekdays 9:30–5, Sat. 9:30–12:30.*

### WHERE TO EAT

$$ MEDITERRANEAN ✕ **Theo's Taverna.** This authentic Greek eatery is one of the nicest surprises in Pinehurst. Located right downtown, it offers a big selection of traditional specialties, including spankopita, pizettes, and gyros. Theo's

For a souvenir that's sure to become a conversation starter, pick up a handmade face jug at one of Seagrove's potteries.

outdoor seating is a fun option, as the concrete statues in the garden make you feel like you're in the Mediterrean. Every drop of olive oil used here comes from owners Elias and Helen Dalitsouris' own olive farm in Sparta, where they also live. You can buy your own bottle on your way out. $ *Average main: $16* ✉ *38 Chinquapin Rd* ☎ *910/295–0780* 🌐 *www.theostaverna.com.*

### WHERE TO STAY

*Hotel reviews have been abbreviated in this book. For expanded reviews, please go to Fodors.com.*

$$$$ RESORT Fodor's Choice ★ **The Carolina.** In business since 1901, this stately hotel has never lost its charm: civilized pleasures await in the spacious public rooms and elegantly traditional accommodations, on the rocker-lined wide verandas, and amid the gardens. **Pros:** historic setting combined with attentive service and luxurious amenities makes staying at the Carolina a special experience. **Cons:** geared to golfers and spa-goers with deep pockets, so bring plenty of cash. $ *Rooms from: $350* ✉ *80 Carolina Vista Dr.* ☎ *910/295–6811, 800/487–4653* 🌐 *www.pinehurst.com* *217 rooms, 13 suites, 44 villas* *Multiple meal plans.*

$$$ HOTEL **The Holly Inn.** The first hotel in the village when it opened in 1895, the Holly has crown molding, elegant lighting, and other architectural features that make that era come back to life. **Pros:** beautiful and more relaxed than its sister property, the Carolina; great in-house restaurants; attentive staff heighten the luxurious experience. **Cons:** folks looking for the ultimate Pinehurst experience might prefer staying closer to the golf course; lacks some modern amenities. $ *Rooms from: $240* ✉ *155*

*Cherokee Rd.* ☎ *910/295–6811, 800/487–4653* ⊕ *www.pinehurst.com* *77 rooms, 5 suites* *Multiple meal plans.*

$$ **Magnolia Inn.** This turn-of-the-20th-century inn is a charming choice
B&B/INN for those looking for something a little more intimate than one of Pinehurst's sprawling resorts. **Pros:** cozy and historic; food is well regarded; great in-town location. **Cons:** older bathrooms may not be up to some travelers' standards; the inn doesn't offer many modern amenities; breakfast is only included on weekends. *Rooms from: $175* ✉ *65 Magnolia Rd.* ☎ *910/295–6900* ⊕ *www.themagnoliainn.com* *11 rooms* *Multiple meal plans.*

$ **Pine Crest Inn.** Nostalgia and mahogany fill the rooms of this slightly
B&B/INN faded gem. **Pros:** popular restaurant; individually decorated rooms are full of character and history; more casual and comfortable than many others inns in the area. **Cons:** if you want a large room, request one, as some are small; rustic interior is not everyone's cup of tea. *Rooms from: $111* ✉ *50 Dogwood Rd.* ☎ *910/295–6121, 800/371–2545* ⊕ *www.pinecrestinnpinehurst.com* *40 rooms* *Multiple meal plans.*

## SPORTS AND THE OUTDOORS

### GOLF

**Beacon Ridge Golf & Country Club.** Located in West End, a few miles from the village of Pinehurst, this well-regarded course boasts a classic layout by Gene Hamm and the biggest lake in Moore County (Lake Autumn). ✉ *102 Lake Way Dr.* ☎ *910/673–2950* ⊕ *www.beaconridgegolfcc.com* *18 holes. 6494 yards. Par 72. Green Fee: $40–$85.* ☞ *Facilities: Driving range, putting green, pitching area, golf carts, rental clubs, pro shop, golf academy/lessons, restaurant, bar.*

**National Golf Club.** Constructed by golfing great Jack Nicklaus, this course features wide fairways and undulating putting surfaces (signature Nicklaus elements). Take note that since it's surrounded by a gated community, you must reserve your tee time in advance. ✉ *1 Royal Troon Dr.* ☎ *910/295–4300, 800/471–4339* ⊕ *www.nationalgolfclub.com* *18 holes. 7144 yards. Par 72. Green Fee: $175–$225.* ☞ *Facilities: Driving range, putting green, pitching area, golf carts, rental clubs, pro shop, golf academy/lessons, restaurant, bar.*

Fodor's Choice ★ **Pinehurst Resort.** Pinehurst has been the site of more championships than any other golf resort in the country. The eight courses—known by their numbers—can bring a tear to a golfer's eye with their beauty. The courses range from the first, designed in 1898 by legendary Donald Ross, to the most recent, designed in 1995 by Tom Fazio to mark the resort's centennial. The hilly terrain of No. 7, completely renovated in 2003, makes it especially tough. ✉ *1 Carolina Vista Dr.* ☎ *910/235–8125, 800/487–4653* ⊕ *www.pinehurst.com* *8 18-hole courses. Average of 6600 yds. Par 70–72. Green Fee: $89–$410.* ☞ *Facilities: Driving range, putting green, pitching area, golf carts, caddies, rental clubs, pro shop, golf academy/lessons, restaurant, bar.*

### TENNIS

**Lawn and Tennis Club of North Carolina.** Visitors come for the club's seven clay courts and swimming pool. ✉ *1 Merrywood Pl.* ☎ *910/692–7270* ⊕ *www.lawnandtennisclub.com.*

## SEAGROVE

★ *35 miles northwest of Pinehurst.*

What golf is to Pinehurst, pottery is to Seagrove. This little town is home to upward of 100 potters, many whose families have been making ceramics for generations. For some, the notoriety extends far beyond the town limits, as Seagrove pottery can be seen as far away as the Smithsonian in Washington, D.C. While exploring Seagrove, expect to see all kinds of work, from decorative to functional, from wall hangings to bowls, pitchers, and vases. "Face jugs" (sometimes called "ugly face jugs") are a local specialty and can be bought in many of the shops and galleries scattered off Route 705 and U.S. 220. To truly immerse yourself in the Seagrove art scene, be in town for one of its two largest pottery events. Most local ceramists show at the huge **Celebration of Seagrove Potters,** held the weekend before Thanksgiving. The newer **Celebration of Spring,** an open-studio tour, is held every April. ■ **TIP→** To learn more about Seagrove happenings and to see a listing of area artists, visit 🌐 *www.discoverseagrove.com,* a site created by a collection of potters.

### GETTING HERE AND AROUND

A chance to meander is part of the Seagrove area's draw. If you're coming from Charlotte, take N.C. 49 or Interstate 85 east to U.S. 64. Take U.S. 64 east to U.S. 220 and follow U.S. 220 south to the town of Seagrove and the North Carolina Pottery Center, which is a good starting point. From the Triangle, take U.S. 64 west, then U.S. 220 south. No matter where you come from, you'll see signs directing you toward pottery before you reach the town of Seagrove. Stop, check the stores out, and see where the traveler's spirit leads.

### EXPLORING

★ **North Carolina Pottery Center.** Start your pottery adventure here. The center exhibits ceramics from Seagrove and all over the state. You can also pick up maps of the various studios around the area. ✉ *233 East Ave.* ☎ *336/873–8430* 🌐 *www.ncpotterycenter.com* 🎫 *$2* ⏲ *Tues.–Sat. 10–4.*

### WHERE TO EAT

$ AMERICAN ✕ **Westmoore Family Restaurant.** Always filled with locals, this all-American diner is a friendly place to grab a quick bite while touring Seagrove's endless pottery studios. Westmoore specializes in seafood, offering dishes like crab cakes, flounder, and shrimp. Be sure to check out the homemade deserts as well. 💲 *Average main: $10* ✉ *2172 Hwy. 705 S* ☎ *910/463–5222* ⏲ *Closed Mon.*

### SHOPPING

**Bulldog Pottery.** This studio's functional and decorative pieces are filled with color and texture, and often are delectably weird. The artists, couple Bruce Gholson and Samantha Henneke, are also known for their iridescent crystalline glazes and nature-inspired subject matter. ✉ *3306 U.S. Hwy. 220* ☎ *336/302–3469* 🌐 *www.bulldogpottery.com* ⏲ *Tues.–Sat. 9–5. For Mon. and Sun. times, call ahead.*

**Crystal King Pottery.** There's nothing in Seagrove quite like Crystal King's folk art sculptures, which she has been crafting since her high school days. Born into a family of Seagrove potters, King makes brightly colored, rustic work, mostly of animals. Her quirky pottery studio also features functional thrown pieces and face jugs, all made in Seagrove by herself, her family, or other famed potters. Folk art from other media is available as well. ✉ *2475 Hwy. 705* ☎ *336/879–6990* 🌐 *www.crystalkingpottery.com* ⏲ *Tues.–Sat. 10–5 and occasionally Mon.*

**McCanless Pottery.** This gallery's ornate work comes from the hands of Will McCanless, who opened his shop in 2006. Expect hand-painted functional ware, zinc silicate crystalline pieces, and a bright "Sea Grove Red" collection, among other offerings. Everything is carefully crafted, intricate, and bursting with color. ✉ *634 Hwy. 705* ☎ *336/879–3610* 🌐 *www.mccanlesspottery.com* ⏲ *Mon.–Sat. 10–5, Sun. 11:30–5.*

## ASHEBORO

*13 miles north of Seagrove; 23 miles south of Greensboro.*

Asheboro, the seat of Randolph County, sits in the Uwharrie National Forest, which is popular with those who like hiking, biking, and horseback riding. At 500 million years old, the Uwharries are the oldest mountain range in North America. This part of the southern Piedmont is a lovely place to view scenery and visit crafts shops.

### GETTING HERE AND AROUND

U.S. 220 and U.S. 64 intersect just south of Asheboro, providing easy access from all directions. The North Carolina Zoo, the area's most popular attraction, is southeast of town. To reach it, follow U.S. 220 south and go east on N.C. 159.

### ESSENTIALS

**Visitor Information** **Randolph County Tourism Development Authority** ✉ *222 Sunset Ave., Suite 108* ☎ *800/626–2672* 🌐 *www.visitrandolphcounty.com.*

### EXPLORING

★ **North Carolina Zoo.** The over 2,200-acre zoo, home to more than 1,100 animals from more than 250 species and with more than 5 miles of walking trails, was the first zoo in the country designed from the get-go as a natural-habitat facility. The park includes the 300-acre African Region, which features the Watani Grasslands elephant exhibit, a 200-acre North American Region with polar bears and grizzlies, and an interactive kids zone. ■ **TIP→ This is a massive park, so take advantage of the tram that connects the various areas.** ✉ *4401 Zoo Pkwy.* ☎ *336/879–7000, 800/488–0444* 🌐 *www.nczoo.org* 🎟 *$12* ⏲ *Apr.–Sept., daily 9–5; Oct.–Mar., daily 9–4.*

OFF THE BEATEN PATH

**Town Creek Indian Mound Historic Site.** About 30 miles south of Asheboro, this historic site is a glimpse into North Carolina's pre-Columbian past. A self-guided tour takes you through reconstructions of buildings that belonged to the Pee Dee people. Guided tours are available on weekends or by appointment. Excavations of the site began in 1937 and are still in progress. ✉ *509 Town Creek Mound Rd., Mt. Gilead* ☎ *910/439–6802* 🌐 *www.nchistoricsites.org/town* 🎟 *Free* ⏲ *Tues.–Sat. 9–5, Sun. 1–5.*

4

# Asheville and the North Carolina Mountains

## WORD OF MOUTH

"To me, part of the charm of Asheville is its downtown's walk-ability so we always try to stay within walking distance of downtown. That way we don't have to worry about driving/parking when enjoying all the great bars and restaurants."

—Brian_in_Charlotte

# WELCOME TO ASHEVILLE AND THE NORTH CAROLINA MOUNTAINS

## TOP REASONS TO GO

★ **Biltmore Estate:** The 250-room Biltmore House, modeled after the great Renaissance châteaux of the Loire Valley in France, is the largest private home in America. It is the most-visited attraction in North Carolina.

★ **Blue Ridge Parkway:** This winding two-lane road, which ends at the edge of the Great Smokies and shows off the highest mountains in eastern America, is the most scenic drive in the South.

★ **Asheville:** Hip, artsy, sometimes funky, with scores of restaurants and active nightlife, Asheville is one of America's coolest places to live, and visit.

★ **Engaging small towns:** You could easily fall in love with the charm, style, and Southern hospitality of Black Mountain, Blowing Rock, Brevard, and Hendersonville, to name a few.

★ **Mountain arts and crafts:** The mountains are a center of handmade art and crafts, with more than 4,000 working craftspeople.

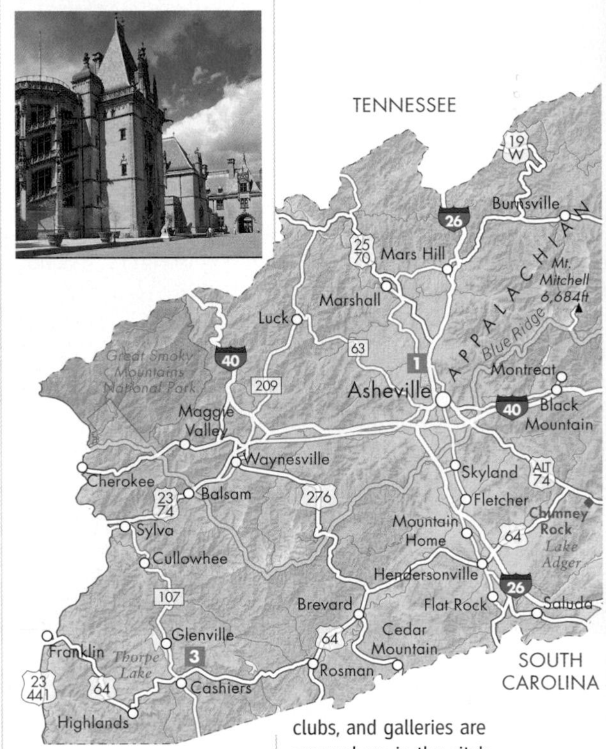


**1 Asheville.** Set in a valley surrounded by the highest mountains in eastern America, Asheville is a base for exploring the region, but it is also a destination unto itself. Here you can tour America's largest home and discover why Asheville has a national reputation for its arts, crafts, and music scenes. Coffeehouses, brewpubs, sidewalk cafés, boutiques, antiques shops, clubs, and galleries are everywhere in the city's art-deco downtown. Just a short drive away are inviting small mountain towns, mile-high vistas that will take your breath away, and enough high-energy outdoor fun to keep your heart rate way up.

**2 The High Country.** The High Country is the snow-skiing area of the mountains. Boone, Beech Mountain (the highest-elevation incorporated community east of the Mississippi River),

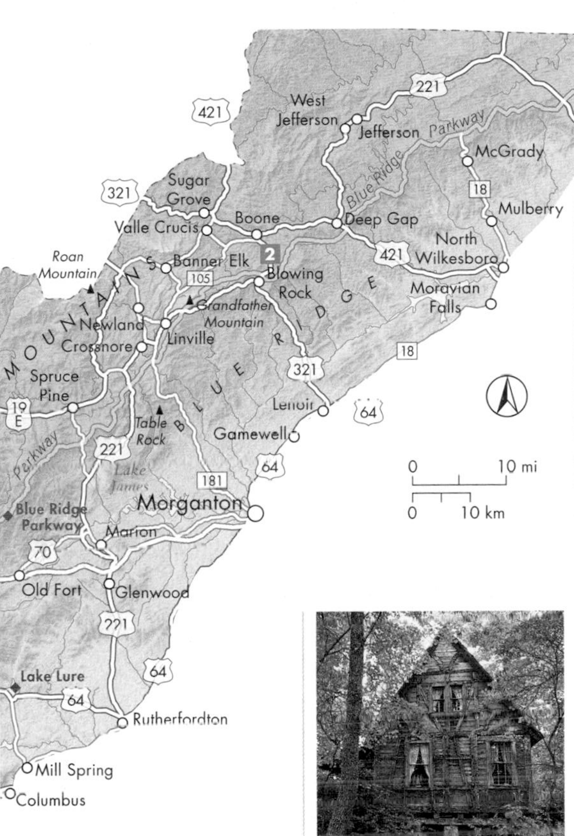

# GETTING ORIENTED

The buzz about the North Carolina Mountains dates back to the early 19th century, when wealthy Lowcountry planters flocked to the highlands to escape the summer heat. Today visitors still come here to enjoy the cool, green mountains and all the activities they provide—hiking, camping, fishing, boating, and just marveling at the scenery. Asheville, the hub of the mountain region, is one of the biggest small cities you'll ever visit, with the artsy élan and dynamic downtown of a much larger burg.

4

Blowing Rock, and Seven Devils together have four ski resorts. Summers here are noticeably cooler than elsewhere in the Southeast, and the mountain scenery notably dramatic.

**3 The Southern Mountains.** The Southern Mountains is comprised of towns in North Carolina southwest of Asheville, including Brevard and the chic enclaves of Lake Toxaway, Cashiers, and Highlands. These towns are diverse in terms of size, elevation, and attractiveness. If they have anything in common, it is high real estate prices and a reputation as summer getaways for well-to-do flatlanders.

# DAY TRIP: BLUE RIDGE PARKWAY

(above) Autumn along the Blue Ridge Parkway is simply breathtaking. (upper right) Sculptures are set in among the gardens at the North Carolina Arboretum.

Often called America's narrowest national park, the Blue Ridge Parkway's two-lane blacktop traverses some of the East's most dramatic scenery, soaring along the ridges of mile-high mountains and then swooping into lush alpine valleys, where restaurants, craft shops, stylish inns, and outdoor fun await.

While the entire 252-mile North Carolina section of the Blue Ridge Parkway is well worth your time, the 90-mile portion between **Blowing Rock** and **Asheville** offers the most appealing combination of dramatic vistas and things to do. Enter the Parkway from U.S. 321/221 between Boone and Blowing Rock. Almost immediately you're at **Moses Cone Park**, where there's a crafts center in the manor house and 25 miles of carriage roads on the former estate, winding through what's left of old apple orchards. Adjoining Moses Cone Park is **Julian Price Park**. You'll recognize it by the lovely small lake adjacent to the parkway. There is a 100-table picnic ground and several hiking trails.

—Lan Sluder

### PLANNING YOUR TIME

April to early November is the best time to drive the Blue Ridge Parkway. (In winter, sections of the Parkway sometimes close due to ice and snow.) This two-lane mountain road has a 45 mph speed limit, so don't plan on a quick trip. With stops you can easily spend a full day. If you want to break up the trip, Asheville and Blowing Rock have great hotels in all price ranges.

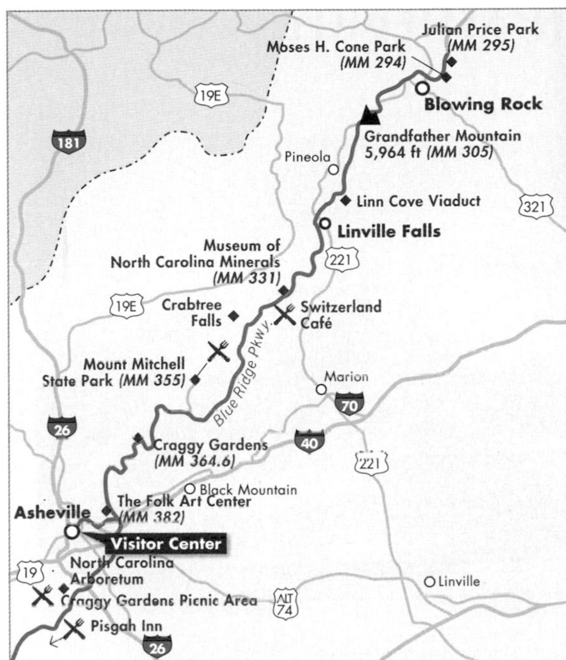

Most of the next 20 miles offers stunning scenery, with spruce and fir forests reminiscent of the more northern climates. The **Linn Cove Viaduct** is a marvel of engineering, and a small visitor center has displays explaining its construction. **Grandfather Mountain,** 2 miles south, has enclosures for black bear, panthers, and other local wildlife, a nature museum, and a mile-high swinging bridge that's a sure winner for kids.

At **Linville Falls** and **Crabtree Falls,** moderate round-trip hikes of 1.6 miles and 2.5 miles get you to the falls and back. Another good spot for kids is the **Museum of North Carolina Minerals,** with displays on gems and minerals of western North Carolina. Take Route 128 to **Mt. Mitchell State Park,** anchored by the 6,684-foot peak. You can hike to the observation tower, enjoy a mile-high picnic, or dine at the highest restaurant east of the Rockies. Even in midsummer, temperatures are almost never higher than the mid-70s. Continue south toward Asheville to the **Craggy Gardens** area in late spring and early summer has stunning views of purple and rosebay rhododendron.

Approaching Asheville, you have an abundance of choices for stops. There's the **Folk Art Center,** with displays of quilts and crafts, the **Parkway Visitor Center,** and the **North Carolina Arboretum,** for colorful displays of local foliage.

## QUICK BITES

**Switzerland Café and General Store.** Enjoy a smoked trout BLT for lunch at the charming Switzerland Café. Dinner is a little more upscale, with rib-eye steak and baby back ribs. ✉ *9440 Hwy. 226A, Little Switzerland* ☎ *828/765–5289* 🌐 *www.switzerlandcafe.com* ⏲ *Closed Dec.–Mar.*

**Mt. Mitchell State Park Restaurant.** Dine in the clouds on mountain trout, chicken fingers, and burgers here. ✉ *2388 NC Hwy. 128, Burnsville* ☎ *828/675–4611* ⏲ *Closed Nov.–Apr.*

**Craggy Gardens Picnic Area.** This is a lovely spot for a picnic and a great place to explore tunnels of rhododendron and heaths covered in wild blueberries. ✉ *Blue Ridge Pkwy. MM 364.5* ☎ *828/298–0398* .

**Pisgah Inn Restaurant.** Near Mt. Pisgah, the inn features a tempting selection of burgers, sandwiches, wraps, and full meals at lunch or dinner. ✉ *Blue Ridge Pkwy., MM 408.6, Waynesville* ☎ *828/235–8228* 🌐 *www.pisgahinn.com* ⏲ *Closed early Nov.–late Mar.*

4

# GOOD EATS IN ASHEVILLE

Asheville's acclaimed diversity is reflected in its dynamic food scene. Central to it all is the local food movement, nourished by scores of organic farms and tailgate markets.

(above) The Popeye's spinach burger at Asheville Pizza & Brewing. (lower right) The North Asheville Tailgate market on the UNCA campus. (upper right) Try a seasonal beer at Craggie Brewing Co.

Within a few blocks, you can nosh on Indian street food, Spanish tapas, French, Italian, Japanese, Thai, Himalayan, Jamaican, Cuban, and, of course, veggie and vegan options. While your choices are eclectic, a modern take on Southern cooking rules at many restaurants.

Beer is Asheville's aqua vitae, with local microbreweries splashing out pale ales and porters. Two large national craft brewers, Sierra Nevada and New Belgium, are opening their East Coast breweries and distribution centers in the area, adding to Asheville's claim as Beer City USA.

The epicenter of Asheville's food scene is downtown, where cafés, bistros, and microbreweries jostle each other for street space. West Asheville (edgy, organic cafés), the River Arts District (coffeehouses, artsy cafés, and microbreweries), Biltmore (upscale bistros and restaurants), and North Asheville (neighborhood restaurants) also have popular eateries.

—Lan Sluder

In the heart of up-and-coming West Asheville, the tattooed staff of **Sunny Point Café** (✉ *626 Haywood Rd.* ☎ *828/252–0055* 🌐 *www.sunnypointcafe.com*) serve breakfast all day. Choose organic, orange-scented, gluten-free cornmeal hotcakes, the best shrimp-and-chipotle-cheese grits north of Charleston, or a build-your-own free-range-egg omelet.

## MICROBREWERIES

Microbreweries have replaced moonshine stills in the North Carolina Mountains. Here are some of the best in Asheville:

**Asheville Brewing Co.** (✉ *77 Coxe Ave.* ☎ *828/255-4077* 🌐 *www.ashevillebrewing.com*) brews at its downtown microbrewery and pub, and also sells its hoppy suds in a converted movie theater in North Asheville, **Asheville Pizza & Brewing** (✉ *675 Merrimon Ave.* ☎ *828/254-1281*). Here you can enjoy a second-run movie and beer, seated on comfy sofas and reclining chairs. Asheville Brewing's most popular beer is Shiva, an India pale ale named after the Hindu god of transformation.

**French Broad Brewing Company** (✉ *101-D Fairview Rd.* ☎ *828/277-0222* 🌐 *www.frenchbroadbrewery.com*) brews lagers and specialty ales. Wee-Heavy Er, a Scottish ale, is a best seller. The tasting room also has live music some nights, usually Thursday, Friday, and Saturday.

**Wedge Brewing Co.** (✉ *125B Roberts St.* ☎ *828/279-6393* 🌐 *www.wedgebrewing.com*) in the River Arts District brews Iron Rail India Pale Ale, named after the railroad tracks nearby, and other artisan beers including Witbier, a Belgian-style wheat beer. In good weather, you can sip and mingle in a picnic area outside, where there are food trucks.

The **Asheville Brews Cruise** (☎ *828/545-5181* 🌐 *www.brewscruise.com*) takes microbrew aficionados on a tour of three or four local breweries for $45 per person (four-person minimum). Van tours, daily except Monday (less frequently in winter), last about three hours and include samples of 12 to 15 beers and ales. Walking tours are sometimes available, also $45 per person.

## CAFFEINATED ASHEVILLE

Downtown Asheville has about a dozen local coffeehouses, with many others nearby. **Clingman Café** (✉ *242 Clingman Ave.* ☎ *828/253-2177*), near many studios in the River Arts District, attracts an arts crowd for its organic and free-trade coffees and tasty meals. The café has rotating shows of paintings, photography, clay, and sculpture. **Double D's Coffees & Desserts** (✉ *41 Biltmore Ave.* ☎ *828/505-2439*) is hard to miss, as it's located in an old red double-decker British bus. **Izzy's Coffee Den** (✉ *74 N. Lexington Ave.* ☎ *828/258-2004*) is an alternative, slightly hipster spot. It serves Counter Culture coffee, of course. **Old Europe** (✉ *13 Broadway St.* ☎ *828/255-5999*) remains vastly popular for its locally roasted Mountain City coffees and Hungarian pastries. **Waking Life** (✉ *976 Haywood Rd.* ☎ *828/505-3240*) in West Asheville arguably has the best espresso in town.

By Lan Sluder

The majestic peaks, meadows, balds, and valleys of the Appalachian, Blue Ridge, and Great Smoky Mountains epitomize the western corner of North Carolina. The Great Smoky Mountains National Park, national forests, handmade-crafts centers, Asheville's eclectic and sophisticated pleasures, the astonishing Biltmore Estate, and the Blue Ridge Parkway are the area's main draws, providing prime opportunities for shopping, skiing, hiking, bicycling, camping, fishing, canoeing, and just taking in the views.

The city of Asheville is one of the stops on the counterculture trail and a center of the New Age movement, as well as being a popular retirement area. Its restaurants regularly make the TV food show circuit. Thanks to their moneyed seasonal residents and long histories as resorts, even smaller towns like Highlands, Cashiers, Flat Rock, and Hendersonville are surprisingly sophisticated, boasting restaurants with daring chefs and professional summer theater. In the High Country, where summer temperatures are as much as 15 degrees cooler than in the flatlands, and where snow skiing is a major draw in winter, affluent retirees and hip young entrepreneurs bring panache to even the most rural enclaves.

Some of the most important arts and culture movements of the 20th century, including Abstract Impressionist painting and the Beat movement, had roots just east of Asheville, at Black Mountain College, where in the 1930s and 1940s the notables included famed artists Josef and Anni Albers, Willem de Kooning, and Robert Motherwell, dancemeister Merce Cunningham, musician John Cage, thinker Buckminster Fuller, architect Walter Gropius, and writers Charles Olson and Paul Goodman.

# PLANNING

## WHEN TO GO

Western North Carolina is a four-season destination. Dates for high season vary from hotel to hotel, but generally it's from Memorial Day through early November. It's most difficult to get a hotel reservation, especially on weekends, in October, which is peak leaf-peeping time. Mid-June to mid-August draws a lot of families, since kids are out of school. Around ski resorts, winter, especially the Christmas season and the months of January and February, is prime time; elsewhere, these winter months are dead, and some hotels are closed.

## PLANNING YOUR TIME

4

The Asheville area makes a convenient base for day visits to Black Mountain and Hendersonville, and even to Brevard, Cashiers, and Highlands in the Southern Mountains. Of course, if you want to see these areas more completely, you're better off spending the night in one or several of these towns. Likewise, it's easy to make day trips to Great Smoky Mountain National Park from Asheville. The Oconaluftee entrance to the Smokies is only an hour and 15 minutes' drive from downtown Asheville. But if you want to spend several days or longer in the Smokies, you'll be better off staying in the park or at one of the small towns at the edge of it, such as Bryson City or Waynesville. ⇨ *For more information about the park, see Chapter 5: Great Smoky Mountains National Park*. The High Country is too far away for a comfortable day visit from Asheville, especially considering the winding mountain roads and possible weather conditions (snow in winter and fog almost anytime). To explore the High Country in detail, you'll want to make your headquarters in the appealing college town of Boone or one of the other towns nearby, such as Blowing Rock or Banner Elk.

## GETTING HERE AND AROUND

### AIR TRAVEL

Asheville Regional Airport (AVL), one of the most pleasant and modern small airports in the South, is served by Allegiant, Delta, United, and US Airways. Most of the flights are on regional jets. A $20-million expansion and improvement project was completed in 2009. There are nonstop flights to and from Atlanta, Charlotte, Chicago, Detroit, Houston, Orlando, Philadelphia, New York's LaGuardia, Newark, and Washington, D.C. Some flights are seasonal.

South Carolina's Greenville-Spartanburg International Airport (GSP), 75 minutes from Asheville, is convenient to parts of the Southern Mountains. It has service by Allegiant, American Eagle, Delta, United, Southwest, and US Airways. Charlotte Douglas International Airport (CLT), a major hub for US Airways with service by about a half dozen other airlines including Air Canada, Lufthansa, and JetBlue, is about a two-hour drive from Asheville and Boone.

**Airport Information Asheville Regional Airport** ✉ *708 Airport Rd., Fletcher* ☎ *828/684–2226* 🌐 *www.flyavl.com.* **Charlotte Douglas International Airport** ✉ *5501 Josh Birmingham Pkwy., Charlotte* ☎ *704/916–2200* 🌐 *www.charlottedouglasintlairport.com.* **Greenville-Spartanburg International**

**Airport** ✉ *2000 GSP Dr., Greer, South Carolina* ☎ *864/989–0788* 🌐 *www.gspairport.com.*

### CAR TRAVEL

The coast-to-coast Interstate 40 runs east–west through Asheville. Interstate 26 runs from Charleston, South Carolina, to Asheville and, partly on a temporary route, continues northwest into Tennessee and the Ohio Valley. Interstate 240 forms a perimeter around the city. U.S. 19/23 is a major north and west route. The Blue Ridge Parkway runs northeast from Great Smoky Mountains National Park to Shenandoah National Park in Virginia, passing Cherokee, Asheville, and the High Country. U.S. 221 runs north to the Virginia border through Blowing Rock and Boone and intersects Interstate 40 at Marion. U.S. 321 intersects Interstate 40 at Hickory and heads to Blowing Rock and Boone.

## RESTAURANTS

You can still get traditional mountain food, served family-style, at inns around the region. Increasingly, though, mountain cooks are offering more-sophisticated fare. Asheville chefs, trained at leading culinary programs, are creating innovative dishes. At many places the emphasis is on "slow food"—made with locally grown, often organic, ingredients. You can find nearly every world cuisine somewhere in the region, from Thai, Cuban, and Jamaican to Nepalese and northern Indian. *Prices in the reviews are the average cost of a main course at dinner or, if dinner is not served, at lunch.*

## HOTELS

Around the mountains, at least in the larger cities and towns such as Asheville, Hendersonville, and Boone, you can find the usual chain motels and hotels. For more of a local flavor, look at the many mountain lodges and country inns, some with just a few rooms with simple comforts, others with upmarket amenities like tennis courts, golf courses, and spas. Bed-and-breakfasts bloom in the mountains like wildflowers, and there are literally scores of B&Bs in the region; Asheville alone has more than three dozen. The mountains also have a few large resorts, of which the Grove Park Inn in Asheville is the prime example. Visiting in the off-season can save you a third or more on hotel rates. Rates are highest during summer weekends and the October leaf-changing season. *Prices in the reviews are the lowest cost of a standard double room in high season.*

## VISITOR INFORMATION

**Contacts Brevard/Transylvania County Chamber of Commerce** ✉ *175 E. Main St., Brevard* ☎ *800/648–4523, 828/883–3700* 🌐 *www.brevardnc.org.* **Cashiers Area Chamber of Commerce** ✉ *202 U.S. 64, Cashiers* ☎ *828/743–5191* 🌐 *www.cashiersnorthcarolina.com.* **Highlands Chamber of Commerce** ✉ *269 Oak St., Highlands* ☎ *828/526–2112, 866/526–5841* 🌐 *www.highlandschamber.org.* **North Carolina High Country Host** ✉ *1701 Blowing Rock Rd., Boone* ☎ *800/438–7500, 828/264–1299* 🌐 *www.visitboonenc.com.*

# ASHEVILLE

Asheville is the hippest city in the South. At least that's the claim of Asheville's fans, who are legion. Visitors flock to Asheville to experience the arts and culture scene, which rivals that of Santa Fe, and to experience the city's blossoming downtown, with its myriad restaurants, coffeehouses, microbreweries, museums, galleries, bookstores, antiques shops, and boutiques.

Named "the best place to live" by many books and magazines, Asheville is also the destination for retirees escaping the cold North, or of "half-backs," those who moved to Florida but who are now coming half the way back to the North. Old downtown buildings have been converted to upmarket condos for these affluent retirees, and, despite the housing slowdown, new residential developments are springing up south, east, and west of town. As a result of this influx, Asheville has a much more cosmopolitan population than most cities of its size (85,000 people in the city; 430,000 in the metro area).



Asheville has a diversity you won't find in many cities in the South. There's a thriving gay community, many aging hippies, and young alternative-lifestyle seekers. People for the Ethical Treatment of Animals (PETA) have named Asheville the most vegetarian-friendly small city in America.

The city really comes alive at night, with the restaurants, sidewalk cafés, and coffeehouses; so visit after dark to see the city at its best. Especially on warm summer weekends Pack Square, Biltmore Avenue, Broadway, Haywood Street, Wall Street, Pritchard Park (site of a popular drum circle on Friday night), and Battery Park Avenue are busy until late.

### GETTING HERE AND AROUND

From the east and west, the main route to Asheville is Interstate 40. The most scenic route to Asheville is via the Blue Ridge Parkway, which meanders between Shenandoah National Park in Virginia and Great Smoky Mountains National Park near Cherokee, North Carolina. Interstate 240 forms a freeway perimeter around Asheville, and Pack Square is the center of the city.

While a car is virtually a necessity to explore Asheville thoroughly, the city does have a metropolitan bus system with 24 routes radiating from the Transit Center in downtown. Asheville also has sightseeing trolley services; tickets are available at the Asheville Convention and Visitors Bureau. The city is highly walkable, and the best way to see downtown is on foot.

### ESSENTIALS

**Visitor Information Asheville Convention and Visitors Bureau** ✉ *36 Montford Ave., Downtown* ☎ *828/258–6129, 828/258–6101* 🌐 *www.exploreasheville.com* ⏲ *Mon.–Sat. 9–5.*

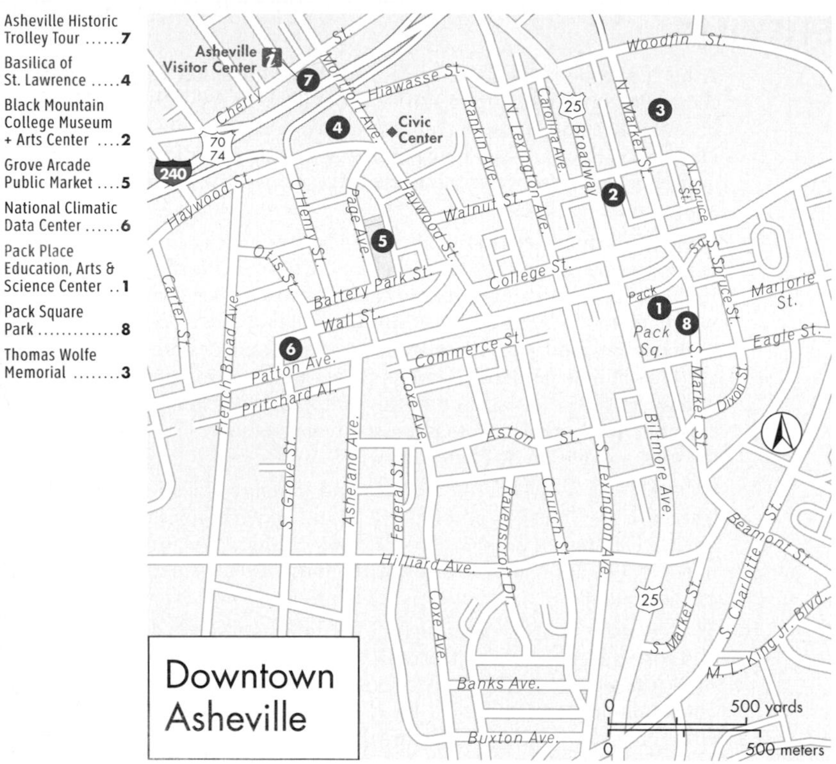


## DOWNTOWN ASHEVILLE

A city of neighborhoods, Asheville rewards careful exploration, especially on foot. You can break up your sightseeing with stops at the more than 100 restaurants and bars in downtown alone, and at any of hundreds of unique shops.

Downtown Asheville has the largest extant collection of art-deco buildings in the Southeast outside of Miami Beach, most notably the S&W Cafeteria (1929), Asheville City Hall (1928), First Baptist Church (1927), and Asheville High School (1929). It's also known for its architecture in other styles: Battery Park Hotel (1924) is neo-Georgian; the Flatiron Building (1924) is neoclassical; the Basilica of St. Lawrence (1909) is Spanish baroque; and Pack Place, formerly known as Old Pack Library (1925), is in the Italian-Renaissance style.

### TOP ATTRACTIONS

**Basilica of St. Lawrence.** A collaboration of Biltmore House head architect Richard Sharp Smith and the Spanish engineer-architect Rafael Gustavin, this elaborate Catholic basilica was completed in 1909. It follows a Spanish-Renaissance design, rendered in brick and polychrome tile, and has a large, self-supporting dome with Catalan-style vaulting. Groups of five or more can request a guided tour by filling out the form on the church's website; walk-in, self-guided tours are available any time the church is open (free brochures available in vestibule). ✉ *97 Haywood St., Downtown* ☎ *828/252–6042* ✉ *basilicatours@gmail.com* 🌐 *www.saintlawrencebasilica.org* *Free, donations requested* ⏲ *Daily, hours vary.*

**Black Mountain College Museum + Arts Center.** Famed Black Mountain College (1933–57), 16 miles east of Asheville, was important in the development of several groundbreaking 20th-century art, dance, and literary movements. Some of the maverick spirits it attracted in its short lifetime include artists Willem and Elaine de Kooning, Robert Rauschenberg, Josef and Anni Albers, Ben Shahn, M. C. Richards, and Franz Kline; dancer Merce Cunningham; musician John Cage; filmmaker Arthur Penn; futurist Buckminster Fuller; and writers Kenneth Noland, Charles Olson, and Robert Creeley. A museum and gallery dedicated to the history of the radical college occupies a small space in downtown Asheville. It puts on exhibits, hosts lectures, and publishes material about the college. Call ahead or visit the museum's Web site to find out what's currently happening. ✉ *56 Broadway, Downtown* ☎ *828/350–8484* 🌐 *www.blackmountaincollege.org* *Varies by exhibit, usually $5–$10* ⏲ *Tues.–Wed. noon–4; Thurs.–Sat. 11–5.*

4

**Grove Arcade Public Market.** Before its official opening in 1929, the Grove Arcade was trumpeted as "the most elegant building in America" by its builder, W. E. Grove, the man also responsible for the Grove Park Inn. Grove envisioned a new kind of retail, office, and residential center, an early version of a mall. Grove died before completing the project, and a planned 14-story tower was never built. The building is an architectural wonder, with gargoyles galore, but after World War II it lost its luster. In late 2002 its polished limestone elegance was restored, and it reopened as a public market patterned in some ways after Pike Place Market in Seattle. (A self-guided architectural tour takes about 45 minutes.) The market covers a full city block and has about 40 locally owned shops and restaurants, along with apartments and office space. The south end of the Arcade has an outdoor market with about a dozen stalls selling local crafts and farm products. ✉ *1 Page Ave., Downtown* ☎ *828/252–7799* 🌐 *www.grovearcade.com* *Free* ⏲ *Mon.–Sat. 10–6, Sun. noon–5; store hrs vary.*

**Pack Place Education, Arts & Science Center.** This 92,000-square-foot complex in downtown Asheville houses the **Asheville Art Museum, Colburn Earth Science Museum,** and **Diana Wortham Theatre.** The **YMI Cultural Center** (also a part of Pack Place), which focuses on the history of African-Americans in North Carolina is just south of Place Place at 39 South Market St. The Asheville Art Museum stages major exhibits several times a year, with some highlighting regional artists. The Colburn Earth Science Museum displays local gems and minerals. The intimate 500-seat Diana Wortham Theatre hosts musical concerts and dance and theater performances year-round. ✉ *2 S. Pack Sq., Downtown* ☎ *828/257–4500* 🌐 *www.packplace.org* *Asheville Art Museum $8, Colburn Earth Science Museum $6, YMI Cultural Center $5* ⏲ *Tues.–Sat. 10–5, Sun. 1–5; YMI Tues.–Fri. 10–5.*

Biltmore, once the home of George Vanderbilt, is the largest private home in the United States; the estate grounds occupy some 8,000 acres.

Fodor's Choice ★ **Thomas Wolfe Memorial.** Asheville's most famous son, novelist Thomas Wolfe (1900–38), grew up in a 29-room Queen Anne–style home that his mother ran as a boardinghouse. In his prime in the 1930s, Wolfe was widely viewed as one of the best writers America had ever produced; his reputation gradually waned, although today he is being rediscovered. The house—memorialized as "Dixieland" in Wolfe's novel *Look Homeward, Angel*—was badly damaged in a 1998 fire; it reopened in 2004 following a painstaking $2.4 million renovation. While about one-fifth of the furniture and artifacts were lost in the fire, the house has been restored to its original 1916 condition, including a light canary-yellow paint on the exterior. You'll find a visitor center and many displays, and there are guided tours of the house and heirloom gardens. ✉ *52 Market St., Downtown* ☎ *828/253–8304* 🌐 *www.wolfememorial.com* 🎟 *$5* ⏲ *Tues.–Sat. 9–5, Sun. 1–5.*

## WORTH NOTING

**Asheville Historic Trolley Tour.** A motorized trolley bus takes you to the main points of interest around Asheville, including the Grove Park Inn, Biltmore Village, the River Arts District, Pack Square, and downtown. You can buy tickets and board the trolley at the Asheville Convention and Visitors Bureau and get on or off at any stop on this 90-minute narrated tour. Family packages at $45 are a good deal if you're traveling with children. Ghost Tours on Thursday, Friday, and Saturday evenings at 7:30, May to October (reduced schedule during the rest of the year) explore Asheville's supernatural side. ✉ *Asheville Convention and Visitors Bureau, 36 Montford Ave.* ☎ *828/681–8585, 888/667–3600* 🌐 *www.ashevilletrolleytours.com* 🎟 *$19, ghost tours $20.*

**Asheville Urban Trail.** This 1.7-mile walk developed by the City of Asheville has 30 "stations" in five areas of downtown, with plaques marking places of historical or architectural interest. The free self-guided tour begins at Pack Square and takes about 2 hours to complete. Pick up free maps at Pack Place and various shops in downtown Asheville, or download the Urban Trail map and brochure from the website. Guided tours must be scheduled in advance. ✉ *2 S. Pack Sq., Downtown* ☎ *828/259–5800* 🌐 *www.ashevillenc.gov/parks* 🎟 *Free, guided tour $5.*

**LaZoom Tour.** If you're looking for something a little different in a tour, try LaZoom comedy tours. You ride in a big, open-air purple bus and watch actors and comics do comedy skits and over-the-top routines about the wacky side of Asheville. If you're 21 or over, you can bring your own wine or beer (no booze) on the bus. In peak periods such as summer and fall weekends, LaZoom has three or four tours a day, including 90-min City Comedy Tours ($23 adults, $20 for Asheville residents) and 60-min Haunted Comedy Tours ($20). Due to adult comedy routines, riders must be at least 17 on the Haunted Comedy Tours and at least 13 on the City Comedy Tours. Haunted tours leave from the Thirsty Monk at 92 Patton Ave.; city tours leave from the French Broad Co-Op at 90 Biltmore Ave. ✉ *Ticket Office, 1 1/2 Battery Park Ave., Downtown* ☎ *828/225–6932* 🌐 *www.lazoomtours.com* ⏲ *No tours Mon. or Jan.–Feb. In slower periods tours may not run daily.*

**National Climatic Data Center (NCDC).** The world's largest active archive of global weather data, the National Climatic Data Center provides weather data to researchers all over the world. The NCDC gathers and maintains weather data from some 10,000 weather stations around the United States, and some of its historical data goes back more than 200 years. Users of the data range from large engineering firms planning energy-efficient development to individuals planning a retirement move. **■ TIP→ At present, only group tours of the center are available and must be arranged in advance.** ✉ *Federal Plaza, 151 Patton Ave., Downtown* ☎ *828/271–4494 for group tours, 828/271–4800* 🌐 *www.ncdc.noaa.gov* 🎟 *Free* ⏲ *Weekdays 8–4:30.*

**Pack Square Park.** Reopened in 2009–2010 after an $18 million renovation, the former City-County Plaza is a great place to relax downtown. At Pack Square there's a stone-and-bronze fountain designed by local sculptor Hoss Haley, and the Zebulon Vance Monument honoring a North Carolina governor. Princeton elms, London plane trees, black gum trees, and hornbeam trees provide plenty of shade. At the eastern edge of the park in Roger McGuire Green is Splashville, a large fountain where in warm weather you'll see hundreds of kids, and even some adults, playing in the water. There's also a stage lined with colorful tiles by local ceramist Kathy Triplett, a grassy amphitheater, and a veterans monument. ✉ *Pack Sq., Downtown* ☎ *828/252–2300 Pack Square Conservancy, 828/259–5800 Asheville Parks* 🌐 *www.packsquarepark.org* 🎟 *Free* ⏲ *Daily 24 hrs.*

## GREATER ASHEVILLE

North Asheville, the historic Montford section (home to more than a dozen B&Bs), and the Grove Park neighborhood all have fine Victorian-era homes, including many remarkable Queen Anne houses. Biltmore Village, across from the entrance to the Biltmore Estate, was constructed at the time that Biltmore House was being built and is now predominantly an area of retail boutiques and galleries. The River Arts District, along the French Broad River, is the up-and-coming arts area, with many studios and galleries, plus cafés and clubs. Across the river, West Asheville has become a hot part of the city, with its main artery, Haywood Road, sporting new restaurants, edgy stores, and popular clubs, though much of West Asheville retains its low-key, slightly scruffy, 1950s ambience.

### TOP ATTRACTIONS

Fodor's Choice ★ **Biltmore Estate.** Built in the 1890s as the private home of George Vanderbilt, the astonishing 250-room French-Renaissance château is America's largest private home. Some of Vanderbilt's descendants still live on the estate, but the bulk of the house and grounds is open to visitors. Richard Morris Hunt designed it, and Frederick Law Olmsted landscaped the original 125,000-acre estate (now 8,000 acres). It took 1,000 workers five years to complete the gargantuan project. On view are the priceless antiques and art collected by the Vanderbilts, including notable paintings by Renoir and John Singer Sargent, along with 75 acres of gardens and formally landscaped grounds. You can also see the state-of-the-art winery, one of the largest in the East, and an 1890s-era farm, River Bend. Candlelight tours of the house are offered at Christmastime. Also on the grounds are a deluxe hotel, seven restaurants, and an equestrian center. A new section called Antler Hill Village, with shops, restaurants, and crafts demonstrations, opened in 2010. Each summer, Biltmore Estate hosts music concerts with nationally known entertainers. Most people tour the house on their own, but guided tours are available. Note that there are a lot of stairs to climb, but much of the house is accessible for guests in wheelchairs or with limited mobility. ■ **TIP→ At busier times, self-guided visits of the interior of the house now require a reservation, so call in advance or book online.** Save money by buying tickets online rather than at the gate, with the lowest prices for tickets purchased seven days in advance. The best deal is the annual pass, allowing unlimited admission for a year and costing only a little more than one-day admission. ✉ *1 Approach Rd., Biltmore Village* ☎ *828/225–1600* 🌐 *www.biltmore.com* 🎫 *Sun.–Fri. $59, Sat. $69 Discounts available with advance purchase online and at certain times of the year.* ⏲ *Late Mar.–early Nov., daily 9–4; late-Nov.–early Mar., hrs vary.*

**Biltmore Village.** Across from the main entrance to the Biltmore Estate, Biltmore Village is a highly walkable collection of restored English village–style houses dating from the turn of the 20th century, along with some newer buildings designed to blend with the original architecture. Stroll the brick sidewalks and tree-lined streets and visit antiques stores, clothing and jewelry shops, art galleries, and restaurants. ✉ *Biltmore Village* 🌐 *www.biltmorevillage.com.*

**All Souls Cathedral.** One of the most beautiful churches in America, All Souls Espiscopal Cathedral was designed by Richard Morris Hunt following the traditional Greek Cross plan and inspired by abbey churches in Northern England. It opened in 1896. ✉ *9 Swan St., Biltmore Village* ☎ *828/274–2681* 🌐 *www.allsoulscathedral.org* 🎫 *Free* 🕑 *Daily, hrs vary.*

Fodor's Choice ★ **North Carolina Arboretum.** Part of the original Biltmore Estate, these 434 acres completed Frederick Law Olmsted's dream of creating a world-class arboretum in the western part of North Carolina. The Arboretum is affiliated with the University of North Carolina. Highlights include southern Appalachian flora in stunning settings, such as the Blue Ridge Quilt Garden, with bedding plants arranged in patterns reminiscent of Appalachian quilts, and sculptures set among the gardens. The Arboretum has a total of 65 acres of cultivated gardens. A 10-mile network of trails is available for walking or mountain biking. A bonsai exhibit features miniature versions of many native trees. The 16,000-square-foot Baker Exhibit Center hosts traveling exhibits on art, science, and history. Dogs are welcome on the grounds but must be leashed. ✉ *100 Frederick Law Olmsted Way, 10 miles southwest of downtown Asheville, at BRP MM 393, near I–26 and I–40, South Metro* ☎ *828/665–2492* 🌐 *www.ncarboretum.org* 🎫 *Free, parking fee $8* 🕑 *Visitor and exhibit center daily 9–5; gardens and grounds Apr.–Oct., daily 8 am–9 pm; Nov.–Mar., daily 8–7.*

**WNC Farmers Market.** The highest-volume farmers' market in North Carolina may be architecturally unappealing, but it's a good place to buy local jams, jellies, honey, stone-ground grits and cornmeal, and, in season, local fruits and vegetables. In spring look for ramps, a wild cousin of the onion with a very strong odor. A wholesale section with large sheds below the main retail section (both are open to all) offers produce in bulk. An herb festival is held annually in the spring. On the grounds of the market are a garden supply store and a restaurant, Moose Café. ✉ *570 Brevard Rd., 5 miles southwest of downtown Asheville, at Exit 47 of I–40, South Metro* ☎ *828/253–1691* 🌐 *www.ncagr.gov/markets/facilities/markets/asheville* 🎫 *Free* 🕑 *Apr.–Oct., daily 8–6; Nov.–Mar., daily 8–5.*

### WORTH NOTING

Fodor's Choice ★ **Grove Park Inn.** This large resort overlooking Asheville is well worth a visit even if you don't stay the night. The oldest section was built in 1913 using locally mined granite stones, some weighing 10,000 pounds, and was modeled after the grand railroad hotels in the American West. Inside you'll find the largest collection of Arts and Crafts furniture in the world. On the grounds are two small but interesting museums: the **North Carolina Homespun Museum** (🌐 *www.grovewood.com/homespun_museum.php*) tells the story of a training school established by the Vanderbilt family to revive interest in native crafts. A collection of antique cars assembled by a local car dealer is the main feature of the **Estes-Winn Memorial Automobile Museum** (🌐 *www.grovewood.com/car_museum.php*). Grovewood Gallery, also on the resort grounds in a 1917 English-style cottage, showcases the work of some 500 craftspeople and artists. If you visit in the cooler months, be sure to warm

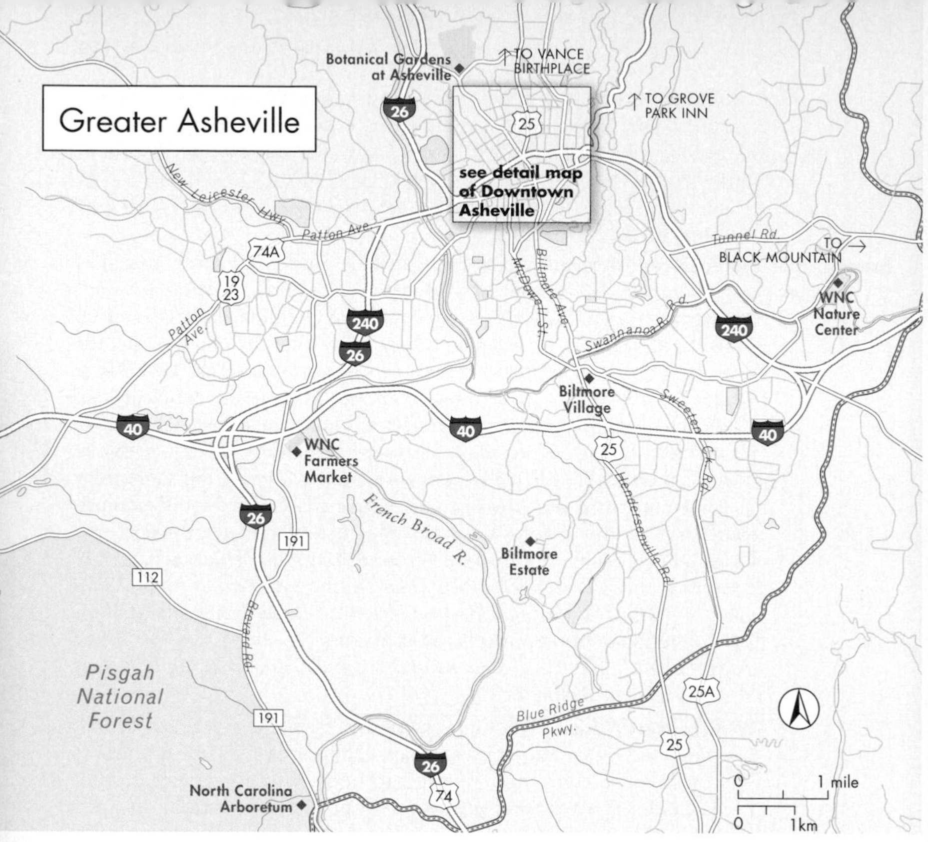


yourself in front of the two enormous stone fireplaces in the inn's lobby. ✉ *290 Macon Ave., North Metro* ☎ *800/438–5800, 828/252–2711* 🌐 *www.groveparkinn.com* 🎫 *Free* 🕑 *Hotel daily 24 hrs; Homespun Museum and Estes-Winn Automobile Museum Apr.–Dec., Mon.–Sat. 10–5, Sun. 11–5.*

**WNC Nature Center.** On a 42-acre Natural Heritage site, the WNC Nature Center is one of the region's most popular attractions for kids. It's basically a zoo focusing on animals native to the region, with cougars, bobcats, black bears, white-tailed deer, gray and red wolves, and gray and red foxes in natural-like settings. The center also has an excellent area on native reptiles and amphibians, plus a petting zoo with farm animals. ✉ *75 Gashes Creek Rd., East Metro* ☎ *828/298–5600* 🌐 *www.wildwnc.org* 🎫 *$8* 🕑 *Daily 10–5.*

## WHERE TO EAT

Because of the large number of visitors to Asheville and the many upscale retirees who've moved here, the city has a dining scene that's much more vibrant and varied than its size would suggest. You'll find everything from Greek to Vietnamese, Moroccan to Southern soul food, and barbecue to sushi. Asheville has more vegetarian restaurants per capita than any other city, and there are coffeehouses on many corners.

## DOWNTOWN

$ INDIAN
**Chai Pani.** Chai Pani serves "Indian street food," but you don't have to buy it from a street stall. In a pleasant small space with photos of India on the walls, enjoy classic snacks like *bhel puri* (puffed rice, flour crisps, and chickpea noodles with tamarind chutney) or green tomato pakoras fried in a curried chickpea batter. Most items are only $5 or $6, so you and your party can order several for a filling meal without spending a lot of rupees. *Average main: $11* ✉ *22 Battery Park Ave., Downtown* ☎ *828/254–4003* 🌐 *www.chaipani.net.*

$$$ SPANISH
**Cúrate.** If you have the blahs, Cúrate, with its extraordinary tapas and fun atmosphere, is the cure. Opened in 2011, Cúrate quickly became the hottest dining ticket in town, with reservations essential. Restaurant owners Ted, Elizabeth, and Katie Button, and Chef Felix Meana, formerly of the famed elBulli restaurant on the Costa Brava, brought truly authentic Spanish tapas to the mountains. There are about four dozen small plates on the menu (ranging from $4 to $20), about 80% of which remain throughout the year, though seasonal dishes are added. Especially notable are the cured Iberian ham dishes, the creamy chilled gazpacho, *berenjenas la taberna* (fried eggplant drizzled with mountain honey), and for dessert, *espuma de chocolate* (warm chocolate mousse with raspberry sorbet and hazelnut praline). *Average main: $23* ✉ *11 Biltmore Ave., Downtown* ☎ *828/239–2946* 🌐 *www.curatetapasbar.com* *Reservations essential* *Closed Mon.*

$ SOUTHERN
**Early Girl Eatery.** Named after an early-maturing tomato variety, Early Girl Eatery is casually Southern, with a cheerfully natural twist. A wall of south-facing windows provides wonderful light most of the day. Early Girl partners with about two dozen local farms for its farm-to-table cuisine. Breakfast is served all day and includes stacks of multigrain pancakes with organic maple syrup, shrimp and grits, and sausage and sweet potato scramble. At lunch and dinner, go for the sandwiches or try the "meat and two" option that includes a main dish such as sauteed local trout with pecan butter or pan-fried free-range chicken, served with a fresh-made biscuit and your choice of a selection of sides such as ginger cole slaw, collard greens, and macaroni and cheese. There's often a wait at breakfast; reservations usually accepted for dinner only. *Average main: $11* ✉ *8 Wall St., Downtown* ☎ *828/259–9292* 🌐 *www.earlygirleatery.com* *No dinner Mon.*

$$$ ECLECTIC Fodor's Choice ★
**Limones.** Though often considered a Mexican restaurant, and the chef is from Mexico City, Limones is not the kind of Mexican you may be thinking of. Instead, the eclectic menu melds French, Italian, and New American influences with modern Mexican ingredients and techniques. The result is an extraordinary fusion of flavors. For example, the beef tenderloin is served on a bed of vinegar-infused organic kale with truffle macaroni and cheese, and a shaved fennel and onion salad. The sea scallops, huge and juicy, come with a bacon and corn risotto, arugula, heirloom tomato salsa, and lemon beurre blanc. Almost two pages of the menu are devoted to various tequila drinks, including a dozen kinds of margaritas, and there's a small but interesting wine list, as well as a nice selection of Mexican and local microbrew beers. Located around the corner from an art movie house, the space—a small, narrow rectangle

CLOSE UP

## Asheville's Slow Food Movement

The Asheville area also has many tailgate markets, usually in parking lots where local growers set up temporary sales stalls on certain days, and farmers' markets, which typically are larger than tailgate markets and often have permanent booths.

**ASAP.** About 500 small family farms in the region belong to Asheville-based ASAP. The Appalachian Sustainable Agriculture Project lists more than 80 local restaurants that buy direct from local farmers. ✉ *306 W. Haywood St., Downtown* ☎ *828/236–1281* 🌐 *www.asapconnections.org.*

**Blue Ridge Food Ventures.** Part of a local economic development organization called Advantage West, Blue Ridge Food Ventures assists entrepreneurs in developing and selling local food products. Around 30 specialty-food producers are members of Blue Ridge Food Ventures, including Carolina Pig Polish (barbecue sauce), Lusty Monk (hot mustards), and Hominy Valley Farms (free-range chicken and beef). ✉ *1461 Sand Hill Rd., Candler* ☎ *828/348–0128* 🌐 *www.advantagewest.com.*

*Below are some Asheville markets, the best of the more than 50 tailgate and farmers' markets in the region.*

**Asheville City Market.** Nearly everything at this downtown market is local. Offerings vary, but usually include farm-fresh produce, free-range eggs, homemade breads, and local cheeses from up to 30 local farms. ✉ *161 S. Charlotte St., Downtown* ☎ *828/348–0340* 🕓 *Sat. 8–1.*

**Asheville City Market–South.** This spin-off from the downtown Asheville City Market is a producer-only market with food from local farmers. ✉ *Biltmore Park Town Square, Town Square Blvd., Metro South* ☎ *828/348–0340* 🕓 *Wed. 2–6.*

Lusty Monk mustards.

**French Broad Food Co-Op Wednesday Market.** Besides organic vegetables and fruits, the market at the French Broad Food Co-Op also has local honey and jams, vegan baked goods, and brick-oven breads. ✉ *76 Biltmore Ave., Downtown* ☎ *828/255–7650* 🕓 *Wed. 2–6.*

**Greenlife Sunday Market.** The focus here is on organically grown produce, as well as herbs, flowers, and seasonal items from local organic farms. ✉ *Greenlife/Whole Foods, 70 Merrimon Ave., Metro North* ☎ *828/243–0222* 🌐 *www.local-farmers-markets.com* 🕓 *May–Oct., Sun. 1–5.*

**North Asheville Tailgate Market.** Asheville's oldest tailgate market has about 40 vendors selling local produce, fruit, meats, breads, and crafts. ✉ *UNC-Asheville, 1 University Heights, Metro North* ☎ *828/776–6286* 🌐 *www.northashevilletailgatemarket.org* 🕓 *Mid-Apr.–Dec., Sat. 8–noon.*

**West Asheville Tailgate Market.** Local natural and organic farms bring their best stuff, including free-range chicken, grass-fed beef, and organic eggs, to this popular tailgate market. ✉ *718 Haywood Rd., Metro West* ☎ *828/216–8102* 🌐 *www.westashevilletailgatemarket.com* 🕓 *Apr.–Nov., Tues. 3:30–6:30.*

Asheville has a thriving restaurant scene and the weather is often mild enough to dine alfresco.

with a high pressed-tin ceiling and exposed ducts—has the feel of a side-street San Francisco bistro. *Average main: $24* *13 Eagle St., Downtown* *828/252–2327* *www.limonesrestaurant.com* *Reservations essential* *Open daily for dinner; brunch Sun.*

$$ INDIAN ★ **Mela Indian.** Mela has established itself as the best Indian restaurant in the city. Rather than specialize in one type of Indian cuisine, it offers dishes from across the country. The tandoori dishes (chicken, salmon, or lamb) are especially delicious. At lunch, there's an extensive buffet selection. Dinner entrées are served with basmati rice, lentil stew, and *papadum* (lentil wafers). Portions are large, making this one of the best values downtown. The space is unexpectedly modern, with rough tile walls and a high ceiling, though accented with woodwork, doors, and furnishings from India. *Average main: $14* *70 N. Lexington, Downtown* *828/225–8880* *www.melaasheville.com.*

$ AMERICAN **Pack's Tavern.** A location overlooking Pack Square Park, bustling with families and downtown workers, helped make Pack's Tavern instantly popular. The multi-million-dollar renovation of a 1907 building, with original brick walls, high ceilings, and big windows with views of the park, provides a pleasant atmosphere for enjoying a menu that includes fried foods like potato skins, onion straws (splashed with lemon pepper and sprinkled with Parmesan), and the signature Mt. Mitchell Burger, an eight-ouncer with bacon, green tomato, a fried egg, and cheddar and Swiss cheese. You can also get steak, local trout, grilled chicken, and various salads. Pack's Tavern promises more than 30 draft beers and a full bar. There's a Sunday brunch in an upstairs meeting room and year-round outdoor dining. *Average main: $11* *20 Spruce St., Downtown* *828/225–6944* *www.packstavern.com.*

$$ CARIBBEAN **Salsa's.** Newly expanded in 2012, Salsa's is the original flagship of Puerto Rico native Hector Diaz's several Asheville restaurants, which include **Chorizo** (Latin), **Modesto** (Italian), and Zambra (Spanish-Moroccan tapas), all recommended. Here, you'll find spicy and highly creative Caribbean-Mexican fusion fare in large portions. Roast pork enchiladas with corn, chilies, coconut-annatto sauce, and queso blanco, and organic chicken quesadillas with peppers, carrots, and curry sauce are among the recommended entrées. At lunch you'll find equally large portions, often enough to carry out for a second meal, at midday prices. *Average main: $15 6 Patton Ave., Downtown 828/252–9805 www.salsasnc.com.*

$$ SOUTHERN ★ **Tupelo Honey Café.** Hello, darlin'! This is the place for down-home Southern cooking with an uptown twist. Chef Brian Sonoskus delivers a lot more than grits, with dishes like Stroganoff, Y'all and mountain trout with spinach beurre blanc. Breakfast is served anytime. The atmosphere is noisy and a little funky. There's some sidewalk seating and often a line. Kids are welcome; they can entertain themselves by drawing on the paper tablecloths. A suburban location on Hendersonville Road in South Asheville has a similar menu, with a little more Southern kitsch in the decor. *Average main: $16 12 College St., Downtown 828/255–4863 www.tupelohoneycafe.com Reservations not accepted.*

$$$ SPANISH ★ **Zambra.** Sophisticated tapas selections, such as grilled scallops with parsnip-potato gratin, prosciutto-wrapped medjool dates with goat cheese, pomegranate and pork spring rolls, and pan-seared local trout, make this one of the most interesting restaurants in Asheville. There are also several varieties of paella and other dishes, influenced by the cuisine of Mediterranean Spain and North Africa, and an award-winning wine list featuring some 200 Spanish wines and sherries. Ingredients are sourced from local organic farms. Voluptuous Moorish colors, dim lighting, a cave-like atmosphere, and live jazz lend an exotic air. *Average main: $20 85 Walnut St., Downtown 828/232–1060 www.zambratapas.com Reservations essential No lunch.*

## GREATER ASHEVILLE

$ BARBECUE Fodor's Choice ★ **12 Bones Smokehouse.** You'll recognize this spot by the long line of customers snaking out the door. Open only weekdays 11 to 4, the wait to place your order is often half an hour. (Even President Barack Obama had to wait during a visit in 2010.) True to the barbecue-joint ethos, with concrete floors and old Formica-top tables, 12 Bones has little atmosphere. What it does have is the smokiest baby-back ribs you've ever tasted, pulled pork, turkey, beef brisket, chicken BBQ plates, and delicious sides including collard greens, corn pudding, and "mashed sweet taters." The crowd ranges from hippie potters from the River District art studios to downtown suits. The staff will call you "Sweetie." A second location is south of Asheville in Arden. *Average main: $7 5 Riverside Dr., River Arts District 828/253–4499 www.12bones.com Closed weekends; no dinner.*

$$$ ECLECTIC ★ **The Admiral.** Don't be put off by the dowdy cinderblock exterior and the low-rent West Asheville neighborhood. Inside this dimly lit, narrow little restaurant with a divey bar atmosphere, you'll find some of the most creative cooking in town. The dinner menu changes daily and features both

small and large plates. Expect dishes such as seared scallops with smoked corn bisque or duck breast with poblano-bacon consommé and pea tendrils. Start with The Admiral's refreshing signature drink, the Cucumbersome, gin infused with fresh cucumber. $ *Average main: $24* ✉ *400 Haywood Rd., Greater Asheville* ☎ *828/252–2541* 🌐 *www.theadmiralnc.com* ✍ *Reservations essential* ⊙ *Closed Sun.; no lunch.*

$$ ECLECTIC ✕ **Chef Mo's.** Mexico City native Mauricio Abreu mixes Mexican, South American, and New Orleans flavors with a variety of traditional ingredients (from scallops, shrimp, and lobster to lamb, veal, and beef) to create his innovative and eclectic menu of tasty treats. For example, Chef Mo's version of lobster is to dip a tail in beer batter, quickly deep-fry it, and serve it with chipotle rémoulade, mashed sweet potatoes, and sauteed kale and spinach. The restaurant, stuck on the second level of a nondescript strip mall with parking around back, is virtually invisible from the street. But once inside, the space is welcoming, with bold abstract paintings by local River Arts District artist Jonas Gerard. Compared with other Asheville restaurants of the same quality, prices here are generally a good value. $ *Average main: $18* ✉ *900 Hendersonville Rd., Ste. 201, South Metro* ☎ *828/274–3533* 🌐 *www.chefmo.com.*

$$ SOUTHERN ★ ✕ **Isis Restaurant & Music Hall.** A classic movie house, the Isis Theater was brought back to life in late 2012 after a two-year total renovation. It's now the most upscale restaurant in West Asheville and a late-night music club. Underneath the movie marquee, the dining room has expansive windows overlooking the busy West Asheville street scene. High ceilings with exposed ducting, wood tables, and polished concrete floors give the space a modern urban feel. The menu of new Southern cuisine includes appetizers like hoppin' John with yellow-eyed peas, shrimp, smoked bacon and red quinoa, and mains like seared local rainbow trout with wilted chard and artichoke beurre blanc. The main music stage is at the back where the movie screen used to be, with a lively bar connecting the two areas. Dinner is served until 10, at which point the Isis starts serving bar snacks and the music—a mix of bluegrass, reggae, jazz, and rock—begins. $ *Average main: $15* ✉ *743 Haywood Rd., West Metro* ☎ *828/575–2737* 🌐 *www.isisasheville.com* ⊙ *No lunch.*

$$ SOUTHERN ★ ✕ **The Junction.** Hip and artsy, The Junction is the quintessential River Arts District dinner spot. With exposed ducting and concrete floors, the main dining space has an industrial vibe, softened by original art on the walls. The noise level can be high, though there's quieter dining on the outdoor patio. Chefs in the open kitchen create locally sourced slow food dishes, often with a Southern twist, such as sweet tea–brined fried chicken on green tomato stew. The cocktail menu is innovative, involving unusual mixtures of premium liquors, herbs, and freshly squeezed juices. There's also an interesting small wine list and a good selection of microbeers, though the best value is draft PBR for $2. Brunch is served Saturday and Sunday. $ *Average main: $16* ✉ *348 Depot St., #190, River Arts District* ☎ *828/225–3497* 🌐 *www.thejunctionasheville.com* ⊙ *Closed Mon.*

$$ ITALIAN ★ ✕ **Nona Mia Ritrovo.** Situated in West Asheville, "My Grandmother" has a full Italian menu, but the pizza's the thing. Choose between thick Sicilian style or thin-crust Napoletana style, both made in wood-fired

ovens and both delicious. In good weather you can escape the noisy din inside by eating on the deck out back or at outdoor tables. For dessert try the freshly made gelato. Waitstaff is super-friendly if sometimes forgetful. Lunch is served on weekends only. *Average main: $15 ✉ 1050 Haywood Rd., West Metro ☎ 828/505–8315 ⊕ www.nonamiaritrovo.com ✍ Reservations not accepted ⊙ Closed Mon.; No lunch Tues.–Fri.*

$ MEXICAN **✕ Papa's & Beer.** Asheville's most popular Mexican spots are known for huge portions at modest prices. With fajita plates sizzling, cervezas popping, and tables packed with hungry families, Papa's & Beer, the most popular of them all, can be noisy. The margaritas here are top-notch. Additional locations include one on Tunnel Road and one on Hendersonville Road. *Average main: $9 ✉ 1000 Brevard Rd., West Metro ☎ 828/665–9070.*

$$ VEGETARIAN **✕ Plant.** Having overcome its location in a former financial loan office a little north of the downtown bustle, Plant has become one of Asheville's best vegan and vegetarian spots, with a sophisticated, frequently changing menu. Look for starters like flamed seitan skewers with fried bananas, and entrées like chanterelle and lobster mushrooms with smoked-jalapeño mashed Yukon potatoes and herbed baby vegetables, or red-curry tofu with kaffir limes, jasmine rice, and teriyaki broccoli. For dessert, the made-on-site ice cream (with coconut milk) is fantastic. Decor is minimalist, with just one window and an open kitchen dominating the narrow dining room. There's outdoor seating on the south end of the building. The staff is amiable. Wine and beer only. *Average main: $16 ✉ 165 Merrimon Ave., North Metro ☎ 828/258–7500 ⊕ www.plantisfood.com ⊙ Closed Mon.*

$$ AMERICAN **✕ Stone House Market.** Situated in an obscure, off-the-beaten path residential area west of Asheville (you may need a GPS to find it), Stone House Market occupies a 1920s service station, renovated with an eye for kitsch. Be prepared to linger over dinner because the only staff is the couple who own it (Dan cooks, Debbie handles the front of the house). You'll definitely get your money's worth—a huge serving of beautifully charred pork ribs in a chipotle sauce with mashed potatoes and vegetables comes with a salad and delicious fresh-baked bread, all for under $20. Accompany it with a glass of house red from Australia. The menu at this little restaurant—it seats only 30—changes weekly, but there's usually a choice of fish, pork, lamb or beef, pasta, and chicken. And, oh yes, the bathroom is outside and around the back, just like it was when this was still a gas station. *Average main: $18 ✉ 301 Old Leicester Hwy., West Metro ☎ 828/252–1200 ⊙ Open for dinner Thurs.–Sun.*

$ SOUTHERN ★ **✕ Sunny Point Café and Bakery.** In a restored storefront in up-and-coming West Asheville, Sunny Point lives up to its name with bright, cheerful decor, heavy on the orange and blue. It's a good spot for breakfast (served all day), where free-range pork sausage shares the menu with granola, herbed potatoes, and some of the biggest biscuits in town. For dinner, try the shrimp and grits; meatloaf with buttermilk mashed potatoes, onion strings, and sauteed greens; or build your own burger. Herbs and some veggies come from the restaurant's organic garden next door. In good weather the best tables are outside on the covered patio. *Average main: $12 ✉ 626 Haywood Rd., West Metro ☎ 828/252–0055* *www.sunnypointcafe.com* *Reservations not accepted* *No dinner Sun. and Mon.*

$ ECLECTIC **White Duck Taco Shop.** Popular with penny-pinching artists and craftspeople in the River Arts District, White Duck Taco stays true to its name with a roast duck taco, but it also has other fusion tacos, including Thai peanut chicken, lamb gyro, and Vietnamese banh mi tofu. Most tacos are under $4, and two make a filling meal. Line up to place your order, then find a seat inside or at the picnic tables outside; food runners will bring your drinks and food. *Average main: $8* *1 Roberts St., #101, River Arts District* *828/258–1660* *www.whiteducktacoshop.com* *Reservations not accepted* *Closed Sun.*



## BILTMORE VILLAGE

$$$ AMERICAN ★ **Corner Kitchen.** One of Asheville's most popular restaurants, Corner Kitchen even hosted President Obama when he and his family vacationed in Asheville. The menu changes regularly, and many dishes are locally sourced, with entrees such as pecan-crusted trout with sweet potatoes, or herb-roasted pork with fingerling potatoes. Be aware that this is not quite fine dining, more on the casual, homey side, and that due to limited space and the crowds from Biltmore Estate nearby, even with a reservation you may have to wait. The charmingly renovated Victorian cottage in Biltmore Village has wood floors, plaster walls painted in serene colors, and a fireplace in one dining room. *Average main: $24* *3 Boston Way, Biltmore Village* *828/274–2439* *www.thecornerkitchen.com* *Reservations essential.*

$$$ BISTRO Fodor's Choice ★ **Fig Bistro.** Though it may be tiny in size, with only around 15 tables, Fig is big in creativity. Many dishes are at least vaguely French, as the chef trained in France, but "eclectic" better describes the selection. The Prince Edward Island mussels in a rich chipotle or tomato broth are a fine way to start the meal. The menu changes frequently, but the locally sourced trout, pork, and duck are always good. Our favorite is the steak frites, with a hearty hangar steak, bordelaise sauce, and superb fries, as authentic as you'd find in Paris. Fig has a true bistro ambience, quite unpretentious, with hardwood floors, pressed-tin ceilings, a near floor-to-ceiling wall of windows (though the view is unappealing), and a well-stocked bar at one end. In good weather, there's seating in an outdoor courtyard. *Average main: $23* *18 Brook St., Biltmore Village* *828/277–0889* *www.figbistro.com* *Reservations essential* *Closed for dinner Sun.*

$$$ MEDITERRANEAN ★ **Rezaz.** With abstract art displayed on the deep red- and apricot-colored walls and waiters (the staff is nearly all male) dressed in black rushing around pouring wine, you'd never know this sophisticated Mediterranean restaurant is located in a former hardware store. The menu is divided into small- and large-plate sections. Definitely go for the fried calamari and crispy shrimp small-plate appetizer with cabbage, scallions, and a sweet-and-sour glaze. For your main course, stick to the simpler seafood and grilled steak dishes as some of the more unusual dishes miss the mark. Enter the restaurant through Enoteca, Rezaz's wine bar, which serves less expensive fare in a casual setting. *Average main: $22* *28 Hendersonville Rd., Biltmore Village* *828/277–1510* *www.rezaz.com* *Reservations essential.*

$$$$ STEAKHOUSE ★ ✕ **Ruth's Chris Steak House.** This outpost of the international restaurant group opened in Biltmore Village at the end of 2011 and quickly sizzled its way to the top of the red-meat venues in Asheville. The U.S. Prime steaks *are* top-notch, the atmosphere is upmarket, the service is doting, and the wine list is sophisticated if pricey. For the Ruth's Chris experience on a budget, join the crowd in the bar at happy hour (4:30–7 except Saturday) for a prime burger with fries at a bargain price. Parking is limited, so use the complimentary valet. *Average main: $40 ✉ 26 All Souls Crescent, Biltmore Village ☎ 828/398–6200 ⊕ www.ruths-chris.com/asheville ⊙ Dinner only.*

## WHERE TO STAY

*Hotel reviews have been abbreviated in this book. For expanded reviews, please go to Fodors.com.*

The Asheville area has a nice mix of B&Bs, motels, and small owner-operated inns. There are more than three-dozen B&Bs, one of the largest concentrations in the South. Most are in the Montford area near downtown and the Grove Park area. At least eight B&Bs in the area promote themselves as gay-owned and actively seek gay and lesbian guests, and others advertise that they are gay-friendly. With the opening of the Aloft and Indigo hotels, and the renovation of Haywood Park and some other older properties, the selection of places to stay downtown (within walking distance of restaurants and bars) has improved.

### DOWNTOWN

$$$ HOTEL **Aloft Asheville Downtown.** New in late summer 2012, this white-hot hotel (part of Starwood's "Style at a Steal" Aloft brand) targets Gens X and Y with the trendy "w xyz" bar and a smashing central location just south of Pack Square. **Pros:** new; great center-of-town location within walking distance of many clubs, restaurants, and attractions. **Cons:** perhaps a bit too trendy and social-networked for some; not designed for young kids or families. *Rooms from: $214 ✉ 51 Biltmore Ave., Downtown ☎ 828/232–2838, 877/462–5638 ⊕ www.starwoodhotels.com/alofthotels 115 No meals.*

$$$ HOTEL **Haywood Park Hotel.** Location is the main draw of this refurbished, all-suite downtown hotel, which is within walking distance of many of Asheville's shops, restaurants, and galleries. **Pros:** great central downtown location; expansive refurbished suites. **Cons:** some street noise; no pool. *Rooms from: $219 ✉ 1 Battery Park Ave., Downtown ☎ 828/252–2522, 800/228–2522 ⊕ www.haywoodpark.com 33 suites No meals.*

$$$$ HOTEL ★ **Hotel Indigo.** The 12-story Hotel Indigo, within easy walking distance of downtown, has a contemporary, boutique vibe with furnishings and artwork crafted by local Asheville artists and views of the Blue Ridge Mountains and downtown. **Pros:** well located; a short walk to most of downtown; free parking in underground garage; friendly service; trendy bar and restaurant on premises. **Cons:** no pool; some street noise from the nearby expressway; pricey in-season. *Rooms from: $299 ✉ 151 Haywood St., Downtown ☎ 828/239–0239, 877/846–3446 ⊕ www.hotelindigo.com 100 rooms No meals.*

## NORTH METRO

$$ B&B/INN Fodor's Choice ★ **1900 Inn on Montford.** Guests are pampered at this Arts & Crafts–style B&B in the Montford section, where most rooms have whirlpool baths, big-screen TVs, and fireplaces. **Pros:** well-run; lovely antiques; modern amenities. **Cons:** not for families with small children. *Rooms from: $178 ✉ 296 Montford Ave., North Metro ☎ 828/254–9569, 800/254–9569 🌐 www.innonmontford.com 4 rooms, 4 suites, 1 cabin Breakfast.*

$$$ B&B/INN ★ **Albemarle Inn.** This quiet B&B in an upscale North Asheville residential area housed famed Hungarian composer Béla Bartók in the early 1940s, when he was creating his "Asheville Concerto"; you can stay in his room on the third floor, although Juliet's Chamber, with its private balcony overlooking lovely gardens, may appeal more to modern Romeos. **Pros:** delightfully upscale and historic; lovely residential neighborhood; excellent breakfasts. **Cons:** old-fashioned claw-foot tubs in some rooms make showering difficult. *Rooms from: $225 ✉ 86 Edgemont Rd., 1 mile north of I–240, North Metro ☎ 828/255–0027, 800/621–7435 🌐 www.albemarleinn.com 11 rooms, 1 suite Breakfast.*

$$$ B&B/INN ★ **Black Walnut Bed and Breakfast Inn.** The Biltmore House supervising architect Richard Sharp Smith built this 1899 home in Asheville's Montford section; today it's a six-room B&B on the National Register of Historic Places. **Pros:** a gem of a B&B; charming antiques-filled house; excellent breakfast. **Cons:** a bit of a walk into town, but closer than many other Asheville B&Bs. *Rooms from: $225 ✉ 288 Montford Ave., North Metro ☎ 828/254–3878, 800/381–3878 🌐 www.blackwalnut.com 6 rooms, 2 suites Breakfast.*

$$$$ RESORT Fodor's Choice ★ **Grove Park Inn Resort & Spa.** The area's premier large resort, an imposing granite edifice celebrating its 100th anniversary in 2013, has grand views of downtown Asheville and the Blue Ridge Mountains and offers all kinds of resort amenities including a Donald Ross-designed golf course, tennis, racquetball, and an amazing spa. **Pros:** imposing historic hotel; wonderful setting; magnificent mountain views; remarkable spa. **Cons:** individual guests sometimes play second fiddle to groups. *Rooms from: $300 ✉ 290 Macon Ave., North Metro ☎ 828/252–2711, 800/438–5800 🌐 www.groveparkinn.com 500 rooms, 12 suites No meals.*

$$ B&B/INN ★ **The Lion and the Rose.** One of the characters in Thomas Wolfe's *Look Homeward, Angel* lived in this house, an 1898 Queen Anne–Georgian in the historic Montford Park area near downtown, and it couldn't have looked any better then than it does now. **Pros:** comfortable small B&B; impressively landscaped grounds; good value. **Cons:** a bit of a walk to downtown, but closer than many other Asheville B&Bs. *Rooms from: $160 ✉ 276 Montford Ave., North Metro ☎ 828/255–6546, 800/546–6988 🌐 www.lion-rose.com 4 rooms, 1 suite Breakfast.*

## SOUTH METRO

$$$ HOTEL ★ **Grand Bohemian Hotel.** This upscale hotel with Tudor-inspired architecture and hunting-lodge decor is as close as you can get to the main Biltmore gate, and steps from all the shops and restaurants in Biltmore Village. **Pros:** recently opened upscale hotel; at Biltmore Estate

4

CLOSE UP

## River Arts District

**River Arts District.** Asheville's River Arts District isn't SoHo—not yet, at least. This former industrial and warehouse section, just southwest of downtown, is the up-and-coming arts-and-crafts center of the region. As industrial companies moved out, artists moved in, seeking cheaper rents for studios and loft apartments. Today the district is home to more than 165 working artists—mainly pottery and ceramics artists, fabric artists, and sculptors—and this doesn't include students taking courses. As many as 70 studios in 18 early-20th-century industrial buildings are open to the public (hours vary but many are open daily from 9–5). You can talk to artists and buy their work, often at lower prices than in galleries. On the second Saturday of each month, studios offer refreshments and demonstrations for visitors. Twice a year, on weekends in mid-June and early November, the District holds a Studio Stroll, when nearly all the studios and galleries are open to the public. Increasingly, restaurants, bars, and coffee houses are opening in the District, and a large national craft brewing company, New Belgium, is opening its East Coast brewery and distribution center here. ✉ *River Arts District* ☎ *828/280–7709* 🌐 *www.riverartsdistrict.com.*

gate and near Biltmore Village. **Cons:** in a congested area; not all will appreciate the stuffed animal heads. $ *Rooms from: $229* ✉ *11 Boston Way, Biltmore Village* ☎ *828/505–2949, 888/717–8756* 🌐 *www.bohemianhotelasheville.com* *104 rooms.*

$$$$ HOTEL Fodor's Choice ★ **Inn on Biltmore Estate.** Many people who visit the Biltmore mansion long to stay overnight; if you're one of them, your wish is granted in the form of this posh hilltop property on the estate. **Pros:** deluxe hotel on Biltmore Estate grounds; exclusive restaurant; top-notch service. **Cons:** very expensive; atmosphere can be a bit formal. $ *Rooms from: $400* ✉ *1 Antler Hill Rd., Biltmore Estate, South Metro* ☎ *828/225–1660, 866/336–1245* 🌐 *www.biltmore.com/inn* *201 rooms, 9 suites* *No meals.*

$$ HOTEL ★ **The Residences at Biltmore.** A short drive from the gates of the Biltmore Estate, these suite-style accommodations are some of the most spacious and attractive in Asheville. **Pros:** fully equipped kitchens; nicely maintained pool and hot tub; accessible to Biltmore Estate and downtown Asheville. **Cons:** no on-site restaurant; limited hotel services. $ *Rooms from: $189* ✉ *700 Biltmore Ave., South Metro* ☎ *866/433–5594* 🌐 *www.residencesatbiltmore.com* *55 suites.*

### NEARBY ASHEVILLE

$$ B&B/INN **Sourwood Inn.** Two miles from the Blue Ridge Parkway, down a narrow winding road, sits one of the most stunning small inns in the mountains, constructed of stone and cedar, in the Arts & Crafts style. **Pros:** stunning mountainside setting; handsome rooms; bathrooms with mountain views. **Cons:** a 20-minute drive to downtown; no in-room TV; no air-conditioning. $ *Rooms from: $169* ✉ *810 Elk Mountain Scenic Hwy., Metro North* ☎ *828/255–0690* 🌐 *www.*

*sourwoodinn.com* 12 rooms, 1 cabin Closed late Dec.–Jan. and weekdays in Feb. Breakfast.*

## NIGHTLIFE AND THE ARTS

For the latest information on nightlife, arts, and entertainment in the Asheville area, get a copy of *Take 5*, an entertainment tabloid in Friday's *Asheville Citizen-Times* or the weekly free newspaper *Mountain Express*.

### THE ARTS

The Asheville area has about 40 theaters and theater companies. Asheville also has a vibrant gallery scene with about three dozen galleries. Many of the galleries are within a block or two of Pack Square, while some, especially those with working studios, are in the River Arts District. Biltmore Village also has several galleries.

4

#### GALLERIES

**ArtEtude Gallery.** New in 2012, ArtEtude is a fine-arts gallery exhibiting the work of a number of local and regional contemporary artists. *89 Patton Ave., Downtown 828/252–1466 www.artetudegallery.com.*

**Blue Spiral 1.** The biggest and arguably the best art gallery in town with 14,000 square feet of exhibit space, Blue Spiral 1 has changing exhibits of sculpture, paintings, fine crafts, and photographs. *38 Biltmore Ave., Downtown 828/251–0202 www.bluespiral1.com.*

**Folk Art Center.** As the headquarters of the prestigious Southern Highland Craft Guild, the Folk Art Center on the Blue Ridge Parkway just east of Asheville regularly puts on exceptional quilt, woodworking, pottery, and other crafts shows and demonstrations. This is a top spot to purchase very high-quality (and often expensive) crafts, such as quilts, baskets, and pottery. *BRP MM 382, East Metro 828/298–7928 www.southernhighlandguild.org.*

**Grovewood Gallery.** On the grounds of the Grove Park Inn, Grovewood Gallery has 9,000 square feet of high-quality ceramic, glass, fiber, wood, and other crafts, along with furniture in what the gallery calls "the Asheville style." *111 Grovewood Rd., Grove Park Inn, Metro North 828/253–7651 www.grovewood.com.*

**Kress Emporium.** In a 1928 landmark building decorated with polychrome terra-cotta tile, Kress Emporium is a place for more than 80 craftspeople to show and sell their crafts. *19 Patton Ave., Downtown 828/281–2252 www.thekressemporium.com.*

**New Morning Gallery.** Owned by arts entrepreneur John Cram, New Morning Gallery has more than 13,000 square feet of exhibit space in a prime location in Biltmore Village. The gallery, which has a national reputation, focuses on more popular and moderately priced ceramics, garden art, jewelry, furniture, and art glass. Nearby, under the same ownership, are art-to-wear galleries Bellagio and Bellagio Everyday. *7 Boston Way, Biltmore Village 828/274–2831, 800/933–4438 www.newmorninggallerync.com.*

**Odyssey Center for Ceramic Arts.** One of the pioneers in Asheville's now-burgeoning River Arts District, Odyssey Center for Ceramic Arts hosts

Grab a glass of wine or bubbly and pore over the thousands of used books for sale at Battery Park Book Exchange and Champagne Bar.

dozens of working potters in rental and student studios, as well as a ceramics gallery. A wide selection of pottery classes and workshops is also available. Under the same ownership is Highwater Clays (nearby at 600 Riverside Drive), the region's largest clay, pottery equipment, and ceramics supplies store. ✉ *236 Clingman Ave., River Arts District* ☎ *828/285–0210* 🌐 *www.odysseyceramicarts.com.*

**Woolworth Walk.** In a 1938 building that housed a five-and-dime, Woolworth Walk features the work of 160 crafts artists in 20,000 square feet of exhibit space on two levels. There's even a soda fountain, built to resemble the original Woolworth luncheonette. ✉ *25 Haywood St., Downtown* ☎ *828/254–9234* 🌐 *www.woolworthwalk.com.*

### THEATER

**Diana Wortham Theatre.** In the Pack Place complex, near many downtown restaurants, the intimate 500-seat Diana Wortham Theatre is home to more than 100 musical, dance, and theatrical events each year. ✉ *2 S. Pack Sq., Downtown* ☎ *828/257–4530* 🌐 *www.dwtheatre.com.*

**North Carolina Stage Company.** In a recently expanded theater space located in an alley off Walnut St., North Carolina Stage Company is a professional company that puts on mostly edgy, contemporary plays. ✉ *15 Stage La., Downtown* ☎ *828/239–0263* 🌐 *www.ncstage.org.*

**Thomas Wolfe Auditorium.** The 2,400-seat Thomas Wolfe Auditorium, in the U.S. Cellular Center Asheville (formerly Asheville Civic Center), hosts larger events, including traveling Broadway shows and performances of the Asheville Symphony. ✉ *87 Haywood St., Downtown* ☎ *828/259–5736 for tickets.*

## NIGHTLIFE

**Asheville Pizza and Brewing Company.** More than a restaurant, more than a movie theater, Asheville Pizza and Brewing Company, also called Brew 'n' View, is a wildly popular place to catch a flick while lounging on a sofa, drinking a microbrew, and scarfing a veggie pizza. ✉ *675 Merriman Ave.* ☎ *828/254–1281* 🌐 *www.ashevillebrewing.com.*

**Barley's Taproom.** In a renovated downtown appliance store, the ever-popular Barley's Taproom has live bluegrass and Americana music three or four nights a week. The bar downstairs has about two dozen microbrew beers on draft, and you can play pool and darts upstairs in the Billiard Room, which has another 19 taps. ✉ *42 Biltmore Ave., Downtown* ☎ *828/255–0504* 🌐 *www.barleystaproom.com/asheville.*

**Battery Park Book Exchange and Champagne Bar.** For a quiet spot, try Battery Park Book Exchange and Champagne Bar. Relax on an overstuffed chair or sofa while sipping one of 80 wines and pondering the 22,000 used books for sale. ✉ *Grove Arcade, 1 Page Ave., Ste. 101* ☎ *828/252–0020* 🌐 *www.batteryparkbookexchange.com.*

**Bywater.** An unusual combination of outdoor picnic grounds and bar, Bywater is close to the French Broad River and near the River Arts District. Baring your own food and cook it on one of the charcoal grills beside the bar, or buy from a rotating food truck. ✉ *796 Riverside Dr., Metro North* ☎ *828/232–6967* 🌐 *www.bywaterbar.com* ⏲ *Daily 2–2.*

**Club Hairspray.** The camp decor at Club Hairspray will make you feel like you're back in 1961, though the dance music and entertainment (often drag shows) is contemporary. Cover charge $3 to $10. The crowd is diverse but with many LGBT folks. Hairspray has taken over two former nearby clubs, Remix (located below Hairspray) and Metropolis (large dance floor, space for 400), so there's more room to party. ✉ *38 N. French Broad Ave.* ☎ *828/258–2027* 🌐 *www.clubhairspray.com.*

**Grey Eagle.** Situated in the River Arts District area, Grey Eagle features popular local and regional bands four or five nights a week, with contra dancing on some other nights. The bar serves wine and beer. ✉ *185 Clingman Ave., River Arts District* ☎ *828/232–5800* 🌐 *www.thegreyeagle.com.*

**Orange Peel Social Aid and Pleasure Club.** This is by far the number-one nightspot in downtown Asheville. Bob Dylan, Hootie and the Blowfish, Modest Mouse, and the Beastie Boys have played here in a smoke-free setting for audiences of up to 1,100. In 2008 *Rolling Stone* named it one of the top-five rock clubs in the United States. For smaller events, it also has a great dance floor, with springy wood slats. There's a private club on the lower level called PULP. ✉ *101 Biltmore Ave.* ☎ *828/225–5851* 🌐 *www.theorangepeel.net.*

**Scandals Nightclub.** Asheville's best-known late-night gay and lesbian club, Scandals has a lively dance floor and drag shows on weekends. ✉ *Grove House, 11 Grove St., Downtown* ☎ *828/505–1612* 🌐 *www.scandalsnightclub.com* ⏲ *Daily 10 pm–3 am.*

**Tressa's Downtown Jazz & Blues.** In a 1913 downtown building, Tressa's has a New Orleans ambience and features a full bar plus sandwiches

4

and bar snacks. There's live jazz or blues most nights. ✉ *28 Broadway, Downtown* ☎ *828/254–7072* 🌐 *www.tressas.com* ⊙ *Closed. Sun.–Tues.*

**Westville Pub.** In happening West Asheville, the smoke-free Westville Pub has about 24 different local beers on draft, and a different band plays nearly every night. ✉ *777 Haywood Rd., West Asheville* ☎ *828/225–9782.*

## SPORTS AND THE OUTDOORS

### BASEBALL

**Asheville Tourists.** A Class A farm team of the Colorado Rockies, the Asheville Tourists play April to early September at historic McCormick Field, which opened in 1924. McCormick Field appears briefly in the 1987 movie *Bull Durham,* starring Kevin Costner and Susan Sarandon. Many well-traveled baseball fans consider McCormick Field one of the most appealing minor-league stadiums in the country. ✉ *McCormick Pl., 30 Buchanan Pl., Downtown* ☎ *828/258–5800* 🌐 *www.milb.com.*

### GOLF

**Asheville Municipal Golf Course.** This municipal course beside the Swannanoa River, owned by the city of Asheville but since 2012 under private management, is known for its firm and fast greens. Designed by famed golf architect Donald Ross, it opened in 1927. ✉ *226 Fairway Dr.* ☎ *828/298–1867* 🌐 *www.ashevillenc.gov* ✍ *Reservations essential* 🏌 *18 holes. 6420 yds. Par 72. Green Fee: $18 weekday/$22 weekend. Monthly non-resident pass $500.* ☞ *Facilities: Putting green, pitching area, golf carts, pull carts, rental clubs, pro shop, snack bar.*

**Grove Park Inn Resort.** Formerly the course for the Country Club of Asheville, this beauty first opened in 1899 and was redesigned by Donald Ross in 1924. It has been played by several U.S. presidents, including Barack Obama. ✉ *Grove Park Inn, 290 Macon Ave.* ☎ *828/252–2711, 800/438–5800* 🌐 *www.groveparkinn.com* ✍ *Reservations essential* 🏌 *18 holes. 6740 yds. Par 70. Green Fee: $129 May.–Oct., $85 Nov.–Apr.* ☞ *Facilities: Putting green, golf carts, pull carts, rental clubs, pro shop, golf lessons, restaurants, bars.*

### HORSEBACK RIDING

**Cataloochee Ranch.** Riders can explore this property's mile-high vistas on horseback. Half-day riding trips are $60. Lower rates available if you're staying in a rental cabin on the ranch. ✉ *119 Ranch Rd., Maggie Valley* ☎ *828/926–1401, 800/868–1401.*

**Pisgah View Ranch.** Trail rides are offered from April through November at Pisgah View Ranch, where you can gallop through 2,000 acres of wooded mountainside. Two-hour rides are $70. If you're not staying at this dude ranch, reserve 24 hours in advance. ✉ *70 Pisgah View Ranch Rd., Candler* ☎ *828/667–9100, 866/252–8361* 🌐 *www.pisgahviewranch.net* ⊙ *Closed Dec.–Mar.*

### SKIING

**Cataloochee Ranch.** In addition to having outstanding skiing and snowboarding, Cataloochee Ranch has cabin rentals and hosts lots of different activities for the whole family. ✉ *119 Ranch Dr., Maggie Valley* ☎ *828/926–1401, 800/868–1401* 🌐 *www.cataloocheerranch.com.*

**Sapphire Valley Ski Area.** At around 3,400 feet, Sapphire Valley offers basic skiing, snowboarding, and a 500-foot tube run. ✉ *4000 U.S. 64 W, Sapphire Valley* ☎ *828/743–1169 for ski lodge, 800/743–1162 for snow report* 🌐 *www.skisapphirevalley.com.*

**Wolf Ridge Ski Resort.** You can "Ski the Wolf" at Wolf Ridge Ski Resort, which has night skiing and excellent snowmaking capabilities. Weekday all-day and evening lift tickets are $46, weekends $69. ✉ *578 Valley View Cir., Mars Hill* ☎ *828/689–4111, 800/817–4111* 🌐 *www.skiwolfridgenc.com* 🕒 *Open Dec.–early Mar., depending on weather and ski conditions.*

4

### ZIPLINING

**Navitat Canopy Adventures.** Zip through the treetops at Navitat, which has 10 zip lines, ranging from 120 to 1100 feet in length. There also are hiking trails, two sky bridges, and two rappelling areas on the 240-acre site. Zip-line tours through the trees, lasting about three hours, cost $89. The zip lines have a 250-pound weight limit. ✉ *242 Poverty Branch Rd., 25 miles north of downtown Asheville, Greater Asheville, Barnardsville* ✣ *From Asheville, take I-26/US Hwy. 19/23 to Jupiter/Barnardsville exit (Exit 15), then take Barnardsville Hwy. (NC 197) east 6 miles to Barnardsville. At Barnardsville post office, turn north on Poverty Branch Road (SR2171) and go 1.5 miles to Navitat (on left).* ☎ *828/626–3700, 855/628–4828* 🌐 *www.navitat.com* 🕒 *Closed Dec.–Mar.*

## SHOPPING

### SHOPPING CENTERS

**Asheville Mall.** About 2 miles southeast of downtown, Asheville Mall, the region's largest mall, has four department stores (Belk, Dillard's, Sears, and JCPenney), and more than 100 specialty shops. ✉ *3 S. Tunnel Rd., East Metro* ☎ *828/298–0012* 🌐 *www.asheville-mall.com* 🕒 *Mon.–Sat. 10–9, Sun. Noon–6.*

**Biltmore Village.** Across from the Biltmore Estate, Biltmore Village is a cluster of specialty shops, restaurants, galleries, and hotels in an early-20th-century English-hamlet-style setting. You'll find everything from children's books to music, antiques, and wearable art. **New Morning Gallery,** a jewelry, crafts, and art gallery at 7 Boston Way, attracts customers from all over the Southeast. ⇨ *All Souls Cathedral is one of the most beautiful churches in America.* ✉ *Hendersonville Rd., Biltmore Village* 🌐 *www.biltmorevillage.com.*

**Downtown Asheville.** Shopping is excellent all over Downtown Asheville, with around 200 stores, including more than 30 art galleries and over a dozen antiques shops. Several streets, notably **Biltmore Avenue, Broadway Street, Lexington Avenue, Haywood Street,** and **Wall Street,** are lined with small, independently owned stores. ✉ *Downtown* 🌐 *www.ashevilledowntown.org.*

**Grove Arcade Public Market.** One of America's first indoor shopping centers, the Grove Arcade Public Market originally opened in 1929. The architecturally remarkable building, which covers an entire city block, includes around 40 local specialty shops and restaurants. ✉ *1 Page Ave., Downtown* ☎ *828/252–7799* 🌐 *www.grovearcade.com.*

### BOOKS

**Captain's Bookshelf.** Since 1976, Captain's Bookshelf has stocked rare books on Western North Carolina, the South, architecture, art, gardening, and other subjects. The collection incldes many first editions. ✉ *31 Page Ave., Downtown* ☎ *828/253–6631* 🌐 *www.captainsbookshelf.com* ⏲ *Tues.–Sat. 10–6.*

**Malaprop's Bookstore and Cafe.** This is what an independent bookstore should be, with an intelligent selection of new books, many author appearances and other events, and a comfortable café. Staffers speak many foreign languages including Hungarian, Russian, Italian, Spanish, French, and German. ✉ *55 Haywood St., Downtown* ☎ *828/254–6734, 800/441–9829* 🌐 *www.malaprops.com* ⏲ *Mon.–Sat. 9–9, Sun. 9–7.*

# SIDE TRIPS FROM ASHEVILLE

## BLACK MOUNTAIN

*16 miles east of Asheville via I–40.*

Black Mountain is a small town that has played a disproportionately large role in American cultural history because it's the site of Black Mountain College. For more than 20 years in the middle of the 20th century, from its founding in 1933 to its closing in 1957, Black Mountain College was one of the world's leading centers for experimental art, literature, architecture, and dance, with a list of faculty and students that reads like a *Who's Who* of American arts and letters.

On a different front, Black Mountain is also the home of evangelist Billy Graham. The Graham organization maintains a training center near Black Mountain, and there are several large church-related conference centers in the area, including Ridgecrest, Montreat, and Blue Ridge Assembly. Downtown Black Mountain is small and quaint, with a collection of little shops and several B&Bs.

Fodor's Choice ★ **Black Mountain College.** Originally housed in rented quarters at nearby Blue Ridge Assembly, southeast of the town of Black Mountain, in 1941 Black Mountain College moved across the valley to its own campus at Lake Eden (today a private summer camp for boys, Camp Rockmont). The school's buildings were originally designed by the Bauhaus architects Walter Gropius and Marcel Breuer, but at the start of World War II the college turned to an American architect, Lawrence Kocher, and several intriguing buildings resulted, including one known as "The Ship," which still stands, with murals by Breuer. Black Mountain College attracted maverick spirits in art, music, and literature, including

CLOSE UP

## Authors of the North Carolina Mountains

They may not be able to go home again, but many famous writers have made their homes in the North Carolina Mountains. The one most closely associated with the terrain is Thomas Wolfe (1900–38), author of *Look Homeward, Angel,* who was born and buried in Asheville. His contemporary F. Scott Fitzgerald visited Asheville and environs frequently in the 1930s, staying for long periods at the Grove Park Inn and at other hotels in the area. Fitzgerald's wife, Zelda, an author and artist in her own right, died in a 1948 fire at Highland Hospital, then a psychiatric facility in North Asheville.

William Sydney Porter, who under the pen name O. Henry, wrote "The Ransom of Red Chief," "The Gift of the Magi," and many other stories, married into an Asheville-area family and is buried in Asheville at Riverside Cemetery. Carl Sandburg, Pulitzer Prize–winning poet and biographer of Lincoln, spent the last 22 years of his life on a farm in Flat Rock. A younger generation of poets, including Jonathan Williams, Robert Creeley, Joel Oppenheimer, Robert Duncan, and Charles Olson, made names for themselves at Black Mountain College, an avant-garde hotbed for literature during the 1940s and early 1950s.

More recently, Jan Karon, Elizabeth Daniels Squire, and Sharyn McCrumb have set popular mystery series in the area. Novelist Charles Frazier, born in Asheville in 1950, made Cold Mountain, in the Shining Rock Wilderness of the Pisgah National Forest, the setting (and the title) for his best-selling Civil War drama. The mountain can be viewed from the Blue Ridge Parkway at mile marker 412. The movie, however, was filmed in Romania. Enka-Candler native Wayne Caldwell writes eloquently of the people of the Cataloochee section of what is now the Great Smokies in 2007's *Cataloochee* and 2009's *Requiem by Fire.* In several books, Canton native and former North Carolina poet laureate Fred Chappell paints powerful images of his hometown and its odiferous paper mill. Novelist Anne Tyler (*The Accidental Tourist*) spent her early years in the small town of Celo, near Mt. Mitchell, and Marjorie Rawlings wrote her classic novel, *The Yearling,* in Banner Elk.

4

Willem and Elaine de Kooning, Robert Rauschenberg, Josef and Anni Albers, Buckminster Fuller, M. C. Richards, Merce Cunningham, John Cage, Kenneth Noland, Ben Shahn, Franz Kline, Arthur Penn, Charles Olson, Robert Creeley, and others. Today the site is a privately owned 550-acre summer camp for boys. During the Lake Eden Festival, held in mid-May and mid-October, you can visit the college. Other times of the year you can rent a cabin on the grounds for overnight stays. ⇨ *Black Mountain College Museum + Arts Center is located in downtown Asheville at 56 Broadway Street.* ✉ *375 Lake Eden Rd., 5 miles west of Black Mountain* ☎ *828/686–3885 Camp Rockmont, 828/350–8484 Black Mountain College Museum* 🌐 *www.blackmountaincollege.org.*

## FLAT ROCK

*3 miles south of Hendersonville; 26 miles south of Asheville via I–26.*

Flat Rock has been a summer resort since the early 19th century. It was a favorite of wealthy planters from Charleston eager to escape the Lowcountry heat. The trip from Charleston to Flat Rock by horse and carriage took as long as two weeks, so you know there must be something here that made the long trek worthwhile. Today, you can tour the home and farm where poet Carl Sandburg spent the last years of his life, take in professional drama at the official state theater of North Carolina, Flat Rock Playhouse, or play a round of golf.

### GETTING HERE AND AROUND

From Asheville, take Interstate 26 East 22 miles to Exit 53. Follow Upward Road about 2½ miles to Flat Rock.

### EXPLORING

★ **Carl Sandburg Home National Historic Site.** This is the farm to which the famed poet and Lincoln biographer Carl Sandburg moved with his wife, Lillian, in 1945. Guided tours of their house, Connemara, where Sandburg's papers still lie scattered on his desk and 12,000 of his books are on bookshelves, are given by the National Park Service. Kids enjoy a walk around the grounds of the farm, which still maintains descendants of the Sandburg family goats. ✉ *81 Carl Sandburg La., or 1800 Little River Rd.* ☎ *828/693–4178* 🌐 *www.nps.gov/carl* 🎟 *$5* ⏲ *Daily 9–5.*

**Flat Rock Playhouse.** This theater is known for its high-quality summerstock productions. It is the State Theatre of North Carolina and holds summer and fall college apprentice programs and classes for aspiring actors. The drama season runs from April to December. Flat Rock Playhouse also puts on plays at a second location in downtown Hendersonville, **Playhouse Downtown**, at 125 Main Street. ✉ *2661 Greenville Hwy.* ☎ *828/693–0731, 866/732–8008* 🌐 *www.flatrockplayhouse.org* ⏲ *Closed Jan.–Mar.*

## HENDERSONVILLE

*23 miles south of Asheville via I–26.*

With about 14,000 residents, Hendersonville has one of the most engaging downtowns of any small city in the South. Historic Main Street, as it's called, extends 10 serpentine blocks, lined with about 40 shops, including antiques stores, galleries, and restaurants. Each year from April through October, Main Street has displays of public art. Within walking distance of downtown are several B&Bs.

The Hendersonville area is North Carolina's main apple-growing area, and some 200 apple orchards dot the rolling hills around town. An apple festival, attracting 200,000 people, is held each year in August.

### GETTING HERE AND AROUND

It is about 25 miles from Asheville to Hendersonville, via Interstate 26 East. From Interstate 26, take Four Seasons Boulevard through the typical suburban mix of motels, strip malls, and fast-food restaurants to downtown Hendersonville. Main Street, where there's free parking, runs through the center of town.

## WHERE TO EAT AND STAY

*Hotel reviews have been abbreviated in this book. For expanded reviews, please go to Fodors.com.*

$ BAKERY **Mountain Pie and Cake Company.** This is primarily a bakery with delicious, freshly made cakes and pies, but it is also a fine place to eat breakfast in a friendly, homey atmosphere. Pancakes come in blueberry, buckwheat, whole-wheat, pecan, and chocolate-chip versions. Try the French toast croissant topped with strawberries and whipped cream. All breakfasts are reasonably priced and come with orange juice and fruit. No meat or eggs served. Try to get a spot on the outdoor deck, with views of the mountains. *Average main: $6 3400 Asheville Hwy., Hendersonville 828/693–0501 www.mountainpiecompany.com Closed Sun. and Mon.*

$ PIZZA **West First Wood-Fired.** Wood-fired, thin-crust pizza from organic flour is the specialty here, but this is no ordinary pizza joint. Besides the usual pies, West First offers more creative options such as potato pizza (with a thin topping of new potatoes and rosemary rather than tomato sauce) and roasted-salmon pizza. It also has Italian dishes like eggplant parmigiana and house-made fennel sausage in a marinara sauce. The main dining room is a large rectangle, anchored at the far end by the open oven blazing away. Dominating one side of the room are two large, striking paintings, portraits inspired by the owner's grandparents. The ceiling is high in the industrial restaurant style with duct work showing. There is also a small dining area in a covered patio outside, and a second-level loft. Prices are surprisingly low. The same owners opearate Flat Rock Village Bakery in nearby Flat Rock. *Average main: $12 101b 1st Ave. W, Hendersonville 828/693–1080 www.flatrockwoodfired.com/restaurant Closed Sun.*

$$$ B&B/INN **1898 Waverly Inn.** On a warm afternoon you'll love to "sit a spell" in a rocking chair on the front porch of Hendersonville's oldest inn. **Pros:** historic building; walking distance to downtown; very well run. **Cons:** quite a bit of traffic; some rooms are on small side. *Rooms from: $175 783 N. Main St., Hendersonville, North Carolina 828/693–9193, 800/537–8195 www.waverlyinn.com 14 rooms, 1 suite Breakfast.*

## SPORTS AND THE OUTDOORS

### GOLF

**Etowah Valley Country Club and Golf Lodge.** Three 9-hole courses and four tee positions let you play several different 18-hole combinations at this semiprivate course. Preference is given to guests of the lodge. Croquet and tennis are also available. *470 Brickyard Rd., Etowah, North Carolina 828/891–7141, 800/451–8174 www.etowahvalley.com Reservations essential Front course: 18 holes. 5253 yds. Par 73. Back course: 18 holes. 6880 yds. Par 73. Green Fee: $29–$49 weekday, depending on time of day and season/$35–$62 weekend. Facilities: Driving range, putting green, pitching area, golf carts, pull carts, rental clubs, pro shop, golf lessons, restaurant, bar.*

# THE HIGH COUNTRY

Here you'll find the highest, steepest, coldest, snowiest, windiest, and, some say, friendliest parts of the mountains. The High Country has not only the tallest mountains east of the Rockies, but the highest average elevation in all of eastern America. With temperatures 10 to 15 degrees cooler than in the foothills and flatlands, even folks from Asheville come to the High Country in the summer to cool down.

Unlike the rest of the mountains, winter is the peak season in much of the High Country. The reason? The white stuff. Towns like Boone, Blowing Rock, and Banner Elk have boomed in the 40 years since the introduction of snowmaking equipment, and the ski resorts of Beach Mountain, Seven Devils, Sugar Mountain, and Appalachian Ski Mountain attract skiers, snowboarders, and snow-tubers from all over the Southeast. A magnificent scenic road, the Blue Ridge Parkway is a highlight of this region.

## BLUE RIDGE PARKWAY

*Entrance 2 miles east of Asheville, off I–40, and at many other points.*

The Blue Ridge Parkway's 252 miles within North Carolina wind down the High Country through Asheville, ending near the entrance of Great

Smoky Mountains National Park. Highlights on and near the parkway include Mt. Mitchell, the highest mountain peak east of the Rockies, Grandfather Mountain, and Mt. Pisgah. Nearly all the towns and cities along the parkway route offer accommodations, dining, and sightseeing. In particular, Boone, Blowing Rock, Burnsville, Asheville, Waynesville, Brevard, and Cherokee are all near popular entrances to the parkway.

**WORD OF MOUTH**

"[L]ove the mountains, love Biltmore, the arts and crafts, the views, and what you can do along the Blue Ridge Parkway." —JJ495



### GETTING HERE AND AROUND

The parkway connects Shenandoah National Park near Waynesboro, Virginia, with Great Smoky Mountains National Park near Cherokee. Entrances to the Parkway are located at many points along Interstate 40 and Interstate 26 as well as along other major highways. In North Carolina, Asheville and Boone are the largest cities along the way.

## EXPLORING

Fodor's Choice ★ **Blue Ridge Parkway.** The beautiful Blue Ridge Parkway gently winds through mountains and meadows and crosses mountain streams for more than 469 miles on its way from Cherokee, North Carolina, to Waynesboro, Virginia, connecting the Great Smoky Mountains and Shenandoah national parks. With elevations ranging from 649 to 6,047 feet, and with more than 250 scenic lookout points, it is truly one of the most beautiful drives in North America. Admission to the Parkway is free. No commercial vehicles are allowed, and the entire parkway is free of billboards, although in a few places residential or commercial development encroaches close to the road. The parkway, which has a maximum speed limit of 45 mph, with some sections lower, is generally open year-round but often closes during inclement weather. In winter, sections can be closed for weeks at a time due to snow, and even in good weather fog and clouds occasionally make driving difficult. Maps and information are available at visitor centers along the highway. Mileposts or mile markers (MM) identify points of interest and indicate the distance from the parkway's starting point in Virginia. A new Park headquarters and visitor center near Asheville at Mile Marker 384 opened in late 2007. It has a "green roof" with plants growing on it. Gas up before you get on the Parkway. Although there are no gas stations on the Parkway itself, you'll find stations at intersecting highways near Parkway exits. ✉ *Blue Ridge Pkwy., 199 Hemphill Knob Rd., Asheville* ☎ *828/298–0398* 🌐 *www.nps.gov/blri* 🎫 *Free.*

### TOP ATTRACTIONS

**Folk Art Center.** Authentic mountain crafts made by members of the Southern Highland Craft Guild are on display and for sale here. Demonstrations are held frequently. This is one of the best places in the region to buy high-quality crafts. ✉ *Blue Ridge Pkwy., MM 382 at Asheville, 382 Blue Ridge Pkwy., East Metro, Asheville* ☎ *828/298–7928* 🌐 *www.southernhighlandguild.org* 🎫 *Free* ⏲ *Jan.–Mar., daily 9–5; Apr.–Dec., daily 9–6.*

A contestant at the Grandfather Mountain Highland Games throws a 22-pound hammer as part of the Scottish Heavy Athletics competition.

**Grandfather Mountain.** Soaring to almost 6,000 feet, Grandfather Mountain is just off the Parkway at mile marker 305. It is famous for its Mile-High Swinging Bridge, a 228-foot-long bridge that sways over a 1,000-foot drop into the Linville Valley. The **Natural History Museum** has exhibits on native minerals, flora and fauna, and pioneer life. There are 12 miles of nature trails and some 100 picnic tables. The annual **Singing on the Mountain** (fourth Sunday in June) is an opportunity to hear old-time gospel music and preaching, and the **Highland Games** (second weekend in July) bring together Scottish clans from all over North America for athletic events and Highland dancing. ✉ *Blue Ridge Pkwy. and U.S. Hwy. 221, Linville* ☎ *828/733–4337, 800/468–7325* 🌐 *www.grandfather.com* 🎟 *$18* ⏲ *Mid-Mar.–mid-Jun., daily 8–6; mid-Jun.–mid-Sep., daily 8–7; mid-Sep.–mid-Dec., daily 8–6; mid-Dec.–mid-Mar., daily 9–5.*

**Mt. Mitchell State Park.** This park includes the highest mountain peak east of the Rockies, 6,684-foot Mt. Mitchell. The summit was named after Elisha Mitchell, who died from a fall while trying to prove the mountain's true height. At the 1,855-acre park you can climb an observation tower and get food (May–October) at a restaurant claimed to be the highest elevation restaurant in the eastern United States. Keep an eye on the weather here, as high winds and snow can occur at almost any time, occasionally even in summer. Clouds obscure the views here for at least parts of 8 days out of 10. ✉ *2388 NC Hwy. 128, off MM 355 Blue Ridge Pkwy., Burnsville* ☎ *828/675–4611* 🌐 *www.ncparks.gov* 🎟 *Free.*

**Mt. Pisgah.** At 5,721 feet, this is one of the most easily recognized peaks due to the television tower installed there in the 1950s. It has walking trails, an amphitheater where nature programs are given most evenings June through October, a campground, inn, restaurant, picnic area, and small grocery. The nearby area called **Graveyard Fields** is popular for blueberry picking in midsummer. ✉ *Blue Ridge Pkwy., MM 408.6* ☎ *828/271–4779 parkway headquarters, 828/235–8228 Pisgah Inn, 828/298–0398 Blue Ridge Parkway Association* 🌐 *www.nps.gov/blri.*

### WORTH NOTING

**Craggy Gardens.** At Blue Ridge Parkway Mile Marker 364, at 5,500 to 6,000 feet, Craggy Gardens has some of the parkway's most colorful displays of rhododendrons, usually in June. You can also hike trails and picnic here. Craggy Pinnacle trail offers stunning 360-degree views. ✉ *Blue Ridge Pkwy., MM 364* ☎ *828/298–0398 parkway information line* 🌐 *www.nps.gov/blri* 🎟 *Free.*

4

**Julian Price Park.** Green spaces along the parkway near Grandfather Mountain include this park, which has hiking, canoeing on a mountain lake, trout fishing, and camping. ✉ *Blue Ridge Pkwy., MM 295–298.1* ☎ *828/298–0398 Parkway information line* 🌐 *www.nps.gov/blri.*

**Linville Falls.** A ½-mile hike from the visitor center leads to one of North Carolina's most-photographed waterfalls. The easy trail winds through evergreens and rhododendrons to overlooks with views of the series of cascades tumbling into Linville Gorge. There are also a campground and a picnic area. ✉ *Blue Ridge Pkwy., MM 316.3, Spruce Pine* ☎ *828/765–1045* 🌐 *www.nps.gov/blri.*

**Moses H. Cone Park.** There is a turn-of-the-20th-century manor house here that's now the **Parkway Craft Center,** which sells fine work by area craftspeople. Here and at the adjoining Julian Price Park near Grandfather Mountain are some 100 picnic sites and the largest campground on the Parkway. ✉ *Blue Ridge Pkwy., MM 292.7–295* ☎ *828/295–7938 parkway information line* 🌐 *www.nps.gov/blri* ⏲ *Apr.–Nov., daily 9–5.*

**Museum of North Carolina Minerals.** At mile marker 331, the museum has hands-on displays about gold, copper, kaolin, and other minerals found nearby. The museum was recently renovated and now includes some interesting exhibits geared toward kids. ✉ *Blue Ridge Pkwy., MM 331 at U.S. Hwy. 226, Spruce Pine* ☎ *828/765–2761* 🌐 *www.nps.gov/blri* 🎟 *Free* ⏲ *Daily 9–5.*

## WHERE TO STAY

$$ B&B/INN ★ **Pisgah Inn.** This inn, run by a park-service concessionaire, has motel-like rooms of little distinction, but the setting is spectacular. **Pros:** on a mile-high mountaintop with incredible 30-mile views; good value; good on-site restaurant. **Cons:** motel-like rooms; remote setting; often fully booked months in advance. [$] *Rooms from: $150* ✉ *Blue Ridge Pkwy., MM 408, Waynesville* ☎ *828/235–8228* 🌐 *www.pisgahinn.com* *51 rooms* ⏲ *Closed early Nov.–late Mar.*

## SPORTS AND THE OUTDOORS

### HIKING

**Figure 8 Trail.** Moses H. Cone Park's (MM 292.7) Figure 8 Trail is an easy and beautiful trail that the Cone family designed for their morning walks. The ½-mile loop winds through a tunnel of rhododendrons and a hardwood forest. ✉ *Blue Ridge Pkwy., MM 292.7, Blowing Rock* 🌐 *www.nps.gov/blri.*

**Waterrock Knob Trail.** Those who tackle the strenuous ½-mile Waterrock Knob Trail (MM 451.2), near the south end of the Parkway, will be rewarded with spectacular views from the 6,300-foot-high Waterrock Knob summit, the highest peak in the Plott Balsams range. ✉ *Blue Ridge Pkwy., MM 451.2, 18 miles from south end of Parkway* 🌐 *www.nps.gov/blri.*

## BLOWING ROCK

*86 miles northeast of Asheville; 93 miles west of Winston-Salem.*

Blowing Rock, a draw for mountain visitors since the 1880s, has retained the flavor of a quiet New England village, with stone walls and buildings with wood shakes or bark siding. About 1,200 people are permanent residents of this town at a 4,000-foot elevation, but the population swells each summer. On summer afternoons it seems as if most of the town's population is sitting on benches in the town park. To ensure that the town would remain rural, the community banded together to prohibit large hotels and motels. Blowing Rock is the inspiration for the small town in resident Jan Karon's novels about country life in the fictional town of Mitford.

#### GETTING HERE AND AROUND

To get here from the Blue Ridge Parkway, take U.S. 221/321 at mile marker 292 near Moses H. Cone Park. U.S. 321 makes a loop around the village of Blowing Rock.

### EXPLORING

**Tweetsie Railroad.** A Wild West theme park built into the side of a mountain between Boone and Blowing Rock, Tweetsie Railroad is centered on a steam locomotive beset by robbers. A petting zoo, carnival amusements, gem panning, shows, and concessions, all mostly of interest to young children, are also here. Several of the attractions are at the top of the mountain and can be reached on foot or by ski lift. ✉ *300 Tweetsie Railroad La., Near U.S. Hwy. 321/221, off Blue Ridge Pkwy. at MM 291* ☎ *828/264–9061, 800/526–5740* 🌐 *www.tweetsie.com* *$35* *Mid-Apr.–May and late Aug–Oct., Fri.–Sun. 9–6; Jun.–late Aug., daily 9–6.*

### WHERE TO EAT AND STAY

*Hotel reviews have been abbreviated in this book. For expanded reviews, please go to Fodors.com.*

$$ SOUTHWESTERN **Canyons.** While oohing over the Linville Gorge scenery, or eyeing the funky artwork on the walls inside, you can munch on freshly made tortilla chips, chimichangas, veggie burritos, or a classic drive-in burger slathered with chili and slaw. At dinner, Canyons also serves steaks, local trout, pork chops and other American fare. On most days the restaurant is one of the busiest in Blowing Rock. Reservations available only for parties of five or more. There's live entertainment some nights and a Sunday brunch. *Average main: $15* ✉ *8960 U.S. Hwy. 321* ☎ *828/295–7661* 🌐 *www.canyonsbr.com.*

DID YOU KNOW?

Linville Falls is a great spot to stop and stretch your legs when driving the Blue Ridge Parkway. The falls are a short hike away from the visitor center at mile marker 316.4.

$$ B&B/INN **Inn at Ragged Gardens.** With a stone staircase in the entry hall, colorful gardens, richly toned chestnut paneling, and High Country–style chestnut-bark siding, it's no wonder that this manor-style house in the heart of Blowing Rock gets many return guests. **Pros:** historic old inn; within walking distance of Blowing Rock shops and restaurants. **Cons:** if you're on the first floor, you may hear guests on floor above. *Rooms from: $175 ✉ 203 Sunset Dr. ☎ 828/295–9703 🌐 www.ragged-gardens.com 6 rooms, 5 suites, 2 cottages Breakfast.*

$$$$ B&B/INN ★ **Westglow Resort & Spa.** If you want to be pampered at a beautiful mountain estate, this resort—housed in an elegant 1916 mansion on 20 acres—may be your cup of herbal tea. **Pros:** rejuvenate yourself in luxury surroundings; complete health spa facilities; healthful meals. **Cons:** expensive rates. *Rooms from: $375 ✉ 224 Westglow Circle, 2845 U.S. 221 S ☎ 828/295–4463, 800/562–0807 🌐 www.westglowresortandspa.com 7 rooms, 1 cottage Multiple meal plans.*

## SPORTS AND THE OUTDOORS

### RAFTING

**High Mountain Expeditions.** You can go white-water rafting on the Nolichucky or Wautaga rivers, or white-water kayaking on Wilson Creek, with High Mountain Expeditions. The rafting and tubing company also has locations in Asheville and Banner Elk, as well as in Tennessee. Rafting trips on the Nolichucky are around $85. *✉ 1380 Hwy. 105 S, Boone ☎ 828/898–9786, 800/262–9036 🌐 www.highmountainexpeditions.com.*

### SKIING

**Appalachian Ski Mountain.** There's downhill skiing and snowboarding at Appalachian Ski Mountain. Also available: cabin rentals and an RV park. *✉ 940 Ski Mountain Rd., High Country ☎ 828/295–7828, 800/322–2373 🌐 www.appskimtn.com.*

## SHOPPING

**Bolick Pottery and Traditions Pottery.** This store sells mountain crafts and pottery handcrafted by fifth-generation potters. *✉ Martin House, Main St. ☎ 828/295–6128 🌐 www.traditionspottery.com.*

# BOONE

*8 miles north of Blowing Rock.*

A fast-growing college town, Boone is home to Appalachian State University and its 17,500 students. Suburban sprawl has arrived, especially along U.S. 321 with its clusters of fast-food restaurants, chain motels, and a small mall, the only enclosed mall in the High Country. Closer to ASU, however, you get more of the college-town vibe, with organic-food stores and boutiques. The town was named for frontiersman Daniel Boone, whose family moved to the area when Daniel was 15.

### GETTING HERE AND AROUND

Boone, about 100 miles northeast of Asheville, is located at the convergence of three major highways—U.S. 321, U.S. 421, and Route 105. From Asheville, take Interstate 40 East to U.S. 64. Follow U.S. 64 to U.S. 321, which leads into Boone.

## EXPLORING

**Daniel Boone Native Gardens.** On 6 acres adjacent to the Horn in the West amphitheater, Daniel Boone Native Gardens highlights local plants and trees in a setting of quiet beauty. The wrought-iron gate to the gardens was a gift of Daniel Boone VI, a direct descendant of the pioneer. ✉ *651 Horn in the West Dr., ¼ mile off U.S. 321* ☎ *828/264–6390* 🌐 *www.danielboonenativegardens.org* 🎫 *$2* 🕒 *May–Oct., daily 9–6.*

## WHERE TO EAT AND STAY

*Hotel reviews have been abbreviated in this book. For expanded reviews, please go to Fodors.com.*

$$ AMERICAN ✕ **Dan'l Boone Inn.** Near Appalachian State University, in a former hospital surrounded by a picket fence and flowers, Dan'l Boone offers old-fashioned food served family-style. You can have any or all of the items on the menu, and seconds and thirds if you want them, for the same price. Warning: the portions of fried chicken, country-style steak, ham biscuits, mashed potatoes, scrambled eggs, bacon, and breads (to name a few) are generous. The dishes certainly aren't of gourmet standard, but it's well-prepared country food. Lunch or dinner, including beverage and dessert, is a bargain at $16.95. Breakfast ($9.95) is served weekends from Memorial Day through October. There's usually a line waiting to get in. No credit cards. No reservations except for groups of at least 15. [$] *Average main: $17* ✉ *130 Hardin St.* ☎ *828/264–8657* 🌐 *www.danlbooneinn.com* ✍ *Reservations not accepted* ▭ *No credit cards* 🕒 *No lunch weekdays Jan.–May.*

$$$$ AMERICAN ★ ✕ **Gamekeeper.** This stone cottage in the woods, off a winding country road between Boone and Blowing Rock surprises newcomers with unusual dishes and sophisticated presentations. Signature game dishes include smoky grilled ostrich fillet, leg of Canadian elk, and hanging loin of buffalo with blue-cheese macaroni. Beef and pork dishes also available. Entrees are expensive for this area, some over $40. For those who don't eat meat, there's a vegetarian plate with delicious grilled vegetables. A nice way to end the meal is with espresso and a selection of freshly made sorbets. On weekends in high season, definitely make a reservation, and while there's no dress code, this isn't a place for grungy shorts and a T-shirt. [$] *Average main: $35* ✉ *3005 Shull's Mill Rd., 6 miles southwest of Boone* ☎ *828/963–7400* 🌐 *www.gamekeeper-nc.com* 🕒 *No lunch. No dinner Sun.–Tues. in Nov. and Dec., Sun.–Wed. in Jan.–Apr.*

$$ MODERN AMERICAN ★ ✕ **Vidalia.** Named for the famous sweet onion, this small bistro in the middle of town brings creative regional American cooking to the High Country. Large paintings dominate the tiny dining area, but it's the food, much of it from local organic farms, that stands out. For dinner, try the chicken and dumplings with sweet potato crisps or the sesame coriander tuna. Lunch on the lighter side offers several interesting salads along with hearty dishes like fried chicken and waffles. There's sidewalk seating also. [$] *Average main: $19* ✉ *831 W. King St.* ☎ *828/263–9176* 🌐 *www.vidaliaofboonenc.com* ✍ *Reservations essential.*

$$ B&B/INN ★ 🏨 **Lovill House Inn.** Built in 1875 and featuring unusual details such as wormy chestnut woodwork, this two-story inn occupies 11 wooded acres in a quiet area just west of downtown. **Pros:** charming rooms;

delicious breakfasts. **Cons:** a bit of a walk into Boone or to App State. *Rooms from: $179 404 Old Bristol Rd. 828/264–4204, 800/849–9466 www.lovillhouseinn.com 6 rooms, 1 cottage Breakfast.*

### NIGHTLIFE AND THE ARTS

**Horn in the West.** A project of the Southern Appalachian Historical Association, *Horn in the West* is an outdoor drama by Kermit Hunter that traces the story of the lives of Daniel Boone and other pioneers, as well as the Cherokee, during the American Revolution. *Amphitheater at 591 Horn in the West Dr., off U.S. 321 828/264–2120 www.hornintheweswest.com $18 Performances mid-June–mid-Aug., Tues.–Sun. at 8 pm.*

### SPORTS AND THE OUTDOORS

#### CANOEING AND RAFTING

Near Boone and Blowing Rock, the New River, a federally designated Wild and Scenic River (Class I and II rapids) provides excitement for canoeists and rafters, as do the Watauga and Toe rivers and Wilson Creek.

**Wahoo's Adventures.** This outfitter offers rafting, kayaking, canoeing, and tubing on several rivers in Western North Carolina (including the Nolichucky, Watauga, and New rivers), and Class V "extreme rafting" trips on Wilson Creek. *3385 S. US Hwy. 321 828/262–5774, 800/444–7238 www.wahoosadventures.com.*

#### GOLF

**Boone Golf Club.** This Ellis Maples–designed course is open to the whole family. *433 Fairway Dr., off U.S. Hwy. 321 828/264–8760, 866/264–8760 www.boonegolfclub.com Reservations essential 18 holes. 6686 yds. Par 71. Green Fee: $32–$37 weekday/$41–$43 weekend, all plus $16 cart fees. Facilities: Putting green, pitching area, golf carts, pull carts, rental clubs, pro shop, golf academy/lessons, restaurant. Closed early Sep.–Apr.*

## VALLE CRUCIS

*5 miles south of Boone.*

This tiny mountain town has the state's first rural historic district; vintage stores line the downtown streets.

### WHERE TO STAY

*Hotel reviews have been abbreviated in this book. For expanded reviews, please go to Fodors.com.*

$$ B&B/INN ★ **Mast Farm Inn.** You can turn back the clock and still enjoy modern amenities at this charming pastoral inn in Valle Crucis, built in the 1800s and now on the National Register of Historic Places. **Pros:** delightful and historic country inn; personalized service; amazing food. **Cons:** a little off the beaten path. *Rooms from: $169 2543 Broadstone Rd. 828/963–5857 www.themastfarminn.com 7 rooms, 8 cottages Breakfast.*

### SHOPPING

**Gallery Alta Vista.** If you're looking for a mountain painting, stop by Gallery Alta Vista, which features the work of more than 100 artists, many from Western North Carolina. ✉ *2839 Broadstone Rd.* ☎ *828/963–5247* 🌐 *www.altavistagallery.com.*

**Mast General Store.** Everything from ribbons and overalls to yard art and cookware is sold in the original Mast General Store. Built in 1882, the store has plank floors worn to a soft sheen and an active old-timey post office. You can take a shopping break by sipping bottled dope (mountain talk for a soda pop) while sitting in a rocking chair on the store's back porch. For more shopping, an annex is just down the road. ✉ *NC Hwy. 194* ☎ *828/963–6511, 866/367–6278* 🌐 *www.mastgeneralstore.com.*

4

## BANNER ELK

*6 miles southwest of Valle Crucis; 11 miles southwest of Boone.*

Banner Elk is a ski-resort town, which bills itself as the "highest town in the East," surrounded by the lofty peaks of Grandfather, Hanging Rock, Beech, and Sugar mountains. The massively ugly condo tower you'll see on top of Little Sugar Mountain (not a part of the Sugar Mountain ski resort) is the only scar on the scenic beauty of the area. At least something good came of the monstrosity—it so outraged local residents that it prompted the passing of a ridge line law preventing such mountaintop development.

### SPORTS AND THE OUTDOORS

#### SKIING

**Beech Mountain Resort.** At about 5,500 feet above sea level, Beech Mountain Resort is the highest ski area in the eastern United States. Full-day weekday lift/slopes tickets are around $30 on weekdays and $60 on weekends. Beech also offers snowboarding and ice skating. In summer, the resort switches to mountain biking. ✉ *1007 Beech Mountain Pkwy., Beech Mountain* ☎ *828/387–2011, 800/438–2093* 🌐 *www.beachmountainresort.com.*

**Hawksnest.** You can no longer ski here but you can try snow tubing on any of 20 tubing lanes. Rates are around $25 for a 1-hour 45-minute session on weekdays, $30 on weekends (discounts for multiple sessions). Children must be at least 3 to snowtube. In warmer weather, Hawksnest also offers zip lining with 19 zip lines. ✉ *2058 Skyland Dr., Seven Devils* ☎ *828/963–6561, 800/822–4295* 🌐 *www.hawksnesttubing.com.*

**Sugar Mountain.** One of the larger ski resorts in the High Country, Sugar Mountain has an equipment shop and lessons, along with snowboarding, tubing, and ice skating. Full-day weekday rates are $41, weekends $68. Lower rates in effect in March. Sugar also offers golf, tennis, and vacation rentals. ✉ *1009 Sugar Mountain Dr., off NC Rte. 184* ☎ *828/898–4521, 800/784–2768 800-SUGARMT* 🌐 *www.skisugar.com.*

## DID YOU KNOW?

The Blue Ridge Parkway has more than 200 overlooks with breathtaking vistas of the Blue Ridge Mountains, old farmsteads, meadows, and valleys. Be sure to stop and smell the wildflowers as you make your way along America's favorite drive.

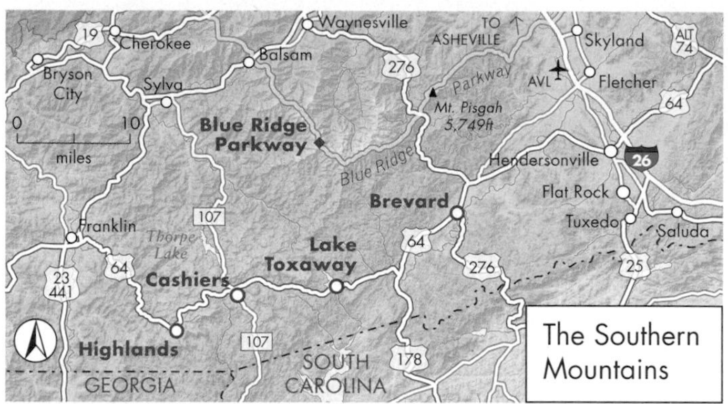


## SHOPPING

**Fred's General Mercantile.** For hardware, firewood, a half gallon of milk, locally grown vegetables, pumpkins for Halloween, snowboard and ski rentals, gourmet bird seed, today's *Wall Street Journal,* and just about anything else you need, Fred's General Mercantile, half general store and half boutique, is the place to go in the Banner Elk and Beech Mountain areas, and has been for more than 30 years. It's at an elevation of 5,049 feet, making it the highest general store in the East. ✉ *501 Beech Mountain Pkwy.* ☎ *828/387–4838* 🌐 *www.fredsgeneral.com.*

# THE SOUTHERN MOUNTAINS

The Southern Mountains encompass a diverse area in nine North Carolina counties south and west of Asheville. They include Brevard in Transylvania County and also Cashiers, Highlands, and Lake Toxaway, chic summer enclaves where some building lots cost a million dollars.

## BREVARD

*40 miles southwest of Asheville on Rte. 280.*

With its friendly, highly walkable downtown, Brevard is Mayberry RFD transported to the Pisgah National Forest. In fact, a popular toy store in town is called O. P. Taylor's—get it?

In summer, more than 400 talented music students from around the country attend the music school at the Brevard Music Center, and the Brevard Music Festival features some 80 classical music concerts, some with such noted visiting artists as cellist Yo-Yo Ma, violinists Joshua Bell and Midori, and pianists André Watts and Emanuel Ax.

Brevard residents go nuts over the white squirrels, which dart around the town's parks. These aren't albinos, but a variation of the eastern gray squirrel. About a quarter of the squirrels in town are white. The white squirrels are thought to have come originally from Hawaii by way of Florida; they possibly were released in Brevard by a visitor in the

1950s. Whatever the truth, today Brevard capitalizes on it by holding a White Squirrel Festival in late May.

**Brevard College.** One of the best places in town to see the rare white squirrels is on the Brevard College campus. ✉ *1 Brevard College Dr.* ☎ *828/883–8292* 🌐 *www.brevard.edu.*

**GETTING HERE AND AROUND**

You can reach Brevard via U.S. 64 from Hendersonville, or from the U.S. 276 exit of the Blue Ridge Parkway. North Broad Street and Main Street are the two primary thoroughfares through Brevard. Brevard Music Center is less than 1 mile west of town—look for directional signs.



## EXPLORING

### TOP ATTRACTIONS

Fodor'sChoice ★ **Cradle of Forestry in America.** The home of the first forestry school in the United States is on 6,500 acres in the Pisgah National Forest. The school, started in 1898 by Carl Schenck, trained some 300 foresters. Here you can visit the school's original log buildings, a restored 1915 steam locomotive, a 1-mile interpretive trail, and a visitor center with many hands-on exhibits of interest to kids and adults. The road from Brevard to the Cradle of Forestry, a scenic byway, continues on to connect with the Blue Ridge Parkway near Mt. Pisgah. ✉ *11250 Pisgah Hwy., off US Hwy. 276 near Brevard, 11 miles from intersection of U.S. 280 and U.S. 276, Pisgah Forest* ☎ *828/877–3130* 🌐 *www.cradleofforestry.com* *$5, free Tues.* ⏲ *Mid-Apr.–early Nov., daily 9–5.*

**DuPont State Forest.** Between Hendersonville and Brevard you'll find this 10,000-acre North Carolina State Forest with six waterfalls and 80 miles of old dirt roads to explore. It's ideal for biking, hiking, or horseback riding. Fishing and hunting also are permitted during the seasons. ✉ *U.S. 64 and Little River Rd., Cedar Mountain* ✈ *From Asheville, take I-26 East to the Asheville Airport (exit 40). Go south on NC 280 for about 16 miles. Turn left on U.S. 64 (heading east) for 4 miles. In Penrose, turn right on Crab Creek Rd. for 4 miles to DuPont Rd. Turn right on DuPont Rd. go 3.1 miles.* ☎ *828/877–6527* 🌐 *www.ncforestservice.gov* *Free* ⏲ *Daily 24 hrs.*

**Pisgah Center for Wildlife Education.** This fish hatchery in Pisgah National Forest produces more than 400,000 brown, rainbow, and native brook trout each year for release in local streams. You can see the fish up close in tanks called raceways and even feed them (approved trout feed is sold for a quarter). There's also a small visitor center with information about the life cycle of trout and an educational nature trail. The Davidson River, which runs by the hatchery, is popular for fly fishing. ✉ *1401 Fish Hatchery Rd., off U.S. Hwy. 276, Pisgah Forest* ☎ *828/877–4423* 🌐 *www.ncwildlife.org* *Free* ⏲ *Mon.–Sat. 8–4:45.*

**Sliding Rock.** In summer you can skid 60 feet on a natural waterslide, fueled by 11,000 gallons of mountain water a minute, into a clear, cold pool in Pisgah National Forest. The pool is 6 to 8 feet deep, so you need to know how to swim. Wear old jeans and tennis shoes and bring a towel. On hot days the parking lot fills up early. No picnicking allowed at the Rock, but there are picnic grounds nearby. Sliding Rock is maintained by the National Forest Service. ✉ *U.S. 276, about 8 miles north of intersection of Hwys. 280 and 276 in Brevard, Pisgah Forest* ☎ *828/877–3265 National Forest Service, 828/257–4200 National Forest Service office in Asheville* 🌐 *www.fs.usda.gov* 🎟 *$1* 🕓 *Late May–early Sept., daily 10–5:30.*

### MOUNTAIN BIKING

The North Carolina Mountains offer some of the best mountain biking in the East. Among the favorite places for mountain biking are **Tsali**, a peninsula sticking out into Lake Fontana near Bruston City, in the Nantahala National Forest; **Dupont State Forest**, just south of Brevard; and the **Bent Creek, Davidson River**, and **Mills River** sections of the Pisgah Ranger District of the Pisgah National Forest.

### WORTH NOTING

**Looking Glass Falls.** Getting to this waterfall is easy, as it's right beside the road in Pisgah National Forest. Water cascades 60 feet into a clear pool. There's a parking area and a walkway down to the falls. ⚠ **Caution! Rocks around waterfalls are extremely slick.** ✉ *U.S. Hwy. 276, 6 miles north of Brevard, Pisgah Forest* ☎ *828/877–3265 Pisgah Ranger District, National Forest Service* 🎟 *Free* 🕓 *Daily 24 hrs.*

### WHERE TO EAT AND STAY

*Hotel reviews have been abbreviated in this book. For expanded reviews, please go to Fodors.com.*

$$ ITALIAN ✕ **Marco Trattoria.** Run by chef Mark Dambax, Marco Trattoria serves northern Italian and Mediterranean dishes. Wood-fired pizzas with such unusual toppings as ricotta cheese with carmelized rosemary onions or Gorgonzola cheese with pine nuts are specialties here. For dinner you can try leg of lamb with cannelini beans or orecchiette pasta with scallops, shrimp, and sundried tomatoes. The restaurant goes out of its way to promote local artists (the wife of the owner designed the restaurant's plates). Dine inside or under umbrellas in the front yard. [$] *Average main: $15* ✉ *204 W. Main St.* ☎ *828/883–4841* 🌐 *www.marcotrattoria.com.*

$ B&B/INN 🏨 **Red House Inn.** One of the oldest houses in Brevard, the Red House Inn was built in 1851 as a trading post and later served as a courthouse, tavern, post office, and school. Now it's an unpretentious but pleasant B&B four blocks from the center of town. **Pros:** B&B in historic house; in the center of town; comfortable; friendly hosts. **Cons:** not for swinging singles. [$] *Rooms from: $125* ✉ *266 W. Probart St.* ☎ *828/884–9349* 🌐 *www.brevardbedandbreakfast.com* *3 rooms, 1 suite, 1 cottage, 2 houses* 🍽 *Breakfast.*

### THE ARTS

**Brevard Music Center.** The nationally known Brevard Music Center hosts a seven-week music festival each summer, with about 80 concerts from mid-June to early August. Boston Pops conductor Keith Lockhart is the artistic director of the Brevard Music Festival. ✉ *349 Andante La.* ☎ *828/862–2100* 🌐 *www.brevardmusic.org.*

### SPORTS AND THE OUTDOORS

**Davidson River Outfitters.** Catch rainbow, brown, or brook trout on the Davidson River, named one of the top 100 trout streams in the United States by Trout Unlimited. Davidson River Outfitters and its guides arrange trips in the Pisgah and Nantahala National Forests and elsewhere. It also has a fly-fishing school and a fly shop. A full-day guided fly fishing trip (wading) for two is around $350. ✉ *26 Pisgah Hwy., Pisgah Forest* ☎ *828/877–4181, 888/861–0111* 🌐 *www.davidsonflyfishing.com.*

## LAKE TOXAWAY

*40 miles southwest of Asheville.*

A century ago a group called the Lake Toxaway Company created a 640-acre lake in the high mountains between Brevard and Cashiers. Nearby, a grand 500-room hotel built with the finest materials, providing the most modern conveniences and serving European cuisine, attracted many of the country's elite. That hotel is long gone, but the scenic area, which some still call "America's Switzerland," has a number of fine resorts and some of the priciest real estate in the North Carolina Mountains.

### GETTING HERE AND AROUND

From Asheville, take Interstate 26 East to Exit 40. Take U.S. 280 South for about 16 miles, where it becomes U.S. 64 West. Continue about 19 miles to Lake Toxaway.

### WHERE TO STAY

*Hotel reviews have been abbreviated in this book. For expanded reviews, please go to Fodors.com.*

$$$$ B&B/INN ★ **Greystone Inn.** In 1915 Savannah resident Lucy Molz built a second home on Lake Toxaway, a Swiss-style mansion that is now a luxurious inn listed on the National Register of Historic Places. **Pros:** deluxe lakeside mountain inn; pampering service; excellent food. **Cons:** very expensive; no elevator. *Rooms from: $440* ✉ *Greystone La.* ☎ *828/966–4700, 800/824–5766* 🌐 *www.greystoneinn.com* *31 rooms, 3 suites* *Some meals.*

## CASHIERS

*63 miles southwest of Asheville via U.S. 74 and NC 107; 14 miles west of Lake Toxaway.*

Cashiers (pronounced CASH-ers) is not a quite a town. Until recently, it was just a crossroads, with a store or two, a summer getaway for wealthy South Carolinians escaping the heat. But with the building of many exclusive gated developments, the Cashiers area, at a cool 3,500-foot elevation, is seeing a bevy of new restaurants and lodges.

### GETTING HERE AND AROUND

From Asheville, take Route 280 to U.S. 64 to get to Cashiers. Everything in Cashiers is within a mile or two of the intersection of Route 107 and U.S. 64.

For a thrilling ride through classes III and IV rapids, take a guided rafting trip on the Nantahala River.

## WHERE TO EAT AND STAY

*Hotel reviews have been abbreviated in this book. For expanded reviews, please go to Fodors.com.*

$$ AMERICAN ★ **Cornucopia.** In the second-oldest building in Cashiers, built in 1892, you can sit on the huge, airy, covered back porch with a metal roof and eat some of the best sandwiches in the region. Lunch specialties include the "Arabian Club," with turkey, bacon, sprouts, and black olives on pita bread. The Black Angus burgers are excellent, and there are several veggie options. Cornucopia has moved upmarket for dinner, with dishes such as bacon-wrapped filet mignon and sesame-seared tuna. No alcohol is sold, but you can bring your own beer, wine, or liquor (there's a set-up charge of $2 for wine and beer and $5 for liquor, per person.) Cornucopia is often packed, especially at lunch. *Average main: $18 ✉ Hwy. 107 S ☎ 828/743–3750 🌐 www.cornucopianc.com ⏲ No dinner Sun.*

$$$ AMERICAN ★ **The Orchard.** Situated in a century-old farmhouse with brown wood shakes, The Orchard is the best restaurant in Cashiers, putting a Southern twist on traditional American dishes. Try the mountain trout, served four different ways, including with almonds, pecans, or herbs, or the rack of venison. While the decor is comfortable rather than fancy, with some kitchy Southern touches such as an old Mail Pouch chewing tobacco sign, dinner prices are higher than you'd expect for a small town. The restaurant now offers wine and beer. Reservations advised in-season. *Average main: $23 ✉ 905 Hwy. 107 S ☎ 828/743–7614 🌐 www.theorchardcashiers.com Reservations essential ⏲ Nightly for dinner only.*

$$$$ RESORT ★ **High Hampton Inn & Country Club.** With rustic rooms and cottages around the 1,400-acre property, the atmosphere at the family-owned High Hampton Inn (listed on the National Register of Historic Places) is unplugged, family-oriented, and pays high respect to tradition. **Pros:** historic property; full of tradition; like resorts used to be. **Cons:** a little old-fashioned and eccentric; few modern conveniences; some rooms are very small and some need to be updated. *Rooms from: $262* ✉ *1525 Hwy. 107 S* ☎ *828/743–2411, 800/334–2551* 🌐 *www.highhamptoninn.com* *116 rooms, 18 cottages; 36 rental houses* ⏲ *Closed late Nov.–mid-Apr.* *Multiple meal plans.*

## HIGHLANDS

4

*85 miles southwest of Asheville; 11 miles south of Cashiers on U.S. 64.*

Highlands is a tony town of only 900 people, but the surrounding area swells to 10,000 or more in summer and fall, when those with summer homes here flock back, like wealthy swallows of Capistrano. Once, Highlands billed itself as the highest town in the East, but it relinquished the title when Banner Elk and other tiny communities a little higher up in the High Country were incorporated as towns. Still, at 4,118 feet it is usually cool and pleasant when even Asheville gets hot. The town's five-block downtown is, not surprisingly given the local demographics, lined with upscale shops, antiques stores, restaurants, and coffeehouses, and there's a sniff of West Palm Beach in the air.

### GETTING HERE AND AROUND

From Asheville, you can get to Highlands by two routes. One is via Interstate 40 West, U.S. 23/74 and 441 to Franklin, then Route 28 and U.S. 64 to Highlands. Alternatively, you can drive Route 280 to U.S. 64.

**Cullasaja Gorge.** West of Highlands via US Hwy. 64 toward Franklin, the Cullasaja Gorge (Cul-lah-SAY-jah) is a 7½-mile gorge passing the Cullasaja River, Lake Sequoyah, and several waterfalls, including **Bridal Veil Falls, Dry Falls, Quarry Falls,** and the 200-foot **Cullasaja Falls.** The gorge and falls are in the Nantahala National Forest. ⚠ Rocks around waterfalls are slippery, and it is dangerous to try to cross the top of the falls. ✉ *U.S. Hwy. 64* *From Highlands follow U.S. Hwy 64 W/28 N to Franklin* ☎ *828/524–6441 Nantahala Ranger Station, Nantahala National Forest* 🌐 *www.fs.usda.gov/recarea/nfsnc.*

### WHERE TO EAT AND STAY

*Hotel reviews have been abbreviated in this book. For expanded reviews, please go to Fodors.com.*

$$$$ AMERICAN ★ **Madison's.** In the Old Edwards Inn, Madison's is Highlands' most upscale restaurant. The dining room is gorgeous, light, and sunny, with windows overlooking Highland's Main Street. The restaurant adheres to a farm-to-table philosophy as much as possible. Try the seared mountain trout with local potatoes and celery root slaw. Save room for one of the excellent desserts, such as a peach crisp or strawberry shortcake with white chocolate mousse and a citrus sorbet. Adjacent to Madison's, the Wine Garden is an outdoor café serving a casual lunch menu of

sandwiches, salads, and wines by the glass. *Average main: $25* *445 Main St.* *828/526–5477* *www.oldedwardsinn.com.*

$$$$ ITALIAN ★ **Ristorante Paoletti.** A fixture on Main Street in Highlands for nearly three decades, Ristorante Paoletti offers sophisticated Italian cuisine with first-rate service, but without a hint of snobbishness. The menu includes a lengthy section of freshly made pastas, along with many excellent seafood dishes. The wine list, one of the largest in the area, includes more than 1,000 selections. *Average main: $30* *440 Main St.* *828/526–4906* *www.paolettis.com* *Reservations essential* *No lunch.*

$$$$ B&B/INN Fodor's Choice ★ **Old Edwards Inn and Spa.** A $40-million renovation turned this 115-year-old inn into the smartest hotel in Highlands by far. **Pros:** deluxe inn with a plethora of amenities; central location; top-notch spa. **Cons:** pricey rates; often booked months in advance. *Rooms from: $290* *445 Main St.* *828/526–8008, 866/526–8008* *www.oldedwardsinn.com* *43 rooms, 19 suites, 7 cottages* *Multiple meal plans.*

## THE ARTS

**Highlands Playhouse.** The well-respected Highlands Playhouse, an equity theater, puts on four or five productions each summer. *362 Oak St.* *828/526–2695* *www.highlandsplayhouse.org.*

## SHOPPING

**Scudder's Galleries.** This high-end antiques dealer and estate liquidator, established in 1925, hosts antiques auctions every night except Sunday between mid-June and November. The auctions are entertaining to see, even if you don't plan on making a purchase. *352 Main St.* *828/526–4111* *www.scuddersgallery.com.*

5

# Great Smoky Mountains National Park

## WORD OF MOUTH

"Whether you delight in the challenge of a strenuous hike to the crest of a mountain or prefer to sit quietly and watch the sun set, Great Smoky Mountains National Park offers a myriad of activities for you to enjoy. The hardest part may be choosing which auto tour, trail, waterfall, overlook, or historic area to explore!"

—gatlinburglover

# WELCOME TO GREAT SMOKY MOUNTAINS NATIONAL PARK

## TOP REASONS TO GO

★ **Witness the wilderness:** This is one of the last remaining big chunks of wilderness in the East. Get away from civilization in more than 800 square miles of tranquility, with old-growth forests, clear streams, meandering trails, wildflowers, and panoramic vistas from mile-high mountains.

★ **Get your endorphins going:** Outdoor junkies can bike, boat, camp, fish, hike, ride horses, white water raft, watch birds and wildlife, and even cross-country ski.

★ **Experience mountain culture:** Visit restored mountain cabins and tour "ghost towns" in the park, with old frame and log buildings preserved much as they were 100 years ago.

★ **Spot wildlife:** Biologists estimate there are more than 1,500 bears, 6,000 deer, and nearly 150 elk now in the park, so your chances of seeing these beautiful wild creatures is quite good.

★ **Learn something new:** Take advantage of the interpretative talks and walks.

**1 North Carolina Side.** The North Carolina (or eastern) side of the park boasts the highest mountain in the park—Clingmans Dome—as well as the historic Cataloochee Valley, many scenic overlooks, and great hiking opportunities. It also connects to the famed Blue Ridge Parkway near Cherokee.

**2 Tennessee Side.** The Tennessee (or western) side of the park offers scenic drives to historic parts of the park such as Cades Cove, fun activities like river tubing, excellent hiking, and the only overnight lodge accommodations in the park, Mt. LeConte.

**3 Nearby North Carolina Towns.** Sometimes called "the quiet side of the park," the North Carolina side of the Smokies is edged with a collection of small, low-key

towns. The most appealing of these are Bryson City and Waynesville. Except for these towns, and the city of Asheville about 50 miles east, most of the area around the east side of the park consists of national forest lands and rural areas. On the southwestern boundary of the park is Lake Fontana, the largest lake in western North Carolina.

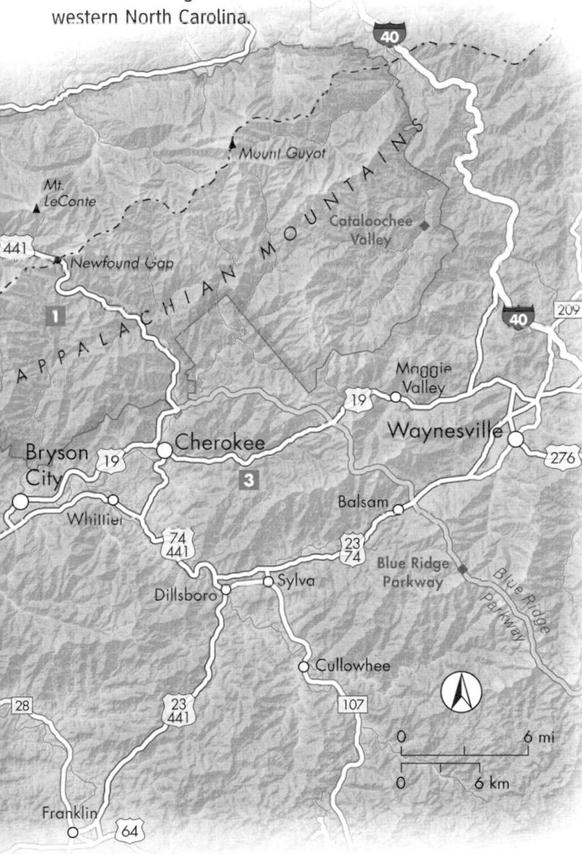


## GETTING ORIENTED

The Great Smoky Mountains National Park straddles parts of two states, North Carolina and Tennessee. The park headquarters is in Gatlinburg, Tennessee, and many people think of the Smokies as being a Tennessee national park. In fact, slightly more of the park is on the eastern, or North Carolina side, than on the Tennessee side—276,000 acres to 245,000 acres. The dividing line is at Newfound Gap. Once inside the park, you may not be aware of which state you're in except for practical considerations of geography and the time it takes to get from point to point.

By Lan Sluder

Great Smoky Mountains National Park is one of the great wild areas of the eastern United States and the most visited national park in the United States. From a roadside lookout or from a clearing in a trail, in every visible direction you can see the mountains march toward a vast horizon of wilderness.

Some of the tallest mountains in the East are here, including 16 peaks over 6,000 feet. The highest in the park, Clingmans Dome, was reputedly the original inspiration for the folk song "On Top of Old Smoky." It rises 6,643 feet above sea level and 4,503 feet above the valley floor. These are also some of the oldest mountains in the world, far older than the Rockies, the Alps, or the Andes. Geologists say the building of what are now the Great Smokies began about a billion years ago.

Today, the park hosts around 9 million visitors each year, more than twice as many as the second-most-visited national park, the Grand Canyon. Even so, with more than 814 square miles of protected land, if you get out of your car you can soon be in a remote cove where your closest neighbors are deer, bobcats, and black bears.

Due to a fortuitous combination of moderate climate and diverse geography, Great Smoky Mountains National Park is one of the most biologically rich spots on Earth. Bears are the most famous animal in the park, but elk are also making the Smokies their home for the first time in 150 years. The Park Service also attempted to reintroduce red wolves to the park, but due to high pup mortality the effort was discontinued in the late 1990s; however, visitors occasionally report seeing what they believe is a wolf. But it is not just large mammals that make it special. The Smokies have been called the "salamander capital of the world," with at least 30 different salamander species. It is also one of the few places on Earth where, for a few evenings in June, you can see synchronous fireflies flashing in perfect unison.

The park offers extraordinary opportunities for other outdoor activities: it has world-class hiking, on more than 850 miles of trails, ranging from easy half-hour nature walks to weeklong backpacking treks. While backcountry hiking has its wonders, some of the most interesting sights in the park are viewable from the comfort of your car or motorcycle. You can explore old farms and mountain homesteads, or watch cornmeal ground at a working gristmill.

For a complete guide to the park, pick up a copy of *Fodor's In Focus Great Smoky Mountains National Park.*

# PLANNING

## WHEN TO GO

There's not a bad time to visit the Smokies, though summer and the month of October are the busiest times. The biggest month for visitation in the park is July, followed by June, and October, which is peak fall-color season. Weekends in October are especially crowded, and you should expect traffic delays on U.S. 441 and traffic jams in Cades Cove. Beat the crowds by coming on weekdays and also early in the day, before 10 am. Late spring is a wonderful time to visit the park, as wildflowers are in bloom, and it's before the heat, humidity, and crowds of summer. Winter in the park can be beautiful, especially when there's snow on the ground or rime frost on the tree limbs. The air is usually clearer in winter, with less haze, and with leaves off the trees the visibility is excellent. Some park roads, including Clingmans Dome Road, are closed in winter due to ice and snow.



## GETTING HERE AND AROUND

Although there are numerous entrances to the North Carolina side of the park, the main entrance is via U.S. Highway 441 near Cherokee and the Oconaluftee Visitor Center.

Another, and much more pleasant (but slower), route to the Smokies is the Blue Ridge Parkway, which has its southern terminus at Cherokee. ⇨ *For more information on the Blue Ridge Parkway, see Chapter 4: Asheville and the North Carolina Mountains.*

You can enter the park by car at nine different places on the Tennessee side. Most of these entrances take you just a short distance into the park to a developed campground or picnic area. The two major entrances to the park on the western side are from Gatlinburg and Townsend.

### AIR TRAVEL

The closest airport on the North Carolina side with national air service is Asheville Regional Airport (AVL), about 60 miles east of the Cherokee entrance. On the Tennessee side, the closest major airport is Knoxville McGhee Tyson Airport (TYS), about 45 miles west of the Sugarlands entrance.

**Airport Information Asheville Regional Airport** *(AVL). ✉ 61 Terminal Dr., off I–26, Fletcher ☎ 828/684–2226, 828/209–3660 guest services 🌐 www.flyavl.com.* **Knoxville McGhee Tyson Airport** *(TYS). ✉ 2025 Alcoa Hwy., Alcoa ☎ 865/342–3000 🌐 www.tys.org.*

### CAR TRAVEL

The nearest sizable city to the park in North Carolina is Asheville. Asheville is about 50 miles east of Cherokee and the Oconaluftee Visitor Center. It takes a little over an hour to get from Asheville to the Cherokee entrance of the park, via Interstate 40 and U.S. Highways 19 and 441. The closest sizable city to the park in Tennessee is Knoxville, about 40 miles west of the Sugarlands entrance, via U.S. Highway 441.

Coming either from the east or west, Interstate 40 is the main interstate access route to the Great Smokies; from the north and south, Interstate 75, Interstate 81, and Interstate 26 are primary arteries.

U.S. 441, also called Newfound Gap Road, is the main road through the park, and the only paved road that goes all the way through. It travels 31 miles between Cherokee and Gatlinburg, crossing Newfound Gap at nearly a mile high.

## RESTAURANTS

The closest thing to fine dining you can find in the park is a hot dog at the snack bar in Cades Cove or a Coke from a vending machine at a visitor center. If you're up to a 14- or 15-mile round-trip hike, there is a dining room at LeConte Lodge, which only offers lunch for day visitors. (Overnight guests get breakfast and dinner at the lodge.) You can create your own gourmet dining with an alfresco picnic at one of the park's 11 attractive picnic areas.

Outside the park you'll find many more dining options, from fast food to fine dining, the latter especially in Asheville. ⇨ *For more information on Asheville, see Chapter 4: The North Carolina Mountains.* On the Tennessee side, both Gatlinburg and Pigeon Forge have myriad fast-food and family dining choices. *Prices in the reviews are the average cost of a main course at dinner or, if dinner is not served, at lunch.*

## HOTELS AND CAMPGROUNDS

The only accommodations actually in the park, besides camping, are at LeConte Lodge. Outside the park, you have a gargantuan selection of hotels of every ilk. On the Tennessee side, in Gatlinburg you'll see a street sign that says "2,000 Hotel Rooms" and points up the hill, and that's just in one section of town. On the North Carolina side, lodging is mostly more low-key, but you can choose from old mountain inns, B&Bs, and motels in the small towns of Bryson City, Waynesville, and Robbinsville. A seemingly ever-expanding number of hotel towers are connected to the giant Harrah's casino in Cherokee, with more than 1,100 rooms, it's the largest hotel in North Carolina. About 50 miles away, in and around Asheville, you can choose from among one of the largest collections of B&Bs in the Southeast, along with hip urban hotels and classic mountain resorts. *Prices in the reviews are the lowest cost of a standard double room in high season.*

Camping is abundant and reasonably priced. The park has nearly 950 tent and RV camping spaces at 10 developed campgrounds, in addition to more than 100 backcountry campsites and shelters. The cost ranges from $4 per person (backcountry sites and shelters, a new fee approved to start in 2013) to $14–$23 per night for front-country sites. All but one of the campgrounds accept RVs and trailers, though most

CLOSE UP

## One Day on the North Carolina Side

If you only have a day to visit the Smokies and are coming from the North Carolina side, start early, pack a picnic lunch, and drive to the **Oconaluftee Visitor Center** to pick up orientation maps and brochures. While you're there, spend an hour or so exploring the **Mountain Farm Museum.** Then drive the ½ mile to **Mingus Mill** and see corn being ground into meal in an authentic working gristmill. Head on up **Newfound Gap Road** and, via Clingmans Dome Road, to **Clingmans Dome.** The 25-mile drive takes you, in terms of the kinds of plants and trees you'll see at the mountain top, all the way to Canada. Stretch your legs and walk the ½-mile paved, but fairly steep, trail to the observation tower on Clingmans Dome, the highest point in the Smokies. If you've worked up an appetite, head back down the mountain and stop for a leisurely picnic at **Collins Creek Picnic Area** (MM 25.4).

If you want a moderate afternoon hike, the 4-mile (round-trip) **Kephart Prong Trail** is nearby and wanders for 2 miles along a stream to the remains of a Depression-era Civilian Conservation Corps camp. Alternatively, and especially if it's a hot summer day, save your picnic and hike and instead drive via the **Blue Ridge Parkway** and Heintooga Ridge Road to the **Heintooga Picnic Area** at Balsam Springs. At a mile high, this part of the Smokies is usually cool even in mid-July. If you're up for it, you can hike all (about 5 miles round-trip) or part of the **Flat Creek Trail**, which begins near the Heintooga picnic area and is one of the hidden jewels of trails in the park. If you decide not to take a long hike, you may have time to drive the one-way, unpaved **Balsam Mountain Road** to Big Cove Road back to Cherokee. Catch the sunset at an overlook on your drive back.

5

have size limits. Immediately outside the park are many commercial campgrounds and RV parks. Permits are required for all backcountry camping.

### VISITOR INFORMATION

There are three main visitor centers in the park: Oconaluftee near Cherokee, Sugarlands near Gatlinburg, and Cades Cove. In addition, there is a visitor contact station at Clingmans Dome, plus four information centers outside the park (in Sevierville and Townsend and two in Gatlinburg).

**Cades Cove.** This visitor center is located about midway on the 11-mile Cades Cove Loop on the Tennessee side. What makes this one especially worth visiting is the Cable Mill, which operates spring through fall, and the Becky Cable House, a pioneer home with farm outbuildings. ✉ *Cades Cove Loop* ☎ *865/436–1200* 🌐 *www.nps.gov/grsm* ⏲ *Dec. and Jan., daily 9–4:30; Feb. and Nov., daily 9–5; Mar., Sept., and Oct., daily 9–6; Apr.–Aug., daily 9–7.*

**Clingmans Dome Visitor Contact Station.** While not a full-fledged visitor information center, Clingmans Dome now has a staffed information kiosk, along wth a small park store and bookshop, at the Clingmans Dome trailhead. ✉ *Clingmans Dome, Great Smoky Mountains National*

*Park* ☎ *865/436–1200* 🌐 *www.nps.gov/grsm* ⏲ *Apr.–Oct., daily 10–6; Nov., daily 9:30–5.*

**Oconaluftee.** The park's only information center on the North Carolina side is 1½ miles from Cherokee. In 2011, it reopened after a major expansion and now features interactive displays, a book and gift store, and live assistance from park rangers and volunteers. Adjoining the visitor center, in a large level field next to the Oconaluftee River, is the ⇨ *Mountain Farm Museum.* ✉ *US Hwy. 441, 1 1/2 miles from Cherokee* ☎ *865/436–1200* 🌐 *www.nps.gov/grsm/planyourvisit/visitorcenters.htm* ⏲ *Jan.–Feb., daily 8–4:30; Mar. and Nov., daily 8–5; Apr.–May and Sep.–Oct., daily 8–6; June–Aug., daily 8–7.*

**Sugarlands.** Here, at the main visitor center on the Tennessee side, you can watch a 20-minute film about the park and take in extensive exhibits about park flora and fauna. ✉ *U.S. Hwy 441, 2 miles south of Gatlinburg* ☎ *865/436–1200* 🌐 *www.nps.gov/grsm/planyourvisit/visitorcenters.htm* ⏲ *Jan.–Feb., daily 8–4:30; Mar. and Nov., daily 8–5; Apr., May, Sept., and Oct., daily 8–6; June–Aug., daily 8–7.*

## FLORA AND FAUNA

A profusion of vegetation defines the Great Smokies; it has one of the richest and most diverse collections of flora in the world. The park is about 95% forested, home to almost 6,000 known species of wildflowers, plants, and trees. Many call the Smokies the "wildflower national park," as it has more flowering plants than any other U.S. national park. In all, typically in October, hundreds of thousands of visitors jam the roads of the park to view the autumn leaf colors.

You can see wildflowers in bloom virtually year-round: ephemerals such as trillium and columbine in late winter and early spring; bright red cardinal flowers, orange butterfly weed, and black-eyed Susans in summer; and Joe-pye weed, asters, and mountain gentian in the fall. However, the best time to see wildflowers in the park is the spring, especially April and early May. The second-best time to see the floral display is early summer. From early to mid-June to mid-July, the hillsides and heath balds blaze with the orange of flame azaleas, the white and pink of mountain laurel, and the purple and white of rhododendron.

Living in Great Smoky Mountains National Park are some 66 species of mammals, more than 200 varieties of birds, 50 native fish species, and more than 80 types of reptiles and amphibians.

The North American black bear is the symbol of the Smokies. Bear populations vary year to year, but biologists think that up to 1,500 bears are in the park, a density of about two per square mile. Many visitors to the park see bears, although sightings are never guaranteed.

The National Park Service has helped reintroduce elk, river otters, and peregrine falcons to the Smokies. Attempts to reintroduce red wolves failed, though visitors occasionally report seeing what they believe is a wolf.

Because of the high elevation of much of the park, you'll see birds here usually seen in more northern areas, including the common raven and the ruffed grouse.

For a few short weeks, usually from late May to mid-June, synchronous fireflies put on an amazing light show. In this illuminated mating dance, the male *Photinus* fireflies blink four to eight times in the air, then wait about six seconds for the females on the ground to return a double-blink response. Inside the park, the Elkmont camping area on the Tennessee side is a popular place to see the fireflies. The Joyce Kilmer Memorial Forest just outside the park near Robbinsville, North Carolina, is another great place to see them.

Altogether, some 17,000 species of plants, animals, and invertebrates have been documented in the park, and scientists believe up to 80,000 additional species of life, as yet unidentified, may exist here.

# NORTH CAROLINA SIDE



The North Carolina side of the park has a variety of sights and experiences, from high peaks to historical houses. Right at the Oconaluftee Visitor Center at the entrance to the park is the Mountain Farm Museum, one of the best-preserved collections of historic log buildings in the region. Cataloochee Cove is a beautiful valley where you can spot deer, wild turkeys, and even elk. Even if you never leave your car, Newfound Gap Road offers plenty of scenic views. If, however, you're ready to lace up your hiking boots, there are hundreds of miles of hiking trails to be explored, including the trail to the top of Clingmans Dome, the highest mountain in the park at 6,643 feet. North Carolina's Mountains to Sea trail starts at Clingmans Dome and ends at Jockey's Ridge on the Outer Banks.

## SCENIC DRIVES

Fodor's Choice ★ **Newfound Gap Road** (*U.S. 441*). Newfound Gap Road is the busiest road in the park by far, with more than a million vehicles making the 16-mile climb from 2,000-foot elevation near Cherokee to almost a mile high at Newfound Gap (and then down to Gatlinburg on the Tennessee side). It's the only road that goes all the way through the center of the park, and the only fully paved road through the park. While it's not a route to escape from the crowds, the scenery is memorable, perhaps more so on the Tennessee than on the North Carolina side. If you don't have time to explore the back roads or to go hiking, Newfound Gap Road will give you a flavor of the richness and variety of the Smokies. Unlike other roads in the park, Newfound Gap Road has mile markers; however, the markers run "backwards" (as far as North Carolinians are concerned), starting at MM 0 at the park boundary near Gatlinburg to MM 31.1 at the border of the park at the entrance to the Blue Ridge Parkway near Cherokee. Among the sites on the road are Oconaluftee Visitor Center and Mountain Farm Museum (MM 30.3); Mingus Mill (MM 29.9); Smokemont Campground and Nature Trail (MM 27.2); Web Overlook (MM 17.7), from which there's a good view almost due west of Clingmans Dome; and Newfound Gap (MM 14.7), the start of the 7-mile road to Clingmans Dome. The speed limit on Newfound Gap Road is 45 mph, and lower in some places. ⇨ *For information on*

At over 6,000 feet high, the observation tower atop Clingmans Dome offers spectacular 360-degree views of the countryside.

*scenic drives on the Tennessee side, see that section below.* ✉ *Newfound Gap Rd. (US Hwy. 441)* ☎ *865/436–1200.*

★ **Cove Creek Road** (*Old Highway 284*). This drive takes you to one of the most beautiful valleys in the Smokies, and to one of the most interesting destinations. The first 7 miles of Cove Creek Road is a mostly paved, winding two-lane road through a scenic rural valley. As you enter the park, the road becomes gravel. Although in the park this is a two-way road, in places it is wide enough only for one vehicle, so you may have to pull over and let the oncoming vehicle pass. At points the curvy road hugs the mountainside, with steep drop-offs, making it unsuitable for large RVs or travel trailers. As you near the Cataloochee Valley, suddenly you're on a nice, paved road again. Follow the paved road, as it is a short cut to the historic old buildings of Cataloochee. (You can also continue on the unpaved Cove Creek Road toward Crosby, Tennessee, and in about 5 miles you can enter Cataloochee from the back side.) Follow the signs for a driving tour of the old houses, barns, churches, a school, and other buildings that are all that remain of the once-thriving Cataloochee community, which at its peak in 1910 had about 1,200 residents. You can stop and walk through most of the buildings. Keep a lookout for elk, wild turkey, deer, and other wildlife here. If you haven't had enough driving for the day, from Cataloochee you can continue on the unpaved Cove Creek Road to Big Creek campground near the North Carolina–Tennessee line, where you can reconnect with I–40 at Exit 451 on the Tennessee side. ✉ *Cove Creek Rd.* ☎ *865/436–1200.*

CLOSE UP

## Bear Facts

Black bear attacks in the Great Smokies or elsewhere in the mountains are extremely rare, but they do happen occasionally. The latest incident in the park was in May 2010, when a man hiking the Laurel Falls Trail was bitten on the foot by a small female bear. Later, the man was taken to court for luring the bear too close so that he could take a photo of it. The last known fatal bear attack in the park was in 2000, when a 50-year-old woman was attacked and killed in the Elkmont section on the Tennessee side.

If you see a bear, and you may—there are about 1,500 black bears in the Smokies—don't approach too closely. Never feed bears or leave food out, as most human-bear conflicts result from bears becoming used to eating human food. Picnic areas and campgrounds in the park have bear-proof garbage cans and food containers. If a bear comes toward you making loud noises or swatting the ground, it's likely demanding more space. Don't run, but back away slowly. If the bear follows, especially if it is not vocalizing or swatting, stand your ground, shout, and intimidate it by throwing rocks or sticks.



## WHAT TO SEE

### HISTORIC SIGHTS

There are five historic districts in the Smokies: Cataloochee, Mountain Farm Museum, Cades Cove, Roaring Fork, and Elkmont. Cataloochee and the Mountain Farm Museum are on the North Carolina side, and the rest are on the Tennessee side. All together, the park contains nearly 100 historical buildings that are being preserved, and about 200 old cemeteries. Some of these, including Cataloochee, Cades Cove, and the Mountain Farm Museum, can be easily reached by car. Others require sometimes strenuous trail hikes.

Fodor's Choice ★ **Cataloochee Valley.** This is one of the most memorable and eeriest sites in all of the Smokies. At one time Cataloochee was a community of more than 1,200 people, in some 200 buildings. After the land was taken over in 1934 for the national park, the community dispersed. Although many of the original buildings are now gone, more than a dozen houses, cabins, and barns, two churches, and other structures have been kept up. You can visit the Palmer Methodist Chapel, a one-room schoolhouse, Beach Grove School, and the Woody and Messer homesteads. It's much like Cades Cove on the Tennessee side, but much less visited. On a quiet day you can almost hear the ghosts of the former Cataloochee settlers. Here you will almost always spot a few elk, reintroduced in 2001, especially in the evening and early morning. Cataloochee is one of the most remote parts of the Smokies reachable by car, via a narrow, winding, gravel road. The novels of Asheville area native Wayne Caldwell, *Cataloochee* and *Requiem by Fire,* bring to life the world of Cataloochee before the coming of the park. ✉ *Cataloochee Community, Cove Creek Rd.* ✧ *Take I–40 W to Exit 20 (U.S. Hwy. 276) near Maggie Valley to*

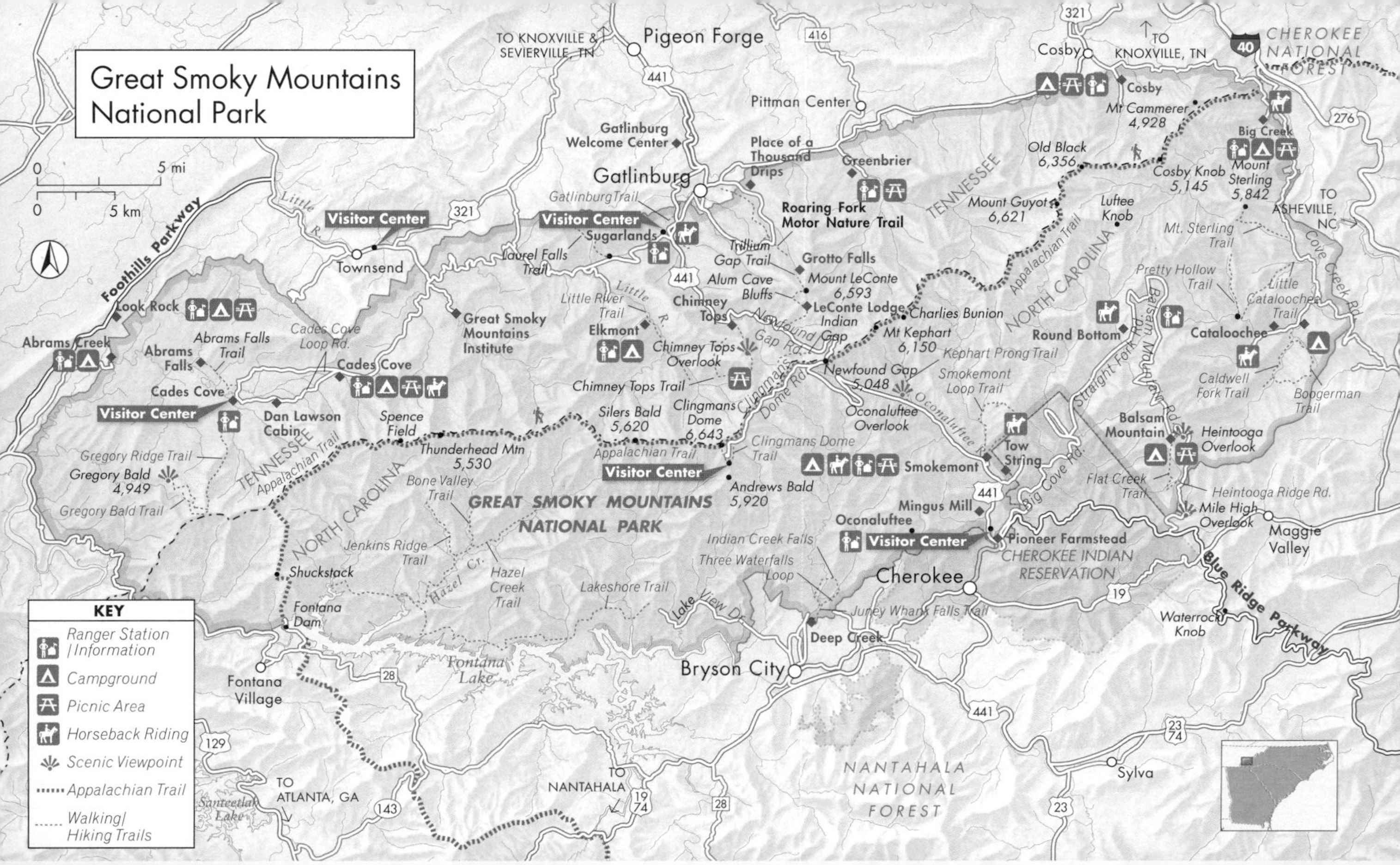

Great Smoky Mountains National Park
0 5 mi
0 5 km
TO KNOXVILLE & SEVIERVILLE, TN
Pigeon Forge
TO KNOXVILLE, TN
CHEROKEE NATIONAL FOREST
Cosby
Pittman Center
Gatlinburg Welcome Center
Gatlinburg
Place of a Thousand Drips
Greenbrier
Roaring Fork Motor Nature Trail
Mt Cammerer 4,928
Big Creek
Old Black 6,356
Cosby Knob 5,145
Mount Sterling 5,842
TO ASHEVILLE, NC
Mount Guyot 6,621
Luftee Knob
TENNESSEE
NORTH CAROLINA
Appalachian Trail
Mt. Sterling Trail
Cove Creek Rd.
Pretty Hollow Trail
Little Cataloochee Trail
Cataloochee
Caldwell Fork Trail
Boogerman Trail
Round Bottom
Straight Fork Rd.
Balsam Mountain Rd.
Balsam Mountain
Heintooga Overlook
Heintooga Ridge Rd.
Flat Creek Trail
Mile High Overlook
Maggie Valley
Blue Ridge Parkway
Waterrock Knob
Sylva
Foothills Parkway
Little R.
Visitor Center
Townsend
GatlinburgTrail
Sugarlands
Laurel Falls Trail
Trillium Gap Trail
Grotto Falls
Mount LeConte 6,593
Alum Cave Bluffs
LeConte Lodge
Charlies Bunion
Mt Kephart 6,150
Kephart Prong Trail
Chimney Tops
Newfound Gap Rd.
Indian Gap
Newfound Gap 5,048
Smokemont Loop Trail
Oconaluftee Overlook
Oconaluftee R.
Tow String
Look Rock
Abrams Creek
Abrams Falls
Abrams Falls Trail
Cades Cove Loop Rd.
Cades Cove
Great Smoky Mountains Institute
Little River Trail
Elkmont
Chimney Tops Overlook
Chimney Tops Trail
Clingmans Dome Rd.
Dan Lawson Cabin
Spence Field
Silers Bald 5,620
Clingmans Dome 6,643
Clingmans Dome Trail
Smokemont
Big Cove Rd.
Gregory Ridge Trail
Gregory Bald 4,949
Gregory Bald Trail
Thunderhead Mtn 5,530
Bone Valley Trail
GREAT SMOKY MOUNTAINS NATIONAL PARK
Andrews Bald 5,920
Mingus Mill
Oconaluftee
Pioneer Farmstead
CHEROKEE INDIAN RESERVATION
Jenkins Ridge Trail
Hazel Cr.
Hazel Creek Trail
Indian Creek Falls
Three Waterfalls Loop
Cherokee
Shuckstack
Lakeshore Trail
Lake View Dr.
Juney Whank Falls Trail
Fontana Dam
Deep Creek
Bryson City
Fontana Lake
Fontana Village
NANTAHALA NATIONAL FOREST
TO NANTAHALA
TO ATLANTA, GA
Santeetlah Lake
KEY
Ranger Station /Information
Campground
Picnic Area
Horseback Riding
Scenic Viewpoint
Appalachian Trail
Walking/ Hiking Trails

*Cove Creek Rd. and follow signs to Great Smoky Mountains National Park and Cataloochee* ☎ *865/436–1200.*

★ **Mountain Farm Museum.** This is perhaps the best re-creation anywhere of a mountain farmstead. The nine farm buildings, all dating from the late 19th century, were moved to this site, next to the Oconaluftee Visitor Center, from locations within the park. Besides a furnished two-story chestnut log cabin, there is a barn, apple house, corn crib, smokehouse, springhouse, chicken coop, and other outbuildings. In season, corn, tomatoes, pole beans, squash, and other mountain crops are grown in the garden, and park staff sometimes put on demonstrations of pioneer activities, such as making apple butter and molasses. Two 1½-mile walking trails (easy) begin near the farm museum. ✉ *U.S. 441 at Oconaluftee Visitor Center, 1½ miles from Cherokee* ☎ *828/497–1904, 865/436–1200 park information line.*

**Mingus Mill.** In its time, the late 19th century, this was the state of the art in gristmills, the two large grist stones powered by a store-bought turbine rather than a hand-built wheel. From mid-March to just after Thanksgiving, you can watch the miller make cornmeal, and even buy a pound of it. ✉ *U.S. Hwy. 441, 2 miles north of Cherokee* ☎ *828/497–1904, 865/436–1200 park information line* ⏲ *Mid-Mar.–late Nov., daily 9–5.*

5

## SCENIC STOPS

★ **Andrews Bald.** Getting to Andrews Bald isn't easy. You have to walk the rocky Forney Ridge Trail some 1.8 miles one-way, with an elevation gain of almost 600 feet, the equivalent of a 60-story skyscraper. The payoff is several acres of grassy bald at more than 5,800 feet, with stunning views of Lake Fontana and the southeastern Smokies. This is one of only two balds in the Smokies (the other is Gregory Bald on the Tennessee side) that the park service keeps clear. ✉ *1.8 miles from the Forney Ridge trailhead parking lot, at the end of Clingmans Dome Rd.* ☎ *865/436–1200.*

**Big Witch Gap Overlook.** The 2-mile drive on the Blue Ridge Parkway between Big Witch Gap Overlook and Noland Divide Overlook offers fine views into the eastern side of the Smokies, and in May and June the roadsides are heavily abloom with rhododendron. ✉ *BRP MM 461.9* ☎ *828/298–0398 BRP information line.*

**Cataloochee Overlook.** Coming from Cove Creek Road onto the paved section of Cataloochee Road, this is your first opportunity to stop and see the broad expanse of Cataloochee Cove. Cataloochee is taken from a Cherokee word meaning "row upon row" or "standing in rows," and indeed you'll see rows of mountain ridges here. The overlook is well marked and has a split-rail fence. ✉ *Cataloochee Rd.* ☎ *865/436–1200.*

★ **Clingmans Dome.** At an elevation of more than 6,600 feet, this is the third-highest peak east of the Rockies, only a few feet shorter than the tallest, Mt. Mitchell. From the parking lot (where there are restrooms) at the end of Clingmans Dome Road, walk up a paved, but steep, ½-mile trail to an observation tower offering 360-degree views from the "top of Old Smoky." There's also a small visitor contact center and bookshop (open April–November). Temperatures here are usually 10–15°F lower than at the entrance to the park near Cherokee or Gatlinburg. Clingmans Dome Road is closed to vehicular traffic in winter (December–March), but if there's snow on the ground you can put on your snowshoes and hike up to the peak. ✉ *Clingmans Dome Rd., 7 miles from U.S. 441* ☎ *865/436–1200.*

★ **Heintooga Overlook.** This is one of the best spots to watch the sunset, with a sweeping view westward of the crest of the Great Smokies. ✉ *Heintooga Ridge Rd.* ✥ *Entrance to Heintooga Ridge Rd. is at BRP MM 458.2. Overlook is 7 miles from BRP.* ☎ *828/298–0398 BRP information line* ⏲ *Often closed in winter due to weather conditions.*

**Mile High Overlook.** This overlook has a panoramic view of much of the eastern side of the Smokies. ✉ *Heintooga Ridge Rd.* ✥ *Entrance to Heintooga Ridge Rd. is at MM 458.2 on the Blue Ridge Pkwy. Overlook is 1.3 miles from BRP.* ☎ *865/436–1200* ⏲ *Often closed in winter due to weather conditions.*

**Oconaluftee Valley Overlook.** From atop the Thomas Divide, just a little below the crest of the Smokies, you can look down and see the winding Newfound Gap Road. This is also a good spot to view sunrise in the Smokies. ✉ *U.S. Hwy. 441 (Newfound Gap Rd.) at MM 15.4* ☎ *865/436–1200.*

## SPORTS AND THE OUTDOORS

### BICYCLING

The North Carolina side of the Smokies offers excellent cycling, and bicycles are permitted on most roads. However, you have to be selective about where you bike. ■ **TIP→** Vehicular traffic on the main roads, especially Newfound Gap Road (U.S. 441), can be very heavy. Steep terrain, and curvy, narrow back roads with narrow shoulders and blind spots make biking difficult or unsafe in some areas.

Two good places for biking on (mostly) paved roads are Lakeview Drive—the so-called Road to Nowhere near Bryson City—and in Cataloochee Cove. Also, Balsam Mountain Road and Cove Creek Road offer pleasant biking with very little auto traffic. Since these roads are unpaved, with mostly gravel surfaces, you should use a mountain bike or an all-terrain hybrid. Helmets are not required by law in the park but are strongly recommended.

### BOATING

**Fontana Lake and Dam.** More than 29 miles long, and comprising around 12,000 acres of reservoir, Fontana Lake and Dam border the southern edge of the Great Smokies. Unlike most other lakes in the mountains, Fontana has a shoreline that is almost completely undeveloped, since about 90% of its 240 miles are owned by the federal government. Fishing here is excellent, especially for small-mouth bass, muskie, and walleye. On the downside, the Tennessee Valley Authority (TVA) manages the lake for power generation, and at the peak visitor period in the fall the lake is drawn down, leaving large areas of mudflats. Fontana Dam, completed in 1944, at 480 feet is the highest concrete dam east of the Rockies. The dam's visitor center gets about 50,000 visitors a year. The

Palmer Methodist Chapel is one of the historic buildings in the once-inhabited Cataloochee Valley.

Appalachian Trail crosses the top of the dam. ✉ *Fontana Dam Visitor Center, off Rte. 28, 3 miles from Fontana Village* ☎ *865/632–2101 TVA headquarters, 865/436–1200 park information line* 💴 *Free* ⏲ *Visitor center May–Oct., daily 9–7.*

### BOAT RENTALS

**Fontana Village Resort Marina.** Boat rentals on Fontana Lake, including kayaks, canoes, pontoon boats, small powerboats, and jet skis, are available at Fontana Village Marina, open April–October. Bass boats go for $35–$40 an hour or $150–$200 a day, pontoon boats for $60 an hour, jet skis for $85, and kayaks for $25–$40 for two hours. ✉ *Fontana Village Resort, 300 Woods Rd., off Hwy. 28 N, Fontana Dam* ☎ *828/498–2211, 800/849–2258* 🌐 *www.fontanavillage.com/marina.*

### FISHING

The North Carolina side of the Smokies has one of the best wild trout fisheries in the East. Deep Creek, Little Cataloochee, and Hazel Creek are streams known to serious anglers all over the country. The North Carolina side has more than 1,000 miles of streams (not all contain trout), and all are open to fishing year-round, except Bear Creek at its junction with Forney Creek, and upstream from there.

Among the best trout streams on this side of the park are Big Creek, Cataloochee Creek, Palmer Creek, Raven Fork, Deep Creek, Hazel Creek, and Noland Creek. Often the best fishing is in higher-elevation streams, in areas that are more difficult to reach. Streams that are easily accessible, such as the Pigeon River, have greater fishing pressure.

## DID YOU KNOW?

The "smoke" the Great Smoky Mountains is named for is a blueish fog created by moisture in the air. Unfortunately, air pollution is taking a toll on the mountains. The whitish haze you see, especially in summer, is more smog than fog and consists of airborne particles from burning fossil fuels.

CLOSE UP

## Fishing Rules

To fish in the park you must possess a valid fishing license or permit from either Tennessee or North Carolina. Either state license is valid throughout the park, and no trout stamp is required. Persons under 16 don't need a license. Fishing licenses are not available in the park but may be purchased in nearby towns or online.

Only artificial flies or lures with a single hook can be used—no live bait. Fishing is permitted from a half hour before official sunrise to a half hour after official sunset. The limit for the combined total of brook, rainbow, or brown trout, or smallmouth bass must not exceed five fish each day. You may not have more than five fish in your possession, regardless of whether they are fresh, stored in an ice chest, or otherwise preserved. Twenty rock bass may be kept in addition to the above limit.

The minimum size is 7 inches for brook, rainbow, brown trout, and smallmouth bass. For rock bass there is no minimum size.

If you fish in the stocked streams of the Qualla Boundary, you'll need a tribal fishing license, available at shops in Cherokee.

#### OUTFITTERS

For backcountry fishing trips, you may want to hire a licensed guide. Full-day trips cost around $225–$300 for one angler, $300–$400 for two. Only guides approved by the National Park Service are permitted to take anglers into the backcountry.

### HIKING

Great Smoky Mountains National Park has more than 850 miles of hiking trails, about equally divided between the North Carolina and Tennessee sides. The trails range from short nature walks to long, strenuous hikes that gain several thousand feet in elevation.

Download a copy of the trail guide from the park's website or buy a hiking guide at park stores. You can also call the park's Backcountry Information office (☎ *865/436–1297*) for information to help plan your backpacking or hiking trip.

#### EASY

**Three Waterfalls Loop.** For the effort of a 2.4-mile hike, this trail will reward you with three pretty waterfalls, Tom Branch, Indian Creek, and Juney Whank. Deep Creek also has a picnic area and campground. Tubing on Deep Creek is fun, too, although it is officially discouraged by the park. Biking also is allowed in this area. ✉ *Deep Creek Rd.* ✣ *Trailhead at end of Deep Creek Rd., near Bryson City entrance to park* ☎ *865/436–1200*.

#### MODERATE

**Clingmans Dome Trail.** If you've been driving too long and want some exercise, along with unbeatable views of the Smokies and an ecological lesson, too, take the ½-mile (1-mile round-trip) trail from the Clingmans Dome parking lot to the observation tower at the top of Clingmans Dome, the highest peak in the Smokies. While paved, the trail is

You'll have fish tales to tell for years to come from a fly fishing trip in the Great Smoky Mountains.

steep, and at well over 6,000 feet elevation you'll probably be gasping for air. Most of the fir trees here are dead, killed by the alien invader, the balsam wooly adelgid. ✉ *Clingmans Dome Rd.* ✣ *Trail begins at Clingmans Dome parking lot* ☎ *865/436–1200* ⊙ *Clingmans Dome Rd. is closed Dec.–Mar.*

**Flat Creek.** This is one of the hidden gems among the park's trails. It's little known, but it's a delightful hike, especially in summer when this higher elevation means respite from stifling temperatures. The path stretches through a pretty woodland, with evergreens, birch, rhododendron, and wildflowers. The elevation gain is about 570 feet. The trail is only 2.6 miles if you use a two-car shuttle, one at the trailhead at mile 5.4 of Heintooga Ridge Road, and the other at the Heintooga picnic area; if you don't do a two-car shuttle, you'll have to walk 3.6 miles along Heintooga Ridge Road to your car, but even this is pleasant, with spruce and fir lining the road and little traffic. ✉ *Flat Creek Trailhead, Heintooga Ridge Rd., MM 5.4* ☎ *865/436–1200* ⊙ *Heintooga Ridge Rd. is closed in winter.*

**Kephart Prong.** A 4-mile (round-trip) woodland trail wanders beside a stream to the remains of a Civilian Conservation Corps camp. ✉ *U.S. 441(Newfound Gap Rd.)* ✣ *Trailhead is 5 miles north of Smokemont Campground on U.S. 441 (Newfound Gap Rd.)* ☎ *865/436–1200.*

★ **Little Cataloochee.** No other hike in the Smokies offers a cultural and historic experience like this one. In the early 20th century Cataloochee Cove had the largest population of any place in the Smokies, around 1,200 people. Most of the original structures have been torn down or succumbed to the elements, but a few historic frame buildings remain, such as a log cabin near Davidson Gap at mile 2.6, an apple house at mile 3.3, and a church at mile 4, preserved by park staff. You'll see several of these, along with rock walls and other artifacts, on the Little Cataloochee Trail. The trail is 5.9 miles (one-way) including about 0.8 mile at the beginning on Pretty Hollow Gap Trail. It is best hiked with a two-car shuttle, with one vehicle at the Pretty Hollow Gap trailhead in Cataloochee Valley and the other at the Little Cataloochee trailhead at Old Highway 284 (Cove Creek Road). Including the time it takes to explore the historic buildings and cemeteries, you should allow at least six hours for this hike. The Pretty Hollow Gap trailhead is near Beech Grove School in the Cataloochee Valley. ✉ *Cataloochee Valley* ☎ *865/436–1200.*

### TIPS FOR HIKING SAFELY

■ Be realistic about your physical condition and abilities.

■ Carry plenty of water and energy-rich foods, like GORP (good old raisins and peanuts), energy bars, and fruit.

■ Dress in layers and be prepared for temperature changes, especially snow in winter. Carry rain gear and expect rain at any time.

■ Be sure to allow plenty of time to complete your hike before dark. As a rule of thumb, when hiking in the Smokies you'll travel only about 1½ miles per hour, so a 10-mile hike will take almost seven hours.

**Smokemont Loop.** A 6.1-mile loop takes you by streams and, in spring and summer, lots of wildflowers, including trailing arbutus. The trail also passes a field with old chestnut trees killed by the chestnut blight decades ago and the old Bradley Cemetery. With access off Newfound Gap Road (U.S. 441) at Smokemont campground near Cherokee, this is an easy trail to get to. ✉ *Smokemont Campground, U.S. 441 (Newfound Gap Rd.)* ✥ *Bradley Fork trailhead is at D section of Smokemont campground; follow Bradley Fork Trail to Smokemont Loop Trail* ☎ *865/436–1200.*

#### DIFFICULT

**Mt. Sterling.** A 5.4-mile hike (round-trip) takes you to an old fire watchtower, which you can climb. The route is steep, with an elevation gain of almost 2,000 feet, so you should consider this a strenuous, difficult hike. ✉ *Cove Creek Rd. (Old Hwy. 284)* ✥ *Trailhead on Cove Creek Rd. (Old Hwy. 284), midway between Cataloochee and Big Creek Campground* ☎ *865/436–1200.*

## HORSEBACK RIDING

Get back to nature and away from the crowds with a horseback ride through the forest. Guided horseback rides are offered by one park concessionaire stable at Smokemont near Cherokee. Rides are at a walking pace, so they are suitable for even inexperienced riders.

Another option is to bring your own horse. Smoky Mountains National Park is one of the best places to ride in the Southeast. There are five horse camps in the Smokies, three on the North Carolina side and two in Tennessee. About 550 miles of the park's hiking trails are open to horses.

#### OUTFITTERS

**Smokemont Riding Stable.** The emphasis here is on a family-friendly horseback riding experience, suitable even for novice riders. Choose either the 1-hour trail ride ($30) or a 2½-hour waterfall ride (departing daily at 9, noon, and 3; $70). There's also a four-hour ride for $100. Riders must be at least five years old and weigh no more than 225 pounds. Smokemont also offers wagon rides ($10). Check with the stable for dates and times. ✉ *135 Smokemont Riding Stable Rd., off U.S. Hwy. 441 near MM 27.2, Cherokee* ☎ *828/497–2373* 🌐 *www.smokemontridingstable.com* ⏲ *Late Mar.–Oct.*

### TUBING

On a hot summer's day there's nothing like hitting the water. On the North Carolina side, you can swim or go tubing on Deep Creek near Bryson City. The upper section is a little wild and woolly, with white water flowing from cold mountain springs. The put-in is at the convergence of Indian Creek and Deep Creek where the sign reads "No tubing beyond this point." The lower section of Deep Creek is more suitable for kids. Put-in for this section is at the swimming hole just above the first bridge on the Deep Creek Trail. There are several tubing outfitters near the entrance of the park at Deep Creek. Some have changing rooms and showers. Wear a swimsuit and bring towels and dry clothes to change into that you can leave in your car. Most tubing outfitters are open April–October.

5

#### OUTFITTERS

You can rent an inner tube for tubing on Deep Creek for around $5 a day at these outfitters, all located near the Deep Creek entrance to the park near Bryson City. Tubes come in a variety of sizes, and some have seats and backrests.

**Creekside Tubing.** On the left near the Deep Creek entrance to the park, Creekside Tubing has hot showers, a game room, and snack bar as well as tubes for rent. It also has rooms and a cabin for rent. ✉ *1881 W. Deep Creek Rd., Bryson City* ☎ *828/488–2587* 🌐 *www.deepcreeklodgetubing.com.*

**Deep Creek Store & Tubes.** About 50 yards from the Bryson City entrance to the park, Deep Creek Store & Tubes is a (highly) commercial operation that rents tubes and sells camping supplies. It also has a campground and rental cabins, with free Wi-Fi. ✉ *1840 W. Deep Creek Rd., Bryson City* ☎ *828/488–9665* 🌐 *www.smokymtncampground.com* ⏲ *Closed Nov.–Mar.*

**Deep Creek Tube Center.** About 1 mile from the park entrance, Deep Creek Tube Center rents tubes with plastic seats ($3–$6 a day) and sells creek shoes and other tubing accessories in its camp store. The Tube Center also has a petting zoo with goats and a campground with more than 50 sites and rental cabins (including two restored log cabins) with Wi-Fi. ✉ *1090 Deep Creek Rd., about 1 mile from downtown Bryson City, Bryson City* ☎ *828/488–6055* 🌐 *www.deepcreekcamping.com.*

## EDUCATIONAL OFFERINGS

Discover the flora, fauna, and mountain culture of the Smokies with scheduled ranger programs and nature walks.

**Interpretive Ranger Programs.** The National Park Service organizes all sorts of orientation activities, such as daily guided hikes and talks. The focus of the programs varies widely from talks on mountain culture to old-time fiddle and banjo music to ranger-led walks through historical areas of the park. Most are free, though a ranger-led hayride in Cades Cove costs $14. Many of the programs are suitable for older children as well as for adults. For schedules, go to the Oconaluftee Visitor Center or other park visitor centers and pick up a free copy of *Smokies Guide* newspaper, or check online for park events. ☎ *865/436–1200* 🌐 *www.nps.gov/grsm/planyourvisit/events.htm* 🎟 *Most are free.*

**Junior Ranger Program for Families.** Children ages 5 to 12 can take part in these hands-on educational programs. Kids can pick up a Junior Ranger booklet ($2.50) at Oconaluftee or at other park visitor centers. They're also available at Elkmont and Cades Cove campgrounds and online through the Great Smoky Mountains Association (🌐 *www.shop.smokiesinformation.org*). After they've completed the activities in the booklet, kids can stop by a visitor center to talk to a ranger and receive a Junior Ranger badge. The badges are available year-round but spring through fall the park offers many age-appropriate demonstrations, classes, and programs for Junior Rangers, such as Blacksmithing, Stream Splashin', Geology, Critters and Crawlies, Cherokee Pottery for Kids, and—our favorite—Whose Poop's on Our Boots? ✉ *Tennessee* ☎ *865/436–1200* 🌐 *www.nps.gov/grsm/forkids/index.htm* 🎟 *$2.50.*

## WHERE TO EAT

There are no restaurants within the park (other than at the remote LeConte Lodge on the Tennessee side). Picnic areas, however, provide amenities such as restrooms and pavilions. Most picnic areas in the park have raised grills for cooking. All picnic areas have restrooms, some with pit toilets and some with flush toilets, but not all have running water in the bathrooms (bring hand sanitizer) or potable drinking water.

### PICNIC AREAS

**Big Creek Picnic Area.** This is the smallest picnic area in the park, with only 10 picnic tables. It's accessible via Exit 451 of Interstate 40, or the unpaved Cove Creek Road from Cataloochee. There's a small campground here and restrooms but no pavilion. Several good hiking trails can be reached from the picnic area. Big Creek has some Class IV rapids nearby. ✉ *Off I–40 at Exit 451, Waterville* ✣ *Follow the road past the Walters Power Generating Station to a four-way intersection. Continue straight through and follow signs.* ☎ *865/436–1200* ⏲ *Closed Nov.–Mar.*

**Collins Creek Picnic Area.** The largest developed picnic area in the park, Collins Creek has 182 picnic tables. Collins Creek, which runs near the picnic area, is a small stream with above-average trout fishing. The site has restrooms with flush toilets, potable water, and a 70-seat

CLOSE UP

## Getting Groceries

Other than a small convenience store at Cades Cove campground, there is no place to buy picnic supplies and groceries in the park. However, you'll find good-size supermarkets near the park entrance. In North Carolina, **Ingles** is the dominant supermarket chain, with stores in Bryson City, Waynesville, Sylva, and Robbinsville, among other towns near the park. **Bi-Lo,** another Southeastern chain supermarket with more than 220 stores, has a location in Waynesville. There are several independent grocers in Cherokee, and **Food Lion,** a regional supermarket, has a location near Cherokee in Whittier. In Asheville, besides many supermarkets, you'll find **Greenlife** (owned by Whole Foods) and **Earth Fare,** two natural-foods supermarkets, and **Fresh Market,** a regional gourmet supermarket chain. The largest farmers' market in North Carolina is in Asheville, too.

In Tennessee, **Food City** has outlets in Pigeon Forge, Sevierville, and Gatlinburg.

5

pavilion for groups that can be reserved in advance for $20. ✉ *US Hwy. 441 (Newfound Gap Rd.) at MM 25.4, about 8 miles from Cherokee* ☎ *865/436–1200* ⏲ *Picnic area early Apr.–Oct.; grounds close at 8 pm May–Aug., at sunset the rest of the yr.*

★ **Deep Creek Picnic Area.** Deep Creek offers more than picnicking. You can go tubing (rent a tube for the day for under $5 at nearby tubing centers), hike about 2 miles to three pretty waterfalls, or go trout fishing. You can even go mountain biking here, as this is one of the few park trails where bikes are allowed. The picnic area, open year-round, has 58 picnic tables, plus a pavilion that seats up to 70. ✉ *1912 E. Deep Creek Rd., Bryson City* ✣ *From downtown Bryson City, follow signs for 3 miles to Deep Creek* ☎ *865/436–1200.*

Fodor's Choice ★ **Heintooga Picnic Area.** This is our favorite developed picnic area in the park. Located at more than a mile high and set in a stand of spruce and fir, the picnic area has 41 tables. Nearby is Mile High Overlook, which offers one of the most scenic views of the Smokies and is a great place to enjoy the sunset. For birders, this is a good spot to see golden-crowned kinglets, red-breasted nuthatches, and other species that prefer higher elevations. You're almost certain to see the common raven here. Nearby are a campground and trailheads for several good hiking trails, including Flat Creek. You can return to Cherokee via an unpaved back road, Balsam Mountain Road, which is one-way, to Big Cove Road. The disadvantage is that due to the high elevation (and the risk of snow and ice) the picnic area is only open from mid-May to early October. ✉ *Heintooga Ridge Rd.* ✣ *From Cherokee, take the BRP 11 miles to the turnoff for Heintooga Ridge Rd. Follow Heintooga Ridge Rd. about 9 miles to picnic area* ☎ *865/436–1200* ⏲ *Closed early Oct.–mid-May.*

# TENNESSEE SIDE

The Tennessee side of the park, like the nearby communities of Pigeon Forge and Gatlinburg, gets a lot of visitors. Some 2 million people a year tour Cades Cove, and on a busy fall weekend the traffic on the Cades Cove Loop may remind you of midtown Manhattan, except more scenic. The Tennessee side also has the largest and busiest campgrounds and picnic areas.

## SCENIC DRIVES

Fodor's Choice ★ **Cades Cove Loop Road.** This 11-mile loop through Cades Cove is the most popular route in the park and arguably the most scenic part of the entire Smokies. The one-way, one-lane paved road (recently resurfaced) starts 7.3 miles from the Townsend entrance. Stop at the orientation shelter at the start of the loop and pick up a Cades Cove Tour booklet ($1.50). The drive begins with views over wide pastures to the mountains at the crest of the Smokies. Few other places in the Appalachians offer such views across wide valley bottoms with hayfields and wildflower meadows, framed by split-rail fences and surrounded by tall mountains. Along the way, you'll pass three 19th-century churches and many restored houses, log cabins, and barns. All are open for exploration. A highlight of the loop road, about midway, is the Cable Mill area, with a visitor center, working water-powered gristmill, and a restored farmstead. The Cades Cove Loop Road is also an excellent place to see wildlife, including black bears (especially in late summer and fall), white-tailed deer, and wild turkeys. The road, open year-round, is closed from sunset to sunrise. On Wednesday and Saturday mornings until 10 am the loop is open only to bicyclists and walkers. On almost any day, and especially on weekends, you can expect traffic delays, as passing points on the one-way road are few and far between, and if just one vehicle stops, scores of vehicles behind it also have to stop and wait. Allow at least two to three hours just to drive the loop, longer if you want to stop and explore the historic buildings. A campground open year-round is in Cades Cove, and a horse camp is nearby. ✉ *Cades Cove Loop Rd.*

**Foothills Parkway.** Foothills Parkway is a long-planned 71-mile scenic parkway that parallels the northern and western edges of the Great Smoky Mountains National Park. Construction began in 1960, but due to funding problems to date only three sections of the parkway have been completed and opened to the public, a 17.5-mile western section from U.S. 321 near Townsend to U.S. 129 at Chilhowee Lake, a 6-mile portion from Cosby (at TN 32) to Interstate 40, plus the Gatlinburg Bypass between Pigeon Forge and the park, which also is considered part of the Parkway. Another 9.5-mile section, as yet unpaved, is open to bikers and pedestrians—it is an excellent place for biking. The 17.5-mile western section is particularly scenic, with stunning views of the western edge of the park. Known as the "Tail of the Dragon" for its 318 curves in 11 miles, U.S. 129 is popular with motorcycle and sports-car enthusiasts. It connects with the end of the Foothills Parkway at Chilhowee. ✉ *Foothills Pkwy.*

## NORTH CAROLINA CAMPGROUNDS

There is no lodging, other than camping, inside the park on the North Carolina side. Two campgrounds on the North Carolina side, Smokemont and Cataloochee, accept reservations. They are required at Cataloochee and advised for Smokemont. Others on the North Carolina side are first-come, first-served.

**Balsam Mountain Campground.** If you like a high, cool campground with a beautiful setting in evergreens, Balsam Mountain is it. It's the highest elevation in the park, at more than 5,300 feet. By evening, you may want a campfire even in summer. The 46 campsites—first-come, first served—are best for tents, but small trailers or RVs up to 30 feet can fit in some sites. Due to its somewhat remote location off the Blue Ridge Parkway, Balsam Mountain Campground is rarely full even on peak summer and fall weekends. ✉ *Near end of Heintooga Ridge Rd., GSMNP, NC* ☎ *865/436–1200* 🌐 *www.nps.gov/grsm.*

**Big Creek Campground.** With just 12 campsites, Big Creek is the smallest campground in the park, and the only one that doesn't accept RVs or trailers—it's for tents only. This is a walk-in, not hike-in, campground. Five of the 12 first-come, first-served sites (unnumbered) are beside Big Creek, which offers good swimming and fishing. Carefully observe bear protection rules, as there have been a number of human-bear interactions nearby. ✉ *Cove Creek Rd. (Old Hwy. 284), GSMNP* ☎ *865/436–1200* 🌐 *www.nps.gov/grsm.*

**Cataloochee Campground.** The appeal of this small campground is its location in the beautiful and historical Cataloochee Valley. Reservations for all of the 27 tent and RV sites are required. Although the campground allows RVs and trailers up to 31 feet, you may want to think twice before driving anything other than a car or truck into the valley—the unpaved Cove Creek Road is narrow with sharp curves, and in some places you hug the mountainside, with a steep drop-off just a few feet away. ✉ *Cataloochee Valley, Cove Creek Rd., Waynesville* ☎ *877/444–6777* 🌐 *www.recreation.gov.*

**Deep Creek Campground.** This campground is near the most popular tubing spot on the North Carolina side of the Smokies. There's also swimming in several swimming holes. Of the 92 first-come, first-served sites here, sites 1–42 are for tents only, and the other sites are for tents and small RVs/trailers up to 26 feet in length. ✉ *1912 E. Deep Creek Rd., Bryson City* ☎ *865/436–1200* 🌐 *www.nps.gov/grsm.*

**Smokemont Campground.** With 142 sites, Smokemont is the largest campground on the North Carolina side of the park, and it's open year-round. Some of the campsites are a little jammed up, but the individual sites themselves are spacious. ✉ *Off U.S. Hwy. 441 (Newfound Gap Rd.), 6 miles north of Cherokee, GSMNP* ☎ *877/444–6777* 🌐 *www.recreation.gov.*

★ **Newfound Gap Road.** In a little more than 14 miles, Newfound Gap Road (U.S. 441) on the Tennessee side of the park climbs more than 3,500 feet from Gatlinburg to the gap through the crest of the Smokies at 5,046 feet. It takes you through Southern cove hardwood, pine-oak, and Northern hardwood forests to the spruce-fir forest at Newfound Gap. Unlike other roads in the park, Newfound Gap Road has mile markers, starting at the park entrance near Gatlinburg. Sugarlands Visitor Center is at mile marker 1.7. It's worth stopping at Chimneys picnic area (MM 6.2), even if you're not picnicking. A lovely stream, with huge boulders, cuts through the picnic area, and an easy 0.75-mile hiking trail takes you through a cove hardwood forest. At around mile marker 7, three overlooks provide a good view of Chimney Tops, two rock spires sticking out of the ridge line. Note the hundreds of dead fir trees, killed by the woolly adelgid, on the mountainsides. You'll probably see a lot of cars parked at Alum Cave trailhead (MM 10.4), which follows Alum Cave Creek to Arch Rock, a natural tunnel caused by weathering, and then to Alum Cave Bluffs, a site of a potash alum and epsomite mine briefly operated by Epsom Salts Company before the Civil War. The trail eventually leads to LeConte Lodge on Mt. LeConte. At Newfound Gap (MM 14.7), you can straddle the Tennessee–North Carolina state line and also hike some of the Appalachian Trail. The two-lane, paved Newfound Gap Road has a 45 mph speed limit, with lower limits in some curvy areas. It is sometimes closed in winter due to ice and snow. ⊠ *U.S. Hwy. 441.*

★ **Roaring Fork Motor Nature Trail.** Roaring Fork offers a dramatic counterpoint to Cades Cove Loop Road. Where Cades Cove Loop meanders through a wide open valley, Roaring Fork closes in, with the forest sometimes literally just inches from your car's fender. The one-way, paved road is so narrow in places that RVs, trailers, and buses are not permitted. The 6-mile Roaring Fork Motor Nature Trail starts just beyond the Noah "Bud" Ogle farmstead and the Rainbow Falls trailhead. Stop and pick up a Roaring Fork Auto Tour booklet ($1) at the information shelter. Numbered markers along the route are keyed to 16 stops highlighted in the booklet. Along the road are many opportunities to stop your car and get closer to nature. Among the sites are several old cabins and the Alfred Reagan place, which is painted in the original blue, yellow, and cream, "all three colors that Sears and Roebuck had," according to a story attributed to Mr. Reagan. At one point the roadside is littered with fallen and now decaying chestnut trees that were killed by the chestnut blight in the early part of the 20th century. There are several good hiking trails starting along the road, including Trillium Gap Trail that leads to Mt. LeConte. The road follows Roaring Fork Creek a good part of the way, and the finale is a small waterfall called "The Place of a Thousand Drips," right beside the road. Roaring Fork Motor Nature Trail is closed in winter (usually December–March). ⊠ *Roaring Fork Motor Nature Tr.* ✥ *To get to Roaring Fork from Gatlinburg from the parkway (U.S. 441), turn onto Historic Nature Trail at stoplight number 8 in Gatlinburg and follow it to the Cherokee Orchard entrance of the park.* ⊙ *Closed Dec.–Mar. (dates vary).*

CLOSE UP

## One Day on the Tennessee Side

If you have one day and are entering the park from the Tennessee side, start early, pack a picnic lunch, and drive to the **Sugarlands Visitor Center** to orient yourself to the park. Head to the **Cades Cove Loop Road** and drive the 11-mile loop, stopping to explore the preserved farmsteads and churches. Spend some time in the **Cable Mill** area, visiting the gristmill, **Gregg-Cable House,** and other outbuildings. Depending on your timing, you can picnic at one of the stops in Cades Cove or Metcalf Bottoms. Take **Newfound Gap Road** up to **Newfound Gap. Clingmans Dome Road** is just over the state line, but if you've come this far you'll want to drive up. Stretch your legs and walk to the observation tower on **Clingmans Dome.** Return down Clingmans Dome and Newfound Gap roads and walk the self-guided trail around the **Noah "Bud" Ogle** farm. Then proceed on to **Roaring Fork Motor Nature Trail.** Stop to explore the preserved cabins and other sites along the trail. At Auto Tour site number 5, park in the parking lot at the Trillium Gap trailhead and—if you have the time and are up to a moderate 2.6-mile (round-trip) hike—walk to **Grotto Falls.**

5

## WHAT TO SEE

### HISTORIC SIGHTS

Fodor'sChoice ★ **Cades Cove.** The Cherokee name for this 6,800-acre valley is *Tsiyahi,* or place of otters. Its English name may have come from a Cherokee chief called Kade. For hundreds of years Cherokee Indians hunted in Cades Cove, but there is no evidence of major settlements. Under the terms of the Calhoun Treaty of 1819, the Cherokee forfeited their rights to Cades Cove, and the first white settlers came in the early 1820s. By the middle of the 19th century, well over 100 families lived in the cove, growing corn, wheat, oats, cane, and vegetables. For a while, when government-licensed distilleries were allowed in Tennessee, corn whiskey was the major product of the valley, and even after Tennessee went dry in 1876 illegal moonshine was still produced. After the establishment of the park in the 1930s, many of the nearly 200 buildings were torn down to allow the land to revert to its natural state. However, in 1940 the Park Service decided that the human history of the valley was worth preserving. Since then, the bottomlands in the cove have been maintained as open fields, and the remaining farmsteads and other structures have been restored to depict life in Cades Cove as it was from around 1825 to 1900. Today, Cades Cove has more historic buildings than any other area in the park. Driving, hiking, or biking the 11-mile Cades Cove Loop Road, you can see three old churches (Methodist, Primitive Baptist, and Missionary Baptist); a working gristmill (Cable Mill); a number of log cabins and houses in a variety of styles; and many outbuildings, including cantilevered barns which used balanced beams to support large overhangs. ✉ *Cades Cove Loop Rd.* ☎ *865/436–1200.*

★ **Elkmont Historic District.** What began as a logging town in the early years of the 20th century evolved into a summer colony for wealthy families from Knoxville, Chattanooga, and elsewhere in Tennessee. In 1910,

*Continued on page 271*

# GREAT SMOKY MOUNTAINS THROUGH THE SEASONS

## SPRING, SUMMER, AND FALL

by Lan Sluder

The changing seasons bring new experiences to the Great Smoky Mountains National Park. In spring you can tiptoe through the wildflowers; in fall a curtain of fiery red and gold leaves sets the trees ablaze; in summer shady paths and cool mountain streams beckon. Throughout the seasons, miles of hiking trails and wilderness await exploration beyond the car window.

Above: Newfound Gap, Great Smoky Mountains

*Spring* arrives at the lower elevations in March and April. With it, the wildflowers—buttercups, columbine, arbutus, and hundreds more—bloom, carpeting meadows and popping up near forest streams. Wildflower walks are a popular activity and the Spring Wildflower Pilgrimage in late April is a must for budding botanists.

The warm, hazy days of *summer* begin in June as do many of the park's best activities. You can hike to a cool, high peak in the clouds, walk part of the Appalachian Trail, splash or tube in a stream, or fish for native brook trout.

In *autumn,* the flaming golds of sugar maples, the rich reds of sumac and sourwoods, and the mellow yellows of birch and poplar make for memorable leaf peeping. Because elevations in the park range from 1,000 to over 6,000 feet, autumn color lasts for up to two months. Fall foliage generally peaks in mid- to late-October.

## TOP SPRING WILDFLOWERS

### ❶ Trillium

The large flowered trillium, with blooms three to four inches across, is the most common of ten trillium varieties in the park. To identify this impressive flower, look for sets of three: three large pointed green leaves, three sepals, and three white petals. Trilliums bloom on woody slopes and along roadsides and trails at elevations up to 3,500 feet from April to May. **See it:** Middle Prong Trail (TN), Oconaluftee River Trail (NC).

### ❷ Lady Slippers

These delicate orchids come in pink, yellow, and white. The slender stalk rises from a pair of green leaves, and then bends a graceful neck to suspend the paper-thin flower, which resembles a woman's slipper. They favor wooded areas in dappled sunlight, often under oaks. **See it:** Cove Hardwood Nature Trail (TN).

### ❸ Fire pink

These brilliant red flowers have five notched petals and bloom in dry rocky areas in April and May. Look for the ruby-throated hummingbirds that pollinate the flowers. **See it:** Chestnut Top Trail (TN).

### ❹ Rhododendron

The park is famous for its displays of rhododendron. The rosebay's big clumps of white flowers appear in June around streams at the lower and middle elevations and as late as July at higher elevations. The Catawba, with stunning purple flowers, blooms at higher elevations in June. **See it:** rosebay, trails below 5,000 feet; Catawba, Newfound Gap Road (NC and TN).

### ❺ Flame azalea

Blooms can be found in white, peach, yellow, and red, but the most striking color is the namesake flame orange. They bloom in April and May at low to mid-elevation, and June to early July on the mountaintops. **See it:** Gregory Bald (TN), Andrews Bald (NC), Balsam Mountain Road (NC).

## TOP TREES FOR FALL COLOR

### ❶ Tulip poplar

With its tall, straight trunk and light yellow leaves in the fall, the tulip poplar is hard to miss. Poplars are among the first to turn and often grow in stands of hundreds of trees, at elevations under 4,500 feet. **See it:** Cove Hardwood Nature Trail (TN), Fontana Lake (NC), Ramsey Cascades Trail (TN).

### ❷ Sugar maple

Sugar maples are the kings of the fall forest with brilliant orange-to-yellow leaves that appear like fire against the blue autumn sky. Each leaf has five multi-pointed lobes. Maples turn early in the season and are found at elevations up to 4,500 feet. **See it:** Sugarlands Valley (TN), Cataloochee (NC), Newfound Gap Road (NC and TN).

### ❸ Sumac

Sumac are small shrubs, but inch for inch they pack more fall color than almost any other tree in the mountains. You'll recognize them for their bright scarlet leaves and oblong clusters of red fruit. Staghorn sumac grows along roadsides at up to 5,500 feet. **See it:** Newfound Gap Road (NC and TN).

### ❹ Sourwood

In the fall, the sourwood leaves are among the first to turn, glowing deep red and orange. At this time the sourwood also bears sprays of small green fruit. The leaves have a slight sour taste. **See it:** low to middle elevations off Parson Branch Road (TN).

### ❺ Sweetgum

The spiny ball-shaped fruits of the American sweetgum can be annoying to step on, but the trees' showy fall colors make up for it. Orange-yellow and red leaves mix with dark purple and smoky brown. Sweetgums turn around the middle of the season. These medium-size hardwoods, grow at the lower elevations, especially near creeks and streams. **See it:** Cades Cove (TN), Lower Little Pigeon River (TN).

● =Common ● =Somewhat Common ● =Rare

# CHOOSE YOUR DAY HIKE

Whether you just want to stretch your legs or you have a yen to climb a mountain, the Smokies has a hike for you. Here are a few of our favorite hikes to waterfalls, scenic overlooks, and historic sites. ⇨ *For detailed information on these hikes and others, see Hiking in Chapter 5.*

Tom Branch waterfall, Deep Creek

## BEST HIKES TO WATERFALLS

### ABRAMS FALLS, TN

Moderate, 5-mi roundtrip, 3 hours

From the trailhead off Cades Cove Loop Road, follow Abrams Creek to Abrams Falls, where you can take a dip in a lovely natural pool below the falls framed by laurel and rhododendron.

### LAUREL FALLS, TN

Easy, 2.6-mi roundtrip, 1.5 hours

Off Little River Road, this popular trail to 75-foot, multi-level Laurel Falls is paved and offers a mostly gentle walk in the woods. It's suitable for kids and strollers, though the trail is narrow in places with steep drop-offs.

### THREE WATERFALLS LOOP, NC

Easy, 2.4-mi roundtrip, 1.5 hours

About 3 mi by car from Bryson City, Deep Creek offers something for the entire family, with river tubing, mountain biking, fishing, and several loop trails including this easy loop, which takes you by three small falls.

### TRILLIUM GAP TRAIL TO GROTTO FALLS, TN

Moderate, 2.6-mi roundtrip, 2 hours

From the trailhead off Roaring Fork Motor Trail, Trillium Gap Trail gains over 400 feet in elevation, crossing several small streams and passing old-growth hemlocks before reaching 30-foot Grotto Falls, the only falls in the park that you can walk behind.

## BEST HIKES TO OVERLOOKS

### CHIMNEY TOPS, TN

Difficult, 4-mi roundtrip, 3.5 hours

From the trailhead off Newfound Gap Road about 9 mi from Gatlinburg, the trail climbs past rhododendrons and tall yellow buckeye trees over 1,300 feet in only 2 mi to the Chimney Tops summit.

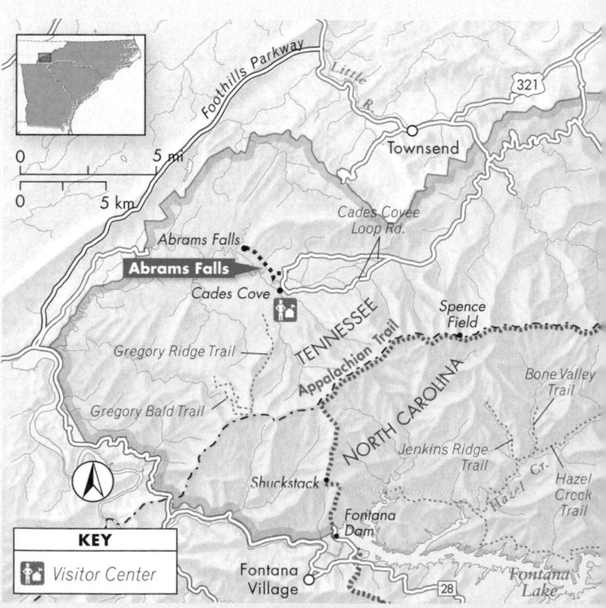

The ascent makes this one of the most strenuous short hikes in the Smokies, though your effort is rewarded by striking views of the Sugarlands Valley.

### CLINGMANS DOME TRAIL, NC

Moderate, 1-mi roundtrip, 1 hour

Paved but steep, this trail leads you to the 6,643-foot Clingmans Dome, crosses the Appalachian Trail, and ends at a 54-foot tall observation tower with stunning views of the Smokies.

Clingmans Dome

Hikers in Great Smoky Mountains National Park

## BEST HIKES TO HISTORIC SITES

### KEPHART PRONG, NC

Moderate, 4-mi roundtrip, 3 hours

Named for Horace Kephart, who was an advocate for the establishment of the park, the trail crosses the Oconaluftee River six times over footbridges, passing remains of a 1930s Civilian Conservation Corps camp that was later used to house conscientious objectors during World War II.

### LITTLE CATALOOCHEE TRAIL, NC

Moderate, 5.9-mi one way, 6 hours

The Little Cataloochee Trail is one of the Smokies' most historically rich hikes, passing several old cabins and houses, cemeteries, a church, school, and other relics of early 20th century life in the Cataloochee Valley before the coming of the national park. We recommend using a two-car shuttle for this hike.

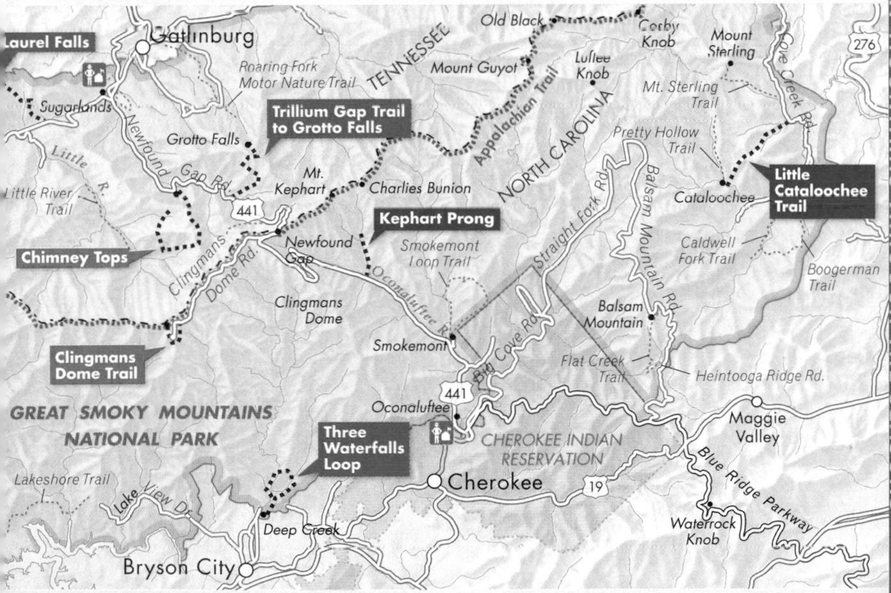

## FUN SUMMER ACTIVITIES

Rafting on the Nantahala River

Summer is prime time for outdoor fun in the park and nearby. ⇨ *For detailed information on these outdoor activities, see Sports and the Outdoors in Chapter 5.*

### BIKING

Main roads have a lot of traffic and lack bike lanes. For safer biking, choose back roads such as Balsam Mountain Road (NC) and Cove Creek Road (NC). A hybrid or mountain bike is best on these unpaved roads. For mountain biking, try the Tsali Recreation Area.

**Best places to bike:** Cades Cove Loop (TN), an 11-mi paved road, is closed to motor vehicles Wednesday and Saturday mornings until 10. Cataloochee Valley (NC) is another good place to bike.

### BOATING

Rent a powerboat or pontoon boat and enjoy a lazy day on the water.

**Best place for boating:** Fontana Lake, bordering the southern edge of the park in North Carolina, has power and pontoon boats for rent.

### FISHING

There's top-notch trout fishing in the 2,100 miles of trout streams in the park. You can catch rainbow, brown, and the native brook trout. Only artificial lures and flies can be used, not live bait.

**Best places to fish:** In North Carolina, Deep Creek, Little Cataloochee, and Hazel Creek are good trout streams. Little River, Abrams Creek, and Little Pigeon River are good choices on the Tennessee side.

### RAFTING

Ride the white water! You can take a guided rafting trip, or rent your own raft on several rivers in and near the Smokies.

**Best places to raft:** The Nantahala just outside the park on the North Carolina side is the most popular river for rafting. On the Tennessee side, the Big Pigeon River offers rafting in mild white water.

### TUBING

Few things are more pleasant than floating down a refreshing stream on a hot day. You can rent a large inner tube for less than $10 a day.

**Best places to tube:** Deep Creek (NC) and Little River (TN).

Little River Lumber Company deeded a tract of 50 acres of land to some prominent Knoxvillians who belonged to a fishing and hunting club called the Appalachian Club. Later, exclusive hunting and fishing rights on a 40,000-acre tract above Elkmont were sold to the club. The Appalachian Club erected a clubhouse, and many cottages were built as summer getaways. Other prominent east Tennessee families bought land here and built the Wonderland Hotel. In the 1920s, a debate broke out among property owners in Elkmont. Some owners wanted to keep the Elkmont area private, but others wanted the land to become part of the proposed national park. Eventually, the park won out and was established in 1934. Parts of the Elkmont community were placed on the National Registry of Historic Places in 1994. Today, Elkmont is primarily a campground, although some of the original 74 cottages remain along Jakes Creek and Little River. Most of the cottages are just south of the campground. The Wonderland Hotel, in disrepair, began to collapse in 2005–06, and the Park Service demolished most of what was left. The remains of the hotel, primarily a chimney, are just northwest of the campground. In recent years, the Park Service has been stabilizing and restoring several homes along Jakes Creek near the Elkmont campground. The rustic Appalachian Clubhouse has been restored and is now open to the public—it is rented for group events April to mid-November. Some 18 cottages in the "Daisy Town" are being restored, but more than 50 other cottages have been, or are slated to be, torn down despite objections from some conservation groups. ✉ *Elkmont Campground, off Little River Rd. 4½ miles west of Gatlinburg entrance to park* ☎ *865/436–1200.*

## PETS IN THE SMOKIES

Pets are allowed in campgrounds, picnic areas, and along roadways in the Great Smoky Mountains National Park; however, they must be on a leash at all times. Dogs and other pets are only allowed on two short walking paths—the Gatlinburg Trail and the Oconaluftee River Trail. They are not allowed on any other park trails or elsewhere in the backcountry. Pet excrement must be immediately collected by the owner and disposed of in a trash receptacle.



**Roaring Fork.** You can visit several preserved mountain cabins and other buildings in the Roaring Fork area near Gatlinburg. Roaring Fork was settled by Europeans in the 1830s and '40s. The land was rocky and steep and not particularly well suited to farming. At its height around the turn of the 20th century, there were about two dozen families in the area. Most lived a simple, even hardscrabble existence, trying to scrape out a living from the rough mountain land. The Noah "Bud" Ogle self-guided nature trail, on Orchard Road just before entering the one-way Roaring Fork Motor Nature Trail, offers a walking tour of an authentic mountain farmstead and surrounding hardwood forest. Highlights include a log cabin, barn, streamside tub mill, and a wooden flume system to bring water to the farm. Among historic structures on the Motor Nature Trail, all open for you to explore, are the Jim Bales cabin, the Ephraim Bales cabin, and the Alfred Reagan house, one of

Deer are a common sight throughout the Great Smoky Mountains, especially in the early morning and at dusk.

the more "upscale" residences at Roaring Fork. ✉ *Orchard Rd. and Roaring Fork Motor Nature Trail* ☎ *865/436–1200.*

## SCENIC STOPS

★ **Chimney Tops Overlook.** From any of the three overlooks grouped together on Newfound Gap Road, you'll have a good view of the Chimney Tops—twin peaks that cap 2,000-foot-high cliffs. You also see hundreds of dead Frazer fir and spruce trees, along with some dead hemlocks, victims of woolly adelgids and air pollution. ✉ *Newfound Gap Rd. (U.S. 441), MM 7.1.*

★ **Dan Lawson Cabin.** From many points along the 11-mile, one-way Cades Cove Loop Road, you'll enjoy iconic views of the broad Cades Cove valley. The Park Service keeps hayfields and pastures cleared, so you can see how the valley may have looked in the late 19th century when it was farmed by more than 100 families. Typical is the view across the valley from the front porch of the Dan Lawson cabin, the original portion of which was built in 1856. ✉ *Cades Cove Loop Rd.*

**Gregory Bald.** From almost 5,000 feet on Gregory Bald, you have a breathtaking view of Cades Cove and Rich Mountain to the north, and the Nantahala and Yellow Creek mountains to the south. You can also see Fontana Lake to the southeast. Many hybrid rhododendrons grow on and around the bald. Gregory Bald is one of only two balds in the Smokies that are being kept cleared of tree growth by the Park Service. This is a view that just a few thousand people a year will see, as it's reachable only by a strenuous hike of more than 11 miles roundtrip. The trailhead is at the end of Forge Creek Road in Cades Cove. ✉ *Hike the Gregory Ridge Trail (5.5 miles one-way) from Cades Cove.*

★ **Look Rock.** The overlooks east on the western section of the Foothills Parkway around Look Rock have remarkable views. This is also a great spot to enjoy the sunrise over the Smokies. Stargazers gather at the five overlooks south of the Look Rock exit where light pollution is especially low. ✉ *Look Rock Overlook, Foothills Pkwy.*

## SPORTS AND THE OUTDOORS

### BICYCLING

Tennessee requires that children age 16 and under wear a helmet, and it's strongly recommended that all riders do so, regardless of age.

★ **Cades Cove.** Arguably the best place to bike, the 11-mile loop road is mostly level, and being on a bike allows you to get around traffic backups. However, traffic can be heavy, especially on weekends in summer and fall, and the road is narrow. ■ **TIP→** **The best time to bike the Cove is from early May to late September on Wednesday and Saturday mornings until 10 am when it is closed to motor vehicles.** Bicycles and helmets can be rented ($20 per day) in summer and fall at an annex behind Cades Cove Campground Store (✉ *Cades Cove Campground* ☎ *865/448–9034*).

**Foothills Parkway West.** The 17.5-mile road has light vehicular traffic and is a scenic and fairly safe place for bicycling. Safe biking also is available on the lightly used access roads to **Greenbrier** picnic area and **Cosby** campground.

### FISHING

There are more than 200 miles of wild trout streams on the Tennessee side of the park. Trout streams are open to fishing year-round. Among the best trout streams on the Tennessee side are Little River, Abrams Creek, and Little Pigeon River.

#### OUTFITTERS

For backcountry trips, you may want to hire a guide. Full-day trips cost about $200–$300 for one angler, $250–$300 for two. Only guides approved by the National Park Service are permitted to take anglers into the park backcountry.

**Little River Outfitters.** This large fly-fishing shop and school has been in business since 1984. It specializes in teaching beginners to fly fish. Although it does not offer guide services, it can hook you up with guides for fishing in the Smokies or elsewhere. ✉ *106 Town Square Dr., Townsend, Tennessee* ☎ *877/448–3474, 865/448–9459* 🌐 *www.littleriveroutfitters.com.*

**Rocky Top Outfitters.** Fly or spin trout-fishing trips are available at Rocky Top Outfitters. A full-day trout fishing trip for two is $250–$270, and a half-day trip for two is $200–$210. ✉ *2611 Ruth Hall Rd., Pigeon Forge, Tennessee* ☎ *865/661–3474* 🌐 *www.rockytopoutfitter.com.*

**Smoky Mountain Angler.** This well-equipped fly-fishing shop also offers equipment rentals, fishing licenses, and half-day and full-day fly- and spin-fishing trips with guide. Full-day guided trout fishing trips in the park are $250 for one person and $300 for two. ✉ *466 Brookside Village Way, Ste. 8, Gatlinburg, Tennessee* ☎ *865/436–8746* 🌐 *www.smokymountainangler.com.*

## HIKING

### EASY

**Elkmont Nature Trail.** This 1-mile loop is good for families, especially if you're camping at Elkmont. Pick up a self-guided brochure (50¢) at the start of the trail. ✉ *Near Elkmont campground.*

**Gatlinburg Trail.** This is one of only two trails in the park (the other one is Oconaluftee River Trail on the North Carolina side) where dogs and bicycles are permitted. Dogs must be on leashes. The trail, which starts at Sugarlands Visitor Center, follows the Little Pigeon River. The first 0.3 mile of the 1.9-mile trail (one-way) is through the park headquarters and on a service road. ✉ *Trailhead at Sugarlands Visitor Center off U.S. Hwy. 441.*

**Laurel Falls.** Mostly paved, this trail is failry easy. It takes you past a series of cascades to a 60-foot waterfall and a stand of old-growth forest. The trail is extremely popular in summer and on weekends almost anytime (trolleys from Gatlingburg stop here), so don't expect solitude. The 1.3-mile paved trail to the falls is wheelchair accessible. Wooden posts mark every one-tenth of a mile, and the total round-trip hike is 2.6 miles. ✉ *Trailhead is on the west side of Little River Rd. between Sugarlands Visitor Center and Elkmont campground, about 3.9 miles west of Sugarlands.*

★ **Little River.** This 5.1-mile loop (if Cucumber Gap and Jakes Creek trails are included) offers a little of everything—historical buildings, fly-fishing, a waterfall, and wildflowers. The first part of the trail wanders past remnants of old logging operations and dilapidated cottages that were once the summer homes of wealthy Tennesseans (currently closed to the public). Huskey Branch Falls appears at about 2 miles. The Little River Trail passes the junction with three other trails, offering the possibility for even longer hikes—Cucumber Gap at 2.3 miles, Huskey Gap at 2.7 miles, and Goshen Prong Trail at 3.7 miles. The trail is normally open even in winter. At any point you can try your hand at fly-fishing for trout in the Little River, one of the best trout streams in the park. Parking at the trailhead has been improved and expanded. This is the habitat of the synchronous fireflies, which put on their light show on June evenings. ✉ *Trailhead is near Elkmont campground.* ✣ *Turn left just before entrance to campground and go 0.6 mile to a fork in the road. The trail is a continuation of the left fork.*

**Noah "Bud" Ogle Nature Trail.** Settlers Noah "Bud" Ogle and his wife, Cindy, built a cabin and started farming here in 1879. Although this is more of a nature walk than a hike, it offers a lot in a 0.75-mile loop. You'll see the Ogle Tub Mill on LeConte Creek, lots of wildflowers, and the Ogle cabin and barn, which you can explore. It's a fine trail for families with kids. ✉ *Cherokee Orchard Rd., just before entering the Roaring Fork Motor Nature Trail.*

**Sugarlands Valley Trail.** The easiest trail in the park, it's only 0.25-mile one-way, virtually level, and paved, so it's suitable for young children, strollers, and wheelchairs. A brochure available at the start (50¢) explains the numbered exhibits and features of the trail. ✉ *Trailhead is*

*0.3 mile south of Sugarlands Visitor Center, U.S. Hwy. 441 (Newfound Gap Rd.).*

**MODERATE**

★ **Abrams Falls.** This 5-mile round-trip trail is one of the most popular in the Smokies, in part due to the trailhead location near stop #10 on the loop road in Cades Cove, which gets more than 2 million visitors a year. Beginning at the wooden bridge over Abrams Creek, the trail first goes along a pleasant course through rhododendron. It becomes somewhat steep at a couple of points, especially near Arbutus Ridge. The path then leads above Abrams Falls and down to Wilson Creek. Though only about 20 feet high, the falls are beautiful, with a good volume of water and a broad pool below. ✉ *Cades Cove Loop Rd., park in the large parking lot on an unpaved side road between signposts 10 and 11.*

**THE APPALACHIAN TRAIL**

Each spring about 1,500 hikers set out to conquer the Appalachian Trail (AT), the 2,175-mile granddaddy of all hikes. The AT celebrated its 75th anniversary in 2012. Most hike north from Springer Mountain, Georgia, toward Mt. Katahdin, Maine. By the time they get to the Great Smokies, 160 miles from the trailhead in Georgia, about half the hikers will already have dropped out. Typically, only about 400 hikers per year complete the entire AT. You can get on it for a short hike from Newfound Gap Road on the North Carolina–Tennessee line.

★ **Appalachian Trail at Newfound Gap.** For those who want to say they hiked part of the AT (www.nps.gov/appa), which celebrated its 75th anniversary in 2012, this section is a great place to start; it's easy to get to and not too steep. Park in the Newfound Gap parking lot and cross the road to the trail. From Newfound Gap to Indian Gap the trail goes 1.7 miles through spruce-fir high-elevation forest, and in late spring and summer there are quite a few wildflowers. The total round-trip distance is 3.4 miles. ✉ *U.S. Hwy. 441 (Newfound Gap Rd.)* ⊕ *Park at Newfound Gap parking lot.*

**Trillium Gap Trail to Grotto Falls.** Grotto Falls is the only waterfall in the park that you can walk behind. The Trillium Gap Trail, off of the Roaring Fork Motor Nature Trail, which leads to Grotto Falls, is primarily through a hemlock forest (many of the hemlocks have been killed by the hemlock woolly adelgid). Only 1.3 miles long, with an easy slope, this trail is suitable for novice hikers and is one of the most popular in the park. The total round-trip distance to Grotto Falls is 2.6 miles. Trillium Gap Trail continues on to LeConte Lodge, a total one-way distance of about 8 miles. It is a horse trail, and llamas resupplying the lodge also use it. The Roaring Fork Motor Trail is closed in winter. ✉ *Roaring Fork Motor Nature Tr.* ⊕ *Take Roaring Fork Motor Nature Trail to stop # 5 on the auto tour, then look for trailhead for Trillium Gap Trail.*

**DIFFICULT**

★ **Chimney Tops.** Pant, wheeze, and gasp. This is a steep trail that will take a lot out of you, but it gives back a lot, too. The payoff for the difficult climb is one of the best views in the Smokies, from the top of Chimney Tops. In places the trail has loose rock, and the elevation gain is 1,350 feet. ⚠ **This trail is not recommended for small children.** The total distance round-trip is 4 miles. The trail had severe storm damage and was closed for much of summer 2012, but has been rehabilitated. ✉ *Trailhead is about halfway between Sugarlands Visitor Center and Newfound Gap, 6.7 miles south of Sugarlands, U.S. Hwy. 441 (Newfound Gap Rd.).*

## HORSEBACK RIDING

Several hundred miles of backcountry trails on the Tennessee side are open to horseback riders. Horses are restricted to trails specifically designated for horse use; check the park trail map ($1) for horse trails and rules and regulations about riding in the backcountry. You can also download a map from 🌐 *www.nps.gov/grsm/planyourvisit/horseriding.htm.*

### OUTFITTERS

**Cades Cove Riding Stables.** This park concessionaire offers carriage rides ($12), hayrides ($12), and ranger-guided hayrides ($14), along with horseback riding ($30 an hour). Call the stables to find out times and dates of ranger-led hayrides. Horseback riders must be at least 6 years old and weigh no more than 250 pounds. ✉ *Cades Cove Campground* ☎ *865/448–9009* 🌐 *www.cadescovestables.com* ⊙ *Closed early Dec.–mid-Mar.*

**Smoky Mountain Riding Stables.** You'll find 40 trained trail horses at Smoky Mountain Riding Stables, a park concessionaire. One-hour rides in the park are $30, and two-hour rides $60. Riders must be at least 5 years old and weigh no more than 225 pounds. ✉ *U.S. Hwy. 321 (East Pkwy.), 4 miles east of downtown Gatlinburg, Tennessee* ☎ *865/436–5634* 🌐 *www.smokymountainridingstables.com* ⊙ *Closed late Nov.–mid-Mar.*

## SKIING

**Ober Gatlinburg Ski Resort & Amusement Park.** Whenever temperatures fall low enough, the resort makes snow for the eight skiing and snowboarding trails. A single-session chairlift ticket is $33 on weekdays and $51 on weekends. There is also a snow-tubing park with 10 lanes and a 50-foot vertical drop and an ice-skating rink. Rates for snow tubing are $20 per person weekdays and $25 weekends for 1½ hours. Ober Gatlinburg's winter season usually begins in mid-December and ends in early March, although the amusement park is open year-round. ✉ *1001 Parkway, Gatlinburg, Tennessee* ☎ *865/436–5423, 800/251–9202 snow report line* 🌐 *www.obergatlinburg.com.*

## TUBING

Tubing requires little skill beyond the ability to let yourself float down a river and can be done at almost any age. Little River is the most popular tubing river on the west side of the Smokies. It flows east to west from its headwaters in the park through the town of Townsend. The Little River is mostly flat water (Class I), with a few mild Class II rapids. Although you can tube on the Little River within the park, several outfitters in Townsend rent tubes and life jackets and provide shuttle buses or vans that drop you at an entry point from which you can float a mile or two downriver to the outfitter's store. Expect to pay from $8 to $13 per person, which includes a full day's tube and life-jacket rental plus unlimited use of the shuttle. Kayak rentals are also offered

Hundreds of miles of trails are open to horseback riding, and several stables offer guided rides.

by some outfitters. Typically the cost is $15 for the kayak rental and the first shuttle trip, and $5 each for additional shuttle trips. Outfitters are generally open May–September or October.

#### OUTFITTERS

**River Rage.** Here you'll find inner tubes available for rent on the Little River, a go-kart track, and a barbecue restaurant. One-day tube and life-vest rental and all-day shuttle service is $9. ✉ *8303 Hwy. 73, Townsend, Tennessee* ☎ *865/448–8000* 🌐 *www.riverragetubing.com.*

**Smoky Mountain River Rat.** This outfitter offers tubing and kayaking on the Little River and white-water rafting on the Pigeon River during warm-weather months. Tube rental, life jacket, and all-day shuttle is $13. Kayak rental is $15 for first trip down the river and $5 for each additional trip. ✉ *205 Wears Valley Rd., Townsend, Tennessee* ☎ *865/448–8888* 🌐 *www.smokymtnriverrat.com* ⏲ *Closed Sept.–Apr.*

## EDUCATIONAL OFFERINGS

**Great Smoky Mountains Institute at Tremont.** Located within the park at Tremont, this residential environmental education center offers a variety of programs year-round for student groups, teachers, and families. The adult programs include photography, crafts, naturalist certification, and backpacking nature trips. Summer camp programs are offered for children 9–17, starting at $523. Family camp weekends for a family of four, including accommodations, meals, and instructional programs cost $422 ($95 for each additional family member). A week-long family program is $1,216 ($304 for each additional family member).

Accommodations at Tremont are in Caylor Lodge, a heated and air-conditioned dormitory that can sleep up to 125 people, and also in tents on platforms. Meals are served family-style in a large dining hall. Some 4,000 students and adults attend programs at the Institute each year. ✉ *9275 Tremont Rd., Townsend, Tennessee* ☎ *865/448–6709* 🌐 *www.gsmit.org.*

**Smoky Mountain Field School.** The University of Tennessee's Smoky Mountain Field School offers non-credit workshops, hikes, and outdoor adventures for adults and families. More than a dozen programs are presented, mostly in the fall, including ones on orienteering (using a map and compass to get from one place to another), mushrooms, nature photography, and edible plants. Classes are held at various locations within the park. Field School programs are generally held on weekends and last from four hours to two days. Fees vary, with most programs $49; overnight guided hikes to LeConte Lodge are $175. ✉ *UT Smoky Mountain Field School, 313 Conference Center Bldg., Knoxville, Tennessee* ☎ *865/974–0150* 🌐 *www.aceweb.outreach.utk.edu.*

## WHERE TO EAT

$ FAST FOOD

✕ **Cades Cove Camp Store Snack Bar.** The only eating establishment in the park, other than the restaurant at LeConte Lodge, is a little snack bar inside the Cades Cove camp store. Here, you can buy hot dogs, pizza, sandwiches, soup, soft-serve ice cream, and other snacks. Breakfast items include coffee and bagels. The camp store, about the size of a small convenience store, also sells canned pork 'n' beans, s'more fixings, soft drinks, chips, and other junk food. Firewood is sold here, and you can rent bicycles. [$] *Average main: $5* ✉ *Cades Cove Campground, Cades Cove Loop Rd.* ☎ *865/448–9034.*

### PICNIC AREAS

**Cades Cove Picnic Area.** This picnic area, near the beginning of the Cades Cove loop, has 81 picnic tables. Its big advantage is that you're near the beautiful Cades Cove valley; the disadvantage is that as many as 2 million people come through this area each year. At only 1,800 feet high, it can be hot and humid here in summer. Potable water and flush toilets are available. Bears are fairly common here, so closely observe food storage precautions. Spence Field, Anthony Creek, and Thunderhead trailheads are at the picnic area. Open year-round. ✉ *9 miles east of Townsend, near the entrance to Cades Cove Loop and near the Cades Cove campground* ⏲ *Sept.–Apr., daily dawn–dusk; May–Aug., daily dawn–8 pm.*

Fodor'sChoice ★

**Chimneys Picnic Area.** Chimneys, just off Newfound Gap Road and a little more than 6 miles from the Sugarlands Visitor Center, may be the most popular picnic area in the park. Along both sides of a well-shaded loop road through the area are 89 picnic tables with grills. Some are wheelchair accessible. The prime spots along the wadeable stream that runs through the site fill up first. Huge boulders in the stream make for a striking view from your table. Potable water and flush toilets are available. ✉ *Newfound Gap Rd. (U.S. 441), MM 6.2* ⏲ *May–Aug., daily*

LeConte Lodge has no electricity, no running water, and the only way to get there is to hike up a mountain; it rewards guests with peace, quiet, and fantastic views.

*dawn–8 pm; Sept.–late Nov. and mid-Mar.–Apr., daily dawn–sunset. Closed late Nov.–mid-Mar.*

## WHERE TO STAY

$$$$ B&B/INN Fodor's Choice ★ **LeConte Lodge.** Set at 6,360 feet near the summit of Mt. LeConte, this hike-in lodge is remote, rustic, and remarkable; it is not, however, luxurious. **Pros:** unique setting high on Mt. LeConte; a true escape from civilization; a special experience available only to a few. **Cons:** books up far in advance; hike-in access only; simplest of accommodations with few modern conveniences. *Rooms from: $252 Mt. LeConte, Great Smoky Mountains National Park, Tennessee 865/429–5704 865/774–0045 www.lecontelodge.com 7 cabins, 3 group sleeping cabins, all with shared bath Closed late Nov.– late Mar. Multiple meal plans.*

$$$$ RESORT Fodor's Choice ★ **Blackberry Farm.** Sprawled over more than 4,200 acres with fantastic views of the Smoky Mountains, this rustic spread, complete with red barn, hides a luxurious country retreat with refined service. **Pros:** wonderful setting and hospitality; activities include children's programs. **Cons:** remote and rural; dedicated urbanites may have difficulty adjusting to the quiet and stillness. *Rooms from: $995 1471 West Millers Cove Rd., Walland, Tennessee 865/984–8166, 800/557–8864, 800/648–2348 www.blackberryfarm.com 62 rooms All meals.*

## FESTIVALS AND EVENTS

**Old Timers' Day at Cades Cove.** Visitors are invited to bring lawn chairs and a picnic along to enjoy Old Timers' Day at Cades Cove. Usually held the third weekend in September at the Cable Mill area of Cades Cove, Old Timers' Day allows former residents of Cades Cove, and their descendants, along with the general public, to reminisce about the old days in the valley. The event usually attracts more than 4,000 people. ✉ *Cades Coves, Great Smoky Mountains National Park, Tennessee* ☎ *865/436–1200* 🌐 *www.nps.gov/grsm* 🎫 *Free.*

Fodor's Choice ★ **Spring Wildflower Pilgrimage.** Each year in mid- to late April, the Great Smoky Mountains National Park hosts the Spring Wildflower Pilgrimage. It attracts wildflower enthusiasts from all over the country for five days of wildflower and natural-history walks, seminars, classes, photography tours, and other events. Instructors include National Park Service staff, along with outside experts. Most activities are at various locations in the park, both on the North Carolina and Tennessee sides, but registration is in Gatlinburg at the Mills Conference Center. Begun in 1951, the pilgrimage has grown to more than 150 different walks, classes, and events. Advance registration online begins in February of the year of the conference, and some events quickly sell out. Check the website for current details and dates. ✉ *Mills Conference Center, 303 Reagan Dr., Gatlinburg, Tennessee* ☎ *865/974–0280 UT Conferences* 🌐 *www.springwildflowerpilgrimage.org* 🎫 *Registration $50 for 1 day, $75 for 2 or more days; some events free.*

**Townsend in the Smokies Spring Festival.** Usually held the first weekend in May, the Townsend in the Smokies Spring Festival is held at the Townsend Visitor Center. It features bluegrass bands, antique tractors, craft booths, and mountain craft demonstrations. Townsend also holds other festivals during the year. ✉ *Townsend Visitor Center, 7906 E. Lamar Alexander Pkwy., Townsend, Tennessee* ☎ *865/448–6134 Townsend visitor center* 🌐 *www.smokymountains.org* 🎫 *Free (parking $8).*

# NEARBY NORTH CAROLINA TOWNS

Whether you're looking for a hot meal and a comfy bed after days of camping out or just want some "unnatural" diversion, these small towns have everything from a big casino to quaint potteries to keep you entertained.

## CHEROKEE

*178 miles east of Charlotte; 51 miles west of Asheville; 2 miles from entrance to Great Smoky Mountains National Park.*

The 56,000-acre Cherokee reservation is known as the Qualla Boundary, and the town of Cherokee is its capital. Truth be told, there are two Cherokees. There's the Cherokee with the often tacky pop culture, with junky gift shops full of cheap plastic "Indian crafts" and caged black bears. These are designed to appeal to the lowest common denominator

## TENNESSEE CAMPGROUNDS

Campgrounds at Cades Cove, Cosby, and Elkmont on the Tennessee side accept reservations, which can be made up to six months in advance.

**Abrams Creek Campground.** This first-come, first-served campground is on the extreme western edge of the park, way off the beaten path. It can be hot and humid here in summer. Several trails, including Gold Mine, Cane Creek, Rabbit Creek, and Little Bottoms begin at or near the campground. ✉ *Off Happy Valley Rd.* ✣ *On the western section of the Foothills Pkwy., turn southeast on Happy Valley Rd. and follow approx. 2 miles to sign at access road to Abrams Creek Campground. GSMNP* ☎ *865/436–1200* 🌐 *www.nps.gov/grsm.*

**Cades Cove Campground.** This is one of the largest campgrounds in the Smokies, the one with the most services on-site, and one of only two in the park open year round (the other is Smokemont on the NC side). It has a small general store with a snack bar, bike rentals, horse stables, hayrides, an amphitheater, picnic area, and an RV dump station. This is a popular campground and often fills up in summer and fall. Reservations must be made at least one day ahead of arrival and can be made up to six months in advance. ✉ *At entrance to Cades Cove Loop Rd., 10042 Campground Dr., GSMNP* ☎ *877/444–6777* 🌐 *www.recreation.gov.*

**Cosby Campground.** This large campground is shadily set among poplars, hemlocks, and rhododendrons, near Cosby and Rock creeks. More than 150 of the campsites are for tents only, and RVs/trailers are limited to just 25 feet. Of the 165 total sites, 26 can be reserved in advance by telephone or online. Bears are in the area, and several campsites may be closed temporarily due to aggressive bear activity. Nearby are many opportunities for hiking, with trailheads for Snake Den Ridge and Gabes Mountain trails. This campground is rarely very busy and nearly always has sites available even when others are full. ✉ *127 Cosby Park Rd., off TN 32, GSMNP* ☎ *877/444–6777* 🌐 *www.recreation.gov.*

**Elkmont Campground.** Easy hiking trails and the ability to wade, tube (bring your own inner tubes), fish, and swim in Little River, which runs through the campground, make Elkmont ideal for kids. the stream. Even though it is the largest campground in the Smokies, it is often fully booked. Rates are $17–$23; reserved in advance by phone or online (reservations must be made at least one week ahead and can be made up to six months in advance). ✉ *434 Elkmont Rd., GSMNP* ☎ *877/444–6777* 🌐 *www.recreation.gov.*

**Look Rock Campground.** At the western edge of the park off Foothills Parkway this first-come, first-served (no reservations) campground is the only camping area in the park with no length limit for RVs and trailers. Set in oak and pine woods, there's not much to do here except hike. Several trails can be accessed from the campground, including Cane Creek, Little Bottoms, and Rabbit Creek. ✉ *Off Flats Rd., GSMNP* ☎ *865/436–1200* 🌐 *www.nps.gov/grsm.*

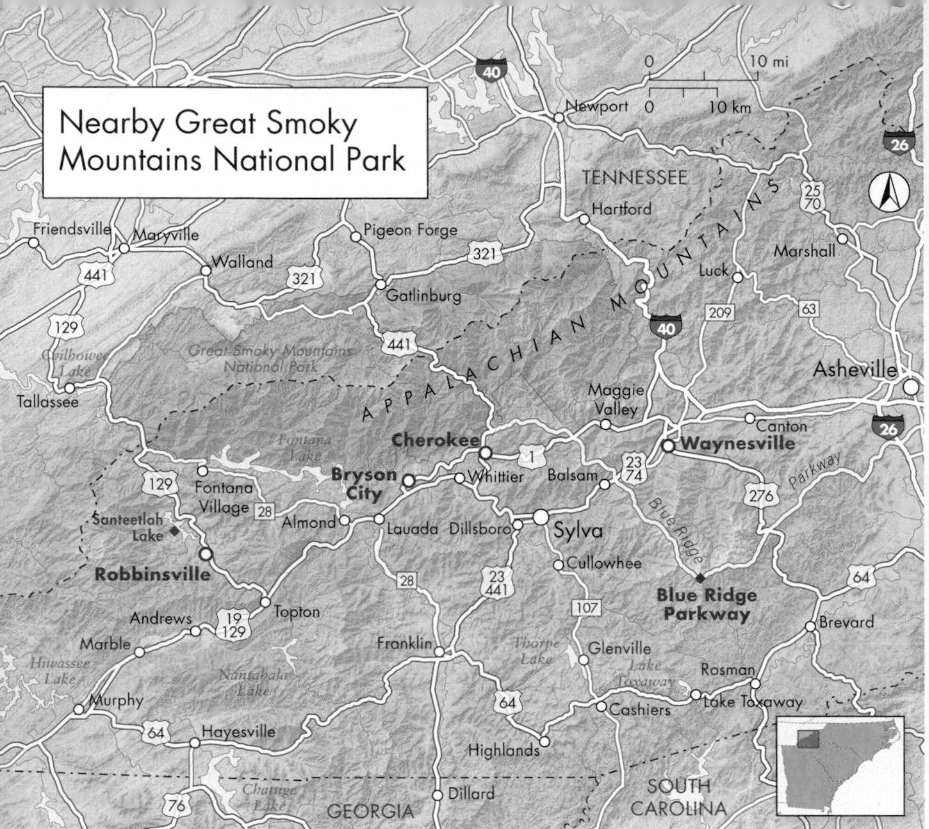


of the tourist masses. But there's another Cherokee that's a window into the rich heritage of the tribe's Eastern Band. Although now relatively small in number—Eastern Band of Cherokee tribal enrollment is 12,500—these Cherokee and their ancestors have been responsible for keeping alive the Cherokee culture. They are the descendants of those who hid in the Great Smoky Mountains to avoid the Trail of Tears, the forced removal of the Cherokee Nation to Oklahoma in the 19th century. They are survivors, extremely attached to the hiking, swimming, trout fishing, and natural beauty of their ancestral homeland. You'll note that due to tribal efforts, all official signs in the Qualla Boundary, and many private commercial ones, are in the Cherokee language as well as in English. The reservation is dry, with no alcohol sales, except at the Harrah's complex. This means that there are few upscale restaurants in the area (since they depend on wine and cocktail sales for much of their profits), just fast-food and mom-and-pop places.

#### GETTING HERE AND AROUND

The Blue Ridge Parkway's southern terminus is at Cherokee, and the parkway is by far the most beautiful route to Cherokee and to Great Smoky Mountains National Park. A faster option is U.S. 23 and U.S. 74/U.S. 441, connecting Cherokee with Interstate 40 from Asheville or from Franklin in the south. The least pleasant route is U.S. 19 from Interstate 40, a mostly two-lane road pocked with touristy roadside shops.

### ESSENTIALS

**Cherokee Visitor Center.** This visitor center partners with and provides tourism information for a number of local organizations including Qualla Arts & Crafts, Museum of the Cherokee Indian, Cherokee Fishing, Cherokee Chamber of Commerce, and the Cherokee Historical Association. ✉ *498 Tsali Blvd.* ☎ *800/438–1601* 🌐 *visitcherokeenc.com.*

## EXPLORING

★ **Museum of the Cherokee Indian.** With displays and artifacts that cover 12,000 years, this is one of the best Native American museums in the United States. Computer-generated images, lasers, specialty lighting, and sound effects help re-create events in the history of the Cherokee: for example, you'll see children stop to play a butter-bean game while adults shiver along the snowy Trail of Tears. The museum has an art gallery, a gift shop, and an outdoor living exhibit of Cherokee life in the 15th century. ✉ *589 Tsali Blvd., at Drama Rd.* ☎ *828/497–3481* 🌐 *www.cherokeemuseum.org* 🎫 *$10* 🕒 *Daily 9–5; late May–early Sept., Mon.–Sat. 9–7.*

**Oconaluftee Indian Village.** At the historically accurate, re-created Oconaluftee Indian Village guides in native costumes lead you through a 1760-era Cherokee village, while others demonstrate traditional skills such as weaving, pottery, canoe construction, and hunting techniques. ✉ *U.S. 441 at Drama Rd.* ☎ *828/497–2315* 🌐 *www.cherokeehistorical.org/OconalufteeVillage.html* 🎫 *$18* 🕒 *May–mid-Oct., Mon.–Sat. 10–5.*

## WHERE TO EAT AND STAY

*Hotel reviews have been abbreviated in this book. For expanded reviews, please go to Fodors.com.*

$ AMERICAN **Peter's Pancakes and Waffles.** Pancake houses are big in Cherokee, and Peter's is at the top of the stack. Many locals are regulars here, and you'll see why when you try the blueberry pancakes with country ham. If you're really hungry, get the Backpacker Pancakes, made with several types of flour and loaded with nuts. Ask for a seat in the dining room overlooking the river. [$] *Average main: $8* ✉ *1384 Tsali Tr. (U.S. Hwy. 441)* ☎ *828/497–5116, 800/697–0752* 🌐 *www.peterspancakeswnc.com* 🕒 *Open daily 6:30 am–2 pm. No dinner.*

$ HOTEL **Baymont Inn.** This 67-room, three-story motel is part of the Wyndham chain, but it's a superior link at the budget end of the chain. **Pros:** pretty good value in a chain motel; away from traffic **Cons:** no fitness room. [$] *Rooms from: $116* ✉ *1455 Acquoni Rd.* ☎ *828/497–2102* 🌐 *www.baymontinns.com* *67 rooms* *Breakfast.*

$ HOTEL **Harrah's Cherokee Casino Hotel.** The 21-story hotel, the tallest in Western North Carolina and the largest in the entire state—with more than 1,200 rooms and suites, towers over the mom-and-pop motels nearby and the huge casino next door, to which it is umbilically attached via a series of escalators and walkways. **Pros:** supersize hotel; convenient to casino. **Cons:** hotel often heavily booked due to comps and deals for gamblers; public areas reek of tobacco smoke. [$] *Rooms from: $139* ✉ *U.S. 19 at U.S. 441 Business, 777 Casino Dr.* ☎ *828/497–7777,*

*800/223–7277 for reservations ⊕ www.harrahscherokee.com ⇨ 1,011 rooms, 107 suites* 🍴 *No meals.*

## NIGHTLIFE AND THE ARTS

### THE ARTS

***Unto These Hills.*** This colorful, well-staged history of the Cherokee begins at the time of Spanish explorer Hernando de Soto's visit in 1540 and continues to the infamous Trail of Tears. The show runs from early June to mid-August, and reserved-seat tickets start at $20 ($10 for children 6–12, free for children 5 and under). First presented in 1950, the drama has been updated with a new script and new costumes. More than 6 million people have seen the play over the years. Contemporary plays are presented in the Mountainside Theater as well. ✉ *Mountainside Theater on Drama Rd., off U.S. 441 N, 564 Tsali Blvd (U.S. 441)* ☎ *828/497–2111, 866/554–4557* ⊕ *www.cherokeehistorical.org/UntoTheseHills.html.*

### NIGHTLIFE

**Harrah's Casino.** Owned by the Eastern Band of the Cherokee, Harrah's Casino now has live blackjack, roulette, craps, and poker games along with some 5,000 electronic gaming machines in a huge casino the size of more than three football fields. At the new entrance, five-story columns surround a 75-foot colored waterfall, highlighting a 140-foot, hi-def TV screen. The casino is truly a great "smoky" experience—except for a small smoke-free area, the casino allows cigarette and cigar smoking. Alcohol also is now available in restaurants, bars, and in the casino at Harrah's, the only place on the Cherokee Indian Reservation where alcohol is sold. Ruth's Chris Steak House, Paula Deen's Kitchen, Johnny Rockets, Brio Tuscany Grille, and other restaurants in the casino (the restaurants are smoke-free) and connected hotel provide a good choice of dining. Big-name stars such as Hank Williams Jr., Willie Nelson, and Scotty McCreery provide entertainment at the casino's new theater, which seats 3,000. A $650 million expansion has doubled the size of the hotel, making it the largest in the state of North Carolina. A new 1,132-space parking deck allows easier access to the casino and hotel, though it can be quite a hike (parking is free, valet parking is $12). ✉ *777 Casino Dr., U.S. 19 at U.S. 441 Business* ☎ *828/497–7777, 800/427–7247* ⊕ *www.harrahscherokee.com.*

## SPORTS AND THE OUTDOORS

### FISHING

**Cherokee Indian Reservation.** There are 30 miles of regularly stocked trout streams on the Cherokee Indian Reservation. To fish in tribal waters you need a tribal fishing permit, available at many reservation businesses or online. (Kids under 12 don't need a permit.) The $10 permit is valid for one day. Also, permits for longer periods are available: $17 for a two-day, $27 for a three-day, and $47 for a five-day. Creel limit is 10 per day per permit holder. A season's permit is available for $250. Fishing is permitted year-round. A North Carolina fishing license and trout stamp are not required for reservation fishing. ✉ *Fisheries & Wildlife Management, 1840 Painttown Rd* ☎ *828/497–1826* ⊕ *www.fishcherokee.com.*

### GOLF

**Sequoyah National Golf Club.** A part of Harrah's Cherokee Casino & Resort, owned by the Eastern Band of the Cherokee Nation, Sequoyah is open to the public. The challenging course was designed by Trent Jones II and opened in 2009. ✉ *79 Cahons Rd., Whittier* ☎ *828/497–3000* 🌐 *www.sequoyahnational.com* ✍ *Reservations essential* 🏌 *18 holes. 6600 yds. Par 72. Green Fee: $85 weekday/$110 weekend* ☞ *Facilities: Driving range, putting green, pitching area, golf carts, pull carts, rental clubs, pro shop, golf academy/lessons, restaurant, bar.*

### SHOPPING

**Qualla Arts and Crafts Mutual.** The Qualla Arts and Crafts Mutual, across the street from the Museum of the Cherokee Indian, is a cooperative that displays and sells items created by 300 Cherokee craftspeople. The store has a large selection of extraordinary high-quality baskets, masks, and wood carvings, which can cost hundreds of dollars. Many items are of museum or near-museum quality, and there's a central gallery with truly wonderful Cherokee arts and crafts on display (items in the gallery are not for sale). ✉ *645 Tsali Blvd. (U.S. 441 at Drama Rd.)* ☎ *828/497–3103* 🌐 *www.quallaartsandcrafts.com.*

5

## BRYSON CITY

*65 miles east of Asheville; 11 miles southwest of Cherokee.*

Bryson City is a little mountain town on the Nantahala River, one of the lesser-known gateways to the Great Smokies. The town's most striking feature is a city hall with a four-sided clock. Since becoming the depot and headquarters of the Great Smoky Mountains Railroad, the downtown shopping area has been rejuvenated, mostly with gift shops and ice-cream stands.

### GETTING HERE AND AROUND

Bryson City is a 15-minute drive from Cherokee on U.S. 19. Near Bryson City are two entrances to the Great Smokies.

### EXPLORING

**Nantahala River.** The most popular river in western North Carolina for rafting and kayaking is Nantahala River, which races through the scenic Nantahala Gorge, a 1,600-foot-deep gorge that begins about 13 miles west of Bryson City on U.S. 19. Class III and Class IV rapids (Class V are the most dangerous) make for a thrilling ride. Several outfitters run river trips or rent equipment. At several points along the river you can park your car and watch rafters run the rapids—on a summer day you'll see hundreds of rafts and kayaks going by. ✉ *U.S. 19, beginning 13 miles west of Bryson City* ☎ *828/524–6441 Nantahala Ranger District, National Forest Service* 🌐 *www.fs.usda.gov.*

★ **Great Smoky Mountains Railroad.** The popular train rides of the Great Smoky Mountains Railroad include excursions from the railroad's Bryson City depot and a number of special trips. Diesel-electric and, occasionally, steam locomotives go 44 miles along the Nantahala Gorge from March through October. The 32-mile Tuckasegee River to Dillsboro and back trip is offered year-round. Open-sided cars or standard coaches are ideal for picture taking as the mountain scenery glides by. There also are refurbished first-class, climate-controlled cars, with deluxe seating. Combination rail excursions and Nantahala River rafting trips are offered in summer and early fall, in conjunction with Nantahala Outdoor Center. The railroad also does special-event excursions at various times during the year, including wine and beer tastings, dinner trains, and mystery theater trips. For kids, the railroad offers a variety of special excursions, including Charlie Brown Peanuts Pumpkin Patch Express trip in fall and Polar Express trips in November and December. Excursion schedules change frequently so check the railroad's website for the latest information. ✉ *225–226 Everett St.* ☎ *800/872–4681* 🌐 *www.gsmr.com* 🎟 *$39–$92 depending on trip, class, and type of car; $5 parking fee at Bryson City depot* ⏲ *Jan.–Feb., weekly departures on Sat.; Mar., departures Fri. and Sat.; Apr.–late May, departures Tues.–Sat.; late May–Dec., daily departures most days (up to three trips daily); check website for exact schedules and changes.*

## WHERE TO EAT AND STAY

*Hotel reviews have been abbreviated in this book. For expanded reviews, please go to Fodors.com.*

$ CAFÉ — ✕ **Bryson City Cork & Bean.** This new café, coffee shop, and wine bar brings cool to Bryson City, with organic coffees, crepes (try the brie crepe with organic spinach and avocado, or the Nutella dessert crepe), wines by the glass or bottle, and microbrew beers. It's in a bright, woody space in a 1908 building that formerly housed Bryson City Bank. $ *Average main: $10* ✉ *16 Everett St.* ☎ *828/488–1934* 🌐 *www.brysoncitycorkandbean.com* ⏲ *No dinner Sun.*

$ FAST FOOD — ✕ **The Filling Station Deli and Sub Shop.** This sandwich shop in downtown Bryson City is a popular place to grab a Cuban, foot-long kosher hot dog, corned beef on rye, or other sandwich—or a bowl of chili. While you're waiting, you can look at the old service-station memorabilia. $ *Average main: $7* ✉ *145 Everett St.* ☎ *828/488–1919* 🌐 *www.thefillingstationdeli.com* ⏲ *Mon.–Sat. 11–4; closed Sun.*

$ AMERICAN — ✕ **River's End at Nantahala Outdoor Center.** The casual riverbank setting and high-energy atmosphere at NOC's eatery draws lots of hungry people just returned from an invigorating day of rafting or hiking. There are salads, soups, pizzas, and sandwiches during the day and a little fancier fixins' in the evening. It's reasonably priced, with only a few items more than $10 or $12. The chili's a winner—there are black- and white-bean, chicken, beef, and vegetarian versions. Also at NOC, **Slow Joe's Café** serves sandwiches by day and becomes a pub at night. $ *Average main: $10* ✉ *13077 Hwy. 19 W* ☎ *828/488–2176* 🌐 *www.noc.com* ✍ *Reservations not accepted* ⏲ *No breakfast Nov.–Feb.*

$ B&B/INN — 🏨 **Fryemont Inn.** An institution in Bryson City for eight decades, the Fryemont Inn, set on the side of a hill above the town, is on the National Register of Historic Places. **Pros:** historic inn; comfortably rustic; charming restaurant with wholesome, simple food. **Cons:** rooms in main lodge are far from posh and without a/c can be warm on a summer day. $ *Rooms from: $135* ✉ *245 Fryemont St.* ☎ *828/488–2159, 800/845–4879* 🌐 *www.fryemontinn.com* 🛏 *37 rooms, 8 suites, 1 cabin* ⏲ *Main lodge closed late Nov.–Mar.* 🍽 *Some meals.*

$$ B&B/INN **Hemlock Inn.** This folksy, friendly mountain inn on 50 acres above Bryson City is the kind of place where you can rock, doze, and play Scrabble. **Pros:** unpretentious, family-oriented inn; delicious Southern-style food; like a visit to Grandma's. **Cons:** no Wi-Fi, TVs, or in-room phones; family-style meals may not suit everyone; no alcohol served; rooms are basic and need updating. *Rooms from: $169* *Galbraith Creek Rd.* *828/488–2885* *www.hemlockinn.com* *22 rooms, 3 cottages* *Breakfast.*

### SPORTS AND THE OUTDOORS

#### RIVER RAFTING AND KAYAKING

**Nantahala Outdoor Center (NOC).** Nantahala Outdoor Center (NOC) guides more than 30,000 rafters every year on the Nantahala and six other rivers: the Chattooga, Cheoah (for the more advanced and experienced rafter), French Broad, Nolichucky, Ocoee, and Pigeon. Rates vary depending on the length of the trip and the river; half-day trips on the Nantahala are $38–$50. Raft rental starts at $22 for a half day. NOC also rents kayaks, ducks, mountain bikes, and other equipment. The bustling NOC complex on the Nantahala River is virtually a tourist attraction itself, especially for young people, with three restaurants, cabin and campground rentals, a zip line, an inn, a fly-fishing shop, and a stop for the Great Smokies Railroad. *13077 Hwy. 19 W* *800/905–7238* *www.noc.com.*

5

## ROBBINSVILLE

*98 miles southwest of Asheville; 35 miles southwest of Bryson City.*

If you truly want to get away from everything, head to the area around Robbinsville in the far southwest corner of North Carolina, a little south of the southern edge of the Great Smokies. The town of Robbinsville offers little, but the Snowbird Mountains, Lake Santeetlah, Fontana Lake, the rugged Joyce Kilmer Slickrock Wilderness, and the Joyce Kilmer Memorial Forest, with its giant virgin poplars and sycamores, definitely are highlights of this part of North Carolina.

### EXPLORING

Fodor's Choice ★ **Joyce Kilmer Memorial Forest.** One of the few remaining sections of the original Appalachian forests, Joyce Kilmer Memorial Forest, a part of the 17,000-acre Joyce Kilmer–Slickrock Wilderness, has incredible 400-year-old yellow poplars that measure as large as 20 feet in circumference, along with huge hemlocks, oaks, sycamores, and other trees. If you haven't seen a true virgin forest, you can't imagine what America must have looked like in the early days of settlement. A 2-mile trail, moderately strenuous, takes you through wildflower- and moss-carpeted areas of great beauty. The forest is named for the early-20th-century poet/soldier, killed in World War I, who is famous for the lines "I think I shall never see / A poem lovely as a tree." During June, the parking lot of the Joyce Kilmer Memorial Forest is an excellent spot to see the light shows of the synchronous fireflies (*Photinus carolinus*), which blink off and on in unison. *15 miles west of Robbinsville, off Cherohala Skyway via Hwy. 143 and Kilmer Rd.* *From Robbinsville,*

Children participate in a dance demonstration at the Smoky Mountain Folk Festival.

*take Hwy. 129 North for 1½ miles to the junction with Hwy. 143 West (Massey Branch Road). Turn left on Hwy. 143 and go 5 miles to a stop sign. Turn right onto Kilmer Rd. Drive 7.3 miles and bear to the right at the junction of Santeetlah Gap and the Cherohala Skyway. Continue another 2.5 miles to the entrance of Joyce Kilmer Memorial Forest.* ☎ *828/479–6431 Cheoah Ranger District, U.S. National Forest* 🌐 *www.fs.usda.gov* 🎫 *Free.*

## WAYNESVILLE

*17 miles east of Cherokee on U.S. 19.*

This is where the Blue Ridge Parkway meets the Great Smokies. Waynesville is the seat of Haywood County. About 40% of the county is occupied by Great Smoky Mountains National Park, Pisgah National Forest, and the Harmon Den Wildlife Refuge. The town of Waynesville is a rival of Blowing Rock and Highlands as a summer and vacation-home retreat for the well-to-do, though the atmosphere here is a bit more countrified.

Folkmoot USA, a two-week international festival that began in Waynesville in 1984 and is held annually in July, brings music and dancing groups from around the world to various venues in Waynesville and elsewhere in western North Carolina.

### GETTING HERE AND AROUND

Waynesville is about 30 miles southwest of Asheville. From Asheville, take Interstate 40 West. At Exit 27, take U.S. Highway 74 West to U.S. Highway 23/Highway 74 West. At Exit 102, take U.S. Highway

276 to Waynesville. If coming from Cherokee, about 19 miles west of Waynesville, you can take U.S. Highway 74 East to U.S. Highway 23 to Waynesville; the longer but much more scenic route is via the Blue Ridge Parkway. South Main Street is the main commercial street in Waynesville, lined for several blocks with small shops.

## EXPLORING

**Cold Mountain.** The vivid best-selling novel by Charles Frazier, *Cold Mountain,* has made a destination out of the real Cold Mountain. About 15 miles from Waynesville in the Shining Rock Wilderness Area of Pisgah National Forest, the 6,030-foot rise had long stood in relative anonymity. But with the success of Frazier's book, people want to see the region that Inman and Ada, the book's Civil War–era protagonists, called home. For a view of the splendid mass, stop at any of a number of overlooks off the Blue Ridge Parkway. Try the Cold Mountain Parking Overlook, just past mile marker 411.9; the Wagon Road Gap parking area, at mile marker 412.2; or the Waterrock Knob Interpretative Station, at mile marker 451.2. You can climb the mountain, but be prepared: the hike to the summit is strenuous. No campfires are allowed in Shining Rock, so you'll need a stove if you wish to cook. ✉ *BRP* ☎ *828/298–0398 BRP information line* 🌐 *www.nps.gov/blri.*

**Museum of North Carolina Handicrafts.** Exhibits of 19th-century heritage crafts are on display at the Museum of North Carolina Handicrafts, located in the Shelton House (circa 1875). ✉ *49 Shelton St., at corner of U.S. Hwy 276 S* ☎ *828/452–1551* 🌐 *www.sheltonhouse.org* 🎫 *$5* ⏲ *May–Oct., Tues.–Sat. 10–4; occasional hrs in winter.*

## WHERE TO EAT AND STAY

*Hotel reviews have been abbreviated in this book. For expanded reviews, please go to Fodors.com.*

$ CAFÉ ✕ **Panacea.** Don't be put off by the location in a gentrifying area beside the railroad tracks called Frog Level. This little café, coffeehouse, and coffee roaster in a renovated brick-front warehouse serves some of the best sandwiches and freshly roasted coffee in the area. Inside you'll find exposed brick walls, burlap bags, and the smell of coffee. For lunch try the panini and wraps. In good weather there's outside seating in the back, overlooking a creek. Free Wi-Fi. $ *Average main: $7* ✉ *66 Commerce St.* ☎ *828/452–6200* 🌐 *www.panaceacoffee.com* ⏲ *Closed Sun. No dinner.*

$$ SOUTHERN ✕ **The Sweet Onion.** This casual restaurant serves delicious Southern comfort food like roast beef, chicken potpie, crab cakes, bacon-wrapped meat loaf, and shrimp and grits. Freshly made cheese biscuits accompany meals. $ *Average main: $15* ✉ *39 Miller St.* ☎ *828/456–5559* 🌐 *www.sweetonionrestaurant.com* ⏲ *Closed Sun.*

$ B&B/INN **Andon-Reid Bed & Breakfast Inn.** Inside this large, 6,000-square-foot 1902 restored Victorian house all is light and comfort: the two suites and three large rooms are nicely decorated in a crafty, early American style. **Pros:** charming B&B; delicious full breakfasts. **Cons:** with a gym, you may feel guilty if you don't work out. $ *Rooms from: $149* ✉ *92 Daisy Ave.* ☎ *828/452–3089, 800/293–6190* 🌐 *www.andonreidinn.com* *3 rooms, 2 suites* 🍽 *Breakfast.*

$$$$ B&B/INN ★ **The Swag Country Inn.** The Swag sits at 5,000 feet, high atop the Cataloochee Divide, with its 250 wooded acres bordering the Great Smoky Mountains National Park, and with guest rooms and cabins assembled from authentic log structures and transported here. **Pros:** small inn with personality; fabulous location on a nearly mile-high mountaintop; delicious meals included. **Cons:** remote; expensive; no TV; no bar. *Rooms from: $500 ⊠ 2300 Swag Rd. ☎ 828/926–0430, 800/789–7672 ⊕ www.theswag.com 9 rooms, 2 suites, 3 cabins ⊗ Closed late Nov.–mid-Apr. All meals.*

$$ B&B/INN **The Yellow House on Plott Creek Road.** Just outside town, this lovely two-story Victorian, painted a sunflower yellow, sits on a low knoll, with colorful surrounding gardens and hammocks under shady trees. **Pros:** well-run B&B; lovely grounds; personal service. **Cons:** not a place for singles looking for action. *Rooms from: $165 ⊠ 89 Oak View Dr., at Plott Creek Rd., 1 mile west of Waynesville ☎ 828/452–0991, 800/563–1236 ⊕ www.theyellowhouse.com 3 rooms, 7 suites Breakfast.*

## SPORTS AND THE OUTDOORS

### FISHING

**Waynesville Fly Shop.** This fly-fishing shop also offers guide services. A full-day wading trip for two with guide costs $350; a float trip costs $395. *⊠ 178 Waynesville Plaza ☎ 828/246–0306 ⊕ www.waynesvilleflyshop.com.*

### GOLF

**Waynesville Inn Golf Resort & Spa.** At this resort course near downtown Waynesville, you can play three 9-hole Donald Ross–designed courses in any combination. Avoid the Cork & Cleaver restaurant at the resort, however. *⊠ 176 Country Club Dr. ☎ 828/452–4617, 800/627–6250 ⊕ www.thewaynesvilleinn.com/golf Reservations essential 27 holes. Dogwood course 2829 yards; Carolina course 2969 yards; Blue Ridge course 2974 yards. Each 9-hole course is par 35. Green Fee (with cart): $79 weekday/$79 weekend (guests at resort: $69 weekday/$69 weekend) ☞ Facilities: Putting green, pitching area, golf carts, pull carts, rental clubs, pro shop, golf academy/lessons, restaurant, bar. ⊗ Closed mid-Nov.–mid-Mar.*

6

# Myrtle Beach, SC, and the Grand Strand

**WORD OF MOUTH**

"Myrtle Beach is very family friendly . . . albeit very much spread out. Most of the family activities are in the central area—water parks, amusement parks, Broadway at the Beach (restaurants, mini-golf, shops etc.) all within a 30–40 block area (short blocks)."

—Wrongfoot

# WELCOME TO MYRTLE BEACH, SC, AND THE GRAND STRAND

## TOP REASONS TO GO

★ **Sixty miles of beach:** From North Myrtle Beach south to Pawleys Island, Grand Strand sand is silky-smooth, perfect for sunbathing and biking.

★ **Golf, golf, and more golf:** More than 100 golf courses for all skill levels meander through pine forests, dunes, and marshes.

★ **Southern culture:** Explore Southern culture and history on a plantation tour; taste it in the form of barbecue and other local foods; bring it home with a hammock woven right in Pawleys Island.

★ **Brookgreen Gardens:** More than 500 works from American artists are set among 250-year-old oaks, palms, and flowers in America's oldest sculpture garden.

★ **Kayak tours:** Paddle a kayak or ride a pontoon boat past the ruins of the rice plantations that line the shores around Georgetown.

**1 The Myrtle Beach Area.** Myrtle Beach has a colorful case of multiple personalities in its makeup, from exclusive resorts to gritty nostalgia and everything in between. And that's what makes it unique. Try local muscadine wine, feed your foodie at any of the renowned restaurants, touch heaven in the SkyWheel, play Skee-Ball at an oceanfront arcade, take in shops and variety shows, and, of course, enjoy the miles of sandy beaches. North Myrtle Beach, including the small, waterfront fishing towns of Little River and Cherry Grove, has a diverse assortment of entertainment options, from casino riverboats to scuba-diving artificial reefs and shipwrecks to fishing off the Cherry Grove Pier. At the Shagger's Hall of Fame, learn about South Carolina's state dance, the shag, born on Ocean Drive.

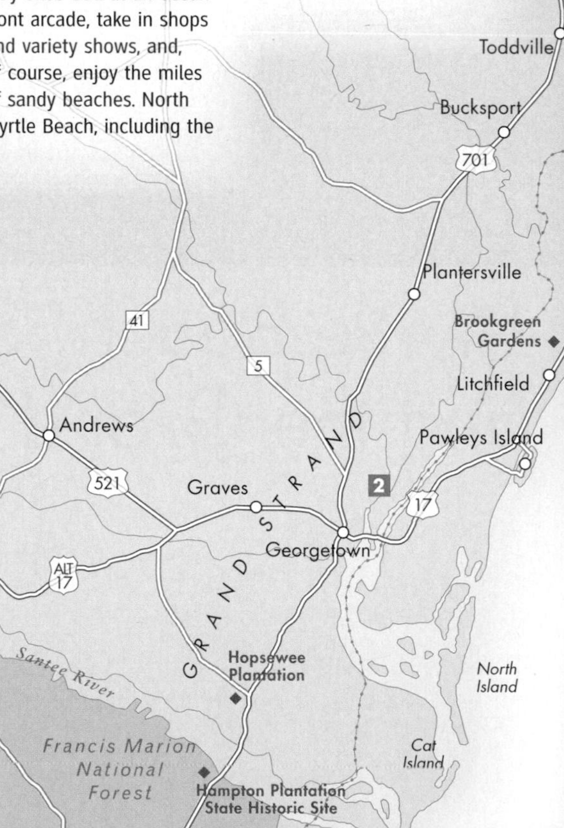

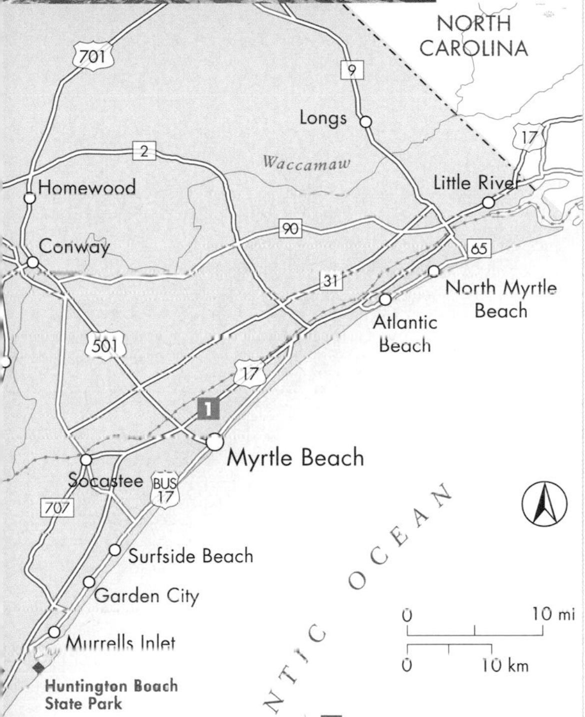

## GETTING ORIENTED

While most resort communities have beaches and water activities, the Grand Strand—the 60-mile stretch of beaches from Little River to Georgetown—is known for much more. Lush botanical gardens, elegant waterfronts, quirky art galleries, high-end and kitschy shopping, and tasty seafood are just some of the Strand's assets. While other coastal communities, such as Charleston or Hilton Head Island, may cater to a wealthier lifestyle, the Grand Strand can accommodate both the budget conscious as well as the high-end traveler.





**2 The Southern Grand Strand.** Where the busy highways and hotel high-rises of Myrtle Beach end at the border of Horry and Georgetown counties, the South Strand begins. The coastal communities of Georgetown County—seafood-centric Murrells Inlet, arrogantly shabby Pawleys Island, and historic Georgetown—boast a slow-paced, rustic elegance. Poke around small shops surrounded by live oaks or sample the fresh catch of the day, with no pretense in sight.

# MYRTLE BEACH AND THE GRAND STRAND BEACHES

(above) Low tide is the perfect time for kids to splash in the waves. (lower right) Family beach days are easy with so many amenities nearby. (upper right) You can rent sailboats along the beach.

The broad, flat beaches along the Grand Strand are a patchwork of colorful coastal scenes—from the high-energy section of Myrtle Beach backed by a wall of hotel high-rises to the laid-back leisure of Pawleys Island, accessible only by two causeway bridges that cross the salt marshes.

The family-oriented Grand Strand is one of the Eastern Seaboard's mega–vacation centers. The main attraction, of course: 60 miles of white sand, stretching from the North Carolina border south to Georgetown, with Myrtle Beach as the hub. From North Myrtle Beach all the way down to Pawleys Island, Grand Strand sand is silky-smooth, perfect between your toes while you're sunbathing and relaxing. Low-tide-packed sand makes way for early-bird joggers, bikers, and dog walkers next to the crashing waves. If you're lucky, you'll see dolphins, which often come in close in the early morning or just before sunset.

—Ashley Morris

## GOLF

If you are looking to combine a beach trip with some golf, the Myrtle Beach area is the place to go. More than 100 golf courses at all skill levels meander through pine forests, dunes, and marshes. The Arrowhead Course in the Briarcliffe Area offers holes and vistas along the intracoastal waterway. Tidewater Plantation and the renowned private Dunes Club course offer breathtaking ocean views.

### MYRTLE BEACH

It's no secret **Myrtle Beach** is a big hit with families. The international praise it has received as a family destination put it on the summer vacation map, so if you're seeking a quiet spot on the sand this isn't the place for you. What you will find here is a buzz of activity, from music spilling out of beachfront tiki bars, to an overflow of excitement from the stretch of boardwalk shops and cafés between the piers at 14th and 2nd avenues north. There is still plenty of natural beauty to be found, with shelling along the water in the morning. The hard-packed sand at low tide is perfect for bicycling. For sun-seekers who prefer more peace, Myrtle Beach's residential section, which boasts minimal beach access parking, between 38th and 48th avenues north is the best bet. **Myrtle Beach State Park,** just south of Springmaid Pier, is another peaceful spot with picnic areas, wooded nature trails, playgrounds, and a fishing pier.

### NORTH MYRTLE BEACH

**North Myrtle Beach** is less crowded, but it's certainly no less appealing. You'll find a hodgepodge of smaller hotels, high-rises, and beach cottages along the coastline. Sunbathers, shellers, and walkers love the wide beaches. North Myrtle's population increases in spring and fall when two national shag-dance gatherings take over the streets. The old shag dance clubs, as well as oodles of cute restaurants, still thrive along North

Myrtle's Main Street. You may even see a few shaggers shuffling the dance steps on the sand, like they first did more than 50 years ago.

### SURFSIDE BEACH AND GARDEN CITY BEACH

**Surfside Beach** is a small, southern suburb of Myrtle Beach, touted as a family beach that has a tight community of locals, parks, and a pier flanked by a block of seafood restaurants for visitors. **Garden City Beach** is south of Surfside off the Atlantic Avenue causeway, which ends at the Garden City Pier, boasting a fun arcade, fishing, and a one of a kind bar that hosts live bands on summer nights. Garden City not only features beaches oceanside, but a popular secluded beach inlet-side, called the Point, accessible by boat.

### LITCHFIELD BEACH AND PAWLEYS ISLAND

When you go to the South Strand's **Litchfield Beach** and **Pawleys Island,** it's time to relax, slow down your stride, and breathe in the fragrance of the saltwater marshes. Pawleys Island was once a summertime retreat for wealthy rice plantation owners who lived inland and remains perfect for quiet relaxation. Kissing the northern cusp of Litchfield is **Huntington Beach State Park,** a coastal haven for hikers, bird-watchers, or history buffs.

# DAY TRIP: MYRTLE BEACH TO PAWLEYS ISLAND

(above) Slow down your pace with a visit to Pawleys Island's uncrowded beaches. (upper right) There are no lifeguards at Pawleys Island beaches, but there are at Myrtle Beach.

The Grand Strand's comely coastline makes for an appealing drive from Myrtle Beach to Pawleys Island. Along the way there are plenty of opportunities to enjoy the beautiful vistas and take in the lights and sights.

Begin on the north end of Myrtle Beach on U.S. 17 Bypass, the main travel artery of the Grand Strand. The bypass is bordered by stately Carolina pines and split by intermediate grass medians populated by pretty palmettos and pineapple palms. Stop by **Broadway at the Beach,** a 350-acre outdoor complex of boutiques, restaurants, bars, nightclubs—there's even a mini amusement park and sky-high zip line—that spans between 21st and 29th avenues north and the bypass. The **Palace Theatre,** which hosts intermittent matinee performances of "Le Grande Cirque," is also here. Turn off the bypass for a bit along 21st Avenue North, head east to the T at Ocean Boulevard, and continue south for a view of the Atlantic. The new, oceanfront **Myrtle Beach Boardwalk** between 14th and 2nd avenues north makes for another worthy stop to stroll, look out at the sea, and get a taste of salt air.

–Ashley Morris

## PLANNING YOUR TIME

Begin your journey at U.S. 17 Bypass and 82nd Avenue North near the posh Grand Dunes area of northern Myrtle Beach. End in the beach town of Pawleys Island, where big beach houses blend with the simple beauty of the barrier island. The stretch is 30 miles long and will take a few hours with stops along the way.

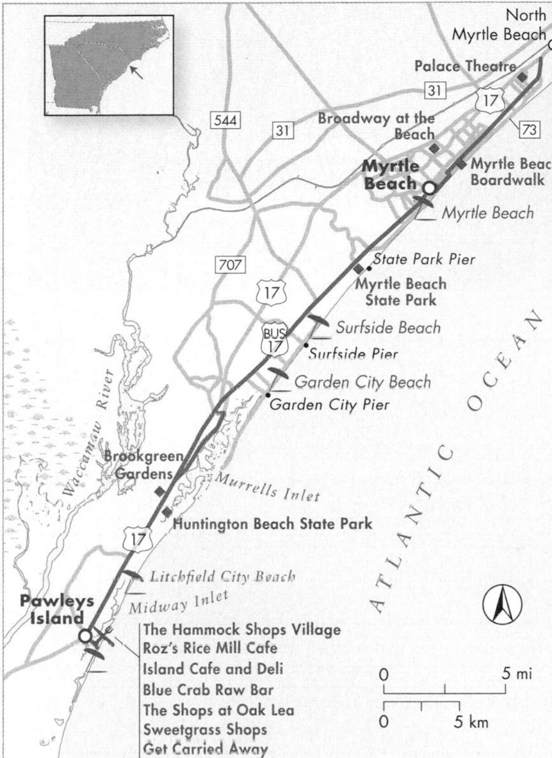

After hitting the boards at the Myrtle Beach Boardwalk, circle back onto U.S. 17 Bypass and continue south through the smaller suburbs of **Surfside Beach** and **Garden City Beach**. The bypass then merges into U.S. 17 Business in **Murrells Inlet**. You can either choose to detour at the large Murrells Inlet sign to drive on the waterfront or remain on the highway and visit the majestic **Brookgreen Gardens** or the sprawling **Huntington Beach State Park** across the highway.

It's from here and points south on this rural route that a beautiful, noncommercial transformation takes place. Stop by local favorite **Litchfield Books** for a good beach read. Visit the **Sweetgrass Shops, Island Shops,** or **Shops at Oak Lea** for great shopping. **The Hammock Shops Village**, a community of 20 specialty shops and Lowcountry restaurants nestled under the shade of ancient live oaks, is another must-stop.

For a final detour, follow Ocean Highway south and cross Pawleys' South Causeway bridge, and turn right onto Myrtle Avenue to the public beach there.

## QUICK BITES

**Blue Crab Raw Bar.** This seafood shack offers loads of surprises, from succulent shellfish from the raw bar to fun surroundings, including a massive playground for the kids. ✉ *9448 Ocean Hwy., Pawleys Island* ☎ *843/979–2722* 🌐 *www.bluecrabrawbar.com.*

**Get Carried Away Southern Takeout.** This is a great spot to stop and pack your picnic basket or to pick up ready-to-heat homemade Southern comforts for dinner. ✉ *10126 Ocean Hwy., 5B, Pawleys Island* ☎ *843/314–3493* 🌐 *www.getcarriedawaypi.com.*

**Island Café and Deli.** Stop in for big sandwiches off the grill at this tiny, roadside café complete with a covered patio. ✉ *10683 Ocean Hwy., Pawleys Island* ☎ *843/237–9527* 🌐 *www.islandcafeanddeli.com.*

**Roz's Rice Mill Cafe.** This cozy cottage serves up creative comfort foods. ✉ *The Hammock Shops, 10880 Ocean Hwy., Pawleys Island* ☎ *843/235–0196* 🌐 *www.rozsricemillcafe.com* ⏲ *Closed Sun. No dinner Mon.*

6

Updated by Ashley Morris

The coastal beauty of the Myrtle Beach area is priceless, but its affordability for families has also ranked this resort area one of the most valuable beach destinations in the world. And, as Myrtle Beach's reputation as a family-friendly destination has grown, so have the size, sophistication, and number of activities available.

The main attraction is the broad, beckoning beach known as the Grand Strand—60 miles of white sand, stretching nearly from the North Carolina border in Little River and North Myrtle Beach south to Surfside Beach, Garden City Beach, Murrells Inlet, Pawleys Island, and Georgetown, with Myrtle Beach centered at the hub. People come to "the Strand" for all of the traditional beach-going pleasures: swimming, sunbathing, sailing, surfing, shell hunting, fishing, jogging, and strolling. Away from the water, golfers have more than 100 courses to choose from, designed by the likes of Arnold Palmer, Robert Trent Jones, and Jack Nicklaus.

Golfing and beaching are far from "it" in Myrtle Beach, however. When it comes to diversions, you could hardly be better served, with critically acclaimed seafood restaurants, giant shopping complexes, trendy markets, factory outlets, Vegas-style live performance and concert venues, nightlife hotspots, amusement and water parks, arcades, a dozen shipwrecks for divers to explore, beachfront campgrounds, antique-car and wax museums, an aquarium, the world's largest outdoor sculpture garden, and a museum dedicated entirely to rice.

# PLANNING

## WHEN TO GO

The Grand Strand was developed as a summer resort, and with its gorgeous beaches, flowering tropical plants and palmetto trees, and warm weather, it continues to shine during the height of the summer season. That said, the fall and spring shoulder seasons may be even better.

Warm temperatures allow for beach activities, but the humidity drops and the heat of summer passes.

Winter—November through February—isn't usually considered a time to visit the beach, but the region can be quite pleasant. There are certainly cold days, but for the most part golfers, tennis players, and other outdoor enthusiasts can enjoy their pursuits during these months—at rock-bottom prices.

■ **TIP→** In the third and fourth weeks of May, most of the South Strand is inhabited by bikers in town for the Harley Davidson Spring Rally and the Atlantic Beach Bike Fest. Traffic and noise problems are common, and hotel space is scarce.

## PLANNING YOUR TIME

Many visitors do Myrtle Beach in a long weekend; beach or golf by day, and nightlife, dining, and shows by night. But with the area's bounty of beaches, amusements parks, mini golf courses, and waterslides, you could easily fill a week, especially if you've got kids in tow. Enjoy the great outdoors by water or land (boardwalk, mini-golf and Market Common festivals year-round) or pass rainy days in indoor playgrounds with aquariums, museums, and arcades galore. If history is your passion, spend at least a day exploring Georgetown on foot, by boat, or with a guided tour. With all this to explore, we recommended you rent a car, as these treasures are widespread.



## GETTING HERE AND AROUND

### AIR TRAVEL

The Myrtle Beach International Airport (MYR) is served by Delta, Porter, US Air, Spirit Air, Allegiant Air, and United Airlines, flying nonstop to more than 25 cities. The terminal is currently undergoing a massive expansion, adding six gates and 240,000 square feet with more shops and restaurants.

**Air Contacts Myrtle Beach International Airport** (*MYR*). ✉ *1100 Jetport Rd.* ☎ *843/448–1580* 🌐 *www.flymyrtlebeach.com.*

### CAR TRAVEL

Midway between New York and Miami, the Grand Strand isn't connected directly to any interstate highways but is within an hour's drive of Interstate 95, Interstate 20, Interstate 26, and Interstate 40 via Route 22 (Veterans Highway), U.S. 501, and the newer Route 31 (Carolina Bays Parkway). U.S. 17 Bypass and U.S. 17 Business are the major north–south coastal routes through the Strand.

■ **TIP→** In summer, to bypass incoming southbound traffic jams on U.S. 501, take Interstate 95 to Interstate 40 to U.S. 17 (at Wilmington) to Route 31, which connects to Myrtle Beach via Route 544 or the tail end of U.S. 501.

### MOPED TRAVEL

Rent a moped for a fun way to travel with the slower traffic along Ocean Boulevard, anywhere along the Grand Strand. Helmets are strongly advised within Myrtle Beach city limits and are required for riders under 21.

**Contacts****East Coast Golf Carts and Scooters** ☎ *843/424–2644* 🌐 *www.eastcoastgolfcarts.com.* **Mopeds, Bikes & Surf** ☎ *843/626–6900.* **Myrtle Beach Moped Rentals** ☎ *843/626–6900* 🌐 *www.mopedrentalsofmyrtlebeach.com.*

#### TAXI TRAVEL

Taxi services are available at several locations along the Grand Strand. Diamond Taxi Transportation serves the North Myrtle Beach area, Pawleys Yellow Cab serves the South Strand, and Ocean Boulevard Shuttle and Taxi Services serves the central Myrtle Beach area.

**Taxi Contacts Diamond Cab** ☎ *843/448–8888* 🌐 *www.myrtlebeachdiamondcab.com.* **Ocean Boulevard Shuttle and Taxi Services** ☎ *843/444–1144* 🌐 *www.oceanboulevardtaxi.com.* **Pawleys Yellow Cab** ☎ *843/237–5599.*

### RESTAURANTS

With the sand at your feet, seafood will most likely be on your mind. The nearly 2,000 restaurants on the Grand Strand boast all types of seafood, whether you're seeking a buffet or a more intimate dining spot. The summer months see an influx of visitors, so waits at popular restaurants can reach up to an hour or more. ■ **TIP→** To avoid long waits, take advantage of early-bird dinner specials, make a reservation, or opt for takeout. Many spots oblige with free delivery to hotels or offer gourmet takeout boxes. *Prices in the reviews are the average cost of a main course at dinner or, if dinner is not served, at lunch.*

### HOTELS

High-rise hotels line the Grand Strand, but kitschy beach motels, beachside camping, luxury resorts, and weekly beach house or cottage rentals are popular choices, too. Most accommodations have pools, and many high-rises up the ante with lazy rivers or water-play areas. Advance reservations are recommended for the majority of beach properties. Ask about special packages that include golf, shows, and shopping. *Prices in the reviews are the lowest cost of a standard double room in high season.*

### DISCOUNTS AND DEALS

Visitor centers and grocery stores throughout the Grand Strand have free coupon books with discounts for mini-golf, 18-hole golf courses, personal watercraft rentals, and parasailing, to name a few.

### TOURS

Palmetto Tour & Travel, Sunway Charters & Tours, and Gray Line offer tour packages and guide services.

**Tour Contacts Gray Line Myrtle Beach** ☎ *843/448–9483, 800/261–5991* 🌐 *www.grayline.com.* **Palmetto Tour & Travel** ☎ *843/626–2431, 800/634–3778* 🌐 *www.palmettotourandtravel.com.* **Sunway Charters & Tours** ☎ *843/293–2100, 800/334–6669* 🌐 *www.sunwaychartersandtours.com.*

# THE MYRTLE BEACH AREA

Myrtle Beach was a late bloomer. Until 1901 it didn't have an official name; that year the first hotel went up, and oceanfront lots were selling for $25. Today, more than 14 million people a year visit the region, and no wonder: lodging, restaurants, shopping, and entertainment choices are varied and plentiful. And the many award-winning golf courses in the area add to the appeal. What's more, Myrtle Beach recently took a big step toward cleaning up its reputation as a frenzied collection of all-you-can-eat buffets, T-shirt shops, and gritty bars with the May 2010 unveiling of an oceanfront boardwalk that meanders between the 14th Avenue North and 2nd Avenue North piers. There is a renewed interest in the oceanfront shops, ice cream parlors, restaurants, and arcades, and the beautiful new boardwalk is recapturing a pedestrian- and family-friendly Myrtle Beach that was alive with the Pavilion amusement park (demolished in 2006) in its 1960s heyday. The Myrtle Beach Boardwalk is constantly expanding; the latest addition is the SkyWheel, the largest Ferris wheel on the East Coast by day (and a sky-high spectacle at night), and there are more plans for restaurant-mini-golf complexes as well.



Neon lights still light up noisy blocks of Ocean Boulevard ("the Strip"), Kings Highway, and Restaurant Row (sometimes called the Galleria area), but the Strip and boardwalk are generally safe and clean. Nearby attractions such as Family Kingdom amusement park and Myrtle Waves Water Park can add a dose of fun to your afternoon.

If a quiet vacation is more your speed, opt for evenings dining in sophisticated restaurants following days lolling on relatively uncrowded beaches. Myrtle Beach State Park, for instance, is a bastion of peace and quiet, as are the beaches adjacent to the residential areas of Myrtle Beach at either end of the Strip.

■ **TIP→** Be sure to take note of whether an establishment is on U.S. 17 Business or U.S. 17 Bypass—confusing the two could lead to hours of frustration. U.S. 17 Business is also referred to as Kings Highway.

## MYRTLE BEACH

*94 miles northeast of Charleston via U.S. 17; 138 miles east of Columbia via U.S. 76 to U.S. 378 to U.S. 501.*

Myrtle Beach, with its high-rises and hyper-development, is the nerve center of the Grand Strand and one of the major seaside destinations on the East Coast. Visitors are drawn here for the swirl of classic vacation activity, from beaches to golf to nightlife to live music and theater shows.

To capture the flavor of the place, take a stroll along the sidewalks or boardwalk of Ocean Boulevard. Here you'll find an eclectic assortment of gift and novelty shops, a wax museum, and a museum of oddities. When you've had your fill, turn east and make your way back onto the beach amid the sunbathers, parasailers, kite fliers, and kids building sand castles.

## THREE DAYS IN MYRTLE BEACH

No time for planning? We've mapped out a fun-filled three-day itinerary.

Spend your first day at the beach. In the evening, choose from an amusement park, like Family Kingdom, or a water park (rates are lower in the evening); a live show at the Palace, Carolina Opry, Pirates Voyage, or Medieval Times; or at Broadway at the Beach, which has hundreds of shops and restaurants, night clubs, speed-boat rides, and a zip line (Pavilion Nostalgia Park is also here).

On your second day, head to Georgetown and take a tour through Winyah Bay on a sightseeing cruise, where you might see dolphins, bald eagles, and even the remains of a Civil War submarine. Brookgreen Gardens, between Pawleys Island and Murrells Inlet, is also a must.

On your last day, check out the shopping and dining and full schedule of outdoor festivals at The Market Common, off Farrow Parkway on the site of the old Myrtle Beach Air Force Base.

### GETTING HERE AND AROUND

Most routes to Myrtle Beach run via Interstates 95 and 40, and connect to either U.S. 501, Route 31, Route 22, or U.S. 17. The main thoroughfares through the Grand Strand are U.S. 17 Bypass and U.S. 17 Business (aka Kings Highway); both run parallel to the beach. Most of the city's main streets are numbered and are designated north or south.

Drivers should also be aware that construction is under way of a grade-separated interchange at the existing U.S. Route 17 Bypass/S.C. Route 707 intersection near The Market Common at the back gate of the former Myrtle Beach Air Force Base. This is to be completed in 2016.

### ESSENTIALS

**Visitor Information Myrtle Beach Area Convention and Visitors Bureau welcome centers** ✉ *1200 N. Oak St.* ☎ *843/626–7444, 800/356–3016* 🌐 *www.visitmyrtlebeach.com* 🕒 *May.–Labor Day, weekdays 8:30–5, Sat. 9–5, Sun. 10–2; Labor Day–April, weekdays 8:30–5, Sat. 10–2.* ✉ *Myrtle Beach International Airport 1100 Jetport Rd.* ☎ *843/626–7444, 800/356–3016* 🌐 *www.visitmyrtlebeach.com* 🕒 *Daily 8–7*

## EXPLORING

### TOP ATTRACTIONS

**Family Kingdom.** Dominated by a gigantic white wooden roller coaster called the Swamp Fox, **Family Kingdom amusement park** is quite an experience, and it's right on the ocean. There are thrill and children's rides, a log flume, go-cart track, old-fashioned carousel, and the Slingshot Drop Zone, which rockets riders straight down a 110-foot tower. It's a bit like going to a state fair that runs all summer long. Bring your bathing suit and cross the street for more fun at **Family Kingdom water park**. Operating hours can vary, so it's worthwhile to call before visiting, especially on Saturday when the parks are sometimes rented by groups. Money-saving bundled tickets and multiday passes are readily available; check the website for more information. ✉ *300 S. Ocean Blvd., The Strip* ☎ *843/626–3447 amusement park, 843/916–0400 water park*

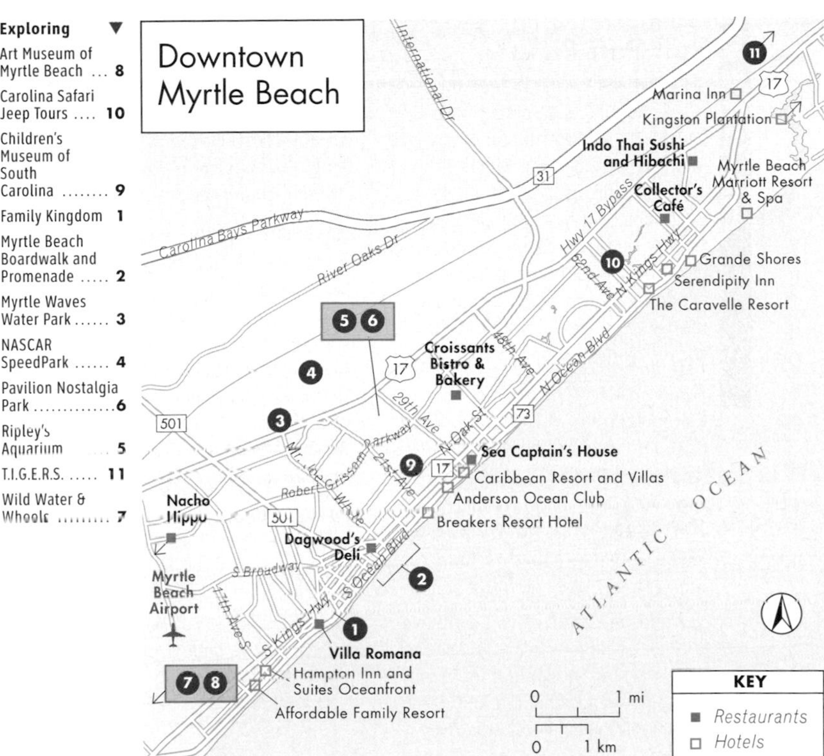


*www.family-kingdom.com Single-ride tickets $1.15 each; 1-day unlimited access to most rides $24.50 amusement park, $18.95 water park; amusement and water park combo pass $35 Amuseument park generally Apr.–Sept. daily; water park generally late May–Aug. daily (closed some weekdays in shoulder season), but hrs vary; call or check website for details.*

**Myrtle Beach Boardwalk and Promenade.** It's a mile-long oceanfront destination in itself, day or night, drawing in visitors of all ages. The boardwalk stretches from the 14th Avenue Pier, where seafood restaurant/café Pier 14 roosts, to the newly renovated 2nd Avenue Pier and its Pier House restaurant and Pier View, an open-air rooftop lounge. Take a sky-high seat on the new SkyWheel, the largest Ferris wheel on the East Coast at 175 feet tall with enclosed gondolas for a smooth ride (don't miss the light show at night), then stop in for a bite to eat at Jimmy Buffett's LandShark restaurant located right at the entrance. You can also take the kids to play in the old-time arcade, zip line across the new Adrenaline Adventure ziplne, break for a soft-serve ice cream cone, shop for a souvenir at the world-famous Gay Dolphin, shuck oysters at Dirty Don's, pull up a stool at the Bowery (the legendary bar that gave country band Alabama its start), or just stroll or sit, taking in the beach scene. A schedule of free live concerts, performances, fireworks,

CLOSE UP

## Putt-Putt Picks

Nearly 50 mini-golf courses, also known as "putt-putt" around here, are in full swing along the Grand Strand. It's practically a subculture of Myrtle Beach that will have you climbing through caverns, scaling volcanic mountains, crossing rapids, and dodging fire-breathing dragons to master the 18-hole mini-greens. Beat the crowds by putt-putting in the morning or before the after-dinner rush.

**Cancun Lagoon Mayan Adventure Golf.** Putt inside or out Cancun's massive Mayan temple. ✉ *2101 S. Kings Hwy., South Myrtle Beach* ☎ *843/444-1098* *$9 (age 5 and up)* ⌚ *Daily 9 am–11:30 pm.*

**Dragon's Lair Fantasy Golf.** Mini-golf goes medieval, as you maneuver through castle lookouts and caverns while dodging the 30-foot fire-breathing dragon that intermittently pops up from his lair. ✉ *Broadway at the Beach, 1197 Celebrity Circle, Central Myrtle Beach* ☎ *843/913-9301* *$9 before 6 pm, $10 after 6* ⌚ *Daily 10 am–11 pm.*

**Hawaiian Rumble.** Host of the U.S. ProMiniGolf Association's Masters Championship, this course takes mini-golf to a whole new level, especially with its centerpiece: a 40-foot-tall, fire-erupting volcano mountain that "rumbles" the ground every 20 minutes. ✉ *3210 U.S. 17 S, North Myrtle Beach* ☎ *843/272-7812* *$9 (age 5 and up)* ⌚ *Daily 9 am–midnight.*

**Mt. Atlanticus Minotaur.** Indoor and outdoor greens race around a giant mountain, past waterfalls, and into lagoons of this popular putt-putt place near the Strip. ✉ *707 N. Kings Hwy., off 7th Ave. N, near U.S. 501, Central Myrtle Beach* ☎ *843/444-1008* *$9–$12* ⌚ *Daily 9 am–midnight.*

and children's carnivals abounds in summer at the boardwalk's Plyler Park. And don't miss the holiday, family-friendly block parties year-round. ⚠ **Bikes, pets, and skateboards are prohibited on the boards May–September.** ✉ *14th Ave. N to 2nd Ave. N and Ocean Blvd.* 🌐 *www.myrtlebeachdowntown.com* *Free* ⌚ *Daily 24 hrs, year-round.*

**Myrtle Waves Water Park.** At South Carolina's largest water park you can shoot through twisty chutes, swim in the Ocean in Motion Wave Pool, float the day away on an inner tube on the LayZee River, or ride a boogie board on the Racer River. Even the toddlers will enjoy splashing in Bubble Bay and Saturation Station playground. There's beach volleyball, too, for when you've had enough water. Shaded areas with lounge chairs offer respite from the sun, and new private cabanas, complete with waitstaff, are available to rent for the day. Soft drinks and sunscreen are included in the admission price, lifeguards on duty are aplenty, and lockers are available to keep money and valuables safe. Admission discounts are available after 3pm daily, and also for early bird season passes. Wear a well-secured swimsuit on the big slides, or you may reach the end of the slide before your suit does. ✉ *3000 10th Ave. N, Central Myrtle Beach* ☎ *843/918-8725* 🌐 *www.myrtlewaves.com* *Full day $27.99, after 3 pm $21.99* ⌚ *Mid-May and mid-Sept.*

Myrtle Beach's mile-long boardwalk is lined with restaurants to grab a bite.

*weekends only; June–Aug. daily. Opens at 10 or 11 am and closes between 5 and 7 pm, but hrs vary; call or check website for details.*

**NASCAR SpeedPark.** Race to the checkered flag on seven different NASCAR-replica tracks. The cars vary in sophistication and speed; to use the most advanced track you need to be a licensed driver. The 26-acre facility also has racing memorabilia, amusement rides, an arcade, and miniature golf. Lines at attractions are shortest on Monday. *1820 21st Ave. N, at U.S. 17 Bypass, Central Myrtle Beach 843/918–8725 www.nascarspeedpark.com Single-ride tickets from $3.50 ($25 for 10), unlimited day pass $23.99, season combo passes with Myrtle Waves start at $79.99 Opens daily at 10 am or noon, closes between 8 pm and 11 pm; call or check website for details.*

**Pavilion Nostalgia Park.** The historic oceanfront Pavilion (razed in 2006) lives on through its amusement rides that were moved to this new section of Broadway at the Beach. Enjoy a classic collection of amusement rides, including the famous Herschell-Spillman Carousel, dating back to 1912. Plus, hit the snack stands vending funnel cakes and snow cones. *Broadway at the Beach, 1171 Celebrity Circle, Central Myrtle Beach 843/918–8725 www.pavilionnostalgiapark.com $3.50 per ride, $25 unlimited ride pass Daily noon–11 pm.*

**Ripley's Aquarium.** Glide underwater (no need for a wet suit) through a winding tunnel exhibit that's longer than a football field, where sharks of all kinds and exotic marine creatures, including poisonous lionfish, moray eels, and an octopus, are the main attractions at this aquarium. Children can examine horseshoe crabs and eels in touch tanks; mermaid shows offered regularly. Special exhibits are often included in the price of aquarium admission. Admission discounts are available when combined with price of Ripley's Ocean Boulevard attractions. ✉ *Broadway at the Beach, U.S. 17 Bypass between 21st Ave. N and 29th Ave. N, Central Myrtle Beach* ☎ *843/916–0888, 800/734–8888* 🌐 *www.ripleyaquariums.com* 🎫 *$21.99* 🕒 *Sun.–Thurs. 9–8, Fri.–Sat. 9–9* .

**SLINGSHOT THRILL RIDE**

If you and a daredevil sidekick want to be catapulted to more heart-pounding heights, go to the Slingshot Thrill Ride on the corner of 12th Avenue North and Ocean Boulevard, which shoots you 300 feet into the air at 100 mph—and captures it all on video.

★ **T.I.G.E.R.S.** A three-hour tour at the Institute of Greatly Endangered and Rare Species transports you away from Myrtle Beach on an African safari. A team of animal handlers, led by nationally renowned trainer Dr. Bhagavan "Doc" Handle, allows you to hold baby tigers, pose with a 900-pound liger, hug orangutans, feed Bubbles the elephant, and more. You leave with a life-changing experience, captured on a personalized DVD, plus a disc with hundreds of professional photos taken of you as you pose with animals throughout the day. The tour is intended to be both entertaining and educational; entrance fees fund conservation of the animals at this sanctuary and conservation projects in Africa. Driving to the sanctuary is not permitted; tour reservations can be made from the T.I.G.E.R.S. Preservation Station at Barefoot Landing, where they will brief you on directions to the sanctuary. Children must be at least six years old. ✉ *Preservation Station: Barefoot Landing, 4898 S. Hwy. 17, North Myrtle Beach* ☎ *843/361–4552* 🌐 *www.tigerfriends.com* 🎫 *$199* 🕒 *Tours Mar.–Oct. at 10 am; days vary.*

**Wild Water & Wheels.** About 9 miles south of Myrtle Beach in Surfside Beach this water park has 24 water-oriented rides and activities, along with go-carts and mini-golf. If your children are old enough to navigate the park on their own, spend a few minutes at the adults-only lounge pool, where you can sit immersed in Jacuzzi-like bubbles, or rest in your own private cabana. ✉ *910 U.S. 17 S, Surfside Beach* ☎ *843/238–3787* 🌐 *www.wild-water.com* 🎫 *Full day $27.98, after 3 pm $17.98* 🕒 *May–Sept., daily 10–6, Fri. 10–9 starting in June.*

### WORTH NOTING

**Art Museum of Myrtle Beach.** A hidden gem in a 1920s beach cottage on the southern cusp of Ocean Boulevard, this museum has a permanent collection that will open your eyes to the art community that thrives on the Grand Strand. Impressive national touring exhibits stop here year-round and KidsArt studio club. ✉ *3100 S. Ocean Blvd., South End* ☎ *843/238–2510* 🌐 *www.myrtlebeachartmuseum.org* 🎫 *Donations accepted* 🕒 *Tues.–Sat. 10–4, Sun. 1–4.*

**Carolina Safari Jeep Tours.** Visit everything from a plantation house to an alligator-laden salt marsh to an 18th-century church on these tours. Along the way, learn fun facts and scary ghost stories, told from a script that keeps even history-phobes entertained. The 3½-hour tour, which includes some walking, provides a surprisingly complete overview of the region and beautiful views of the Grand Strand's varied ecosystem. Call to make a reservation; you'll be picked up at your hotel in a jeep that seats about a dozen people. ✉ *725 Seaboard St., Unit E* ☎ *843/497–5330, 843/272–1177* 🌐 *www.carolinasafari.com* 🎫 *$40* ⏲ *Call to reserve and arrange tour time.*

## MARKET FRESH

If you'd rather gather fresh ingredients to cook up some lunch or dinner in your condo, stop by Myrtle's Market, an outdoor farmers' market at the corner of Oak Street and Mr. Joe White Avenue in Myrtle Beach that's open Wednesday, Friday, and Saturday from 9 to 3. You'll find fish, fruit, vegetables, cheese, homemade jam, and more.

**Children's Museum of South Carolina.** Bring the kids here to beat the heat or take cover on a rainy day. Create giant bubbles, pet turtles, and play dentist or doctor. It's educational, it's hands-on, and it's entertaining for parents, too. ✉ *2501 N. Kings Hwy., Central Myrtle Beach* ☎ *843/946–9469* 🌐 *www.cmsckids.org* 🎫 *$8* ⏲ *Mon.–Sat. 9–4.*

OFF THE BEATEN PATH

**Conway.** For a break from the beach, or as a pleasant way to spend a cool or cloudy day, take a day trip to the historic town of Conway. Conway is a 15-mile trip inland on Route 501 North to Route 501 Business across the bridge that arches over the Waccamaw River and onto the town's Main Street. A huge source for lumber in the 1870s, the town is now an eclectic hub for art studios and the arts, antiques stores, and a growing number of foodie hotspots. Conway's Riverwalk, along the Waccamaw River, offers a peaceful respite for walkers, joggers, and bikers.

### WHERE TO EAT

$$$ ECLECTIC ★ **Collectors Café.** A successful restaurant, art gallery, and coffeehouse rolled into one, this unpretentiously artsy spot has bright, funky paintings and tile work covering its walls and tabletops. The cuisine is among the most inventive in the area. Although the menu changes with the seasons, a standby for patrons is the delectable scallop cakes. All in all, it's a far cry from standard Myrtle Beach fish-house fare. [$] *Average main: $20* ✉ *7740 N. Kings Hwy., North End* ☎ *843/449–9370* 🌐 *www.collectorscafeandgallery.com* ⏲ *Closed Sun.*

$$ FRENCH **Croissants Bistro & Bakery.** Myrtle Beach's cake-baking goddess, Heidi Vukov, has expanded her renowned bakery, breakfast, and lunch offerings into a French-Southern-fused dinner bistro and wine menu. Like its food, Croissants is comfy and elegant, drawing a classy crowd. Lunch on pimento cheese on a croissant; from the dinner menu, try the Bistro chicken, which is stuffed with herbed Boursin cheese, sundried tomatoes, and prosciutto. [$] *Average main: $18* ✉ *3751 Grissom Pkwy., Central Myrtle Beach* ☎ *843/448–2253* 🌐 *www.croissants.net* ⏲ *Closed Sun.*

$ AMERICAN **Dagwood's Deli.** Comic-strip characters Dagwood and Blondie could split one of the masterful meat-packed sandwiches at Dagwood's Deli, where locals line up on their lunch break. There are the usual suspects—ham, turkey, and homemade chicken salad—but you won't regret trying one of the more distinctive creations, such as blackened mahimahi with homemade pineapple-cilantro salsa, or the grilled chicken breast with bacon, provolone, and ranch dressing. Salads and burgers round out the menu, and they deliver (for $1) to most of Myrtle Beach. Dagwood's also has a sports-bar location in Surfside Beach. *Average main: $8 ✉ 400 Mr. Joe White Ave., Central Myrtle Beach ☎ 843/448–0100 Reservations not accepted ⏲ Closed Sun. No dinner* *Average main: $8 ✉ 600 U.S. 17 Business, Surfside Beach ☎ 843/828–4600 ⊕ www.dagwoodsdeli.com.*

### FABULOUS FISH

With ocean on one side and tidal marsh and rivers on the other, the Grand Strand isn't at a loss for fresh seafood. Local shrimp, oysters, and fish—particularly grouper—are good bets. For a real treat, try she-crab soup, a creamy bisquelike creation served with a cruet of sherry on the side. Don't drink the sherry—add a splash to the soup, along with a dash of hot sauce.

$$ ASIAN **Indo Thai Sushi & Hibachi.** Owner Laura Heryadi is legendary in Myrtle Beach for her sushi artistry. In addition to sushi masterpieces she creates a slew of authentic Thai noodle dishes and signature seafood creations like sea bass curry, Coco Shrimp (coconut-battered colossal shrimp with vegetables in chili sauce), and pad thai. Inside, the sleek eatery is more metro than Myrtle Beach. A sister location is located in Pawleys Island. *Average main: $18 ✉ 980 82nd Pkwy., North End ☎ 843/692–7000 ⊕ www.indothaidining.com.*

$ MODERN MEXICAN **Nacho Hippo.** If you're a hungry hippo, then slide a stool over to a maximo plate of nachos here at this hip corner cantina in The Market Common. It's bold, fresh and fun—from the funky wall and ceiling decor to the creative Mexican dishes like The Donald, nachos piled with Maine lobster meat, and the Kamikaze and Freakin Vegan tacos. If you're thirsty, there are $3 freshly made house margaritas every day. *Average main: $10 ✉ The Market Common, 1160 Farrow Pkwy., South End ☎ 843/839–9770 ⊕ www.nachohippo.com Reservations not accepted.*

$$$ SEAFOOD **Sea Captain's House.** The windowed porch overlooking the ocean houses the best seats at this nautical-themed restaurant in a 1930s beach cottage. The fireplace inside the wood-panel dining room is warmly welcoming on cool off-season evenings. Menu highlights include the crab casserole and the Avocado Sea Fare salad with crabmeat and boiled shrimp. Breads and desserts are baked on the premises. *Average main: $22 ✉ 3000 N. Ocean Blvd., The Strip ☎ 843/448–8082 ⊕ www.seacaptains.com.*

$$$ ITALIAN ★ **Villa Romana.** It's all about family at Villa Romana, where owners Rinaldo and Franca come in early to make the gnocchi and stick around to greet customers. It's hard to resist filling up on the *stracciatella* (Italian egg-drop) soup, bruschetta, salad, and rolls (perhaps the best on the Strand) that accompany every meal, but try. The gnocchi is a perfect foil for any of the homemade sauces, and the veal Absolut (sautéed veal in a sauce of cream, mushrooms, and vodka) is a specialty. Michael the accordion player entertains diners with songs ranging from "Mack the Knife" to "Stairway to Heaven." *Average main: $20 ✉ 707 S. Kings*

## HOME SWEET HOME

If a hotel just won't suit the size of your crew, the Grand Strand can accommodate with beach-house or cottage rentals aplenty.

Here are a few agencies to check out before you check in:

**Beachcomber Vacations** *800/334–3798 www.beachcombervacations.com.*

**Dunes Realty** *888/889–0312, 843/651–2116 www.dunes.com.*

**Elliott Realty** *888/669–7853 www.northmyrtlebeachtravel.com.*

**Garden City Realty** *Garden City Beach 877/767–7737 www.gardencityrealty.com.*

**Grand Strand Vacation Rentals Inc.** *North Myrtle Beach 800/722–6278 www.grandstrandvacations.com.*

**Seaside Rentals** *Surfside Beach 866/252–9930 www.seasiderentalsonline.com.*

**Surfside Realty Company** *Surfside Beach 800/833–8231 www.surfsiderealty.com.*

*Hwy. 843/448–4990 www.villaromanamyrtlebeach.com Reservations essential No lunch.*

6

### WHERE TO STAY

*Hotel reviews have been abbreviated in this book. For expanded reviews, please go to Fodors.com.*

$ HOTEL **Affordable Family Resort.** With suites and cottages large enough to house three generations of family members, this spot is both budget-conscious and family-friendly. **Pros:** pets are welcome for an extra charge per night; arcade for the kids. **Cons:** rooms are not rented to anyone under 25. *Rooms from: $125 2300 S. Ocean Blvd., South End 888/839–4330 www.affordablefamilyresort.com 66 suites, 6 cottages.*

$$$ RESORT **Anderson Ocean Club and Spa.** Heavenly Moroccan luxury greets you from the start, with a fountain in the front plaza, through the stately double-door entrance flanked by large lanterns, inside to the two-story lobby. **Pros:** upscale furnishings will wow you; central location convenient to Broadway at the Beach dining and entertainment options. **Cons:** proximity of Magnolia's restaurant is only a plus if you love country cookin'. *Rooms from: $225 2600 N. Ocean Blvd., Central Myrtle Beach 843/213–5340, 866/578–8494 www.andersonoceanclub.com 289 suites and condos.*

$$$ RESORT **Breakers Resort Hotel.** The rooms in this oceanfront hotel are airy and spacious, with contemporary furnishings. **Pros:** excellent views from the tower rooms; rooms renovated in 2009. **Cons:** pool areas are on the small side for the potential number of guests. *Rooms from: $225 2006 N. Ocean Blvd., Central Myrtle Beach 843/444–4444, 800/952–4507 www.breakers.com 288 rooms, 384 suites.*

$$$ HOTEL **The Caravelle Resort.** She may be over the hill (at 52 years old), but she's as youthful and tropically trendy as ever, with a bright yellow exterior, super-chic condos, and the Wild Water pool area running the length of one side of the hotel, which receives rave giggles and shrieks

of delight from kids. **Pros:** on-site Santa Maria Restaurant is a Myrtle Beach institution; breezy seventh-floor oceanfront sundeck; one of only five Myrtle Beach hotels with access to private Dunes Club Golf & Beach Club. **Cons:** since lobby and concierge are located across the street, check-in can be confusing, especially during heavy summertime traffic. *Rooms from: $225 6900 N. Ocean Blvd., North End 800/507–9145 www.thecaravelle.com 540 condos.*

$$$ HOTEL **Caribbean Resort and Villas.** The Caribbean actually consists of four different properties, each offering access to the other's amenities. **Pros:** floor-to-ceiling windows in the Cayman Tower afford expansive views of the beach and the ocean from most rooms; great family-geared water facilities. **Cons:** not for couples looking for a quiet romantic stay: children in wet bathing suits are a regular sight in the elevators, and the pools and water-activity areas are designed for families. *Rooms from: $225 30th Ave. N, The Strip 800/552–8509 www.caribbeanresort.com 465 rooms and suites.*

$$ RESORT **Grande Shores.** Grande Shores, built in 2001, is a combination of rentable condos with full kitchens and standard hotel rooms outfitted with refrigerators, coffeemakers, and, in a few cases, kitchenettes. **Pros:** water features for all age groups; spacious rooms with full kitchens are great for families. **Cons:** only a select group of rooms actually faces the ocean, most either face north or south, offering glimpses rather than views. *Rooms from: $160 201 77th Ave. N, North End 843/692–2397, 877/798–4074 www.grandeshores.com 136 rooms.*

$$$$ HOTEL **Hampton Inn and Suites Oceanfront.** This property, completely refurbished in 2009, combines the reliability of an established hotel chain with the joys of a beach resort. **Pros:** crisp white bed linens lend rooms a tropical, beachy feel; on-site day spa. **Cons:** immediate neighborhood isn't the best at night. *Rooms from: $270 1803 S. Ocean Blvd., South End 843/946–6400, 877/946–6400 www.hamptoninnoceanfront.com 227 rooms and suites Breakfast.*

$$$$ RESORT **Kingston Plantation.** On 145 acres of oceanside woodlands, this complex includes two hotels, as well as restaurants, shops, and one- to three-bedroom condominiums and villas. **Pros:** lushly landscaped property; award-winning restaurant, Café Amalfi, on-site. **Cons:** some condos may include a sleeper sofa in the bed count; only the Embassy Suites includes breakfast. *Rooms from: $260 9800 Queensway Blvd., North End 843/449–0006, 800/876–0010 www.kingstonplantation.com 385 rooms, 255 suites, 414 villas, 414 condos Breakfast.*

$$$ HOTEL **Marina Inn at Grande Dunes.** Geared to families, business travelers, and golf enthusiasts, this hotel oozes luxury. **Pros:** exemplary service; waterway and golf greens on the western bank. **Cons:** too close to U.S. 17; no easy way to get to the beach. *Rooms from: $225 8121 Amalfi Pl., North End 866/437–4113 www.marinainnatgrandedunes.com 210 rooms.*

$$$$ RESORT ★ **Myrtle Beach Marriott Resort & Spa.** Entering this plantation-chic high-rise resort, with its airy wicker furniture, giant palms, and mahogany details, will take you away from the hubbub of Myrtle Beach and straight to a tropical locale. **Pros:** striped hammocks swing near the dunes with views of the ocean; several pools and water features are

## INLAND HOTELS

While landlocked Myrtle Beach hotels may not have the ocean views, several do have easy access to other attractions, making them well worth recommending for both business and family stays.

**Hampton Inn at Broadway at the Beach.** Hampton Inn at Broadway at the Beach is on the grounds of the entertainment, nightlife, dining, and shopping hub for all ages, Broadway at the Beach. *Rooms from: $225 1140 Celebrity Circle, Central Myrtle Beach 843/916–0600 www.hamptoninnbroadway.com.*

**Hilton Garden Inn.** Right down the street from Myrtle Beach International Airport and within walking distance to Coastal Grand Mall and its Restaurant District, the Hilton Garden Inn has tons of on-site meeting space and a 24-hour business center. *Rooms from: $200 2383 Coastal Grand Circle, South Myrtle Beach 843/839–1200 www.hiltongardeninn.hilton.com.*

**Sheraton Myrtle Beach Convention Center Hotel.** The plush Sheraton Myrtle Beach Convention Center Hotel is next door to the area's prime location for conventions, banquets, and formal occasions. *Rooms from: $225 2101 N. Oak St., Central Myrtle Beach 843/918–5000 www.sheratonmyrtlebeach.com.*

**Suites of The Market Common.** Suites of The Market Common is reservation central for posh by-the-week condo rentals overlooking The Market Common skyline. *Rooms from: $200 1232 Farrow Pkwy., South Myrtle Beach 877/593–0205 www.myrtlebeachhotels.com/resorts/suites-of-the-market-common.com.*

6

available. **Cons:** it's a bit of a drive south to the hub of Myrtle Beach shopping. *Rooms from: $270 8400 Costa Verde Dr. 843/449–8880 www.myrtlebeachmarriott.com 400 rooms Breakfast.*

$ B&B/INN **Serendipity Inn.** This cozy Spanish-villa-style B&B is about 300 yards from the beach. **Pros:** the tranquil setting helps you forget the hustle and bustle of busy Myrtle Beach. **Cons:** some amenities are dated, but still pleasant; don't expect brand-new lounge chairs or a sleekly designed pool. *Rooms from: $149 407 71st Ave. N, North End 843/449–5268, 800/762–3229 www.serendipityinn.com 15 rooms, 2 suites Breakfast.*

## SPORTS AND THE OUTDOORS

### BASEBALL

**Myrtle Beach Pelicans Baseball.** Catch a minor-league baseball game April–September with this proud Texas Rangers–affiliated team at TicketReturn.com Field. Look for specials and promos, like the "all-you-can-eat" seats and Thirsty Thursdays. Distractions include a super-size playground and inflatable rides for kids, and contests and entertainment between innings. A sandy beach section can be reserved for groups. *1251 21st Ave. N, Central Myrtle Beach 843/918–6000 www.myrtlebeachpelicans.com.*

Beach volleyball can be just as entertaining as a spectator sport.

### BEACHES

Regardless of whether you're staying on the beach, you shouldn't have too much trouble getting to a spot of sand. There are nearly 150 public-beach-access points in the city, all marked with signs. Most are located off Ocean Boulevard and have parking and "shower towers" for cleaning up; few have restroom facilities. Parking can be scarce, but in summer the city allows metered parallel parking on Ocean Boulevard.

Since much of Myrtle Beach's coastline is dominated by high-rise hotels, there are plenty of places to get lunch or a cool drink without having to get back in your car. Many of these hotels also rent beach chairs, umbrellas, and boogie boards. Some have nets set up for games of beach volleyball. ■ **TIP→** For a quieter beach experience, look for beach accesses away from the high-rise hotels. The Strand's residential section between 30th and 48th avenues north are good bets.

Dogs, kayaks, and surfboards are limited on many beaches from May through September. Be sure to read the ordinances posted at each access point for details. ⚠ Summer heat can be brutal and the sand can scorch: don't step out of the hotel barefoot.

★ **Garden City Beach.** In Horry County's southernmost coastal town of the same name, this diverse landscape of beachfront along the Atlantic is backed by a causeway that crosses creeks and tributaries feeding into marinas and the southern village of Murrells Inlet. The coastline is a curious collection of a few high-rise hotels, older condo buildings, and cute, stilted beach houses. Beachfront disappears at high tide farther south, so much so that it slaps up against the pilings and sea wall. The Garden City Pier is a must for fishing (free), strolling, playing arcade games, or dancing on the boards to live music at the fun, partially covered bar perched at the very end. Other beach activities include kayaking, Jet Skiing, kiteboarding, parasailing, ATV-ing, banana-boat rides, and boogie boarding. **Amenities:** food and drink, lifeguards (sometimes), parking, showers, water sports. **Best for:** solitude, surfing, swimming. ✉ *Atlantic Ave. and S. Waccamaw Dr., Garden City Beach.*

★ **Myrtle Beach.** The beachfront of the city of Myrtle Beach stretches from the Springmaid Pier at the south end up to 82nd Avenue North. That's a lot of real estate to choose from for your chair or blanket, especially since the 2007 beach renourishment project pumped more sand from the sea to the coastline, which is beneficial at high tide. Expect the entire length of this popular family beach to be busy from May to October with people fishing, boogie boarding, parasailing, surfing (only allowed after 5 pm), and sunbathing. In the off-season (November–February) you can take horseback rides on the beach. Restaurants and shops line the boardwalk section of 2nd to 14th avenues here. **Amenities:** food and drink, lifeguards (May–September; no lifeguards in residential section of 38th–48th avenues north), parking (free at north-end beach access areas; metered on street along Ocean Boulevard; pay daily or hourly at Pavilion Parking Garage at 8th Avenue North), showers, water sports. **Best for:** partiers, swimming. ✉ *32nd Ave. S to 82nd Ave. N, Central Myrtle Beach.*

## HELICOPTER RIDES

For a bird's-eye view of the beach, take to the sky in a helicopter to scoot along the coastline or explore more customized tours and mileage inland. The tours are great for aerial photo ops.

**Huffman Helicopters** ✉ *3000 S. Kings Highway, Myrtle Beach (U.S.-17-Business-side of Myrtle Beach Airport)* ☎ *843/946–0022* 🌐 *www.huffmanhelicopters.com.*

**Helicopter Adventures** ✉ *1860 21st Ave. North, Myrtle Beach (near Broadway at the Beach entrance)* ☎ *1-800/FLY-4-FUN* 🌐 *www.helicopteradventures.com.*



★ **Myrtle Beach State Park.** This state-protected parcel of land has a mile-long beach, camping facilities, picnic pavilions, nature hiking trails in the woods beyond the dunes, a fishing pier complete with an ice cream shop, playgrounds, and a quaint boardwalk. You could sign up for year-round family or children's activities offered through the park, like crabbing or learning more about turtles. Note that there are no lifeguards. **Amenities:** food and drink, parking (free with $4 admission to park), showers, toilets. **Best for:** solitude, swimming, walking. ✉ *4401 S. Kings Hwy., South Myrtle Beach.*

★ **Surfside Beach.** Dubbed "the Family Beach," this small strand just south of Myrtle Beach offers up about 2 miles of white sand. Here, the hotel high-rises, bright lights, and big city of Myrtle Beach disappear, replaced by beach houses, cottages, and peaceful views. The centerpiece Surfside Pier is the site of most of the town's festivals, a family-owned breakfast spot, and a kickin' karaoke bar. **Amenities:** food and drink, lifeguards (May–September), parking (lots with meters at 12 out of 36 beach access areas), showers, toilets. **Best for:** surfing, swimming. ✉ *17th Ave. N to Melody La., Surfside Beach.*

#### FISHING

The Gulf Stream makes for good fishing from early spring through December. Anglers can fish from 10 piers and jetties for amberjack, sea trout, and king mackerel. Surf-casters may snare bluefish, whiting, flounder, pompano, and channel bass. In the South Strand, salt marshes, inlets, and tidal creeks yield flounder, blues, croakers, spots, shrimp, clams, oysters, and blue crabs.

> **MYRTLE BEACH MARATHON**
>
> Ranked nationally as one of the top-10 winter marathons, the Myrtle Beach Marathon lures thousands of runners from across the country to Myrtle Beach each year around Valentine's Day weekend. Myrtle Beach has the right combination of a flat course, mild weather, and plenty to do at the beach, even in winter.

⚠ Swimmers, steer clear of the piers. Fishermen's bait is known to lure unwelcome sharks to the water as well.

**Grand Strand Fishing Rodeo.** Held each year, for more than 50 years, from April through October, the Grand Strand Fishing Rodeo holds a fish-of-the-month contest, with prizes for the largest catch of a designated species. There's no registration fee; entrants must take their catch to designated weigh stations for consideration. A $2,000 grand prize is handed out at the end. ☎ *800/356–3016.*

#### GOLF

Many of the Grand Strand's more than 100 courses are championship layouts; most are public.

⚠ Alligators have taken up residence in many of the Strand's golf courses. If you see one, don't investigate: they're faster than they look.

**Tee Time Central.** This service makes it easy to book tee times and special golf packages at nearly all the Strand's courses. ☎ *843/347–4653, 800/344–5590* 🌐 *www.ambassadorgolf.com.*

**Arrowhead Country Club.** Known for its top-notch condition regardless of the season, Arrowhead is the only Raymond Floyd–designed course in the region. Many of the scenic 27 holes, uniquely grouped into 9-hole themes, run along the intracoastal waterway. All greens are MiniVerde Bermudagrass, a grass species developed to tolerate high temperatures. Chomping at the bit? Arrowhead offers a free shuttle from the airport to its first tee. ✉ *1269 Burcale Rd., West Myrtle Beach* ☎ *800/236–3243* 🌐 *www.arrowheadcc.com* ✍ *Reservations essential* ⛳ *27 holes. 6180 yds. Par 72. Green Fee: $79/$69* ☞ *Facilities: Driving range, putting green, pitching area, golf carts, pro shop, golf academy/lessons for juniors, restaurant.*

**Indigo Creek Golf Club.** Beauty and bargains await at Indigo Creek, a course cut through forests of huge oaks and pines that once surrounded an indigo plantation. The Willard Byrd design often takes home national awards. ✉ *9480 Indigo Club Dr., Murrells Inlet* ☎ *843/650–1809, 800/718–1830* 🌐 *www.indigocreekgolfclub.com* ✍ *Reservations* *essential 18 holes. 6747 yds. Par 72. Green Fee: $72/$62 Facilities: Driving range, putting green, pitching area, pull carts, golf academy/lessons, restaurant, bar.*

**Pine Lakes Country Club.** Built in 1927 and listed on the National Register of Historic Places, Pine Lakes is reputed as the Grand Strand's "Granddaddy" of courses. The patriarch is carefully maintained and was redesigned in 2009, unveiling new holes near the new north-end entrance off Grissom Parkway. The course's classic Scottish theme is untouched, as are traditions like cups of clam chowder served on the 10th tee. New traditions have begun as well, with the establishment of the Myrtle Beach Golf Hall of Fame here in 2009, in the Hall of Fame Garden near the clubhouse, a glorious venue for weddings and holiday gatherings. *5603 Granddaddy Dr., Central Myrtle Beach 843/315–7700, 800/446–6817 www.pinelakes.com Reservations essential 18 holes. 6675 yds. Par 70. Green Fee: $125/$99 Facilities: Putting green, pitching area, golf carts, golf academy/lessons, restaurant, bar.*

**Resort Club at Grande Dunes.** This course has some of the widest and purportedly fairest fairways in Myrtle Beach, a veritable kingdom of golf, with majestic, national award–winning views of the tranquil waterway. *8700 Golf Village Lane, North End 888/886–8877, 843/315–0333 www.grandedunesgolf.com Reservations essential 18 holes. 7618 yds. Par 72. Green Fee: $149/$129 Facilities: Putting green, pitching area, golf carts, golf academy/lessons, restaurant, bar.*

6

**The Tournament Players Club Myrtle Beach.** Designed by the legendary Tom Fazio, this former home to the Senior PGA Tour Championship has also been solid training grounds for PGA Tour star and Myrtle Beach local Dustin Johnson. The scenery is both beautiful and challenging, with plenty of towering pines, wetlands, and water hazards. *1199 TPC Blvd., Murrells Inlet 843/357–3399, 888/742–8721 www.tpcmyrtlebeach.com Reservations essential 18 holes. 6950 yds. Par 72. Green Fee: $129/$112 Facilities: Driving range, putting green, pitching area, pull carts, golf academy/lessons, restaurant, bar.*

**The Witch.** Dan Maples–designed, this course is off the beaten Myrtle Beach path amid the pines along Route 544. True to its name, it can be quite bewitching throughout its 500-acre rolling layout over higher elevations and the lower wetlands connected by a mile of bridges. *1900 Hwy. 544, East Conway 843/347–2706 www.mysticalgolf.com Reservations essential 18 holes. 6796 yds. Par 71. Green Fee: $129/$112 Facilities: Driving range, putting green, golf carts, rental clubs, pro shop, golf academy/lessons.*

### SCUBA DIVING

You don't have to go far off the coast of the Grand Strand to explore the underwater world. Man-made reefs boast an array of fish including sea fans, sponges, reef fish, anemones, urchins, and crabs. A number of shipwrecks are also worth exploring under the waves. Paddle wheelers, freighters, and cargo ships lie in ruins off the coast, and are popular scuba spots. ■ **TIP→ Always wanted to dive but never learned how? Most dive shops can have you PADI-certified in a weekend.**

**Nu Horizons Dive and Travel.** Instruction and equipment rentals, as well as an indoor dive tank, are available in the Sports Corner shopping center from Nu Horizons Dive and Travel. ✉ *515 U.S. 501, Suite A, Central Myrtle Beach* ☎ *843/839–1932, 800/505–2080* 🌐 *www.southcarolinadive.com.*

### TENNIS

There are more than 200 courts on the Grand Strand. Facilities include hotel and resort courts, as well as free municipal courts in Myrtle Beach, North Myrtle Beach, and Surfside Beach. ■ **TIP→** Many tennis clubs offer weekly round-robin tournaments that are open to players of all levels.

**Grande Dunes Tennis.** Grande Dunes Tennis is a full fitness facility with 10 lighted Har-Tru courts; the club also offers lessons, clinics, camps, and match opportunities. ✉ *U.S. 17 Bypass at Grande Dunes Blvd., North End* ☎ *843/449–4486* 🌐 *www.grandedunes.com.*

**Prestwick Country Club.** Prestwick Country Club offers court time, instruction, and tournament opportunities; clay and hard courts are lighted for nighttime play. ✉ *1001 Links Rd., South End* ☎ *843/828–1000, 888/250–1767.*

### WATER SPORTS

Don't forget to bring your own towels and sunscreen when you head out.

**Downwind Sails.** Hobie Cats, personal watercraft, Jet Skis, ocean kayaks, and sailboats are available for rent at Downwind Sails, a trusted company here at the beach since 1981; they also have banana-boat rides (where you're towed in a long, yellow inflatable raft) and parasailing. ✉ *2915 S. Ocean Blvd., next to Damon's, South End* ☎ *843/448–7245* 🌐 *www.downwindsailsmyrtlebeach.com.*

**Ocean Watersports.** Ocean Watersports rents water-sports equipment. ✉ *3rd Ave. S and beach, between Family Kingdom amusement park and Westgate Resort, The Strip* ☎ *843/445–7777* 🌐 *www.parasailmyrtlebeach.com.*

**Village Surf Shoppe.** Learn how to ride the waves with a surfing lesson from the crew at Village Surf Shoppe, led by Kelly Richards and his son Cam. Richards even shapes his own Perfection Surfboards at the shop, while his national surf champion sons and staff take aspiring surfers out for camps and some hands-on action near the Garden City Pier. ✉ *500 Atlantic Ave., Garden City Beach* ☎ *843/651–6396* 🌐 *www.villagesurf.com.*

## NIGHTLIFE AND THE ARTS

### CLUBS AND LOUNGES

**2001 Entertainment Complex.** A triple threat, this entertainment venue has live beach-music bands, a mainstream club, and a live rock-blues-country music area called The Stage that was undergoing renovations at press. ✉ *920 Lake Arrowhead Rd., North End* ☎ *843/449–9434, 877/662–0016* 🌐 *www.2001nightclub.com.*

**Boathouse Waterway Bar & Grill.** If you're up for a rowdy night of entertainment (and a worthy basket of grub for dinner), grab a spot in the backyard at the Boathouse Waterway Bar & Grill during its annual

Summer Concert Series every Sunday, April–September. It's quite a sight, as fleets of boats anchor for a waterway view of the stage and the land-locked crowd packs the bank. ✉ *201 Fantasy Harbour Blvd., Fantasy Harbor* ☎ *843/903–2628* 🌐 *www.boathousemb.com.*

**Broadway at the Beach.** South Carolina's only Hard Rock Cafe, Jimmy Buffett's Margaritaville restaurant, daiquiri bar Fat Tuesday, dueling piano bar Crocodile Rocks, and karaoke haven Broadway Louie's are just a few of the hotspots at Broadway at the Beach, which also has shopping and recreational activities like an amusement park, WonderWorks interactive museum, speed boat rides on the lakes and a towering zip line over Lake Broadway. ✉ *U.S. 17 Bypass, between 21st and 29th Aves. N, Central Myrtle Beach* ☎ *843/444–3200* 🌐 *www.broadwayatthebeach.com.*

### FILM

**BigD . . . Ultimate Movie Experience.** Former site of IMAX 3D Theatre at Broadway at the Beach, BigD features large-format digital movies on a giant three-story-high screen, plus new luxury leather seating. ✉ *Broadway at the Beach, U.S. 17 Bypass between 21st and 29th Aves. N, Central Myrtle Beach* ☎ *843/445–1600* 🌐 *www.carmike.com.*

6

### MUSIC AND LIVE SHOWS

**Carolina Opry.** This family-oriented variety show features country, light rock, show tunes, and gospel, plus a new "Good Vibrations" show that pays tribute to the '60s, '70s and '80s. ✉ *8901A U.S. 17 Business N, North End* ☎ *800/843–6779* 🌐 *www.thecarolinaopry.com.*

**Comedy Cabana.** The hottest comedians on cable and on the road make their way to Comedy Cabana, a little comedy club on the north side of town. ✉ *9588 N. Kings Hwy., North End* ☎ *843/449–4242* 🌐 *www.comedycabana.com.*

**Legends in Concert.** Impersonators of Elvis, Garth Brooks, Michael Jackson, and the Blues Brothers, plus more current pop stars like Britney Spears and Lady Gaga play high-energy shows at this Broadway-at-the-Beach venue. ✉ *2925 Hollywood Drive, Central Myrtle Beach* ☎ *843/238–7827, 800/960–7469* 🌐 *www.legendsinconcert.com.*

**Medieval Times Dinner & Tournament.** Watch knights on horseback battle for their kingdom, followed by a real jousting tournament. ✉ *2904 Fantasy Way* ☎ *843/236–4635, 888/935–6878* 🌐 *www.medievaltimes.com.*

**Palace Theatre.** The elegant Palace Theatre hosts the acrobatic feats of Le Grande Cirque, as well as a full lineup of nationally touring acts and musicals. ✉ *Broadway at the Beach, U.S. 17 Bypass between 21st and 29th Aves. N, Central Myrtle Beach* ☎ *843/448–0588, 800/905–4228* 🌐 *www.palacetheatremyrtlebeach.com.*

**Pirates Voyage.** Dolly Parton transformed her indoor Dixie Stampede horse corral into a 15-foot-deep water lagoon staged with the Crimson and Sapphire pirate ships. Families will enjoy swashbuckling fights, acrobats and mermaids in flight, a five-course feast, and more. ✉ *8901B U.S. 17 Business N, North End* ☎ *843/497–9700, 800/433–4401* 🌐 *www.piratesvoyage.com.*

Jimmy Buffett's Margaritaville restaurant is one of the hot spots at Broadway at the Beach.

## SHOPPING

**Broadway at the Beach.** For recreational shopping, Broadway at the Beach has more than 100 shops selling everything from high-end apparel to Harley Davidson–themes gifts. ✉ *U.S. 17 Bypass between 21st and 29th Aves. N, Central Myrtle Beach* ☎ *800/386–4662, 843/444–3200* 🌐 *www.broadwayatthebeach.com.*

**Coastal Grand Mall.** The Myrtle Beach area's main indoor mall with department stores is also the second largest in the state. What's more, the blocks surrounding the mall contain a cool restaurant district, a movie theater, and tons of specialty shops. ✉ *2000 Coastal Grand Circle, Central Myrtle Beach* ☎ *843/839–9100* 🌐 *www.coastalgrand.com.*

**The Market Common.** Combining high-end shopping with upscale living and dining spaces, The Market Common features stores like Banana Republic, Anthropologie, and Tommy Bahama. A movie theater, playgrounds, bountiful year-round outdoor festivals, and a park with a man-made lake and bike path make it a day-trip destination. ✉ *4017 Deville St., off Farrow Pkwy., between U.S. 17 Business and U.S. 17 Bypass, South End* ☎ *843/839–3500* 🌐 *www.marketcommonmb.com.*

### DISCOUNT OUTLETS

**Tanger Factory Outlet Center.** This large outlet center has two locations in Myrtle Beach. Nike, Polo, Brooks Brothers, and J. Crew are some of the stores found at the location on U.S. 501. The North End location has 75 factory outlet stores, including Gap, Banana Republic, and Old Navy. ✉ *4635 Factory Stores Blvd., off U.S. 501, East Conway* ☎ *843/236–5100* ✉ *10785 Kings Rd., at U.S. 17, North End* ☎ *843/449–0491* 🌐 *www.tangeroutlet.com.*

## NORTH MYRTLE BEACH

*5 miles north of Myrtle Beach via U.S. 17.*

North Myrtle Beach, best known as the site where the shag, South Carolina's state dance, originated, is made up of the beach towns Cherry Grove, Crescent Beach, Windy Hill, and Ocean Drive. Entering North Myrtle Beach from the south on U.S. 17, you'll see Barefoot Landing, a huge shopping and entertainment complex that sits on the intracoastal waterway. As you make your way east toward the ocean, then north on Ocean Boulevard South, high-rises give way to small motels, then to single beach houses, many of which are available for rent. This end of the Strand marks the tip of a large peninsula, and there are lots of little islands, creeks, and marshes between the ocean and the intracoastal to explore by kayak or canoe. ■ **TIP→** Mosquitoes can be a problem on the marsh, especially in the early evening. Be sure to pack repellent.

#### GETTING HERE AND AROUND

North Myrtle Beach is an easy jaunt up U.S. 17 or Route 31 from Myrtle Beach (Route 22 or Main Street exits) or just south of Little River. Once inside the city limits, the numbered cross streets connect to Ocean Drive, the beachfront road.

6

#### ESSENTIALS

**Visitor Information North Myrtle Beach Chamber of Commerce Convention and Visitor's Bureau.** North Myrtle Beach Chamber of Commerce Convention and Visitor's Bureau ✉ *270 U.S. 17 N* ☎ *843/281–2662, 877/332–2662* 🌐 *www.northmyrtlebeachchamber.com* ⏲ *Weekdays 8:30 am–5:30 pm, weekends 10–4.*

### EXPLORING

★ **Alligator Adventure.** Interactive reptile shows, including an alligator-feeding demonstration, are the main attractions at this wildlife park. Boardwalks lead through marshes and swamps on the 15-acre property, where you'll see wildlife of the wetlands, including a pair of rare white albino alligators, the largest known crocodile in captivity, giant Galápagos tortoises, river otters, and all manner of reptiles, including boas, pythons, and anacondas. Unusual plants and exotic birds, as well as tigers, lemurs, bats and bobcats also thrive here. ✉ *U.S. 17 at Barefoot Landing* ☎ *843/361–0789* 🌐 *www.alligatoradventure.com* 🎫 *$18.99* ⏲ *Daily 9 am–11 pm.*

**Hawaiian Rumble.** The crown jewel of Myrtle Beach miniature golf, Hawaiian Rumble hosts the U.S. ProMiniGolf Association championship tournament and is best known for its smoking volcano, which rumbles and belches fire at timed intervals. ✉ *3210 33rd Ave. S, at U.S. 17* ☎ *843/272–7812* 🌐 *www.prominigolf.com* 🎫 *One round $9* ⏲ *Daily 9 am–midnight.*

### SPORTS AND THE OUTDOORS

#### BEACHES

★ **Cherry Grove Oceanfront Park.** In the quiet community of Cherry Grove, this small oceanfront park with pretty, budding landscaping has amenities for families, like a shaded gazebo, bench swings, and a ramp to the sand for strollers. **Amenities:** lifeguards, parking, showers, toilets. **Best**

**for:** swimming. ✉ *2108 N. Ocean Blvd., near 21st Ave. N.*

★ **North Myrtle Beach.** Choose from more than 240 access points to this beach, which is populated with fewer sunbathers than Myrtle Beach—especially farther south and north of Main Street's stretch of beachfront. Ocean Park, on the beach at 101 South Ocean Boulevard, is a nice setting, with a beachfront picnic shelter and its giant, 36-foot-tall inflatable waterslide, dubbed the Hippo, open in summer. **Amenities:** food and drink, lifeguards, parking (metered), showers, toilets. **Best for:** swimming. ✉ *Ocean Blvd. from 63rd Ave. N to 47th Ave. S.*

**RIP TIDES**

Occasional riptides, especially during hurricane season, are something to take seriously around here. Heed lifeguards' warnings about sticking to shallow water.

### FISHING

**Cherry Grove Fishing Pier.** A two-story observation deck and a 985-foot reach into the ocean makes this the place to catch pompano, bluefish, and mackerel. You can rent tackle and buy bait at the pier. Early morning and late afternoon are the best time to catch fish. ✉ *3500 N. Ocean Blvd.* ☎ *843/249–1625* 🌐 *www.cherrygrovepier.com.*

**Little River Fishing Fleet.** The fleet offers half- and full-day excursions, including night fishing. ✉ *1901 U.S. 17* ☎ *843/361–3323, 800/249–9388* 🌐 *www.littleriverfleet.com.*

### GOLF

**Barefoot Resort and Golf.** The four 18-hole championship courses at Barefoot were designed by Tom Fazio, Davis Love III, Pete Dye, and Greg Norman with all skill levels in mind. Notable details include a replica of plantation ruins on the Love course and only 60 acres of mowable grass among the natural vegetation on the Norman course. The Dye course is the chosen site of the annual Monday After the Masters celebrity tournament, hosted by Hootie and the Blowfish. ✉ *4980 Barefoot Resort Bridge* ☎ *843/390–3200, 866/638–4818* 🌐 *www.barefootgolf.com* ✍ *Reservations essential* 🏌 *72 holes. Dye: 7343 yds. Par 71. Fazio: 6834 yds. Par 71. Love: 7000 yds. Par 72. Norman: 7200 yds. Par 72. Green Fee: $140/$125* ☞ *Facilities: Driving range, putting green, pitching area, golf carts, pull carts, golf academy/lessons, restaurants, bar.*

**Tidewater Golf Club and Plantation.** Designed by Ken Tomlinson, the magnificent Tidewater peninsula is one of only two courses in the area with an ocean view; the marshes and waterway border other well-crafted parts of the course. The challenging fairways and high bluffs are reminiscent of Pebble Beach. ✉ *1400 Tidewater Dr.* ☎ *843/913–2424, 800/446–5363* 🌐 *www.tidewatergolf.com* ✍ *Reservations essential* 🏌 *18 holes. 7044 yds. Par 72. Green Fee: $94/$112* ☞ *Facilities: Driving range, putting green, pitching area, golf carts, golf academy/lessons, bar.*

### WATER SPORTS

**Coastal Scuba.** Learn to scuba dive, take a dive trip, or just rent equipment at Coastal Scuba, which is PADI-certified. It also has a ropes course and a tiki bar. ✉ *1901 U.S. 17 S* ☎ *843/361–3323, 800/249–9388* 🌐 *www.coastalscuba.com.*

**Myrtle Beach Water Sports, Inc.** You can rent your own pontoon boats or Jet Skis at Myrtle Beach Water Sports, Inc., or try parasailing or a ride on *Sea Screamer,* touted, at 72 feet, as the world's largest speedboat. ✉ *4495 Mineola Ave., on the docks, Little River* ☎ *843/280–7777* 🌐 *www.myrtlebeachwatersports.com.*

## WHERE TO EAT

$$$ ECLECTIC ★ ✕ **Greg Norman's Australian Grille.** Overlooking the Intracoastal Waterway, this large restaurant in Barefoot Landing has leather booths, Australian aboriginal art on the walls, an extensive wine list, an outdoor patio with a fire pit, and a classy bar, the Shark Pub. The menu features grilled meats and seafood, and many of the selections have an Asian flair. The Australian rock lobster is a highlight, but the Australian theme comes through more strongly in the decor and the Greg Norman merchandise for sale than in the food. 💲 *Average main: $22* ✉ *4930 U.S. 17 S* ☎ *843/361–0000* 🌐 *www.gregnormansaustraliangrille.com* ✍ *Reservations essential.*

$$$ AMERICAN ★ ✕ **Parson's Table.** It's a heavenly experience at this Little River staple housed in an old country church that dates back to 1885. Stained glass windows add to the charm; renowned chef/owner Ed Murray brings the finest in food to the table. You'll be praying for more after you try Murray's marvel of meats, like prime rib and braised short ribs. 💲 *Average main: $22* ✉ *4305 McCorsley Ave., Little River* ☎ *843/249–3702* 🌐 *www.parsonstable.com* ✍ *Reservations essential.*

$$$ SEAFOOD ✕ **Rockefellers Raw Bar.** Yes it's a raw bar—and a good one, with a bounty of fresh seafood—but don't sell the cooked items short at this small, casual locals' joint. The oysters Rockefeller, with a splash of Pernod and fresh spinach, are the real deal, and the iron pot of steamed mussels, clams, scallops, and other goodies is a terrific version of a Lowcountry staple. 💲 *Average main: $20* ✉ *3613 U.S. 17 S* ☎ *843/361–9677* ✍ *Reservations not accepted.*

$$$$ AMERICAN ✕ **Sea Blue.** Don't let the strip-mall location put you off; the restaurant's cuisine stands out. Blue mood lighting, a glowing aquarium, and abstract art combine to give this restaurant more of a Miami Beach than Myrtle Beach feel. The VIP vibe begs a cocktail; try the pomegranate martini, which is a touch tart. The extensive wine list includes flights and wines by the glass. Dine on dishes like Kobe beef sliders or duck with fresh berries and organic greens. The swanky blue-tiled bar hops on Friday nights, often to the beat of a live band. There is also a patio for outdoor seating, albeit facing a parking lot. 💲 *Average main: $25* ✉ *501 Hwy. 17 N* ☎ *843/249–8800* 🌐 *www.seablueonline.com* 🕒 *No lunch.*

CLOSE UP

## The Shag Dance

Contrary to views on the other side of the pond, "shag" isn't dirty word in North Myrtle Beach; it's a dance that has defined the area since the first pitter-patter-shuffle of footwork on Ocean Drive in the 1940s. A slower-paced sister of the swing, the shag is still celebrated today nightly in a number of clubs, biannually with the Society of Stranders citywide festivals in April and September, and annually with the National Shag Dance Championships held in North Myrtle Beach in March.

**Duck's Beach Club.** You can dance the shag and take lessons from the pros at Duck's Beach Club. The club often hosts shag events throughout the year for dedicated and novice dancers. ✉ *229 Main St.* ☎ *843/249–3858* 🌐 *www.ducksatoceandrive.com.*

**Fat Harold's Beach Club.** Fat Harold's Beach Club is a hip-movin' shag spot and is constantly hosting shag contests. ✉ *212 Main St.* ☎ *843/249–5779* 🌐 *www.fatharolds.com.*

**OD Arcade & Lounge.** This small club is big on the moves. ✉ *100 S. Ocean Blvd.* ☎ *843/249–6460* 🌐 *www.shagtour.com.*

**Pirate's Cove.** Pirate's Cove always has a crowded dance floor. ✉ *205 Main St.* ☎ *843/249–1047* 🌐 *www.piratescovelounge.com.*

**Shagger's Hall of Fame.** There's even a Shagger's Hall of Fame within the Ocean Drive Beach & Golf Resort. ✉ *98 N. Ocean Blvd.* ☎ *800/438–9590.*

**The Spanish Galleon Beach Club.** Live bands are on regular rotation at The Spanish Galleon Beach Club. ✉ *Ocean Drive Beach & Golf Resort, 98 N. Ocean Blvd.* ☎ *843/249–1436* 🌐 *www.spanishgalleonbeachclub.com.*

### WHERE TO STAY

*Hotel reviews have been abbreviated in this book. For expanded reviews, please go to Fodors.com.*

$$ HOTEL **Best Western Ocean Sands Resort.** One of the few fairly small, family-owned properties left in North Myrtle Beach, the Ocean Sands has a beachfront tiki bar and rooms that were remodeled in 2008. **Pros:** friendly, available staff; Continental breakfast included. **Cons:** annex building is down the street away from the central hotel. *Rooms from: $140* ✉ *1525 S. Ocean Blvd.* ☎ *843/272–6101, 800/588–3570* 🌐 *www.oceansands.com* *116 suites* *Breakfast.*

$$$ RESORT **Myrtle Beach Barefoot Resort.** This luxury golf resort includes more than 160 one- to four-bedroom condominium units along fairways as well as in the 62-unit, 14-story North Tower, which overlooks the Intracoastal Waterway. **Pros:** pretty views of the Intracoastal Waterway surround the resort; Barefoot Landing shopping and entertainment center is just across the inlet. **Cons:** getting to the beach and the ocean requires driving across a busy highway. *Rooms from: $200* ✉ *4898 U.S. 17 S* ☎ *800/548–9904, 843/692–2299* 🌐 *www.myrtlebeachbarefootresort.com* *322 condos.*

$$$$ RESORT **North Beach Plantation.** Built in 2009, the Plantation's towering design rises above White Point Swash and turns heads everywhere along the

coast. **Pros:** sky-high surroundings make you feel like royalty; Cinzia Spa and fitness center are incomparable on the Grand Strand. **Cons:** spa and fitness center are not in the towers, but are approximately ½ mile from the entrance. $ *Rooms from: $250* ✉ *719 N. Beach Blvd., North Myrtle Beach* ☎ *800/615–3598* 🌐 *www.northbeachrentals.com* *300 condos.*

### LITTLE RIVER WATERFRONT

The quiet fishing village of Little River throws a bounty of big Southern-style parties throughout the year, including the well-known Shrimp & Jazz Festival held in October, usually on Columbus Day weekend. Live jazz music and a shrimp cook-off proves to be a delicious combination.

## NIGHTLIFE AND THE ARTS

### CLUBS AND LOUNGES

**Dick's Last Resort.** Sassy and saucy, but with live music that ranges from R&B to classic rock to beach favorites, Dick's Last Resort is big and loud, and the beer is cold. ✉ *Barefoot Landing, 4700 U.S. 17 S* ☎ *843/272–7794.*

### MUSIC AND LIVE SHOWS

Live acts, and country-and-western shows in particular, are a big draw on the Grand Strand. Music lovers have many family-oriented shows to choose from.

**Alabama Theatre.** The 2,250-seat Alabama Theatre has a regular variety show with a wonderful patriotic closing; the theater also hosts guest music and comedy artists during the year. ✉ *Barefoot Landing, 4750 U.S. 17 S* ☎ *843/272–1111* 🌐 *www.alabama-theatre.com.*

**House of Blues.** Big names and up-and-coming talent in blues, rock, jazz, country, and R&B headline at The House of Blues in its 2,000-seat concert hall and on stages in its Southern-style restaurant and patio. The gospel brunch is a great deal. ✉ *Barefoot Landing, 4640 U.S. 17 S* ☎ *843/272–3000 for tickets* 🌐 *www.houseofblues.com.*

## SHOPPING

### MALLS

**Barefoot Landing.** This mall has more than 100 specialty shops, along with numerous entertainment activities, including children's amusement rides. In summer, check out fireworks displays here every Monday night. ✉ *4898 U.S. 17 S* ☎ *843/272–8349.*

**Myrtle Beach Mall.** The indoor Myrtle Beach Mall, formerly Colonial Mall, sits in the Briarcliffe section just north of Tanger Outlets and just south of Barefoot Landing, offering department store and boutique standards, as well as the monstrous Bass Pro Shops, a movie theater, and an improv comedy club. ✉ *10177 N. Kings Hwy.* ☎ *843/272–4040* 🌐 *www.mymallmyrtlebeach.com.*

### SPECIALTY STORES

**Judy's House of Oldies.** Beach-music lovers have been finding their long-lost favorites at Judy's House of Oldies for years. Find classics on cassette and CD at this small but packed-to-the-gills music emporium. ✉ *300 Main St.* ☎ *843/249–8649* 🌐 *www.judyshouseofoldies.com.*

# THE SOUTHERN GRAND STRAND

Unlike the more developed area to the north, the southern end of the Grand Strand—Murrells Inlet, Litchfield, Pawleys Island, and Georgetown—has a barefoot, laid-back vibe that suits its small restaurants, shops, galleries, outdoor outfitters, and natural beauty. Locals pride themselves on their "shabby chic" mentality.

## MURRELLS INLET

*15 miles south of Myrtle Beach via U.S. 17.*

Murrells Inlet, a fishing village with some popular seafood restaurants, is a perfect place to rent a fishing boat or join an excursion. A notable garden and state park provide other diversions from the beach. Though there are a few chain hotels, they aren't anywhere near the water. The village makes a fine day trip, unless you've rented a waterfront cottage.

#### GETTING HERE AND AROUND

Driving south on U.S. 17 takes you through Murrells Inlet. If you stay on U.S. 17 Bypass, though, you'll miss some of the town's character. Try taking U.S. 17 Business to get a taste of the real Murrells Inlet. Most cross streets connect to the bypass if you get turned around.

#### ESSENTIALS

**Visitor Information Myrtle Beach Area Chamber of Commerce and Information Center** ✉ *3401 U.S. 17 Business S* ☎ *843/651–1010, 800/356–3016* 🌐 *www.visitmyrtlebeach.com* 🕓 *Apr.–Labor Day, weekdays 8:30–5, Sat. 10–5, Sun. noon–5; early Sept.–Mar., weekdays 8:30–5, Sat. 10–1.*

### EXPLORING

Fodor's Choice ★ **Brookgreen Gardens.** One of the Grand Strand's most magnificent hidden treasures, Brookgreen Gardens is the oldest and largest sculpture garden in the United States, with more than 550 examples of figurative American sculpture by such artists as Frederic Remington and Daniel Chester French. Each sculpture is carefully set within garden rooms and outdoor galleries graced by sprawling live oak trees, colorful flowers, and peaceful ponds. The gardens are lush and full in spring and summer, and in winter splashes of color from winter-blooming shrubs are set off against the stark surroundings.

The 9,000-acre property was purchased as a winter home for industrialist Archer Huntington and his wife Anna Hyatt Huntington in 1929, but they quickly decided to open it to the public as a sculpture garden and wildlife sanctuary. Today their legacy endures in this center for not only American art, but Lowcountry culture and nature preservation. You'll find a wildlife park, an aviary, a cypress swamp, nature trails, an education center, and a butterfly house. Several tours, including a boat tour of tidal creeks and a jeep excursion into the preserve, leave from Brookgreen. Summer concerts under the stars and the garden's breathtaking Night of a Thousand Candles during Christmas season are Brookgreen traditions. The gardens are just beyond *The Fighting Stallions*, the Anna Hyatt Huntington sculpture alongside U.S. 17. ✉ *West of U.S. 17, 3 miles south of Murrells Inlet* ☎ *843/235–6000,*

800/849–1931 www.brookgreen.org $14, good for 7 days June–Sept., Wed.–Fri. 9:30–9, Sat.–Tues. 9:30–5; Oct.–May, daily 9:30–5.*

**Huntington Beach State Park.** This 2,500-acre former estate of Archer and Anna Huntington lies east of U.S. 17, across from Brookgreen Gardens. The park's focal point is **Atalaya** (circa 1933), their Moorish-style 30-room home. There are nature trails, ample areas for biking, fishing, an education center with aquariums and a loggerhead sea turtle–nesting habitat, picnic areas, bird-watching expeditions, a playground, concessions, and a campground. *East of U.S. 17, 3 miles south of Murrells Inlet 843/237–4440 www.huntingtonbeachsc.org $5 Daily 6 am–10 pm.*

## WHERE TO EAT

$$$ SEAFOOD **The Crab Cake Lady.** A weathered yellow shack with a hand-lettered sign heralds this unassuming spot in Murrells Inlet. While you can't sit down and eat, you can order the famous creations of An, known as the Crab Cake Lady, who fishes daily for crab to go into her handmade cakes. Creek Rolls, a twist on the classic egg roll, feature baby shrimp caught daily in the inlet. *Average main: $20 4368 Highway 17 843/651–5707 www.thecrabcakelady.com Closed Sun.*

$$$ SEAFOOD ★ **Divine Fish House.** Whether you choose to sit inside the contemporary confines of this casual, fine-dining waterfront restaurant or outside at the tropical-tiki Wahoo's Raw Bar, you can't go wrong with atmosphere or exquisite food, from sushi to seafood entrées. The menu whispers of international influences to its Lowcountry cuisine in dishes like pesto sea bass and Asian barbecued pork ribs. *Average main: $22 3993 U.S. 17 Business 843/651–5800 www.divinefishhouse.com Reservations essential No lunch.*

$$$$ SEAFOOD **Lee's Inlet Kitchen.** They're closed at lunchtime, on Sunday, and in winter; they don't take reservations or have a view, but nobody fries up a mess of seafood like Lee's, which is something they've been doing since 1948. Even the biggest eaters will get their fill when they order the Shore Dinner: fried or broiled flounder, shrimp, oysters, scallops, deviled crab, and lobster, along with a shrimp cocktail, clam chowder, hush puppies, fries, and coleslaw. Sure, you can get your fish broiled or grilled, but why mess with deep-fried perfection? *Average main: $25 4660 U.S. 17 Business 843/651–2881 www.leesinletkitchen.com Reservations not accepted Closed Sun., Dec., and Jan. No lunch.*

$$$ SEAFOOD ★ **Nance's Creekfront Restaurant.** You can smell the brine and Old Bay seasoning the minute you leave your car and head toward the front door of Nance's. Atmosphere is somewhat lacking, but that's okay—so is any inkling of pretension. Oysters, the small local ones that taste of saltwater and seaweed, are the specialty, available raw or steamed in an iron pot and served with butter. There are other selections on the menu, but it's really all about the oysters—and the 10-layer chocolate cake, made specially for Nance's by a local baker. *Average main: $20 4883 U.S. 17 Business 843/651–2696 www.nancescreekfrontrestaurant.com Reservations not accepted No lunch.*

$ AMERICAN **Prosser's Bar-B-Que.** This ain't your four-star fine-dining eatery, and it's practically a requirement to lick your fingers clean. Most times, the line for Prosser's lunch buffet will weave outside the clapboard house after church on Sunday. Lip-smacking pulled pork is served along with Lowcountry goodies like collard greens, mashed potatoes, fried chicken, macaroni and cheese, banana pudding, and peach cobbler. And the price will have you coming back for more. *Average main: $12 3750 U.S. 17 Business 843/357–6146 Reservations not accepted.*

$$ AMERICAN **Salt Water Creek.** It may not have that typical inlet view, but this café certainly isn't typical, set under a giant live oak tree along the bypass and beyond a lovely brick patio. Cool, coastal inspirations are cleverly combined with comforting Southern hospitality. On the menu, fresh-rolled sushi and blackened shrimp Alfredo meshes with musts like the turkey and stuffing sandwich and, for brunch (10–2 on weekends), the stuffed lobster omelet. *Average main: $18 4660 U.S. 17 Bypass 843/357–2433 www.saltwatercreekcafe.com.*

## NIGHTLIFE

**Murrells Inlet Marshwalk.** You can have a drink, watch boats come back from a day of fishing, hear a blend of live music, and enjoy the evening breeze with a stroll along the Murrells Inlet Marshwalk, a picturesque boardwalk that connects eight waterfront bars and restaurants, from Drunken Jack's on the north end to Spud's at the Crazy Sister Marina

While stunning year-round, Brookgreen Gardens kicks it up a notch during the Nights of a Thousand Candles in December.

on the south end. On the Fourth of July, the Marshwalk serves as your front-row seat to the wildly popular Boat Parade. Also included along the way are colorful waterfront stops with fanciful names like Dead Dog Saloon, Creek Ratz, Bubba's Love Shak, and Wahoo's. 🌐 *www.marshwalk.com*.

**Hot Fish Club.** This happening spot has a great view. ✉ *4911 U.S. 17 Business* ☎ *843/357–9175*.

### SPORTS AND THE OUTDOORS

**Capt. Dick's.** Capt. Dick's runs half- and full-day fishing and sightseeing trips. You can also rent boats and kayaks and go parasailing. The evening ghost-story cruise is scary fun. ✉ *4123 U.S. 17 Business* ☎ *843/651–3676* 🌐 *www.captdicks.com*.

## PAWLEYS ISLAND

*10 miles south of Murrells Inlet via U.S. 17.*

About 4 miles long and a half mile wide, Pawleys, sometimes referred to as "arrogantly shabby," began as a resort before the Civil War, when wealthy planters and their families summered here. It's mostly made up of weathered old summer cottages nestled in groves of oleander and oak trees. You can watch the famous Pawleys Island hammocks being made and bicycle around admiring the beach houses, many dating to the early 1800s. Golf and tennis are nearby. **■TIP→** **Parking is limited on Pawleys and facilities are nil, so arrive early and bring what you need.**

### GETTING HERE AND AROUND

Pawleys Island is located south of Murrells Inlet on U.S. 17. Take North Causeway Drive off the main highway to experience the natural beauty of the island. A 2-mile-long historic district is home to rustic beach cottages, historic buildings, and even a church.

### WHERE TO EAT

$$$ AMERICAN ★ **Frank's.** This local favorite serves dishes that give traditional cooking methods and ingredients a new twist. The former 1930s grocery store has transformed into fine dining, with wood floors, framed French posters, and cozy fireside seating. Diners indulge in large portions of fish, seafood, beef, and lamb cooked over an oak-burning grill. The local grouper with mustard-bacon butter, served with a side of stone-ground grits, is a star. Behind Frank's is the casual (but still pricey) Outback, a lush candlelit garden with a huge stone fireplace. Enjoy a before- or after-dinner drink at Outback's bar. Heaters will keep you warm in winter. *Average main: $22 10434 U.S. 17 843/237–3030 Closed Sun. No lunch.*

$ MEXICAN **Habaneros.** The fish tacos here are to die for, but the full menu of Mexican favorites at this colorful cantina proves that Pawleys Island is not just about seafood. Take a seat inside or on the festive deck, which is the place to be on Cinco de Mayo, and order a burrito with secret sauce and a margarita each for under $3. *Average main: $10 11151 Ocean Hwy. 866/679–2514 www.habanerospi.com.*

$ BARBECUE ★ **Hog Heaven BBQ and Raw Bar.** Part barbecue joint, part raw bar (after 5), Hog Heaven has a wonderful smoky aroma that perfumes U.S. 17 for miles. Pulled-pork barbecue has the tang of vinegar and the taste of long hours in the pit. Although sandwiches are available, the buffet, which includes fried chicken, greens, and sweet-potato casserole, is the main event. In the evening try the seafood tray, an assortment of shellfish steamed to order and served piping hot. *Average main: $10 7147 Ocean Hwy. 843/237–7444 www.hogheaveninc.com Reservations not accepted.*

$ CAFÉ **Landolfi's.** This fourth-generation-owned Italian pastry shop, deli, and restaurant has excellent coffee, hearty hoagies, pizzas, homemade sorbet, and delicious and authentic pastries, including cannoli and *pasticciotti* (a rich cookielike pastry filled with jam). Both counter and table service is available. It's open until 5 Tuesday and Wednesday and until 9 Thursday through Saturday. *Average main: $10 9305 Ocean Hwy. 843/237–7900 Closed Sun. and Mon.*

### WHERE TO STAY

*Hotel reviews have been abbreviated in this book. For expanded reviews, please go to Fodors.com.*

$$ HOTEL **Hampton Inn Pawleys Island/Litchfield.** Ongoing upgrades keep this hotel in tip-top condition. **Pros:** cute turtles populate a pond outside and beg for treats; look for the remodeled lobby and breakfast dining area. Continental breakfast included. **Cons:** the beach isn't close by. *Rooms from: $175 150 Willbrook Blvd. 843/235–2000 www.pawleysislandhamptoninn.com 66 rooms Breakfast.*

$$ RESORT Fodor's Choice ★ **Litchfield Beach & Golf Resort.** This beautifully landscaped 4,500-acre resort runs along both sides of U.S. 17. **Pros:** geared to all kinds of traveler; beautiful natural surroundings; modern amenities. **Cons:** some properties are as much as a 15-minute walk to the beach. *Rooms from: $200 ✉ 14276 Ocean Hwy. ☎ 843/237–3000, 888/766–4633 🌐 www.litchfieldbeach.com 140 rooms; 216 suites; 200 condominiums, cottages, and villas.*

$$$ B&B/INN Fodor's Choice ★ **Litchfield Plantation.** From the regal live oak-lined driveway to the Pawleys Island hammock placed by the river, you know you've arrived in the Old South. **Pros:** historic property; beautiful grounds; shared cottages are good for groups; beach house is a huge bonus. **Cons:** rugs and furniture a little worn; loud chorus of frogs at night; box TVs are an eyesore; no Wi-Fi in the rooms. *Rooms from: $225 ✉ 300 Avenue of Live Oaks or 4 Avenue of the Oaks ☎ 843/237–9121, 800/869–1410 🌐 www.litchfieldplantation.com 19 rooms, 2 suites, 7 two- and three-bedroom cottages Breakfast.*

$$ B&B/INN **Sea View Inn.** A "barefoot paradise," Sea View is a no-frills beachside boardinghouse (there are no TVs or in-room phones) with long porches. **Pros:** live oak trees and a nearby nature preserve keep you insulated from resort hustle and bustle. **Cons:** not wheelchair-accessible; only 6 of the 15 rooms have air-conditioning; some showers are outside the room. *Rooms from: $175 ✉ 414 Myrtle Ave. ☎ 843/237–4253 🌐 www.seaviewinn.com 15 rooms, 1 cottage No credit cards Closed Dec.–Mar. All meals.*

6

## THE ARTS

**Pawleys Island Festival of Music & Art.** Pawleys Island comes alive each September and early October during the Pawleys Island Festival of Music & Art, which brings national and local artists together for a month of concerts, exhibitions, and readings. Past performers have included David Sanborn and Delbert McClinton. *☎ 843/626–8911 🌐 www.pawleysmusic.com.*

## SPORTS AND THE OUTDOORS

### BEACHES

★ **Litchfield Beach/Pawleys Island.** Three miles of tranquil and natural beach runs along the shoreline just north of Pawleys Island. The surrounding architecture consists only of beach cottages and low-lying resorts, so it's a peaceful retreat. Lack of crowds allows for bicycling on packed sand, shelling, or napping on a hammock. Note that there aren't any lifeguards. **Amenities:** parking (limited, on side streets). **Best for:** solitude, sunrises, swimming. *✉ 16148 Ocean Hwy.*

### GOLF

**Caledonia Golf & Fish Club.** Designed by Mike Strantz, this course on a former Southern rice plantation is a stunning Lowcountry beauty, from its entrance avenue of live oaks, continuing around pretty streams, and ending with an 18th hole that borders the old rice field. *✉ 369 Caledonia Dr. ☎ 843/237–3675 🌐 www.fishclub.com Reservations essential 18 holes. 6526 yds. Par 70. Green Fee: $165/$160 Facilities: Driving range, putting green, pitching area, golf carts, pull carts, gold academy/lessons, restaurant, bar.*

**Pawleys Plantation Golf & Country Club.** This Jack Nicklaus–designed course demands respect from golfers for its several tricky holes surrounded by saltwater marshes. Off the course, many reserve the posh clubhouse and patio for four-course wedding receptions, with the 18th as a backdrop. ✉ *70 Tanglewood Dr.* ☎ *843/237–6100, 800/367–9959* 🌐 *www.pawleysplantation.com* ✍ *Reservations essential* 🏌 *18 holes. 7026 yds. Par 72. Green Fee: $76/$64* ☞ *Facilities: Driving range, putting green, pitching area, golf carts, pull carts, golf academy/lessons, restaurant, bar.*

**Tradition Golf Club.** Rated as one of the best-maintained courses on the Grand Strand, this Ron Garl–designed beauty is also affordable. ✉ *1027 Willbrook Blvd.* ☎ *877/599–0888* 🌐 *www.traditiongolfclub.com* ✍ *Reservations essential* 🏌 *18 holes. 6313 yds. Par 72. Green Fee: $80/$60* ☞ *Facilities: Driving range, putting green, pitching area, golf carts, pull carts, golf academy/lessons, restaurant, bar.*

**Willbrook Plantation.** Dan Maples designed this course with nature in mind, on two former rice plantations that now wind past historical markers, a slave cemetery, and a tobacco shack. Polls have ranked Willbrook high on the list with women, in particular, for its Southern hospitality and leafy surrounds. ✉ *379 Country Club Dr.* ☎ *843/237–4900* 🌐 *www.mbn.com* ✍ *Reservations essential* 🏌 *18 holes. 6704 yds. Par 72. Green Fee: $90/$76* ☞ *Facilities: Driving range, putting green, pitching area, golf carts, pull carts, golf academy/lessons, restaurant, bar.*

#### TENNIS

**Litchfield Country Club.** You can get court time, rental equipment, and instruction at Litchfield Country Club. ✉ *U.S. 17 S* ☎ *843/235–4653.*

### SHOPPING

**Hammock Shops Village.** This outdoor complex of two dozen boutiques, gift shops, and restaurants was built with old beams, timber, and ballast brick under the canopy of live oaks. Outside the Original Hammock Shop, in the Hammock Weavers' Pavilion, craftspeople demonstrate the 19th-century art of weaving the famous cotton-rope Pawleys Island hammocks. Also look for jewelry, toys, antiques, and designer fashions. ✉ *10880 Ocean Hwy.* ☎ *843/237–9122* 🌐 *www.thehammockshops.com.*

**Litchfield Books.** This independent bookstore is the place to pick up a beach read or regional-interest book. And it's also the home base for authors who want to return home after making it on the bestsellers'

#### PAWLEYS ISLAND HAMMOCK

Created in 1889 by a riverboat captain tired of sleeping on his grain-filled mattress, the original Pawleys Island rope hammock is handcrafted in Pawleys Island exactly as it was by Captain Ward. More than 1,000 feet of rope are knitted by hand, pulled between oak stretcher bars, and tied with bowline knots to the body. In the 1930s Captain Ward's brother-in-law began selling the hammocks at a general store called the Hammock Shop. Still standing at the same location on U.S. Highway 17, the shop's weaving room is open to visitors most Saturdays.

list during the store's Moveable Feast series. ✉ *14427 Ocean Hwy., Litchfield Landing* ☎ *843/237–8138* 🌐 *litchfieldbooks.com.*

## GEORGETOWN

*13 miles south of Pawleys Island via U.S. 17.*

Founded on Winyah Bay in 1729, Georgetown became the center of America's colonial rice empire. A rich plantation culture developed on a scale comparable to Charleston's, and the historic district is among the prettiest in the state. Today oceangoing vessels still come to Georgetown's busy port, and the **Harborwalk,** the restored waterfront, hums with activity. ■ **TIP→ Many of the restaurants along the riverside of Front Street have back decks overlooking the water that come alive in the early evening for happy hour.**

### GETTING HERE AND AROUND

Georgetown is accessible from U.S. 17, as well as Route 701. The heart of the town is located near the waterfront—an easy trip off the highway down any side street is worth it. Take Cannon Street to Front Street to see the harbor.

### ESSENTIALS

**Visitor Information Georgetown County Chamber of Commerce.** ✉ *531 Front St.* ☎ *843/546–8436, 800/777–7705* 🌐 *www.visitgeorge.com.*

6

## EXPLORING

### TOP ATTRACTIONS

**Hobcaw Barony Visitors Center.** Discover this historic landmark at the entrance of Hobcaw Barony, on the vast estate of the late Wall Street financier Bernard M. Baruch. Franklin D. Roosevelt and Winston Churchill came here to confer with him. A small interpretive center has exhibits on coastal ecology and history, with special emphasis on the Baruch family. There are aquariums, touch tanks, and video presentations, and guided three-hour tours of the 17,500-acre wildlife refuge take place Tuesday, Wednesday, and Friday mornings and Thursday afternoon. ✉ *22 Hobcaw Rd., off U.S. 17, 2 miles north of Georgetown* ☎ *843/546–4623* 🌐 *www.hobcawbarony.org* 🎫 *Visitors center free, tours $20* ⏲ *Weekdays 10–5; reservations necessary for tour.*

**Kaminski House Museum.** Overlooking the Sampit River from a bluff is this sprawling historic town house (circa 1769) that's notable for its collections of regional antiques and furnishings, its Chippendale and Duncan Phyfe furniture, Royal Doulton vases, and silver. Events at the Kaminski House include summer outdoor concerts on the lawn. ✉ *1003 Front St.* ☎ *843/546–7706* 🌐 *www.kaminskihousemuseum.org* 🎫 *$7* ⏲ *Mon.–Sat. 10–4, Sun. 1–4.*

**Rice Museum.** A graceful market and meeting building in the heart of Georgetown, topped by an 1842 clock and tower, has been converted into a most unique museum, with maps, tools, and dioramas that outline the history of rice in Georgetown. At the museum's Prevost Gallery next door is the Brown's Ferry river freighter, the oldest American-built water-going vessel in existence. The museum gift shop has local pine needle baskets, African dolls, and art (including baskets made from

Learn about the fascinating history of rice cultivation in Georgetown at the Rice Museum.

whole cloves), as well as South Carolina rice and honey. ✉ *633 Front St.* ☎ *843/546–7423* 🌐 *www.ricemuseum.org* 🎟 *$7* 🕓 *Mon.–Sat. 10–4:30.*

### WORTH NOTING

**Hampton Plantation State Historic Site.** The home of Archibald Rutledge, poet laureate of South Carolina for 39 years until his death in 1973, this 18th-century plantation house is a fine example of a Lowcountry mansion. The exterior has been restored; cutaway sections in the finely crafted interior show the changes made through the centuries. The grounds are landscaped, and there are picnic areas. ✉ *1950 Rutledge Rd., McClellanville* ☎ *843/546–9361* 🌐 *www.southcarolinaparks.com* 🎟 *Mansion $7.50, grounds free* 🕓 *Grounds Nov.–Mar. 9–5, Apr.–Oct. 9–6. Mansion tours Sat.–Tues. at 1, 2, and 3.*

**Hopsewee Plantation.** If you're up to a drive south of Georgetown, make a trip to this amazing plantation overlooking the North Santee River and surrounded by moss-draped live oaks, magnolias, and tree-size camellias. The circa-1740 mansion has a fine Georgian staircase and hand-carved lighted-candle moldings. ✉ *494 Hopsewee Rd., off U.S. 17, 12 miles south of Georgetown* ☎ *843/546–7891* 🌐 *www.hopsewee.com* 🎟 *Mansion tour $15, grounds-only $5 per car* 🕓 *Mansion and grounds Feb.–Nov., Tues.–Fri 10–4, Sat noon–4; mansion tours on the hr, Dec. and Jan. by appointment.*

**Prince George Winyah Episcopal Church.** Named after King George II, this church still serves the parish established in 1721. It was built in 1737 with bricks brought from England. ✉ *Broad and Highmarket Sts.* ☎ *843/546–4358* 🌐 *www.pgwinyah.org* 🎟 *Donations accepted* 🕓 *Mar.–Oct., weekdays 11:30–4:30.*

## WHERE TO EAT

$ CAFÉ Fodor's Choice ★ **Kudzu Bakery.** Come here for the justifiably famous key lime pie and red velvet cake, both of which are available whole or by the slice, and can be eaten in the garden. Kudzu is also a great source for ready-to-cook specialties such as cheese biscuits, macaroni and cheese, and quiche. In addition, you'll find fresh bread, deli items, and a terrific selection of wines. A sister Kudzu is located to the north in Litchfield Beach on Willbrook Boulevard. *Average main: $12 120 King St. 843/546–1847 www.kudzubakery.com Closed Sun. No dinner.*

$$$$ AMERICAN **Rice Paddy.** At lunch, locals flock to this Lowcountry restaurant for the shrimp and bacon quesadilla and the creative salads and sandwiches. Dinner in the Victorian building—which actually dates back to pre-Revolutionary days—overlooking Front Street is more relaxed. Grilled local tuna with a ginger-soy glaze is a winner, as are the crab cakes, which you can get uncooked to go. *Average main: $25 732 Front St. 843/546–2021 www.ricepaddyrestaurant.com Reservations essential Closed Sun.*

$$ SEAFOOD **River Room.** This restaurant on the Sampit River specializes in char-grilled fish, Cajun fried oysters, seafood pastas, and steaks. For lunch you can have shrimp and grits or your choice of sandwiches and salads. The dining room has river views from most tables. It's especially romantic at night, when the oil lamps and brass fixtures cast a warm glow on the dark wood and brick interior of the early-20th-century building. *Average main: $18 801 Front St. 843/527–4110 www.riverroomgeorgetown.com Reservations not accepted Closed Sun.*

$ SOUTHERN **Thomas Café.** Though it might look the part, this isn't a greasy spoon: the luncheonette dishes up great fried chicken, homemade biscuits, and pie, plus grits, eggs, country ham, and other breakfast favorites. Join the regulars at the counter, or sit in one of the booths or café tables in the 1920s storefront building. Breakfast is served Monday through Saturday. *Average main: $10 703 Front St. 843/546–7776 www.thomascafe.net Closed Sun. No dinner.*

## WHERE TO STAY

*Hotel reviews have been abbreviated in this book. For expanded reviews, please go to Fodors.com.*

$ HOTEL **Hampton Inn Georgetown Marina.** Watch boats cruise up and down the river at this riverside resort; spectacular views of the waterway, marina, and sunsets are an easy trade for being a little farther from the beach (about 12 miles to Pawleys). **Pros:** there is a marina outside the hotel if you'd like to arrive by boat. **Cons:** as a chain hotel, it lacks the unique aspects of some other hotels. *Rooms from: $149 420 Marina Dr. 843/545–5000, 800/426–7866 www.georgetownhamptoninn.com 90 rooms, 8 suites.*

$ B&B/INN **Harbor House Bed and Breakfast.** Watch the shrimp boats come into the harbor from the front porch of Georgetown's only waterfront B&B; if you're lucky, innkeeper Meg Tarbox will turn some of the catch into shrimp and grits for breakfast. **Pros:** great views of Winyah Bay; home-away-from-home feel; gourmet breakfasts each morning. **Cons:** guests typically socialize, so those who prefer to keep to themselves might be turned off; closed during the winter. *Rooms from: $150 15 Cannon*

*St.* ☎ *843/546–6532, 877/511–0101* 🌐 *www.harborhousebb.com* ⇨ *4 rooms* ⏲ *Closed mid-Dec.–mid-Feb.* 🍽 *Breakfast.*

## SPORTS AND THE OUTDOORS

### BOATING

**Cap'n Rod's Lowcountry Plantation Tours.** Cruise past abandoned rice plantations and hear stories about the belles who lived there with Captain Rod of Cap'n Rod's Lowcountry Plantation Tours; other tours include a lighthouse expedition and a ghost-stories cruise. ✉ *Front St. on the harbor* ☎ *843/477–0287* 🌐 *www.lowcountrytours.com.*

**Rover Boat Tours.** Book a three-hour tour with Rover Boat Tours, sailing the high seas since 1995, to an untouched barrier island past the Winyah Bay Lighthouse for an exclusive afternoon of shelling. Pack snacks for the nearly hour-long trip to and from the island. ✉ *735 Front St., on the harbor* ☎ *843/546–8822, 800/705–9063* 🌐 *roverboattours.com.*

**Wallace Sailing Charters.** Feel the spray on your face as you explore Winyah Bay aboard a 40-foot yacht with Captain Dave of Wallace Sailing Charters. Each trip is limited to six passengers, so it feels like you're touring on a private yacht. ✉ *Front St. on the harbor* ☎ *843/902–6999* 🌐 *www.wallacesailingcharters.com.*

### CANOEING AND KAYAKING

★ **Black River Outdoor Center and Expeditions.** Black River Outdoor Center and Expeditions offers naturalist-guided canoe and kayak morning, evening (including moonlight tours) and now afternoon tours of the tidelands of Georgetown. Guides are well versed not just in the wildlife but also in local lore. Tours take kayakers past settings such as Drunken Jack's (the island that supposedly holds Blackbeard's booty), and Chicora Wood plantation, where dikes and trunk gates mark canals dug by slaves to facilitate rice growing in the area. It's said that digging the canals required as much manual labor as Egypt's pyramids. Black River also rents and sells equipment. Wildlife tends to be more active during the early morning or late afternoon; there's a good chance you'll hear owls hooting on the evening tours, especially in fall. ✉ *21 Garden Ave., off U.S. 701* ☎ *843/546–4840* 🌐 *www.blackriveroutdoors.com.*

### GOLF

**Wedgefield Plantation.** This premier Georgetown course on a former rice plantation has a ghost story: People have reported sightings of the ghost of a Revolutionary War–era British soldier, who lost his head to Francis Marion while guarding valuable prisoners in the plantation house. The spirit's appearance near the house is accompanied by the sound of horses' hooves. The 18th hole is surrounded by remnants from the original home. Most of the course is flat, a result of the rice fields' terrain. ✉ *129 Club House La., off U.S. 701* ☎ *843/448–2124* 🌐 *www.wedgefield.com* ✍ *Reservations essential* 🏌 *18 holes. 7072 yds. Par 71. Green Fee: $65/$50* ☞ *Facilities: Driving range, putting green, pitching area, golf carts, pull carts, golf academy/lessons, restaurant, bar.*

# Charleston, SC

**WORD OF MOUTH**

"Charleston . . . could become an addiction—we were there 2X last year and would go again in a heartbeat. There are so many top restaurants there that eating in a different one for every meal in a long weekend would just give you a sampling."

—basingstoke2

# WELCOME TO CHARLESTON, SC

## TOP REASONS TO GO

★ **Dining out:** Charleston has become a culinary destination, with talented chefs who offer innovative twists on the city's traditional Lowcountry cuisine.

★ **Seeing art:** The city is home to more than 100 galleries, so you'll never run out of places to see remarkable art.

★ **Spoleto Festival USA:** If you're lucky enough to visit in late May and early June, you'll find a city under a cultural siege: Spoleto's flood of indoor and outdoor performances (opera, music, dance, and theater) is impossible to miss and almost as difficult not to enjoy.

★ **The Battery:** The views from the point—both natural and man-made—are the loveliest in the city. Look west to see the harbor; to the east you'll find elegant Charleston mansions.

★ **Historic homes:** Step back in time in Charleston's preserved 19th-century houses like the Nathaniel Russell House, or visit plantations like Boone Hall outside the city.

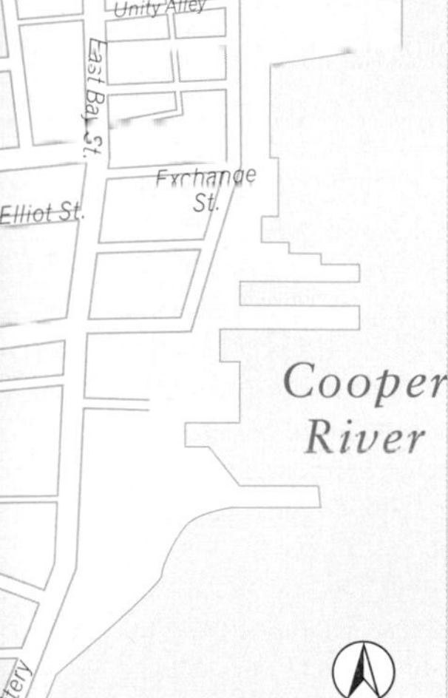


# GETTING ORIENTED

The heart of the city is on a peninsula, sometimes just called "downtown" by the nearly 60,000 residents who populate the area. Walking Charleston's peninsula is the best way to get to know the city.

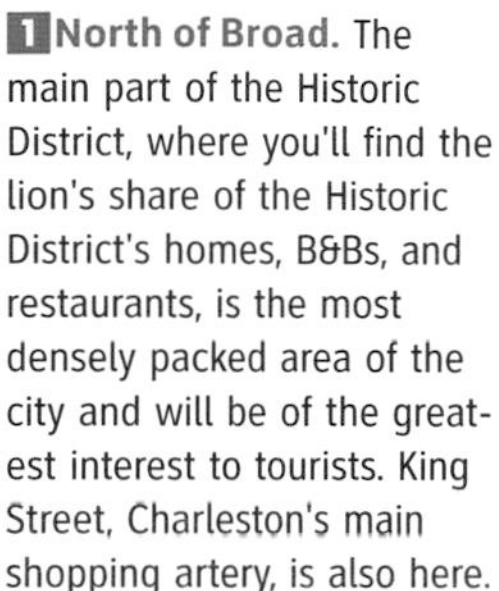

**1 North of Broad.** The main part of the Historic District, where you'll find the lion's share of the Historic District's homes, B&Bs, and restaurants, is the most densely packed area of the city and will be of the greatest interest to tourists. King Street, Charleston's main shopping artery, is also here.

**2 The Battery and South of Broad.** The southern part of the Historic District is heavily residential, but it still has a few important sights and even some B&Bs, though fewer restaurants and shops than North of Broad.

**3 Mount Pleasant and Vicinity.** East of Charleston, on the other side of the Arthur Ravenel Jr. Bridge, which spans the Cooper River, is Mount Pleasant, an affluent suburb with some interesting sights (such as Boone Hall Plantation). There are several good hotels in Mount Pleasant itself.

**4 West of the Ashley River.** Beyond downtown, the area of Charleston west of the Ashley River, beckons to visitors because it is home to three major historic plantations on Ashley River Road.

# GOOD EATS IN CHARLESTON

Time was, visitors could turn to Charleston for Southern standards: expertly fried fish and chicken, pimento cheese sandwiches, and gorgeous suppertime spreads.

*(above) McCrady's is known for its innovative food pairings. (lower right) Hominy Grill specializes in upscale Southern classics. (upper right) FIG takes a farm-to-table approach.*

Only now, Charleston has cast its eye toward sustainability, and smarter, healthier, and more refined dining options.

Chefs and restaurants have increasingly turned to local fishermen who plumb surrounding waters for shrimp, flounder, and grouper, and to farmers supplying bounties of vegetables and produce. Not to say Charleston has forsaken tradition—it's still easy to find a white-tablecloth setting and Lowcountry classics—but only now those same tables might be chocked with indigenous delicacies.

Younger chefs have proven themselves to be catalysts, scouring local markets and developing relationships with growers and purveyors. Their gain is ours, with menus dressed with offerings such as house-made charcuterie, pasture-raised pork, stone-ground grits, and heirloom tomatoes. It's a progressive turn, one that doesn't sacrifice Charleston's heritage, but rather improves upon it.

—Rob Young

### FARMERS' MARKET

Beneath shaded trees, lining the brick walkways of Marion Square at the downtown Charleston Farmers Market. Set in a green space at the intersection of King and Calhoun streets, the market runs from 8 am to 2 pm every Saturday from April through mid-December. Here you can find organic produce and vegetables, homemade pickles, boiled peanuts, and more. Breakfast and lunch options are plentiful, too.

## TASTE OF THE CITY

Holly Herrick
**Writer**

Holly Herrick is a classically trained chef, former restaurant critic at Charleston's *Post and Courier*, and the author of the book, *The Charleston Chef's Table*. Here, she talks with Fodor's about some of her favorite places in the Holy City.

**Q:** She-crab soup is probably the most iconic Charleston dish. Where do you go for the best version?
**A:** My personal favorite is at **Virginia's on King** (✉ *412 King St.* ☎ *843/735–5800*). What I love about it is that they use the blue crab, which is local and seasonal. To me it's just really delicious. It's a perfect dish to make for New Year's Eve or for the holidays. There are several good variations around town, but that's my personal favorite.

**Q:** Where do you go for the best shrimp and grits?
**A:** I happen to love the shrimp and grits at **Hominy Grill.** In fact I love Hominy Grill in general. He uses local shrimp. There's really a difference in taste in Lowcountry shrimp, unlike any other. It's got a real, briney sweetness to it that makes it exceptional. It's fabulous.

**Q:** Are there any new places that you're excited about?
**A:** There's a place that I'm just over-the-moon crazy about. It's a patisserie called **Macaroon Boutique** (✉ *45 John St.* ☎ *843/577–5441* 🌐 *www.macaroonboutique.com*). It's just this cool, boutique-y place with glass counters and the most beautiful pastries and breads, and then the macaron case, which looks too beautiful to eat. The pastry crème and the ganache that fill the macarons are just impeccable. It's impossible not to feel happy when you go there. It feels like you are in Paris, the second you open the door.

**Q:** Do you have a favorite local's joint?
**A:** My current favorite is **The Glass Onion** (✉ *1219 Savannah Hwy., West Ashley* ☎ *843/225–1717* 🌐 *www.ilovetheglassonion.com*). It's about 12 to 14 minutes from the heart of downtown, so it's really easy to get to. It's just casual and they just do amazing, hearty, Southern food, like a really great oyster po'boy or really fabulous meat loaf. It's just a feel-good place. The people are really friendly, and there are a lot of local regulars.

## AWARD-WINNING CHARLESTON

Charleston has long enjoyed an impressive reputation among gastronomes, branded as *the* source for shrimp and grits and she-crab soup. More recently, a trio of chefs, Robert Stehling of the **Hominy Grill** (✉ *207 Rutledge Ave.* ☎ *843/937–0930* 🌐 *www.hominygrill.com*), Mike Lata of **FIG** (✉ *232 Meeting St.* ☎ *843/805–5900* 🌐 *www.eatatfig.com*), and Sean Brock of **Husk** (✉ *2 76 Queen Street* ☎ *843/577–2500* 🌐 *www.huskrestaurant.com*) were, in consecutive years, each named best chef in the Southeast by the esteemed James Beard Foundation, widely hailed as the Oscars of the culinary world. All three chefs have advanced the city's standing, leading a movement built on seasonality, locality, and freshness. At the Hominy Grill, Stehling serves classic dishes like okra and shrimp beignets and farm-raised catfish. Lata offers a sustainable menu at FIG, and Brock is feted for his farm-to-table approach at Husk.

7

Updated by Melissa Bigner and Anna Evans

Wandering through the city's famous Historic District, you would swear it is a movie set. Dozens of church steeples punctuate the low skyline, and horse-drawn carriages pass centuries-old mansions and town houses, their stately salons offering a crystal-laden and parquet-floored version of Southern comfort. Outside, magnolia-filled gardens overflow with carefully tended heirloom plants. At first glance, the city resembles an 18th-century etching come to life—but look closer and you'll see that block after block of old structures have been restored. Happily, after three centuries of wars, epidemics, fires, and hurricanes, Charleston has prevailed and is now one of the South's best-preserved cities.

Although home to Fort Sumter, where the bloodiest war in the nation's history began, Charleston is also famed for its elegant houses. These handsome mansions are showcases for the "Charleston style," a distinctive look that is reminiscent of the West Indies, and for good reason. Before coming to the Carolinas in the late 17th century, many early British colonists first settled on Barbados and other Caribbean islands. In that warm and humid climate they built homes with high ceilings and rooms opening onto broad "piazzas" (porches) at each level to catch welcome sea breezes. As a result, to quote the words of the Duc de La Rochefoucauld, who visited in 1796, "One does not boast in Charleston of having the most beautiful house, but the coolest."

Preserved through the hard times that followed the Civil War and an array of natural disasters, many of Charleston's earliest public and private buildings still stand. Thanks to a rigorous preservation movement and strict Board of Architectural Review guidelines, the city's new structures blend in with the old. In many cases, recycling is the name of the game—antique handmade bricks literally lay the foundation for new homes. But although locals do dwell—on certain literal levels—in the past, the city is very much a town of today.

Take, for instance, the internationally heralded Spoleto Festival USA. For 17 days every spring, arts patrons from around the world come to enjoy international concerts, dance performances, operas, and plays at various venues citywide. Day in and day out, diners can feast at upscale restaurants, shoppers can look for museum-quality paintings and antiques, and lovers of the outdoors can explore Charleston's outlying beaches, parks, and marshes. But as cosmopolitan as the city has become, it's still the South, and just beyond the city limits are farm stands cooking up boiled peanuts, the state's official snack.

# PLANNING

## WHEN TO GO

There really is no bad time to visit Charleston. Spring and fall are high season, when the temperatures are best and hotel rates and occupancy are at their highest. Spring and fall temperatures are delightful during the day, and mild at night. Art shows, craft fairs, and music festivals (including the famous Spoleto USA festival) take place in summer. In fall, golfers are out in full force, and though it may be too cool to swim, beachcombing is a popular activity out on the sea islands. During the high season it's important to make your reservations as far in advance as possible for both hotels and restaurants.



## PLANNING YOUR TIME

The best way to get acquainted with Charleston is to take a carriage ride or walking tour, especially one that takes you through the South of Broad neighborhood. You can get acquainted with Charleston's Historic District at your leisure, especially if you can devote at least three days to the city, which will allow time to explore some of the plantations west of the Ashley River. With another day, you can explore Mount Pleasant, and if you have even more time, head out to the coastal islands, where golf and beach activities are the order of the day.

## GETTING HERE AND AROUND

### AIR TRAVEL

Charleston International Airport is about 12 miles west of downtown. Charleston Executive Airport on John's Island is used by private (noncommercial) aircraft as is Mount Pleasant Regional Airport.

Airport Ground Transportation arranges shuttles, which cost $12 per person to downtown. You can be picked up by the same service when returning to the airport by making advance reservations with the driver.

**Airport Information Charleston Executive Airport** ✉ *2742 Fort Trenholm Rd., John's Island* ☎ *843/559–2401.* **Charleston International Airport** ✉ *5500 International Blvd., North Charleston* ☎ *843/767–1100.* **Mount Pleasant Regional Airport** ✉ *700 Faison Rd., Mount Pleasant* ☎ *843/884–8837.*

**Airport Transfers Airport Ground Transportation** ☎ *843/767–1100.*

### BOAT AND FERRY TRAVEL

Boaters—many traveling the intracoastal waterway—dock at Ashley Marina and City Marina, in Charleston Harbor, or at Wild Dunes Yacht Harbor, on the Isle of Palms. The Charleston Water Taxi is a delightful way to travel between Charleston and Mount Pleasant. Some people take the $10 round-trip journey just for fun. It departs from the Charleston Maritime Center. Do not confuse its address at 10 Wharfside as being near the area of Adger's Wharf, which is on the lower peninsula. The water taxi departs daily every hour from 10 am to 7 pm. It also offers dolphin cruises and harbor boat rides.

**Boat and Ferry Contacts Charleston Water Taxi** ✉ *Charleston Maritime Center, 10 Wharfside St., Upper King* ☎ *843/330–2989* 🌐 *www.charlestonwatertaxi.com.*

### CAR TRAVEL

You'll need a car in Charleston if you plan on visiting destinations outside the city's Historic District, or if you plan to take trips to Walterboro, Edisto Island, Beaufort, or Hilton Head.

Interstate 26 traverses the state from northwest to southeast and terminates at Charleston. U.S. 17, the coastal road, also passes through Charleston. Interstate 526, also called the Mark Clark Expressway, runs primarily east–west, connecting the West Ashley area, North Charleston, Daniel Island, and Mount Pleasant.

### PUBLIC TRANSPORTATION

The Charleston Area Regional Transportation Authority (CARTA), the city's public bus system, takes passengers around the city and to the suburbs. Bus 11, which goes to the airport, is convenient for travelers. CARTA operates DASH, which runs buses that look like vintage trolleys along three downtown routes. All trips are free on DASH. CARTA buses go to James Island, West Ashley, and Mount Pleasant. From Mount Pleasant you can catch CARTA's Flex Service to the beach at Sullivan's Island for $3.

**Public Transportation Contacts CARTA** ✉ *3664 Leeds Ave., North Charleston* ☎ *843/747–0922* 🌐 *www.ridecarta.com.*

### TAXI TRAVEL

Fares within the city average about $5 per trip with the regular cab companies. The newer Green Taxis, using hybrid vehicles (and one minivan), run $7. Other taxis include Yellow Cab, available 24 hours a day.

The bike-pedaling companies will take you anywhere in the Historic District for $4.50 per person per 10 minutes. It is a fun way to get around in the evening especially if you are barhopping. They stay available until the bars close. Three can squeeze into the one pedicab seat.

**Taxi Contacts Charleston Bike Taxi** ☎ *843/532–8663.* **Charleston Black Cab Company** ☎ *843/216–2627, 843/216–1206.* **Charleston Ped-Cab** ☎ *843/577–7088.* **Charleston Rickshaw Company** ☎ *843/723–5685.* **Green Taxis** ☎ *843/819–0846.* **Safety Cab** ☎ *843/722–4066.* **Yellow Cab** ☎ *843/577–6565.*

## DISCOUNTS AND DEALS

A $45.95 Charleston Heritage Passport, sold at the Charleston Visitor Center, gets you into the Charleston Museum, the Gibbes Museum of Art, the Nathaniel Russell House, the Edmondston-Alston House, the Aiken-Rhett House, Drayton Hall, and Middleton Place (stableyards and grounds). It's good for two days.

## TOURS

### BOAT TOURS

Charleston Harbor Tours offers tours that give the history of the harbor; it's the oldest harbor tour boat company (since 1908) in Charleston and gives a good narrated tour of the harbor; however, these tours do not stop at Fort Sumter. Spiritline Cruises, which runs the ferry to Fort Sumter, also offers harbor tours and dinner cruises ($49–$55). The dinner cruises leave from Patriots Point Marina in Mount Pleasant and include a three-course dinner and dancing to music by a local radio DJ. Each table has a water view. Sandlapper Tours has tours focused on regional history, coastal wildlife, and nocturnal ghostly lore; you must make reservations by phone in advance since there is no ticket office where the harbor tours depart. All harbor cruises range between $22 and $30. On the authentic, 84-foot-tall schooner *Pride* (capacity 49 people), you can enjoy a diesel-free sail and the natural sounds of Charleston harbor on a two-hour harbor cruise, a dolphin cruise, a sunset cruise, romantic full-moon sails, and special events; tours range from $34 to $55.

**Boat Tour Contacts Charleston Harbor Tours** ✉ *Charleston Maritime Center, 10 Wharfside St., Upper King* ☎ *843/722–1112, 800/979–3370, 212/209–3370* 🌐 *www.charlestonharbortours.com.* **Sandlapper Tours** ✉ *Charleston Maritime Center, 10 Wharfside St., Upper King* ☎ *843/849–8687* 🌐 *www.sandlappertours.com.* **Schooner Pride** ✉ *Aquarium Wharf, Upper King* ☎ *843/559–9686, 843/722–1112* 🌐 *www.schoonerpride.com.* **Spiritline Cruises** ✉ *360 Concord St., Aquarium Wharf, Upper King* ☎ *843/881–7337, 800/789–3678* 🌐 *www.spiritlinecruises.com.*

### CARRIAGE TOURS

Carriage tours are a great way to see Charleston. The going rate is $22 for an adult. Carolina Polo and Carriage Company, Old South Carriage Company (where drivers wear mock Confederate uniforms), and Palmetto Carriage Works run horse- and mule-drawn carriage tours of the Historic District. Each tour, which follows one of four routes, lasts about one hour. Most carriages queue up at North Market and Anson streets. Charleston Carriage and Polo, which picks up passengers at the Doubletree Guest Suites Historic Charleston on Church Street, has a historically authentic carriage that is sought after for private tours and wedding parties. Palmetto offers free parking at their big red barn and has combo tickets for harbor tours.

**Carriage Tour Contacts Charleston Carriage & Polo Company** ☎ *843/577–6767* 🌐 *www.cpcc.com.* **Old South Carriage Company** ☎ *843/723–9712* 🌐 *www.oldsouthcarriagetours.com.* **Palmetto Carriage Works** ☎ *843/723–8145.*

### ECOTOURS

Barrier Island Ecotours, at the Isle of Palms Marina, runs three-hour pontoon-boat tours to a barrier island. Coastal Expeditions has half-day and full-day naturalist-led kayak tours on local rivers. Coastal Eco Tours offers a wide variety of two- and three-hour water tours of the Lowcountry.

**Ecotour Contacts Barrier Island Ecotours** ✉ *Isle of Palms Marina off U.S. 17, Isle of Palms* ☎ *843/886–5000* 🌐 *www.nature-tours.com.* **Charleston Explorers** ✉ *40 Patriots Point Rd., Mount Pleasant* ☎ *843/723–5656* 🌐 *www.charlestonexplorers.org.* **Coastal Expeditions** ✉ *514-B Mill St., Mount Pleasant* ☎ *843/884–7684* 🌐 *www.coastalexpeditions.com.*

### WALKING TOURS

Walking tours on various topics—horticulture, slavery, or women's history—are given by Charleston Strolls and the Original Charleston Walks. Bulldog Tours has walks that explore the city's supernatural side. Listen to the infamous tales of lost souls with Ghosts of Charleston, which travel to historic graveyards. They have expanded their offerings to include a sunset cruise and a culinary tour. They explore culinary strongholds where you can watch food artisans at work while sampling and shopping along the way.

Let Mary Coy, a fourth-generation Charlestonian and former teacher, bring the history and architecture of Charleston's back alleys and noble streets to life on her two-hour Charleston 101 Tour. Pay attention—there may be a quiz at the end.

Culinary Tours of Charleston is a foodie adventure that stops at a variety of restaurants in the Historic District, where you'll experience the area's rich culinary history and Southern hospitality.

**Walking Tour Contacts Bulldog Tours** ✉ *40 N. Market St., Market area* ☎ *843/568–3315* 🌐 *www.bulldogtours.com.* **Charleston 101 Tours.** ✉ *Tours start at the Powder Magazine on Cumberland St., one block from the City Market, Market area* ☎ *843/556–4753* 🌐 *www.charleston101tours.com* 🎫 *$16.* **Charleston Strolls** ✉ *Charleston Pl., 130 Market St., Market area* ☎ *843/766–2080* 🌐 *www.charlestonstrolls.com.* **Ghosts of Charleston** ✉ *184 E. Bay St., French Quarter* ☎ *843/723–1670, 800/723–1670.* **Original Charleston Walks** ✉ *58½ Broad St., South of Broad* ☎ *843/577–3800, 800/729–3420.* **Pat Conroy Tours** ✉ *115 Meeting St. (Mills House Hotel), Market area* ☎ *843/722–7033.*

## VISITOR INFORMATION

The Charleston Area Convention & Visitors Bureau runs the Charleston Visitor Center, which has information about the city as well as Kiawah Island, Seabrook Island, Mount Pleasant, North Charleston, Edisto Island, Summerville, and the Isle of Palms. The Historic Charleston Foundation and the Preservation Society of Charleston have information on house tours.

**Visitor Information Charleston Visitor Center** ✉ *375 Meeting St., Upper King* ☎ *843/853–8000, 800/868–8118* 🌐 *www.charlestoncvb.com.* **Historic Charleston Foundation** ☎ *843/723–1623* 🌐 *www.historiccharleston.org.* **Preservation Society of Charleston** ☎ *843/722–4630* 🌐 *www.preservationsociety.org.*

The Joseph Manigault House is one of the finest examples of Federal-style architecture in Charleston.

## EXPLORING CHARLESTON

Everyone starts a tour of Charleston in Downtown's famous Historic District. Roughly bounded by Lockwood Boulevard on the Ashley River to the west, Calhoun Street to the north, East Bay Street on the Cooper River to the east, and the Battery to the south, this fairly compact area of 800 acres contains nearly 2,000 historic homes and buildings. The peninsula is divided up into several neighborhoods, starting from the south and moving north, including the Battery, South of Broad, Lower King Street, and Upper King Street ending near the "Crosstown," where U.S. 17 connects downtown to Mount Pleasant and West Ashley.

Beyond downtown, the Ashley River hugs the west side of the peninsula; the region on the far shore is called West Ashley. The Cooper River runs along the east side of the peninsula, with Mount Pleasant on the opposite side and Charleston Harbor in between. Lastly, there are outlying sea islands: James Island, John's Island, Wadmalaw Island, Kiawah Island, Seabrook Island, Isle of Palms, and Sullivan's Island. Each has its own appealing attractions. Everything that entails crossing the bridges is best explored by car or bus.

### NORTH OF BROAD

During the early 1800s, large tracts of land were available North of Broad—as it was outside the bounds of the original walled city—making it ideal for suburban plantations. A century later the peninsula had been built out, and today the resulting area is a vibrant mix of residential neighborhoods and commercial clusters, with verdant parks

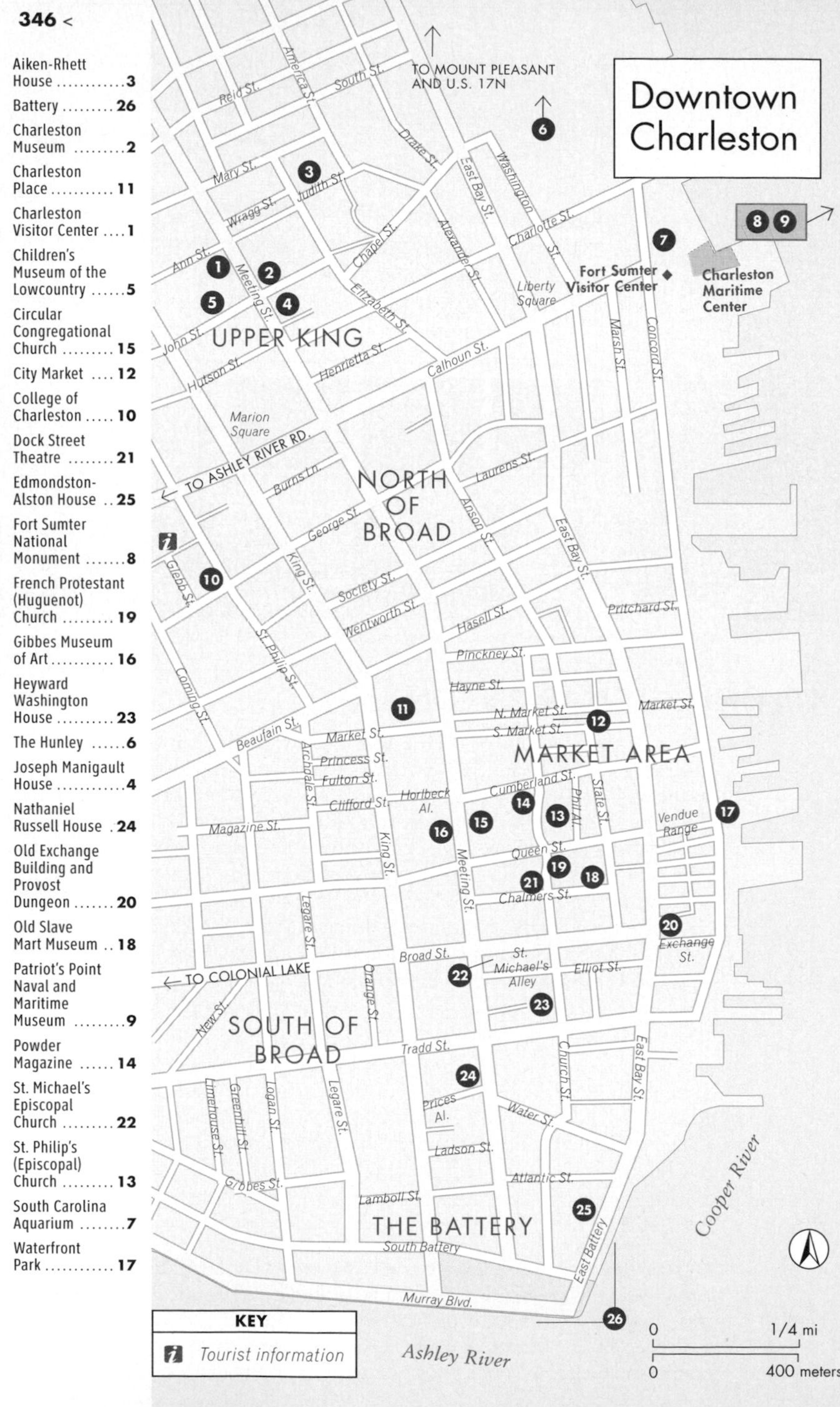


Aiken-Rhett House ............ 3
Battery ......... 26
Charleston Museum ......... 2
Charleston Place ........... 11
Charleston Visitor Center .... 1
Children's Museum of the Lowcountry ...... 5
Circular Congregational Church ......... 15
City Market .... 12
College of Charleston ..... 10
Dock Street Theatre ........ 21
Edmondston-Alston House .. 25
Fort Sumter National Monument ....... 8
French Protestant (Huguenot) Church ......... 19
Gibbes Museum of Art ........... 16
Heyward Washington House .......... 23
The Hunley ...... 6
Joseph Manigault House ............ 4
Nathaniel Russell House . 24
Old Exchange Building and Provost Dungeon ....... 20
Old Slave Mart Museum .. 18
Patriot's Point Naval and Maritime Museum ......... 9
Powder Magazine ...... 14
St. Michael's Episcopal Church ......... 22
St. Philip's (Episcopal) Church ......... 13
South Carolina Aquarium ........ 7
Waterfront Park ............ 17

scattered throughout. The district comprises three primary neighborhoods: Upper King, the Market area, and the College of Charleston. Though there are a number of majestic homes and pre-Revolutionary buildings in this area (including the Powder Magazine, the oldest public building in the state), the main draw is the rich variety of stores, museums, restaurants, and historic churches.

As you explore, note that the farther north you travel (up King Street in particular), the newer and more commercial development becomes. Although pretty much anywhere on the peninsula is considered prime real estate these days, the farther south you go, the more expensive the homes become. In times past, Broad Street was considered the cutoff point for a coveted address. Those living in the area Slightly North of Broad were referred to as SNOBs, and, conversely, their wealthier neighbors South of Broad were nicknamed SOBs.

### TOP ATTRACTIONS

Fodor's Choice ★ **Aiken-Rhett House.** One of Charleston's most stately mansions, built in 1820 and virtually unaltered since 1858, has been preserved rather than restored, meaning visitors can see its original wallpaper, paint schemes, and some furnishings. Two of the former owners, Governor Aiken and his wife, Harriet—lovers of all things foreign and beautiful—bought many of the chandeliers, sculptures, and paintings in Europe. Out back, the kitchen, slave quarters, and work yard are much as they were when the original occupants lived here, making this the most intact mansion and accompanying outbuildings to showcase urban life in antebellum Charleston. Take the audio tour, as it vividly describes both the ornate rooms and the slaves' quarters, giving historical and family details throughout. ✉ *48 Elizabeth St., Upper King* ☎ *843/723–1159* 🌐 *www.historiccharleston.org* 🎫 *$10; $16 with admission to Nathaniel Russell House* 🕑 *Mon.–Sat. 10–5, Sun. 2–5; last tour at 4:15.*

★ **Charleston Museum.** Although housed in a modern-day brick complex, this institution was founded in 1773 and is the country's oldest museum. To the delight of fans of *Antiques Roadshow,* the collection is especially strong in South Carolina decorative arts, from silver to snuffboxes. There's also a large gallery devoted to natural history (don't miss the giant polar bear). Children love the permanent Civil War exhibition, with plenty of Confederate uniforms, and the interactive "Kidstory" area, where they can try on reproduction clothing in a miniature historic house. A recent addition is the Historic Textiles Gallery, featuring changing displays that showcase everything from couture gowns to antique quilts. Combination tickets that give you admission to the Joseph Manigault House and the Heyward-Washington House are a bargain at $22. ✉ *360 Meeting St., Upper King* ☎ *843/722–2996* 🌐 *www.charlestonmuseum.org* 🎫 *$10* 🕑 *Mon.–Sat. 9–5, Sun. 1–5.*

**Charleston Place.** The city's most renowned hotel is flanked by upscale boutiques and specialty shops. Stop in for cocktails and tapas at the classy Thoroughbred Club. The city's finest public restrooms are downstairs near the shoeshine station. Entrances for the garage and reception area are just past the intersection of Hasell and Meeting streets. ✉ *205 Meeting St., Market area* ☎ *843/722–4900* 🌐 *www.charlestonplace.com.*

**Charleston Visitor Center** ✉ *375 Meeting St., Upper King* ☎ *843/853–8000, 800/868–8118* 🌐 *www.charlestoncvb.com* 🎟 *Free* 🕐 *Apr.–Oct., daily 8:30–5:30; Nov.–Mar., daily 8:30–5.*

★ **Children's Museum of the Lowcountry.** Hands-on interactive environments at this top-notch museum will keep kids—from toddlers on up to age eight—occupied for hours. They can climb aboard a Lowcountry pirate ship, drive an antique fire truck, race golf balls down a roller coaster, and create masterpieces in the art center. ✉ *25 Ann St., Upper King* ☎ *843/853–8962* 🌐 *www.explorecml.org* 🎟 *$7* 🕐 *Tues.–Sat. 9–5, Sun. noon–5.*

**Circular Congregational Church.** The first church building erected on this site in the 1680s gave bustling Meeting Street its name. The present-day Romanesque structure, dating from 1890, is configured on a Greek-cross plan and has a breathtaking vaulted ceiling. While the church is not open to drop-in visitors, guests are welcome to explore the graveyard, which is the oldest in the city, with records dating back to 1696. ✉ *150 Meeting St., Market area* ☎ *843/577–6400* 🌐 *www.circularchurch.org* 🕐 *Graveyard open weekdays 8–6, Sun. 9–6.*

**City Market.** Most of the buildings that make up this popular attraction were constructed between 1804 and the 1830s to serve as the city's meat, fish, and produce market. These days, you'll find the open-air portion packed with stalls selling jewelry, crafts, handmade clothing, jams and jellies, and regional souvenirs. In 2011, a major renovation transformed the market's indoor section, creating a beautiful backdrop for 20 desirable new stores and eateries. Local "basket ladies" weave and sell sweetgrass, pine-straw, and palmetto-leaf baskets—a craft passed down through generations from their West African and Caribbean ancestors. This shopping mecca's perimeters (North and South Market streets) are lined with restaurants and shops selling everything from pralines and other candies to high-end sportswear, hats, and Charleston gifts and collectibles. ✉ *N. and S. Market Sts. between Meeting and E. Bay Sts., Market area* 🌐 *www.thecharlestoncitymarket.com* 🕐 *Daily 9:30–dusk.*

**College of Charleston.** With a majestic Greek revival portico, Randolph Hall—an 1828 building designed by Philadelphia architect William Strickland—presides over the college's central Cistern area. Draping oaks envelop the lush green quad, where graduation ceremonies and concerts, notably during the Spoleto Festival, take place. Scenes from films including *Cold Mountain* have been filmed on the historic campus of this liberal arts college, founded in 1770. ✉ *Cistern Yard, 66 George St., College of Charleston Campus* ☎ *843/805–5507* 🌐 *www.cofc.edu.*

**Dock Street Theatre.** Incorporating the remains of the Old Planter's Hotel (circa 1809), this theater is hung with green velvet curtains and has wonderful woodwork, giving it a New Orleans French Quarter feel. After a three-year closure and a $20 million restoration, it reopened with fanfare in the spring of 2010 and now looks grand! ✉ *135 Church St., Market area* ☎ *843/720–3968* 🌐 *www.charleston-sc.gov.*

Women in Charleston keep alive the art of sweetgrass basket weaving brought over by enslaved people from Africa.

QUICK BITES

**Baked Charleston. Try the incredible spiced carrot cake with cream-cheese frosting at Baked Charleston or opt for their heavenly sweet 'n' salty brownies or cupcake (chocolate with a salty caramel filling). The secret is in the frosting, which is light, fluffy, and always flavorful. Soft as a pillow, the homemade marshmallows make great take-away treats. A Wi-Fi hotspot, this also has "real" food lunch items, which, like the sweets, change according to the chef's whims. Check out the *Baked* cookbook for drool-worthy photos and great recipes.** ✉ ***160 E. Bay St.*** ☎ ***843/577–2180.***

Fodor's Choice ★

**Fort Sumter National Monument.** Set on a man-made island in Charleston's harbor, this is the hallowed spot where the Civil War began. On April 12, 1861, the first shot of the war was fired at the fort from Fort Johnson (now defunct) across the way. After a 34-hour battle, Union forces surrendered and Confederate troops occupied Sumter, which became a symbol of Southern resistance. The Confederacy managed to hold it, despite almost continual bombardment, from August 1863 to February of 1865. When it was finally evacuated, the fort was a heap of rubble. Today, the National Park Service oversees it, and rangers give interpretive talks and conduct guided tours. To reach the fort, you have to take a ferry or a private boat; ferries depart from the Fort Sumter Visitor Education Center, downtown, and from Patriots Point in Mount Pleasant. There are six trips daily between mid-March and mid-August. The schedule is abbreviated the rest of the year, so call ahead for details. For those using a GPS to find the boat departure points for Fort Sumter, remember to use the address for Patriots Point and the Visitor Education Center, not the mailing address for the fort.

☎ *843/883–3123* 🌐 *www.nps.gov/fosu* 🎫 *Fort free, ferry $17* ⏲ *Mid-Mar.–early Sept., daily 10–5:30; early Sept.–mid-Mar., daily 10–4; Dec.–Feb., daily 11:30–4. Closed Christmas wk.*

**Fort Sumter Visitor Education Center.** Next to the South Carolina Aquarium, the visitor center contains exhibits on the antebellum period and the causes of the Civil War. This is a departure point for ferries headed to Fort Sumter. ✉ *340 Concord St., Upper King* ☎ *843/577–0242* 🌐 *www.nps.gov/fosu* 🎫 *Free* ⏲ *Daily 8:30–5*

### HISTORY LESSON

A ferry ride to Fort Sumter is a great way to sneak in a history lesson for the kids. For about the same price as a standard harbor cruise you get a narrated journey that points out the historic sites and explains how the Civil War began.

**French Protestant (Huguenot) Church.** The circa-1845 Gothic-style church is home to the only practicing Huguenot congregation in the nation. English-language services are held Sunday at 10:30. ✉ *136 Church St., Market area* ☎ *843/722–4385* 🌐 *www.frenchchurch.org* ⏲ *Mid-Mar.–mid-June and mid-Sept.–mid-Nov., Mon.–Thurs. 10–4, Fri. 10–1.*

Fodor's Choice ★ **Gibbes Museum of Art.** Experience Charleston's history through art. Housed in a beautiful Beaux-Arts building, the Gibbes boasts a collection of 10,000 works, principally American with a local connection. Each year a dozen special exhibitions, often of contemporary art, attract a more youthful audience. Different objects from the museum's permanent collection are always on view in "The Charleston Story," offering a nice overview of the region's history, and the gift shop is exceptional. The museum is slated to close for renovations in 2014, so call ahead before visiting. ✉ *135 Meeting St., Market area* ☎ *843/722–2706* 🌐 *www.gibbesmuseum.org* 🎫 *$9* ⏲ *Tues.–Sat. 10–5, Sun. 1–5.*

Fodor's Choice ★ **Joseph Manigault House.** Considered by many to be the finest example of Federal-style architecture in the South, this 1803 home was built for a rich rice-planting family of Huguenot heritage. Having toured Europe as a gentleman architect, Gabriel Manigault returned to design this residence for his brother Joseph as the city's first essay in neoclassicism. The house glows in red brick and is adorned with a two-story piazza balcony. Inside, marvels await: a fantastic "flying" staircase in the central hall; a gigantic Venetian window; elegant plasterwork and mantels; notable Charleston-made furniture; and a bevy of French, English, and American antiques, including some celebrated tricolor Wedgwood pieces. Outside, note the garden "folly." ✉ *350 Meeting St., Upper King* ☎ *843/723–2926* 🌐 *www.charlestonmuseum.org* 🎫 *$10* ⏲ *Mon.–Sat. 10–5, Sun. 1–5.*

Fodor's Choice ★ **Old Slave Mart Museum.** This is likely the only building still in existence in South Carolina that was used for slave auctioning, a practice that ended here in 1863. It was once part of a complex called Ryan's Mart, which also contained a slave jail, kitchen, and morgue. It is now a museum that recounts the history of Charleston's role in the slave trade, an unpleasant story but one that is vital to understand. Charleston once served as the center of commercial activity for the South's plantation economy,

Take the ferry to Fort Sumter National Monument to see where the first shots of the Civil War were fired.

and slaves were the primary source of labor both within the city and on the surrounding plantations. Galleries are outfitted with some interactive exhibits, including push buttons that allow you to hear voices relating stories from the age of slavery. The museum is on one of the few remaining cobblestone streets in town. ✉ *6 Chalmers St., Market area* ☎ *843/958–6467* 🌐 *www.charlestoncity.info* 🎫 *$7* 🕒 *Mon.–Sat. 9–5.*

Fodor's Choice ★ **St. Philip's Church.** One of the three churches that gave Church Street its name, this graceful Corinthian-style building is the second one to rise on its site: the first one burned down in 1835 and was rebuilt in 1838. A shell that exploded in the churchyard while services were being held one Sunday during the Civil War didn't deter the minister from finishing his sermon (the congregation gathered elsewhere for the remainder of the war). Notable Charlestonians such as John C. Calhoun are buried in the eastern and western churchyards. If you want to tour the church, call ahead, as open hours depend upon volunteer availability. ✉ *142 Church St., Market area* ☎ *843/722–7734* 🌐 *www.stphilipschurchsc.org* 🕒 *Churchyard weekdays 9–4.*

Fodor's Choice ★ **South Carolina Aquarium.** The 385,000-gallon Great Ocean Tank houses the tallest aquarium window in North America. Along with sharks, moray eels, and sea turtles, exhibits include more than 7,000 creatures, representing 350-plus species. In 2011, the 2,500-square-foot Saltmarsh Aviary opened, offering views of Charleston Harbor and allowing you to catch sight of herons, diamondback terrapins, puffer fish, and stingrays. The latest exhibit is Madagascar Journey, filled with exotic animals including ring-tailed lemurs—a favorite among visitors, who can step inside an observation bubble within the primates' habitat. The

4-D theater shows popular family films complete with special effects such as wind gusts and splashes of water. ✉ *100 Aquarium Wharf, Upper King* ☎ *843/720–1990, 800/722–6455* 🌐 *www.scaquarium.org* 🎫 *$29.95* ⏲ *Mar.–Aug., daily 9–5; Sept.–Feb., daily 9–4.*

> **IF THE SHOE FITS**
>
> Wear good walking shoes, because the sidewalks, brick streets, and even Battery Promenade are very uneven. Take a bottle of water, or take a break to sip from the fountains in White Point Gardens, as there are practically no shops south of Broad Street.

★ **Waterfront Park.** Enjoy the fishing pier's "front-porch" swings, stroll along the waterside path, or relax in the gardens overlooking Charleston Harbor. Two fountains can be found here: the much acclaimed Pineapple Fountain and the Vendue Fountain, which children love to run around in on hot days. The park is at the foot of Vendue Range, along the east side of Charleston Harbor and the Cooper River. ✉ *Vendue Range at Concord St., Market area* ☎ *843/724–7321* 🎫 *Free* ⏲ *Daily 6 am–midnight.*

### WORTH NOTING

**Powder Magazine.** Completed in 1713, the oldest public building in South Carolina is the only one that remains from the time of the Lords Proprietors. The city's volatile—and precious—gunpowder was kept here during the Revolutionary War, and the building's thick walls were designed to contain an explosion if its stores were detonated. Today it's a museum with a new permanent exhibit focusing on colonial warfare. ✉ *79 Cumberland St., Market area* ☎ *843/722–9350* 🌐 *www.powdermag.org* 🎫 *$3* ⏲ *Mon.–Sat. 10–4, Sun. 1–4.*

## SOUTH OF BROAD

The heavily residential area south of Broad Street brims with beautiful private homes, many of which have plaques bearing brief descriptions of the property's history. Mind your manners, but feel free to peek through iron gates and fences at the verdant displays in elaborate gardens. Although an open gate once signified that guests were welcome to venture inside, that time has mostly passed—residents tell stories of how they came home to find tourists sitting in their front-porch rockers. But you never know when an invitation to have a look-see might come from a friendly owner-gardener. Several of the city's lavish house museums call this famously affluent neighborhood home.

### TOP ATTRACTIONS

Fodor's Choice ★ **Battery.** During the Civil War, the Confederate army mounted cannons in the Battery, at the southernmost point of Charleston's peninsula, to fortify the city against Union attack. Cannons and piles of cannonballs still line the oak-shaded park known as White Point Gardens—kids can't resist climbing them. Where pirates once hung from the gallows, strollers now take in the serene setting from Charleston benches (small wood-slat benches with cast-iron sides). Stroll the waterside promenades along East Battery and Murray Boulevard and you can enjoy views of Charleston Harbor, the Ravenel Bridge, and Fort Sumter on

To experience Charleston in high style, opt for a carriage ride around the historic district.

one side, with some of the city's most photographed mansions on the other. You'll find Gullah oldsters dangling their fishing lines, waiting for a catch. ✉ *East Bay St. at Murray Blvd., South of Broad.*

**Heyward-Washington House.** Thomas Heyward, rice king, patriot leader, and signer of the Declaration of Independence, lived in this house, built in 1772. The city rented the house from Heyward for George Washington's use when Washington stayed in Charleston in May 1791. The salons have mid-18th-century Charleston furniture, notably the Withdrawing Room's Chippendale-style Holmes Bookcase, which is considered among the top 10 pieces of furniture in America. The original kitchen building is also significant, as it is the only such structure open to public view in Charleston. The three-story brick house is near Cabbage Row, a neighborhood central to Charleston's African American history and the setting for the book *Porgy* (and the Gershwin opera based on it), written by Heyward descendant DuBose Heyward. ✉ *87 Church St., South of Broad* ☎ *843/722–0354* 🌐 *www.charlestonmuseum.org* 🎟 *$10* ⏲ *Mon.–Sat. 10–5, Sun. 1–5.*

Fodor's Choice ★ **Nathaniel Russell House.** One of the nation's finest examples of Federal-style architecture, the Nathaniel Russell House was built in 1808, when Russell was 70 years old. Its grand beauty is proof of the immense wealth he accumulated as one of the city's leading merchants. In addition to the famous "free-flying" staircase that spirals up three stories with no visible support, the ornate interior is distinguished by fine, Charleston-made furniture as well as paintings and works on paper by well-known American and European artists, including Henry Benbridge, Samuel F. B. Morse, and George Romney. The extensive

*Continued on page 362*

### DID YOU KNOW?

The original steeple bells of St. Philip's (Episcopal) Church were given to the Confederate army to be melted into cannon. Four of the eleven bells were replaced in 1976 and now chime from 8 in the morning to 8 at night.

# WALKING CHARLESTON'S HISTORIC DISTRICT

by Mary Coy

Charleston is picturesque from a car window and beguiling from a horse-drawn carriage, but the best way to experience its gracious homes and stately public buildings, hidden gardens, and lofty church steeples is on foot. The city's Historic District is one of the best preserved in the South, and a walking tour of this National Historic Landmark reveals layers of 18th- and 19th-century history.

Fires, earthquakes, hurricanes, economic downturns, and major wars have all struck mighty blows, but Charleston's original grace has endured. Although many buildings were neglected during the very difficult century after the Civil War, a new spirit of community activism helped to rescue the old homes. In 1920 citizens formed the Society for the Preservation of Old Dwellings (the first such group in the nation), now the Preservation Society of Charleston. Today the Preservation Society awards the prestigious Carolopolis Award to buildings that merit recognition for restoration and conservation, and a city-run Board of Architectural Review oversees alterations to buildings in the Historic District.

As you explore, stop to notice the details, peek into well-tended gardens, explore the alleyways. Keep an eye out for features like old fire insurance plaques, earthquake bolts, and wrought ironwork, and appreciate the painstaking efforts of today's residents to preserve what was built centuries ago.

Above, City Market

## CHARLESTON'S KEY ARCHITECTURAL FEATURES

### ❶ Carriage blocks

Also called mounting blocks, these large stones were used in the 19th century as stepping stones to get into carriages or mount horses. **See it:** Dock Street Theatre, 132 Church St., 16 Chalmers St., 59 Meeting St.

### ❷ Carolopolis seal

Since 1953, this prestigious award has been given annually by the Preservation Society of Charleston to buildings that exemplify outstanding achievement in exterior restoration and preservation. More than 1,300 buildings display this seal. **See it:** County Courthouse, Pink House, Rainbow Row.

### ❸ Charleston brick

The brick used to build most 18th- and 19th-century buildings in the city was manufactured by slaves on local plantations and is often referred to as plantation brick. **See it:** Dock Street Theatre, 8 Chalmers St., 26 Queen St.

### ❹ Charleston green

Shutters and doors are often painted with this very dark color, which is a cross between green and black. The green hue is most noticeable when the sunlight hits it. **See it:** 10 State St., Rainbow Row.

### ❺ Charleston single house

These long, narrow houses are turned sideways, so that only one room on each floor faces the street. When Charleston was laid out, it was necessary to position most homes this way so that they could fit into the deep, narrow lots. Wider lots allowed for gardens and porches (piazzas) to capture the breeze. **See it:** 134 and 132 Church St.; 64, 69, and 76 Meeting St.

### ❻ Chevaux de frise

Many white homeowners installed this unusual form of protection after the fear of a slave uprising in 1822. **See it:** 27 King St., 18 Meeting St., 38 Chalmers St.

5

10

11

**7 Earthquake bolts**

Following the earthquake of 1886, which damaged about 8,000 buildings, metal rods were inserted into floor joists of damaged homes. The exposed bolts were tightened, essentially straightening the house and giving it stability. Bolt heads and washers are often disguised with different shapes. **See it:** Dock Street Theatre (circles), 8 ½ State St. (crosses), 11 St. Michael's Alley (stars), 9 E. Battery (lion heads).

**8 Fire marks**

Before the city established a fire department in 1885, private cooperatives provided a homeowner's best hope in a catastrophe. Members paid to join but were also required to volunteer to extinguish fires. Marks (plaques) representing the 12 different companies adorn facades. **See it:** 7 and 19 State St., 100 Church St., 22–24 Queen St.

**9 Haint blue**

The popular trend of painting the ceilings of piazzas blue is borrowed from the Gullah culture's use of the color blue to keep away haunts, or ghosts. **See it:** 16 and 69 Meeting St., 59 Tradd St.

**10 Joggling boards**

These benches are prevalent on Charleston piazzas and in gardens. Made from a beam of pine measuring roughly 20 feet long and a foot wide, the wood is supported between posts that rest on rockers. If a courting couple sat on opposite ends of the board and bounced, they would eventually be bounced closer together. **See it:** 38 Chalmers St., 42 and 215 Meeting St.

**11 Wrought iron**

Although much of the ironwork in the city dates to the 18th and 19th centuries, the work of Philip Simmons (1912–2009), a renowned African American blacksmith, adorns homes, gardens, and churches. His home and workshop at 30 ½ Blake Street is now a museum. **See it:** 72, 74, and 91 Anson St.; 34, 36 and 45 Meeting St.; 2, 5, and 9 Stoll's Alley; 313 King St.; 2 St. Michael's Alley.

# CHARLESTON BY FOOT

U.S. Post Office, Four Corners of Law

This one-mile walking tour offers the best of the Historic District. Begin and end your tour in the thick of things at the "Four Corners of Law," whose nickname is derived from its four buildings representing three branches of secular government (federal, county, and city) along with "God's Law." This walk will take approximately an hour, depending on stops. It is best to stroll through Charleston in the early morning or early evening to enjoy the serenity of quiet streets and cooler temperatures. Restrooms are available in most city parking garages.

## FOUR CORNERS OF LAW TO DOCK STREET THEATRE

**St. Michael's Episcopal Church** (1752) is the oldest church in the city and one of the finest colonial churches in the country. The white 186-foot octagonal steeple dominates the city's skyline, even though the earthquake of 1886 caused it to sink eight inches. Note the elaborate gates to the churchyard, which depict funerary urns.

The **U.S. Post Office** was constructed in 1896 and exemplifies the Renaissance Revival style with its stone window trims, quoins (cornerstones), and arches. It is one of only a few buildings made with real stone as opposed to stuccoed brick.

St. Michael's Episcopal Church

**City Hall** was designed by native son Gabriel Manigualt. Built in 1801, this building typifies Adamesque architecture with its graceful marble stairs, circular windows, and recessed wall arches. Notice the city's seal in the pedimented gable, proclaiming in Latin, "The Body Politic, She Guards Her Buildings, Customs and Laws."

Legend has it that George Washington so admired the Neoclassical-style **County Courthouse** (1790) that he had the original White House modeled after it.

Cross Broad Street and continue up Meeting Street to **No. 108.** The plans to build a gas station on this spot in 1930 caused a public outcry prompting a redesign. This Colonial Revival–style building was the result. A gas station for 50 years, it is now the gift shop of the Historic Charleston Foundation. ■ **TIP→ This is a good place to purchase a bottle of water.** **The Mills House Hotel** (1968) across the street was a cornerstone of the revitalization of the Historic District.

A Protestant "meeting house" once stood on the site of the **Circular Congregational Church** (1892), giving Meeting Street its name. This Victorian Romanesque structure resembles Boston's Trinity Church. The oldest cemetery in the city is here, with some gravestones dating to the late 1600s.

Turn right at Cumberland Street to reach the **Old Powder Magazine.** Built in 1713 as a depot for storing gunpowder, the three-foot-thick walls kept the interior cool and dry. The vaulted attic was equipped with over two tons of sand which would drop to extinguish a fire. ■ **TIP→ Don't miss the map of the original walled city displayed on the fence.**

Turn right at Church Street for a view of one of the Holy City's

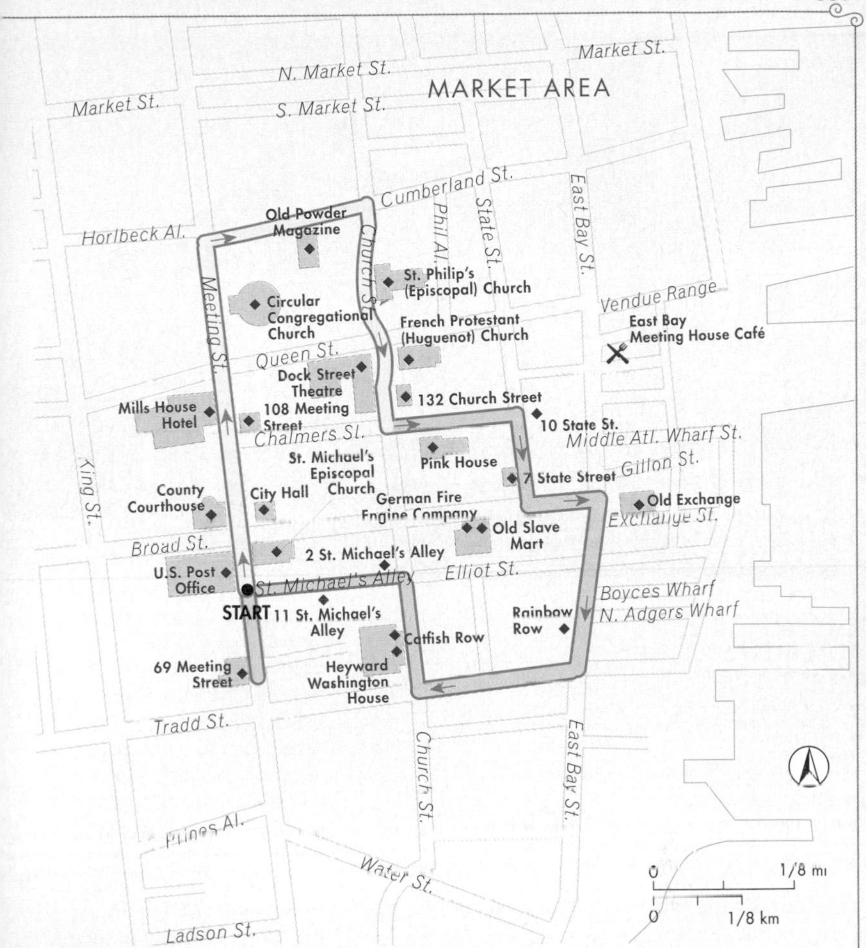

St. Philip's (Episcopal) Church

best-loved steeples at **St. Philip's (Episcopal) Church** (1835). Crossing Queen Street, the 1845 **French Protestant (Huguenot) Church** was designed by renowned Charleston architect Edward Brickell White. It has typical Gothic Revival features such as cast-iron spires, pointed windows, and a steep roof.

In 1736, the first theater in America was built on the corner of Church and Dock streets (now Queen Street). However, most of the current **Dock Street Theatre** stems from the early 19th century, when the Planters' Hotel stood here. Note the spectacular balcony and brownstone columns. **■ TIP→ Walk through the iron gate to visit the delightful courtyard.**

Built around 1800, the house at **132 Church Street** typifies the Charleston single-house style.

Dock Street Theatre

The Pink House

## CHALMERS STREET TO ST. MICHAEL'S ALLEY

Turn left onto Chalmers Street, continuing to the **Pink House.** At more than 300 years old, this is one of the oldest buildings in the city. Originally a tavern, the structure was made of Bermuda stone, giving it its pinkish appearance and a nickname that has been reinforced today with a coat of pink paint. The gambrel (two-sloped) roof is covered with pantiles (terra cotta) which date to the mid-1700s.

The **German Fire Engine Company** (1851) was one of the original cooperative fire insurance companies in Charleston. It abuts the **Old Slave Mart** (1859), which was once the rear entrance of Ryan's Slave Mart located a block over on Queen Street. It is the only known building still in existence that was used for slave auctions in South Carolina. The museum currently housed here tells the history of Charleston's role in the slave trade.

Turn right onto State Street to **No. 10.** Because it has no piazza, this 1810 house allows a good perspective of the sideways positioning of a Charleston single house. The stucco covering the Charleston brick has been scored to look like blocks of stone. The shutters are painted Charleston green.

Built in 1811–19 as one of Charleston's earliest office buildings, the oversized fire mark in the gable of **7 State Street** announces that the company's headquarters were here.

Turn left onto Broad Street. Built in the Georgian Palladian style, the original custom house, or **Old Exchange,** was acclaimed as one of the largest and grandest public buildings in America in 1767. The basement was used as a dungeon during the Revolutionary War. **■ TIP→ Take a slight detour to the left for a snack at the East Bay Meeting House Café and Bar, on the corner of East Bay and Gendron, where you can enjoy a cheese and fruit plate, a slice of quiche, or delightful desserts.**

Turn right onto East Bay Street. Built early in the 18th

Old Exchange

century, the rowhouses on **Rainbow Row** (Nos. 79–107) became the first homeowner-funded rehabilitation project in the city in the 1930s. The Caribbean colors gave the area its well-known identity.

Turn right onto Tradd Street to view 18th-century iron gates and balconies reminiscent of New Orleans' French Quarter. A right onto Church Street will take you to an example of the double house, the **Heyward Washington House**, built in 1772. Its square symmetrical design is typical of the Georgian style. **■ TIP→ Across the street, peek into the garden at 86 Church Street to glimpse camellias bloom, and smell tea olive trees in the fall.**

Rainbow Row

Heyward Washington House

Built in 1783, **Catfish Row** (Nos. 89–91 Church Street) was made famous in the early 20th century as the setting for the novel *Porgy* and subsequent operetta *Porgy and Bess*. Note the elaborate scrollwork in the original wrought-iron lunette above the central breezeway. **■ TIP→ Dip into the breezeway to see the lovely courtyard designed by renowned landscape architect Loutrel Briggs.**

Turn left onto St. Michael's Alley to **No. 2**. The gate was made in the 1970s by renowned African American blacksmith Philip Simmons.

Typical of many smaller homes in the city, **11 St. Michael's Alley** (c. 1780) began as a carriage house. The space upstairs served as slave quarters. Notice the star-shape earthquake bolts.

You are back near the Four Corners of Law, where you began. Take a quick left on Meeting Street to see ceilings of the piazzas on **69 Meeting Street** painted Haint Blue. **■ TIP→ Public restrooms are available in City Hall.**

## CHARLESTON'S HOUSE AND GARDEN TOURS

The popular **Spring Festival of Houses & Gardens** (☎ *843/720–1183* 🌐 *www.historiccharleston.org*) provides the rare opportunity to look inside some of Charleston's most impressive historic residences and gardens. The event is held annually mid-March to mid-April during the peak of the city's blooming season.

Annual **Fall Tours of Homes and Gardens** (☎ *843/722–4630* 🌐 *www.preservationsociety.org*) feature the interiors of architecturally significant privately owned homes, gardens, churches, and public buildings. Tours run from the end of September through the end of October. All proceeds benefit the Preservation Society of Charleston.

The delightful, free self-guided **Gateway Walk** encompasses churchyards and gardens in a three-block area of the city. You can pick up a map of the route at the Charleston Visitor Center at 375 Meeting Street or just let the wrought-iron gates along the way guide you. Start at St. John's Lutheran Church on Archdale Street. This lovely trail is maintained by the Garden Club of Charleston (🌐 *www.thegardenclubofcharleston.org*).

formal garden is worth a leisurely stroll. ✉ *51 Meeting St., South of Broad* ☎ *843/724–8481* 🌐 *www.historiccharleston.org* 🎟 *$10; $16 with admission to Aiken-Rhett House Museum* ⏲ *Mon.–Sat. 10–5, Sun. 2–5.*

**St. Michael's Episcopal Church.** Topped by a 186-foot steeple, Charleston's most famous, this is the city's oldest surviving church. The first cornerstone was set in place in 1752 and, through the years, other elements were added: the steeple clock and bells (1764); the organ (1768); the font (1771); and the altar (1892). The pulpit—original to the church—was designed to maximize natural acoustics. Washington worshipped here in 1791. ✉ *78 Meeting St., South of Broad* ☎ *843/723–0603* 🌐 *www.stmichaelschurch.net* ⏲ *Weekdays 9–4:30, Sat. 9–noon.*

### BASKET LADIES

Drive along U.S. 17 North, through and beyond Mount Pleasant, to find the basket ladies set up at rickety roadside stands, weaving the traditional sweetgrass, pine-straw, and palmetto-leaf baskets for which the area is known. Be braced for high prices, although baskets typically cost less on this stretch than in downtown Charleston. Each purchase supports the artisans, whose numbers are dwindling year by year.

### WORTH NOTING

**Edmondston-Alston House.** In 1825, Charles Edmondston built this house in the Federal style, with Charles Alston transforming it into the imposing Greek Revival structure you see today beginning in 1838. Tours of the home—furnished with antiques, portraits, silver, and fine china—are informative. ✉ *21 E. Battery, South of Broad* ☎ *843/722–7171* 🌐 *www.edmondstonalston.com* 🎟 *$12; $44 with admission to Middleton Place* ⏲ *Tues.–Sat. 10–4:30, Sun. 1–4:30.*

**Old Exchange Building and Provost Dungeon.** Originally a customs house with a waterside entrance, this building was used by the British to house prisoners during the Revolutionary War, an ordeal detailed in a new exhibit. Costumed interpreters bring history to life on guided tours, and kids are both fascinated and scared by the period mannequins on display in the dungeon. But happier events also occurred here: the state ratified the Constitution in 1788, and Washington attended a ball in 1791 (remarking in a letter on the 400 grand ladies that attended). ✉ *122 E. Bay St., South of Broad* ☎ *843/727–2165* 🌐 *www.oldexchange.com* 🎟 *$8* ⏲ *Daily 9–5.*

## MOUNT PLEASANT AND VICINITY

East of Charleston, across the Arthur Ravenel Jr. Bridge—the longest cable-stay bridge in North America—is the town of Mount Pleasant, named not for a mountain but for a plantation founded there in the early 18th century. In its Old Village neighborhood are antebellum homes and a sleepy, old-time town center with a drugstore where patrons still amble up to the soda fountain and lunch counter for egg-salad sandwiches and floats. Along Shem Creek, where the local fishing fleet brings in the daily catch, several seafood restaurants serve the area's freshest (and most deftly fried) seafood. Other attractions in the

Boone Hall is one of the country's oldest working plantations and continues to grow crops like strawberries, tomatoes, and pumpkins.

area include military and maritime museums, plantations, and, farther north, the Cape Romain National Wildlife Refuge.

### TOP ATTRACTIONS

Fodor's Choice ★ **Boone Hall Plantation and Gardens.** A drive through a ½-mile-long live-oak alley draped in Spanish moss introduces you to this still-functioning plantation, the oldest of its kind. Tours take you through the 1935 mansion, the butterfly pavilion, and the heirloom rose garden. Eight slave cabins on the property have recently been transformed into the Black History in America exhibit, displaying life-size figures, recorded narratives, audiovisual presentations, photos, and historical relics. Seasonal Gullah culture performances in the theater are perennial crowd favorites. Stroll along the winding river, or pick your own strawberries, pumpkins, or tomatoes in the fields. Across the highway is Boone Hall's Farm Market, with fresh local produce, a lunch café, and a gift shop. *North and South*, *Queen*, and Nicholas Sparks's *The Notebook* were filmed here. ■ **TIP→** **Plan your visit to coincide with annual events like the Lowcountry Oyster Festival in January, the Strawberry Festival in the spring, and the Scottish Games & Highland Gathering in September.** *✉ 1235 Long Point Rd., off U.S. 17 N, Mount Pleasant, Charleston ☎ 843/884–4371 ⊕ www.boonehallplantation.com $19.50 ⊙ Jan.–early Feb., Sat. 9–5, Sun. noon–5; early Feb.–mid-Mar. and Labor Day–Dec., Mon.–Sat. 9–5, Sun. noon–5; mid-Mar.–Labor Day, Mon.–Sat. 8:30–6:30, Sun. noon–5; call ahead to confirm hours.*

**Fort Moultrie.** A section of the Fort Sumter National Monument, this is the site where Colonel William Moultrie's South Carolinians repelled a British assault in one of the first patriot victories of the Revolutionary

DID YOU KNOW?

Magnolia Plantation and Gardens has massive informal gardens that include a 30-acre Audubon Swamp Garden, which can be explored through a series or boardwalks and bridges.

War. Completed in 1809, the fort is the third fortress on this site on **Sullivan's Island** (reached on Route 703 off U.S. 17 North, 10 miles southeast of Charleston). Set across the street, the companion museum is an unsung hero. Although much is made of Fort Sumter, this smaller, historical site is creatively designed, with mannequins in various uniforms and other creative visuals that make military history come alive. A well-done, 20-minute educational film that spans several major wars tells the colorful history of the fort. There's also an exhibit focusing on the slave trade and Sullivan's Island's role in it. ■ **TIP→** Plan to spend the day bicycling through Sullivan's Island, which is characterized by its cluster of early-20th-century beach houses (fuel up at Dunleavy's Pub on Sullivan's, on Middle Street). ✉ *1214 Middle St., Sullivan's Island* ☎ *843/883–3123* 🌐 *www.nps.gov/fosu* 🎫 *$3* 🕓 *Daily 9–5.*

★ **Patriots Point Naval and Maritime Museum.** Climb aboard the USS *Yorktown* aircraft carrier—which contains the Congressional Medal of Honor Museum—as well as the submarine USS *Clamagore* and the destroyer USS *Laffey*. A life-size replica of a Vietnam support base camp showcases naval air and watercraft used in the military action. ✉ *40 Patriots Point Rd., Mount Pleasant, Charleston* ☎ *843/884–2727* 🌐 *www.patriotspoint.org* 🎫 *Museum $18, parking $5* 🕓 *Daily 9–6:30; last tickets sold at 5.*

## WORTH NOTING

**Cape Romain National Wildlife Refuge.** A grouping of barrier islands and salt marshes, this refuge of 66,287 acres was established in 1932 as a migratory bird haven. The **Sewee Visitor & Environmental Education Center** has information and exhibits on the refuge and its trails, as well as an outdoor enclosure housing four red wolves. Currently, the refuge is aiding the recovery of the threatened loggerhead sea turtles, and a turtle-hatchling video details the work. ■ **TIP→** From the mainland refuge, take a ferry ride ($40) with Coastal Expeditions from Garris Landing to Bulls Island. There are also four scheduled tours each year to Lighthouse Island—call the Sewee Center for dates and cost. ✉ *Sewee Center, 5821 U.S. 17 N, Awendaw* ☎ *843/928–3368* 🌐 *www.fws.gov/caperomain/* 🎫 *Free* 🕓 *Tues.–Sat. 9–5.*

**Charles Pinckney National Historic Site.** This site is comprised of the last 28 acres of the plantation of Charles Pinckney, a drafter and signer of the U.S. Constitution. You can tour an 1820s coastal cottage, constructed after Pinckney's death. It features interpretive exhibits about the man, the Constitution, and slave life. A nature trail includes the archaeological foundations of three slave houses. ✉ *1254 Long Point Rd., off U.S. 17 N* ☎ *843/881–5516* 🌐 *www.nps.gov/chpi* 🎫 *Free* 🕓 *Daily 9–5.*

**Old Village.** The historic nucleus of Mount Pleasant, this neighborhood is distinguished by white picket fences, storybook cottages, antebellum manses, tiny churches, and waterfront homes. Prices run to the millions. It's a lovely area for a stroll or bike ride, and Pitt Street offers a couple locally loved eateries and boutiques. Follow that street south until it ends in the Pickett Street Recreation Area (which residents call the Pitt Street Bridge), an old bridge-turned-greenway that's popular for picnicking, fishing, and enjoying sunset views. ✉ *Pitt St. and Venning St.*

## WEST OF THE ASHLEY RIVER

Ashley River Road, Route 61, begins a few miles northwest of downtown Charleston, over the Ashley River Bridge. Sights are spread out along the way, and those who love history, old homes, and gardens may need several days to explore places like Drayton Hall, Middleton Place, and Magnolia Plantation and Gardens. Spring is a peak time for the flowers, although many of them are in bloom throughout the year.

### EXPLORING

**Drayton Hall.** Considered the nation's finest example of unspoiled Palladian-inspired architecture, this mansion is the only plantation house on the Ashley River to have survived the Civil War intact. A National Trust Historic Site built between 1738 and 1742, it's an invaluable lesson in history as well as in architecture. The home has been left unfurnished to highlight the original plaster moldings, opulent hand-carved woodwork, and other ornamental details. Regular tours, with guides known for their in-depth knowledge, depart on the half hour and give wonderful insight into the people who once inhabited and built this fabled house. Visitors can also see the African-American graveyard and even take part in the 45-minute "Connections" program that uses maps, historic documents, and artifacts to trace the story of Africans from their journey to America, through slavery, and into the 20th century. ✉ *3380 Ashley River Rd., West Ashley, Charleston* ☎ *843/769–2600* 🌐 *www.draytonhall.org* 🎟 *$18; $24 with admission to Magnolia Plantation* ⏲ *Mon.–Sat. 9–3:30, Sun. 11–3:30.*

7

**Magnolia Plantation and Gardens.** Owner Thomas Drayton came from Barbados in 1671 and created this garden, the oldest public one in the country. The extensive informal garden, established in 1685, has evolved into an overflowing collection of plants, including a vast array of azaleas and camellias, along with some themed areas (a biblical garden, for example). Take a train or boat to tour the grounds, travel through the 125-acre Waterfowl Refuge (originally rice fields), or explore the 30-acre Audubon Swamp Garden by foot, compliments of a network of boardwalks and bridges. You can traverse more than 500 acres of trails, or bring your bike if you're inclined. Also here are a petting zoo, a nature center, and a reptile house. Five pre- and post-Emancipation cabins have been restored, and a new tour by interpreters is called From Slavery to Freedom. And be sure to tour the 19th-century plantation house, which originally stood in Summerville. The home was taken apart, floated down the Ashley River, and reassembled here. ✉ *3550 Ashley River Rd., West Ashley, Charleston* ☎ *843/571–1266, 800/367–3517* 🌐 *www.magnoliaplantation.com* 🎟 *all-inclusive pass $47; grounds $15; tram $8; boat $8; house tour $8; Audubon Swamp Garden $8; From Slavery to Freedom $8; combo ticket with Drayton Hall $24* ⏲ *Apr.–Oct., daily 8–5:30; Nov.–Mar., daily 9–5.*

Fodor's Choice ★ **Middleton Place.** This former plantation is home to America's oldest landscaped gardens, begun in 1741 by Henry Middleton, second president of the First Continental Congress. From camellias to roses, blooms of all seasons form floral *allées* (alleys) along terraced lawns and around a pair of ornamental lakes that are shaped like butterfly wings. As

A red bridge leads you over a pond at Magnolia Plantation and Gardens.

for the house, a large part of the three-building residential complex was destroyed during the Civil War, but the "flanker" that contained the gentlemen's guest quarters was restored. It now serves as a house museum, displaying impressive silver, furniture, paintings, and historic documents. In the Stableyards, craftspeople use authentic tools to demonstrate spinning, weaving, blacksmithing, and other skills from the plantation era. Heritage-breed farm animals, such as water buffalo and cashmere goats, are housed here, along with peacocks. If all this leaves you feeling peckish, head over to the Middleton Place Restaurant for excellent Lowcountry specialties for lunch and dinner. It has a cozy character and a real sense of history, and is a charming, tranquil spot. You do not have to pay admission to have dinner, and dinner guests can walk the grounds from 5 until dusk. There is also a high-end (but not overpriced) museum gift shop that carries local arts, crafts, and tasteful souvenirs, plus a wonderful garden shop with lunch café. Finally, you can stay overnight at the contemporary Middleton Inn, where floor-to-ceiling windows splendidly frame the Ashley River. Kayaking excursions depart from the inn, and the Middleton Equestrian Center offers trail rides in the surrounding woods. ✉ *4300 Ashley River Rd., West Ashley, Charleston* ☎ *843/556–6020, 800/782–3608* 🌐 *www.middletonplace.org* 🎟 *General admission $25, house tour $12, carriage tours $18; all-inclusive day pass $49; $45 combination ticket with Edmondston-Alston House* 🕒 *Gardens daily 9–5; house museum Mon. noon–4:30, Tues.–Sun. 10–4:30.*

# WHERE TO EAT

Updated by Rob Young

Yes, to eat. Of course, to eat. This is, after all, Charleston, which is blessed with a bevy of Southern-inflected selections, from barbecue parlors to fish shacks to traditional, white-tablecloth restaurants. The attention to Southern foods has increased in recent years, largely because of improved exposure, large food festivals like Big Apple Barbecue Block Party in New York, and regional emphases. Charleston, to its credit, rests at distinguished crossroads, benefiting from established stock, and newer flourishes, such as the nationally recognized Charleston Wine & Food Festival.

As for attire, Charleston invites a casual atmosphere, appropriate for jeans or slacks, sundresses or skirts, and in many cases, even flip-flops. Don't forget, Charleston was recognized as the Most Mannerly City in the union by Marjabelle Young Stewart. Which means that residents are slow to judge (or, at the least, that they're doing so very quietly). But on the whole, the city encourages comfort and unhurried, easy pacing. The result is an idyllic setting in which to enjoy shrimp and grits, oysters on the half shell, and other homegrown delicacies from the land and sea that jointly grant the city its impressive culinary standing.

### PRICES

Fine dining in Charleston can be expensive. One option to keep costs down might be to try several of the small plates that many establishments offer. To save money, drive over the bridges or go to the islands, including James and Johns islands. *Prices in the reviews are the average cost of a main course at dinner or, if dinner is not served, at lunch. Use the coordinate (✥ B2) at the end of each listing to locate a site on the Where to Eat and Stay in Charleston map.*

7

## NORTH OF BROAD

$$ FRENCH

✕ **39 Rue de Jean.** With a backdrop of classic French-bistro style—gleaming wood, cozy booths, and white-papered tables—Charleston's trendy set wines and dines until the wee hours on such favorites as steamed mussels in a half dozen preparations. Order them with pommes frites, as the French do. Each night of the week there's a special, such as the bouillabaisse on Sunday. Rabbit with a whole-grain mustard sauce was so popular it jumped to the nightly menu, while Rue's burgers have a well-established following. If you're seeking quiet, ask for a table in the dining room on the right. It's noisy—but so much fun—at the bar, especially since it has the city's best bartenders. *$ Average main: $18 ✉ 39 John St., Upper King ☎ 843/722–8881 ⊕ www.39ruedejean.com ✍ Reservations essential ✥ B2.*

$$ SOUTHERN

✕ **Alluette's Cafe.** Alluette Jones has coined a new genre of cuisine—"holistic soul food"—which she fixes at her eponymously named restaurant. It's simple, fresh, local, and organic, drawing from Geechee-Gullah origins, and it has earned well-deserved praise. And guess what? You won't be able to find any pork products here. Her hearty soups (lima bean, for instance) contain nary a trace of the traditional Southern accoutrement: ham hock. Plus, Alluette cooks some of the city's best

# BEST BETS FOR CHARLESTON DINING

**Fodor'sChoice**

**Basil,** p. 370
**Charleston Grill,** p. 371
**FIG,** p. 371
**The Grocery,** p. 374
**Hall's Chophouse,** p. 375
**Husk,** p. 376
**The Macintosh,** p. 376
**Martha Lou's Kitchen,** p. 377
**McCrady's,** p. 377
**Peninsula Grill,** p. 378
**Recovery Room,** p. 379
**The Tattooed Moose,** p. 380
**Trattoria Luca,** p. 380
**Two Boroughs Larder,** p. 380
**The Wreck of the Richard & Charlene,** p. 382
**Sesame Burgers & Beer,** p. 383
**Tomato Shed Café,** p. 384

## By Price

**$**

**Hominy Grill,** p. 375

**$$**

**39 Rue de Jean,** p. 369
**Alluette's Cafe,** p. 369

**$$$**

**La Fourchette,** p. 376

**$$$$**

**Charleston Grill,** p. 371
**McCrady's,** p. 377
**Peninsula Grill,** p. 378
**Slightly North Of Broad (SNOB),** p. 379

## By Cuisine

**SOUTHERN**

**Anson,** p. 370
**FIG,** p. 371
**Hominy Grill,** p. 375
**Husk,** p. 376
**McCrady's,** p. 377

## By Experience

**BRUNCH**

**The Glass Onion,** p. 382
**High Cotton,** p. 375
**Hominy Grill,** p. 375

fried shrimp, which arrive butterflied and lightly battered after simmering in organic oil. It's a pleasant, newfound perspective on Southern food. $ *Average main: $15* ✉ *80 Reid St., Upper King* ☎ *843/577–6926* 🌐 *www.alluettes.com* ✣ *B1.*

$$$$ SOUTHERN ✕ **Anson.** Nearly a dozen windows here afford picturesque views of the passing horse-drawn carriages. The softly lighted, gilt-trimmed dining room is ideal for romantic occasions, though some locals prefer the more casual scene downstairs. Cuisine is traditional Lowcountry, including shrimp with grits, and oysters fried in cornmeal (both served as appetizers). The she-crab soup is one of the best around. The chef takes liberties with some classics, including the whole crispy flounder in apricot sauce and the roasted red snapper with succotash and shrimp, giving them a more contemporary spin. Gooey, molten chocolate cake with house-made peanut butter ice cream is a favorite. $ *Average main: $27* ✉ *12 Anson St., Market area* ☎ *843/577–0551* 🌐 *www.ansonrestaurant.com* ⏲ *No lunch* ✣ *G5.*

$$ ASIAN Fodor'sChoice ★ ✕ **Basil.** This corner restaurant in the heart of downtown enjoys the best reputation for Thai food in the city. Need proof? Dinner hours generate extended wait times—no reservations allowed—as patrons angle for an outdoor or window table. From the exposed glassed-in kitchen emerge popular specialties such as *tom aban talay*, a hot-and-sour mixed seafood soup flavored with Kaffir lime leaves, lemongrass, and button

mushrooms; red curry duck, a boneless half bird, deep-fried; and the tilapia served with shrimp and ginger sauce. And seriously, don't fret over the line. It's always worth the wait. But if you're farther afield, try hitting Basil's newest locations in Charlotte, N.C., and Mount Pleasant. *Average main: $16* ✉ *460 King St., Upper King* ☎ *843/724–3490* *www.eatatbasil.com* ✣ *A1.*

$$$$ SOUTHERN Fodor's Choice ★ **Charleston Grill.** Quite simply, this restaurant continues to provide what many think of as the city's highest gastronomic experience. Chef Michelle Weaver has succeeded her former boss, the estimable Bob Waggoner, and carries on the Grill's groundbreaking New South cuisine. The dining room is a soothing backdrop, highlighted by pale wood floors, flowing drapes, and elegant Queen Anne chairs. A jazz ensemble adds a hip, yet unobtrusive, element. As it was hoped, the Grill, which has been reborn in a more relaxed form, attracts a younger and more vibrant clientele than its original incarnation. The menu is now in four quadrants: simple, lush (foie gras and other delicacies), cosmopolitan, and Southern. A nightly tasting menu offers a way to sample it all. And don't skip the extra indulgences: Sommelier Rick Rubel has 1,300 wines in his cellar, with many served by the glass. And the pastry chef sends out divine creations like chocolate caramel ganache. *Average main: $30* ✉ *Charleston Place Hotel, 224 King St., Market area* ☎ *843/577–4522* *www.charlestongrill.com* *Reservations essential* *No lunch* ✣ *C4.*

$$$$ SOUTHERN **Circa 1886.** Near Wentworth Mansion, in a former residential home full of hand-carved marble fireplaces and Tiffany stained-glass windows, rests the intimate Circa 1886 restaurant. The award-winning eatery sets a sophisticated tone with low lighting and a yellow rose atop each table. Executive chef Marc Collins emphasizes seasonal offerings, highlighted by the menu's heirloom-tomato salad, a deconstructed BLT made with bacon gelée, Romaine *espuma* (foam), and white-grain toast. Collins also shows off his Texan extraction with an antelope dish, the free-range game procured from the Broken Arrow Ranch in Texas hill country. The tender variation spiced with horseradish is a must-eat for the adventurous. *Average main: $28* ✉ *149 Wentworth St., Lower King* ☎ *843/853–7828* *www.circa1886.com* *Reservations essential* *Closed Sun. No lunch* ✣ *A4.*

$ SOUTHERN **Dixie Supply Bakery and Cafe.** It might be a lil' eatery buttressed by a Lil' Cricket convenience store, but don't be fooled by its size. Dixie Supply Bakery and Cafe belongs to an old Charlestonian family (and by old, we mean they arrived here in 1698 or so) that seeks to honor its roots through food. It's here you'll find Lowcountry and Southern classics: shrimp and creamy stone-ground grits, fried chicken, and a mighty fine tomato pie. Daily alternating blue-plate specials abound, including fried green tomatoes, shrimp from nearby Wadmalaw Island, summer-squash-and-ricotta-cheese ravioli, and a steady assortment of locally plucked vegetables. *Average main: $7* ✉ *62 State St., Market area* ☎ *843/722–5650* *www.dixiecafecharleston.com* ✣ *G5.*

$$$$ SOUTHERN Fodor's Choice ★ **FIG.** Spend an evening here for fresh-off-the-farm ingredients cooked with unfussy, flavorful finesse. Chef and partner Mike Lata has won awards for keeping it simple at FIG. The menu changes frequently, but the family-style vegetables might be as simple as young beets in sherry

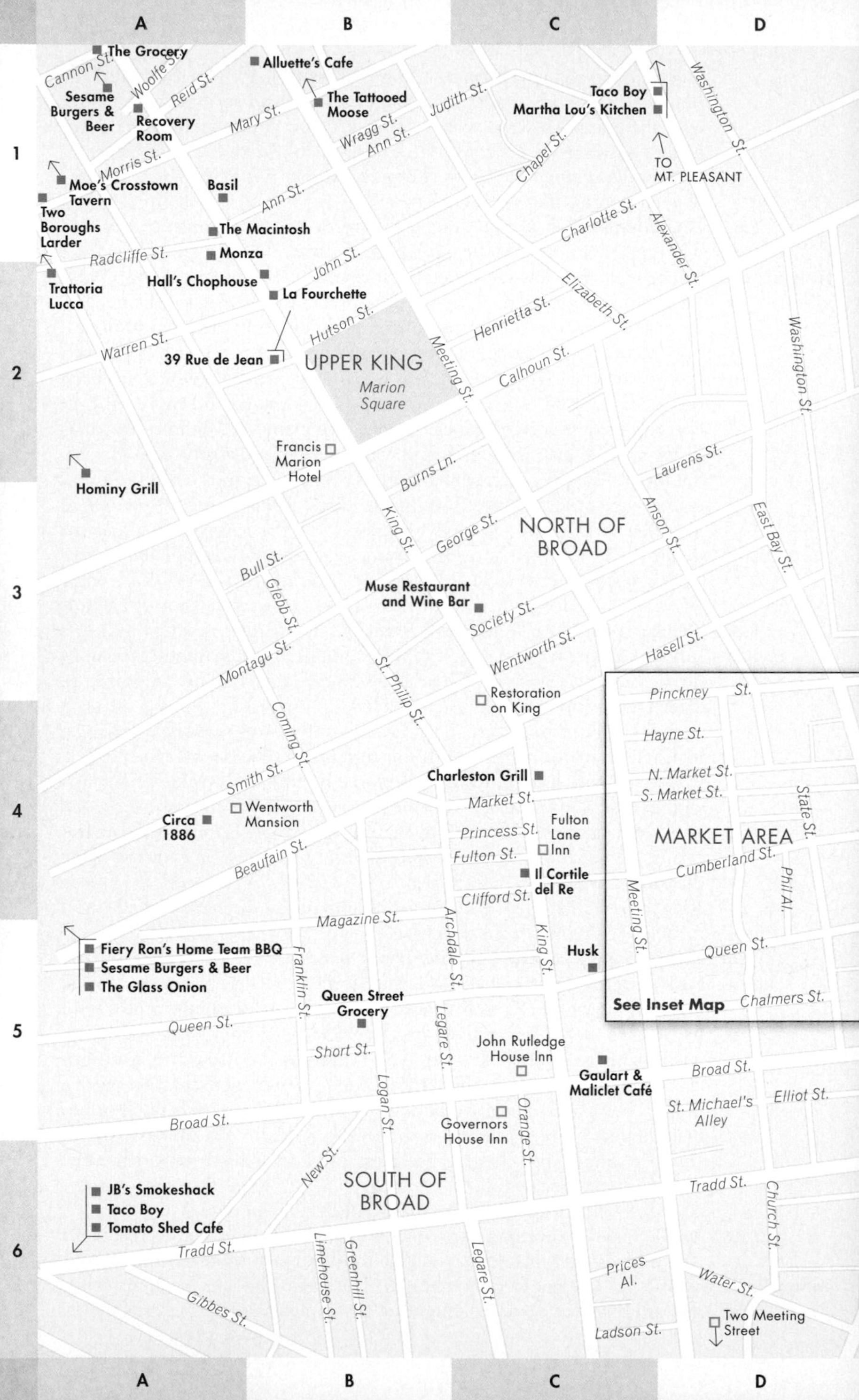

A
B
C
D
1
2
3
4
5
6
The Grocery
Cannon St.
Woolfe St.
Sesame Burgers & Beer
Recovery Room
Reid St.
Alluette's Cafe
The Tattooed Moose
Mary St.
Wragg St.
Ann St.
Judith St.
Taco Boy
Martha Lou's Kitchen
Washington St.
TO MT. PLEASANT
Chapel St.
Morris St.
Moe's Crosstown Tavern
Two Boroughs Larder
Basil
Ann St.
The Macintosh
Monza
Radcliffe St.
Charlotte St.
Alexander St.
John St.
Hall's Chophouse
La Fourchette
Trattoria Lucca
Elizabeth St.
Hutson St.
Henrietta St.
Washington St.
Warren St.
39 Rue de Jean
UPPER KING
Marion Square
Meeting St.
Calhoun St.
Francis Marion Hotel
Hominy Grill
Burns Ln.
Laurens St.
King St.
George St.
NORTH OF BROAD
Anson St.
East Bay St.
Bull St.
Glebb St.
Muse Restaurant and Wine Bar
Society St.
Montagu St.
St. Philip St.
Wentworth St.
Hasell St.
Restoration on King
Pinckney St.
Hayne St.
Coming St.
Smith St.
Charleston Grill
N. Market St.
S. Market St.
Market St.
State St.
Circa 1886
Wentworth Mansion
Princess St.
Fulton Lane Inn
MARKET AREA
Beaufain St.
Fulton St.
Cumberland St.
Il Cortile del Re
Clifford St.
Phil Al.
Meeting St.
Magazine St.
Archdale St.
King St.
Fiery Ron's Home Team BBQ
Sesame Burgers & Beer
The Glass Onion
Franklin St.
Husk
Queen St.
Queen Street Grocery
See Inset Map
Chalmers St.
Queen St.
Legare St.
Short St.
John Rutledge House Inn
Gaulart & Maliclet Café
Broad St.
Logan St.
St. Michael's Alley
Elliot St.
Broad St.
Governors House Inn
Orange St.
New St.
SOUTH OF BROAD
JB's Smokeshack
Taco Boy
Tomato Shed Cafe
Tradd St.
Church St.
Tradd St.
Limehouse St.
Greenhill St.
Legare St.
Prices Al.
Water St.
Gibbes St.
Ladson St.
Two Meeting Street

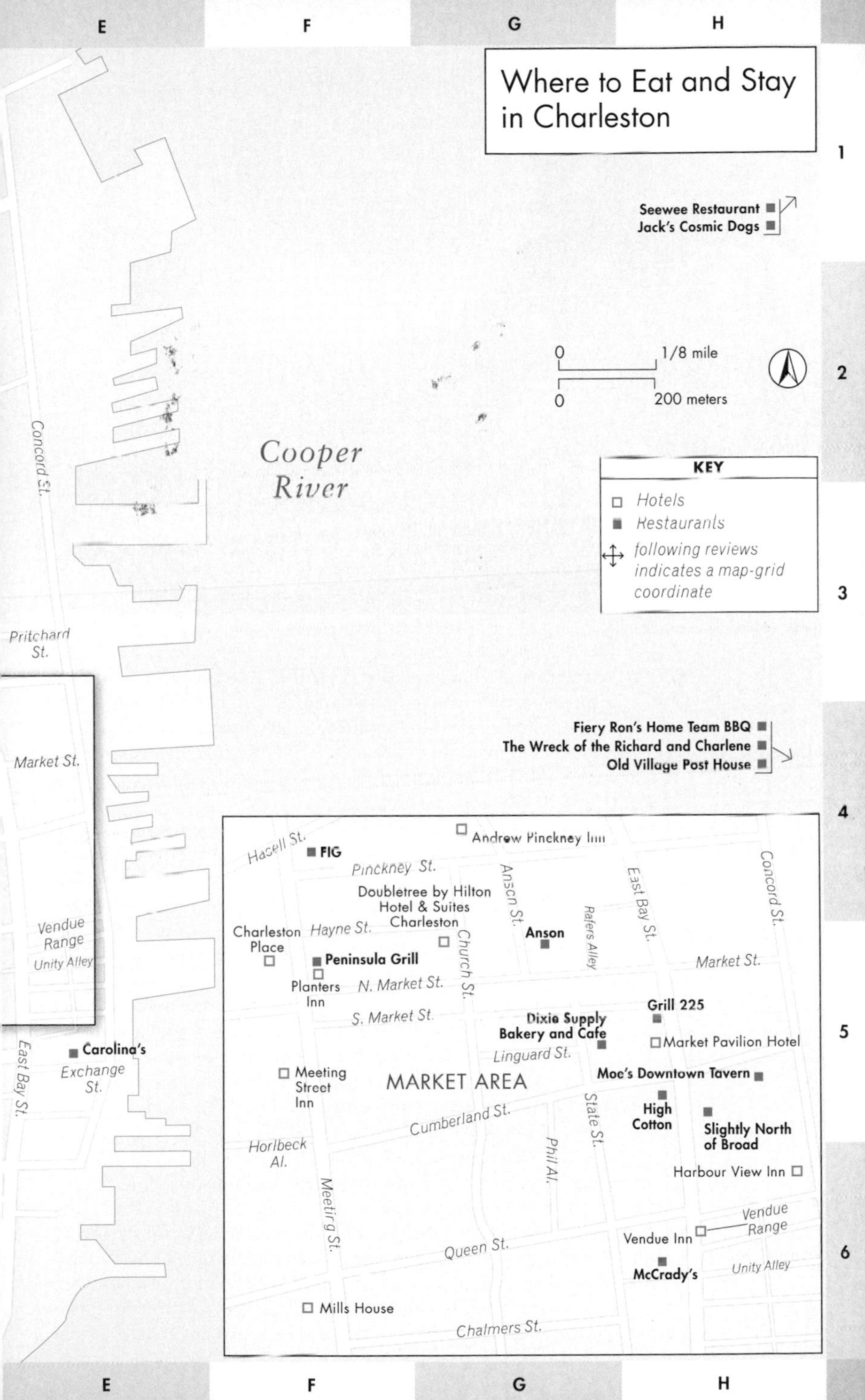
E
F
G
H
Where to Eat and Stay in Charleston
1
Seewee Restaurant
Jack's Cosmic Dogs
0
1/8 mile
0
200 meters
2
Concord St.
Cooper River
KEY
Hotels
Restaurants
following reviews indicates a map-grid coordinate
3
Pritchard St.
Market St.
Fiery Ron's Home Team BBQ
The Wreck of the Richard and Charlene
Old Village Post House
4
Andrew Pinckney Inn
Hasell St.
FIG
Pinckney St.
Doubletree by Hilton Hotel & Suites Charleston
Anson St.
East Bay St.
Concord St.
Charleston Place
Hayne St.
Church St.
Anson
Rafers Alley
Vendue Range
Unity Alley
Peninsula Grill
Market St.
Planters Inn
N. Market St.
Grill 225
S. Market St.
Dixie Supply Bakery and Cafe
Market Pavilion Hotel
5
Carolina's
Linguard St.
Exchange St.
East Bay St.
Meeting Street Inn
MARKET AREA
Moe's Downtown Tavern
State St.
High Cotton
Slightly North of Broad
Cumberland St.
Horlbeck Al.
Phil Al.
Harbour View Inn
Meeting St.
Vendue Range
Vendue Inn
6
Queen St.
McCrady's
Unity Alley
Mills House
Chalmers St.
E
F
G
H

Try the crispy pork trotters with a sunny-side-up egg and heirloom peppers at FIG.

vinegar placed in a plain white bowl. His dishes do get more complex: there's the pureed cauliflower soup with pancetta, incredible veal sweetbreads with smoked bacon and escarole, and grouper with a perfect golden crust accompanied by braised artichokes. Hit the lively bar scene for a nightcap. *Average main: $30* ✉ *232 Meeting St., Market area* ☎ *843/805–5900* 🌐 *www.eatatfig.com* ⏲ *No lunch* ✣ *F4.*

$$$$ STEAKHOUSE **Grill 225.** This atmospheric establishment has been stockpiling accolades over the years, and it's never been better. The cuisine combined with a staggering array of excellent wines and professional, caring service make Grill 225 a popular special-occasion spot. Take the opportunity to dress up; the elegant wood floors, white linens, and red-velvet upholstery call for it. If you eat red meat, indulge in the prime USDA, wet-aged steaks; the filet with foie gras with a fig demi-glace is equally excellent. But don't miss sharing a side or two, such as the mashed sweet potatoes with Boursin cheese. Presentation is at its best with appetizers like the tuna-tower tartare. Expect hefty portions, but save room for the pastry chef's shining creations, which include a contemporized version of baked Alaska with a nutty crust, flambéed table-side. *Average main: $40* ✉ *Market Pavilion Hotel, 225 E. Bay St., Market area* ☎ *843/266–4222* 🌐 *www.marketpavilion.com* ✣ *H5.*

$$$ MODERN AMERICAN Fodor's Choice ★ **The Grocery.** Executive chef and owner Kevin Johnson's new restaurant sits in impressive quarters near the corner of Cannon and King streets. Cast in dim lighting and painted concrete, the spacious Grocery projects an earthy, unassuming presence. The high wainscoting and tall shelving filled with jams, pickled vegetables, and vintage kitchenware match the restaurant's aim—and title. Similarly, the menu suggests a humble, considerate approach, as the dishes represent local flavors:

liver mousse mixed with ripe persimmons provides a light, fluffy taste smeared on crunchy, buttered bread. Wood-roasted clams offer native appeal, emboldened with merguez sausage and a light chili. A rich pot roast is made from grass-fed beef, and the delicate scamp grouper crowns a bed of field peas, crab, and perloo (made from Charleston Gold rice). If you visit during the hot months, try the watermelon gazpacho with stone crab, too. It tastes like summer in a bowl. $ *Average main: $22* ✉ *4 Cannon St., Market area* ☎ *843/302–8825* 🌐 *www.thegrocerycharleston.com* ✣ *A1.*

$$$$ STEAKHOUSE Fodor's Choice ★

✕ **Hall's Chophouse.** Hall's Chophouse set down in early 2009 in the old Artist and Craftsman Supply digs on upper King Street, plying a different brand of craftsmanship: 28-day-aged USDA steaks. In plush, two-story environs, the restaurant has swiftly made good, establishing itself as one of the top three steakhouses in town (Oak and Grill 225 being the others). Recommended are the 28-ounce, long-bone Tomahawk rib eye, the New York strip, and the dry aged, slow-roasted prime rib. A heads-up, too: Hall's service borders on excessive, or is it obsessive? Staff takes uncommon heed of its guests, though the lavishly prepared steaks offer the restaurant's greatest source of hospitality. $ *Average main: $40* ✉ *434 King St., Upper King* ☎ *843/727–0090* 🌐 *www.hallschophouse.com* ✍ *Reservations essential* ✣ *B2.*

$$$$ SOUTHERN

✕ **High Cotton.** The styling here remains unchanged by time: lazily spinning paddle fans, palm trees, and exposed brick walls. Clearly Joe Palma's appointment as chef has not affected the nature of this classic venue; rather, his selection has ramped up the restaurant to new heights. The picnic plate allows a pleasant introduction, displaying delicately fried green tomatoes, pillowy pimento cheese, pickled okra and peaches, a bit of the restaurant's house-made charcuterie, and a selection of BBQ Lowcountry peanuts. Smothered in a sticky sauce, the peanuts seem a modernized, much improved version of Cracker Jack. If you want a traditional dinner, the restaurant still offers thick cuts of steaks and chops with choice of sauce and side dishes like fried brussels sprouts and the timeless creamy white corn grits. Then for dessert: a Southern-style pecan pie baked with bourbon brown sugar caramel, or a high-rising peanut butter pie. Choose both if you feel bold. They're like rich Southern blessings. $ *Average main: $27* ✉ *199 E. Bay St., Market area* ☎ *843/724–3815* 🌐 *www.mavericksouthernkitchens.com/highcotton* ✍ *Reservations essential* ⏲ *No lunch weekdays* ✣ *H5.*

$ SOUTHERN

✕ **Hominy Grill.** The wooden barber poles from the last century still frame the door of this small, homespun café. Chalkboard specials are often the way to go here, whether you are visiting for breakfast, lunch, or dinner. Chef Robert Stehling is a Carolina boy who lived in New York; that dichotomy shows in his "uptown" comfort food. Here, you can have the perfect soft-shell-crab sandwich with homemade fries, but leave room for the tangy buttermilk pie or the chocolate peanut butter pie. The bottom line: whatever Stehling cooks tastes good. Renovations in recent years include a new patio and roomier indoor seating. Both are lovely improvements. $ *Average main: $13* ✉ *207 Rutledge Ave., Canonboro* ☎ *843/937–0930* 🌐 *www.hominygrill.com* ⏲ *No dinner Sun.* ✣ *A2*

7

$$$$ SOUTHERN Fodor's Choice ★

✕ **Husk.** Welcome to Husk, home to celebrated chef Sean Brock, a host of ingredients indigenous to the region, and an abundance of accolades. Named Best New Restaurant in America by *Bon Appetit* magazine in 2011, Husk serves an ambitious menu steeped in the South—and the South alone. Seriously. Brock forbids the inclusion of items from other regions or provinces, even olive oil. A large chalkboard inside the restaurant accounts for an offering of ever-changing artisanal foods, as the menu sometimes varies twice daily. Supper favorites include seafood such as snapper, catfish, and flounder, frequently paired with heirloom vegetables. Try the Southern fried chicken skins or skillet of smoky bacon corn bread, too—both are terrifically popular. The building itself, balcony intact, dates to the late 19th century, and the freestanding bar beside the restaurant is lined with 100-year-old exposed brick and several Kentucky bourbons and whiskeys. $ *Average main: $26* ✉ *76 Queen St., Market area* ☎ *843/577–2500* 🌐 *www.huskrestaurant.com* ✣ *C5.*

## CHITTERLINGS

Do not be afraid, be informed. Chitterlings, better known as chitlins (and sometimes chit'lins), can be sampled from several soul-food establishments in Charleston, including Martha Lou Gadsden's eponymously named restaurant. A quick primer: chitterlings are made up of the small intestines of a pig, and usually served fried or steamed after being boiled for several hours. They're not for everyone, but try to withhold judgment before tasting (possibly with cider vinegar or hot sauce).

$$$ FRENCH

✕ **La Fourchette.** French owner Perig Goulet moves agilely through the petite dining room of this unpretentious bistro. With back-to-back chairs making things cozy (and noisy), this place could easily be in Paris. Kevin Kelly chooses the wines—predominantly French and esoteric—and they befit the authentic fare. Goulet is especially proud of his country pâté, from a recipe handed down from his grand-mère. Other favorites include duck salad, scallops sautéed in cognac, and shrimp in a leek sauce. Dieters may be shocked by the golden frites fried in duck fat and served with aioli, but they keep putting their hands in the basket. Check the blackboard for fish straight off the boats. $ *Average main: $22* ✉ *432 King St., Upper King* ☎ *843/722–6261* 🌐 *www.lafourchettecharleston.com* ⏲ *Closed Sun. No lunch Aug.–Mar.* ✣ *B2*

$$$ AMERICAN Fodor's Choice ★

✕ **The Macintosh.** Here's another name to tuck into your sweetgrass basket filled with great Charleston chefs: Jeremiah Bacon. And what a perfect name, right? As the former chef at Carolina's and Oak Steakhouse, Bacon enjoys free reign at The Macintosh, named one of *Bon Appetit*'s 50 Best New Restaurants in America in 2012. The Macintosh continues in the traditions of restaurants like FIG, offering comfy quarters and homespun victuals to a stylish crowd. Here, Bacon shows off his fondness for the little-regarded deckle, a highly-marbled, delicious piece of rib eye, as well as local cobia, clams, and grouper, and bone marrow bread pudding. Already exceedingly popular, The Mac's aiming to take its place among Charleston's best. $ *Average main: $24* ✉ *478 King*

*St., Upper King* ☎ *843/788–4299* 🌐 *www.themacintoshcharleston.com* ✥ *A1.*

$ SOUTHERN Fodor's Choice ★ ✕ **Martha Lou's Kitchen.** You may not delight in the decor—vinyl booths repaired with duct tape and walls muddled with old photographs—but for those venturing inside Martha Lou's Kitchen, a bit of Charleston heritage awaits. Of course, the chicken, perfectly cooked to golden brown, and those fried pork chops aren't bad, either. Martha Lou Gadsden has made her pink cinder-block building into a palace of soul food, serving some of the city's finest. The tireless octogenarian works all day, preparing collard greens, giblet rice, lima beans, and, yes, even chitterlings. Just a chat with Miss Martha Lou is enough to make the trip worthwhile. $ *Average main: $8* ✉ *1068 Morrison Dr.* ☎ *843/577–9583* ▬ *No credit cards* ⏲ *Closed Sun.* ✥ *C1*

## COLD-PRESSED COFFEE

Though not exclusive to Charleston, cold-pressed coffee is considered more potent than regular coffee. The basis: cold-pressed coffee requires extended brewing times, which removes some of the bite or acidity, while ramping up natural caffeine levels. Queen Street Grocery supplies the hooch downtown.

$$$$ AMERICAN Fodor's Choice ★ ✕ **McCrady's.** Executive chef Sean Brock may spend the majority of his time at his new enterprise, Husk, but the unswerving McCrady's still delivers thanks to talented chef de cuisine Jeremiah Langhorne and his crackerjack restaurant staff. Originally constructed in 1788, the structure features heart pine flooring, two fireplaces, exposed brick walls, and a pair of handsome brick archways. Its impressive legacy is supported by cuisine still ranking among Charleston's best. Bear witness to the short rib, set with sweet corn and green tomatoes, or the beef tartare featuring small discs of egg yolk, ramps, and frisee. Or enjoy fresh fish from local waters, such as grilled cobia or flounder crusted with green peppercorn. Meats include Berkshire pork so tender your fork leaves indentions, and aged duck roasted on the bone. A four-course menu featuring smaller dishes allows diners to taste several items. The only trouble: it may leave you craving more. $ *Average main: $30* ✉ *2 Unity Alley, Market area* ☎ *843/577–0025* 🌐 *www.mccradysrestaurant.com* ✍ *Reservations essential* ⏲ *No lunch* ✥ *H6.*

$ AMERICAN ✕ **Moe's Taverns.** First things first: no, it's not a burrito joint, far from it. Moe's Tavern is decidedly old-school, earning a perennial place on the area's best-burger list. They're big, half-pound, Angus beef chuck patties, cooked to order. And they're not even the best thing on the menu. Give it up for Moe's BLT, containing a sizable disc of mozzarella cheese, fried tomato, and, of course, plenty of bacon. Visit the original location on Rutledge Avenue near Hampton Park, or the newer, downtown installation. The first is preferable, as much for its nostalgic charm as its heady selection of beers. $ *Average main: $30* ✉ *Moe's Crosstown Tavern, 714 Rutledge Ave., Hampton Park* ☎ *843/722–3287* $ *Average main: $7* ✉ *Moe's Downtown Tavern, 5 Cumberland St., Market area* ☎ *843/577–8500* 🌐 *www.moestaverns.com* ✥ *A1.*

$ PIZZA ✕ **Monza.** An homage to the Italian city of the same name, Monza provides genuine Neapolitan-style pizza and an introduction to one of the

7

world's most historic motor-sport racing circuits: the Autodromo Nazionale Monza. The restaurant takes its cue after several Formula One greats, naming its pizzas for Emilio Materassi, Felice Nazzaro, Giuseppe Campari, Wolfgang Von Trips, Ronnie Peterson, and "El Maestro," Juan Manuel Fangio. Like the sport the restaurant celebrates, service is quick-paced, the setting modish. As for the pizza, baked in a wood-fired oven, all specialties boast a thin, crisp crust, and toppings such as house-made sausage, pepperoni, eggplant, roasted red peppers, and locally farmed eggs. *Average main: $13 ✉ 451 King St., Upper King ☎ 843/720–8787 🌐 www.monzapizza.com ⊕ A1.*

$$$ MEDITERRANEAN **Muse Restaurant & Wine Bar.** Set in an older, pale yellow home on Society Street, Muse lays bare Mediterranean stylings in sophisticated, relaxed quarters. The bar functions as a drawing room, permitting easy introductions and closer inspection of the restaurant's impressive, 100-plus-bottle wine list. Nature provides ideal lighting, as sunlight spills into the dining rooms during evenings in spring and summer. The restaurant serves standout plates, such as tuna carpaccio, sweetbreads, swordfish, and its signature dish: a delicious, scarcely fried sea bass, served with head and tail intact, over saffron rice and roasted-pepper puree. *Average main: $24 ✉ 82 Society St., Lower King ☎ 843/577–1102 🌐 www.charlestonmuse.com ✍ Reservations essential ⏲ No lunch ⊕ C3.*

$$$$ SOUTHERN Fodor's Choice ★ **Peninsula Grill.** Graham Dailey has successfully filled the post formerly occupied by longtime chef Bob Carter, incorporating Lowcountry produce and seafood into traditional Peninsula dishes, at once eyeing the past and the future. The dining room looks the part: the walls are covered in olive-green velvet and dotted with 18th-century-style portraits, and the ceiling supports black-iron chandeliers. These fixtures serve as an excellent backdrop for "sinfully grilled" Angus steaks, as well as jumbo sea scallops, and Berskhire pork chops. Palate-cleanse with the homemade sorbet, or try the signature three-way chocolate dessert that comes with a shot of ice-cold milk. The servers, who work in tandem, are pros; the personable sommelier makes wine selections that truly complement your meal, anything from bubbly to clarets and dessert wines. The atmosphere is animated and convivial, and Carter's famous coconut cake still graces the menu. *Average main: $35 ✉ Planters Inn, 112 N. Market St., Market area ☎ 843/723–0700 🌐 www.peninsulagrill.com ✍ Reservations essential ⏲ No lunch ⊕ F5.*

$ AMERICAN **Queen Street Grocery.** For crepes and cold-pressed coffee, most folks turn to a venerable Charleston institution: Queen Street Grocery. Established in 1922, the corner shop has endured several guises through the years: butchery, candy shop, and late-night convenience store. Back in 2008, new owners returned the store to its roots as a neighborhood grocery store, sourcing much of the produce and other goods from local growers. It's a great preservation act, improved upon by QSG's newest offerings: sweet and savory crepes named for the islands surrounding Charleston. *Average main: $9 ✉ 133 Queen St., Market area ☎ 843/723–4121 🌐 www.qsg29401.com ⊕ B5.*

The pastel houses of Rainbow Row on East Bay Street are a popular photo-op.

$ AMERICAN Fodor's Choice ★ **Recovery Room.** The graffiti-splashed walls and tongue-in-cheek title make the Recovery Room a favorite for hipsters and college kids. In addition to cans of PBR, the watering hole, set underneath the U.S. Highway 17 bridge, serves up brunch, lunch, a late-night menu, and even amateur pole dancing on Monday night. Go for the tater tachos, tater tots covered in shredded cheeses, jalapeños, tomatoes, and onions, or the wings in 12 sauces. The windows may be few and the view muted, but look at it this way: at least nobody will see you scarf down an order of "chicken biscuits"—fried chicken tenders sopping with honey or gravy over a homemade biscuit. *Average main: $6* ✉ *685 King St., Upper King* ☎ *843/722–4220* *www.recoveryroomtavern.com* ✣ *A1.*

$$$$ SOUTHERN **Slightly North of Broad.** This former warehouse with brick-and-stucco walls has a chef's table that looks directly into the open kitchen. It's a great place to perch if you can "take the heat," as chef Frank Lee, who wears a baseball cap instead of a toque, is one of the city's culinary characters. He is known for his talent in prepping game, and his venison is exceptional. Many of the items come as small plates, which makes them perfect for sharing. The braised lamb shank with a ragout of white beans, arugula, and a red demi-glace is divine. Lunch can be as inexpensive as $9.95 for something as memorable as mussels with spinach, grape tomatoes, and smoked bacon. *Average main: $28* ✉ *192 E. Bay St., Market area* ☎ *843/723–3424* *www.mavericksouthernkitchens.com/snob* *No lunch weekends* ✣ *H5.*

$ MEXICAN **Taco Boy.** Accommodating visitors and locals alike, Taco Boy delivers tasty Mexican treats to a bustling patio crowd. The restaurant belongs to Revolutionary Eating Ventures (REV), the talented gang behind Monza and Moe's Tavern, two other restaurants found in this guide.

REV casts an eye toward sustainability at Taco Boy, constructing the restaurant (in its previous life an old bread-distribution warehouse) with rehabbed or reclaimed materials—right down to the bar counter, carved from a fallen North Carolina walnut tree. It's a forward-thinking and fun joint, perfect for downing margaritas and *micheladas* (beer with lime juice, tomato juice, and chilies) or sharing a sampler trio of house-made guacamole and salsas. *Average main: $7 ✉ 217 Huger St., North of Broad ☎ 843/789–3333 🌐 www.tacoboy.net ✥ C1.*

$ AMERICAN Fodor's Choice ★

**The Tattooed Moose.** It only seems like a cross between a veterans' hall and a dive bar, but the Tattooed Moose's decidedly unpretentious look was thoughtfully put together by the owners of the Voodoo Tiki Bar in West Ashley. With 90-plus beers on the menu, and a large moose head behind the counter, the Tattooed Moose cuts a distinctive figure. The bar's famous duck club is a menu showstopper. Priced at twice the amount as the other sandwiches, it relies on duck confit, apple-smoked bacon, garlic aioli, and ripened tomatoes bounded by sweet, Hawaiian bread. Homey eats like house-smoked barbecue brisket, chicken salad, jumbo chicken wings, and fried turkey breast round out the offerings. *Average main: $10 ✉ 1137 Morrison Dr., Market area ☎ 843/277–2990 🌐 www.tattooedmoose.com ✥ B1.*

$$$ ITALIAN Fodor's Choice ★

**Trattoria Lucca.** The naysayers scoffed when chef Ken Vedrinski opened Trattoria Lucca back in 2008. Not because of Vedrinski; the well-heeled chef manned the kitchen of the bygone Sienna restaurant on Daniel Island. Rather, the whispers were from Lucca's unlikely location, deep on the peninsula in a neighborhood in need of TLC. And now, well, now they flock, visiting Lucca for his warm cauliflower *sformatino* (with soft organic egg, pancetta, and parmigiano cheese), organic Mezze Maniche and Chitarra pastas, and, on Sunday evening, family-style suppers with communal seating. *Average main: $24 ✉ 41 Bogard St., North of Broad ☎ 843/973–3323 🌐 www.luccacharleston.com ⚠ Reservations essential ✥ A2.*

$$$ AMERICAN Fodor's Choice ★

**Two Boroughs Larder.** Husband and wife Josh and Heather Keeler ventured down from Philadelphia to open up their restaurant and market in the Cannonborough-Elliotborough neighborhoods. The menu changes daily, featuring an eclectic but irrepressible mix. You can opt for a breakfast sandwich any time of the day, only with pepperonata and egg, Neueske's bacon, or pork scrapple—a traditional heap of pork mush of Pennsylvania Dutch and Amish descent. But the restaurant supplies other pleasing mains, too, like grouper brodetto, oven-roasted trout, and veal sweetbreads along with plentiful sides such as marrow-roasted cauliflower, braised heirloom beans, and buffalo pig tails. The restaurant is already prized by the community, so much so that Josh Keeler nabbed one of the seven seats at the 2012 Critics' Dinner, an annual event affiliated with the Charleston Wine & Food Festival. *Average main: $20 ✉ 186 Coming St., Cannonborough ☎ 843/637–3722 🌐 www.twoboroughslarder.com ✥ A1.*

## SOUTH OF BROAD

$$$$ SOUTHERN

**Carolina's.** On a quiet side street between East Bay Street and Waterfront Park, this longtime favorite occupies a former wharf building. The smartened-up decor includes romantic banquettes, and an evolving menu under chef Jill Mathias has a strong emphasis on healthful ingredients. (Owner Richard Stoney also owns Kensington Plantation, where most of the produce is grown.) Lowcountry favorites stand next to original dishes like scallops with roasted cauliflower. Local grouper works amazingly well with a port-wine broth. Ask about the special prix-fixe dinners, including those with beer pairings. On Sunday and Monday bottles of wine are half-price. The free valet parking is another nice touch. *Average main: $30* *10 Exchange St., South of Broad* *843/724–3800* *www.carolinasrestaurant.com* *Reservations essential* *No lunch weekends* *E5.*

$$ FRENCH

**Gaulart and Maliclet Café.** Sharing high, family-style tables for breakfast, lunch, or dinner leads to camaraderie at this bustling bistro also known as Fast 'n' French. Thursday brings a crowd for fondue. The cheese version can be disappointing, but the seafood, which you cook in broth yourself, is better. Opt to get your cheese fix with the wonderful Bucheron cheese salad. Nightly specials, such as bouillabaisse or couscous, are reasonably priced and come with a petite glass of wine. And a subtly sweet chocolate-mousse cake is the best way to end your meal. The service is often imperfect but fun, and prices have stayed reasonable (while others downtown have soared). Although not as popular as it once was, the restaurant still has a loyal following. *Average main: $15* *98 Broad St., South of Broad* *843/577–9797* *www.fastandfrenchcharleston.com* *Closed Sun. No dinner Mon.* *C5*

## MOUNT PLEASANT AND VICINITY

$$$$ SOUTHERN

**Old Village Post House.** If you've been on the road too long, this circa 1888 inn will provide warmth and sustenance. Many residents of this tree-lined village consider this their neighborhood tavern. The second, smaller dining room is cozy, and the outdoor space under the market umbrellas is open and airy. Expect contemporary takes on Southern favorites like lump crab cakes, shrimp and grits, and especially the fresh vegetables, like a butter beans mélange. From the open kitchen, the chefs can perfectly sauté the catch of the day. Here, pork tenderloin may have a ginger-peachy glaze. In season, plump softshell crabs are deftly fried. Frank Sinatra serenades as you cleanse your palate with a tart, key lime pie with a crunchy crust and passion-fruit coulis. *Average main: $25* *101 Pitt St., Mount Pleasant* *843/388–8935* *www.mavericksouthernkitchens.com* *No lunch Mon.–Sat.* *H4*

$$$ SOUTHERN

**Seewee Restaurant.** This throwback to the 1950s (or earlier) was once a general store. Some 20 minutes from downtown, it's worth the trip to the country for this Southern-style flashback. You pull open the screen door and the shelves are still lined with canned goods, and there are a few tables for four. Outdoors on the screened porch is more seating, and that is also where the bands (really good blues, bluegrass, etc.) set up come Saturday night when the weather is warm. The veteran

7

waitresses will call you "hon" and caringly recommend their favorites, a lot of which are Southern-fried: pickles, green tomatoes, chicken, oysters, and fresh local shrimp. Look on the blackboard to find the more-contemporary, less-caloric (and more expensive) dishes. For breakfast or lunch, you will love the traditional shrimp and grits. *$ Average main: $25 ✉ 4808 Hwy. 17 N, Awendaw ☎ 843/928–3609 🌐 No Web site ⏲ No dinner Sun. ✣ H1*

$$$ SEAFOOD Fodor's Choice ★ **✕ The Wreck of the Richard & Charlene.** At first glance the name appears to refer to the waterfront restaurant's look, topped off with a shabby, screened-in porch. (In actuality, the *Richard and Charlene* was a trawler that slammed into the building during a hurricane in 1989.) But looks aren't the thing here—it's all about the food. Located in the old village of Mount Pleasant, the kitchen serves up Southern tradition on a plate: boiled peanuts, fried shrimp, and stone-crab claws. The best option is the most expensive: the mixed seafood platter with fried flounder, shrimp, oysters, and scallops. Know that it closes by 8:30 Tuesday through Thursday, and at 9:15 on Friday and Saturday night. *$ Average main: $22 ✉ 106 Haddrell St., Mount Pleasant ☎ 843/884–0052 🌐 www.wreckrc.com ✍ Reservations not accepted ▭ No credit cards ⏲ No lunch. Closed Sun. and Mon. ✣ H4*

## GREATER CHARLESTON

$ SOUTHERN **✕ Fiery Ron's Home Team BBQ.** Home Team, as the bar and restaurant is called, has swiftly earned the endorsement of even the old-school barbecue set (the restaurant's newfangled pork tacos notwithstanding). And they've done so with time-honored adherence to the oft-preferred technique of low-and-slow grilling, producing St. Louis–style ribs, and traditional smoked pork and chicken. Dress up your meal with three tableside sauces, including vinegar flavored, tomato tinged, and a mustard-based concoction, befitting South Carolina's German heritage. Side offerings are a good measuring stick for any barbecue joint, and Home Team delivers with mashed potatoes, mac 'n' cheese, collards, red rice, baked beans, Brunswick stew, poppy-seed slaw, and potato salad. A second location is on Sullivan's Island at 2209 Middle Street. *$ Average main: $8 ✉ 1205 Ashley River Rd., West Ashley ☎ 843/225–7427 $ Average main: $8 ✉ 2209 Middle St., Sullivan's Island ☎ 843/883–3131 🌐 www.hometeambbq.com ✣ H4.*

$ SOUTHERN **✕ The Glass Onion.** Established by a trio of New Orleans ex-pats, the Glass Onion fashions a taut bond between Charleston and its sister city, dishing up beaucoup seasonable, Southern eats. Take a peek at the menu: deviled eggs, overstuffed pimiento-cheese sandwiches, meat loaf, and fried catfish po'boys, and sweets like bread pudding with whiskey sauce. Yep, it's decidedly Southern, and decidedly dreamy. The Saturday brunch (10–3) is a must, with fluffy buttermilk biscuits and gravy, and pork tamales, but get there early, as they often sell out. The meals are set on sheets of brown paper that drape the restaurant's wooden tabletops, another clever touch. *$ Average main: $12 ✉ 1219 Savannah Hwy., Johns Island ☎ 843/225–1717 🌐 www.ilovetheglassonion.com ✣ A5.*

$ SOUTHERN **✕ JB's Smokeshack.** When you come to the sign of the pig (not to mention other rudimentary signs stuck in the ground like "Catfish"), turn

Broad Street divides Charleston's historic district into North and South of Broad.

in for one of the area's best barbecue joints. At this funky find, you will see evidence of the diverse crowd, beat-up pickup trucks to new BMWs—the latter often driven by guests at nearby Kiawah Island. (JB's will deliver out there for $35.) Most people have the buffet, which consists of barbecue pork, apple-wood-smoked chicken, and all of the Southern veggies—usually including okra gumbo, butter beans, and coleslaw—plus desserts like banana pudding; it's all for one (very) low price. Barbecue connoisseurs know that JB's takes the big prizes at the competitions and that the ribs and the Angus beef brisket are top-shelf. To further flavor the smoky meats, sauces are served on the side. Just come early, because dinner is over by 8:30. [$] *Average main: $9* ✉ *3406 Maybank Hwy., Johns Island* ☎ *843/577–0426* 🌐 *www.jbssmokeshack.com* ⏲ *Closed Sun.–Tues.* ✣ *A6*

$ AMERICAN Fodor's Choice ★

✕ **Sesame Burgers & Beer.** Sesame's secret? The burger-and-beer joint makes just about everything on the premises—from its house-ground burgers right down to the mustard, ketchup, and mayonnaise. Sample the South Carolina, topped with homemade pimiento cheese; the Southwestern, with guacamole and chipotle sour cream; or the Park Circle, with cheddar cheese, coleslaw, barbecue sauce, and tomatoes. Also garnering special mention: Blue's Corn on the Cob, which is charred on the grill, then slathered in chipotle butter and Cotija cheese. Sesame's devotion to beer is strong, too, with selections running at least 30-deep. Two other locations can be found in North Charleston at 4726 Spruill Avenue and in Mount Pleasant at 675-E Johnny Dodds Boulevard. [$] *Average main: $8* ✉ *2070 Sam Rittenberg Blvd.* ☎ *843/766–7770* ✣ *A5.*

$ SOUTHERN Fodor's Choice ★ ✕ **Tomato Shed Cafe.** Open only for lunch on weekdays, the Tomato Shed Cafe presents a banquet of locally raised delicacies. Owners and farmers Pete and Babs Ambrose maintain a 135-acre farm on Wadmalaw Island, sourcing grounds for the restaurant. The menu emphasizes seasonal choices, allowing for fresh butter beans, cabbage, collards, cucumber salad, and rutabaga casserole. These veggies sit well with the Tomato Shed's other offerings, such as peel-and-eat shrimp from local waters, barbecue, crab cakes, and roast pork. Be sure to grab a bag of boiled peanuts on your way out. *Average main: $10* ✉ *842 Main Rd., Johns Island* ☎ *843/599–9999* 🌐 *www.stonofarmmarket.com/tomatoshedcafe.html* ⊙ *Closed Sun.* ✥ *A6*

# WHERE TO STAY

Updated by Anna Evans

*Hotel reviews have been abbreviated in this book. For expanded reviews, please go to Fodors.com.*

Charleston is a city known for its lovingly restored mansions that have been converted into atmospheric bed-and-breakfasts, as well as deluxe inns, all found in the residential blocks of the Historic District. Upscale, world-class hotels are in the heart of downtown as are boutique hotels that provide a one-of-a-kind experience. Chain hotels pepper the busy, car-trafficked areas (like Meeting Street). In addition, there are chain properties in the nearby areas of West Ashley, Mount Pleasant, and North Charleston. Mount Pleasant is considered the most upscale suburb; North Charleston is the least, but if you need to be close to the airport, are participating in events in its Coliseum, or aim to shop the outlet malls there, it is a practical, less expensive alternative.

## RENTAL AGENCIES

**ResortQuest.** Call for condo and house rentals on Kiawah Island or Seabrook Island. For those on Isle of Palms, Sullivan's Island, or Wild Dunes Resort, also call ResortQuest (✉ *1400 Palm Blvd., Isle of Palms* ☎ *800/870–4078* 🌐 *www.resortquestcharleston.com.*) ✉ *2 Beachwalker Dr., Kiawah Island* ☎ *800/544–8222* 🌐 *www.resortquestcharleston.com.*

**Historic Charleston Bed & Breakfast.** As prices escalate, more and more downtown residents are renting out a room or two through the reservation service Historic Charleston Bed & Breakfast. They can be in up-and-coming revitalized neighborhoods or even on the Battery. Handsomely furnished, these rooms can be less expensive than commercial operations. However, since the owners or families are usually on-site, they may not offer the same level of privacy as more traditional B&Bs or small inns. ☎ *800/743–3583* 🌐 *www.historiccharlestonbedandbreakfast.com.*

## PRICES

Charleston's downtown lodgings have three seasons: high season (March–May and September–November), mid-season (June–August), and low season (late November–February). Prices drop significantly during the short low season, except during holidays and special events. High season is summer at the island resorts. You should factor in the cost of downtown parking; if a hotel offers free parking, that is a huge

# BEST BETS FOR CHARLESTON LODGING

**Fodor's Choice**

**Charleston Place,** p. 385
**Kiawah Island Golf Resort,** p. 390
**Market Pavilion Hotel,** p. 387
**Mills House,** p. 387
**Planters Inn,** p. 387
**Wentworth Mansion,** p. 388
**Wild Dunes Resort,** p. 390

## By Price

**$**

**Aloft Charleston Airport & Convention Center,** p. 390
**Old Village Post House,** p. 389

**$$**

**Francis Marion Hotel,** p. 386
**Mills House,** p. 387

**$$$**

**Two Meeting Street Inn,** p. 388

**$$$$**

**Market Pavilion Hotel,** p. 387
**Restoration on King,** p. 388

## By Experience

**BEST B&BS**

**Governors House Inn,** p. 386
**John Rutledge House Inn,** p. 387

**BEST BEDS**

**Restoration on King,** p. 388
**Wentworth Mansion,** p. 388

**BEST LOCATION**

**Charleston Place,** p. 385
**Francis Marion Hotel,** p. 386

**BEST FOR ROMANCE**

**John Rutledge House Inn,** p. 387
**Wentworth Mansion,** p. 388

**BEST VIEWS**

**HarbourView Inn,** p. 386
**Two Meeting Street Inn,** p. 388

plus. In the areas "over the bridges," parking is generally free. *Prices in the reviews are the lowest cost of a standard double room in high season. Use the coordinate (↔ B2) at the end of each listing to locate a site on the Where to Eat and Stay in Charleston map.*

## DOWNTOWN CHARLESTON

$$$ B&B/INN **Andrew Pinckney Inn.** Nestled in the heart of Charleston, this West Indies-inspired inn offers charming rooms as well as two-story town-house suites that sleep four. **Pros:** the town houses are ideal for longer stays; afternoon gourmet tea and coffee service with fresh-baked cookies; iPod docks in each room. **Cons:** elevator accesses regular rooms only, not town houses; near the horse stables, which can smell; can tend toward the loud side due to the bustling neighborhood. *Rooms from: $229 ✉ 40 Pinckney St., Market area ☎ 843/937–8800, 800/505–8983 🌐 www.andrewpinckneyinn.com 37 rooms, 3 town houses, 1 suite Breakfast ↔ G4.*

$$$$ HOTEL Fodor's Choice ★ **Charleston Place.** Even casual passersby enjoy gazing up at the immense handblown Murano glass chandelier in the hotel's open lobby, clicking across the Italian marble floors, admiring the antiques from Sotheby's, and browsing the gallery of upscale shops that completes

the ground-floor offerings of this hotel with deluxe day spa. **Pros:** three fantastic restaurants; on the best shopping street in the Historic District; pet-friendly. **Cons:** rooms aren't as big as one would expect for the price; much of the business is conference groups in shoulder seasons; built in 1986, it lacks the charm of area historic properties. *Rooms from: $375 205 Meeting St., Market area 843/722–4900, 888/635–2350 www.charlestonplace.com 435 rooms, 48 suites No meals F5.*

$$$ HOTEL **DoubleTree by Hilton Hotel & Suites Charleston–Historic District.** Housed in a onetime bank with a restored entrance portico from 1874, this property has clean, spacious suites with nice touches like antique reproductions and canopy beds. **Pros:** in the Market; it's an easy walk to King Street shopping and a charming one to the South of Broad residential area. **Cons:** no breakfast; Internet is expensive; can be noisy because of the location. *Rooms from: $209 181 Church St., Market area 843/577–2644 www.doubletree.com 47 rooms, 165 suites No meals G5.*

$$ HOTEL **Francis Marion Hotel.** Wrought-iron railings, crown moldings, and decorative plasterwork speak of the elegance of 1924, when the Francis Marion was the largest hotel in the Carolinas, and in the guest rooms—many of which have views of Marion Square—bountiful throw pillows and billowy curtains add flair. **Pros:** architecturally and historically significant building; in the midst of the peninsula's best shopping, yet still near the College of Charleston; some of the best city views. **Cons:** rooms are small, as is closet space; on a busy intersection. *Rooms from: $169 387 King St., Upper King 843/722–0600, 877/756–2121 www.francismarioncharleston.com 217 rooms, 16 suites No meals B2.*

$$$ B&B/INN **Fulton Lane Inn.** This inn is both lovely and quirky: its Victorian-dressed rooms (some with four-poster beds, fireplaces, and spa baths) are laid out in a bit of a floor-creaking maze, but it adds to the inn's individuality. **Pros:** location is tops; Room 317 is a cute spot off an alley; privately owned. **Cons:** what's character to one guest can be annoying to another; street noise does seep in; the free breakfast can be paltry. *Rooms from: $219 202 King St., Lower King Street 843/720–2600 www.fultonlaneinn.com 45 rooms Breakfast C4.*

$$$$ B&B/INN ★ **The Governor's House Inn.** The stately architecture of this quintessential Charleston lodging radiates the grandeur, romance, and civility of the city's bountiful colonial era. **Pros:** you can take breakfast on the piazza, in the dining room, or have it delivered; pets are allowed in some rooms; free bicycles make exploring the centrally located area a breeze. **Cons:** older children are welcome in the former kitchen-house rooms, but the main house is not the appropriate environment; busy commercial and government street location. *Rooms from: $265 117 Broad St., South of Broad 843/720–2070, 800/720–9812 www.governorshouse.com 11 rooms Breakfast C5.*

$$$$ B&B/INN **HarbourView Inn.** This is the only hotel on the harbor, and if you ask for a room facing the harbor, you can gaze out onto the kid-friendly fountain and 8 acres of Waterfront Park. **Pros:** Continental breakfast can be delivered to the room or the rooftop; service is notable. **Cons:**

rooms are off long, modern halls; rooms are not particularly spacious. *Rooms from: $279* *2 Vendue Range, Market area* *843/853–8439, 888/853–8439* *www.harbourviewcharleston.com* *52 rooms* *Breakfast* *I16.*

$$$$ B&B/INN ★ **John Rutledge House Inn.** In 1791, George Washington visited this elegant, grand mansion, then residence of one of South Carolina's most influential politicians, John Rutledge, and now a National Historic Landmark with spacious accommodations within the main house. **Pros:** at night, when you "go home" and pour a sherry, it's like being a blue-blood Charlestonian; nice, quiet back courtyard; friendly staff. **Cons:** you can hear some street and kitchen noise in the first-floor rooms; the two carriage houses are not as grand as the main house. *Rooms from: $279* *116 Broad St., South of Broad* *800/476–9741* *www.johnrutledgehouseinn.com* *16 rooms, 3 suites* *Breakfast* *C5.*

$$$$ HOTEL Fodor's Choice ★ **Market Pavilion Hotel.** The melee of one of the busiest corners in the city vanishes as soon as the uniformed bellman opens the lobby door to reveal dark, wood-paneled walls, antique furniture, and chandeliers hung from high ceilings; it resembles a European grand hotel from the 19th century, and you feel like you're visiting royalty. **Pros:** opulent furnishings; architecturally impressive, especially the tray ceilings; conveniently located for everything. **Cons:** the gym is small; those preferring a minimalist or understated decor may find the interior over the top and perhaps a touch nouveau riche. *Rooms from: $279* *225 E. Bay St., Market area* *843/723–0500, 877/440–2250* *www.marketpavilion.com* *61 rooms, 9 suites* *Breakfast* *H5.*

$$$ B&B/INN **Meeting Street Inn.** Rooms in this 1870s stucco house with porches on the second, third, and fourth floors overlook a lovely courtyard with fountains and a garden as well as a larged heated spa tub. **Pros:** all rooms have free Wi-Fi, and some of the more expensive rooms have desks and piazza access; bathrooms sport nice marble fixtures. **Cons:** rooms have 19th-century-style reproductions but could use some updated decor; parking in a nearby lot is $12 a day. *Rooms from: $239* *173 Meeting St., Market area* *843/723–1882, 800/842–8022* *www.meetingstreetinn.com* *56 rooms* *Breakfast* *F5.*

$$ HOTEL Fodor's Choice ★ **Mills House.** A favorite local landmark, from which several historic tours depart, the Mills House is the reconstruction of an 1853 hotel where Robert E. Lee once waved from the wrought-iron balcony. **Pros:** convenient to business district, Historic District, and art galleries; a popular Sunday brunch spot; a concierge desk so well regarded that locals have long called on the Mills House for neighborly assistance and advice. **Cons:** rooms are rather small, which is typical of hotels of this time period; it's on a busy street. *Rooms from: $179* *115 Meeting St., Market area* *843/577–2400, 800/874–9600* *www.millshouse.com* *199 rooms, 16 suites* *No meals* *F6.*

$$$$ B&B/INN Fodor's Choice ★ **Planters Inn.** Part of the Relais & Châteaux group, this boutique property with well-appointed and beautifully maintained rooms is a stately sanctuary amid the bustle of Charleston's Market. **Pros:** double-pane and interior shuttered windows render the rooms soundproof; the same front-desk people take your initial reservation and know your name upon arrival; exceptional full breakfast (included only as part of

a package). **Cons:** no pool; no fitness center. *Rooms from: $399 ✉ 112 N. Market St., Market area ☎ 843/722–2345, 800/845–7082 🌐 www.plantersinn.com 64 rooms, 2 penthouse king suites, 6 governor suites No meals ✣ F5.*

### DOGGY DAY CARE

**Dog Daze.** If you have brought your dog along but don't want to leave him in your room all day, call Dog Daze. Services are $20 a day. *✉ 307 Mill St., Mount Pleasant ☎ 843/884–7387, 843/324–6945.*

$$$$ B&B/INN **Restoration on King.** Charleston architect Neil Stevenson is known for his modern buildings, streamlined interiors, and being something of a stylish scenester about town. **Pros:** wine and water when you arrive is a nice touch, as is the stock-the-refrigerator option; room service comes via neighboring restaurants; iHome stations and Blu-ray players help technophiles feel at home; the location is ideal for those who want to explore all aspects of the city. **Cons:** no gym on the premises, but there are complimentary passes to nearby workout facilities within easy walking distance; prices are steep; no on-site restaurant. *Rooms from: $399 ✉ 75 Wentworth St., Market area ☎ 877/221–7202 🌐 www.restorationonking.com 16 suites Breakfast ✣ C4.*

$$$ B&B/INN ★ **Two Meeting Street Inn.** As pretty as a wedding cake, this 1892 Queen Anne–style mansion wears overhanging bays, colonnades, balustrades, and a turret; Tiffany-stained-glass windows, carved-oak paneling, and a crystal chandelier dress up the public spaces inside. **Pros:** free on-street parking; community refrigerator on each floor; ringside seat for a Battery view and horse-drawn carriages clipping by. **Cons:** no credit cards accepted; some rooms have thick walls and make Wi-Fi spotty; the decor is on the grandmotherly side. *Rooms from: $225 ✉ 2 Meeting St., South of Broad ☎ 843/723–7322 🌐 www.twomeetingstreet.com 9 rooms No credit cards Breakfast ✣ D6.*

$$$$ B&B/INN **Vendue Inn.** Two 19th-century warehouses have been transformed into an inn with nooks and crannies filled with antiques. **Pros:** soundproofing masks street noise; pets allowed for a $50 fee; the Library Restaurant on the first floor is well regarded. **Cons:** popular local hangouts nearby can be noisy; $250 fine for smoking in rooms; complimentary breakfast is only for those who book directly through the inn. *Rooms from: $355 ✉ 19 Vendue Range, Market area ☎ 843/577–7970, 800/845–7900 🌐 www.vendueinn.com 31 rooms, 35 suites Breakfast ✣ H6.*

$$$$ B&B/INN Fodor's Choice ★ **Wentworth Mansion.** Guests at the most grand inn in town admire the Second Empire antiques and reproductions, the rich fabrics, inset wood paneling, and original stained-glass windows, as well as the views from the roofop cupola. **Pros:** luxury bedding, including custom-made mattresses, down pillows, and Italian linens; each room has a whirlpool tub and iPod docking station. **Cons:** Second Empire style can strike some people as forbidding; the building has some of the woes of an old building, including loudly creaking staircases; location deems pedicab, bike, or car advisable to reach tourist areas. *Rooms from: $379 ✉ 149 Wentworth St., College of Charleston Campus ☎ 888/466–1886 🌐 www.wentworthmansion.com 21 rooms Breakfast ✣ A4.*

Rocking chairs on the porch of Two Meeting Street transport guests to a more genteel time.

## MOUNT PLEASANT

$ RESORT **Charleston Harbor Resort & Marina.** Mount Pleasant's finest hotel sits on Charleston Harbor, so you can gaze at the city's skyline, just a 10-minute water-taxi ride away from the marina. **Pros:** the most accessible hotel to downtown that's not in downtown (approximately 6 miles away); a "trolley" runs to the Market from 10 to 10 daily; some rooms have fireplaces. **Cons:** no gym on-site (guests are offered complimentary use of an area gym 10 minutes away); the lobby and the restaurant are not memorable. *Rooms from: $129 ✉ 20 Patriots Point Rd., Mount Pleasant ☎ 843/856–0028, 888/856–0028 🌐 www.charlestonharborresort.com 127 rooms, 6 suites.*

$ B&B/INN **Old Village Post House.** This white wooden building anchoring Mount Pleasant's Historic District on the Cooper River is three-in-one—an excellent restaurant, a neighborly tavern, and a cozy inn, the last of which is set at the top of a high staircase and has rooms with hardwood floors and reproduction furnishings that will remind you of Cape Cod. **Pros:** prices are as affordable as some chain motels on the highway; set on the "Main Street" of the most picturesque and walkable neighborhood in Mount Pleasant; close to Sullivan's Island and Isle of Palms. **Cons:** the inn shares some public spaces with the downstairs restaurant, detracting from privacy; some minor old-building woes, including creaky wood floors; not a traditional hotel, so service can be quirky. *Rooms from: $142 ✉ 101 Pitt St., Mount Pleasant ☎ 843/388–8935 🌐 www.oldvillageposthouse.com 6 rooms Breakfast.*

## ELSEWHERE IN CHARLESTON

$ HOTEL **Aloft Charleston Airport & Convention Center.** Designed with the young, hip, and high-tech traveler in mind, this hotel is retro-meets-the-Jetsons. **Pros:** high concept design; convenient for airport and convention center; inexpensive. **Cons:** noise from planes taking off; small, somewhat cramped rooms; far from downtown. *Rooms from: $139 ✉ 4875 Tanger Outlet Blvd., North Charleston ☎ 843/566–7300 ⊕ www.starwoodhotels.com/alofthotels 136 rooms.*

$$$ RESORT Fodor's Choice ★ **Kiawah Island Golf Resort.** Choose from one- to four-bedroom villas, three- to eight-bedroom private homes, or the Sanctuary at Kiawah Island, an amazing 255-room luxury waterfront hotel and spa that is one of the most prestigious resorts in the country, yet still kid-friendly. **Pros:** the smaller condo-villas are still fairly affordable; the Ocean Room is an ideal venue for an anniversary or a proposal; the golf courses and tennis programs are ranked among the country's best. **Cons:** not all hotel rooms have a view of the ocean; it is pricey and a substantial drive from town. *Rooms from: $225 ✉ 1 Sanctuary Beach Dr., Kiawah Island ☎ 843/768–2121, 800/654–2924 ⊕ www.kiawahresort.com 242 rooms, 13 suites, 400 villas, 90 homes No meals.*

$$$$ RESORT Fodor's Choice ★ **Wild Dunes Resort.** Guests, which include many families in the summer, have a long list of recreational options—such as Tom Fazio golf courses and nationally ranked tennis programs—at this 1,600-acre island resort. **Pros:** golf courses and marina are appealing; free shuttle runs from 7 am to 11 pm to wherever you need to go within the complex. **Cons:** in peak summer season, kids dominate the pool areas and the boardwalk, as children's programs run predominantly in summer; a congested, high-density feel exists in all the main facilities. *Rooms from: $299 ✉ 4600 Palm Blvd., Isle of Palms ☎ 843/886–6000, 888/845–8926 ⊕ www.wilddunes.com 396 units, 93 rooms No meals.*

# NIGHTLIFE AND THE ARTS

Updated by Rob Young

For a midsize city, Charleston has a surprisingly varied and sophisticated arts scene, though the city really shines during its major annual arts festival, Spoleto Festival USA. The nightlife scene is similarly comprehensive, with nocturnal venues for all ages and tastes.

## THE ARTS

### FESTIVALS

Spoleto USA is only the beginning—there are dozens of festivals held throughout the city each year. Some focus on food and wine, whereas others are concerned with gardens and architecture. Charleston is one of the few American cities that can claim a distinctive regional cuisine.

**BB&T Charleston Food + Wine Festival.** In just a few years, the BB&T Charleston Wine + Food Festival has become a four-day, favored culinary playground for the nation's leading chefs (including several already from Charleston), food writers, and, of course, foodies. Held in late February and early March, events emphasize the Lowcountry's foodways

End a perfect Charleston day with drinks at the classy Pavilion Bar atop the Market Pavilion Hotel.

and heritage, as well as restaurant dinners exclusive to the festival that pair Charleston-area chefs with national colleagues. ☎ *843/763–0280, 866/369–3378* 🌐 *charlestonwineandfood.com/.*

★ **MOJA Arts Festival.** During the last week of September and first week of October, the MOJA Arts Festival celebrates African heritage and Caribbean influences on African-American culture. It includes theater, dance, and music performances, art shows, films, lectures, and tours of the Historic District. ☎ *843/724–7305* 🌐 *www.mojafestival.com.*

**Piccolo Spoleto.** The spirited companion festival of Spoleto Festival USA, Piccolo Spoleto showcases the best in local and regional talent from every artistic discipline. There are as many as 700 events—from jazz performances to puppet shows, military band concerts, and expansive art shows in Marion Square—from mid-May through early June. Many of the performances are free or priced democratically. Hundreds of these cultural experiences are kid-friendly. ☎ *843/724–7305* 🌐 *www.piccolospoleto.org.*

**Southeastern Wildlife Exposition.** Held in mid-February, the Southeastern Wildlife Exposition is one of Charleston's biggest annual events, with fine art by renowned wildlife artists, live animals, an oyster roast, and a gala. ☎ *843/723–1748, 800/221–5273* 🌐 *www.sewe.com.*

### VENUES

**Charleston Music Hall.** Bluegrass, blues, and country musicians step onto the historic stage of the Charleston Music Hall, especially for Piccolo Spoleto performances. It's within walking distance of several popular bars and restaurants. ✉ *37 John St., Upper King* ☎ *843/853–2252* 🌐 *www.charlestonmusichall.com.*

CLOSE UP

## Spoleto Festival USA

Spoleto Festival USA performance.

**Spoleto Festival USA.** For 17 glorious days in late May and early June, Charleston gets a dose of culture from the Spoleto Festival USA. This internationally acclaimed performing-arts festival features a mix of distinguished artists and emerging talent from around the world. Performances take place in magical settings, such as beneath a canopy of ancient oaks or inside a centuries-old cathedral.

Some 45 events—which cost between $10 (for balcony seats) to $130 (good orchestra seats), with most averaging between $25 and $50—include everything from improv to Shakespeare, from rap to chamber music, from ballet to salsa. A mix of formal concerts and casual performances is what Pulitzer Prize–winning composer Gian Carlo Menotti had in mind when, in 1977, he initiated the festival as a complement to his opera-heavy Italian festival. He chose Charleston because of its European look and because its residents love the arts—not to mention any cause for celebration. He wanted the festival to be a "fertile ground for the young" as well as a "dignified home for the masters." Mayor Joseph Riley has diligently worked to renew that Italian connection with the original mother festival in Spoleto, Italy (🌐 *www.festivaldispoleto.it*). This reaffirmation of sister-city partnership and the sharing of ideas has encouraged and increased tourism between the two cities for both festivals and beyond.

The finale is a must-do, particularly for the younger crowd. Staged outdoors at Middleton Place, the plantation house and lush landscaped gardens provide a dramatic backdrop. The inexpensive seating is unreserved and unlimited. The lawn is covered with blankets and chairs, and many cooks prepare lavish spreads. For decades the Spoleto Festival Orchestra has played a spirited concert of contemporary and classical pieces, followed by spectacular fireworks exploding over the Ashley River. Tradition was broken in 2010 when the Carolina Chocolate Drops, an African-American string band performed. Because events sell out quickly, insiders say you should buy your Spoleto tickets several months in advance. (Tickets to mid-week performances are a bit easier to secure.) Hotels definitely fill up quickly, so book a room at the same time and reserve your tables for the trendy downtown restaurants. ☎ *843/722–2764* 🌐 *www.spoletousa.org.*

**North Charleston Performing Art Center.** Dance, symphony, and theater productions are among those staged at the North Charleston Performing Art Center. In recent years, performers such as Hall & Oates, Edward Sharpe and the Magnetic Zeroes, and Greg Allman have taken the stage. ✉ *5001 Coliseum Dr., North Charleston* ☎ *843/529–5050* 🌐 *www.northcharlestoncoliseumpac.com.*

**Simons Center for the Arts.** Performances by the College of Charleston's theater department and musical recitals are presented here during the school year. ✉ *54 St. Phillips St., College of Charleston Campus* ☎ *843/953–5604* 🌐 *www.cofc.edu.*

## NIGHTLIFE

You can find it all here, across the board, for Charleston loves a good party. The more mature crowd goes to the sophisticated spots, and there are many: piano bars, wine bars, lounges featuring jazz groups or a guitarist/vocalist, and cigar lounges. Rooftop bars are a particular Charleston tradition, and the city has several good ones. Many restaurants offer live entertainment on at least one weekend night, and these tend to cater to an older crowd. The Upper King area especially has grown in recent years, overtaking the Market area in terms of popularity and variety. ⚠ A city ordinance mandates that bars must close by 2 am and that patrons must be out of the establishment and doors locked by that hour. Last call is usually 1:30.

### NORTH OF BROAD

#### BARS AND PUBS

**Club Habana.** Located above the Tinder Box tobacco store and cigar shop, Club Habana thrives as a chic martini and cognac bar known for its mixology and classic cocktails. Additionally, it's one of the few establishments in town where you can still smoke inside the club. ✉ *177 Meeting St., Market area* ☎ *843/853–5900, 843/853-5008* 🌐 *www.tinderboxcharleston.com/habana.*

**Gin Joint.** The cocktails here—frothy Ramos fizzes, Sazeracs, slings, smashes, and juleps—are retro, some pre-Prohibition. The bartenders don bowties and suspenders, but the atmosphere is utterly contemporary, with slick gray walls and subtle lighting. The bar is named after Humphrey Bogart's famous line in *Casablanca*: "Of all the gin joints, in all the towns, in all the world, she walks into mine." The kitchen serves up small plates like foie gras torchon, pheasant potpie, sweets, and cheeses. ✉ *182 East Bay St., Market area* ☎ *843/577–6111* 🌐 *www.theginjoint.com.*

**The Griffon.** Pin a dollar to the wall, or a dart to the board bull's-eye. In the tradition of similar Irish pubs, dollar bills cover just about every inch of real estate at the Griffon, helping the bar achieve institutional status within the city. It's dark, dusty, and well worn, and somehow still seems charming. A rotating draft selection includes beers from local breweries like Westbrook, Coast, and Holy City, providing additional appeal. ✉ *18 Vendue Range, Market area* ☎ *843/723–1700* 🌐 *www.griffoncharleston.com.*

Fodor's Choice ★ **Pavilion Bar.** Atop the Market Pavilion Hotel, the outdoor Pavilion Bar offers panoramic views of the city and harbor. Enjoy appetizers, delicacies created with lobster and duck, with a signature martini, like a pomegranate Paviliontini. This is Charleston's best rooftop bar. The dress code dictates no flip-flops, baseball caps, visors, or tank tops. ✉ *225 E. Bay St., Market area* ☎ *843/266–4218* ⊕ *www.marketpavilion.com.*

**Rooftop at Vendue.** Have a cocktail and appetizer as you watch the colorful sunset behind the church steeples. There are actually two bars at this venue, and the lower Deck Bar has tables and chairs shaded by umbrellas, but the view of the water is partially obscured by condo high-rises. The second, higher-level bar, called the Bridge Bar, offers a 360-degree panorama, tables and chairs, but no umbrellas. You'll find live music by local and regional talent nightly from 6 to 9, and select appetizers are half off during happy hour. ✉ *23 Vendue Range, Market area* ☎ *843/577–7970* ⊕ *www.vendueinn.com.*

**The Royal American.** A relatively new addition to the North Morrison corridor, the Royal American isn't really a dive bar—it's just positioned to look like one. The establishment features dim lighting, decorative top hats, and an expansive front deck. Even better, the bar serves up a gallery of cheap, canned beers and a trio of tasty, 32-ounce signature punches with rum, bourbon, or vodka poured over crushed ice. Hungry? Feast on blue-collar eats like Frito pie, loaded baked potatoes, cheddar cheeseburgers, and house-made beef jerky. ✉ *970 Morrison Dr., North Morrison* ☎ *843/817–6925* ⊕ *theroyalamerican.com.*

**Social Restaurant & Wine Bar.** If you need help choosing from among 60 wines by the glass, as well as bottles and flights of everything from Tempranillo to Prosecco, knowledgeable sommelier and owner Brad Ball is your man. The restaurant also features terrific homespun pizzas. ✉ *188 E. Bay St., Market area* ☎ *843/577–5665* ⊕ *www.socialwinebar.com.*

### JAZZ CLUBS

★ **Charleston Grill.** The elegant Charleston Grill has live jazz from 7 to 10 on Friday and 8 to midnight on Saturday. Shows range from the internationally acclaimed, Brazilian-influenced Quentin Baxter Ensemble to the Bob Williams Duo, a father and son who play classical guitar and violin. It draws a mature, upscale clientele, hotel guests, well-known locals, and more recently an urbane thirtysomething crowd. ✉ *Charleston Place Hotel, 224 King St., Market area* ☎ *843/577–4522* ⊕ *www.charlestongrill.com.*

### WINE BARS

**Bin 152.** Husband-and-wife Patrick and Fanny Panella ply their guests with selections from more than 100 bottles of wine and 35 varieties of cheeses and charcuterie, freshly baked breads, artwork, and antique furniture. All of it is imminently available, too, from the Sauvignon Blanc and Shiraz to the tables and chairs. Cast in low lighting, the wine bar serves as a comfortable backdrop for a pre- or postdinner drink or an entire evening. ✉ *152 King St., Lower King* ☎ *843/577–7359* ⊕ *www.bin152.com.*

## UPPER KING

### BARS AND PUBS

**The Belmont.** The Belmont doesn't seek attention—heck, the place won't even list its phone number. But with a high, tin ceiling, exposed-brick walls, and a penchant for screening black-and-white films, the charisma comes naturally. An inventive cocktail menu helps, too. Try their take on the spicy-sweet Brown Derby, a bourbon drink made with jalapeño-infused honey, or the Bells of Jalisco, featuring reposado tequila, more jalapeño honey, and lime juice. ✉ *511 King St., Upper King* 🌐 *www.thebelmontcharleston.com.*

**Closed for Business.** Closed for Business bills itself as a draught emporium—and we're happy to agree. The downtown bar showcases 42 taps, including several seasonal and local brews. Typified by its light-colored woods and unique markings—lightbulbs flickering in a fireplace, for instance—CFB also features a tasty menu containing fresh-ground burgers, Chicago-style hot dogs, and a special fried pork cutlet sandwich called the Pork Slap. ✉ *453 King St., Upper King* ☎ *843/853–8466* 🌐 *www.closed4business.com* ⏲ *Mon.–Sat. 11 am–2 am, Sun. 10 am–2 am.*

**The Cocktail Club.** Perhaps no other Charleston establishment characterizes the craft cocktail movement like the Cocktail Club. The bar showcases exposed-brick walls and wooden beams inside its lounge areas, though warm evenings are best spent outside on the rooftop patio. Inside, some of Charleston's best (and best-looking) bartenders concoct clever mixtures like Safety Word, made from habañero-spiked tequila, muddled kiwi, and lime juice, and the Double Standard, a serrano-pepper-infused gin and cucumber vodka blend. The menu says it best: it's a true farm-to-shaker approach. ✉ *479 King St., #200, Upper King* ☎ *843/724–9411* 🌐 *www.thecocktailclubcharleston.com.*

7

### DANCE CLUBS

**Trio Club.** Funky 1970s and '80s sounds are perennially popular at this dance club, which starts late and runs hard until closing. Listen to the house band downstairs or head upstairs for the dance party. Cover is usually $5. ✉ *139 Calhoun St., Upper King* ☎ *843/965–5333.*

### GAY AND LESBIAN

**Club Pantheon.** Charleston's only gay dance club is a large, unadorned space with a stage where drag shows are performed on Friday and Sunday nights. Male go-go dancers shake their stuff on the bar and there's a DJ every night. The club offers a good dance space with lots of action. Although the crowd is primarily gay, straight folks and bachelorette parties come here, too, and are made welcome. **■ TIP➔** Eighteen- to twenty-year-olds are allowed in but they are given a special bracelet and are not allowed to drink alcohol. The cover charge is $5. ✉ *28 Anne St., Upper King* ☎ *843/557–2582* 🌐 *www.clubpantheon.net.*

**Dudley's on Ann.** Charleston's landmark gay bar has classic, old-timey tavern decor and a poolroom in the back. It can be mellow or hopping and has happy-hour specials from 4 to 9. There is karaoke on Wednesday. ✉ *42 Ann St., Upper King* 🌐 *dudleysonann.com.*

### LIVE MUSIC

**Music Farm.** Once a train depot and now a live music venue, Music Farm has a warehouse capacity filled to the max when popular bands like Galactic, the North Mississippi Allstars, and Passion Pit play. Tickets typically range from $15 to $25. ✉ *32 Ann St., Upper King* ☎ *843/577–6969* 🌐 *www.musicfarm.com.*

**The Torch Velvet Lounge.** This martini and hookah bar offers tobacco in flavors such as mint and passion fruit, and if that's not enough, small bands ranging from bluegrass to rock to beach music play seven nights a week. The back room has semiprivate booths. ✉ *545 King St., Upper King* ☎ *843/723–9333* 🌐 *www.torch-lounge.com.*

### BEACH SAFETY

The *"no swimming"* signs by the Isle of Palms bridge over Breach Inlet are there because the current is treacherous and sadly people drown every year.

It may seem inviting to walk out to a sandbar at low tide, but the tide sweeps in fast and it can disappear, leaving people stranded far from shore.

## SPORTS AND THE OUTDOORS

Updated by Kinsey Gidick

Charleston is a great place to get outdoors. The region's beaches are taupe sand, and the Carolina sun warms them some nine months out of the year. You'll find an amazing number of low-cost options, from biking to canoeing and kayaking and nature walks. Area golf courses are reasonably priced compared to, say, Hilton Head, the public courses being the least expensive.

## BASEBALL

Fans who like to hear the crack of the bat and the cheers of the crowd can plan on attending a game at "the Joe" (Joseph P. Riley Jr. Stadium).

**Charleston Riverdogs.** The local minor-league baseball team plays at "the Joe," on the banks of the Ashley River near the Citadel. Kids love their mascot, Charlie T. Riverdog. After games, fireworks often illuminate the summer sky in honor of this all-American pastime. The season runs from April through September. Tickets cost a reasonable $7 to $12. ✉ *Joseph P. Riley Jr. Stadium, 360 Fishburne St., Hampton Park Terrace* ☎ *843/577–3647* 🌐 *www.riverdogs.com.*

## BEACHES

There are glorious beaches just outside the Charleston city limits. You and your kids can build sand castles, gather seashells after high tide, or bring a kite and let it loose on a long lead. The Charleston area's mild climate means you can swim from March through October.

**Isle of Palms County Park.** Play beach volleyball or quietly sunbathe in a lounge chair at this 600-foot-long beach. This beach is as good as the island's idyllic name. The sands are golden, the water is temperate, and the waves are gentle. It's great for little children, seniors with limited mobility, or those who seek peace. It is also the only lifeguard-protected area on the Isle of Palms. **Amenities:** lifeguards; toilets; food and drink; showers (seasonal). **Best for:** surfing; walking; swimming. ✉ *1 14th Ave., U.S. 17 north to I–517, the Isle of Palms connector; once on the island go through the traffic light and then straight ahead; the parking lot is on the left, Isle of Palms* ☎ *843/886–3863, 843/768–4386* 🌐 *www.ccprc.com* 🎫 *$8 per car* ⏲ *Nov.–Feb., daily 10–5; Mar.–Apr. and Sept.–Oct., daily 10–6; May–Labor Day, daily 9–7.*

Fodor's Choice ★ **Kiawah Beachwalker Park.** The public park about 28 miles southwest of Charleston has an ample 500-foot-wide beach. Kiawah is one of the Southeast's most physically beautiful and largest barrier islands, with 10 miles of wide, immaculate ocean beach. Crime is a rarity here, and you can walk safely for miles, shelling and beachcombing. The beach is complemented by the Kiawah River, with lagoons filled with birds and wildlife, and golden marshes that make the sunsets even more glorious. **Amenities:** lifeguards (seasonal); food and drink; toilets; showers. **Best for:** solitude; sunset; swimming; walking. ✉ *1 Beachwalker Dr., Kiawah Island* ☎ *843/768–2395* 🌐 *www.ccprc.com* 🎫 *$8 per car* ⏲ *Jan. and Feb., daily 10–5; Mar. and Apr., daily 10–6; May–Labor Day, daily 9–7; Sept., daily 10–6; Oct., weekdays 9–5, weekends 10–6; Nov. and Dec., daily 10–5.*

★ **Sullivan's Island Beach.** This is one of the most noncommercialized, pristine beaches in the greater Charleston area. The beachfront lands are owned by the town—some 190 acres of infant maritime forest with coastal wildlife, held in a perpetual land easement by the Lowcountry Open Land Trust. The downside is that there are no amenities that make beach-going easier, like public toilets and showers. There are, however, a number of good small restaurants for lunch or drinks on nearby Middle Street, the island's main drag. There are approximately 30 public-access paths (4 are wheelchair accessible) that lead to the beach. Alcohol and glass containers are not allowed. "Sully's" is a delightful island with a rich historic background that includes a lighthouse and Fort Moultrie National Monument. The island is home to some 2,000 people, whose numbers swell in summer with vacationers occupying the many beach houses and rentals. **Amenities:** none. **Best for:** sunrise; swimming; walking; windsurfing. ✉ *Station 9–Station 22½ (stations radiate off Middle St.), Sullivan's Island* 🌐 *www.sullivansisland-sc.com.*

## BIKING

The historic district is ideal for bicycling as long as you stay off the busier roads. Many of the city's green spaces, including Colonial Lake and Palmetto Islands County Park, have bike trails. If you want to rent a bike, expect to pay about $20 for a half day (three hours) and $25 for a full day. Most of the shops charge the same price, but exceptions are noted.

**Affordabike.** This shop sells and rents bikes. Rentals are a mere $20 for a 24-hour day ($45 a week), which includes a helmet, lock, and basket. Conveniently located in the Upper King area, it is also open on Sunday from noon to 5—the best day for riding in downtown Charleston and/

or across the Ravenel Bridge. ✉ *534 King St., Upper King* ☎ *843/789–3281* 🌐 *www.affordabike.com.*

**Bicycle Shoppe.** You can rent bikes at the Bicycle Shoppe seven days a week. The typical rental is a simple beach cruiser for $7 an hour or $28 a day, and includes a helmet. For those wanting to tackle the Ravenel Bridge, the store offers hybrid-geared bikes for $10 an hour or $40 a day. ✉ *281 Meeting St., Market area* ☎ *843/722–8168* ✉ *1539 Johnnie Dodds Blvd., Mount Pleasant* ☎ *843/884–7433* 🌐 *www.thebicycleshoppecharleston.com.*

**Island Bike and Surf Shop.** Rent island cruisers (beach bikes) for a very moderate weekly rate of $34.95, or check out tandem bikes, bicycles built for two, hybrids, mountain bikes, Burley trailers, cargo trailers, adult tricycles with large baskets, joggers' children's strollers, baby strollers, and more. The shop will even deliver to Kiawah and Seabrook Islands. If you just want a bike for a day or two ($20 per day), you have to pick it up and return it. Kayak rental costs $40 for a double kayak and $30 for an individual. ✉ *3665 Bohicket Rd., Johns Island* ☎ *843/768–1158, 800/323–0579* 🌐 *www.islandbikeandsurf.com.*

## BOATING

Kayak through isolated marsh rivers and estuaries to outlying islands, or explore Cape Romain National Wildlife Refuge.

★ **AquaSafaris.** If you want a sailing or motor yacht charter, perhaps a beach barbecue, an ecotour, or just to go offshore fishing, contact AquaSafaris. Captain John takes seaworthy sailors out daily, leaving from Shem Creek and Isle of Palms. A sunset cruise on the *Palmetto Breeze* catamaran offers guests panoramic views of Charleston Harbor serenaded by the sounds of Jimmy Buffett. Enjoy beer and cocktails as you cruise in one of the smoothest sails in the Lowcountry. ✉ *24 Patriots Point Rd., Mount Pleasant* ☎ *843/886–8133* 🌐 *www.aqua-safaris.com.*

**Charleston Kayak Company.** Guided kayak tours with Charleston Kayak Company depart from the grounds of the Inn at Middleton Place. Kayakers glide down the Ashley River and through brackish creeks, in an area that is the Lowcountry's only State Scenic River Corridor (22-mile stretch). Naturalist guides interpret the surrounding wetlands and tell of the river's cultural history. It's not uncommon to spot an American alligator but thankfully they take no interest in kayakers. Tours last two hours (reservations essential) and cost $45 per person. Both single and tandem kayaks are available for rent at $40 for a tandem and $30 for a single, including all safety gear. If visiting January through April, inquire about cypress swamp tours. ✉ *Middleton Place Plantation, 4290 Ashley River Rd., West Ashley* ☎ *843/556–6020, 843/628–2879* 🌐 *www.charlestonkayakcompany.com.*

**Coastal Expeditions.** Outings for individuals, families, and groups are provided by Coastal Expeditions. They have additional kayak outlets at Crosby's Seafood on Folly Road and at Isle of Palms Marina. A kayak tour with a naturalist guide is $58 per person, and they rent kayaks for $38 (single) or $48 (tandem) for a half day. They provide exclusive access to Cape Romain National Wilderness Area on Bull Island via the Bull Island Ferry. The ferry departs from Garris Landing and runs Tuesday and Thursday–Saturday from April through November. It costs $30 round-trip. Bull Island has rare natural beauty, a "boneyard beach," shells galore, and 277 species of migrating birds. ✉ *Shem Creek Maritime Center, 514B Mill St., Mount Pleasant* ☎ *843/884–7684* 🌐 *www.coastalexpeditions.com.*

**Island Bike & Surf Shop.** Rent surfboards and bicycles, or have them delivered to the resort islands. Boards cost $20 a day, $15 after four days. Bikes are $34.95 plus tax for a weeklong rental including delivery and pickup. ✉ *3665 Bohicket Rd., Johns Island* ☎ *843/768–1158* 🌐 *www.islandbikeandsurf.com.*

**Thriller.** Take a high-powered, adrenaline-spiking tour for Charleston. This brightly painted catamaran is propelled by two turbo-diesel engines, and it can clock 25 mph. It runs from Charleston harbor to the Morris Lighthouse and back, passing another lighthouse and five forts. The live narration is broken up by rock music. Tours cost $35 per adult. ✉ *1529 Strathmore La., Mount Pleasant* ☎ *843/276–4203* 🌐 *www.thrillercharleston.com.*

## FISHING

**Fodor's Choice** ★ Fishing can be a real adventure here, and if you go offshore with an experienced fishing guide, you can have enough fish stories to tell until the next trip.

**Bohicket Marina.** Bohicket Marina has half- and full-day charters on 24- to 48-foot boats. Small boat rentals are also available, as well as sunset dolphin-watching cruises. This marina is the closest to Kiawah and Seabrook, and this charter company has a long-standing reputation. For inshore fishing, expect to pay about $375 for three hours minimum for one to three people, and $400–$600 for four or more people, including bait, tackle, and licenses. ✉ *1880 Andell Bluff Blvd., Johns Island* ☎ *843/768–1280* 🌐 *www.bohicket.com.*

**Captain Richard Stuhr.** Saltwater fly-fishers looking for an Orvis-endorsed guide do best by calling Captain Richard Stuhr, who has been fishing the waters of Charleston, Kiawah, and Isle of Palms since 1991. He'll haul his 19-foot Action Craft to you and take you on a half-day tour through Charleston's harbor and tributaries for $375. ✉ *547 Sanders Farm La.* ☎ *843/881–3179* 🌐 *www.captstuhr.com.*

## GOLF

With fewer golfers than in Hilton Head, the courses around Charleston have more prime starting times available. Nonguests can play at private island resorts, such as Kiawah Island, Seabrook Island, and Wild Dunes. There you will find breathtaking ocean views within a pristine setting. Municipal golf courses are a golfing bargain, from $27 to $39 for 18 holes.

7

Check out the shrimp boats and spot bottlenose dolphins from a kayak tour on Shem Creek.

**Charleston Area Golf Guide.** For anything from green fees to course statistics and golf vacation packages in the area, contact the Charleston Area Golf Guide. ☎ *800/774–4444* 🌐 *www.charlestongolfguide.com.*

**Charleston Municipal Golf Course.** This walker-friendly public course isn't gorgeous like some of the resort courses—a highway bisects it—but it does have a lot of shade trees and the price is right. About 20 miles from the resort islands of Kiawah and Seabrook and about 6 miles from downtown, the course has a simple snack bar serving breakfast, lunch, and beer and wine. ✉ *2110 Maybank Hwy., James Island* ☎ *843/795–6517* 🌐 *www.charleston-sc.gov* *18 holes. 6450 yds. Par 72. Green Fee: $27/$39* ☞ *Facilities: Driving range, putting green, pitching area, golf carts, pull carts, rental clubs, lessons, restaurant, bar.*

**Charleston National Golf Club.** The best nonresort golf course in Charleston is well maintained and tends to be quiet on weekdays, which translates to lower prices. The setting is captivating, with the course carved along the intracoastal waterway, traversing wetlands, lagoons, and pine and oak forests. Finishing holes are set along golden marshland. Diminutive wooden bridges and a handsome, salmon-colored clubhouse that looks like an antebellum mirage add to the natural beauty. ✉ *1360 National Dr., Mount Pleasant* ☎ *843/884–7799, 843/884–4653* 🌐 *www.charlestonnationalgolf.com* *18 holes. 6412 yds. Par 72. Green Fee: $48/$58* ☞ *Facilities: Driving range, putting green, pitching area, golf carts, pull carts, rental clubs, pro shop, golf academy/lessons, restaurant, bar.*

**Dunes West Golf & River Club.** This semiprivate, championship golf course was designed by Arthur Hill. It has great marshland and river views and lots of modulation on the Bermuda-covered greens shaded by centuries-old oaks. The generous fairways with greens that may be considered small by today's standards make approach shots very important to scoring low. Located about 15 miles from downtown Charleston, it is in a gated residential community with an attractive antebellum-style clubhouse. ✉ *3535 Wando Plantation Way, Mount Pleasant* ☎ *843/856–9000* 🌐 *www.duneswestgolfclub.com* *18 holes. 6871 yds. Par 72. Green Fee: $46/$95* ☞ *Facilities: Driving range, putting green, pitching area, golf carts, rental clubs, pro shop, golf academy/lessons, restaurant, bar.*

**Patriots Point Links.** A partly covered driving range and spectacular harbor and bridge views make this golf experience special. It is just across the spectacular Ravenel Bridge, with free public parking. You could also take the water taxi from downtown to the nearby Hilton and arrange for a Links staffer to pick you up. Four pros instruct, and there are lessons and clinics, as well as a junior camp during the summer. ✉ *1 Patriots Point Rd., Mount Pleasant* ☎ *843/881–0042* 🌐 *www.patriotspointlinks.com* *18 holes. 6900 yds. Par 72. Green Fee: $60/$85* ☞ *Facilities: Driving range, putting green, pitching area, golf carts, rental clubs, pro shop, golf academy/lessons, restaurant, bar.*

### RESORT GOLF COURSES

**Kiawah Island Golf Resort.** Kiawah is home to five championship courses: the world-famous **Ocean Course,** designed by Pete Dye; **Turtle Point,** designed by Jack Nicklaus; **Osprey Point,** designed by Tom Fazio; **Cougar Point,** designed by Gary Player; and **Oak Point,** redesigned by Clyde Johnston, is just outside the Kiawah gate. ✉ *Kiawah Island Golf Resort, 1000 Ocean Course Dr., Kiawah Island* ☎ *843/266–4670* 🌐 *www.kiawahresort.com.*

**Wild Dunes Resort.** This 1,600-acre oceanfront resort on the tip of the Isle of Palms is some 30 minutes from downtown Charleston. It has two nationally renowned Tom Fazio–designed courses, the **Links** and the **Harbor** courses. Groups frequent this family-friendly resort because of its meeting facilities, and many resort guests opt for the golf package. ✉ *Wild Dunes Resort, 10001 Back Bay Dr., Isle of Palms* ☎ *843/886–2002* 🌐 *www.wildunes.com.*

## SPAS

Unlock your senses, breathe in the aromatherapy, indulge your body, and let the pampering begin. Prices vary, depending on whether you chose a facial or a salt scrub or some other exotic treatment. As a rule of thumb, prices here are lower than a major metropolis.

**Charleston Place Spa.** Charleston Place Spa, a truly deluxe day spa, has nine treatment rooms and a wet room where exotic body wraps like their signature magnolia blossom wrap and other treatments like the Moroccan-oil scalp, neck, and shoulder massage with hot stones, are administered. Four-handed massages for couples are a popular option. ✉ *130 Market St., Market area* ☎ *843/722–4900* 🌐 *www.charlestonplacespa.com.*

Fodor's Choice ★ **Seeking Indigo.** Seeking Indigo is 6,000 square feet of delightful, positive sensory overload. Behind the carved wooden Indonesian doors, a tranquil day spa, a Pilates studio, and a holistic wellness center await. Here, ancient healing meets modern technology with everything from detox footbaths to Ayurvedic treatments and Thai massage. Stressed professionals stop by for a 20-minute ($30) thermal massage on the Migun Bed, donning meditative headphones. Ladies, book ahead for the Japanese face-lift massage ($155). A holistic naturopath conducts metabolic assessments, and there is detoxing, Reiki, and a state-of-the-art hyperbaric oxygen chamber. ✉ *445 King St., Upper King St.–Design District* ☎ *843/725–0217* 🌐 *www.seekingindigo.com.*

**Stella Nova.** In a historic Charleston "single house," Stella Nova is just off King Street. It's serious about all of its treatments, from waxing to salt scrubs. If anti-aging is a priority, the collagen masque and massage can erase years. For couples, there are aromatherapy massages and men's services, too. Enjoy refreshments on the breezy verandas. ✉ *78 Society St., Lower King–Fashion District* ☎ *843/723–0909* 🌐 *www.stella-nova.com.*

## TENNIS

Whether your interest in tennis is casual or serious, the Charleston area, especially its resort islands, offers tennis options for every skill level. Spring and fall are simply ideal for play. You can play for free at neighborhood courts, including several near Colonial Lake and at the Isle of Palms Recreation Center. Others owned by the city charge a mere $4 to $9 an hour for nonresidents. The resort islands are the most costly, depending on whether or not you are a guest.

**Charleston Tennis Center.** Appropriate clothes and tennis shoes are required on the center's 15 hard courts, which at $8 an hour are inexpensive even for nonresidents. The courts are lighted at night, and there are restrooms on the premises. Tennis balls and racquets are also for sale. ✉ *19 Farmfield Ave., West Ashley* ☎ *843/769–8258* 🌐 *www.charleston-sc.gov.*

Fodor's Choice ★ **Family Circle Tennis Center.** World class, the Family Circle Tennis Center is, without question, one of the top facilities in the Southeast. The 17 courts (13 clay, 4 hard) are all lighted for night play and open to the public. Rates are $10 for the hard courts, $15 for clay. Four Quick Starts, miniature courts for children four to eight years old, have been added. The Instinctive Tennis Academy has private lessons (prices vary) and clinics for adults and children as young as four years old. It has one of the best-qualified teaching staffs in the country. The women's tennis Family Circle Cup is hosted here each April. A signature event for women's tennis, this tourney has brought in the sport's top names. Not incidentally, it is the city's top year-round outdoor arena and a venue for music concerts under the stars. ✉ *161 Seven Farms Dr., Daniel Island* ☎ *843/856–7900* 🌐 *www.familycirclecup.com.*

# SHOPPING

Updated by Kinsey Gidick

One-of-a-kind, locally owned boutiques, where the hottest trends in fashion hang on the racks, make up an important part of the contemporary Charleston shopping experience. Charleston has more than 25 fine-art galleries, making it one of the top art towns in America. Local Lowcountry art, which includes both traditional landscapes of the region as well as more contemporary takes, is among the most prevalent styles here.

## SHOPPING DISTRICTS

**City Market.** The Market area is a cluster of shops and restaurants centered on the City Market. Sweetgrass basket weavers work here, and you can buy the resulting wares, although these artisan crafts have become expensive. There are T-shirt and souvenir stores here as well as upscale boutiques. In the covered, open-air market, shops are open daily and vendors have stalls with everything from jewelry to dresses and purses. And, thanks to a beautiful 2011 remodel, you can peruse the middle section of the market in enclosed, air conditioned comfort. ✉ *E. Bay and Market Sts., Market area* 🌐 *www.thecharlestoncitymarket.com.*

**Tanger Outlet.** If you are a dedicated outlet shopper, head to Tanger Outlet in North Charleston. This spiffy, contemporary mall is not far from the airport. It houses 80 name-brand outlets, like Loft, Kenneth Cole, J. Crew, Timberland, and Saks Fifth Avenue OFF 5TH. ✉ *I–26 eastbound Exit 213A, or westbound Exit 213; left on Montague Ave., right on International Dr., North Charleston* ☎ *843/529–3095* 🌐 *www.tangeroutlet.com* ⏲ *Mon.–Sat. 10–9, Sun. 11–6.*

**Fodor's Choice ★** **King Street.** King Street is Charleston's main street and the major shopping corridor downtown. The latest lines of demarcation divide the street into districts: Lower King (from Broad Street to Market Street) is the Antiques District, lined with high-end antiques dealers; Middle King (from Market Street to Calhoun Street) is now called the Fashion District and is a mix of national chains like Banana Republic and Pottery Barn, alternative shops, and locally owned landmark stores and boutiques; and Upper King (from Calhoun Street to Spring Street) has been dubbed the Design District, an up-and-coming area becoming known for its furniture and interior-design stores selling home fashion. Check out Second Sundays on King, when the street closes for pedestrian use from Calhoun Street to Queen Street, and visit the Farmers' Market in Marion Square throughout the summer months. 🌐 *www.kingstreetantiquedistrict.com, www.kingstreetfashiondistrict.com, or littleworksofheart.typepad.com/upperkingcharleston.*

7

King Street is the perfect place to go antiquing in Charleston.

## NORTH OF BROAD

### LOWER KING

#### ANTIQUES

**George C. Birlant & Co.** You'll find mostly 18th- and 19th-century English antiques here, but keep your eye out for a Charleston Battery bench (which you can spot at White Point Garden), for which they are famous. Founded in 1922, Birlant's is fourth-generation family-owned. ✉ *191 King St., Lower King* ☎ *843/722–3842* 🌐 *www.birlant.com* 🕒 *Mon.–Sat. 9–5:30.*

**Jacques' Antiques.** As the name suggests, most of the antiques here are imported from France, but all are either European or English, from the 17th to the 20th centuries. Decorative arts include ceramics, porcelains, and crystal. From the candlesticks to the armoires, all are in exquisite taste. ✉ *160 King St., Lower King* ☎ *843/577–0104* 🌐 *www.jacantiques.com* 🕒 *Mon.–Sat. 10–5.*

#### CLOTHING

**Berlin's Clothing Store.** Family-owned for four generations since 1883, this Charleston landmark has clothing and sporting goods for men and is known as a destination for special-occasion clothing. The store, which for generations sold the preppy, Charlestonian look, has now added European designer styles. There is a complimentary parking lot across the street for customers. ✉ *114–116 King St., Lower King* ☎ *843/722–1665 men's shop, 843/723–5591 ladies' shop* 🌐 *www.berlinsclothing.com* 🕒 *Mon.–Sat. 9:30–6.*

**Christian Michi.** This shop carries tony women's clothing and accessories. Designers from Italy, such as Piazza Sempione, are represented, as is Hoss Intropia from Spain. Known for its evening wear, it has pricey but gorgeous gowns and a fine selection of cocktail dresses. High-end fragrances add to the luxurious air. ✉ *220 King St., Lower King* ☎ *843/723–0575* 🌐 *www.christianmichi.com* ⏲ *Mon.–Sat. 10–6, Sun. noon–6.*

### FOODSTUFFS

**Robot Candy Co.** Willy Wonka ain't got nothing on Charleston. This divine confectionery is a child's dream, chock-full of tasty treats and toys. ✉ *322 King St., Lower King* ☎ *843/608–8090* 🌐 *www.robotcandyco.com* ⏲ *Mon.–Thurs. 11–6, Fri. and Sat. 11–8, Sun. noon–6.*

### JEWELRY

**Dixie Dunbar Studio.** Dealing in artistic, unique jewelry, this contemporary jewelry shop has been here for decades. The handmade pieces can be delightfully unpredictable. ✉ *192 King St., Lower King* ☎ *843/722–0006* 🌐 *www.dixiedunbar.com* ⏲ *Mon.–Sat. 10–5:30.*

### SHOES AND ACCESSORIES

**Bob Ellis.** In business for more than 60 years, this Charleston landmark sells some gorgeous shoes from Prada, Manolo Blahnik, YSL, Jimmy Choo, and Christian Louboutin, among other high-end designers. ✉ *332 King St., King St.–Fashion District* ☎ *843/722–2515* 🌐 *www.bobellisshoes.com* ⏲ *Mon.–Sat. 10–6; selected Sun.*

7

## MARKET AREA

### ART GALLERIES

**City Gallery on Waterfront Park.** This city-owned art gallery, with handsome contemporary architecture and a delightful location within Waterfront Park, rotates paintings and sculpture shows and showcases predominately Charleston and South Carolina artists. Young and emerging talents exhibit, and residents and visitors alike love the many opening receptions and artist lectures. From the second floor, particularly, one has a privileged riverfront view. ✉ *34 Prioleau St. A, Market area* ☎ *843/958–6484* 🌐 *www.charlestonarts.sc* ⏲ *Tues.–Fri. 11–6, weekends noon–5.*

**Horton Hayes Fine Art.** This gallery carries the sought-after Lowcountry paintings depicting coastal life by Mark Kelvin Horton, who also paints architectural and figurative works. Shannon Rundquist is among the other Lowcountry artists shown; she has a fun, whimsical way of painting local life and is known for her blue-crab art. ✉ *30 State St., Market area* ☎ *843/958–0014* 🌐 *www.hortonhayes.com* ⏲ *Mon.–Sat. 10–5:30, Sun. 12:30–5.*

**Robert Lange Studio.** The most *avant* of the contemporary galleries, this striking, minimalist space is a working studio for Robert Lange and the other exceptionally talented young artists who are on exhibit and who come by to paint. Most of the work has a hyper-realistic style with surreal overtones. Belgian Fred Jamar is the senior anchorman here, and his "bubble tree" Charleston cityscapes are whimsical, even cartoonlike. ✉ *2 Queen St., Market area* ☎ *843/805–8052* 🌐 *www.robertlangestudios.com* ⏲ *Daily 11–5.*

**Smith-Killian Fine Art.** This gallery exhibits contemporary paintings and Lowcountry-scapes by Betty Smith and her talented triplets, Jennifer, Shannon, and Tripp. Her son, Tripp, is a nature photographer specializing in black-and-white images. The bronze wildlife sculpture is by nationally recognized Darrell Davis; the acclaimed oil paintings by Kim English are attention-getters. ✉ *9 Queen St., Market area* ☎ *843/853–0708* 🌐 *www.smithkillian.com* ⏲ *Mon.–Sat. 10–6, Sun. by appt.*

Fodor's Choice ★ **Wells Gallery.** Showcasing the talents of many fine artists, Wells Gallery shows Lowcountry-scapes, still lifes, black-and-white photographs, bronze sculpture, and hand-blown glass sculpture. Everything here is done in excellent taste, from the contemporary decor to its meet-the-artist receptions. Felice Designs, one-of-a-kind jewelry art, mainly of Italian Murano glass beads, is on exhibit, too. ✉ *125 Meeting St., Market area* ☎ *843/853–3233* 🌐 *www.wellsgallery.com* ⏲ *Mon.–Sat. 10–5.*

### CLOTHING

**The Trunk Show.** This upscale consignment shop sells designer dresses, handbags and shoes, and vintage apparel. The back room has been converted into a men's department, with mostly new clothes but some vintage items as well. The shop has become known for its estate jewelry and also custom-made jewelry from semiprecious stones. It has an excellent selection of gowns and evening wear. Many items now come in new from other shops. ✉ *281 Meeting St., Market area* ☎ *843/722–0442* 🌐 *www.charlestontrunkshow.com* ⏲ *Mon.–Sat. 11–6.*

### FOODSTUFFS

**Charleston Candy Kitchen.** This sweets shop sells freshly made fudge, Charleston chews, and benne-seed (sesame-seed) wafers. It has a bigger sister in Savannah. ✉ *32A N. Market St., Market area* ☎ *843/723–4626* 🌐 *www.savannahcandy.com* ⏲ *Daily 9:30 am–10 pm.*

**Market Street Sweets.** Make time to stop at Market Street Sweets for the melt-in-your-mouth pralines, bear claws, fudge, and their famous glazed pecans—cinnamon and sugar is the favorite. Its mother-store is in Savannah. ✉ *100 N. Market St., Market area* ☎ *843/722–1397* 🌐 *www.riverstreetsweets.com* ⏲ *Tues.–Sun. 9 am–11 pm.*

**Ted's Butcherblock.** In addition to gourmet meals to go, you can buy wines, cheeses, cold meats, and olive oil, attend one of the frequent wine tastings, or stop by to see what's cooking on Ted's Big Green Egg grill. ✉ *334 E. Bay St., Ansonborough* ☎ *843/577–0094* 🌐 *www.tedsbutcherblock.com* ⏲ *Tues.–Sat. 11–7.*

### FURNITURE

**Historic Charleston Foundation.** Bring home superb replicas of Charleston furniture, china, and decorative accessories. The variety and quality of these Charleston mementos, from the high-end pieces to the bags of Carolina Rice, make treasured gifts. Royalties from sales contribute to restoration projects. ✉ *108 Meeting St., Market area* ☎ *843/723–1623* 🌐 *www.historiccharleston.org* ⏲ *Mon.–Sat. 9–6, Sun. noon–5.*

### GIFTS

**Charleston Cooks/Maverick Kitchen Store.** You'll find just about every gourmet kitchen tool and accessory you can think of here. Regional food and cookbooks, as well as culinary gifts, abound. And you can also enjoy cooking classes and demonstrations. ✉ *194 E. Bay St., Market area* ☎ *843/722–1212* 🌐 *www.charlestoncooks.com* ⏲ *Mon.–Sat. 10–9, Sun. noon–6.*

**Indigo.** Indigo stocks funky home and garden accessories. In addition, there are both locally made and handmade products that come from unique vendors, from quirky clothes to artisan jewelry. ✉ *4 Vendue Range, Market area* ☎ *843/723–2983* 🌐 *www.indigohome.com* ⏲ *Mon.–Sat. 10–9, Sun. 10–7.*

## MIDDLE KING

### CLOTHING

**Bits of Lace.** When this exclusive lingerie shop opened in 1977 with its sexy French imports, no one thought it would make it in such a conservative town. It's still here and now stocks beautiful maternity sleepwear and Eres swimsuits. It has become known for its bra-fitting service, especially for bigger cup sizes—up to K. ✉ *302 King St., Middle King* ☎ *843/266–6985* 🌐 *www.bitsoflace.com* ⏲ *Mon.–Sat. 10–6.*

**Copper Penny.** Shop Copper Penny for trendy dresses and names like Trina Turk, Millie, Tibi, and Diane Von Furstenberg. ✉ *311 King St., Middle King* ☎ *843/723–2999* 🌐 *www.shopcopperpenny.com* ⏲ *Mon.–Sat. 10–7, Sun. noon–6.*

**Everything But Water.** In the Shops at Charleston Place, this store has one of the town's largest and finest collections of swimwear for all ages. ✉ *130 Market St., Shops at Charleston Place, Middle King* ☎ *843/722–5884* 🌐 *www.everythingbutwater.com* ⏲ *Mon.–Wed. 10–6, Thurs.–Sat. 10–8, Sun. noon–5.*

**Finicky Filly.** Boutique favorite Finicky Filly carries exceptional women's apparel and accessories by such designers as Lela Rose, Schumacher, All Dressed Up, and Etro. The Filly appeals to women from college age to seniors. ✉ *303 King St., Middle King* ☎ *843/534–0203* 🌐 *thefinickyfilly.com* ⏲ *Mon.–Sat. 10–5:30, Sun. 1–5.*

**Hampden Clothing.** One of the city's trendiest boutiques attracts the young and well heeled, who come here for an edgier style. The shop's sophisticated sensitivity and hot new designers such as Yigal Azrouël, Vena Cava, Alexander Wang, and Jenni Kayne help make it a premier destination for the latest in fashion. ✉ *314 King St., Middle King* ☎ *843/724–6373* 🌐 *www.hampdenclothing.com* ⏲ *Mon.–Sat. 10–6, Sun. noon–5.*

### FOODSTUFFS

**Caviar and Bananas.** This upscale specialty market and café features not-so-ordinary supermarket items like epicurean prepared foods and artisanal cheeses. Note the locally made items such as Callie's Pimento Cheese. ✉ *51 George St., Middle King* ☎ *843/577–7757* 🌐 *www.caviarandbananas.com* ⏲ *Weekdays 7 am–8:30 pm, Sat. 8:30–8:30, Sun. 8–8.*

7

### GIFTS

**Worthwhile.** Artsy and hip baby gear, women's clothes and shoes, housewarming gifts, jewelry, books, and even office supplies make the mundane fun at Worthwhile. ✉ *268 King St., Middle King* ☎ *843/723–4418* 🌐 *www.shopworthwhile.com* ⏲ *Mon.–Sat. 10–6, Sun. noon–5.*

## UPPER KING

### ANTIQUES

**Haute Design.** This shop sells antiques, chandeliers, and French and Italian furniture, as well as custom-designed pieces like tables and mirrors. Belgian linen and hand-screen-printed fabrics are a specialty, and available accessories include Vinnini blown glass and "antique" pillows. Interior-design services are available. ✉ *489 King St., Upper King* ☎ *843/577–9886* 🌐 *www.hautedesign.com.*

### ART GALLERIES

**Gallery Chuma.** This gallery showcases Gullah (Lowcountry African-American) art from inexpensive mini-prints to the work of its primary artist, Jonathan Green. The popularity of Gullah art and its growth as a genre is attributed to this highly successful South Carolina artist. ✉ *188 Meeting St., Upper King* ☎ *843/722–1702* 🌐 *www.gallerychuma.com* ⏲ *Daily 9:30–6.*

### BOOKS

**Blue Bicycle Books.** Look for out-of-print and rare books, including hardcover classics, at Blue Bicycle Books. It has a large selection of everything from fiction to military history and cookbooks. Check their website for frequent book signings by the likes of Pat Conroy and Dorothea Benton Frank. ✉ *420 King St., Upper King* ☎ *843/722–2666* 🌐 *www.bluebicyclebooks.com* ⏲ *Mon.–Sat. 10–7:30, Sun. 1–6.*

### CLOTHING

**Ellington.** Chic and classy, this shop is known for its washable, packable travel pieces, its flowing tops, its feel-good fabrics like silk, linen, and cashmere. Its fashions have classic styles, but with new arrangements. ✉ *473 King St., Upper King* ☎ *843/722–7999* ⏲ *Mon.–Sat. 10:30–5:30.*

### FURNITURE

**Old Charleston Joggling Board Co.** As the name suggests, this shop sells joggling boards, historic Lowcountry oddities on which young, courting couples once bounced toward each other. Nowadays, they are simply used for sitting, usually on front verandas. ✉ *652 King St., Upper King* ☎ *843/723–4331* 🌐 *www.oldcharlestonjogglingboard.com* ⏲ *Mon.–Thurs. 8:30–4, Fri. 8:30–noon.*

### JEWELRY

**Felice Designs.** Owner Felice Killian forms Italian Murano glass into beads to create her mesmerizing jewelry collection. She also pairs the beads with crystals and pearls. Many designs mirror sea life such as sea anemones and jellyfish. ✉ *424 King St., Upper King* ☎ *843/853–3354* 🌐 *www.felicedesigns.com* ⏲ *Weekdays 10–5:30, Sat. 10–5.*

### SHOES AND ACCESSORIES

**Magar Hatworks.** Selling handcrafted headgear, young milliner Leigh Magar has stood the test of some time now and has introduced her love of hats to the young and fashionable. Her wholesale business includes sales to Barneys New York, and she has received national attention and media coverage, with celebs from Eartha Kitt to Sean Lennon buying her wares. ✉ *57 Cannon St., Upper King* ☎ *843/345–4483* 🌐 *www.magarhatworks.com* ⏲ *By appt.*

## SOUTH OF BROAD

### ART GALLERIES

**Ann Long Fine Art.** Serious art collectors head to Ann Long Fine Art for neoclassical and modern works. This elite, world-class gallery has some outstanding, albeit pricey work, by both gifted American and European artists. Many are painted with Old Master techniques. In addition, the gallery manages the estate of Otto Neumann. ✉ *54 Broad St., South of Broad* ☎ *843/577–0447* 🌐 *www.annlongfineart.com* ⏲ *Weekdays 10–5; summer hours vary.*

**Ellis-Nicholson Gallery.** Showcasing artists and sculptors who span many levels, from emerging artists to those with international recognition, this gallery has a premier selection of oils, acrylics, mixed media, bronze, clay, glass, wood, and handcrafted jewelry. ✉ *1½ Broad St., South of Broad* ☎ *843/722–5353* 🌐 *www.ellis-nicholsongallery.com* ⏲ *Mon.–Sat. 10–6, Sun. by appt.*

Fodor's Choice ★ **Martin Gallery.** In a former bank building, this is the city's most impressive gallery, selling art by nationally and internationally acclaimed artists, sculptors, and photographers. The gallery is known especially for its bronzes and large wooden sculptures, as well as glass sculpture and custom-designed jewelry. ✉ *18 Broad St., South of Broad* ☎ *843/723–7378* 🌐 *www.martingallerycharleston.com* ⏲ *Mon.–Sat. 10–6, Sun. 11–5.*

7

### JEWELRY

**Paulo Geiss Jewelers.** Paulo Geiss Jewelers has been a family tradition for more than 90 years and is a member of the American Gem Society. The shop features the work of couture jewelry designers as well as high-end timepieces by Rolex and some custom designs. ✉ *116 E. Bay St., South of Broad* ☎ *843/577–4497* 🌐 *www.geissjewelers.com* ⏲ *Mon.–Sat. 9:30–5:30.*

## GREATER CHARLESTON

### CANNONBOROUGH

#### CLOTHING

**Indigo & Cotton.** This Cannonborough men's store is the go-to boutique for the latest in gentlemen's tailoring featuring brands such as Gitman Vintage, Filson Red Label bags, and Raleigh Denim, along with bow ties, handkerchiefs, and other accessories. ✉ *79 Cannon St., Cannonborough* ☎ *843/718–2980* 🌐 *www.indigoandcotton.com* ⏲ *Weekdays 11–6, Sat. 11–5.*

#### GIFTS

**Mac & Murphy.** This Cannonborough hole-in-the-wall is for the lover of traditional snail-mail letters, with the trendiest in notepads, pens, note cards, wrapping paper, and stationery, including Cheree Berry, Crane &

Co., Dude and Chick. ✉ *74 Cannon St., Cannonborough* ☎ *843/576–4394* 🌐 *www.macandmurphy.com* ⏲ *Weekdays 10:30–6, Sat. 10:30–5.*

## WEST ASHLEY

### ANTIQUES

**Livingston Antiques.** This shop deals in 18th- and 19th-century English and Continental furnishings, clocks, and bric-a-brac. Moderate pricing can be found here, as it is in a suburb. ✉ *2137 Savannah Hwy., West Ashley* ☎ *843/556–6162* 🌐 *www.livingstonantiques.com* ⏲ *Tues.–Sat. 10–4.*

8

# Hilton Head, SC, and the Lowcountry

## WORD OF MOUTH

"Hilton Head is a nice family vacation place for those who want lots of variety. There's great golf, biking, horseback riding, restaurants, and outlet shopping."

—willowjane

# WELCOME TO HILTON HEAD, SC, AND THE LOWCOUNTRY

## TOP REASONS TO GO

★ **Beachcombing:** Hilton Head Island has 12 miles of beaches. You can swim, soak up the sun, or walk along the sand.

★ **Challenging golf:** Hilton Head's nickname is "Golf Island," and its many challenging courses have an international reputation.

★ **Serving up tennis:** Home to hundreds of tennis courts, Hilton Head is one of the nation's top tennis destinations.

★ **Staying put:** This semitropical island has been a resort destination for decades, and it has all the desired amenities for visitors: a vast array of lodgings, an endless supply of restaurants, and excellent shopping.

★ **Beaufort:** This small antebellum town offers large doses of heritage and culture; nearly everything you might want to see is within its downtown historic district.

**1 Hilton Head Island.** One of the Southeast coast's most popular tourist destinations, Hilton Head is known for its golf courses and tennis courts. It's a magnet for time-share owners and retirees. Bluffton is Hilton Head's neighbor to the west. The old-town area is laden with history and charm.

**2 Beaufort.** This charming town just inland from Hilton Head is a destination in its own right, with a lively dining scene and cute bed-and-breakfasts.

**3 Daufuskie Island.** A scenic ferry ride from Hilton Head, Daufuskie is now much more developed than it was during the days when Pat Conroy wrote *The Water Is Wide*, but it's still a beautiful island to explore, even on a day trip. You can stay for a few days at a variety of fine rental properties, tool down shady dirt roads in a golf cart, and delight in the glorious, nearly deserted beaches.

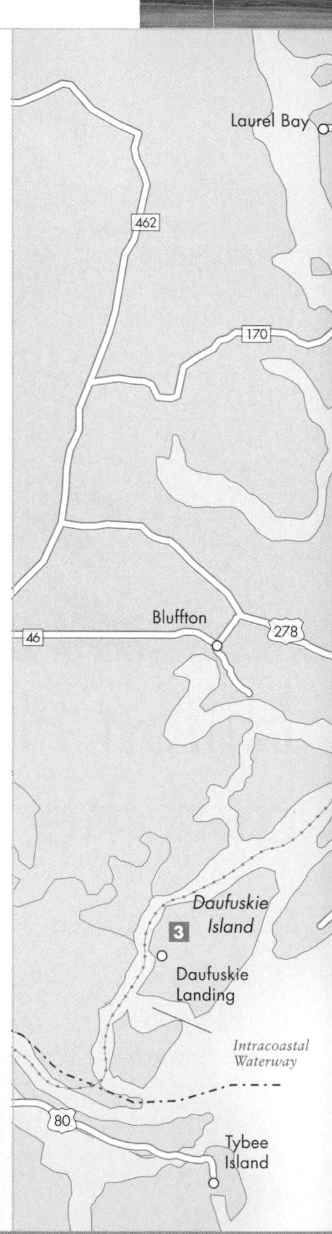

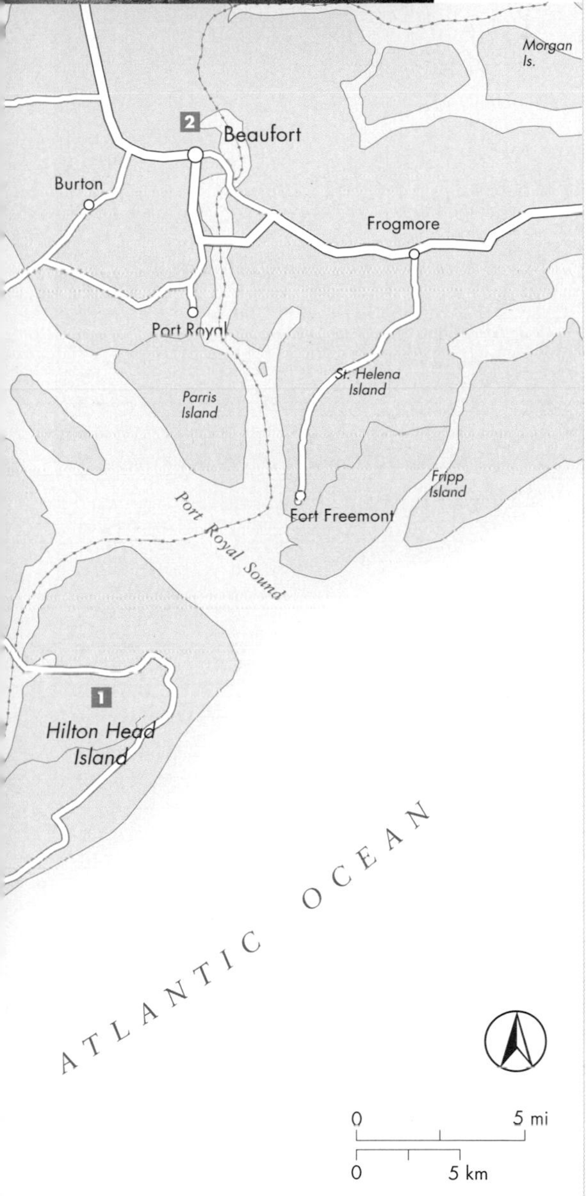

# GETTING ORIENTED

Hilton Head is just north of South Carolina's border with Georgia. This part of South Carolina is best explored by car, as its points of interest spread over a flat coastal plain that is a mix of wooded areas, marshes, and sea islands, the latter of which are sometimes accessible only by boat or ferry. The 42-square-mile island is shaped like a foot, hence the reason locals often describe places as being at the "toe" or "heel" of Hilton Head. Hilton Head's neighbor, Bluffton, is a quirky, artsy town rich with history. In the last several years it has grown from 1 square mile to about 50 square miles. South of Hilton Head is the city of Savannah, which is about a 45-minute drive from the island. North of Hilton Head is Beaufort, a cultural treasure and a graceful antebellum town. Beaufort is also about 45 minutes from Hilton Head.



Morgan Is.
2 Beaufort
Burton
Frogmore
Port Royal
St. Helena Island
Parris Island
Fripp Island
Fort Freemont
Port Royal Sound
1 Hilton Head Island
ATLANTIC OCEAN
0 5 mi
0 5 km

# HILTON HEAD BEACHES

(above and upper right) With 12 miles of beaches on Hilton Head Island, there are plenty of wide-open spaces. (lower right) Conservation efforts assure critters large and small a home.

Hilton Head's beaches are good for the soul. The 12 glorious miles of white-sand beaches are perfect for sunbathing, bike riding, or simply taking a peaceful walk. The Atlantic Ocean waters are generally smooth thanks to the island's geographic location.

There are several beaches on Hilton Head Island that range from the bucolic and peaceful to ones perfect for families. All beaches are open to the public, but many access points are open only to resort or hotel guests. There are several public access points that take beachgoers over small walkways or boardwalks surrounded by sand dunes and sea oats. Beachgoers might see a variety of critters, including crabs, sand dollars, starfish, pelicans, great blue herons, and many other species. The beaches are wide, particularly at low tide, and the sand at the mid-tide point is packed hard, making it great for bike riding. The waters are generally tame, although under certain weather conditions you'll see surfers riding the waves.

—Sally Mahan

## SEA TURTLES

Between May and August, loggerhead sea turtles build their nests and lay their eggs on the beaches of Hilton Head. The hatchlings emerge from their nests at night and are guided by the light on the horizon to the ocean. Any artificial light will disorient them, causing them to go toward the dunes instead of into the water. Due to this, all light sources along the beaches must be off by 10 pm.

## HILTON HEAD'S BEST BEACHES

### ALDER LANE BEACH PARK

**Alder Lane Beach Park** is a nice spot for a swim or a romantic walk. This beach, which has lifeguards on patrol during the summer months, is less crowded than some of the more popular areas, like Coligny Beach. There are restrooms, outdoor showers, and vending machines. The beach, like almost all public beaches on Hilton Head, is wheelchair accessible. Alder Lane Beach Park is on the south end (near the toe) of Hilton Head Island, next to the Marriott Vacation Club Grande Ocean off South Forest Beach Drive.

### BURKES BEACH

If you're looking to get away from the crowds, **Burkes Beach** is a great choice. It's located midisland, adjacent to the Chaplin Community Park at the end of Burkes Beach Road off William Hilton Parkway (U.S. 278). There are no lifeguards, so it's quieter than many of the other Hilton Head beaches. It's a great place for a quiet walk along the shore. If you get up early it's also a perfect spot to catch an amazing sunrise.

### COLIGNY BEACH PARK

This south-end beach, located off Coligny Circle, is by far the most popular beach on Hilton Head Island. The entrance to the beach has choreographed fountains for children to play

under, showers and changing rooms, large restroom facilities, swinging benches, and a boardwalk to the beach. Throughout the summer months there is children's entertainment starting at 6:30 pm weekdays at Coligny Plaza, which is within walking distance to the beach. There are chairs and umbrellas for rent, volleyball nets, and even Wi-Fi. For the grown-ups, the outdoor Tiki Hut bar at the Holiday Inn Oceanfront is a local favorite spot to drink a cool beverage while enjoying the ocean view. Parking is free at **Coligny Beach Park.**

### DRIESSEN BEACH AND FOLLY FIELD BEACH

These beaches are near the heel of Hilton Head Island and are great spots for families. In fact, on many summer days you'll see bicyclists enjoying the day, beachgoers flying colorful kites, and children building sand castles. **Driessen Beach** is accessible at Bradley Beach Road off William Hilton Parkway. Follow along a wooden boardwalk, which weaves over a small tidal marsh, to get to the beach. It's a hike, but the beach is worth the walk. There are barbecue grills, a playground, outdoor showers, restrooms, and a picnic pavilion. **Folly Field Beach** is next to Driessen Beach off Folly Field Road, and also boasts outdoor showers, restrooms, and lifeguards during the summer months.

# LOWCOUNTRY CUISINE

(above) Shrimp po'boys are menu staples in the Lowcountry. (lower right) Once you taste shrimp and grits you may crave it morning, noon, and night. (upper right) Hoppin' John is often topped with salsa.

To understand Lowcountry cuisine, you have to dig in to the "what" and the "where" of its historic culinary conglomeration.

Although you can find Lowcountry cuisine along most of coastal South Carolina all the way down to Savannah, the food's foundation feeds off the pulse of Lowcountry, the Holy City of Charleston, where, centuries ago, European aristocrats would share kitchens with their African slaves. The result was a colonial European fusion with Caribbean and West African, otherwise known as Gullah, influences.

Seafood—shrimp, crabs, fish and oysters—from the marshlands, combined with rice pulled from the countless coastal rice plantations' paddies, are the core ingredients of this specific cuisine. Add to that a twist of exotic African spices and citrus zest, as well as locally grown okra, corn, and benne seeds and you have Lowcountry staples like shrimp and grits, she-crab soup, hoppin' John, and Perlau.

First-time visitors to the area will quickly realize that Lowcountry cuisine is pure Southern comfort.

—Ashley Morris

## A SWEET SIDE

While, it's true, you can't eat this Lowcountry must with a fork, sweet tea is an undoubtedly essential sidekick to South Carolina cuisine. Sugar is added to the brew before it cools, which makes this supersaturated beverage all the more sweet. Lowcountry visitors beware: when ordering at a restaurant, iced tea will most likely arrive as sweet tea.

*Here are some Lowcountry staples:*

**SHRIMP AND GRITS**

If you're not convinced that South Carolina is serious about grits, consider this: in 1976, it declared grits the official state food. In the South, grits are most commonly paired with its coastal-waters counterpart, making shrimp and grits a standard dish for breakfast, lunch, and dinner. Today, foodies will delight in discovering the dish to be dressed up with everything from sausage, bacon, and Cajun seasoning to cheese, gravy, and tomato-based sauces.

**SHE-CRAB SOUP**

Rich and creamy, with lumps of crabmeat and a splash of dry sherry, she-crab soup is to the Lowcountry as chowder is to New England. The "she" of this signature dish actually comes from the main ingredient, a female crab's orange crab roe. It is delicious as an appetizer, and quite filling as an entrée.

**STEAMED OYSTERS**

Oyster beds are plentiful in the creeks and inlet waters along the Lowcountry coast. Also plentiful are those who can't get enough of shucking the fresh meat out of clasped shells and dipping it into warm, drawn butter or cocktail sauce. Oysters are usually served by the half dozen, with a side of Saltine crackers.

**HOPPIN' JOHN**

This rice-and-bean concoction is not only a favorite Lowcountry dish, but a lucky one at that. Families throughout the Lowcountry prepare hoppin' John on New Year's Day for lunch or dinner in hopes that it will provide them with a year's worth of good luck. It's all in the classic Lowcountry ingredients: black-eyed peas symbolize pennies (a side of collard greens adds to the wealth in the new year). Rice, chopped onions, bacon (or ham), and peppers are added to the peas. Add garnishes like a spoonful of salsa or a dollop of sour cream for an interesting Southwest spin.

**PERLAU**

South Carolina takes great pride in its perlau, more lovingly known at the table as chicken bog. This rice-based dish is cooked with chunks of tender chicken and sausage slices, simmered in the chef's choice of Southern seasonings. For more than 30 years, in fact, the tiny town of Loris has been hosting its annual Loris Bog-off Festival, where hundreds of chefs compete to be awarded with the best bowl of bog.

8

Updated by Sally Mahan

Hilton Head Island is a unique and incredibly beautiful resort town that anchors the southern tip of South Carolina's coastline. What makes this semitropical island so unique? At the top of the list is the fact that visitors won't see large, splashy billboards or neon signs. What they will see is an island where the environment takes center stage, a place where development is strictly regulated.

There are 12 miles of sparkling white sand beaches, amazing world-class restaurants, top-rated golf courses—Harbour Town Golf Links annually hosts the Heritage Golf Tournament, a PGA Tour event—and a thriving tennis community. There are also many animals, including loggerhead sea turtles, alligators, snowy egrets, wood storks, great blue heron, and, in the waters, dolphins, manatees, and various species of fish. There are lots of activities offered on the island, including parasailing, charter fishing, kayaking, and many other water sports.

The island has several large, private, gated communities. They include Sea Pines, Hilton Head Plantation, Shipyard, Wexford, Long Cove, Port Royal, Indigo Run, Palmetto Hall, and Palmetto Dunes. Within most of the plantations are vacation rentals, upscale housing, golf courses, shopping, and restaurants. For instance, Sea Pines has a shopping center, restaurants, three golf courses, and the iconic candy-cane-striped Hilton Head Lighthouse. There are also many housing and shopping areas on the island that are not behind security gates.

## PLANNING

### WHEN TO GO

The high season follows typical beach-town cycles, with June through August and holidays year-round being the busiest and most costly. Mid-April, during the annual Heritage Golf Tournament, is when rates tend to be highest. Thanks to the Lowcountry's mostly moderate year-round temperatures, tourists are ever-present. Spring is the best time to visit, when the weather is ideal for tennis and golf. Autumn is almost as active for the same reason.

## PLANNING YOUR TIME

No matter where you stay, spend your first day relaxing on the beach or hitting the links. After that, you'll have time to visit some of the area's attractions, including the Coastal Discovery Museum or the Sea Pines Resort. You can also visit the Tanger outlet malls on U.S. 278 in Bluffton. Old-town Bluffton is a quaint area with many quirky, locally owned shops and art galleries. If you have a few more days, visit Beaufort or even spend the night there. This historic antebellum town is rich with history. Savannah is also a short day trip away.

## GETTING HERE AND AROUND

### AIR TRAVEL

Most travelers use the Savannah/Hilton Head International Airport, less than an hour from Hilton Head, which is served by American Eagle, Delta, United, and US Airways. Hilton Head Island Airport is served by US Airways.

**Air Contacts Hilton Head Island Airport** ✉ *120 Beach City Rd., North End, Hilton Head* ☎ *843/255–2950* 🌐 *www.hiltonheadairport.com.* **Savannah/Hilton Head International Airport** ✉ *400 Airways Ave., Northwest, Savannah, Georgia* ☎ *912/964–0514* 🌐 *www.savannahairport.com.*

### BUS TRAVEL

The Lowcountry Regional Transportation Authority, known as the Palmetto Breeze, has a transportation-on-demand service that ranges from $6 to $10 one way. The service also has buses that leave Bluffton in the morning for Hilton Head, Beaufort, and some of the Sea Islands. The fare is $2. Exact change is required.

**Bus Contacts The Lowcountry Regional Transportation Authority** ✉ *25 Benton Field Rd., Bluffton* ☎ *843/757–5782* 🌐 *www.palmettobreezetransit.com.*

### CAR TRAVEL

Driving is the best way to get onto Hilton Head Island. Off Interstate 95, take Exit 8 onto U.S. 278 East, which leads you through Bluffton and then onto Hilton Head proper. Once on Hilton Head, U.S. 278 forks. On the right is William Hilton Parkway and on the left is the Cross Island Parkway, which is a toll road ($1.25 each way). If you take the Cross Island (as the locals call it) to the south side where Sea Pines and many other resorts are, it will take about 10 to 15 minutes to get to Sea Pines Circle, depending on traffic. If you take William Hilton Parkway (business U.S. 278), it will take about 30 minutes, again depending on traffic. Be aware that at check-in and checkout times on Friday, Saturday, and Sunday, U.S. 278 can slow to a crawl. ■**TIP→ Be careful of putting the pedal to the metal, particularly on the Cross Island Parkway. The speed limits change dramatically, and it is patrolled regularly.**

Once on Hilton Head Island, signs are small and blend in with the trees and landscaping, and nighttime lighting is kept to a minimum. The lack of streetlights makes it difficult to find your way at night, so be sure to get good directions.

8

### TAXI TRAVEL

There are several taxi services available on Hilton Head, including Hilton Head Taxi and Limousine, Yellow Cab HHI, and Diamond Transportation of Hilton Head, which has SUVs and passenger vans available for pickup to and from Savannah/Hilton Head International Airport and Hilton Head Airport. Prices range from $20 to $110.

**Taxi Contacts Diamond Transportation** ✉ *5 Gumtree Rd., Mid-island, Hilton Head* ☎ *843/247–2156* 🌐 *hiltonheadrides.com.* **Hilton Head Taxi and Limousine** ✉ *374 Spanish Wells Rd., Mid-island, Hilton Head* ☎ *843/785–8294.* **Yellow Cab HHI** ☎ *843/686–6666* 🌐 *www.yellowcabhhi.com.*

### TRAIN TRAVEL

Amtrak gets you as close as Savannah or Yemassee.

**Train Contacts Savannah Amtrak Station** ✉ *2611 Seaboard Coastline Dr., Savannah, Georgia* ☎ *800/872–7245* 🌐 *www.amtrak.com.*

## TOURS

Hilton Head's Adventure Cruises hosts dolphin-watching cruises, sport crabbing, and more. Several companies, including H2O Sports, Live Oac, Outside Hilton Head, and Low Country Nature Tours in Hilton Head, run dolphin-watching, shark-fishing, kayak, sunset, and delightful environmental trips. Low Country Nature Tours offers a family-friendly fireworks tour during the summer, as well as educational and fun bird-watching tours that children are sure to enjoy.

Gullah Heritage Trail Tours gives a wealth of history about slavery and the Union takeover of the island during the Civil War; tours leave from the Coastal Discovery Museum at Honey Horn Plantation and cost $32.

There's a wide variety of tours available at Harbour Town Yacht Basin, including sunset cruises, fireworks, and dolphin tours; Vagabond Cruise runs a cruise on the *Stars & Stripes* of America's Cup fame. Pau Hana & Flying Circus Sailing Charters offers tours on a catamaran sailboat, and fireworks and sunset cruises. The captains provide an interactive, educational adventure, and the catamaran makes for smooth sailing.

**Tour Contacts Adventure Cruises** ✉ *Shelter Cove Marina, 9 Harbourside La., Mid-Island, Hilton Head Island* ☎ *843/785–4558* 🌐 *www.hiltonheadisland.com/adventure.* **Gullah Heritage Trail Tours** ✉ *Coastal Discovery Museum, 70 Honey Horn Dr., North End, Hilton Head* ☎ *843/681–7066* 🌐 *www.gullaheritage.com.* **H2O Sports** ✉ *Harbour Town Marina, 149 Lighthouse Rd., South End, Hilton Head Island* ☎ *843/671–4386, 877/290–4386* 🌐 *www.h2osportsonline.com.* **Harbour Town Yacht Basin** ✉ *Sea Pines, 149 Lighthouse Rd., South End, Hilton Head Island* ☎ *843/363–2628* 🌐 *harbourtownyachtbasin.com.* **Live Oac** ✉ *Hilton Head Harbor, 43A Jenkins Rd., North End, Hilton Head Island* ☎ *888/254–8362* 🌐 *www.liveoac.com.* **Low Country Nature Tours** ✉ *Shelter Cove Marina, 1 Shelter Cove La., Mid-Island, Hilton Head Island* ☎ *843/683–0187* 🌐 *www.lowcountrynaturetours.com.* **Outside Hilton Head** ✉ *Shelter Cove Marina, 1 Shelter Cove La., Mid-Island, Hilton Head Island* ☎ *843/686–6996* 🌐 *www.outsidehiltonhead.com.* **Pau Hana & Flying Circus Sailing Charters** ✉ *Palmetto Bay Marina, 86 Helmsman Way, South End, Hilton Head Island* ☎ *843/686–2582* 🌐 *www.hiltonheadislandsailing.com.*

### RESTAURANTS

The number of fine-dining restaurants on Hilton Head Island is extraordinary, given the size of the island. Because of the proximity to the Atlantic and small farms on the mainland, most locally owned restaurants are still heavily influenced by the catch of the day and seasonal field harvests. Most of the fine-dining restaurants open at 11 and don't close until 9 or 10, but some take a break between 2 and 4. Most of the more expensive restaurants have an early dining menu, and this is a popular time to dine. During the height of the summer season, reservations are a good idea, though in the off-season you may need them only on weekends. Smoking is prohibited in restaurants and bars in Bluffton, Beaufort, and on Hilton Head Island. Beaufort's restaurant scene has certainly evolved, with more trendy restaurants serving contemporary cuisine moving into the immediate downtown area. *Prices in the reviews are the average cost of a main course at dinner or, if dinner is not served, at lunch.*

### HOTELS

Hilton Head is known as one of the best vacation spots on the East Coast, and its hotels are a testimony to its reputation. The island is awash in regular hotels and resorts, not to mention beachfront or golf-course-view villas, cottages, and luxury private homes. You can expect the most modern conveniences and world class service at the priciest places. Clean, updated rooms and friendly staff are everywhere, even at lower-cost hotels—this is the South, after all. Staying in cooler months, for extended periods of time, or commuting from nearby Bluffton can save money. *Prices in the reviews are the lowest cost of a standard double room in high season.*



# HILTON HEAD ISLAND

Hilton Head Island is known far and wide as a vacation destination that prides itself on its top-notch golf courses and tennis programs, world-class resorts, and beautiful beaches. But the island is also part of the storied American South, steeped in a rich, colorful history. It has seen Native Americans and explorers, battles from the Revolutionary War to the Civil War, plantations and slaves, and development and environmentally focused growth.

## EXPLORING

### GETTING HERE AND AROUND

Hilton Head Island is 19 miles east of I–95. Take Exit 8 off I–95 and then U.S. 278 east, directly to the bridges. If you're heading to the southern end of the island, your best bet to save time and avoid traffic is the Cross Island Parkway toll road. The cost is $1.25 each way.

### TOP ATTRACTIONS

Fodor's Choice ★ **Coastal Discovery Museum.** This wonderful museum has a variety of art and historical exhibits that tell the story of the Lowcountry and Hilton Head Island's history. For instance, visitors will learn about the early development of Hilton Head as an island resort from the Civil War to

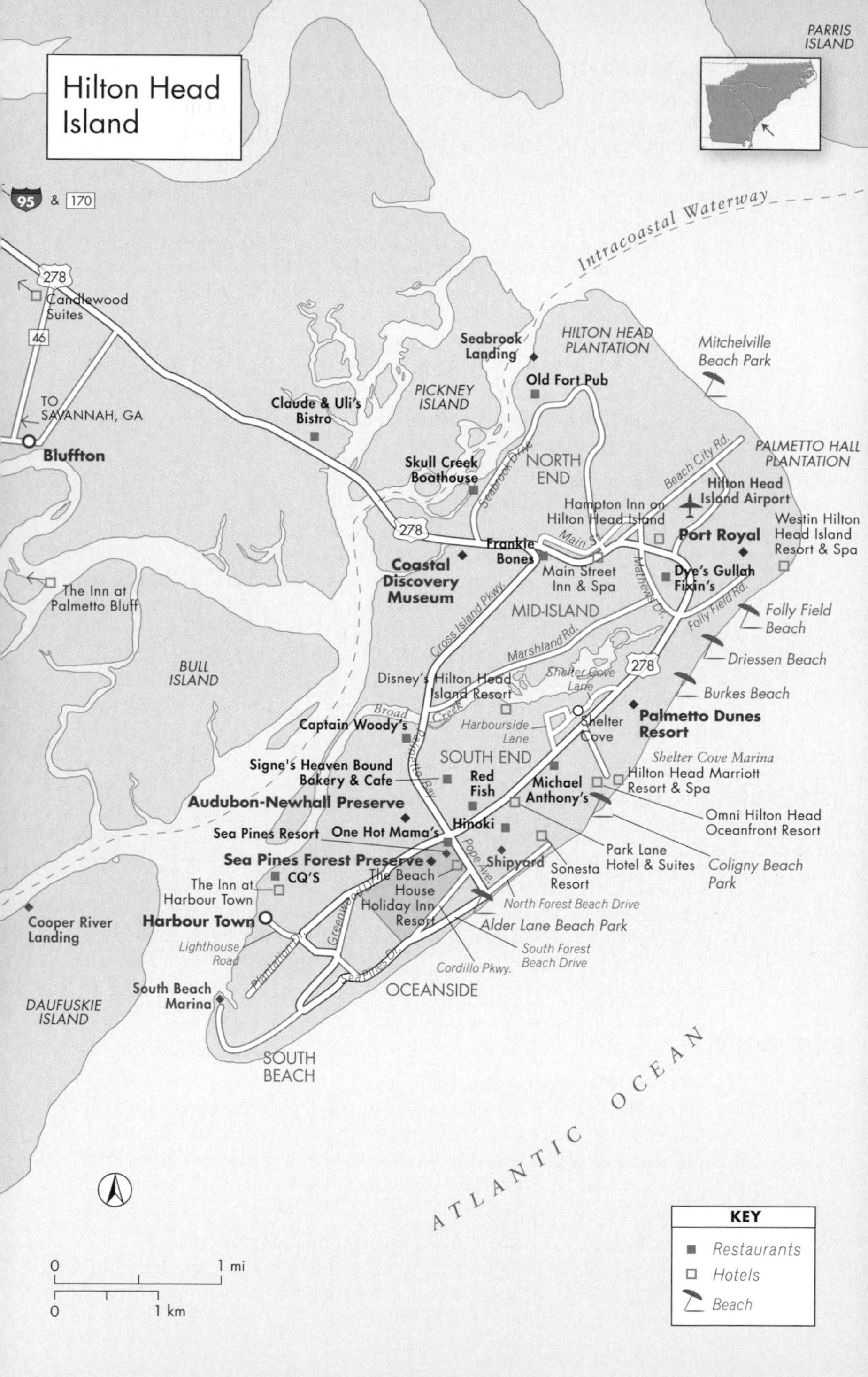

Hilton Head Island
PARRIS ISLAND
95 & 170
Intracoastal Waterway
278
Candlewood Suites
46
TO SAVANNAH, GA
Bluffton
Seabrook Landing
HILTON HEAD PLANTATION
Mitchelville Beach Park
PICKNEY ISLAND
Old Fort Pub
Claude & Uli's Bistro
Skull Creek Boathouse
Seabrook Drive
NORTH END
Beach City Rd.
PALMETTO HALL PLANTATION
Hilton Head Island Airport
Hampton Inn on Hilton Head Island
Westin Hilton Head Island Resort & Spa
Main St.
Port Royal
Frankie Bones
Coastal Discovery Museum
Main Street Inn & Spa
Mathews Dr.
Dye's Gullah Fixin's
The Inn at Palmetto Bluff
Folly Field Rd.
Folly Field Beach
Cross Island Pkwy.
MID-ISLAND
Marshland Rd.
Driessen Beach
BULL ISLAND
Disney's Hilton Head Island Resort
Shelter Cove Lane
278
Burkes Beach
Broad Creek
Harbourside Lane
Shelter Cove
Palmetto Dunes Resort
Captain Woody's
SOUTH END
Shelter Cove Marina
Signe's Heaven Bound Bakery & Cafe
Palmetto Bay
Red Fish
Michael Anthony's
Hilton Head Marriott Resort & Spa
Audubon-Newhall Preserve
Omni Hilton Head Oceanfront Resort
Hinoki
Sea Pines Resort
One Hot Mama's
Park Lane Hotel & Suites
Sea Pines Forest Preserve
Pope Ave.
Shipyard
Sonesta Resort
Coligny Beach Park
CQ'S
The Beach House Holiday Inn Resort
The Inn at Harbour Town
Greenwood Dr.
North Forest Beach Drive
Cooper River Landing
Harbour Town
Alder Lane Beach Park
Lighthouse Road
Plantation
South Forest Beach Drive
Cordillo Pkwy.
Sea Pines Dr.
South Beach Marina
OCEANSIDE
DAUFUSKIE ISLAND
SOUTH BEACH
ATLANTIC OCEAN
0
1 mi
0
1 km
KEY
Restaurants
Hotels
Beach

the 1930s. There is also a new butterfly enclosure, various hands-on programs for children, guided walks, and much more. Admission is free; lectures and tours on subjects both historical and natural cost $7 and up. Although the museum is just off the Cross Island Parkway, the peaceful grounds make it feel a century away. ■ **TIP→ Take a walk around the grounds to see marshes, open fields, old live-oak trees dripping with Spanish moss, and South Carolina's largest southern red cedar tree, which dates to 1595.** ✉ *Hwy. 278 at Gumtree Rd., 70 Honey Horn Dr., North End* ☎ *843/689–6767* 🌐 *www.coastaldiscovery.org* 🎟 *Free.*

**Sea Pines Forest Preserve.** Walking trails take you past a stocked fishing pond, a waterfowl pond, and a 3,400-year-old Native American shell ring at this 605-acre public wilderness tract. Pick up the extensive activity guide at the Sea Pines Welcome Center to take advantage of goings-on—moonlight hayrides, storytelling around campfires, and alligator- and bird-watching boat tours. The preserve is part of the grounds at Sea Pines Resort. ■ **TIP→ Head to the preserve's outdoor chapel for some quiet meditation.** The chapel overlooks a small lake and has five wooden pews and a lectern, all with the Prayer of St. Francis engraved in the wood. You can get directions at the Sea Pines Welcome Center. ✉ *Sea Pines Resort, South End* ☎ *843/363–4530* 🌐 *www.seapines.com* 🎟 *$5 per car* ⏲ *Daily dawn–dusk.*

## WORTH NOTING

**Audubon-Newhall Preserve.** There are trails, a self-guided tour, and seasonal walks on this 50-acre preserve. Native plant life is tagged and identified in this pristine forest. ✉ *Palmetto Bay Rd. near southern base of Cross Island Pkwy., South End* 🌐 *www.hiltonheadaudubon.org.*

8

**Bluffton.** Tucked away from the resorts, charming Old Town Bluffton has several historic homes and churches, an active artists' colony in the Calhoun Street area, good restaurants (including the fun-named Squat 'n' Gobble, Sippin' Cow, and Pepper's Porch), and oak-lined streets dripping with Spanish moss. At the end of Wharf Street in Old Town Bluffton is the Bluffton Oyster Company, a place to buy fresh raw local shrimp, fish, and oysters. Grab some picnic fixings from the Downtown Deli (✉ *27 Dr. Mellichamp Dr.*) and head to the boat dock at the end of Pritchard Street for a meal with a view. ■ **TIP→ Another incredibly beautiful spot for a picnic is the grounds of the Church of the Cross on the May River at 60 Calhoun Street.** Bluffton's chain hotels—including Candlewood Suites, Holiday Inn Express, and the Comfort Inn—a few miles from the Old Town district provide a nearby alternative to Hilton Head's higher prices. ✉ *S.C. 46 and May River Rd., Old Town, Bluffton.*

**Sea Pines Resort.** The oldest and best known of Hilton Head's developments, this resort occupies 4,500 thickly wooded acres with three golf courses, tennis clubs, stables, a fine beach, and shopping plazas. The focus of Sea Pines is **Harbour Town,** a charming marina with a luxury hotel, shops, restaurants, condominiums and vacation rental homes, and the landmark candy-cane-stripe Hilton Head Lighthouse. A free trolley shuttles visitors around the resort. ■ **TIP→ Check out the Stoney-Baynard Ruins, the remnants of a plantation home and slave quarters built in**

the 1700s by Captain John "Saucy Jack" Stoney. On the National Register of Historic Sites, they're not easy to find, so ask for directions at the Sea Pines Welcome Center at the Greenwood Drive gate. ✉ *32 Greenwood Dr., South End* ☎ *866/561–8802* 🌐 *www.seapines.com* 🎟 *$5 per car for nonguests.*

## WHERE TO EAT

$$ SEAFOOD

✕ **Captain Woody's.** If you're looking for a fun, casual, kid-friendly restaurant with terrific seafood and reasonable prices, Captain Woody's is the place to go. The restaurant has two locations, one in Hilton Head and one in Bluffton. The Hilton Head location overlooks Palmetto Bay Marina and has a beach-y feel with ceiling fans, aquariums, and outdoor seating. Start with a dozen oysters on the half shell or the sampler platter, which includes crab legs, shrimp, and oysters. The grouper sandwiches are a staple of Captain Woody's, and include the buffalo grouper, grouper melt, and grouper Reuben. Also available are salads, burgers, and homemade soups—the crab bisque is creamy and delicious. $ *Average main: $19* ✉ *Palmetto Bay Marina, 86 Helmsman Way, South End* ☎ *843/785–2400* 🌐 *www.captainwoodys.com* ✍ *Reservations not accepted.*

$$ SOUTHERN

✕ **Dye's Gullah Fixin's.** It's often hard to find the real thing, but this is true Gullah food: decadent, delicious, and comforting. Owner Dye Scott-Rhodan uses recipes handed down by generations of her Gullah family. Those recipes include dishes like fried chicken, pork ribs, macaroni and cheese, collard greens, and Lowcountry boil (shrimp, smoked sausage, potatoes, corn, and seasonings). Wash it down with the South's most popular beverage: sweet tea. There is also a full bar, and a Sunday buffet from noon to 3. The small restaurant has occasional entertainment, including karaoke. It is located in the Pineland Station shopping center. $ *Average main: $18* ✉ *Pineland Station, 430 William Hilton Pkwy., Mid-Island* ☎ *843/681–8106* 🌐 *www.dyesgullahfixins.com* ✍ *Reservations essential* ⏲ *No lunch Sat.*

$$$ ITALIAN

✕ **Frankie Bones.** Since this restaurant is dedicated to the loving memory of Frank Sinatra, you might assume that its name is also one of the handles of "ol' blue eyes." But you'd be wrong. "Bones" was a Chicago gangster before Prohibition. This place appeals to an older set of regulars who like the traditional parmigianas and marsalas on the early dining menu. But during happy hour, the bar and tall cocktail tables are populated with younger patrons who order flat-bread pizzas and small portions of pasta. It's especially popular with guys who prefer the substantial and familiar, but some dishes have more innovative twists, including a 16-ounce rib eye with a sweetened coffee rub. Be an honorary Italian and just drink your dessert, something Amaretto-based such as a Godfather or a Burnt Almond. $ *Average main: $22* ✉ *1301 Main St., North End, Hilton Head* ☎ *843/682–4455* 🌐 *www.frankieboneshhi.com* ✍ *Reservations essential* ⏲ *Closed Sun. No lunch.*

$$$ JAPANESE Fodor's Choice ★

✕ **Hinoki.** A peaceful oasis awaits you at Hinoki, which has repeatedly been voted best sushi on Hilton Head Island. As you make your way into the restaurant, fishponds and Japanese flora flank the boardwalk. The interior has an intimate feel, and includes a bar, regular seating, a

**DID YOU KNOW?**

Bluffton, 12 miles west of Hilton Head Island, is a quaint town with historic homes, an active artists' colony, and several good restaurants.

sushi bar, and a few sunken tables, with bamboo touches throughout. Try the Hilton Head roll, which is white fish tempura and avocado, or the Hinoki roll of asparagus and spicy masago (Capelin roe), topped with tuna and avocado. The sushi chef will also make specialty rolls as requested. One of the specialties of the house is a to-die-for tuna sashimi salad with spicy mayo, cucumbers, onions, salmon roe, and crabmeat. There are more than 50 sushi and sashimi choices, along with udon noodle dishes and bento boxes. There's also an extensive sake menu. $ *Average main: $22* ✉ *Orleans Plaza, 37 New Orleans Rd., South End* ☎ *843/785–9800* 🌐 *hinokihhi.com* ⏲ *Closed Sun.*

### COOKING CLASS

Learn to prepare Italian cuisine in a hands-on cooking class at Michael Anthony's. Classes include samples of the dishes and wine. Demonstration classes, wine tastings, and programs for visiting corporate groups are also available. There is a high demand for these classes, so reserve your place as far in advance as possible on Michael Anthony's website (🌐 *www.michael-anthonys.com*).

$$$$ ITALIAN Fodor's Choice ★

**Michael Anthony's.** A throwback to the days when the most exotic ethnic restaurant in town was a family-owned Italian spot, Michael Anthony's is more upscale, with fresh, top-quality ingredients, simple yet elegant sauces, and waiters who know and care about the food they serve. Owned by a talented, charismatic Philadelphia family, the restaurant has a convivial spirit, and its innovative pairings and plate presentations are au courant. Added bonus: The restaurant offers cooking demonstrations/classes and wine tastings in their upstairs dining room, which has a Tuscan farmhouse feel. $ *Average main: $30* ✉ *Orleans Plaza, 37 New Orleans Rd., Suite L, South End* ☎ *843/785–6272* 🌐 *www.michael-anthonys.com* *Reservations essential* ⏲ *Closed Sun. No lunch.*

$$$$ EUROPEAN

**Old Fort Pub.** Overlooking the sweeping marshlands of Skull Creek, this romantic restaurant has almost panoramic views. It offers one of the island's best overall dining experiences: the building is old enough to have some personality, and the professional waiters do their duty. More important, the kitchen serves flavorful food, including a great appetizer of roasted calamari with sun-dried tomatoes and olives. Entrées like the bouillabaisse and filet mignon with chanterelles hit the spot. The wine list is extensive, and there's outdoor seating plus a third-floor porch for toasting the sunset. Sunday brunch is celebratory and includes a mimosa. $ *Average main: $30* ✉ *Hilton Head Plantation, 65 Skull Creek Dr., North End* ☎ *843/681–2386* 🌐 *www.oldfortpub.com* ⏲ *No lunch.*

$ BARBECUE

**One Hot Mama's.** In the South, heaven is barbecue, and at One Hot Mama's, the barbecue makes the angels sing. This Hilton Head institution, with its graffiti-strewn walls and upbeat atmosphere, is known for its melt-in-the-mouth pulled pork and fall-off-the-bone ribs. But it also offers some unusual choices. The wings, which have won multiple awards at Hilton Head's Rib Burnoff and Wing Fest, come in tasty sauces ranging from strawberry-jalapeño to Sriracha to "Devil Caution." The winning rib sampler includes hot Asian, chocolate barbecue, and "Mama's Perfect 10." In addition to food that will wake up your taste buds, there are also 15 beers on tap, about a dozen flat-screen TVs, and an outdoor patio with a big brick fireplace for the cooler months. *Average main: $14 7A Greenwood Dr., South End 843/682–6262 onehotmamas.com.*

$$$$ AMERICAN Fodor's Choice ★ **Red Fish.** The "naked" catch of the day—seafood grilled with olive oil, lime, and garlic—is a low-cal, heart-healthy specialty that many diners opt for. Caribbean and Cuban flavors permeate the rest of the menu in dishes such as Latin ribs and a Cajun shrimp-and-lobster burger. The restaurant's wine cellar is filled with some 1,000 bottles, and there's also a retail wine shop on-site. Although the location in a commercial strip isn't inspired, the lively crowd sitting amid candlelight, subdued artwork, dark furniture, and white linens more than makes up for it. *Average main: $28 8 Archer Rd., South End 843/686–3388 www.redfishofhiltonhead.com No lunch Sun.*

$ AMERICAN Fodor's Choice ★ **Signe's Heaven Bound Bakery & Café.** Every morning locals roll in for the deep-dish French toast, crispy polenta, and whole-wheat waffles. Since 1972, European-born Signe has been feeding islanders her delicious soups, curried chicken salad, quiches, and loaded hot and cold sandwiches. The beach bag ($12 for a cold sandwich, pasta or fresh fruit, chips, a beverage, and cookie) is a great deal. The melt-in-your-mouth cakes and the rave-worthy breads are amazing. *Average main: $8 93 Arrow Rd., South End 843/785–9118 www.signesbakery.com Dec.–Feb., closed Sun. No dinner.*

$$ AMERICAN Fodor's Choice ★ **Skull Creek Boathouse.** The Skull Creek Boathouse invites patrons to soak up the salty, casual atmosphere. In the two indoor dining areas, almost every table has a view of the water. Outside is a dining area and a bar called the Buoy Bar at Marker 13. Adirondack chairs invite you to sit back, relax, and catch the sunset. The Dive Bar features seafood raw, in sushi, and as carpaccio. A wide variety of other options include chilled seafood, salads, sandwiches, po'boys, burgers, and hot dogs. The dinner offerings include salmon, mahimahi, tuna, steaks, chicken, ribs, and more. Patrons can also bring in their freshly caught fish and the chef will prepare it to order. The problem with the Skull Creek Boathouse is deciding what to order, but you can take your time and enjoy the beautiful view. *Average main: $16 397 Squire Pope Rd., North End 843/681–3663 www.skullcreekboathouse.com.*

8

## BLUFFTON

$$$ EUROPEAN ★ **Claude & Uli's Bistro.** It's hard to go wrong with a chef who has cooked at Maxim's in Paris, the Connaught Hotel in London, and Ernie's in San Francisco. Chef Claude Melchiorri, who grew up in Normandy, France, and his wife, Uli, offer divine food at this atmospheric restaurant tucked away in a strip mall right before the bridges to Hilton Head Island. Candles and fresh flowers top the white linen–covered tables. Parisian art lines the walls; a large painting of dogs at a French bar adds a touch of humor. The French-European cuisine is simply irresistible. Before ordering appetizers and dinner, order the Souffle Grand Marnier with chocolate sauce ahead for dessert, then start with the seafood crepe with white-wine sauce. For the entrée, try the veal Normandy with brandied mushroom cream sauce. All the seafood is fresh, and all the sauces are

handmade. *Average main: $22 Moss Creek Village, 1533 Fording Island Rd., Suite 302, Bluffton 843/837–3336 claudebistro.com No lunch in summer.*

## WHERE TO STAY

$$$ RESORT **The Beach House Holiday Inn Resort.** This high-rise on one of the island's most popular beaches and within walking distance of major South End shops and restaurants underwent $5 million in renovations in 2012 and has a very upscale yet beach-y feel. **Pros:** the location cannot be beat; the renovations have made this once-tired property a very desirable vacation destination; strong professional management and corporate standards. **Cons:** in summer the number of kids raises the noise volume; small front desk can back up. *Rooms from: $249 1 S. Forest Beach Dr., South End 843/785–5126 www.hihiltonhead.com 202 rooms No meals.*

$$$$ RESORT **Disney's Hilton Head Island Resort.** The typical cheery colors and whimsical designs of Disney create a look that's part Southern beach resort, part Adirondack hideaway, and the villas here have fully furnished dining, living, and sleeping areas, as well as porches with rocking chairs and picnic tables. **Pros:** it is all about kids; young and friendly staffers. **Cons:** many guests actually think that there is a theme park here and are disappointed; it is a time-share property; not inexpensive. *Rooms from: $325 22 Harbourside La., Mid-Island 843/341–4100 www.disneybeachresorts.com/hilton-head-resort/ 102 villas, 21 deluxe studios No meals.*

$ HOTEL **Hampton Inn on Hilton Head Island.** Although it's not on the beach, this recently renovated and attractive hotel is a good choice for those traveling on a budget. **Pros:** good customer service; clean; moderate prices. **Cons:** not on a beach; view is often the parking lot. *Rooms from: $149 1 Dillon Rd., Mid-Island 843/681–7900 www.hamptoninn.com 95 rooms, 8 suites, 12 studios Breakfast.*

$$$$ HOTEL **Hilton Head Marriott Resort & Spa.** The Marriott's standard rooms get a tropical twist at this palm-enveloped resort: sunny yellow-and-green floral fabrics and cheery furnishings are part of the peppy decor. **Pros:** steps from the beach; three superb golf courses; 25 tennis courts; one of the best-run operations on the island. **Cons:** rooms could be larger; in summer kids are everywhere; in-room Wi-Fi costs $9.95 a day. *Rooms from: $299 1 Hotel Circle, Palmetto Dunes, Mid-Island 843/686–8400 www.hiltonheadmarriott.com 476 rooms, 36 suites No meals.*

$$$ HOTEL Fodor's Choice ★ **The Inn at Harbour Town.** At the most buzz-worthy of Hilton Head's properties, this European-style boutique hotel has a proper staff, clad in kilts, to pamper you with British service and a dose of Southern charm; butlers are on hand any time of the day or night, and the kitchen delivers around the clock. **Pros:** a service-oriented property; central Sea Pines address; unique, it is one of the finest hotel operations on island; complimentary parking. **Cons:** no water views; two-day minimum on most weekends in season. *Rooms from: $249 Sea Pines, 32 Greenwood Dr., South End 843/785–3333 www.seapines.com 60 rooms No meals.*

$$$$ B&B/INN **Fodor's Choice** ★ **The Inn at Palmetto Bluff.** Fifteen minutes from Hilton Head and a member of the Leading Small Hotels of the World, the Lowcountry's most luxurious resort sits on 20,000 acres that have been transformed into a perfect replica of a small island town, complete with its own clapboard church. **Pros:** the tennis-bocce-croquet complex has an atmospheric, impressive retail shop; the river adds both ambience and boat excursions; pillared ruins dotting the grounds are like sculpture. **Cons:** the mock Southern town is not the real thing; not that close geographically to the amenities of Hilton Head. *Rooms from: $556 ✉ 1 Village Park Sq., Bluffton ☎ 843/706–6500, 866/706–6565 www.palmettobluffresort.com 50 cottages No meals.*

$$ B&B/INN **Fodor's Choice** ★ **Main Street Inn & Spa.** This Italianate inn has stucco facades ornamented with lions' heads, elaborate ironwork, and shuttered doors: staying here is like being a guest at a rich friend's estate. **Pros:** pampering and indulgence is the order of the day; the service, the atmosphere and the rooms are all excellent. **Cons:** weddings can overwhelm the resort, especially on weekends and throughout June; regular rooms are small. *Rooms from: $159 ✉ 2200 Main St., North End ☎ 843/681–3001, 800/471–3001 www.mainstreetinn.com 29 rooms, 4 suites Breakfast.*

$$$ RESORT **Omni Hilton Head Oceanfront Resort.** At this five-story beachfront hotel with a Caribbean sensibility, the smallest accommodations are large, commodious studios with a kitchenette and the largest are two-bedroom suites; many rooms face the ocean, and all are decorated with elegant wood furnishings, such as hand-carved armoires. **Pros:** competes more with condos than hotels because of the size of its accommodations; lots of outdoor dining options. **Cons:** wedding parties can be noisy; cell phone service is spotty. *Rooms from: $229 ✉ Palmetto Dunes, 23 Ocean La., Palmetto Dunes, Mid-Island ☎ 843/842–8000 www.omnihilton.com 303 studios, 20 suites No meals.*

$ HOTEL **Park Lane Hotel & Suites.** The island's only all suites property has a friendly feel, since many guests settle in for weeks, enjoying the private balcony and full kitchen in every suite; most suites have a fireplace. **Pros:** this is one of the island's most reasonably priced lodgings; the bigger the unit, the nicer the condition and decor; flat-screen TVs; playground. **Cons:** not high-end; more kids mean more noise, especially around the pool area. *Rooms from: $99 ✉ 12 Park Lane, South End ☎ 843/686–5700 www.hiltonheadparklanehotel.com 156 suites.*

$$$$ RESORT **Sonesta Resort.** Decorated in a classy nautical theme and set in a luxuriant garden, the Sonesta is the centerpiece of Shipyard Plantation, which means guests have access to all its amenities, including golf and tennis. **Pros:** close to all the restaurants and nightlife in Coligny Plaza; parking is free, although valet parking costs $10. **Cons:** Wi-Fi and cell service problematic because of low-rise, older concrete structures; large and sometimes impersonal. *Rooms from: $289 ✉ Shipyard Plantation, 130 Shipyard Dr., South End ☎ 843/842–2400, 800/334–1881 www.sonesta.com/hiltonheadisland 331 rooms, 9 suites No meals.*

$$$$ RESORT **Westin Hilton Head Island Resort & Spa.** A circular drive winds around a metal sculpture of long-legged marsh birds as you approach this beachfront resort, whose lush landscape lies on the island's quietest, least

8

inhabited stretch of sand. **Pros:** a great destination wedding hotel, ceremonies can be performed on the beach and other outdoor or indoor venues; the beach here is absolutely gorgeous. **Cons:** in the off-season, the majority of its clientele are large groups; hotel's phone service can bog down. *Rooms from: $279 Port Royal Plantation, 2 Grass Lawn Ave., North End 800/933–3102, 843/681–4000 www.westinhiltonheadisland.com 412 rooms, 29 suites No meals.*

### BLUFFTON

$ HOTEL **Candlewood Suites.** At this suites-only hotel, opened in 2010, every room has a dishwasher, full-size refrigerator, microwave, and two-burner stove, as well as big, cozy leather recliners and flat-screen TVs. **Pros:** location makes it convenient to Hilton Head, Beaufort, and Savannah. **Cons:** cell phone service inside the hotel is hit-or-miss; set back from road and difficult to find (it's just past Sun City Hilton Head on U.S. 278). *Rooms from: $109 5 Young Clyde Court, Bluffton 843/705–9600, 877/226–3539 www.ichotelsgroup.com 124 suites.*

### PRIVATE VILLA RENTALS

Hilton Head has some 6,000 villas, condos, and private homes for rent, almost double the number of the island's available hotel rooms. Villas and condos seem to work particularly well for families with children, especially if they want to avoid the extra costs of staying in a resort.

#### RENTAL AGENTS

**Hilton Head Rentals and Golf.** With more than 250 vacation rentals on Hilton Head ranging in size from one to seven bedrooms, Hilton Head Rentals and Golf offers a wide variety of options. Many of its villas, condos, and homes for rent have oceanfront views. It also offers various packages that include golf and other activities. Rentals are generally for three to seven days. *578 William Hilton Pkwy. 843/785–8687 www.hiltonheadvacation.com.*

**Resort Rentals of Hilton Head Island.** This company represents some 275 homes and villas island-wide, from the gated communities of Sea Pines, Palmetto Dunes, and Shipyard to some of the older nongated areas that have the newest homes such as North and South Forest Beach and the Folly Field, Singleton Beach area. Stays are generally Saturday to Saturday during the peak summer season; three- or four-night stays may be possible off-season. Most of the properties are privately owned, so decor and amenities can vary. In addition to the rental fee, you'll pay 10% tax, an $85 reservation fee, and a 7% resort fee. Linens and departure cleaning are included in the quoted rates, but daily maid service or additional cleaning is not. *32 Palmetto Bay Rd., Suite 1B, Mid-Island 843/686–6008, 800/845–7017 www.hhivacations.com.*

## NIGHTLIFE

Bars, like everything else on Hilton Head, are often in plantations or shopping centers.

**Big Bamboo.** Decked out like a World War II–era South Pacific officers' club, this bar and restaurant features live music most nights of the week.

*Coligny Plaza, 1 N. Forest Beach Dr., South End 843/686–3443 www.bigbamboocafe.com.*

**Hilton Head Comedy Club.** This lounge brings top-flight comedic talent to Hilton Head Island Wednesday through Sunday. The red-and-black candlelit room is dark and intimate, and there are fantastic waterfront views. Start off with dinner and drinks downstairs at the Kingfisher, which serves some of the best crab in town. Stick around for music and dancing, and then head up to the "Top of the Kingfisher" for the comedy. Tickets are $12 per person. **TIP→** Make reservations, because the shows sell out fairly quickly. *Shelter Cove, 18 Harbourside La., South End 843/681–7757 www.hiltonheadcomedyclub.com.*

**Hilton Head Plaza.** Dubbed "the Barmuda Triangle" by locals, the bars at this plaza include One Hot Mama's, Reilley's, the Hilton Head Brew Pub, the Lodge Martini, and Jump & Phil's Bar & Grill. The plaza is near the Sea Pines Circle, and it's where the kids go. It's the closest thing Hilton Head Island has to a raging club scene. *Hilton Head Plaza, Greenwood Dr. right before gate to Sea Pines, South End.*

Fodor's Choice ★ **The Jazz Corner.** The intimate, elegant supper-club atmosphere at this popular spot is a wonderful setting in which to enjoy an evening of world-class entertainment and great food. The Jazz Corner is known for its jazz, swing, blues, and Motown performances. Owner, jazz historian, and horn player Bob Masteller sometimes takes the stage, too. The Jazz Corner offers a signature martini menu, extensive wine list, full bar, and late-night menu. It fills up quickly, so make reservations. *The Village at Wexford, 1000 William Hilton Pkwy., Suite C-1, South End 843/842–8620 www.thejazzcorner.com.*

**Remy's Bar & Grill.** Off-duty food and beverage workers love this spot, which is an island institution. Plus, it serves food until the sun comes up. Bonus: shag lessons are on Friday night. *Arrow Center, 130 Arrow Rd., Suite 104, South End 843/842–3800 remysbarandgrill.com Closed Sun.*

**The Salty Dog Cafe.** If there's one thing you shouldn't miss on Hilton Head Island, it's the iconic Salty Dog Cafe. It's the ideal place to escape, sit back, and enjoy the warm nights and ocean breezes in a tropical setting at the outdoor bar. There's music à la Jimmy Buffett seven nights a week during the summer and five nights a week in the off-season. Bring the family along for kids' entertainment, including music, magic, and face painting at 7 pm throughout the summer. *South Beach Marina, 224 S. Sea Pines Dr., South End 843/671–5199 www.saltydog.com.*

**Santa Fe Cafe.** A sophisticated spot to grab some cocktails in the early evening, it's also a great place to lounge in front of the fireplace or sip top-shelf margaritas on the rooftop cantina. *807 William Hilton Pkwy., Mid-Island 843/785–3838 www.santafecafeofhiltonhead.com.*

## SPORTS AND THE OUTDOORS

Hilton Head Island is a mecca for the sports enthusiast and for those who just want a relaxing walk or bike ride on the beach. There are 12 miles of beaches, more than 50 miles of public bike paths, 24 public golf courses, and more than 300 tennis courts. There's also tons of water sports, including kayaking and canoeing, parasailing, fishing, sailing, and much more.

### SAND DOLLARS

Hilton Head Island's beaches hold many treasures, including starfish, sea sponges, and sand dollars. Note that it is strictly forbidden to pick up any live creatures on the beach, especially live sand dollars. How can you tell if they are alive? Live sand dollars are brown and fuzzy and will turn your fingers yellow and brown. You can take sand dollars home only if they're white. Soak them in a mixture of bleach and water to remove the scent once you get home.

### BEACHES

A delightful stroll on the beach can end with an unpleasant surprise if you don't put your towels, shoes, and other earthly possessions way up on the sand. Tides here can fluctuate as much as 7 feet. Check the tide chart at your hotel.

**Alder Lane Beach Park.** A great place for solitude during the summer season and especially during the off-season, the beach has hard-packed sand at low tide, making it great for walking. Accessible from the Marriott Grand Ocean Resort. **Amenities:** lifeguards; showers; toilets. **Best for:** solitude; walking; swimming. ✉ *South Forest Beach Rd. at Alder La., 2 Woodward Ave., South End.*

**Burkes Beach.** This beach is usually not crowded, mostly because it is a bit hard to find and there are no lifeguards on duty. **Amenities:** none. **Best for:** solitude, sunrise, swimming, windsurfing. ✉ *60 Burkes Beach Rd., at William Hilton Pkwy. (U.S. 278), Mid-Island.*

Fodor's Choice ★ **Coligny Beach.** The most popular beach on the island is a lot of fun, but can get very crowded. Accessible from the Holiday Inn Oceanfront, Comfort Inn, Hilton Head Metropolitan Hotel, and Players Club Hotel, it has choreographed fountains for children to play under, Wi-Fi, bench swings, and beach umbrellas and chaise longues for rent. **Amenities:** lifeguards; food and drink; parking; showers; toilets. **Best for:** windsurfing; swimming. ✉ *1 Coligny Circle, at Pope Ave. and South Forest Beach Dr., South End.*

**Driessen Beach.** A good beach for families, Driessen is peppered with people flying kites, making it colorful and fun. There is a long boardwalk to the beach. **Amenities:** parking; lifeguards; toilets; showers. **Best for:** walking; sunrise; swimming. ✉ *43 Bradley Beach Rd., at William Hilton Pkwy., Mid-Island.*

**Folly Field Beach Park.** Next to Driessen Beach, Folly Field is also very nice for families. It can get crowded in season, but it's a wonderful spot for a day of sunbathing and swimming. The first beach cottages on Hilton Head Island were built here in the mid-1950s. **Amenities:** lifeguards, parking, toilets, outdoor showers. **Best for:** swimming, sunrise, walking. ✉ *55 Starfish Dr., off Folly Field Rd., North End.*

**Mitchelville Beach Park.** Not good for swimming due to the many sharp shells and rocks on the beach and in the water, but it is a terrific spot for a walk or shelling. It is not on the Atlantic Ocean, but rather on Port Royal Sound. **Amenities:** parking; toilets. **Best for:** solitude; walking. ✉ *Hilton Head Plantation, 124 Mitchelville Rd., North End.*

Biking is popular on the hard-packed sand at low tide.

## BIKING

Bikes with wide tires are a must if you want to ride on the beach. They can save you a spill should you hit loose sand on the trails. More than 50 miles of public paths crisscross Hilton Head Island. ■ **TIP→ For a map of trails, visit ⊕ www.hiltonheadislandsc.gov and click on "Our Island."**

**Hilton Head Bicycle Company.** You can rent bicycles, helmets and adult tricycles from the Hilton Head Bicycle Company. ✉ *112 Arrow Rd., South End* ☎ *843/686 6888, 800/995–4319* ⊕ *www.hiltonheadbicycle.com.*

**Pedals Bicycles.** Rent beach bikes for adults and children, kiddy karts, jogging strollers, and mountain bikes at Pedals. ✉ *71A Pope Ave., South End* ☎ *843/842–5522, 888/699–1039* ⊕ *www.pedalsbicycles.com.*

**South Beach Cycles.** Rent bikes, helmets, tandems, and adult tricycles at this spot in Sea Pines. ✉ *Sea Pines, 230 South Sea Pines Dr., South End* ☎ *843/671–2453* ⊕ *www.south-beach-cycles.com.*

## CANOEING AND KAYAKING

This is one of the most delightful ways to commune with nature on this commercial but physically beautiful island. Paddle through the creeks and estuaries and try to keep up with the dolphins.

**Outside Hilton Head.** Boats, canoes, kayaks, and paddleboards are available for rent. The company also runs nature tours and dolphin-watching excursions. ✉ *Shelter Cove Marina, 1 Shelter Cove La., Mid-Island* ☎ *843/686–6996, 800/686–6996* ⊕ *www.outsidehiltonhead.com.*

## FISHING

Anglers can fish year-round in island waters, with April starting to crank up the season and May heavily booked. May is the season for cobia, especially in Port Royal Sound. In the Gulf Stream you can hook king mackerel, tuna, wahoo, and mahimahi. **■ TIP→ A fishing license is necessary if you are fishing from a beach, dock, or pier. For nonresidents, they are $11 for seven days.** Licenses aren't necessary on charter fishing boats because they already have their licenses. For more information, visit *www.dnr.sc.gov*.

**Bulldog Fishing Charters.** Captain Christian offers his guests 4-, 6-, 8-, and 10-hour fishing tours on his 32-foot boat. *Departs from docks at the Chart House, 2 Hudson Rd., Mid-Island 843/422–0887 bulldogfishingcharters.com.*

**Capt. Hook Party Boat.** Shark and deep-sea fishing tours are available on this large party boat, which sells concessions as well. The friendly crew helps teach children how to bait and reel in fish. *Shelter Cove Marina, 1 Shelter Cove La., Mid-Island 843/785–1700.*

**Fishin' Coach.** Captain Dan Utley offers a variety of fishing tours on his 22-foot boat to catch redfish and other species year-round, and cobia, shark, and other species by season. *1640 Fording Island Rd., Mid-Island 843/368–2126 www.fishincoach.com.*

**Palmetto Bay Charters.** Palmetto Bay Charters offers a wide variety of charters on various size boats. *Palmetto Bay Marina, 86 Helmsman Way, South End 843/785–7131 www.palmettobaymarinahhi.com.*

**Palmetto Dunes.** Fishing trips are available on the 34-foot *Gullah Gal* (six people), the 34-foot *True Grits* (six people), the 24-foot *Bayrunner* (four people), and at Palmetto Lagoon Charters in Shelter Cove. *Departs from Shelter Cove Marina, 4 Queens Folly Rd., Mid-Island 866/380–1778 www.palmettodunes.com/south-carolina-fishing-charters.php.*

## GOLF

Hilton Head is nicknamed "Golf Island" for good reason: the island itself has 24 championship courses (public, semiprivate, and private), and the outlying area has 16 more. Each offers its own packages, some of which are great deals. Almost all charge the highest green fees in the morning and lower fees as the day goes on. Lower rates can also be found in the hot summer months. It's essential to book tee times in advance, especially in the busy spring and fall months; resort guests and club members get first choices. Most courses can be described as casual-classy, so you will have to adhere to certain rules of the greens. **■ TIP→ The dress code on island golf courses does not permit blue jeans, gym shorts, or jogging shorts. Men's shirts must have collars.**

**The Heritage PGA Tour Golf Tournament.** The most internationally famed golf event in Hilton Head is the annual Heritage PGA Tour Golf Tournament, which is held mid-April. *Sea Pines Resort, 2 Lighthouse La., South End www.theheritagegolfsc.com.*

### GOLF SCHOOLS

**Golf Academy at Sea Pines Resort.** The academy offers one- to three-day schools, hourly private lessons by PGA-trained professionals, and comprehensive analysis. ✉ *Sea Pines, 100 North Sea Pines Dr., South End* ☎ *843/785–4540* 🌐 *www.golfacademy.net.*

**Palmetto Dunes Golf Academy.** There's something for golf-lovers of all ages at the academy. Lessons are offered for ages 3 and up, and there are ladies' programs, instructional videos, daily clinics, and multiday schools. Free demonstrations are held at 4 pm each Monday with Doug Weaver, former PGA Tour pro and director of instruction for the academy. Free club-fittings are also available. ✉ *Palmetto Dunes Oceanfront Resort, 7 Trent Jones La., Mid-Island* ☎ *843/785–1138* 🌐 *www.palmettodunes.com.*

> **TEE OFF ON A BUDGET**
>
> Golfing on Hilton Head can be very expensive after you tally up the green fee, cart fee, rental clubs, gratuities, and so on. But there are ways to save money. There are several courses in Bluffton that are very popular with the locals, and some are cheaper to play than the courses on Hilton Head Island. Another way to save money is to play late in the day. At some courses, a round in the morning is more expensive than 18 holes in the late afternoon.

**The PGA Tour Academy of Palmetto Hall Plantation.** Affiliated with the PGA, the academy is one of only six in the country. It is known for its teaching technologies that include video analysis, which compares one's swing on a split-screen with the best golfers in the world. Students can choose from a one-hour private lesson to up to five days of golf instruction. ✉ *Palmetto Hall Plantation, 108 Fort Hollow Dr., North End* ☎ *843/342–2582* 🌐 *www.palmettohallgolf.com.*

8

### GOLF COURSES

**Arthur Hills and Robert Cupp at Palmetto Hall.** There are two prestigious courses at Palmetto Hall Plantation: Arthur Hills and Robert Cupp. Arthur Hills is a player favorite, with trademark undulating fairways punctuated with lagoons, and winding around moss-draped oaks and towering pines. Robert Cupp is a very challenging course, but is great for the higher handicappers as well. ✉ *Palmetto Hall, 108 Fort Howell Dr., North End* ☎ *843/689–9205* 🌐 *www.palmettohallgolf.com* ✍ *Reservations essential* 🏌 *Arthur Hills: 18 holes. 6257 yds. Par 72. Green Fee: $145. Robert Cupp: 18 holes. 6025 yds. Par 72. Green Fee: $145* ☞ *Facilities: Driving range, 2 putting greens, pitching area, golf carts, rental clubs, pro shop, lessons, restaurant, bar.*

**Country Club of Hilton Head.** Although it's part of a country club, the course is open for public play. A well-kept secret, it's rarely overcrowded. This 18-hole Rees Jones–designed course is a more casual environment than many of the other golf courses on Hilton Head. ✉ *Hilton Head Plantation, 70 Skull Creek Dr., North End* ☎ *843/681–4653, 866/835–0093* 🌐 *www.clubcorp.com/Clubs/Country-Club-of-Hilton-Head* 🏌 *18 holes. 6162 yds. Par 72. Green Fee: $85–$105* ☞ *Facilities: Driving range, putting green, pitching area, golf carts, rental clubs, pro shop, golf academy/lessons, restaurant (for members), snack bar for guests.*

**Golden Bear Golf Club at Indigo Run.** On an island renowned for its exceptional golf, Jack Nicklaus, the golf legend and course designer, created another must-play course for Hilton Head. Located in the upscale Indigo Run community, its natural woodlands setting offers easygoing rounds. It is a course that requires more thought than muscle, yet you will have to earn every par you make. Though fairways are generous, you may end up with a lagoon looming smack ahead of the green on the approach shot. And there are the fine points—the color GPS monitor on every cart and women-friendly tees. After an honest, traditional test of golf, most golfers finish up at the plush clubhouse with some food and drink at Just Jack's Grille. ✉ *Indigo Run, 100 Indigo Run Dr., North End* ☎ *843/689–2200* 🌐 *www.goldenbear-indigorun.com* 🏌 *18 holes. 6184 yds. Par 72. Green Fee: $79–$99* ☞ *Facilities: Driving range, putting green, pitching area, golf carts, rental clubs, pro shop, golf academy/lessons, restaurant, bar.*

Fodor's Choice ★ **Harbour Town Golf Links.** This is considered by many golfers to be one of those must-play-before-you-die courses. It's extremely well known because it has hosted the Heritage Golf Tournament every spring for the last four decades. Designed by Pete Dye, the layout is reminiscent of Scottish courses of old. The Golf Academy at the Sea Pines Resort is ranked among the top 10 in the country. ✉ *Sea Pines Resort, 11 Lighthouse La., South End* ☎ *843/842–8484, 800/732–7463* 🌐 *www.seapines.com/golf* ✍ *Reservations essential* 🏌 *18 holes. 6603 yds. Par 71. Green Fee: $200–$250* ☞ *Facilities: Driving range, putting green, pitching area, golf carts, pull carts, caddies, rental clubs, pro shop, golf academy/lessons, restaurant, bar.*

**The May River Golf Club.** An 18-hole Jack Nicklaus course, this has several holes along the banks of the scenic May River and will challenge all skill levels. The greens are Champion Bermuda grass and the fairways are covered by Paspalum, the latest eco-friendly turf. A distinction of this classy operation is that caddy service is always required, even if you choose to rent a golf cart, and then no carts are allowed earlier than 9 am to encourage walking so golfers will enjoy the beauty of the course. ✉ *Palmetto Bluff, 476 Mount Pelia Rd., Bluffton* ☎ *843/706–6500* 🌐 *www.palmettobluffresort.com/golf* ✍ *Reservations essential* 🏌 *18 holes. 7171 yds. Par 72. Green Fee: $175–$260* ☞ *Facilities: Driving range, putting green, golf carts, pull carts, caddies, rental clubs, pro shop, golf academy/lessons, restaurant, bar.*

**Old South Golf Links.** There are many scenic holes with marshland and intracoastal waterway views at this Clyde Johnson–designed course. It was named one of the Top Ten New Public Courses by *Golf Digest* in 1992. Reservations are recommended. ✉ *50 Buckingham Plantation Dr., Bluffton* ☎ *843/785–5353* 🌐 *www.oldsouthgolf.com* 🏌 *18 holes. 6772 yds. Par 72. Green Fee: $65–$95* ☞ *Facilities: Driving range, putting green, pitching area, golf carts, pull carts, rental clubs, pro shop, golf academy/lessons, restaurant, bar.*

**Robert Trent Jones at Palmetto Dunes.** One of the island's most popular layouts, this course's beauty and character are accentuated by the par-5 10th hole, which offers a panoramic view of the ocean. ✉ *Palmetto*

If you golf, playing a round at Harbour Town Golf Links—home to The Heritage Golf Tournament—is probably already on your bucket list.

*Dunes, 7 Robert Trent Jones La., North End* ☎ *843/785–1138* 🌐 *www.palmettodunes.com* ✍ *Reservations essential* 🏌 *18 holes. 6122 yds. Par 72. Green Fee: $55–$155* ☞ *Facilities: Driving range, putting green, pitching area, golf carts, pull carts, rental clubs, pro shop, golf academy/lessons, restaurant, bar.*

8

### TENNIS

There are more than 300 courts on Hilton Head. Tennis comes in at a close second as the island's premier sport after golf. It is recognized as one of the nation's best tennis destinations. Hilton Head has a large international organization of coaches. ■ **TIP→ Spring and fall are the peak seasons for cooler play, with numerous tennis packages available at the resorts and through the schools.**

Fodor's Choice ★ **Palmetto Dunes Tennis Center.** This facility has 23 clay and 2 hard courts and welcomes nonguests. In 2010, the resort was ranked #7 in the world by Tennis Resorts Online. ✉ *Palmetto Dunes Oceanfront Resort, 6 Trent Jones La., Mid-Island* ☎ *843/785–1152* 🌐 *www.palmettodunes.com.*

**Port Royal Racquet Club.** The club has 10 clay and 4 hard courts. ✉ *Port Royal Plantation, 15 Wimbledon Court, Mid-Island* ☎ *843/686–8803* 🌐 *www.heritagegolfgroup.com.*

**Sea Pines Racquet Club.** The club has 23 clay courts, instructional programs, and a pro shop. There are special deals for registered guests of Sea Pines. In 2010, the resort was ranked #16 in the world by Tennis Resorts Online. ✉ *Sea Pines Resort, 5 Lighthouse La., South End* ☎ *843/363–4495* 🌐 *www.seapines.com.*

**Shipyard Racquet Club.** Play on 4 hard courts, 3 indoor courts, and 13 clay courts at this club. ✉ *Shipyard Plantation, 116 Shipyard Dr., South End* ☎ *843/686–8804* 🌐 *www.vandermeertennis.com.*

**Van der Meer Tennis Center.** Recognized for its tennis instruction, this club has 17 hard courts, 4 of which are covered and lighted. ✉ *Shipyard Plantation, 19 DeAllyon Ave., South End* ☎ *843/785–8388* 🌐 *www.vandermeertennis.com.*

## SHOPPING

Hilton Head is a great destination for those who love shopping, starting with the Tanger outlet malls. Although they're officially in Bluffton, visitors drive by the outlets on U.S. 278 to get to Hilton Head Island. Tanger Outlet I has been completely renovated and recently reopened with many high-end stores, including Saks OFF 5th.

### MALLS AND SHOPPING CENTERS

**Coligny Plaza.** Things are always humming at this shopping center, which is within walking distance of the most popular beach on Hilton Head. Coligny Plaza has more than 60 shops and restaurants, including large grocery store Piggly Wiggly, unique gift boutiques, clothing stores, souvenir shops, and more. There are also bike rentals, beauty salons, and free family entertainment throughout summer. ✉ *Coligny Circle, 1 North Forest Beach Dr., South End* ☎ *843/842–6050* 🌐 *www.colignyplaza.com.*

★ **Harbour Town, Shops at Sea Pines Center, South Beach Marina.** The three shopping areas in Sea Pines include boutiques, unique gift shops, restaurants, pro shops, and much more. ✉ *Sea Pines, 32 Greenwood Dr., South End* ☎ *866/561–8802* 🌐 *www.seapines.com.*

Fodor's Choice ★ **Tanger Outlets.** Reopened in 2011 after extensive renovations, Tanger Outlet I is anchored by Saks OFF 5th and has 40 other stores, many of them upscale. It also has an Olive Garden, Panera Bread, and Longhorn Steakhouse. Tanger Outlet II has more than 60 stores, including Abercrombie & Fitch, Banana Republic, the Gap, Nike, and Loft. There are also several children's stores, including Gymboree, Carter's, and Baby Gap. Dine at Food Network star Robert Irvine's restaurant, Nosh. There are almost always great outlet-wide coupons on the website. ✉ *1414 Fording Island Rd. (U.S. 278), Bluffton* ☎ *843/837–5410, 866/665–8679* 🌐 *www.tangeroutlet.com/hiltonhead.*

### ART GALLERIES

**Arts Center of Coastal Carolina.** This gallery showcases local artists. ✉ *Walter Greer Gallery at the Arts Center of Coastal Carolina, 14 Shelter Cove La., Mid-Island* ☎ *843/681–5060* 🌐 *www.artleaguehhi.org.*

Fodor's Choice ★ **Images by Ben Ham.** The extraordinary photography of Ben Ham focuses on Lowcountry landscapes and is very popular with locals. ✉ *90 Capital Dr., Suite 104, Mid-Island* ☎ *843/842–4163* 🌐 *www.benhamimages.com.*

### GIFTS

★ **Markel's.** You'll find unique Lowcountry gifts and a very helpful and friendly staff who are known for wrapping gifts with giant bows at Markel's. Pick up hand-painted wineglasses and beer mugs, Christmas decorations, pottery, lawn ornaments, baby gifts, greeting cards, and more. ✉ *1008 Fording Island Rd. (U.S. 278), Bluffton* ☎ *843/815–9500.*

★ **Salty Dog T-Shirt Factory.** It's a rule that tourists cannot leave Hilton Head Island without a Salty Dog T-shirt, but hit this factory store for the best deals. The iconic Salty Dog T-shirts can be seen all over the country and are hard to resist. There are lots of choices for kids and adults in various colors and styles. ✉ *69 Arrow Rd., South End* ☎ *843/842–6331* 🌐 *www.saltydog.com/stores/shop.*

### JEWELRY

Fodor's Choice ★ **Bird's Nest.** Local handmade jewelry, accessories, and island-themed charms are available at this popular spot. ✉ *Coligny Plaza, 1 N. Forest Beach Dr., #21, South End* ☎ *843/785–3737.*

**Forsythe Jewelers.** This is the island's leading jewelry store. ✉ *Sea Pines, 71 Lighthouse Rd., South End* ☎ *843/671–7070* 🌐 *www.forsythejewelers.biz.*

**Goldsmith Shop.** Classic jewelry and island charms are on sale at the Goldsmith Shop. ✉ *3 Lagoon Rd., South End* ☎ *843/785–2538* 🌐 *www.thegoldsmithshop.com.*

### SPAS

Spa visits have become a recognized activity on the island, and for some people they are as popular as golf and tennis. The quality of therapists island-wide is noteworthy—their training, certifications, and expertise.

**Auberge Spa at Palmetto Bluff.** Dubbed the "celebrity spa" by locals, this two-story facility is the ultimate pamper palace. It is as creative in its names, which often have a Southern accent, as it is in its treatments. There are Amazing Grace and High Cotton body therapies, sensual soaks and couples massage, special treatments for gentlemen and golfers, and Belles and Brides package. Nonguests are welcome. ✉ *Palmetto Bluff, 1 Village Park Sq., Bluffton* ☎ *843/706–6500* 🌐 *www.palmettobluffresort.com/spa.*

**Faces.** Faces has been pampering loyal clients for more than 20 years, with body therapists and cosmetologists who do what they do well. It has a fine line of cosmetics and does makeovers or evening makeups. It is open seven days a week. Monday night is geared to guys, who get 15% off services. ✉ *The Village at Wexford, 1000 William Hilton Pkwy., South End* ☎ *843/785–3075* 🌐 *www.facesdayspa.com.*

Fodor's Choice ★ **Heavenly Spa by Westin.** This is the quintessential sensorial spa experience. Known internationally for its innovation and latest in therapies and decor, Westin's Heavenly Spa brand also brings the treatments home. Prior to a treatment, clients are told to put their worries in a Gullah (a sweetgrass burden-basket); de-stressing is a major component here. Unique is a collection of treatments based on the energy from the color indigo, once a cash crop in the Lowcountry. The full-service salon, the relax room with its teas and healthy snacks, and the adjacent retail area with products like sweetgrass scents are heavenly, too. In-room spa services are available as are romance packages. Major renovations to the spa and hotel should be complete by spring of 2013. ✉ *Westin*

*Resort Hilton Head Island, Port Royal Plantation, 2 Grasslawn Ave., North End* ☎ *843/681–4000* 🌐 *www.westinhiltonhead.com.*

**Main Street Inn and Spa.** The holistic massages will put you in another zone at this petite facility. It offers deep-muscle therapy, couples massage, and hydrotherapy soaks. In-room spa services are also available. ✉ *2200 Main St., North End* ☎ *843/681–3001* 🌐 *www.mainstreetinn.com.*

# BEAUFORT

Updated by Sally Mahan

*38 miles north of Hilton Head via U.S. 278 and Rte. 170; 70 miles southwest of Charleston via U.S. 17 and U.S. 21.*

Charming homes and churches grace this old town on Port Royal Island. Come here on a day trip from Hilton Head, Savannah, or Charleston, or to spend a quiet weekend at a B&B while you shop and stroll through the historic district. Beaufort continues to gain recognition as an art town and supports a large number of galleries for its diminutive size.

More and more transplants have decided to spend the rest of their lives here, drawn to Beaufort's small-town charms, and the area is burgeoning. A truly Southern town, its picturesque backdrops have lured filmmakers here to shoot *The Big Chill*, *The Prince of Tides,* and *The Great Santini,* the last two being Hollywood adaptations of best-selling books by author Pat Conroy. Conroy has waxed poetic about the Lowcountry and calls the Beaufort area home.

### GETTING HERE AND AROUND

Beaufort is 25 miles east of Interstate 95, on U.S. 21. The only way here is by private car or Greyhound bus.

### ESSENTIALS

Well-maintained public restrooms are available at the Beaufort Visitors Center. You can't miss this former arsenal; a crenellated, fortlike structure, it is now beautifully restored and painted ochre.

The Beaufort County Black Chamber of Commerce (🌐 *www.bcbcc.org*) puts out an African-American visitor's guide, which takes in the surrounding Lowcountry. The Beaufort Visitors Center gives out copies.

**Visitor Information Beaufort Visitors Center** ✉ *713 Craven St.* ☎ *843/525–8500* 🌐 *www.beaufortsc.org.* **Regional Beaufort Chamber of Commerce** ✉ *1106 Carteret St.* ☎ *843/986–5400* 🌐 *www.beaufortchamber.org.*

## EXPLORING

Fodor'sChoice ★ **Henry C. Chambers Waterfront Park.** Off Bay Street, this park is a great place to survey the scene. Trendy restaurants and bars overlook these 7 landscaped acres along the Beaufort River. At night everyone walks the river walk. ✉ *1006 Bay St.* ☎ *843/525–7000* 🌐 *www.cityofbeaufort.org.*

**St. Helena Island.** Nine miles southeast of Beaufort via U.S. 21, St. Helena is the site of the Penn Center Historic District. Established in the middle of the Civil War, Penn Center was the South's first school for freed slaves; now open to the public, the center provides community services, too. This island is both residential and commercial, with nice beaches, cooling ocean breezes, and a great deal of natural beauty. It continues to be a stronghold of the Gullah culture, with several African-American-owned businesses in its "downtown" Frogmore, which is actually getting to be quite the tourist magnet. ✉ *St. Helena Island.*

**York W. Bailey Museum.** The museum at the Penn Center has displays on the heritage of Sea Island African-Americans; it also has pleasant grounds shaded by live oaks. The Penn Center (1862) was the first school for the newly emancipated slaves. These islands are where Gullah, a musical language that combines English and African languages, developed. This is a major stop for anyone interested in the Gullah history and culture of the Lowcountry. ✉ *30 Penn Center Circle West, St. Helena Island* ☎ *843/838–2432* 🌐 *www.penncenter.com* *$5* ⏲ *Mon.–Sat. 11–4.*

## WHERE TO EAT

$$$ SEAFOOD Fodor's Choice ★

✕ **11th Street Dockside.** Start with the fried green tomatoes or crab-stuffed shrimp. The succulent fried oysters, shrimp, and fish are some of the best around. More healthful options are also available, including a steamed seafood hot pot filled with crab legs, oysters, and shrimp. Everything is served in a classic wharfside environment, where you can eat on a screened porch and have water views from nearly every table. [$] *Average main: $21* ✉ *6 miles southwest of Beaufort, 1699 11th St. W, Port Royal* ☎ *843/524–7433* 🌐 *www.11thstreetdockside.com* *Reservations not accepted* ⏲ *No lunch.*

$$$ ECLECTIC

✕ **Breakwater Restaurant & Bar.** This downtown restaurant offers small tasting plates such as tuna tartare, rack of lamb, and fried oysters, with mains like lamb meat loaf and filet mignon with truffle demi-glace. The artistic plate presentation is as contemporary as the decor. There's a friendly bar scene, with tapas like pimento cheese, fried shrimp, and crab stack, and an impressive and affordable wine list. [$] *Average main: $23* ✉ *203 Carteret St., Downtown Historic District* ☎ *843/379–0052* 🌐 *www.breakwatersc.com* ⏲ *Closed Sun. No lunch.*

$$ AMERICAN

✕ **Plums.** This hip restaurant began its life in 1986 in a homey frame house with plum-color awnings shading the front porch. The name-sake awnings facing the riverwalk are still here, but a major renovation has more than doubled its seating, giving it a contemporary open space. An oyster bar that looks out to Bay Street, Plums still uses old family recipes for its soups, crab-cake sandwiches, and curried chicken salad served at lunch, but now it also offers inventive burgers, po'boys, and wraps. Dinner is more sophisticated with creative pairings and artistic plate presentations, particularly on the pasta and seafood dishes. There's live music Tuesday through Saturday, starting at around 10 pm. [$] *Average main: $19* ✉ *904 Bay St., Downtown Historic District* ☎ *843/525–1946* 🌐 *www.plumsrestaurant.com.*

$$$$ AMERICAN Fodor's Choice ★

✕ **Saltus River Grill.** The hippest eatery in Beaufort, with a classy sailing motif, wins over diners with its cool design, patio, and modern Southern menu. The bar opens at 4 pm, as does the raw bar with its tempting oyster varieties and sushi. Take in the sunset from outdoor seating overlooking the riverfront park. From 5 to 6, the early dining menu is a steal

8

CLOSE UP

## The World of Gullah

Drummers at a Gullah festival.

In the Lowcountry, Gullah refers to several things: a language, a people, and a culture. Gullah (the word itself is believed to be derived from *Angola*), an English-based dialect rooted in African languages, is the unique language, more than 300 years old, of the African-Americans of the Sea Islands of South Carolina and Georgia. Most locally born African-Americans of the area can understand, if not speak, Gullah.

Descended from thousands of slaves who were imported by planters in the Carolinas during the 18th century, the Gullah people have maintained not only their dialect but also their heritage. Much of Gullah culture traces back to the African rice-coast culture and survives today in the art forms and skills, including sweetgrass basketmaking, of Sea Islanders. During the colonial period, when rice was king, Africans from the West African rice kingdoms drew high premiums as slaves. Those with basketmaking skills were extremely valuable because baskets were needed for agricultural and household use. Made by hand, sweetgrass baskets are intricate coils of marsh grass with a sweet, haylike aroma.

Nowhere is Gullah culture more evident than in the foods of the region. Rice appears at nearly every meal—Africans taught planters how to grow rice and how to cook and serve it as well. Lowcountry dishes use okra, peanuts, *benne* (a word of African origin for sesame seeds), field peas, and hot peppers. Gullah food reflects the bounty of the islands: shrimp, crabs, oysters, fish, and such vegetables as greens, tomatoes, and corn. Many dishes are prepared in one pot, a method similar to the stewpot cooking of West Africa.

On St. Helena Island, near Beaufort, Penn Center is the unofficial Gullah headquarters, preserving the culture and developing opportunities for Gullahs. In 1852 the first school for freed slaves was established at Penn Center. You can delve into the culture further at the York W. Bailey Museum.

On St. Helena, many Gullahs still go shrimping with hand-tied nets, harvest oysters, and grow their own vegetables. Nearby on Daufuskie Island, as well as on Edisto, Wadmalaw, and John's islands near Charleston, you can find Gullah communities. A famous Gullah proverb says, *If oonuh ent kno weh oonuh dah gwine, oonuh should kno weh oonuh come f'um.* Translation: If you don't know where you're going, you should know where you've come from.

with three courses for $19 and select wines for $5. A flawless dinner might start off with the signature crab-and-lobster bisque, then segue to the seared sea scallops with curry oil, pea puree, and orange salad. The wine list is admirable, and desserts change nightly. *Average main: $30* *802 Bay St., Downtown Historic District* *843/379–3474* *www.saltusrivergrill.com* *No credit cards* *No lunch.*

## WHERE TO STAY

Even though accommodations in Beaufort have increased in number, prime lodgings can fill up fast, so do call ahead. The Best Western Sea Island Inn is still the only downtown property with a swimming pool.

$$ B&B/INN **Beaufort Inn.** This coral 1890s Victorian inn charms you with its gables and wraparound verandas; pine-floor guest rooms have period reproductions, striped wallpaper, and comfy chairs, and several have fireplaces and four-poster beds. **Pros:** in the heart of the historic district; beautifully landscaped, green events space; light afternoon refreshments are complimentary. **Cons:** atmosphere in the main building may feel too dated for those seeking a more contemporary hotel; no water views. *Rooms from: $165* *809 Port Republic St., Downtown Historic District* *843/379–4667* *www.beaufortinn.com* *7 queen rooms, 7 queen or king luxury suites, 8 2-BR cottages, 1 2-BR loft apartment, 2 flats, 1 4-BR house* *Breakfast.*

$$ B&B/INN **Beaulieu House.** From the French for "beautiful place," Beaulieu House is the only waterfront bed-and-breakfast in Beaufort, a quiet, relaxing inn with airy rooms brightly decorated in Caribbean colors. **Pros:** great views; scrumptious gourmet hot breakfast; about 7 miles from Beaufort Historic District. **Cons:** thin walls; hot water can be a problem; a bit off the beaten path. *Rooms from: $179* *3 Sheffield Ct.* *843/770–0303* *beaulieuhouse.com* *4 rooms, 1 suite* *Breakfast.*

$$ HOTEL **City Loft Hotel.** Cleverly transformed into a boutique property, this former motel built in the '60s was bought and resuscitated by the McAlhaneys, a young, hip Beaufort couple, who have infused it with their sense of high-tech, minimalist style. **Pros:** guests can use the adjacent gym around the clock; very accommodating staff. **Cons:** the sliding Asian screen that separates the bathroom doesn't offer full privacy; no lobby or public spaces. *Rooms from: $179* *301 Carteret St., Downtown Historic District* *843/379–5638* *www.cityloftbotel.com* *22 rooms, 1 suite.*

$$ ★ B&B/INN **Cuthbert House Inn.** Named after the original Scottish owners, who made their money in cotton and indigo, this 1790 home is filled with 18th- and 19th-century heirlooms and retains the original Federal fireplaces and crown and rope molding. **Pros:** owners are accommodating; they and other guests provide good company during the complimentary wine and hors d'oeuvres service; great walk-about location. **Cons:** some furnishings are a bit busy; some artificial flower arrangements; stairs creak. *Rooms from: $179* *1203 Bay St., Downtown Historic District* *843/521–1315, 800/327–9275* *www.cuthberthouseinn.com* *6 rooms, 3 suites* *Breakfast.*

8

$$ B&B/INN **Two Suns.** With its unobstructed bay views and wraparound veranda complete with porch swing, this historic home—built in 1917 by an immigrant Lithuanian merchant, whose grandson is now the mayor—offers a distinctive Beaufort experience. **Pros:** most appealing is the Charleston room, with its own screened-porch and water views; it's truly peaceful. **Cons:** decor is unsophisticated; although on Bay Street it's a bike ride or short drive downtown; third-floor skylight room is cheapest but least desirable. *Rooms from: $169* ✉ *1705 Bay St., Downtown Historic District* ☎ *843/522–1122, 800/532–4244* 🌐 *www.twosunsinn.com* *6 rooms* *Breakfast.*

### FRIPP ISLAND

$ RESORT ★ **Fripp Island Resort.** On the island made famous in *Prince of Tides,* with 3½ miles of broad, white beach and unspoiled sea island scenery, this resort has long been known as one of the more affordable and casual on the island and ideal for families. **Pros:** fun for all ages; the beach bar has great frozen drinks and live music. **Cons:** distance from Beaufort; some of the infrastructure and less expensive units, like the Sun Suites, are dated and even tired from so many children; could use another restaurant with contemporary cuisine. *Rooms from: $121* ✉ *1 Tarpon Blvd., 19 miles south of Beaufort, Fripp Island* ☎ *843/838–3535, 877/374–7748* 🌐 *www.frippislandresort.com* *210 units* *No meals.*

## NIGHTLIFE AND THE ARTS

**Emily's Restaurant & Tapas Bar.** This fun hangout is populated with locals who graze on tapas while eyeing one of the four wide-screen TVs. The piano sits idle until a random patron sits down and impresses the crowd. The bar is full of local characters. Reservations are suggested. ✉ *906 Port Republic St., Downtown Historic District* ☎ *843/522–1866* 🌐 *www.emilysrestaurantandtapasbar.com* *No lunch.*

**Hallelujah Singers.** The Gullah group, which was founded by Marlena Smalls, performs at Lowcountry venues, foot-stomping, clapping hands, and singing spirituals. ✉ *806 Elizabeth St., Port Royal* 🌐 *www.marlenasmalls.net.*

**Luther's.** A late-night waterfront hangout, Luther's is casual and fun, with a young crowd dancing to the beats of rock n' roll by live bands on Thursday, Friday, and Saturday nights. Luther's also has big-screen TVs, drink specials, and a terrific late-night menu. The decor features exposed brick, pine paneling, and cool 1940s and '50s posters. ✉ *910 Bay St., Downtown Historic District* ☎ *843/521–1888.*

**Nippy's Fish.** The mood is laid back at this simple café. There's outdoor seating under shade trees and live music—often a vocalist with a guitar—usually on Thursday and Friday night from 6 to 8:30 and Saturday afternoon from 2 to 3. ✉ *310 West St., Downtown Historic District* ☎ *843/379–8555.*

## SPORTS AND THE OUTDOORS

### BEACHES

★ **Hunting Island State Park.** This secluded park 18 miles southeast of Beaufort via U.S. 21 has 4 miles of public beaches—some dramatically eroding. The light sand beach decorated with driftwood and the raw, subtropical vegetation is breathtaking. The state park was founded in 1938 to preserve and promote its natural existence, and it harbors 5,000 acres of rare maritime forests. You can kayak in the tranquil lagoon; stroll the 1,300-foot-long fishing pier, which is among the longest on the East Coast; and go fishing or crabbing. For sweeping views, climb the 167 steps of the **Hunting Island Lighthouse** (built in 1859 and abandoned in 1933). It costs $2, and kids must be at least 44 inches tall. Bikers and hikers can enjoy 8 miles of trails. **Barefoot Bubba's** (✉ *2135 Sea Island Pkwy., St. Helena* ☎ *843/838–9222*), less than 1 mile from Hunting Island, rents bikes and kayaks and will deliver them to the park or anywhere in the area. The nature center has exhibits, an aquarium, and lots of turtles; there is a resident alligator in the pond. The campground has 200 sites, about 180 of which are for RVs and tents; 20 are for tents only. Expect to pay about $25 for campsites with electricity, $21 without. **Amenities:** none. **Best for:** solitude, sunrise, swimming, walking. ✉ *2555 Sea Island Pkwy., off St. Helena Island, Hunting Island* ☎ *843/838–2011* 🌐 *www.southcarolinaparks.com* 🎫 *$5* ⏲ *Park Apr.–Oct., daily 6 am–9 pm; Nov.–Mar., daily 6–6. Lighthouse daily 10–4.*

### BIKING

Beaufort looks different from two wheels. In town, traffic is moderate, and you can cruise along the waterfront and through the historic district. However, if you ride on the sidewalks or after dark without a headlight and a rear red reflector, you run the risk of a city fine of nearly $150.

**Lowcountry Bicycles.** If you want a decent set of wheels, call Lowcountry Bicycles. For just $5 you can rent bike headlights for your rental bike, which will cost just $8 an hour, $25 a full day, $75 a week. Adult bicycles only are available. ✉ *102 Sea Island Pkwy.* ☎ *843/524–9585* 🌐 *www.lowcountrybicycles.com.*

### CANOE AND BOAT TOURS

★ Beaufort is where the Ashepoo, Combahee, and Edisto rivers form the A.C.E. Basin, a vast wilderness of marshes and tidal estuaries loaded with history. For sea kayaking, tourists meet at the designated launching areas for fully guided, two-hour tours.

**A.C.E. Basin Tours.** This outfitter might be the best bet for the very young, or anyone with limited mobility, as it operates a 38-foot pontoon boat tour. A tour with Captain Stan Lawson at the helm costs $35, $15 for kids 12 and under. ✉ *1 Coosaw River Dr.* ☎ *843/521–3099* 🌐 *www.acebasintours.com.*

**Beaufort Kayak Tours.** Owner-operators Kim and David Gundler of Beaufort Kayak Tours are degreed naturalists and certified historical guides. Adults pay $40 and children under 18 pay $30 for half-day interpretive/

educational trips. The large cockpits in the kayaks make for easy accessibility and the tours go with the tides, not against them, so paddling isn't strenuous. Tours meet at various public landings throughout Beaufort County. ☎ *843/525–0810* 🌐 *www.beaufortkayaktours.com.*

### GOLF

Most golf courses are about a 10- to 20-minute scenic drive from Beaufort.

**Fripp Island Golf & Beach Resort.** This resort has a pair of championship courses. Ocean Creek Golf Course, designed by Davis Love, has sweeping views of saltwater marshes. Designed by George Cobb, Ocean Point Golf Links runs along the ocean the entire way. This is a wildlife refuge, so you'll see plenty of it, particularly marsh deer. In fact, the wildlife and ocean views may make it difficult for you to keep your eyes on the ball. Nonguests should call the golf pro to make arrangements to play. One must belong to a private golf club, and its head golf pro must call to arrange a tee time. Both are rated among the top 50 courses in South Carolina. ✉ *201 Tarpon Blvd., Fripp Island* ☎ *843/838–3535, 843/838–1576* 🌐 *www.frippislandresort.com* 🏌 *Ocean Creek: 18 holes. 6643 yds. Par 71. Green Fee: $75–$99. Ocean Point: 18 holes. 6556 yds. Par 72. Green Fee: $75–$99* ☞ *Facilities: Driving range, putting green, pitching area, golf carts, pull carts, rental clubs, pro shop, golf academy/lessons, restaurant, bar.*

## SHOPPING

### ART GALLERIES

**Bay Street Gallery.** A variety of Southern artists who use a variety of mediums to convey the feel of the Lowcountry are featured at Bay Street Gallery, including Lana Hefner, Susan Graber, Denise Choppin, Roger Steele, Jim Draper, Susan West, and Mandy Johnson. ✉ *719 Bay St., Downtown Historic District* ☎ *843/525–1024, 843/522–9210* 🌐 *baystgallery.com.*

**The Gallery.** One of the best galleries for contemporary art features a litany of artists' exhibitions. There are oils, collages, wood sculpture, jewelry, stained and fused glass, humorous Lowcountry scenes, and whimsical pieces with catchy titles. Pricing is democratic and goes up to high-end. ✉ *802 Bay St., Downtown Historic District* ☎ *843/470–9994* 🌐 *www.thegallery-beaufort.com.*

**Longo Gallery.** The colorful designs of Suzanne and Eric Longo decorate the Longo Gallery. Suzanne creates ceramic sculpture—couples dancing, mothers with children, and even works in concrete, while Eric's whimsical paintings often feature fish. ✉ *103 Charles St., Downtown Historic District* ☎ *843/522–8933* 🌐 *longogallery.com.*

Fodor's Choice ★ **Red Piano Too Gallery.** More than 150 Lowcountry artists are represented at the Red Piano Too Gallery, which is considered one of the best (if not the best) art gallery in the area. It carries folk art, books, fine art, and much more. The gallery is in the Corner Store, the first store in South Carolina to pay people of color with money rather than barter for goods. The gallery is ¼ mile from the National Historic

Landmark District of Penn Center, famous as a former school for freed slaves, whose culture is known as "Gullah." Much of the art at the gallery represents the Gullah culture. ✉ *870 Sea Island Pkwy., St. Helena* ☎ *843/838-2241* 🌐 *redpianotoo.com.*

**Rhett Gallery.** The Rhett Gallery sells Lowcountry art by four generations of the Rhett family, including remarkable wood carvings, as well as antique maps, books, Civil War memorabilia, and Audubon prints. ✉ *901 Bay St., Downtown Historic District* ☎ *843/524-3339* 🌐 *rhettgallery.com.*

### FOOD

**Barefoot Farm.** Check out this farm stand for perfect watermelons, rhubarb, and strawberry jam. Jacky "Barefoot" Frazier, the owner, is a local celebrity. ✉ *939 Sea Island Pkwy., St. Helena Island* ☎ *843/838-7421.*

## DAUFUSKIE ISLAND

*13 miles (approximately 45 minutes) from Hilton Head via ferry.*

From Hilton Head you can take a 45-minute ferry ride to nearby Daufuskie Island, the setting for Pat Conroy's novel *The Water Is Wide,* which was made into the movie *Conrack*. The boat ride may very well be one of the highlights of your vacation. The Lowcountry beauty unfolds before you, as pristine and unspoiled as you can imagine. The island is in the Atlantic, nestled between Hilton Head and Savannah. Many visitors do come just for the day, to play golf and have lunch or dinner; kids might enjoy biking or horseback riding. On summer Sunday afternoons from 2 to 6, the little tiki hut at Freeport Marina whirrs out frozen concoctions as a vocalist sings or a band plays blues and rock and roll. On weekend nights when there are bands at Marshside Mama's, the hip crowd even boats in from Hilton Head.

### GETTING HERE AND AROUND

The only way to Daufuskie is by boat, as it is a bridgeless island. The public ferry departs from Broad Creek Marina on Hilton Head Island several times a day. On arrival to Daufuskie you can rent a golf cart (not a car) or bicycle or take a tour. If you are coming to Daufuskie Island for a multiday stay with luggage and/or groceries, and perhaps a dog, be absolutely certain that you allow a full hour to park and check in for the ferry, particularly on a busy summer weekend. Whether you are staying on island or just day-tripping, the ferry costs $28 round-trip. Usually the first two pieces of luggage are free, and then it is $10 apiece.

### TOURS

Calibogue Cruises runs the public ferries at Freeport Marina. The marina includes the Freeport General store, a restaurant, overnight cabins, and more. A two-hour bus tour of the island by local historians will become a true travel memory. The ferry returns to Hilton Head Island on Tuesday night in time to watch the fireworks at Shelter Cove at sundown.

Daufuskie Discoveries sets you up for adventure, whether it's a three- or six-hour self-guided tour or a two-hour guided tour in one of its gas golf carts. It also offers an eight-hour "Fuskie Beach Day," which includes a round-trip water taxi from Hilton Head Island to 3 miles of secluded beaches, as well as golf excursions, overnight golf cart rentals, a guided cruise on a high-speed water taxi, and charter fishing and dolphin watching with its Unreel Expeditions.

Live Oac, based on Hilton Head, is an owner-operated company that offers Lowcountry water adventures such as nature tours, fishing excursions, and dolphin cruises. On its first-class hurricane-deck boats you are sheltered from sun and rain; tours, usually private charters, are limited to six people. Captains are interpretive naturalist educators and U.S. Coast Guard licensed.

Take a narrated horse-drawn carriage tour of historic Beaufort with Southurn Rose Buggy Tours and learn about the city's fascinating history and its antebellum and Victorian architecture.

**Tour Contacts Calibogue Cruises** ✉ *Broad Creek Marina, 18 Simmons Rd., Mid-Island, Hilton Head Island* ☎ *843/342-8687* ✉ *Freeport Rd., Freeport Marina* ☎ *843/785-8242* 🌐 *www.daufuskiefreeport.com.* **Daufuskie Discoveries** ☎ *843/384-4354* 🌐 *www.daufuskiediscoveries.com.* **Live Oac** ✉ *43 Jenkins Rd., North End, Hilton Head Island* ☎ *888/254-8362* 🌐 *www.liveoac.com.* ★ **Southurn Rose Buggy Tours** ✉ *1002 Bay St., Downtown Historic District, Beaufort* ☎ *843/524-2900* 🌐 *www.southurnrose.com.*

## WHERE TO EAT

$$ SEAFOOD Fodor's Choice ★

**Old Daufuskie Crab Company Restaurant.** Everyone calls this restaurant the Freeport Marina because of its location in the marina. A cold beer may be in order at the colorful bar that plays reggae and rock tunes, especially after a warm-water boat ride. This outpost, with its rough-hewn tables facing the water, serves up surprisingly good fare. The specialties are deviled crab and chicken salad on grilled, buttery rolls. Many also enjoy the Lowcountry buffet with its pulled pork and sides like butter beans and potato salad. Dinner entrées include shrimp, rib eyes, blackboard specials, and the catch of the day. *Average main: $17* ✉ *Freeport Marina, 1 Cooper River Landing Rd.* ☎ *843/785-6652* 🌐 *www.daufuskiefreeport.com* *Closed Mon.*

## NIGHTLIFE

**Marshside Mama's.** A bar, restaurant, and grocery store, this is *the* hot spot on the island, especially on Friday and Saturday nights when bands play everything from blues to bluegrass. The decor and the vibe here are funky and colorful. ✉ *At the dead end of Old Haig Point Rd., across from a public boat landing, 15 Haig Point Rd., South End* ☎ *843/785-4755* 🌐 *marshsidemamas.com.*

9

# The Midlands and the Upstate, SC

## WORD OF MOUTH

"Downtown Greenville is one of the great urban success stories. Lots of restaurants and plenty of people-watching. Check out minor league baseball as well."

—Ackislander

# WELCOME TO THE MIDLANDS AND THE UPSTATE, SC

## TOP REASONS TO GO

★ **Small-town charm:** Small towns—most complete with shady town squares, jewel-box shops, and a café—dot this region. Abbeville and Aiken are a couple of the nicest.

★ **Rafting the Chattooga:** The fact that the movie *Deliverance* was filmed here doesn't scare away rafting enthusiasts from some of the best white water in the country.

★ **Antiquing in Camden:** Camden's Art and Antique District, which comprises most of the downtown area, is a trove of well-priced furniture, ironwork, and high-quality paintings.

★ **Congaree Swamp National Park:** Wander through 20 miles of trails or follow the 2½-mile boardwalk that meanders over lazy creeks and under massive hardwoods.

★ **Waterfalls:** There are more than 25 waterfalls in the Upstate; some, like 75-foot Twin Falls, are an easy walk from the road. Others, such as Raven Cliff Falls, are a 2-mile hike away.

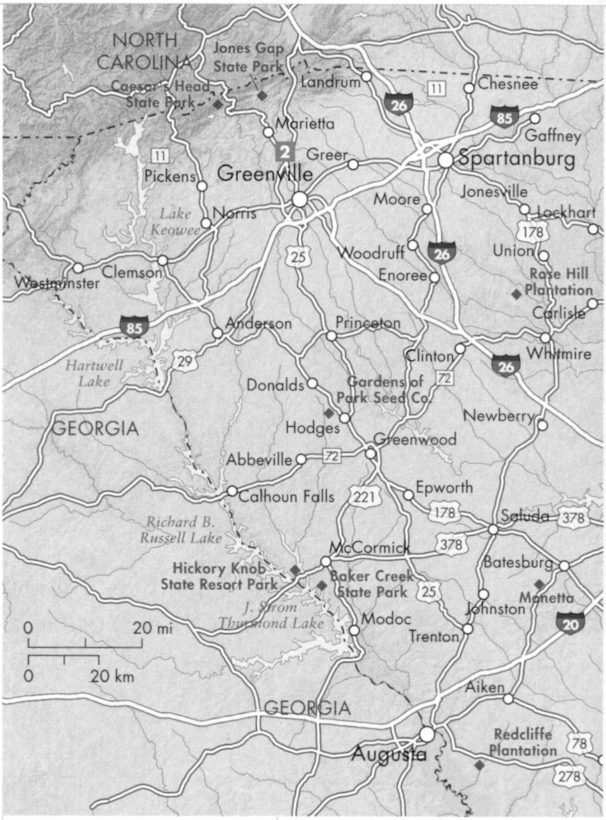

**1 Columbia and the Midlands.** Columbia is swarming with activity, from the University of South Carolina campus to the halls of the State House. Day or night, there is always something to do. It's worth it, though, to slow down the pace and take a drive out of town. With thick forests, quaint towns, and scores of local home-cooking restaurants, the Midlands will not disappoint.

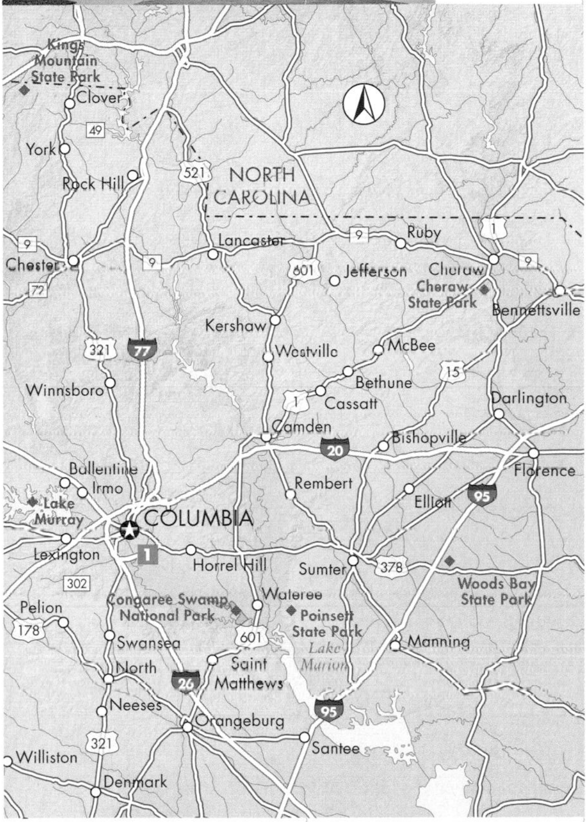

## GETTING ORIENTED

South Carolina's gleaming coasts and rolling mountains are linked by its lush Midlands. Swells of sandy hills mark where the state's coastline once sat, and as you drive farther inland you'll be greeted by the beauty of the Smoky Mountain foothills. What lies between is a mixture of Southern living—in cities and rural farms—that is truly remarkable.

**2 The Upstate.** The Upstate is a treasure trove of natural and historic sites. Hiking trails and waterfalls abound for visitors of all fitness levels. Even the most robust will enjoy the river and falls in Falls Park, right in the heart of downtown Greenville. History buffs will love following the South Carolina National Heritage Corridor through the area. The drive stretches through lush landscapes, making stops at historic sites and homes along the way.

Updated by Christine Anderson

South Carolina's Midlands, between the coastal Lowcountry and the mountains, is a varied region of swamps and flowing rivers, fertile farmland—perfect for horse-raising—and hardwood and pine forests. Lakes have wonderful fishing, and the many state parks are popular for hiking, swimming, and camping. Small old towns with mansions-turned-bed-and-breakfasts are common, and the many public gardens provide islands of color during most of the year.

At the center of the region is the state capital, Columbia, an engaging contemporary city enveloping cherished historic elements. Just outside town, Congaree Swamp National Park has the largest intact tract of old-growth floodplain forest in North America. Aiken, the center of South Carolina's Thoroughbred country, is where champions Sea Hero and Pleasant Colony were trained. Towns such as Abbeville and Camden preserve and interpret the past, with old house museums, history re-creations, and museum exhibits.

The Upstate of South Carolina is a land of waterfalls and wide vistas, cool pine forests, and fast rapids. Camping, hiking, white-water rafting, and kayaking are less than an hour from downtown Greenville and a paddle's throw from the small hamlets that are scattered about. Greenville itself, artsy and refined, is a modern Southern city with a thriving downtown full of trendy restaurants, boutiques, and galleries.

# PLANNING

## WHEN TO GO

Central South Carolina comes alive in spring, beginning in early March, when the azaleas, dogwoods, wisteria, and jasmine turn normal landscapes into fairylands of pink, white, and purple shaded by a canopy of pines. The heat of late May through September can be oppressive, particularly in the Midlands. Festivals celebrating everything from peaches to okra are held in summer. Fall will bring the state fair in Columbia,

SEC and ACC football to the University of South Carolina and Clemson University, rich yellows and reds of the changing trees in the mountains, and a number of art and music festivals.

## PLANNING YOUR TIME

The Midlands and Upstate have a wonderful mix of larger cities and small towns and villages. Columbia and Greenville are destinations on their own, with plenty of sites, stores, and high-end eateries. However, the dozens of surrounding towns offer great day trips and shopping excursions, especially if you're looking to go antiquing. Aiken offers a chance to spend the day with the horses at major events like the Triple Crown each spring and Sunday polo matches every fall.

Miles of forested land and winding rivers offer plenty of reasons to stay outdoors. With options covering everything from hiking and mountain biking to motorcycle paths and bridle trails, it's easy to find an excuse to head into the woods. The Palmetto Trail stretches across the entire state and can be walked in segments. The South Carolina National Heritage Corridor allows visitors to take a driving tour of some of South Carolina's major historic sites from the foothills of the Smokies to the coast of Charleston. The Ninety Six National Historic Site offers a mile-long loop through the woods, past Revolutionary War battlegrounds.

## GETTING HERE AND AROUND

### AIR TRAVEL

Columbia Metropolitan Airport (CAE), 10 miles west of downtown Columbia, is served by American Eagle, Delta, United, and US Airways. Greenville-Spartanburg Airport (GSP), off Interstate 85 between the two cities, is served by American Eagle, Delta, Independence, Southwest, United Express, and US Airways/Express.

**Air Contacts Columbia Metropolitan Airport (CAE)** ✉ *3250 Airport Blvd., West Columbia* ☎ *803/822–5000* 🌐 *www.columbiaairport.com.* **Greenville-Spartanburg International Airport (GSP)** ✉ *2000 G.S.P. Dr., Greer* ☎ *864/877–7426* 🌐 *www.gspairport.com.*

### CAR TRAVEL

Interstate 77 leads into Columbia from the north, Interstate 26 runs through north–south, and Interstate 20 east–west. Interstate 85 provides access to Greenville, Spartanburg, Pendleton, and Anderson. Interstate 26 runs from Charleston through Columbia to the Upstate, connecting with Interstate 385 into Greenville. Car rental by all the national chains is available at the airports in Columbia and Greenville.

### TAXI TRAVEL

Companies providing service in Columbia include Blue Ribbon and Checker-Yellow. VIP Transportation provides citywide service as well as service to other cities statewide. It's about $20 to $25 from the airport to downtown Columbia. Greenville services include Budget Cab Company, Yellow Cab of Greenville, and Greenville Metro Cab. Fares from the Greenville airport to downtown Greenville will run around $25.

**Taxi Contacts Blue Ribbon** ☎ *803/754–8163.* **Budget Cab Company** ☎ *864/233–4200.* **Checker-Yellow** ☎ *803/799–3311.* **Jay R's Taxi Service** ☎ *864/553-5469.* **VIP Transportation** ☎ *803/238–6669.* **Yellow Cab of Greenville** ☎ *864/233–6666.*

### TRAIN TRAVEL

Amtrak makes stops at Camden, Columbia, Denmark, Florence, Greenville, Kingstree, and Spartanburg.

**Train Contacts Amtrak** ☎ *800/872–7245* 🌐 *www.amtrak.com.*

### RESTAURANTS

Most of the smaller towns have at least one dining choice that might surprise you with its take on sophisticated fare. Larger cities such as Columbia and Greenville have both upscale foodie haunts and ultracasual grits-and-greens joints. Plan ahead: many places close on Sunday. *Prices in the reviews are the average cost of a main course at dinner or, if dinner is not served, at lunch.*

### HOTELS

Your best bet is to stay in an area inn or B&B. Count on just a handful of rooms, family favorites for breakfast, and, if you're lucky, a garden for wandering and a restored town square just steps away. What you gain in charm, however, you may have to give up in convenience. *Prices in the reviews are the lowest cost of a standard double room in high season.*

# COLUMBIA AND THE MIDLANDS

The wide swath of land that comprises the Midlands may have only one large city—the state capital, Columbia—but its profusion of small and medium-size towns makes this area a patchwork quilt of history and activity. The local museums and historic homes that line the shady streets often house surprisingly deep collections on everything from Civil or Revolutionary War battles to the lifestyle on 1850s plantations. Well-informed and friendly docents are happy to share stories, not to mention some tips on who's got the best peach pie that day.

## COLUMBIA

*112 miles northwest of Charleston via I–26; 101 miles southeast of Greenville via I–385 and I–26.*

Old as Columbia may be, trendy and collegiate neighborhoods have given the city an edge. The symphony, two professional ballet companies, several theaters that stage live—and often locally written—productions, and a number of engaging museums keep culture alive. The city is a sprawling blend of modern office blocks, suburban neighborhoods, and the occasional antebellum home. Here, too, is the expansive main campus of the University of South Carolina. Out of town, 550-acre Lake Murray is full of pontoon boats and Jet Skis, and Congaree Swamp National Park is waiting to be explored.

In 1786 South Carolina's capital was moved from Charleston to Columbia, along the banks of the Congaree River. One of the nation's first planned cities, Columbia has streets that are among the widest in America, because it was then thought that stagnant air in narrow streets fostered the spread of malaria. The city soon grew into a center of political, commercial, and cultural activity, but in early 1865 General William

Tecumseh Sherman invaded South Carolina and incinerated two-thirds of Columbia. A few homes, public buildings, and historic sights were spared. The First Baptist Church, where secession was declared, still stands because a janitor directed Sherman's troops to a Presbyterian church instead.

### GETTING HERE AND AROUND

Columbia lies in the heart of the state. It's two hours from the coast and just a little more than that from the mountains. Major interstates, along with airport, train, and bus terminals, make the city very accessible. Most of the action happens in the downtown neighborhoods of the Vista and Five Points. Devine Street, in the Shandon neighborhood, also offers plenty of boutique shopping and fine dining, and the university's football stadium, fairground, zoo, and gardens are all a short drive away. Historic Columbia runs guided tours of Columbia and rents out old properties.

### ESSENTIALS

**Visitor Information Columbia Metropolitan Convention Center and Visitors Bureau** ✉ *1101 Lincoln St.* ☎ *803/545–0000* 🌐 *www.columbiaconventioncenter.com.*

**Tour Contacts Historic Columbia Foundation** ☎ *803/252–7742* 🌐 *www.historiccolumbia.org.*

## EXPLORING

### TOP ATTRACTIONS

**Columbia Museum of Art.** This museum contains art from the Kress Foundation collection of Renaissance and baroque treasures, sculpture, decorative arts. There are plenty of prominent paintings by European and American masters, including a Monet and a Botticelli. Guided tours are offered on Saturday, Sunday, and the first Friday of each month. ✉ *1515 Main St., Main Street area* ☎ *803/799–2810* 🌐 *www.columbiamuseum.org* 🎟 *$10, free Sun.* ⏲ *Tues.–Fri. 11–5, Sat. 10–5, Sun. noon–5.* 9

Fodor's Choice ★ **EdVenture Children's Museum.** With more than 90,000 square feet for climbing, exploring, painting, playing, building—oh, and learning, too—this museum is a full day of hands-on fun. Eddie, a 40-foot-tall statue of a boy that can be climbed on and in by children and adults, is the centerpiece. Each of nine galleries has a theme, such as Body Detectives, Wags & Whiskers, and Mission Imagination. Kids can shop in their own grocery store, act as firefighters in a full-size fire truck, and pretend to be newscasters. The annual Beakers and Broomsticks Halloween party is a blast. On the second Tuesday evening of each month, admission is only $1. ✉ *211 Gervais St., Vista* ☎ *803/779–3100* 🌐 *www.edventure.org* 🎟 *$11.50* ⏲ *Tues.–Sat. 9–5, Sun. noon–5.*

★ **Riverbanks Zoological Park and Botanical Garden.** This zoo contains more than 2,000 animals and birds in natural habitats. Walk along pathways and through landscaped gardens to see elephants, Siberian tigers, koalas, and penguins. The South American primate collection has won international acclaim, and the park is noted for its success in breeding endangered species. The Aquarium–Reptile Complex has South Carolina, desert, tropical, and marine specimens. At the Bird Pavilion you

A tour of the South Carolina State House reveals the six cannon hits made by General Sherman's army during the Civil War.

view birds and wildlife under a safari-like tent. You can ride the carousel and also take a tram over the Saluda River to the 70-acre botanical gardens. A forested section with walking trails has spectacular views of the river and passes Civil War ruins. Stop by the Saluda Factory Interpretive Center for more information about the site's history and its connection to the Civil War. ✉ *500 Wildlife Parkway at I–126 and U.S. 76, West Columbia* ☎ *803/779–8717* 🌐 *www.riverbanks.org* 🎟 *$11.75* ⏲ *Daily 9–5.*

**South Carolina State Museum.** Exhibits in this refurbished textile mill explore the state's natural history, archaeology, and historical development, as well as technological and artistic accomplishments. An iron gate made for the museum by Phillip Simmons, the "dean of Charleston blacksmiths," is on display, as is an exhibit on South Carolina's astronauts. In the Stringer Discovery Center, children can check out microorganisms under microscopes and climb inside a tree to observe the animals that live in the branches. Other objects include a reproduction of a Confederate submarine and artifacts from the state's cotton industry and slavery. Admission on the first Sunday of each month is only $1. ✉ *301 Gervais St., Vista* ☎ *803/898–4921* 🌐 *www.southcarolinastatemuseum.org* 🎟 *$7* ⏲ *Tues.–Sat. 10–5, Sun. 1–5.*

★ **State House.** Six bronze stars on the western wall mark where direct hits were made by General Sherman's cannons. The Capitol building, started in 1851 and completed in 1907, is made of native blue granite in the Italian-Renaissance style. The interior is richly appointed with brass, marble, mahogany, and artwork. Guided tours are available throughout the day. ✉ *1100 Gervais St., Main Street area* ☎ *803/734–2430* 🌐 *www.southcarolinaparks.com* 🎟 *Free* ⏲ *Weekdays 9–4:30.*

**WORTH NOTING**

**Hampton-Preston Mansion.** Dating from 1818, this grand home is filled with lavish furnishings collected by three generations of two influential families. Buy tickets at the Robert Mills House. ✉ *1615 Blanding St., Main Street area* ☎ *803/252–1770* 🌐 *www.historicalcolumbia.org* 🎟 *$6* ⏲ *Tues.–Sat. 10–4, Sun. 1–5.*

**Lake Murray.** This 41-mile-long lake has swimming, boating, picnicking, and superb fishing. There are many marinas and campgrounds in the area. A 1.7-mile pedestrian walkway stretches across the Dreher Shoals Dam offering panoramic views. The lake is off Interstate 26, 15 miles west of Columbia. In summer a massive flock of purple martins turns the sky nearly black at sunset when the birds return to their roost on Bomb Island. ✉ *2184 N. Lake Dr.* ☎ *803/781–5940* 🌐 *www.scjewel.com.*

**Mann-Simons Cottage.** This was the home of Celia Mann, one of only 200 free African-Americans in Columbia in the mid-1800s. Buy tickets at the Robert Mills House. ✉ *1403 Richland St., Main Street area* ☎ *803/252–1770* 🎟 *$6* ⏲ *Tues.–Sat. 10–4, Sun. 1–5.*

**Riverfront Park and Historic Columbia Canal.** Where the Broad and Saluda rivers form the Congaree River is the site of the city's original waterworks and hydroelectric plant. Interpretive markers describe the area's plant and animal life and tell the history of the buildings. A 2½-mile paved trail weaves between the river and the canal and is filled with runners and walkers. ✉ *312 Laurel St., Vista* ☎ *803/733–8613* 🎟 *Free* ⏲ *Daily dawn–dusk.*

**Robert Mills House.** The classic, columned 1823 house was named for its architect, who later designed the Washington Monument. It has opulent Regency furniture, marble mantels, and spacious grounds. This is the home of the Historic Columbia Foundation, where you can get maps of walking and driving tours of historic districts and buy tickets to the Hampton-Preston Mansion and Gardens and the Mann-Simons Cottage. ✉ *1616 Blanding St., Main Street area* ☎ *803/252–1770* 🎟 *$6* ⏲ *Tues.–Sat. 10–4, Sun. 1–5.*

**Tunnelvision.** Make sure it's dark out when you drive by this glowing optical illusion painted on the wall of the Federal Land Bank Building by local artist Blue Sky. ✉ *Taylor and Marion Sts., Main Street area.*

**University of South Carolina.** A highlight of the sprawling university is its original campus with its scenic, tree-lined streets. ✉ *Sumter St., USC Campus* ☎ *803/777–0169* 🌐 *www.sc.edu/visitorcenter.*

Horseshoe. Listed on the National Register of Historic Places, the Horseshoe dates to 1801 and features fullyrestored 19th century buildings, beautiful gardens, and century-old trees. ✉ *Bull St. at Pendleton St., USC Campus* ☎ *800/922–9755* 🌐 *www.sc.edu/visitorcenter.*

South Caroliniana Library. Explore the special collections on state history and genealogy at the South Caroliniana Library, established in

1840. ✉ *Sumter St., USC Campus* ☎ *803/777–3131* 🌐 *library.sc.edu* ⏲ *Weekdays 8:30–5, Sat. 9–1.*

## WHERE TO EAT

$$$ SEAFOOD Fodor's Choice ★ ✕ **Garibaldi's.** Although the name is Italian, locals flock here for the creative fish dishes that might include crispy flounder, or almond-crusted tilapia—the seafood menu changes slightly with the season. Creative dinner salads make interesting starters, and the ice cream in an almond basket makes a crunchy-smooth finale to a meal. Don't miss the chocolate martini for a very grown-up dessert. [$] *Average main: $25* ✉ *2013 Greene St., Five Points* ☎ *803/771–8888* 🌐 *www.garibaldicolumbia.com* ✍ *Reservations essential* ⏲ *No lunch.*

$$$ AMERICAN ✕ **Hampton Street Vineyard.** Tucked into one of the first buildings constructed in the city after Sherman's infamous march, Hampton Street Vineyard is a cozy spot. Exposed brick walls, arched windows, and original wide-plank floors set the tone. Dinners are creative but never over the top, featuring upscale American fare such as seared breast of duck and sautéed crab cakes. The 650-bottle wine list was the first in the state to receive *Wine Spectator*'s Best Award of Excellence. [$] *Average main: $19* ✉ *1201 Hampton St., Downtown* ☎ *803/252–0850* 🌐 *www.hamptonstreetvineyard.com* ⏲ *Closed Sun. No lunch Sat.*

### MIDLANDS BARBECUE

Barbecue in the Midlands, as elsewhere in the Carolinas and Georgia, means pork (or on rare occasion, chicken), roasted all day and basted with sauce, not just cooked on a grill. What makes Midlands barbecue distinctive is the sauce, which has a mustard base, rather than the vinegar or tomato commonly used elsewhere. The result is a flavor that's pungent but not spicy, and meat that lacks the red tint often associated with Southern barbecue. (Some places serve a variety of sauces, so you can do a taste test and see what you think of the native style.)

$ SOUTHERN ✕ **Little Pigs Barbecue.** Grab a plate, get in the buffet line and load up on barbecue, fried chicken, ribs, and fried fish, along with fixings such as collards, coleslaw, and macaroni and cheese. Since Little Pigs uses mustard-, tomato-, and vinegar-base barbecue sauces, you can sample all three and pick your favorite. [$] *Average main: $10* ✉ *4927 Alpine Rd., Northeast Columbia* ☎ *803/788–8238* 🌐 *www.littlepigs.biz* ✍ *Reservations not accepted* ⏲ *Closed Mon.–Tues. No dinner Sun. and Wed.*

$ MIDDLE EASTERN ✕ **Mediterranean Tea Room.** The name is something of a misnomer, since this friendly little restaurant serves Middle Eastern food. The marinated chicken breast keeps people coming back, but the *kofta* (spiced meatball), hummus, and vegetarian dishes offer patrons a break from traditional rich Southern cooking. [$] *Average main: $10* ✉ *2601 Devine St., Shandon* ☎ *803/799–3118* ✍ *Reservations not accepted* ⏲ *Closed Sun. No lunch Sat.*

$$ SOUTHERN ★ ✕ **Mr. Friendly's New Southern Café.** Who knew that barbecue sauce could be the base for such tasty salad dressing or that lowly pimiento cheese could elevate a fillet to near perfection? Appetizers of fried pickles and country ham and spinach dip only add to the creative thinking that makes Mr. Friendly's such a treasure; the ever-changing wine-by-the-glass menu that's pulled from an eclectic list is another. [$] *Average main: $14*

*2001 A Greene St., Five Points 803/254–7828 www.mrfriendlys.com Reservations not accepted No lunch Sat. Closed Sun.*

## WHERE TO STAY

*Hotel reviews have been abbreviated in this book. For expanded reviews, please go to Fodors.com.*

$ HOTEL **Comfort Suites.** A short drive down the access road from a mall, shopping center, and cinema complex, the Comfort Suites is off Interstate 26 just west of downtown Columbia. **Pros:** great for avoiding heavy downtown traffic. **Cons:** too far away to go anywhere on foot. *Rooms from: $80 750 Saturn Pkwy., Exit 103, Harbison 803/407–4444, 800/426–6423 www.comfortinn.com 82 suites Breakfast.*

$ HOTEL **Embassy Suites Hotel Columbia–Greystone.** In the spacious seven-story atrium lobby—with skylights, fountains, pool, and live plants—you can enjoy your complimentary breakfast and evening cocktails. **Pros:** across from the zoo and botanical gardens. **Cons:** not close to restaurants or nightlife. *Rooms from: $149 200 Stoneridge Dr., Greystone 803/252–8700, 800/362–2779 www.columbiagreystone.embassysuites.com 218 suites Breakfast.*

$ B&B/INN **Hampton Inn Downtown Historic District.** This classy chain is within walking distance of restaurants and nightlife in the Vista neighborhood. **Pros:** free reception Monday through Thursday afternoon. **Cons:** rooms along Gervais Street can be noisy. *Rooms from: $139 822 Gervais St., Vista 803/231–2000 www.hamptoninncolumbia.com 122 rooms Breakfast.*

$$ B&B/INN **The Inn at Claussen's.** An old bakery warehouse in the heart of Five Points makes for a great small hotel. **Pros:** breakfast is served in-room; plenty of parking; complimentary glass of wine or Scotch. **Cons:** no workout room or pool. *Rooms from: $199 2003 Greene St., Five Points 803/765–0440, 800/622–3382 www.theinnatclaussens.com 20 rooms, 8 suites Breakfast.*

$ HOTEL **Whitney Hotel.** Because they were originally built as condos, the large rooms in the Whitney have full kitchens, dining rooms, bedrooms with doors, and, in the two-bedroom models, two full baths. **Pros:** peaceful setting; within walking distance of shops and restaurants; airport shuttle. **Cons:** health club is off-site. *Rooms from: $100 700 Woodrow St., Shandon 803/252–0845 www.whitneyhotel.com 74 suites Breakfast.*

## NIGHTLIFE AND THE ARTS

### THE ARTS

**Colonial Life Arena.** The largest arena in the state, Colonial Life Arena hosts major entertainment events as well as University of South Carolina basketball games. *801 Lincoln St., Vista 803/576–9200 www.coloniallifearena.com.*

**Cultural Council of Richland and Lexington Counties.** This council provides information by phone or on their website about local cultural events, including the ballet and symphony. *803/799–3115 www.smartarts.info.*

**Koger Center for the Arts.** This performing arts center presents national and international theater, ballet, and musical groups, as well as

Kayaking is popular in this region along the calm Congaree and the thrilling Saluda and Chattooga rivers.

individual performers. ✉ *1051 Greene St., at Assembly St.* ☎ *803/777–7500* 🌐 *www.koger.sc.edu.*

**Town Theatre.** Founded in 1919, the Town Theatre stages seven plays a year. ✉ *1012 Sumter St., USC Campus* ☎ *803/799–2510* 🌐 *www.towntheatre.com.*

**Trustus.** This local professional theater group presents new and original plays throughout the year. ✉ *520 Lady St., Vista* ☎ *803/254–9732* 🌐 *www.trustus.org.*

**Workshop Theatre of South Carolina.** A number of plays are produced by the Workshop Theatre of South Carolina. ✉ *1136 Bull St., USC Campus* ☎ *803/799–4876* 🌐 *www.workshoptheatre.com.*

## NIGHTLIFE

**Art Bar.** In the hopping Vista neighborhood, the Art Bar is funky, with neon-painted walls, lighted lunch boxes, and live music for dancing. ✉ *1211 Park St., Vista* ☎ *803/929–0198* 🌐 *artbarsc.com.*

**Blue Tapas Bar and Cocktail Lounge.** An ice bar and multiple water features help create the big-city feel of Blue Tapas Bar and Cocktail Lounge, while free valet parking and a delicious menu only add to the cool atmosphere. ✉ *721A Lady St., Vista* ☎ *803/251–4447.*

**Goatfeathers.** A bohemian bar-café that's popular with university and law-school students, Goatfeathers also appeals to late-night coffee and dessert seekers. ✉ *2017 Devine St., Five Points* ☎ *803/256–3325.*

★ **Hunter-Gatherer Brewery & Alehouse.** If you're more into rock, Hunter-Gatherer Brewery & Alehouse has it on tap most nights, along with an excellent selection of beers, some made in-house. ✉ *900 Main St., USC Campus* ☎ *803/748–0540.*

**Mac's on Main.** Jazz is king at Mac's on Main, where local groups often jam into the night and patrons enjoy true Southern cuisine. ✉ *1710 Main St., Main Street area* ☎ *803/929–0037* 🌐 *www.macsjazznblues.com.*

## SPORTS AND THE OUTDOORS

### CANOEING AND KAYAKING

The Saluda River near Columbia has challenging Class III and IV rapids. Saluda access is out of town in Gardendale and Saluda Shoals Park, as well as at the Riverbanks Zoo. The Broad and the Saluda rivers meet in the center of town to become the calmer Congaree River. There's public access for the Congaree behind EdVenture on Senate Street at the Senate Street Landing.

**Adventure Carolina.** Guided Saluda, Broad, and Congaree river (Saluda and Broad have rapids, Congaree is calm) trips and swamp canoeing excursions can be arranged, as can canoe rentals, at Adventure Carolina. ✉ *1107 State St., 1 mile southwest of Columbia, Cayce* ☎ *803/796–4505* 🌐 *www.adventurecarolina.com.*

**Congaree National Park.** Self-guided canoe trails traverse Congaree National Park, 20 miles southeast of Columbia. Free guided trips are offered throughout the year and there is a 2.5-mile boardwalk through the swamp. ✉ *100 National Park Rd., Hopkins* ☎ *803/776–4396* 🌐 *www.nps.gov/cong.*

**River Runner Outdoor Center.** You can rent canoes and kayaks or sign up for guided river or swamp expeditions at the River Runner Outdoor Center. ✉ *905 Gervais St., Vista* ☎ *803/771–0353* 🌐 *www.riverrunner.us.*

**Saluda Shoals Park.** Canoe and kayak rentals are available at Saluda Shoals Park. ✉ *5605 Bush River Rd., 12 miles northwest of downtown Columbia* ☎ *803/731-5208, 803/213-2050* 🌐 *www.icrc.net.*

9

### HIKING

Fodor's Choice ★ **Congaree National Park.** Congaree National Park has 22 miles of trails and a 2.5-mile boardwalk for people with disabilities. The alluvial floodplain, bordered by high bluffs, in the 22,200-acre park contains many old-growth bottomland hardwoods (the oldest and largest trees east of the Mississippi River). The water and trees are beautifully eerie. Hiking and canoe trails line the park, which is full of wildlife, including otters, deer, and woodpeckers, as well as the occasional wild boar. When darkness falls, join park naturalists for a hike deep into the forest to search for owls and other nighttime wildlife Friday at 8:30. Call for nighttime walk reservations. ✉ *100 National Park Rd., 20 miles southeast of Columbia, Hopkins* ☎ *803/776–4396* 🌐 *www.nps.gov/cong* 🎫 *Free* ⏲ *Visitor center weekdays 8:30–5, weekends 9–1.*

**Sesquicentennial State Park.** The 1,419-acre Sesquicentennial State Park is not far from downtown but feels like you're in the country. A 30-acre lake sits at the heart of the park, allowing for fishing and nonmotorized boating. Enjoy picnicking areas, playgrounds, and miles of nature, hiking, and mountain-biking trails. ✉ *9564 Two Notch Rd., Northeast* ☎ *803/788–2706* 🌐 *www.southcarolinaparks.com* 🎫 *$2* 🕑 *Daily 8–6.*

### SHOPPING

Many of Columbia's antiques outlets, boutique shops, and restaurants are in the ever-growing Vista neighborhood around Huger and Gervais streets, between the State House and the river. A number of intriguing shops and cafés are in Five Points, around Blossom at Harden streets, as well as along Devine Street in the Shandon neighborhood to the east. There are also antiques shops across the river on Meeting and State streets in West Columbia.

**Old Mill Antique Mall.** You'll find items from many dealers, including furniture, glassware, jewelry, and books, at Old Mill Antique Mall. ✉ *310 State St., West Columbia* ☎ *803/796–4229* 🌐 *oldmillantiquemall.com.*

**State Farmers' Market.** One of the 10 largest in the country, the State Farmers' Market features fresh vegetables, along with flowers, plants, seafood, and more, Monday to Saturday 6 am to 9 pm and Sunday 1 to 6. ✉ *3483 Charleston Hwy., West Columbia* ☎ *803/737–4664* 🌐 *www.scstatefarmersmarket.com.*

## CAMDEN

*35 miles northeast of Columbia via I–20.*

A town with horse history and grand colonial homes, charming Camden has never paved some of its roads for the sake of the hooves that regularly trot over them. The Carolina Cup and Colonial Cup are run here.

Camden is South Carolina's oldest inland town, dating from 1732. British General Lord Cornwallis established a garrison here during the Revolutionary War and burned most of Camden before evacuating it. A center of textile trade from the late 19th century through the 1940s, Camden blossomed when it became a refuge for Northerners escaping the cold winters. Because General Sherman spared the town during the Civil War, most of its antebellum homes still stand.

#### GETTING HERE AND AROUND

A roughly 40-minute drive northeast of Columbia will take you to Camden. A great day trip, this town is a prime location for antiquing. Once you're in the antiques and art district, you'll have easy access to stores carrying antiques, collectibles, and one-of-a-kind art. Outside the downtown area you will find historical homes, museums, and horse-race courses. Camden Carriage Company takes you on a tour on a horse-drawn carriage through Camden's loveliest neighborhood and down unpaved roads.

#### ESSENTIALS

**Tour Information Camden Carriage Company** ☎ *803/425–5737* 🌐 *www.camdencarriage.com.*

### EXPLORING

**Bonds Conway House.** This home was built by the first black man in Camden to buy his freedom. The circa-1812 home has the fine details of a skilled craftsman, including wonderful woodwork and heart-pine floors. ✉ *811*

**DID YOU KNOW?**

Rangers provide free, guided canoe trips on weekends along Cedar Creek in Congaree Swamp National Park. The trips are an excellent way to experience the floodplain forest, which contains some of the tallest trees in eastern North America. You might also spot river otters, turtles, snakes, and wild pigs.

*Fair St.* ☎ *803/425–1123* 🌐 *www.kershawcountyhistoricalsociety.org* 🎟 *Free* ⏲ *Thurs. 1–5 or by appointment.*

**Historic Camden Revolutionary War Site.** This 107-acre outdoor museum complex puts emphasis on the period surrounding the British occupation of 1780. Several structures dot the site, including the 1789 **Craven House,** the **Blacksmith Shed,** and the **Kershaw House,** a reconstruction of the circa-1770 home of Camden's founder, Joseph Kershaw, which also served as Cornwallis's headquarters; it's furnished with period pieces. A nature trail, fortifications, powder magazine, picnic area, and crafts shop are also here. Guided tours are available. ✉ *U.S. 521, 1½ miles north of I–20* ☎ *803/432–9841* 🌐 *www.historic-camden.net* 🎟 *Free, guided tours $5* ⏲ *Tues.–Sat. 10–5, Sun. 2–5.*

**Kershaw County Chamber of Commerce.** When you stop in for brochures and information, take note of the Chamber's building: it was designed by Robert Mills, the architect of the Washington Monument. Upstairs, the old courthouse is open for viewing. ✉ *607 S. Broad St.* ☎ *803/432–2525, 800/968–4037* 🌐 *www.kershawcountychamber.org* ⏲ *Weekdays 9–5, Sat. 9-1.*

**National Steeplechase Museum.** Located at the historic Springdale Race Course, this museum contains the largest collection of racing memorabilia in the United States. The Equisizer, a training machine used by jockeys for practice, lets you experience the race from the jockey's perspective; don't stay on too long, unless you want to feel the race all day. ✉ *200 Knights Hill Rd.* ☎ *800/780–8117* 🌐 *www.nationalsteeplechasemuseum.org* 🎟 *Free* ⏲ *Sept.–May, Mon.–Sat. 10–4, Sun. and other months by appointment.*

## WHERE TO EAT AND STAY

*Hotel reviews have been abbreviated in this book. For expanded reviews, please go to Fodors.com.*

$$$$ STEAKHOUSE ★ **Mill Pond Steak House.** It's all about steak here, and what steaks they are: aged for at least 35 days before they're cut, the fillets, rib eyes, and strips are juicy, tender, and packed with flavor. You can dine alfresco overlooking the sprawling millpond or inside a trio of old buildings. The wood paneling was reclaimed from the Boykin Tractor Shed after it was destroyed by Hurricane Hugo. The more casual side of the restaurant has a vintage saloon-style bar, which, in its first life, was the soda fountain at Zemps, a drugstore in Camden. Area farmers provide most of the produce; grits for the "shrimp and grits" are ground at the mill next door. There is a limousine service available to and from Camden. Save room for homemade mixed-berry cobbler with ice cream. $ *Average main: $26* ✉ *84 Boykin Mill Rd., 10 miles south of Camden, Rembert* ☎ *803/425–8825* 🌐 *www.themillpondsteakhouse.com* ⏲ *Closed Sun. and Mon. No lunch.*

$$$ SEAFOOD **Sam Kendall's.** This storefront restaurant has high-back booths that make for cozy dining. The exposed brick wall and modern furnishings offer the perfect backdrop for a delicious menu of steak or seafood. The seafood pasta is a great way to experience gulf shrimp, and the fried shrimp has developed its own cult following. The menu also features an extensive list of more than 100 wines. $ *Average main: $15*

⊠ *1043 Broad St., Downtown* ☎ *803/424–2005* 🌐 *www.samkendalls.com* ⏲ *Closed Sun. No lunch.*

$$ B&B/INN **Bloomsbury Inn.** Noted Civil War diarist Mary Boykin Chestnut wrote much of her famous account in this home—now a lovely 4-room inn—that was built in 1849 by her husband's family. **Pros:** breakfast is a full gourmet event, with two to three courses each morning. **Cons:** no elevator; no phone in room. *Rooms from: $159* ⊠ *1707 Lyttleton St.* ☎ *803/432–5858* 🌐 *www.bloomsburyinn.com* *4 rooms* *Breakfast.*

## SPORTS AND THE OUTDOORS

**Springdale Race Course.** You're likely to see Thoroughbreds working out most mornings October through April at the Springdale Race Course. Camden puts on two steeplechase events here: the Carolina Cup, in late March or early April; and the Colonial Cup, in November. ⊠ *200 Knights Hill Rd.* ☎ *803/432–6513, 800/780-8117* 🌐 *www.carolina-cup.org.*

## SHOPPING

Camden is known for its antiques shopping, with the heart of the antiques and arts district along Broad Street, as well as on neighboring Rutledge, DeKalb, and Market streets.

**Andries Van Dam Investment Arts and Antiques.** Shop for Dutch impressionist paintings at Andries Van Dam Investment Arts and Antiques—it's as much a gallery as an antiques shop. ⊠ *914 Market St.* ☎ *803/432–0850.*

**Camden Antiques Market.** Find well-priced furniture and decorative art from the 18th, 19th, and 20th centuries at Camden Antiques Market. ⊠ *830 S. Broad St.* ☎ *803/432–0818* ⏲ *Mon.–Sat. 10–6, Sun. 1–6.*

**Granary.** Though it specializes in English, French, and American antiques, the Granary also has whimsical garden furniture. ⊠ *830A S. Broad St.* ☎ *803/432–8811* 🌐 *www.thegranaryantiques.com.*

**Mulberry Market Bake Shop.** Sample almond Danish pastries, lemon bars, and macaroons at the delightful Mulberry Market Bake Shop. European-style butter is key to the divine cheese sticks. ⊠ *536 E. DeKalb St.* ☎ *803/424–8401.*

**Rutledge Street Gallery.** If modern pieces are more your style, stroll over to Rutledge Street Gallery for sophisticated paintings, textiles, and sculpture. ⊠ *508 Rutledge St.* ☎ *803/425–0071* 🌐 *www.rutledgestreetgallery.com* ⏲ *Closed Sun.–Mon.*

**TenEleven Galleria.** Browse through the antiques mall, bookstore, and other shops that comprise the TenEleven Galleria, housed in a restored warehouse. ⊠ *1011 Broad St.* ☎ *803/424–1011* 🌐 *www.tenelevengalleria.com* ⏲ *Closed Sunday.*

9

# AIKEN

*89 miles southwest of Camden via I–20; 56 miles southwest of Columbia via I–20 and U.S. 1.*

This is Thoroughbred country, and Aiken first earned its fame in the 1890s, when wealthy Northerners wintering here built stately mansions and entertained one another with horse shows, hunts, and lavish parties.

Small-town Aiken is delightful during local festivals and antique car shows.

Many up-to-60-room homes stand as a testament to this era of opulence. The town is still a center for all kinds of outdoor activity, including the equestrian events of the Triple Crown, as well as tennis and golf.

### GETTING HERE AND AROUND

An hour's drive southwest of Columbia will take you to the rolling green horse country of Aiken. Though not a concise town square, Laurens Street and the surrounding streets offer plenty in the way of shopping, dining, and entertainment. If you're headed to the polo matches or races, the horse district is only a five-minute drive outside the downtown area.

The City of Aiken runs a nearly two-hour tour of the historic district ($12) and will customize tours to suit individual interests.

### ESSENTIALS

**Visitor Information City of Aiken** ☎ *888/245–3672* 🌐 *www.aikenis.com.* **Greater Aiken Chamber of Commerce** ✉ *121 Richland Ave. E, PO Box 892* ☎ *803/641–1111* 🌐 *www.aikenchamber.net.*

## EXPLORING

**Aiken County Historical Museum.** One wing of this 1860 estate is devoted to early regional culture. It has Native American artifacts, firearms, an authentically furnished 1808 log cabin, a schoolhouse, and a miniature circus display. ✉ *433 Newberry St. SW* ☎ *803/642–2015* 🌐 *www.aikencountyhistoricalmuseum.org* 🎫 *Donations suggested* ⏲ *Tues.–Sat. 10–5, Sun. 2–5.*

**Aiken Thoroughbred Racing Hall of Fame and Museum.** The area's horse farms have produced many national champions, which are commemorated here. Exhibits include horse-related decorations, paintings, and sculptures, plus racing silks and trophies. The Hall of Fame is on the grounds of the 14-acre **Hopelands Gardens,** where you can wind along paths past quiet terraces and reflecting pools. There's a Touch and Scent Trail with Braille plaques. Open-air free concerts and plays are presented on Monday evening May through August. ✉ *135 Dupree Pl., at Whiskey Rd.* ☎ *803/642–7631* 🌐 *www.aikenracinghalloffame.com* 🎫 *Free* 🕙 *Museum Sept.–May, Tues.–Fri. and Sun. 2–5, Sat. 10–5; June–Aug., Sat. 10–5, Sun. 2–5. Grounds daily 10–dusk.*

**Hitchcock Woods.** Three times the size of New York's Central Park, this is the largest urban forest in the country and is listed on the National Register of Historic Places. Make use of the maps available at the entrances. The park's size makes it easy to get lost. ✉ *Enter from junction of Clark Rd. and Whitney Dr., Berrie Rd., and Dibble Rd.* ☎ *803/642-0528* 🌐 *www.hitchcockwoods.org.*

**Old Edgefield Pottery.** Stephen Ferrell has an extensive collection of Edgefield pottery on display at this shop operated by the Edgefield County Historical Society. Ferrell, like his father, is an accomplished potter in his own right. Ask to see original pieces crafted by Dave, a literate slave who created some of the first "face vessels." ✉ *230 Simpkins St., 15 miles northwest of Aiken, Edgefield* ☎ *803/637–2060* 🕙 *Tues.–Sat. 10–5.*

**Redcliffe Plantation.** Home to James Hammond, who is credited with being first to declare that "Cotton is King," this wood frame house remained in the family until 1975. The 13,000-square-foot mansion (which sits on 369 acres) remains just as it was, down to the 19th-century books on the carved shelves. Slave quarters contain photograph and textile exhibits. Once you've toured the house (starting at 11, 1, or 3), be sure to explore the grounds on the 1-mile trail. ■ **TIP→** Take note: the house has no central heat or air-conditioning. ✉ *181 Redcliffe Rd., 15 miles southwest of Aiken, Beech Island* ☎ *803/827–1473* 🌐 *www.southcarolinaparks.com* 🎫 *$5* 🕙 *Grounds Thurs.–Mon. 9–5, house tours Thurs.–Mon. at 11, 1, and 3.*

9

## WHERE TO EAT

$$ EUROPEAN ✕ **Linda's Bistro.** Chef Linda Rooney elevates traditional European favorites, turning out excellent mushroom-Gruyère tarts, risotto with roasted mushrooms and Asiago cheese, and steak frites. Main courses come with a salad, a vegetable, and potatoes. It's all served in an open, café-like environment. 💲 *Average main: $16* ✉ *135 York St. SE* ☎ *803/648–4853* 🌐 *www.lindasbistro-aiken.com* 🕙 *Closed Sun. and Mon. No lunch.*

$$$ ECLECTIC ✕ **Malia's.** Locals love this busy contemporary restaurant, with dim lighting and dark fabrics that convey a cool class. The menu changes monthly and serves up a wide variety of international cuisine that includes American, Caribbean, French, and Italian entrées. Dinner reservations are recommended. 💲 *Average main: $20* ✉ *120 Laurens St. SW* ☎ *803/643–3086* 🌐 *www.maliasrestaurant.com* 🕙 *Closed Sun. and Mon. No dinner Tues.*

$ AMERICAN ✕ **New Moon.** Here you can pair Aiken's best coffee (the coffee beans are roasted right next door) with freshly baked muffins and sweet rolls, panini sandwiches and salads, and homemade soups. The crab bisque is particularly good. *Average main: $7 ⊠ 116 Laurens St. ☎ 803/643–7088 ⊕ www.newmoondowntown.com ⚠ Reservations not accepted ⊗ No dinner.*

### WHERE TO STAY

*Hotel reviews have been abbreviated in this book. For expanded reviews, please go to Fodors.com.*

$ B&B/INN **Briar Patch.** You can learn plenty about both the Old and New Souths from the knowledgeable innkeepers of this terrific B&B, made up of former tack rooms in Aiken's stable district. **Pros:** close to the polo fields; Continental breakfast. **Cons:** tennis courts and surrounding yards are overgrown. *Rooms from: $95 ⊠ 544 Magnolia La. SE ☎ 803/649–2010 ⊕ www.bbonline.com/sc/briar ⇨ 2 rooms ▭ No credit cards ǀ○ǀ Breakfast.*

$$ B&B/INN Fodor's Choice ★ **The Willcox.** Winston Churchill, Franklin D. Roosevelt, and the Astors have slept at this 19th-century inn where luxurious facilities—including a spa, restaurant, and outdoor pool—and authentic Southern hospitality come together for an outstanding getaway experience. **Pros:** breakfast is a huge step above normal fare. **Cons:** there is no business center and no drinks are served poolside. *Rooms from: $185 ⊠ 100 Colleton Ave. ☎ 803/648–1898, 877/648–2200 ⊕ www.thewillcox.com ⇨ 15 rooms, 7 suites ǀ○ǀ Breakfast.*

### SPORTS AND THE OUTDOORS

**Triple Crown.** Three weekends in late March and early April are set aside for the famed Triple Crown, which includes Thoroughbred trials of promising yearlings, a steeplechase, and harness races by young horses making their debut. *⊠ Horse district off Whiskey Rd., U.S. 19 ☎ 803/641–1111.*

**Whitney Field.** In Aiken, polo matches are played at Whitney Field Sunday at 3, September through November and March through June. *⊠ 200 Mead Dr., off Whiskey Rd., U.S. 19 ☎ 803/643–3611 ⊕ www.aikenpoloclub.org.*

## NINETY SIX

*53 miles northwest of Aiken via Rte. 19, U.S. 25, and Rte. 24; 73 miles west of Columbia via U.S. 378, U.S. 178, and Rte. 248.*

The town of Ninety Six, on an old Native American trade route, is so named for being 96 miles from the Cherokee village of Keowee in the Blue Ridge Mountains—the distance a young Cherokee maiden, Cateechee, is supposed to have ridden to warn her English lover of a threatened Native American massacre.

**Ninety Six National Historic Site.** This park commemorates two Revolutionary War battles. The visitor center's museum has descriptive displays, along with a 10-minute historical film. Along the mile-long paved path through the woods and surrounding fields there are remnants of the old village, a reconstructed French and Indian War stockade, and Revolutionary-era fortifications. The gates close promptly at 5, but if you park outside you're allowed to stay until sunset. *⊠ 1103 Hwy. 248*

*S., 2 miles south of Ninety Six* ☎ *864/543–4068* 🌐 *www.nps.gov/nisi* 🎫 *Free* 🕒 *Daily 9–5.*

## ABBEVILLE

★ *25 miles west of Ninety Six via Rte. 34 and Rte. 72; 102 miles west of Columbia.*

Abbeville may well be one of inland South Carolina's most satisfying lesser-known towns. An appealing historic district includes the old business areas, early churches, and residential areas. What was called the "Southern cause" by supporters of the Confederacy was born and died here: it's where the first organized secession meeting was held and where, on May 2, 1865, Confederate president Jefferson Davis officially disbanded the defeated armies of the South in the last meeting of his war council.

#### GETTING HERE AND AROUND

Abbeville is a little more than an hour west of Columbia. Most of the sites, including the opera house, are around its quaint town square, with shopping and eateries all within walking distance. A short drive—or a long walk—past the square is the historic Burt-Stark Mansion.

#### ESSENTIALS

**Visitor Information Greater Abbeville Chamber of Commerce** ✉ *107 Court Sq.* ☎ *864/366–4600* 🌐 *www.abbevillescchamber.com.*

### EXPLORING

**Abbeville Opera House.** Built in 1908 along the old town square, this auditorium has been renovated to reflect the grandeur of the days when lavish road shows and stellar entertainers took center stage. Current productions range from contemporary light comedies to local renderings of Broadway musicals. Self-guided tours available. ✉ *100 Court Sq.* ☎ *864/366–2157* 🌐 *www.theabbevilleoperahouse.com.*

9

**Burt-Stark Mansion.** It was here that Jefferson Davis disbanded the Confederate armies, effectively ending the Civil War. Built in 1820, the house was a private residence until 1971, when Mary Stark Davis died. She willed the house to the Abbeville County Historic Preservation Commission, with a provision that nothing be added or removed from the house. It's filled with lovely antiques, carved-wood surfaces, and old family photos. Her clothing is still in the dresser drawers. ✉ *400 N. Main St.* ☎ *864/366–0166* 🌐 *www.burt-stark.com* 🎫 *$10* 🕒 *Fri. and Sat. 1-5 or by appointment.*

**Trinity Episcopal Church.** Built in 1860, this is the town's oldest church. Complete with a 125-foot spire, an original chancery window imported from England, and a rare working 1860 John Baker tracker organ, Trinity is an example of Gothic Revival architecture. ✉ *200 Church St.* ☎ *864/366–4600* 🌐 *www.trinityabbesc.org* 🎫 *Free* 🕒 *Daily 10–5.*

### WHERE TO EAT

$$ AMERICAN ★ ✕ **Village Grille.** The menu spans a wide variety, from hamburgers to fillets, but many locals frequent the Village Grille because of the herb rotisserie chicken. As much of the food preparation as possible is done

in house, meaning burgers are ground on the spot and salads consist of locally grown organic veggies. Antique mirrors hang on pomegranate-color walls below high ceilings. *Average main: $10 ✉ 110 Trinity St. ☎ 864/366–2500 ⊕ www.abbevillevillagegrill.com ⊙ Closed Sun. and Mon.*

$ AMERICAN ✕ **Yoder's Dutch Kitchen.** Try some authentic Pennsylvania-Dutch home cooking in this unassuming South Carolina redbrick building. There's a lunch buffet and evening smorgasbord with fried chicken, stuffed cabbage, Dutch meat loaf, breaded veal Parmesan, and plenty of vegetables. Shoofly pie is great to go. *Average main: $10 ✉ 809 E. Greenwood St., east of downtown ☎ 864/366–5556 ⊙ Closed Sun.–Tues. No dinner Wed. and Thurs.*

# THE UPSTATE

The Upstate, also known as the Upcountry, in the northwest corner of the state, has long been a favorite for family vacations because of its temperate climate and natural beauty. The abundant lakes and waterfalls and several state parks (including Caesar's Head, Keowee-Toxaway, Oconee, Table Rock, and the Chattooga National Wild and Scenic River) provide all manner of recreational activities. Beautiful anytime, the 130-mile Cherokee Foothills Scenic Highway (Route 11), which goes through the Blue Ridge Mountains, is especially delightful in spring (when the peach trees are in bloom) and autumn.

## GREENVILLE

*100 miles northwest of Columbia via I–26 and I–385.*

Once known for its textile and other manufacturing plants, Greenville has reinvented itself as a trendy and sophisticated city able to support a surprising number of restaurants, galleries, and boutiques along a tree-lined Main Street that passes a stunning natural waterfall. Anchored by two performance centers, the city's business district is alive well into most evenings with couples and families enjoying the energy of this revitalized Southern city. Downtown development has been so successful that many young professionals are moving here and creating interesting living spaces from old warehouses and retail establishments. Downtown festivals are held most weekends along tree-lined Main Street.

### GETTING HERE AND AROUND

Greenville is a little over two hours northwest of Columbia. While Columbia sits in a valley of sorts, the Greenville area is more mountainous. There is plenty of hiking and numerous waterfalls just outside town. The revitalized Main Street area is a great base camp for your stay. The street is a long tree-lined stretch of shops, restaurants, and hotels. To the south, the road runs through Falls Park and passes the Greenville Drive Stadium. The northern end runs close to the Heritage Green neighborhood, which is a block of museums, theaters, and a library. Be prepared when driving around the outskirts of Greenville—Interstate 185, a connector loop of Interstate 85 and Interstate 385, is a toll road, so have your dollars ready.

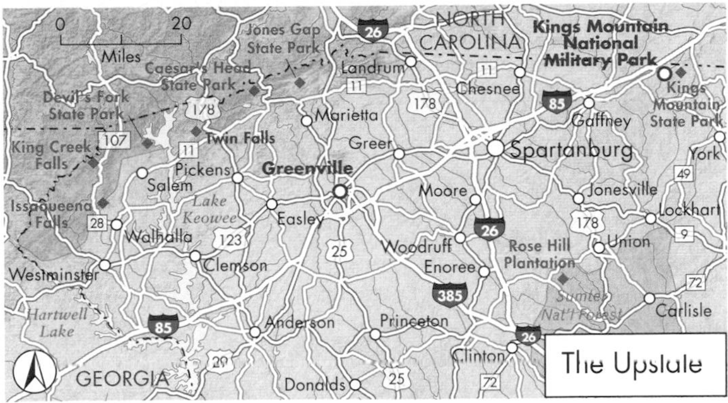


ESSENTIALS

**Visitor Information Discover Upcountry Carolina Association** ☎ *800/849-4766, 800/849-4766* 🌐 *www.theupcountry.com.* **Greater Greenville Convention and Visitors Bureau** ✉ *206 S. Main St.* ☎ *864/233-0461, 800/717-0023* 🌐 *www.greenvillecvb.com.*

## EXPLORING

★ **Bob Jones University Museum & Gallery.** The renowned international collection of religious art includes works by Botticelli, Rembrandt, Rubens, and van Dyck. Children younger than six are not permitted. Guided tours are available. ✉ *Bob Jones University, 1700 Wade Hampton Blvd.* ☎ *864/770-1331* 🌐 *www.bjumg.org* 🎫 *$5* ⏲ *Tues.–Sun. 2–5.*

**Children's Museum of the Upstate.** This 80,000-square-foot facility is packed with hands-on exhibits that cover everything from science and music to construction and race cars. There are also special areas for kids five and under. ✉ *300 College St., Heritage Green* ☎ *864/553-7911* 🌐 *www.tcmupstate.org* 🎫 *$10* ⏲ *Tues.–Sat. 9–5, Sun. 11–5.*

**Devils Fork State Park.** Located on Lake Jocassee, this park has luxurious villas and camping facilities, hiking, boating, and fishing. Lower Whitewater Falls plunges more than 200 feet over huge boulders to splash into the lake waters. The falls can be viewed from an overlook or from a boat on the lake. ✉ *161 Holcombe Cr., off Rte. 11, north of Salem, 45 miles northwest of Greenville* ☎ *864/944-2639* 🌐 *www.southcarolinaparks.com* 🎫 *$2* ⏲ *Daily 9–7 during daylight saving time; daily 9–5 rest of yr.*

**Greenville County Museum of Art.** American paintings dating from the colonial era are on display, along with modern works by Andy Warhol, Georgia O'Keeffe, Andrew Wyeth, Jasper Johns. ✉ *420 College St., Heritage Green* ☎ *864/271-7570* 🌐 *www.greenvillemuseum.org* 🎫 *Free* ⏲ *Wed.–Sat. 10–5; Sun. 1–5. Closed Mon. and Tues.*

**Fodor's Choice** ★ **Mountain Bridge Wilderness Area.** About 30 miles north of Greenville, these two state parks boast more than 50 miles of hiking trails.

**Raven Cliff Falls.** The trail leading to 420-foot-tall Raven Cliff Falls can be accessed 1 mile north of the main entrance to **Caesar's Head**

CLOSE UP

## The Palmetto Trail

Beginning in Oconee State Park in the Upstate and ending along the coast just north of Charleston, the Palmetto Trail is the perfect way to travel the state on foot or by mountain bike. Marked for travel in both directions by way of standard trail blazes and occasional signs, the route spans 425 miles of South Carolina's natural resources. That mileage is broken into more than 20 passages that vary in length from a short 7-mile section to a multiday hike that's roughly 50 miles. The trail winds through state parks and national forests and past Revolutionary War battlefields—all with glorious views.

**Palmetto Conservation.** The best place to begin your Palmetto Trail journey is at the Palmetto Conservation's main office in downtown Columbia. Guided hikes on some of the Midlands' passages are offered on a weekly basis, as are children's weekly trailblazer programs. They also have an entire facility dedicated to outdoor recreation at the Glendale Outdoor Leadership School in Spartanburg. ✉ *722 King Street, Columbia* ☎ *803/771–0870* 🌐 *www.palmettoconservation.org.*

**State Park.** Along the way there are spectacular views of river gorges and pine-covered mountains. Cross Matthews Creek on a suspension bridge; the view of the falls is worth the terror of knowing you're held in the air by nothing but wire. Register at Park Headquarters before you head out on the trail. Near the headquarters are Table Rock and Devil's Kitchen, a geological phenomenon that stays cool even in the heat of summer. ✉ *8155 Geer Hwy., U.S. 276, Cleveland* ☎ *864/836–6115* 🌐 *www.southcarolinaparks.com* 🎫 *Overlook is free, $2 for use of hiking trails* ⏲ *Office daily 9–5, overlook daily until dark.*

**Jones Gap State Park.** Famous for the Rim of the Gap trail, which has views of Rainbow Falls, Jones Gap State Park is 6 miles east of U.S. 276. Access several trails from the Park Headquarters, or pick up a map and drive to one of the well-marked trailheads. Be sure to pick up your trail map and register before venturing into the wilderness; some of the trails are long and strenuous. ✉ *303 Jones Gap Rd., 6 miles east off U.S. 276, Marietta* ☎ *864/836–3647* 🌐 *www.southcarolinaparks.com* 🎫 *$2* ⏲ *Daily 9–9 during daylight saving time; daily 9–6 rest of yr.*

**Shoeless Joe Jackson Museum and Baseball Library.** This collection is housed in the former home of baseball great Joe Jackson. Jackson, along with seven other White Sox players, was accused of throwing the 1919 World Series. Though he was found not guilty, Jackson was banned from playing baseball. The museum has records, artifacts, photographs, and a film, along with a library of baseball books donated from fans around the country. At the end of each summer, staffers challenge their peers at Georgia's Ty Cobb Museum to a vintage baseball game. ✉ *356 Field St., across from Fluor Field, Historic West End* ☎ *864/235–6280* 🌐 *www.shoelessjoejackson.org* 🎫 *Free* ⏲ *Sat. 10–2, home-game nights 5:30–7.*

The unique Twin Falls, 24 miles outside of Greenville, is also one of the easiest falls to get to.

OFF THE BEATEN PATH

**Twin Falls.** The white water swooshes over wide gray boulders on the right; the falls on the left are higher. Don't give in to the temptation to climb the rocks leading to the top of the falls; not only is the view not much better but the stones are very slippery. The trail is on public property, a ¼-mile hike one-way. ✉ *Cleo Chapman Rd., off Rte. 178, north of Pickens 24 miles east of Greenville* ☎ *800/849-4766, 864/233-2690* 🌐 *www.upcountrysc.com.*

9

**Upcountry History Museum.** Exhibits focus on the history of the 15 counties of the South Carolina Upstate. There are two floors of interactive displays and a small theater where special programs are regularly presented. ✉ *540 Buncombe St., Heritage Green* ☎ *864/467–3100* 🌐 *www.upcountryhistory.org* 🎫 *$5* 🕒 *Tues.–Sat. 10–5, Sun. 1–5.*

## WHERE TO EAT

$$$ AMERICAN

✕ **Augusta Grill.** Depending on what's in season, and on the whims of the chef, menu selections change daily. Seafood such as triggerfish with creamy crabmeat beurre blanc and beef with one of chef Bob Hackell's made-from-scratch sauces are typical. You can also order dinner as a series of small plates. The crab-cake special on Wednesday night packs the house. Order ahead to be sure the kitchen hasn't run out of its signature blackberry cobbler. $ *Average main: $19* ✉ *1818 Augusta St.* ☎ *864/242–0316* 🌐 *www.augustagrill.com* 🕒 *Closed Sun.–Mon. No lunch Tues.–Sat.*

$$ SOUTHERN

✕ **Devereaux's.** The exposed brick walls and wood beams are telltale signs of the building's former life as a 1902 cigar factory. Completely refurbished, it's now home to award-winning chef Steven Devereaux Greene's restaurant. The contemporary menu has a Southern flair, and you can expect such main dishes as barbecue glazed pork loin and pine-nut-crusted rack of lamb. There are also unique desserts like the goat-cheese cheesecake with lavender ice cream. The kitchen is open so patrons can watch the chef in action. The dress code calls for upscale or business casual attire. *Average main: $19 25 E. Court St., Downtown 864/241–3030 www.devereauxsdining.com Closed Mon. No lunch.*

$$$ SOUTHERN **Soby's New South Cuisine.** The palette of plums and golds is a stunning contrast to the original brick and wood that was uncovered during the renovation of this 19th-century cotton exchange building. Although the menu changes seasonally, perennial favorites—a layered appetizer of fried green tomatoes and jalapeño pimiento cheese, shrimp, and locally ground grits, and the famous mind-numbing white-chocolate banana-cream pie—are always available. Brunch is a local favorite. *Average main: $19 207 S. Main St., Downtown 864/232–7007 www.sobys.com No lunch.*

$ ECLECTIC **Stax's Omega Diner.** This contemporary diner has both booths and a half-circle counter with stools. The menu lists a little of everything: bacon and eggs, burgers, souvlaki, Greek-style chicken, shrimp, and grits. When you're done with your meal, check out the dessert menu from the Stax bakery next door. *Average main: $10 72 Orchard Park Dr. 864/297–6639 www.staxs.net.*

$ AMERICAN **Two Chefs Delicatessen.** Mix and match from the deli's selection of delicious homemade sandwiches and salads. Try the roasted-potato salad, dried-cranberry-and-grilled-chicken salad, or pepper-crusted turkey on rosemary sourdough. There are a lot of tempting desserts, too, including apple-brandy cake, flourless chocolate cake, and fruit tarts. There's a second, to-go location on the east side. *Average main: $7 104 S. Main St., Suite 105 864/370–9336 www.twochefsdeli.com Closed weekends. Average main: $7 8590 Pelham Rd. 864/284–9970 www.2chefs2go.com Closed Sun. No dinner Sat.*

## WHERE TO STAY

*Hotel reviews have been abbreviated in this book. For expanded reviews, please go to Fodors.com.*

$ HOTEL **Hyatt Regency Hotel.** This upscale-chain offering's best asset is its location in the midst of the revitalized downtown of shops and restaurants. **Pros:** convenient in-room dining. **Cons:** some guests have complained bathrooms are too small. *Rooms from: $139 220 N. Main St., Downtown 864/235–1234, 800/233–1234 www.greenville.hyatt.com 328 rooms No meals.*

$ HOTEL **Phoenix Greenville's Inn.** Ask for a room overlooking the courtyard gardens and pool at this accommodating Southern inn. **Pros:** award-winning restaurant; free airport shuttle by appointment. **Cons:** far from the downtown area; no elevator. *Rooms from: $79 246 N. Pleasantburg Dr. 800/257–3529, 864/233–4651 www.phoenixgreenvillesinn.com 184 rooms, 2 suites Breakfast.*

$ HOTEL **Westin Poinsett Hotel.** This 1925, 11-story hotel in Greenville's downtown area has a unique historic feel with the luxury of Westin-style modern upgrades. **Pros:** great location; three rooms have exercise machines. **Cons:** there is a daily fee to park in the garage. *Rooms* *from: $169 ✉ 120 S. Main St. ☎ 864/421–9700 🌐 www.westin.com ⇒ 200 rooms, 23 suites 🍴 No meals.*

## NIGHTLIFE AND THE ARTS

**Bi-Lo Center.** The 15,000-seat Bi-Lo Center hosts major concerts and sporting events. *✉ 650 N. Academy St. ☎ 864/241-3800 🌐 www.bilocenter.com.*

**Handlebar.** Since 1994, the Handlebar has been bringing small-stage live music to Greenville. Monday is known for local bands, while Tuesday brings a bluegrass jam to the bar and a swing dance to the concert hall. *✉ 304 E. Stone Ave. ☎ 864/233–6173 🌐 www.handlebar-online.com ⊙ Closed Sun.*

**The Peace Center.** Situated along the Reedy River, The Peace Center presents star performers, touring Broadway shows, dance companies, chamber music, and local groups. *✉ 300 S. Main St. ☎ 864/467–3000, 800/888-7768 🌐 www.peacecenter.org.*

## SPORTS AND THE OUTDOORS

South Carolinians sometimes prefer Upstate golf courses to those on the coast, as they're less crowded and enjoy a slightly cooler climate. The area's rolling hills provide an added challenge.

**Links O'Tryon.** This 18-hole course with stunning views of the Blue Ridge Mountains and fieldstone bridges and walls features a Tom Jackson–design layout. *✉ 11250 New Cut Rd., Campobello ☎ 864/468-4995 🌐 www.linksotryongc.com 🏌 18 holes. 6877 yds. Par 72. Green Fee: $35/$45 ☞ Facilities: Driving range, putting green, short game area, golf carts, pro shop, golf lessons, restaurant, bar.*

**Rock at Jocassee.** This mountain course features plenty of water hazards; its signature hole has a waterfall view. *✉ 171 Sliding Rock Rd., Pickens ☎ 864/878–2030 🌐 www.golfattherock.com 🏌 18 holes. 6710 yds. Par 72. Green Fee: $25/$35 ☞ Facilities: Driving range, putting green, pitching area, golf carts, rental clubs, proshop, golf lessons, restaurant.*

## SHOPPING

The shopping area along Greenville's Main Street and adjoining West End may be just a mile or so long, but it's chockablock with interesting shops.

**Augusta Twenty.** The shop is hip, but the service is so friendly at Augusta Twenty that you won't feel uncomfortable browsing the racks of designer duds. *✉ 20 Augusta St., at S. Main St., Downtown ☎ 864/233–2600 🌐 www.augustatwenty.com.*

**O. P. Taylors.** Even adults love O. P. Taylors, a super-cool toy emporium. *✉ 117 N. Main St. ☎ 864/467–1984 🌐 www.optaylors.com.*

**Perdue's Mountain Fruit Farm.** Open from mid-June until the first of November, Perdue's Mountain Fruit Farm sells an always-changing selection of locally grown fruits such as peaches, blackberries, pears, apples, and raspberries. Owner Dick Perdue also makes the jams, jellies, applesauce, and ciders that fill the shelves, along with local honey. *✉ 2400 SC Hwy 11, Travelers Rest ☎ 864/895–0608.*

**Postcard from Paris.** Filling two floors with French linens, furniture, and home accessories, Postcard from Paris is a slice of the Left Bank in the deep South. ✉ *631 S. Main St.* ☎ *864/233-6622* 🌐 *www.postcardfromparis.com.*

## KINGS MOUNTAIN NATIONAL MILITARY PARK

*70 miles northeast of Greenville via I-85.*

**Kings Mountain National Military Park.** A Revolutionary War battle considered an important turning point was fought here on October 7, 1780. Colonial Tories commanded by British major Patrick Ferguson were soundly defeated by ragtag patriot forces from the southern Appalachians. Visitor center exhibits, dioramas, and an orientation film describe the action. A paved self-guided trail leads through the battlefield. ✉ *Off Exit 2, I-85, Blacksburg* ☎ *864/936-7921* 🌐 *www.nps.gov/kimo* *Free* *Daily 9-5.*

OFF THE BEATEN PATH

**Chattooga National Wild and Scenic River.** Designated as a Wild and Scenic River by Congress in 1974, the Chattooga River can test the skills of even the most experienced rafters with Class V-plus runs that have names like "Crack-in-the-Rock," "Corkscrew," and "Sock-Em Dog" (which includes a stomach-sinking 7-foot drop).

Commercial rafting outfitters also run shorter, more gentle rides (Class II and below) that are appropriate for senior citizens and children as young as eight years old. The river is on the border of South Carolina and Georgia, about 38 miles northeast of Pendleton via U.S. 76 or Route 28, and is part of Sumter National Forest. ☎ *864/638-9568* 🌐 *www.discoversouthcarolina.com.*

**Nantahala Outdoor Center** ☎ *888/905-7238* 🌐 *www.noc.com.*

**Southeastern Expeditions** ☎ *800/868-7238* 🌐 *www.southeasternexpeditions.com.*

**Wildwater Ltd** ☎ *800/451-9972, 866/319-8870* 🌐 *www.wildwaterrafting.com.*

# Savannah, GA

10

**WORD OF MOUTH**

"The natural beauty in Savannah is astounding. I think it is the prettiest city in the U.S. and really underrated. The parks every other block or so are stunning. It had a much more eclectic and laid-back feel than Charleston."

—ilford2121

# WELCOME TO SAVANNAH, GA

## TOP REASONS TO GO

★ **Intriguing architecture:** Savannah has no shortage of architectural or historical marvels. The many building styles make strolling the tree-lined neighborhoods a delight.

★ **Midnight in the Garden of Good and Evil:** John Berendt's famous 1994 book about a local murder and the city's eccentric characters still draws travelers to the places mentioned.

★ **Famous Southern restaurants:** Savannah's elegant restaurants, notably Elizabeth's on 37th and the Olde Pink House, have exquisite Southern cuisine. And, of course, there's celebrity chef Paula Deen's restaurant, The Lady & Sons.

★ **Historic inns and bed-and-breakfasts:** One of Savannah's unique pleasures is the opportunity to stay in a historic home fronting a prominent square.

★ **Savannah by night:** Ubiquitous "to-go" cups make bar-hopping a popular pastime. Ghost tours are another fun nocturnal activity.

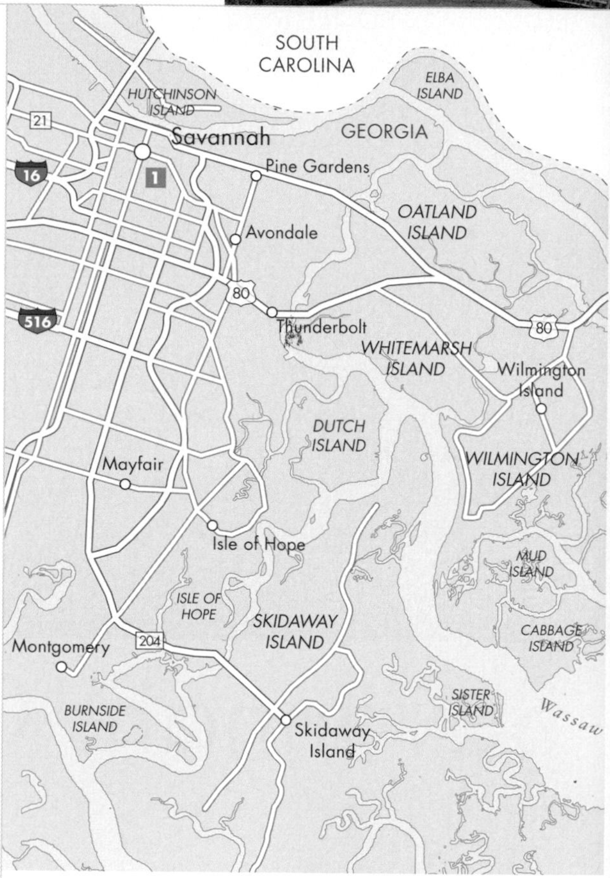

**1 The Historic District.** A link to the past is a big part of Savannah's allure. The 2½-square-mile landmark Historic District is the nation's largest. It is where the city's historic squares and most of its accommodations, restaurants, and shops are located.

## GETTING ORIENTED

Although it's commonly referred to as "downtown," the Historic District lies on the northern edge of Savannah, just across the river from Hutchinson Island and South Carolina. The borders of the district are River Street to the north, Gaston Street to the south, and East Broad Street and Martin Luther King Jr. Boulevard to the east and west. Tybee Island is 18 miles east of Savannah via Victory Drive (U.S. 80).

**2 Tybee Island.** Formerly known as Savannah Beach, has been a destination since the 1920s, when a train connected downtown to the beach pavilion where jazz bands played. These days the island is a mix of kitschy shops and interesting restaurants. Whether you're looking to work on your tan, spend a day on a fishing charter, or maneuver a Jet Ski, this is a must-see during the summer months.

# GOOD EATS IN SAVANNAH

(above and upper right) The sampler at Wiley's Championship BBQ lets you try just about everything on the menu. (lower right) You haven't lived until you've tried red velvet cake in Savannah.

John Berendt's *Midnight in the Garden of Good and Evil* fueled Savannah tourism in the mid- to late 1990s The surge of new visitors and their varied tastes knocked Savannah's culinary scene off its genteel Southern pedestal.

Certainly, menus inspired by plantation days—dirty rice, collard greens, hearty pork dishes, and shrimp—still sway romantic notions of curious foodies. But the new diners expect Savannah chefs to step up to the trends and flavors of today. Not only do menus pay homage to the past with contemporary versions of shrimp and grits, but also reach out to more adventurous diners with seafood caught fresh in the morning and regionally sourced meats, cheeses, and produce that represent the area's unique terroir.

Downtown restaurants embrace both tradition and exploration; dockside eateries are casual destinations for fresh-caught fish and shrimp; the growing Midtown and Southside bring an array of ethnic dishes to the table.

—Tim Rutherford

## INTERNATIONAL EATS

Savannah's food offerings run deeper than just traditional southern cooking. **John's Jamaican BBQ Jerk City** (✉ *205 East Montgomery Crossroads* ☎ *912/921-7140*) serves up favorites like jerk chicken and rice. For Korean flavors, make your way to **Kim Chi II** (✉ *149 E. Montgomery Cross Rd.* ☎ *912/920-7273*) for the fiery kimchi banchan, and the bubbling hot pork and tofu stew.

## SOUTHERN SOUL FOOD

Soul food has evolved from plantation and sharecropper kitchens, where the cheapest cuts of meat, boniest fish, and home garden vegetables fed many mouths for very little money. Today, those same cuts of meat grace fine-dining menus, but savvy foodies know the best interpretations come from authentic soul-food restaurants. Here are some of our favorites:

**Marandy's**. At Marandy's, chef Cynthia is famous for her tender oxtails, crisp fried whiting, and red velvet cake. Saturday is "Soul Food Spaghetti" day, when the week's leftover meats and seafood are combined in a giant pot of red sauce and tender pasta—it usually sells out during the first hour. ✉ *7010 Skidaway Rd.* ☎ *912/692–0036* ⏲ *Closed Sun. and Mon.*

**Masada Café at the United House of Prayer**. If you find yourself in a busy church parking lot at lunchtime, you're likely at Masada Café. Proceeds fund church mission work and the daily changing cafeteria-style menu always offers several meat and vegetable options. You can't go wrong with juicy meat loaf or braised pork chops smothered in cream gravy; stewed cabbage, baked squash, and buttery field peas are among a handful of daily changing sides. ✉ *2301 W. Bay St.* ☎ *912/236–9499* ⏲ *Closed Sun. and Mon.*

**Sisters of the New South Café.** Favorites here include smothered shrimp over rice, slow-cooked oxtails, and homemade desserts like gooey peach cobbler, decadent red velvet cake with cream cheese frosting, and tangy key lime pie. ✉ *2607 Skidaway Rd.* ☎ *912/335–2761* ⏲ *Closed Sun. and Mon.*

## SAVANNAH BBQ

Low and slow is the mantra of Savannah's barbecue pit masters who have perfected the region's tender, juicy, and mildly smoky style of pulled pork, traditionally served with sauce on the side. At **Wiley's Championship BBQ** (✉ *4700 U.S. Hwy. 80 E* ☎ *912/201–3259* 🌐 *www.wileyschampionshipbbq.com*) a wall of awards testifies to Wiley's skill. The pulled pork and beef brisket are must-haves; make sure to save room for the bread pudding. **Sandfly BBQ** (✉ *8413 Ferguson Ave.* ☎ *912/356–5464*) is mecca for 'cue lovers. The ribs are influenced by a Memphis-style dry rub. **Angel's BBQ** (✉ *21 W. Oglethorpe La.* ☎ *912/495–0902* 🌐 *www.angels-bbq.com*) seats only 12 but prepares 10 times that of its juicy pulled-pork sandwiches for carryout.

Updated by Patrick Rodgers and Summer Teal Simpson

Savannah is such a warm, welcoming city that you may find it especially easy to get acquainted with the "Hostess City," as it is known to those smitten by its hospitality and charm. As America's first planned city, Savannah is perhaps most recognized for its 22 squares, the diverse group of parks that dot the Historic District. The city also remains connected with its namesake river; it is home to a busy commercial port, and towering cargo ships are a common sight along River Street.

Savannah, Georgia's oldest city, began its modern history on February 12, 1733, when Oglethorpe and 120 colonists arrived at Yamacraw Bluff on the Savannah River to what would be the last British colony in the New World. For a century and a half the city flourished as a bustling port, and was the departure point for cotton being shipped around the world.

Although Savannah was spared during the Civil War, the city fell onto hard times soon afterward. Cobwebs replaced cotton in the dilapidated riverfront warehouses. Historic buildings languished; many were razed or allowed to decay. The tide finally turned in the 1950s, when residents began a concerted effort—which continues to this day—to restore and preserve the city's unique architectural heritage.

The past plays an important role in Savannah. Standing in a tranquil square surrounded by historic homes, it's easy to feel as if you have stumbled through a portal into the past. Don't be fooled though, as the city offers much more than antebellum nostalgia for moonlight and magnolias. Savannah is home to several colleges and universities, including the prestigious Savannah College of Art and Design, and in the last decade in particular has seen a surge of creative energy. A new crop of cultural events lends a youthful vibe to the Hostess City.

# PLANNING

## PLANNING YOUR TIME

Savannah is not large, but it is atmospheric, and you want to make sure you allow sufficient time to soak in the ambience. You'll need a minimum of two or three days to fully appreciate the Historic District and its many sights, not to mention the food, which is an integral part of the Savannah experience. You'll need another day or two to see the sights in the surrounding area, including a jaunt out to Tybee Island for a fishing trip, kayaking tour, or relaxing on the beach. Some travelers head north to Hilton Head or Charleston to round out their Lowcountry experience.

## GETTING HERE AND AROUND

You can fly into Savannah and catch a cab into downtown, but you'll probably need a car if you want to explore beyond the Historic District.

### AIR TRAVEL

Savannah and Hilton Head share an airport. Savannah/Hilton Head International Airport (SAV) is 11 miles west of downtown. The airport is only 20 minutes by car from the Historic District and around 40 minutes from Hilton Head Island. There are plenty of taxis waiting outside the baggage claim area, and some of the larger hotels offer shuttles. **■ TIP→** If the flights into Savannah/Hilton Head International Airport aren't convenient, consider Jacksonville International Airport. The drive time to Savannah is just shy of two and a half hours.

**Airport Information Savannah/Hilton Head International Airport** ✉ *400 Airways Ave., Pooler, North Carolina* ☎ *912/964–0514* 🌐 *www.savannahairport.com.*

### CAR TRAVEL

Interstate 95 slices north–south along the Eastern Seaboard, intersecting 10 miles west of town with east–west Interstate 16, which dead-ends in downtown Savannah. U.S. 17, the Coastal Highway, also runs north–south through town. U.S. 80 another east–west route through Savannah.

This is one city where it is to your advantage not to rent a car unless and until you plan on leaving the immediate area. Downtown parking can be a challenge, but it is often easier in the residential neighborhoods. Tourists may purchase one- and two-day parking passes for $7 and $12 from the Savannah Visitor Information Center, the Parking Services Department, and various hotels and inns (several properties give you this pass for free if you're staying with them). Rates vary at local parking garages, but you should expect to pay at least $1 for the first hour and 75¢ for each additional hour. Rates vary at local parking garages, but in a City of Savannah–owned lot you should expect to pay at least $1 per hour during business hours weekdays, a $2 flat rate in the evenings, and a flat rate of $5–$10 on the weekends.

### PUBLIC TRANSPORTATION

Chatham Area Transit (CAT) operates buses in Savannah and Chatham County Monday through Saturday from 6 am to just shy of midnight, Sunday from 7 am to 9 pm. (Some lines stop running earlier or may not run on Sunday.) A free shuttle runs a loop throughout the Historic District. The Riverfront Trolley—a refurbished 1930s streetcar—runs the length of River Street Wednesday to Sunday.

**Public Transit Contacts Chatham Area Transit (CAT)** ☎ *912/233–5767* 🌐 *www.catchacat.org.*

### TAXI TRAVEL

AAA Adam Cab is a reliable 24-hour taxi service. Calling ahead for reservations could yield a flat rate. Yellow Cab Company is another dependable taxi service. Average cost for both companies is $1.92 per mile. MC Transportation is a taxi and shuttle service that operates 24 hours a day and will go anywhere, anytime.

You can hail these cabs on the street if they do not have riders and if they are not "on a mission." Most cab services offer flat rates to and from the airport, usually in the range of $31, plus $5 for each additional person.

**Contacts AAA Adam Cab** ☎ *912/927–7466.* **Savannah Pedicab** ☎ *912/232–7900* 🌐 *www.savannahpedicab.com.* **Yellow Cab** ☎ *912/236–1133* 🌐 *www.yellowcabofsavannah.com.*

## TOURS

### BUS, CARRIAGE, AND TROLLEY TOURS

Carriage Tours of Savannah, with tours departing from City Market, takes you through the Historic District by day or by night at a 19th-century clip-clop pace, with coachmen spinning tales and telling ghost stories along the way. A romantic evening tour in a private carriage costs $85 (add $20 per person over two); regular tours are a modest $20 per person.

Old Savannah Tours is the city's award-winning company with years of experience and the widest variety of tours, including the following popular options: the hop-on/hop-off trolley tour; the 90-minute Historic District tour in a van with air-conditioning; and the ghost tour with dinner at Pirates' House, among others. The on-off pass starts at $25 per person.

Old Town Trolley Tours has narrated 90-minute tours traversing the Historic District. Trolleys stop at 15 designated stops every 30 minutes daily from 9 to 4:30; you can hop on and off as you please. The cost is $26.

**Bus and Trolley Tour Contacts Carriage Tours of Savannah** ☎ *912/236–6756* 🌐 *www.carriagetoursofsavannah.com.* **Old Savannah Tours** ☎ *912/234–8128, 800/517–9007* 🌐 *www.oldsavannahtours.com.* **Old Town Trolley Tours** ☎ *912/233–0083* 🌐 *www.trolleytours.com.*

### WALKING TOURS

For those interested in something a little unusual, consider these creative tour companies to take you off the beaten path. A must-experience tour is **Savannah Rambles**, led by Dirk, the former architectural consultant for the Historic Savannah Foundation. A treasure trove of information, he provides tour-goers with intimate, professional knowledge of the city's structural history (☎ *912/704-8170* 🌐 *savannahrambles.com,* tours start at $15, times listed on website). Lastly, take the family on one of the evening **Blue Orb Ghost Tours.** They offer the "City of the Dead' walking tour through the old cemeteries, or the "Zombies Tour," which is ages 18 and up and is guaranteed to give you chill bumps (☎ *912/665-4258*, 🌐 *www.blueorbtours.com/savannah-ghost-tours*, reservations required, "City" tour is $25 for 90 minutes, "Zombies" tour is $35 for 2 hours).

### VISITOR INFORMATION

The Savannah Area Convention & Visitors Bureau is easily accessed from all major thoroughfares, and is open daily weekdays 8:30 to 5 and weekends 9 to 5. The center has a useful audiovisual overview of the city and a staff of knowledgeable trip counselors. For detailed information about Tybee Island, drop by the island's visitor center, just off Highway 80. It's open daily 10 to 6.

Visitor Information Contacts **Savannah Visitor Information Center** ✉ *301 Martin Luther King Jr. Blvd.* ☎ *912/944–0455* 🌐 *www.savannahvisit.com.* **Tybee Island Visitor Information Center** ✉ *Campbell Ave. and Hwy. 80, Tybee Island* ☎ *912/786–5444, 800/868–2322* 🌐 *www.tybeevisit.com.*

# EXPLORING

With an eclectic array of shops, restaurants, museums, and monuments spread across the Historic District, the best way to explore downtown Savannah is by foot. Whether you plan a route ahead of time or just wander aimlessly, a leisurely stroll will always result in unique discoveries. If your feet start to ache, flag down a pedicab driver—these people-powered vehicles are a great way to get around, and the drivers usually tell a good story or two.

## THE HISTORIC DISTRICT

Georgia's sage founder, General James Oglethorpe, laid out the city on a grid as logical as a geometry solution. The Historic District is neatly hemmed in by the Savannah River, Gaston Street, East Broad Street, and Martin Luther King Jr. Boulevard. Streets are arrow-straight, and public squares are tucked into the grid at precise intervals. Bull Street, anchored on the north by City Hall and the south by Forsyth Park, charges down the center of the grid and maneuvers around the five public squares that stand in its way. The squares all have some historical significance; many have elaborate fountains, monuments to war heroes, and shaded resting areas with park benches. Beautiful homes and mansions speak lovingly of another era.



### TOP ATTRACTIONS

★ **City Market.** Although the 1870s City Market was razed years ago, its atmosphere and character are still evident. Adjacent to Ellis Square, the area is a lively destination because of its art galleries, boutiques, street music, and open-air cafés. City Market is also a good spot to purchase trolley tickets or take a ride in a horse-drawn carriage. ✉ *W.*

### DID YOU KNOW?

*Midnight in the Garden of Good and Evil* by John Berendt brought so much fame to Savannah, it is known simply as "the book" here. Fans make the pilgrimage to the Mercer House on Monterey Square, where Jim Williams once had his antique business.

Savannah Historic District
Bonaventure Cemetery ...... 20
Cathedral of St. John the Baptist ..... 16
City Market ....... 3
Colonial Park Cemetery ...... 14
Ellis Square ...... 5
Factors Walk ..... 6
First African Baptist Church ... 2
Forsyth Park ... 19
Fort Pulaski National Monument ....... 8
Jepson Center for the Arts .... 10
Juliette Gordon Low Birthplace/ Girl Scout National Center 11
Mighty Eighth Air Force Heritage Museum .......... 1
Monterey Square ......... 18
Oatland Island Wildlife Center .. 7
Owens-Thomas House and Museum ........ 13
Savannah Children's Museum ........ 17
SCAD Museum of Art .......... 13
Ships of the Sea Maritime Museum .......... 4
Telfair Museum of Art ............ 9
Tricentennial Park and Battlefield ..... 15
Savannah River
Riverfront Plaza
River St.
Factors Walk
Williamson St.
W. Bay St.
E. Bay St.
W. Bryan St.
E. Bryan St.
W. Julian
E. Julian
Johnson Sq.
Reynolds Sq.
Warren Sq.
W. Congress St.
E. Congress St.
W. Broughton St.
E. Broughton St.
Whitaker St.
Lincoln St.
Prince St.
W. State St.
E. State St.
Telfair Sq.
W. President
Wright Sq.
E. President
Oglethorpe Sq.
Columbia Sq.
W. York St.
E. York St.
W. Oglethorpe Ave.
E. Oglethorpe St.
Montgomery St.
Jefferson St.
Barnard St.
Drayton St.
Colonial Park Cemetery
W. Hull
E. Hull
Orleans Sq.
Chippewa Sq.
Abercorn St.
Habersham St.
W. Perry
E. Perry
W. Liberty St.
E. Liberty St.
Bull St.
W. Harris St.
E. Harris St.
Pulaski Sq.
Madison Sq.
Lafayette Sq.
E. Macon St.
Troup Sq.
W. Charlton
E. Charlton
St. John's Episcopal Church
Tattnall St.
W. Jones St.
E. Jones St.
W. Taylor St.
E. Taylor St.
Chatham Sq.
W. Wayne St.
E. Wayne St.
Monterey Sq.
Calhoun Sq.
Whitefield Sq.
W. Gordon St.
E. Gordon St.
Price St.
W. Gaston St.
E. Gaston St.
Forsyth Park
W. Huntingdon St.
E. Huntingdon St.
King-Tisdell Cottage
W. Hall St.
E. Hall St.
W. Gwinett St.
E. Gwinett St.
W. Park Ave.
E. Park Ave.
W. Park Avenue Ln.
E. Park Avenue Ln.
0
1/4 mile
0
400 meters

*St. Julian St. between Barnard and Montgomery Sts., Historic District* ☎ *912/232–4903* 🌐 *www.savannahcitymarket.com.*

★ **Colonial Park Cemetery.** Stroll the shaded pathways and read some of the old tombstone inscriptions in this park, the final resting place for Savannahians who died between 1750 and 1853. Many of those interred here died during the yellow fever epidemic in 1820. Notice the dramatic entrance gate on the corner of Abercorn and Oglethorpe streets. Local legend tells that when Sherman's troops set up camp here, they moved some headstones around and altered inscriptions for their own amusement. This spooky spot is a regular stop for ghost tours. ✉ *Oglethorpe and Abercorn Sts., Historic District* ⏲ *Daily 8–8.*

Fodor's Choice ★ **Ellis Square.** Converted from public square to parking garage in the 1970s, Ellis Square has been restored in recent years and is once again one of Savannah's most popular squares. Near the western end stands a statue of legendary songwriter Johnny Mercer, a Savannah native. A great treat for youngsters (and the young at heart) is the square's interactive fountain, which is entertaining and refreshing in the warmer months. Ellis Square also has a visitors center with travel brochures, a touch-screen city guide, and public restrooms. ✉ *Barnard St. between W. Congress and W. Bryan Sts., Historic District.*

**Factors Walk.** A network of iron crosswalks and steep stone stairways connects Bay Street to Factors Walk below. The congested area of multistory buildings was originally the center of commerce for cotton brokers, who walked between and above the lower cotton warehouses. Cobblestone ramps lead pedestrians down to River Street. ■ **TIP→ This area is paved in cobblestones, so wear comfortable shoes.** ✉ *Bay St. to Factors Walk, Historic District.*

Fodor's Choice ★ **Forsyth Park.** The heart of the city's outdoor life, Forsyth Park hosts a number of popular cultural events, including film screenings, sporting events, and the annual Savannah Jazz Festival. A glorious white fountain dating to 1858, Confederate and Spanish-American War memorials, multiple playgrounds, and an old fort are spread across this grand park. Recently restored, the fort now contains a café, an open-air stage, and lovely fountains. The park's one-mile perimeter is among the prettiest walks in the city and takes you past many beautifully restored historic homes. ✉ *Gaston St. between Drayton and Whitaker Sts., Historic District.*

Fodor's Choice ★ **Jepson Center for the Arts.** This contemporary building is one-of-a-kind among the characteristic 18th- and 19th-century architecture of historic Savannah. The modern art extension of the Telfair Museum of Art, the Jepson was designed by renowned architect Moshe Safdie and opened in 2006. Within the marble-and-glass edifice are rotating exhibits, on loan and from the permanent collection, ranging from European masters to contemporary locals. There's also an outdoor sculpture terrace and a kid-friendly interactive area called the ArtZeum. ✉ *207 W. York St., Historic District* ☎ *912/790–8802* 🌐 *www.telfair.org/jepson* 🎟 *$12, $20 with admission to the Owens-Thomas House and Museum and the Telfair Museum of Art* ⏲ *Sun.–Mon. noon–5, Tues.–Wed. and Fri.–Sat. 10–5, Thurs. 10–8.*

10

A beautiful fountain adorns Forsyth Park.

★ **Juliette Gordon Low Birthplace/Girl Scout National Center.** This early 19th-century townhouse, attributed to William Jay, was designated in 1965 as Savannah's first National Historic Landmark. "Daisy" Low, founder of the Girl Scouts, was born here in 1860, and the house is now owned and operated by the Girl Scouts of America. Mrs. Low's paintings and other artwork are on display in the house, restored to the style of 1886, the year of Mrs. Low's marriage. Droves of Girl Scout troops make the regular pilgrimmage to Savannah to see their founder's birthplace and earn merit badges. ✉ *142 Bull St., Historic District* ☎ *912/233–4501* 🌐 *www.juliettegordonlowbirthplace.org* 🎫 *$8, $18 with admission to the Andrew Low House and the Isaiah Davenport House* ⏲ *Mon.–Sat. 10–4, Sun. 11–4. Nov.–Feb., closed Wed.*

Fodor's Choice ★ **Owens-Thomas House and Museum.** Designed by William Jay, the Owens-Thomas House is widely considered to be one of the finest examples of English Regency architecture in America. Built in 1816–19, the house was constructed with local materials. Of particular note are the curving walls of the house, Greek-inspired ornamental molding, half-moon arches, stained-glass panels, original Duncan Phyfe furniture, and the hardwood "bridge" on the second floor. The carriage house includes a gift shop and rare urban slave quarters, which have retained the original furnishings and "haint-blue" paint made by the slave occupants. This house had indoor toilets before the White House and the Palace of Versailles. If you have to choose just one or two house museums, let this be one. Owned and administered by the Telfair Museum of Art, this home gives an inside perspective on Savannah's history. ✉ *124 Abercorn St., Historic District* ☎ *912/790–8880* 🌐 *telfair.org/owens-thomas*

*$15 $20 with admission to Jepson Center for the Arts and the Telfair Museum of Art ⊙ Mon. noon–5, Tues.–Sat. 10–5, Sun. 1–5; last tour at 4:30.*

★ **Savannah Children's Museum.** The newest addition to the Coastal Heritage Society's impressive selection of historical and cultural museums, the Savannah Children's Museum opened its doors in the summer of 2012. Adhering to the principle of learning through play, the first of two phases of the open-air museum features two vintage railcars, one serving as a group space for birthday parties and the other as a nursing/changing station. In the open green space are several stations geared for sensory play, including a water/sand play excavation station, sound station of percussion instruments, and an organic sensory garden. The storybook nook is a partnership with the Savannah public library and encourages visiting youngsters to balance physical play with mental. Phase II, due for completion in 2013, will more than double the size of the museum. Call for the latest hours and admission. **■ TIP→ Enter through the Georgia State Railroad Museum.** ✉ *655 Louisville Rd., Historic District* ☎ *912/651–6840* 🌐 *www.savannahchildrensmuseum.org* *$7.50* ⊙ *Mon. and Thurs.–Sat. 9–5, Sun. noon–5.*

Fodor's Choice ★ **SCAD Museum of Art.** This architectural marvel rose from the ruins of the oldest surviving railroad building in the U.S. Appropriately, the architect chosen for the lofty design and remodel project was Christian Sottile, the valedictorian of Savannah College of Art and Design's 1996 graduating class and the current dean of the School of Building Arts. Sottile rose to the hearty challenge of merging the past with the present, preserving key architectural details of the original structure, while introducing contemporary design elements, gallery functionality, and cohesive relevance for the city and the cultural arts district of the historic MLK corridor. SCAD Museum of Art (MOA) houses two main galleries with rotating exhibits by some of the most acclaimed figures in contemporary art: the Evans Gallery features works of African-American arts and culture, while the André Leon Talley Gallery is devoted to fashion and high style. Completed in 2011, SCAD MOA has brought the global art-world conversation to Savannah and to SCAD students, and elevated the city to an international level. ✉ *601 Turner Blvd., Historic District* ☎ *912/525–7191* 🌐 *scadmoa.org* *$10* ⊙ *Tues., Weds., and Fri. 10–5, Thurs. 10–8, weekends noon–5.*

★ **Ships of the Sea Maritime Museum.** This exuberant Greek-revival mansion was the home of William Scarborough, a wealthy merchant in the early 19th century. The structure, with its portico capped by half-moon windows, is another of architect William Jay's notable contributions to the Historic District. These days, it houses the Ships of the Sea Museum, with displays of model ships and exhibits detailing maritime history. Already home to the largest garden in the Historic District, Ships of the Sea recently completed the ambitious addition of the North Garden, nearly doubling the walled courtyard's size and providing ample space for naturalist walking tours, relaxation, and outdoor concerts. ✉ *41 Martin Luther King Jr. Blvd., Historic District* ☎ *912/232–1511* 🌐 *www.shipsofthesea.org* *$8* ⊙ *Tues.–Sun. 10–5.*

CLOSE UP

## Moss Mystique

Spanish moss—the silky gray garlands that drape over the branches of live oaks—has come to symbolize the languorous sensibilities of the Deep South. A relative of the pineapple, the moisture-loving plant requires an average year-round humidity of 70%, and thus thrives in subtropical climates—including Georgia's coastal regions.

Contrary to popular belief, Spanish moss is not a parasite; it's an epiphyte, or "air plant," taking water and nutrients from the air and photosynthesizing in the same manner as soil-bound plants. It reproduces using tiny flowers. When water is scarce, it turns gray, and when the rains come it takes on a greenish hue. Although it is tempting to grab handfuls of Spanish moss as a souvenir, be careful. It often harbors the biting menaces commonly known as chiggers.

★ **Telfair Museum of Art.** The oldest public art museum in the Southeast was designed by William Jay in 1819 for Alexander Telfair. Within its marble rooms are a variety of paintings from American and European masters, plaster casts of the Elgin Marbles and other classical sculptures, and some of the Telfair family furnishings, including a Duncan Phyfe sideboard and Savannah-made silver. It is the permanent home of the notable Bird Girl statue, made famous on the cover of John Berendt's *Midnight in the Garden of Good and Evil*. The Telfair hosts classical music performances during spring's Savannah Music Festival. ✉ *121 Barnard St., Historic District* ☎ *912/790–8871* 🌐 *www.telfair.org* 🎟 *$12, $20 with admission to the Jepson Center for the Arts and the Owens-Thomas House and Museum* ⏲ *Mon. noon–5, Tues.–Sat. 10–5, Sun. 1–5.*

★ **Tricentennial Park and Battlefield.** This 25-acre complex is home to the **Savannah History Museum,** the Georgia State Railroad Museum, Battlefield Memorial Park, and the newest addition, the Savannah Children's Museum. This site offers an unbeatable introduction to the city and a full day of fun for the whole family. Located behind the Visitors Center, the history museum houses exhibits on Savannah's cultural and military history and includes a new temporary exhibit, "Women of Merit," honoring Savannahian Juliette Gordon Low and the 2012 Girl Scout Centennial. The **Georgia State Railroad Museum** preserves the legacy of the Central of Georgia Railway terminal facilities and support buildings. On site are numerous railcars and boxcars, working diesel and steam locomotives, a rare functioning railroad turntable, an iconic 125-foot smokestack, expansive model-train exhibit, and even original homes of the Railroad Ward District. The two museums are separated by the park, site of the 1779 Siege of Savannah. Visitors can lunch inside an old dining car at the Whistle Stop Café. ✉ *303 Martin Luther King Jr. Blvd., Historic District* ☎ *912/651–6825* 🌐 *www.chsgeorgia.org* 🎟 *Savannah History Museum $7;* ⏲ *Weekdays 8:30–5, weekends 9–5.*

### WORTH NOTING

★ **Cathedral of St. John the Baptist.** Soaring over the city, this French Gothic–style cathedral, with pointed arches and free-flowing traceries, is the seat of the Catholic diocese of Savannah. It was founded in 1799 by the first French colonists to arrive in Savannah. Fire destroyed the early structures; the present cathedral dates from 1876. Its architecture, gold-leaf adornments, and the entire edifice give testimony to the importance of the Catholic parishioners of the day. The interior spaces are grand and dramatic, including incredible stained glass and an intricately designed altar. ✉ *222 E. Harris St., at Lafayette Sq., Historic District* ☎ *912/233–4709* 🌐 *www.savannahcathedral.org* ⏲ *Weekdays 9–5.*

★ **First African Baptist Church.** Slaves constructed this church at night by lamplight after having worked the plantations during the day. It is one of the first organized black Baptist churches on the continent. The basement floor still shows signs of its time as a stop on the Underground Railroad. Designs drilled in the floor are thought to actually have been air holes for slaves hiding underneath, waiting to be transported to the Savannah River for their trip to freedom. It was also an important meeting place during the civil rights era. ✉ *23 Montgomery St., Historic District* ☎ *912/233–6597* 🌐 *firstafricanbc.com/* 🎫 *$7* ⏲ *Tours Tues. and Thurs. at 11 and 1, Weds., Fri., and Sat. at 11 and 2.*

★ **Monterey Square.** Commemorating the victory of General Zachary Taylor's forces in Monterrey, Mexico in 1846, this is the fifth and southernmost of Bull Street's squares. A monument honors General Casimir Pulaski, the Polish nobleman who lost his life in the Siege of Savannah during the Revolutionary War. On the square sits Temple Mickve Israel (one of the country's oldest Jewish congregations) and some of the city's most beautiful mansions, including the infamous Mercer House. ✉ *Bull St. between Taylor and Gordon Sts., Historic District.*

## THE SAVANNAH AREA

10

★ **Bonaventure Cemetery.** The largest of Savannah's municipal cemeteries, Bonaventure spreads over 160 acres and sits on a bluff above the Wilmington River. Once a plantation, the land became a private cemetery in 1846 and the public cemetery was established in 1907. The scenescape is one of lush natural beauty transposed against the elegant and almost eerie backdrop of lavish marble headstones, monuments, and mausoleums. John Muir reportedly camped at Bonaventure in 1867 on his legendary "thousand-mile walk." Local photographer Jack Leigh, novelist and poet Conrad Aiken, and singer/songwriter Johnny Mercer are among those interred here. ✉ *330 Bonaventure Rd., Thunderbolt* ⏲ *Daily 8–5.*

★ **Fort Pulaski National Monument.** Named for Casimir Pulaski, a Polish count and Revolutionary War hero, this must-see sight for Civil War buffs was designed by Napoléon's military engineer and built on Cockspur Island between 1829 and 1847. Robert E. Lee's first assignment after graduating from West Point was as an engineer here. The fort was thought to be impervious to attack, but as weapons advanced, it proved penetrable. During the Civil War, the fort fell after bombardment by

### DID YOU KNOW?

Live oak allées draped with Spanish moss are a symbol of Savannah, but have you ever wondered why these trees are called "live" oaks? Evergreen oaks appear to stay alive during the winter while other oaks lose their leaves. Hence the term "live" to refer to Southern evergreen oaks.

newfangled rifled cannons. The restored fortification, operated by the National Park Service, has moats, drawbridges, massive ramparts, and towering walls. The park has trails and picnic areas. ✉ *U.S. Hwy. 80* ☎ *912/786–5787* 🌐 *www.nps.gov/fopu* 🎟 *$5* ⏲ *Daily 9–5.*

**Mighty Eighth Air Force Heritage Museum.** Famous World War II squadron the Mighty Eighth Air Force was formed in Savannah in January 1942. Within one month, they answered the call to arms and shipped out to the United Kingdom. Flying Royal Air Force aircraft, the Mighty Eighth became the largest air force of the period. Exhibits at this museum begin with the prelude to World War II and the rise of Adolf Hitler, and continue through Desert Storm. You can see vintage aircraft, fly a simulated bombing mission with a B-17 crew, test your skills as a waist gunner, and view interviews with courageous World War II vets. The museum also has three theaters, an art gallery, a 7,000-volume library, archives, a memorial garden, a chapel, and a museum store. ✉ *175 Bourne Ave., I–95, Exit 102, to U.S. 80, 14 miles west of Savannah, Pooler, North Carolina* ☎ *912/748–8888* 🌐 *www.mightyeighth.org* 🎟 *$10* ⏲ *Daily 9–5.*

★ **Oatland Island Wildlife Center.** Located a few miles east of the Historic District, this wildlife preserve is home to a variety of animal habitats spread along a 2-mile path. Several coastal habitats are represented, including the wetlands habitat of the alligators, herons, and cranes. Bobcats, buffalo, wolves, armadillo, and assorted birds of prey are on exhibit in the Center. ■ **TIP→** Be sure to bring a camera and comfortable shoes. ✉ *711 Sandtown Rd.* ☎ *912/395–1212* 🌐 *www.oatlandisland.org* 🎟 *$5* ⏲ *Daily 10–4.*

**Tybee Island.** *Tybee* is an Indian word meaning "salt." The Yamacraw Indians came to this island in the Atlantic Ocean to hunt and fish. These days, the island is chock-full of seafood restaurants, chain motels, condos, and shops—most of which sprang up during the 1950s and haven't changed much since. Fun-loving locals still host big annual parties like fall's Pirate Festival and spring's Beach Bum Parade. Tybee Island's entire expanse of taupe sand is divided into three public beach stretches: North Beach, the Pier and Pavillion, and the south end. Beach activities abound, including swimming, boating, fishing, Jet Skiing, sea kayaking, and parasailing. Newer water sports have gained popularity, including kiteboarding and stand-up paddle boarding. ✉ *U.S. 80, 18 miles east of Savannah, Tybee Island* ☎ *800/868–2322* 🌐 *tybeeisland.com.*

**Tybee Island Lighthouse and Museum.** Well restored and considered one of North America's most beautifully renovated lighthouses, the Tybee Light Station has been guiding Savannah River mariners for more than 270 years. This is actually the fourth lighthouse on this site; the original was built on orders of General Oglethorpe in 1732. You can walk up 178 steps for amazing views at the top. The lighthouse keeper's cottage houses a small theater showing a video about the lighthouse. The nearby museum is housed in a gun battery constructed for the Spanish-American War. Check their website for information on the monthly Friday Sunset Tours. ✉ *30 Meddin Dr., Tybee Island*

*912/786–5801 www.tybeelighthouse.org $9 Daily 9–5:30, last tickets sold at 4:30*

# WHERE TO EAT

Southern cuisine is rich in tradition, but the dining scene in Savannah is more than just fried chicken and barbecue. Many of the city's restaurants have been exploring locally sourced ingredients as a way to tweak their usual homespun offerings, a change that is now attracting chefs and foodies alike. While the farm-to-table trend was first spotted at upscale spots like the Sapphire Grill, Cha Bella or Local 11Ten, more neighborhood restaurants are now getting in on the action. Places like the Green Truck Pub utilize locally raised, grass fed beef for their burgers, and after-dinner options now even include locally roasted coffee.

The arrival of some new kids on the block doesn't mean the old standbys have ridden off into the sunset just yet. For traditional, exquisitely prepared menus, be sure to visit Elizabeth's on 37th or the Olde Pink House, both of which have been pleasing local palates for decades. Or follow the crowds to either Paula Deen's famous Lady & Sons or the ever-popular Mrs. Wilkes' Dining Room (which even President Obama once visited), where you'll find all the fried chicken, collard greens, and mac 'n' cheese you can handle.

That's just a few ideas to get you started. While exploring Savannah, you're sure to find any number of other exciting options as well whether you're craving fresh sushi or a simple sandwich.

### HOURS, PRICES, AND DRESS

Most popular restaurants serve both lunch and dinner, usually until 8 or 9, later on Friday and Saturday nights. Sunday brunch is a beloved institution, but be prepared to wait for a table at most of the popular spots. Prices, although on the rise, are less than in most major cities, especially on either coast. *Prices in the reviews are the average cost of a main course at dinner or, if dinner is not served, at lunch.*

Some locals and restaurant owners have a laid-back attitude about dressing for a night out. And if you are hitting a River Street tourist restaurant, a small neighborhood eatery, or a barbecue joint, jeans are just fine. However, if you are going to an upscale restaurant, dress in keeping with the environment, especially on weekend nights.

*Use the coordinate (✣ B2) at the end of each listing to locate a site on the Where to Eat and Stay in Savannah map.*

10

## HISTORIC DISTRICT

$$ ECLECTIC ★ **B. Matthews Eatery.** The freshly updated and expanded kitchen here offers a great menu that ranges from familiar to unexpected. Breakfast (starting at 8) is a highlight, while lunch (until 3) is known as a great value, with most of their well-portioned sandwiches around $8. Few can resist the fried-green-tomato and black-eyed-pea cakes, served up with Cajun rémoulade and oregano aioli. Dinner entrées are more-upscale fare that won't break the ban, and the best bets include the inventive seafood

# BEST BETS FOR SAVANNAH DINING

**Fodor's Choice**

**Café 37**, p. 498
**Circa 1875**, p. 499
**Elizabeth on 37th**, p. 499
**Garibaldi's**, p. 499
**Green Truck Pub**, p. 504
**Leoci's Trattoria**, p. 500
**Local 11ten**, p. 501
**Mrs. Wilkes' Dining Room**, p. 501
**Olde Pink House**, p. 501
**Papillote**, p. 502
**Sapphire Grill**, p. 502
**Wiley's Championship BBQ**, p. 505

## By Price

**$**

**Vinnie VanGoGo's**, p. 504
**Wiley's Championship BBQ**, p. 505

**$$**

**B. Matthews Eatery**, p. 497
**Leoci's Trattoria**, p. 500
**Mrs. Wilkes Dining Room**, p. 501

**$$$**

**Cha Bella**, p. 498
**Olde Pink House**, p. 501

**$$$$**

**Elizabeth on 37th**, p. 499
**Sapphire Grill**, p. 502

## By Cuisine

SOUTHERN

**Elizabeth on 37th**, p. 499
**Mrs. Wilkes Dining Room**, p. 501
**Wiley's Championship BBQ**, p. 505

## By Experience

MOST ROMANTIC

**Elizabeth on 37th**, p. 499
**Planter's Tavern (Olde Pink House)**, p. 501
**Sapphire Grill**, p. 502

dishes and the divine braised lamb shank. *Average main: $19 ✉ 325 E. Bay St., Historic District ☎ 912/233–1319 🌐 www.bmatthewseatery.com ⏲ Brunch only on Sun. 10–3. No dinner Sun. ✣ D2.*

$$$ ECLECTIC  ★ **Café 37.** This small, unassuming spot is tucked away behind 37th Street @ Abercorn Antiques and Design store in the Thomas Square neighborhood. Although it's a bit outside the downtown Historic District, this little café is worth the trip, and for antiques shoppers it's a great place to grab lunch after checking out the wealth of antiques stores in the Victorian District (just south of the Historic District). Chef-owner Blake Elsinghorst is a Georgia boy who graduated from Le Cordon Bleu in Paris and, fittingly, his lunch menu runs the gamut from Southern contemporary (a pork sandwich with Gruyère cheese, champagne vinaigrette, and Dijon mustard on herbed sourdough) to French classics (crepes or escargot). Tip for the thrifty: small plates are served on Thursday evenings, so you can sample all the flavors at a lower price point. The artwork in the café is an oversized takeoff on Southern country landscapes and lends the place a fun and funky vibe. *Average main: $30 ✉ 205 E. 37th St., at Abercorn St., Thomas Square ☎ 912/236–8533 🌐 www.cafe37.com ⏲ No dinner Sun.–Wed. ✣ C6.*

$$$ AMERICAN ★ **Cha Bella.** "Organic is the only way," says chef-owner Matthew Roher, who does everything possible to conform his restaurant to this maxim by serving only the finest locally grown ingredients. Surrounding the outdoor seating, sheltered by a tin roof, you'll find an aromatic

herb garden; the restaurant also has two plots of land nearby where they grow much of their produce. The menu includes some excellent dishes, including amazing seafood and risottos, but it changes regularly based on what's fresh and available, so even if you've been there recently, there may be some new surprises waiting for you. A local, seared black grouper makes regular appearances with seasonal veggies, and is a definite highlight. Among recent additions are a delightful array of cocktail specialties, including the light and refreshing cucumber mojito. The interior decor is contemporary and comfortable. *Average main: $26* ✉ *102 E. Broad St., Historic District* ☎ *912/790–7888* 🌐 *www.cha-bella.com* *Closed Monday. No lunch* ✣ *D2.*

$$$ FRENCH Fodor's Choice ★ ✕ **Circa 1875.** The closest thing you can find to Parisian bistro dining in Georgia, this intimate gastropub has introduced Franco-fare to Savannah thanks to a menu rich in traditional dishes like the escargot and pâté starters, and the steak frites, ragout, and cassoulet entrées. Don't miss the mussels lovingly steeped in fennel, shallots, and white wine (and be sure to ask for extra bread to sop up the heavenly juice in the bowl). Trust the well-trained staff to suggest a wine pairing for your meal. Head next door to the adjacent bar either for an apertif after your meal or if you're in the mood for a late-night bite, as the kitchen stays open late for orders from the bar wing. *Average main: $24* ✉ *48 Whitaker St., Historic District* ☎ *912/443–1875* 🌐 *www.circa1875.com* *No lunch. Closed Sundays* ✣ *B2.*

$$$$ SOUTHERN Fodor's Choice ★ ✕ **Elizabeth on 37th.** Set within the Victorian District, this elegant turn-of-the-20th-century mansion has been feeding Savannah's upper crust for decades. Regional specialties are the hallmark at this acclaimed restaurant that goes so far as to credit local produce suppliers on its menu. Although original chef and owner Elizabeth Terry retired in 1996, Kelly Yambor has helmed the kitchen ever since, and she replicates the blue-crab cakes that sit comfortably beside Southern-fried grits and honey-roasted pork tenderloin with roasted shiitake and oyster mushrooms over dried tomatoes, black-eyed peas, and carrot ragout. Splurge for the chef's seven-course tasting menu; you won't regret it. Don't be afraid to ask for wine recommendations, because their wine cellar is massive, and the staff is knowledgeable. As might be imagined, service is impeccable. *Average main: $35* ✉ *105 E. 37th St., Thomas Square* ☎ *912/236–5547* 🌐 *www.elizabethon37th.net* *Reservations essential* *No lunch* ✣ *D6.*

$$$ ECLECTIC Fodor's Choice ★ ✕ **Garibaldi's.** This well-appointed restaurant is well known to locals and travelers alike for its contemporary cuisine. The original tin ceilings are a burnished gold, the bar and its fixtures are opulent, and the circular maple tables have leather booth seats. Renowned for their well-priced Italian classics, the kitchen also sends out some much more ambitious offerings, albeit at slightly higher prices. There are such unforgettable appetizers as lamb ribs slow-cooked with a sweet ginger sauce and pear-cabbage relish, or a salad with poached pear, arugula, walnuts, and goat-cheese fritters with a port-wine vinaigrette. The crispy flounder entrée is the stuff of local legend; the full fish presentation drizzled with apricot and shallot sauce is incredible. Have your knowledgeable and professional server offer wine pairings from the intelligent and

Forgo the buffet and try the delectable chicken pot pie from the à la carte menu at the Lady & Sons.

global wine cart. *Average main: $21 ✉ 315 W. Congress, Historic District ☎ 912/232–7118 ⊕ www.garibaldisavannah.com ⚠ Reservations essential ⊗ No lunch ↔ A2.*

$$$ SOUTHERN **✕ The Lady & Sons.** Put some South in your mouth! Expect to take your place in line simply to get reservations for either lunch or dinner because, y'all, this is the place that Paula Deen, high priestess of southern cooking, made famous. Alas, the quality can sometimes suffer because of the volume these days (locals will tell you that in the early days, when Paula was doing her own cooking, it was decidedly better). Nevertheless, everyone patiently waits to attack the buffet, which is stocked for both lunch and dinner with crispy fried chicken, mashed potatoes, collard greens, lima beans, and other Southern favorites. Peach cobbler and banana pudding round off the offerings. Although most fans jump on the buffet when their name is called, you can order off the menu, too. The fried green tomatoes are a great starter, and long-time fans vouch that the crab-cake burger at lunch or chicken pot pie or barbecue grouper at dinner are sometimes better than the buffet fixings. *Average main: $23 ✉ 102 W. Congress St., Historic District ☎ 912/233–2600 ⊕ www.ladyandsons.com ⚠ Reservations essential ⊗ No dinner Sun. ↔ A2.*

$$ ITALIAN Fodor's Choice ★ **✕ Leoci's Trattoria.** Chef Roberto Leoci learned his unique take on traditional Italian dishes the old-fashioned way, while spending time with his grandmother in Sicily. He worked behind the line at several prestigious spots around the Southeast before opening up this place, a block east of Forsyth Park. Although a little off the beaten path, Leoci's became an instant hit with local food fanatics. Few can resist the carpaccio starter or the beet salad with blue cheese and champagne tarragon vinaigrette.

The Bari Bari—orecchiette pasta tossed with broccoli and sausage—and the Fettucini Frutti di Mare are both great entrée choices (if you think there's no difference between fresh pasta and store-bought dry pasta, prepare to learn an important lesson). Save room for homemade gelato for dessert. The relatively small dining room is complemented by a large outdoor patio, which is great when the weather's nice. *$ Average main: $18 ✉ 606 Abercorn St., Historic District ☎ 912/335–7027 ⊕ www.leocis.com ✍ Reservations essential ✣ C5.*

$$$$
SOUTHERN
Fodor's Choice ★

**Local 11ten.** Light years away from the neighborhood watering hole, this stark, minimalist place looks like it was transported from a much bigger, more sophisticated city. That also goes for the upbeat and contemporary menu, another reason why several top young chefs in Savannah head here on their nights off. Seasonally driven, the menu is continually changing depending on the local harvest and the chef's vision but, regardless of availability, most dishes are perfectly prepared and presented. When available, the fried oyster salad, charcuterie selection, and venison medallions are highly recommended. Local has perfected their sea scallops, however prepared, but when served over black rice with pickled watermelon rind, they are as fantastic as they come. With dessert, take in the fine art installations on the walls, which rotate regularly to feature Savannah's talented creatives. *$ Average main: $29 ✉ 1110 Bull St., Historic District ☎ 912/790–9000 ⊕ www.local11ten.com ✍ Reservations essential ⊗ No lunch ✣ B6.*

$$
SOUTHERN
Fodor's Choice ★

**Mrs. Wilkes' Dining Room.** Locals can tell you that this is the city's best Southern cuisine, and when President Obama was visiting Savannah, he and his entourage had lunch here. Luckily, he didn't have to join the rest of the folks lined up around the corner to enjoy the orgy of fine Southern fare, served here family-style at big tables. It's been family-owned for decades, and the original Miz Wilkes really did run this historic home as a boarding house, serving three meals a day. These days, you can expect fried or roasted chicken, beef stew, collard greens, okra, mashed potatoes, macaroni and cheese, sweet-potato soufflé, and corn bread, with favorites like banana pudding for dessert. No alcohol is served, but you can get a lot of sweet tea. Mrs. Wilkes made this place somewhat of a legend, and her granddaughter and great-grandson are keeping it a family affair in more ways than one (kids under age 12 eat for half-price). *$ Average main: $18 ✉ 107 W. Jones St., Historic District ☎ 912/232–5997 ⊕ www.mrswilkes.com ✍ Reservations not accepted ▭ No credit cards ⊗ Closed weekends and Jan. No dinner ✣ B4.*

$$$
SOUTHERN
Fodor's Choice ★

**Olde Pink House.** This pink-brick Georgian mansion was built in 1771 for James Habersham, one of the wealthiest Americans of his time, and the historic atmosphere comes through in the original Georgia pine floors of the tavern, the Venetian chandeliers, and the 18th-century English antiques. Looking to contemporize a cherished landmark, the owners added a "new" dining room with vintage pine floors and walls. A lovely bar, The Arches, is adjacent with curvaceous doors that can open on balmy nights for outdoor seating. Expect great service and amazing food. The menu has no shortage of delicious choices, but some of the best-reviewed dishes are the simple items with a twist. How about a classic chicken potpie with roasted veggies, porcini cream sauce, and a sweet-potato biscuit? ■ **TIP→ If you want some the best ambience in Savannah, head downstairs to the Planter's Tavern, where the menu from upstairs is available, but in a more intimate space flanked by two large fireplaces and piano jazz.** *$ Average main: $26 ✉ 23 Abercorn St., Historic District ☎ 912/232–4286 ⏲ No lunch Sun. and Mon. ✥ C1.*

## MONEY-SAVING TIPS

Order a Visitor VIP Dining Club Card for culinary savings during your stay in the Big S. It's plastic, just like a credit card, and costs $29.95 for six months ($39.95 for 12 months). Some of the top restaurants are included in the list of more than 100 that honor the card. You might get a free appetizer or dessert, a bottle of wine, or a half-price entrée. Order the card online at 🌐 *www.savannahmenu.com*, or stop by Destination Savannah to purchase one after you arrive.

$ FRENCH Fodor's Choice ★

✕ **Papillote.** This quaint little bistro is a great place to grab something quick and delicious. Its focus is mostly to-go items, which makes it an amazing resource for a fresh picnic meal one of Savannah's parks and squares. The menu is divided between savory and sweet, so be ready to try at least one of each. The traditional French sandwich, the *croque monsieur,* is a great savory option that pairs salty ham with melted swiss with mouth-watering results. Finish it off with a selection of macarons, perfectly crisp and chewy in flavors like pistachio, lavender, and chocolate. Keep an eye out for a creative selection of daily specials as well. Don't miss their crepes specials at Sunday brunch. *$ Average main: $9 ✉ 218 W. Broughton St., Historic District ☎ 912/232–1881 🌐 www.papillote-savannah.com ✍ Reservations not accepted ⏲ Closed Mon. and Tues. ✥ A2.*

$$$$ AMERICAN Fodor's Choice ★

✕ **Sapphire Grill.** Savannah's foodies pack this trendy haunt with its surprisingly chic interior and artistic culinary creations. Downstairs, the decor is hip—think converted industrial loft—with gray brick walls alongside those painted a deep sapphire and a stone bar; upstairs is quieter and a little more romantic. Chef Chris Nason focuses his seasonal menus on local ingredients, such as Georgia white shrimp, crab, and fish prepared with care and creative flare. The Grill features succulent choices of steak, poultry, and fish, with myriad interesting à la carte accompaniments such as jalapeño tartar sauce, sweet soy-wasabi sauce, and lemongrass butter. The six-course chef's tasting menu, with fresh seafood and top-quality meats, is $100 and worth every penny. Chocoholics Alert: you will find your bliss in the miniature cocoa gâteau with lavender-almond ice cream. From the bar, the hand-muddled mojito is a thing of beauty and delicious fortitude. Don't forget that if you and, say, nine of your favorite people want to celebrate, reserve the private wine room on the third floor. *$ Average main: $33 ✉ 10 W. Congress St., Historic District ☎ 912/443–9962 🌐 www.sapphiregrill.com ✍ Reservations essential ⏲ No lunch ✥ B2.*

$ ECLECTIC ★

✕ **SoHo South Cafe.** Originally a mechanic's garage, then an art gallery and, finally, a restaurant, this spot shares aesthetic hallmarks of all its previous incarnations. Inside, the art gallery roots are still strong thanks to the eclectic collection of paintings and sculptures still on view (and available). But the food is the reason why people still make this a

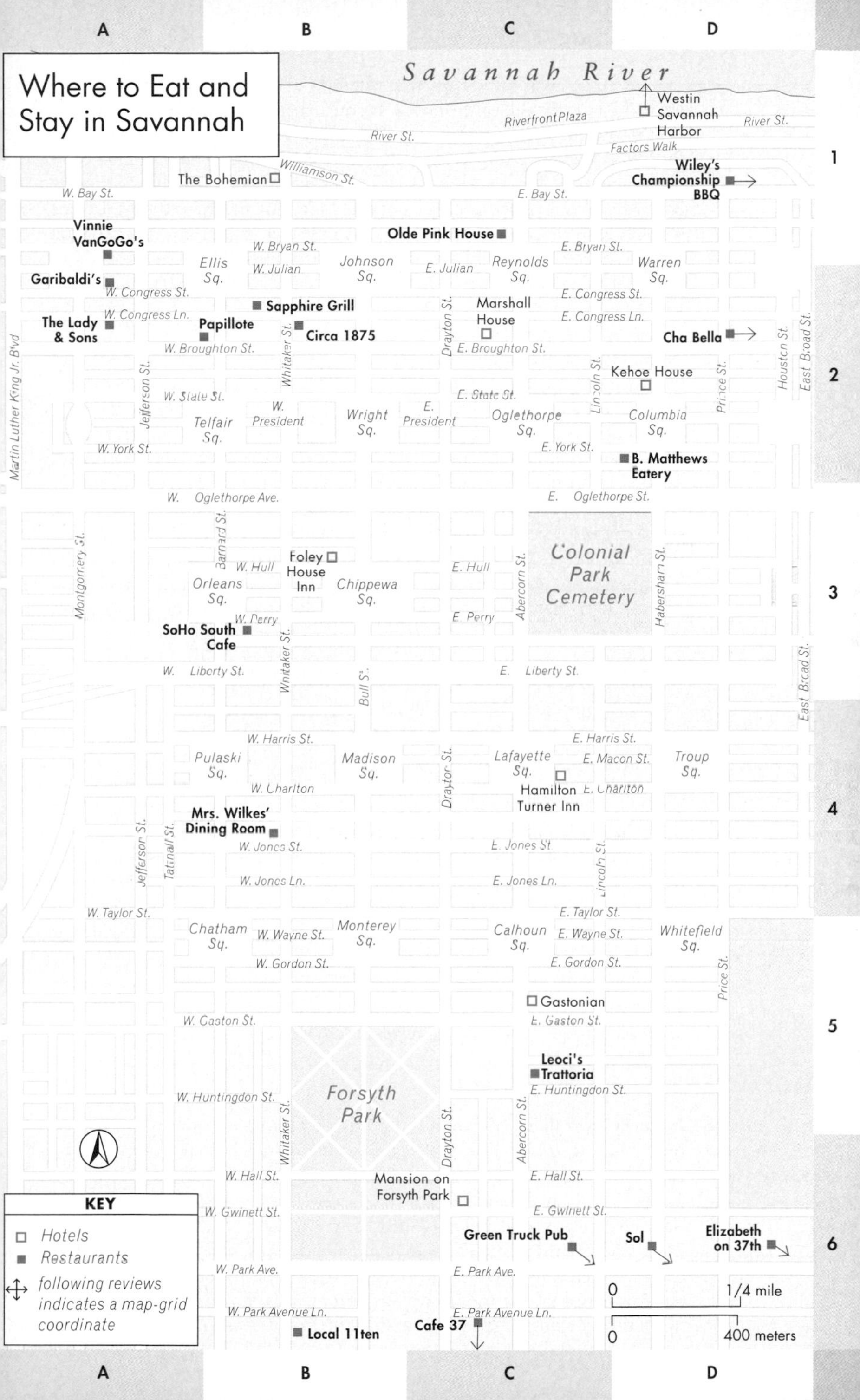

Where to Eat and Stay in Savannah
Savannah River
Westin Savannah Harbor
Riverfront Plaza
River St.
Factors Walk
Wiley's Championship BBQ
The Bohemian
Williamson St.
W. Bay St.
E. Bay St.
Vinnie VanGoGo's
Olde Pink House
Garibaldi's
W. Bryan St.
E. Bryan St.
Ellis Sq.
Johnson Sq.
Reynolds Sq.
Warren Sq.
W. Julian
E. Julian
W. Congress St.
E. Congress St.
Sapphire Grill
Marshall House
The Lady & Sons
W. Congress Ln.
E. Congress Ln.
Papillote
Circa 1875
Cha Bella
W. Broughton St.
E. Broughton St.
Kehoe House
W. State St.
E. State St.
Telfair Sq.
W. President
Wright Sq.
E. President
Oglethorpe Sq.
Columbia Sq.
W. York St.
E. York St.
B. Matthews Eatery
W. Oglethorpe Ave.
E. Oglethorpe St.
Foley House Inn
Colonial Park Cemetery
W. Hull
E. Hull
Orleans Sq.
Chippewa Sq.
W. Perry
E. Perry
SoHo South Cafe
W. Liberty St.
E. Liberty St.
W. Harris St.
E. Harris St.
Pulaski Sq.
Madison Sq.
Lafayette Sq.
E. Macon St.
Troup Sq.
W. Charlton
E. Charlton
Hamilton Turner Inn
Mrs. Wilkes' Dining Room
W. Jones St.
E. Jones St.
W. Jones Ln.
E. Jones Ln.
W. Taylor St.
E. Taylor St.
Chatham Sq.
W. Wayne St.
Monterey Sq.
Calhoun Sq.
E. Wayne St.
Whitefield Sq.
W. Gordon St.
E. Gordon St.
Gastonian
W. Gaston St.
E. Gaston St.
Leoci's Trattoria
W. Huntingdon St.
E. Huntingdon St.
Forsyth Park
W. Hall St.
E. Hall St.
Mansion on Forsyth Park
W. Gwinett St.
E. Gwinett St.
Green Truck Pub
Sol
Elizabeth on 37th
W. Park Ave.
E. Park Ave.
W. Park Avenue Ln.
E. Park Avenue Ln.
Local 11ten
Cafe 37
Martin Luther King Jr. Blvd
Montgomery St.
Jefferson St.
Tatnall St.
Barnard St.
Whitaker St.
Bull St.
Drayton St.
Abercorn St.
Lincoln St.
Habersham St.
Price St.
Houston St.
East Broad St.
0 1/4 mile
0 400 meters
KEY
Hotels
Restaurants
following reviews indicates a map-grid coordinate
A B C D
1 2 3 4 5 6

regular stop, with Sunday brunch being the most popular time of the week. Check out the salmon BLT if you're leaning toward lunch, or the sumptuous brioche French toast. The menu is playful at times, but never too experimental, and even picky eaters will find something to love here. The meat-loaf sandwich with Russian dressing, or the "Ultimate Roast Beef" sandwich are both best bets for lunchtime patrons, or opt for the signature tomato-basil bisque, a perfect accompaniment for the grilled cheese on sourdough with pimiento aioli. There's also a small but well-rounded selection of craft beers and wine. $ *Average main: $11* ✉ *12 W. Liberty St., Historic District* ☎ *912/233–1633* 🌐 *www.sohosouthcafe.com* ⏲ *No dinner* ✣ *B3.*

$ MEXICAN FUSION ★ ✕ **Sol.** Once a mechanic's garage, Sol occupies the charmed space that was formerly the local staple Queeny's Cafe. The dining room is mostly outdoors, which can present challenges during the more extreme summer and winter months, but it makes for a delightful dining experience during Savannah's many months of temperate weather. Enjoy an Asian-Latino fusion menu and affordable, gourmet specials with flair. Don't miss their salsa sampler served with their addicting homemade tortilla chips. The bahn-mi shrimp tacos are highly recommended, as is the skirt steak salad, served over a head of seared romaine lettuce. The bar pumps out some seriously tasty cocktails, including the Sol Punch and the best margarita in town. Opt for the spicy rendition, mixed up with jalapeño tequila that is steeped in-house starting each Monday; it gets spicier as the week goes on! $ *Average main: $10* ✉ *1611 Habersham St., Historic District* ☎ *912/232–1874* 🌐 *solfusionrestaurant.com* ⏲ *Closed Sun. and Mon.* ✣ *D6.*

$ PIZZA ✕ **Vinnie VanGoGo's.** With a secret dough recipe and homemade sauce, Vinnie's is critically acclaimed by pizza and calzone enthusiasts from around the Southeast, and was once featured on Paula Deen's TV show. The place has now been a revered local institution downtown for more than 20 years. There are only a few tables inside, along with a long stretch of stools at the bar. The heart of the restaurant is its plentiful outdoor seating, great for people-watching. Lots of visitors get a kick out of watching the cooks throw the dough in the air in the big open kitchen. Because of its prime City Market location, the wait for a table can be an hour or more, but you'll understand why with one bite of your pizza. $ *Average main: $12* ✉ *317 W. Bryan St., City Market* ☎ *912/233–6394* 🌐 *www.vinnievangogo.com* *Reservations not accepted* *No credit cards* ⏲ *No lunch Mon.–Thurs.* ✣ *A1.*

## ELSEWHERE IN SAVANNAH

$ VEGETARIAN Fodor's Choice ★ ✕ **Green Truck Pub.** Routinely voted as best burger in town and noted in a 2012 *Southern Living* for being one of the best in Georgia, this casual haunt is a burger joint redefined. Located in the remodeled skeleton of an old fast-food restaurant, Green Truck is widely patroned for its gourmet grassfed burgers and hearty meatless patties. Everything from coffee and beef to cheese and produce is sourced locally, and even the ketchup and veggie burgers are made in-house. Little wonder this is one of the most popular restaurants in town. **TIP→ At any given time, be prepared to wait at least 30 minutes for a table.** $ *Average*

Victorian homes in Savannah's Historic District.

*main: $10* ✉ *2430 Habersham St., Thomas Square* ☎ *912/234–5885* 🌐 *greentruckpub.com* ⏲ *Closed Sun. and Mon.* ✢ *C6.*

$ BARBECUE Fodor's Choice ★ **Wiley's Championship BBQ.** Tucked away in a strip mall on the way out to Tybee Island, this relative newcomer to the local BBQ scene has become an instant favorite with locals. The pulled pork is moist and flavorful, and the brisket is the best you'll find outside Texas. Try the BBQ sampler, which is enough to feed two people, and will let you sample just about everything they make. The small space is intimate and friendly and the staff is like long-lost family. There are only a few tables though, so you may have to choose between waiting for a seat and grabbing something to go. Be aware that Wiley's will close early if they run out of barbecue—so it doesn't hurt to show up early. $ *Average main: $13* ✉ *4700 U.S. Hwy. 80 E, Wilmington Island* ☎ *912/201–3259* 🌐 *www.wileyschampionshipbbq.com* *Reservations not accepted* ⏲ *Closed Sun.* ✢ *D1.*



## WHERE TO STAY

*Hotel reviews have been abbreviated in this book. For expanded reviews, please go to Fodors.com.*

Savannah is best known for its many inns and B&Bs, which have moved into the stately antebellum mansions, renovated cotton warehouses, and myriad other historic buildings stretching from the river out to the Victorian neighborhoods in the vicinity of Forsyth Park. Most are beautifully restored with the requisite high ceilings, ornate carved millwork, claw-foot tubs, and other quaint touches. Some stay in close touch with the past and do not offer televisions or telephones; others have mixed in the modern luxuries that many travelers have grown accustomed to, including flat-screen TVs, Wi-Fi, and upscale bath amenities. Oftentimes, Southern hospitality is served up in the form of evening wine-and-cheese socials, decadent breakfasts, and pillow-top pralines.

A flush of newer boutique hotels has shaken some of the dust out of Savannah's lodging scene and raised the bar for competing properties. Properties like the Bohemian, and the luxurious Mansion on Forsyth Park would be at home in a much larger city, but all have figured out how to introduce a sleek, cosmopolitan edge without bulldozing over Savannah's charm.

### HOTEL PRICES

The central location and relatively high standards of quality in Savannah's Historic District hotels do drive-up room rates, especially during peak seasons, holidays, and special events like St. Patrick's Day. The number of hotel rooms has doubled since 2000, and occupancy rates have grown accordingly, even in the former slow season from September through January. October is another relatively busy time thanks to the pleasant temperatures and packed events calendar. *Prices in the reviews are the lowest cost of a standard double room in high season.*

*Use the coordinate (✣ B2) at the end of each listing to locate a site on the Where to Eat and Stay in Savannah map.*

## HISTORIC DISTRICT

$$$$ HOTEL Fodor's Choice ★ **The Bohemian.** Clustered among River Street's commercial hustle and bustle but in a class of its own, this boutique hotel opened its doors in 2009 and proved to be a much-needed addition to Savannah's hotel landscape: you won't find the feminine, floral Victorian decor that's so prevalent in Savannah; a stay at the Bohemian is like settling into a gentleman's study in a regal English manse. **Pros:** river-view rooms offer lovely Savannah River vistas; upscale setting; pets under 80 pounds are allowed for a nonrefundable fee of $100; courtesy transportation to those amenities at the Bohemian's stunning sister property, the Mansion on Forsyth Park, and access to their spa. **Cons:** decor is a little over-the-top; the rooftop lounge stays open late, and the noise can sometimes be heard in guest rooms; proximity to River Street also means the occasional noise disturbance; not very kid-friendly. *Rooms from: $253* ✉ *102 W. Bay St., Historic District* ☎ *912/721–3800, 888/213–4024* 🌐 *www.bohemianhotelsavannah.com* *75 rooms* *No meals* ✣ *B1.*

$$$ B&B/INN ★ **Foley House Inn.** Set in an extremely central location in the Historic District, two town houses, built 50 years apart, form this elegant inn with stunning architecture and beautifully appointed accommodations, including four rooms with whirlpool tubs and three with balconies. **Pros:** pets of all breeds and sizes allowed for $50 cleaning fee; Aveda bath products; complimentary cocktails at night. **Cons:** no Wi-Fi in the carriage house; not wheelchair accessible; four floors but no elevator; fee for two-day parking pass ($12). *Rooms from: $249* ✉ *14 W. Hull St., Historic District* ☎ *912/232–6622, 800/647–3708* 🌐 *www.foleyinn.com* *19 rooms* *Breakfast* ✣ *B3.*

# BEST BETS FOR SAVANNAH LODGING

**Fodor's Choice**

**The Bohemian,** p. 506
**Gastonian,** p. 507
**Hamilton Turner Inn,** p. 507
**Kehoe House,** p. 507
**Mansion on Forsyth Park,** p. 508
**Marshall House,** p. 508
**Westin Savannah Harbor Golf Resort & Spa,** p. 508

## By Price

**$$$**

**Foley House Inn,** p. 506
**Gastonian,** p. 507
**Kehoe House,** p. 507
**Mansion on Forsyth Park,** p. 508

**$$$$**

**The Bohemian,** p. 506

## By Experience

**BEST HOTEL BARS**

**The Bohemian,** p. 506
**Mansion on Forsyth Park,** p. 508

**BEST FOR ROMANCE**

**Gastonian,** p. 507
**Kehoe House,** p. 507
**Mansion on Forsyth Park,** p. 508

**BEST B&BS**

**Gastonian,** p. 507
**Kehoe House,** p. 507

**BEST INTERIOR DESIGN**

**The Bohemian,** p. 506

**BEST LOCATION**

**Foley House Inn,** p. 506

$$$ B&B/INN Fodor's Choice ★

**Gastonian.** Guest rooms—many of which are exceptionally spacious—in this atmospheric Italianate inn, built in 1868, all have fireplaces and are decorated with a mix of funky finds and antiques from the Georgian and Regency periods and most have whirlpool tubs. **Pros:** cordial and caring staff; hot breakfast; afternoon tea, and wine and cheese at night. **Cons:** accommodations on the third floor are a hike; some of the furnishings are less than regal. *Rooms from: $200 ✉ 220 E. Gaston St., Historic District ☎ 912/232–2869, 800/322–6603 ⊕ www.gastonian.com 15 rooms, 2 suites Breakfast ✧ C5.*

10

$$$ B&B/INN Fodor's Choice ★

**Hamilton-Turner Inn.** With bathrooms the size of New York City apartments, this French-Empire mansion is celebrated, if not in song, certainly in story, and certainly has a "wow" effect, especially the rooms that front Lafayette Square. **Pros:** the carriage house is the most private room, though not as atmospheric; pets are allowed in the four brick-walled, ground-level rooms ($50 deposit). **Cons:** sedate, not for young kids or party types; no guest elevator (except for accessible Room 201) and some rooms are on the fourth floor; street parking only (at a charge). *Rooms from: $239 ✉ 330 Abercorn St., Historic District ☎ 912/233–1833, 888/448–8849 ⊕ www.hamilton-turnerinn.com 11 rooms, 6 suites, 1 carriage house Breakfast ✧ C4.*

$$$ B&B/INN Fodor's Choice ★

**Kehoe House.** Widely considered one of the better B&B choices in Savannah given the high-class accommodations and remarkably friendly and attentive staff, this handsomely appointed house, dating from the 1890s, was originally the family manse of William Kehoe. **Pros:** made-to-order Southern breakfast; afternoon tea and desserts, and an evening wine and hors d'oeuvres reception; B&B is wheelchair accessible, with two elevators. **Cons:** only one king or queen bed per room; a few rooms have the sink and shower in the room, separated by drapes; soundproofing in guest rooms could be better. *Rooms from: $229* ✉ *123 Habersham St., Historic District* ☎ *912/232–1020, 800/820–1020* 🌐 *www.kehoehouse.com* *13 rooms* *Breakfast* ✣ *D2.*

**BREAKFAST INCLUDED**

When you are trying to decide on what kind of accommodation to reserve in Savannah, consider that B&Bs include breakfast (sometimes a lavish one), complimentary wine and cheese nightly, and even free bottled water. Hotels, particularly the major ones, usually do not even give you a small bottle of water.

$$$ HOTEL Fodor's Choice ★ **Mansion on Forsyth Park.** Sitting on the edge of Forsyth Park, this Kessler property has dramatic design, opulent interiors with a contemporary edge, and a magnificently diverse collection of some 400 pieces of American and European art, all of which create a one-of-a-kind experience—sophisticated, chic, and artsy only begin to describe it. **Pros:** an exciting, stimulating environment that transports you from the workaday world; full-service spa; complimentary shuttle to fellow downtown Kessler hotel, The Bohemian, on River Street. **Cons:** very pricey, particularly for room service and phone calls; some of the art from the early 1970s is not appealing. *Rooms from: $239* ✉ *700 Drayton St., Historic District* ☎ *888/213–3671, 912/238–5158* 🌐 *www.mansiononforsythpark.com* *125 rooms* *No meals* ✣ *C6.*

$$ B&B/INN Fodor's Choice ★ **Marshall House.** This restored hotel, with original pine floors, woodwork, exposed brick, and swanky rooms featuring flat-screen TVs and work desks, caters to business travelers as well as families, yet it provides the intimacy of a B&B. **Pros:** great location near stores and restaurants; exceptional restaurant on-site; balconies offer great bird's-eye views of Broughton Street. **Cons:** no free parking; no room service; the sounds of bustling Broughton Street can be noisy. *Rooms from: $179* ✉ *123 E. Broughton St., Historic District* ☎ *912/644–7896, 800/589–6304* 🌐 *www.marshallhouse.com* *65 rooms, 3 suites* *Breakfast* ✣ *C2.*

## ELSEWHERE IN SAVANNAH

$$$ RESORT Fodor's Choice ★ **Westin Savannah Harbor Golf Resort & Spa.** Within its own fiefdom, this major high-rise property with more resort amenities than any other property in the area—including tennis courts, a full-service spa, and a golf course—presides over small Hutchinson Island, five minutes by water taxi from River Street and just a short drive over the Talmadge Bridge. **Pros:** outdoor pool is heated and boasts a great view of River Street; dreamy bedding; great program of kids activities throughout the week. **Cons:** you are close, but still removed, from downtown; this is a major chain hotel, not an atmospheric, historic inn; hotel charges an expensive and annoying resort fee. *Rooms from: $199* ✉ *1 Resort Dr., Hutchinson Island* ☎ *912/201–2000, 800/937–8461* 🌐 *www.westinsavannah.com* *390 rooms, 13 suites* *No meals* ✣ *D1.*

Bluegrass legends, the Del McCoury Band play at the Savannah Music Festival.

## TYBEE ISLAND

$ RENTAL **Tybee Vacation Rentals.** If renting a five-star beach house, a pastel island cottage, or a waterfront condo in a complex with a pool and tennis courts is your coastal-Georgia dream stay, check out Tybee Vacation Rentals. *Rooms from: $129* *1010 Hwy. 80 E, Tybee Island* *912/786–5853, 866/359–0297* *www.tybeevacationrentals.com* *10+ properties* *Mon.–Sat. 9–6, Sun. 10–4.*

# NIGHTLIFE AND THE ARTS



As the old saying goes, "In Atlanta, they ask you what you do. In Macon, they ask what church you go to. And in Savannah, they ask you what you drink." Congress Street and River Street have the highest concentrations of bars with live music, especially if you're looking for rock, heavy metal, or the blues. Many of the most popular dance clubs are scattered across the same area. If you're in the mood for something more sedate, there are plenty of chic enclaves known for their creative cocktails and cozy nooks that encourage intimate conversation.

## THE ARTS

### FESTIVALS AND SPECIAL EVENTS

Fodor's Choice ★ **Savannah Music Festival.** Georgia's largest and most acclaimed musical arts festival, the Savannah Music Festival brings together musicians and music lovers from around the world for more than two weeks' worth of unforgettable performances. The multigenre entertainment ranges from foot-stomping gospel to moody blues to classical to mainstream rock. Performances take place in Savannah's premier music venues, as well as nontraditional venues like area churches, industrial spaces, and even the rotunda of the Telfair Museum of Art. Festival honcho Rob Gibson spent several years with Jazz at Lincoln Center, so there is no shortage of amazing jazz players. ✉ *Downtown* 🌐 *www.savannahmusicfestival.org*.

**St. Patrick's Day Parade.** The city's largest annual festival has evolved over the past two centuries to be one of the largest of its kind in the country. Each March, roughly 700,000 participants tip their hats (and their glasses) to the rolling hills of Ireland. Though they no longer color the river itself, River Street is a sea of green; clothing, beer, food, and even the water in city fountains is dyed the color of the clover. ■ **TIP→** Hotel rates during this period can be as much as three times the norm, that is if you can get a room (most are reserved well in advance). 🌐 *www.savannahsaintpatricksday.com*.

## NIGHTLIFE

### THE HISTORIC DISTRICT

#### BARS AND PUBS

★ **Lulu's Chocolate Bar.** This laid-back spot invites you to indulge your sweet tooth. When you walk through the door, you're immediately greeted by the dessert case, full of freshly baked specialties. Try some of the homemade truffles. The menu also includes a spectacular list of specialty drinks, including delectable champagne cocktails, alongside a modest selection of beers and wines. ✉ *42 Martin Luther King Jr. Blvd., Historic District* ☎ *912/238–2012* 🌐 *www.luluschocolatebar.net*.

**Moon River Brewing Company.** The longstanding lone microbrewery in town since 1999, Moon River occupies a multilevel historic building on Bay Street that once served as the City Hotel and later as a lumber and coal warehouse. Check out the amazing variety of handcrafted lagers, ales, and wheat beers, compliments of award-winning brewmaster John Pinkerton. Pinkerton monitors the large steel vats of beer, which you can see through the glass partition. Soak up the first few rounds with a good variety of pub food. ✉ *21 W. Bay St., Historic District* ☎ *912/447–0943* 🌐 *www.moonriverbrewing.com*.

**Pinkie Masters.** It might not be the oldest bar in Savannah, but Pinkie Masters could be the most historically significant. This dive bar's biggest claim to fame is that Georgia's own Jimmy Carter stood up on the bar to announce that he would run for president. Photos of Southern politicians and public figures adorn the walls. Under new management, onetime regulars have complained of increased prices and a different vibe, but newer patrons seem to appreciate the upgrades and sprucing. ✉ *318 Drayton St., Lafayette Sq., Historic District* ☎ *912/238–0447*.

Fodor's Choice ★ **Planters Tavern.** Lighted by flickering candles, the Planters Tavern, in the basement of the Olde Pink House, is one of Savannah's most romantic late-night spots. There's a talented piano player setting the mood, two stone fireplaces, and an array of fox-hunt memorabilia. The upstairs menu is available, with the same quality of service but a slightly less formal approach. ■ TIP→ There is only a handful of tables and they fill up fast. ✉ *23 Abercorn St., Historic District* ☎ *912/232–4286.*

Fodor's Choice ★ **Rocks on the Roof.** Located on the top floor of the trendy Bohemian Hotel, this rooftop bar offers some of the city's best sunset and river views. Taking full advantage of Savannah's beautiful weather, the north and south walls of the bar open onto well-appointed outdoor areas with comfortable seating. The bar serves a limited menu that includes pizzas, sandwiches, and a cheese plate. ✉ *102 W. Bay St., Historic District* ☎ *912/721–3901* 🌐 *www.bohemianhotelsavannah.com.*

★ **Sparetime.** This highly anticipated bar opened its doors in 2012 to an enthusiastic reception by locals familiar with owner Clara Fishel's past successful establishments. Sparetime is a classy, minimalist space with local fine art and careful attention to details. The cocktail and bites menus are alike in the limited, yet finely crafted, selections. Try the house gin or one of their popular rye drinks. The arugula and prosciutto flatbread pizza is particularly delightful with a fried egg on top. Don't miss an opportunity to dance with the crowd on a DJ night. ✉ *36 Martin Luther King Jr. Blvd., at Congress St., Historic District* ☎ *912/232–7094* 🌐 *sparetimesavannah.com* ⊙ *Closed Sun.*

#### GAY AND LESBIAN

**Club One.** This gay bar wins praise from locals as one of the city's best dance clubs. The notorious Lady Chablis (famous for her role in *Midnight in the Garden of God and Evil*) makes appearances here, lip-synching disco tunes, shimmering in sequins, and bumping and grinding her way down the catwalk. ✉ *1 Jefferson St., Historic District* ☎ *912/232–0200* 🌐 *www.clubone-online.com.*

#### LIVE MUSIC CLUBS

**Casimir Lounge.** This sleek nightspot regularly features live jazz and blues—keep an eye out for local favorites like vocalist Roger Moss. The decor is luxe, albeit somewhat over the top. There's a great balcony on the side where you can have a drink while enjoying a view of the park. ✉ *Mansion on Forsyth Park, 700 Drayton St., Historic District* ☎ *912/721–5002* 🌐 *www.mansiononforsythpark.com/700drayton/casimirs.asp* ⊙ *Closed Sun.–Tues.*



## SPORTS AND THE OUTDOORS

The area around Savannah and the barrier islands of the Lowcountry is conducive to nearly all types of water sports. The waters of Savannah are generally warm enough for swimming from May through September. For those who would prefer to stay on land, bicycling, jogging, golf, tennis, Ultimate Frisbee, and arena sports dominate.

### BEACHES

**Pier and Pavilion.** This is Tybee's "grand strand," the center of the summer beach action. Anchored by a 700-foot pier that is sometimes host to summer concerts, this stretch of shoreline is your best bet for people-watching and beach activities. Just off the sand at the bustling

Tybee Island's 700-foot pier plays host to summer concerts.

intersection of Tybrisa Street and Butler Avenue, a cluster of watering holes, souvenir shops, bike shacks, and oyster bars makes up Tybee's main business district. Parking is not quite as plentiful as North Beach, but there is metered street parking as well as two good-size lots. ■ **TIP→ Both fill up fast during the high season, so arrive early.** There are public restrooms at the Pier and at 15th and Tybrisa streets. The pier is popular for fishing and is also the gathering place for fireworks displays. **Amenities:** food and drink, lifeguard, parking (fee), toilets. **Best for:** partiers, sunrise, surfing, swimming. ✉ *Tybrisa St. at Butler Ave., Tybee Island.*

## BIKING

Savannah is table-flat, perfect for biking. Forsyth and Daffin parks are favored by locals. Rails-to-Trails, a 3-mile route, starts 1 mile east of the Bull River Bridge on Highway 80 and ends at the entrance to Fort Pulaski. Tom Triplett Park, east of town on U.S. 80, offers three bike loops—3.5 miles, 5 miles, and 6.3 miles.

**Bicycle Link.** Rent single-speed beach cruisers for $20 for a full day or $40 for three days. The shop provides helmets, locks, and trailers that will hold one child. A deposit of $150 is required, and all major credit cards are accepted. The shop will sometimes pick up and deliver to the inns, but they prefer that customers pick up bikes at the shop. ✉ *210 W. Victory Dr.* ☎ *912/233–9401* 🌐 *www.bicyclelinksav.com* ⏲ *Mon.–Sat. 10–6.*

★ **Motorini.** See the sights of Savannah aboard a Vespa—a fun, stylish, and efficient transportation alternative. Motorini rents Piaggio scooters, an iconic Italian company that includes Vespas among their classic fleet. Rates start at $30 for the first hour; overnight rental is $90. ✉ *236 Drayton St., Historic District* ☎ *912/201–1899* 🌐 *www.vespasavannah.com* ⏲ *Daily 10–6.*

## BOATING AND FISHING

**Miss Judy Charters.** Captain Judy Helmey, a longtime fishing guide and legendary local character, heads up Miss Judy Charters, which provides packages ranging from 4-hour sightseeing tours to 16-hour deep-sea fishing expeditions. Inshore rates start at around $350 for two people for four hours; offshore rates start at $500 for up to six people for four hours. ✉ *124 Palmetto Dr., Wilmington Island* ☎ *912/897–4921* 🌐 *www.missjudycharters.com.*

**North Island Surf & Kayak.** North Island Surf & Kayak has sit-on-top kayaks that are virtually unsinkable. Stable and safe on inland rivers, they allow you to navigate the shallowest of creeks where no other boats can go. You can put in at the company's floating dock or launch wherever you want. All rentals include paddles, lifejackets, and seat backs. Prices are $40 per day for a single, $55 for a double. For $5 you can rent a "dry bag" to stow your important items while you kayak. Paddle to the beautiful uninhabited island of Little Tybee or to Cockspur Beacon. If you've always wanted to learn how to surf, $50 will get you a board rental and a one-hour lesson. ✉ *1C Old Hwy. 80, Tybee Island* ☎ *912/786–4000* 🌐 *www.northislandkayak.com.*

## GOLF

Fodor's Choice ★ **The Club at Savannah Harbor.** Savannah's only PGA course, this is the resort property of the Westin Savannah Harbor resort on Hutchinson Island, a free ferry ride from Savannah's riverfront. The lush championship course winds through pristine wetlands and has unparalleled views of the river and downtown Savannah. It is also home to the annual Liberty Mutual Legends of Golf tournament, which attracts golfing's finest each spring. A bit pricier than most local clubs, it's packed with beauty and amenities. ✉ *2 Resort Dr., Hutchinson Island* ☎ *912/201–2007* 🌐 *www.theclubatsavannahharbor.com* *Reservations essential* *18 holes. 7288 yds. Par 72. Green Fee: $95–$170 (seasonal)* ☞ *Facilities: Driving range, putting green, pitching area, golf carts, rental clubs, pro shop, lessons, restaurant, bar.*

10

# SHOPPING

You would have to make a concerted effort to leave Savannah empty-handed. Whether you're on a quest for designer clothing or handmade candy, Savannah offers up a potent dose of shopping therapy on a silver platter.

## SHOPPING DISTRICTS

**Broughton Street.** Savannah's "main street" has long served as a shopping and social hub, and so an indicator of the changing economic and demographical trends over the city's history. The first of Savannah's department stores, Adler's and Levy's, emerged on Broughton, followed by the post-WWII introduction of national chains Sears & Roebuck, JCPenney, and Kress. During the 1950s, ladies donning white gloves and heels did their shopping, while kids gathered at the soda counter or caught the matinee. Downtown's decline began in the late 1950s and continued through the '70s, during which time for-sale signs and boarded-up storefronts were the norm rather than the exception. Today, Broughton is again thriving, not only with local boutiques and world-class shops, but with theaters, restaurants, and coffeehouses. A handful of new and renovated storefronts open for business each year, as the retail thoroughfare continues to reemerge. *Vogue*'s annual Fashion's Night Out, a grand fete for retailers that takes place in early September, began here in 2011. Broughton closes to vehicle traffic for the premier event; highlights include a series of in-street runway shows and concert performances. ✉ *Between Congress and State Sts., Historic District.*

**City Market.** Originally Savannah's farmers' market in the 1700s, City Market is a four-block, pedestrian-friendly emporium that has seen a magnificent renaissance. The area contains an eclectic and concentrated mix of artists' studios, sidewalk cafés, bars, shops, and art galleries. On weekends, the sounds of live music drift throughout the market. City Market is also ground zero for trolley and horse-carriage tours. ✉ *W. St. Julian St. between Ellis and Franklin Sqs., Historic District* ☎ *912/232–4903* 🌐 *www.savannahcitymarket.com.*

**Downtown Design District.** Renowned for its array of the city's finest antiques shops and interior design boutiques, the Downtown Design District is worth a visit. Stop in some of Savannah's trendier fashion stores housed in charming historic storefronts. Nearby are the famed Mercer-Williams House and the landmark Mrs. Wilkes' Dining Room for some of the area's best family-style Southern food. ✉ *Whitaker St. between Charlton and Gaston Sts., Historic District.*

## THE HISTORIC DISTRICT

### ANTIQUES

Fodor's Choice ★ **Alex Raskin Antiques.** This shop is located inside the Noble Hardee Mansion, a gilded, four-story Italianate home. You can wander through almost all 12,000 square feet of the former grand residence and see how Savannah's gentry once lived. The building is a bit musty, with peeling wallpaper and patches of leaky ceiling, but the antiques within are in great condition and represent a colorful scrapbook of Savannah's past. They specialize in furniture, rugs, and paintings, but take note of more rare artifacts like tramp art frames and antique doll furniture. Be sure to take in the view of Forsyth Park from one of the upper-level porches. ✉ *441 Bull St., Historic District* ☎ *912/232–8205* 🌐 *www.alexraskinantiques.com* ⏲ *Mon.–Sat. 10–5.*

### BOOKS

**"The Book" Gift Shop and Midnight Museum.** Paying dutiful homage to John Berendt's novel *Midnight in the Garden of Good and Evil,* this shop, affectionately termed "The Book," offers souvenirs related to that best seller, autographed copies of the novel, and reproductions of the iconic "Bird Girl" statue. **TIP→** For a more behind-the-scenes look at the best-seller, take one of the daily bus or walking tours from the shop. ✉ *127 E. Gordon St., Historic District* ☎ *912/233–3867* 🌐 *www.midnightinsavannah.com* ⏲ *Mon.–Sat. 10:30–5, Sun. 12:30–4.*

Fodor's Choice ★ **E. Shaver Booksellers.** Among the most beloved bookshops in town, E. Shaver is the source for 17th- and 18th-century maps and new books on regional subjects, as well as books on local history, recipes, artists, and authors. This shop occupies 12 rooms of a historic building, which alone is something to see. The booksellers are welcoming and knowledgeable about their wares. ✉ *326 Bull St., Historic District* ☎ *912/234–7257* 🌐 *eshaverbooks.com* ⏲ *Mon.–Sat. 9:30–5:30.*

### CLOTHING

**ARC.** Opened in 2012, ARC has quickly made a name for itself. The curated boutique offers men's and women's vintage and designer clothing and accessories, leather goods, and specialty books and stationery. Store merchandise is as meticulously displayed as it is selected. The space is aesthetically minimalist yet inviting. Oddities pop up along well-organized shelves of high-end, apothecary-influenced bath and beauty products. ✉ *320 W. Broughton St., Historic District* ☎ *912/721–7745* ⏲ *Mon.–Sat. 11–7, Sun. noon–6.*

**James Hogan.** Savannah's resident fashion designer and his shop, tucked in a storefront in the Historic District, have brought a touch of glamour to the city. Featured here is apparel designed by Hogan himself, as well as upscale women's fashions from well-regarded American and European designers like Etro and Charles Chang Lima. ✉ *412B Whitaker St., Historic District* ☎ *912/234–0374* 🌐 *www.jameshogan.com* ⏲ *Weekdays 10–5:30, Sat. 10–5, Sun. noon–4.*

**Red Clover.** This shop is the place to be if you want fashionable and affordable apparel, shoes, and handbags. They feature sharp looks from indie and local designers alike, all at under $100. It's a great place to search for gifts and jewelry, too. Visit their online boutique for a quick peek at this season's best looks. ✉ *244 Bull St., Historic District* ☎ *912/236–4053* 🌐 *www.shopredclover.com* ⏲ *Mon.–Sat. 10:30–6, Sun. noon–5.*



### FOOD

Fodor's Choice ★ **Savannah Bee Company.** Local Ted Dennard's Savannah Bee Company has been featured in such national magazines as *O, Vogue, InStyle,* and *Newsweek*, and with good reason—the locally cultivated honey and bath products are simply wonderful. You can sample and buy multiple varieties of honey, including Tupelo, Acacia, and raw honeycombs. Don't miss the hot and fresh biscuits and honey, as well as decadent honey lattes, which were recently featured on the Travel Channel. Though there is a new location on River Street, be sure to stop in their flagship store on Broughton Street. Children enjoy the life-size bee hive.

✉ *104 W. Broughton St., Historic District* ☎ *912/233–7873* 🌐 *www.savannahbee.com* 🕐 *Mon.–Sat. 10–7, Sun. 11–5.*

### GIFTS

Fodor's Choice ★ **ShopSCAD.** The recently renovated ShopSCAD sells amazing works by faculty, alumni, and students of Savannah College of Art and Design, including handcrafted jewelry, clothing, furniture, glasswork, and original postcards. Handmade and hand-dyed silk accessories are cutting edge, as are the original fashion pieces and experimental purses by design students. Just remember that these originals do not come cheap. ✉ *340 Bull St., Historic District* ☎ *912/525–5180* 🌐 *www.shopscadonline.com* 🕐 *Weekdays 9–5:30, Sat. 10–5:30, Sun. noon–5.*

### HOME FURNISHINGS

Fodor's Choice ★ **The Paris Market & Brocante.** A Francophile's dream from the time you open the antique front door and take in the intoxicating aroma of lavender, this two-story emporium with chandeliers and other lighting fixtures is a classy reproduction of a Paris flea market, selling furniture, vintage art, garden planters and accessories, and home fashions like boudoir items and bedding. Although the store will ship, there are numerous treasures that can be easily carried away, like soaps, candles, vintage jewelry, kitchen and barware, and dried lavender. ✉ *36 W. Broughton St., Historic District* ☎ *912/232–1500* 🌐 *www.theparismarket.com* 🕐 *Mon.–Sat. 10–6, Sun. noon–5.*

### SHOES, HANDBAGS, AND LEATHER GOODS

Fodor's Choice ★ **Satchel.** As featured in *Southern Living*, Satchel is an artisan leather studio and shop owned by Elizabeth Seegar, a New Orleans native and graduate of the Savannah College of Art and Design. The store specializes in handmade and custom leather clutches, handbags, travel bags, and accessories and offers a wide selection of leathers to choose from, including metallics, python, embossed alligator, and cork. At lower price points are their sharp and handy beverage cozies, cuff bracelets, and wallets. ✉ *311 W. Broughton St., Historic District* ☎ *912/233–1008* 🌐 *shopsatchel.com* 🕐 *Mon.–Sat. 10–6.*

## ELSEWHERE IN SAVANNAH

### FOOD

**Byrd Cookie Company & Gourmet Marketplace.** Founded in 1924, this shop sells picture tins of Savannah and gourmet foodstuffs such as condiments and dressings. Their newly renovated gift shop is the best place to get benne wafers ("the seed of good luck") and trademark Savannah cookies, notably key lime, and other house-made crackers. Free samples of all are available. As this is a drive, look for their products in numerous gift shops around town. ✉ *6700 Waters Ave., Southside* ☎ *912/355–1716* 🌐 *www.byrdcookiecompany.com.*

# Georgia's Coastal Isles and the Okefenokee

## WORD OF MOUTH

"Jekyll Island is a state park and one of which Georgia can be rightly proud. It has the most excellent bike paths, all off road, all flat as a board and most paved. It could not be more friendly to biking."

—cmcfong

# WELCOME TO GEORGIA'S COASTAL ISLES AND THE OKEFENOKEE

## TOP REASONS TO GO

★ **Saltwater marshes:** Fringing the coastline, waist-high grasses transform both sunlight and shadow with their lyrical textures and shapes.

★ **Geechee culture:** Vestiges of Georgia's Black Republic, an independent state of freed slaves established on the barrier islands in the mid-19th century, remain at the Sapelo Island settlement of Hog Hammock.

★ **Horses of Cumberland:** Some 200 feral horses, descendants of horses abandoned by the Spanish in the 1500s, roam the wilderness of Cumberland Island.

★ **Jekyll Island:** Originally the exclusive winter retreat of America's exceptionally rich, this village of mansion-size "cottages" is now open to all.

★ **Go for a ride:** Jekyll Island has 20 miles of paved bike paths that traverse salt marshes, maritime forests, beaches, and the island's National Historic Landmark District.

**1 Sapelo Island.** Reachable only by ferry from Meridien, less developed Sapelo is a protected state wildlife preserve and home to the Geechee, direct descendants of freed African slaves. You must have a reservation for a day tour or to camp or stay at one of the island's small hotels in order to take the ferry over.

**2 Little St. Simons Island.** Little St. Simons, a private island with accommodations for a limited number of overnight guests and day-trippers, is accessible by private launch from the northern end of St. Simons.

**3 Sea Island.** One of the wealthiest private communities in the United States, Sea Island is accessible only to residents and guests at the Cloister, the island's swanky resort hotel.

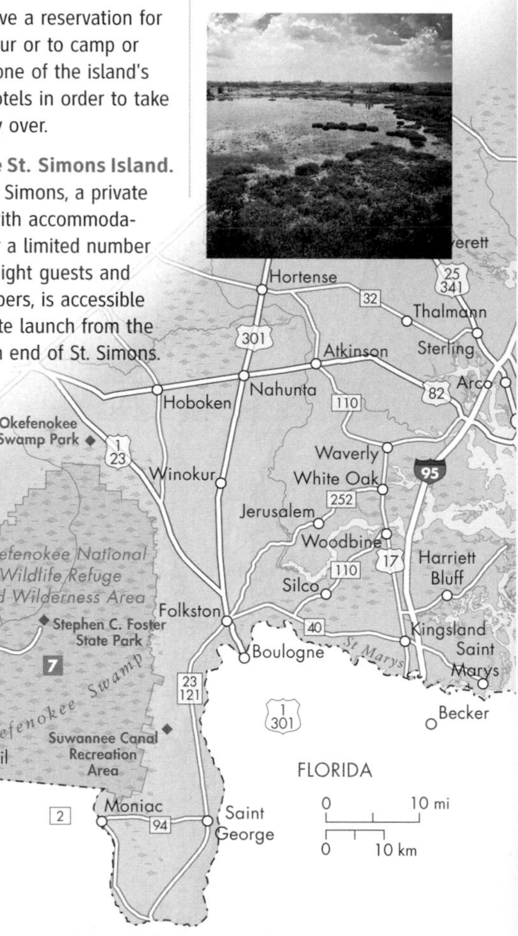

**4 St. Simons Island.** The most developed of the Golden Isles is a well-rounded vacation destination with a variety of hotels and restaurants in varying price ranges.

**5 Jekyll Island.** Once the playground for the rich and famous, Jekyll is now more egalitarian. Its pristine beaches are uncommercialized and open to all, and the range of resorts and restaurants appeals to a wide range of travelers.

**6 Cumberland Island.** Reachable only by ferry, this virtually pristine island is a national seashore and has only one accommodation (a former Carnegie family mansion) and a few campgrounds.

**7 Okefenokee National Wildlife Range.** The Okefenokee is a mysterious world where, as a glance at a map will indicate, all roads disappear. A large, interior wetland navigable only by boat, it can be confusing and intimidating to the uninitiated. None of the individual parks within the area give a sense of the total Okefenokee experience—each has its own distinct natural features. Choose the park that best aligns with your interests and begin there.

## GETTING ORIENTED

Coastal Georgia is a complex jigsaw wending its way from the ocean and tidal marshes inland along the intricate network of rivers. U.S. 17, the old coastal highway, gives you a taste of the slower, more rural South. But because of the subtropical climate, the lush forests tend to be dense along the mainland, and there are few opportunities to glimpse the broad vistas of salt marsh and islands. To truly appreciate the mystique of Georgia's coastal salt marshes and islands, make the 40-minute ferry crossing from Meridian to Sapelo Island.

# GEORGIA'S COASTAL ISLES BEACHES

Remote and largely untouched, the beaches on Georgia's barrier islands sit at the confluence of rich salt marshes and the Atlantic Ocean. Nature-watching on foot or by canoe or kayak is the biggest draw, with dolphins, manatees, nesting sea turtles, more than 300 bird species, and much more found along these shores.

(above) Enjoy a sunset stroll on Georgia's remote beaches. (lower right) Bring your camera to Driftwood Beach—the downed trees make great photo-ops. (upper right) Wild horses roam Cumberland Island.

Of all the islands, only two—Jekyll and St. Simons—have undergone significant development. East Beach on St. Simons has the most facilities and is the place to go for sunbathing, swimming, and water sports, while Jekyll's beaches are both accessible and uncrowded. Driftwood Beach, at Jekyll's northern end, is arguably the most picturesque beach on the coast, and dolphins frolic off St. Andrews Beach, at the island's southern tip. Exploring the farther-flung beaches of Sapelo or Cumberland islands requires advance planning and a ferry ride, as both are protected parklands and access is limited. Beachcombing is especially good here.

—Travis Marshall

## BEACH CAMPING

Experience the solitude and rich wildlife of Georgia's beaches by pitching a tent right on the shore. Cumberland Island has wonderful camping, with standard campgrounds as well as backcountry campsites that can be reached only by hiking trails 5½ to 10½ miles from the ferry dock. There are no stores on the island, so bring all necessary food and supplies. Camping costs $2 to $4 per night; reservations are recommended.

## GEORGIA'S COASTAL ISLES BEST BEACHES

### NANNY GOAT BEACH (SAPELO ISLAND)

Used as an outdoor classroom by the Sapelo Island National Estuarine Research Reserve, this remote beach, accessible only by boat, offers ample beachcombing and wildlife-watching opportunities. Look for sand dollars and conch shells on its 2 miles of sandy shore while pelicans and osprey fish among the shallows, or bring a seine net to dip for shrimp and crabs. Coastal dunes give way to protected maritime forest, and a ¾-mile trail leads to the historic Reynolds Mansion.

### EAST BEACH (ST. SIMONS ISLAND)

The Golden Isles' liveliest stretch of sand occupies the southeastern edge of St. Simons Island, from the Coast Guard station at the end of 1st Street to Massengale Park, both of which offer facilities and access to the hard-packed sand beach. Here you can swim and sun, boogie board in the mild shore break, or kite surf past the offshore sandbars. This is one of the few beaches in the area with lifeguards, making it a good family destination.

### DRIFTWOOD BEACH (JEKYLL ISLAND)

The pristine northern end of Jekyll Island offers beautiful views of St. Simons against a stark and dramatic backdrop.

Accessible by trail from the Clam Creek Picnic Area or from North Beachview Drive, near the campground (there's a small parking area on the shoulder) the beach has a graveyard of coastal trees slowly succumbing to the sea, reeling at odd angles as the encroaching tide loosens their roots. Drained of color by the sun and saltwater, they create a maze of craggy limbs, gray against the bright white sand. Come here for the view and the unique scenery, but use caution swimming among the grasping branches.

### DUNGENESS BEACH (CUMBERLAND ISLAND)

Nearly 18 miles of unspoiled beach fringe the eastern edge of this national-park island, off the coast of St. Marys. At the southern end, Dungeness Beach is accessible via the *Cumberland Queen*, a reservations-only, 146-passenger ferry that stops here and at Sea Camp Beach to the north. Beachcombers can potentially find shells and sharks' teeth on the sand here, and Pelican Flats, off the island's southern tip, offers good shore fishing. From the beach it's an easy hike to Thomas Carnegie's great estate, Dungeness. Keep an eye out for the wild horses that roam the area.

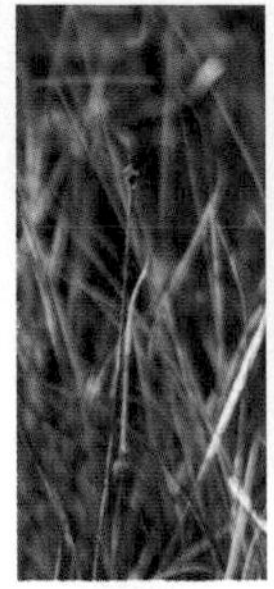

Updated by Stina Sieg

Georgia's lush barrier islands meander down the Atlantic coast from Savannah to the Florida border. Notable for their subtropical beauty and abundant wildlife, the isles strike a unique balance between some of the country's wealthiest communities and some of its most jealously protected nature preserves. Until recently, large segments of the coast were in private hands, and as a result much of the region remains as it was when the first Europeans set eyes on it 450 years ago. Though the islands have long been a favorite getaway of the rich and famous, they no longer cater only to the well heeled.

St. Simons, Jekyll, Little St. Simons, and Sea islands are known collectively as Georgia's Golden Isles. And while even today Little St. Simons Island and Sea Island remain privately owned—each with its own exclusive resort catering to the very wealthy—St. Simons and Jekyll islands have morphed into relaxed beach communities. These more developed islands (although by Georgia law, only 35% of Jekyll's land can be developed) have become diverse havens with something for everyone, from beach bums to family vacationers to the suit-and-tie crowd.

Sapelo Island and the Cumberland Island National Seashore are the least developed and, as protected nature preserves, the most ecologically intact of all the islands. With their miles of untouched beaches, forests of gnarly live-oak trees draped with Spanish moss, and rich swamps and marshlands, both islands are ideal camping destinations, with sites ranging from primitive to (relatively) sophisticated. Non-camping accommodations are available, but limited, and require booking well in advance. More commonly, many visitors opt to stay on the mainland and make day trips by ferry, private boat, or kayak.

The Okefenokee National Wildlife Refuge, 60 miles inland from St. Marys, near Folkston, is one of the largest freshwater wetlands in the

United States. Spread over 700 square miles of southeastern Georgia and northeastern Florida, the swamp is a trove of flora and fauna that naturalist William Bartram called a "terrestrial paradise" when he visited in the 1770s. From towering cypress swamps to alligator- and snake-infested waters and prairielike wetlands, the Okefenokee is a mosaic of ecosystems, much of which has never been visited by humans.

# PLANNING

## WHEN TO GO

Early spring and late fall are ideal for visiting the coastal isles and the Okefenokee. By February, temperatures often reach into the 70s, while nights remain cool and even chilly, which keeps the bugs at bay. Because of the high demand to visit these areas before the bugs arrive and after they depart, you should book ferry reservations to Sapelo Island and Cumberland Island National Seashore months in advance for spring and fall: without a reservation, you risk having to wait days for a cancellation. If you plan to stay in the immediate vicinity of St. Marys or Meridian, the docking points for the Cumberland and Sapelo ferries, or Folkston, the gateway to the Okefenokee, it's advisable to book rooms for these areas well in advance for spring, as accommodations are scarce and the demand is high. The Cumberland Island ferry accepts reservations six months in advance. If you go during the warmer months, always bring water because these areas generally offer minimal services.

By May, deerflies and mosquitoes swarm the coast and islands in abundance. Don't underestimate their impact: during peak times in some areas they are so thick they sound like hail hitting your car. And though many localities spray, it's imperative to have a good repellent handy, especially when traveling to outlying areas. Despite the subtropical heat and humidity, summer is busy and you can count on crowds flocking to the beaches, so you'll want to make reservations at least a couple of months in advance. The season lasts until Labor Day, but you can still expect many travelers making weekend getaways until October or late November, when the weather begins to turn cooler. Hurricane season officially runs from June through the end of November, but August and September are typically the peak months.

## PLANNING YOUR TIME

Although Georgia's coastal islands are along a strip of coastline that is less than 60 miles long, each has a different feel, and a visit requires at least a day. The complications of ferries to Sapelo or Cumberland make it difficult to visit either of those in less than a day, and these visits must generally be planned far in advance. It's possible to base yourself on busy St. Simons Island (or any of the Golden Isles for that matter) and visit much of the region on a series of day trips. The Okefenokee is a bit farther out of the way, but can be visited on a day trip from almost any of the islands; if you have more time, it can be an overnight trip.

## GETTING HERE AND AROUND

Visiting the region is easiest by car, because many of the outer reaches of Georgia are remote places with little in the way of alternate transportation. Touring by bicycle is an option for most of the region, but note that the ferries at Sapelo and Cumberland do not allow bicycles on board. Except for Little St. Simons, the Golden Isles are connected to the mainland by bridges around Brunswick and are the only coastal isles accessible by car. Sapelo Island and the Cumberland Island National Seashore can be reached only by ferry from Meridian and St. Marys, respectively.

### AIR TRAVEL

The coastal isles are served by the Brunswick Golden Isles Airport, 6 miles north of Brunswick, and the McKinnon St. Simons Airport on St. Simons Island. McKinnon accommodates light aircraft and private planes. The closest major airports are in Savannah, Georgia, and Jacksonville, Florida.

**Air Contacts The Brunswick Golden Isles Airport** ✉ *295 Aviation Pkwy., off I- 95, Brunswick* ☎ *912/265–2070* 🌐 *www.glynncountyairports.com.* **McKinnon St. Simons Island Airport** ✉ *Airport Rd. off Demere Rd., St. Simons Island* ☎ *912/265–2070* 🌐 *www.glynncountyairports.com.*

### BOAT AND FERRY TRAVEL

Cumberland Island, Sapelo Island, and Little St. Simons are accessible only by ferry or private launch. The *Cumberland Queen* serves Cumberland Island, and the *Katie Underwood* serves Sapelo Island. (The National Park Service has a Cumberland Island ferry schedule at 🌐 *www.nps.gov/cuis/reservations.htm.*) The Lodge on Little St. Simons Island operates a private launch that is available only to overnight or day-trip guests by prior arrangement.

**Boat and Ferry Contacts *Cumberland Queen.*** ✉ *101 Wheeler St., St. Marys* ☎ *912/882-4335, 877/860-6787* 🖷 *912/673–7747* 🌐 *www.nps.gov/cuis.* ***Katie Underwood.*** ✉ *Sapelo Island Visitors Center, Rte. 1, Darien* ☎ *912/437-3224* 🌐 *www.sapelonerr.org/visitorcenter.htm.* **The Lodge on Little St. Simons Island** ☎ *912/638–7472, 888/733–5774* 🖷 *912/634–1811* 🌐 *www.littlessi.com.*

### CAR TRAVEL

From Brunswick take the Jekyll Island Causeway ($5 per car) to Jekyll Island and the Torras Causeway to St. Simons and Sea Island. You can get by without a car on Jekyll Island and Sea Island, but you'll need one on St. Simons. You cannot bring a car to Cumberland Island, Little St. Simons, or Sapelo.

### TAXI TRAVEL

Courtesy Cab provides taxi service from Brunswick to and from the islands for a set rate that ranges from $15 to $30 to St. Simons and from $27 to Jekyll Island with a $2 per person surcharge. Island Cab Service can shuttle you around St. Simons for fares that range between $7 and $15 depending on your destination.

**Taxi Contacts Island Cab Service** ☎ *912/634–0113* 🌐 *www.islandtransportandtaxi.com.*

### RESTAURANTS

Restaurants range from fish camps—normally rustic dockside affairs—to the more upscale eateries that tend to spawn around the larger towns. And though there's still room for growth, the area now has several menus gaining not only local but nationwide attention. The rising tide of quality has begun to lift all boats. Some restaurants still serve food family-style. *Prices in the reviews are the average cost of a main course at dinner or, if dinner is not served, at lunch.*

### HOTELS

Hotels run the gamut from Victorian mansions to Spanish-style bed-and-breakfasts to some of the most luxurious hotel/spa accommodations found anywhere. Since options are somewhat limited, make your reservations as far in advance as possible. Most hotels offer the full range of guest services, but as a matter of philosophy many B&Bs do not provide televisions or telephones in the rooms. Lodging prices quoted here may be much lower during non-peak seasons, and specials are often available on weekdays even in high season. *Prices in the reviews are the lowest cost of a standard double room in high season.*

### TOURS

Coastal Georgia Charters and Tours offers year-round bus and boat tours from St. Simons Island and Jekyll Island that explore the surrounding marshes and rivers and get you up close and personal with dolphins, manatees, and other marine life. Kayaks and canoes are also a great way to explore the creeks; Southeast Adventure Outfitters has locations on St. Simons Island and in Brunswick.

**Coastal Georgia Charters and Tours** ✉ *4111 Knight St., Brunswick* ☎ *912/264–9808* 🌐 *www.goldenislesfun.com.*

**SouthEast Adventure Outfitters** ✉ *313 Mallory St., St. Simons Island* ☎ *912/638–6732* 🌐 *www.southeastadventure.com* ✉ *1200 Glynn Ave., Hwy. 17, Brunswick* ☎ *912/638–6732* 🌐 *www.southeastadventure.com.*

## SAPELO ISLAND

*8 miles northeast of Darien.*

The fourth-largest of Georgia's coastal isles—and bigger than Bermuda—Sapelo Island is a unique community in North America. It still bears evidence of the Paleo-Indians who lived here some 4,500 years ago, and is home to the Geechee, direct descendants of African slaves who speak a creole of English and various African languages. This rapidly dwindling community maintains many traditional African practices, including the making of sweetgrass baskets and the use of herbal medicines made from recipes passed down for generations. It's also a nearly pristine barrier island with miles of undeveloped beaches and abundant wildlife. To take the 40-minute ferry ride from Meridian on the mainland through the expanse of salt marshes to Sapelo Island is to enter a world seemingly forgotten by time.

CLOSE UP

## The Geechee, a Culture Apart

Georgia's Geechee, like the Gullah people of South Carolina, are descendants of African slaves who have preserved a distinct culture and language, in large part due to the isolation of the remote coastal areas, such as Sapelo Island, where they live.

The Geechee take their name from the Ogeechee River in north coastal Georgia. Geechee ancestry includes a variety of African tribes, but is particularly marked by the language and traditions of slaves from Sierra Leone, who were brought to work the vast coastal plantations because of their expertise in rice cultivation. Their native tongue, Krio, is still evident in the Geechee language of the region today: *tief/tif* (steal), *ooman/uman* (woman), and *enty/enti* (isn't it so?) are just a few of the easily recognizable words that are similar in Geechee and Krio, respectively. The two languages share similar sentence structures and grammatical elements as well. Geechee, not English, was the first language of Supreme Court Justice Clarence Thomas, who was born and raised in Savannah.

#### GETTING HERE AND AROUND

You can explore many historical periods and natural environments here, but facilities on the island are limited. Note that you can't simply walk up to the dock and catch the ferry—you need to have a reservation for a tour, a campsite, or one of the island's lodgings (or have prearranged plans to stay with island residents). Bring insect repellent, especially in summer, and leave your pets at home. You can rent a bicycle on the island, but you cannot bring a bicycle on the ferry.

## EXPLORING

**Hog Hammock Community.** This small settlement near the southern end of Sapelo Island is one of the few remaining Gullah/Geechee communities on the south Atlantic Coast. The Saltwater Geechee people, Georgia's sea-island equivalent to the Gullah of South Carolina, are descendants of slaves who worked the island's plantations during the 19th century. Hog Hammock's roughly 50 residents still maintain their distinct language and customs, which share many characteristics with their West African origins.

The Spirit of Sapelo Tours. These private, guided bus tours are led by an island native who discusses island life, culture, and history. ☎ *912/266-4848* 🌐 *www.gacoast.com/geecheetours.html.*

Sapelo Cultural Day. This celebration of Geechee folklore, music, food, handcrafts, and art, takes place in Hog Hammock every year on the third weekend in October. Reservations are required. ☎ *912/485-2197* 🌐 *www.sapeloislandga.org/culturalday/index.html.*

**Sapelo Island Visitor Center.** Start your visit here, on the mainland near the Sapelo Island ferry docks. You can see exhibits on the island's history, culture, and ecology, and you can purchase tickets for a round-trip ferry ride and bus tour of the island. The sights that make up the

A ferry leads to Sapelo Island, one of Georgia's most pristine barrier islands.

bus tour vary depending on the day of the week, but always included are the marsh, the sand-dune ecosystem, and the wildlife management area. On Friday and Saturday the tour includes the 80-foot-tall **Sapelo Lighthouse,** built in 1820, a symbol of the cotton and lumber industry once based out of Darien, a prominent shipping center of the time. To see the island's **Reynolds Mansion** schedule your tour for Wednesday or Saturday. To get to the visitor center and Meridian Ferry Dock from downtown Darien, go north on Route 99 for 8 miles, following signs for the Sapelo Island National Estuarine Research Reserve. Turn right onto Landing Road at the Elm Grove Baptist Church in Meridian. The visitor center is about ½ mile down the road. ✉ *1766 Landing Rd. SE, Darien* ☎ *912/437–3224, 912/485–2300 for group tours* 🌐 *www.sapelonerr.org* ⏲ *Closed Sun.–Mon.*

## WHERE TO EAT

$$ SEAFOOD ★ ✕ **Mudcat Charlie's.** This tabby-and-wood restaurant on the Altamaha River sits right in the middle of the Two Way Fish Camp and is a favorite haunt of locals from nearby Darien. The restaurant overlooks the boats moored in the marina, and the seafood is local. Crab stew, fried oysters, and shrimp are the specialties, and the desserts are made in-house. It's just over 1 mile south of Darien on U.S. 17, just after the fourth bridge. Look for the Two Way Fish Camp sign. $ *Average main: $15* ✉ *250 Ricefield Way, Brunswick* ☎ *912/261–0055.*

$$$ SEAFOOD ★ ✕ **Skipper's Fish Camp.** This upscale take on the fish camp theme lies at the foot of a public dock on the Darien River, where working shrimp boats moor. It has a beautiful courtyard pond and an open-air oyster

bar. Popular menu items include Georgia white shrimp, ribs, and fried flounder. There's usually a wait on weekends, so get there early. At the southern end of Darien, turn right at Broad just before the river bridge, then take the first left down to the waterfront. *Average main: $20 ✉ 85 Screven St., Darien ☎ 912/437–3474 ⊕ www.skippersfishcamp.com Reservations not accepted.*

## WHERE TO STAY

*Hotel reviews have been abbreviated in this book. For expanded reviews, please go to Fodors.com.*

$ B&B/INN **The Blue Heron Inn.** Bill and Jan Chamberlain's airy, Mediterranean-style home sits on the edge of the marsh and is only minutes from the ferry at the Sapelo Island Visitor Center. **Pros:** deliciously inventive breakfasts; decks provide great views. **Cons:** the small number of rooms means the place can book up fast. *Rooms from: $125 ✉ 1346 Blue Heron La., Darien ☎ 912/437–4304 ⊕ www.blueheroninngacoast.com 4 rooms Breakfast.*

$ B&B/INN ★ **Open Gates Bed and Breakfast.** Built by a timber baron in 1876, this two-story, Italianate house on Darien's Vernon Square is filled with antiques and Victorian atmosphere. **Pros:** easy walking distance to Darien's restaurants and waterfront; the library has an excellent collection of books of local historical interest; setting is so lovely that the home's exterior was featured on the cover of *Southern Living* magazine. **Cons:** not a good choice for singles. *Rooms from: $125 ✉ 301 Franklin St., Box 662, Darien ☎ 912/437–6985 ⊕ www.opengatesbnb.com 5 rooms, 4 with bath Breakfast.*

$ B&B/INN **The Wallow Lodge.** A stay at this historic inn at Hog Hammock offers a chance to experience the island's distinct Geechee culture. **Pros:** unique decor; next door to the Trough, the town's only bar. **Cons:** the lodge has a communal kitchen, so unless you make prior arrangements for meals, you must bring your own supplies from the mainland. *Rooms from: $70 ✉ Downtown Hog Hammock ☎ 912/485–2206 ⊕ www.gacoast.com/geecheetours 6 rooms, 5 with bath No credit cards.*

## SPORTS AND THE OUTDOORS

### BEACHES

**Cabretta Beach.** Just north of Nanny Goat Beach, Cabretta Beach stretches along Sapelo's eastern shore, with its northern terminus at the outflow of Blackbeard Creek. This remote expanse of hard-packed sand is sometimes visited by fishermen or kayakers on their way to Blackbeard Island, and it's also the site of the Cabretta group campsite, a wilderness camp that can be reserved via Georgia's Department of Natural Resources—there are showers and bathrooms here for campers. **Amenities:** showers, toilets. **Best for:** sunrise, walking. ✉ *End of Cabretta Rd.*

**Nanny Goat Beach.** On the southeastern edge of the island, this beach sits at the heart of the rich ecological zones for which the island is known and protected. Naturalists with the Sapelo Island National Estuarine Research Reserve use this beach as an outdoor classroom, sometimes bringing groups here for beach walks. Visitors can hunt for sand dollars and whelk shells along nearly 2 miles of sandy shore; bird sightings include blue herons, egrets, ospreys, bald eagles, and the occasional plain chachalaca. A 1-mile trail connects this beach with the historic R. J. Reynolds House, crossing five ecological zones along the way. **Amenities:** bathrooms. **Best for:** solitude, walking. ✉ *End of Beach Rd.*

### CAMPING ON SAPELO ISLAND

**Comyam's Campground.** The name of Hog Hammock's only campground comes from the Geechee word meaning "come here." The campground has marsh views and is great for backpackers looking for a more rustic taste of the island life. Campsite reservations are essential. ✉ *Next to the Wallow Lodge in Hog Hammock, Sapelo Island, Georgia* ☎ *912/266–4848* 🌐 *www.gacoast.com/geecheetours.*

### CANOEING AND KAYAKING

**Altamaha Coastal Tours.** The Altamaha River, the largest undammed river on the East Coast, runs inland from near Darien. You can take expeditions along it with Altamaha Coastal Tours, which rents equipment and conducts guided trips from the waterfront in Darien. With them you can explore tidal swamps, marshlands, and Queen and Sapelo islands. ✉ *229 Fort King George Dr., Darien* ☎ *912/437–6010* 🌐 *www.altamaha.com.*

## NIGHTLIFE

**Trough.** It seems appropriate that the only watering hole in Hog Hammock is named the Trough. It's a small, barebones, belly-up-to-the-bar establishment, but owner Julius Bailey serves his beer ice cold, and there's usually a good conversation going on. It's next to the Wallow Lodge (operated by Julius's wife, Cornelia) right "downtown." A store on the backside of the bar offers basic supplies and souvenirs. ✉ *1 Main Rd.* ☎ *912/485–2206* ⏲ *Closed Sun.*

EN ROUTE

**Hofwyl-Broadfield Plantation.** Rice, not cotton, dominated Georgia's coast in the antebellum years, and the Hofwyl-Broadfield Plantation is the last remaining example of a way of life that fueled an agricultural empire. The main farmhouse, in use since the 1850s when the original house burned, is now a museum with family heirlooms accumulated over five generations, including extensive collections of silver and Canton china. A guide gives an insightful talk on rural plantation life. Though grown over, some of the original dike works and rice fields remain, as do some of the slave quarters. A brief film at the visitor center complements exhibits on rice technology and cultivation, and links to Sierra Leone, from where many slaves were taken because of their expertise in growing rice. ✉ *5556 U.S. 17 N, 5 miles south of Darien* ☎ *912/264–7333* 🌐 *www.gastateparks.org/info/hofwyl* 🎟 *$6.50* ⏲ *Thurs.–Sat. 9–5.*

Stroll along the live oak allées at St. Simons Island.

## ST. SIMONS ISLAND

*22 miles south of Darien, 4 miles east of Brunswick.*

St. Simons may be the Golden Isles' most developed vacation destination: here you can swim and sun, golf, hike, fish, ride horseback, tour historic sites, and feast on local seafood at more than 50 restaurants. (It's also a great place to bike and jog, particularly on the southern end, where there's an extensive network of trails.) Despite the development, the island has managed to maintain some of the slow-paced Southern atmosphere that made it such a draw in the first place. Upscale resorts and restaurants are here for the asking, but this island the size of Manhattan has only 20,000 year-round residents, so you can still get away from it all without a struggle. Even down in the village, the center of much of St. Simons's activity, there are unpaved roads and quiet back alleys of chalky white sand that seem like something out of the past.

### GETTING HERE AND AROUND

Reach the island by car via the causeway from Brunswick.

### ESSENTIALS

**Tours St. Simons Trolley Tours.** In the village area, at the more developed south end of the island, you can find shops, several restaurants, pubs, and a popular public pier. For $23, a quaint trolley from the 1930s takes you on a 1½-hour guided tour of the island, leaving from near the pier at 11 am daily. ☎ *912/638–8954*.

**Visitor Information The Golden Isles Convention and Visitors Bureau** ✉ *I–95 southbound between Exits 42 and 38, Brunswick* ☎ *912/265–0620, 800/933–2627* 🌐 *www.goldenisles.com* ✉ *530 Beachview Dr.* ☎ *912/638–9014,*

*800/809–1790* ⊕ *www.goldenisles.com.* **St. Simons Visitors Center** ✉ *St. Simons, F.J. Torras Causeway at U.S. 17* ☎ *912/638–9014* ⊕ *www.goldenisles.com.*

## EXPLORING

**Christ Episcopal Church.** This white-frame, Gothic-style church was built by shipwrights and consecrated in 1886 following an earlier structure's desecration by Union troops. It's surrounded by historic live oaks, dogwoods, and azaleas. The interior has beautiful stained-glass windows and several handmade pews. ✉ *6329 Frederica Rd.* ☎ *912/638–8683* ⊕ *www.ccfssi.org* 🎫 *Donations suggested* ⏲ *Tue.–Sun. 2–5.*

**Fort Frederica National Monument.** Built by English troops in the mid-1730s, Fort Frederica was constructed to protect the southern flank of the new Georgia colony against a Spanish invasion from Florida. At its peak in the 1740s, it was the most elaborate British fortification in North America. Around the fort today are the foundations of homes and shops and the partial ruins of the tabby barracks and magazine. Start your visit at the National Park Service Visitors Center, which has a film and displays. ✉ *6515 Frederica Rd., north end of the island* ☎ *912/638–3639* ⊕ *www.nps.gov/fofr* 🎫 *$3* ⏲ *Daily 9–5.*

**Maritime Center at the Historic St. Simons Coast Guard Station.** Set in the restored 1936 station, this museum—geared as much to kids as adults—features the life of a "Coastie" in the early 1940s through personal accounts of the military history of St. Simons Island and has illustrative displays on the ecology of the islands off the coast of Georgia. ■ **TIP→ Your ticket also covers the lighthouse and is good for more than one day.** ✉ *4201 1st St.* ☎ *912/638–4666* ⊕ *www.saintsimonslighthouse.org* 🎫 *$10* ⏲ *Daily 10–noon and 1–5.*

**Neptune Park.** Named after St. Simons slave Neptune Small, this park in the village on the island's south end has picnic tables, beach access, and a large recreation area meant to delight families. The Neptune Park Fun Zone has a free playground, a swimming pool ($7 per person) that opens in the warmer months, and a year-round miniature golf course ($7 per round). A newly renovated pier, good for fishing or watching ships roll in, is adjacent to the park. Restrooms are in the library beside the visitor center. ✉ *550 Beachview Dr.* ☎ *912/279–2836* ⊕ *www.glynncounty.org* ⏲ *Daily dawn to dusk.*

★ **St. Simons Lighthouse.** One of only five surviving lighthouses in Georgia, St. Simons Lighthouse has

### GEECHEE RESISTANCE

**Ebo Landing.** In May 1803 an Igbo chief and his West African tribesmen became Geechee folk legends when they "walked back to Africa," drowning en masse rather than submitting to a life of slavery. Captured in what is modern-day Nigeria, the tribesmen disembarked their slave ship at Ebo Landing and headed straight into Dunbar Creek, chanting a hymn. Though the site is now private property, it can be seen from the road. ✉ *From the F.J. Torras Causeway, turn left on Sea Island Rd. After Hawkins Island Dr., look left (north) just before crossing small bridge at Dunbar Creek. The landing is at a bend in the creek.*

become a symbol of the island. It's been in use since 1872; a predecessor was blown up to prevent its capture by Union troops in the Civil War. The **St. Simons Lighthouse Museum,** occupying two stories of the lightkeeper's dwelling, tells of the history of the island, the lighthouse, and James Gould, the first lightkeeper of the original lighthouse. The keeper's second-floor quarters contain a parlor, kitchen, and two bedrooms furnished with period pieces, including beds with rope mattress suspension. The last climb of the lighthouse is at 4:30. ⊠ *101 12th St.* ☎ *912/638–4666* 🌐 *www.saintsimonslighthouse.org* 🎟 *$10* ⏲ *Daily 10–5.*

---

## WHERE TO EAT

$ BARBECUE ✕ **The Beachcomber BBQ and Grill.** No shoes, no shirt, no problem in this small, rustic eatery where the walls are covered with reed mats and the barbecue smokes away on a cooker right beside the front door. Despite the name, it doesn't have a beachfront location. However, it's one of the best barbecue joints on the island, offering everything from sandwiches to pulled pork, ribs, and brisket by the pound. Food Network fans might recognize The Beachcomber from an edition of *The Best Thing I Ever Ate,* in which famed chef Alton Brown raved about the place. ■ **TIP→** The freshly squeezed lemonade is to die for. [$] *Average main: $8* ⊠ *319 Arnold Rd.* ☎ *912/634–5699* 🌐 *www.beachcomberbbq.com.*

$$$ AMERICAN ✕ **Bennie's Red Barn.** The steaks are cut fresh daily and cooked over an oak fire in this barn of a restaurant that has been serving St. Simons for more than 50 years. Though there's room for 200 people, it feels just like family with the checkered tablecloths and the big open fireplace. There's also fresh local seafood and homemade pies. The Club at Bennie's, which is connected to the restaurant, is a large event space with a stage that is often used for group functions. [$] *Average main: $22* ⊠ *5514 Frederica Rd.* ☎ *912/638–2844* 🌐 *www.benniesredbarn.com* ⏲ *No lunch.*

$ AMERICAN ✕ **Gnat's Landing.** There's more than a little bit of Margaritaville in this Key West–style bungalow catering to the flip-flop crowd. Seafood is their specialty, with a gumbo that's outta sight. Besides being the strangest item on the menu, the fried dill pickle is also the most popular. Sandwiches and salads are also offered. And, of course, there's the "$8,000 margarita," which is about how much owner Robert Bostock spent in travel and ingredients coming up with the recipe. There's live music most Sunday nights, and once a year there's "Gnatfest," a party blowout with live bands for all those pesky regulars. [$] *Average main: $13* ⊠ *310 Redfern Village* ☎ *912/638–7378* 🌐 *www.gnatslanding.com.*

$$$$ AMERICAN ★ ✕ **Halyards.** This elegant restaurant with a laid-back attitude makes everything except the ketchup right on the premises. Chef-owner Dave Snyder's devotion to quality has earned a faithful following of discerning locals. Slide into a cozy, tufted booth or sit at a table or the sophisticated bar lined with photos of yachts. Headliners include the seared, sushi-grade tuna with a plum-wine reduction; the Asian-style diver scallops; and the Georgia white shrimp and grits. The signature coffee hits the mark, accompanied by a vanilla bean crème brûlée with fresh strawberries. [$] *Average main: $28* ⊠ *55 Cinema La.* ☎ *912/638–9100*

*www.halyardsrestaurant.com* *Reservations essential* *Closed Sun. No lunch.*

$ AMERICAN **Mullet Bay.** After 9 pm the older beach-bar crowd has this place hopping, and on weekends the bar and wraparound porches can be standing-room only until the wee hours. By day, however, this spacious and casual restaurant is great for families, serving a good selection of burgers, pastas, and salads. The kids' menu starts at $1.95. The platters of fried popcorn shrimp are delicious and perfect for sharing. *Average main: $11* *512 Ocean Blvd.* *912/634–9977* *www.mulletbayrestaurant.com.*

$$ ITALIAN **Tramici.** This is the Italian offering of David Snyder, owner of the more refined Halyards. Tramici is billed as a neighborhood restaurant, although it's in a shopping center. It certainly is kid-friendly, with spaghetti and meatballs and pizzas piled with favorite toppings. There's a remarkable antipasto with prosciutto and asparagus and a superb take on veal marsala over pasta, with sun-dried tomatoes as the mystery ingredient. *Average main: $17* *75 Cinema La.* *912/634–2202* *www.tramicirestaurant.com.*

### LODGING ALTERNATIVES

**By the Sea Vacations.** Do-it-yourselfers and families on a budget have many options beyond inns and hotels. *Rooms from: $110* *411 Longview Plaza, Suite 108* *912/638–6610, 866/639–6610* *www.bytheseavacations.com.*

**Parker-Kaufman Realty.** This realty firm manages a range of rental homes on St. Simon. *Rooms from: $150* *912/638–3368, 888/227–8573* *www.parker-kaufman.com.*

## WHERE TO STAY

*Hotel reviews have been abbreviated in this book. For expanded reviews, please go to Fodors.com.*

$ HOTEL **Holiday Inn Express.** With clean, simple, brightly decorated rooms at great prices, this chain hotel is an attractive option in this price category. **Pros:** good value; nonsmoking. **Cons:** guests have complained that walls are too thin. *Rooms from: $129* *Plantation Village, 299 Main St.* *912/634–2175, 888/465–4329* *www.hiexpress.com/stsimonsga* *60 rooms* *Breakfast.*

$$$ RESORT **King and Prince Beach & Golf Resort.** Your accommodation options at this cushy retreat are spacious guest rooms, two- and three-bedroom apartment-style "villas," and stand-alone guesthouses. **Pros:** sprawling suites; golf-course access; speedy room service. **Cons:** amenities are fairly basic. *Rooms from: $249* *201 Arnold Rd.* *912/638–3631, 800/342–0212* *www.kingandprince.com* *145 rooms, 2 suites, 44 villas, 7 guesthouses.*

$$$$ B&B/INN Fodor's Choice ★ **The Lodge at Sea Island Golf Club.** This small resort overlooking the sea is one of the top golf and spa destinations in the country. **Pros:** fantastic golfing; elegant interiors. **Cons:** high price; meals aren't included. *Rooms from: $395* *100 Retreat Ave.* *800/732–4752* *www.seaisland.com* *38 rooms, 2 suites.*

$$ RESORT **Sea Palms Resort and Conference Center.** If you're looking for an active getaway, this contemporary complex could be the place for you—it has golf, tennis, a fitness center loaded with state-of-the-art equipment, a beach club, sand-pit volleyball, horseshoes, and bicycling. **Pros:** guests have beach-club privileges; large. **Cons:** somewhat unimaginative furnishings. *Rooms from: $179 5445 Frederica Rd. 912/638–3351, 800/841–6268 www.seapalms.com 115 rooms, 26 suites.*

$$ B&B/INN **St. Simons Inn.** In a prime spot by the lighthouse, and only minutes on foot from the village and the beaches, this European-style inn is made up of privately owned guest rooms—nothing fancy, but they're clean, comfortable, and individually decorated, many with furnishings and art that give off a beachy vibe. **Pros:** excellent location; affordable rates. **Cons:** some rooms are small; individually decorated rooms means some are not as nice as others. *Rooms from: $159 609 Beachview Dr. 912/638–1101 www.stsimonsinn.com 34 rooms Breakfast.*

$$ B&B/INN **The Village Inn & Pub.** What was once a cinder-block beach house has since won awards for its environmentally friendly design that incorporated the original structure and preserved the surrounding live oaks. **Pros:** great location; owners have taken care to preserve the mossy live oaks. **Cons:** basic rooms. *Rooms from: $160 500 Mallery St. 912/634–6056, 888/635–6111 www.villageinnandpub.com 28 rooms Breakfast.*

## SPORTS AND THE OUTDOORS

### BEACHES

**East Beach.** The only public beach on St. Simons is also one of the most popular in all of the Golden Isles. Entrances sit on either end of the beach: at the Coast Guard Station on 1st Street to the north and Massengale Park on Oak Street to the south. Between the two entrances, this ½-mile stretch of hard-packed white sand is vacation central, with calm, shallow water perfect for swimming, boogie boarding, or windsurfing. Plenty of parking is available, lifeguards watch the waves all summer, and drinking is allowed in plastic containers (no glass bottles). **Amenities:** food and drink, lifeguards, parking, showers, toilets. **Best for:** swimming, windsurfing. *Ocean Blvd. from 1st to Oak Sts. www.goldenisles.com/listing/east-beach.*

### BIKING

**Ocean Motion Surf Co.** St. Simons has an extensive network of bicycle trails, and you can ride on the beach as well. Ocean Motion rents bikes for the entire family, from trail bikes to beach bikes to seats for infants. *1300 Ocean Blvd. 912/638–5225, 800/669–5215 www.stsimonskayaking.com.*

### CRABBING AND FISHING

**St. Simons Island Bait and Tackle.** There's no simpler fun for the kids than to grab a crab basket or fishing pole and head to St. Simons Island Pier next to Neptune Park. This bait shop is near the foot of the pier and is open 364½ days a year. Owners Mike and Trish Wooten have everything from crabbing and fishing gear to snacks and cold drinks.

A couple watches the sunrise at St. Simons Island.

They also sell one-day, three-day, and yearly licenses. ✉ *121 Mallory St.* ☎ *912/634–1888.*

## GOLF

The top-flight golf facilities at the Lodge at Sea Island are available only to members and guests, but St. Simons has two other high-quality courses open to the general public.

**The King and Prince Golf Course.** At the north end of St. Simons, on the site of the Hampton Plantation—an 18th-century cotton, rice, and indigo plantation—is a *Golf Digest* "Places to Play" four-star winner. The course, originally designed by Joe Lee, was restored in 2009, and it lies amid towering oaks, salt marshes, and lagoons. ✉ *100 Tabbystone* ☎ *912/634–0255* 🌐 *www.kingandprince.com* *18 holes. 6462 yds. Par 72. Green Fee: $79 King and Prince Resort guests, $115 non-guests.* ☞ *Facilities: Driving range, putting green, pitching area, golf carts, rental clubs, pro shop, golf academy/lessons, restaurant, bar.*

**Sea Palms Resort and Conference Center.** On a former cotton and indigo plantation, this resort offers 27 holes of golf on a standard 18-hole course and a 9-hole executive course, and a driving range. ✉ *5445 Frederica Rd.* ☎ *912/638–3351, 800/841–6268* 🌐 *www.seapalmsgolf.com* *27 holes. 18-hole course: 6477 yds. Par 71. 9-hole course: 2400 yds. Par 34. Green Fee: $79/$29.* ☞ *Facilities: Driving range, putting green, pitching area, golf carts, rental clubs, pro shop, golf academy/lessons, restaurant, bar.*

### KAYAKING AND SAILING

**Ocean Motion.** After an instructional clinic, head off to explore the marsh creeks, coastal waters, and beaches with Ocean Motion, which has been giving kayaking tours of St. Simons for more than 30 years. The shop also does bike rentals. ✉ *1300 Ocean Blvd.* ☎ *912/638–5225, 800/669–5215.*

**Barry's Beach Service.** If sailing is your thing, check out this shop in front of the King and Prince Beach and Golf Resort on Arnold Road for its Hobie Cat rentals and sailing lessons. Barry's also rents kayaks, boogie boards, stand-up paddle boards, beach chairs and umbrellas, and beach funcycles (low, reclining bikes), and conducts guided kayak tours. ✉ *On the beach near the Beach Club North Breaker Condominiums* ☎ *912/638–8053, 800/669–5215* 🌐 *www.stsimonskayaking.com.*

### SCUBA DIVING

**Island Dive Center.** Gray's Reef, off Sapelo island, is one of only 14 National Marine Sanctuaries. It's home to loggerhead turtles and part of the northern right whale breeding grounds, all of which makes it an attractive place for diving. Island Dive Center is the place to go for scuba and snorkeling instruction, equipment rental, and charter trips. ✉ *101 Marina Dr., in Morningstar Marina on F.J. Torras Causeway* ☎ *912/638–6590, 800/940–3483.*

---

# LITTLE ST. SIMONS ISLAND

*10–15 minutes by ferry from Hampton River Club Marina on St. Simons Island.*

Little St. Simons Island is 15 minutes by boat from St. Simons Island, but in character it's a world apart. The entire island is a privately owned resort. The only habitations comprise a rustic former hunting lodge on the riverfront, three upscale cottages, and two river houses; none have telephones or televisions. This compound is so at one with its surroundings that the deer graze in the open. "Luxury" on Little St. Simons Island means having the time and space to get in tune with the rhythms of nature.

The island's forests and marshes are inhabited by deer, armadillos, raccoons, gators, otters, and more than 280 species of birds, some of which migrate to and from the island at various times during the year. As a guest at the resort, you can take part in guided activities with on-site naturalists, including birding walks, beachcombing, kayak trips, and fishing excursions, all for no additional charge. You're also free to walk the 7 miles of undisturbed beaches, swim in the mild surf, fish from the dock, and seine for shrimp and crab along the shore.

#### GETTING HERE AND AROUND

Day-trippers can visit the island and the lodge without an overnight reservation for a fee of $75, which includes the ferry to and from the island, a naturalist-led tour on the island, lunch at the lodge or the beach gazebo, and an afternoon on the beach. *Contact the Lodge on Little St. Simons Island for more information.*

## WHERE TO STAY

$$$$ B&B/INN **Lodge on Little St. Simons Island.** Privacy and simplicity are the star attractions on this 10,000-acre island with 7 mile of undisturbed beachfront and this rustic 1917 lodge and five cottages with capacity for only 32 guests. **Pros:** secluded location; friendly, attentive staff. **Cons:** close quarters and family-style meals might not suit those looking for more alone time. *Rooms from: $600 Hampton River Marina, 1000 Hampton Point Dr. 888/733–5774, 912/638–7472 www.littlessi.com 16 rooms All meals.*

# SEA ISLAND

*East of St. Simons Island, connected by a 1-mile causeway.*

Tiny Sea Island—with a full-time population of less than 400—is one of the nation's wealthiest communities. Established by Howard Coffin, the wealthy Detroit auto pioneer who also owned Sapelo Island in the early 20th century, Sea Island has been a getaway for the well-heeled since 1928, when Coffin opened the elegant Cloister hotel that sits at the heart of this posh island retreat. Today Sea Island is a gated community accessible only to registered guests of the hotel and Sea Island Club members.

### GETTING HERE AND AROUND

Though accessible by causeway, the island is restricted to owners and guests of the single hotel.

## WHERE TO STAY

$$$$ RESORT Fodor's Choice ★ **The Cloister.** This Mediterranean-style, waterside resort—tucked behind a secure gate and impeccably appointed with tropical landscaping, rich rococo fabrics, and stained glass—is fit for dignitaries (and hosted them during the 2004 G8 Summit). **Pros:** elegant getaway; golfing galore; horseback riding; pristine beach; sprawling guest rooms. **Cons:** the winding paths and property layout may be a bit confusing for first-time visitors. *Rooms from: $395 100 Cloister Dr. 912/638–3611, 800/732–4732 www.seaisland.com 113 rooms, 62 suites No meals.*

# JEKYLL ISLAND

*18 miles south of St. Simons Island; 90 miles south of Savannah.*

For 56 winters, between 1886 and 1942, America's rich and famous faithfully came south to Jekyll Island. Through the Gilded Age, World War I, the Roaring '20s, and the Great Depression, Vanderbilts and Rockefellers, Morgans and Astors, Macys, Pulitzers, and Goodyears shuttered their 5th Avenue castles and retreated to elegant "cottages" on their wild coastal island. It's been said that when the island's distinguished winter residents were all "in," a sixth of the world's wealth was represented. Early in World War II the millionaires departed for the last time. In 1947 the state of Georgia purchased the entire island for the bargain price of $675,000.

Jekyll Island is still a 7½-mile playground, but it's no longer restricted to the rich and famous. A water park, picnic grounds, and facilities for golf, tennis, fishing, biking, and jogging are all open to the public. One side of the island is lined by nearly 10 miles of hard-packed Atlantic beaches; the other by the intracoastal waterway and picturesque salt marshes. Deer and wild turkey inhabit interior forests of pine, magnolia, and moss-veiled live oaks. Egrets, pelicans, herons, and sandpipers skim the gentle surf. Jekyll Island's clean, mostly uncommercialized public beaches are free and open year-round. Bathhouses with restrooms, changing areas, and showers are open at regular intervals along the beach.

### GETTING HERE AND AROUND

Jekyll Island is connected to the mainland by the Sidney Lanier Bridge. Visitors coming to the island by car must stop at the greeting station to pay a parking fee of $5 per vehicle, per day. Once on the island, you'll need a car or a bicycle to get around.

### ESSENTIALS

**Visitor Information Jekyll Island Welcome Center** ✉ *901 Downing Musgrove Causeway* ☎ *912/635–3636* 🌐 *www.jekyllisland.com.*

## EXPLORING

**Georgia Sea Turtle Center.** A must-see on Jekyll Island, this center aims to increase awareness of habitat and wildlife conservation challenges for the endangered loggerhead turtles through turtle rehabilitation, research, and education programs. The center includes educational exhibits and a "hospital," where visitors can view rescued turtles and read their stories. The loggerheads lay their eggs along Jekyll Island beaches from May through August. ✉ *214 Stable Rd.* ☎ *912/635–4444* 🌐 *www.georgiaseaturtlecenter.org* *$7* *Mar.–Nov., Mon. 10–2, Tue.–Sun. 9–5; Dec.–Feb., Tue.–Sun. 9–5.*

**Jekyll Island National Historic Landmark District.** Tram tours of this 240-acre historic district include two millionaires' residences. Call ahead to see if the tour will visit **Faith Chapel,** built in 1904, which is illuminated by stained-glass windows, including one Tiffany original. The chapel is open daily 2–4 unless it has been reserved for a wedding.

**Jekyll Island Museum.** Tours ($16) originate at this little museum, departing daily at 11, 1, and 3, weather permitting. ✉ *100 Stable Rd., off I–95, Exit 29* ☎ *912/635–4036* 🌐 *www.jekyllisland.com.*

**Summer Waves.** At this 11-acre park more than a million gallons of water are used in the 18,000-square-foot wave pool, waterslides, children's activity pool with two slides, splash zone, and circular river for tubing and rafting. Inner tubes and life vests are provided at no extra charge. ✉ *210 S. Riverview Dr.* ☎ *912/635–2074* 🌐 *www.summerwaves.com* *$19.95* *Late May–early Sept., weekdays 10–6, Sat. 10–8, Sun. 11–7; hrs vary at beginning and end of season.*

Learn about Jekyll Island's history as the playground of the rich and famous at the Jekyll Island Museum.

## WHERE TO EAT

$$$$ MEDITERRANEAN **Courtyard at Crane.** When it was built in 1917, Crane Cottage—actually an elegant Italianate villa—was the most expensive winter home on Jekyll Island. Now, as part of the Jekyll Island Club Hotel, the Courtyard at Crane offers casual alfresco dining in quirky little dining areas. The menu, which changes twice a year, has a Mediterranean flair with salads and sandwiches at lunch and more substantial dishes in the evening. Previous dinner offerings have included a bacon-wrapped filet mignon and a pan-seared duck breast with plum cherry chutney. The bread served at dinner, a warm loaf speckled with vegetables, is especially tasty and made in-house. *Average main: $31* *Jekyll Island Club Hotel, 375 Riverview Dr.* *912/635–2600* *www.jekyllclub.com* *No dinner Fri. and Sat.*

$$$$ SOUTHERN ★ **Grand Dining Room.** This colonnaded restaurant inside the Jekyll Club maintains a tradition of fine dining first established in the 19th century. The huge fireplace, views of the pool, and sparkling silver and crystal all contribute to the sense of old-style elegance. Signature dishes are the rack of lamb, duck breast, and the filet mignon, all seasoned differently depending on the seasons. The menu also includes local seafood and upscale takes on regional dishes such as shrimp and grits. Note that while there is a "jacket preference" for male dining guests, there is not a dress code. *Average main: $29* *Jekyll Island Club, 371 Riverview Dr.* *912/635-5155* *www.jekyllclub.com* *Reservations essential* *Jacket required.*

$$$ SEAFOOD **Latitude 31.** Right on the Jekyll Island Club Wharf, in the middle of the historic district, Latitude 31 wins the prize for best location.

The interior is understated and beach-chic, with hard-wood floors and huge windows overlooking the sea. This is definitely the place to be for a romantic sunset. The menu has lots of seafood, from wild Georgia shrimp to jumbo crab cakes, but there are also several meat and pasta dishes. There is a kids' menu to boot. *Average main: $23 Jekyll Island Club Wharf, 1 Pier Rd. 912/635–3800 www.latitude31jekyllisland.com Closed Mon.*

$$ SEAFOOD ★ **The Rah Bar.** A tiny swamp shack right on the end of the Jekyll Island Club Wharf (connected to Latitude 31), the Rah Bar is the place for a hands-on experience. It's elbow-to-elbow dining—unless you eat at the tables outside on the wharf—with "rah" oysters (get it?), "crawdaddies," and "u peel 'em" shrimp. As you eat, you look out on the beautiful salt-marsh sunsets. Live bands on the weekends. *Average main: $17 Jekyll Island Club Wharf, 1 Pier Rd. 912/635–3800 www.latitude31jekyllisland.com.*

$$ SEAFOOD **SeaJay's Waterfront Cafe & Pub.** A casual tavern overlooking the Jekyll Harbor Marina, SeaJay's serves delicious, inexpensive seafood, including a crab chowder and Brunswick stew that locals love. This is also the home of the wildly popular, nightly Lowcountry boil buffet: an all-you-can-eat feast of local shrimp, corn on the cob, smoked sausage, and red potatoes. There's live music Thursday through Saturday night. **TIP→** Bring the kids—special menus run from $5.95. *Average main: $19 Jekyll Harbor Marina, 1 Harbor Point Rd. 912/635–3200 www.seajays.com.*

## WHERE TO STAY

*Hotel reviews have been abbreviated in this book. For expanded reviews, please go to Fodors.com.*

$$ HOTEL **Beachview Club.** Grand old oak trees shade the grounds of this luxury lodging. **Pros:** friendly and eager staff; property on the beach. **Cons:** not much for kids to do here. *Rooms from: $169 721 N. Beachview Dr. 912/635–2256, 800/299–2228 www.beachviewclub.com 27 rooms, 11 suites.*

$$$ RESORT ★ **Jekyll Island Club Hotel.** This sprawling 1887 resort was once described as "the richest, the most exclusive, the most inaccessible club in the world." **Pros:** on the water; Old-World charm, with traditional room keys; close proximity to restaurants, shopping, and sea-turtle center. **Cons:** room decor and some appliances could use an update. *Rooms from: $209 371 Riverview Dr. 912/635–2600, 800/535–9547 www.jekyllclub.com 138 rooms, 19 suites.*

$ HOTEL **Oceanside Inn and Suites.** This two-story, motel-style property directly on the ocean has been around for more than 50 years, thanks in no small part to its fantastic location. **Pros:** lovely views; laundry facilities; good value. **Cons:** some guests have complained about the bathrooms being small and needing updating. *Rooms from: $105 711 N. Beachview Dr. 912/635–2211 www.oceansideinnandsuites.com 80 rooms, 94 suites.*

## SPORTS AND THE OUTDOORS

### BEACHES

**Driftwood Beach.** For a firsthand look at the effects of erosion on barrier islands, head at low tide to this oceanfront boneyard on North Beach, where live oaks and pines are being consumed by the sea at an alarming rate. The snarl of trunks and limbs and the dramatic, massive root systems of upturned trees are an eerie and intriguing tableau of nature's slow and steady power. It's been estimated that nearly 1,000 feet of Jekyll's beach have been lost since the early 1900s. ■ **TIP→** Bring your camera; the photo opportunities are terrific, and this is the best place to shoot St. Simons Lighthouse. The snarling branches of submerged trees can make this a dangerous place to swim, however, so use caution in the water. Restrooms and other facilities are at the Clam Creek Picnic Area. **Amenities:** parking, showers, toilets. **Best for:** solitude, sunrise. ✉ *Walk from the trailhead at the east side of the Clam Creek Picnic Area or from the roadside parking area on N. Beachview Dr.*

#### CAMPING ON JEKYLL ISLAND

**Jekyll Island Campground.** At the northern end of Jekyll across from the entrance to the fishing pier, this campground lies on 18 wooded acres with more than 200 closely packed sites that can accommodate everything from backpackers looking for primitive sites to RVs needing full hookups. Pets are welcome, but there's a $3 fee. It's within walking distance to Driftwood Beach but far from the main activity of the island. ✉ *1197 Riverview Dr., Jekyll Island, Georgia* ☎ *866/658–3021.*

**Great Dunes Park.** The newest addition to Jekyll Island's beach facilities (only partially constructed at this writing) is this centrally located park next to the convention center on South Beachview Drive. A beach deck and multiple dune crossovers provide access to the hard packed beach, and a boardwalk offers beachfront bike parking. Facilities include ample parking, restrooms and changing areas, and a pavilion for local events and festivals. **Amenities:** parking, showers, toilets. **Best for:** swimming. ✉ *S. Beachview Dr. on the north side of the convention center* 🌐 *www.jekyllisland.com.*

**Great Dunes Beach.** Starting just south of the entrance road on South Beachview Drive, this strand runs from the beach deck, next to the convention center, to Glory Boardwalk (built when the final battle scene of the film *Glory* was shot here) at the soccer complex. This is one of the most accessible beaches on the island, with parking at both ends and good shower/restroom facilities at the beach deck. The white-sand beach is backed by dunes, which are protected wildlife areas, while calm, shallow water, and a mild shore break make this a good spot to swim and play in the surf. **Amenities:** parking, showers, toilets. **Best for:** swimming. ✉ *S. Beachview Dr. from the beach deck to the Glory Boardwalk.*

**St. Andrews Beach.** Stretching south of the Glory Boardwalk to the St. Andrews Picnic Area at the very southern end of the island, this narrow beach backs up to dense maritime forest, making it a quiet, secluded bit of coast and a great spot for wildlife viewing or beachcombing. At the picnic area, a short trail leads to a viewing platform overlooking the outflow of Jekyll Creek—keep an eye out for dolphins cruising near the shoreline. **Amenities:** parking, toilets. **Best for:** solitude. ✉ *Take S. Beachview Dr. or S. Riverview Dr. to the southernmost end of the island.*

## BIKING

The best way to see Jekyll is by bicycle: a long, paved trail runs right along the beach, and there's an extensive network of paths throughout the island.

**Beachside Bike Rentals.** Located at Days Inn, this one-stop rental shop offers everything from multispeed bikes to double surreys with Bimini tops that look like antique cars and carry up to six adults and two children. The shop also has beach chairs, umbrellas, stand-up paddle boards, and kayaks. ✉ *60 S. Beachview Dr.* ☎ *912/635–9801* 🌐 *www.beachsidebikerentals.com.*

**Jekyll Island Mini-Golf and Bike Rentals.** Play minigolf or choose from a wide selection of rental bikes, including surrey pedal cars that can hold four people, recumbent bikes, and traditional bikes at this shop located next to the Red Bug. ✉ *N. Beachview Dr. at Shell Rd.* ☎ *912/635–2648.*

## FISHING

**Coastal Expeditions.** With 40 years of experience in local waters, Captain Vernon Reynolds provides half-day and full-day trips in-shore and offshore for fishing, dolphin-watching, and sightseeing. ✉ *Jekyll Harbor Marina* ☎ *912/265–0392* 🌐 *www.coastalcharterfishing.com.*

**Jekyll Fishing Center.** Larry Crews runs in-shore and offshore fishing trips and dolphin-watching and sightseeing tours on four charter boats. He also offers his services as captain to tie the knot for couples with their sea legs. ✉ *Jekyll Island Fishing Pier, 10 Clam Creek Rd.* ☎ *912/270–7474* 🌐 *www.offshore-charters.com.*

## GOLF

**Jekyll Island Golf Club.** A golf destination for nearly 90 years, today this club has four courses: the original 9-hole course called Oceanside Nine (now known as Great Dunes), built in 1926, and three beautifully designed 18-hole courses, plus a clubhouse. ✉ *322 Capt. Wylly Rd.* ☎ *912/635–2368* 🌐 *www.golf.jekyllisland.com* 🏌 *63 holes. 6458–6700 yds. Par 72 (all 18-hole courses). Green Fee: $45 (18 holes), $25 (9 holes)* ☞ *Facilities: Driving range, putting green, pitching area, golf carts, pull carts, rental clubs, pro shop, golf academy/lessons, restaurant, bar.*

## HORSEBACK RIDING

**Three Oaks Carriage and Trail Company.** See Jekyll by horseback with this well-regarded livery company, in business for more than 30 years. Trail rides include visits to the salt marsh and Driftwood Beach, a boneyard of live oaks and pine trees being reclaimed by the sea; narrated carriage tours explore the sights of the historic district. Rides leave from the Clam Creek picnic area across from the Jekyll Island Campground, and the carriages leave from the Island History Center.

Perks for families include a horse camp for children and riding lessons for all ages. Three Oaks is located in a historic building that has been used as a livery for over 100 years. ✉ *Jekyll Island History Center, 100 Stable Rd.* ☎ *912/635–9500* 🌐 *www.threeoakscarriageandtrail.com.*

### TENNIS

**Jekyll Island Tennis Center.** The center offers 13 clay courts, with 7 lighted for nighttime play, and provides lessons for all ages and summer camps for juniors. Courts cost $6 per person, per session, daily 9 am to 10 pm. Reservations for lighted courts are required and must be made before the shop closes at 6 the day of play. ✉ *400 Capt. Wylly Rd.* ☎ *912/635–3154.*

## CUMBERLAND ISLAND

**Fodor's Choice** ★ *47 miles south of Jekyll Island; 115 miles south of Savannah to St. Marys via I–95; 45 minutes by ferry from St. Marys.*

Cumberland, the largest of Georgia's coastal isles, is a national treasure. The 18-mile spit of land off the coast of St. Marys is a nearly unspoiled sanctuary of marshes, dunes, beaches, forests, lakes, and ponds. And although it has a long history of human habitation, it remains much as nature created it: a dense, lacework canopy of live oak shades, sand roads, and foot trails through thick undergrowths of palmetto. Wild horses roam freely on pristine beaches. Waterways are homes for gators, sea turtles, otters, snowy egrets, great blue herons, ibises, wood storks, and more than 300 other species of birds. And in its forests are armadillos, wild horses, deer, raccoons, and an assortment of reptiles.

In the 16th century the Spanish established a mission and a garrison, San Pedro de Mocama, on the southern end of the island. But development didn't begin in earnest until the wake of the American Revolution, with timbering operations for shipbuilding, particularly construction of warships for the early U.S. naval fleet. Cotton, rice, and indigo plantations were also established. In 1818 Revolutionary War hero General "Lighthorse" Harry Lee, father of Robert E. Lee, died and was buried near the Dungeness estate of General Nathaniel Greene. Though his body was later moved to Virginia to be interred beside his son, the gravestone remains. During the 1880s, the family of Thomas Carnegie (brother of industrialist Andrew) built several lavish homes here. In the 1950s the National Park Service named Cumberland Island and Cape Cod as the most significant natural areas on the Atlantic and Gulf coasts. And in 1972, in response to attempts to develop the island by Hilton Head developer Charles Fraser, Congress passed a bill establishing the island as a national seashore. Today most of the island is part of the national park system.

### GETTING HERE AND AROUND

The only access to the island is via the *Cumberland Queen,* a reservations-only, 146-passenger ferry based near the National Park Service Information Center at St. Marys. The round-trip ticket price is $17. The $4 entry fee to the Cumberland Island National Seashore (⇨ *Exploring*) applies to all island visitors. There are two Park Service docks at the

Wild horses roam freely on Cumberland Island.

island's south end: the main ferry dock is the Sea Camp Dock, with a secondary stop at Dungeness Dock farther south.

Ferry bookings are heavy in spring and early summer. Cancellations and no-shows often make last-minute space available, but don't rely on it. You can make reservations up to six months in advance. The ferry operates twice (October–February) or three times (March–September) a day in both directions between St. Marys and Cumberland Island. ■ **TIP→ Note that the ferry does not transport pets, kayaks, or cars.**

Getting around the island is solely by foot or bicycle, which can be rented at the Sea Camp dock.

**ESSENTIALS**

**Ferry *Cumberland Queen.*** ✉ *101 Wheeler St, St. Marys* ☎ *912/882–4335* 🌐 *wwww.nps.gov/cuis.*

## EXPLORING

**Cumberland Island National Seashore.** Encompassing the vast majority of Cumberland Island, this 36,347-acre preserve has pristine forests and marshes marbled with wooded nature trails, 18 miles of undeveloped beaches, and opportunities for fishing, bird-watching, and viewing the ruins of Thomas Carnegie's great estate, **Dungeness.** You can also join history and nature walks led by Park Service rangers. Bear in mind that summers are hot and humid and that you must bring everything you need, including your own food, soft drinks, sunscreen, and insect repellent. The only public access to the island is via the *Cumberland Queen* ferry (⇨ *Getting Here and Around*). ✉ *101 Wheeler St., St.*

*Marys* ☎ *912/882–4335* 🌐 *www.nps.gov/cuis* 🎟 *Preserve $4, ferry $20* ⏲ *Year-round, 24 hrs; ferry departures 2–3 times per day.*

WORD OF MOUTH

"BEST BEACH and most unique = Cumberland Island. Our very own (almost) deserted island. For overnights you can either camp or splurge and stay at the Greyfield Inn."

—starrs

OFF THE BEATEN PATH

**The First African Baptist Church.** This small, one-room church on the north end of Cumberland Island is where John F. Kennedy Jr. and Carolyn Bessette were married on September 21, 1996. Constructed of whitewashed logs, it's simply adorned with a cross made of sticks tied together with string and 11 handmade pews seating 40 people. It was built in 1937 to replace a cruder 1893 structure used by former slaves from the High Point–Half Moon Bluff community. The Kennedy–Bessette wedding party stayed at the Greyfield Inn, built on the south end of the island in 1900 by the Carnegie family. ✉ *North end of Cumberland, near Half Moon Bluff, about 12 miles from Sea Camp dock.*

**St. Marys Aquatic Center.** If the heat has you, and the kids are itching to get wet, head to this full-service water park on the mainland, where you can get an inner tube and relax floating down the Continuous River, hurtle down Splash Mountain, or corkscrew yourself silly sliding down the Orange Crush. ✉ *301 Herb Bauer Dr., St. Marys* ☎ *912/673–8118* 🌐 *www.funatsmac.com* 🎟 *$9.95* ⏲ *Summer daily; hrs vary.*

## WHERE TO STAY

*Hotel reviews have been abbreviated in this book. For expanded reviews, please go to Fodors.com.*

### ON THE ISLAND

$$$$ B&B/INN ★ **Greyfield Inn.** Once described as a "Tara by the sea," this turn-of-the-last-century Carnegie family home is Cumberland Island's only accommodation. **Pros:** air-conditioned in summer; lack of telephone service means complete solitude. **Cons:** no stores on Cumberland; communications to the mainland are limited. $ *Rooms from: $475* ✉ *Southern end of the island, accessible by private boat from Fernadina Beach, FL* ☎ *904/261–6408, 866/401–8581* 🌐 *www.greyfieldinn.com* *12 rooms, 4 suites* 🍽 *All meals.*

### ON THE MAINLAND

$ HOTEL **Cumberland Island Inn & Suites.** Children under 18 stay free at this modern, moderately priced hotel 3½ miles from the St. Marys waterfront. **Pros:** clean, large rooms; affordable rates. **Cons:** not in historic area; not in walking distance to the beach. $ *Rooms from: $79* ✉ *2710 Osborne Rd., St. Marys* ☎ *912/882–6250, 800/768–6250* 🌐 *www.cumberlandislandinn.com* *79 rooms* 🍽 *Breakfast.*

$ B&B/INN **Riverview Hotel.** The front door to the Riverview could be a time machine transporting you straight to the Old West, circa 1916, the year the hotel was built. **Pros:** old-time touches; excellent location. **Cons:** some rooms seem a little bit shabby; some common areas are

CLOSE UP

## Georgia's Black Republic

After capturing Savannah in December 1864, General William Tecumseh Sherman read the Emancipation Proclamation at the Second African Baptist Church and issued his now famous Field Order No. 15, giving freed slaves 40 acres and a mule. The field order set aside a swath of land reaching 30 miles inland from Charleston to northern Florida (roughly the area east of Interstate 95), including the coastal islands, for an independent state of freed slaves.

Under the administration of General Rufus Saxton and his assistant, Tunis G. Campbell, a black New Jersey native who represented McIntosh County as a state senator, a black republic was established with St. Catherines Island as its capital. Hundreds of former slaves were relocated to St. Catherines and Sapelo islands, where they set about cultivating the land. In 1865 Campbell established himself as virtual king, controlling a legislature, a court, and a 275-man army. Whites called Campbell "the most feared man in Georgia."

Congress repealed Sherman's directive and replaced General Saxton with General Davis Tillison, who was sympathetic to the interests of former plantation owners, and in 1867 federal troops drove Campbell off St. Catherines and into McIntosh County, where he continued to exert his power. In 1876 he was convicted of falsely imprisoning a white citizen and sentenced, at the age of 63, to work on a chain gang. After being freed, he left Georgia for good and settled in Boston, where he died in 1891. Every year on the fourth Saturday in June, the town of Darien holds a festival in Campbell's honor.

not air-conditioned. *Rooms from: $80* ✉ *105 Osborne St., St. Marys* ☎ *912/882–3242* 🌐 *www.riverviewhotelstmarys.com* *18 rooms* *Breakfast.*

$ B&B/INN **Spencer House Inn.** At the heart of St. Mary's historic district, this pink, three-story Victorian inn, built in 1872, is a perfect base for touring the town and Cumberland Island. **Pros:** short walk to the ferry; big balconies with rocking chairs. **Cons:** not recommended for young singles in search of a party. *Rooms from: $135* ✉ *101 E. Bryant St., St. Marys* ☎ *912/882–1872, 888/840–1872* 🌐 *www.spencerhouseinn.com* *13 rooms, 1 suite* *Breakfast.*

## SPORTS AND THE OUTDOORS

### BEACHES

★ **Dungeness Beach.** From the Dungeness ferry dock to the southern tip of the island, Dungeness Beach covers nearly 2 miles of pristine, remote coast. This wild stretch of sand attracts beachcombers—sharks' teeth are a sought-after find—and fishermen, who cast for redfish and flounder at the southernmost point, called Pelican Flats. Trails lead to Thomas Carnegie's historic estate, Dungeness, and this is also a good area to spot Cumberland's famed wild horses that roam the beach and inland

## CAMPING ON CUMBERLAND ISLAND

**Brickhill Bluff Campground.** Way off the beaten path, this primitive campsite is a favorite spot to see manatees and dolphins. For those looking for adventure (and not amenities), Brickhill is worth the long hike from the dock. ✉ *Cumberland Island* ☎ *912/882–4336* 🌐 *www.nps.gov/cuis.*

**Hickory Hill Campground.** Located in the heart of the island, this primitive camping area is about 1 mile from the beach. Though still in the trees, its canopy is more open than at some of the other sites. ✉ *5½ miles from Sea Camp ferry dock, Cumberland Island* ☎ *912/882–4336* 🌐 *www.nps.gov/cuis.*

**Sea Camp Campground.** Close to the ferry dock and with plenty of amenities, this is an ideal spot for first-timers, families, and groups. Expect a fire pit, food cage, and picnic table at each site. ✉ *½ mile from Sea Camp ferry dock, Cumberland Island* ☎ *912/882–4336* 🌐 *www.nps.gov/cuis.*

**Stafford Beach Campground.** Located behind the dunes, 3½ miles from the ferry dock, this is the only backcountry site not considered to be in the wilderness. It has more amenities than most of the other, more primitive sites. Expect good tree cover, bathrooms, showers, and a water source. ✉ *3½ miles from Sea Camp ferry dock, Cumberland Island* ☎ *912/882–4336* 🌐 *www.nps.gov/cuis*

**Yankee Paradise Campground.** Surrounded by palmettos, this forested and secluded spot is protected from the wind. It's a long hike back to the ferry dock, but the remoteness could be a big draw for some. ✉ *7½ miles from Sea Camp ferry dock, Cumberland Island* ☎ *912/882–4336* 🌐 *www.nps.gov/cuis.*

areas here. **Amenities:** none. **Best for:** solitude, sunrise. ✉ *Dungeness ferry dock to Pelican Flats.*

**Sea Camp Beach.** Proximity to the ferry makes this beach fronting the Sea Camp campground the most popular beach among day-trippers, though with only 300 visitors allowed on-island daily, it's never very crowded. Hard-pack trails and a boardwalk allow short nature walks, and the beach has good beachcombing. **Amenities:** showers, toilets. **Best for:** solitude, sunrise. ✉ *½ mile north of Sea Camp dock.*

### KAYAKING

**Up the Creek Xpeditions.** Whether you're a novice or skilled paddler, Up the Creek can guide you on kayak tours through some of Georgia and Florida's most scenic waters. Classes include navigation, tides and currents, and kayak surfing and racing. Trips include Yulee, the St. Marys River, Cumberland Sound, and the Okefenokee Swamp. ✉ *111 Osborne St., St. Marys* ☎ *912/882–0911* 🌐 *www.upthecreekx.com.*

## NIGHTLIFE

**Seagle's Saloon and Patio Bar.** The closer you get to borders, the more pronounced allegiances become. A case in point is Seagle's Saloon and Patio Bar, a smoky watering hole not far from the Florida state line

Sea Camp, one of five campgrounds on Cumberland Island, is closest to the ferry dock.

that's festooned with University of Georgia memorabilia. Bawdy bartender Cindy Deen is a local legend, so expect some Southern sass. ✉ *105 Osborne St., St. Marys* ☎ *912/882–1807.*

## OKEFENOKEE NATIONAL WILDLIFE REFUGE

Larger than all of Georgia's barrier islands combined, the Okefenokee National Wildlife Refuge covers 700 square miles of southeastern Georgia and northeastern Florida. From the air, all roads and almost all traces of human development almost disappear into this vast, seemingly impenetrable landscape, the largest intact freshwater wetlands in the contiguous United States. The rivers, lakes, forests, prairies, and swamps all teem with seen and unseen life: alligators, otters, bobcats, raccoons, opossums, white-tailed deer, turtles, bald eagles, red-tailed hawks, egrets, muskrats, herons, cranes, red-cockaded woodpeckers, and black bears all make their home here. The term "swamp" hardly does the Okefenokee justice. It's the largest peat-producing bog in the United States, with numerous and varied landscapes, including aquatic prairies, towering virgin cypress, sandy pine islands, and lush subtropical hammocks.

None of the parks encompass everything the refuge has to offer; you need to determine what your highest priorities are and choose your gateway on that basis. Day trips and boat rentals can be arranged at any of the parks, and more adventurous visitors can take guided or independent overnight canoe-camping trips into the interior. The refuge offers permits for 14 multiday itineraries along the nearly 120 miles of boat trails. Paddlers camping in the swamp must spend their nights in designated wooden shelters built on stilts over the water.

**■ TIP→ Visit between September and April to avoid the biting insects that emerge in May, especially in the dense interior.**

### GETTING HERE AND AROUND

To get around the Okefenokee swamplands you will need a motorboat, canoe, or kayak, or you'll have to book a tour. Rentals and tours are arranged through individual parks and local outfitters.

Three gateways provide access to the refuge: the eastern (and main) entrance at the Suwannee Canal Recreation Area, near Folkston; a northern entrance at the privately owned Okefenokee Swamp Park near Waycross; and a western entrance at Stephen C. Foster State Park, outside the town of Fargo. There are also two small boat launches (no facilities) at Kingfisher Landing and the Suwannee River Sill on the eastern and western sides, respectively.

The surrounding towns of Folkston, Waycross, and Fargo don't offer much as destinations themselves—they primarily serve as bases from which to visit the swamp.

## SUWANNEE CANAL RECREATION AREA

*8 miles southwest of Folkston via Rte. 121.*

**Suwannee Canal Recreation Area.** Extensive open areas at the core of the refuge—like Chesser, Grand, and Mizell prairies—branch off the man-made Suwanee Canal, accessed via the main entrance to the Okefenokee National Wildlife Refuge, and contain small natural lakes and gator holes. The prairies are excellent spots for sport fishing and birding, and it's possible to take guided boat tours of the area leaving from the Okefenokee Adventures concession, near the visitor center. The concession also has equipment rentals, and food is available at the Camp Cornelia Cafe. The visitor center has a film, exhibits, and a mechanized mannequin that tells stories about life in the Okefenokee (it sounds hokey but it's surprisingly informative). A boardwalk takes you over the water to a 50-foot observation tower. Hikers, bicyclists, and private motor vehicles are welcome on the Swamp Island Drive; several interpretive walking trails may be taken along the way. Picnicking is permitted. ✉ *Visitor center, 4155 Suwannee Canal Rd.* ☎ *912/496–7836* 🌐 *www.fws.gov/okefenokee* 🎫 *$5 per car* 🕑 *Refuge Mar.–Oct., daily ½ hr before sunrise–7:30 pm; Nov.–Feb., daily ½ hr before sunrise–5:30 pm.*

### WHERE TO EAT AND STAY

*Hotel reviews have been abbreviated in this book. For expanded reviews, please go to Fodors.com.*

$ SOUTHERN ✕ **Okefenokee Restaurant.** Everything's home-cooked at this half-century-old, local institution—and from the fried shrimp to the black-eyed peas, it's all good. They open early for breakfast and have a daily lunch and dinner buffet, which includes tea or coffee, for $8.50. Ⓢ *Average main: $9* ✉ *1596 S. 3rd St.* ☎ *912/496–3263* 🕑 *Closed Sun.*

$ B&B/INN **The Folkston House.** This white, two-story B&B built in 1900 has rooms with names like Victorian Lace, Suite Destiny, and Jardin de

Canoe trips into the Okefenokee Swamp Park reveal its unique ecology.

Lune that are filled with antiques and period furniture, though the overall effect is contemporary country. **Pros:** elegantly furnished; excellent breakfast. **Cons:** no children under age eight permitted. *Rooms from: $110 264 Kingsland Dr. 904/219–4240 www.folkstonhouse.com 7 rooms Breakfast.*

$ B&B/INN **The Inn at Folkston.** This Craftsman-style inn with a huge front veranda, porch swings, and rocking chairs is filled with antiques, and each room is uniquely decorated. **Pros:** inn is beautifully restored; owners make you feel like welcome relatives. **Cons:** the many trains that pass by can be noisy. *Rooms from: $120 3576 W. Main St. 912/496–6256, 888/509–6246 www.innatfolkston.com 4 rooms Breakfast.*

## SPORTS AND THE OUTDOORS

### CANOEING AND CAMPING

**Okefenokee Wildlife Refuge.** Wilderness camping, by canoe or kayak, in the Okefenokee's interior is allowed by permit only (for which there's a $10 fee per person, per night). Availability is limited and can fill

### CAMPING NEAR OKEFENOKEE SWAMP

**Laura S. Walker State Park.** One of the few state parks named for a woman, this 626-acre park honors a Waycross teacher who championed conservation. The park, 9 miles northeast of the Okefenokee Swamp Park, has campsites with electrical and water hookups. Be sure to pick up food and supplies on the way. Boating, skiing, and fishing are permitted on the 120-acre lake, and there's an 18-hole golf course with a restaurant. *5653 Laura Walker Rd., Waycross 800/864–7275 www.gastateparks.org/lauraswalker.*

up fast, especially in the cooler seasons. During March and April, the most popular months, trips are limited to two nights. Reservations can be made only by phone. Call the Okefenokee Wildlife Refuge headquarters weekdays between 7 am and 10 am within two months of your desired starting date to make a reservation. ☎ *912/496–3331* ⊕ *www.fws.gov/okefenokee.*

**Okefenokee Adventures.** Guided overnight canoe trips can be arranged by this rental and guiding business. They also do 90-minute interpretive boat tours ($18) and have boat, canoe, and kayak rentals. ✉ *4159 Suwannee Canal Rd.* ☎ *912/496–7156* ⊕ *www.okefenokeeadventures.com.*

## OKEFENOKEE SWAMP PARK

*8 miles south of Waycross via U.S. 1.*

**Okefenokee Swamp Park.** This privately owned and operated park serves as the northern entrance to the Okefenokee National Wildlife Refuge, offering exhibits and orientation programs for the entire family. The park has observation areas, wilderness walkways, an outdoor museum of pioneer life, and boat tours into the swamp that reveal its unique ecology. The 90-foot-tall observation tower is an excellent place to glimpse cruising gators and birds. A 1½-mile train tour (included in the admission price) passes by a Seminole village and stops at Pioneer Island, a re-created pioneer homestead, for a 15-minute walking tour. ✉ *5700 Okefenokee Swamp Park Rd.* ☎ *912/283–0583* ⊕ *www.okeswamp.com* *$15, $25 with 45-min boat tour* ⏲ *Daily 9–5:30.*

### WHERE TO STAY

*Hotel reviews have been abbreviated in this book. For expanded reviews, please go to Fodors.com.*

$ HOTEL **Quality Inn and Suites.** What makes this chain hotel stand out is its bargain package deal: for $90 you get a double room and two adult admissions to the Okefenokee Swamp Park. **Pros:** affordable rooms; convenient location; good breakfast. **Cons:** older hotel; fairly standard chain experience. $ *Rooms from: $69* ✉ *1725 Memorial Dr.* ☎ *912/283–4490, 800/424–6423* ⊕ *www.qualityinn.com* *141 rooms* *Breakfast.*

$ B&B/INN **Pond View Inn.** Though the pond is long gone, everything else is just as it should be here at one of the more elegant lodgings in Waycross. **Pros:** beautiful, with historic decor; reasonably priced. **Cons:** only four rooms, so it might be full on a busy weekend. $ *Rooms from: $95* ✉ *311 Pendleton St.* ☎ *912/283–9300, 866/582–5149* ⊕ *www.pondviewinn.com* *4 rooms* *Breakfast.*

## STEPHEN C. FOSTER STATE PARK

**Stephen C. Foster State Park.** Named for the songwriter who penned "Swanee River," this 80-acre island park is the southwestern entrance to the Okefenokee National Wildlife Refuge and offers trips to the headwaters of the Suwannee River, Billy's Island—site of an ancient Indian village—and a turn-of-the-20th-century town built to support logging efforts in the swamp. The park is home to hundreds of species of birds and a large cypress-and-black-gum forest, a majestic backdrop for one of the thickest growths of vegetation in the southeastern United States. Park naturalists lead boat tours and recount a wealth of Okefenokee lore while you observe alligators, birds, and native trees and plants. You may also take a self-guided excursion in a rental canoe or a motorized flat-bottom boat. ✉ *17515 Hwy. 177* ☎ *912/637–5274, 800/864–7275* 🌐 *www.gastateparks.org/info/scfoster* 🎟 *$5 per vehicle* ⏲ *Daily 7 am–10 pm.*

## EXPLORING

**Suwannee River Visitors Center.** A high-definition film and exhibits on swamp, river, and timbering history are part of the fare at this visitor center in Fargo. The 7,000-square-foot facility is eco-friendly, employing solar-powered fans, composting toilets that use no water, decking made from recycled plastic, insulation from recycled newspapers, and a retaining wall made from recycled dashboards and electrical cables. ✉ *125 Suwannee River Dr., at U.S. 441 bridge over Suwannee River* ☎ *912/637–5156* 🌐 *www.gastateparks.org/info/scfoster* 🎟 *Free* ⏲ *Wed.–Sun. 9–5.*

### CAMPING IN STEPHEN C. FOSTER STATE PARK

**Stephen C. Foster State Park.** The park has sites for all types of camping as well as basically equipped, two-bedroom cabins that can sleep up to eight. Be aware that the gates of the park are closed between sunset and sunrise—there's no traffic in or out for campers, so you need to stock up on supplies before the sun goes down. You can book sites and cabins up to 13 months in advance. ✉ *17515 Hwy. 177, Fargo* ☎ *800/864–7275* 🌐 *www.gastateparks.org/info/scfoster.*

# Southwest Georgia

**WORD OF MOUTH**

"I was fortunate to attend the Fantasy in Lights last week [at Callaway Gardens], it was spectacular. Worth every penny. Do take a blanket; it is freezing on the wagon trains."

—Lynn Clayton

# WELCOME TO SOUTHWEST GEORGIA

## TOP REASONS TO GO

★ **Callaway Gardens Resort and Preserve:** 14,000 acres of gardens and parkland make this the raison d'être for visiting Pine Mountain. In spring the rhododendrons and wild azaleas take your breath away.

★ **Thomasville plantations:** Nowhere is the lore of the Deep South better understood than in and around the plantations of Thomasville. Because many have been restored as country inns or are open to the public, they are almost like living museums.

★ **FDR's Little White House:** The cottage where President Franklin Delano Roosevelt stayed while taking in the healing waters of Warm Springs looks much as it did in his day. You can even see the pools where he was treated for polio.

★ **Jimmy Carter's home town:** President Jimmy Carter and First Lady Rosalynn Carter still live in Plains, Georgia, and still worship at the Maranatha Baptist Church. There are a number of museums and historic sites in Plains dedicated to Carter's legacy.

**1 Western Foothills and Farmland.** Take a walk through the past with a visit to Franklin Roosevelt's Little White House retreat or tiptoe through the tulips at the 14,000-acre Callaway Gardens. This area also is home to Georgia's largest state park, and massive Fort Benning.

**2 The Southwest Corner.** Antiques shopping, peach picking, golf courses, and country inns are abundant in this part of the state, particularly in Thomasville, which is celebrated most for its Victorian homes, plantations, and historic churches.

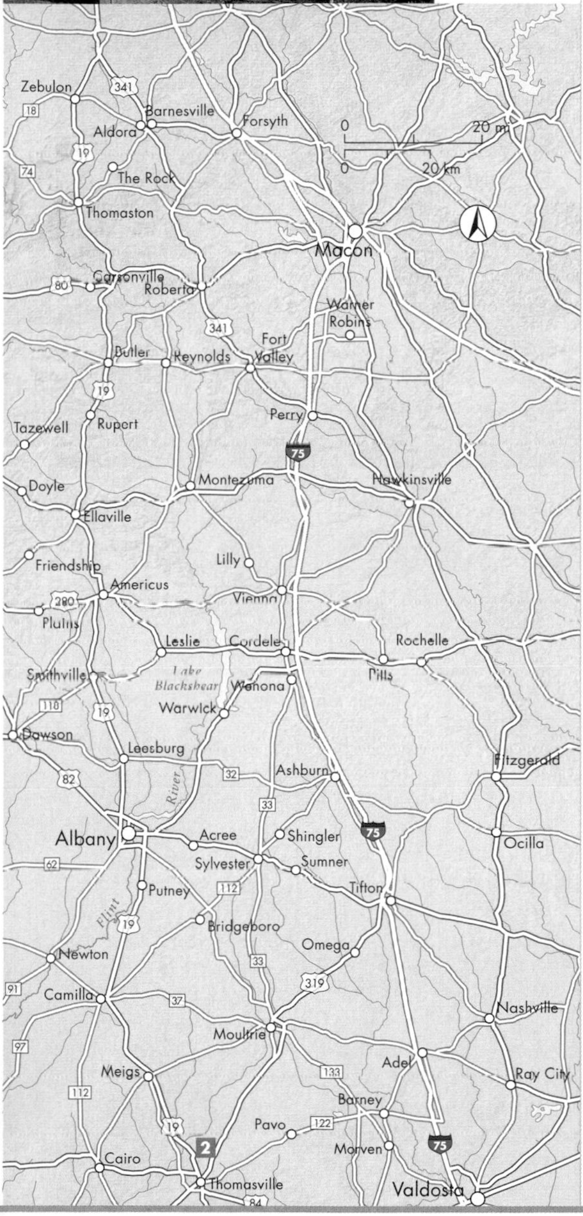

# GETTING ORIENTED

Scattered along a vast coastal plain that covers much of the southern part of the state, the small towns of southwest Georgia are best explored by car or by the SAM Shortline. The touring train chugs through the countryside between Cordele and Archery.

# SOUTHERN SNACKS

Collards, grits, mac and cheese—the list of snacks originating from the South is long with a storied history that dates back to the plantation days and the Civil War.

(above) Collard greens with bacon. (lower right) A bowl of grits isn't complete without a pat of butter. (upper right) Boiled peanuts are at their best piping hot.

Many of the dishes, which have influences from cuisines as varied as African-American, Native American, and French, were of a spontaneous nature, and born of necessity in times of poverty and slavery. Stale bread was turned into bread pudding. Leftover fish became croquettes. Liquid left behind by cooked greens became gravy. The discarded tops of turnips, beets, and dandelions became the stars of a vegetable plate. The unwanted parts of a pig were used to flavor cooked vegetables. Biscuits were used to sop up sauces, so nothing went to waste. And a great emphasis was placed on sharing among family and friends.

Today, you likely won't find boiled peanuts on a mainstream menu in the South. And chitlins, the viscera intestines of a pig, aren't often seen outside of Grandma's country kitchen. But other regional snacks are now sold at gourmet markets and sophisticated restaurants.

—Christine Van Dusen

## SAY CHEESE

Pimento cheese, the orange mix of cheddar cheese, mayonnaise, pimentos, and salt and pepper, has long been considered a Southern comfort food. It is traditionally served as a spread on crackers or between two pieces of soft, white bread, and variations on the classic recipe may include ingredients like Worcestershire sauce, jalapeños, and dill pickles.

### BOILED PEANUTS

Take a drive out of the city and you'll most likely see many a roadside sign advertising this decidedly Southern snack, which—according to legend—has been on the scene since Union General William T. Sherman marched through Georgia. Freshly harvested or raw peanuts are boiled in salted water for four to seven hours, until the shells get soft and the nuts get mushy. They're usually served in a paper bag, which can get soggy, so eat 'em while they're hot.

### COLLARD GREENS

Similar to kale and spring greens, collards have thick, large leaves and a slightly bitter taste. Their origins as a Southern food are traced back to the slaves, who would cook them with the scraps from the kitchen: ham hocks, pork neckbones, fatback, and pig's feet. Seasonings typically include onions, salt, pepper, and vinegar. Nowadays it's a Southern tradition to serve collards on New Year's Eve, along with black-eyed peas, for wealth in the new year.

### MAC AND CHEESE

In the South, this dish is a vegetable. It's true. Though in these creamy, top-browned bowls of noodles and cheese there's not a veggie in sight, many meat-and-three restaurants list mac and cheese as one of the three vegetables you can get on the side. And who are we to argue? Whether we're talking about traditional mac and cheese or a fancier version with homemade shells, truffle oil, and Gouda, it's a rich and sinful Southern snack.

### HUSH PUPPIES

Legend has it that this snack got its name from an African cook in Atlanta. She was frying catfish and croquettes when her puppy began to howl. To quiet the dog she gave him a plate of the croquettes, saying, "Hush, puppy." Really, though, a dog's dish is far too lowly a place for these delicious fried cornmeal dumplings. Today you'll find them on the South's simple country menus and in the breadbaskets of fine-dining establishments.

### SWEETS

Southerners have a sweet tooth, bless their hearts. And it's satisfied by a number of indigenous desserts. There's chess pie, a simple pie with just eggs, sugar, butter, and flour that supposedly got its name when a Southern cook said she was making "jes' pie." Then there's pecan pie, created by French settlers in New Orleans. And of course there is peach cobbler, a favorite in the South, where the climate allows for early peach harvests and few frosts.

Updated by Rachel Roberts Quartarone

The rolling agricultural landscapes of a slower, older South, where things remain much the same as they were for generations, can be found within a couple of hours' drive of Atlanta's high-rise bustle. Here small towns evoke a time when the world was a simpler place, where people lived close to the land and life was measured on a personal scale. In southwest Georgia, peanuts, corn, tobacco, and cotton are the lifeblood of the local economies, and you're as likely to see a tractor on a country road as a car.

People here live far from the hassles of Atlanta's modernity—the daily grind of traffic jams and suburban sprawl. The accents are slow and seductive. Small towns and petite country hamlets beckon with their charming town squares and elegant bed-and-breakfasts. In southwest Georgia the inclination simply to relax is contagious—it can saturate you slowly but completely, like syrup on a stack of pancakes. And the Southern pride is palpable: sometimes seen in yellow ribbons scattered throughout entire communities or heard in conversations that still refer to "the War between the States" rather than the Civil War.

Despite the quiet pace of life here, this is the land of such greats as President Jimmy Carter, writers Erskine Caldwell and Carson McCullers, singers Ma Rainey and Otis Redding, and baseball legend Jackie Robinson. For a time even Franklin Delano Roosevelt was drawn here; he returned again and again for the healing mineral waters of Warm Springs.

## PLANNING

### WHEN TO GO

Because many of the towns in the region are off the beaten path, crowds are rarely a problem, though spring (which comes early) and fall (which comes late) are the most popular seasons. If you're not fond of the heat,

March to May and September to December are the best times to visit. During this time, book well in advance for the more popular hotels and B&Bs in Pine Mountain, Warm Springs, and Thomasville.

## PLANNING YOUR TIME

A traveler could easily get lost on the backroads of southwest Georgia, so perhaps the best way to take in the sites of this region is to park your car and board the SAM Shortline Southwest Georgia Excursion Train in Cordele. The ride will take you to Georgia Veterans State Park, the Rural Telephone Museum, Habitat for Humanity's Global Village, the Rylander Theatre, Windsor Hotel, and Plains. This way you'll get a sense of what spots deserve more time and which are suited for a drive-by.

Many of southwest Georgia's attractions are ideal day trips from Atlanta. Warm Springs, Callaway Gardens, and Pine Mountain are a 90-minute drive from Atlanta. Thomasville is a little over four hours from Atlanta, so plan on an overnight stay.

## GETTING HERE AND AROUND

### AIR TRAVEL

Delta Airlines has daily flights into Columbus Metro Airport (CSG) from Atlanta. American Eagle also flies into Columbus, offering direct flights from the airline's hub in Dallas.

**Air Contacts Columbus Metro Airport (CSG)** ✉ *3250 W. Britt David Rd., Columbus* ☎ *706/324–2449* 🌐 *www.flycolumbusga.com.*

### CAR TRAVEL

A car is the best way to tour this part of Georgia. Interstate 75 runs north–south through the eastern edge of the region and connects to several U.S. and state highways that traverse the area. Interstate 85 runs southwest through LaGrange and Columbus. Do explore backcountry roads—they offer the landscapes and ambience of the real South. Just be sure to travel with a good road map or GPS, and expect detours for photo opportunities.

### TRAIN TRAVEL

A great means of seeing the countryside, the SAM Shortline Southwest Georgia Excursion Train originates in Cordele and runs west through Georgia Veteran's State Park, Leslie, Americus, Plains, and Archery. You can get on or off at any of the stations, stop over for the night, and take the train again the next morning (check the schedule to be sure there's a train running the next day).

**Train Contacts SAM Shortline Southwest Georgia Excursion Train** ✉ *105 E. 9th Ave., Cordele* ☎ *229/276–0755, 877/427–2457* 🌐 *www.samshortline.com.*

## RESTAURANTS

This region of Georgia does lovely things by slow-cooking pork over green oak. Pit barbecue joints in the area are homey, hands-on, and relatively inexpensive. *Prices in the reviews are the average cost of a main course at dinner or, if dinner is not served, at lunch.*

### HOTELS

Lodging in the area runs the gamut from elegant, luxurious properties to low-profile but unique B&Bs to reliable and inexpensive chain hotels. RV parks and campgrounds are also available. *Prices in the reviews are the lowest cost of a standard double room in high season.*

## WESTERN FOOTHILLS AND FARMLAND

You won't be able to visit this slice of Georgia without feeling the influence of two generations of American presidents, Franklin Roosevelt and Jimmy Carter. About 100 miles south of Atlanta, near the Alabama border, Pine Mountain and Warm Springs are the rural retreats they have always been since FDR used to visit, and have retained much of their ambience from yesteryear. The Little White House is among its historical highlights. Plains (Jimmy Carter country) seems cut from the pages of the past.

## WARM SPRINGS

*97 miles southwest of Atlanta via I–85 and U.S. 27.*

Renowned for centuries for the supposed healing properties of its thermal waters, Warm Springs is where the Creek Indians brought their wounded warriors when all other treatments had failed. In the early 1920s news spread that a young Columbus native and polio victim, Louis Joseph, had made a dramatic recovery after extensive therapy in the springs. Word reached Franklin Delano Roosevelt (1882–1945), who had contracted polio, and a 20-year relationship began between him and this remote mountain village, where he built a cottage for his visits that came to be known as the Little White House. Roosevelt's experiences here led to the effort to eradicate polio around the world through the founding of the March of Dimes, and his encounters with his poor rural neighbors fueled ideas for his Depression-era New Deal recovery programs. After Roosevelt's death, the town fell on hard times, but an influx of crafts and antiques shops in the 1980s has revitalized Warm Springs.

#### GETTING HERE AND AROUND

The best way to visit Warm Springs is to travel from Atlanta on Interstate 85 South to Exit 41. Take a left turn onto Highway 27A/41, then continue for 35 miles to Warm Springs. Columbus is another good point to embark from; Warm Springs is about 40 miles south on Georgia 85 North. Much of Warm Springs is walkable, but a car is necessary if you want to hit all the high points.

#### ESSENTIALS

**Visitor Information Warm Springs Welcome Center** ✉ *1 Broad St.* ☎ *706/655–3322, 800/337–1927* 🌐 *www.visitmeriwether.com.*

Franklin Delano Roosevelt used to stay in this modest cottage, nicknamed the Little White House, during his trips to Warm Springs.

## EXPLORING

Fodor'sChoice ★ **Little White House Historic Site/FDR Memorial Museum.** Located on the southern end of town, this fascinating historic site contains the modest three-bedroom cottage in which Roosevelt stayed during his visits. The cottage, built in 1932, remains much as it did the day he died here (while having his portrait painted) and includes the wheelchair Roosevelt designed from a kitchen chair. The unfinished portrait is on display, along with the 48-star American flag that flew over the grounds when Roosevelt died. The FDR Memorial Museum includes an interesting short film narrated by Walter Cronkite (last screening at 4 pm), exhibits detailing Roosevelt's life and New Deal programs, and some of Roosevelt's personal effects, such as his 1938 Ford, complete with the full hand controls he designed. Admission here allows you to also visit the nearby pools where Roosevelt took his therapy. ✉ *401 Little White House Rd.* ☎ *706/655–5870* 🌐 *www.fdr-littlewhitehouse.org* 🎟 *$10* ⏲ *Daily 9–4:45.*

## WHERE TO STAY

*Hotel reviews have been abbreviated in this book. For expanded reviews, please go to Fodors.com.*

$ B&B/INN **Hotel Warm Springs Bed & Breakfast Inn.** In downtown Warm Springs, this historic hotel has plenty of character—the guest rooms have oak furniture and 12-foot ceilings with crown molding. **Pros:** convenient to Warm Springs' sights; storied history. **Cons:** no elevator; sometimes harried staff; not large enough for group travel. 💲 *Rooms from: $110* ✉ *47 Broad St.* ☎ *706/655–2114, 800/366–7616* 🌐 *www.hotelwarmspringsbb.org* 🛏 *10 rooms, 3 suites* 🍽 *Breakfast.*

## PINE MOUNTAIN

*14 miles west of Warm Springs via Rte. 18 and Rte. 194.*

Pine Mountain Ridge is the last foothill of the Appalachian chain, and the town of Pine Mountain rests at the same elevation as Atlanta, making it generally cooler than the surrounding communities. The flora and fauna here reflect the town's Appalachian connections. Most visitors are lured by the surrounding area's large-scale attractions—such as Callaway Gardens Resort and Preserve—and are then pleasantly surprised that the small-town burg has a folksy, inviting downtown square. Antiques figure prominently in the area economy, and shops abound in the town center.

#### GETTING HERE AND AROUND

Pine Mountain can be reached by car from Atlanta via Interstate 85 South and sits 14 miles west of Warm Springs, via Routes 18 and 194. A 90-minute drive from Atlanta, it's a popular destination for day-trippers.

#### ESSENTIALS

**Visitor Information Pine Mountain Welcome Center** ✉ *101 E. Broad St.* ☎ *706/663–4000, 800/441–3502* 🌐 *www.pinemountain.org.*

### EXPLORING

**Callaway Gardens Resort and Preserve.** South of Pine Mountain Village lies the area's main draw: a 14,000-acre golf, tennis, and spa resort with a combination of elaborate, cultivated gardens and natural woodlands. This family-friendly destination was developed in the 1930s by textile magnate Cason J. Callaway and his wife, Virginia, as a way to breathe new life into the area's dormant cotton fields. With more than 1,000 varieties, the **Day Butterfly Center** is one of the largest free-flight conservatories in North America. **Mountain Creek Lake** is well stocked with largemouth bass and bream. **Ida Cason Callaway Memorial Chapel**—a favorite wedding venue—is a lovely stone chapel nestled in the woods alongside a lake and babbling stream. During the holidays, Callaway lights up with the popular "Fantasy in Lights." ✉ *17800 U.S. Hwy. 27* ☎ *706/663–2281, 800/225–5292* 🌐 *www.callawaygardens.com* *$18; free to overnight guests* *Mid-Mar.–early Sept., daily 9–6; mid-Sept.–early Mar., daily 9–5.*

**Wild Animal Safari.** You'll hardly believe you're still in Georgia at this quirky animal preserve northwest of Pine Mountain. Camels, llamas, antelopes, and hundreds of other exotic animals traipse around freely, often coming close to vehicles for a close-up view. You can either drive your own car, rent a Zebra Van, or take a guided bus tour through the 500-acre animal preserve. An added plus is the **Walk-About,** which operates more like a traditional zoo with monkeys, kangaroos, bears, and reptiles on display. **TIP→** The park sells special food for you to offer the animals, and some will scamper over your car to get it. ✉ *1300 Oak Grove Rd.* ☎ *706/663–8744, 800/367–2751* 🌐 *www.animalsafari.com* *$19.95* *Mar. and Apr., daily 10–6:30; May–Labor Day, daily 10–7:30; Labor Day–Feb., daily 10–5:30; call to confirm hrs and tour-bus schedule.*

## WHERE TO EAT AND STAY

*Hotel reviews have been abbreviated in this book. For expanded reviews, please go to Fodors.com.*

$$$$ ECLECTIC **Carriage & Horses.** International cuisine is served in this Victorian house north of town and overlooking the horse pastures of Grey Eagle Farm. The eclectic menu includes escargots, alligator with mushroom and lemon sauce, grilled trout (a house specialty), and filet mignon served with garlicky mashed potatoes. The restaurant's wide windows and patio make it a local favorite for sunset dining, and often local artists play assorted easy-listening '40s and '50s music. *Average main: $25 607 Butts Mill Rd. 706/663–4777 www.cometodagher.com Reservations essential.*

$ RESORT **Callaway Gardens Resort and Preserve.** Stay at this sprawling resort and your room key gains you access to its famous gardens from dawn until dusk. **Pros:** access to gardens; choice of accommodations. **Cons:** some guests say the decor is dated, and housekeeping is slow to respond. *Rooms from: $139 17800 U.S. 27 706/663–2281, 800/225–5292 www.callawaygardens.com 453 rooms, 20 suites, 155 cottages, 50 villas.*

$ B&B/INN **Chipley Murrah House B&B.** One mile from Callaway Gardens and near downtown Pine Mountain, this lavish inn occupies a high-style Queen Anne Victorian dating to 1895. **Pros:** welcoming owners; clean accommodations; spectacular stained glass. **Cons:** breakfast is not included with the cottages; no pets allowed; kids under 12 allowed only in the cottages. *Rooms from: $95 207 W. Harris St. 706/663–9801, 888/782–0797 www.chipleymurrah.com 4 rooms, 3 cottages Closed Jan. Breakfast.*

$ HOTEL **Days Inn.** There are no surprises at this old standby, but it's clean and close to downtown Pine Mountain and area attractions. **Pros:** good Continental breakfast; inexpensive option; close to Callaway Gardens. **Cons:** small rooms; sometimes iffy customer service. *Rooms from: $69 368 S. Main Ave. 706/663–2121, 800/325–2525 www.daysinn.com 60 rooms Breakfast.*

## SPORTS AND THE OUTDOORS

### CANOEING AND KAYAKING

**Flint River Outdoor Center.** About 45 minutes from Pine Mountain between Thomaston and Columbus is the Flint River Outdoor Center, with 10 miles of river courses where you can test your skills in everything from a float tube to kayaks running Class II rapids. Some expeditions include an overnight stay at their campsite. *4429 Woodland Rd., Rte. 36 at Flint River, Thomaston 706/647–2633 www.flintriveroutdoorcenter.com.*

### HORSEBACK RIDING

**Roosevelt Stables.** The mountain terrain makes the Pine Mountain area an interesting place for horseback riding. Roosevelt Stables, in Franklin D. Roosevelt State Park, has 28 miles of trails and offers everything from one-hour rides to overnight trips complete with cowboy breakfasts. *1063 Group Camp Rd. 706/628–7463 www.rooseveltstables.com.*

A ferry transports bikers across Mountain Creek Lake back to the start of the Discovery Bike Trail at Callaway Gardens Resort and Preserve.

## COLUMBUS

*35 miles south of Pine Mountain via U.S. 27.*

During the Civil War, Columbus supplied uniforms, weapons, and other goods to the Confederate army, making the city a prime target for Union troops. But it wasn't until April 16, 1865—a week after the war had ended at Appomattox—that the 13,000 cavalrymen known as "Wilson's Raiders" attacked Columbus and burned all the war industries to the ground. The textile mills soon recovered, however, and grew to a prominence that dwarfed their prewar significance. Textiles still play a major role in the Columbus economy.

Today, Columbus is perhaps best known as the home of Fort Benning, the largest infantry-training center in the world; it's also the site of Columbus College's Schwob School of Music, one of the finest music schools in the South. A project to rejuvenate the downtown area has included the renovation of old manufacturing and ironworks buildings and the creation of the 15-mile **Riverwalk** to highlight the city's river origins; this linear park along the Chattahoochee is ideal for jogging, strolling, biking, and rollerblading.

### ESSENTIALS

**Visitor Information Columbus Convention and Visitors Bureau** ✉ *900 Front Ave.* ☎ *706/322–1613, 800/999–1613* 🌐 *www.visitcolumbusga.com.*

## EXPLORING

**Columbus Museum.** The state's largest art and history museum focuses heavily on American art ranging from colonial portraiture to provocative contemporary works. Other exhibits concentrate on science and the history of the Chattahoochee Valley. ✉ *1251 Wynnton Rd.* ☎ *706/748–2562* 🌐 *www.columbusmuseum.com* 🎫 *Free* ⏲ *Tues.–Wed. and Fri.–Sat. 10–5, Thurs. 10–8, Sun. 1–5. Closed Mon.*

### STRETCH YOUR LEGS

**Pine Mountain Trail** is a favorite of the nearly 40 miles of trails in Franklin D. Roosevelt State Park that are designated for hikers only. Although each part of the trail is interesting in its own right, Dowdell's Knob Loop, near the center, makes a great day hike at 4.7 miles. The 6.5-mile Wolfden Loop is another beautiful part of the trail, traveling past beaver dams, over Hogback Mountain, and along the Mountain Creek Nature Trail, which features all manner of plant life. Trail maps are available at the State Park office and at Callaway Gardens Country Store.

**Heritage Corner.** You can visit four historic buildings in a single block on a guided walking tour given by the Historic Columbus Foundation, including the 1840 four room **Pemberton House,** home to Columbus native John Pemberton (1831–88), the pharmacist who created Coca Cola. Other structures are the one-room early-19th-century **log cabin** that is said to be the oldest extant structure in Muscogee County, the 1828 Federal-style **Walker-Peters-Langdon House,** and the 1840s **Woodruff Farm House.** ✉ *708 Broadway* ☎ *706/322–0756* 🌐 *www.historiccolumbus.com* 🎫 *$5* ⏲ *By appointment only.*

**Ma Rainey House.** The child of minstrel-show performers, blues singer Gertrude Pridgett (1886–1939), more famously known as Ma Rainey, the "mother of the blues," toured in tent shows, levee camps, and cabarets throughout the South and Midwest. She recorded more than 100 songs and entertained with the greats, including Louis Armstrong, Bessie Smith, and Tommy Dorsey. She's buried in **Porterdale Cemetery,** an extension of an old slave cemetery, on 10th Avenue. The Ma Rainey House, listed on the National Register of Historic Places, is now open to the public as a museum. ✉ *805 5th Ave.* ☎ *706/653–4960* 🎫 *Free* ⏲ *Tues.–Sat. 9–3.*

**National Civil War Naval Museum at Port Columbus.** Anybody interested in the nation's Civil War past should make it a point to visit this innovative military museum lauded for its interactive approach and high-tech exhibits. The museum is focused on the Confederate navy and its influence on the U.S. Navy's subsequent development. You can walk the decks of partially reconstructed Civil War ships and get a glimpse of what combat was like in a full-scale replica of the CSS *Albermarle.* ✉ *1002 Victory Dr.* ☎ *706/327–9798* 🌐 *www.portcolumbus.org* 🎫 *$7.50* ⏲ *Tues.–Sat. 10–4:30, Sun.–Mon. 12:30–4:30.*

**National Infantry Museum and Soldier Center.** Located outside the gates of Fort Benning, this newly constructed museum examines the role of the U.S. infantry through every war in the nation's history. A must for military buffs, the facility has more than 30,000 artifacts, including weaponry, uniforms, and equipment from the Revolutionary War to the present day. The Family Support Gallery focuses on the sacrifices made by military families and features a children's area where youngsters can try on uniforms and sit in the re-created interior of a Bradley fighting vehicle. For an additional fee, you can test your skills at the very realistic Rifle Range Simulator that uses the same high-tech technology the military uses to train soldiers. The center also features an IMAX theater that shows both documentaries and Hollywood blockbusters. ✉ *1775 Legacy Way* ☎ *706/685–5800* 🌐 *www.nationalinfantrymuseum.com* 🎟 *Free* 🕒 *Mon.–Sat. 9–5, Sun. 11–5.*

**Springer Opera House.** Since its opening in 1871, this National Historic Landmark has been known as one of the finest opera houses in the South. In its heyday, its stage boasted of legends such as Lillie Langtry and Will Rogers. Today the theater hosts musicals, dramas, and regional talent. Tours are offered Monday and Wednesday at 3:30 or by appointment. ✉ *103 10th St.* ☎ *706/327–3688* 🌐 *www.springeroperahouse.org* 🎟 *Tours $5* 🕒 *Tours Mon. and Wed. at 3:30.*

## WHERE TO EAT

$$$ STEAKHOUSE

✕ **Buckhead Grill.** At this upscale Southern-style steak house, beef plays a prominent role on the menu with USDA Prime Angus and natural, hormone-free prime rib, N.Y. strip, and rib eye as headliners. Seafood is also done well here, in such entrées as cedar-planked Norwegian salmon and shrimp linguine. The wine list is said to be the most extensive in Columbus. You can dine inside or on the heated patio. While upscale, the restaurant is also family-friendly and accommodating of large groups. Brunch is served on Sunday. $ *Average main: $24* ✉ *5010 Armour Rd.* ☎ *706/571–9995* 🌐 *www.buckheadbarandgrill.com* 🕒 *No lunch.*

$ BARBECUE ★

✕ **Country's On Broad.** In a land where barbecue reigns supreme, Country's cooks with taste and style. You can eat inside the restaurant, a converted bus terminal decorated with '50s flair, or sit at a table in the 1946 bus-turned-diner. The barbecue, cooked over hickory and oak, includes not only pork, but also chicken, beef, turkey, ribs, and brisket; buttermilk fried chicken is also on the menu. $ *Average main: $9* ✉ *1329 Broadway* ☎ *706/596–8910* 🌐 *www.countrysbarbecue.com.*

## WHERE TO STAY

*Hotel reviews have been abbreviated in this book. For expanded reviews, please go to Fodors.com.*

$$ HOTEL

**Marriott Columbus.** On the site of a vast 1860s complex of warehouses, factories, mills, and a Confederate arsenal, this hotel is a key component of the Columbus Ironworks Convention and Trade Center just across the street. **Pros:** excellent location; modern amenities; historic space. **Cons:** large facility may be a turnoff to some; service can be spotty. $ *Rooms from: $164* ✉ *800 Front Ave.* ☎ *706/324–1800* 🌐 *www.marriott.com* *172 rooms, 5 suites* 🍽 *No meals.*

$$ B&B/INN

**Rothschild-Pound House Inn & Village.** At this acclaimed B&B, the main inn offers a glimpse of old Columbus' elegance—with four-poster mahogany beds, hardwood floors, and period antiques—while the separate cottages offer tranquil retreats. **Pros:** beautiful architecture;

lots of privacy. **Cons:** no pool or spa. *Rooms from: $175 ✉ 201 7th St. ☎ 706/322–4075 🌐 www.thepoundhouseinn.com ⇨ 21 rooms, 6 cottages 🍽 Breakfast.*



## PLAINS

*85 miles southeast of Pine Mountain via U.S. 27.*

This rural farming town—originally named the Plains of Dura after the biblical story of Shadrach, Meshach, and Abednego—is the birthplace and current home of former president Jimmy Carter and his wife, Rosalynn. Although it's the hub of a thriving farming community, the one-street downtown paralleling the railroad tracks resembles a 1930s movie set.

### GETTING HERE AND AROUND

From Interstate 85 or Interstate 75, look for the exit to Route 280, then exit for Plains.

### ESSENTIALS

**Visitor Information Plains Welcome Center** ✉ *1763 U.S. 280* ☎ *229/824–7477* 🌐 *www.plainsgeorgia.com.*

### EXPLORING

★ **Jimmy Carter National Historic Site.** Here you can see the late-1880s **railroad depot** that housed Jimmy Carter's 1976 presidential campaign headquarters. Vintage phones play recordings of Carter discussing his grassroots run for the White House. A couple of miles outside town on the Old Plains Highway is the 360-acre **Jimmy Carter Boyhood Farm,** where the Carter family grew cotton, peanuts, and corn; it has been restored to its original appearance before electricity was introduced. Period furniture fills the house, and the battery-powered radio plays Carter's reminiscences of growing up on a Depression-era farm. **Plains High School,** in which the Carters were educated, is now a museum and the headquarters of the historic site. Start your visit here with a short orientation film, and pick up a self-guided tour book that explains the sites. ✉ *Plains High School, 300 N. Bond St.* ☎ *229/824–4104* 🌐 *www.nps.gov/jica* 🎫 *Free* 🕘 *Daily 9–5.*

**Maranatha Baptist Church.** The Carters still live in a ranch-style brick house on the edge of town—the only home they have ever owned, and they still worship at the Maranatha Baptist Church. President Carter teaches Sunday school here some Sundays at 10 am; doors open at 8:30 and the class fills up fast, so arrive early. Call or check the Web site for the schedule. ✉ *148 GA 45 N* ☎ *229/824–7896* 🌐 *www.mbcplains.org.*

**WORD OF MOUTH**

"We arrived in Plains about four in the afternoon.... We immediately came across signs for President Jimmy Carter's boyhood farm. We stopped in and took a look at President Carter's very humble beginnings. When we arrived in downtown Plains it was interesting to see the train station that housed the campaign headquarters, the high school that President Carter attended, and Billy Carter's gas station. We enjoyed strolling around and taking several photos." —tdelano

QUICK BITES

For a local spot to refuel, try one of these casual eateries.

**Dylan's Diner.** Taking over the old Mom's Kitchen spot, Dylan's Diner offers buffet-style Southern specialties for lunch daily and dinner on the weekends. ✉ *203 E. Church St.* ☎ *229/824–5458.*

**Buffalo Cafe at the Old Bank.** This local favorite offers soup, salads, burgers and sandwiches in a cozy hometown setting. ✉ *118 Main St.* ☎ *229/824–4520.*

**Plains Peanut Festival.** Each September the town comes alive with the Plains Peanut Festival, which includes a parade, live entertainment, arts and crafts, food vendors, and races. The annual softball game pitting President Carter and Secret Service agents against alumni from Plains High School is always a festival highlight.

OFF THE BEATEN PATH

**Andersonville National Historic Site.** About 20 miles northeast of Plains, Andersonville National Historic Site is a solemn reminder of the Civil War's tragic toll. Andersonville, also known as Camp Sumter, was the war's deadliest prisoner-of-war camp. Some 13,000 Union prisoners died here, mostly from disease, neglect, and malnutrition. Photographs, artifacts, and high-tech exhibits detail not just the plight of Civil War prisoners, but also prison life and conditions affecting all of America's 800,000 POWs since the Revolutionary War. ✉ *496 Cemetery Rd., Andersonville* ☎ *229/924–0343* 🌐 *www.nps.gov/ande/index.htm* 🎫 *Free* ⏲ *Daily 8–5.*

### WHERE TO STAY

*Hotel reviews have been abbreviated in this book. For expanded reviews, please go to Fodors.com.*

$ HOTEL ★ **Best Western Windsor Hotel.** Located in nearby Americus, this ornate jewel of a hotel has garnered awards from the National Trust for Historic Preservation. **Pros:** unique historical property; recently renovated. **Cons:** recent transition to a national chain may be a turnoff for some. $ *Rooms from: $100* ✉ *125 W. Lamar St., Americus* ☎ *229/924–1555* 🌐 *www.windsor-americus.com* *45 rooms, 8 suites.*

$ B&B/INN **Plains Historic Inn.** Each spacious room of this inn, set in a century-old furniture store above an antiques mall, is decorated to reflect the aesthetics of a particular decade between the 1920s and the 1980s. **Pros:** close to tourist attractions; cozy and comfortable; claw-foot tubs in some bathrooms. **Cons:** breakfast is self-serve; not many eateries nearby. $ *Rooms from: $85* ✉ *106 Main St.* ☎ *229/824–4517* 🌐 *www.plainsinn.net* *7 suites* 🍴 *Breakfast.*

EN ROUTE

**Westville Village.** Warp back in time to the mid-19th century at Westville Village. In Lumpkin, 7 miles east of Plains, this replica of an 1850s town has more than 30 pre–Civil War buildings, relocated and authentically restored. Costumed tour guides show you the town. The village comes alive with hearth-cooked food, mules and wagons, and period-dressed townspeople and tradesmen demonstrating skills such as candle making, quilting, and cotton baling. ✉ *9294 Singer Pond Rd., Lumpkin* ☎ *229/838–6310, 888/733–1850* 🌐 *www.westville.org* 🎫 *$10* ⏲ *Thurs.–Sat. 10–5.*

Andersonville National Cemetery is the final resting place for soldiers who died at Andersonville Prison, the Civil War's deadliest prisoner-of-war camp.

**Providence Canyon State Outdoor Recreation Area.** Known as "Georgia's Little Grand Canyon," Providence Canyon State Outdoor Recreation Area is actually made up of 16 canyons whose earthen walls display at least 43 different colors of sand. Providence Canyon is a favorite of geologists, photographers, and hikers, who enjoy peering over the canyon's rim and traversing its 10 miles of trails. ✉ *8930 Canyon Rd., Lumpkin* ☎ *229/838–6870* 🌐 *www.gastateparks.org* 💰 *$5 parking* ⏲ *Daily 7–6.*

## THE SOUTHWEST CORNER

Thomasville is the highlight of Georgia's southwest corner. It's among the nation's most appealing small towns, thanks to an inviting town square, shaded glens, and an easygoing air; you can also find some fine country inns here.

### THOMASVILLE

*236 miles south of Atlanta via I–75 and U.S. 319.*

The early fortunes of this appealing small town in the Tallahassee Red Hills paralleled the rise and fall of the antebellum cotton plantations that lined the region's famed "Plantation Trace." Following the Civil War, thousands of Union prisoners who had been evacuated from the nearby Andersonville prison to Thomasville brought home stories of the curative effects of the balsam breezes of the pine-scented air. These stories fueled the second boom in the region's fortunes, during which

CLOSE UP

## King Cotton

Such was Georgia's preeminence in world cotton production at the turn of the 20th century that the international market price was set at the Cotton Exchange in Savannah. And the huge plantations of southwest Georgia were major players in the engine driving the state's economic prosperity. For more than 100 years, from the first time it was planted in Georgia in 1733 until the beginning of the Civil War, cotton was the most commercially successful crop in the state. But because the seeds had to be separated from the lint by hand, production was laborious and output was limited. In 1793 a young Yale graduate named Eli Whitney (1765–1825) came to Savannah's Mulberry Grove Plantation as a tutor to the children of Revolutionary War hero Nathaniel Greene. After watching the difficulty workers were having separating the seeds from the cotton, he invented a simple machine of two cylinders with combs rotating in opposite directions. The "gin," as he called it (short for engine), could do the work of 50 people and revolutionized the cotton industry. So significant was its immediate impact on the U.S. economy that President George Washington personally signed the patent issued to Whitney.

In 1900 the boll weevil came to the United States via Mexico and quickly undermined cotton production. The weevil was a major cause of the onset of the economic depression that spread throughout the South. Cotton production was at an all-time low in Georgia by 1978; in 1987 the state began a boll weevil eradication program that has all but wiped out the threat. And the result is that today Georgia is once again one of the top producers in the nation.

Northerners fleeing the cold wintered here. The wealthier among them built elegant estates in and around the town.

Although Thomasville's golden era has long since ended and there's little left of the old-growth forests that brought winter vacationers south, the distinct pine-scented air remains, as does the Victorian elegance of the town's heyday. Thomasville retains the stately vestiges of a once-posh resort, but without the crowds. Known as the "City of Roses," it draws thousands of visitors each spring to its annual Rose Festival (the fourth weekend in April). And during the Victorian Christmas, locals turn out in period costumes to enjoy horse-drawn carriage rides, caroling, and street theater.

### GETTING HERE AND AROUND

Thomasville, with its rich atmosphere of a bygone era, sits 55 miles south of Tifton and can be reached from Atlanta via Interstate 75 and U.S. 319.

### ESSENTIALS

**Visitor Information Thomasville Welcome Center** ✉ *144 E. Jackson St.* ☎ *229/228–7977, 866/577–3600* 🌐 *www.thomasvillega.com.*

You can tour the main house, school, fire station, stable, gardens, and more at Pebble Hill Plantation.

## EXPLORING

**Birdsong Nature Center.** With 565 acres of lush fields, forests, swamps, and butterfly gardens, this nature center is a wondrous haven for birds and scores of other native wildlife. Miles of walking trails meander through the property, and nature programs are offered year-round. *2106 Meridian Rd 229/377–4408 www.birdsongnaturecenter.org $5 Wed., Fri., and Sat. 9–5; Sun. 1–5.*

**Lapham–Patterson House.** When it was built by Chicago shoe manufacturer Charles W. Lapham in 1884, this three-story Victorian house was state of the art, with gas lighting and indoor plumbing with hot and cold running water. But the most curious feature of this unusual house is that Lapham, who had witnessed the Great Chicago Fire of 1871, had 45 exit doors installed because of his fear of being trapped in a burning house. The house is now a National Historic Landmark because of its unique architectural features. *626 N. Dawson St. 229/226–7664 www.gastateparks.org/info/lapham $5 Fri. 1–5, Sat. 10–5, Sun. 2–5.*

★ **Pebble Hill Plantation.** On the National Register of Historic Places, Pebble Hill is the only plantation in the area open to the public. The property dates to 1825, although most of the original house was destroyed in a fire in the 1930s. Highlights of the current two-story main house include a dramatic horseshoe-shape entryway, a wraparound terrace on the upper floor, and an elegant sunroom decorated with a wildlife motif. Surrounding the house are 34 acres of immaculately maintained grounds that include gardens, a walking path festooned with jasmine, a log-cabin school, a fire station, a carriage house, kennels, and a hospital for the plantation's more than 100 dogs (prized dogs were buried with full funerals, including a minister). The sprawling dairy-and-horse-stable complex resembles an English village. ✉ *5 miles south of Thomasville, 1251 U.S. Hwy. 319 S* ☎ *229/226–2344* 🌐 *www.pebblehill.com* 🎟 *Grounds $5, house tour $15* 🕓 *Tues.–Sat. 10–5, Sun. 1–5; last tour at 4.*

## WHERE TO EAT AND STAY

*Hotel reviews have been abbreviated in this book. For expanded reviews, please go to Fodors.com.*

$ SOUTHERN ✕ **George & Louie's.** The fresh gulf seafood served at this airy Key West–style restaurant is as good as you can find anywhere. Try the broiled shrimp, cooked in olive oil with a smattering of fresh garlic; fresh mullet dinner; or combination platter with homemade deviled crab, shrimp, oysters, scallops, and flounder for one, two, or three people. The fried green tomatoes sprinkled with feta are cooked to perfection, and the burgers are a local favorite. Vintage music from the '40s plays on the sound system, and there's outdoor dining under umbrellas. [$] *Average main: $13* ✉ *217 Remington Ave.* ☎ *229/226–1218* 🌐 *www.georgeandlouies.com* 🕓 *Closed Sun.*

$$$ ECLECTIC ✕ **Liam's.** With a flair for the unexpected, this bistro turns out a rotating seasonal menu with such updated Southern dishes as pork tenderloin with mashed root vegetable, duck with dumplings, and prime beef tenderloin. Liam's also serves a full cheese cart of various artisan cheeses from Europe, as well as local selections. It's especially proud of its humongous European brunch served every Saturday. An open kitchen, garden dining, and paintings by local artists create a cozy dining room. [$] *Average main: $24* ✉ *113 E. Jackson St.* ☎ *229/226–9944* 🌐 *www.liamsofthomasville.com* 🕓 *Closed Sun. and Mon. No dinner Tues. and Wed.*

$$ ITALIAN ✕ **Mom and Dad's.** That's definitely oregano you smell when entering Mom and Dad's—but also expect to hear a Southern drawl. These go together perfectly at this restaurant, a great place for Italian food made with rich cheeses and thick red tomato sauce. The garlic bread is served warm and strong enough to turn your breath into a blowtorch. [$] *Average main: $15* ✉ *1800 Smith Ave.* ☎ *229/226–6265* 🌐 *www.momanddadsitalian.com* 🕓 *Closed Sun. and Mon. No lunch.*

$$ B&B/INN ★ 🏨 **1884 Paxton House Inn.** Each room is unique in this immaculate property, a stately blue Victorian mansion with a wraparound veranda. **Pros:** private lap pool and hot tub; friendly innkeeper; old-time charm. **Cons:** no kids; modern amenities may spoil mood. [$] *Rooms from: $175* ✉ *445 Remington Ave.* ☎ *229/226–5197* 🌐 *www.1884paxtonhouseinn.com* 🛏 *10 rooms* 🍽 *Breakfast.*

# Atlanta, GA

## WORD OF MOUTH

"[The Georgia Aquarium] was a wonderfully surprising experience for me. I really didn't believe all the hype about 'best aquarium in the world' but . . . I was blown away."

—amyb

# WELCOME TO ATLANTA, GA

## TOP REASONS TO GO

★ **The Georgia Aquarium:** This wildly successful draw, the world's largest aquarium, draws visitors from all over the globe.

★ **A stroll through the park:** April in Paris has nothing on Atlanta, especially when the azaleas and dogwoods are blooming in the Atlanta Botanical Garden and Piedmont Park.

★ **Following in Dr. King's footsteps:** Home of Martin Luther King Jr., Atlanta was a hub of the civil rights movement. Tour the King Center and his childhood home on Auburn Avenue.

★ **Civil War history:** Artifacts in the city's museums—as well as at historic sites in nearby Kennesaw, Marietta, and Roswell—give you the chance to revisit those difficult times.

★ **Southern cooking, and then some:** Good Southern food has always been easy to find here, but Atlanta's proliferation of young, talented chefs and its ethnic diversity makes it a great place to sample a wide range of cuisines.

**1 Downtown.** Although tourists flock to sites like the Georgia Aquarium and more residents are moving to the city center, this area still has at least a partially earned reputation for being desolate and a bit dangerous.

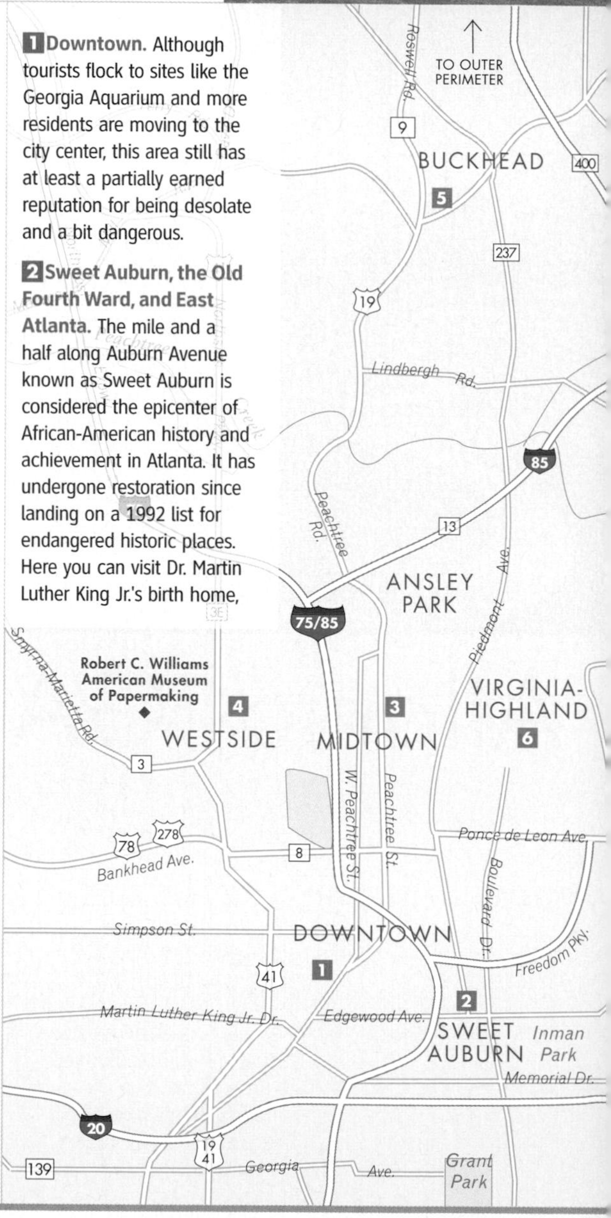

**2 Sweet Auburn, the Old Fourth Ward, and East Atlanta.** The mile and a half along Auburn Avenue known as Sweet Auburn is considered the epicenter of African-American history and achievement in Atlanta. It has undergone restoration since landing on a 1992 list for endangered historic places. Here you can visit Dr. Martin Luther King Jr.'s birth home,

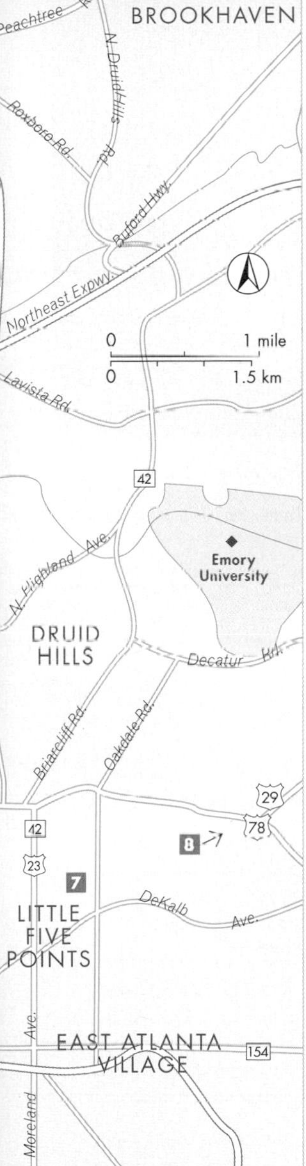


church, and grave. The neighboring Old Fourth Ward is one of Atlanta's hippest nightlife destinations, and after a wave of revitalization, East Atlanta has some beautiful and restored housing stock.

**3 Midtown.** Picturesque and very walkable Midtown is home to many of Atlanta's major cultural institutions, including the High Museum, and lots of luxurious high-rise condos.

**4 Westside.** In recent years, chefs, restaurateurs and designers have flocked to this once-barren industrial expanse opposite the highway from Midtown and transformed it into one of the city's best neighborhoods for shopping and dining.

**5 Buckhead.** Known for its glamorous condos, majestic homes, and moneyed residents like Elton John, the bars that used to draw crowds here are now largely gone, replaced by ritzy boutiques and stores.

**6 Virginia-Highland and the Emory Area.** Stroll through the leafy neighborhood at the intersection of Virginia and North Highland avenues to find trendy stores, patio bars, cozy music venues, and some great food. The area has a sunny disposition, and sits not far from the venerable Emory University.

## GETTING ORIENTED

Atlanta, the state's capital and seat of Fulton County, was founded in 1837 and sits on the Piedmont Plateau in northern Georgia. Though the metro area spans 8,000 square miles, don't let the sprawling size—or all the transplanted Yankees—fool you into thinking Southern hospitality is dead. It's alive and well in Atlanta's pith-helmeted Downtown ambassadors, drawling coffee-mug fillers, waving neighbors, and good ol' boy politicians.

**7 Little Five Points and Inman Park.** There's a lively mix here, with the majestic old mansions and adorable bungalows of Inman Park just down Euclid Avenue from the gritty bars, comfy restaurants, tattoo parlors, vintage-clothing shops, and street characters of Little Five Points.

**8 Decatur.** This suburb is about 10 miles east of Downtown. Its charming town square is always buzzing thanks to its many vibrant restaurants, pubs, and stores.

# ATLANTA'S CIVIL RIGHTS LEGACY

(above) Fountains at the King Center. (lower right) Dr. Martin Luther King Jr. and President Lyndon B. Johnson. (upper right) Stained-glass windows at Ebenezer Baptist Church.

To some, Atlanta's location in the South may have made it seem an unlikely hotbed for social change, but the city earned an important place in the history of civil rights, particularly through the work and words of Dr. Martin Luther King Jr. Many of the monuments to this rich legacy—including the birth home and church of Dr. King—are open to the public.

Tracing back to 1862, when the first African-American property owner sold her land for $500 to purchase her enslaved husband's freedom, Atlanta has been a civil rights city. Though many important activists have called this city home, Dr. Martin Luther King Jr. stands apart. He was born here, preached here, and raised a family here before he was assassinated in 1968. His legacy is kept alive at the King Center—a living memorial to his work in leading the nation's nonviolent movement for equality and peace.

—Christine Van Dusen

### KING QUOTES

"Freedom is never voluntarily given by the oppressor; it must be demanded by the oppressed."

"I look to a day when people will not be judged by the color of their skin, but by the content of their character."

"All labor that uplifts humanity has dignity and importance and should be undertaken with painstaking excellence."

—Dr. Martin Luther King Jr.

## CIVIL RIGHTS WALK

A great way to take a tour of Atlanta's civil rights history is to walk through the Sweet Auburn neighborhood. To get here, take the MARTA train to the Five Points station Downtown and switch to either of the two eastbound lines (the Green/Edgewood/Candler Park or the Blue/Indian Creek line). Get off at the King Memorial stop. All tours are self-guided, and you can download a free audio tour from the Center for Civil & Human Rights Partnership.

Spend time at the Martin Luther King Jr. National Historic Site, also known as **The King Center,** established in 1968 by Coretta Scott King and housing Reverend King's library, a resource center, the Eternal Flame, and the Kings' final resting place. Pause at King's white marble tomb to see its inscription: "Free at last, free at last, thank God almighty I'm free at last."

Stroll along the **International Civil Rights Walk of Fame,** created in 2004 and set up along the National Park Service's Visitor Center to recognize civil rights heroes and cultural icons like Rosa Parks, Stevie Wonder, Hank Aaron, and President Jimmy Carter with 2-foot-square granite markers.

Stop by **Ebenezer Baptist Church,** which was founded in 1886 and moved to Auburn Avenue in 1914. King was baptized here and took the pulpit in 1960 as co-pastor with his father. Visit on a Sunday to see the recent renovation and hear Senior Pastor Raphael G. Warnock lead a service.

Then stop by the **Sweet Auburn Curb Market,** which was established in 1918 in a tent before moving in 1924 to its current brick-and-concrete building. The market was segregated, and only white people were permitted to shop inside while black people shopped from stalls lining the curb. That's where the market got its name. Today the market welcomes everyone with two sculptures at its front door by Atlanta artist Carl Joe Williams. Inside are stalls featuring fruits, vegetables, and meats, and small cafés.

## ATLANTA IN CIVIL RIGHTS HISTORY

**1800s:** The first African-American congressman from Georgia is elected; Booker T. Washington's "Atlanta Compromise" speech is given here.
**1900–1940:** Atlanta Life Insurance Co. is founded by former slave Alonzo Herndon; 25 black people die during the Atlanta Race Riots; Martin Luther King Jr. is born in Atlanta.
**1950–1960:** Atlanta's segregated bus system is ruled unconstitutional; members of the Student Nonviolent Coordinating Committee stage a sit-in at segregated lunch counters; public pools and parks integrate.
**1954:** U.S. Supreme Court declares school segregation unconstitutional in *Brown v. Board of Education of Topeka* ruling.
**1973:** Maynard Holbrook Jackson Jr. is elected as the city's first African-American mayor.
**1980s:** The King Center is named a national historic site.
**2000:** Shirley Franklin is Atlanta's first female African-American mayor; Tyler Perry opens his movie studios in Atlanta.

# GOOD EATS IN ATLANTA

(above) Hugh Acheson's Empire State South is a must for Southern food lovers. (lower right) Sushi at Tomo Japanese restaurant. (upper right) Braised beef shortribs at Empire State South.

Some cities are best known for their museums, their architecture, or their culture. While Atlanta boasts a solid assortment of all three, what locals celebrate—and debate, and pontificate about—most is its food.

Though you can find grits, BBQ, and "meat-and-three" in many low-budget and wallet-busting restaurants, Atlanta's not only about down-home Dixie cooking. There are burger boutiques for the choosy carnivore, organic-only slow-food havens for the dedicated locavore, and enough fish, tofu, and offal to suit the most discerning omnivore. Prices in Atlanta restaurants can be significantly cheaper than those in other metropolitan areas, and most places don't enforce dress codes, so you can just come as you are. Today, the stars of Atlanta's food scene, chefs like Richard Blais, Kevin Gillespie, and Hugh Acheson, are getting their due on the national stage and putting Atlanta on the culinary map. The same goes for the city's cocktail scene, thanks to innovative mixologists and barkeeps, such as Holeman & Finch's Greg Best.

—Debbie Michaud

## MARKET TO MARKET

Every Saturday from 9 am to 1 pm, dozens of local farmers, cheese mongers, popsicle makers, and bakers line the path inside Piedmont Park's 12th Street gate for the weekly **Green Market** (✉ *12th St. and Piedmont Ave.* ☎ *404/875-7275*). It's fun to wander the stalls to admire the local produce, enjoy the live music, and sample some of the fresh goodies.

## ATLANTA TWO WAYS

Sampling Atlanta's gastronomic delights doesn't have to cost a mint—though it certainly can. Here, high-end and low-end choices from some of the city's favorite food categories.

### SUSHI

**Low end:** Many locals swear by **Ru San's** (✉ *1529 Piedmont Rd., Midtown* ☎ *404/875–7042* 🌐 *www.rusans.com*), a Georgia chain with strangely named maki ("Gone With the Wind" roll?), a hectically fun atmosphere, and reasonable prices.

**High end: Tomo Japanese Restaurant** (✉ *3630 Peachtree Rd., Buckhead* ☎ *404/835–2708* 🌐 *www.tomorestaurant.com*) is a spectacular splurge for sushi lovers. The chef's choice *omakase*, a 10-course tasting menu, starts at $100.

### BAR FOOD

**Low end:** One of the best sandwiches in town is at **The Earl** (✉ *488 Flat Shoals Ave., East Atlanta* ☎ *404/522–3950* 🌐 *www.badearl.com*). Order the "Greenie Meanie Chicken," a char-grilled Cajun chicken breast topped with roasted poblano peppers and salsa verde.

**High end: Holeman & Finch** (✉ *2277 Peachtree Rd., Suite B, Buckhead* ☎ *404/948–1175* 🌐 *www.holeman-finch.com*), a small and cozy public house, made a name for itself with an impressive cocktail program and a signature burger. The kitchen serves small plates that include creamy farm-egg-and-pancetta carbonara and a tiny 4-ounce N.Y. strip steak.

### SOUTHERN

**Low end: Carver's Country Kitchen** (✉ *1118 W. Marietta St., Westside* ☎ *404/794–4410* 🌐 *www.carverscountrykitchen.com*) is where locals go for huge portions of meat loaf, turnip greens, baked ham, and fried catfish for budget prices.

**High end: Empire State South** (✉ *999 Peachtree St., Midtown* ☎ *404/541–1105* 🌐 *www.empirestatesouth.com*) serves modern, sophisticated versions of Southern classics. The house charcuterie and "In Jars" appetizer shouldn't be missed.

## INTERNATIONAL DELIGHTS

Buford Highway, which stretches northeast from Buckhead to outside the perimeter, is packed with all manner of ethnic food, shopping, and nightlife. Check out the Buford Highway Farmers Market for hard-to-find Asian foodstuffs and Plaza Fiesta for everything from tacos to *quinceañera* dresses. There's no shortage of cheap, delicious Mexican food along the international thoroughfare, but **Taquería El Rey del Taco** (✉ *5288 Buford Hwy., Doraville* ☎ *770/986–0032*) stands out for its carnitas tacos on homemade tortillas.

There are a number of Korean BBQ restaurants to match the burgeoning Korean population. One of the area's oldest and best, **Hae Woon Dae BBQ** (✉ *5805 Buford Hwy., Doraville* ☎ *770/451–7957*) serves outstanding bibimbap and grilled marinated meats on charcoal tabletop barbecues.

Head to **Sushi House Hayakawa** (✉ *5979 Buford Hwy., Doraville* ☎ *770/986–0010*) for authentic Japanese dining.

13

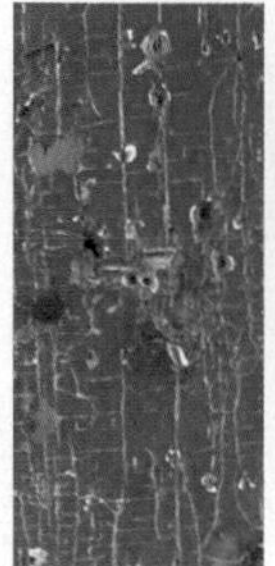

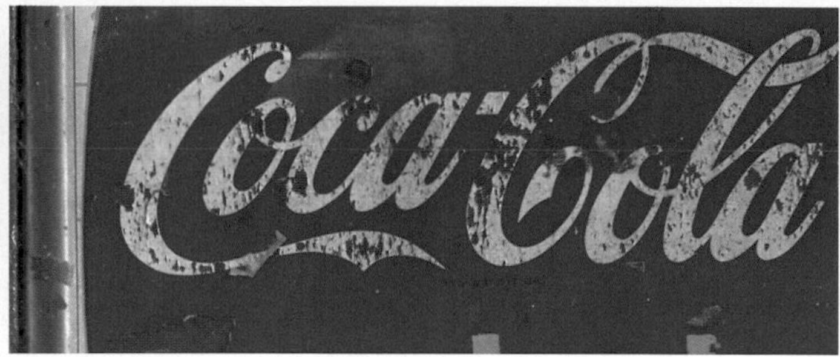


Updated by Debbie Michaud

Originally built as the terminus of the Western & Atlantic Railroad, Atlanta remains a hub for transportation (with the world's busiest airport), industry (with the headquarters for Coca-Cola), art (with treasures from on display at the High Museum of Art), and natural wonders (with the world's largest aquarium). The city's half million residents enjoy a mix of old-fashioned Southern charm, offbeat artistic funkiness, chic luxury shopping, superb dining, and major attractions.

In the past, many of the city's big draws—Stone Mountain Park, for example—were outside the city limits. Today there's plenty in town to keep you occupied. The Georgia Aquarium draws visitors who want to get up-close and personal with whale sharks. At the Woodruff Arts Center, you can catch a performance by the Atlanta Symphony Orchestra or watch films projected onto the exterior of the High Museum of Art. And the fizzy World of Coca-Cola is dedicated to the hometown beverage.

Atlanta continues to experience explosive growth. A good measure of the city's expansion is the ever-changing skyline; condominium developments appear to spring up overnight, while run-down properties seem to disappear in a flash. In Buckhead—once home to a noisy, raucous bar district—most of the taverns have been razed as developers hope to bring a Rodeo Drive of the South into being. Office and residential towers have risen throughout Midtown, Downtown, and the outer perimeter (fringing Interstate 285, especially to the north). Residents, however, are less likely to measure the city's growth by skyscrapers than by the increase in the already bad traffic, crowds, higher prices, and the ever-burgeoning subdivisions that continue to push urban sprawl farther and farther into surrounding rural areas.

Known as "the city too busy to hate," Atlanta has become the best example of the New South, a fast-paced modern city proud of its heritage. Transplanted Northerners and those from elsewhere account for more than half the population, and they have undeniably affected the mood of the city, as well as the mix of accents of its people. Irish immigrants played a major role in the city's early history, along with Germans and Austrians. Since the 1980s, Atlanta has seen spirited growth in its Asian and Latin-American communities. The newcomers' restaurants, shops, and institutions have become part of the city's texture.

# PLANNING



## WHEN TO GO

Atlanta isn't called "Hotlanta" for nothing—in the late spring and summer months the mosquitoes feast and the temperatures can reach a sticky and humid 99 degrees F (thankfully, almost every place in the city is air-conditioned). July 4 weekend can be particularly hectic, due to the influx of runners for the annual 10K Peachtree Road Race. Labor Day weekend also sees major crowds thanks to dozens of popular national festivals, including Dragon*Con and the Decatur Book Festival. The best time to visit is in fall and early winter. When many other cities are beginning to get cold and gray, Atlanta typically maintains a steady level of sunshine and cool breezes. Airfares are fairly reasonable at most times of the year, given that the city is a transportation hub and most Atlanta attractions aren't seasonal.

## PLANNING YOUR TIME

Because it would take too long to explore the city end-to-end in one fell swoop, consider discovering Atlanta one pocket at a time. In Downtown you can stroll through the Georgia Aquarium, tour the CNN Center, and meander through the World of Coca-Cola, then finish off the day with dinner and a beer at Marietta Street sports bar Stats or with a glass of wine outside at the historic Ellis Hotel's Terrace restaurant. Another good pocket includes three adjoining, very walkable neighborhoods, all known for their canopies of trees, cute shops, and fun bistros: Virginia-Highland, Little Five Points, and Inman Park. From there you can drive to East Atlanta and check out its casual bars, tattoo shops, restaurants, and live music. Your third pocket should be Buckhead, and depending on when you go you will either see a neighborhood in metamorphosis or, if all goes according to plan, a shopper's mecca. Two constants there are Lenox Mall and Phipps Plaza, great shopping spots in their own right. Finally, there's the beer-loving, literary hotspot of Decatur (home to the 2012–13 U.S. Poet Laureate, Natasha Trethewey), which is increasingly being recognized for its top-notch restaurants.

## GETTING HERE AND AROUND

### AIR TRAVEL

Hartsfield-Jackson Atlanta International (ATL), the busiest passenger airport in the world, is served by more than 26 airlines, including AirTran, Continental, and Delta. Although an underground train and moving walkways help you reach your gate more quickly, budget a little extra time for negotiating the massive facility. Because of the airport's size, security lines can be long, especially during peak travel periods. The airport typically suggests arriving two hours before your flight.

The airport is 13 miles south of Downtown. There are large parking facilities, but they tend to fill up quickly. Check their current capacity, which is available on ATL's website. Locals know that MARTA, the regional subway system, is the fastest and cheapest way to and from the airport, but taxis are available. The fare to Downtown is about $35 for one person. From the airport to Buckhead, the fare is $38 for one person (though some politicians are trying to raise it). Buckhead Safety Cab and Checker Cab offer 24-hour service.

**Airport Contacts Hartsfield-Jackson Atlanta International Airport (ATL)** ✉ *6000 N. Terminal Pkwy.* ☎ *404/530–7300* 🌐 *www.atlanta-airport.com.*

AIRPORT SHUTTLES

Atlanta Airport Superior Shuttle & Limo vans run daily every 30 minutes between 6 am and 11:30 pm to Perimeter Center offices, hotels, and residences. The trip can take 30 to 45 minutes, depending on the traffic. A one-way trip costs $35.

Atlanta Airport Shuttle operates vans every 15 minutes to Downtown, Midtown, and Buckhead. Vans heading Downtown cost $16.50 for the 20-minute trip. Vans to Midtown cost $18.50 for the 30-minute trip, and vans to Buckhead cost $20.50 for the 45-minute trip. Reservations are recommended at least 24 hours in advance for return trips.

Airport Metro Shuttle operates shuttles around the clock to destinations around the region. It's recommended that you make reservations 24 hours in advance. Typical shuttle fees range from $35–$45 for one passenger to Marietta.

**Shuttle Contacts Airport Metro Shuttle** ☎ *404/766–6666* 🌐 *airportmetro.com.* **Atlanta Airport Superior Shuttle & Limo** ☎ *404/457–4794* 🌐 *atlsuperiorshuttle.com.*

### BUS TRAVEL

MARTA operates more than 90 routes covering more than 1,000 miles, but the bus system isn't popular among visitors. The fare is $2.50, and a Breeze Card ($1 and reusable) is required. Service is limited outside the perimeter of Interstate 285, except for a few areas in Clayton, DeKalb, and north Fulton counties.

### CAR TRAVEL

The city is encircled by Interstate 285. Three interstates also crisscross Atlanta: Interstate 85, running northeast–southwest from Virginia to Alabama; Interstate 75, running north–south from Michigan to Florida; and Interstate 20, running east–west from South Carolina to Texas.

Some refer to Atlanta as the "Los Angeles of the South," because driving is virtually the only way to get around. Atlantans have grown accustomed to frequent delays at rush hour—the morning and late-afternoon commuting periods seem to get longer every year. ■ **TIP→ The South as a whole may be laid-back, but Atlanta drivers are not; they tend to drive faster and more aggressively than drivers in other Southern cities, and they rarely slow down at a yellow light.**

If you plan to venture beyond the neighborhoods served by MARTA, you will want to rent a car. Many national agencies have branch offices all over the city, as well as at Hartsfield-Jackson Atlanta International Airport.

#### SUBWAY TRAVEL

MARTA has clean and safe subway trains with somewhat limited routes that link Downtown with many major landmarks, like the CNN Center and the Martin Luther King Jr. Memorial. The system's two main lines cross at the Five Points station. MARTA uses a smart-card fare system called Breeze. The cards are available at RideStores and from vending machines at each station by using cash or credit cards. The one-way fare is $2.50, but the cards offer several options, including weekend, weekly, and monthly passes.



Trains generally run weekdays 5 am to 1 am and weekends and holidays 6 am to 12:30 am. Most trains operate every 15 to 20 minutes; during weekday rush hours, trains run every 10 minutes.

■ **TIP→ Locals take MARTA to and from Hartsfield-Jackson International Airport, which has the traffic snarls common with larger airports. The $2.50 fare is a fraction of the amount charged by shuttles or taxis.** Airport travelers should be careful about catching the right train. One line ends up at North Springs station to the north. The other at Doraville station, to the northeast. Daily parking is free at MARTA parking facilities. Long-term parking rates range from $5 to $8 daily. Not all stations have lots, however.

**Subway Contact MARTA** ☎ *404/848–5000* 🌐 *www.itsmarta.com.*

#### TAXI TRAVEL

Taxi service in Atlanta can be uneven. Drivers often lack correct change, so bring along plenty of small bills. You can also charge your fare, as many accept credit cards. Drivers may be as befuddled as you are by the city's notoriously winding streets, so if your destination is somewhere other than a major hotel or popular sight, bring along printed directions, or have your smartphone's GPS set up.

In Atlanta taxi fares begin at $2.50, then add $2 for each additional mile. Additional passengers are $2 each, and there's a $2 gas surcharge added to every trip. You generally need to call for a cab, as Atlanta is not a place where you can hail one on the street. Buckhead Safety Cab and Checker Cab offer 24-hour service.

**Taxi Contacts Buckhead Safety Cab** ☎ *404/233–1152.* **Checker Cab** ☎ *404/351–1111* 🌐 *www.atlantacheckercab.com.*

#### TRAIN TRAVEL

Amtrak operates daily service from Atlanta's Brookwood Station to New York; Philadelphia; Washington, D.C.; Charlotte, North Carolina; and New Orleans.

**Train Contacts Amtrak** ✉ *Brookwood Station, 1688 Peachtree St., Buckhead* ☎ *800/872–7245* 🌐 *www.amtrak.com.*

### DISCOUNTS AND DEALS

Visitors can take advantage of the deal offered with **Atlanta CityPass**, "the ticket to a New and Old South vacation." As of this writing, an adult pass—which is valid for a nine-day period—cost $69 and provided access to six attractions: Georgia Aquarium, World of Coca-Cola, Inside CNN Atlanta Studio Tour, and a choice between the Fernbank Museum of Natural History or High Museum of Art, and Zoo Atlanta or the Atlanta History Center. Visit *www.citypass.com/city/atlanta.html.*

### VISITOR INFORMATION

The Atlanta Convention & Visitors Bureau, which provides information on Atlanta and the outlying area, has several information centers in Atlanta: Hartsfield-Jackson Atlanta International Airport, in the Atrium; Underground Atlanta; and the Georgia World Congress Center.

**Visitor Information Atlanta Convention & Visitors Bureau** *233 Peachtree St., Suite 1400, Downtown 404/521-6600 Underground Atlanta, 50 Upper Alabama St., Downtown 404/523-2311 Georgia World Congress Center, 285 Andrew Young International Blvd., Downtown 404/223-4000 www.atlanta.net.*

## EXPLORING ATLANTA

The greater Atlanta area embraces several different counties. The city of Atlanta is primarily in Fulton and DeKalb counties, although its southern end and the airport are in Clayton County. Outside Interstate 285, which encircles the city, Cobb, Gwinnett, and northern Fulton counties are experiencing much of Atlanta's population increase.

Atlanta's lack of a grid system confuses many drivers, even locals. Some streets change their names along the same stretch of road, including the city's most famous thoroughfare, Peachtree Street, which follows a mountain ridge from Downtown to suburban Norcross, outside Interstate 285: it becomes Peachtree Road after crossing Interstate 85 and then splits into Peachtree Industrial Boulevard beyond the Buckhead neighborhood and the original Peachtree Road, which heads into Chamblee. Adding to the confusion, dozens of other streets in the metropolitan area use "Peachtree" in their names. ■ **TIP→** Before setting out anywhere, get the complete street address of your destination, including landmarks, cross streets, or other guideposts. Street numbers and even street signs are often difficult to find.

Atlanta proper has three major areas—Downtown, Midtown, and Buckhead—as well as many smaller commercial districts and in-town neighborhoods. Atlanta's Downtown is filled with government staffers and office workers by day, but at night the visiting conventioneers—and, as city improvements take hold, residents—come out to play. Midtown, Virginia-Highland, Buckhead, the Westside, and Decatur are the best places to go for dinner, nightclubs, and shows. Other neighborhoods like East Atlanta, Grant Park, Little Five Points, and Kirkwood have unique characteristics that merit exploration.

The city's public transportation system, the Metropolitan Atlanta Rapid Transit Authority (MARTA), operates bus and rail networks in Atlanta and Fulton and DeKalb counties. The two major rail lines, which run east–west and north–south (there's a northern spur, so consult a map before you jump on board), extend roughly to the edges of Interstate 285. ■ **TIP→** MARTA is best for traveling to and from the airport and within Downtown, Midtown, Buckhead, and Decatur; if you plan to venture beyond those regions, call a taxi or rent a car.

The Georgia Aquarium is the world's largest aquarium, with 10 million gallons of water and more than 80,000 animals.

## DOWNTOWN

Downtown Atlanta clusters around the hub known as Five Points. You'll find the MARTA station that intersects the north–south and east–west transit lines, both of which run underground here. On the surface, Five Points is formed by the intersection of Peachtree Street with Marietta, Broad, and Forsyth streets. It's a crowded area, and traffic can be snarled in the early morning and late afternoon. With the opening of the Georgia Aquarium and the World of Coca-Cola, which join the Imagine It! Children's Museum and the CNN Center, Downtown has taken on greater interest for travelers. Lush Centennial Olympic Park—built for the 1996 Olympic Games—is a great place to let your children play in the Fountain of Rings or to enjoy a take-out lunch.

### TOP ATTRACTIONS

Fodor's Choice ★ **Centennial Olympic Park.** This 21-acre swath of green was the central venue for the 1996 Summer Olympics. The benches at the Fountain of Rings allow you to enjoy the water and music spectacle—eight tunes are timed to coincide with water displays that shoot sprays 15 feet to 30 feet high. The All Children's Playground is designed to be accessible to kids with disabilities. Nearby is the world's largest aquarium and Imagine It! Children's Museum. The park also has a café, restrooms, and a playground, and typically offers ice skating in winter. Don't miss seeing Centennial Olympic Park at night, when eight 65-foot-tall lighting towers set off the beauty of the park. They represent the markers that led ancient Greeks to public events. ⊠ *Marietta St. and Centennial Olympic Park*

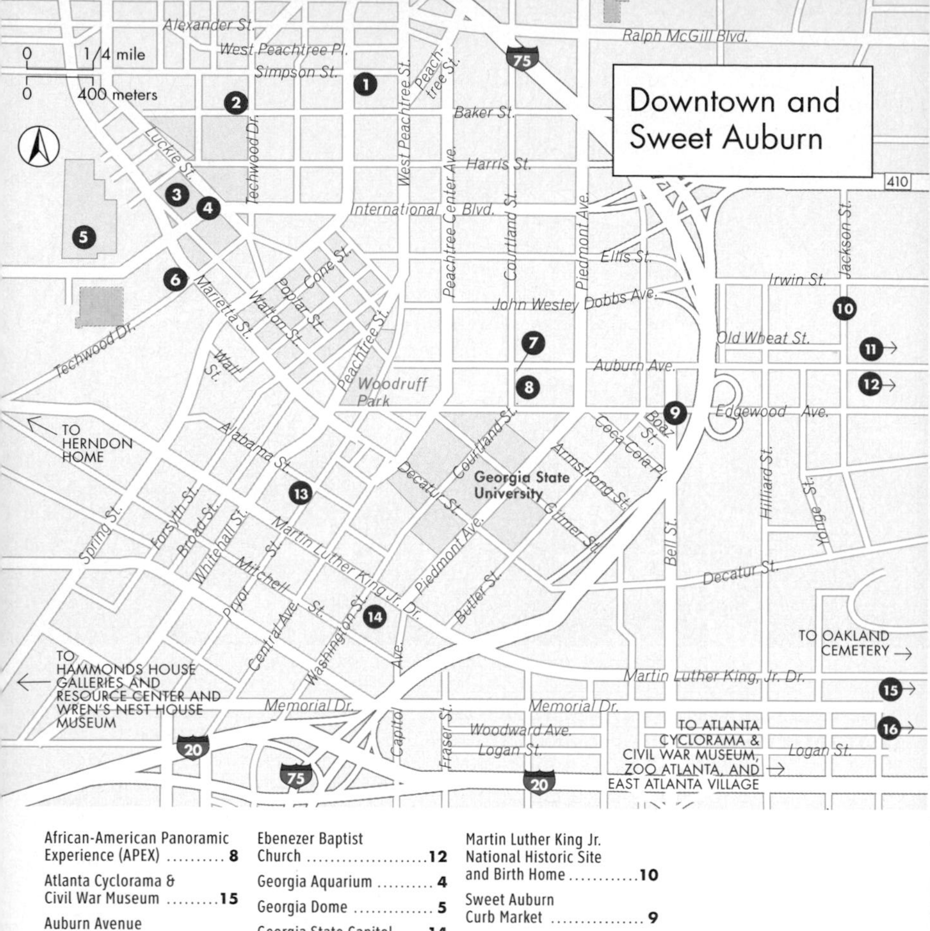


African-American Panoramic Experience (APEX) .......... **8**

Atlanta Cyclorama & Civil War Museum ......... **15**

Auburn Avenue Research Library on African-American Culture and History ......... **7**

Centennial Olympic Park ............... **3**

CNN Center ................. **6**

Ebenezer Baptist Church ..................... **12**

Georgia Aquarium .......... **4**

Georgia Dome .............. **5**

Georgia State Capitol ..... **14**

Imagine It! The Children's Museum of Atlanta ................... **1**

Martin Luther King Jr. Center for Nonviolent Social Change ............. **11**

Martin Luther King Jr. National Historic Site and Birth Home ............ **10**

Sweet Auburn Curb Market ................ **9**

Underground Atlanta ...... **13**

World of Coca-Cola .................. **2**

Zoo Atlanta ................ **16**

*Dr., Downtown* ☎ *404/223–4412* 🌐 *www.centennialpark.com* ⏲ *Daily 7 am–11 pm.*

★ **CNN Center.** The home of Cable News Network occupies all 14 floors of this dramatic structure on the edge of Downtown. The 55-minute CNN studio tour—difficult for some people because it descends eight flights of stairs—is a behind-the-scenes glimpse of the control room, newsrooms, and broadcast studios. Tours depart approximately every 20 minutes. A limited number of tours have elevator access. You can make reservations by telephone or online. ✉ *1 CNN Center, Downtown* ☎ *404/827–2300* 🌐 *www.cnn.com/tour/atlanta* 🎫 *Tour $15* ⏲ *Daily 9–5.*

WORD OF MOUTH

"Fox Theatre tour—fantastic! Amazing architecture, beautiful building, great story of its survival." –jill_h

13

Fodor's Choice ★ **Georgia Aquarium.** With more than 10 million gallons of water, this wildly popular attraction is the world's largest aquarium. The 604,000-square-foot building, an architectural marvel resembling the bow of a ship, has tanks of various sizes filled with more than 80,000 animals, representing 500 species. The aquarium's 6.3-million-gallon Ocean Voyager Gallery is the world's largest indoor marine exhibit, with 4,574 square feet of viewing windows. But not everything has gills: there are also penguins, sea lions, sea otters, river otters, sea turtles, and giant octopi. The much-anticipated 84,000-square-foot AT&T Dolphin Tales exhibit, which opened in 2011, includes a 25-minute show (reservations required). Hordes of kids—and many adults—can always be found around the touch tanks. Admission includes entry to all public exhibits, shows and galleries. One-hour behind-the-scenes tours are $50. Cafe Aquaria serves sandwiches, salads, and other light fare. There are often huge crowds, so arrive early or late for the best chance of getting a close-up view of the exhibits. Try to buy your tickets at least a week ahead. Online ticketing is best, as you are e-mailed tickets you can print out at home. ✉ *225 Baker St., Downtown* ☎ *404/581–4000* 🌐 *www.georgiaaquarium.org* 🎫 *$34.95* ⏲ *Sun.–Fri. 10–5, Sat. 9–6; hrs may vary on holidays.*

★ **Imagine It! The Children's Museum of Atlanta.** In this colorful and joyfully noisy museum for children ages eight and younger, kids can build sand castles, watch themselves perform on closed-circuit TV, operate a giant ball-moving machine, and get inside an imaginary waterfall (after donning raincoats, of course). Other exhibits rotate every few months. ✉ *275 Centennial Olympic Park Dr. NW, Downtown* ☎ *404/659–5437* 🌐 *www.childrensmuseumatlanta.org* 🎫 *$12.75* ⏲ *Weekdays 10–4, weekends 10–5.*

**World of Coca-Cola.** This shrine to the brown soda's image, products, and marketing is, at 62,000 square feet, twice the size of its previous building and features more than 1,200 artifacts never before displayed to the public. You can sip samples of 60 different Coca-Cola products from around the world and peruse more than a century's worth of memorabilia from the corporate archives. The gift shop sells everything from refrigerator magnets to evening bags. ✉ *121 Baker St.*

*NW, Downtown* ☎ *404/676–5151* 🌐 *www.worldofcoca-cola.com* 🎫 *$16* 🕑 *Mon.–Sat. 9–6, Sun. 10–6.*

## WORTH NOTING

**Georgia Dome.** This arena, opened in 1992, accommodates 71,250 spectators, with good visibility from every seat; it's the site of Atlanta Falcons football games and other sporting events, conventions, and trade shows. The white, plum, and turquoise 1.6-million-square-foot, seven-level facility is crowned with the world's largest cable-supported oval, giving the roof a circus-tent top. ✉ *1 Georgia Dome Dr., Downtown* ☎ *404/223–4636* 🌐 *www.gadome.com* 🎫 *Tours $6* 🕑 *Tours Mon., Wed., and Fri. 10–2.*

**Georgia State Capitol.** The capitol, a Renaissance-style edifice, was dedicated on July 4, 1889. The gold leaf on its dome was mined in nearby Dahlonega. Inside, the **Georgia Capitol Museum** houses exhibits on its history. On the grounds, state historical markers commemorate the 1864 Battle of Atlanta, which destroyed nearly the entire city. Statues memorialize a 19th-century Georgia governor and his wife (Joseph and Elizabeth Brown), a Confederate general (John B. Gordon), and a former senator (Richard B. Russell). Former governor and president Jimmy Carter is depicted with his sleeves rolled up, a man at work. Those who wish to honor Martin Luther King Jr. should visit the governor's wall, where a portrait of the civil rights leader was unveiled in 2006. Visit the Web site for tour information and reservations. ✉ *206 Washington St. SW, Downtown* ☎ *404/656–2846* 🌐 *www.sos.georgia.gov/archives/state_capitol* 🕑 *Museum weekdays 8–5; guided tours Jan.–Mar., weekdays at 10, 10:30, 11, and 11:30; Apr.–Dec., weekdays at 9:30, 10:30, and 11:30.*

**Underground Atlanta.** Underground has seen more than its share of ups and downs. It was created from the web of subterranean brick streets, ornamental facades, and tunnels that fell into disuse in 1929, when the city built viaducts over the train tracks. The six-block district opened in 1969 as a retail and entertainment center and remained fairly popular until it was closed in 1980 for the MARTA train project. After a $142 million renovation, it reopened with eateries, retail, and specialty shops. AtlanTIX, a half-price ticket outlet theater and cultural attractions, is in Underground Atlanta. It's open 11 to 6 Tuesday to Saturday, noon to 4 Sunday. ✉ *50 Upper Alabama St., Downtown* ☎ *404/523–2311* 🌐 *www.underground-atlanta.com.*

### HELP AT HAND

Need a helping hand—or simply directions—while exploring Downtown? Watch for a member of the **Atlanta Ambassador Force** (🌐 *www.atlantadowntown.com/initiatives/ambassadors*). The members, easily recognized by their pith helmets, are a traveler's best friends.

## SWEET AUBURN, THE OLD FOURTH WARD, AND EAST ATLANTA



Between 1890 and 1930, the Sweet Auburn district was Atlanta's most active and prosperous center of black business, entertainment, and political life. Following the Depression, the area went into an economic decline that lasted until the 1980s, when the residential area where civil rights leader Reverend Martin Luther King Jr. (1929–68) was born, raised, and later returned to live was declared a National Historic District. Nearby, the Old Fourth Ward and the East Atlanta area have mostly benefited from slow gentrification. The former is now a nightlife hotspot and the latter is home to some beautifully restored houses.

### TOP ATTRACTIONS

**African American Panoramic Experience (APEX).** The museum's quarterly exhibits chronicle the history of black people in America. Videos illustrate the history of Sweet Auburn, the name bestowed on Auburn Avenue by businessman John Wesley Dobbs, who fostered business development for African-Americans on this street. ✉ *135 Auburn Ave., Sweet Auburn* ☎ *404/523–2739* 🌐 *www.apexmuseum.org* 🎟 *$6* 🕒 *Tues.–Sat. 10–5.*

★ **Atlanta Cyclorama & Civil War Museum.** A building in Grant Park (named for a New England–born Confederate colonel, not the U.S. president) houses a huge circular painting depicting the 1864 Battle of Atlanta, during which 90% of the city was destroyed. A team of expert European panorama artists completed the painting in Milwaukee, Wisconsin, in 1887; it was donated to the city of Atlanta in 1897. On the second level, a display called "Life in Camp" displays rifles, uniforms, and games soldiers played to pass the time. An outstanding bookstore has dozens of volumes about the Civil War. Guided tours are available every hour on the half hour except for 12:30 pm. To get here by car, take Interstate 20 east to Exit 59A, turn right onto Boulevard, and then follow signs to the Cyclorama. The museum shares a parking lot and entrance walkway with Zoo Atlanta. ✉ *800 Cherokee Ave., Grant Park* ☎ *404/658–7625* 🌐 *www.atlantacyclorama.org* 🎟 *$10* 🕒 *Tues.–Sat. 9:15–4:30.*

Fodor's Choice ★ **Ebenezer Baptist Church.** A Gothic Revival–style building completed in 1922, the church came to be known as the spiritual center of the civil rights movement. Members of the King family, including the slain civil rights leader, preached at the church for three generations. The congregation itself now occupies the building across the street. ✉ *407 Auburn Ave. NE, Sweet Auburn* ☎ *404/331–5190* 🌐 *www.nps.gov/malu* 🎟 *Free.*

**Martin Luther King Jr. Center for Nonviolent Social Change.** The Martin Luther King Jr. National Historic District occupies several blocks on Auburn Avenue, a few blocks east of Peachtree Street in the black business and residential community of Sweet Auburn. Martin Luther King Jr. was born here in 1929; after his assassination in 1968, his widow, Coretta Scott King, established this center, which exhibits such personal items as King's Nobel Peace Prize, bible, and tape recorder, along with memorabilia and photos chronicling the civil rights movement. In the courtyard in front of Freedom Hall, on a circular brick pad in the

Martin Luther King Jr. was born and raised in this modest Queen Anne–style house.

middle of the rectangular Meditation Pool, is Dr. King's white-marble tomb. The inscription reads, "Free at last, Free at last, Thank God Almighty I'm Free at last." Nearby, an eternal flame burns. A chapel of all faiths sits at one end of the reflecting pool. Mrs. King, who passed away in 2006, is also entombed at the center. ✉ *449 Auburn Ave. NE, Sweet Auburn* ☎ *404/526–8900* 🌐 *www.thekingcenter.org* 🎫 *Free* ⏲ *Daily 9–5.*

Fodor's Choice ★ **Martin Luther King Jr. National Historic Site and Birth Home.** The modest Queen Anne–style residence is where Martin Luther King Jr. was born and raised. Besides items that belonged to the family, the house contains an outstanding multimedia exhibit focused on the civil rights movement. A limited number of visitors are allowed to tour the house each day. Advance reservations are not possible, so sign up early in the day. ✉ *501 Auburn Ave., Sweet Auburn* ☎ *404/331–6922* 🌐 *www.nps.gov/malu* 🎫 *Free* ⏲ *Tours daily 10–5.*

**Zoo Atlanta.** This zoo has more than 1,500 animals and 200 species from around the world living in naturalistic habitats. The gorillas and tigers are always a hit, as are giant pandas named Yang Yang, Lun Lun, and Xi Lan. Children can ride the Nabisco Endangered Species Carousel and meet new friends at the petting zoo; the whole family can take a ride on the Georgia Natural Gas Blue Flame Express Train. To reach the zoo by car, take Interstate 20 east to Exit 59A and turn right on Boulevard. Follow the signs to the zoo, which is right near the Atlanta Cyclorama & Civil War Museum. ✉ *800 Cherokee Ave. SE, Grant Park* ☎ *404/624–5600* 🌐 *www.zooatlanta.org* 🎫 *$20.99* ⏲ *Weekdays 9:30–5:30, weekends 9:30–6:30; sometimes closes earlier in winter.*

### WORTH NOTING

**Auburn Avenue Research Library on African-American Culture and History.** An extension of the Atlanta-Fulton Public Library, this unit houses a noncirculating collection of about 60,000 books of African-American interest. The archives contain art and artifacts, transcribed oral histories, and rare books, pamphlets, and periodicals. There are frequent special events, all of them free. ✉ *101 Auburn Ave. NE, Sweet Auburn* ☎ *404/730–4001* 🌐 *www.afpls.org/aarl* ⏲ *Mon. 10–6, Tues.–Thurs. noon–8, Fri. and Sat. noon–6, Sun. 2–6.*

13

**Sweet Auburn Curb Market.** The market, an institution on Edgewood Avenue since 1923, sells flowers, fruits, and vegetables, and a variety of meat—everything from fresh catfish to foot-long oxtails. Vendors also include the popular Bell Street Burritos, an organic coffee shop, and the local favorite Grindhouse Killer Burgers lunch counter. Individual stalls are run by their owners, making this a true public market. Don't miss the splendid totemic sculptures by Atlanta artist Carl Joe Williams. ✉ *209 Edgewood Ave., Sweet Auburn* ☎ *404/659–1665* 🌐 *www.sweetauburncurbmarket.com* ⏲ *Mon.–Sat. 8–6.*

OFF THE BEATEN PATH

**East Atlanta Village.** This earthy outpost of edgy-cool shops, restaurants, bars, and concert venues started growing, beginning in 1996, thanks to a group of proprietors with dreams much bigger than their bank accounts. Spurning the high rents of fancier parts of town, they set up businesses in this then-blighted but beautiful ruin of a neighborhood 4 miles southeast of Downtown. Soon artists and others came to soak up the creative atmosphere. East Atlanta, which is centered at Flat Shoals and Glenwood avenues, just southeast of Moreland Avenue at Interstate 20, has had its ups and downs, but after new streetscapes were installed in 2005, it experienced a resurgence. Many of the majestic homes have been renovated, and what remains unrestored seems to romanticize the area's gritty appeal. ✉ *Flat Shoals and Glenwood Aves., East Atlanta.*

**Kaboodle Home.** Check out the funky furniture and gifts here. ✉ *485-B Flat Shoals Ave., East Atlanta* ☎ *404/522–3006.*

## MIDTOWN AND WESTSIDE

Midtown Atlanta—north of Downtown and south of Buckhead—is four miles and has a skyline of gleaming office towers that rivals Downtown's. Its renovated mansions and bungalows have made it a city showcase, and so has Piedmont Park and the Atlanta Botanical Garden. It's also the location of the Woodruff Arts Center, one of the largest performing-arts centers in the country, and roughly 20 other arts and cultural venues, including the recently relocated Museum of Design Atlanta. The neighborhood is the hub for the city's sizable gay community.

The Westside, once considered a part of Midtown, has earned its own identity. Here you'll find some of the city's best and most sophisticated restaurants, including high-end Bacchanalia, as well as the Atlanta Contemporary Art Center and other top galleries.

CLOSE UP

## In Search of the Old South

*Gone With the Wind* enthusiasts coming to Atlanta for the first time are often disappointed to discover that Scarlett O'Hara's beloved plantation, Tara, was no more real than Scarlett herself. But history buffs can find antebellum treasures in towns like Marietta and Kennesaw (about 20 miles northwest of Atlanta) and Roswell (about 23 miles north of Atlanta).

**Marietta Museum of History.** On the second floor of the historic 1845 Kennesaw House, this museum traces the history of Cobb County. ✉ *1 Depot St., Marietta* ☎ *770/794–5710* 🌐 *www.mariettahistory.org* 🎫 *$7* 🕑 *Mon.–Sat. 10–4.*

**Marietta Gone With the Wind Museum.** Props, costumes, and artifacts here pay homage to the movie and Margaret Mitchell's 1936 novel. ✉ *18 Whitlock Ave.* ☎ *770/794–5576* 🌐 *www.gwtwmarietta.com* 🎫 *$7* 🕑 *Mon.–Sat. 10–5.*

**Kennesaw Mountain National Battlefield.** The 2,884-acre park was the site for crucial battles in 1864. The National Park Service maintains 16 miles of well-used hiking trails. A small museum has uniforms, weapons, and other items from the era. ✉ *900 Kennesaw Mountain Dr., Kennesaw* ☎ *770/427–4686* 🌐 *www.nps.gov/kemo* 🎫 *Free* 🕑 *Park: Dawn to dusk. Visitor center: Daily 8:30–5.*

**Southern Museum of Civil War and Locomotive History.** This fascinating museum is the home of the *General*, a locomotive stolen by Union forces from the Confederates during the Civil War. ✉ *2829 Cherokee St., Kennesaw* ☎ *770/427–2117* 🌐 *www.southernmuseum.org* 🎫 *$7.50* 🕑 *Mon.–Sat. 9:30–5, Sun. 11–6.*

**Barrington Hall.** Completed in 1842, Barrington Hall is widely recognized as one of the nation's best examples of Greek Revival architecture. ✉ *535 Barrington Dr., Roswell* ☎ *770/640–3253* 🌐 *www.barringtonhall-roswell.com* 🎫 *$8* 🕑 *Mon.–Sat. 10–3, Sun. 1–3. Tours on the hour.*

**Bulloch Hall.** Mittie Roosevelt, mother of President Teddy Roosevelt and grandmother of Eleanor Roosevelt, lived in this Greek Revival house (1839) as a child. It has a nice museum shop. ✉ *180 Bulloch Ave., Roswell* ☎ *770/992–1731* 🌐 *www.bullochhall.org* 🎫 *$8* 🕑 *Mon.–Sat. 10–3, Sun. 1–3. Tours on the hour.*

**Archibald Smith Plantation.** The original furniture of the Archibald Smith family fills the plantation house here. ✉ *935 Alpharetta St., Roswell* ☎ *770/641–3978* 🎫 *$18* 🕑 *Mon.–Sat. 10–3, Sun. 1–3. Tours on the hour.*

### TOP ATTRACTIONS

Fodor's Choice ★

**Atlanta Botanical Garden.** Occupying 30 acres inside Piedmont Park, the grounds contain acres of display gardens, including a 2-acre interactive children's garden; a hardwood forest with walking trails; the Fuqua Conservatory, which has unusual flora from tropical and desert climates; and the award-winning Fuqua Orchid Center. The Canopy Walk, a 600-foot suspension bridge through Storza Woods, was recently added. A variety of special exhibits take place throughout the year. ✉ *1345 Piedmont Ave. NE, Midtown* ☎ *404/876–5859* 🌐 *www.*

The Atlanta Botanical Garden is a 30-acre oasis inside Piedmont Park.

*atlantabotanicalgarden.org* 🎟 *$18.95* ⏲ *Apr., Tues.–Sun. 9–7; May–Oct., Tues., Wed., and Fri.–Sun., 9–7, Thurs. 9 am—10 pm; Nov.–Mar., Tues.–Sun. 9–5.*

**Center for Puppetry Arts.** The largest puppetry organization in the country houses a museum where you can see more than 350 puppets from around the world. Make sure to check out the furry and funny creatures from Jim Henson's productions. The elaborate performances include original works and classics adapted for stage. Kids also love the create-a-puppet workshops. The Jim Henson Museum at Center for Puppetry Arts houses most of the famed puppeteer's collection. ✉ *1404 Spring St. NW, at 18th St., Midtown* ☎ *404/873–3391* 🌐 *www.puppet.org* 🎟 *$16.50* ⏲ *Tues.–Fri. 9–3, Sat. 9–5, Sun. 11–5.*

**Fodor's Choice** ★ **Fox Theatre.** One of a dwindling number of vintage movie palaces in the nation, the Fox was built in 1929 in a fabulous Moorish-Egyptian style. The interior's crowning glory is its ceiling, complete with moving clouds and twinkling stars above Alhambra-like minarets. Threatened by demolition in the 1970s, the Fox was saved from the wrecking ball by community activists. Today it hosts musicals, rock concerts, dance performances, and film festivals. Tours should be scheduled in advance. ✉ *660 Peachtree St. NE, Midtown* ☎ *404/881–2100 for box office, 404/688–3353 for tours* 🌐 *www.foxtheatre.org* 🎟 *Tour $10* ⏲ *Tours Mon. and Thurs. at 10, Sat. at 10 and 11.*

★ **High Museum of Art.** This museum's permanent collection includes 19th- and 20-century American works, including many by African-American artists. It also has some stellar examples of contemporary and outsider art—don't miss the works by the self-taught artist Rev. Howard

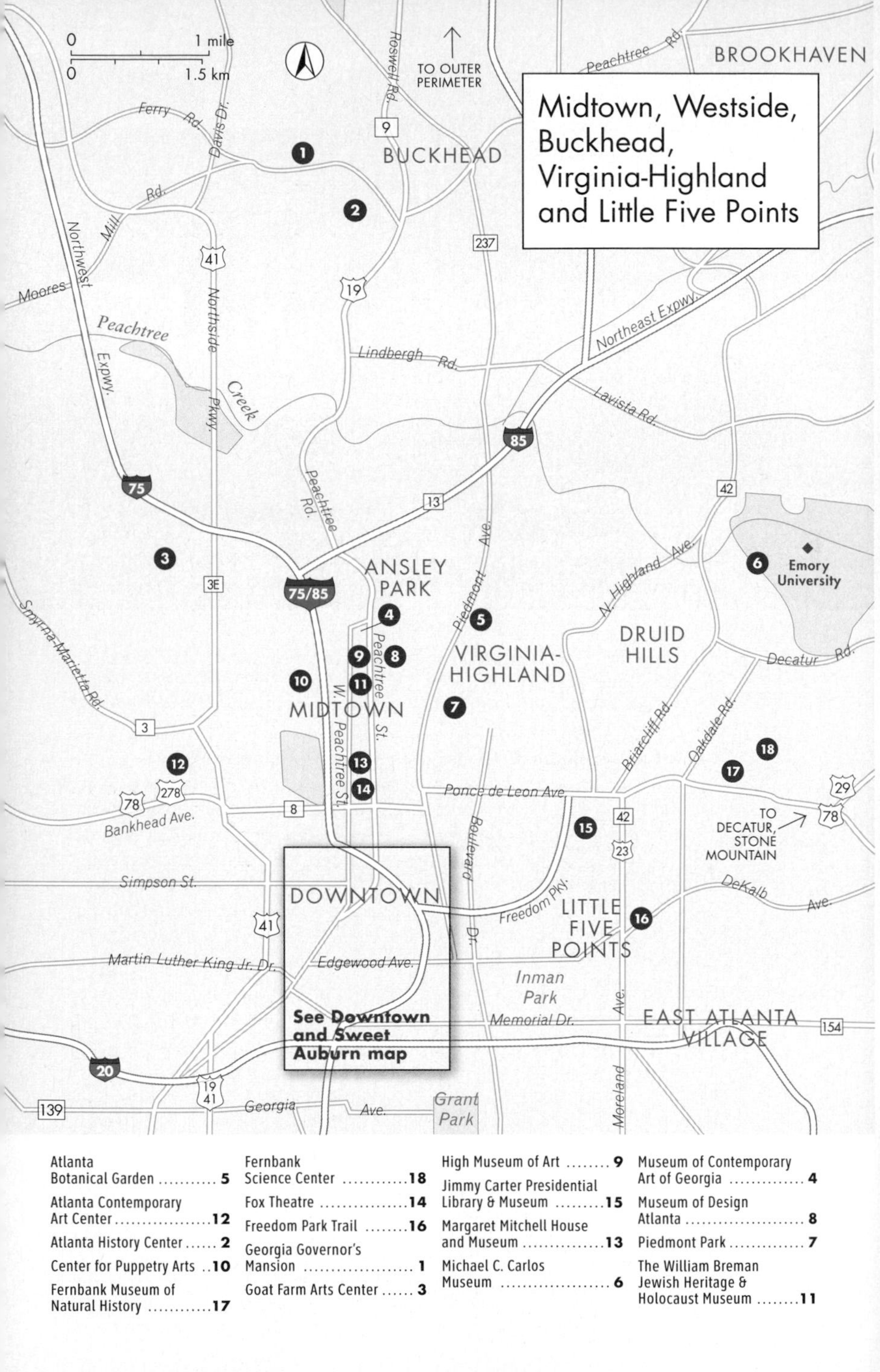
Midtown, Westside, Buckhead, Virginia-Highland and Little Five Points
0
1 mile
0
1.5 km
TO OUTER PERIMETER
BROOKHAVEN
BUCKHEAD
ANSLEY PARK
VIRGINIA-HIGHLAND
MIDTOWN
DRUID HILLS
Emory University
DOWNTOWN
LITTLE FIVE POINTS
Inman Park
EAST ATLANTA VILLAGE
Grant Park
TO DECATUR, STONE MOUNTAIN
See Downtown and Sweet Auburn map
Peachtree Rd.
Roswell Rd.
Ferry Rd.
Davis Dr.
Mill Rd.
Northwest Expwy.
Moores
Peachtree Creek
Northside Pkwy.
Lindbergh Rd.
Northeast Expwy.
Lavista Rd.
Peachtree Rd.
Piedmont Ave.
N. Highland Ave.
Decatur Rd.
Smyrna-Marietta Rd.
Peachtree St.
W. Peachtree St.
Briarcliff Rd.
Oakdale Rd.
Ponce de Leon Ave.
Bankhead Ave.
Boulevard Dr.
Simpson St.
Freedom Pky.
DeKalb Ave.
Martin Luther King Jr. Dr.
Edgewood Ave.
Memorial Dr.
Moreland Ave.
Georgia Ave.
9
237
41
19
85
75
13
42
3E
75/85
3
278
78
8
23
29
154
20
139
Atlanta Botanical Garden ........... 5
Atlanta Contemporary Art Center .................. 12
Atlanta History Center ...... 2
Center for Puppetry Arts .. 10
Fernbank Museum of Natural History ............ 17
Fernbank Science Center ............ 18
Fox Theatre ................ 14
Freedom Park Trail ........ 16
Georgia Governor's Mansion .................... 1
Goat Farm Arts Center ...... 3
High Museum of Art ........ 9
Jimmy Carter Presidential Library & Museum ......... 15
Margaret Mitchell House and Museum .............. 13
Michael C. Carlos Museum .................... 6
Museum of Contemporary Art of Georgia .............. 4
Museum of Design Atlanta ...................... 8
Piedmont Park .............. 7
The William Breman Jewish Heritage & Holocaust Museum ........ 11

### GARDEN SPOTS

Atlantans love their gardens—and the chance to show them off. **Garden tours** are plentiful in spring, so check the *Atlanta Journal-Constitution* (🌐 *www.ajc.com*) for listings. December brings tours of the inside of many similar houses, all done up for the holidays.



Finster. The building itself is a work of art; the American Institute of Architects listed the sleek structure, designed by Richard Meier, among the 10 best works of American architecture of the 1980s. A 2005 expansion designed by Renzo Piano doubled the museum's size to 312,000 square feet with three new aluminum-paneled buildings. The roof features a system of 1,000 "light scoops" that filter light into the skyway galleries. The High often partners with other major museums, including the Louvre and New York's Museum of Modern Art. ✉ *Woodruff Arts Center, 1280 Peachtree St. NE, Midtown* ☎ *404/733–4444* 🌐 *www.high.org* 🎟 *$19.50* ⏲ *Tues., Wed., Fri., and Sat. 10–5, Thurs. 10–8, Sun. noon–5.*

**Margaret Mitchell House and Museum.** While she wrote her masterpiece, the author of *Gone With the Wind* lived in an apartment house built in 1899 that she called "the Dump." Volunteers gathered the funds necessary to restore the building in the early 1990s. To many Atlantans, the Margaret Mitchell House symbolizes the conflict between promoting the city's heritage and respecting its roots. The house has been struck by fire twice, in 1994 and 1996. Arson was strongly suspected but no one was ever caught. The visitor center exhibits photographs, archival material, and personal possessions. ✉ *990 Peachtree St., at Peachtree Pl., Midtown* ☎ *404/249–7015* 🌐 *www.gwtw.org* 🎟 *$13* ⏲ *Mon.–Sat. 10–5:30, Sun. noon–5:30. Tours every half hour.*

**Museum of Design Atlanta.** The only museum in the Southeast devoted exclusively to design mounts exhibits on fashion, graphics, architecture, furniture, and product design. In 2011, MODA relocated to a high-profile and eco-friendly new location across the street from the High Museum of Art. ✉ *1315 Peachtree St., Midtown* ☎ *404/979–6455* 🌐 *www.museumofdesign.org* 🎟 *$10* ⏲ *Tues.–Sat. 10–5, Sun. noon–5.*

## WORTH NOTING

**Atlanta Contemporary Art Center.** Established by a group of photographers in the '70s as the arts co-op Nexus, the ACAC exhibits edgy contemporary art. It anchors the vibrant Westside Arts District (WAD), a group of contemporary art spaces that have flourished in this once-industrial area. ■ **TIP→ The lively WAD art walk takes place the third Saturday of every month.** ✉ *535 Means St. NW, Westside* ☎ *404/688–1970* 🌐 *www.thecontemporary.org* 🎟 *$5* ⏲ *Tues., Wed., Fri., and Sat. 11–5, Thur. 11–8, Sun. noon–5.*

**The Goat Farm Arts Center.** In 2008, a complex of cotton-factory buildings from the 19th century was transformed into a 12-acre group of studios and performance and rehearsal spaces for some of Atlanta's most exciting artists and performers. There's a nice on-site coffee shop called the Warhorse, and the Goat Farm also hosts concerts by local and national touring acts. ✉ *1200 Foster St., Westside* 🌐 *www.facebook.com/TheGoatFarmArtsCenter.*

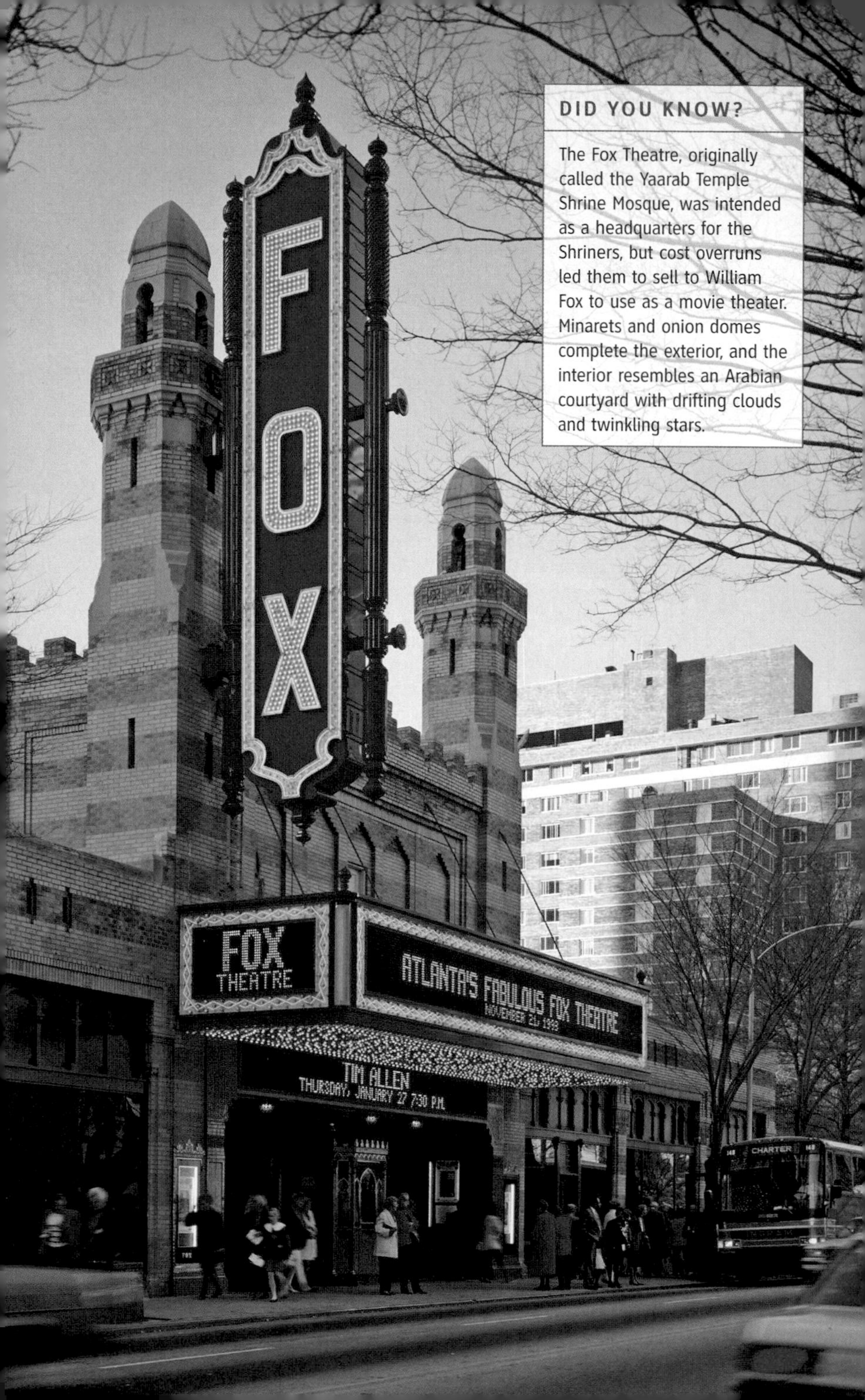


**DID YOU KNOW?**

The Fox Theatre, originally called the Yaarab Temple Shrine Mosque, was intended as a headquarters for the Shriners, but cost overruns led them to sell to William Fox to use as a movie theater. Minarets and onion domes complete the exterior, and the interior resembles an Arabian courtyard with drifting clouds and twinkling stars.

Fodor'sChoice ★ **Piedmont Park.** A popular destination since the late 19th century, Piedmont Park is still expanding: 35 acres complete with a fountain and new sports facilities were added in 2011, and another 15 were tacked on in 2012. Tennis courts, a swimming pool, a popular dog park, and paths for walking, jogging, and rollerblading are part of the attraction, but many retreat to the park's great lawn for picnics with a smashing view of the Midtown skyline. ✉ *10th St. and Monroe Dr., Midtown* 🌐 *www.piedmontpark.org* ⏲ *Daily 6–11.*

**The William Breman Jewish Heritage & Holocaust Museum.** The history of the Jewish community in Atlanta is told through a permanent exhibit called *Creating Community*. Other exhibits document the Holocaust and the immigrant experience in America. The facility—the largest archive of Georgia Jewish history—also contains a research library and an education center. ✉ *1440 Spring St. NW, Midtown* ☎ *678/222–3700* 🌐 *www.thebreman.org* 🎟 *$12* ⏲ *Mon.–Thurs. 10–5, Fri. 10–3, Sun. 1–5.*

## BUCKHEAD

Atlanta's sprawl doesn't lend itself to walking between major neighborhoods, so take a car or MARTA to reach this neighborhood, which has some great stores and restaurants. Lenox Square and Phipps Plaza malls are loaded with hundreds of upscale shops. Finding a parking spot on the weekends and at night can be a real headache, and long waits are common in the hottest restaurants.

Fodor'sChoice ★ **Atlanta History Center.** Life in Atlanta and the rest of the South during and after the Civil War are a major focus of this fascinating museum. Displays are provocative, juxtaposing *Gone With the Wind* romanticism with the grim reality of Ku Klux Klan racism. Located on 33 acres in the heart of Buckhead, this is one of the Southeast's largest history museums, with a research library and archives that annually serve more than 10,000 patrons. Visit the elegant 1928 **Swan House** mansion and the plantation house that is part of **Tullie Smith Farm.** The Kenan Research Center houses traveling exhibitions and an extensive archival collection. Lunch is served at the Swan Coach House, which also has a gallery and a gift shop. ✉ *130 West Paces Ferry Rd. NW, Buckhead* ☎ *404/814–4000* 🌐 *www.atlantahistorycenter.com* 🎟 *$16.50* ⏲ *Museum Mon.–Sat. 10–5:30, Sun. noon–5:30; Swan House & Smith Family House tours Mon.–Sat. 11–4, Sun. 1–4.*

**Georgia Governor's Mansion.** This 24,000-square-foot 1967 Greek Revival mansion contains 30 rooms with Federal-period antiques. It sits on 18 acres that originally belonged to the Robert Maddox family (no relation to Georgia governor Lester Maddox, who was its first occupant). Reservations are necessary for parties of 10 or more. ✉ *391 W. Paces Ferry Rd. NW, Buckhead* ☎ *404/261–1776* 🌐 *mansion.georgia.gov* 🎟 *Free* ⏲ *Tours Tues.–Thurs. 10–11:30.*

★ **Museum of Contemporary Art of Georgia (MOCA GA).** Georgia's visual artists are showcased in a small gallery housed in an office-building lobby. More than 500 paintings, sculptures, and other works are part of the permanent collection. ✉ *75 Bennett St., Suite A2, Buckhead* ☎ *404/367–8700* 🌐 *www.mocaga.org* 🎟 *$5* ⏲ *Tues.–Sat. 10–5.*

## VIRGINIA-HIGHLAND AND THE EMORY AREA

Restaurants, bars, and boutiques are sprinkled throughout Virginia-Highland/Morningside, northeast of Midtown. Like Midtown, this residential area was down-at-the-heels in the 1970s. Reclaimed by writers, artists, and a few visionary developers, Virginia-Highland (as well as bordering Morningside) is a great place to explore. To the east, the Emory University area is studded with enviable mansions. Near the Emory University campus is Druid Hills, used for film locations for *Driving Miss Daisy,* by local playwright Alfred Uhry. The neighborhood was designed by the firm of Frederick Law Olmsted, which also landscaped Asheville's Biltmore and New York's Central Park.

### TOP ATTRACTIONS

★ **Fernbank Museum of Natural History.** One of the largest natural history museums south of the Smithsonian Institution in Washington, D.C., this museum offers 17 galleries and an on-site IMAX theater. The "Giants of the Mesozoic" exhibit includes an exact replica of the world's largest dinosaur. The café, with an exquisite view of the forest, serves great food. ■ **TIP→** On Friday nights, the museum hosts Martinis & IMAX, which also includes food and live music. ✉ *767 Clifton Rd., Emory* ☎ *404/929–6300* 🌐 *www.fernbankmuseum.org* 🎟 *$17.50, IMAX $13, Martinis & IMAX $12* ⏲ *Museum Mon.–Sat. 10–5, Sun. noon–5; Martinis & IMAX Fri. 6:30–11.*

★ **Jimmy Carter Presidential Library & Museum.** This complex occupies the site where Union General William T. Sherman orchestrated the Battle of Atlanta (1864). The museum and archives detail the political career of former president Jimmy Carter. The adjacent Carter Center, which is not open to the public, focuses on conflict resolution and human-rights issues. Outside, the Japanese-style garden is a serene spot to unwind. Both Carter and former First Lady Rosalynn Carter maintain offices here. ✉ *441 Freedom Pkwy., Virginia-Highland* ☎ *404/865–7100* 🌐 *www.jimmycarterlibrary.org* 🎟 *$8* ⏲ *Mon.–Sat. 9–4:45, Sun. noon–4:45.*

**Michael C. Carlos Museum.** Housing a permanent collection of more than 16,000 objects, this excellent museum, designed by the architect Michael Graves, exhibits artifacts from Egypt, Greece, Rome, the Near East, the Americas, and Africa. European and American prints and drawings cover the Middle Ages through the 20th century. The gift shop sells rare art books, jewelry, and art-focused items for children. The museum's Caffe Antico is a good lunch spot. ✉ *Emory University, 571 S. Kilgo Circle, Emory* ☎ *404/727–4282* 🌐 *www.carlos.emory.edu* 🎟 *$8* ⏲ *Tues.–Fri. 10–4, Sat. 10–5, Sun. noon–5.*

### WORTH NOTING

**Fernbank Science Center.** The museum, in the 65-acre Fernbank Forest, focuses on ecology, geology, and space exploration. In addition to the exhibit hall, there's a planetarium as well as an observatory, which is open Thursday and Friday nights from 9–10:30. ✉ *156 Heaton Park Dr., Emory* ☎ *678/874–7102* 🌐 *fsc.fernbank.edu* 🎟 *Free* ⏲ *Mon.–Wed. 9–5, Thurs. and Fri. 9–9, Sat. 10–5.*

From the creation of the cotton gin to the premiere of *Gone With the Wind*, the Civil War to the civil rights movement, you can learn all about it at the Atlanta History Center.

## LITTLE FIVE POINTS AND INMAN PARK

About 4 miles east of Downtown, this neighborhood was laid out by famous developer Joel Hurt in 1889. Since then it has faded and flourished a number of times, which explains the vast gaps in opulence evident in much of the architecture here. Huge, ornate Victorian mansions sit next to humble bungalows. But no matter the exact address or style of home—be it modest or massive—Inman Park now commands considerable cachet among many different constituents, including young families, empty nesters, and gays and lesbians. Nearby you'll also find the delightfully countercultural Little Five Points section, with funky boutiques, neighborhood bars, and gritty music venues.

### EXPLORING

**Freedom Park Trail.** One of the neighborhood's best features is the Freedom Park Trail, a particularly pleasant stretch of the PATH Foundation's more-than-160-mile trail system in the metro area. It gives runners, bikers, and dog-walkers a peaceful thoroughfare inside the 210-acre Freedom Park. The PATH is the largest public green space in a major metro area in the United States in the last century. ✉ *Moreland Ave. and Freedom Pkwy, Little Five Points* ☎ 404/875–7284 🌐 *www.pathfoundation.org*.

## OTHER AREA ATTRACTIONS

It's essential to drive to most of these venues, so plan your visits with Atlanta's notorious rush hours in mind.

**Six Flags Over Georgia.** The heart-stopping roller coasters, family rides, and water attractions (best saved for last so you won't be damp all day), make Georgia's major theme park a child's ideal playground. At at 200 feet, the Goliath is a giant among roller coasters. The heart-clenching ride hits speeds of 70 mph. In early 2013, the park added its tallest ride yet—the 24-story SkyScreamer. The park also has well-staged musical revues and concerts by top-name artist. To get here, take MARTA's west line to the Hamilton Homes station and then hop aboard the Six Flags bus. ✉ *I–20 W at, 275 Riverside Pkwy., Austell* ☎ *770/948–9290* 🌐 *www.sixflags.com/overgeorgia* 🎟 *$56.99* 🕒 *June–mid-Aug., daily; mid-Aug.–Oct. and Mar.–May, weekends; hrs vary.*

### NAMING ATLANTA

Founded in 1837 by the Western & Atlantic Railroad, Atlanta has changed names several times. It was nicknamed Terminus, for its location at the end of the tracks. Marthasville was its first official name, in honor of the then-governor's daughter. It switched soon afterward to Atlanta, the feminine of Atlantic—another nod to the railroad.

★ **Stone Mountain Park.** At this 3,200-acre state park you'll find the largest exposed granite outcropping on Earth. The Confederate Memorial, on the north face of the 825-foot-high mountain, is the world's largest sculpture, measuring 90 feet by 190 feet. There are several ways to see the sculpture, including a cable car that lifts you to the mountaintop and a steam locomotive that chugs around the mountain's base. Summer nights are capped with the **Lasershow Spectacular,** an outdoor light display set to music and projected onto the side of Stone Mountain—attendance is a rite of passage for new Atlantans. A recent $4 million renovation included the addition of Mountainvision (3D effects without the glasses) to the show. There's also a wildlife preserve, an antebellum plantation, a swimming beach, two golf courses, a campground, a hotel, a resort, several restaurants, and two Civil War museums. Crossroads, an entertainment complex with an 1870s-Southern-town theme, offers costumed interpreters and a movie theater. The Sky Hike is a family-friendly ropes course at 12 feet, 24 feet, or 40 feet high. ✉ *U.S. 78 E, Stone Mountain Pkwy., Exit 8, Stone Mountain* ☎ *770/498–5690* 🌐 *www.stonemountainpark.com* 🎟 *$10 per car, $28 per adult for an Adventure Pass* 🕒 *Daily 6 am–midnight; Lasershow spectacular Mar.–Oct., attraction hrs. vary.*

## WHERE TO EAT

This is a city known for its food; many a trip to Atlanta is planned around meals in its barbecue shacks, upscale diners, and chic urban eateries. Traditional Southern fare—including Cajun and creole, country-style and plantation cuisine, coastal and mountain dishes—thrives, as do Asian fusion, Peruvian tapas, creative vegan, and mouth-scorching Indian food. Catch the flavor of the South at breakfast and lunch in diners and other modest establishments that serve only these meals.

Hike the 1.3-mile trail or ride a cable car to the top of Stone Mountain for views of downtown Atlanta and the North Georgia mountains.

Many restaurants will accept you just as you are; dress codes are extremely rare in this casual city, except in the chicest of spots. While many restaurants accept reservations, some popular spots operate on a first-come, first-served basis on weekends. Waits at some hot dining locales can exceed an hour, especially if you arrive after 7 pm.

### PRICES

Eating in Atlanta is surprisingly affordable, at least when compared with cities like New York and Chicago. Some of the pricier restaurants offer early-bird weeknight specials and prix-fixe menus. Ask when you call to make reservations. *Prices in the reviews are the average cost of a main course at dinner or, if dinner is not served, at lunch. Use the coordinate (⊕ 1:B2) at the end of each listing to locate a site on the corresponding map.*

## DOWNTOWN

$$$$ STEAKHOUSE ✕ **BLT Steak.** Located on the ground floor of the W's downtown location, this chain entry serves excellent steaks and decadent sides (macaroni and cheese with bacon and truffle oil), all with the flourishes of a high-end business dinner destination. Almost as mouthwatering as the steaks are the complimentary Gruyère-infused popovers that come with every meal. Not into steak? Try the Dover sole, served with soy-caper brown butter. Ⓢ *Average main: $40* ✉ *W Atlanta-Downtown, 45 Ivan Allen Junior Blvd.* ☎ *404/577–7601* 🌐 *www.c2hospitality.com* ⊕ *1:B1.*

$ TAPAS ✕ **Lunacy Black Market.** One of the city's quirkiest and most fun dining experiences is tucked away behind a small storefront on Mitchell Street. At this tapas restaurant, the chef-owner Paul Luna is often as involved in your dining selections as you are, stopping to pull up a chair and chat up patrons in the small dining room. The menu changes regularly, but Luna always does well with seafood, soups, and fresh, seasonal vegetables. Note that the restaurant is not child-friendly. *Average main: $9 ✉ 231 Mitchell St. SW, Downtown ☎ 404/736–6164 ⊕ www.lunacyblackmarket.com ✍ Reservations not accepted ⊙ Closed Mon. and Tues. No lunch ✣ 1:A3.*

$$ AMERICAN

✕ **Ted's Montana Grill.** The Ted in question is CNN founder Ted Turner, who has left a significant mark on this city. That's why Atlantans feel a sense of ownership for this chain specializing in bison meat. Chicken, beef, and salmon also play a role on the menu. Tin ceilings, a cheerful waitstaff, and mahogany paneling add to the comfortable feel. Ted himself is known to stop by this location a lot; he lives in the building's penthouse. *Average main: $19 ✉ 133 Luckie St. NW, Downtown ☎ 404/521–9796 ⊕ www.tedsmontanagrill.com ✍ Reservations not accepted ✣ 1:B1.*

## SWEET AUBURN, THE OLD FOURTH WARD, AND EAST ATLANTA

$$$$ SOUTHERN

✕ **4th & Swift.** The industrial-chic decor of 4th & Swift's cavernous dining space offers a cool visual contrast to its impeccably plated offerings—comfort foods like pork belly, butternut squash, and homemade grits. Slide into a cream-color banquette and try the "Three Little Pigs," a delectable combination of sausage, pork belly, and pork loin. The bar here has made a reputation for itself with its fine cocktail program. *Average main: $25 ✉ 621 North Ave. NE, Old Fourth Ward ☎ 678/904–0160 ⊕ www.4thandswift.com ⊙ No lunch ✣ 1:D1.*

$ AMERICAN

✕ **The Earl.** Scrappy and lots of fun, this East Atlanta bar has a hearty menu of classic pub food, as well as a few entrées that are more innovative, such as jerk tuna. A favorite here is the "Greenie Meanie Chicken," a grilled chicken breast topped with roasted poblano peppers and salsa verde. In the back bar you'll see the country's best up-and-coming indie acts. *Average main: $8 ✉ 488 Flat Shoals Ave., East Atlanta ☎ 404/522–3950 ⊕ badearl.com ✍ Reservations not accepted ✣ 2:D4.*

$$ JAPANESE ★

✕ **Miso Izakaya.** Chef-owner Guy Wong's *izakaya* (Japanese pub) has gathered a following for his well-executed menu of mostly small plates. Skip the sushi bar for a sampling of crispy duck buns and a noodle bowl with pork belly. Waits can be long on Saturday, as the dining room is small, and the waitstaff can be inconsistent: order a drink immediately in case it takes a while for the food to arrive. **■ TIP→ Wong likes to run specials, such as the ramen he recently made from scratch and served for lunch, when the restaurant's usually closed. Check the website for details.** *Average main: $15 ✉ 619 Edgewood Ave. SE, Old Fourth Ward ☎ 678/701–0128 ⊕ www.misoizakaya.com ⊙ Closed Sun. No lunch ✣ 1:D3.*

$ MEXICAN Fodor's Choice ★

✕ **Holy Taco.** Don't fill up on the tortilla chips at this Tex-Mex joint. They are so tasty—deep fried and super-crispy—that you might miss the rest of the inventive menu. Best bets include the dessertlike arepas topped with queso fresco and dulce de leche. There are surprises, too, like tacos with roasted beef tongue or buttermilk-fried chicken hearts. Don't miss

13

# BEST BETS FOR ATLANTA DINING

**★ Fodor's Choice**

**Antico Pizza Napolitana,** p. 607
**Bacchanalia,** p. 607
**Cakes & Ale,** p. 614
**Empire State South,** p. 604
**Holeman and Finch Public House,** p. 609
**Holy Taco,** p. 602
**West Egg Cafe,** p. 608

## By Price

**$**

**The Earl,** p. 602
**Lunacy Black Market,** p. 601
**Taquería del Sol,** p. 608
**Thumb's Up Diner,** p. 603
**Victory Sandwich Bar + Emporium,** p. 614

**$$**

**Leon's Full Service,** p. 614
**Miso Izakaya,** p. 602
**No. 246,** p. 614

**$$$**

**Bocado,** p. 607
**The Optimist,** p. 608

**$$$$**

**Miller Union,** p. 607
**Rathbun's,** p. 613
**Watershed on Peachtree,** p. 611

## By Cuisine

**BEST ASIAN**

**Miso Izakaya,** p. 602

**BEST MEXICAN**

**Holy Taco,** p. 602
**Taquería del Sol,** p. 608

## By Experience

**BEST BRUNCH**

**Canoe,** p. 600
**Flying Biscuit,** p. 612
**Gato Bizco,** p. 613
**Thumb's Up Diner,** p. 603

**MOST ROMANTIC**

**Bacchanalia,** p. 607
**Lunacy Black Market,** p. 601

the *elote asado*, a grilled corncob smeared with spiced mayo and queso fresco. A big patio makes this a big sunny-day draw. $ *Average main: $12 ✉ 1314 Glenwood Ave., East Atlanta ☎ 404/230–6177 🌐 www.holy-taco.com ✣ 2:D4.*

$ SOUTHERN ✕ **Thelma's Kitchen.** Head to this cheerful spot for favorites like okra pancakes, fried catfish, slaw, and macaroni and cheese, all of which are among the best in town. Thelma Grundy's desserts, including lemon cheese pound cake, sweet-potato pie, red velvet cake, and pecan pie, are worth the trip. $ *Average main: $8 ✉ 302 Auburn Ave., Sweet Auburn ☎ 404/688–5855 ✍ Reservations not accepted ⏲ Closed Sun. No dinner ✣ 1:D2.*

$ AMERICAN ✕ **Thumb's Up Diner.** You haven't really lived, or at least tested the limits of your heart's health, until you've tried The Heap: a sizzling skillet full of eggs, buttery veggies, and potatoes. Add a fluffy biscuit on the side and this is one of the city's best breakfasts. With five locations around town, Thumb's Up also has good lunch options, and some might be better for your ticker, including tamari-flavored tofu served on a bed of raw spinach. The place gets packed on weekends, so bring something to read while you wait. $ *Average main: $7 ✉ 573 Edgewood Ave. SE, Old Fourth Ward ☎ 404/223–0690 🌐 www.thumbsupdiner.com ▭ No credit cards ⏲ No dinner ✣ 2:D3.*

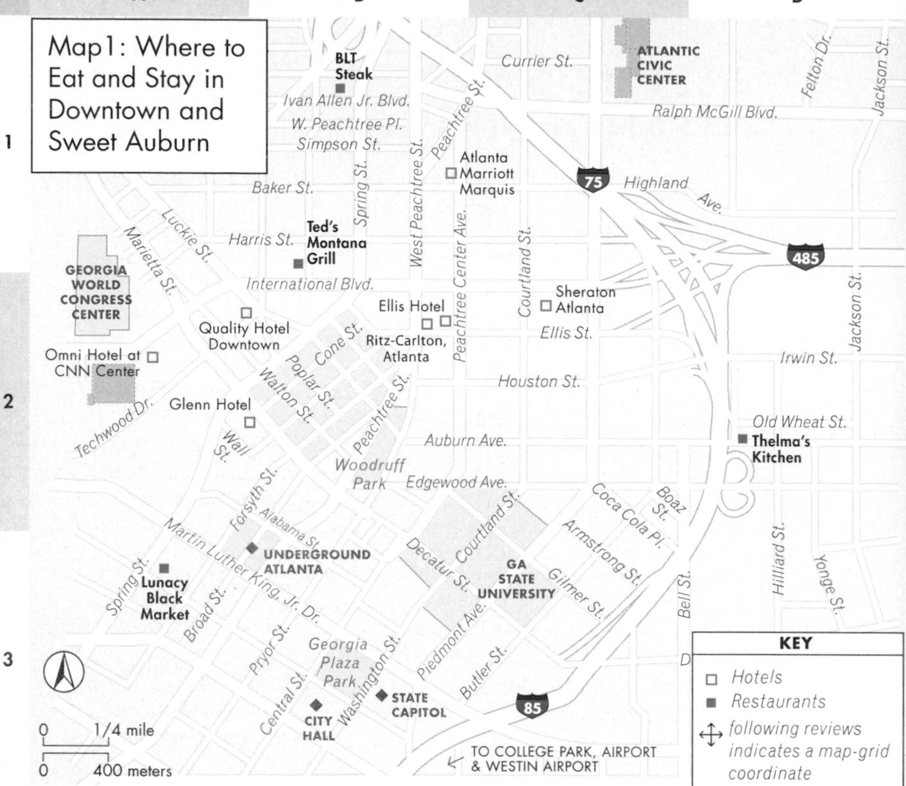


## MIDTOWN

**$$$$** SOUTHERN Fodor's Choice ★ **Empire State South.** Southern ingredients get the fine-dining treatment without the pretension at celebrity chef Hugh Acheson's Midtown favorite. Empire State South does it all: towering build-your-own breakfast biscuits, *tiffin* (Indian lunchbox) daily lunch specials (these must be ordered by 11 am), beautifully prepared Georgia trout with green beans and pimentos at dinner, and the perfect espresso. For a lunchtime protein boost, order the Super Food entrée, a protein-and nutrient-rich plate of hanger steak, radish, pickled beets, squash, field peas, wheat berries, pickled pimentos, and apples. The wine list is one of the most diverse in the city. *Average main: $29* *999 Peachtree St., Midtown* *404/541–1105* *empirestatesouth.com* *2:B2.*

**$$** AMERICAN **The Lawrence.** The noncorporate upscale pub food at the Lawrence was a very welcome addition to Midtown when it opened in early 2012. Dinner options such as crispy duck-tongue carnitas, heirloom tomato panzanella, and pho-style oxtail with corn velouté and gnocchi reflect the range available at this buzzing young establishment. Speaking of buzz, the bar offers a wide selection of gin, in some ways a nod to its location on Juniper Street. *Average main: $18* *905 Juniper St. NE, Midtown* *404/961–7177* *www.thelawrenceatlanta.com* *Closed Mon. No lunch* *2:B2.*

$ SOUTHERN ✕ **Mary Mac's Tea Room.** Local celebrities and ordinary folks line up for the country-fried steak, fried chicken, and fresh vegetables here. In the Southern tradition, waitresses will call you "honey" and pat your arm to assure you that everything's all right. It's a great way to experience Southern food and hospitality all at once. *Average main: $14 224 Ponce de Leon Ave., Midtown 404/876–1800 www.marymacs.com 2:C3.*

$$ AMERICAN ✕ **One Midtown Kitchen.** An unassuming warehouse entrance down a side street near Piedmont Park leads to a seductively lighted, industrial-chic restaurant. The dining room is energetic but can be loud; the back porch, on the other hand, is quieter and offers a serene view of the park and the city skyline. The wood-roasted pizzas are outstanding, as is the price-tiered wine list. Order a glass or bottle and choose several small plates (maybe the salmon crudo?) for the table to share. *Average main: $19 559 Dutch Valley Rd., Midtown 404/892–4111 www.onemidtownkitchen.com No lunch 2:A3.*

$$$$ AMERICAN ✕ **Park 75.** This swanky hotel restaurant features a seasonal menu that includes standouts like whole branzino and Angus beef tenderloin; all sides are à la carte. The Sunday brunch—featuring dishes like an egg-white frittata, chocolate waffles, and mac and cheese with rock shrimp and jumbo lump crabmeat—is very popular. *Average main: $30 Four Seasons, 75 14th St., Midtown 404/253–3840 www.fourseasons.com/atlanta/dining/restaurants/park_75.*

$$$ SOUTHERN ✕ **South City Kitchen.** The culinary traditions of South Carolina inspire the dishes served at this cheerful restaurant. This is the place to get fried green tomatoes with goat cheese, she-crab soup, or buttermilk fried chicken. The chef prepares catfish in many intriguing ways. Crab hash, served with poached eggs and chive hollandaise, is a classic. Don't miss the chocolate pecan tart. In the heart of the Crescent Avenue entertainment district, the spare, art-filled restaurant attracts a hip crowd. *Average main: $22 1144 Crescent Ave., Midtown 404/873–7358 www.southcitykitchen.com 2:A2.*

$$ THAI ✕ **Tamarind Seed.** All that is good about Thai flavors—refreshing lime, spicy basil, hot peppers, cooling coconut, and smoky fish sauces—comes through at this standout known for excellent service. Favorite dishes include chicken with green curry and sea bass with three-flavor sauce. Meals are served in a simple, subdued, but elegant setting. *Average main: $18 1197 Peachtree St. NE, Midtown 404/873–4888 www.tamarindseed.com No lunch Sat. 2:C3.*

$ AMERICAN ★ ✕ **Top Flr.** Young Atlantans flock to this stylish Midtown eatery for its creative menu, interesting wines, and good-looking bartenders. Get the white bean hummus to start, and then try the duck confit pizza (it's big enough for two to share) or the orange-apple tofu bowl. The bar staff likes to experiment: instead of ordering a cocktail from the menu, describe the kind of drink you want and they'll customize one just for you. *Average main: $13 674 Myrtle St., Midtown 404/685–3110 www.topflr.com No lunch 2:C3.*

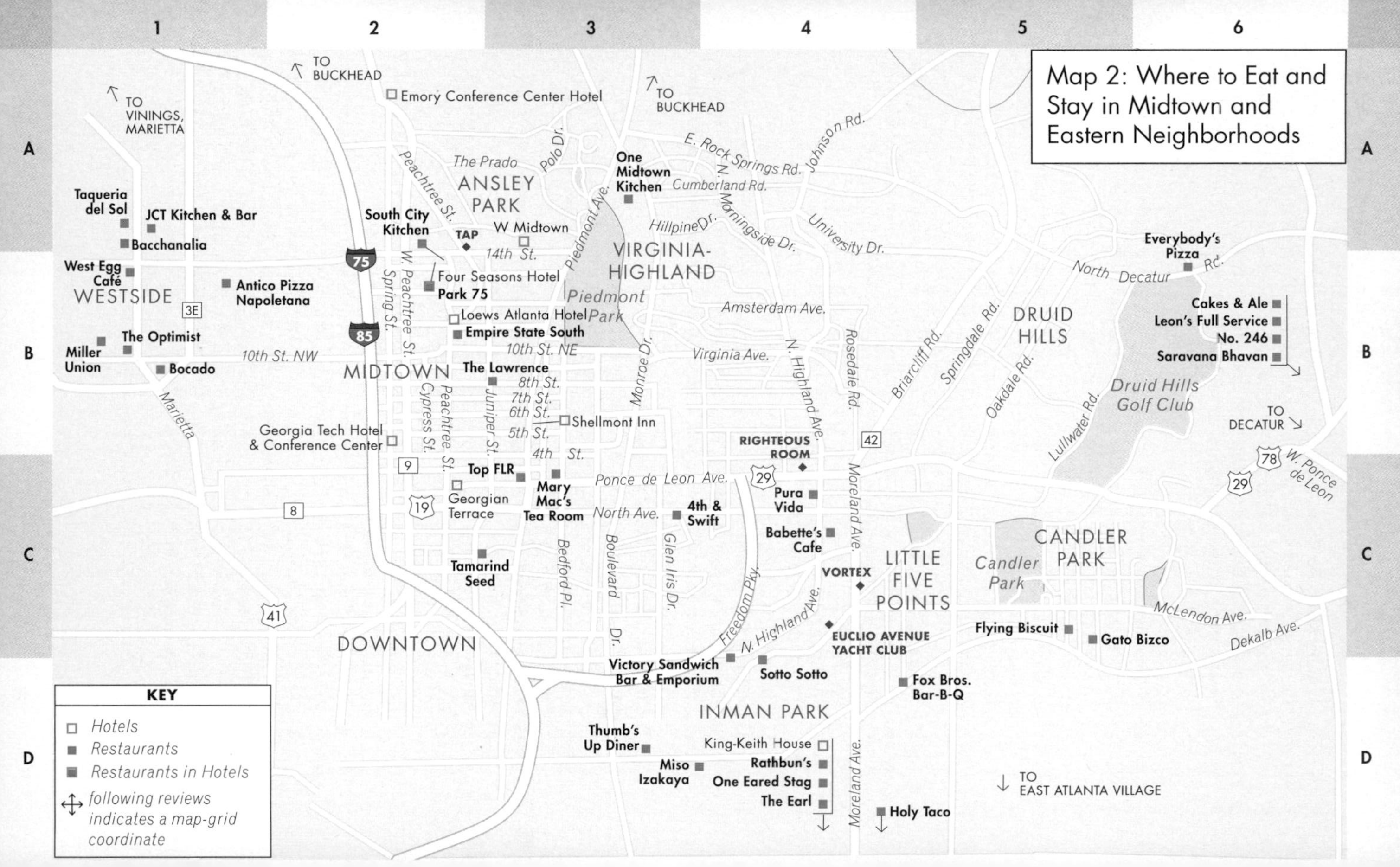

Map 2: Where to Eat and Stay in Midtown and Eastern Neighborhoods
1
2
3
4
5
6
A
B
C
D
TO VININGS, MARIETTA
TO BUCKHEAD
Emory Conference Center Hotel
TO BUCKHEAD
Taqueria del Sol
JCT Kitchen & Bar
Bacchanalia
West Egg Café
WESTSIDE
3E
Antico Pizza Napoletana
Miller Union
The Optimist
Bocado
10th St. NW
Marietta
South City Kitchen
TAP
W Midtown
14th St.
Four Seasons Hotel
Park 75
Loews Atlanta Hotel
Empire State South
10th St. NE
MIDTOWN
The Lawrence
8th St.
7th St.
6th St.
5th St.
4th St.
Shellmont Inn
Georgia Tech Hotel & Conference Center
Top FLR
Mary Mac's Tea Room
Georgian Terrace
Tamarind Seed
The Prado
ANSLEY PARK
Peachtree St.
W. Peachtree St.
Spring St.
Cypress St.
Juniper St.
Polo Dr.
Piedmont Ave.
Piedmont Park
One Midtown Kitchen
VIRGINIA-HIGHLAND
Hillpine Dr.
N. Morningside Dr.
Cumberland Rd.
E. Rock Springs Rd.
Johnson Rd.
University Dr.
Amsterdam Ave.
Virginia Ave.
Monroe Dr.
N. Highland Ave.
Rosedale Rd.
Briarcliff Rd.
Springdale Rd.
Oakdale Rd.
Lullwater Rd.
DRUID HILLS
Druid Hills Golf Club
North Decatur Rd.
Everybody's Pizza
Cakes & Ale
Leon's Full Service
No. 246
Saravana Bhavan
TO DECATUR
W. Ponce de Leon
78
29
42
RIGHTEOUS ROOM
29
Ponce de Leon Ave.
North Ave.
4th & Swift
Pura Vida
Babette's Cafe
Moreland Ave.
9
8
19
41
Bedford Pl.
Boulevard Dr.
Glen Iris Dr.
Freedom Pky.
N. Highland Ave.
VORTEX
LITTLE FIVE POINTS
EUCLIO AVENUE YACHT CLUB
CANDLER PARK
Candler Park
Flying Biscuit
Gato Bizco
McLendon Ave.
Dekalb Ave.
DOWNTOWN
Victory Sandwich Bar & Emporium
Sotto Sotto
Fox Bros. Bar-B-Q
INMAN PARK
Thumb's Up Diner
Miso Izakaya
King-Keith House
Rathbun's
One Eared Stag
The Earl
Moreland Ave.
Holy Taco
TO EAST ATLANTA VILLAGE
KEY
Hotels
Restaurants
Restaurants in Hotels
following reviews indicates a map-grid coordinate

## WESTSIDE

$$ NEAPOLITAN Fodor's Choice ★ **Antico Pizza Napoletana.** Antico offers a big slice of cheesy, saucy, chewy, Naples-style heaven. The communal tables, as well as the Italian opera on the stereo, give the place a convivial vibe. The best seats are inside the kitchen, where you can watch the wood-burning ovens. Try the enormous Pomodorini pie, with cherry tomatoes, mozzarella, garlic, and basil. The Vesuvio calzone is a pillow full of cheese, spicy sopressata, and prosciutto. This place is popular, so be prepared for long lines. *Average main: $19 1093 Hemphill Ave., Westside 404/724–2333 www.anticopizza.it Closed Sun. 2:B1.*

$$$$ AMERICAN Fodor's Choice ★ **Bacchanalia.** Often called the city's best restaurant, Bacchanalia has been a destination since it opened in Buckhead in 1993. The current Westside location, a renovated warehouse with 20-foot ceilings, is decorated in deep, inviting tones. The kitchen focuses on locally grown organic produce and seasonal ingredients. Items on the prix-fixe menu change frequently, but could include crab fritters, wood-grilled prime NY strip, and warm chocolate cake. *Average main: $85 1198 Howell Mill Rd., Westside 404/365–0410 www.starprovisions.com Reservations essential Closed Sun. No lunch 2:A1.*

$$$ MODERN AMERICAN ★ **Bocado.** It's rare to see the dining room of this classy Westside staple empty. Local professionals out for casual business lunches dominate the place by day, while at dinnertime friends gather around the bar for cocktails, and couples make a beeline for the cozy tables. Much of Bocado's reputation is wrapped up in its burger—two patties covered in cheese and house-made pickles—widely thought of as the city's best. Order a side of the garlic herbed fries. The lunch menu's roasted cauliflower sandwich packs a punch with roasted eggplant and jalapeño mayo. At dinner lamb Bolognese accompanies hand-cut pappardelle, ricotta, mint, and chilies. *Average main: $20 887 Howell Mill Rd., Suite 2, Westside 404/815–1399 www.bocadoatlanta.com No lunch weekends. Closed Sun. 2:B1.*

$$$ SOUTHERN **JCT Kitchen & Bar.** This comfortable, airy restaurant—with pale wood, white, and silver accents—is part of the now-bustling Westside Urban Market. JCT, a "farmstead bistro" with Southern flair, is a great place for a business-casual lunch or a dinner date. The deviled eggs are to die for, as are the perfectly crisp truffle-Parmesan fries. The upstairs bar has a comfortable outdoor patio with fantastic views of the Midtown skyline. The bar's only downside is the oppressively loud live music often playing during happy hour. *Average main: $20 1198 Howell Mill Rd., Suite 18, Westside 404/355–2252 www.jctkitchen.com No lunch Sun. 2:A1.*

$$$$ AMERICAN ★ **Miller Union.** Miller Union's farm egg baked in celery cream with rustic bread is one of the best dishes in town. It's just the right mix of rich, smooth, and salty. The rest of the Southern-inflected menu is almost as good, with locally sourced foods and a delicious grilled pork loin and seasonal-vegetable plate. For dessert, try the ice cream sandwich, which is served only at lunch. *Average main: $26 999 Brady Ave. NW, Westside 678/733–8550 www.millerunion.com Closed Sun. No lunch Mon. 2:B1.*

13

$$$ SEAFOOD ★ **The Optimist.** Named *Esquire* magazine's Best New Restaurant of 2012, the Optimist lives up to the hype, serving top-notch seafood in a dazzingly refurbished warehouse space. To start, slurp on raw oysters on the half-shell from the oyster bar—also a fun place to hang out and have a beer. Then try the seafood gumbo, which has dark complex gravy and is full of meaty hunks of crab. The black grouper is savory and served atop all the delicious components of a Lowcountry boil; the breaded redfish with pepper jelly provides bite after bite of sweet, crunchy, flaky fish. The restaurant has a lively atmosphere (there's a putting green out front) and can get a bit noisy in the middle of dinner. *Average main: $23 914 Howell Mill Rd., Westside 404/477–6260 theoptimistrestaurant.com No lunch weekends 2:B1.*

$ MEXICAN **Taquería del Sol.** Don't let the long lines outside this counter-service eatery discourage you. They move quickly, and once you get in you'll be rewarded with a full bar, a wide selection of tacos and enchiladas, unusual sides like spicy collard greens and jalapeño coleslaw, a fabulous trio of salsas, and not-to-be-missed chunky guacamole. Don't grab a table before you order or you'll get glares from those waiting in line. *Average main: $6 1200–B Howell Mill Rd., Westside 404/352–5811 taqueriadelsol.com Reservations not accepted Closed Sun. No dinner Mon. 2:A1.*

$ AMERICAN Fodor's Choice ★ **West Egg Cafe.** A great place to come for one of the city's best breakfasts, especially if you're staying in Midtown: this industrial-chic spot is right across the highway. West Egg serves breakfast all day—locals swear by the blue-plate special and the old-fashioned oatmeal. For lunch or dinner, be sure to try the pimento cheese, particularly good on the fried green tomato BLT. The dining room is popular, so either try to come early to avoid a wait, or opt to eat at the spacious bar. *Average main: $11 1100 Howell Mill Rd., Westside 404/872–3973 westeggcafe.com 2:B1.*

## BUCKHEAD

$$$$ AMERICAN **Aria.** Chef Gerry Klaskala's talent is best captured by his love of rustic and hearty "slow foods"—braises, stews, roasts, and chops cooked over a roll-top French grill. Pork shoulder is presented with a delicious red pepper and white corn succotash and crisp Vidalia onions. Signature dishes include a lobster cocktail and zinfandel-braised beef short ribs. Don't miss renowned pastry chef Kathryn King's mouthwatering dessert menu, including Valrhona-chocolate-cream pie with Drambuie sauce. *Average main: $30 490 E. Paces Ferry Rd., Buckhead 404/233–7673 www.aria-atl.com Reservations essential Closed Sun. No lunch 3:B4.*

$$$$ AMERICAN **Canoe.** This popular spot on the bank of the Chattahoochee River has built a reputation based on such seasonal dishes as oysters on the half shell; cornmeal-crusted rainbow trout with eggplant hummus; and slow-roasted rabbit with bacon ravioli and Swiss chard. Sunday brunch—with smoked-salmon eggs Benedict, house-made English muffins with citrus hollandaise, and other offerings—is superb. **TIP→ The restaurant's tagline, "tucked away, not far away," is no joke—call for direc-**

If Southern soul food is what you crave, head to Mary Mac's Tea Room for a taste of her famous fried chicken, collard greens, hoppin' John, and fried okra.

tions. *Average main: $25 ✉ 4199 Paces Ferry Rd. SE, Buckhead ☎ 770/432–2663 🌐 www.canoeatl.com ⊙ No lunch Sat. ⊕ 3:A3.*

$ SOUTHERN **Colonnade.** For traditional Southern food—fried chicken, ham steak, and turkey with dressing—insiders head to Colonnade, a local institution since 1927 and a magnet for gay men and the elderly. The interior, with patterned carpeting and red banquettes, is a classic version of a 1950s restaurant. *Average main: $13 ✉ 1879 Cheshire Bridge Rd., Buckhead ☎ 404/874–5642 🌐 colonnadeatl.com Reservations not accepted No credit cards ⊙ No lunch weekdays ⊕ 3:C6.*

$$ MEDITERRANEAN **Eclipse di Luna.** Twentysomethings flock to this bustling place on weekends. The lunch menu includes sandwiches and salads; evening fare consists of tapas such as *patatas bravas con romesco* (potatoes with olive oil and a spicy sauce). The only real entrées are a roasted whole fish and a traditional paella overflowing with fresh seafood, chicken, and chorizo (a vegetarian version is available). The restaurant is at the very end of the Miami Circle design center. *Average main: $15 ✉ 764 Miami Circle, Buckhead ☎ 404/846–0449 🌐 www.eclipsediluna.com ⊙ No lunch Sun. or Mon. ⊕ 3:C4.*

$ AMERICAN Fodor's Choice ★ **Holeman and Finch Public House.** Started in part by a Restaurant Eugene alum, Holeman and Finch helped revitalize Atlanta's drink scene with its custom "tinctures" and classic cocktails. It also unleashed a local appetite for house-made charcuterie (the city's best might be right here)—and had a big hand in the burger craze that swept the city a few years back, thanks to the limited availability of its popular double-patty cheeseburger. Only 24 are offered each night, starting at 10 pm. Show up early and order quickly if you want one. *Average main: $11 ✉ 2277*

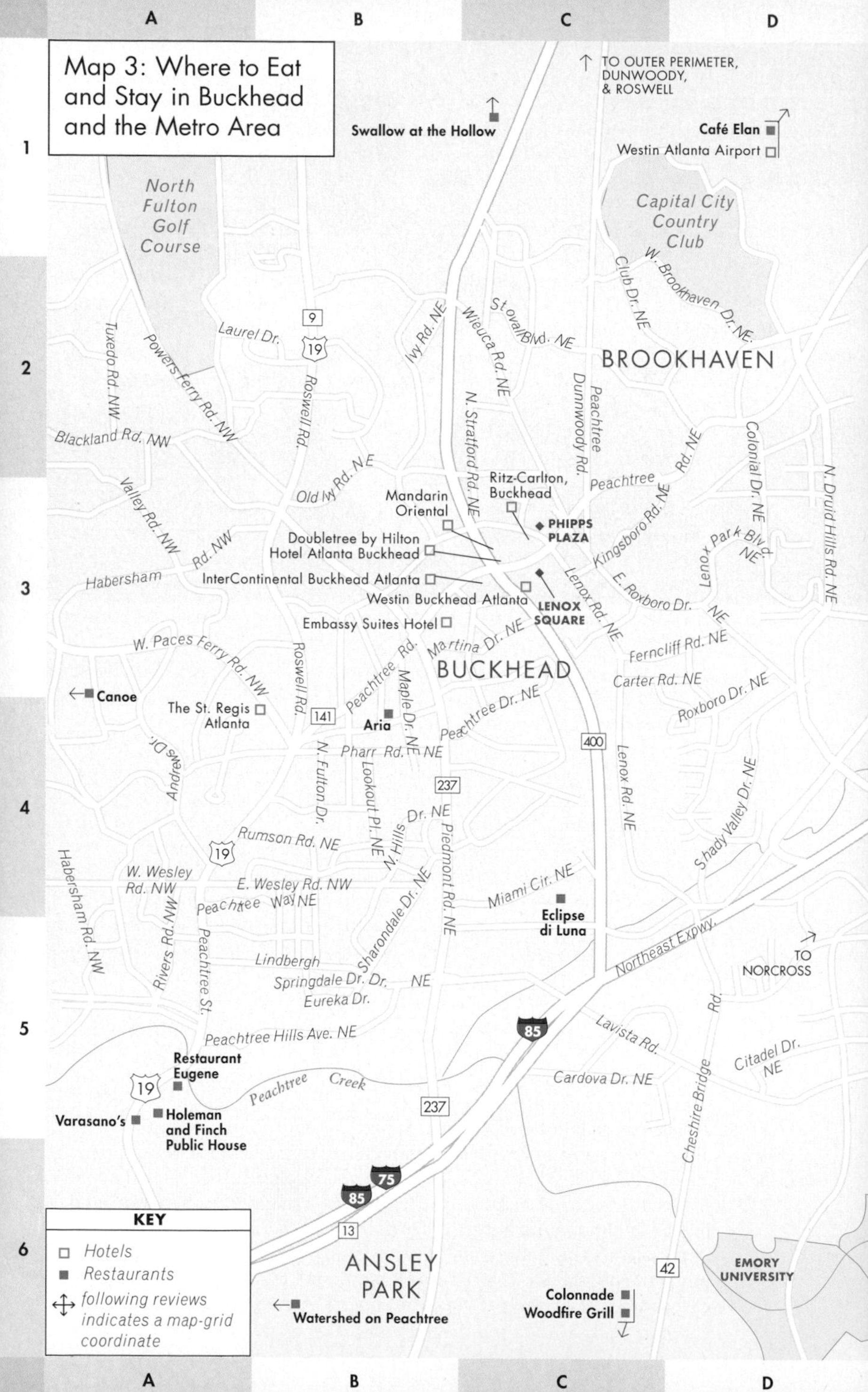

Map 3: Where to Eat and Stay in Buckhead and the Metro Area
A
B
C
D
1
2
3
4
5
6
TO OUTER PERIMETER, DUNWOODY, & ROSWELL
Swallow at the Hollow
Café Elan
Westin Atlanta Airport
North Fulton Golf Course
Capital City Country Club
BROOKHAVEN
Mandarin Oriental
Ritz-Carlton, Buckhead
PHIPPS PLAZA
Doubletree by Hilton Hotel Atlanta Buckhead
InterContinental Buckhead Atlanta
Westin Buckhead Atlanta
LENOX SQUARE
Embassy Suites Hotel
BUCKHEAD
Canoe
The St. Regis Atlanta
Aria
Eclipse di Luna
TO NORCROSS
Restaurant Eugene
Varasano's
Holeman and Finch Public House
ANSLEY PARK
Watershed on Peachtree
Colonnade
Woodfire Grill
EMORY UNIVERSITY
KEY
Hotels
Restaurants
following reviews indicates a map-grid coordinate

*Peachtree Rd., Suite B, Buckhead ☎ 404/948–1175 ⊕ holeman-finch.com ✍ Reservations not accepted ⊙ No lunch. No dinner Sun. ↔ 3:A5.*

$$$$ MODERN AMERICAN ✕ **Restaurant Eugene.** Linton Hopkins, the 2012 James Beard Award winner for best chef in the Southeast, is behind this quiet and sophisticated homage to local ingredients. The "vegetable tasting" is one of the menu's best dishes (and the city's best vegetable plate); its components vary with what's freshest. There's plenty of meat on the menu as well (this is the South after all), including sweetbreads, pork belly, and a rib eye seared in an iron skillet. Desserts range from classic to cerebral—try the fried padrón pepper with peanut butter, caramelized milk, and chocolate ricotta; or the chocolate financier cake with roast beets, blackberry sorbet, and lavender. [$] *Average main: $30 ✉ 2277 Peachtree Road NE, Buckhead ☎ 404/355–0321 ⊕ www.restauranteugene.com ⊙ No lunch. ↔ 3:A5.*

$$ ITALIAN ✕ **Varasano's.** Jeff Varasano was 14 when he set the country's Rubik's Cube record. Though this makes the software engineer proud, it barely registers when compared to his most recent feat: building the perfect pizza. After experimenting at home, configuring his oven so it could shoot up to 800 degrees without burning down his house, he wrote a 22,000-word manifesto on the process. It quickly became an Internet sensation and led to a series of tastings with pizza fanatics from around the world. Now Varasano has a restaurant that serves thin, lightly charred pies along with pastas, salads, and rich Italian donuts. [$] *Average main: $16 ✉ 2171 Peachtree Rd. NE, Buckhead ☎ 404/352–8216 ⊕ www.varasanos.com ⊙ No lunch Mon.–Thurs. ↔ 3:A5.*

$$$$ SOUTHERN ✕ **Watershed on Peachtree.** Indigo Girl Emily Saliers and three of her friends originally launched this casual restaurant in a converted Decatur gas station; it became an Atlanta classic renowned for its fried chicken. Chef Joe Truex has maintained the farm-to-table theme and a menu full of updated Southern comfort food in the current Buckhead location. Think Sapelo Island clams, pimento cheese toast with a smoked ham hock, and jambalaya. And don't forget about the Wednesday-night fried chicken—get there while the gettin' is good. [$] *Average main: $25 ✉ 1820 Peachtree Rd. NW, Buckhead ☎ 404/809–3561 ⊕ www.watershedrestaurant.com ⊙ No dinner Sun. Closed Mon. ↔ 3:C6.*

$$$ AMERICAN ✕ **Woodfire Grill.** The menu at this cozy upscale bistro changes almost daily, and it's kept short and sweet. Think chilled cucumber and almond soup followed by wood-grilled duck. The five- and seven-course tasting menus feature exceptionally flavorful surprises (literally—they don't tell you what's in store). A recent chef's tasting included wood-smoked pork belly and lacquered quail with smoky greens, caramelized onion grits, and crackling pork skins. [$] *Average main: $24 ✉ 1782 Cheshire Bridge Rd., Buckhead ☎ 404/347–9055 ⊕ www.woodfiregrill.com ✍ Reservations essential ⊙ Closed Sun. and Mon. No lunch ↔ 3:C6.*

## VIRGINIA-HIGHLAND AND THE EMORY AREA

$ PIZZA ✕ **Everybody's Pizza.** This restaurant and bar feels like a neighborhood joint. Traditional slices and pies are available, but what Everybody's is most known for are its pizza-crisps, with very thin crusts and inventive topping combos, like shrimp and artichoke or Thai chicken. The

13

The Clara Meer in Piedmont Park offers fantastic views of Midtown's skyscrapers.

salads are a standout, too—build your own with goat cheese, roasted peanuts, and the creamy Italian dressing. *Average main: $14* *1593 N. Decatur Rd., Emory* *404/377–7766* *www.everybodyspizza.com* *Reservations not accepted.*

$ LATIN AMERICAN **Pura Vida.** Latin-American tapas are served up in a vibrant atmosphere at this small and busy Poncey-Highland establishment, which is helmed by "Top Chef" alum Hector Santiago. Pura Vida offers a wide selection of cheeses and charcuterie, in addition to entrées such as Georgia trout ceviche con leche, charred mushrooms in a chipotle-garlic butter, and shrimp that have been marinated in garlic and rosemary. The coconut bun with pork belly glazed with tamarind sauce is a must. And the bar makes a mean mojito. *Average main: $9* *656 N. Highland Ave. NE, Poncey-Highland* *404/870–9797* *www.puravidatapas.com* *Closed on Sun. No lunch* *2:C4.*

## LITTLE FIVE POINTS AND INMAN PARK

$$$ EUROPEAN **Babette's Cafe.** Sunny yellow walls and back-porch seating add to the homey charm of this renovated bungalow. The restaurant, which describes its cuisine as rustic European, offers such seasonal dishes as New England sole with grilled fennel, and beef tenderloin with Gorgonzola sauce. Loyal locals love the Sunday brunch. *Average main: $21* *573 N. Highland Ave., Inman Park* *404/523–9121* *Closed Mon. No lunch* *2:C4.*

$ SOUTHERN **Flying Biscuit.** There's a long wait on weekends at this spot, which is famous for its biscuits served with cranberry-apple butter. Other huge hits include sausage made with free-range chicken and sage, and bean cakes with tomatillo salsa. Fancier dinners include roasted chicken and turkey meat loaf with pudge (mashed potatoes). There are also plenty of vegetarian options. Next door is a bakery serving biscuits to go, as well as freshly baked muffins and cookies. *Average main: $9 1655 McLendon Ave., Candler Park 404/687–8888 www.flyingbiscuit.com Reservations not accepted 2:C5.*

$ BARBECUE ★ **Fox Bros. Bar-B-Q.** Here's what pays the bills here: brisket, pulled pork, fried pickles, fried mac-and-cheese, and an artery-cloggin' take on tater tots, served smothered in Brunswick stew and melted cheese. Try to get a seat on the patio, a great place to soak up sun and sip a cold beer. *Average main: $13 1238 Dekalb Ave., Candler Park 404/577–4030 www.foxbrosbbq.com Reservations not accepted 2:D4.*

$ AMERICAN **Gato Bizco.** Brunch is big business in Atlanta, and sometimes the waits at the best spots can span an hour. But this little eatery, across the street from the always-packed Flying Biscuit, somehow always seems to have room on a stool or in one of the six booths. Sitting at the counter is like sitting in your friend's kitchen while she cooks; the work is done right there in front of you by the easygoing, tattooed staff. The food may take some time to arrive, but it's worth the wait for fluffy omelets and great pancakes—locals rave about the sweet-potato variety. Hours are limited—9 am to 2:30 pm—so plan accordingly. *Average main: $10 1660 McLendon Ave., Candler Park 404/371–0889 Reservations not accepted Closed Mon. and Tues. No dinner 2:C5.*

$$$ MODERN AMERICAN **One Eared Stag.** The adventurous menu at this upscale bistro is tweaked daily to accommodate the freshest, most interesting ingredients. Chef Robert Phalen loves to play with expectations and flavor combinations, as with the shrimp heads in a romesco-sauce aioli, or the strawberry grouper that's been poached in duck fat and served with gazpacho, cucumber salad, and roe from the hackleback sturgeon. The space occupies a quiet corner in residential Inman Park, but patrons from all over the city come to dine at communal tables in front of the open kitchen. *Average main: $24 1029 Edgewood Ave. NE, Inman Park 404/525–4479 www.oneearedstag.com 2:D4.*

$$$$ AMERICAN ★ **Rathbun's.** This hot spot is helmed by local super-chef Kevin Rathbun, who once bested Bobby Flay on *Iron Chef*. The space's high ceilings, white tablecloths, exposed brick, and expensive dishes described as "second mortgage" plates could seem high-falutin', but Rathbun's maintains a coziness with its fine cuisine. Go for a signature steak or stick to the "small plates" menu for a more complete tour of the kitchen. The well-sauced lamb scaloppine with cubes of pancetta is divine, as is the side of charred corn and gouda. *Average main: $30 112 Krog St. NE, Suite R, Inman Park 404/524–8280 www.rathbunsrestaurant.com Reservations essential Closed Sun. No lunch 2:D4.*

$$$ ITALIAN **Sotto Sotto.** This hot spot close to Downtown has an adventurous take on Italian cuisine. The former commercial space hops with young, hip patrons dining on seafood risotto, spaghetti with sun-dried mullet roe, and utterly perfect *panna cotta* (custard). Next door is Fritti, its sister restaurant, which specializes in gourmet pizza and fried calamari and mushrooms. *Average main: $21 313 N. Highland Ave., Inman Park 404/523–6678 www.urestaurants.net No lunch 2:C4.*

13

$ AMERICAN

**Victory Sandwich Bar + Emporium.** Word spread quickly when Victory first opened: not only did it sell Jack (Daniels) and Coke slushies, but it also had a Ping-Pong table. As if that weren't enough to attract plenty of twenty- and thirty-somethings living in the neighborhood, the bar-restaurant also offers super-cheap ($4) and delicious sandwiches. The Castro is a take on the classic Cuban, with slow-roasted pork, ham, pickles, fontina cheese, and yellow mustard; the Hambo is a salty-sweet Italian treat, with prosciutto, mozzarella, arugula, apple, and a balsamic reduction. The prices are small, but so are the portions: you may want to order two sandwiches if you're really hungry. *Average main: $4* *280 Elizabeth St., Inman Park* *770/676–7287* *vicsandwich.com* *2:C4.*

## DECATUR

$$$$ SOUTHERN Fodor's Choice ★

**Cakes & Ale.** Fresh, seasonal veggies frequently take center stage at this crisp, upscale farm-to-table restaurant, and they often come from chef-owner Billy Allin's own garden. The roast chicken is a classic dish here. Or try the halibut with *fregula* (small toasted balls of pasta), peppers, pink-eyed peas, clams, and shrimp in a saffron broth. There's a large patio with plenty of seating and a view of the sleepy town square, for those who like to dine outdoors. The restaurant itself isn't open for lunch, but the nearby **Bakery at Cakes & Ale** is: it serves hearty grain bowls, sandwiches, and homemade breads and sweets. The bakery is also open for breakfast. *Average main: $29* *155 Sycamore St., Decatur* *404/377–7994* *cakesandalerestaurant.com* *Closed Sun. and Mon. No lunch* *2:B6.*

$$ MODERN AMERICAN

**Leon's Full Service.** In a neighborhood flush with craft beer options, Leon's introduced an inventive specialty cocktail menu (as well as its own long list of craft beers). The food menu is full of fun snacks to share while drinking, including fries served with an array of sauces such as garlic aioli and massaman curry; a warm chickpea and cherry salad; and bacon, which comes served in a glass, with the option of peanut butter on the side. For an entrée, try the pan-roasted trout or flatiron steak. The restaurant, and L-shape former service station in the heart of downtown Decatur, borders a popular patio on one side and is lined by a busy bocce court on the other. *Average main: $19* *131 E. Ponce de Leon Ave., Decatur* *404/687–0500* *www.leonsfullservice.com* *Reservations not accepted* *No lunch Mon.* *2:B6.*

$$ ITALIAN

**No. 246.** It's fun to come sit at the oversized bar and sample any number of the smaller plates on this happening Italian eatery's menu, such as the variety of toasts, including ones served with pâté-like pork rillette or roasted tomatoes; or the house meatball, served with a plate of fresh red sauce and basil. If you'd rather stay closer to the food, request a seat facing the wood-fire oven and watch the *pizzaiolas* (pizza guys) slide fresh pies in and out of the oven while you eat. The pastas are delicate and delicious, and the pizzas are thin, charred, and chewy—the classic margherita is a great choice. *Average main: $18* *129 E. Ponce de Leon Ave., Decatur* *678/399–8246* *www.no246.com* *2:B6.*

13

$ **Saravana Bhavan.** The vegetarian food is fantastic, flavorful, and filling at this ever-popular chain restaurant, whose headquarters are in South India. Favorites include cheese *masala dosai* (lentil flour crepe with spiced potatoes), mango *lassi* (yogurt smoothie), and *chaat samosas* (vegetable turnovers topped with onions, chickpeas, crispy noodles, sweet-and-sour sauces, and cilantro). The service is fast and the restaurant is spacious, if a little bit cafeterialike. *Average main: $9* *2179 Lawrenceville Hwy., Decatur* *404/636–4400* *www.saravanabhavan.com* *2:B6.*

INDIAN ★

## METRO ATLANTA

$ **The Swallow at the Hollow.** Bring your biggest appetite when visiting this legendary barbecue restaurant and country-music venue, where everything is homemade, from the sausages to the pickles. Belly up to the long picnic tables for some of the region's best ribs, smoked meats, and cabin bread. There's even a delicious vegetarian option: the pit-cooked portabello mushroom sandwich with smoked Gouda and fried green tomatoes. The place gets packed, so be prepared to wait on the homey front porch. If you want to catch the music, call ahead for a reservation. *Average main: $13* *1072 Green St., Roswell* *678/352–1975* *swallowatthehollow.com* *Reservations essential* *Closed Mon. and Tues.* *3:C1.*

BARBECUE

# WHERE TO STAY

*Hotel reviews have been abbreviated in this book. For expanded reviews, please go to Fodors.com.*

One of America's most popular convention destinations, Atlanta offers plenty of variety in terms of lodgings. More than 76,000 rooms are in metro Atlanta, with more than 12,000 Downtown, close to the Georgia World Congress Center, Atlanta Civic Center, and Philips Arena. Other clusters are in Buckhead, in the north Interstate 285 perimeter, and around Hartsfield-Jackson Atlanta International Airport.

### PRICES

Atlanta lodging facilities basically have two seasons: summer and convention (conventions are generally held year-round, though there are fewer in summer). *Prices in the reviews are the lowest cost of a standard double room in high season.*

*Use the coordinate (1:B2) at the end of each listing to locate a site on the corresponding map.*

## DOWNTOWN

$$ **Atlanta Marriott Marquis.** Immense and coolly contemporary, the building seems to go up forever as you stand under the lobby's huge fabric sculpture, which hangs from the skylighted roof 47 stories above. **Pros:** great views; convenient to public transportation. **Cons:** lobby noise can carry to the lower floors; parking is over $30 a day. *Rooms from: $179* *265 Peachtree Center Ave., Downtown* *404/521–0000,*

HOTEL

# BEST BETS FOR ATLANTA LODGING

**Fodor's Choice ★**

**Emory Conference Center Hotel,** p. 621
**Loews Atlanta Hotel,** p. 618
**The St. Regis Atlanta,** p. 619

## By Price

**$**

**King-Keith House,** p. 621

**$$**

**Ellis Hotel,** p. 616
**Shellmont Inn,** p. 618
**Westin Atlanta Airport,** p. 621

**$$$**

**Emory Conference Center Hotel,** p. 621
**Georgian Terrace,** p. 618

**$$$$**

**Mandarin Oriental,** p. 619
**Ritz-Carlton Atlanta,** p. 617
**The St. Regis Atlanta,** p. 619
**Westin Buckhead Atlanta,** p. 619

## By Experience

**BEST AMENITIES**

**Loews Atlanta Hotel,** p. 618
**Mandarin Oriental,** p. 619
**St. Regis,** p. 619

**BEST VALUE**

**Doubletree Hotel Atlanta/Buckhead,** p. 618
**Quality Hotel Downtown,** p. 617

**BEST LOCATION**

**Shellmont Inn,** p. 618
**Loews Atlanta Hotel,** p. 618
**Omni Hotel,** p. 616

**MOST ROMANTIC**

**King-Keith House,** p. 621
**Mandarin Oriental,** p. 619
**Shellmont Inn,** p. 618

**PET-FRIENDLY**

**InterContinental Buckhead Atlanta,** p. 619
**Loews Atlanta Hotel,** p. 618

*888/855–5701 ⊕ www.marriott.com ⇆ 1,569 rooms, 94 suites 🍴 Multiple meal plans ✣ 1:B1.*

$$ HOTEL **Ellis Hotel.** This renovated boutique hotel provides Southern hospitality in a restored 1913 historic landmark, and each of the rooms has pillow-top mattresses, flat-screen televisions, and Wi-Fi. **Pros:** 24-hour fitness and business centers; free in-room Wi-Fi; near MARTA stop. **Cons:** small rooms with considerable street noise. *[$] Rooms from: $163 ✉ 176 Peachtree St. NE, Downtown ☎ 404/602–0563 ⊕ www.ellishotel.com ⇆ 114 rooms, 13 suites 🍴 No meals ✣ 1:B2.*

$$$ HOTEL **Glenn Hotel.** This boutique hotel is a mix of New York sophistication and Miami sex appeal; the rooms are small, but they makes the best of the space. **Pros:** business center; free Wi-Fi; rooftop bar with great city views. **Cons:** lighting might be a bit dim for some guests. *[$] Rooms from: $229 ✉ 110 Marietta St. NW, Downtown ☎ 404/521–2250, 888/717–8851 ⊕ www.glennhotel.com ⇆ 93 rooms, 17 suites 🍴 Multiple meal plans ✣ 1:B2.*

$$$$ HOTEL **Omni Hotel at CNN Center.** An ultramodern marble lobby overlooks Centennial Olympic Park through floor-to-ceiling windows in this sleek two-tower hotel next to CNN's headquarters. **Pros:** convenient location for Downtown tourists; near public transportation. **Cons:** panhandlers often outside. *[$] Rooms from: $259 ✉ 100 CNN Center, Downtown*

404/659–0000, 800/444–6664 *www.omnihotels.com* 1,038 *rooms, 32 suites* *No meals* *1:A2.*

$ HOTEL **Quality Hotel Downtown.** This quiet, older Downtown hotel two blocks off Peachtree Street is priced reasonably for its location. This, along with the hotel's proximity to the Georgia World Congress Center and the AmericasMart complex, makes the hotel popular during conventions. **Pros:** good breakfast; convenient to Downtown attractions; early check-in. **Cons:** one elevator; few amenities. *Rooms from: $120* *89 Luckie St., Downtown* *404/524–7991, 888/729–7705* *www.qualityinn.com* *75 rooms* *Breakfast* *1:A2.*

**WORD OF MOUTH**

"We stayed at the Georgian Terrace.... It is very 'southern' in history and location. There were a few weddings going on, and we got to watch all the excitement, which was a lot of fun. We toured the aquarium, and it was a short walk to the MARTA station from the hotel and an easy trip." —willowjane

$$$$ HOTEL **Ritz-Carlton, Atlanta.** You can opt for the traditional experience, with afternoon tea served English-style with loose tea steeped in individual teapots, or enjoy a fancy cocktail at the chic Lumen lobby bar: whatever you choose, the experience will be top-notch at this luxurious hotel. **Pros:** top-notch restaurant; ideal for doing business Downtown; impeccable service. **Cons:** the standard rooms can feel small and dated compared to newer options; very expensive. *Rooms from: $395* *181 Peachtree St., Downtown* *404/659–0400* *www.ritzcarlton.com* *422 rooms, 22 suites* *No meals* *1:B2.*

$$$$ HOTEL **Sheraton Atlanta.** In this business-friendly hotel, there's a grand porte-cochère entrance as well as ample meeting and exhibit space, a tropical-looking indoor pool under a retractable roof, and amenities like flat-screen televisions and big work desks. **Pros:** convenient location; kid-friendly vibe; nicely refurbished rooms. **Cons:** fairly high rates; doesn't have big-name restaurants like its more upscale counterparts, but the food is good. *Rooms from: $300* *165 Courtland St. NE, Downtown* *404/659–6500* *www.sheratonatlantahotel.com* *746 rooms, 17 suites* *No meals* *1:C2.*

## MIDTOWN

$$$ HOTEL **Four Seasons Hotel.** Amenities abound throughout this luxury hotel: marble bathrooms with extra-large soaking tubs, comfy mattresses, and brass chandeliers. **Pros:** great dining options; top-notch service. **Cons:** heavily trafficked area during rush hour. *Rooms from: $250* *75 14th St. NE, Midtown* *404/881–9898* *www.fourseasons.com* *226 rooms, 18 suites* *No meals* *2:B2.*

$$ HOTEL **Georgia Tech Hotel & Conference Center.** In the heart of Midtown, this gleaming building gets kudos for its comfortable, contemporary decor, pleasing rooms, and a staff that understands the needs of business travelers and meeting organizers. **Pros:** pleasant views of the skyline; walking distance to eateries and attractions. **Cons:** short on charm; some guests say service can be hit or miss. *Rooms from: $189* *800 Spring St. NW, Midtown* *404/347–9440, 866/395–1376* *www.*

*gatechhotel.com* 247 *rooms, 5 suites* No meals 2:C2.

$$$ HOTEL ★ **Georgian Terrace.** Enrico Caruso and other stars of the Metropolitan Opera once stayed in this fine 1911 hotel that's across the street from the Fox Theatre. **Pros:** the front terrace is a great place for people-watching; proximity to the Fox makes upscale in-house restaurant Livingston a convenient pre-theater choice; rooftop pool offers an incredible 360-degree city view. **Cons:** some rooms are a little bit old-fashioned; not many rooms with ensuite kitchens; parking is $25 per night to self-park or $30 per night to valet. *Rooms from: $229* *659 Peachtree St., Midtown* *404/897–1991* *www.thegeorgianterrace.com* *32 rooms, 294 suites* *No meals* *2:C2.*

### THE BUC STOPS HERE

**The Buc.** This free bus shuttle service links two MARTA stations, the Buckhead station and the Lenox station, during peak commute and lunchtime hours on weekdays. It also stops at major hotels in central Buckhead, making it an easy way to get to the subway. Route maps are available at all stops. *404/812–7433* *www.bucride.com.*

$$$$ HOTEL Fodor's Choice ★ **Loews Atlanta Hotel.** Georgia's booming film industry brings plenty of celebs to Atlanta, and many of them stay in this sleek glass tower in the heart of bustling Midtown. **Pros:** huge and modern gym and spa; bright, modern rooms; safe, central location. **Cons:** no pool. *Rooms from: $270* *1065 Peachtree St. NE, Midtown* *404/745–5000* *www.loewshotels.com/atlanta* *370 rooms, 44 suites* *No meals* *2:B2.*

$$ B&B/INN **Shellmont Inn.** Designed in 1891 by architect Walter T. Downing, this distinctive lodging is named for its recurring shell motif; the mansion has antique, stained, leaded, and beveled glass, enhanced by artfully carved woodwork and charming stencils. **Pros:** homey touches like stenciling in rooms; verandas overlook gardens and fishpond; modern, updated bathrooms. **Cons:** not ideal for people with disabilities. *Rooms from: $200* *821 Piedmont Ave. NE, Midtown* *404/872–9290* *www.shellmont.com* *3 rooms, 2 suites, 1 carriage house* *Breakfast* *2:B3.*

$$$$ HOTEL **W Midtown.** A trip to this trendy hotel in Midtown feels less like Atlanta and more like New York City, with slick details and more black-suited security guards and velvet ropes than seem necessary. **Pros:** beautiful people; beautiful views; Manhattan-style chic. **Cons:** self-consciously hip; customer service can be spotty. *Rooms from: $299* *188 14th St., Midtown* *404/892–6000* *www.starwoodhotels.com* *433 rooms, 33 suites* *No meals* *2:A3.*

## BUCKHEAD

$$ HOTEL **DoubleTree by Hilton Hotel Atlanta - Buckhead.** If the complimentary fresh-baked chocolate-chip cookies that welcome you don't convince you to stay here, maybe the excellent location, spacious rooms, and reasonable rates will. **Pros:** a warm welcome; comfortable beds; next to MARTA. **Cons:** small bar; pay to park. *Rooms from: $159* *3342 Peachtree Rd., Buckhead* *404/231–1234* *doubletree3.hilton.com* *230 rooms* *No meals* *3:B3.*

$$ HOTEL **Embassy Suites Hotel.** Just blocks from the shopping meccas of Lenox Square and Phipps Plaza you'll find this modern suites-only high-rise. **Pros:** convenient to shopping; indoor and outdoor pools. **Cons:** Internet is not free. *Rooms from: $189 3285 Peachtree Rd., Buckhead 404/261–7733 embassysuites3.hilton.com 316 suites Breakfast 3:B3.*

$$$$ HOTEL **InterContinental Buckhead Atlanta.** Marble bathrooms with separate soaking tubs and glass showers, 300-thread-count Egyptian-cotton linens, plush bathrobes and slippers, and twice-daily housekeeping are some of the highlights of the traditionally styled rooms in this hotel, the flagship for the Atlanta-based chain. **Pros:** 24-hour fitness center. **Cons:** small spa. *Rooms from: $269 3315 Peachtree Rd. NE, Buckhead 404/946–9000 www.ichotelsgroup.com 401 rooms, 21 suites No meals 3:B3.*

13

$$$$ HOTEL **Mandarin Oriental.** Sophisticated glamour with a touch of Zen characterizes this upscale 42-story Buckhead hotel: guests are offered bottled water and cool towels on arrival, and most of the spacious guest rooms offer great views and ample balconies thanks to the building's eight-sided tower. **Pros:** attentive staff; quiet atmosphere; high-end but not stuffy. **Cons:** Peachtree Road is often congested and in various states of construction; not much within walking distance besides Buckhead malls and other shopping; very expensive. *Rooms from: $455 3376 Peachtree Rd. NE, Buckhead, 404/995–7500 www.mandarinoriental.com/atlanta 117 rooms, 10 suites 3:C3.*

$$$$ HOTEL **Ritz-Carlton, Buckhead.** Decorated with 18th- and 19th-century antiques, this elegant hotel is a regular stopover for visiting celebrities. **Pros:** elegant; convenient to shopping; occasional celeb sightings. **Cons:** drab exterior doesn't seem very ritzy. *Rooms from: $429 3434 Peachtree Rd. NE, Buckhead 404/237–2700 www.ritzcarlton.com/buckhead 397 rooms, 56 suites No meals 3:C3.*

$$$$ HOTEL **Westin Buckhead Atlanta.** Behind the chic glass-and-white-tile exterior of this hotel overlooking Lenox Square is a correspondingly chic interior. **Pros:** wonderful beds; plenty of restaurants nearby. **Cons:** small pool. *Rooms from: $299 3391 Peachtree Rd., Buckhead 404/365–0065 www.westin.com/buckhead 354 rooms, 11 suites 3:C3.*

$$$$ HOTEL Fodor's Choice ★ **The St. Regis Atlanta.** By far Atlanta's most prestigious and regal hotel, the St. Regis is adorned with impressive touches, including the etching on the elevator doors and the crystals dangling from the hotel's many chandeliers. **Pros:** 40,000-square-foot Pool Piazza with Jacuzzi and waterfall; lots of spaces for eating, drinking, and relaxing; within walking distance of high-end shops and galleries. **Cons:** can sometimes feel overly formal; very expensive. *Rooms from: $440 88 W. Paces Ferry Rd., Buckhead 404/563–7900 www.starwoodhotels.com 120 rooms, 31 suites No meals 3:B4.*

## VIRGINIA HIGHLAND AND THE EMORY AREA

$$$ HOTEL Fodor's Choice ★ **Emory Conference Center Hotel.** Done in a modified Prairie Style, this hotel is surrounded by 26 acres of forest preserve near Emory University and about six miles from downtown Atlanta. **Pros:** indoor pool is fun for kids; green. **Cons:** some small bathrooms. *Rooms from: $239 1615*

## DID YOU KNOW?

The sculpture *Phoenix Rising from the Ashes* by Gamba Quirino represents Atlanta's rebirth after its burning during the Civil War. It's at the Five Points entrance of Woodruff Park.

*Clifton Rd., Emory* ☎ *404/712–6000* 🌐 *www.emoryconferencecenter.com* 318 *rooms, 6 suites* 🍴 *No meals.*

## LITTLE FIVE POINTS AND INMAN PARK

**$** B&B/INN **King-Keith House.** Built in 1890 by hardware magnate George E. King, this Victorian mansion gives guests the full bed-and-breakfast experience. **Pros:** close to Downtown; near public transportation. **Cons:** two-night minimum stay. $ *Rooms from: $150* ✉ *889 Edgewood Ave. NE, Inman Park* ☎ *404/688–7330, 800/728–3879* 🌐 *www.kingkeith.com* *2 rooms, 1 suite* 🍴 *Breakfast* ⊕ *2:D4.*

13

## METRO ATLANTA

**$$** HOTEL **Westin Atlanta Airport.** Following a major renovation, this former airport pit stop has been transformed into a high-class accommodation, with some rooms that rival any W Hotel. **Pros:** incredibly convenient to the airport. **Cons:** not near any restaurants or attractions. $ *Rooms from: $189* ✉ *4736 Best Rd., Airport* ☎ *404/762–7676* 🌐 *www.westin.com* *476 rooms, 24 suites* 🍴 *No meals* ⊕ *3:D1.*

# NIGHTLIFE AND THE ARTS

## THE ARTS

For the most complete schedule of cultural events, check the weekly Access Atlanta section of the *Atlanta Journal-Constitution* (🌐 *www.ajc.com*) or the city's lively and free alternative weekly, *Creative Loafing* (🌐 *clatl.com*). The *Atlanta Daily World* (🌐 *www.atlantadailyworld.com*), serving the African-American community, is also published weekly.

**AtlanTIX Ticket Services.** Head to the Underground Atlanta mall for half-price same-day tickets for performances as well as half-price same-day and next-day tickets for cultural events. ✉ *Underground Atlanta, Visitors Center, 65 Upper Alabama St. SW, Downtown* ☎ *404/588–9890* 🌐 *www.atlantaperforms.com* ⊙ *Tues.–Sat. 11–6, Sun. noon–4.*

**Ticket Alternative.** Tickets to local festivals, events, plays, concerts, and more. ☎ *800/725–8849* 🌐 *www.ticketalternative.com.*

**Ticketmaster.** Ticketmaster sells tickets for Fox Theatre, Atlanta Civic Center, Philips Arena, and other venues. ☎ *800/745–3000* 🌐 *www.ticketmaster.com.*

### CONCERTS

**Atlanta Symphony Orchestra (ASO).** The Atlanta Symphony Orchestra, under the musical direction of Robert Spano since 2001, has 27 Grammy awards to its credit. It performs the fall–spring subscription series in the 1,800-seat Symphony Hall at Woodruff Arts Center. In summer the orchestra regularly plays with big-name popular and country artists in the outdoor Chastain Park Amphitheatre. ✉ *Woodruff Arts*

*Center, Symphony Hall, 1280 Peachtree St., Midtown* ☎ *404/733–4900* 🌐 *www.atlantasymphony.org.*

**Emory University.** On its idyllic campus surrounded by picturesque houses, Emory University has five major venues where internationally renowned artists perform. ✉ *N. Decatur and Clifton Rds., Emory* ☎ *404/727–6123* 🌐 *www.emory.edu.*

**Florence Kopleff Recital Hall.** Georgia State University hosts concerts that are free and open to the public. The hall's entrance is on Gilmer Street, and there's parking in the lot at the corner of Edgewood and Peachtree Center avenues. ✉ *10 Peachtree Center Ave., at Gilmer St., Downtown* ☎ *404/413–5900* 🌐 *www.music.gsu.edu.*

## DANCE

**Atlanta Ballet.** The Atlanta Ballet, founded in 1929, is the country's oldest continuously operating ballet company. It has been internationally recognized for its productions of classical and contemporary works. Artistic director John McFall brings a constant stream of innovative ideas and vision to the group. Most performances, except for the annual *Nutcracker,* are held at the Cobb Energy Performing Arts Centre. ✉ *Michael C. Carlos Dance Centre, 1695 Marietta Boulevard NW, Westside* ☎ *404/873–5811* 🌐 *www.atlantaballet.com.*

**gloATL.** A contemporary dance company helmed by visionary choreographer Lauri Stallings and founded in 2009, gloATL has entranced Atlantans with its site-specific dance performances and collaborations with local artists, which have included Outkast's Big Boi and the Atlanta Ballet. ✉ *The Goat Farm Arts Center, Goodson Yard, 1200 Foster St. NW, Westside* 🌐 *gloatl.org.*

## FESTIVALS

**Atlanta Food & Wine Festival.** This festival, which debuted in 2011, takes place over a four-day weekend every May in and around Midtown's Loews Hotel. It not only offers incredible food from some of the country's best chefs but also smart seminars on a variety of subjects. ✉ *1065 Peachtree St. NE, Midtown* ☎ *404/474–7330* 🌐 *atlfoodandwinefestival.com.*

**Decatur Book Festival.** The Decatur Book Festival, launched in 2006, is the largest independent book festival in the nation. It takes over Decatur's historic square every Labor Day weekend, with readings, signings, and other literary events. Past keynote speakers have included the novelist Jonathan Franzen and the Decatur resident and Emory University professor Natasha Trethewey, the 19th U.S. Poet Laureate. ✉ *E. Ponce de Leon and Clairemont Aves., Decatur* 🌐 *www.decaturbookfestival.com.*

**Dragon*Con.** Swarms of sci-fi and fantasy fans from around the world descend on Downtown Atlanta every Labor Day weekend to celebrate everything from zombies to *Star Trek*. The popular Saturday morning Parade is not to be missed. ✉ *Downtown* ☎ *770/909–0115* 🌐 *www.dragoncon.org.*

**National Black Arts Festival.** Celebrating black literature, dance, visual arts, theater, film, and music, this fesival is held in venues throughout the city the third week in July. Maya Angelou, Cicely Tyson, Harry

Belafonte, Spike Lee, Tito Puente, and Wynton Marsalis have all appeared at past events. There is also year-round programming. ✉ *730 Peachtree St., Midtown* ☎ *404/730–7315* 🌐 *www.nbaf.org.*

## OPERA

**Atlanta Opera.** Major roles at the Atlanta Opera are performed by national and international guest artists; the chorus and orchestra come from the local community. ✉ *Cobb Energy Perforing Arts Centre, 2800 Cobb Galleria Pkwy.* ☎ *404/881–8885* 🌐 *www.atlantaopera.org.*



## PERFORMANCE VENUES

**Buckhead Theatre.** This restored 1931 Spanish baroque theater has sloped floors that make it ideal for the comedy, rock, jazz, and hip-hop shows hosted here. ✉ *3110 Roswell Rd., Buckhead* ☎ *404/843–2825* 🌐 *www.thebuckheadtheatre.com.*

**Chastain Park Amphitheatre.** Home to Atlanta Symphony Orchestra's summer series and other pop concerts, this theater feels more like an outdoor nightclub than a typical performance venue. Pack a picnic, bring a blanket if you've snagged some seats on the lawn, and prepare to listen to your favorite performers over the clink of dishes and the chatter of dinner conversation. ✉ *4469 Stella Dr. NW, Buckhead* ☎ *404/233–2227* 🌐 *www.classicchastain.com.*

**Ferst Center for the Performing Arts.** Georgia Institute of Technology's arts center hosts classical, jazz, dance, and theatrical performances. There's ample free parking on weekends. ✉ *Georgia Tech, 349 Ferst Dr., Westside* ☎ *404/894–9600* 🌐 *www.ferstcenter.org.*

**Fox Theatre.** This dramatic faux-Moorish theater is the principal venue for touring Broadway shows, national productions, concerts, and the Coca-Cola Summer Film Festival. ✉ *660 Peachtree St., Midtown* ☎ *404/881–2100* 🌐 *www.foxtheatre.org.*

**Philips Arena.** With a seating capacity of 21,000, Philips Arena is the major venue Downtown. In addition to hosting the biggest musical acts, it's also the home of NBA Atlanta Hawks and WNBA Atlanta Dream. The Philips Arena MARTA station makes getting here a snap. ✉ *1 Philips Dr., Downtown* ☎ *404/878–3000* 🌐 *www.philipsarena.com.*

**Rialto Center for the Performing Arts.** Developed by Georgia State University in a beautifully renovated and restructured former movie theater, the Rialto hosts film, theater, and dance, as well as musical performances by local and international performers. ✉ *Georgia State University, 80 Forsyth St. NW, Downtown* ☎ *404/413–9849* 🌐 *www.rialtocenter.org.*

**Tabernacle.** This former church hosts top acts of all genres in an intimate setting. Seating is limited; the main floor is standing-room only. ✉ *152 Luckie St., Downtown* ☎ *404/659–9022* 🌐 *www.tabernacleatl.com.*

**Variety Playhouse.** What was once a movie theater is now one of the cultural anchors of the hip Little Five Points neighborhood. Music lovers come for rock, bluegrass and country, blues, reggae, folk, jazz, and pop. ✉ *1099 Euclid Ave. NE, Little Five Points* ☎ *404/524–7354* 🌐 *www.variety-playhouse.com.*

**Woodruff Arts Center.** The Alliance Theatre, the Atlanta Symphony Orchestra, the High Museum of Art, and Young Audiences are all housed

Centennial Olympic Park hosts free outdoor concerts April through October.

in this complex. ⊠ *1280 Peachtree St. NE, Midtown* ☎ *404/733–4200* 🌐 *www.woodruffcenter.org.*

## THEATER

**14th Street Playhouse.** Local and touring musicals, plays, and sometimes opera are performed here. ⊠ *Woodruff Arts Center, 173 14th St. NE, Midtown* ☎ *404/733–4750* 🌐 *www.14thstplayhouse.org.*

**Actor's Express.** This acclaimed theater group presents an eclectic selection of classic and cutting-edge productions in its 150-seat theater at King Plow Arts Center, a stylish artists' complex hailed by local critics as a showplace of industrial design. ⊠ *King Plow Arts Center, 887 W. Marietta St. NW, Westside* ☎ *404/607–7469* 🌐 *www.actors-express.com.*

**Alliance Theatre.** Atlanta's Tony award–winning professional theater, presents everything from Shakespeare to the latest Broadway and off-Broadway hits. ⊠ *Woodruff Arts Center, 1280 Peachtree St. NE, Midtown* ☎ *404/733–4650* 🌐 *www.alliancetheatre.org.*

**Atlanta Shakespeare Company.** The Atlanta Shakespeare Company stages plays by the Bard and his peers, as well as by contemporary dramatists. Performances vary in quality but are always fun. The Elizabethan-style playhouse is a real tavern, so alcohol and pub-style food are available. ⊠ *New American Shakespeare Tavern, 499 Peachtree St. NE, Midtown* ☎ *404/874–5299* 🌐 *www.shakespearetavern.com.*

**Dad's Garage Theatre Company.** Founded in 1995, this scrappy playhouse with a sense of humor offers a variety of comedy and improv classes and performances as well as original theatrical works. ⊠ *280 Elizabeth St., Suite C–101, Inman Park* ☎ *404/523–3141* 🌐 *www.dadsgarage.com.*

★ **Georgia Shakespeare.** An Atlanta tradition since 1986, Georgia Shakespeare brings classic plays to a 509-seat theater from June to November. In the spring, the company gives open-air performances at Piedmont Park's Legacy Fountain during the Shakespeare in the Park series. ✉ *Conant Performing Arts Cener, Oglethorpe University, 4484 Peachtree Rd. NE, Buckhead* ☎ *404/504–1473* 🌐 *www.gashakespeare.org.*

**Horizon Theatre Co.** This professional troupe, established in 1983, debuts provocative and entertaining contemporary plays in its 175-seat theater. ✉ *1083 Austin Ave., Little Five Points* ☎ *404/584–7450* 🌐 *www.horizontheatre.com.*

### GAY AND PROUD

**Atlanta Pride.** Since 1971, Atlanta has put on one of the most vibrant and popular gay festivals in the country. Thousands of people gather in Piedmont Park every October for Atlanta Pride, which includes a long lineup of entertainers and a market with vendors and organizations from around the area. The main event is the parade, with festive floats and dancers and folks of all stripes marching through the streets of the city. ✉ *Piedmont Park, Midtown* 🌐 *www.atlantapride.org.*

13

## NIGHTLIFE

Atlanta has long been known for having more bars than churches, and in the South that stands out. Atlanta's vibrant nightlife includes everything from cerebral cocktail lounges to dive bars, from country line dancing to high-energy dance clubs.

If you're looking for a gay or lesbian club, you'll find most of them in Midtown, although a few can be found in Buckhead and the suburbs. For up-to-the-minute information on the scene, pick up a free copy of the *GA Voice* (🌐 *www.thegavoice.com*) throughout the city.

### SWEET AUBURN, THE OLD FOURTH WARD, AND EAST ATLANTA

#### BARS

**Sister Louisa's Church of the Living Room & Ping Pong Emporium.** Ping-pong meets folk art meets gay pride meets sangria at Church, as this popular Old Fourth Ward dive bar is referred to by locals. Nun mannequins in full habit dangle from the ceiling, and choir robes are available for patrons should the spirit move them. Less unusually, there's also an outdoor patio and a spacious second floor. ✉ *466 Edgewood Ave. SE, Old Fourth Ward* ☎ *404/522–8275* 🌐 *www.sisterlouisaschurch.com.*

**Soundtable.** Incredible food and some of the city's best drinks are served at the Soundtable, which turns into a dance club once the kitchen closes. ✉ *483 Edgewood Ave., Old Fourth Ward* ☎ *404/835–2534* 🌐 *www.thesoundtable.com.*

#### GAY AND LESBIAN

**The Cockpit.** This laid-back, smoke-free gay bar has specials or events every night. ✉ *465 Boulevard, Grant Park* ☎ *404/343–2450* 🌐 *www.thecockpit-atlanta.blogspot.com.*

★ **Mary's.** One of the best gay bars in Atlanta, the divey and fun Mary's is known for its "Mary-oke" karaoke night. ✉ *1287 Glenwood Ave., East Atlanta* ☎ *404/624–4411* 🌐 *marysatlanta.com.*

★ **My Sister's Room.** Billing itself as the city's "most diverse ladies' bar," this lesbian club brings the party with hip-hop, DJs, and karaoke. ✉ *1271 Glenwood Ave., East Atlanta* ☎ *678/705–4585* 🌐 *www.mysistersroom.com.*

#### ROCK

**529.** A cavelike live music venue with great sound, a full bar, and a patio, 529 hosts local and national emerging indie bands. ✉ *529 Flat Shoals Ave., East Atlanta* ☎ *404/228–6769* 🌐 *www.529atl.com.*

### MIDTOWN

#### BARS

**Clermont Lounge.** You may have heard of the infamous Clermont Lounge, a strip club unlike any other—the women who rule the roost at this local landmark are older, sassier, and less concerned about personal appearance than your average exotic dancer. And really, they're just a sideshow on Saturday nights, when the dance floor opens up and the DJ plays old-school disco, funk, pop and R&B. The well drinks are strong, the bathrooms are dirty, and the clientele is cool—all making for a very entertaining night out in Atlanta. ✉ *789 Ponce de Leon Ave. NE, Midtown* ☎ *404/874–4783* 🌐 *clermontlounge.net* ⏲ *Closed Sun.*

**TAP.** One of the best features at this pub is the patio—typically populated with after-work execs and trendy Midtowners—which sits out on busy Peachtree Street and provides ample opportunity for people-watching. TAP serves upscale food, such as a mahi sandwich and watercress and cornichon salad, alongside a variety of specialty brews and wine. The kitchen closes one hour before the bar. ✉ *1180 Peachtree St., Midtown* ☎ *404/347–2220* 🌐 *www.tapat1180.com.*

#### COMEDY

**Laughing Skull Lounge.** These 73 seats in the back of the Vortex restaurant and bar are Atlanta's most popular destination for local and national touring comedians. Part-time Atlantan Margaret Cho heads here when she's in town to watch and perform. ✉ *878 Peachtree St., Midtown* ☎ *877/523–3288* 🌐 *laughingskulllounge.com.*

#### DANCE

**El Bar.** Behind the El Myr restaurant on Ponce de Leon Avenue, El Bar has a tightly packed dance room with live DJs, cold drinks, and a refreshingly unpretentious clientele. It's open Thursday to Saturday. ✉ *939 Ponce de Leon Ave., Midtown.*

**Opera.** Head to this sleek dance club for a theater-like main lounge, balcony VIP boxes, and banquettes with personal cocktail service. The outdoor area looks like it's straight out of South Beach, with private cabanas and bottle service. Parking in this area can be tricky—street parking often leads to break-ins—so be prepared to pay garage fees. ✉ *1150B Peachtree St., Midtown* ☎ *404/874–0428* 🌐 *www.operaatlanta.com.*

### GAY AND LESBIAN

**Blake's on the Park.** Weekly drag shows, a diverse crowd, and plenty of people-watching all help keep this place near the southwest corner of Piedmont Park popular. ✉ *227 10th St. NE, Midtown* ☎ *404/892–5786* 🌐 *www.blakesontheparkatlanta.com.*

**Burkhart's.** Gay men come to this neighborhood hangout for pool, karaoke, and drag shows. ✉ *1492 Piedmont Ave. NE, Midtown* ☎ *404/872–4403* 🌐 *www.burkharts.com.*

**Woofs.** Atlanta's first and only gay sports bar has pool and darts as well as 25 TVs. A menu of bar food is also available—perfect for the big game. ✉ *2425 Piedmont Rd. NE, Midtown* ☎ *404/869–9422* 🌐 *www.woofsatlanta.com.*

### JAZZ AND BLUES

**Churchill Grounds.** Weekly jam sessions and great local and national jazz acts are on the calendar here. ✉ *660 Peachtree St. NE, Midtown* ☎ *404/876–3030* 🌐 *www.churchillgrounds.com.*

### ROCK

**Drunken Unicorn.** Indie bands play in Drunken Unicorn's small performance space. Pull an all-nighter at the neighboring underground dance club MJQ. ✉ *736 Ponce De Leon Ave. NE, Midtown* 🌐 *www.thedrunkenunicorn.net.*

**Smith's Olde Bar.** Smith's Olde Bar schedules different kinds of talent, both local and regional, in its acoustically fine performance space. Food is available in the downstairs restaurant. Covers vary depending on the act, but are usually $5 to $15. ✉ *1578 Piedmont Ave., Midtown* ☎ *404/875–1522* 🌐 *www.smithsoldebar.com.*

## WESTSIDE

### GAY AND LESBIAN

**Swinging Richards.** A gay male strip club, Swinging Richards draws a fun party crowd. Women are welcome, but bachelor and bachelorette parties are not. ✉ *1400 Northside Dr. NW, Westside* ☎ *404/352–0532* 🌐 *www.swingingrichards.com.*

## BUCKHEAD

### JAZZ AND BLUES

**Dante's Down the Hatch.** Resembling a ship, Dante's Down the Hatch is as popular for its music as it is for its kitschy design. Most nights, the music is provided by a jazz trio, which conjures silky-smooth tunes. ✉ *3380 Peachtree Rd. NE, Buckhead* ☎ *404/266–1600* 🌐 *www.dantesdownthehatch.com.*

## VIRGINIA-HIGHLAND AND THE EMORY AREA

### BARS

**Manuel's Tavern.** The food's OK at Manuel's Tavern, a local landmark and a favorite of left-leaning politicos and media gadflies. The crowd gathers around the wide-screen TVs when the Atlanta Braves play. ✉ *602 N. Highland Ave., Virginia-Highland* ☎ *404/525–3447* 🌐 *www.manuelstavern.com.*

### JAZZ AND BLUES

**Blind Willie's.** New Orleans and Chicago blues groups are the main thing here, although Cajun and zydeco are also on the agenda from time to time. The name honors Blind Willie McTell, a native of Thomson, Georgia; his original compositions include "Statesboro Blues," made popular by the Georgia-based Allman Brothers. ✉ *828 N. Highland Ave., Virginia-Highland* ☎ *404/873–2583* 🌐 *www.blindwilliesblues.com.*

## LITTLE FIVE POINTS AND INMAN PARK

### BARS

**Euclid Avenue Yacht Club.** If you're looking for a spot at which to become a "regular," here's a great candidate. Euclid Avenue Yacht Club is the kind of place where everybody knows your name. The cans of PBR and friendly staff make everyone feel welcome. ✉ *1136 Euclid Ave. NE, Little Five Points* ☎ *404/688–2582* 🌐 *www.theeayc.com.*

**Porter Beer Bar.** Try the salt-and-vinegar popcorn or the hush puppies with smoked bacon and applesauce at the Porter Beer Bar. ✉ *1156 Euclid Ave., Little Five Points* ☎ *404/223–0393* 🌐 *www.theporterbeerbar.com.*

### ROCK

★ **Star Community Bar.** Highly recommended for those who enjoy grunge and rockabilly. Bands play almost nightly, with covers of $5 to $8, depending on the act. The bar used to be a bank—the Elvis shrine in the vault must be seen to be believed. ✉ *437 Moreland Ave., Little Five Points* 🌐 *starbaratlanta.com.*

## DECATUR

### BARS

**Brick Store Pub.** At the Brick Store Pub, you can choose from hundreds of bottled and draft brews—including high-altitude beers—along with some very good burgers, salads, and sandwiches. Upstairs, the popular Belgian beer bar is cave-like and cramped but worth it for the selection. ✉ *125 E. Court Sq., Decatur* ☎ *404/687–0990* 🌐 *www.brickstorepub.com.*

### ROCK

**Eddie's Attic.** Close to the Decatur MARTA station, this bar and restaurant is a good spot for catching local and some national rock, folk, and country-music acts. Cover charges typically range from $5 to $20. ✉ *515B N. McDonough St., Decatur* ☎ *404/377–4976* 🌐 *www.eddiesattic.com.*

## METRO ATLANTA

### COMEDY

**Punchline.** The city's oldest comedy club books major national acts. It's ages 21 and up only. ✉ *Balconies Shopping Center, 280 Hilderbrand Dr.* ☎ *404/252–5233* 🌐 *punchline.com.*

### COUNTRY MUSIC

**Wild Bill's.** Billing itself as the nation's largest country-music dance club and concert hall, Wild Bill's has room for 5,000 dancin', drinkin', partyin' cowpokes. Line dancing lessons are offered early in the evening. There's usually a cover, and you must be at least 18 to attend. ✉ *2075 Market St., Duluth* ☎ *678/473–1000* 🌐 *wildbillsatlanta.com.*

### GAY AND LESBIAN

**The Jungle.** Located off of Atlanta's seedy Cheshire Bridge Road, this nightclub has a popular dance floor and drag stage. ✉ *2115 Faulkner Rd., Cheshire Bridge* ☎ *404/844–8800* 🌐 *www.jungleclubatlanta.com.*

## SPORTS AND THE OUTDOORS



At almost any time of the year, in parks, private clubs, and neighborhoods throughout the city, you'll find Atlantans pursuing everything from tennis to soccer to rollerblading.

### BASEBALL

**Atlanta Braves.** Atlanta's most beloved team, Major League Baseball's Atlanta Braves, plays in Turner Field, once the Olympic Stadium. ✉ *755 Hank Aaron Dr., Downtown* ☎ *404/522–7630* 🌐 *braves.mlb.com.*

### BASKETBALL

**Atlanta Hawks.** The Hawks play Downtown in Philips Arena. ✉ *1 Philips Dr., Downtown* ☎ *866/715–1500* 🌐 *www.nba.com/hawks.*

### BIKING

**Piedmont Park.** Closed to traffic, Atlanta's beloved Piedmont Park is popular for biking, running, dog walking, and other recreational activities. ✉ *10th Street between Piedmont Ave. and Monroe Dr., Midtown* ☎ *404/876–4024* 🌐 *www.piedmontpark.org.*

**Silver Comet Trail.** Connecting Atlanta with the Alabama state line, the Silver Comet Trail is very popular with bikers. The trail is asphalt and concrete. ✉ *Highland Station trailhead, South Cobb Dr. and Cumberland Pkwy., Smyrna* ☎ *404/875–7284* 🌐 *www.pathfoundation.org.*

**Skate Escape.** Bikes and in-line skates are for sale and for rent here. ✉ *1086 Piedmont Ave., across from Piedmont Park, Midtown* ☎ *404/892–1292* 🌐 *www.skateescape.com.*

**Stone Mountain/Atlanta Greenway Trail.** Part of the Atlanta–DeKalb trail system, the Stone Mountain/Atlanta Greenway Trail is a mostly off-road paved path that follows Ponce de Leon Avenue east of the city into Stone Mountain Park. The best place to start the 17-mile trek is the Jimmy Carter Presidential Library & Museum. ☎ *404/875–7284* 🌐 *www.pathfoundation.org.*

### FOOTBALL

**Atlanta Falcons.** The Atlanta Falcons play at the Georgia Dome. In July and August, training camp is held in Flowery Branch, about 40 miles north of Atlanta. There's no charge to watch an open practice session. ✉ *1 Georgia Dome Dr., Downtown* ☎ *404/223–8000* 🌐 *www.atlantafalcons.com.*

### GOLF

Golf is enormously popular here, as the numerous courses attest.

**Bobby Jones Golf Course.** Named after the famed golfer and Atlanta native and occupying a portion of the site of the Civil War's Battle of Peachtree Creek, this is the only public course within sight of downtown Atlanta. Despite having some of the area's worst fairways and greens, the immensely popular course is always crowded. ✉ *384 Woodward*

*Way, Buckhead* ☎ *404/355–1009* 🌐 *bobbyjones.americangolf.com* *18 holes. 6455 yds. Par 71. Green Fee: $27–$50.* ☞ *Facilities: Putting green, pitching area, golf carts, pull carts, rental clubs, pro shop, golf academy/lessons.*

**North Fulton Golf Course.** This course has one of the best layouts in the area. It's at Chastain Park, within the Interstate 285 perimeter. ✉ *216 W. Wieuca Rd. NW, Buckhead* ☎ *404/255–0723* 🌐 *northfulton.americangolf.com* *18 holes. 6570 yds. Par 71. Green Fee: $24–$27.25.* ☞ *Facilities: Pro shop, golf carts, rental clubs, golf academy/lessons.*

**Stone Mountain Golf Club.** Stonemont, with several challenging and scenic holes, is the better of the two courses here (the other is Lakemont). ✉ *1145 Stonewall Jackson Dr., Stone Mountain* ☎ *770/465–3272* 🌐 *www.stonemountaingolf.com* *18 holes. 6837 yds. Par 70. Green Fee: $49–$64.* ☞ *Facilities: Driving range, putting green, golf carts, pull carts, rental clubs, pro shop, golf academy/lessons.*

## HOCKEY

**Gwinnett Gladiators.** The Gwinnett Gladiators, a farm team for the NHL's Phoenix Coyotes, play in the ECHL, a nationwide hockey league. Games are played October to April. ✉ *Arena at Gwinnett Center, 6400 Sugarloaf Pkwy., Duluth* ☎ *770/497–5100* 🌐 *www.gwinnettgladiators.com.*

## RUNNING

Check the **Atlanta Track Club's** website (🌐 *www.atlantatrackclub.org*) for weekly Atlanta-area group runs.

**Chattahoochee River National Recreation Area.** Crisscrossed by 70 miles of trails, this rec area contains different parcels of land that lie in 16 separate units spread along the banks of the Chattahoochee River. Much of it has been protected from development. ✉ *Visitor Center, 1978 Island Ford Pkwy.* ☎ *678/538–1200* 🌐 *www.nps.gov/chat* ⏲ *Visitors Center daily 9–5.*

**Piedmont Park.** The longest running path in Piedmont Park is the Park Loop, which circles the park in 1.68 miles. ✉ *10th St. between Piedmont Ave. and Monroe Ave., Midtown* ☎ *404/875–7275* 🌐 *www.piedmontpark.org.*

## TENNIS

**Bitsy Grant Tennis Center.** Named after one of Atlanta's best-known players, this is the area's best public facility. There are 13 lighted clay courts and 10 lighted hard courts. Before 6 pm it costs $3 per hour for the hard courts and $6 for the clay courts (seniors age 55 and up get 50 percent off). After 6 pm and on weekends the prices bump up to $5 and $6.50. ✉ *2125 Northside Dr., Buckhead* ☎ *404/609–7193* 🌐 *www.bitsytennis.com.*

# SHOPPING

Atlanta's department stores, specialty shops, malls, and antiques markets draw shoppers from across the Southeast. Most stores are open Monday through Saturday 10 to 9, Sunday noon to 6. The sales tax is 8% in the city of Atlanta and 6% to 7% in Fulton County and the suburbs.



## WESTSIDE

Most of the high-end restaurants and design shops here are located in and around the Westside Provisions District, a complex of former meatpacking warehouses transformed into bustling stores.

### ART GALLERIES

The city overflows with art galleries. For more on the local scene, including openings, events, and criticism, consult the sites 🌐 *ArtsATL.com* and 🌐 *BurnAway.org*.

**Get This! Gallery.** This mid-range gallery concentrates on contemporary art in all media by emerging and mid-career artists. ✉ *662 11th St. NW, Westside* ☎ *678/596–1151* 🌐 *getthisgallery.com* 🕒 *Wed.–Sat. noon–5.*

### CLOTHING

**Sid Mashburn.** This upscale source for classic men's clothing is on the Westside. Next door, Ann Mashburn sells chic ladies' duds. ✉ *1198 Howell Mill Rd. NW, Westside* ☎ *404/350–7135* 🌐 *www.sidmashburn.com.*

### FOOD

**Toscano & Sons Italian Market.** With fine oils, vinegars, wines, meats, cheeses, there's little that Italian and tasty that you can't find here. And panini are top-notch and inexpensive. ✉ *1000 Marietta St., Suite 106, Westside* ☎ *404/815–8383* 🌐 *www.toscanoandsons.com* 🕒 *Mon. 10–6, Tues.–Fri. 10–7, Sat. 10–4.*

## BUCKHEAD

Anchored by Lenox Square and Phipps Plaza, Buckhead is one of the city's centers for good consumption. Boutiques, gift shops, and some fine restaurants line East and West Paces Ferry roads, Pharr Road, East Shadowlawn Avenue, and East Andrews Drive. Cates Center has similar stores. Others are on Irby Avenue and Paces Ferry Place.

### ANTIQUES AND DECORATIVE ARTS

**Bennett Street.** Home-decor stores, such as John Overton Oriental Rugs-Antiques, and art galleries, including the TULA art center and galleries, join the Stalls on Bennett Street and other antiquing destinations on this street. ✉ *Buckhead* 🌐 *www.buckhead.net/bennettstreet.*

**Miami Circle.** Upscale antiques and decorative-arts shops are the draw here. ✉ *Miami Circle and Piedmont Rd., Buckhead* 🌐 *miamicircleshops.com.*

### ART GALLERIES

**Jackson Fine Art Gallery.** The specialty here is fine-art photography. ✉ *3115 E. Shadowlawn Ave., Buckhead* ☎ *404/233–3739* 🌐 *www.jacksonfineart.com* 🕒 *Tues.–Sat. 10–5.*

### MALLS

**Lenox Square.** One of Atlanta's oldest and most popular shopping centers, Lenox Square has branches of Neiman Marcus, Bloomingdale's, and Macy's looming next to specialty shops such as Cartier and Mori. Valet parking is available at the front of the mall, but free parking is nearby. You'll do better at one of the several good restaurants in the mall—even for a quick meal—than at the food court. The shopping behemoth recently expanded by opening the nearby Shops Around Lenox. ✉ *3393 Peachtree Rd., Buckhead* ☎ *404/233–6767* 🌐 *www.simon.com/mall/?id=207.*

**Phipps Plaza.** Branches of Tiffany & Co., Saks Fifth Avenue, and Gucci are here, as are such shops as Lilly Pulitzer and Teavana. ✉ *3500 Peachtree Rd. NE, Buckhead* ☎ *404/262–0992* 🌐 *www.simon.com.*

## VIRGINIA-HIGHLAND AND THE EMORY AREA

The window-shopping's great in Virginia-Highland, thanks to the boutiques, antiques shops, and art galleries. Parking can be tricky in the evening, so be prepared to park down a side street and walk a few blocks.

### ART GALLERIES

**Young Blood Gallery and Boutique.** Young Blood is an edgy hangout with artwork, crafts, and gifts created by indie artists. ✉ *636 N. Highland Ave., Virginia-Highland* ☎ *404/254–4127* 🌐 *youngbloodgallery.com* ⏲ *Tues.–Sat. noon–8, Sun. noon–6.*

## LITTLE FIVE POINTS AND INMAN PARK

Vintage-clothing emporiums, used-record stores and bookshops, and some stores that defy description are what draw thrifters and others to Little Five Points.

### ART GALLERIES

**Whitespace Gallery.** An Inman Park staple, Whitespace exhibits contemporary paintings and installations in its renovated carriage house and a smaller satellite gallery, Whitespec. ✉ *814 Edgewood Ave., Inman Park* ☎ *404/688–1892* 🌐 *whitespace814.com* ⏲ *Wed.–Sat. 11–5.*

### BOOKS

**A Cappella Books.** New and out-of-print titles are sold here; the store hosts regular author appearances. ✉ *208 Haralson Ave. NE, Inman Park* ☎ *404/681–5128* 🌐 *www.acappellabooks.com.*

**Charis Books.** This is the South's oldest and largest feminist bookstore. ✉ *1189 Euclid Ave. NE, Little Five Points* ☎ *404/524–0304* 🌐 *www.charisbooksandmore.com* ⏲ *Mon.–Sat. 11–7, Sun. noon–6.*

### CLOTHING

**Clothing Warehouse.** The Clothing Warehouse is one of the many colorful vintage-clothing stores in Little Five Points. ✉ *420 Moreland Ave., Little Five Points* ☎ *404/524–5070* 🌐 *www.theclothingwarehouse.com.*

**Junkman's Daughter.** Kooky wigs, rubber corsets, and water pipes are all sold at this funky-junky department store. ✉ *464 Moreland Ave. NE, Little Five Points* ☎ *404/577–3188* 🌐 *www.thejunkmansdaughter.com.*

Clothing Warehouse is one of the many vintage-clothing stores and funky boutiques that line Little Five Points.

## DECATUR

Busy downtown Decatur, 8 miles east of Midtown Atlanta, is one of the metro area's favorite spots for dining, sidewalk strolling, and window shopping. Its town quad, with a sophisticated, artistic vibe, teems with interesting restaurants, specialty shops, and delectable coffeehouses and cafés.

## METRO ATLANTA

### ANTIQUES AND DECORATIVE ARTS

**Chamblee Antique Row.** You'll find this browser's delight in the suburban town of Chamblee. It's just north of Buckhead and about 10 miles north of Downtown. ✉ *Peachtree Industrial Blvd. and Broad St., Chamblee* ☎ *770/458–6316* 🌐 *www.antiquerow.com.*

### FOOD

**Buford Highway Farmers Market.** Originally started more than 25 years ago as a specialty Asian grocery, the Buford Highway Farmers Market has grown into a full-blown international marketplace; a turn down each aisle is like a trip to a different country. Make sure to stop at the Eastern European deli counter. ✉ *5600 Buford Hwy., Doraville* ☎ *770/455–0770* 🌐 *www.aofwc.com* ⏲ *Daily 8 am–10 pm.*

**Plaza Fiesta.** A 350,000-square-foot Latino shopping mall with more than 280 storefronts, Plaza Fiesta's got everything from cowboy boots to handmade tortillas to quinceañera dresses. ✉ *4166 Buford*

*Hwy.* ☎ *404/982–9138* 🌐 *www.plazafiesta.net* ⏲ *Weekdays 11–8:30, weekends 10:30–9.*

**Your DeKalb Farmers Market.** It may not be a true farmers market, this is truly a market experience to remember. In a sprawling warehouse store 9 mi east of Atlanta, some 175,000 square feet are given over to exotic fruits, cheeses, seafood, sausages, breads, and delicacies from around the world. You'll find root vegetables from Africa, greens from Asia, wines from South America, and cheeses from Europe. The store also has one of the largest seafood departments in the country (some species still swimming) and sizable meat, deli, and wine sections. The cafeteria-style buffet, with a selection of earthy and delicious hot foods and salads ranging from lasagna to goat stew, alone is worth the trip. The market is accessible by MARTA bus from the Avondale rail station. ✉ *3000 E. Ponce de Leon Ave., Decatur* ☎ *404/377–6400* 🌐 *www.dekalbfarmersmarket.com.*

## MALLS

**Perimeter Mall.** Known for upscale family shopping, Perimeter Mall has Nordstrom, Macy's, Dillard's, Von Maur, and a plentiful food court. Its restaurants include the Cheesecake Factory, Goldfish, and Maggiano's Little Italy. ✉ *4400 Ashford-Dunwoody Rd., Dunwoody* ☎ *770/394–4270* 🌐 *www.perimetermall.com.*

## OUTLETS

The interstate highways leading to Atlanta have discount malls similar to those found throughout the country. About 60 miles north of the city on Interstate 85 at Exit 149 is a huge cluster of outlets in the town of Commerce.

**Discover Mills Mall.** Twenty-five miles northeast of downtown Atlanta, this outlet mall has stores that include Off 5th Saks Fifth Avenue and Last Call by Neiman Marcus. ✉ *5900 Sugarloaf Pkwy., Lawrenceville* ☎ *678/847–5000* 🌐 *www.simon.com.*

**North Georgia Premium Outlets.** Here you'll find 140 stores, including Williams-Sonoma, OshKosh B'Gosh, Bose, and numerous designer outlet shops like Coach, Ann Taylor, and Polo Ralph Lauren. For the true shopper, it's worth the 45 minutes it takes to get here from Atlanta's northern perimeter. ✉ *800 Hwy. 400 S, at Dawson Forest Rd., Dawsonville* ☎ *706/216–3609* 🌐 *www.premiumoutlets.com/northgeorgia.*

# Central and North Georgia

**WORD OF MOUTH**

"Tallulah Falls is definitely worth a stop. There's a nice trail that skirts the rim of the gorge. Gorgeous views. Detour a block west to the little town of Clayton for some good restaurant options and some cute shops."

—starrs

# WELCOME TO CENTRAL AND NORTH GEORGIA

## TOP REASONS TO GO

★ **The Antebellum Trail:** Traveling this picturesque trail between Macon and Athens will cast you back in time and introduce you to the elegance of the Old South.

★ **Surround yourself in Civil War history:** The second-bloodiest battle of the Civil War was fought for two days at Chickamauga and Chattanooga National Military Park.

★ **Take a hike:** The starting point of the more than 2,100-mile Appalachian Trail is at Springer Mountain, a few miles north of Amicalola Falls, the tallest cascading waterfall east of the Mississippi.

★ **Lovely lakes:** Lake Oconee, Lake Allatoona, Lake Hartwell, and Lake Rabun provide numerous recreational opportunities.

★ **Explore the Native American past:** Visit New Echota, the former capital of the Cherokee Nation, which offers tribute to the proud tribe. Nearby is the historic Vann House, a beautiful three-story residence of Cherokee Chief James Vann.

**1 The Northwest.** A trip to Northwest Georgia reveals its fascinating history, from its Native American heritage to the state's critical role in the Civil War (sometimes called the War Between the States here). The Cherokee Nation once had its capital in New Echota, before the federal government forced members of the tribe on a long, tragic resettlement march to Oklahoma, marking the infamous "Trail of Tears." The first gold strike in U.S. history was discovered in the region. A few years later, the Civil War's second-bloodiest battle was fought at Chickamauga & Chattanooga National Military Park, which is now commemorated by hundreds of monuments and markers in the country's first Civil War battlefield park.

**2 The North Georgia Mountains.** North Georgia has become a fascinating meld of the past and the present. Its residents wholeheartedly cherish their Appalachian roots at attractions such as the Foxfire Museum and Heritage Center and the Folk Pottery Museum of Northeast Georgia. They take pride in introducing visitors to their music, as well as their natural surroundings: mountains, hiking trails (including the Appalachian Trail), and waterfalls. But residents are

embracing the mountains' potential for new ventures, as well. Award-winning wineries are springing up across the region, and a passion for fine dining is a natural accompaniment.

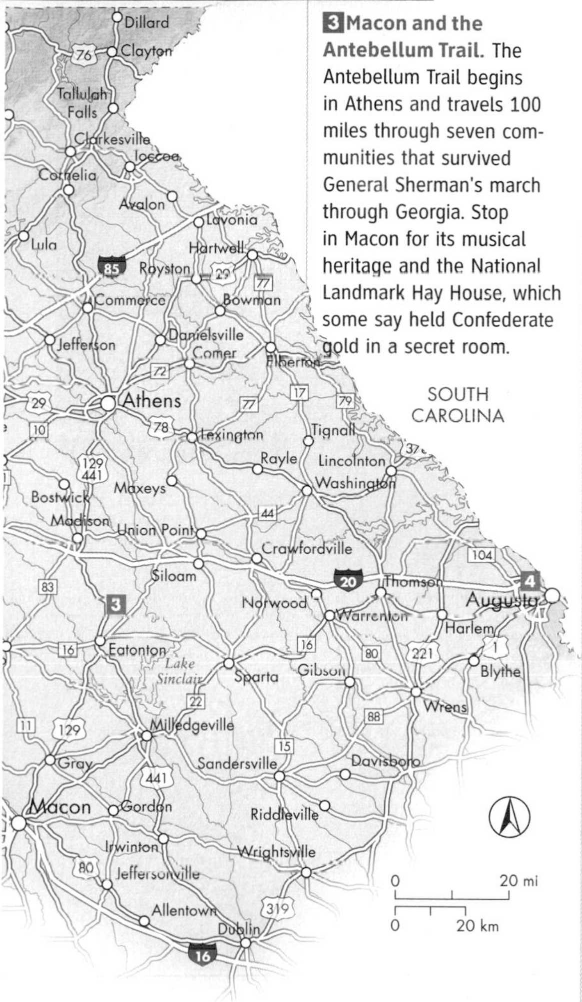

**3 Macon and the Antebellum Trail.** The Antebellum Trail begins in Athens and travels 100 miles through seven communities that survived General Sherman's march through Georgia. Stop in Macon for its musical heritage and the National Landmark Hay House, which some say held Confederate gold in a secret room.

**4 Augusta.** Though the Masters Tournament of Golf put this 200,000-person city on the map, Augusta also charms with its antebellum mansions and tree-lined streets dotted with shops.

## GETTING ORIENTED

North Georgia's tree-lined mountain roads are a relief from the traffic jams of metro Atlanta. You can spot critters from wild turkeys to deer, and stop off for refreshing visits to waterfalls or savor shopping, lodging, and meals in quaint—and quiet—towns. The area's proximity to metro Atlanta makes it ideal for day trips and overnight stays. Central Georgia roughly forms a triangle defined by Athens, Macon, and Augusta, which together give you a real flavor of Georgia's elegant past and vibrant future. Madison epitomizes small-town America with its charming antebellum and Victorian architecture. Eatonton, 20 miles down the highway, also has its share of stately historic houses, although your attention will be drawn to the statue of the giant rabbit on the courthouse lawn. It's part of the town's tribute to favorite son Joel Chandler Harris, creator of Br'er Rabbit and Uncle Remus.

# DAY TRIP: ANTEBELLUM TRAIL

(above) A statue of Br'er Rabbit adorns the Eatonton County Courthouse lawn. (upper right) Grab a hot dog at landmark Nu-Way Weiners in Macon.

Grand, columned mansions, rolling hills, and scenic small towns far off the beaten path are just a few reasons to explore the Antebellum Trail. This route takes you through the center of the state, where you'll find some of the finest pre–Civil War architecture in the Southeast.

Athens is the northern gateway to the Antebellum Trail. Broad Street takes you through the heart of downtown past the **University of Georgia.** Peek inside the arches to see the Greek Revival buildings of the original campus. Head to **Church-Waddel-Brumby House** on East Dougherty Street. The 1820 home, headquarters of the Athens Welcome Center, is a great place to stop for information about the Antebellum Trail. Make your way to "the Loop," which is what locals call the Athens Perimeter Highway, and then to U.S. 441 South. Only 8 miles from Athens is Watkinsville, home of the **Eagle Tavern Museum.** The stagecoach stop dates back to the late 1700s when Watkinsville was a frontier town bordering Cherokee and Creek lands.

—Rachel Quartarone

### PLANNING YOUR TIME

The Antebellum Trail can begin in Athens in the north or Macon in the south. The main artery is U.S. 441, which connects Athens, Madison, Eatonton, and Milledgeville. Route 22/129 runs from Milledgeville to Macon. The 100-mile trip takes a little more than two hours, not counting stops.

U.S. 441 between Watkinsville and Madison—dotted with forests, pastures, and cotton patches—is the most scenic stretch of the Antebellum Trail. Farm stands offering peaches, tomatoes, and boiled peanuts are plentiful. Downtown Madison is full of quaint shops. From Madison, it's 22 miles to Eatonton. Just off Madison Avenue is the **Plaza Arts Center**, home to the Eatonton-Putnam Chamber of Commerce Welcome Center. Pick up a self-guided tour of Madison Avenue's immaculately restored white-columned Antebellum mansions and Victorian masterpieces. On the way out of town, the **Uncle Remus Museum** recounts Joel Chandler Harris's folktales.

Back on U.S. 441, it's 20 miles to the college town of Milledgeville, once the state capital. The **Old Governor's Mansion**, built in 1839, is pristinely restored and certainly worth a stop. From Milledgeville, take Route 22/129 south through the tiny towns of Haddock, Gray, and Old Clinton. The scenery is dramatic, with rolling hills, sweeping pastures, and forests. Just after Old Clinton the road forks—take U.S. 129 and follow along to Macon. Cross the Ocmulgee River and make your way to the **Downtown Visitor Center** on Martin Luther King Jr. Boulevard for a proper introduction. Don't miss the Italianate **Hay House** perched high on Georgia Avenue. Plan on spending at least a couple of hours in Macon, as there are more than enough attractions to hold your interest.

## NEED A BREAK?

**Weaver D's Delicious Fine Foods.** This Athens soul-food staple was made famous by R.E.M.'s album *Automatic for the People*, which is the restaurant's slogan. ✉ *1016 E. Broad St., Athens* ☎ *706/353–7797* ⏲ *Closed Sun.*

**Antique Sweets.** This locally owned candy shop offers handmade fudge, truffles, pralines, and more. ✉ *127 South Main St., Madison* ☎ *706/342–0034* 🌐 *www.antiquesweets.com.*

**Blackbird Coffee.** This coffee shop offers small-batch roasted coffee and fresh baked goods. ✉ *114 W. Hancock St., Milledgeville* ☎ *478/454–2473* 🌐 *www.blackbirdcoffee.com.*

**Trish Ann's Antiques & Tearoom.** A charming antiques store with a tearoom in back, head here for sandwiches and quiches. ✉ *102 Bowen Hill Rd., Haddock* ☎ *478/932–5885* ⏲ *Closed Sun. and Mon.*

**Nu-Way Weiners.** Opened in 1916, this landmark serves acclaimed hot dogs, onion rings, and chocolate malts. ✉ *430 Cotton Ave., Macon* ☎ *478/743–1368* ⏲ *Closed Sun.*

14

Updated by Rachel Quartarone

It is often said there are two Georgias: Atlanta and the rest of the state. While Atlanta offers bright lights and big-city action, the regions to the north and southeast are filled with farms, lush forests, sleepy hamlets, and larger towns boasting vibrant arts and cultural scenes. In either direction, there is no shortage of beautiful scenery from the mountains to the north to the rolling hills and rivers to the south.

North Georgia is known for its abundant natural wonders and its cool mountain air. The region is home to the 750,000-acre Chattahoochee National Forest, where several bold rivers, including the Chattahoochee, Oconee, Toccoa, and Chattooga, have their headwaters. Rabun, Burton, Nottley, and Chatuge lakes offer recreational opportunities and camping. To the northwest are two important Georgia historic sites: New Echota State Historic Site and the Chickamauga & Chattanooga National Military Park.

Whether planning a day trip from Atlanta or a longer exploration, there is plenty to do and see in Central Georgia. Head down U.S. 441—the Antebellum Trail—from Athens to Macon and you'll quickly see that the elegance of the Old South is new again, with many historic buildings returned to their original splendor. Athens, home of the University of Georgia, pulses with college life, especially when the Bulldogs are playing. For a taste of old Georgia, Macon's historical architecture is unmatched. Farther east, Augusta is home of the Masters Tournament. Even if you're not drawn to the tees, this city—like so many in Georgia—is undergoing a renaissance of its waterfront and historic districts.

## PLANNING

### WHEN TO GO

Summer in the South can be unpleasant; temperatures of 90 degrees or higher (plus humidity) cause even the most Southern of Southerners to wilt. The best times to visit Central Georgia are fall and spring, when temperatures are in the 60s and 70s and there are plenty of recreational activities to enjoy. Springtime is particularly lovely in Macon, as the cherry trees are in full bloom.

Spring, summer, and fall are prime times for travel in North Georgia. Weekends are far busier than weekdays, since many visitors drive up from nearby Atlanta for a short getaway. For the mountains, the ideal time is October and early November, when fall color is at its peak. Don't arrive without reservations during spring and early fall festival weekends, when visitors head north to enjoy the spring wildflowers, fall apple and pumpkin harvests, and absolutely blissful weather.



## PLANNING YOUR TIME

As a transportation hub, Atlanta is the jumping-off point for this region. In fact, many of North and Central Georgia's attractions are little more than an hour's drive from the city, making them perfect for a day trip. Panning for gold in Dahlonega, apple picking in Ellijay, and sampling North Georgia wines are worthy excursions. For a more relaxed pace, plan to stay overnight in the beautiful North Georgia mountains.

The bustling college town of Athens is a great place to start if you are interested in exploring the Antebellum Trail winding through Madison, Milledgeville, and Macon. With so much to do and see, consider breaking up the trip with an overnight stay. These cities also stand alone as day-trip destinations or overnight trips, particularly if history and architecture are of interest.

## GETTING HERE AND AROUND

### AIR TRAVEL

If you're headed to Central Georgia, GeorgiaSkies airline offers nonstop daily service from Atlanta's Hartsfield-Jackson International Airport to Athens Ben Epps Airport (AHN) and Macon's Middle Georgia Regional Airport (MCN). Augusta Regional Airport (AGS) is served by Delta Airlines and US Airways Express.

The gateway airports for North Georgia are Hartsfield-Jackson International Airport in Atlanta and Chattanooga Metropolitan Airport in Chattanooga, Tennessee.

**Airline Contacts GeorgiaSkies** ☎ *877/849-4997* 🌐 *www.flygeorgiaskies.com.*

**Airport Contacts Athens Ben Epps Airport (AHN)** ✉ *1010 Ben Epps Dr., Athens* ☎ *706/613-3420* 🌐 *www.athensairport.net.* **Augusta Regional Airport (AGS)** ✉ *1501 Aviation Way, Augusta* ☎ *706/798-3236* 🌐 *www.flyags.com.* **Chattanooga Metropolitan Airport (CHA)** ✉ *1001 Airport Rd., Chattanooga, Tennessee* ☎ *423/855-2202* 🌐 *www.chattairport.com.* **Hartsfield-Jackson Atlanta International Airport (ATL)** ✉ *6000 N. Terminal Pkwy., Atlanta* ☎ *404/530-7300* 🌐 *www.atlanta-airport.com.* **Middle Georgia Regional Airport (MCN)** ✉ *1000 Terminal Dr., Macon* ☎ *478/788-3760.*

### CAR TRAVEL

U.S. 441, known as the Antebellum Trail, runs north–south, merging with U.S. 129 for a stretch and connecting Athens, Madison, Eatonton, and Milledgeville. Macon is on Route 49, which splits from U.S. 441 at Milledgeville. Washington lies at the intersection of U.S. 78, running east from Athens to Thomson, and Route 44, running south to Eatonton. Interstate 20 runs east from Atlanta to Augusta, which is about 93 miles east of U.S. 441.

Plan on using your car—or renting one—to get around North Georgia. U.S. 19 runs north–south, passing through Dahlonega and up into the North Georgia mountains. U.S. 129 travels northwest from Athens, eventually merging with U.S. 19. GA 75 stems off of U.S. 129 and goes through Helen and up into the mountains. U.S. 23/441 will take you north through Clayton; U.S. 76 runs west from Clayton to Dalton, merging for a stretch with GA 5/515. GA 52 runs along the edge of the Blue Ridge Mountains, passing through Ellijay. Interstate 75 is the major artery in the northwesternmost part of the state and passes near the New Echota State Historic Site and the Chickamauga and Chattanooga National Military Park.

### RESTAURANTS

Central and North Georgia offer an abundance of dining options from hole-in-the-wall barbecue joints to upscale eateries serving sophisticated cuisine. The culinary specialty is Southern food, of course, and a heaping plate of fried chicken washed down with sweet tea is a must. Aside from traditional local fare, plenty of other options are available in larger towns like Athens and Macon. In the North Georgia mountains, you'll find quite a bit of culinary sophistication at many of the charming little bistros on the town squares and near the scenic wineries that dot the Wine Highway. *Prices in the reviews are the average cost of a main course at dinner or, if dinner is not served, at lunch.*

### HOTELS

The most attractive lodging options here tend to have been around for a long time; the structures often date from the 19th century. At such places—most commonly B&Bs but sometimes larger inns—you're likely to find big porches with rocking chairs and bedrooms decorated with antiques. If that's more Southern charm than you're after, you can choose from a smattering of chain hotels. In the North Georgia mountains and near the recreational areas of Central Georgia there is also a large variety of cabins and home rentals. *Prices in the reviews are the lowest cost of a standard double room in high season.*

### DISCOUNTS AND DEALS

**North Georgia Premium Outlets.** It's hard not to bring back antiques and crafts from North Georgia. But those in the know also make time for a stop at the popular North Georgia Premium Outlets, which offers 140 name-brand stores. ✉ *800 GA 400 S, Dawsonville* ☎ *706/216–3609* 🌐 *www.premiumoutlets.com.*

### VISITOR INFORMATION

**Georgia Welcome Center** ☎ *706/737–1446* 🌐 *www.exploregeorgia.org.*

## THE NORTHWEST

Northwest Georgia is rich in history. Chickamauga & Chattanooga National Military Park reminds visitors of the devastation of the Civil War and the determination of both Southern and Northern soldiers

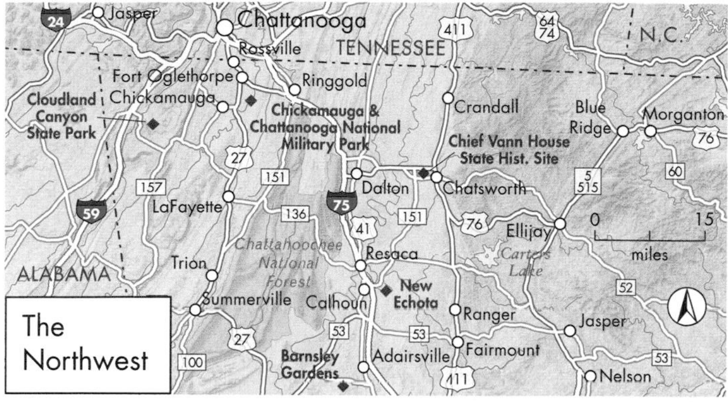




participating in its bloodiest two-day battle. The area also pays homage to Georgia's former Cherokee residents, driven from their verdant homeland in New Echota—once the capital of the Cherokee nation—to dusty Oklahoma on the Trail of Tears. Northwest Georgia lies along the Cumberland Plateau, with its flat-top sandstone mountains.

## NEW ECHOTA

*71 miles northwest of Atlanta via I–75 north to GA 225; 41 miles southwest of Ellijay via U.S. 76 to GA 382W/GA 136.*

From 1825 to 1838, New Echota was the capital of the Cherokee Nation, whose constitution was patterned after that of the United States. The public buildings and houses in town were generally log structures, among them a council house, a printing office, a Supreme Court building, and the *Cherokee Phoenix* newspaper. The first newspaper established (in 1828) by Native Americans, it utilized the 86-character alphabet developed by Sequoyah, who spent 12 years developing the written Cherokee language despite having no formal education. He is the only known person in history to have single-handedly created a written language.

The Treaty of 1835, signed in New Echota by a small group of Cherokee leaders, relinquished Cherokee claims to lands east of the Mississippi. Most Cherokees considered the treaty fraudulent. A few years later 7,000 federal and state troops began removing Cherokee from their homes in Georgia, North Carolina, and Tennessee and put them in stockades, including one in New Echota. About 15,000 Cherokee were then forced to travel west to Oklahoma on foot, horseback, and in wagons, along what is known as the "Trail of Tears." Thousands died along the way. After reaching Oklahoma in 1839, the three principal signers of the Treaty of 1835 were assassinated by Cherokee who considered them traitors.

Following the removal of the Cherokee, New Echota reverted to farmland. Today one original building remains, some buildings have been reconstructed and furnished, and other structures have been moved to the site. The visitor center has a movie and a variety of books about Cherokee history. When visiting New Echota, you can stay in Calhoun, the nearest town, or in Dalton, Rome, Chickamauga, or even in Chattanooga.

### GETTING HERE AND AROUND

This is a good day trip from Atlanta. Take Interstate 75 to Exit 317, GA 225, for a tour of New Echota, near Calhoun, then travel 17 miles north on GA 225 to the Chief Vann House.

## EXPLORING

Fodor's Choice ★ **Chief Vann House.** This beautifully restored, three-story brick home was commissioned in 1804 by a leader of the Cherokee Nation. Moravian artisans helped construct the intricately carved interior mantles and other woodwork. The well-decorated home is furnished as it would have been when Chief Vann lived there. Of mixed Scottish and Cherokee parentage, Chief James Vann owned numerous slaves who also worked on the construction of the house. His son, Cherokee statesman Joseph Vann, lived in the house until he was evicted by the Georgia Militia in 1835 and forced to move to Cherokee Territory, in what is now Oklahoma. ✉ *82 GA 225, at GA 52A, Chatsworth* ✣ *17 miles north of New Echota* ☎ *706/695–2598* 🌐 *www.gastateparks.org/info/chiefvann* 🎟 *$6* ⏲ *Thurs.–Sat. 9–5.*

★ **New Echota State Historic Site.** At this collection of a dozen original and reconstructed buildings, you can discover the rich history of the Cherokee nation. Worcester House, a home and Presbyterian mission station, is an original building, restored in the late 1950s. The Cherokee Council House is a reconstruction of the 1819 building where the legislature met. The Supreme Court building is also a reconstruction, as is the print house, where thousands of books translated in Cherokee and the weekly *Cherokee Phoenix* were published. Other buildings—including the 1805 Vann Tavern—and outbuildings were relocated to the site. ✉ *1211 Chatsworth Hwy., GA 225, 1 mile east of I–75 near Calhoun* ☎ *706/624–1321* 🌐 *www.georgiastateparks.org/newechota* 🎟 *$6.50* ⏲ *Thurs.–Sat. 9–5.*

## WHERE TO STAY

*Hotel reviews have been abbreviated in this book. For expanded reviews, please go to Fodors.com.*

$$$$ RESORT ★ **Barnsley Gardens Resort.** This award-winning resort features luxurious and comfortable accommodations, a championship golf course, spa, restaurant, horseback riding, and miles of nature trails. **Pros:** beautiful grounds; tastefully decorated rooms. **Cons:** pricey; not easy to find at night. *Rooms from: $225* ✉ *597 Barnsley Gardens Rd., Adairsville* ☎ *770/773–7480, 877/773–2447* 🌐 *www.barnsleyresort.com* *90 rooms and suites, 36 cottages.*

Continued on page 651

# A CIVIL WAR TOUR
## CHICKAMAUGA BATTLEFIELD

By Rickey Bevington

Chickamauga Battlefield today

A visit to the South isn't complete without an encounter with the history of the "War Between the States." With nearly a million visitors a year, Chickamauga & Chattanooga National Military Park is one of the most popular battlefields in the country. Here you can gain a fuller sense of one of the Confederacy's greatest military victories by touring the battle lines, standing where the soldiers faced the pain and intensity of war, and imagining the cacophony produced by cannons, gunfire, and battle cries.

Lithograph of Battle of Chickamauga, 1890

## UNDERSTANDING THE BATTLE

Left and center, commanding generals William S. Rosecrans (Union) and Braxton Bragg (Confederacy). Right, General George H. Thomas (Union), also known as the Rock of Chickamauga

Why was the September 19–20, 1863, Battle of Chickamauga so important? To the war-weary people and soldiers of the Confederacy, it was a morale-boosting victory on the heels of terrible losses at Gettysburg and Vicksburg only months before. To the equally fatigued Union states, it was an important test of their use of Chattanooga, Tennessee, as a supply center from which to launch their advance into the Deep South. Union forces had captured the nearby city less than a month before in a bloodless advance. As they continued their push south into the far northwest corner of Georgia, Atlanta was in their sights. But Confederate soldiers were ready. Over two days of some of the war's fiercest fighting, 16,170 Union and 18,454 Confederate men and boys fell or were injured at the Battle of Chickamauga, named for the nearby creek where hostilities began. On the second day, the Confederates managed to send the Union soldiers into full retreat back to Chattanooga. It would take nine more months of fighting before U.S. General William Tecumseh Sherman was finally able to reach his original objective, Atlanta.

"Stars and Bars" Conferderate flag, popular during the beginning of the Civil War.

## CIVIL WAR TIMELINE

Civil War Union Flag

President Abraham Lincoln

**1861**

March 4, Abraham Lincoln is inaugurated.

March 11, Confederate Constitution is signed.

April 12, American Civil War begins.

July 21, First Battle of Bull Run.

**1862**

September 17, Battle of Antietam.

December 13, Battle of Fredricksburg.

**1863**

January 1, Lincoln issues the Emancipation Proclamation.

July 1-3, Battle of Gettysburg.

## 1863: A PIVOTAL YEAR IN THE CIVIL WAR

### DECISIVE UNION VICTORIES

On January 1, 1863, President Lincoln issued the Emancipation Proclamation, which declared "that all persons held as slaves" within the seceded states "are, and henceforth shall be free."

Three strategic victories in this year proved crucial to the north's eventual victory over the south. The July 1863 battle of Gettysburg was Confederate General Robert E. Lee's last major offensive; 170,000 men fought over three days with 51,000 casualties, after which Lee retreated to Virginia. The following day, July 4, Vicksburg, MS, surrendered to Union forces laying siege under the command of Union General Ulysses S. Grant. For the north, taking Vicksburg soon meant controlling the Mississippi River south to New Orleans, cutting the Confederacy in half. In early September, Union forces marched into Chattanooga and seized its river, railroads, and a major Confederate supply center. A vital railroad junction, Chattanooga would become the crucial supply center for Union troops advancing south toward Atlanta.

Confederate troops advancing at Chickamauga, drawing by Alfred R. Waud, Civil War correspondant.

### BATTLE OF CHICKAMAUGA

In September 1863 Union forces followed Confederates retreating into Georgia after abandoning Chattanooga. Morale was low among southern forces after the summer's defeats, but a chance skirmish launched what would be the largest battle and final Confederate victory in the war's western theater. The two-day clash ended with Union forces rapidly retreating north to safer ground at Chattanooga. Confederates were ecstatic, but this battle did little but buy the south time. One month later, U.S. General William Tecumseh Sherman took command of the Union force at Chattanooga and set his sights on Atlanta.

Sherman's March to Sea

July 4, Confederates surrender Vicksburg.

September 19-20, Battle of Chickamauga.

**1864**

September 2, Sherman captures Atlanta.

November 15, Sherman begins his "March to the Sea."

**1865**

April 9, Lee surrenders to Grant at Appomattox Courthouse.

April 14, President Lincoln is shot.

December 6, The Thirteenth Amendment abolishes slavery.

U.S. General William Tecumseh Sherman

## TOURING CHICKAMAUGA BATTLEFIELD

Left, Snodgrass house. Right, replica of Confederate soldier, visitor center

### GETTING HERE

From Atlanta, take I–75 north; the 110 mile-drive takes about two hours. Take exit 350 (Battlefield Parkway) to Fort Oglethorpe and follow signs to the National Military Park.

### PLANNING YOUR TIME

Plan to spend from one hour to an afternoon here. Start with the a visit to the excellent **Chickamauga Battlefield Visitor Center** (☎ *706/866–9241* 🌐 *www.nps.gov/chch* 🎫 *Free* 🕓 *Daily 8:30–5*), which offers a timeline of the battle, a film on the military strategy, a collection of more than 300 antique military rifles, and a well-stocked bookstore. Pack a picnic lunch and go for a hike along one of the park's designated nature trails.

Left, 10th Wisconsin Infantry monument

### THE AUTO TOUR

Imagine crawling out of a dense wood into an open field only to see a uniform line of thousands of enemy soldiers marching steadily toward you. That's just one of the battle scenes described in the seven-mile auto tour of the battle's most significant events. Pick up a free map and brochure at the visitor center with information on the sights. You can also call ☎ *585/672–2619* at each stop for the free cell phone tour. From Memorial Day to Labor Day rangers lead free two-hour auto caravan tours at 10 and 2.

## TOUR HIGHLIGHTS

❶ Starting just outside the visitor center heading south from Stop 1 (where the Florida monument now stands), follow the road that on the second day of battle separated a force of 65,000 Confederates firing from your left toward 62,000 Union troops trying to regain position on your right. The tour follows this battle line nearly the length of the battlefield. Unlike most Civil War engagements, this one did not take place in an open field, and the forested landscape has been preserved much as it was on the day of battle.

❺ Once you veer west at Viniard Field, you are beginning to follow the steps of the retreating Union forces as they succumbed to Confederates pushing them back toward Chattanooga.

❻ The Wilder Brigade Monument is an 85-foot high stone tower honoring Union

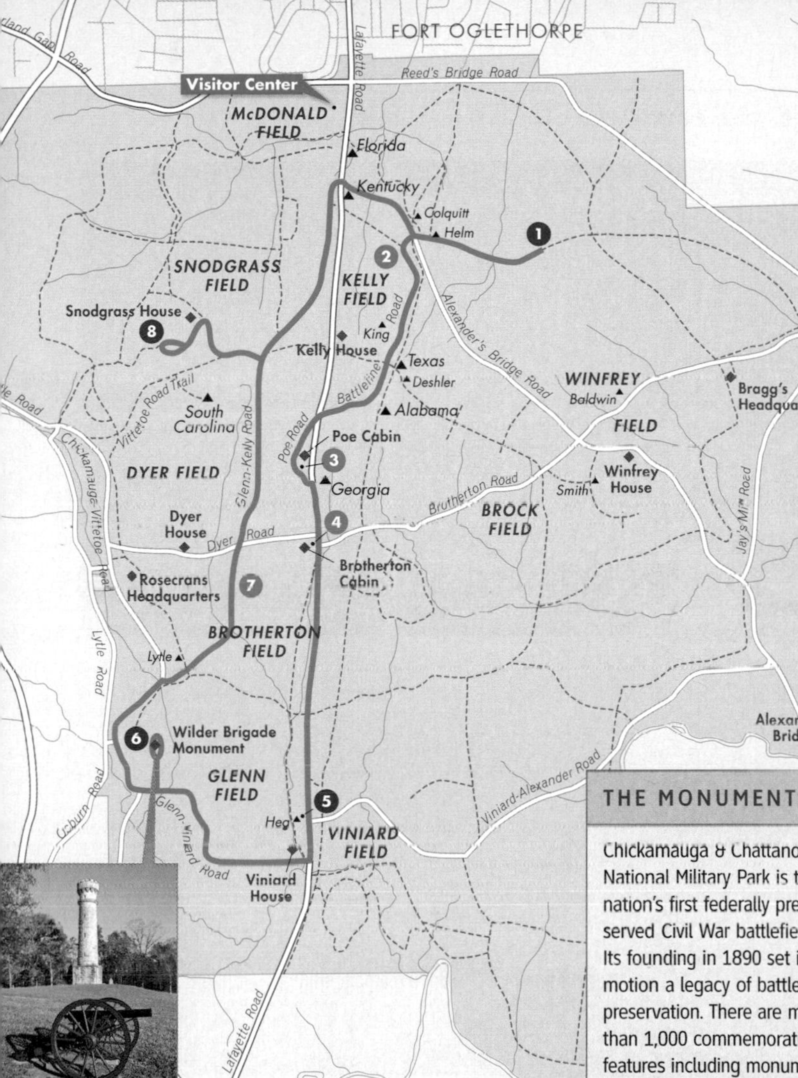


Battlefield and cannon

Colonel John Wilder and his "Lightning Brigade," a group of fast-moving cavalrymen known for their rare but deadly Spencer-7 carbine repeating rifles.

❽ The tour's final stop is Snodgrass Hill. This is the high ground where U.S. General George H. Thomas stayed behind his retreating army to thwart pursuing Confederates, giving Union forces enough time to reach Chattanooga safely. Many of Thomas' men were killed or captured and taken to the notorious Camp Sumter at Andersonville.

## THE MONUMENTS

Chickamauga & Chattanooga National Military Park is the nation's first federally preserved Civil War battlefield. Its founding in 1890 set in motion a legacy of battlefield preservation. There are more than 1,000 commemorative features including monuments, markers, and tablets placed by veterans and by states whose citizens saw combat here. Take time to admire the monuments' design and inscription, and look for monuments from your home state. Red tablets describe Confederate action and blue mark Union activity. Large pyramids of naval shells indicate where a brigade commander was mortally wounded in combat.

## OTHER GEORGIA CIVIL WAR SITES

Left, Andersonville Prisoner of War Museum. Top, Atlanta Cyclorama Museum. Below, Kennesaw Battlefield.

To experience more Civil War history in Georgia, check out these sites.

**RESACA CONFEDERATE CEMETERY.** This intimate, shaded cemetery is the final resting place for more than 450 Confederate soldiers. After the Battle of Resaca in May 1864, resident Mary J. Green returned to her farm to find hundreds of Confederates buried haphazardly where they had fallen. She raised the money to re-inter them on 2 1/2 acres in a corner of the family farm. ✉ *40 miles southeast of Chickamauga, take I-75 to exit 318 for U.S. 41 to Confederate Cemetery Rd.*

**ATLANTA CYCLORAMA & CIVIL WAR MUSEUM.** Experience the July 1864 Battle of Atlanta through what's said to be the world's largest mural—42 feet tall and 358 feet in circumference. Begin your visit with a film detailing events that led to the battle. Guides conduct a 40-minute "tour" of the painting and diorama. The adjoining museum has Civil War artifacts. ⇨ *See Chapter 13.*

**ANDERSONVILLE NATIONAL HISTORIC SITE.** The infamous Civil War–era Camp Sumter, commonly called Andersonville, was one of the largest prisons built in the Confederacy. Over 14 months, 45,000 Union soldiers were confined within a 26 1/2-acre open-air stockade; 13,000 died from disease and exposure—a rate of more than 30 a day. You can tour the rebuilt stockade walls and historic prison grounds here. The National Prisoner of War Museum, which also serves as the site's visitor center, is dedicated to the American men and women who have suffered as POWs. Andersonville National Cemetery is the final resting place for those who perished here. ⇨ *See Chapter 12.*

**KENNESAW MOUNTAIN NATIONAL BATTLEFIELD PARK.** More than 160,000 Union and Confederate soldiers battled here from June 19, 1864, until July 2, 1864. This popular mountain park attracts history enthusiasts as well as runners, hikers, cyclists, and families. ⇨ *See Chapter 13.*

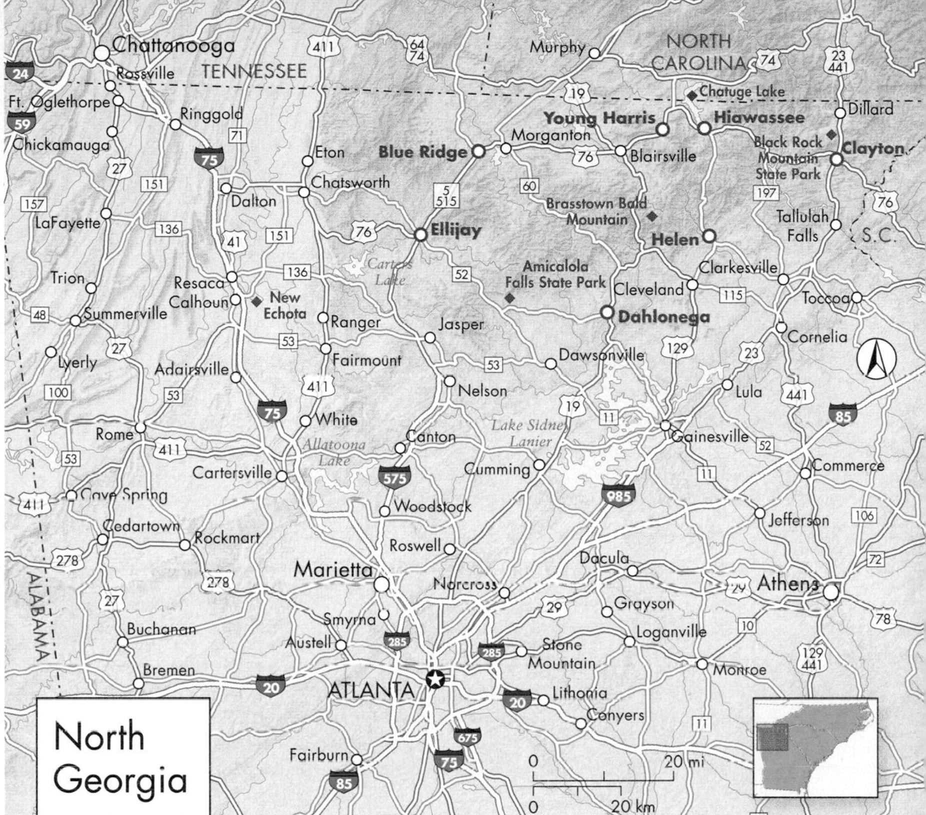


*110 miles northwest of Atlanta via I–75 and GA 2; 42 miles north of New Echota State Historic Site via I–75; 12 miles south of Chattanooga, TN, via U.S. 27.*

## THE NORTH GEORGIA MOUNTAINS

To most Georgians, "North Georgia" means the northeast and north central mountains and foothills—from Clayton and Dillard in the east to Hiawassee and Lake Chatuge in the north, and Blue Ridge and Ellijay and the Cohutta Wilderness to the west. Dahlonega, Helen, and several state parks—Black Rock Mountain, Moccasin Creek, Unicoi, Vogel, and Amicalola Falls—are contained within the broad arc of this scenic mountain region.

### DAHLONEGA

**Fodor's Choice** ★

*65 miles northeast of Atlanta via GA 400 and GA 60.*

Hoards of fortune seekers stormed the town of Dahlonega (pronounced Dah-LON-eh-gah) in the 1820s after the discovery of gold in the nearby hills. The town's name comes from the Cherokee word for "precious yellow metal." But the boom didn't last long; by 1849 miners were starting to seek riches elsewhere. In fact, the famous call "There's gold in them thar hills!" originated as an enticement to miners in the Georgia mountains to keep their minds away from the lure of the Western gold rush. It worked for a while, but government price fixing eventually made gold mining unprofitable, and by the early 1920s Dahlonega's mining operations had halted completely.

Many former mining settlements became ghost towns, but not Dahlonega. Today it thrives with an irresistible town square filled with country stores, art galleries, gem shops, old small-town businesses, and several sophisticated restaurants. Gold Rush Days, a festival held the third weekend in October and celebrating the first gold rush in 1828, attracts about 200,000 weekend visitors.

#### GETTING HERE AND AROUND

It's easy to spend your entire visit in Dahlonega's quaint town square. But a short drive out of town will allow you to climb down into a gold mine, or to taste wine at the local vintners.

#### ESSENTIALS

**Visitor Information Dahlonega-Lumpkin Chamber of Commerce and Visitors Center** ✉ *13 Park St. S* ☎ *706/864–3711, 800/231–5543* 🌐 *www.dahlonega.org.*

### EXPLORING

★ **Consolidated Gold Mine.** Take a guided tour of a real mine, which ceased operations in 1904. With 5 miles of underground tunnels, Consolidated is said to be the largest gold mine east of the Mississippi. Enter the mine (which has been reconstructed for safety), pass through a breathtaking stone passage, and then begin a descent of 120 feet into the mine's geological wonders. Guides, a few of them former miners, expound on historical mining techniques and give demonstrations of tools, such as the "widowmaker," a drill that kicks up mining dust and caused lung disease in many miners. After the tour, guests are invited to pan for gold, prospector-style, from a long wooden sluice. ✉ *185 Consolidated Gold Mine Rd.* ☎ *706/864–8473* 🌐 *www.consolidatedgoldmine.com* *$15* *Daily 10–5 (last tour at 4).*

**Dahlonega Gold Museum.** Located in the center of the town square, this museum has coins, tools, and several large nuggets on display. Built in 1836, this former courthouse is the oldest public building in the state. If you look closely at the bricks that form the building's foundation, you'll notice a sprinkling of gold dust in their formation. Along with two floors of exhibits, the museum features a high-definition film called *America's First Gold Rush.* Arrive an hour before closing to be sure and catch the film. ✉ *1 Public Sq.* ☎ *706/864–2257* 🌐 *www.gastateparks.org/dahlonega* *$6* *Mon.–Sat. 9–4:45, Sun. 10–4:45.*

OFF THE BEATEN PATH

**Amicalola Falls.** This is claimed to be the highest cascading waterfall east of the Mississippi, with waters plunging an eye-popping 729 feet through a cluster of seven cascades. The surrounding 1,021-acre state park contains a visitor's center and is dotted with scenic campsites and cottages strategically situated near a network of nature trails, picnic sites, and fishing streams. The southern starting point of the more than 2,100-mile Appalachian Trail begins near Amicalola Falls. ✉ *418*

Dahlonega's town square is worth a stroll with country stores, art galleries, and restaurants.

*Amicalola Falls Lodge Rd., off GA 52, 18 miles west of Dahlonega, Dawsonville* *706/265–4703* *www.gastateparks.org/AmicalolaFalls* *Parking $5* *Daily 7 am–10 pm.*

**VINEYARDS**

In the Dahlonega area, visitors can find the largest concentration of wineries in Georgia.

**BlackStock Vineyards and Winery.** On 90 acres, BlackStock offers more than a dozen traditional European premium-quality wines. The large outdoor deck overlooks both the vineyards and the mountains. The lodge pulls in elements from the setting, with a stacked stone three-sided fireplace and handcrafted wrought-iron work replicating the look of the grapevines. A waterfall is a highlight of the wine cellar. The winery's ACE—a family reserve blend of Touriga, Mourvèdre, and the winery's best Merlot—is named for owners David and Trish Harris's three children: Austin, Chandler, and Eliza. Check the website for information on regular wine dinners, grape stomps during harvest, and live music. *5400 Town Creek Rd.* *706/219–2789* *www.bsvw.com* *Mon.–Fri. 12–6, Sat. 10–6, Sun. 12:30–6.*

**Frogtown Cellars.** This 50-acre vineyard and winery offers picturesque mountain views from its deck as well as a dramatic dining room. The winery features an underground, gravity-flow wine-making facility on three floors, which utilizes gravity in place of pumps, with wine crush on the first level, fermentation on the second, and storage in wine barrels on the third and lowest level. Since 2005, the winery has won more than 70 medals in major competitions worldwide. Lunch is available Friday to Sunday; Sunday brunch and wine-tasting dinners

CLOSE UP

## Georgia Wine Highway

Grapevines and wineries are popping up all over North Georgia, and burgundy-color signs lead the way to vineyards along the **Georgia Wine Highway.** A listing of current wineries is available at *www.georgiawine.com.*

**Crane Creek Vineyards.** This winery produces 12 regional artisanal wines based on the 10 grape varieties it grows. The most popular choices are Vidal Blanc, Seyval, and Norton. *916 Crane Creek Rd., off GA 515, Young Harris 706/379–1236 www.cranecreekvineyards.com Tues.–Sat. 11–6, Sun. 1–5.*

**Habersham Vineyards & Winery.** One of the oldest wineries in the state, Habersham Vineyards & Winery started producing in 1983. Its tasting room also includes an eclectic shop full of wine-related accessories. *7025 S. Main St. on GA 75, Helen 706/878–9463 www.habershamwinery.com.*

**Sharp Mountain Vineyards.** Fourteen wines from 12 varietals are produced at Sharp Mountain Vineyards. Visitors get great mountain vistas from the property. *110 Rathgeb Trail, Jasper 770/735–1210 www.sharpmountainvineyards.com.*

**Tiger Mountain Vineyards.** Started on a five-generation-old family farm in 1995 by Dr. John and Martha Ezzard, Tiger Mountain Vineyards is known for unusual varietals of French and Portuguese grapes such as Touriga Nacional and Tannat, as well as the native Norton grape—grown on the slopes of Tiger Mountain. Tastings are available for a small fee. Lunch and dinner are served on the weekends (April–November) in their lovely restored Red Barn Cafe. *2592 Old Hwy. 441, 8 minutes south of Clayton, Tiger 706/782–4777 www.tigerwine.com.*

require reservations. *700 Ridge Point Dr., northeast of Dahlonega 706/865–0687 www.frogtownwine.com Mon.–Fri. 12–5, Sat. 12–6, Sun. 12:30–5.*

**Montaluce Winery.** Reminiscent of a grand Tuscan villa, Dahlonega's newest winery features a 20-acre vineyard and state-of-the-art, 25,000-square-foot wine-making facility. Montaluce's spacious dining room/restaurant and multilevel terraces provide breathtaking views of mountain scenery. The Mediterranean-inspired Wine Bar offers tastings of the winery's 11 vintages. The Honey and Wildflower Mead and Super Georgian, a blend of Montaluce's red grape varietals, are especially popular in the tasting room. Complimentary winery tours are offered Tuesday–Sunday at 2. Tastings are available for a fee. *501 Hightower Church Rd. 866/991–8466, 706/867–4060 www.montaluce.com Tues.–Sat. 11–5, Sun. 12–5.*

**Three Sisters Vineyards.** Dahlonega's first family-farm winery has 18 acres of plantings including Cabernet Franc, Cabernet Sauvignon, Pinot Blanc, and Chardonnay, along with American varietals such as Cynthiana-Norton. The relaxed winery is named for nearby Three Sisters Mountain, visible from the farm's gazebo. Deli meats and cheeses are available,

Three Sisters Vineyards has a friendly, down-to-earth tasting room. Be sure to try the Fat Boy Red if it's available.

and a deck provides a comfortable spot for a picnic. The tasting room is decorated with folk art and pottery from the area, including a poster that proclaims "Thar's Wine in Them Thar Hills." A favorite from the winery is the robust "Fat Boy Red." Special events, including the Georgia Wine Country Festival the first weekend in June, occur monthly. ✉ *439 Vineyard Way, northeast of Dahlonega* ☎ *706/865–9463* 🌐 *www.threesistersvineyards.com* ⏲ *Thurs.–Sat. 11–5, Sun. 1–5.*

**Wolf Mountain Vineyards & Winery.** This 25-acre vineyard has hillside plantings of Cabernet Sauvignon, Syrah, Mourvèdre, and Touriga Nacional. The Craftsman-style lodge housing the winery and café offers tastings for a fee and serves lunch Thursday through Saturday from noon to 3, and a Sunday brunch between 12:30 and 2:30. Reservations are required. Wolf Mountain also offers quarterly gourmet dinners and guided tours of the grounds on weekends at 2. Some of the winery's acclaimed labels include Plenitude, a 70% Chardonnay and 30% Viognier blend; Claret, an estate reserve Cabernet and Malbec; and Instinct, a Rhone-style red blend. Call for tour or tasting information. ✉ *180 Wolf Mountain Trail, off U.S. 19/60, north of Dahlonega* ☎ *706/867–9862* 🌐 *www.wolfmountainvineyards.com* ⏲ *Mar.–mid-Dec., Thurs.–Sun. noon–5.*

## WHERE TO EAT

$$$ AMERICAN ★ ✕ **Corkscrew Café.** This cozy and intimate restaurant has terra-cotta-color walls covered with photography from a local artist and a large covered patio. Specialties include hand-carved steaks with a portobello mushroom demi-glace, seared sashimi-grade tuna, and rack of lamb with a curry-orange glaze. Locals love the curry squash bisque and

French onion soup as well as a macadamia-crusted mahi with a grilled pineapple-and-mango salsa and eggplant mascarpone. Inexpensive lunch entrées, also available for dinner, include sandwiches, salads, and soup. *Average main: $24* *51 W. Main St.* *706/867–8551* *www.thecorkscrewcafe.com* *Closed Mon.*

$ AMERICAN ★ **Crimson Moon Café.** Set in the historic Parker-Nix Storehouse, a general store built in the 1850s, this funky spot offers everything from a cheesesteak wrap with roasted red peppers, mushrooms, and onions to Southern-style veggies. Breakfast is served Friday through Sunday, and affordable salads, sandwiches, and snacks are available alongside dinner entrées. The intimate venue features live acoustic music, from blues and bluegrass to Celtic, folk rock, and country, five nights a week. *Average main: $10* *24 N. Park St., Suite A, Dahlonega* *706/864–3982* *www.thecrimsonmoon.com* *Closed Mon. and Tues.*

$$$ MODERN AMERICAN ★ **Le Vigne.** Sweeping vistas of mountain scenery and lush vineyards from its dining room and terrace make Montaluce Winery's restaurant worth the drive. Open for lunch Tuesday to Sunday throughout the week and dinner on weekends, Le Vigne's cuisine is designed to pair well with wine and emphasize local ingredients, including fruits and vegetables grown nearby. Local artisan meats and cheeses are the heart of the menu. The restaurant is a favorite for Sunday brunch and romantic dinners. **TIP→ Call ahead, as the winery is sometimes closed for private events.** *Average main: $22* *501 Hightower Church Rd.* *706/867–4060, 866/991–8466* *www.montaluce.com* *Closed Mon. No dinner Tues.–Thurs. and Sun.*

## WHERE TO STAY

*Hotel reviews have been abbreviated in this book. For expanded reviews, please go to Fodors.com.*

$ HOTEL Fodor's Choice ★ **Amicalola Falls Lodge.** One of the most appealing mountain lodges in Georgia is part of the state park system and features panoramic views over the mountains from the massive glass-windowed lobby. **Pros:** Amicalola Falls is five minutes away; stunning views of the mountains. **Cons:** no swimming pool. *Rooms from: $110* *418 Amicalola Falls Lodge Rd., 20 miles west of Dahlonega, Dawsonville* *706/265–8888, 800/573–9656* *www.amicalolafalls.com* *56 rooms, 4 suites, 14 cottages.*

$ B&B/INN **Historic Worley Bed & Breakfast.** This B&B occupies an 1845 antebellum home with two garden courtyards and is within walking distance of the Dahlonega town square. **Pros:** the only historic B&B in the area; private baths. **Cons:** no elevator; rooms can feel small. *Rooms from: $139* *168 Main St. W* *706/864–7002* *www.bbonline.com/ga/worley* *7 rooms* *Breakfast.*

$ B&B/INN ★ **Len Foote Hike Inn.** A love of the environment is clearly evident at the Len Foote Hike Inn; a 5-mile hike of moderate difficulty (three hours each way), leads visitors to this backcountry pack-it-in-and-pack-it-out inn at Amicalola State Park. **Pros:** lots of puzzles, board games, and books are available; guests need only backpack in with their toothbrushes, toothpaste, overnight clothes, and water bottles. **Cons:** rooms book quickly, especially on weekends and in October. *Rooms from: $140* *240 Amicalola Falls State Park Rd., 20 miles west of Dahlonega* *via GA 52, Dawsonville* ☎ *800/581–8032* 🌐 *www.hike-inn.com* ⇄ *20 rooms* 🍴 *Some meals.*

$ B&B/INN **Lily Creek Lodge.** This eclectic B&B appears slightly Bavarian on the outside, and some of the rooms echo Venice, Africa, Morocco, and Argentina with their decor. **Pros:** lovely grounds; close to Dahlonega, Montaluce, and Wolf Mountain Vineyards. **Cons:** narrow stairs to the uppermost room; no elevator. *Rooms from: $129* ✉ *2608 Auraria Rd.* ☎ *706/864–6848, 888/844–2694* 🌐 *www.lilycreeklodge.com* ⇄ *10 rooms, 3 suites* 🍴 *Breakfast.*

$$ B&B/INN Fodor's Choice ★ **The Smith House.** Just a block from the town square, the family-owned Smith House has been serving guests for generations. **Pros:** luxurious amenities; handicap access on the main floor. **Cons:** the North Georgia College and State University parking lot and recreation facility is next door. *Rooms from: $179* ✉ *84 S. Chestatee St.* ☎ *800/852–9577, 706/867–7000* 🌐 *www.smithhouse.com* ⇄ *9 rooms in main house, 6 in carriage house, 3 villas nearby* 🍴 *Breakfast.*

### NIGHTLIFE AND THE ARTS

**Historic Holly Theater.** This well-restored classic small-town movie theater, built in 1946, stages live theater, movies, children's performances, and special events. "The Mountain Music and Medicine Show," a live production featuring bluegrass and gospel music and humorous tales from Dahlonega's past, is presented regularly. ✉ *69 W. Main St.* ☎ *706/864–3759* 🌐 *www.hollytheater.com.*

### SPORTS AND THE OUTDOORS

**Appalachian Outfitters.** Stop here to pick up equipment and maps for self-guided canoeing and kayaking trips on the Chestatee and Etowah rivers. Tube rentals and shuttle service are also available for tubing trips on the Chestatee. ✉ *2084 S. Chestatee, Hwy. 60 S* ☎ *706/864–7117, 800/426–7117* 🌐 *www.canoegeorgia.com* ⏱ *Nov.–Feb.*

## HELEN AND SAUTEE-NACOOCHEE VALLEY

*32 miles northeast of Dahlonega; 88 miles northeast of Atlanta.*

Helen was founded at the turn of the 20th century as a simple lumber outpost. In the 1960s, when logging declined, business leaders came up with a plan to transform the tiny village of 300 into a theme town, and "Alpine Helen" was born. Today many businesses along Helen's central streets sport a distinctive German facade, giving an initial impression that you've stumbled on a Bavarian vista in the middle of Appalachia. ■ **TIP→** Don't expect small-town prices for anything from parking to ATM charges. This is clearly not Bavaria, but the effect can be briefly contagious, making you feel as if you've stepped into a fairy tale. If it's too touristy, visit nearby areas for delightful crafts, shopping, and dining. Sautee and Nacoochee are the home of the Habersham Winery, the Folk Pottery Museum of North Georgia, and a number of other pottery and craft shops.

Amicalola Falls State Park has a lovely lodge with excellent views of the mountains.

### GETTING HERE AND AROUND

While the quirky town of Helen may merit a quick stop, other nearby attractions a short drive away are also well worth visiting. Try the Folk Pottery Museum of Northeast Georgia to check out the area's centuries-old pottery tradition and Georgia's famous "face jugs." The Sautee and Nacoochee areas are accessible just south of Helen off GA 75.

### ESSENTIALS

**Visitor Information Helen Welcome Center** ✉ *726 Bruckenstrasse* ☎ *706/878–2181, 800/858–8027* 🌐 *www.helenga.org.*

## EXPLORING

**Charlemagne's Kingdom.** This child-friendly museum recreates sections of Germany, from the North Sea to the Alps, all in HO model-train scale (one eighty-seventh of the actual size). The Autobahn is depicted, as is the entire walled town of Rothenburg (there are 350 building replicas) and moving hot-air balloons. There are six running trains, thousands of hand-painted figurines, and sound effects including the ocean, a carnival, and German music. The shop sells Lionel trains, Thomas the Tank Engines, and John Deere toys. Willi Lindhorst, a native of Oldenburg, Germany, created the train layout and its trappings and owns the shop with his wife, Judi. ✉ *8808 N. Main St.* ☎ *706/878–2200* 🌐 *www.georgiamodelrailroad.com* 🎫 *$5* 🕒 *Apr.–Dec., Thurs.–Tues. 10–5; Jan.–Mar., call for hrs.*

**Chattahoochee National Forest.** Covering about 750,000 acres of land in North Georgia, the headwaters of the Chattahoochee River are found at this nature preserve. The forest was created piecemeal, beginning in 1911, from bits and pieces of often environmentally degraded and abused land, and was officially established in 1936. About 15% of the Chattahoochee is wilderness. The national forest supports an estimated 500 species of fish and wildlife, including black bears, white-tailed deer, and wild turkeys. In 1959, 96,000 acres of land in middle Georgia were added, and the combined forests are called the Chattahoochee-Oconee National Forests and total more than 865,000 acres. The forest offers a wide range of recreational opportunities such as camping, hiking, and fishing (from native trout to largemouth bass and bream). ✉ *1755 Cleveland Hwy., Gainesville* ☎ *770/297–3000* 🌐 *www.fs.fed.us/conf.*

Fodor's Choice ★ **Folk Pottery Museum of Northeast Georgia.** Located 4 miles southeast of Helen, this museum showcases a 200-year unbroken tradition of folk pottery in Northeast Georgia (especially in nearby Mossy Creek and the Gillsville-Lula area). Part of the 5,000-square-foot facility outlines how pottery is made and how it was used for essential household purposes. Exhibits showcase a 200-piece collection donated to the museum, including the whimsical face jugs that have become an emblem of Southern folk art. Demonstrations of pottery making are offered one Saturday a month. Call ahead for dates and times. ✉ *283 Hwy. 255, Sautee Nacoochee* ☎ *706/878–3300* 🌐 *www.folkpotterymuseum.com* *$5* *Mon.–Sat. 10–5, Sun. 1–5.*

14

### WHERE TO EAT AND STAY

*Hotel reviews have been abbreviated in this book. For expanded reviews, please go to Fodors.com.*

$$ ECLECTIC **Nacoochee Grill.** Beef, chicken, and fish grilled on a wood-fired grill are the focus at this casual restaurant set in a cheerful old house in Nacoochee Village, just outside town. The roasted corn, trout, and salmon chowder is a specialty. Chicken pot pie is another favorite, along with crab cakes. It's also a great place to try local wines. *Average main: $15* ✉ *7277 S. Main St.* ☎ *706/878–8020* 🌐 *www.nacoocheegrill.com.*

$$$$ RENTAL ★ **The Cottages at Smithgall Woods.** As part of a 5,600-acre park run by the state of Georgia, these five cottages, set in old-growth hardwoods, offer a peaceful retreat. **Pros:** a luxurious and secluded retreat; hiking trails nearby. **Cons:** must bring your own fishing equipment; no food service. *Rooms from: $304* ✉ *61 Tsalaki Trail* ☎ *706/878–3087, 800/318–5248* 🌐 *www.gastateparks.org/SmithgallWoods* *5 cottages.*

$ RESORT **The Lodge at Unicoi.** Choose either the comfortable mountain lodge, with 100 attractive lodge rooms, or a one-, two-, or three-bedroom cottage (some with a fireplace) at this state-run accommodation. **TIP→ The lodge and restaurant will be closed for renovations until late 2013. The campground and cabins will remain open.** **Pros:** live bluegrass and gospel music; less than 3 miles from Helen. **Cons:** breakfast isn't included in the rate; not all cottages have TVs. *Rooms from: $135* ✉ *1788 GA 356, 3 miles north of Helen* ☎ *706/878–2201, 800/573–9659* 🌐 *www.gastateparks.org/Unicoi* *100 rooms, 30 cottages, 82 campsites.*

## SPORTS AND THE OUTDOORS

**Cool River Tubing.** "Tube the Hootch" with Cool River Tubing, which shuttles you on a bus upriver to begin the float back to town. Choose the short (one hour) or long (two hours) float trip. Prices are $5 for a single trip of either length or $9 all day. Cool River also operates a waterslide. A combination all-day ticket for tubing and waterslide is $13. ✉ *590 Edelweiss Strasse* ☎ *706/878–2665, 800/896–4595* 🌐 *www.coolrivertubing.com* ⏲ *Late May–early Sept.*

## SHOPPING

**Georgia Heritage Center for the Arts.** A wide variety of quality local arts and crafts items, such as jewelry, paintings, pottery, stained glass, and wood carvings, are offered at Georgia Heritage Center for the Arts. ✉ *8016 S. Main St.* ☎ *706/892–1033* ⏲ *Closed Jan. and Feb.*

**The Gourd Place.** This unique museum and gourd and pottery store is filled with colorful gourd collections from around the world. Owners Priscilla Wilson and Janice Lymburner sell gourds and supplies to preserve dried gourds (a Southern specialty). They also produce attractive natural-glazed stoneware and porcelain dinnerware, vases, bowls, and luminaries using liquid clay poured into gourd molds. ✉ *2319 Duncan Bridge Rd., Sautee* ☎ *706/865–4048* ⏲ *Apr.–late Dec., Mon.–Sat. 10–5, Sun. 1–5; late Dec.–Mar., by appointment.*

**Hickory Flat Pottery.** This working pottery studio in a large 116-year-old roadside farmhouse is filled with lots more than "just" beautiful pottery. Vibrant stained glass, a variety of jewelry, fiber art, and copper art are featured, along with the vivid, decorative, and functional stoneware of shop owner Cindy Angliss, who enjoys sharing her craft by sending little bags of clay home with children. ✉ *13664 U.S. 197 N, 4 miles north of Mark of the Potter, Clarkesville* ☎ *706/947–0030* 🌐 *www.hickoryflatpottery.com* ⏲ *Jan.–Mar., Mon., Fri., and Sat. 10–5, Sun. noon–5; Apr.–Dec., Mon. and Wed–Sat. 10–6, Sun. noon–6.*

Fodor's Choice ★ **Mark of the Potter.** In an old gristmill with beautiful views of the Soque River, Mark of the Potter offers an outstanding selection of pottery from more than 30 artisans. The emphasis is on functional pieces, with a great variety of clay and firing techniques and glazes in every imaginable color. Items range from coffee scoops to lamps, mugs to elaborate vases and casserole dishes. The shop is legendary among Georgia-pottery lovers. Children and adults alike will enjoy sitting on the porch and feeding the huge pet trout. A potter works on the wheel at the shop on Saturday and Sunday. ✉ *9982 GA 197 N, Clarkesville* ☎ *706/947–3440* 🌐 *www.markofthepotter.com.*

**Old Sautee Store.** This unique shop has been operating continuously since 1872. The front part of the store operates more as a museum, with antique farming implements, old-timey tonics and soaps, and even caskets on display. The retail store, influenced by an earlier owner's Scandinavian heritage, continues to sell Swedish farmer's cheese and Norwegian flat bread. Shoppers can also pick up old-time candy and toys. ✉ *2315 GA 17, 5 miles south of Helen, Sautee* ☎ *706/878–2281* 🌐 *www.oldsauteestore.com.*

Hike the rim trails at Tallulah Gorge State Park for spectacular views of the canyon below.

EN ROUTE

**Russell-Brasstown Scenic Byway.** Beginning and ending in Helen, the Russell-Brasstown Scenic Byway is a 41-mile loop through some of the most dramatic mountain scenery in northeastern Georgia. Start the counterclockwise drive from GA17/74 north of Helen, turn left on GA 180, left again at GA 348, and another left at GA 75 Alternate back to Helen. The loop passes the Raven Cliff Wilderness, wildlife management areas, the headwaters of the Chattahoochee River, a section of the Appalachian Trail, and goes near the state parks of Vogel, Unicoi, Smithgall Woods, and Brasstown Bald Mountain.

## CLAYTON

*35 miles northeast of Helen via GA 356, GA 197, and U.S. 76.*

The town of Clayton, with a downtown filled with shops, is a gateway to North Georgia's mountains. The beautiful lakeshore and the grandeur of Black Rock Mountain State Park and Tallulah Gorge make a day tour of this area a memorable experience. Plenty of shopping and dining is available in Clayton and Clarkesville.

### GETTING HERE AND AROUND

Clayton makes a good base to explore Tallulah Gorge State Park and its falls and Black Rock Mountain State Park. A short drive northwest on U.S. 76 will take you to several of the region's most appealing lakes, including Rabun and Chatuge.

### ESSENTIALS

**Visitor Information Rabun County Welcome Center** ✉ *232 U.S. 441 N* ☎ *706/782–4812* 🌐 *www.gamountains.com.*

## EXPLORING

### TOP ATTRACTIONS

★ **Chattooga River.** The first river in the Southeast to be designated a Wild and Scenic River by Congress, the Chattooga River begins at Whiteside Mountain in North Carolina and forms the border between Georgia and South Carolina. With Class II to Class V rapids, the Chattooga is popular for white-water rafting, especially in spring and summer. Movie buffs should note that this was one of the locations for *Deliverance*. ✉ *From Clayton drive east 7 miles on U.S. 76 to Hwy. 76 Bridge at Georgia–South Carolina state line.*

> **HIKING TIPS**
>
> **Tallulah Gorge.** Each day, 100 hiking permits are issued at the interpretive center for spectacular Tallulah Gorge, considered one of the most stunning gorges in the eastern United States. The hike to the floor of the 1,000-foot gorge with its lush vegetation, scenic waterfalls, and rocky bottom takes three to four hours. Tennis shoes, hiking boots, or river sandals are required for the strenuous hike. Damp walkways and riverbeds can be slick, so use extreme caution. Rim trails to overlooks are also open to visitors.

Fodor's Choice ★ **Foxfire Museum and Heritage Center.** In 1966, students at the Rabin Gap-Nacoochee School wrote articles for a magazine based on generations-old family stories. Their excitement in chronicling life in the Appalachians has led to more than a dozen Foxfire books, which have sold nearly 9 million copies. The nonprofit foundation behind Foxfire opened the center to students and teachers worldwide, inviting them to the Foxfire Course for Teachers. A collection of authentic and reconstructed log cabins, a gristmill, a blacksmith's shop, and a church, accessible by a rough gravel road, re-create Appalachian life before the days of electricity and running water. ✉ *200 Foxfire La., off U.S. 441 at Black Rock Mountain Pkwy., Mountain City* ☎ *706/746–5828* ⊕ *www.foxfire.org* 🎫 *$6* ⏲ *Mon.–Sat. 8:30–4:30.*

Fodor's Choice ★ **Tallulah Gorge State Park.** The 1,000-foot-deep Tallulah Gorge is one of the most impressive in the country. In the late 1800s this area was one of the most visited destinations in the Southeast, with 17 hotels to house tourists who came to see the roaring falls on the Tallulah River. Then, in 1912, to provide electric power, the "Niagara of the South" was dammed, and the falls and tourism dried up. Today the state of Georgia has designated more than 20 miles of the state park as walking and mountain-biking trails. There's also a 16,000-square-foot interpretive center, a 63-acre lake with a beach, a picnic shelter, and 50 tent and RV sites. ✉ *U.S. 441, 338 Jane Hurt Yarn Dr., Tallulah Falls* ☎ *706/754–7970* ⊕ *www.gastateparks.org/TallulahGorge* 🎫 *Parking $5* ⏲ *Daily 8 am–dusk.*

### WORTH NOTING

★ **Black Rock Mountain State Park.** At more than 3,600 feet, Black Rock Mountain is the highest state park in Georgia. Named for the black gneiss rock visible on cliffs in the area, the 1,738-acre park has 10 miles of trails, a 17-acre lake, 44 campsites, a pioneer group campsite, and 10 cottages. The park offers majestic overlooks and a trail that leads visitors along the Eastern Continental Divide, from which water flows south and east to eventually reach the Atlantic Ocean, and on the other side, north and west to the mighty Mississippi River. The ranger station has information on trails. ✉ *Black Rock Mountain Pkwy., 3 miles northwest of Clayton, Mountain City* ☎ *706/746–2141, 800/864–7275 for camping and cottage reservations* 🌐 *www.gastateparks.org/BlackRockMountain* 🎫 *Daily-use fee $5* ⏲ *Daily 7 am–10 pm.*

**Lake Rabun.** Built in 1915, the first of six lakes in the state built by Georgia Railway and Power Company, Lake Rabun covers only 834 acres. Its small size is misleading, as its narrow fingers dart through mountain valleys. Lightly visited by tourists and populated with weekend homes and old boathouses, it has a low-key charm. The lake offers boating, fishing, and camping. There's a small beach at Rabun Beach Recreation Area at the east end of the lake available for day use for a fee. ✉ *West of U.S. 23/441 via Old Hwy. 441 S and Burton Lake Rd., 2 miles southwest of Clayton* ☎ *888/472–5253* 🌐 *www.lakerabun.com.*

14

**Lake Burton.** Another of the six lakes built by Georgia Railway and Power Co., this 2,700-acre lake is in the Chattahoochee National Forest. On the lake, at GA 197, is the **Lake Burton Fish Hatchery,** alongside Moccasin Creek State Park. It has trout raceways (used to raise trout from fingerlings) and a kids-only trout-fishing area. In extremely hot weather, the hatchery is sometimes closed. ✉ *3655 Hwy. 197, off U.S. 76, west of Clayton, Clarkesville* ☎ *706/947–3194* 🌐 *www.gastateparks.org/MoccasinCreek* 🎫 *Parking $5 for park, free parkingfor hatchery.*

## WHERE TO EAT AND STAY

*Hotel reviews have been abbreviated in this book. For expanded reviews, please go to Fodors.com.*

$$$$ MODERN AMERICAN Fodor's Choice ★ **Glen-Ella Springs Inn & Meeting Place.** This gourmet restaurant serves meals in two cozy dining rooms in the more-than-100-year-old lodge. Dishes are prepared with fresh herbs grown on the premises and local microgreens and produce. EntrÈes range from boneless fillet of rainbow trout and herb-crusted rack of New Zealand lamb to macadamia-crusted chicken breast. For lighter fare, try crab cakes, portobello mushrooms, sea scallops, or a variety of creative salads. $ *Average main: $25* ✉ *1789 Bear Gap Rd., Clarkesville* ☎ *706/754–7295, 888/455–8786* 🌐 *www.glenella.com* *Reservations essential.*

$ HOTEL ★ **Dillard House.** An inviting cluster of cottages and motel-style rooms, this establishment sits on a plateau near the state border. **Pros:** a half hour from Smoky Mountain Railway; fly-fishing and horseback riding available; stone fireplaces. **Cons:** on-site restaurant relies too much on its past reputation. $ *Rooms from: $99* ✉ *768 Franklin St., Dillard* ☎ *706/746–5348, 800/541–0671* 🌐 *www.dillardhouse.com* *90 rooms, 25 chalets, 4 cottages, 6 suites.*

$$ B&B/INN Fodor's Choice ★ **Glen-Ella Springs Inn & Meeting Place.** This restored country inn, constructed in 1875 and listed on the National Register of Historic Places, has a rustic but polished charm. **Pros:** eager staff; picturesque perennial and herb gardens; family movie nights. **Cons:** pool can be quite chilly; on a gravel road; limited number of rooms can accomodate families with children. $ *Rooms from: $175* ✉ *1789 Bear Gap Rd., Clarkesville*

☎706/754–7295, 888/455–8786 🌐*www.glenella.com* ⇨ *12 rooms, 4 suites* 🍽 *Breakfast.*

$ B&B/INN **Lake Rabun Hotel.** Set in shady hemlocks across the road from Lake Rabun, this elegant yet rustic hotel has rough-hewn wood paneling and a fieldstone fireplace. **Pros:** furniture is handmade; visitors can take a sunset cruise, rent a pontoon boat, fish, or swim in the lake; gourmet breakfast included in rate. **Cons:** no room TVs, no children under 10 [$] *Rooms from: $129* ✉ *35 Andrea La., Lakemont* ☎ *706/782–4946* 🌐 *www.lakerabunhotel.com* ⇨ *8 rooms and 1 cottage.*

### CLOSED SUNDAY?

Planning on shopping and eating out? Call ahead. Many smaller town shops—such as those in Clayton, Ellijay, Blue Ridge, and Blairsville—are closed Sunday. But Dahlonega and Helen shops are open daily.

### SPORTS AND THE OUTDOORS

WHITE-WATER RAFTING **Nantahala Outdoor Center.** The North Carolina–based Nantahala Outdoor Center, the largest rafting company in the region, runs part-day, daylong, and overnight white-water rafting trips on the Chattooga, Nantahala, and Ocoee Rivers, from $89 per person. ✉ *13077 Highway 19 W, Bryson City, North Carolina* ☎ *888/905–7238* 🌐 *www.noc.com.*

**Southeastern Expeditions.** Guided full-day trips on the Chatooga, starting at $85 per person, are available at Southeastern Expeditions. ✉ *7350 U.S. 76 E* ☎ *800/868–7238* 🌐 *www.southeasternexpeditions.com.*

### SHOPPING

★ **Main Street Gallery.** One of the state's best sources for folk art, Main Street Gallery carries works by more than 75 regional artists. The store also carries jewelry, pottery, paintings, and sculptures. ✉ *51 N. Main St.* ☎ *706/782–2440.*

## HIAWASSEE, YOUNG HARRIS, AND LAKE CHATUGE

*26 miles northwest of Clayton, via U.S. 76; 21 miles north of Helen via GA 75/17.*

The little town of Hiawassee, population 750, and nearby Young Harris, population 600, are near the largest lake in North Georgia, Lake Chatuge, and the tallest mountain in the state, Brasstown Bald. The lake has excellent boating and other water-themed recreation. Appealing mountain resorts are nearby as well. A half-hour drive leads to Brasstown Bald, where temperatures even on the hottest summer day rarely rise above 80∞F. The Georgia Mountain Fairgrounds has a permanent location on the shores of Lake Chatuge. A number of festivals are held at the fairgrounds, including the Fall Festival, and State Fiddler's Convention in October and the Georgia Mountain Fair held in July.

### ESSENTIALS

**Visitor Information Towns County Chamber of Commerce** ✉ *1411 Jack Dayton Circle, Young Harris* ☎ *706/896–4966, 800/984–1543* 🌐 *www.mountaintopga.com.*

### EXPLORING

Fodor's Choice ★ **Brasstown Bald.** In the Chattahoochee National Forest, Brasstown Bald reaches 4,784 feet, the highest point in Georgia. Below the Bald is Georgia's only cloud forest, an area of lichen-covered trees often kept wet by clouds and fog. From the observation platform at the top of the Bald on a clear day you can see Georgia, North Carolina, South Carolina, and Tennessee. A paved but steep foot trail leads from the parking lot (where there are restrooms and a picnic area) to the visitor center, which has exhibits and interpretative programs. You also can ride a bus ($3) to the visitor center. ✉ *GA 180 Spur, 18 miles southwest of Hiawassee via U.S. 76, GA 75, GA 180, and GA 180 Spur* ☎ *706/896–2556* 🌐 *www.fs.fed.us/conf* *Day-use fee $3, shuttle $3* ⏲ *Mid-Mar.–late Nov., daily 10–5.*

### CABIN RENTALS

The Blue Ridge area offers a variety of cabin rentals. Try one of these rental companies or do some browsing on rent-from-owner sites like 🌐 *www.vrbo.com.*

**Cabin Rentals of Blue Ridge** ✉ *Blue Ridge* ☎ *706/632–6600, 877/229–8585* 🌐 *www.cabinrentalsofblueridge.com.*

**Mountain Getaway Cabin Rentals** ✉ *Blue Ridge* ☎ *866/862–2246* 🌐 *www.mtngetawaycabins.com.*

**Mountain Top Cabin Rentals** ✉ *Blue Ridge* ☎ *706/250–6220, 866/402–2246* 🌐 *www.mountaintopcabinrentals.com.*

### WHERE TO STAY

*Hotel reviews have been abbreviated in this book. For expanded reviews, please go to Fodors.com.*

$$ RESORT ★ **Brasstown Valley Resort and Spa.** For upscale, lodge style accommodations, this resort is a great option. **Pros:** elegant but rustic rooms. **Cons:** far-flung location. *Rooms from: $179* ✉ *6321 U.S. 76, Young Harris* ☎ *706/379–9900, 800/201–3205* 🌐 *www.brasstownvalley.com* *97 rooms, 32 cottages, 5 suites* *Breakfast.*

$$ RESORT **The Ridges Resort and Club.** Many of the beautifully appointed rooms in this lodge are decorated with leather furnishings, stone steps, and rustic wood and have gorgeous views of Lake Chatuge. **Pros:** great for outdoors lovers, two restaurants on-site. **Cons:** some say rooms need an update *Rooms from: $189* ✉ *3499 U.S. 76* ☎ *706/896–2262, 888/834–4409* 🌐 *www.theridgesresort.com* *62 rooms, 4 suites, 13 villas* *Breakfast.*

## BLUE RIDGE

*39 miles southwest of Hiawassee via U.S. 76/GA 515; 53 miles northwest of Dahlonega via GA 52 and U.S. 76/GA 515.*

Blue Ridge is one of the most pleasant small mountain towns in North Georgia. After you've eaten breakfast or lunch and shopped for antiques, gifts, or crafts at Blue Ridge's many small shops, you can ride the revived Blue Ridge Scenic Railway to McCaysville, a town at the Tennessee line, and then back through the mountains.

### ESSENTIALS

**Visitor Information** Fannin County Chamber of Commerce and Welcome Center ✉ *152 Orvin Lance Dr.* ☎ *706/632–5680, 800/899–6867* 🌐 *www.blueridgemountains.com.*

### EXPLORING

**Blue Ridge Scenic Railway.** Ride the rails on a four-hour, 26-mile round-trip excursion along the Toccoa River. The trip includes a stop in **McCaysville,** smack on the Georgia–Tennessee state line. Several restaurants, shops, and galleries are open during the two-hour layover. The train, which has open Pullman cars and is pulled by diesel engines, is staffed with friendly volunteer hosts. The ticket office, now on the National Register of Historic Places, dates from 1905 and was originally the depot of the L&N Railroad. Children of all ages enjoy the ride. In summer you may want to consider the air-conditioned coaches. Raft-and-rail ($68–$83) and raft-and-tubing ($50) packages are available. ✉ *241 Depot St.* ☎ *706/632–8724, 877/413–8724* 🌐 *www.brscenic.com* *$27–$43, depending on season* ⏲ *Mid-Mar.–late Dec. Call for hrs.*

**Swan Drive-In Theater.** Originally opened in 1955, this is one of only four drive-in movie theaters operating in Georgia. You can take in a movie under the stars and fill up on corn dogs, pickled eggs, funnel cakes, and popcorn from the concession stand. ✉ *651 Summit St.* ☎ *706/632–5235.*

### WHERE TO EAT

$$ SOUTHERN **Serenity Garden CafÈ.** A relaxing spot for breakfast, lunch, and dinner, this café is a charming hideaway in Blue Ridge's shopping district. Choose between umbrella-shaded tables outside or a bright and cheerful dining room. Breakfast offerings include grits and biscuits with sausage gravy. Homemade soups are popular for lunch and dinner, as are the more than two dozen sandwiches. Dinner favorites are homemade meat lasagna and a handcut rib eye steak. Takeout is available. *Average main: $15* ✉ *657 E. Main St., Blue Ridge* ☎ *706/258–4949.*

## ELLIJAY

*84 miles west of Clayton via U.S. 76; 37 miles northwest of Dahlonega via GA 52; 80 miles north of Atlanta via I–75, I–575, and GA 5/515.*

Billed as "Georgia's apple capital," Ellijay is also popular among antiques aficionados. The town, on the site of what had been a Cherokee village called Elatseyi (meaning "place of green things"), has a colorful cluster of crafts shops and antiques markets.

The most popular time to visit Ellijay is in fall, when roadside stands brimming with delicious ripe apples dot the landscape. The annual Georgia Apple Festival takes place the second and third weekends of October. In addition to showcasing the many manifestations of the crisp fruit—apple butter, apple pie, apple cider, and so on—the very popular festival offers a host of arts-and-crafts exhibitions.

On a clear day, you can see Georgia, North Carolina, South Carolina, and Tennessee from the observation tower at Brasstown Bald.

## ESSENTIALS

**Visitor Information Gilmer County Chamber of Commerce and Welcome Center** ✉ *696 First Ave., East Ellijay* ☎ *706/635–7400* 🌐 *www.gilmerchamber.com.*

## EXPLORING

**Fort Mountain State Park.** This 3,712-acre state park has a 17-acre lake with sandy beach, 14 miles of hiking trails, and 30 miles of mountain biking trails. The gem of the park is a mysterious wall of rock, 855 feet long, thought to have been built by Native Americans around AD 500. Tent and RV sites ($25–$28) and rental cottages ($125–$145) are available. The park also offers a unique primitive site for camping with horses. ✉ *181 Fort Mountain Park Rd., Chatsworth* ☎ *706/422–1932* 🌐 *www.gastateparks.org/fortmountain* *Free, parking $5* *Daily 7 am–10 pm.*

**Hillcrest Orchards.** Buy freshly picked apples (usually early September to late November) at this 80-acre farm. Homemade jellies, jams, breads, and doughnuts are available at the farm's market and bakery. On September and October weekends, the Apple Pickin' Jubilee features live music, wagon rides, apple picking, and other activities. There's also a petting zoo and a picnic area. ✉ *9696 GA 52E* ☎ *706/273–3838* 🌐 *www.hillcrestorchards.net* *$6 for special events including Apple Pickin' Jubilee; $3 for petting zoo* *Sept.–Oct., daily 9–6; Nov., daily 9–5.*

### WHERE TO STAY

*Hotel reviews have been abbreviated in this book. For expanded reviews, please go to Fodors.com.*

$ HOTEL **Best Western Mountain View Inn.** This two-story motel sits on a hilltop above East Ellijay and half of its rooms have mountain views. **Pros:** close to eating and shopping areas, indoor heated pool. **Cons:** entrance is hard to find. *Rooms from: $89 43 Coosawattee Dr., East Ellijay 706/515–1500, 866/515–4515 www.bwmountainviewinn.com 50 rooms, 4 suites Breakfast.*

$ RENTAL **Whitepath Lodge.** From nearly every 2- or 3-bedroom villa at this scenic lodge you get panoramic vistas of the North Georgia mountains. **Pros:** well-appointed accommodations; lovely landscaped grounds. **Cons:** off the beaten track; no elevator. *Rooms from: $120 987 Shenandoah Dr. 706/276–7199 www.whitepathlodge.com 14 villas.*

### SPORTS AND THE OUTDOORS

There are plenty of options for fishing, canoeing, and kayaking on the Cartecay River, which runs through town.

# MACON AND THE ANTEBELLUM TRAIL

The antebellum South, filtered through the romanticized gauze of *Gone With the Wind*, evokes graciousness, gentility, and a code of honor that saw many a duel between dashing gentlemen. Certainly, the historic architecture along the Antebellum Trail would endorse this picture, and even though many of the white-column mansions were built with the sweat of slaves, there is much to appreciate. Anchored between Macon and Athens, the trail was designated a state trail in 1985, and links the historical communities of Watkinsville, Madison, Eatonton, Milledgeville, and Old Clinton, all of which escaped the rampages of General Sherman's army on his march in 1864 from Atlanta to Savannah.

## MACON

*85 miles southeast of Atlanta via I–75.*

At the state's geographic center, Macon, founded in 1823, has more than 100,000 flowering cherry trees, which it celebrates each March with a knockout festival. With 5,500 individual structures listed on the National Register of Historic Places, its antebellum and Victorian homes are among the state's best preserved, and an ongoing program of restoration is revitalizing the downtown core. Following a $1.2 million restoration, the Capitol Theatre (originally founded as a bank in 1897) is open for movies and concerts; after a three-year renovation, St. Joseph's Catholic Church is more impressive than ever; and the old Armory, complete with its first-floor dance hall, is finding new life as an office and retail complex.

Daily news is reported in the *Telegraph. The Georgia Informer, The 11th Hour,* and the upscale *Macon Magazine* are good sources of information on local arts and cultural events.

### GETTING HERE AND AROUND

Poet Raymond Farr, in his piece "Back Roads to Macon," writes of a cozy roadside diner, the sprawling farmland, and a folksy bit of wisdom scrawled on a mailbox in the nearby town of Cordele: "Whatever your destination, thank God you arrive." These kinds of small touches add charm to the back roads to Macon. Or, for a speedier and somewhat less scenic route, jump on U.S. 441.

### ESSENTIALS

**Visitor Information Macon-Bibb County Convention and Visitors Bureau** ✉ *450 Martin Luther King Jr. Blvd.* ☎ *478/743–1074, 800/768–3401* 🌐 *www.maconga.org.*

## EXPLORING

### TOP ATTRACTIONS

★ **Hay House.** Designed by the New York firm T. Thomas & Son in the mid-1800s, Hay House is a study in fine Italianate architecture prior to the Civil War. The marvelous stained-glass windows and many technological advances, including indoor plumbing, make a tour worthwhile. The home's dining room has recently been restored to its 1870s appearance. ✉ *934 Georgia Ave.* ☎ *478/742–8155* 🌐 *www.hayhouse.org* 🎟 *$9* 🕒 *Mon.–Sat. 10–4, Sun. 1–3.*

**Ocmulgee National Monument.** Located 3 miles east of downtown Macon, Ocmulgee is a significant archaeological site. It was occupied for more than 10,000 years; at its peak, between AD 900 and AD 1100, it was populated by the Mississippian peoples. There's a reconstructed earth lodge and displays of pottery, effigies, and jewelry of copper and shells discovered in the burial mound. ✉ *1207 Emery Hwy., take U.S. 80 E* ☎ *478/752–8257* 🌐 *www.nps.gov/ocmu* 🎫 *Free* 🕒 *Daily 9–5.*

**ON THE TRAIL**

A meander along the new **Ocmulgee Heritage Trail** is a delightful diversion. The trailhead is at Gateway Park, at the corner of MLK Boulevard and Riverside Drive. The trail connects the Ocmulgee National Monument along the river to a park and recreation area at the old Macon Waterworks.

★ **Tubman African American Museum.** This museum honors Harriet Tubman, the former slave who led more than 300 people to freedom as one of the conductors of the Underground Railroad. A mural depicts several centuries of black culture. Permanent galleries are focused on African American history, Middle Georgia history, and fine arts. Rotating exhibits showcase African American arts and culture. ✉ *340 Walnut St.* ☎ *478/743–8544* 🌐 *www.tubmanmuseum.com* 🎫 *$8* 🕒 *Tues.–Fri. 9–5, Sat. 11–4.*

### WORTH NOTING

**Georgia Sports Hall of Fame.** With its old-style ticket booths, this shrine to Georgia sports has the look and feel of an old ballpark. Exhibits include a variety of interactive, touch-screen kiosks, and honor sports—including baseball, golf, track and field, and football—at all levels, from prep and college teams to professional. It's open only for group tours on Monday. ✉ *301 Cherry St.* ☎ *478/752–1585* 🌐 *www.gshf.org* 🎫 *$8* 🕒 *Tues.–Sat. 9–5.*

**Macon Museum of Arts and Sciences and Mark Smith Planetarium.** Displaying everything from a whale skeleton to fine art, this museum appeals to adults and children alike. The Discovery House, an interactive exhibit for children, is modeled after an artist's garret. ✉ *4182 Forsyth Rd.* ☎ *478/477–3232* 🌐 *www.masmacon.com* 🎫 *$10* 🕒 *Tues.–Sat. 10–5, Sun. 1–5.*

**Sidney Lanier Cottage.** America has more tributes to Sidney Lanier, famous poet and musician of the Old South, than the years he lived. And it all starts at his birthplace, this charming 1840 structure that features much of Lanier's writings among the period furnishings. Even his bride's tiny wedding gown is on show. Lanier died of tuberculosis at 39 after he was captured during the Civil War. ✉ *935 High St.* ☎ *478/743–3851* 🌐 *www.historicmacon.org* 🎫 *$5* 🕒 *Mon.–Sat. 10–4.*

OFF THE BEATEN PATH

**Museum of Aviation.** This museum at Robins Air Force Base has an extraordinary collection of 90 vintage aircraft and missiles, including a MiG, an SR-71 (Blackbird), a U-2, and assorted other flying machines from past campaigns. From Macon take Interstate 75 south to Exit 146 (Centerville/Warner Robins) and turn left onto Watson Boulevard, 7

Ocmulgee National Monument, just outside of Macon, includes a reconstructed meeting place, the Earth Lodge, and artifacts of the Mississippian peoples who lived here 1,000 years ago.

miles to Route 247/U.S. 129, then right for 2 miles. ✉ *Rte. 247/U.S. 129 at Russell Pkwy., 20 miles south of Macon, Warner Robins* ☎ *478/926 6870* 🌐 *www.museumofaviation.org* 🎟 *Free* ⏲ *Daily 9–5.*

## WHERE TO EAT AND STAY

*Hotel reviews have been abbreviated in this book. For expanded reviews, please go to Fodors.com.*

$$$ AMERICAN ✕ **Downtown Grill.** In the heart of a city block of renovated warehouses, this popular restaurant can be hard to find. But it's well worth the search. The old Georgian brick gives a romantic flair to the decor, and the menu has many classic favorites such as pork tenderloin, filet mignon, and a tasty mixed grill with options for fish lovers and vegetarians. Be prepared to walk a block; the approach alleys aren't always accessible by car. $ *Average main: $24* ✉ *562 Mulberry St. La.* ☎ *478/742–5999* 🌐 *www.macondowntowngrill.com* ⏲ *Closed Sun.*

$$$$ AMERICAN ✕ **Tic Toc Room.** Upscale and stylish, this downtown restaurant serves New American fare with Asian and Italian influences. Sushi is a staple of the menu, which includes such dishes as tuna-spinach rolls. Don't pass up signature dishes like smoked chicken ravioli. At the bar, which is open late into the evening, martinis are a favorite. Perhaps the coolest thing about the Tic Toc Room is its history. The building was once home to Anne's Tic Toc, a popular 1950s nightclub where Little Richard, James Brown, and Otis Redding performed. $ *Average main: $25* ✉ *408 Martin Luther King Jr. Blvd.* ☎ *478/744–0123* ⏲ *Closed Sun.*

$$ B&B/INN 🏨 **1842 Inn.** With its white-pillar front porch and period antiques, it's easy to see why this place is considered to be one of the region's top inns. **Pros:** a taste of antebellum grandeur. **Cons:** no suites available.

CLOSE UP

## Flannery O'Connor

Novelist and short-story writer Flannery O'Connor is one of Milledgeville's most famous residents. The author of novels *Wise Blood* and *The Violent Bear It Away* spent the last 13 years of her life at her family farm just north of town.

**Andalusia.** A picturesque farm with peacocks, a pond, and a lofty barn, Andalusia inspired much of Flannery O'Connor's work. The 1850s farmhouse, untouched since her death in 1964, provides incredible insight into the life of this prolific writer. The home and grounds are open for self-guided tours, and the gift shop sells her books and other memorabilia. ✉ *2628 N. Columbia St.* ☎ *478/445–4391* 🌐 *www.andalusiafarm.org* 🎫 *$5 (suggested donation)* 🕙 *Mon., Tues., and Thurs.–Sat. 10–4.*

**Flannery O'Connor Room.** Fans of Southern literature will want to visit the Flannery O'Connor Room at Georgia College and State University's Museum. Many of the author's handwritten manuscripts and a few furniture items are on display. A highlight is viewing the typewriter where she wrote many of her famous tales. ✉ *221 N. Clarke St., Milledgeville* ☎ *478/445–4391* 🌐 *www.gcsu.edu/library/museum* 🎫 *Free* 🕙 *Mon.–Sat. 10–4.*

**Memory Hill Cemetery.** Flannery O'Connor, who suffered from lupus and died at age 39, is buried at historic Memory Hill Cemetery Literary scholars from around the world come here to pay their respects. ✉ *300 W. Franklin St.*

---

💲 *Rooms from: $189* ✉ *353 College St.* ☎ *478/741–1842, 800/336–1842* 🌐 *www.1842inn.com* 🛏 *19 rooms* 🍴 *Breakfast.*

$ B&B/INN **Henderson Village.** At this retreat, 38 miles south of Macon, you can find stunning 19th- and early-20th-century Southern homes and refurbished tenant cottages clustered around a green. **Pros:** the 1838 Langston House restaurant has three dining rooms and a lovely glassed-in veranda. **Cons:** no fitness center on-site. 💲 *Rooms from: $130* ✉ *125 S. Langston Circle, Perry* ☎ *478/988–8696, 888/615–9722* 🌐 *www.hendersonvillage.com* 🛏 *19 rooms, 5 suites* 🍴 *Breakfast.*

## MILLEDGEVILLE

*32 miles northeast of Macon on GA 49.*

Locals believe ghosts haunt what remains of the antebellum homes in Milledgeville. Laid out as the state capital of Georgia in 1803 (a title it held until Atlanta assumed the role in 1868), the town was not as fortunate as Madison in escaping being torched during the Civil War. Sherman's troops stormed through here with a vengeance after the general heard hardship stories from Union soldiers who had escaped from a prisoner-of-war camp in nearby Andersonville. Quite a few antebellum buildings remain, including the Old Governor's Mansion and old statehouse.

### GETTING HERE AND AROUND

Travel by car to Milledgeville, then park and hop aboard the Milledgeville Trolley Tour. This red coach will take you through the city's landmark historic district, with stops at such spots as the Old Governor's Mansion and the Stetson-Sanford House. The tour leaves from the Convention & Visitors Bureau and is available weekdays at 10 and Saturday at 2 for $12.

### ESSENTIALS

**Visitor Information Milledgeville Convention & Visitors Bureau** ✉ *200 W. Hancock St.* ☎ *478/452–4687, 800/653–1804* 🌐 *www.milledgevillecvb.com.*

## EXPLORING



**Georgia's Old Capital Museum.** Located on the ground floor of the Old State Capitol, this museum tells the story of Milledgeville and the surrounding region from prehistory to post Civil War. A great deal of community pride has gone into this museum, and the majority of its artifacts came from local residents. The Gothic structure, unusual for a statehouse of its time, was built in 1807. Take a peek upstairs at the recently restored legislative chamber. ✉ *201 E. Greene St.* ☎ *478/453–1803* 🌐 *www.oldcapitalmuseum.org* *$5.50* *Tues.–Fri. 10–4, Sat. noon–4.*

★ **Old Governor's Mansion.** This grand 1838 Greek Revival mansion became Sherman's headquarters during the war. His soldiers are said to have tossed government documents out of the windows and fueled their fires with Confederate money. Home to 10 Georgian governors, the mansion has undergone a painstaking $10 million restoration. Guided tours of the building, now a museum, are given daily, on the hour. A special tour, "Labor Behind the Veil," highlights the daily lives of slaves in the mansion, and is available by request with advanced reservation. ✉ *120 S. Clark St.* ☎ *478/445–4545* 🌐 *www.gscu.edu/mansion* *$10* *Tues.–Sat. 10–4, Sun. 2–4.*

## WHERE TO EAT AND STAY

*Hotel reviews have been abbreviated in this book. For expanded reviews, please go to Fodors.com.*

$ PIZZA ✕ **The Brick.** This eatery has a comfortable, worn-at-the-elbows appeal—which is all-important when you're about to consume massive pizzas with tasty toppings like feta cheese and spinach. Vegetarians will appreciate the "environmentally correct" pizza platter with its all-vegetable topping. The menu's pasta selection boasts endless combinations, and also offers salads and calzones. [$] *Average main: $9* ✉ *136 W. Hancock St.* ☎ *478/452–0089* 🌐 *www.thebrick.info.*

$ B&B/INN **Antebellum Inn.** Each room in this pre–Civil War mansion has beautiful period antiques. **Pros:** excellent home-cooked breakfasts; Southern hospitality at its best. **Cons:** books up quickly. [$] *Rooms from: $139* ✉ *200 N. Columbia St.* ☎ *478/453–3993* 🌐 *www.antebelluminn.com* *5 rooms, 1 cottage* *Breakfast.*

# EATONTON

*20 miles north of Milledgeville on U.S. 129/441.*

Right in the middle of the Antebellum Trail, Eatonton is a historic trove of houses that still retains the rare Southern antebellum architecture that survived Sherman's torches. But this isn't the only source of pride for this idyllic town. Take a look at the courthouse lawn; it's not your imagination—that really is a giant statue of a rabbit.

The **Eatonton-Putnam Chamber of Commerce** provides printed maps detailing landmarks from the upbringing of Eatonton native Alice Walker, who won the Pulitzer Prize for her novel *The Color Purple*. It also has information on the many fine examples of antebellum architecture in Eatonton, including descriptions and photographs of the town's prize antebellum mansions, and a walking tour of Victorian homes.

### GETTING HERE AND AROUND

As with most cities along the Antebellum Trail, Eatonton is best reached by car. As you travel there via U.S. 441, check out the scenic views of pastures, mountain valleys, and rivers.

### ESSENTIALS

**Visitor Information Eatonton-Putnam Chamber of Commerce** ✉ *Plaza Arts Center, 305 N. Madison Ave.* ☎ *706/485–7701* 🌐 *www.eatonton.com.*

## EXPLORING

★ **Uncle Remus Museum.** Eatonton is the birthplace of celebrated novelist Joel Chandler Harris, of Br'er Rabbit and Uncle Remus fame. This museum, built from authentic slave cabins, houses countless carvings, paintings, first-edition books, and other artwork depicting the characters made famous by the imaginative author. It's on the grounds of a park. Note the museum closes for lunch from 12–1 daily, so plan your visit accordingly. ✉ *Turner Park, U.S. 441, 214 Oak St.* ☎ *706/485–6856* 🌐 *www.uncleremusmuseum.org* 🎟 *$3* 🕐 *Mon.–Sat. 10–12 and 1–5, Sun. 2–5. Closed some Tuesdays, call ahead.*

## SPORTS AND THE OUTDOORS

Eatonton sits in the center of Georgia's Lake Country. Lake Oconee and Lake Sinclair, both created and maintained by Georgia Power, are nearby.

**Lake Sinclair Recreational Area.** The site of an annual fishing tournament, Lake Sinclair is a favorite of anglers. Georgia Power maintains several parks with boat ramps, fishing piers, and campgrounds. About 11 miles from Eatonton, Lake Sinclair Recreational Area, maintained by the U.S. Forestry Service, has a beach, boat ramp, and campsites. ✉ *Twin Bridges Rd., Eatonton* ☎ *770/297–3000* 🌐 *www.fs.usda.gov.*

**Lawrence Shoals Park.** On the shores of Lake Oconee, the second-largest body of water in Georgia, Lawrence Shoals Park offers a boat ramp, beach area, picnic shelter, and camping facilities. ✉ *123 Wallace Dam Rd., Eatonton* ☎ *706/485–5494* 🌐 *www.georgiapower.com/lakes.*

Spend an afternoon strolling through Eatonton's historic district, which is full of antebellum homes.

## MADISON

*22 miles north of Eatonton on U.S. 129/144.*

In 1809 Madison was described as "the most cultured and aristocratic town on the stagecoach route from Charleston to New Orleans," and today, that charm still prevails, in large part because General Sherman's Union Army deliberately bypassed the town, thus saving it for posterity. From the picturesque town square, with its specialty shops and businesses, you can walk to any number of antebellum and other residences that make up one of the largest designated historic areas in Georgia.

### ESSENTIALS

**Visitor Information Madison/Morgan County Chamber of Commerce** ✉ *115 E. Jefferson St.* ☎ *706/342–4454, 800/709–7406* 🌐 *www.madisonga.org.*

### EXPLORING

★ **Heritage Hall.** Madison is the historic heart of Georgia, and although many of the lovely homes are privately owned, this Greek Revival mansion, circa 1811, is open to the public. Rooms are furnished in the 19th-century style and are an elegant insight as to the lifestyle of an average well-to-do family. Combo tickets are available to tour Heritage Hall along with two other historic homes within walking distance. ✉ *277 S. Main St.* ☎ *706/342–9627* 🌐 *www.friendsofheritagehall.org* 💵 *$7* 🕐 *Mon.–Sat. 11–4, Sun. 1:30–4:30.*

**Madison-Morgan Cultural Center.** This 1895 Romanesque Revival building was one of the first brick schools in the area. A museum features a restored 1895 classroom and a replica of an antebellum-era parlor. There are also art galleries and other exhibits. ✉ *434 S. Main St.* ☎ *706/342–4743* 🌐 *www.mmcc-arts.org* *$3* *Tues.–Sat. 10–5, Sun. 2–5.*

## WHERE TO EAT AND STAY

*Hotel reviews have been abbreviated in this book. For expanded reviews, please go to Fodors.com.*

$$ AMERICAN **Madison ChopHouse Grille.** Popular with locals, this casual eatery in the heart of the downtown shopping district is always busy. The menu offers bar-and-grill classics like sandwiches (called "sammies" here), burgers, steaks, and such Southern specialties as fried pork chops and ribs. While the bar is a focal point, it's a family-friendly joint. Everyone is rewarded with a Tootsie Pop at the end of the meal. *Average main: $15* ✉ *202 S. Main St.* ☎ *706/342–9009.*

$ SOUTHERN **Ye Olde Colonial Restaurant.** Housed in an old bank, this casual eatery is a Madison institution. Food is no-nonsense comfort for the soul—macaroni and cheese, fried chicken, barbecue pork, and squash casserole. Breakfast is quite popular, too. For fun, try to grab a seat in the original bank vault; its walls are plastered with money that was used back in 1867 to fund railroad construction after the war. *Average main: $7* ✉ *108 E. Washington St.* ☎ *706/342–2211* *Reservations not accepted* *Closed Sun. and Mon.*

$$ B&B/INN **The Farmhouse Inn.** On a sprawling plot, this inn offers 5 miles of wooded trails to explore, well-stocked ponds to fish, goats and chickens to feed, and a grassy picnic area to enjoy beside the Apalachee River. **Pros:** a great family destination. **Cons:** fills up often for weddings and events *Rooms from: $170* ✉ *1051 Meadow La.* ☎ *706/342–7933, 866/253–0023* 🌐 *www.thefarmhouseinn.com* *5 rooms, 1 house* *Breakfast.*

$$$ B&B/INN **The James Madison Inn.** In the heart of the historic district, this new building across from Town Park has rooms named for Madison's historic homes. **Pros:** comfortable lodging; excellent service. **Cons:** expensive for the size of the rooms. *Rooms from: $199* ✉ *260 W. Washington St.* ☎ *706/342–7040* 🌐 *www.jamesmadisoninn.com* *17 rooms, 2 suites* *Breakfast.*

## SPORTS AND THE OUTDOORS

**Southern Cross Guest Ranch.** A short drive from Madison you'll see miles of rolling pastures—an ideal landscape for horses. There are numerous horseback-riding outfits in the area, but one of the best is Southern Cross Guest Ranch. Located 7 miles outside Madison, it offers excursions for $40 to $70 per person. For the horse lovers who can't bear to leave, there are comfy bed-and-breakfast-style accommodations. The ranch offers all-inclusive packages, which include lodging, horseback riding, and meals starting at $180 per person, per night. ✉ *1670 Bethany Church Rd., Madison* ☎ *706/342–8027* 🌐 *www.southcross.com.*

# ATHENS

*30 miles northeast of Madison via U.S. 129/441; 70 miles east of Atlanta via I–85 north to Rte. 316.*

Athens, an artistic jewel of the American South, is known as a breeding ground for famed rock groups such as the B-52s and R.E.M. Because of this distinction, creative types from all over the country flock to its trendy streets in hopes of becoming, or catching a glimpse of, the next big act to take the world by storm. At the center of this artistic melee is the University of Georgia (UGA). With more than 30,000 students, UGA is an influential ingredient in the Athens mix, giving the quaint but compact city a distinct flavor that falls somewhere between a misty Southern enclave, a rollicking college town, and a smoky, jazz club–studded alleyway. Of course, this all goes "to the Dawgs" if the home team is playing on home turf; although, even then, Athens remains a truly fascinating blend of Mayberry R.F.D. and MTV. The effect is as irresistible as it is authentic.

To find out what's on in Athens, check out the *Athens Banner-Herald* (daily) and the weekly *Flagpole*.

14

### GETTING HERE AND AROUND

Parking can be scarce on the city streets. Leave yourself extra time to find a spot, then take in the city and its shopping, nightlife, campus, and culture on foot.

The Athens Welcome Center runs historic tours of downtown and surrounding neighborhoods daily at 2 pm. Tours are 90 minutes long and $15 per person.

### ESSENTIALS

**Visitor Information Athens Convention & Visitors Bureau** ✉ *300 N. Thomas St.* ☎ *706/357–4430, 800/653–0603* 🌐 *www.visitathensga.com.*

### TOURS

**Athens Food Tours.** Athens is not a small town when it comes to food. Downtown alone boasts 55 eateries. To sample some of Athen's best cuisine, contact Athens Food Tours. Offered five times a week, the tours focus on specific neighborhoods such as Normaltown, Downtown, and Five Points, and feature stops at five or six locally owned, uniquely Athens eateries. ☎ *706/338–8054* 🌐 *www.athensfoodtours.com.*

## EXPLORING

**Church-Waddel-Brumby House.** The streets of Athens are lined with many gorgeous old homes, some of which are open to the public. Most prominent among them is the Federal-style Church-Waddel-Brumby

### ROOTED IN HISTORY

In Athens the large white oak at the corner of Dearing and Finely streets, surrounded by an enclosure of granite posts and an iron chain, is the **Tree That Owns Itself**. The original tree, which fell in 1942, was granted emancipation by Colonel W. H. Jackson, who wrote: "For and in consideration of the great love I bear this tree and the great desire I have for its protection for all time, I convey entire possession of itself and the land within eight feet of it on all sides." The current tree was grown from an acorn of the original.

A concert at the State Botanical Gardens of Georgia.

House. Built in 1820, it is the town's oldest surviving residence. The museum is home to the Athens Welcome Center, where you can pick up information and arrange for tours. ✉ *280 E. Dougherty St.* ☎ *706/353–1820* 🌐 *www.athenswelcomecenter.com.*

**Georgia Museum of Art.** On the campus of the University of Georgia, the museum serves a dual purpose as an academic institution and the official public art museum of the state of Georgia. The permanent collection contains a wealth of 19th- and 20th-century paintings—some from noted American artists like Georgia O'Keefe and Winslow Homer. It also houses a portion of the Samuel H. Kress Study Collection of Italian Renaissance art. Special exhibitions display cherished works of art from around the world. ✉ *90 Carlton St., University of Georgia* ☎ *706/542–4662* 🌐 *www.georgiamuseum.org* 🎟 *Free, suggested donation $3* ⏲ *Tue.–Wed. and Fri.–Sat. 10–4:45, Thu. 10–8:45, Sun. 1–4:45.*

Fodor's Choice ★ **State Botanical Gardens of Georgia.** Just outside the Athens city limits, you'll find this tranquil, 313-acre wonderland of aromatic gardens and woodland paths. It has a massive conservatory overlooking the **International Garden** that functions as a welcome foyer and houses an art gallery, gift shop, and cafÈ. ✉ *2450 S. Milledge Ave., off U.S. 129/441* ☎ *706/542–1244* 🌐 *www.uga.edu/botgarden* 🎟 *Free* ⏲ *Grounds: Apr.–Sept., daily 8–8; Oct.–Mar., daily 8–6. Visitor center: Tues.–Sat. 9–4:30, Sun. 11:30–4:30.*

**Taylor-Grady House.** Constructed in 1844, the Taylor-Grady House gives a fine sense of history. It has been restored to its 1860s appearance to accurately represent the time when Henry Grady resided there. Grady, a famed newspaper man and booster of the "New South," lived here while he attended the University of Georgia. ✉ *634 Prince Ave.* ☎ *706/549–8688* 🌐 *www.taylorgradyhouse.com* 🎫 *$3* ⏲ *Mon., Wed., and Fri. 9–3, Tues. and Thurs. 9–1* ⏲ *Closed weekends.*

**T. R. R. Cobb House.** Once home to a key author of the Confederate Constitution, T. R. R. Cobb, this historic home has had quite a journey. The Greek Revival structure, with its signature octagonal wings, stands about two blocks from its original location. The house was moved in the 1980s to Stone Mountain, where it sat untouched for 20 years. In 2005, the house was moved back to Athens and meticulously restored. Now open to the public, it details 19th-century Southern life. ✉ *175 Hill St.* ☎ *706/369–3513* 🌐 *www.trrcobbhouse.org* 🎫 *Free* ⏲ *Tues.–Sat. 10–4.*



**University of Georgia.** Athens has several splendid Greek Revival buildings, including two on campus: the **university chapel** built in 1832, just off North Herty Drive, and the **university president's house** that was built in the late 1850s. Easiest access to the campus in downtown Athens is off Broad Street onto either Jackson or Thomas streets, both of which run through the heart of the university. Maps are available at the visitor center. ✉ *570 Prince Ave.*

## WHERE TO EAT

$$ ECLECTIC

✕ **East–West Bistro.** This popular bistro—one of the busiest spots downtown—has a bar, formal dining upstairs, and casual dining downstairs. The most interesting selections downstairs are the small plates that allow you to sample cuisines from around the world—from wasabi-crusted tilapia to salmon in rice paper to roasted-garlic pork chop. The room upstairs is much quieter, and the booths are very romantic. 💲 *Average main: $20* ✉ *351 E. Broad St.* ☎ *706/546–9378* 🌐 *www.eastwestbistro.com.*

$$$ AMERICAN Fodor's Choice ★

✕ **Farm 255.** Many restaurants talk about "farm to table," but Farm 255 actually lives it. Most of the staff also works at the restaurant's organic farm outside town. The result is amazingly fresh, seasonal dishes simply prepared. The airy dining room and open kitchen are in keeping with the restaurant's philosophy of reconnecting people with their food. The menu changes frequently, but two staples are the harvest plate featuring the day's best vegetables, and the burger made from the farm's own grass-fed beef. 💲 *Average main: $21* ✉ *255 W. Washington St.* ☎ *706/549–4660* 🌐 *www.farm255.com* ⏲ *Closed Mon.*

$$$$ ECLECTIC Fodor's Choice ★

✕ **Five & Ten.** Ottawa native Hugh Acheson honed his culinary skills in classical French kitchens in Ontario and San Francisco before opening this cozy restaurant just south of downtown in 2000. His blending of European cuisine with down-home Southern cooking has garnered numerous regional and national accolades, including a James Beard award. The seasonal menu draws from local sources and includes updated Southern classics such as pimento cheese crostini; watermelon salad with feta cheese and pickled watermelon rind; veal sweetbreads with Red Mule grits custard and succotash; and Lowcountry Frogmore stew with shrimp, Andouille sausage, fingerling potatoes, and corn in a tomato-leek broth. Sunday brunch is served 10:30–2:30. 💲 *Average main: $26* ✉ *1653 S. Lumpkin St.* ☎ *706/546–7300* 🌐 *www.fiveandten.com* ✍ *Reservations essential* ⏲ *No lunch.*

$ VEGETARIAN ★ ✕ **The Grit.** This vegetarian paradise has been a favorite in Athens for more than two decades, serving freshly made non-meat food even carnivores adore in the casual comfort of a historic building. A popular dish of browned tofu cubes and brown rice may sound bland, but it's far from it—even the tofu-fearful say it's yummy. Pick up the cookbook for 130 of The Grit's best dishes. *Average main: $7 ✉ 199 Prince Ave. ☎ 706/543–6592 www.thegrit.com Reservations not accepted.*

AN ONION A DAY

Although they originated in Vidalia, about 90 miles southeast of Macon, Vidalia onions are grown throughout Central Georgia. Because of unique soil conditions, the onions are so sweet you can eat them like apples. Watch for them on menus and at roadside stands.

$$ AMERICAN ✕ **Last Resort Grill.** A favorite of locals and tourists alike, the Last Resort is popular for Sunday brunch. EntrÈes like crab cakes, stuffed French toast, and breakfast enchiladas please a variety of palettes. Lunch and dinner are equally appealing, featuring Southern cooking with a Southwestern and Mediterranean bent. Exposed brick walls create a cozy bistro feel. Reminders of the building's history as a 1970s music club line the walls. The restaurant does not accept reservations, but you can call ahead for priority seating. *Average main: $14 ✉ 174–184 W. Clayton St. ☎ 706/549–0810 www.lastresortgrill.com Reservations not accepted.*

$$$ AMERICAN ✕ **The National.** Little sister to widely acclaimed Five and Ten, the National is more casual, evoking the atmosphere of a European café. The kitchen produces Mediterranean-inspired dishes that make creative use of local ingredients. Prosciutto-wrapped grilled figs, cucumber gazpacho, and grilled hanger steak with panzanella salad are a few favorites. Wine is a focus at the bar, with flights available for those craving variety. Prix-fixe "dinner and a movie" deals offered in conjunction with the cinema next door are a steal. *Average main: $24 ✉ 232 W. Hancock Ave. ☎ 706/549–3450 www.thenationalrestaurant.com.*

### WHERE TO STAY

*Hotel reviews have been abbreviated in this book. For expanded reviews, please go to Fodors.com.*

$ HOTEL **Best Western Athens.** A half mile from the UGA campus, this hotel is a favorite among relatives who come to attend graduation. **Pros:** friendly staff; good value. **Cons:** long walk to downtown. *Rooms from: $70 ✉ 170 N. Milledge Ave. ☎ 706/546–7311 www.bestwestern.com 70 rooms Breakfast.*

$$ HOTEL **Hotel Indigo.** Sleek and modern, Hotel Indigo is downtown Athen's newest accommodation. **Pros:** spacious guest rooms; large bathrooms; pet-friendly. **Cons:** fee for parking; pet-friendly aspect may not appeal to all. *Rooms from: $159 ✉ 500 College Avenue ☎ 706/546–0430 www.indigoathens.com 117 rooms, 13 suites.*

$ HOTEL **The Foundry Park Inn.** More than a hotel, this boutique village includes luxury rooms, a full-service spa, two restaurants, and a lively nightclub. **Pros:** quaint setup; great bar and club. **Cons:** live music at The Melting Point, the nightime restaurant and bar, can bring a late crowd. *Rooms* *from: $135* ✉ *295 E. Dougherty St.* ☎ *706/549–7020, 866/928–4367* 🌐 *www.foundryparkinn.com* *113 rooms, 5 suites.*

EN ROUTE

Along U.S. 78 you'll find **Washington,** a picturesque community that exudes a bustling turn-of-the-last-century charm and is a great stopover en route to Augusta. The first city chartered in honor of the country's first president, Washington is a living museum of Southern culture. Brick buildings, some of which date to the American Revolution, line the lively downtown area, which bustles with people visiting cafÈs and antiques shops. The Confederate treasury was moved here from Richmond in 1865, and soon afterward the half-million dollars in gold vanished. This mysterious event has been the inspiration for numerous treasure hunts, as many like to believe the gold is still buried somewhere in Wilkes County.

**Callaway Plantation.** Be sure to stop by historic Callaway Plantation, 4 miles west of downtown Washington. Here, at a site dating to 1785, you can experience the closest thing to an operating plantation. Among a cluster of buildings on the estate you can find a blacksmith's house, schoolhouse, and weaving house. An ancient family cemetery is also fun to explore. During the second week of both April and October the estate comes alive with Civil War reenactments and activities such as butter-churning and quilting demonstrations. ✉ *U.S. 78, Washington* ☎ *706/678–7060* *$4* *Tues.–Sat. 10–5.*

14

# AUGUSTA

*97 miles southeast of Athens via GA 10 and I–20; 150 miles east of Atlanta via I–20.*

Although Augusta escaped the ravages of Union troops during the Civil War, nature itself was not so kind. On a crossing of the Savannah River, the town was flooded many times before modern-day city planning redirected the water into a collection of small lakes and creeks. Now the current is so mild that citizens gather to send bathtub toys downstream every year in the annual Rubber Duck Race.

Check out the *Augusta Daily Chronicle* and the *Metro Spirit* for up-to-the-minute information of what's going on in town.

## GETTING HERE AND AROUND

Explore this part of the classic South via car, then park to wander the streets full of shops and restaurants. You can also canoe on the river or along the 1845 tree-lined Augusta Canal, a natural habitat for herons and other birds.

The Augusta Cotton Exchange (also known as the Augusta Convention & Visitors Bureau) conducts free tours of its historic brick building, with exhibits from its past as an arbiter of cotton prices. It also has Saturday trolley tours throughout the historic district of Augusta ($12).

## ESSENTIALS

**Visitor Information Augusta Convention & Visitors Bureau** ✉ *560 Reynolds St.* ☎ *706/724–4067, 877/284–8782* 🌐 *www.augustaga.org.*

## EXPLORING

### TOP ATTRACTIONS

**Augusta Canal Interpretive Center.** Housed in a converted mill, this museum traces Augusta's important role in developing Georgia's textile industry. The looms are still powered by the building's original turbines (which you can see in action); they also provide the power to juice up the museum's Petersburg canal boats. Tours of the **canal,** usually one hour long, start here and are a fascinating trip through history. Guides are well versed in the passing sights, which include assorted wildlife, a working 19th-century textile mill, and two of Georgia's only remaining 18th-century houses. ✉ *1450 Greene St.* ☎ *706/823–0440* 🌐 *www.augustacanal.com* 🎟 *$6 admission only, $12.50 with boat tour* ⏲ *Apr.–Nov., Mon.–Sat. 9:30–5:30, Sun. 1–5:30; Dec.–Mar., Tue.–Sat. 9:30–5:30.*

**Augusta Riverwalk.** The well-maintained pathways of the Riverwalk (between 5th and 10th streets) curve along the Savannah River and are the perfect place for a leisurely stroll. The upper brick portion connects downtown attractions like St. Paul's Church and the Morris Museum of Art. There are a few shops and restaurants along the way, but not as many as you might expect. On Saturday mornings between April and November, look out for the Saturday River Market at the 8th Street Plaza. The lower paths offer a close-up of wildlife and a peek at the graceful homes of North Augusta, South Carolina. ✉ *5th to 10th Sts.*

**Morris Museum of Southern Art.** This is a splendid collection of Southern art, from early landscapes, antebellum portraits, and Civil War art through neo-impressionism and modern contemporary art. In March 2010, the museum reopened after extensive renovation, revealing refreshed galleries with new installations. ✉ *Riverfront Center, 1 10th St., 2nd fl.* ☎ *706/724–7501* 🌐 *www.themorris.org* 🎟 *$5* ⏲ *Tues.–Sat. 10–5, Sun. noon–5.*

### WORTH NOTING

**Meadow Garden.** Augusta's oldest residence, Meadow Garden was the home of George Walton, one of Georgia's three signers of the Declaration of Independence. At age 26, he was its youngest signer. ✉ *1320 Independence Dr.* ☎ *706/724–4174* 🌐 *www.historicmeadowgarden.org* 🎟 *$4* ⏲ *Weekdays 10–4, weekends by appointment.*

**Olde Town.** Along Telfair and Greene streets, Olde Town is a restored neighborhood of Victorian homes, although many are still very much works in progress. A drive along Olde Town's streets provides a glimpse of many popular 19th-century architectural styles. ✉ *Telfair and Greene Sts.*

## WHERE TO EAT AND STAY

*Hotel reviews have been abbreviated in this book. For expanded reviews, please go to Fodors.com.*

$ AMERICAN **Boll Weevil Cafe and Sweetery.** Named for the insect that ruined the cotton industry, this quirky little café offers some of the best desserts in Augusta. Step inside the former warehouse and you'll find a pastry case filled with at least 30 decadent desserts, all made on the premises. Of course, there are savory items on the menu as well. Sandwiches on fresh-baked bread and seafood bisque are crowd-pleasers. The vibe here is low-key and relaxed—perfect for lunch or a casual dinner. *Average main: $12 10 James Brown Blvd. 706/722–7772 www.thebollweevil.com.*

$$$$ EUROPEAN **La Maison on Telfair.** Augusta's finest restaurant, operated by chef-owner Heinz Sowinski, presents a classic menu of game, sweetbreads, and, with a nod to the chef's heritage, Wiener schnitzel. The experience is enhanced by the quiet and elegant room. The wine and tapas bar is more casual. *Average main: $28 404 Telfair St. 706/722–4805 www.lamaisontelfair.com Reservations essential Closed Sun. No lunch.*

$$ HOTEL **Augusta Marriott at the Convention Center.** Just off the Riverwalk, the Marriott is the city's only full-service downtown hotel. **Pros:** excellent location; prompt and courteous service. **Cons:** large and confusing layout. *Rooms from: $159 2 10th St. 706/722–8900 www.marriott.com 349 rooms, 23 suites.*

$ HOTEL **Partridge Inn.** A National Trust Historic Hotel, this restored inn sits at the gateway to Summerville, a hilltop neighborhood of summer homes dating to 1800. **Pros:** excellent breakfast buffet; lovely atmosphere. **Cons:** lots of stairs and occasionally uneven floors. *Rooms from: $129 2110 Walton Way 706/737–8888, 800/476–6888 www.partridgeinn.com 134 rooms, 12 suites, 1 penthouse.*

## SPORTS AND THE OUTDOORS

### GOLF

**Masters Tournament.** In early April, Augusta hosts the much-celebrated annual Masters Tournament, one of pro golf's most distinguished events. It's broadcast in 180 countries. Tickets for actual tournament play are extremely limited for the general public, but you can try to get tickets for one of the practice rounds earlier in the week—which, for golf addicts, is still hugely entertaining.

The Augusta National Golf Club, home of the Masters Tournament, is known for its exclusivity. Membership is handed down through families, so unless you know someone, you aren't going to get to play there, much less get a glimpse of the grounds. However, there are plenty of other golf courses in this golfer's town. *www.masters.com.*

**Masters Tournament Practice Rounds office.** Masters Tournament practice-round tickets are awarded on a lottery basis; apply online at *www.masters.com* by July 30 of the year preceding the tournament.

14

**Forest Hills Golf Club.** Founded in 1926, Bobby Jones made his "grand slam of golf" here in 1930. The well-kept public course offers tee times seven days a week. *Augusta Magazine* continually names it the "Best Public Golf Course" in the area. Reservations are suggested. ✉ *1500 Comfort Rd.* ☎ *706/733–0001* 🌐 *www.theforesthillsgolfcourse.com* *18 holes. 7231 yds. Par 72. Green Fee: $35/$45* ☞ *Facilities: Driving range, putting green, pitching area, golf carts, pull carts, rental clubs, pro shop, lessons, restaurant.*

WORD OF MOUTH

"If someone were attending the Masters, I'd highly recommend the practice rounds, even over the actual tournament. The players are more relaxed and friendly. You can take all the photos you want when you want, and maybe even get an autograph or two, neither of which is permitted during the tournament. We camped out at the 16th, where the players attempt to skip their shots across the water and onto the green. Fun stuff that you'll never see at the tournament." —k9korps

## SWIMMING

**J. Strom Thurmond Lake.** Located 20 miles northwest of Augusta, 71,000-acre J. Strom Thurmond Lake is where locals head for swimming, boating, camping, and hiking. ✉ *510 Clarks Hill Hwy.* ☎ *800/533–3478* 🌐 *www.sas.usace.army.mil/lakes/thurmond.*

# Travel Smart Carolinas and Georgia

**WORD OF MOUTH**

"Because it is a major hub I would suggest [flying into] Atlanta. From Atlanta, go north on U.S. 19 into western North Carolina to see the mountains and forests. Head east through North Carolina through cities and the Piedmont until you come to the Outer Banks. See Kitty Hawk and Cape Hatteras lighthouse and anything else you want to see on the Outer Banks. From there, head south to Charleston by way of Myrtle Beach."

—tomfuller

# GETTING HERE AND AROUND

## AIR TRAVEL

Flying time to Atlanta is 4 hours from Los Angeles, 2 hours from New York, 2 hours from Chicago, 2 hours from Dallas, and 9 hours from London. By plane, Charlotte is an hour northeast of Atlanta, Raleigh 75 minutes northeast, Wilmington 1½ hours east, Asheville 1 hour north, and Charleston, Hilton Head, and Savannah an hour east–southeast.

Travelers flying into the Carolinas or Georgia are likely to pass through Hartsfield-Jackson Atlanta International Airport. It's by far the most popular airport in the region, and is the busiest in the world, at least in terms of number of passengers—more than 89 million annually.

**Airlines and Airports Airline and Airport Links.com** 🌐 *www.airlineandairportlinks.com.*

**Airline Security Issues Transportation Security Administration** 🌐 *www.tsa.gov.*

### AIRPORTS

The sheer number of flights at Hartsfield-Jackson Atlanta International Airport (ATL)—more than 2,500 arriving and departing flights daily—makes it an obvious, if sometimes hectic, choice. With some 250 concessionaires at the airport, it's easy to find a bite to eat or something to read, and Wi-Fi is available throughout, as are laptop plug-in stations. Hartsfield-Jackson has three interfaith chapels; the chapel in the domestic terminal Atrium is open from 6 am until 11 pm, and the chapels on concourses E and F are open 24 hours a day. A customer-service office and staffed customer-service desks answer questions. Waiting passengers can also check out museum exhibits throughout the airport, including a display of Martin Luther King Jr. memorabilia on International Concourse E. The brand new international terminal, Concourse F, has several art installations to explore. Smoking areas are located on Concourse B, C, E, F, and T. Overnight visitors can choose from 70 hotels and motels near the airport, most with free shuttle service. Give yourself extra time, as you'll have to tackle crowds whether waiting to buy a burger, get through security, or board the underground train to other concourses. The airport's website regularly updates estimates of waits at security areas and on-site parking areas. Arrive 90 minutes before a flight in the United States and allow two hours for international flights. Allow enough time to be at the gate 30 minutes before boarding. Those returning rental cars need to allow time for that process and a short ride on the ATL SkyTrain (to the domestic terminal) or a shuttle bus (to the international terminal) from the rental car center. Keep track of laptops and be ready to collect suitcases as soon as they arrive at the carousels for security's sake.

North Carolina's Charlotte Douglas International Airport (CLT), near the border of North Carolina and South Carolina, is a US Airways hub. Although not as vast as Hartsfield-Jackson, Charlotte Douglas is quite large, and its people-moving systems work well. Tired travelers can plop down in one of the trademark, handcrafted white rocking chairs in the Atrium, a tree-lined indoor crossroads between airport concourses that also offers a food court with mostly fast-food outlets. Within a few miles are more than a dozen hotels, most with free airport shuttles. In the center of the state, right off Interstate 40, is Raleigh-Durham International Airport (RDU), a prime gateway into central and eastern North Carolina. It sometimes feels like the airport is constantly under construction. With Terminal 2 completed, the airport is now embarking on a major construction project to modernize Terminal 1.

Those who live in the western reaches of the Triangle are just as likely to use the Piedmont Triad International Airport (GSO), at the convergence of four interstates in North Carolina. It primarily serves the Triad area—Greensboro, Winston-Salem, and High Point—as well as some cities in southwestern Virginia.

The portal to western North Carolina is Asheville Regional Airport (AVL), which recently expanded to include new amenities like boarding ramps, a gallery featuring regional art, and a guest-services center. It provides nonstop flights to Atlanta, Charlotte, Chicago, Fort Lauderdale, Detroit, Houston, New York, and Orlando.

For visits to the North Carolina coast, fly into Wilmington International Airport (ILM), a small facility with service by two carriers. Upstate South Carolina has the small but user-friendly Greenville–Spartanburg International Airport (GSP), which sometimes has lower fares than either the Charlotte or Asheville airports.

**Airport Information Asheville Regional Airport** ✉ *61 Terminal Dr., Fletcher* ☎ *828/684–2226* 🌐 *www.flyavl.com.* **Charlotte Douglas International Airport** ✉ *5501 Josh Birmingham Pkwy., Charlotte* ☎ *704/359–4000* 🌐 *www.charlotteairport.com.* **Greenville–Spartanburg International Airport** ✉ *2000 GSP Dr., Ste. 1, Greer* ☎ *864/877–7426* 🌐 *www.gspairport.com.* **Hartsfield-Jackson Atlanta International Airport** ✉ *6000 N. Terminal Pkwy., Atlanta, Georgia* ☎ *404/530–7300* 🌐 *www.atlanta-airport.com.* **Piedmont Triad International Airport** ✉ *1000 A Ted Johnson Pkwy., Greensboro* ☎ *336/665–5600* 🌐 *www.flyfrompti.com.* **Raleigh-Durham International Airport** ✉ *2400 John Brantley Blvd., Morrisville* ☎ *919/840–7700* 🌐 *www.rdu.com.* **Wilmington International Airport** ✉ *1740 Airport Blvd., Wilmington* ☎ *910/341–4125* 🌐 *www.flyilm.com.*

## GROUND TRANSPORTATION

Of all the airports in the region, only Hartsfield-Jackson Atlanta International is well served by public transportation. The Metropolitan Atlanta Rapid Transit Authority, better known as MARTA, has frequent service to and from the airport. It's the quickest, cheapest, and most hassle-free way into the city. MARTA's north–south line will get you downtown in 15 to 20 minutes for just $2.50. MARTA riders can also travel to Midtown, Buckhead, Sandy Springs, and Doraville—reaching into north suburban Atlanta. MARTA's Airport Station is located inside the terminal and can be accessed from the north and south sides of the terminal near the baggage claim area. Trains run weekdays 4:45 am to 1 am, and weekends and holidays 6 am to 1 am. Most trains operate every 15 to 20 minutes; during weekday rush hours, trains run every 10–15 minutes. You can print out a copy of the rail map before your trip from the MARTA website or pick one up at any station.

Express bus service is available between the Charlotte Transportation Center in Uptown Charlotte and Charlotte Douglas International Airport weekdays from 5:50 am to 12:02 am and on weekends 6 am to 1 am. The Triangle Transit Authority (TTA) has an airport bus-shuttle service that connects to Raleigh Durham International Airport, but the shuttle does not operate on Sunday. The airport shuttle meets TTA regional buses at the TTA Bus Center in Research Triangle Park.

Most of the airports in the region are served by taxi, limo, and shuttle services. Private limousine or van services also serve the major airports. In Atlanta, use only approved vehicles with the airport decal on the bumper, to ensure the drivers are charging legal fares and have knowledge of local destinations.

## TRANSFERS BETWEEN AIRPORTS

**Contacts Charlotte Area Transit System** ☎ *704/336–7433* 🌐 *www.charmeck.org.* **Metropolitan Atlanta Rapid Transit Authority** ☎ *404/848–5000* 🌐 *www.itsmarta.com.* **Triangle Transit Authority** ☎ *919/485–7433* 🌐 *www.triangletransit.org.*

### FLIGHTS

Hartsfield-Jackson Atlanta International Airport is the primary hub of Delta Airlines and a focus city for AirTran Airways and Southwest Airlines. At press time, Southwest was in the process of gradually taking over service on AirTran flights. Altogether, more than 30 domestic and international airlines, including their regional carriers, fly into Atlanta. US Airways has a hub at North Carolina's Charlotte Douglas International Airport, which is also served by more than a dozen other airlines. Raleigh-Durham International is not a hub for any carrier but is serviced by more than a dozen airlines. Commuter airlines, including US Airways Express, Delta Connection, American Eagle, and United Express have service between many smaller North Carolina airports as well as those in South Carolina. United Express also serves Georgia, New York, Washington, D.C., Chicago, and major Florida airports.

**Airline Contacts AirTran** ☎ *678/254–7999, 800/247–8726* 🌐 *www.airtran.com.* **American Airlines** ☎ *800/433–7300* 🌐 *www.aa.com.* **Continental Airlines** ☎ *800/523–3273 for U.S. reservations, 800/231–0856 for international reservations* 🌐 *www.continental.com.* **Delta Airlines** ☎ *800/221–1212 for U.S. reservations, 800/241–4141 for international reservations* 🌐 *www.delta.com.* **Southwest Airlines** ☎ *800/435–9792* 🌐 *www.southwest.com.* **USAirways** ☎ *800/428–4322 for U.S. and Canada reservations, 800/622–1015 for international reservations* 🌐 *www.usairways.com.*

## BIKE TRAVEL

Throughout coastal Georgia and the Carolinas, hills are few and the scenery remarkable. Many bike routes are marked on North Carolina's Outer Banks, around Savannah and Georgia's coastal islands, and in greater Charleston and coastal South Carolina's Lowcountry. Mountain bikers take to North Carolina's Great Smoky Mountains and the North Georgia mountains. Larger cities in the region, especially Atlanta, can prove difficult for getting around by bicycle. While bike paths are available, riding on streets is often necessary and can prove daunting.

DeLorme's *Atlas & Gazeteer* state maps, available in bike shops and drugstores, contain useful topographic detail. Many tourist boards and local bike clubs also distribute bike maps.

Websites can also be helpful. Southeastern Cycling (🌐 *www.sadlebred.com*) has information on road and trail riding throughout the Southeast and has free ride maps. Mountain Biking in Western North Carolina (🌐 *www.mtbikewnc.com*) has information on mountain trails. Trails.com (🌐 *www.trails.com*) offers information on more than 30,000 bike trails, including many in Georgia and the Carolinas. A year's subscription costs $49.95; a trial subscription is free.

**Bike Maps DeLorme** ✉ *2 DeLorme Dr., Yarmouth, Maine* ☎ *800/561–5105* 🌐 *www.delorme.com.* **Georgia Bikes** ☎ *404/441–9355, 404/634–6745* 🌐 *www.georgiabikes.org.* **North Carolina Division of Bicycle and Pedestrian Transportation** ✉ *1552 Mail Service Center, Raleigh* ☎ *919/707-2600* 🌐 *www.ncdot.gov/bikeped.* **South Carolina Trails Program** ✉ *1205 Pendleton St., Columbia* ☎ *803/734–0173* 🌐 *www.sctrails.net/trails.*

## BOAT TRAVEL

Ferries are a common, and often necessary, way to get around coastal areas, and especially to visit North Carolina's Outer Banks and Georgia's Sea Islands.

The Ferry Division of the North Carolina Department of Transportation operates seven ferry routes over five separate bodies of water: the Currituck and Pamlico sounds and the Cape Fear, Neuse, and Pamlico rivers. Travelers use the three routes between Ocracoke and Hatteras Island, Swan Quarter, and Cedar Island; between Southport and Fort Fisher; and between Cherry Branch and Minnesott

Beach. Ferries can accommodate any car, trailer, or recreational vehicle. Pets are permitted if they stay in the vehicle or are on a leash. Telephone and online reservations for vehicles are available for the Cedar Island–Ocracoke and Swan Quarter–Ocracoke routes; on other routes space is on a first-come, first-served basis. Schedules generally vary by season, with the largest number of departures from May through October.

Ferries are the only form of public transportation to Sapelo and Cumberland islands in Georgia. The Georgia Department of Natural Resources operates a ferry between Meridian and Sapelo. Advance reservations are required, and can be made by phone or at the Sapelo Island Visitor Center in Meridian. From March to November a privately run passenger ferry runs daily between St. Marys and Cumberland Island. The rest of the year the ferry does not operate on Tuesday and Wednesday. Reservations are essential, especially in March and April.

In North Carolina the Cedar Island–Ocracoke and Swan Quarter–Ocracoke ferries cost $1 for pedestrians, $3 for bicycles, $10 for motorcycles, and $15 for cars, and up to $45 for other vehicles (trailers, boats, motor homes). The Southport–Fort Fisher ferry costs $1 for pedestrians, $2 for bicycles, $3 for motorcycles, and $5 to $15 for vehicles. Tickets can be purchased with cash or traveler's checks. Personal checks are not accepted. The other North Carolina ferries are free.

In Georgia the pedestrian ferry to Sapelo Island costs $10 round-trip and includes a guided tour of island historical sites. Advanced reservations are required. The pedestrian ferry to Cumberland Island costs $20 round-trip, plus a $4 national park fee.

**Boat Information Cumberland Island National Seashore** ✉ *113 St. Marys St., St. Marys, Georgia* ☎ *912/882-4335, 877/860-6787* 🌐 *www.nps.gov/cuis.* **North Carolina Department of Transportation Ferry Division** ✉ *8550 Shipyard Rd., North Carolina* ☎ *800/293-3779* 🌐 *www.ncferry.org.* **Sapelo Island Visitor Center** ✉ *1766 Landing Road, S.E., DarienGeorgia* ☎ *912/437-3224* 🌐 *www.sapelonerr.org.*

## CAR TRAVEL

A car is the most practical and economical means of traveling around the Carolinas and Georgia. Atlanta, Savannah, Charleston, Myrtle Beach, and Asheville can also be explored fairly easily on foot or by using public transit and cabs, but a car is helpful to reach many of the most intriguing attractions, which are not always downtown. **TIP→ When returning rental cars to airports, always allow extra time to check in vehicles.**

Although drivers make the best time traveling along the South's extensive network of interstate highways, keep in mind that U.S. and state highways offer some delightful scenery and the opportunity to stumble on funky roadside diners, leafy state parks, and historic town squares. Although the area is rural, it's still densely populated, so travelers rarely drive for more than 20 or 30 miles without passing roadside services, such as gas stations, restaurants, and ATMs.

Among the most scenic highways in the Carolinas and Georgia are **U.S. 78**, running east–west across Georgia; **U.S. 25, 19, 74,** and **64,** traveling through the Great Smoky Mountains of western North Carolina; **U.S. 17** from Brunswick, Georgia, along the coast through South Carolina and North Carolina; and the **Blue Ridge Parkway** from the eastern fringes of the Great Smoky Mountains through western North Carolina into Virginia.

Unlike some other areas of the United States, the Carolinas and Georgia have very few toll roads. Currently, only Georgia State Route 400 in Atlanta, the Cross Island Parkway on Hilton Head, South Carolina, the Southern Connector in Greenville, South Carolina, and the

| TRAVEL TIMES AROUND THE CAROLINAS AND GEORGIA BY CAR | | |
|---|---|---|
| From | To | Time/Distance |
| Atlanta, GA | Savannah, GA | 4 hours / 248 mi |
| Asheville, NC | Great Smoky Mountains National Park, Cherokee entrance | 1 hour / 50 mi |
| Charlotte, NC | Atlanta, GA | 4 hours / 244 mi |
| Charleston, SC | Raleigh, NC | 4 hours / 279 mi |
| Durham, NC | Asheville, NC | 3½ hours / 224 mi |
| Hilton Head, SC | Columbia, SC | 2½ hours / 167 mi |
| Winston-Salem, NC | Charlotte, NC | 1½ hours / 84 mi |

Triangle Expressway in Wake and Durham counties, North Carolina, are toll roads.

## RENTAL CARS

It's important to reserve a car well in advance of your expected arrival. Rental rates vary from city to city, but are generally lowest in larger cities where there's a lot of competition. Economy cars cost between $27 and $61 per day, and luxury cars go for $70 to $198. Weekend rates are generally much lower than those on weekdays, and weekly rates usually offer big discounts. Rates are also seasonal, with the highest rates coming during peak travel times, including Thanksgiving and Christmas holiday seasons. Local factors can also affect rates; for example, a big convention can absorb most of the rental-car inventory and boost rates for those remaining.

Don't forget to factor in the taxes and other add-ons when figuring up how much a car will cost. At Atlanta's Hartsfield-Jackson International Airport, add the 7% sales tax, 11.11% airport concession-recovery fee, 3% city rental car tax, $5 daily customer facility charge, and $0.80 to $1.30 vehicle license-recovery charge. These "miscellaneous charges" mean that a weekly rental can jump in price far higher than the rental agency cost.

Some off-airport locations offer lower rates, and their lots are only minutes from the terminal via complimentary shuttle. Also ask whether certain frequent-flyer, American Automobile Association (AAA), corporate, or other such promotions are accepted and whether the rates might be lower for other arrival and departure dates. In addition to the national agencies, Triangle Rent A Car serves Georgia and the Carolinas.

### CAR RENTAL RESOURCES

**Local Agencies Triangle Rent A Car** ☎ *919/851-2556* 🌐 *www.trianglerentacar.com.*

**Major Agencies Alamo** ☎ *877/222-9075* 🌐 *www.alamo.com.* **Avis** ☎ *800/331-1212* 🌐 *www.avis.com.* **Budget** ☎ *912/964-4600 Airport Location* 🌐 *www.budget.com.* **Dollar** ☎ *800/800-4000* 🌐 *www.dollar.com.* **Enterprise** ☎ *912/964-0171 Airport Location* 🌐 *www.enterprise.com.* **Hertz** ☎ *912/964-1781 Airport Location* 🌐 *www.hertz.com.* **National Car Rental** ☎ *800/227-7368* 🌐 *www.nationalcar.com.*

## ROADSIDE EMERGENCIES

Travelers in Georgia and the Carolinas have help as close as their cell phones in case of emergencies on roadways. The Georgia Department of Transportation's Intelligent Transportation System works on three levels. First, drivers statewide can call 511 to report problems, get directions, information on traffic, MARTA, and Hartsfield airport. Next, on the 300 miles of metro Atlanta interstate highways, Highway Emergency Response Operators (HEROs) help motorists with everything from empty gas tanks to medical emergencies. Finally, the Georgia Navigator system provides statewide information on the Internet on roadway conditions and, in Atlanta, everything from drive times to incident locations to roadway conditions. Welcome centers statewide can also access that information.

In an emergency, drivers in North Carolina should call 911. In metro areas such as Raleigh, Durham, Burlington, Greensboro, Winston-Salem, Charlotte, and Asheville, and in the Pigeon River Gorge area, drivers on major U.S. highways and interstates receive roadside assistance through the Department of Transportation's Incident Management Assistance Patrols (IMAPs). The IMAP staff remove road debris, change tires, clear stalled vehicles, and can call a private tow truck. Motorists should dial *HP to reach the highway patrol and have an IMAP truck dispatched. In North Carolina's congested metro and construction areas, use the NCDOT Traveler Information Management System (TIMS) on the Internet or via cell phone. Go to *www.ncdot.org* and click on the link for "Travel Information." Search for travel updates by region, roadway, or county. Both the Great Smoky Mountains National Park and the Blue Ridge Parkway lure travelers to the state. The state's western area has many narrow, steep, and winding roads near such towns as Asheville, Boone, Sylva, and Waynesville. Use extra caution there, and pay extra attention to winter weather reports for snow and ice when roads may be closed.

South Carolina's Incident Response program operates on interstate highways in urban areas including Charleston, Columbia, Florence, and the constantly busy Myrtle Beach area (specifically the Highway 17 bypass and U.S. 501). Stranded motorists can call *HP for help and reach the local highway patrol dispatch system. The state operates hundreds of traffic cameras to monitor traffic flow and identify accident sites on all five interstates and in the Myrtle Beach area. They also have a camera at Interstate 95 and Interstate 26, in case of hurricane evacuations.

**Roadside Assistance Contacts Georgia Department of Transportation's Intelligent Transportation System** *511, 877/694–2511* *www.georgia-navigator.com.* **Department of Transportation's Incident Management Assistance Patrols (IMAPs)** *www.ncdot.org/traffictravel.* **South Carolina Incident Response Program** *www.scdot.org/getting/shep.aspx.*

## RULES OF THE ROAD

Currently there are no restrictions on the use of handheld cell phones by adults while driving in South Carolina. Georgia and North Carolina prohibit all drivers from texting while driving, and drivers under 18 from using cell phones for any purpose. (North Carolina allows them to answer calls from parents or report emergencies.)

Unless otherwise indicated, motorists may turn right at a red light after stopping if there's no oncoming traffic. When in doubt, wait for the green. In Atlanta, Asheville, Charleston, Columbia, Charlotte, Savannah, and the Triangle and Triad cities of North Carolina, be alert for one-way streets, "no left turn" intersections, and blocks closed to vehicle traffic.

In Georgia, always strap children under age six or under 40 pounds (regardless of age) into approved child-safety seats or booster seats appropriate for their height and weight in the backseat. Children younger than age eight and weighing less than 80 pounds must be properly secured in child restraints or booster seats in North Carolina. Child-safety seats or booster seats are required for children younger than six and weighing less than 80 pounds in South Carolina.

Watch your speed, as police are more than happy to write tickets to speedy out-of-towners. In Georgia, a "Super Speeder Law" allows the state to issue an additional $200 fine to drivers exceeding 75 mph on a two-lane road or 85 mph on any roadway.

## CRUISE SHIP TRAVEL

Carnival and Celebrity have ships to Bermuda, the Bahamas, and the Caribbean that depart from Charleston primarily in spring and fall. Princess Cruises, Holland America, Regent Seven Seas Cruises, and Crystal Cruises occasionally call at Charleston. Savannah, Charleston, Beaufort, and Wilmington are spring destinations for Jacksonville-to-Alexandria trips operated by Cruise West.

**Cruise Lines American Cruise Lines** ☎ *800/460-4518* 🌐 *www.americancruiselines.com.***Carnival** ☎ *305/599-2600, 800/764-7419* 🌐 *www.carnival.com.* **Crystal Cruises** ☎ *310/785-9300, 800/446-6620* 🌐 *www.crystalcruises.com.* **Holland America** ☎ *206/286-3900, 877/932-4259* 🌐 *www.hollandamerica.com.* **Princess Cruises** ☎ *661/753-0000, 800/774-6237* 🌐 *www.princess.com.* **Regent Seven Seas Cruises** ☎ *954/776-6123, 877/505-5370* 🌐 *www.rssc.com.*

## TRAIN TRAVEL

Several Amtrak routes pass through the Carolinas and Georgia; however, many areas are not served by train, and those cities that do have service usually only have one or two arrivals and departures each day. The *Crescent* runs daily through Greensboro, Charlotte, and Atlanta as it travels between New York and New Orleans. Three trains, the *Palmetto,* the *Silver Meteor,* and the *Silver Star* make the daily run between New York and Miami via Raleigh, Charleston, Columbia, and Savannah. The *Carolinian* runs daily from New York to Charlotte, via Raleigh.

Amtrak offers rail passes that allow for travel within certain regions, which can save a lot over the posted fare. Amtrak has several kinds of USA Rail Passes, offering unlimited travel for 15 or 30 days, with rates of $429 to $829, depending on the area traveled, the time of year, and the number of days. Amtrak has discounts for students, seniors, military personnel, and people with disabilities.

**Train Information Amtrak** ☎ *800/872-7245* 🌐 *www.amtrak.com.*

# ESSENTIALS

## ACCOMMODATIONS

With the exception of Atlanta, Savannah, Charleston, Asheville, and Charlotte, most lodging rates in the region fall at or below the national average. They do vary a great deal seasonally; however, coastal resorts and mountainous areas tend to have significantly higher rates in summer. Fall color creates demand for lodging in the mountains. Expect high-season rates. All major chains are well represented in this part of the country, both in cities and suburbs, and interstates are lined with inexpensive to moderate chains.

In many places consider forgoing a modern hotel in favor of a historic property. There are dozens of fine old hotels and mansions that have been converted into inns, many of them lovingly restored. Some may offer better rates than chain hotels. Bed-and-breakfasts are big in some cities, notably Charleston, Savannah, and Asheville. Each of these cities has two dozen or more B&Bs. There also are loads of B&Bs in many small towns along the coast and in the North Georgia and western North Carolina Mountains.

In many coastal resort areas, vacation-home and condo rentals dominate the lodging scene. The North Carolina Outer Banks, Myrtle Beach, and Hilton Head are major rental areas, each with several thousand rental properties. Rental prices vary by season, with peak summer rental rates that can double or more over off-season rates.

In the North Carolina and Georgia mountains, cabins are popular. These are usually owner-operated businesses with only a few cabins. In Georgia many state parks rent cabins, and they're often excellent values. In the mountains a number of lodges are available. These vary from simple accommodations to deluxe properties with spas, golf courses, and tennis courts. Many attract families that come back year after year. Mountain lodges are closed for several months in winter.

**WORD OF MOUTH**

"In Atlanta, I'd stay in Midtown. It's nicer for getting out and walking around. Lots of restaurant options. Several nice hotel options. I like the W (formerly the Sheraton) because it's just a block from Piedmont Park—great for walking around and a great farmers' market on Saturday mornings." —starrs

Thousands of families camp in the Carolinas and Georgia. The North Carolina Outer Banks, the Sea Islands of Georgia, and the Great Smoky Mountains National Park and Pisgah and Nantahala national forests in western North Carolina are especially popular with campers.

The lodgings listed are the cream of the crop in each price category. Facilities that are available are listed—but not any extra costs associated with those facilities. When pricing accommodations, always ask what's included and what costs extra.

### APARTMENT AND HOUSE RENTALS

The far-flung resort areas of the Carolinas and Georgia are filled with rental properties—everything from cabins to luxury homes. Most often these properties, whether part of a huge corporation or individually owned, are professionally managed; such businesses have become an industry unto themselves.

Carolina Mornings and Carolina Mountain Vacations rent cabins in the high country of North Carolina. Homestead Log Cabins has properties in the Pine Mountain area of Georgia. Intracoastal Realty has long-term as well as off-season rentals on the coast of Cape Fear. Hatteras Realty, Midgett Realty, and Sun Realty handle properties on North Carolina's Outer Banks. Island Realty focuses on the Charleston and Isle of Palms area in South Carolina. Hilton Head Rentals and Resort Rentals of Hilton Head Island offer rentals on Hilton Head. Sandy's by the Shore handles properties on Georgia's tiny Tybee island.

**Apartment and House Contacts Carolina Mornings** ☎ *855/398-0712* 🌐 *www.asheville-cabins.com.* **Carolina Mountain Vacations** ☎ *877/488-8500, 877/488-7501* 🌐 *www.carolinamountainvacations.com.* **Hatteras Realty** ☎ *800/428-8372* 🌐 *www.hatterasrealty.com.* **Hilton Head Rentals** ☎ *800/368-5975* 🌐 *www.hiltonheadrentals.com.* **Homestead Log Cabins** ☎ *706/663-4951* 🌐 *www.homesteadcabins.com.* **Intracoastal Realty** ☎ *855/346-2463* 🌐 *www.intracoastalrentals.com.* **Island Realty** ☎ *843/886-8144, 866/380-3983* 🌐 *www.islandrealty.com.* **Midgett Realty** ☎ *252/986-2841, 866/348-8819* 🌐 *www.midgettrealty.com.* **Resort Rentals of Hilton Head Island** ☎ *800/845-7017, 843/686-6008* 🌐 *www.hhivacations.com.* **Sandy's by the Shore** ☎ *866/512-0531, 912/786-0531* 🌐 *www.sandysbytheshore.com.* **Sun Realty, Outer Banks** ☎ *888/853-7770* 🌐 *www.sunrealtync.com.*

## BED-AND-BREAKFASTS

Historic B&Bs and inns are found in just about every region in the Carolinas and Georgia and include quite a few former plantation houses and lavish Southern estates. In many rural or less touristy areas, B&Bs offer an affordable and homey alternative to chain properties. In tourism-dependent destinations, expect to pay about the same as or more than for a full-service hotel. Many of the South's finest restaurants are also found in country inns.

**Reservation Services Asheville Bed & Breakfast Association** ☎ *877/262-6867* 🌐 *www.ashevillebba.com.* **Association of Historic Inns of Savannah** ☎ *912/232-5678* 🌐 *www.historicinnsofsavannah.com.* **Bed & Breakfast.com** ☎ *512/322-2710, 800/462-2632* 🌐 *www.bedandbreakfast.com.* **Bed & Breakfast Inns Online** ☎ *800/215-7365* 🌐 *www.bbonline.com.* **BnB Finder.com** ☎ *888/469-6663* 🌐 *www.bnbfinder.com.* **Romantic Inns of Savannah** 🌐 *www.romanticinnsofsavannah.com.* **South Carolina Bed & Breakfast Association** 🌐 *www.southcarolinabedandbreakfast.com.*

## CAMPING

The Carolinas and Georgia are popular for trailer and tent camping, especially in state and national parks. Georgia offers camping sites at more than 40 state parks, including three along its Atlantic coastline: Skidaway Island, Fort McAllister, and Crooked River. In South Carolina a similar number of state parks offer campsites. Hammocks Beach State Park offers primitive beach camping on Bear Island in North Carolina, and 29 other state parks offer campsites. For detailed information on the state parks and to reserve a site, visit the state parks' website.

A variety of camping experiences are available at the Great Smoky Mountains National Park, including backcountry and horse camping. Reservations for Elkmont, Smokemont, Cades Cove, and Cosby, the park's most popular developed campgrounds (with flush toilets and running water), are required from May 15 to October 31. Camping outside those dates or at the parks' other campgrounds is first-come, first-served.

**Camping Contacts Georgia State Parks** ☎ *800/864-7275* 🌐 *www.gastateparks.org.* **Great Smoky Mountains National Park** ☎ *877/444-6777* 🌐 *www.nps.gov/grsm.* **North Carolina State Parks** ☎ *877/722-6762* 🌐 *www.ncparks.gov.* **South Carolina State Parks** ☎ *866/345-7275* 🌐 *www.southcarolinaparks.com.*

## HOME EXCHANGES

With a direct home exchange you stay in someone else's home while they stay in yours. Some outfits also deal with vacation homes, so you're not actually staying in someone's full-time residence, just their vacant weekend place.

**Exchange Clubs Home Exchange.com.** $119 for a one-year online listing. ☎ *800/877–8723* 🌐 *www.homeexchange.com.* **HomeLink International.** $119 yearly. ☎ *800/638–3841* 🌐 *www.homelink.org.*

### HOTELS

In summer, especially July and August, hotel rooms in coastal areas and the mountains can be hard to come by unless you book well in advance. In the mountains, the autumn leaf-peeping season, typically early October to early November, is the busiest time of the year, and on weekends nearly every room is booked. Lodging in North Carolina's Triad area is difficult during the twice-yearly international furniture shows: in April and October all rooms are booked within a 30-mile radius of the show's location in High Point. Lodging in downtown Atlanta, despite its density of hotels, can be problematic during trade shows at the Georgia World Congress Center and the AmericasMart complex.

*Our local writers vet every hotel to recommend the best overnights in each price category, from budget to expensive. Unless otherwise specified, you can expect private bath, phone, and TV in your room. For expanded reviews, facilities, and current deals, visit Fodors.com.* Some of the most interesting hotels in the region are housed in historic buildings, particularly in well-preserved old cities like Charleston and Savannah. To find notable historic hotels throughout the region, visit the National Trust for Historic Preservation's Historic Hotels of America site at 🌐 *www.historichotels.org.*

Prices in the reviews are the lowest cost of a standard double room in high season.

## EATING OUT

The increase of international flavors in the region reflects the tastes and backgrounds of the people who have flooded into the Carolinas and Georgia over the past couple of decades. Bagels are as common nowadays as biscuits, and, especially in urban areas, it can be harder to find country cooking than a plate of hummus. For the most part, though, plenty of traditional Southern staples—barbecue, fried chicken, greens, and the like—are available.

Atlanta now has a big-city mix of neighborhood bistros, ethnic eateries, and expense-account restaurants. A new wave of restaurants in Charleston and Savannah serves innovative versions of Lowcountry cooking, with lighter takes on traditional dishes. In North Carolina you can find some nationally recognized restaurants in Charlotte, Asheville, and elsewhere. Outside the many resort areas along the coast and in the mountains, dining costs in the region are often lower than those in the North.

Vegetarians will have no trouble finding attractive places to eat in any of the larger metropolitan areas, although in small towns they may have to stick with pizza. Asheville is a haven for vegetarians; it has been named in many lists of the top vegetarian cities, including being named the most vegetarian-friendly city in the United States by People for the Ethical Treatment of Animals.

For some of the best food in the region, seek out restaurants that specialize in "farm to table" cuisine and frequently change their menus to feature the season's best produce. In the coastal regions, try the seafood shacks by the docks where fresh seafood is virtually guaranteed.

**WORD OF MOUTH**

Did the resort look as good in real life as it did in the photos? Did you sleep like a baby, or were the walls paper thin? Did you get your money's worth? Rate hotels and write your own reviews in Travel Ratings, or start a discussion about your favorite places in the Forums on 🌐 *www.fodors.com.* Your comments might even appear in our books. Yes, you, too, can be a correspondent!

Prices in the reviews are the average cost of a main course at dinner or, if dinner is not served, at lunch.

### MEALS AND MEALTIMES

The Southern tradition of Sunday dinner—usually a midday meal—has morphed to some degree, at least in urban areas, to Sunday brunch. For many people this meal follows midmorning church services, so be advised that restaurants will often be very busy through the middle of the day. In smaller towns many restaurants are closed Sunday. On weekdays in larger cities, restaurants will be packed with nearby workers from before noon until well after 1:30 PM. On Saturday, eateries in cities can be packed from morning through night. In small towns and big cities, weekday nights—when crowds are less likely and the staff can offer diners more time—can be the most pleasant for fine dining.

Southerners tend to eat on the early side, with lunch crowds beginning to appear before noon. The peak time for dinner is around 7. However, late-evening dining is not unusual in big cities, college towns, and tourist destinations.

Unless otherwise noted, the restaurants listed here are open daily for lunch and dinner.

### RESERVATIONS AND DRESS

For the most part, restaurants in the Carolinas and Georgia tend to be informal. A coat and tie are rarely required, except in a few of the fanciest places. Business-casual clothes are safe almost anywhere.

**Reservation Contacts OpenTable** 🌐 *www.opentable.com.*

### WINES, BEER, AND SPIRITS

Blue laws—legislation forbidding sales on Sunday—have a history in this region dating to the 1600s. These bans are still observed in many rural areas, particularly with regard to alcohol sales. Liquor stores are closed Sunday in the Carolinas. Beer and wine can't be sold anywhere before noon in North Carolina and South Carolina on Sunday. There are entire counties in the Carolinas and Georgia that prohibit the sale of alcoholic beverages in restaurants. Some cities and towns allow the sale of beer and wine in restaurants, but not mixed drinks. In North Carolina, bottled distilled spirits are sold only through "ABC" (Alcoholic Beverage Control) outlets; beer and wine are available in most grocery and convenience stores.

Although the Carolinas and Georgia will never be the Napa Valley, the last decade has seen a huge increase in the number of vineyards. North Carolina now has more than 60 wineries, and the Yadkin Valley is the state's first federally recognized American Viticultural Area, with more than 400 acres of vineyards in production. Asheville Biltmore Estate Wine Company is the most popular winery in the United States, with about 1 million visitors each year. Georgia's Wine Highway, which guides visitors to a number of wineries, runs from just north of Atlanta up through the North Georgia mountains. Muscadine and scuppernong grapes are native to warmer parts of the region; the sweetish wine from these grapes is gaining more respect. Traditional wine grapes are also widely grown.

Microbreweries are common all over the region, with hot spots being Atlanta, Asheville, Wilmington, Charlotte, and Charleston, as well as the Triangle of Raleigh, Durham, and Chapel Hill. There are more than 40 microbreweries in North Carolina, some two dozen in South Carolina, and about a half dozen in Georgia, where state laws on alcohol distribution have crimped their growth.

## HEALTH

With the exception of the mountains of North Georgia and western North Carolina, in the Carolinas and Georgia, it's hot and humid for at least six months of the year. Away from the coast, midsummer temperatures can reach the high 90s, making heat exhaustion and heatstroke real possibilities. Heat exhaustion is marked by muscle cramps, dizziness, nausea, and profuse sweating. To counter its effects, lie down in a cool place with the head slightly lower than the rest of the body. Sip cool, not cold, fluids. Life-threatening heatstroke is caused by a failure of the body to effectively regulate its temperature. In the early stages, heatstroke causes fatigue, dizziness, and headache. Later the skin becomes hot, red, and dry (due to lack of sweating), and body temperatures rise to as high as 106° F. Heatstroke requires immediate medical care.

At the beach or anywhere in the sun, slather on the sunscreen. Reapply it every two hours, or more frequently after swimming or perspiring. Remember that many sunscreens block only the ultraviolet light called UVB, but not UVA, which may be a big factor in skin cancer. Even with sunscreen it's important to wear a hat and protective clothing and to avoid prolonged exposure to the sun.

The coastal areas of the Carolinas and Georgia, especially the swamps and marshes of the Lowcountry, are home to a variety of noxious bugs: mosquitoes, sandflies, biting midges, black flies, chiggers, and no-see-ums. Most are not a problem when the wind is blowing, but when the breezes die down—watch out! Experts agree that DEET is the most effective mosquito repellent, but this chemical is so powerful that strong concentrations can melt plastic. Repellents with 100% DEET are available, but those containing 30% or less should work fine for adults; children should not use products with more than 10%. Products containing the chemical picaridin are effective against many insects, and don't have the strong odor or skin-irritating qualities of those with DEET. The plant-based oil of lemon eucalyptus, used in some natural repellents, performed well in some studies. Mosquito coils and citronella candles will also help ward off mosquitoes.

For sandflies or other tiny biting bugs, repellents with DEET alone are often not effective. What may help is dousing feet, ankles, and other exposed areas with an oily lotion, such as baby oil, which effectively drowns them.

The mountains of western North Carolina and North Georgia generally have few mosquitoes or other biting bugs, but in warm weather hikers may pick up chiggers or ticks. Use repellents with DEET on exposed skin. Wasps, bees, and small but ferocious yellow jackets are common throughout the region.

Feel free to drink tap water everywhere in the region, although in coastal areas it may have a sulfur smell. Many visitors to the beaches prefer to buy bottled water.

## MONEY

Although the cost of living remains fairly low in most parts of the South, travel-related costs (such as dining, lodging, and transportation) have become increasingly steep in Atlanta. And tourist attractions are pricey, too. For example, a tour of CNN Center is $15, admission to the High Museum of Art in Atlanta is $19.50, and getting into Georgia Aquarium is a steep $32.35. Costs can also be dear in resort communities throughout the Carolinas and Georgia.

If you plan on seeing multiple attractions in a city, look for money-saving passes sold at local visitor centers. Atlanta, for instance, participates in the national CityPASS program. The pass includes admission to six key attractions for $74, which is half of what you'd pay if buying individual admissions. Check out *www.citypass.com* for more information.

Prices throughout this guide are given for adults. Substantially reduced fees are almost always available for children, students, military personnel, and senior citizens.

## PACKING

Smart but casual attire works fine almost everywhere. A few chic restaurants in the cities prefer more elegant dress, and tradition-minded lodges in the mountains and resorts along the coast still require jackets and ties for men for dinner. For colder months pack a lightweight coat, slacks, and sweaters; bring along heavier clothing in some mountainous areas, where cold, damp weather prevails and snow is not unusual. Keeping summer's humidity in mind, pack absorbent natural fabrics that breathe; bring an umbrella, but leave the plastic raincoat at home. A jacket or sweater is useful for summer evenings and for too-cool air-conditioning. And don't forget insect repellent and sunscreen.

## SAFETY

In general, the Carolinas and Georgia are safe destinations for travelers. Most rural and suburban areas have low crime rates. However, some of the region's larger cities, such as Atlanta, have high crime rates.

In urban areas, follow proven traveler's precautions: don't wander onto deserted streets after dark, avoid flashing large sums of money or fancy jewelry, and keep an eye on purses and backpacks. If walking, even around the historic district, ask about areas to avoid at a hotel or a tourist information center; if in doubt, take a taxi.

In the Smoky Mountains the greatest concerns are driving on some of the curving and narrow roads—sometimes in heavy traffic—and theft of property and credit cards from vehicles in parking lots. Sometimes thieves will watch for motorists locking valuables in their trunks before leaving their cars. Single-car collisions, with motorists hitting trees or rocky outcroppings, are the cause of most accidents. Stolen property is rare in campsites. Drivers should also keep in mind that cell phones don't often work in the park. If visitors encounter bears, they are advised not to move suddenly, but to back away slowly.

**Contact Transportation Security Administration** (*TSA*). 🌐 *www.tsa.gov.*

## TAXES

Sales taxes are: Georgia 4%, North Carolina 4.75%, and South Carolina 6%. Some counties or cities may impose an additional sales tax of 1% to 3%. Most municipalities also levy a lodging tax (usually exempting small inns) and sometimes a restaurant tax. The hotel taxes in the South can be rather steep: as much as 8% in some places in Georgia and many counties in North Carolina. Taxes and fees on car rentals, especially if rented from an airport, can easily add 30% or more to the bill.

## TIME

Georgia and the Carolinas fall in the eastern standard time (EST) zone, which is the same as New York and Florida, making it three hours ahead of California.

**Time Zones Timeanddate.com.** This website will provide the correct time for any location. 🌐 *www.timeanddate.com/worldclock.*

## TIPPING

Tipping in the Carolinas and Georgia is essentially the same as tipping anywhere else in the United States. A bartender typically receives from $1 to $5 per round of drinks, depending on the number of drinks. Tipping at hotels varies with the level of the hotel, but here are some general guidelines: bellhops should be tipped $1 to $5 per bag; if doormen help to hail a cab tip $1 to $2; maids should receive $1 to $3 in cash daily; room-service waiters get $1 to $2 even if a service charge has been added; and tip concierges $5 or more depending on what service they perform.

Taxi drivers should be tipped 15% to 20% of the fare, rounded up to the next dollar amount. Tour guides receive 10%

of the cost of the tour. Valet parking attendants receive $1 to $2 when you get your car back. Tipping at restaurants varies from 15% to 20% by level of service and level of restaurant, with 20% being the norm at high-end restaurants.

## TOURS

The Carolinas and Georgia predominantly attract visitors traveling independently, usually by car. But some areas—notably Savannah, Charleston, Asheville, and the Great Smoky Mountains—get a number of escorted bus tours. Collette Vacations offers a seven-day "Southern Charm" tour featuring stops in Charleston, Savannah, and Jekyll Island. The escorted tour prices start at $1,499 per person. You stay at first-class hotels, such as the Jekyll Island Club, and the price includes most breakfasts and some dinners. Tauck has an eight-day tour of Charleston, Savannah, Jekyll Island, and Hilton Head, staying at such high-end hotels as the Omni Oceanfront Resort on Hilton Head. The cost is $2,690 per person. For one-stop-shopping, check with specialty travel agencies like Affordable Tours, which offers a variety of tour operators and discounted prices.

**Recommended Companies Affordable Tours** ☎ *800/935–2620* 🌐 *www.affordabletours.com.* **Collette Vacations** ☎ *800/340–5158* 🌐 *www.collettevacations.com.* **Tauck** ☎ *800/788–7885* 🌐 *www.tauck.com.*

## VISITOR INFORMATION

Going online is the fastest way to get visitor information. All of the state tourism offices listed below have excellent websites, with maps and other travel information.

**Contacts Georgia Department of Economic Development** ✉ *75 5th St., Technology Square, Suite 1200, Atlanta* ☎ *404/962–4000, 800/847–4842* 🌐 *www.exploregeorgia.org.* **North Carolina Travel & Tourism Division** ✉ *301 N. Wilmington St., Raleigh* ☎ *919/733-8372, 800/847–4862* 🌐 *www.visitnc.com.* **South Carolina Department of Parks, Recreation, and Tourism** ✉ *1205 Pendleton St., Room 248, Columbia* ☎ *803/734–1700, 866/224–9339* 🌐 *www.discoversouthcarolina.com.*

### FODORS.COM CONNECTION

Before your trip, be sure to check out what other travelers are saying in the Forums on 🌐 *www.fodors.com.*

### ONLINE TRAVEL TOOLS

#### ALL ABOUT THE CAROLINAS AND GEORGIA

**Civil War Traveler.** This website has information about Civil War sites in the Carolinas and Georgia, as well as in other states. 🌐 *www.civilwartraveler.com.*

**Doc South.** At this website you'll find a vast collection of historical documents and archives on Southern history, culture, and literature. 🌐 *docsouth.unc.edu.*

**Dr. Beach.** Dr. Stephen Leatherman offers his take on the best beaches nationwide. In 2012, two Carolina beaches made his top 10 beaches list. Cape Hatteras, on the Outer Banks in North Carolina, was No. 10. In South Carolina, Kiawah Island's Beachwalker Park was No. 9. 🌐 *www.drbeach.org.*

**Garden & Gun.** The online version of this popular magazine focused on Southern culture features travel and food articles on many Georgia and Carolinas destinations. 🌐 *www.gardenandgun.com.*

**Southern Living.** The online edition of Southern Living has many articles on travel, attractions, gardens, and people in the region. 🌐 *www.southernliving.com.*

#### ART AND CULTURE

**Gullah Culture.** From the PBS program with Bill Moyers, this is a good introduction to Gullah life and culture. 🌐 *www.pbs.org/now/arts/gullah.html.*

**Handmade in America.** The goal of this community organization is to establish western North Carolina as the nation's center of handmade objects. 🌐 *www.handmadeinamerica.org.*

**Penland School of Crafts.** This website is devoted to the famous crafts school in the North Carolina Mountains, but it also has a wealth of information on crafts in the region. 🌐 *www.penland.org.*

**Southern Highland Craft Guild.** The guild represents more than 900 craftspeople in the Southeast. 🌐 *www.southernhighlandguild.org.*

## GOLF

**Georgia State Park Golf Courses.** Search this website for detailed information on Georgia's public golf courses. 🌐 *www.georgiagolf.com.*

**Golf Guide.** This online guide has links to most golf courses in the Carolinas and Georgia. 🌐 *www.golfguideweb.com.*

**Golf Link.** This website offers information on nearly all the golf courses in the region. 🌐 *www.golflink.com.*

**Golf North Carolina.** Search a database of North Carolina's 600 golf courses on this website. In addition to the usual course information, this site has sections on golf tips and area information. 🌐 *www.golfnorthcarolina.com.*

## OUTDOORS

**Appalachian Trail Conservancy.** The conservancy is dedicated to preserving the nation's longest footpath, which runs from Georgia all the way to Maine. 🌐 *www.appalachiantrail.org.*

**Blue Ridge Parkway Association Guide.** Log on to this site for detailed information on one of the most beautiful roads in America. 🌐 *www.blueridgeparkway.org.*

**Georgia State Parks.** The parks' website covers accommodations, recreational activities, and special activities at one of the best state park systems in the United States. 🌐 *www.gastateparks.org.*

**National Forests in North Carolina.** A comprehensive guide to the state's national forests. 🌐 *www.fs.usda.gov/nfsnc.*

**National Park Service.** The website offers information on all of the national parks in the region, including the Great Smoky Mountains, the country's most popular national park. 🌐 *www.nps.gov/grsm.*

**North Carolina State Parks.** Basic information on state parks is available on the website. 🌐 *www.ncparks.gov.*

**South Carolina State Parks.** This colorful site features information on accommodations, outdoor activities, and even discounts offered at the parks. 🌐 *www.southcarolinaparks.com.*

## WINE

**Georgia Wine Country.** The excellent site for Georgia Wine Country has information on almost 50 wineries in Georgia. 🌐 *www.georgiawinecountry.com.*

**North Carolina Wines.** This comprehensive site offers facts on more than 90 wineries in North Carolina. 🌐 *www.visitncwine.com.*

**Winegrowers Association of Georgia.** A guide to touring and tasting Georgia's wineries. 🌐 *www.georgiawine.com.*

# INDEX

## A



## B

## C

## E



## F

## G

## H

## P



## R



## S

## U



## V



## W



## Y



## Z

## PHOTO CREDITS

1, Robb Helfrick. 3, Pat & Chuck Blackley /Alamy. Chapter 1: Experience the Carolinas and Georgia. 6-7, Bill Russ/NC Tourism. 9 (left), betsyweber/Flickr. 9 (right) and 10, Bill Russ/NC Tourism. 11 (left), National Park Service. 11 (right), Palmetto Dunes Oceanfront Resort. 12, Georgia Department of Economic Development. 13 (left), Jekyll Island Museum and Jekyll Island Club Hotel. 13 (right), Jo Jakeman/Flickr. 16 (all), Bill Russ/NC Tourism Bill Russ/NC Tourism. 17 (left, top center and right), Bill Russ/NC Tourism. 17 (bottom center), John Barreiros/Flickr. 18 (left), William Struhs. 18 (top center), wjarrettc/Flickr. 18 (bottom center), Michael G Smith/Shutterstock. 18 (right), Brian Stansberry/Wikimedia Commons. 19 (left), Middleton Place. 19 (top center), Tim Brown Architects/Flickr. 19 (bottom center), Riverbanks Zoo and Garden.19 (right), Lorie McGraw/iStockphoto. 20 (left), Robb Helfrick. 20 (top center), Rickey Bevington. 20 (bottom center), Georgia Department of Economic Development. 20 (right), Brittany Somerset. 21 (left), Georgia Department of Economic Development. 21 (top right), Georgia Department of Economic Development 21 (bottom right), Georgia Department of Economic Development. 22, Thomas Salley. 23 (left), Myrtle Beach Area CVB. 23 (right), Bill Russ/NC Tourism. 24, Philip Scalia / Alamy. 25, Tatiana Gribanova /Alamy. 26, Library of Congress Prints and Photographs Division. 27 (left), Bill Russ/NC Tourism. 27 (right), Tony Crescibene/Flickr. 28-29 and 30, Blaine Harrington / age fotostock. 31 (left), IMAGE ASSET MANAGEMEN / age fotostock. 31 (top right), Brian Stansberry/Wikipedia Commons. 31 (bottom right), Brady & Co., Washington, D.C./ Wikimedia Commons. 32 (bottom), Jeffrey M. Frank/Shutterstock.32 (top), Corey Ann/Corey Balazowich/Flickr. 33 (top left), Robb Helfrick. 33 (top right), Jeffrey M. Frank/Shutterstock. 33 (bottom), Cotinis/Wikimedia Commons. 34 (top), Charleston Area CVB. 34 (bottom), Drayton Hall. 35 (top left), Middleton Place. 35 (top right), Blaine Harrington / age fotostock. 35 (bottom), Middleton Place. 36 (bottom), Georgia Department of Economic Development. 36 (top), Archibald Smith Plantation Home. 37 (left and right), Georgia Department of Economic Development. 38, Bill Russ/NC Tourism. 39, Georgia Department of Economic Development. 42, Sean Busher and NASCAR Hall of Fame. 44, William Struhs. Chapter 2: The North Carolina Coast. 47, Jim West / age fotostock. 48-49, Bill Russ/ NC Tourism. 50, Brian Leon/ Flickr. 51 (top and bottom) and 52-53, Bill Russ/NC Tourism. 54, Robb Helfrick. 55, Rusty's Surf &Turf. 56, Bill Russ/NC Tourism. 62, Library of Congress Prints and Photographs Division. 65 and 69, Bill Russ/NC Tourism. 72, Robb Helfrick. 76, John Elk III / Alamy. 78-79, Marvin Newman / age fotostock. 81, Pat & Chuck Blackley / Alamy. 86, Bill Russ/NC Tourism. 88, wikipedia.org. 91, Bill Russ/NC Tourism. 96, Gianna Stadelmyer/Shutterstock. 101 and 106, Bill Russ/ NC Tourism. Chapter 3:Central North Carolina. 111, Don Klumpp / age fotostock. 112, Jeff Cravotta Photography. 113 (top),Visit Charlotte. 113 (bottom), Bill Russ/NC Tourism. 114, Southern Foodways/ Flickr. 115 (top), David P. Smith/Shutterstock. 115 (bottom), Southern Foodways/Flickr. 116, Thomas Salley. 117 (bottom), RayLen Vineyards & Winery/Torrey Ferrell. 117 (top), Raffaldini Vineyards. 118 and 124, Bill Russ/NC Tourism. 128, Charles L Harris. 130-44, Bill Russ/NC Tourism. 153, Andre Jenny / Alamy. 158, Johnny Stockshooter / age fotostock. 164,nickledford/Flickr. 168, Historic Latta Plantation. 177, Robb Helfrick. Chapter 4: Asheville and the North Carolina Mountains. 181 and 182-84, Bill Russ/NC Tourism.185, Veri Similitude/Flickr. 186, Leigh Santen Lewis. 187 (top), Sara Gray/ iStockphoto. 187 (bottom), Appalachian Sustainable Agriculture Project (ASAP). 188 and 194, Bill Russ/NC Tourism. 200, Kathi Petersen, courtesy Blue Ridge Food Ventures, Asheville NC. 201, Bill Russ/NC Tourism. 210, Trip Huxley. 220 and 223, Bill Russ/NC Tourism. 228-29 and 234, Robb Helfrick. Chapter 5: Great Smoky Mountains National Park. 237, Buddy Mays / Alamy. 238 (bottom), gary718/Shutterstock. 238 (top), Wayne James/Shutterstock. 239 (top), National Park Service photo. 239 (center), Thomas Takacs/iStockphoto. 239 (bottom), cwwycoff1/Flickr. 240, keith011764/Flickr. 246, Oliver Gerhard / age fotostock. 251, Jason Langley / Alamy. 252-53, Oliver Gerhard / age fotostock. 255, Daniel Dempster Photography / Alamy. 264-65, Bill Russ/NC Tourism. 266 (left), Jlaessle/ Wikimedia Commons. 266 (top center), Bernard B. ILarde/Wikimedia Commons. 266 (bottom center), Mary Terriberry/Shutterstock. 266 (bottom right), rjones0856/Flickr. 266 (top right), pellaea/Flickr. 267, Jean-Pol GRANDMONT/WIkimedia Commons. 267 (top center), Steffen Foerster Photography/ Shutterstock. 267 (bottom center), WiZZiK/Wikimedia Commons. 267 (bottom right), Derek Ramsey/ Wikimedia Commons. 267 (top right), John Seiler/iStockphoto. 268, Kord.com / age fotostock. 269 (left), Thomas Takacs/iStockphoto. 269 (right), Jeff Greenberg / age fotostock. 270, Pat & Chuck Blackley / Alamy. 272, Heeb Christian / age fotostock. 277, Jeff Greenberg / age fotostock. 279, M Blankenship/Shutterstock. 288, NC Tourism. Chapter 6: Myrtle Beach, SC, and the Grand Strand. 291, Myrtle Beach Area CVB. 292, Brookgreen Gardens. 293 (top), Stacie Stauff Smith Photography/Shutterstock.293 (bottom left and bottom right) and 294, Myrtle Beach Area CVB. 295 (top), Stacie Stauff Smith Photography/Shutterstock. 295 (bottom), Myrtle Beach Area CVB. 296, brt COMM / Alamy. 297, Stacie Stauff Smith Photography/Shutterstock. 298, Brookgreen Gardens. 305, Bob Pardue - SC /

Alamy. 312, Peter Horree/ Alamy. 318, Andre Jenny / Alamy. 327, Brookgreen Gardens. 332, Andre Jenny / Alamy. Chapter 7:Charleston, SC. 335, Robb Helfrick. 336, Charleston Area CVB. 337 (top), William Struhs. 337 (bottom),Charleston Area CVB for / www.Explorecharleston.com. 338, McCradyís Restaurant. 339 (bottom),Peter Frank Edwards. 339 (top), Squire Fox. 340, Charleston Area CVB. 345, Richard Cummins /age fotostock. 349, David R. Frazier Photolibrary, Inc. / Alamy. 351, Gabrielle Hovey/Shutterstock. 353, Robb Helfrick. 354, Richard Cummins / age fotostock. 355 and 356 (left and right), Brittany Somerset. 357 (left), Mary Coy. 357 (top right), Richard Ellis / Alamy. 357 (bottom right), Charleston Area CVB. 358 (top), nik wheeler / Alamy. 358 (bottom), Heeb Christian / age fotostock. 359 (left), Brittany Somerset. 359 (right), Robb Helfrick. 360 (top), Stephen Saks Photography / Alamy. 360 (bottom),Richard Cummins/age fotostock. 361 (top), rjones0856/Flickr. 361 (bottom), Blaine Harrington/age fotostock. 363, Rainer Kiedrowski / age fotostock. 364-65, Dennis Hallinan / Alamy. 368, Blaine Harrington / age fotostock. 374, Squire Fox. 379, Beth Whitcomb/Shutterstock. 383, Richard Cummins/age fotostock. 389, H. Mark Weidman Photography / Alamy. 391, The Leading Hotels of the World. 392, William Struhs. 400, Robb Helfrick. 404, Jeff Greenberg / age fotostock. Chapter 8: Hilton Head, SC, and the Lowcountry. 411, Hilton Head Island Visitor & Convention Bureau. 412 (bottom), Hilton Head Island Visitor & Convention Bureau. 412 (top), aceshot1/Shutterstock. 413, 414, and 415 (top), Hilton Head Island Visitor & Convention Bureau. 415 (bottom), Alison Lloyd, Fodors.com member. 416, Hilton Head Island Visitor & Convention Bureau. 417 (bottom), Otokimus/Shutterstock. 417 (top), Ron Diggity/Flickr. 418, Kendra Natter, Fodors.com member. 425, Eric Horan/age fotostock. 433, Hilton Head Island Visitor & Convention Bureau. 437, Bill Bachmann / Alamy. 442, Hilton Head Island CVB. Chapter 9: The Midlands and the Upstate, SC. 449, SuperStock/ age fotostock. 450, rocknroll_guitar/Flickr. 451 (top and center), L Barnwell/Shutterstock. 451 (bottom), Tony Crescibene/Flickr. 452, Richard Cummins / age fotostock. 456, Gabrielle Hovey/Shutterstock. 460, Zach Holmes / Alamy. 463, Clint Farlinger / Alamy. 466, carlfbagge/Flickr. 473, Spring Images / Alamy. Chapter 10: Savannah, GA. 477, Robb Helfrick. 478 (top), Lawrence Roberg/Shutterstock. 478 (bottom), David S. Baker/Shutterstock. 479 (top and center), Georgia Department of Economic Development. 479 (bottom), William Britten/iStockphoto. 480 and 481 (top), Wiley's Championship BBQ. 481 (bottom), kimberlykv/Flickr. 482, Katherine Welles/iStockphoto.486-87, Robb Helfrick. 490, Heeb Christian / age fotostock. 494-95, trinum/iStockphoto. 500, Robb Helfrick. 505, Georgia Department of Economic Development. 509, Savannah Music Festival/Frank Stewart. 512, Clicksy/Flickr. Chapter 11: Georgia's Coastal Isles and the Okefenokee. 517, Robb Helfrick. 518, Jo Jakeman/Flickr. 519, Barbara Kraus/iStockphoto. 520, Georgia Department of Economic Development. 521 (bottom), Jo Jakeman/Flickr. 521 (top), Brandon Laufenberg/iStockphoto. 522, Robb Helfrick. 527 and 530, Georgia Department of Economic Development. 535, Zach Holmes / Alamy. 539, Jekyll Island Museum and Jekyll Island Club Hotel. 544, dougandme/Flickr. 548 and 550, Robb Helfrick. Chapter 12: Southwest Georgia. 553, Cyrille Gibot / age fotostock. 554 (center), Georgia Department of Economic Development. 554 (bottom), divemasterking2000/Flickr. 554 (top), Tony Crescibene/ Flickr. 555 (top), Jeffrey M. Frank/Shutterstock. 555 (bottom), Georgia Department of Economic Development. 556, Mona Makela/Shutterstock. 557 (bottom), Jaimie Duplass/Shutterstock. 557 (top), Yuan Tian/iStockphoto. 558, Georgia Department of Economic Development. 561, Greg Wright / Alamy. 564 and 569, Georgia Department of Economic Development. 571, Robb Helfrick. Chapter 13: Atlanta, GA. 573, Walter Bibikow / age fotostock. 574 and 575 (left), Georgia Department of Economic Development. 575 (right), Kevin Rose/AtlantaPhotos.com. 576 and 577 (top), Georgia Department of Economic Development. 577 (bottom), Wikimedia Commons. 578, Sarah Dorio. 579 (top), Sara Hanna579 (bottom), James Camp. 580, Georgia Department of Economic Development. 585, Kevin Rose/AtlantaPhotos.com. 590,Georgia Department of Economic Development. 593, John E Davidson / age footstock. 596, Kevin Rose/AtlantaPhotos.com. 599, Atlanta History Center. 601, Georgia Department of Economic Development. 609, San Rostro / age fotostock. 612, Kevin Rose/AtlantaPhotos.com. 620, Marvin Newman / age fotostock. 624, Martin Thomas Photography/ Alamy. 633, limaoscarjuliet/ Flickr. Chapter 14: Central and North Georgia. 635-37, Georgia Department of Economic Development. 638, Robb Helfrick. 639, Walter Elliott. 640, Robb Helfrick. 645 (top), divemasterking2000/ Flickr. 645 (bottom), Library of Congress Prints and Photographs Division. 646 (top left and top center), Wikimedia Commons. 646 (top right, center, bottom left, and bottom right) and 647 (top and bottom left), Library of Congress Prints and Photographs division. 647 (bottom right), Wikimedia Commons. 648 (top left), Blair Howard/iStockphoto. 648 (bottom), Legacy Images by Violet Clark/ Flickr. 648 (top right), divemasterking2000/Flickr. 649, Jeffrey M. Frank/Shutterstock. 650 (all) Georgia Department of Economic Development. 653, Ian Dagnall / Alamy. 655, Three Sisters Vineyards. 658-67, Georgia Department of Economic Development. 671, Robb Helfrick. 675 and 678, Georgia Department of Economic Development.

# NOTES

# NOTES

# NOTES

# NOTES

# NOTES